BENSON and HEDGES
CRICKET YEAR

TWELFTH EDITION

Catch the Action

WORLD OF CRICKET

THE CRICKET MAGAZINE ON VIDEO

TCCB

In association with the TCCB

WORLD OF CRICKET

the new cricket magazine on video, month by month,
10 issues a year brings you the complete cricket
picture from around the world.

WORLD OF CRICKET

builds into an invaluable visual library, with each issue
running for 75 minutes – and all for as little as
£9.50 (inc p&p) per issue on an annual subscription.

In addition to the action, leading commentators
present features on all aspects of the game, including
interviews with past and current top players.

CURRENT ACTION
Reviews of all top International, County and Trophy matches

INTERVIEWS WITH LEADING PLAYERS
Profiles and insights into past and present players and views on
the upcoming stars

NEW DEVELOPMENTS IN THE GAME
Analysis of major innovations affecting cricket

OLD FLANNELS
Historic footage of memorable matches from the past

CRICKETABILITY
Leading players discuss various technical aspects

COMPETITIONS
Regular chances to win major prizes

Back issues are available – 1st issue June 1993

UK rates: 1 issue £9.99, 5 issues £48, 10 issues £95 *(overseas rates available by request),*
beginning with the .... issue
Name & address to where the tapes should be sent ....

....

....

Payment by cheque or postal order payable to **World of Cricket**
Payment by credit card (Access/Mastercard or Visa only)

Card number ☐☐☐☐☐☐☐☐☐☐☐☐☐☐☐☐☐☐

Expiry Date......................... Signature...

If cardholders name & statement address is different than that given please include
these details separately. *For Betamax, Secam or NTSC formats please contact us.*

☎ **Credit card hotline 071-924 4362** ☎

World of Cricket, Freepost (SW5087/1), 143 Chatham Road, London SW11 6BR *(no stamp required).*
Tel: 071-924 4362. Fax: 071-924 2208.

BHA93/94

BENSON and HEDGES
CRICKET YEAR

TWELFTH EDITION
SEPTEMBER 1992 to SEPTEMBER 1993

EDITOR—DAVID LEMMON
FOREWORD by GRAHAM GOOCH

HEADLINE

Editor's note

The aim of *Benson and Hedges Cricket Year* is that the cricket enthusiast shall be able to read through the happenings in world cricket, from each October until the following September (the end of the English season). Form charts are printed and a player's every appearance will be given on these charts, and date and place allow these appearances to be readily found in the text.

The symbol * indicates 'not out' or 'wicket-keeper' according to the context.

The editor would like to express his deepest thanks to Brian Croudy, Sudhir Vaidya, John R. Ward, Anthony Lalley, Les Hatton, Victor Isaacs, Ian Smith, Richard Lockwood, Philip Bailey and Qamar Ahmed.

First published in 1993
by HEADLINE BOOK PUBLISHING

10 9 8 7 6 5 4 3 2 1

A CIP catalogue record for this book is available from the British Library

ISBN 0-7472-0898-0

Designed and produced by Book Production Consultants Plc, 25–27 High Street, Chesterton, Cambridge CB4 1ND

Printed and bound in Great Britain by BPCC Hazell Books Ltd, Aylesbury Member of BPCC Ltd

HEADLINE BOOK PUBLISHING
A division of Hodder Headline PLC
Headline House
79 Great Titchfield Street
London W1P 7FN

CONTENTS

Sponsor's message

The twelfth *Benson and Hedges Cricket Year* embraces a season that for England at international level was, at best, not glorious. As the Test series unfolded – with England losing the first two, drawing the third, losing the fourth and fifth – virtually every cricket fan in the country declared him or herself able to do a better job than the selectors. The media bayed for blood with the result that the Chairman of Selectors, Ted Dexter, stood down before his contract had run its term. Was Ted Dexter the culprit, or scapegoat? I suspect the latter. Plainly, it makes little sense to blame any one person, or group of people, for the national side's inability to win games. The problem is more complicated and runs deep.

Graham Gooch expresses some typically forthright views on this very subject in his foreword to this edition. I found his thoughts compelling reading, as I'm sure will many others. The truth is that there is no quick-fix answer to England's difficulties. At – or certainly very near – the root of the problem is the fact that cricket is no longer played in the majority of schools: it's an expensive game and it's time-consuming. It makes great demands on teachers. And specialist coaching is essential to develop potential. In most – if not all – other countries where international cricket is played, the game is part of the school curriculum. This is no longer the case in Britain, except in private schools. If this position continues, it seems likely that cricket will assume the mantle of an elitist sport. I have no interest in making political points, but surely nobody wants cricket to be merely a minority pastime for the privileged few.

The series ended on a high note with a win for the home side at The Oval under Mike Atherton, newly in charge for only the second time. England actually looked like a Test side. There were some fine batting performances, most notably from Graham Gooch who overtook David Gower to become England's most prolific run-maker. Devon Malcolm made his re-appearance in the national side – and made a big difference to it. He was joined in the attack by Angus Fraser, back after prolonged injury problems, bowling his impeccable line and length and leaving Australia's batsmen never a moment to let concentration lapse. Australia deserved to win the series and keep the Ashes. Besides out-playing England in every department, the Aussies also kept crowds roundly entertained wherever they went. The Falstaffian Merv Hughes – 18 stones of undiluted enthusiasm and unbridled moustaches – won cult hero status. And 23-year-old Shane Warne – spinner extraordinary – looks certain to be a feature of the Aussie side for many years to come.

The 22nd Benson and Hedges Cup final at Lord's on 10 July was, by any measure, an absolute cracker. According to the pundits, Derbyshire's chances of beating Lancashire were less than remote. Put in to bat, Derbyshire looked to be proving the pundits correct when at 66 for 4. Then some strong middle-order resistance – including a Gold Award-winning 92 not out from Dominic Cork – changed Derbyshire's fortunes. Their total after 55 overs was a creditable 252. With just nine runs on the board, Lancashire lost Titchard. But sturdy innings from Atherton, Speak and Fairbrother put them firmly back in the game, so that with an over to go, 11 runs were needed for victory. This proved too tall an order for Lancashire, but only just. The rain-interrupted game finished at 8.30 pm – a great day to remember.

There's at least one other thing for which the 1993 season will be noted. A new piece of pantomime has been added to the umpires' repertoire. It involves him turning to the pavilion and describing a screen shape in the air, as he might do if about to mime a TV title in the game of charades. The third umpire is with us.

You hold a particularly meaty *Benson and Hedges Cricket Year* in your hands. As ever, the standard of photography is of the highest and there are statistics, charts and data in sufficient volume to satisfy even those of Frindallesque persuasion.

All cricket lovers will enjoy the feast. Bon appetit!

DEREK STOTHARD
Marketing Manager
Benson and Hedges

Comment

Few cricket years can claim to have had the significance of 1993. For many, it was not simply the end of an act, but the end of the play. Within weeks of each other, Graham Gooch resigned the England captaincy and Ted Dexter announced that he was giving up the post of 'supremo' of English cricket. It was the season which saw the last in the county game of Botham, Randall, Foster, Richards, Marshall, Tavaré and Mendis. Their successors in personality and ability are not easily discernible at this stage.

Richards delighted until the last day of the season. Sadly, Botham's going was uncharacteristically quiet – a whimper rather than a bang. Since the days of W.G. Grace, no cricketer, save Denis Compton, has been more capable of filling a ground. While speaking to the Oxford University Cricket Society some years ago I mentioned his name, and the response was the expected mixture of adulation and character assassination. A young lady undergraduate from Leeds ended the argument when she got to her feet and said, 'I had no interest in cricket until my father took me to see Botham in 1981. Since that day I have loved every minute of the game.' In whatever he did, Ian Botham demanded a response, and for that we should be ever grateful. It is probable that it will be many years before we look upon his like again.

A fit and younger Botham would certainly have been an asset against Border's Australians, a side of great resilience who, with an attack of decided limitations, trounced England and, as Graham Gooch underlines, exposed woeful weaknesses in our cricket.

One of the attempts to eradicate those weaknesses was, of course, the restructuring of the domestic season for 1993, but already the changes that were made are under fire. It is unlikely that the Sunday League will retain its 50-over format and earlier start beyond 1994 – even if it retains them for that long – and there is a strong movement among the counties for bringing back the zonal matches in the Benson and Hedges Cup. A county like Kent finds no joy in losing its interest in one of the most lucrative of competitions after the third week in April; and all counties have now realised with horror that they could go for several seasons without a home tie in either the Benson and Hedges Cup or the NatWest Trophy.

The four-day championship matches still provoke the strongest argument. England's best batsman and former captain asserts that they are here to stay, but the Hampshire captain Mark Nicholas is less certain, seeing the four-day format as 'a less palatable diet for the spectator but at present a more realistic one for the player'. Nicholas echoes what we wrote in these pages last year when he says 'most of England's finest players were educated on uncovered pitches where both method and mind were examined'. The debate is far from over. The four-day game has taken much of the heart out of the county championship, and the real argument revolves around whether the competition has an integral worth of its own or whether, as some – in our view mistakenly – contend, its sole purpose is to produce players for England. Whatever the outcome of this debate, one thing seems certain, and that is that a format which leaves Saturday as the third day of a game has little consideration for the paying customer.

The other significant change in the cricket year which this annual celebrates was, of course, the introduction of the third umpire, the recourse to the television replay. Human fallibility is a vital part of cricket. To attempt to eradicate it is to rid the game of much of its romance and charm. It is an attempt to turn an art into a science, and therefore to take away the mystery. One might also say that the reliance on the monitor is an abnegation of responsibility on the part of the umpire in the middle. At Lord's, the call for a television decision in the second Test brought a two-minute delay and a slow hand-clap from the crowd.

What if next year's Benson and Hedges Cup final or NatWest Trophy final ends as some of these encounters have done in the past, with a single needed from the last ball and a dive for the line and a cloud of dust? Is the crowd to wait for two minutes before they are to be told who has won the cup? That way danger lies.

But to concentrate on what is past and on what is wrong would be a mistake. Youth is at the helm, and there is wisdom and joyful hope. Atherton and his young side may well return from the Caribbean battered, bruised and beaten, but – at least and at last – we will have looked to the future, and that in itself is a welcome and positive step.

On the day after the NatWest final, I saw the Mobil youth finals at Chelmsford with some 120 under-11s playing in the morning and the under-16 final in the afternoon. It was glorious stuff. There is hope in our hearts.

DAVID LEMMON

Benson and Hedges Cricket Year World XI, 1993

1	G.A. Gooch (England)	(2)
2	D.C. Boon (Australia)	(4)
3	B.C. Lara (West Indies)	(6)
4	V.G. Kambli (India)	(13)
5	S.R. Tendulkar (India)	(6)
6	A.R. Border (Australia) (capt)	(10)
7	*I.A. Healy (Australia)	(43 in batting)
8	A.R. Kumble (India)	(3)
9	S.K. Warne (Australia)	(5)
10	C.E.L. Ambrose (West Indies)	(2)
11	Waqar Younis (Pakistan)	(1)

Coopers & Lybrand ratings are in brackets.

Gooch, Boon, Healy, Ambrose and Waqar Younis are the only survivors from last year's side. The eleven is chosen on consistency of form shown in first-class cricket throughout the world in the period covered by this annual.

Foreword

by Graham Gooch, OBE

Champagne flowed after England's victory over Australia at The Oval – and deservedly so. Mike Atherton had his first Test win as captain. Devon Malcolm and – even more crucially – Angus Fraser were back. And, on a personal level, I had become England's leading run-scorer in Tests. But this euphoria at the end of the summer could not disguise the fact that 1993 was a disastrous year for England's international cricketers. That success in the sixth Test and the Ashes draw at Trent Bridge were the only respite from eight heavy defeats against India, Sri Lanka and Australia. There was no consolation from our one-day performances either: England led India 3–1 at one stage in the winter series, but the remaining seven internationals in the year were lost.

It must be of concern to English cricket that years like 1993 are likely to become a common occurrence unless certain problems are confronted. The overall standard of our cricket is not good enough. Our players are not hard enough, or competitive enough, or mentally tough enough. The raw talent is there, but the system is not producing cricketers equipped to compete consistently with the rest of the Test countries. I have no doubt that England's first-class game is over-populated and there is not enough competition for places. Only four counties have won the championship since Essex took their first title in 1979. So what can be done? Maybe one way of introducing more competitiveness in the English first-class game would be to have a two-division County Championship. That might seem a radical step, but these are desperate times. We are going to have to be fully professional in our attitude and performance if we are to stop the rot. How long are supporters going to fill the Test grounds to watch mediocre displays from the home country? It's time some counties looked beyond their own boundaries; there is too much self-interest in English cricket.

The last weeks of my time as England captain were depressing – and not just because we were losing. Winning is not the be-all and end-all, but not all our players seemed aware of what is necessary to achieve success. To put it bluntly, I got fed up telling people what to do. Although my own form had not suffered, the pressure of having to do well every time I went to the crease was becoming unbearable. It was certainly time for a change of captain.

I decided to stay in charge after our disastrous tour of India because I felt England had made real progress since I took over at the end of 1989. In 1990, we won a Test in the Caribbean and took the home series against New Zealand and India. The following year, we drew the series with the West Indies. In 1992, England won in New Zealand, reached the final of the World Cup and only lost the series against Pakistan in the final Test. The problems of touring India are legion. Last winter, the England team had to cope with violent civil unrest and an air strike, illnesses and dodgy prawns – all of which contributed to us losing all the Tests. I felt we had a realistic chance of winning the Ashes and I still had something to offer as captain. I was wrong on both counts. I enjoyed my time as captain and never once regretted accepting the role. But captaincy is not a job you can do for ever.

It's Mike Atherton's era now. He's the right choice and that win at The Oval will have done his confidence the world of good. Mike is a talented batsman and I have enjoyed the time I have spent batting with him. The biggest pressure initially as a Test captain is to succeed as a player. Mike has made a good start and life for him in the Caribbean will be much easier if he is scoring runs. Mike has a big job on his hands – and not only this winter. The best advice I can give him is: 'Just enjoy the job.'

Middlesex played the best cricket of the summer to take the county title. Mike Gatting benefited from career bests from both his spinners, John Emburey and Phil Tufnell. The four-day championship is here to stay; it is a better game with more natural results. The cricket is superior technically and that will help the Test team in future years. The resurgence of Glamorgan was the most welcome news of the summer, plus the return to form of Angus Fraser – the only world-class fast bowler England has produced since Bob Willis.

This has been a year of goodbyes: no more Ian Botham, Viv Richards, Malcolm Marshall or Derek Randall. The game will be less exciting, if quieter, for their absence, although as soon as one Botham departs, another appears. Liam, who has joined Hampshire, has much to live up to. Life for 'sons of' is never easy in the sporting world, though Nigel Clough, Damon Hill and Alec Stewart have all followed their fathers to the top.

Ted Dexter decided to call it a day as Chairman of the England Committee. Ted took a lot of stick for England's poor performances, but that was very unfair. Much of his contribution was made behind the scenes, the importance of which will become more obvious with the passing of time. Keith Fletcher had a torrid debut year as England team manager, but he has long-term plans from which he won't be diverted for short-term gains.

'Fletch' and Mike Atherton have plumped for youth for the Caribbean tour. England must stick with that nucleus of young players and give Mike time to develop his England team. I just hope there's room for one old-timer next summer, form permitting!

SECTION A
India

Duleep Trophy
Deodhar Trophy
Irani Cup
England tour, Test and one-day international series
Ranji Trophy
Zimbabwe tour, Test match and one-day internationals
First-class averages

The spin trio who destroyed England – Chauhan, Kumble and Venkatapathy Raju. (David Munden/Sports-Line)

DULEEP TROPHY

With a tour of South Africa beginning in October, India began the 1992–3 cricket season in late August in an attempt to offer players a chance to find form and win places in the touring party. The Duleep Trophy, India's second major domestic competition, was condensed into some three weeks in late August and early September and was quickly followed by the Irani Cup, after which the side to tour South Africa was named.

QUARTER-FINAL

21, 22, 23, 24 and 25 August 1992 *at SE Railway Stadium, Vishakhapatnam*

South Zone 226 (W.V. Raman 91, S. Mukherjee 6 for 77, Abinash Kumar 4 for 94) and 341 (W.V. Raman 85, A.R. Kumble 67, Robin Singh 65, R. Biswal 5 for 76, Abinash Kumar 5 for 108)

East Zone 254 (P. Sunil Kumar 90, S.S. Karim 79, Venkatapathy Raju 6 for 71) and 141 (Venkatapathy Raju 6 for 46)

South Zone won by 172 runs

Batting first, South Zone were given an excellent start by Raman and Srikkanth with a stand of 111, but thereafter the innings fell apart against the bowling of Abinash Kumar and Mukherjee. East Zone's first innings was founded upon a fourth-wicket stand of 125 between Sunil Kumar and Karim, and, in spite of the magnificent bowling of Venkatapathy Raju and Arshad Ayub, East Zone took a first-innings lead. Their joy was short-lived as Robin Singh and Kumble added 132 for South Zone's sixth wicket, and East Zone then fell apart against the combined spin of Raju and Ayub. The Test pair claimed 18 wickets in the match between them.

SEMI-FINALS

28, 29, 30, 31 August and 1 September 1992 *at M.A. Chidambaram Stadium, Madras*

Central Zone 347 (P.K. Amre 83, S.A. Ankola 5 for 67) and 256 (S.A. Ankola 4 for 41)

West Zone 261 for 8 dec. (R.J. Shastri 62, R.K. Chauhan 6 for 62) and 163 (P.K. Gandhe 6 for 65)

Central Zone won by 179 runs

at M. Chinnaswamy Stadium, Bangalore

North Zone 317 (A.K. Sharma 61, V.S. Yadav 56, M. Prabhakar 55) and 356 for 9 dec. (K.P. Bhaskar 101 retired hurt, Maninder Singh 66 not out, V.S. Yadav 66, Venkatapathy Raju 4 for 110)

South Zone 367 (M. Azharuddin 153, C.M. Sharma 5 for 87) and 106 (Maninder Singh 6 for 23)

North Zone won by 200 runs

The off-spin bowling of Chauhan prompted Central Zone to a surprise victory over the strong West Zone side. Central went from 122 for 1 to 131 for 5, but they were saved by a fine innings from Amre. Chauhan then struck, and Shastri declared West Zone's innings closed when they were still 86 runs adrift, in an attempt to gain quick wickets. Central batted solidly in spite of Ankola's match figures of 9 for 108, and West Zone succumbed to the spinners for a second time.

India's captain Mohammad Azharuddin hit the first century of the season as South Zone took a 50-run lead over the North. Bhaskar Pillai responded with a century for North Zone and, crucially, shared a ninth-wicket stand of 104 with Maninder Singh before being forced to retire hurt. Maninder routed South Zone in their second innings to take North Zone into the final.

FINAL
NORTH ZONE *v.* CENTRAL ZONE
at Hyderabad

The Duleep Trophy final was played as a benefit match for V. Ramnarain of Hyderabad, but the game was ruined when rain prevented any play on the last two days.

Put in to bat in difficult conditions, North Zone struggled against the medium pace of Sanjeev Sharma, but a spirited last-wicket stand between Chetan Sharma and Maninder Singh took them to a creditable 268. The North Zone pace attack, containing three experienced Test players, revelled in the conditions and routed Central Zone who managed only 68 runs from the bat.

Batting a second time, North Zone emphasised their superiority before the rains came.

North Zone retained the trophy by virtue of their first-innings lead.

DEODHAR TROPHY

15 September 1992 *at Corporation Stadium, Calicut*

West Zone 137 (V.G. Kambli 56 not out, M. Prabhakar 4 for 13)

North Zone 138 for 5

North Zone won by 5 wickets

SEMI-FINALS

17 September 1992 *at M. Chinnaswamy Stadium, Bangalore*

Central Zone 214 for 8 (Yusuf Ali Khan 77, S. Banerjee 5 for 40)

East Zone 217 for 4 (J. Arun Lal 90)

East Zone won by 6 wickets

18 September 1992 *at Forest College Ground, Coimbatore*

South Zone 75 (C.M. Sharma 5 for 16)

North Zone 76 for 8

North Zone won by 2 wickets

FINAL

20 September 1992 *at Priyadarshini Municipal Stadium, Vishakhapatnam*

North Zone 254 for 4 (M. Prabhakar 117 not out, A.K. Sharma 62, K.P. Bhaskar 52)

East Zone 257 for 9 (L.S. Rajput 75, C.S. Pandit 52, S. Banerjee 50 not out)

East Zone won by 1 wicket

North Zone failed to add the one-day trophy to the Duleep Trophy in somewhat bizarre circumstances. Prabhakar played a sparkling innings after two wickets had gone for 7 and shared century stands with Ajay Sharma and Bhaskar Pillai. East Zone reached 248 for 9 in their 50 overs, but North Zone had bowled one over short in the allotted time span and were penalised 9 runs, so giving East Zone victory.

IRANI CUP
DELHI v. REST OF INDIA, at Delhi

Kirti Azad must have regretted his decision to ask Rest of India to bat first when he won the toss. In an innings lasting 343 minutes, Raman, captaining the Rest, hit 5 sixes (off Maninder Singh) and 23 fours as he savaged the

---

DULEEP TROPHY FINAL – NORTH ZONE v. CENTRAL ZONE
9, 10, 11, 12 and 13 September 1992 at Lal Bahadur, Hyderabad

NORTH ZONE

	FIRST INNINGS		SECOND INNINGS	
A. Jadeja	c A. Sharma, b Zaidi	25	c Pandey, b S. Sharma	40
N.S. Sidhu	c A. Sharma, b S. Sharma	20	c Gautam, b S. Sharma	17
Rajesh Puri	c Gautam, b Vaidya	10	c Pandey, b Zaidi	2
K.P. Bhaskar	c K.K. Patel, b Chauhan	5	(5) c S. Sharma, b Gandhe	24
A.K. Sharma	c Pandey, b S. Sharma	50	(4) lbw, b S. Sharma	0
A. Kaypee	c A. Sharma, b Zaidi	19	not out	14
M. Prabhakar	c Pandey, b S. Sharma	11	not out	15
Kapil Dev (capt)	lbw, b S. Sharma	18		
*V. Yadav	c A. Sharma, b S. Sharma	16		
C.M. Sharma	not out	37		
Maninder Singh	c and b Gandhe	31		
Extras	b 6, lb 2, w 1, nb 13	22	b 11, nb 8	19
	Penalty runs	4		16
		268	(for 5 wickets)	147

CENTRAL ZONE

	FIRST INNINGS	
Yusuf Ali Khan	c Yadav, b Kapil Dev	2
*K.K. Patel	c Puri, b Kapil Dev	3
A. Gautam	c Yadav, b Jadeja	1
P.K. Amre (capt)	c Bhaskar, b C.M. Sharma	14
Abhay Sharma	c Yadav, b Prabhakar	14
G.K. Pandey	lbw, b C.M. Sharma	0
P.V. Gandhe	c Bhaskar, b C.M. Sharma	24
Sanjeev Sharma	run out	0
R.K. Chauhan	c and b Prabhakar	10
A.W. Zaidi	not out	0
P.S. Vaidya	b Prabhakar	0
Extras	b 1, lb 3, nb 6	10
	Penalty runs	19
		97

	O	M	R	W	O	M	R	W
Vaidya	14.3	3	37	1	7	2	15	–
Zaidi	33	4	73	2	15	6	38	1
Sanjeev Sharma	25.3	6	66	5	16	1	33	3
Chauhan	19	4	38	1	3	–	14	–
Gandhe	14.1	3	21	1	8	2	20	1
Pandey	14	4	21	–				

	O	M	R	W
Kapil Dev	10	4	15	2
Prabhakar	11	3	31	3
C.M. Sharma	9	3	24	3
Jadeja	2	–	4	1

FALL OF WICKETS

1–52, 2–59, 3–72, 4–88, 5–145, 6–145, 7–173, 8–187, 9–203
1–28, 2–33, 3–34, 4–91, 5–106

FALL OF WICKETS

1–8, 2–9, 3–13, 4–34, 5–34, 6–57, 7–63, 8–78, 9–78

Umpires: S.K. Bansal & D.K. Sharma

Match drawn – North Zone won Trophy by virtue of first-innings lead

Ranji Trophy holders' attack. He shared stands of 117 with Sidhu and 198 with Kambli. The two left-handers routed Delhi's bowlers, and Kambli hit 14 fours in his 164-minute innings. The Rest ended the first day on 388 for 3, and some exciting batting by Amre and Yadav took them to 638 on the second day.

Chauhan took the wicket of Nayyar before the close, and Kumble's leg-breaks proved too much for Delhi on the third day. Forced to follow-on, they again fell to Kumble who finished with 13 for 138 in the match and ensured himself of a place in the side to tour South Africa. Azharuddin was named as captain of the side and, not surprisingly, there were places for Raman, Amre and Yadav, but – to the astonishment and anger of many – Kambli, who had shown good early-season form and had been the leading run-scorer in 1991–2, was not selected. He was to answer the selectors later in the season.

ENGLAND TOUR

3, 4 and **5** January 1993 *at Nahar Singh Stadium, Faridabad*

Delhi 286 (H. Sharma 88) and 140 for 2 dec. (A.K. Sharma 61 not out, Bantoo Singh 50 not out)
England XI 194 (M.A. Atherton 59, Kirti Azad 6 for 30) and 62 for 3

Match drawn

There was no happy beginning to England's tour of India. The party arrived in Delhi with storms still raging in England at the omission of David Gower, with Robin Smith injured, with news of Graham Gooch's domestic problems and with political and religious strife in various parts of India. On the field, things were no better. Put in to bat, Ranji Trophy holders Delhi blunted England's attack on a dead pitch for two sessions before showing more enterprise late in the day to end on 190 for 3. Hitesh Sharma, out early on the second morning for 88, was the backbone of the Delhi batting. At the close of the second day England fell apart against the off-spin of Delhi skipper Kirti Azad who enjoyed a spell of 3 for 8 in seven overs. He claimed three more wickets on the last morning after which Ajay Sharma and Bantoo Singh, once of Ealing CC, displayed some exciting shots. Delhi finally completed their moral victory by dismissing Gooch, Atherton and Stewart in the last two hours of the match.

8, 9 and **10** January 1993 *at K.D. Singh Babu Stadium, Lucknow*

Board President's XI 223 (V.G. Kambli 61 retired hurt, N.R. Mongia 55, J.P. Taylor 5 for 46) and 107 for 1 (N.S. Sidhu 57 not out)
England XI 307 for 9 dec. (M.W. Gatting 115, G.A. Gooch 77, N.D. Hirwani 4 for 78)

Match drawn

England gained more confidence from their second first-class match than they had done from their first. The opening day was reduced by bad light and was notable for the excitement caused by the fact that Chris Lewis caused two batsmen to retire hurt. One of them, Kambli, had shown a thrilling array of strokes, and a slight vulnerability outside the off stump, in scoring 61 off 84 balls. He suffered a bruised arm and did not play again in the match. Ajay Sharma returned, but the President's XI collapsed against Taylor on the second morning. Gooch and Gatting hit 131 for the visitors' first wicket, and Gatting hit England's first century of the tour. Hirwani and Maninder Singh troubled England with their spin. There was some exuberant hitting from Navjot Singh Sidhu who was particularly severe on John Emburey.

Ian Salisbury, originally selected to be a net bowler for the first few weeks of the tour of India before joining the England 'A' side in Australia, was asked to remain in India as a full member of the touring side.

13 January 1993 *at Ferozeshah Kotla Ground, Delhi*

England XI 245 for 8 (G.A. Gooch 85)
Board President's XI 246 for 1 (N.S. Sidhu 130 not out, A.K. Sharma 75 not out)

Board President's XI won by 9 wickets

Eight wickets in the Duleep Trophy final for Sanjeev Sharma. (David Munden/Sports-Line)

IRANI CUP – DELHI v. REST OF INDIA
27, 28, 29 and 30 September 1992 at Ferozeshah Kotla Ground, Delhi

REST OF INDIA

FIRST INNINGS

W.V. Raman (capt)	c Kirti Azad, b Prabhakar	184
N.S. Sidhu	c Nayyar, b Maninder Singh	59
V.G. Kambli	c Lamba, b A.K. Sharma	94
P.K. Amre	lbw, b Prabhakar	86
S. Banerjee	c Kirti Azad, b Wassan	26
Saurav Ganguly	c Vinayak, b Maninder Singh	13
*V. Yadav	c Vinayak, b Kirti Azad	82
A.R. Kumble	c Razdan, b Kirti Azad	20
R.K. Chauhan	b Kirti Azad	0
V. Prasad	not out	0
A. Kuruvilla	lbw, b Maninder Singh	0
Extras	b 2, lb 12, nb 20	34
	Penalty runs	40
		—
		638

DELHI

	FIRST INNINGS		SECOND INNINGS	
M. Nayyar	lbw, b Chauhan	42	run out	33
R. Lamba	c Ganguly, b Kumble	89	st Yadav, b Chauhan	39
Bantoo Singh	b Kumble	17	(5) c Kambli, b Kumble	69
A.K. Sharma	c and b Kumble	0	c Amre, b Chauhan	15
Sanjay Sharma	b Kuruvilla	7	(6) c Kambli, b Kumble	8
Kirti Azad (capt)	c Yadav, b Kumble	7	(7) c Kambli, b Kumble	14
M. Prabhakar	not out	27	(3) c Kambli, b Kumble	62
V. Razdan	lbw, b Kumble	0	b Kumble	2
*R. Vinayak	b Kumble	0	c Kambli, b Kumble	19
Maninder Singh	c and b Chauhan	24	(11) not out	2
A.S. Wassan	c Prasad, b Kumble	8	(10) c Banerjee, b Chauhan	9
Extras	b 7, nb 1	8	b 10, lb 5	15
		—		—
		229		287

	O	M	R	W		O	M	R	W	O	M	R	W
Prabhakar	31	4	117	2	Kuruvilla	15	2	44	1	10	–	34	–
Wassan	28	2	93	1	Prasad	11	2	32	–	9	1	38	–
Maninder Singh	49.1	8	218	3	Banerjee	8	2	26	–	2	–	8	–
Razdan	11	1	47	–	Chauhan	25	8	56	2	37	8	118	3
Kirti Azad	8	2	26	3	Kumble	21	4	64	7	35	10	74	6
A.K. Sharma	17	2	75	1									
Nayyar	2	–	8										

FALL OF WICKETS

1–117, 2–315, 3–367, 4–426, 5–465, 6–532, 7–597, 8–598, 9–598

FALL OF WICKETS

1–79, 2–144, 3–144, 4–152, 5–167, 6–167, 7–167, 8–167, 9–218

1–59, 2–127, 3–155, 4–157, 5–203, 6–219, 7–235, 8–268, 9–285

Umpires: V.K. Ramaswamy & P.D. Reporter

Rest of India won by an innings and 122 runs

England received a terrible battering in the 50-over game against a select eleven captained by Maninder Singh. Gooch and Stewart put on 83 for England's first wicket without dominating the bowling, but of the later batsmen, only Reeve and Emburey batted with authority. The President's XI lost Bhave at 54, and Ganguly retired hurt for 7. After this Sidhu and Ajay Sharma slaughtered the England bowling. Sidhu hit 130 off 154 balls, and Emburey again came in for severe punishment. His savaging in this match meant that he had been hit for 12 sixes in three innings. The President's XI won with 14 balls to spare.

15 January 1993 *at Ferozeshah Kotla Ground, Delhi*

Bishen Bedi's XI 202 for 6 (S. Chopra 50 not out)
England XI 203 for 8 (G.A. Hick 93)

England XI won by 2 wickets

The religious tension and disturbances in Ahmedabad brought about the cancellation of the first one-day international which was due to be played in the city on 16 January. In an attempt to offer the England party some practice, Bishen Bedi hastily got together a side to play a 50-over game in Delhi. The match was 'friendly' in every sense, with Kapil Dev batting but not bowling or fielding.

 ONE-DAY INTERNATIONAL SERIES
Matches One and Two

After considerable debate it was decided that the one-day international which had been scheduled for Ahmedabad would be replaced by a game at Gwalior, which would be the last in the series, to be played on 5 March. The game in the most beautiful settings at Jaipur now became the first of the series.

Gooch won the toss and asked India to bat. There was immediate success when Jarvis bowled Sidhu with his second ball of the morning. Jarvis also had Kambli

FIRST ONE-DAY INTERNATIONAL – INDIA *v.* ENGLAND
18 January 1993 at Sawai Mansingh Stadium, Jaipur

INDIA

M. Prabhakar	b Jarvis	25
N.S. Sidhu	b Jarvis	0
V.G. Kambli	not out	100
M. Azharuddin (capt)	lbw, b Lewis	6
S.R. Tendulkar	not out	82
P.K. Amre		
Kapil Dev		
*V. Yadav		
J. Srinath		
A.R. Kumble		
Venkatapathy Raju		
Extras	b 2, lb 7, w 1	10
(48 overs)	(for 3 wickets)	223

ENGLAND

G.A. Gooch (capt)	lbw, b Kapil Dev	4
*A.J. Stewart	c Yadav, b Kapil Dev	91
R.A. Smith	c and b Prabhakar	16
M.W. Gatting	b Kumble	30
N.H. Fairbrother	not out	46
G.A. Hick	run out	13
D.A. Reeve	lbw, b Prabhakar	2
C.C. Lewis	not out	6
J.E. Emburey		
P.A.J. DeFreitas		
P.W. Jarvis		
Extras	b 3, lb 8, w 3, nb 2	16
(48 overs)	(for 6 wickets)	224

	O	M	R	W
DeFreitas	9	3	40	–
Jarvis	10	–	49	2
Reeve	10	–	37	–
Lewis	9	–	26	1
Emburey	8	–	49	–
Gooch	2	–	13	–

	O	M	R	W
Kapil Dev	10	1	36	2
Prabhakar	10	–	41	2
Srinath	10	–	47	–
Venkatapathy Raju	8	1	35	–
Kumble	10	–	54	1

FALL OF WICKETS
1–0, 2–31, 3–59

FALL OF WICKETS
1–29, 2–83, 3–145, 4–161, 5–200, 6–203

Umpires: S. Venkataraghavan & S.K. Bansai   Man of the Match: V.G. Kambli   *England won by 4 wickets*

SECOND ONE-DAY INTERNATIONAL – INDIA *v.* ENGLAND
21 January 1993 at Chandigarh

ENGLAND

G.A. Gooch (capt)	c Tendulkar, b Srinath	7
*A.J. Stewart	c Azharuddin, b Kapil Dev	7
R.A. Smith	lbw, b Kumble	42
M.W. Gatting	c and b Srinath	0
N.H. Fairbrother	lbw, b Venkatapathy Raju	7
G.A. Hick	b Kapil Dev	56
D.A. Reeve	not out	33
C.C. Lewis	not out	16
P.A.J. DeFreitas		
I.D.K. Salisbury		
P.W. Jarvis		
Extras	lb 13, w 13, nb 4	30
(50 overs)	(for 6 wickets)	198

INDIA

N.S. Sidhu	c Reeve, b DeFreitas	76
M. Prabhakar	c Reeve, b Lewis	36
V.G. Kambli	c and b Jarvis	9
M. Azharuddin (capt)	lbw, b Reeve	36
S.R. Tendulkar	lbw, b DeFreitas	1
P.K. Amre	not out	24
Kapil Dev	not out	5
*V. Yadav		
A.R. Kumble		
J. Srinath		
Venkatapathy Raju		
Extras	lb 3, w 5, nb 6	14
(45.1 overs)	(for 5 wickets)	201

	O	M	R	W
Kapil Dev	10	2	40	2
Prabhakar	8	–	30	–
Srinath	10	2	34	2
Tendulkar	3	–	16	–
Venkatapathy Raju	9	–	28	1
Kumble	10	–	37	1

	O	M	R	W
DeFreitas	10	1	31	2
Jarvis	10	1	43	1
Reeve	6.1	–	33	1
Lewis	10	–	47	1
Salisbury	8	1	42	–
Gatting	1	–	2	–

FALL OF WICKETS
1–19, 2–20, 3–22, 4–49, 5–132, 6–153

FALL OF WICKETS
1–79, 2–99, 3–148, 4–161, 5–195

Umpires: R.V. Ramani & V.K. Ramaswamy   Man of the Match: N.S. Sidhu   *India won by 5 wickets*

dropped by Hick at slip before he bowled Prabhakar with an in-swinger in his fifth over. The opener offered no shot. When Lewis trapped Azharuddin – a captain on trial – leg before, India were 59 for 3 in 20 overs.

There now followed an exhilarating stand of 164 in 28 overs between Tendulkar and Kambli. Tendulkar, in splendid form, hit 82 off 81 deliveries; and Kambli, celebrating his 21st birthday, survived an uncertain start against the moving ball to hit his first century in a one-day international. He faced 146 balls and hit 9 fours and a six, off Emburey.

Gooch was dropped off Kapil Dev in the first over of the England innings before being lbw in the 11th. Smith struggled a little until he was well caught and bowled off Prabhakar's slower ball. Gatting suggested more permanence and belligerence, but he chopped on to Kumble who bowled with cunning variation.

Slow to find his touch, Alec Stewart had begun to accelerate when Kapil Dev returned to have him caught behind. England needed 63 runs to win and had less than 12 overs in which to get them. Fairbrother played some of his ingenious swats and shots to keep the score moving, but Hick was stranded, then run out and Reeve went immediately. With two overs left, England wanted 19 runs and, remarkably, Kapil Dev, who had bowled admirably, conceded 13 runs in the penultimate. It still seemed that Prabhakar, bowling a full length, would clinch victory for India. His fifth ball went through to the wicket-keeper, and Fairbrother and Lewis went for a suicidal bye. Yadav's throw missed the stumps, and Prabhakar, following through, gathered the ball and shied at the stumps at the bowler's end, only to concede an overthrow. Two runs had come where none should have been given. Lewis and Fairbrother conjured the winning run from the last ball of the match. Fairbrother had turned the match with his 46 off 40 balls.

Kambli had injured a hamstring towards the end of his innings in the first one-day international and had been unable to field, but he was declared fit for the second match, and India were unchanged. England brought in Salisbury for Emburey, who was unfit.

Azharuddin won an important toss, and England batted on a pitch that was damp, green and, initially, difficult. Stewart square-cut and was caught low down at point. Gooch played a poor shot and was caught at mid-wicket, while Gatting misjudged the pace and skied the ball. When Fairbrother played across the line and was leg before, England were 49 for 4 and sinking fast, but Azharuddin failed to press home the advantage, and Hick and Smith added 83 in 21 overs without ever being subjected to too much pressure. Reeve and Lewis plundered in the unorthodox manner which has become the norm in the later stages of the one-day game, and England reached 198.

The inadequacy of this total was soon apparent as Sidhu and Prabhakar began the Indian innings with 79 in 21 overs. Kambli was dropped and lasted only briefly after his escape, but Sidhu hit Salisbury for 2 sixes as he rushed to 76 off 107 balls. Although Azharuddin and Tendulkar fell in quick succession, there was never any doubt as to who would win.

23, 24 and **25** January 1993 *at BOS Engineering College Ground, Cuttack*

England XI 408 for 4 dec. (R.A. Smith 149 not out, G.A. Gooch 102 not out) and 146 for 2 dec. (M.A. Atherton 80 not out)

Indian Under-25 XI 273 (A.R. Khurasia 103, G. Pandey 54) and 53 for 1

Match drawn

On Saturday, 23 January 1993, Graham Gooch hit what the cricket world believed to be his 100th hundred. Some days later, however, the ICC decreed that the century he scored for the *rebel* touring side against South Africa in 1982 was not to be considered as first-class, although the runs he scored for Western Province during South Africa's period of isolation were to be recognised. It has generally been accepted that the status of a match is determined by the home control board, and the eleven which Gooch represented in 1982 was invited to go to South Africa by the South African Board. The present writer deplored Gooch's decision to go to the Republic at the time, although Gooch was breaking no ICC code by doing so, but one accepted that the runs scored on that tour were first-class, for all runs scored in the Currie Cup and Bowl during South Africa's period of exile are considered first-class. Now, 11 years on, a petulant, political decision has decreed that the runs scored in the representative matches in that tour are not to be so regarded. The sufferers – and the only sufferers – are Gooch, McEwan, Rice, Kirsten and the others who played at that time. The anger and despair that one feels towards those who have been entrusted with administering a great game grow daily.

To return to Cuttack, Robin Smith also hit a welcome century, and Khurasia, having retired hurt early in his innings, returned to respond with 2 sixes and 15 fours for the Young Indians. Devon Malcolm ended the home side's innings with three wickets in four balls, having earlier been laid low by a virus.

 FIRST TEST MATCH
INDIA *v.* ENGLAND, at Calcutta

In assessing India's recent moderate record in Test cricket, it was easy to forget that the series against England was, in fact, their first home series for five years. They had played just one home Test in that time, against Sri Lanka in November 1990. This Test match had been the one match in which Azharuddin had led India to victory. He had captained India on 17 occasions, but only the aforesaid match against Sri Lanka had been at home.

Azharuddin had returned from South Africa amid severe criticism and calls for his deposition. The selectors had named him as captain for the first Test only, and gave first Test caps to Kambli, controversially omitted from the

The second one-day international at Chandigarh. (Ben Radford/ Allsport)

TOP: *Alec Stewart guides England to victory in the first one-day international in Jaipur. (Ben Radford/Allsport)*

ABOVE: *Azharuddin hits Salisbury for six during his breathtaking innings of 182. (David Munden/Sports-Line)*

side that toured South Africa, and to the young off-spinner Rajesh Chauhan. In the absence of Shastri, convalescing, Prabhakar was promoted to open the innings, so giving India the chance to play three spinners.

In contrast, England – whose original selection and preparation had given a disturbing hint of inflexibility and lack of imagination – chose to field four seam bowlers of moderate accomplishment. Ian Salisbury, not named in the original party, was the only spinner included, and the front-line spinners, Tufnell and Emburey – whose selection for the tour will for ever remain a mystery – were not chosen. Neither had bowled well on the tour, but they were all that England had to fall back on in the conditions.

This was Gooch's 100th Test match, but he was not to

enjoy a match of celebration. Azharuddin won the toss, and India batted.

England had given a first Test cap to Taylor, but the Northamptonshire pace bowler's line was depressingly wayward, and Stewart spent much time scrambling at wides outside the off stump. Taylor was finally rewarded with a first Test wicket when Sidhu, who had played with rigid concentration for 101 minutes, edged to slip. Sidhu had already been dropped in this position by Gatting when on 4. At lunch, India were 61 for 1 from 29 overs.

Kambli had looked uncertain outside the off stump where Jarvis pitched most of his deliveries, and he finally edged a wide ball to second slip. Prabhakar, who had done an admirable job, slashed at Salisbury's fifth ball and was splendidly caught by Lewis at slip. At this stage, England could be well satisfied, but then came Tendulkar and Azharuddin. Having first established themselves, they tore the England attack apart, adding 123 at a run a minute. At tea, India were 144 for 3 from 57 overs, and in the 15 overs after tea, India's captain and heir apparent scored 69.

Tendulkar had just completed 50 off 117 balls when he played a careless shot at a ball wide of the off stump and became Hick's third victim at slip. That was England's last success of the day. Azharuddin, 79 when Tendulkar departed, continued to shred the bowling. He reached his 12th Test century, his sixth against England – a record – in 174 minutes off 114 balls. When bad light ended play early he was on 114, and India were 263 for 4.

There was a fourth slip catch for Hick early on the second morning when Amre drove at an out-swinger. Nothing could subdue Azharuddin, however, who dominated a stand of 68 in 70 minutes with a rather hesitant Kapil Dev. Kapil edged Hick to slip, and Azharuddin's glorious knock came to an end when he flicked the same bowler to mid-wicket. The Indian captain was in majestic form and was particularly impressive with his drives square of the wicket and with the manner in which he whipped the ball off his legs. Azharuddin's innings had lasted for 326 minutes and he had faced 197 balls, hitting 26 fours and a six.

Malcolm and Hick, whose off-spin brought him 3 for 19, underlining the errors in the England selection, quickly finished off the tail.

Facing a total of 371 which had been scored at more than three runs an over, England had a dreadful start. Eight runs came from Kapil Dev's opening over, but the first ball of Prabhakar's over saw Stewart, who had been

Indian off-spinner Chauhan captures his first Test wicket. Gatting is bowled. (Patrick Eagar)

FIRST TEST MATCH – INDIA v. ENGLAND
29, 30 and 31 January, 1 and 2 February 1993 at Eden Gardens, Calcutta

INDIA

	FIRST INNINGS			SECOND INNINGS	
M. Prabhakar	c Lewis, b Salisbury	46	b Hick		13
N.S. Sidhu	c Hick, b Taylor	13	st Stewart, b Hick		37
V.G. Kambli	c Hick, b Jarvis	16	not out		18
S.R. Tendulkar	c Hick, b Malcolm	50	not out		9
M. Azharuddin (capt)	c Gooch, b Hick	182			
P.K. Amre	c Hick, b Jarvis	12			
Kapil Dev	c Lewis, b Hick	13			
*K.S. More	not out	4			
A.R. Kumble	b Malcolm	0			
R.K. Chauhan	b Malcolm	2			
Venkatapathy Raju	c Salisbury, b Hick	1			
Extras	b 6, lb 6, w 10, nb 10	32	lb 4, nb 1		5
		371	(for 2 wickets)		**82**

ENGLAND

	FIRST INNINGS			SECOND INNINGS	
G.A. Gooch (capt)	c Azharuddin, b Raju	17	st More, b Kumble		18
*A.J. Stewart	b Prabhakar	0	c Tendulkar, b Kumble		49
M.W. Gatting	b Chauhan	33	b Chauhan		81
R.A. Smith	c Amre, b Kumble	1	c More, b Chauhan		8
G.A. Hick	b Kumble	1	lbw, b Raju		25
N.H. Fairbrother	c More, b Kumble	17	c sub (Raman), b Kumble		25
I.D.K. Salisbury	c More, b Chauhan	28	(9) c More, b Kapil Dev		26
C.C. Lewis	b Venkatapathy Raju	21	(7) c Amre, b Raju		16
P.W. Jarvis	c Prabhakar, b Raju	4	(8) lbw, b Raju		6
J.P. Taylor	st More, b Chauhan	17	not out		17
D.E. Malcolm	not out	4	lbw, b Kapil Dev		0
Extras	b 8, lb 8, w 4	20	lb 13, nb 2		15
		163			**286**

	O	M	R	W	O	M	R	W
Malcolm	24	3	67	3	6	1	16	–
Jarvis	27	5	72	2	5.2	1	23	–
Lewis	23	5	64	–	3	1	5	–
Taylor	19	2	65	1	3	1	9	–
Salisbury	17	2	72	1	6	3	16	–
Hick	12.5	5	19	3	6	1	9	2

	O	M	R	W	O	M	R	W
Kapil Dev	6	1	18	–	8.2	5	12	2
Prabhakar	9	3	10	1	9	4	26	–
Kumble	29	8	50	3	40	16	76	3
Venkatapathy Raju	27	14	39	3	35	9	80	3
Chauhan	29.1	15	30	3	45	17	79	2

FALL OF WICKETS

1–49, 2–78, 3–93, 4–216, 5–278, 6–346, 7–362, 8–368, 9–370
1–51, 2–62

FALL OF WICKETS

1–8, 2–37, 3–38, 4–40, 5–87, 6–89, 7–111, 8–119, 9–149
1–48, 2–111, 3–145, 4–192, 5–192, 6–216, 7–234, 8–254, 9–286

Umpires: P.D. Reporter & S. Venkataraghavan

India won by 8 wickets

keeping wicket for nine hours and was now opening the batting, attempt to withdraw his bat from an in-swinger, only to touch it into his stumps.

Gooch and Gatting batted placidly until tea when the score was 29, but on the resumption, the England innings began to fall apart. In the 20th over, Gooch, leaden-footed, prodded at Venkatapathy Raju and was caught at slip. Three overs later, having already revealed a total incomprehension as to the mysteries of spin, Robin Smith pushed forward to Kumble and was taken at short-leg. Four overs and two runs later, Hick fatally played back to a ball from Kumble that hurried through, and England were 40 for 4, with only one recognised batsman remaining to partner Gatting.

The former England captain had batted for nearly 2¾ hours and faced 143 deliveries when he played back to Chauhan and was bowled off his pads, a first Test wicket for the young off-spinner. The light faded, and Salisbury remained with Fairbrother for the last two overs. England, 88 for 5, could only hope for a miracle and salvation. Thoughts of victory had long since departed.

England's sorry state had been caused in part by the passive way in which Gooch and Gatting, in particular, had allowed the Indian spinners to dominate. In his maiden Test, off-spinner Chauhan conceded just one run an over, and, indeed, the scoring rate throughout the England innings was barely 1.5.

In the second over of the third day, Fairbrother drove at a wide-ish ball from Kumble and was caught behind. All energy now had to be focused on saving the follow-on. Salisbury did his share with unerring defence; Lewis chose the belligerent manner. He batted for over an hour, hit 4 fours and looked set until he went only half-forward to Venkatapathy Raju, who quickly had Jarvis taken at slip also. Taylor and Salisbury held out for more than an hour and Taylor played some robust shots before losing patience and charging down the wicket at Chauhan.

Salisbury batted heroically for over three hours and displayed superb temperament before being last out when he edged to the keeper. England followed-on 208 runs in arrears.

Gooch and Stewart scored 48 in 52 minutes before Gooch was out in bizarre manner. Kumble got a leg-break to turn and bounce sharply, and Gooch overbalanced. He lifted his toe fractionally and held his position as if frozen. More, reacting to the situation, pulled off a slow-motion stumping. Stewart batted with some confidence before playing slightly across the line at Kumble to be caught bat-and-pad at silly point. Gatting was determined, and England closed with hope in their hearts at 128 for 2.

Those hopes diminished when Smith, ponderous against the turning ball, offered More a catch off Chauhan, and Gatting, having swept purposefully and positively, swept once too often and was bowled by the off-spinner. Hick had learned from Gatting's decisive approach, but once again he promised more than he achieved, falling leg before to a tentative shot on the first ball he faced after Gatting's departure.

There was determined resistance from Fairbrother, Salisbury, Lewis and Taylor, but these were brave gestures as England sank more and more quickly to defeat.

Needing 79 to win, Prabhakar and Sidhu hit 36 in 12 overs before the end of the day, and both fell victim to Hick before victory was achieved on the last morning.

Azharuddin took the individual award for his brilliant innings and was confirmed as India's captain for the rest of the series. For England, serious problems had come to the fore, not the least of which was the inability of their batsmen to play the Indian spinners on a pitch which offered slow turn.

The umpiring had been of an impressive standard, and former Test cricketer Venkataraghavan had made an excellent debut. He was the first former Indian player to umpire a Test match. In search of excuses for the ineptitude of the England display, Ted Dexter commissioned a study into the levels of pollution in Indian cities, an action which brought an official government rebuke.

5, 6 and 7 February 1993 *at Vishakhapatnam*

England XI 253 for 6 dec. (R.A. Smith 82, R.J. Blakey 63 not out, J.E. Emburey 53) and 150 for 2 (N.H. Fairbrother 78 not out)

Rest of India XI 345 for 9 dec. (S.V. Manjrekar 96, J. Paranjpe 64, S.R. Tendulkar 61, A. Kapoor 54, P.C.R. Tufnell 4 for 95)

Match drawn

A somewhat tedious display of batting by the tourists, justified in view of their need for as much practice as possible before the second Test, was followed by some sparkling hitting from the Indians and by dissent. Blakey missed a straightforward stumping in Tufnell's first over, an over which also included two no-balls. Tufnell, who suffered at the hands of Tendulkar and the cultured Manjrekar, later reacted petulantly, had an exchange of words with the umpire and was fined £500 by the tour manager, Bob Bennett. Happily, Tufnell showed his better side on the final day when he took four wickets and made his recall to the Test side a certainty.

SECOND TEST MATCH
INDIA *v.* ENGLAND, at Madras

Not surprisingly, India fielded an unchanged side for the second Test match; for England, selection was not so simple. Tufnell replaced Taylor, a sensible change, but problems were compounded when Gooch, who had not been in the best of health during the first Test, withdrew from the side shortly before the start with stomach problems. He, Gatting and Smith had eaten prawns in a Chinese restaurant on the evening before the match. All three were laid low, and both Gatting and Smith were unable to field for periods on the opening day. With Gooch incapacitated, Stewart took over the captaincy and opened the innings with Smith. Atherton had not been fit for the first Test, but he was fit for selection for the

Madras match. Nevertheless, although he was the only regular opener in the party apart from Gooch, he was not chosen. Blakey was brought in to relieve Stewart of the wicket-keeping duties. What must Hegg, Metson, Krikken, Marsh, Russell and several others have thought? The stupidity of the original selection of the England party was once more exposed.

Azharuddin won the toss, India batted and by the end of the first day, having scored at three runs an over, they were immune from defeat. Malcolm tested Prabhakar with some short-pitched bowling, but the all-rounder again did a most capable job. In 16 overs, he and Sidhu scored 41 before Prabhakar edged a lifting ball to Blakey. Any hopes that this success would bring about a collapse soon disappeared. India lost only the wicket of Kambli in the afternoon session while 101 runs were scored. Kambli, again impressive, was leg before when he played only half-forward to Hick. In the final session of the day, Sidhu and Tendulkar added 104. Sidhu, shedding the character of the one-day batsman, played with unrelenting concentration to close the day on 104, made out of 275 in 373 minutes. It was an invaluable innings, providing the rock on which an Indian victory could be built. Tendulkar, not surprisingly, was more expansive and was particularly severe on the England spinners.

The drop of the century? Gatting misses More off the simplest of chances. (Patrick Eagar)

SECOND TEST MATCH – INDIA *v.* ENGLAND
11, 12, 13, 14 and 15 February 1993 at M.A. Chidambaram Stadium, Madras

INDIA

	FIRST INNINGS	
M. Prabhakar	c Blakey, b Lewis	27
N.S. Sidhu	c Hick, b Jarvis	106
V.G. Kambli	lbw, b Hick	59
S.R. Tendulkar	c and b Salisbury	165
M. Azharuddin (capt)	c Smith, b Jarvis	6
P.K. Amre	c Jarvis, b Salisbury	78
Kapil Dev	not out	66
*K.S. More	not out	26
A.R. Kumble		
R.K. Chauhan		
Venkatapathy Raju		
Extras	lb 10, w 2, nb 15	27
	(for 6 wickets, dec.)	560

ENGLAND

	FIRST INNINGS		SECOND INNINGS	
R.A. Smith	lbw, b Kumble	17	c Amre, b Kumble	56
A.J. Stewart (capt)	c sub (Raman), b Raju	74	lbw, b Kapil Dev	0
G.A. Hick	lbw, b Chauhan	64	c Tendulkar, b Kapil	0
M.W. Gatting	run out	2	lbw, b Raju	19
N.H. Fairbrother	c Kapil Dev, b Chauhan	83	c Prabhakar, b Kumble	9
*R.J. Blakey	b Venkatapathy Raju	0	b Kumble	6
C.C. Lewis	c Azharuddin, b Raju	0	c and b Kumble	117
I.D.K. Salisbury	lbw, b Kumble	4	b Kumble	12
P.W. Jarvis	c sub (Raman), b Raju	8	c Tendulkar, b Kumble	2
P.C.R. Tufnell	c Azharuddin, b Chauhan	2	not out	22
D.E. Malcolm	not out	0	c sub (Raman), b Raju	0
Extras	b 14, lb 16, nb 2	32	b 4, lb 5	9
		286		252

	O	M	R	W
Malcolm	27	7	87	–
Jarvis	28	7	72	2
Lewis	11	1	40	1
Tufnell	41	3	132	–
Hick	29	2	77	1
Salisbury	29	1	142	2

	O	M	R	W	O	M	R	W
Prabhakar	3	2	7	–	3	2	4	–
Kumble	25	9	61	2	21	7	64	6
Chauhan	39.3	16	69	3	21	4	59	–
Venkatapathy Raju	54	21	103	4	23.1	3	76	2
Kapil Dev	4	–	11	–	11	5	36	2
Tendulkar	2	1	5	–	2	1	4	–

FALL OF WICKETS

1–41, 2–149, 3–296, 4–324, 5–442, 6–499

FALL OF WICKETS

1–46, 2–157, 3–166, 4–175, 5–179, 6–179, 7–220, 8–277, 9–279
1–10, 2–12, 3–71, 4–82, 5–88, 6–99, 7–172, 8–186, 9–241

Umpires: V.K. Ramaswamy & Prof. R.S. Rathore

India won by an innings and 22 runs

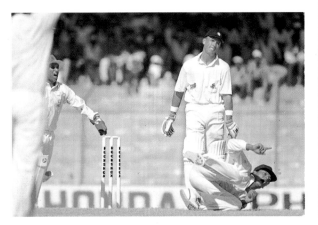

TOP: *The bizarre second-innings dismissal of Gooch – stumped More, bowled Kumble. (Patrick Eagar)*

ABOVE: *Stewart is taken at silly point by Raman. (Chris Cole/Allsport)*

ABOVE: *Sachin Tendulkar launches his blistering attack on the England bowling in the second Test, at Madras. (Patrick Eagar)*

BELOW: *A maiden Test century for Chris Lewis, but all in vain. (Chris Cole/Allsport)*

Sidhu lasted only half an hour on the second morning, and Azharuddin mis-hooked to square-leg after 25 minutes at the crease. By then, however, Tendulkar had reached his fifth Test century, a brilliant innings, studded with shots of exquisite timing and rare power and beauty. He and Amre added 118. Amre was dropped by Emburey fourth ball, but he played some fine shots, hitting one of Tufnell's 12 no-balls for six and clouting 8 fours in his 154-ball innings. He finally fell to a running catch at deep extra cover.

Tendulkar had been dismissed for 165, his highest Test score, when the score had been 442. He had faced 296 balls and hit a six and 24 fours. Following the departure of Amre, Kapil Dev reached 66 off 75 balls, with a six and 8 fours. During the course of his innings, he became the first man in Test history to achieve 5,000 Test runs and 400 Test wickets. As he has done for most of his wonderful career, Kapil enjoyed himself.

On the first day, England had fielded four substitutes on occasions, and on the second day, they were greatly handicapped in that Lewis was unable to bowl because of a thigh strain.

Azharuddin's declaration left England nine overs to negotiate at the end of the second day. Stewart and Smith managed them safely and scored 19 runs.

Bemused by the spinners who pose problems to which he has no answers, Smith played back to Kumble's top-spinner and was leg before. Hick and Stewart scored 47 in the first hour after lunch, but thereafter the innings began to grind to a halt. Hick was adjudged leg before as he offered no shot and moved back; and Stewart now retreated into his shell, playing almost every other ball with his pad and, astonishingly, escaping any appeal from the Indian spinners.

Gatting had had a dreadful match. He had dropped More off the simplest chance one has seen offered in Test cricket, and now he contrived to get out in extraordinary manner. He went down the wicket to Venkatapathy Raju, got an inside edge onto his pad from whence the ball squirted to short-leg. Amre quickly picked the ball up and hit the stumps before Gatting could complete his U-turn.

Nine runs – but 14 overs – later, Stewart was caught bat/pad at silly point. He had played a strange innings, the pushes with the pad being punctuated by some graceful shots. He faced 269 balls in his 312-minute stay. Blakey lasted 21 minutes before dragging the 17th ball he faced onto his stumps. He had kept wicket tidily but as a batsman, the initial reason for his selection, he looked well short of Test class.

Lewis was taken at slip off a fine, spitting delivery from Venkatapathy Raju, and Salisbury got a harsh decision from umpire Rathore when he played back to a googly. England closed at 221 for 7, still 140 short of avoiding the follow-on. All hopes rested on Fairbrother, unbeaten on 38.

At last playing his natural game in a Test match, Fairbrother reached 83 on the fourth morning. In all, he faced 159 balls and hit a six and 10 fours before edging to slip. His heroics could not save England from having to follow-on, and disaster tumbled upon disaster.

Stewart played across the line and was hit on the back foot. Hick went in Kapil Dev's first over after lunch, driving at an out-swinger, and the great Indian all-rounder had smoothed the way for the spinners.

Gatting was dropped by More off Kapil Dev before he had scored, but he fell sweeping at Venkatapathy Raju. Fairbrother tried to repeat the fireworks of the morning but skied to mid-off, by which time both Smith, after a gritty innings of 89 balls, and Blakey had become Kumble's first victims. Smith pushed a low catch to short-leg, and Blakey offered no shot. England were 99 for 6 and facing humiliation.

As Salisbury again showed fine temperament and resolve, Lewis took the attack to India. On a pitch which was offering turn, Lewis hit his first Test century off 112 balls. He reached 95 and went down the pitch to hit Venkatapathy Raju into the crowd for six. It was a glorious and fitting climax to an excitingly defiant knock.

Both Salisbury, beaten by the top-spinner, and Jarvis, brilliantly taken at leg slip, fell to Kumble before the close which came with England on 231 for 8.

It took India only 10 overs to finish the game on the last morning. Lewis mis-timed a drive to give Kumble his sixth wicket of the innings, and Malcolm was taken at silly point off the left-arm spin of Venkatapathy Raju. This gave India their biggest ever win over England. They had outclassed England in every department of the game, having supported their excellent bowling with outstanding fielding. Their batting was a class above England's, and Tendulkar, rightly, took the individual award.

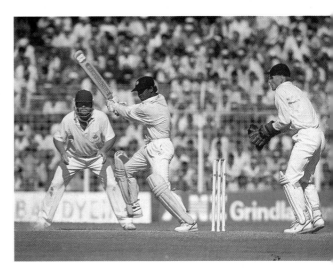

ABOVE RIGHT: *Graeme Hick comes of age. He pulls a ball to the boundary during his innings of 178 in the third Test in Bombay. (Ben Radford/Allsport)*

RIGHT: *Vinod Kambli in all his glory – 224 in the third Test match. (David Munden/Sports-Line)*

The beginning of the collapse – Atherton and Stewart come to rest at the same end. (Patrick Eagar)

THIRD TEST MATCH
INDIA *v.* ENGLAND, at Bombay

India fielded the same side for the third Test in succession. Gooch returned to lead England and Atherton was recalled, but Blakey was retained and kept wicket although Stewart had come on the tour as the first-choice keeper. Emburey replaced Salisbury who, like Tufnell, had suffered great punishment at Madras, and DeFreitas came in for Malcolm while Jarvis, rather unluckily, was also omitted.

Some commentators on the game had conjectured that if England had won the toss at Madras, they might well have won the game. At Bombay, India were to disprove that theory. Gooch won the toss, England batted and, at lunch, they were 62 for 4. Gooch was the first to go, edging Kapil Dev to the keeper. Low comedy followed. Stewart and Atherton found themselves at the same end. More missed the return from the field, but the ball was recovered and the wicket broken while Stewart and Atherton continued their disagreement as to who was to blame. Smith was very well caught, low off an inside

THIRD TEST MATCH – INDIA *v.* ENGLAND
19, 20, 21, 22 and 23 February 1993 at Wankhede Stadium, Bombay

ENGLAND

	FIRST INNINGS		SECOND INNINGS	
G.A. Gooch (capt)	c More, b Kapil Dev	4	b Prabhakar	8
A.J. Stewart	run out	13	lbw, b Prabhakar	10
M.A. Atherton	c Prabhakar, b Kumble	37	c More, b Prabhakar	11
R.A. Smith	c More, b Raju	2	b Kumble	62
M.W. Gatting	c Kapil Dev, b Raju	23	st More, b Chauhan	61
G.A. Hick	c Kapil Dev,		c Amre, b Kumble	47
	b Prabhakar	178		
*R.J. Blakey	lbw, b Kumble	1	b Kumble	0
C.C. Lewis	lbw, b Kumble	49	c More, b Raju	3
J.E. Emburey	c More, b Kapil Dev	12	c Tendulkar, b Kumble	1
P.A.J. DeFreitas	lbw, b Kapil Dev	11	st More, b Raju	12
P.C.R. Tufnell	not out	2	not out	2
Extras	b 4, lb 5, w 2, nb 4	15	b 4, lb 6, w 1, nb 1	12
		347		229

INDIA

	FIRST INNINGS	
N.S. Sidhu	c Smith, b Tufnell	79
M. Prabhakar	c Blakey, b Hick	44
V.G. Kambli	c Gatting, b Lewis	224
S.R. Tendulkar	lbw, b Tufnell	78
M. Azharuddin (capt)	lbw, b Lewis	26
P.K. Amre	c DeFreitas, b Hick	57
Kapil Dev	c DeFreitas, b Emburey	22
*K.S. More	c Lewis, b Emburey	0
A.R. Kumble	c Atherton, b Tufnell	16
R.K. Chauhan	c Atherton, b Tufnell	15
Venkatapathy Raju	not out	0
Extras	b 5, lb 14, w 5, nb 6	30
		591

	O	M	R	W	O	M	R	W		O	M	R	W
Kapil Dev	15	3	35	3	7	1	21	–	DeFreitas	20	4	75	–
Prabhakar	13	2	52	1	11	4	28	3	Lewis	42	9	114	2
Venkatapathy Raju	44	8	102	2	26.5	7	68	2	Emburey	59	14	144	2
Kumble	40	4	95	3	26	9	70	4	Tufnell	39.3	6	142	4
Chauhan	23	7	54	–	12	5	32	1	Hick	29	3	97	2

FALL OF WICKETS

1–11, 2–25, 3–30, 4–58, 5–116, 6–118, 7–211, 8–262, 9–279
1–17, 2–26, 3–34, 4–155, 5–181, 6–181, 7–206, 8–214, 9–215

FALL OF WICKETS

1–109, 2–174, 3–368, 4–418, 5–519, 6–560, 7–560, 8–563, 9–591

Umpires: P.D. Reporter & S. Venkataraghavan

India won by an innings and 15 runs

edge, and Gatting, trying to turn a ball to leg, was taken at slip, a very poor shot.

At lunch, Atherton was 14 and Hick had not scored. In the afternoon, they had seemed to be reviving England when Atherton, losing patience, hit Kumble to deep mid-on. Blakey went immediately and, at 118 for 6, England were in deep trouble. The response offered by Hick and Lewis was initially passive, but Lewis' innings was, in many respects, even more praiseworthy than his innings at Madras. With the century partnership in sight, Lewis played back to Kumble and was gone. Hick was then 77, and with Emburey giving typically stubborn support, he now proceeded to move with greater confidence and ease of rhythm. At the close, England had climbed to 239 for 7, and Hick, 99, remained their abiding hope.

England's adopted son duly came of Test age on the second morning. He pushed the third ball of the day, bowled by Chauhan, wide of cover and went through for the single which brought him his first Test hundred.

Emburey sparred at Kapil Dev with the score on 262, and DeFreitas went four overs later, but Hick and England were far from done. When Tufnell joined him Hick was on 117, and England were 279. Eighty-one minutes later, Hick skied to square-leg where Kapil Dev took an excellent catch – England were 347, and Hick had made 178 off 319 balls in 390 minutes with a six and 20 fours. It was an innings of different shades and moods but the end product, and many of the shots along the way, were heartening to England. Bravely, Tufnell had supported him with the slowest two in Test cricket.

Azharuddin had enjoyed a good series, and the praise now heaped upon him was as extravagant as had been the abuse he had received on his return from South Africa, but surely in this encounter he had erred in his underuse of his pace bowlers. Hick faced only spin until he was comfortably past three figures.

On paper, the Indian openers had seemed the most vulnerable part of the batting line-up, yet once again England failed to break through as Prabhakar and Sidhu gave the home side an admirable start. When Hick was brought into the attack he was hit for 14 in his first over. In his second over Prabhakar came down the wicket, heaved and missed, but Blakey failed to complete the stumping. Tufnell had begun with a no-ball, and Prabhakar had clouted him for six. Emburey had shown a depressing lack of variety, and one was reminded of the former England captain who described the Middlesex off-break man as a boring bowler.

Success came at last when Prabhakar was well caught at the wicket off Hick, but Kambli was unrestrained, and India closed on 144.

On the third morning, Sidhu added 10 to his overnight score before being taken at silly point. This brought the two Bombay protégés, Kambli and Tendulkar, together. There should have been immediate reward for Emburey who persuaded Kambli to hit high to long-off, but De-Freitas completely misjudged the catch. It was a most costly error. At lunch, the score was 225; at tea, 311. In his third Test match, Kambli had completed his first Test century, and he showed no sign of relinquishing his wicket, although he was badly dropped by Gooch at slip on 119 off the persevering Lewis, the best of the England bowlers.

The young Indians tended to build rather than to blaze, but there was some exquisite cricket. They had added 194 in 285 minutes when Tendulkar played back to Tufnell and was leg before. The day ended with India in total command: Kambli 164, Azharuddin 14, and the score 397 for 3.

At the start of the fourth day, Azharuddin continued his delightful cameo of an innings, and his 50-run partnership with Kambli came in 15 overs. It ended when the Indian skipper played back to the deserving Lewis. This provided no respite for England as Amre and Kambli now added 101 in 99 minutes.

The full power and capabilities of Amre had not yet been seen in the series, for the limelight had shone on Sidhu, Tendulkar, Azharuddin, and on Kambli, but now he asserted the immense talent that had been waiting in the wings, as it were. He drove Tufnell through the off side for 4 three-balls in succession. Fifty came in nine overs, and Amre's fifty came off 58 balls. He hit 9 fours before uncharacteristically cutting limply to backward point.

Kambli had been in full flow since early morning. Like Amre, he danced down the wicket and drove fluently. He could sway back and cut and pull, and Bombay roared to a local hero as he moved past 200. With Kapil Dev, runs continued to come at one a minute, but More went second ball. Finally, after 608 minutes at the crease, Kambli drove lazily – or tiredly – at Lewis and was very well caught by Gatting in the gully. The 21-year-old left-hander had faced 411 balls and hit 23 fours. His 224 was the highest score by an Indian batsman against England, and only 12 runs short of Gavaskar's record score. It was a magnificent achievement in every way.

Kumble and Chauhan clouted sixes off Emburey before falling to successive balls from Tufnell, both caught at deep mid-wicket. The wickets flattered Tufnell, but India

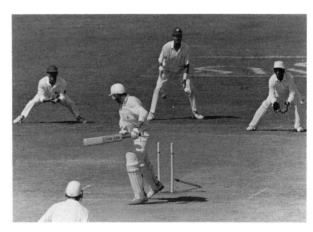

Gooch has his middle stump removed by Prabhakar at the start of England's second innings. (Patrick Eagar)

were not flattered by their 591, the highest score they had made against England in a home Test. England were left needing to score 244 runs in a day, a session and 20 minutes if they were to avoid an innings defeat.

On the stroke of tea, Stewart was beaten by Prabhakar's in-swinger and was palpably lbw. Stewart himself showed obvious dissent to umpire Reporter. He owes Reporter an apology.

Prabhakar beat Gooch with a well-disguised slower ball and knocked the England captain's middle stump out of the ground. This had been the unhappiest of tours for Gooch. England lost a third wicket, again to Prabhakar, when Atherton touched an out-swinger to the keeper. The first three batsmen gone, and Azharuddin had not yet turned to his spinners. When he did, Smith and Gatting survived to the end of the day, 108 for 3, although Gatting had a very close call for a run out.

There was an optimistic start to the last day for England as both Gatting and Smith reached fifty, and 41 runs were scored in an untroubled first hour. Following a drinks break, Chauhan replaced Kumble and, in his second

Smith runs a ball from Chauhan past Azharuddin during his innings of 62. Hick is the other batsman. (David Munden/Sports-Line)

over, he beat Gatting through the air as the batsman came down the wicket. The ball hit More on the chest, but the keeper recovered quickly to bring off a smart stumping. It was a close decision but, unquestionably, it was out. Seven overs later, Kumble returned in place of Venkata-pathy Raju and, in his first over, he beat Smith's correct-looking forward defensive stroke with a leg-break and hit the off stump. Blakey's misery continued as he played down a line that bore no relation to the flight or pitch of the delivery and was bowled first ball. England lunched at 198 for 6.

There was to be no salvation. Lewis received a ball that turned sharply and lifted nastily and was caught behind. Hick was adjudged caught at short-leg, the one debatable decision of the match, and DeFreitas, having hit Venkata-pathy Raju for six, missed when he tried to repeat the shot and was stumped. India had won every match in a series for the first time and had inflicted the heaviest defeats on England in the 61-year history of series between the two countries.

From start to finish England had been handicapped by ill-judged selections, poor tactics and poor mental atti-tudes. The team worked hard and maintained pro-fessional standards, but they were never suitably equipped nor properly prepared for the task at hand. They offered no excuses. With the exception of some hasty decisions by Rathore in the second Test, the um-piring was of a very high standard, certainly of a better quality than much that had been offered to Pakistan in England in 1992.

Rather than dwell on England's failings, which can be attributed in the main to the way in which the game in

DeFreitas is stumped by More off Venkatapathy Raju. Tufnell looks on. The series is over. (Patrick Eagar)

this country is being managed, one should dwell upon the quality of the Indian performance. They lost only 28 wickets in the three Tests. Their narrowest victory was by eight wickets, and they won each match well within the distance. These figures are a true reflection of the difference between the two sides.

The Indian batting was thrilling, and it must be remembered that Manjrekar, a batsman of real class, did not play in the series and Amre's opportunities were limited by the success of Kambli, Tendulkar and Azharuddin.

The recovery in morale after the trials and tribulations of South Africa was remarkable, and the standard of fielding was phenomenal. This has long been an area where India have not shown to advantage, and the work that has been done to bring about the extraordinary lift in standards is to be warmly commended.

Given wickets which offered slow turn, Kumble, Venkatapathy Raju and Chauhan exploited the conditions to the full. Kumble, Man of the Series, was masterly in his control of variations of pace and in the subtlety of his spin, but the achievements of Prabhakar and Kapil Dev, who made early breakthroughs in every match, should not be forgotten.

It has been believed that had England won the toss at Madras, their spinners would have done to India what Kumble and his partners did to England. The Bombay Test exposed the fallacy of that argument. In bowling, as in all else, England were miles behind India in class.

India's three young batsmen of genius – Kambli, Amre and Tendulkar. (Patrick Eagar)

There was some consolation for England in the performances of Hick and Lewis. Hick was named Man of the Match in the final Test, which was a little hard on Kambli, who can draw comfort from the fact that, like his friend Tendulkar, he has some 15 years and more than 100 Tests lying ahead of him.

TEST MATCH AVERAGES – INDIA *v.* ENGLAND

INDIA BATTING

	M	Inns	NO	Runs	HS	Av	100s	50s
V.G. Kambli	3	4	1	317	224	105.66	1	1
S.R. Tendulkar	3	4	1	302	165	100.66	1	2
M. Azharuddin	3	3	–	214	182	71.33	1	–
N.S. Sidhu	3	4	–	235	106	58.75	1	1
Kapil Dev	3	3	1	101	66*	50.50	–	1
P.K. Amre	3	3	–	147	78	49.00	–	2
M. Prabhakar	3	4	–	130	46	32.50	–	–
K.S. More	3	3	2	30	26*	30.00	–	–
R.K. Chauhan	3	2	–	17	15	8.50	–	–
A.R. Kumble	3	2	–	16	16	8.00	–	–
Venkatapathy Raju	3	2	1	1	1	1.00	–	–

ENGLAND BATTING

	M	Inns	NO	Runs	HS	Av	100s	50s
G.A. Hick	3	6	–	315	178	52.50	1	1
M.W. Gatting	3	6	–	219	81	36.50	–	2
C.C. Lewis	3	6	–	206	117	34.33	1	–
N.H. Fairbrother	2	4	–	134	83	33.50	–	1
P.C.R. Tufnell	2	4	3	28	22*	28.00	–	–
R.A. Smith	3	6	–	146	62	24.33	–	2
A.J. Stewart	3	6	–	146	74	24.33	–	1
I.D.K. Salisbury	2	4	–	70	28	17.50	–	–
G.A. Gooch	2	4	–	47	18	11.75	–	–
P.W. Jarvis	2	4	–	20	8	5.00	–	–
D.E. Malcolm	2	4	2	4	4*	2.00	–	–
R.J. Blakey	2	4	–	7	6	1.75	–	–

Played in one Test: J.P. Taylor 17 & 17*; M.A. Atherton 37 & 11; J.E. Emburey 12 & 1; P.A.J. DeFreitas 11 & 12.

INDIA BOWLING

	Overs	Mds	Runs	Wkts	Av	Best	10/m	5/inn
Kapil Dev	51.2	15	133	7	19.00	3-35	–	–
A.R. Kumble	181	53	416	21	19.80	6-64	–	1
M. Prabhakar	48	17	127	5	25.40	3-28	–	–
Venkatapathy Raju	210	62	468	16	29.25	4-103	–	–
R.K. Chauhan	169.4	64	323	9	35.88	3-30	–	–
S.R. Tendulkar	4	1	9	–	–	–	–	–

ENGLAND BOWLING

	Overs	Mds	Runs	Wkts	Av	Best	10/m	5/inn
G.A. Hick	76.5	11	202	8	25.25	3-19	–	–
P.W. Jarvis	60.2	13	167	4	41.75	2-72	–	–
D.E. Malcolm	57	11	170	3	56.66	3-67	–	–
P.C.R. Tufnell	80.3	9	274	4	68.50	4-142	–	–
J.P. Taylor	22	3	74	1	74.00	1-65	–	–
C.C. Lewis	79	16	223	3	74.33	2-114	–	–
I.D.K. Salisbury	52	6	230	3	76.66	2-142	–	–

Bowled in one innings: P.A.J. DeFreitas 20–4–75–0; J.E. Emburey 59–14–144–2.

INDIA FIELDING FIGURES

13 — K.S. More (ct 9/st 4); 4 – S.R. Tendulkar, P.K. Amre and sub (W.V. Raman); 3 – M. Prabhakar, M. Azharuddin and Kapil Dev; 1 – A.R. Kumble

ENGLAND FIELDING FIGURES

5 – G.A. Hick; 3 – C.C. Lewis; 2 – R.A. Smith, I.D.K. Salisbury, R.J. Blakey, M.A. Atherton and P.A.J. DeFreitas; 1 – G.A. Gooch, M.W. Gatting, P.W. Jarvis and A.J. Stewart (st 1)

ONE-DAY INTERNATIONAL SERIES
Matches Three to Six

England's tour of India ended with four one-day internationals which allowed the visitors some opportunity to regain their pride. They took the chance in the third match of the series. Worn by criticism, ill-health and lack of form, Gooch dropped down the order to number six. Smith opened with Stewart, and the pair put on 42 in 10 overs before Stewart fell to Srinath.

Javagal Srinath was to return his best figures in international cricket, taking 3 for 16 in his first six-over spell. The newly-found confidence of Hick was the counter to Srinath, and the Worcestershire batsman hit 56 off 81 balls to give the England innings both purpose and substance. Gooch looked to be taking his side to a comfortable score, but he was bowled by Prabhakar, and DeFreitas and Jarvis went in quick succession, which meant that Malcolm had three balls to face from Kapil Dev. Had Kapil dismissed Malcolm, India would have had a full 50 overs to reach 219, but the great all-rounder bowled with a surprising lack of intelligence, and India had only 47 overs to score the runs they needed.

India were to be fined for their slow over rate, but England were worse. India had an early set-back when Prabhakar was run out by Lewis' direct hit from gully, but Sidhu and Kambli seemed untroubled as they added 58. Then the introduction of Paul Jarvis turned the match completely. In his first over, the 17th, he had Kambli

caught behind; in his next over, he had Azharuddin leg before. In between, Lewis had had Tendulkar caught at slip so three wickets had fallen for six runs, and the heart of India's batting had gone. In spite of the efforts of Sidhu, Kapil Dev and Kumble, there was no reprieve as Jarvis finished with 5 for 35, the best analysis for a match between the two sides and a just reward for some fine bowling.

Stewart suffered a muscle spasm and withdrew from the England side shortly before the start of the fourth match. Gatting was taken ill during the match and could not bat. Atherton had been left in Bangalore, and Blakey again found himself in the England side. Rain delayed the start of the match, which was reduced to 26 overs.

England won the toss, asked India to bat first and bowled more tightly and fielded better than they had done previously on the tour. There were some encouraging cameos from India's batsmen: Azharuddin hit 23 off 22 balls, Amre 19 off 13 with 3 fours, but nobody stayed long enough to play the innings that would decide the match.

England's task seemed easy enough, but Gooch and Smith looked far from secure. Gooch was caught behind, and Smith was run out by Ankola as he attempted a ridiculous third run. Ankola had Hick caught low at slip and hit Fairbrother a painful blow on the knee. Smith returned as runner for Fairbrother who played the bravest of innings. Lewis helped him to add 50 in 10 overs, and Reeve then stayed with Fairbrother who completed his fifty and won the match with a boundary off the fourth ball of the last over.

The blemish on the match was the behaviour of the crowd who invaded the pitch and threw missiles, a dangerous exercise.

Behaviour was better at Gwalior where, on a perfect pitch, England were put in to bat. Again there was controversy with regard to the selection of the England side. Gatting was unwell, but Stewart returned although he did not keep wicket. This meant another match for Blakey at the expense of Atherton who, two seasons ago, was being spoken of as England's next captain.

Robin Smith began positively, but Stewart was less certain, offering chances when he was on 3 and 4. The pair gave England a most encouraging start, posting 100 in the 24th over, but, almost immediately, Stewart cut Kumble onto his stumps. Hick skied a mis-hook after adding 53 with Smith, and Fairbrother, who again batted with spirit, hitting 37 off 39 balls, was third out at 227 in the 46th over. By then, Smith had reached his first century in an international match for England outside England. He was fourth out as he played across the line at Srinath. He hit 129 off 145 balls, with 4 sixes and 12 fours. Three of his sixes were off Maninder Singh who had troubled him earlier, and the fourth was off Ajay Sharma. This was a quite splendid innings from Smith, and its value was shown when England lost their last seven wickets for 10 runs in 20 balls.

Five wickets in the third one-day international for pace bowler Srinath, but he finished on the losing side. (David Munden/Sports-Line)

THIRD ONE-DAY INTERNATIONAL – INDIA *v.* ENGLAND
26 February 1993 at M. Chinnaswamy Stadium, Bangalore

ENGLAND

R.A. Smith	c More, **b** Srinath	29
*A.J. Stewart	lbw, **b** Srinath	14
G.A. Hick	c Amre, **b** Prabhakar	56
M.W. Gatting	**b** Srinath	7
N.H. Fairbrother	run out	5
G.A. Gooch (capt)	**b** Prabhakar	45
C.C. Lewis	c Tendulkar, **b** Srinath	19
D.A. Reeve	not out	13
P.A.J. DeFreitas	c Prabhakar, **b** Srinath	2
P.W. Jarvis	c Azharuddin, **b** Kapil Dev	1
D.E. Malcolm	not out	0
Extras	lb **15**, w **4**, nb **8**	27
(47 overs)	(for 9 wickets)	218

INDIA

M. Prabhakar	run out	0
N.S. Sidhu	c Gooch, **b** DeFreitas	40
V.G. Kambli	c Stewart, **b** Jarvis	33
S.R. Tendulkar	c Hick, **b** Lewis	3
M. Azharuddin (capt)	lbw, **b** Jarvis	1
P.K. Amre	c Hick, **b** Jarvis	16
Kapil Dev	c Gooch, **b** Malcolm	32
*K.S. More	lbw, **b** Jarvis	0
A.R. Kumble	**b** Jarvis	24
J. Srinath	c Hick, **b** Malcolm	2
Venkatapathy Raju	not out	1
Extras	lb **4**, w **11**, nb **3**	18
(41.4 overs)		170

	O	M	R	W
Kapil Dev	8	1	27	1
Prabhakar	10	–	50	2
Srinath	9	1	41	5
Venkatapathy Raju	10	–	46	–
Kumble	10	1	39	–

	O	M	R	W
Malcolm	9	1	47	2
DeFreitas	8	–	27	1
Lewis	10	–	32	1
Jarvis	8.4	1	35	5
Reeve	6	–	25	–

FALL OF WICKETS
1–42, 2–65, 3–79, 4–102, 5–157, 6–185, 7–210, 8–213, 9–218

FALL OF WICKETS
1–3, 2–61, 3–66, 4–67, 5–100, 6–114, 7–115, 8–160, 9–166

Umpires: V.K. Ramaswamy & M.R. Singh   *Men of the Match:* P.W. Jarvis & J. Srinath   *England won by 48 runs*

FOURTH ONE-DAY INTERNATIONAL – INDIA *v.* ENGLAND
1 March 1993 at Keenan Stadium, Jamshedpur

INDIA

N.S. Sidhu	c DeFreitas, **b** Malcolm	18
M. Prabhakar	c Blakey, **b** DeFreitas	2
V.G. Kambli	run out	23
S.R. Tendulkar	**b** Jarvis	24
M. Azharuddin (capt)	c Fairbrother, **b** Lewis	23
Kapil Dev	not out	15
P.K. Amre	c Gooch, **b** Jarvis	19
S.A. Ankola	run out	2
*K.S. More	not out	1
A.R. Kumble		
J. Srinath		
Extras	lb **6**, w **3**, nb **1**	10
(26 overs)	(for 7 wickets)	137

ENGLAND

G.A. Gooch (capt)	c More, **b** Kapil Dev	15
R.A. Smith	run out	17
G.A. Hick	c Azharuddin, **b** Ankola	1
N.H. Fairbrother	not out	53
C.C. Lewis	lbw, **b** Prabhakar	25
D.A. Reeve	not out	17
M.W. Gatting		
*R.J. Blakey		
P.A.J. DeFreitas		
P.W. Jarvis		
D.E. Malcolm		
Extras	lb **8**, w **5**	13
(25.4 overs)	(for 4 wickets)	141

	O	M	R	W
DeFreitas	4	–	17	1
Malcolm	6	–	17	1
Lewis	5	–	25	1
Reeve	6	–	32	–
Jarvis	5	–	40	2

	O	M	R	W
Kapil Dev	4	1	10	1
Prabhakar	5.4	–	34	1
Srinath	6	–	38	–
Ankola	6	–	28	1
Kumble	4	–	23	–

FALL OF WICKETS
1–11, 2–46, 3–51, 4–96, 5–99, 6–122, 7–127

FALL OF WICKETS
1–27, 2–33, 3–43, 4–93

Umpires: L. Narasimhan & C.S. Sathe   *Man of the Match:* N.H. Fairbrother   *England won by 6 wickets*

FIFTH ONE-DAY INTERNATIONAL – INDIA *v.* ENGLAND
4 March 1993 at Roop Singh Stadium, Gwalior

ENGLAND			INDIA		
R.A. Smith	lbw, **b** Srinath	129	N.S. Sidhu	not out	134
A.J. Stewart	**b** Kumble	33	M. Prabhakar	lbw, **b** DeFreitas	0
G.A. Hick	c More, **b** Prabhakar	18	V.G. Kambli	c Gooch, **b** Malcolm	2
N.H. Fairbrother	c Maninder Singh, **b** Srinath	37	M. Azharuddin (capt)	c Stewart, **b** Malcolm	74
C.C. Lewis	lbw, **b** Prabhakar	4	S.R. Tendulkar	**b** Jarvis	5
G.A. Gooch (capt)	run out	1	A.K. Sharma	run out	0
D.A. Reeve	run out	3	Kapil Dev	c Hick, **b** Jarvis	2
*R.J. Blakey	lbw, **b** Srinath	0	*K.S. More	c Hick, **b** Malcolm	1
P.A.J. DeFreitas	not out	2	A.R. Kumble	not out	19
P.W. Jarvis	**b** Prabhakar	0	Maninder Singh		
D.E. Malcolm	**b** Prabhakar	0	J. Srinath		
Extras	b 1, lb 16, w 8, nb 4	29	Extras	b 2, lb 9, w 8, nb 1	20
(50 overs)		256	(48 overs)	(for 7 wickets)	257

	O	M	R	W		O	M	R	W
Kapil Dev	9	–	39	–	DeFreitas	10	–	52	1
Prabhakar	10	–	54	4	Malcolm	10	–	40	3
Srinath	10	–	41	3	Lewis	10	–	56	–
Kumble	10	–	41	1	Jarvis	10	–	43	2
A.K. Sharma	3	–	18	–	Reeve	6	–	37	–
Maninder Singh	8	–	46	–	Hick	2	–	18	–

FALL OF WICKETS

1–101, **2**–154, **3**–227, 4–246, **5**–246, **6**–251, 7–251, 8–256, 9–256

FALL OF WICKETS

1–1, **2**–4, **3**–179, 4–189, **5**–190, **6**–202, 7–205

Umpires: A.V. Jayaprakash & P.D. Reporter   *Man of the Match:* N.S. Sidhu   **India won by 3 wickets**

SIXTH ONE-DAY INTERNATIONAL – INDIA *v.* ENGLAND
5 March 1993 at Roop Singh Stadium, Gwalior

ENGLAND			INDIA		
R.A. Smith	c Sharma, **b** Maninder Singh	72	M. Prabhakar	**b** Jarvis	73
*A.J. Stewart	c More, **b** Srinath	11	N.S. Sidhu	c Hick, **b** Lewis	19
G.A. Hick	not out	105	V.G. Kambli	c Reeve, **b** DeFreitas	22
N.H. Fairbrother	c Kapil Dev, **b** Srinath	41	M. Azharuddin (capt)	not out	95
M.W. Gatting	c Sidhu, **b** Srinath	6	S.R. Tendulkar	c sub (Taylor), **b** Lewis	34
C.C. Lewis	not out	3	Kapil Dev	c Reeve, **b** Jarvis	2
G.A. Gooch (capt)			A.K. Sharma	c Gooch, **b** Jarvis	2
D.A. Reeve			*K.S. More	not out	10
P.A.J. DeFreitas			A.R. Kumble		
P.W. Jarvis			Maninder Singh		
D.E. Malcolm			J. Srinath		
Extras	lb 8, w 17, nb 2	27	Extras	lb 1, w 7, nb 2	10
(48 overs)	(for 4 wickets)	265	(46.4 overs)	(for 6 wickets)	267

	O	M	R	W		O	M	R	W
Kapil Dev	10	2	48	–	Malcolm	8	–	56	–
Prabhakar	9	–	52	–	Lewis	10	1	51	2
Srinath	9	–	37	3	Jarvis	10	–	39	3
Maninder Singh	10	–	62	1	Reeve	8.4	–	64	–
Kumble	10	–	58	–	DeFreitas	10	–	56	1

FALL OF WICKETS

1–42, **2**–158, **3**–246, 4–258

FALL OF WICKETS

1–41, **2**–99, **3**–166, 4–245, **5**–252, **6**–253

Umpires: S. Venkataraghavan & S.K. Bansai   *Man of the Match:* M. Azharuddin   **India won by 4 wickets**

It is hard to think that England could have had a better start when they took the field. Prabhakar was out first ball in the first over of India's innings. Unfortunately, he showed obvious dissent with the decision. Then Kambli skied Malcolm to mid-off, and India were 4 for 2. What followed was pulsating stuff. In 29 overs, Sidhu and Azharuddin added 175 runs with some dazzling stroke-play. Azharuddin hit a six and 6 fours in his 74 off 72 balls as the England bowlers were savaged mercilessly. His dismissal, caught at deep square-leg, heralded a collapse, five wickets falling for 26 runs. Shortly before the dismissal of the Indian captain, Sidhu had edged Jarvis to Blakey, but the wicket-keeper dropped the simplest of chances.

Sidhu continued to destroy the England bowlers, and Kumble helped him to end the collapse. With 15 fours in his 160-ball innings, Sidhu lashed India to victory with two overs to spare. In all forms of cricket against the tourists, Sidhu had scored 656 runs, average 72.88, and there was still one match remaining.

The sixth match in the series followed a pattern very similar to the fifth. For England, Gatting returned to the exclusion of Blakey. India won the toss, and England batted on another lovely pitch. Srinath was once more in good form and had Stewart caught behind playing at a wide-ish delivery. Smith and Hick then added 116, but both batsmen should have been stumped by More. Wicket-keeping had not been the most proficient department of the cricket played between the two countries.

Smith was finally out when he hit the deserving Maninder high to mid-on. Smith's 72 included a six and 7 fours and came off 106 balls. He had shown a defiantly encouraging flourish at the end of a tour which had threatened to be a disaster for him.

Hick and Fairbrother added 88 in 13 overs, and Hick followed his maiden Test hundred with his first century in one-day international cricket. He faced only 109 balls and hit 2 sixes and 7 fours. His advance had been the most positive aspect of England's disappointing trip to the sub-continent.

England's 265 in 48 overs looked a more defendable total than the 256 had looked the previous day, but India were given a most workmanlike start by Prabhakar and Sidhu who scored 41 in 10 overs. Kambli was out of touch and took 14 overs for his 22, so that when Azharuddin joined Prabhakar 167 runs were needed from 24 overs, and the odds seemed very much in England's favour.

The Test series had begun with a memorably glorious innings from the Indian captain; now the one-day series was to end the same way. Malcolm was removed from the attack when 19 runs were taken from two overs, and Reeve was to suffer a similar fate once Azharuddin began to hit him to all parts of the ground. Prabhakar's admirable supporting innings ended after 112 balls, but this only brought in Tendulkar, and 79 runs came in nine overs before the young genius skied to mid-on. The quick dismissal of Kapil Dev and Sharma failed to unsettle Azharuddin, particularly as More was confident from the start.

Victory for India came with eight balls to spare. Azharuddin finished with 95 which had come off 63 balls. He

A sight all too familiar to England – Navjot Singh Sidhu in full cry – 134 not out in the fifth one-day international. (Ben Radford/Allsport)

had hit 12 fours and a six, off Reeve to bring up his fifty. Azharuddin had stamped himself indelibly on this glorious Indian summer.

Bruised and battered, England now had a draw in the one-day series to contemplate alongside their drubbing in the Tests. At home, there was mounting criticism of tactics, dress and selection. The shabby dress of the England side at presentation ceremonies brought the most criticism, but this, surely, should be related to the demands of the sponsor – or to the demands that the marketing department say that the sponsor made. In any case, the brewery sponsoring the England side could not have been happy with the image that they were getting for their money.

More importantly, there were some miserable performances by England players on the tour. Neither Gatting nor Emburey had justified their recall. The choice of Blakey remained incomprehensible, particularly since Stewart's role in the side had become ambivalent as a result. DeFreitas and Malcolm had been hugely disappointing, and it was hard to justify the selection of Reeve, a so-called one-day specialist, ahead of cricketers who would have offered positive alternatives for the Test side.

Gooch returned home to England. Stewart took the rest of the party to Sri Lanka in search of better things. India and Indian cricket rejoiced.

RANJI TROPHY

SOUTH ZONE

6, 7, 8 and 9 November **1992** *at Lal Bahadur Shastri Stadium, Hyderabad*

Hyderabad 395 (Vanka Pratap 86, M.V. Ramanamurthy 64, R. Yadav 61)
Goa 182 (P. Rivenkar 57) and 157 (Arshad Ayub 4 for 26)
Hyderabad won by an innings and 56 runs
Hyderabad 23 pts., Goa 3 pts.

at MCV Stadium, Vishakhapatnam

Kerala 227 for 5 (B. Ramprakash 71 not out, F.V. Rashid 50 not out)
***v.* Andhra**
Match abandoned
Andhra 4 pts., Kerala 2 pts.

Hyderabad began their challenge for the Ranji Trophy with the expected innings win over Goa, while rain prevented any play on the last three days at Vishakhapatnam.

12, 13, 14 and 15 November 1992 *at Mahatma Gandhi Stadium, Salem*

Andhra 128 (M. Venkataramana 5 for 24)
Tamil Nadu 115 for 2
Match drawn
Tamil Nadu 7 pts., Andhra 5 pts.

at Thapar Stadium, AOC Centre Ground, Secunderabad

Hyderabad 448 (M.V. Sridhar 176, V. Jaisimha 67, M.V. Ramanamurthy 61) and 229 for 8 dec. (V. Jaisimha 72 not out, Abdul Azeem 51, B. Ramprakash 4 for 107)
Kerala 409 (V. Narayan Kutty 125, B. Ramprakash 56, Arshad Ayub 4 for 116) and 111 for 3
Match drawn
Hyderabad 17 pts., Kerala 13 pts.

at Panaji Gymkhana Stadium, Panaji

Karnataka 362 (C. Saldanha 71, S.M.H. Kirmani 63, R.S. Dravid 54, A. Shetty 4 for 81, N. Kambli 4 for 88)

Goa 102 (K.A. Jeshwanth 6 for 24, A.R. Bhat 4 for 38) and 187
Karnataka won by an innings and 73 runs
Karnataka 23 pts., Goa 4 pts.

Rain again destroyed Andhra's match while Hyderabad piled up points against Kerala. Maturi Sridhar shared in two century partnerships. Narayan Kutty hit a maiden first-class century as Kerala fought their way back into the game and earned a draw.

Goa suffered another innings defeat as Karnataka batted consistently and bowled steadily.

20, 21, 22 and 23 November 1992 *at Panaji Gymkhana Stadium, Panaji*

Goa 108 and 150 (S. Subramaniam 4 for 24, M. Venkataramana 4 for 40)
Tamil Nadu 404 for 9 dec. (K. Srikkanth 104, Ashish Kapoor 73 not out, D. Vasu 54, V.B. Chandrasekhar 52)
Tamil Nadu won by an innings and 146 runs
Tamil Nadu 25 pts., Goa 4 pts.

at REC Ground, Kozhikode

Karnataka 329 (S.M.H. Kirmani 53, B. Ramprakash 5 for 96)
Kerala 103 (A.R. Bhat 5 for 27) and 152 (A.R. Bhat 4 for 24)
Karnataka won by an innings and 74 runs
Karnataka 22 pts., Kerala 3 pts.

Tamil Nadu asserted their Ranji Trophy challenge with victory over Goa, and Karnataka maintained their strong challenge with another innings victory. The left-arm spin of Raghuram Bhat proved as decisive as ever in the rout of Kerala.

27, 28, 29 and 30 November 1992 *at CRL Ground, Kachi*
Goa 177 (S. Mahadevan 69, B. Ramprakash 4 for 41, P. Jayaraj 4 for 42) and 99
Kerala 163 and 114 for 5
Kerala won by 5 wickets
Kerala 17 pts., Goa 7 pts.

at M. Chinnaswamy Stadium, Bangalore

Karnataka 531 for 6 dec. (R.S. Dravid 200 not out, S.M.H. Kirmani 77, A. Vaidya 65, K.A. Jeshwanth 53, K. Srinath 51) and 259 for 2 dec. (P.V. Shashikanth 102 not out, C. Saldanha 66, R.S. Dravid 56 not out)
Andhra 356 (K.V.S.D. Kamaraju 112, D. Johnson 4 for 115) and 216 for 6 (K. Veerbrahman 90 not out, R. Ananth 5 for 53)
Match drawn
Karnataka 20 pts., Andhra 12 pts.

Tamil Nadu 290 (D. Vasu 78, Robin Singh 51) and 322 for 9
 dec. (Robin Singh 101 not out, Arshad Ayub 6 for 90)
Hyderabad 414 (R.A. Swaroop 72, Arshad Ayub 63,
 R. Yadav 52, D. Vasu 4 for 125) and 113 for 1 (Abdul
 Azeem 71 not out)

Match drawn

Hyderabad 15 pts., Tamil Nadu 9 pts.

Goa led Kerala on the first innings, but they were still
beaten inside three days and so became assured of the
wooden spoon in the South Zone yet again. There was an
abundance of runs at Bangalore where Rahul Dravid
reached the first double century of his career. He and
Kirmani added 173 for Karnataka's fifth wicket, and
Dravid shared a 142-run stand with Vaidya for the sixth
wicket. Andhra began badly, but Kamaraju led their
recovery.

 Electing to bat first against Hyderabad, Tamil Nadu
could gain only one batting point against some accurate
bowling. Hyderabad were also well served by debutant
wicket-keeper Yuvaraj who held five catches in the
innings. In contrast, Hyderabad's batting was consistent,
and their lead over Tamil Nadu in bonus points gave
them every advantage in claiming a place in the quarter-
finals.

5, 6, 7 and **8** December 1992 *at Nehru Stadium, Hubli*

Karnataka 503 (K. Srinath 125, S. Joshi 83 not out, S.M.H.
 Kirmani 81, K.A. Jeshwanth 61, R.S. Dravid 55, Arshad
 Ayub 4 for 191)
Hyderabad 5 for 0

Match abandoned

Karnataka 4 pts., Hyderabad 3 pts.

Kerala 116 (M.V. Venkataramana 5 for 43, S. Subramaniam 5 for 49) and 228 (M.V. Venkataramana 6 for 73)
Tamil Nadu 353 for 8 dec. (Robin Singh 108, V.B. Chandrasekhar 58, S. Subramaniam 50 not out, K.N.A.
 Padmanabhan 5 for 120)

Tamil Nadu won by an innings and 9 runs

Tamil Nadu 23 pts., Kerala 4 pts.

Two days' play at Hubli had seen Karnataka move to a
strong position thanks to Srinath's maiden first-class
hundred, and excellent support batting from the veteran
Kirmani and the late order. Unfortunately, this vital
match was then abandoned because of widespread riots
which caused the implementation of a curfew. This abandonment gave a reprieve to Tamil Nadu who were now
able to close the gap on their rivals. They owed much to
Robin Singh, who hit his second hundred of the season,
and a great deal to their bowlers. Venkataramana may
have failed in his one Test appearance but his off-breaks

Arshad Ayub (Hyderabad). (David Munden/Sports-Line)

still cause havoc in domestic cricket as he proved with
match figures of 11 for 116, while Subramaniam performed the hat-trick in Kerala's first innings.

12, 13, 14 and **15** December 1992 *at Rajendra Prasad Stadium,
Margao*

Goa 247 (M. Sawkar 77, G.V.V. Gopala Raju 4 for 45) and
 222 (M. Sawkar 60, A. Shetty 60)
Andhra 462 (A. Pathak 145, N. Veerbramhan 80, Mohammad F. Rehman 79) and 8 for 0

Andhra won by 10 wickets

Andhra 19 pts., Goa 3 pts.

Goa just managed to force Andhra to bat a second time,
but still lost their fifth match in succession. Amit Pathak
hit the highest score of his career and shared a second-
wicket stand of 175 with Rehman.

17, 18, 19 and **20** December 1992 *at M.A. Chidambaram Stadium,
Madras*

Karnataka 295 (R.S. Dravid 79, P.V. Shashikanth 76,
 K. Srinath 64, M.V. Venkataramana 4 for 61, S. Subra-
 maniam 4 for 67) and 291 (K.A. Jeshwanth 101,
 P.V. Shashikanth 74, S. Subramaniam 6 for 50)

Tamil Nadu 358 (K. Srikkanth 104) and 229 for 4 (Robin Singh 77 not out, M. Senthilnathan 68)

Tamil Nadu won by 6 wickets

Tamil Nadu 21 pts., Karnataka 10 pts.

19, 20, 21 and 22 December 1992 *at Priyadarshini Municipal Stadium, Vishakhapatnam*

Andhra 130 (R. Yadav 4 for 43) and 291 (K.V.S.D. Kamaraju 98, V. Vinay Kumar 62, P. Prakash 57 not out, M.V. Ramanamurthy 4 for 62)

Hyderabad 555 (R.A. Swaroop 140, V. Pratap 122 not out, Abdul Azeem 120, V. Jaisimha 68, P. Prakash 5 for 170)

Hyderabad won by an innings and 134 runs

Hyderabad 22 pts., Andhra 2 pts.

Inspired by the bowling duo of Subramaniam and Venkataramana, the all-round cricket of Robin Singh and the aggression of skipper Srikkanth, Tamil Nadu gained the vital victory that not only put them into the knock-out stages of the competition but ousted Karnataka from second place. Tamil Nadu scored at five runs an over to win the match. Hyderabad bagged a place in the quarter-finals by crushing Andhra. Abdul Azeem and Swaroop began the run feast with an opening partnership of 195.

SOUTH ZONE FINAL TABLE

	P	W	L	D	Pts.
Tamil Nadu	5	3	–	2	85
Hyderabad	5	2	–	3	80
Karnataka	5	2	1	2	79
Andhra	5	1	1	3	42
Kerala	5	1	2	2	39
Goa	5	–	5	–	21

WEST ZONE
20, 21, 22 and 23 November 1992 *at Wankhede Stadium, Bombay*

Baroda 347 (J.J. Martin 64 not out, A.C. Bedade 62, T.B. Arothe 52) and 385 for 5 dec. (A.C. Bedade 102, N.R. Mongia 78 not out, T.B. Arothe 69, J.J. Martin 53 not out)

Bombay 510 (V.G. Kambli 168, Z. Bharuacha 100, J.V. Paranjpe 69, T.B. Arothe 6 for 122) and 81 for 2

Match drawn

Bombay 15 pts., Baroda 9 pts.

at Sardar Patel Stadium, Valsad

Gujarat 159 (N. Mody 56, R.R. Garsondia 4 for 37) and 278 (Maqbul Malam 87, H. Thakkar 60, B.M. Radia 4 for 73)

Saurashtra 290 (B. Dutta 107, V. Sharma 5 for 87, D.T. Patel 4 for 83) and 118 for 5

Match drawn

Saurashtra 11 pts., Gujarat 10 pts.

Salil Ankola (Bombay). (Patrick Eagar)

Bombay's ability to produce batsmen of exceptional quality continues unabated. They asked Baroda to bat first and found the visitors' batsmen particularly stubborn. In reply, Bombay scored consistently and Kambli gave further evidence of his class and further ammunition to those who were waging war against his omission from the side to tour South Africa. The Bombay hero, however, was Bharuacha who hit a century on the occasion of his first-class debut. Bedade and Arothe ended any hopes of victory for Bombay, however, when they added 160 for Baroda's fourth wicket in the second innings.

There were fewer runs at Valsad where Saurashtra needed 148 in 29 overs to win the match on the last day but fell short of their target.

27, 28, 29 and 30 November 1992 *at University Ground, Bhavnagar*

Maharashtra 591 for 5 dec. (S.S. Bhave 220, S.S. Sugwekar 131, H.A. Kinikar 110) and 234 for 8 dec. (M.D. Gunjal 62)

Saurashtra 325 (A.N. Pandya 75, B.N. Jadeja 55, M.H. Parmar 52, S.J. Jadhav 5 for 83) and 41 for 2

Match drawn

Maharashtra 17 pts., Saurashtra 9 pts.

at Pithawala Stadium, Bhimpore

Baroda 214 and 425 for 8 dec. (T.B. Arothe 154, J.J. Martin 86 not out, N.R. Mongia 63)

Gujarat 196 (M.H. Parmar 102, T.B. Arothe 6 for 75) and 248 (M.H. Parmar 52, B.H. Mistry 51, T.B. Arothe 5 for 102, D. Soni 4 for 55)

Baroda won by 195 runs

Baroda 16 pts., Gujarat 6 pts.

Bhave and Kinikar began the match at Bhavnagar with a partnership of 216. Kinikar hit a century on his first-class debut, and skipper Surendra Bhave reached a double century. Sugwekar later plundered runs, but Saurashtra were undaunted, and Bhave's cautious declaration allowed them to escape with a draw.

Some outstanding all-round cricket by Tushar Arothe took Baroda to victory over Gujarat. The left-hander hit the highest score of his career and then returned the best figures of his career for match and innings with his off-breaks.

4, 5, 6 and 7 December 1992 *at GSFC Ground, Baroda*

Baroda 265 (A.C. Bedade 111 not out, T.B. Arothe 51) and 180 (A.H. Palkar 51, M. Kulkarni 5 for 85)

Maharashtra 187 (M.S. Narula 4 for 51) and 259 for 2 (S.V. Jedhe 105 not out, H.A. Kinikar 69)

Maharashtra won by 8 wickets

Maharashtra 19 pts., Baroda 7 pts.

With Bedade hitting his second century of the season, Baroda appeared in command against Maharashtra, but a second-innings collapse put them in jeopardy. Jedhe seized the initiative and took his side to a surprise win.

19, 20, 21 and 22 December 1992 *at Municipal Ground, Rajkot*

Saurashtra 294 (S. Kotak 76, B.M. Radia 52 not out, S.S. Patil 4 for 84) and 204 for 4 dec. (N.R. Odedra 104, B.M. Jadeja 65)

Bombay 426 (J.V. Paranjpe 88, S. More 80, S.S. Dighe 71, Iqbal Khan 59, D. Chudasama 6 for 125) and 40 for 0

Match drawn

Bombay 11 pts., Saurashtra 4 pts.

In spite of a consistent batting display, Bombay were thwarted by Saurashtra who showed fine powers of recovery after being 35 for 4 in their first innings.

26, 27, 28 and 29 December 1992 *at IPCL Sports Complex, Baroda*

Saurashtra 341 (S.S. Tanna 161, M.S. Narula 6 for 92) and 221 for 3 dec. (S. Kotak 60 not out, A.M. Pandya 53 not out)

Baroda 495 for 6 dec. (N.R. Mongia 111 not out, R.B. Parikh 101, R. Naik 87, A.C. Bedade 69, M.S. Narula 58 not out)

Match drawn

Baroda 13 pts., Saurashtra 8 pts.

at Poona Club, Pune

Bombay 408 (S.S. Dighe 100, J.V. Paranjpe 66) and 399 for 4 dec. (V.G. Kambli 202 not out, Z. Bharuacha 96)

Maharashtra 373 (S.V. Jedhe 106, S.J. Jadhav 74 not out, S.S. Sugwekar 58, S.S. Patil 5 for 94, S.A. Ankola 4 for 61) and 116 for 5

Match drawn

Bombay 18 pts., Maharashtra 10 pts.

Sudhir Tanna played a lone hand against the medium pace of Mukesh Narula to help Saurashtra to a commendable 341 against Baroda. The home side responded with centuries from Mongia and Parikh, but did not gather runs quickly enough to claim more than two batting points.

Santosh Jedhe hit his second century in succession as Maharashtra matched Bombay's run glut. With point-winning the only concern, Kambli hit a double century to give further indication of his brilliance.

2, 3, 4 and 5 January 1993 *at Wankhede Stadium, Bombay*

Gujarat 331 (P. Patel 123, Maqbul Malam 52) and 188 (M.H. Parmar 61, B.H. Mistry 55, A. Kuruvilla 6 for 61)

Bombay 635 for 9 dec. (J.V. Paranjpe 218, S.V. Bahutule 123 not out, Z. Bharuacha 79, S. More 71)

Bombay won by an innings and 116 runs

Bombay 24 pts., Gujarat 4 pts.

Parashar Patel of Gujarat hit a century in his debut first-class match, but Bombay swept to a massive victory. Jatin Paranjpe, in only his second season in Ranji Trophy cricket, hit his first double century as Bombay ran riot.

8, 9, 10 and 11 January 1993 *at Railway Stadium, Bhusawal*

Gujarat 277 (M.H. Parmar 127 not out) and 219 (M.H. Parmar 73, M. Kulkarni 4 for 83)

Maharashtra 284 (H.A. Kinikar 114, S.V. Jedhe 58, S.D. Lande 58, T. Varsania 6 for 96) and 216 for 5 (J. Narse 57)

Maharashtra won by 5 wickets

Maharashtra 17 pts., Gujarat 5 pts.

As expected, Maharashtra beat Gujarat, but they found the resistance much harder than anticipated. Varsania, left-arm medium pace, bowled particularly well for Gujarat, returning match figures of 9 for 161.

WEST ZONE FINAL TABLE

	P	W	L	D	Pts.
Bombay	4	1	–	3	68
Maharashtra	4	2	–	2	63
Baroda	4	1	1	2	45
Saurashtra	4	–	–	4	32
Gujarat	4	–	3	1	25

NORTH ZONE

20, 21, 22 and 23 November 1992 *at Palam 'A', Delhi*

Services 111 for 7 dec. (Shakti Singh 6 for 30)
Himachal Pradesh 114 for 8 (M.V. Rao 5 for 52)

Match drawn

Himachal Pradesh 8 pts., Services 6 pts.

No play was possible on the first and third days. Services were 99 for 7 at the end of the second day, declared and gained 12 penalty runs. Shakti Singh followed his six-wicket haul with an innings of 36 which gave Himachal Pradesh first-innings lead after they had been 68 for 7 with only four overs remaining.

25, 26, 27 and 28 November 1992 *at Palam Ground, Delhi*

Services 156 (Kamal Batra 4 for 53) and 207
Haryana 515 (R. Puri 150, Dhanraj Singh 86)

Haryana won by an innings and 152 runs

Haryana 23 pts., Services 3 pts.

at Ferozeshah Kotla Ground, Delhi

Delhi 495 for 7 dec. (A.K. Sharma 150, Bantoo Singh 103, M. Nayyar 68, A. Sen 4 for 128)
Himachal Pradesh 243 (R. Nayyar 72, A.K. Sharma 4 for 43, Maninder Singh 4 for 45) and 128 (Maninder Singh 5 for 38)

Delhi won by an innings and 124 runs

Delhi 25 pts., Himachal Pradesh 2 pts.

Medium-pacer Kamal Batra took four wickets on the occasion of his debut and helped bowl out Services on the first day, at the end of which Haryana were in total command. Dhanraj Singh made a rather painful maiden fifty in his 11th Ranji Trophy match, but Rajesh Puri hit powerfully. Boosted by 60 penalty runs, Haryana won in three days.

Delhi won after only 13 deliveries on the fourth day against Himachal Pradesh. Bantoo Singh and Ajay Sharma batted with spirit, and, after some worthy resistance in the first innings, Himachal Pradesh wilted against the left-arm spin of Maninder Singh in the second.

1, 2, 3 and 4 December 1992 *at Una*

Punjab 415 (V. Rathore 159, Bhupinder Singh jnr 116)
Himachal Pradesh 205 (K. Mohan 6 for 39) and 165 (B. Vij 7 for 67)

Punjab won by an innings and 45 runs

Punjab 23 pts., Himachal Pradesh 2 pts.

With Jammu and Kashmir having been forced to withdraw from the tournament because of political unrest, it was essential that the stronger sides in the North Zone should gather as many points as possible against Services

and Himachal Pradesh. Rathore and Bhupinder Singh jnr duly set Punjab on the right course with a fourth-wicket partnership of 282 against Himachal Pradesh, and the combined talents of Mohan and left-arm spinner Bharati Vij completed a resounding victory.

7, 8, 9 and 10 December 1992 *at Ferozeshah Kotla Ground, Delhi*

Services 198 (K.M. Roshan 71, F. Ghayas 7 for 53) and 210 (F. Ghayas 6 for 57)
Delhi 450 (Sanjay Sharma 103, G. Vadera 95, M. Nayyar 88, P. Maitreya 4 for 67)

Delhi won by an innings and 42 runs

Delhi 22 pts., Services 4 pts.

at Burlton Park, Jalandhar

Punjab 346 (K. Mohan 129 not out, Arun Sharma 80, P. Jain 7 for 119) and 119 for 4 dec. (S. Chopra 63)
Haryana 427 (Amarjeet Kaypee 122, R. Puri 115, N. Goel 76, Jaideep Singh 5 for 89) and 12 for 0

Match drawn

Haryana 11 pts., Punjab 6 pts.

Feriz Ghayas, a 19-year-old trainee from India's pace foundation project, was the hero of Delhi's win over Services. With a mixture of out-swing and off-cutters, the young bowler returned match figures of 13 for 110 on his debut in first-class cricket. Having bowled out Services on the opening day, Delhi scored heavily on the second when Sanjay Sharma hit his first century in the Ranji Trophy, and Gautam Vadera narrowly missed a century on his debut.

Punjab showed great character on a treacherous pitch at Jalandhar. Krishnan Mohan and Arun Sharma came together at 140 for 6 and added 155. Mohan displayed some particularly fine stroke-play on the second morning, and Pradeep Jain completed 100 wickets in his 39th Ranji Trophy match in which he also returned career-best bowling figures. Haryana adopted defensive measures in their batting and, with the exception of Rajesh Puri, who hit his sixth Ranji Trophy century, they were dour.

13, 14, 15 and 16 December 1992 *at Paddal Ground, Mandi*

Haryana 320 (N. Goel 102, Amarjeet Kaypee 101, Shakti Singh 4 for 39) and 203 for 9 dec. (Sukhdev Singh 60, Shakti Singh 5 for 82)
Himachal Pradesh 237 (R. Nayyar 78, P. Jain 6 for 74) and 172 (Deepak Sharma 5 for 54, P. Jain 5 for 80)

Haryana won by 114 runs

Haryana 20 pts., Himachal Pradesh 9 pts.

at Palam Ground, Delhi

Services 132 (Bhupinder Singh snr 5 for 47, B. Vij 4 for 30) and 192 (A. Bedi 5 for 53)
Punjab 447 for 5 dec. (N.S. Sidhu 147, S. Chopra 114, Gursharan Singh 101)

Ajay Sharma (Delhi) won a place in the Indian one-day side with some fine all-round cricket. (Adrian Murrell/Allsport)

Punjab won by an innings and 123 runs

Punjab 25 pts., Services 3 pts.

Amarjeet Kaypee hit his second century in succession and shared a third-wicket stand of 185 with another centurion, Goel, as Haryana demolished Himachal Pradesh. Punjab also overwhelmed their opponents, with Sidhu and Chopra scoring 181 for the first wicket against Services. Put in to bat, Services were 66 for 3 at lunch, but collapsed to 132 all out. Punjab ended the day on 97 for 0, and next day both openers completed centuries. Chopra hit a six and 18 fours while Sidhu, showing great concentration and restraint, hit a six and 16 fours. The stage was set for Gursharan Singh to hit his 13th Ranji Trophy hundred and to pass 3,000 runs in the competition, and Punjab won in three days.

19, 20, 21 and **22** December 1992 *at Ferozeshah Kotla Ground, Delhi*

Punjab 390 (Gursharan Singh 95, Bhupinder Singh snr 53, K. Mohan 51) and 65 for 3

Delhi 235 (Bantoo Singh 68, Bhupinder Singh snr 4 for 51, B. Vij 4 for 61) and 289 for 5 dec. (A.K. Sharma 149 not out, Kirti Azad 50)

Match drawn

Punjab 14 pts., Delhi 9 pts.

Punjab completed their programme with the better of a draw against Delhi. Winning the toss, they reached 262 for 6 on the opening day. Gursharan Singh drove young Ghayas out of the attack, but Maninder Singh dismissed the Punjab captain and Mohan. Delhi seemed likely to take a first-innings lead, but Bantoo Singh suddenly lost

patience, and nine wickets fell for 67 runs in a sensational collapse. In spite of being boosted by 41 penalty runs, Delhi were forced to follow-on, but were saved by Ajay Sharma's century.

24, 25, 26 and **27** December 1992 *at Nehru Stadium, Gurgaon*

Delhi 250 (Maninder Singh 102 not out, A.K. Sharma 57) and 266 for 5 dec. (A.K. Sharma 74, Bantoo Singh 60, K.P. Bhaskar 56)

Haryana 226 (N. Goel 58, Ashok Singh 52, Maninder Singh 7 for 54) and 137 for 7

Match drawn

Delhi 14 pts., Haryana 9 pts.

On a pitch that was full of cracks, Delhi were reduced to 138 for 8 at tea on the first day. In the final session, Maninder Singh hit 5 sixes and 4 fours, and on Christmas Day he raced to his maiden first-class century after losing Chaturvedi to the fifth ball of the morning. He then proceeded to bowl 18 overs and take 5 for 19 as Haryana slipped to 166 for 6. Leading by 24 on the first innings, Delhi were indebted to Bantoo Singh and Ajay Sharma who tamed the Haryana spinners. Bhaskar Pillai, who was having a poor season, hit 56 and reached 4,000 runs in the Ranji Trophy. Set to score 291 in 161 minutes and 15 overs, Haryana came close to defeat as Maninder Singh finished with match figures of 10 for 76 from 49.3 overs. Under the new ruling, three teams from North Zone went forward to the knock-out stage of the competition.

NORTH ZONE FINAL TABLE

	P	W	L	D	Pts.
Delhi	4	2	–	2	70
Punjab	4	2	–	2	68
Haryana	4	2	–	2	63
Himachal Pradesh	4	–	3	1	21
Services	4	–	3	1	16

EAST ZONE

21, 22, 23 and **24** November 1992 *at Tinsukia Stadium, Tinsukia*

Assam 259 (L.S. Rajput 92, C.S. Pandit 58, Avinash Kumar 5 for 69)

Bihar 120 and 146 for 3 (B.S. Gosain 59 not out)

Match drawn

Assam 11 pts., Bihar 6 pts.

at Polytechnic Ground, Agartala

Bengal 432 (A.O. Malhotra 89, S.J. Kalyani 81, Saurav Ganguly 64, A. Saha 5 for 69)

Tripura 88 (U. Chatterjee 6 for 24, S. Mukherjee 4 for 28) and 141 (U. Chatterjee 7 for 63)

Bengal won by an innings and 203 runs

Bengal 23 pts., Tripura 3 pts.

Forced to follow-on against Assam for whom Rajput and Chakraborty scored 153 for the first wicket, Bihar batted 95 overs to score 146 for 3 and save the match. The left-arm spin of Utpal Chatterjee twice demolished Tripura and gave Bengal an overwhelming victory. Chatterjee returned best figures for innings and match.

27, 28, 29 and 30 November 1992 *at Barbatti Stadium, Cuttack*

Orissa 491 for 9 dec. (B.D. Mohanty 100 not out, R. Biswal 84, Abakash Khatua 71, P. Mohapatra 59, C. Dey 4 for 89)
Tripura 110 (S. Mohapatra 6 for 38, R. Biswal 4 for 40) and 255 (R. Deb Burman 72)

Orissa won by an innings and 126 runs

Orissa 20 pts., Tripura 2 pts.

at Eden Gardens, Calcutta

Bengal 293 (Saurav Ganguly 80, S. Mukherjee 56, A.O. Malhotra 51, Avinash Kumar 7 for 60) and 305 for 6 dec. (A.O. Malhotra 100 not out, A. Sheikh 67 not out)
Bihar 163 (U. Chatterjee 4 for 36) and 149 (S.R. Sinha 51, U. Chatterjee 4 for 36)

Bengal won by 286 runs

Bengal 22 pts., Bihar 7 pts.

With wicket-keeper Mohanty hitting a century at number eight, Orissa swept aside Tripura. Avinash Kumar's career-best bowling performance failed to save Bihar against Bengal for whom Malhotra and Sheikh shared an unbroken seventh-wicket partnership of 151 in the second innings.

4, 5, 6 and 7 December 1992 *at Nehru Stadium, Guwahati*

Orissa 166 (Amiya Roy 67, R.C. Thakkar 4 for 53) and 219 for 5 dec. (Amiya Roy 61 not out)
Assam 358 for 8 dec. (L.S. Rajput 125, C.S. Pandit 54, Sushil Kumar 5 for 98) and 1 for 0

Match drawn

Assam 14 pts., Orissa 6 pts.

at MECON, Ranchi

Tripura 102 (Avinash Kumar 7 for 43) and 159 (Avinash Kumar 6 for 73)
Bihar 366 (S.S. Karim 180, S.R. Sinha 51, P. Kumar 4 for 63, A. Saha 4 for 91)

Bihar won by an innings and 105 runs

Bihar 24 pts., Tripura 4 pts.

No play was possible on the first day in Guwahati and, with Orissa's first innings occupying 91 overs, Assam were unable to force victory. Rajput and Pandit shared a third-wicket stand of 103. Avinash Kumar improved on his career-best performance of the previous match and veteran keeper Syed Karim hit 180 as Bihar crushed Tripura.

19, 20, 21 and 22 December 1992 *at Nehru Stadium, Guwahati*

Assam 322 (R.C. Thakkar 92, Javed Khan 73, U. Chatterjee 5 for 84) and 148 (Sen Sharma 5 for 38)
Bengal 429 (S.J. Kalyani 140, A.O. Malhotra 109, Rajinder Singh 5 for 81) and 42 for 1

Bengal won by 9 wickets

Bengal 21 pts., Assam 7 pts.

Bengal assured themselves of a place in the final stages of the competition with their third win in as many matches. They encountered strong resistance from Thakkar and Javed Khan who added 146 for Assam's eighth wicket. Kalyani and skipper Malhotra put on 231 for Bengal's fourth wicket after three wickets had fallen for 47.

25, 26, 27 and 28 December 1992 *at Eden Gardens, Calcutta*

Bengal 636 for 7 dec. (J. Arun Lal 169, S.J. Kalyani 143, A.O. Malhotra 100 not out, I.B. Roy 73, U. Chatterjee 54, R. Biswal 5 for 164)
Orissa 86 (P.S. Vaidya 4 for 31) and 212 (U. Chatterjee 5 for 91)

Bengal won by an innings and 338 runs

Bengal 25 pts., Orissa 4 pts.

at Nehru Stadium, Guwahati

Tripura 80 and 127 (R.C. Thakkar 4 for 35)
Assam 263 (L.S. Rajput 50, A. Saha 4 for 45, P. Kumar 4 for 88)

Assam won by an innings and 56 runs

Assam 22 pts., Tripura 4 pts.

Bengal swept into the pre-quarter-finals with a 100 per cent record in the East Zone. Put in to bat at Eden Gardens, they began with a stand of 159 between Arun Lal and Roy, and Arun Lal was then joined by Kalyani in a stand worth 238. Malhotra and Chatterjee shared another century stand for the seventh wicket, and Orissa faced a daunting 636. Not surprisingly, they were beaten in three days.

Assam, too, won in three days after Tripura had been bowled out for 80 in 40.1 overs on the first day.

31 December 1992, 1, 2 and 3 January 1993 *at Digwadih Stadium, Dhanbad*

Orissa 384 (Amiya Roy 107, Abakash Khatua 93 not out, Hilali Khan 5 for 67) and 340 for 5 dec. (Manas Roy 112, R. Biswal 97, P. Mohapatra 72)
Bihar 519 (S.S. Karim 169, I. Bose 80, Avinash Kumar 50, S. Mohapatra 4 for 170) and 1 for 0

Match drawn

Bihar 13 pts., Orissa 10 pts.

With three teams to qualify from the East Zone, both Orissa and Bihar entered the last match with a chance of a place in the pre-quarter-finals. Put in to bat, Orissa scored heavily but, inspired by another formidable hundred from wicket-keeper Karim, Bihar claimed first-innings lead and third place in the table.

EAST ZONE FINAL TABLE

	P	W	L	D	Pts.
Bengal	4	4	–	–	91
Assam	4	1	1	2	54
Bihar	4	1	1	2	50
Orissa	4	1	1	2	40
Tripura	4	–	4	–	13

CENTRAL ZONE

18, 19, 20 and 21 November 1992 *at VCA, Nagpur*

Vidarbha 160 (O. Kamal 6 for 51) and 230 for 7 dec. (M.G. Gogte 88, U.I. Ghani 51 not out)

Uttar Pradesh 276 (Rizwan Shamshad 102) and 23 for 1

Match drawn

Uttar Pradesh 12 pts., Vidarbha 6 pts.

21, 22, 23 and 24 November 1992 *at Jayanti Stadium, Bhilai*

Rajasthan 144 (H. Joshi 65, N.D. Hirwani 6 for 34) and 106 (N.D. Hirwani 5 for 40)

Madhya Pradesh 319 (M.S. Sahni 74, P.K. Dwivedi 63, A.R. Khurasia 55, A. Rathore 7 for 110)

Madhya Pradesh won by an innings and 69 runs

Madhya Pradesh 21 pts., Rajasthan 4 pts.

No play at all was possible on the first day at Nagpur, and there was much time lost on the following days so that there was never much chance of a result. Asked to bat first, Vidarbha struggled in difficult conditions, and Rizwan Shamshad's century assured first-innings points for the visitors.

Much time was also lost at Bhilai, but the leg-spin bowling of Test player Hirwani brought Madhya Pradesh a comfortable victory.

28, 29, 30 November and 1 December 1992 *at NTPC Ground, Korba*

Madhya Pradesh 563 (A.R. Khurasia 238, A. Vijayvirgiya 142, P.V. Gandhe 4 for 124) and 234 (S.M. Patil 58, K.K. Patel 50)

Vidarbha 194 (H.S. Sodhi 6 for 24) and 317 for 5 (Y.T. Ghare 121, S. Gujar 87)

Match drawn

Madhya Pradesh 18 pts., Vidarbha 4 pts.

at Mansarovar, Jaipur

Railways 410 (K. Bharatan 107, K.K. Sharma 83, Yusuf Ali Khan 52, R.S.P. Rathore 5 for 79)

Rajasthan 158 (K. Bharatan 7 for 39) and 223 (V. Yadav 58, M. Majithia 4 for 46, K. Bharatan 4 for 58)

Railways won by an innings and 29 runs

Railways 20 pts., Rajasthan 4 pts.

A second-wicket stand of 251 between Vijayvirgiya and Khurasia was the backbone of Madhya Pradesh's massive score against Vidarbha. Amay Khurasia hit the first double century of his career and, in effect, put the game out of Vidarbha's reach. Madhya Pradesh were content not to enforce the follow-on and simply amassed bonus points.

Railways beat Rajasthan shortly after lunch on the last day. The match was an all-round triumph for Krishnamachari Bharatan who followed the second century of his career with career-best bowling performances for match and innings.

5, 6, 7 and 8 December 1992 *at Palam Ground, Delhi*

Railways 194 (N.D. Nilose 4 for 60) and 582 (Yusuf Ali Khan 203, Abhay Sharma 106, K. Bharatan 65, Yashpal Sharma 56, S. Sawant 50 not out, N.D. Hirwani 5 for 156)

Madhya Pradesh 407 (A.R. Khurasia 110, P.K. Dwivedi 91, S.M. Patil 82) and 300 for 5 (K.K. Patel 101, M.S. Sahni 75 not out)

Match drawn

Madhya Pradesh 20 pts., Railways 14 pts.

at MB College Ground, Udaipur

Uttar Pradesh 193 (R.S.P. Rathore 6 for 69) and 271 for 7 dec. (R. Sapru 144, A. Gautam 55, Mohammad Aslam 5 for 94)

Rajasthan 255 (A. Sinha 100, S. Kesarwani 4 for 76) and 153 (V. Yadav 161, O. Kamal 6 for 21)

Uttar Pradesh won by 56 runs

Uttar Pradesh 17 pts., Rajasthan 7 pts.

Bowled out for 194 on the opening day, Railways struck back by capturing two Madhya Pradesh wickets for 55 runs before the close, but on the second day Khurasia's second century in succession helped Madhya Pradesh to a commanding lead. On the third day, Yusuf Ali Khan's double century, made in 283 minutes with 28 fours, and an equally belligerent hundred from wicket-keeper Abhay Sharma brought Railways back into the game and deemed that it would be drawn.

Rajasthan shocked Uttar Pradesh by taking a first-innings lead through the bowling of Rathore and the

Regained confidence and form for leg-spinner Hirwani (Madhya Pradesh) who was the leading wicket-taker in Indian cricket. (Simon Bruty/Allsport)

batting of Anil Sinha, but the glory was short-lived. Gautam and Sapru put on 166 for Uttar Pradesh's fourth wicket when they batted again, and Obaid Kamal bowled them to victory.

20, 21, 22 and 23 December 1992 at Karnail Singh Stadium, Delhi

Vidarbha 352 (S.K. Kulkarni 91, P.B. Hingnikar 52, I. Thakur 5 for 113) and 180 (S.K. Kulkarni 67, M. Majithia 6 for 57)

Railways 277 (K.K. Sharma 61, Manvinder Singh 53, T. Gonsalves 4 for 67) and 90 (P.B. Hingnikar 5 for 25, P.V. Gandhe 4 for 27)

Vidarbha won by 165 runs

Vidarbha 20 pts., Railways 9 pts.

Iqbal Thakur's fine debut for Railways was overshadowed by the batting of Kulkarni and Hingnikar who played decisive roles in holding Vidarbha's first innings together. Railways were struggling at 130 for 7 in reply when K.K. Sharma hit a six and 9 fours in a brilliant 61 off 47 deliveries. Boosted by 61 penalty runs, Railways finished only 75 runs short of Vidarbha. The left-arm spin of Manish Majithia kept Railways in the game but, on the last day, they collapsed before the off-spin of Pritam Gandhe and the occasional medium pace of skipper Praveen Hingnikar.

28, 29, 30 and 31 December 1992 at VCA Ground, Nagpur

Vidarbha 338 (V.I. Ghani 94, H.R. Wasu 79, Shamsher Singh 5 for 72, R.S.P. Rathore 4 for 61) and 204 (Y.T. Ghare 74)

Rajasthan 266 (V. Joshi 86, V. Yadav 62) and 231 (Parvinder Singh 108, P.V. Gandhe 5 for 74, H.R. Wasu 4 for 72)

Vidarbha won by 45 runs

Vidarbha 17 pts., Rajasthan 10 pts.

at Nehru Stadium, Ghaziabad

Railways 298 (Abhay Sharma 100, S. Sawant 62, O. Kamal 6 for 69) and 432 (Yusuf Ali Khan 110, Abhay Sharma 53, Manvinder Singh 51)

Uttar Pradesh 416 (G.K. Pande 152, M. Mudgal 90, R. Sapru 67, Rizwan Shamshad 54 not out, K. Bharatan 6 for 126) and 318 for 7 (S.S. Khandkar 100, A. Gautam 87, Rizwan Shamshad 52)

Uttar Pradesh won by 3 wickets

Uttar Pradesh 25 pts., Railways 13 pts.

The injustice of the Ranji Trophy points system was again in evidence. Vidarbha beat lowly Rajasthan but, as victory by runs counts for only eight points, they took just 17 points from the final match of their programme. They remained unbeaten, having won two of their four matches. At Ghaziabad, however, Railways were beaten for the second time in four matches, but took 13 points from the match which clinched their place in the pre-quarter-finals. Railways gained 32 and 106 penalty runs respectively through Uttar Pradesh bowling six and nine overs short in the two innings. The runs were much needed for, having ended the first day on 215 for 5, Railways lost their last five wickets for 66 runs on the second morning in spite of Abhay Sharma's century. A second-wicket partnership of 195 between Pande and Mudgal put Uttar Pradesh on top. Gyanendra Pande hit 18 fours in his fine innings, and Uttar Pradesh took a first-innings lead of 118. Yusuf Ali Khan played a captain's innings to effect a recovery, but it was only the penalty runs conceded in the second innings that gave Uttar Pradesh such a big target, which they reached thanks to Khandkar's century.

18, 19, 20 and 21 January 1993 at K.D. Singh 'Babu' Stadium, Lucknow

Madhya Pradesh 257 and 309 (D.K. Nilose 91, K.K. Patel 69)

Uttar Pradesh 307 (Rizwan Shamshad 109, R. Sapru 56, D.K. Nilose 5 for 101) and 193 (N.D. Hirwani 5 for 60)

Madhya Pradesh won by 66 runs

Madhya Pradesh 17 pts., Uttar Pradesh 10 pts.

As both teams had already qualified for the knock-out stage, the final match in the Central Zone had little significance. Rizwan Shamshad continued his exciting form with a fluent hundred, and there were more signs of regained confidence as Hirwani bowled Madhya Pradesh to victory on the last day.

CENTRAL ZONE FINAL TABLE

	P	W	L	D	Pts.
Madhya Pradesh	4	2	–	2	76
Uttar Pradesh	4	2	1	1	64
Railways	4	1	2	1	56
Vidarbha	4	2	–	2	47
Rajasthan	4	–	4	–	25

PRE-QUARTER-FINALS

5, 6, 7, 8 and **9** February 1993 *at M. Chinnaswamy Stadium, Nabgalore*

Madhya Pradesh 406 (P.K. Dwivedi 174, S.M. Patil 95, A.R. Bhat 4 for 116) and 173 (D.K. Nilose 69 not out, A.R. Bhat 5 for 47, R. Ananth 4 for 50)

Karnataka 342 (K. Srinath 144, R.S. Dravid 89, N.D. Hirwani 6 for 123) and 232 (K.A. Jeshwanth 87, S. Somsunder 59, S.S. Lahore 6 for 95)

Madhya Pradesh won by 5 runs

6, 7, 8, 9 and **10** February 1993 *at Railway Stadium, Madras*

Tamil Nadu 547 (M. Senthilnathan 189, S. Sharath 102, S. Subramaniam 68, D. Vasu 55, M. Sanjay 55 not out)

Assam 251 (Rajinder Singh 91, L.S. Rajput 60, S. Subramaniam 7 for 61) and 224 (L.S. Rajput 105, S. Subramaniam 7 for 57)

Tamil Nadu won by an innings and 72 runs

12, 13, 14, 15 and **16** February 1993 *at Nehru Stadium, Pune*

Maharashtra 405 (S.S. Bhave 93, S.D. Lande 56, S.A. Inamdar 55, I. Siddiqi 51) and 393 for 1 dec. (H.A. Kinikar 205 not out, S. Jedhe 121 not out)

Railways 399 (Abhay Sharma 170, Yusuf Ali Khan 54, P. Shepherd 50, S. Jedhe 6 for 119) and 124 for 2

Match drawn

Maharashtra won on first-innings lead

at IPCL Ground, Baroda

Hyderabad 416 (Abdul Azeem 158, V. Pratap 72, M.A. Narula 4 for 82) and 320 (R.A. Swaroop 125, V. Jaisimha 73, M.A. Narula 4 for 77)

Baroda 431 for 9 dec. (T.B. Arothe 171, J. Martin 82, K.S. Chavan 65, Arshad Ayub 6 for 147) and 254 (N.R. Mongia 91, R.A. Swaroop 5 for 91)

Hyderabad won by 51 runs

at Punjab Agricultural University, Ludhiana

Bengal 209 (J. Arun Lal 60, A. Bedi 4 for 31, B. Vij 4 for 62) and 327 (I.B. Roy 119, S.J. Kalyani 63, B. Vij 5 for 95, Bhupinder Singh snr 4 for 82)

Punjab 196 (P.S. Vaidya 4 for 64, U. Chatterjee 4 for 74) and 344 for 4 (V. Rathore 169 not out, Gursharan Singh 82)

Punjab won by 6 wickets

at Nehru Stadium, Ghaziabad

Haryana 283 (V. Yadav 86, Amarjeet Kaypee 64, A.W. Zaidi 5 for 92, O. Kamal 4 for 72) and 505 for 6 dec. (V. Yadav 191, Amarjeet Kaypee 109, D. Sharma 62, N. Goel 56)

Uttar Pradesh 454 (S.S. Khandkar 137, M. Mudgal 107, Rizwan Shamshad 83, C.M. Sharma 5 for 137) and 263 for 6 (A. Gautam 63 not out, Rizwan Shamshad 61)

Match drawn

Uttar Pradesh won on first-innings lead

at Brabourne Stadium, Bombay

Bihar 182 (T. Kumar 50, M. Karanjkar 4 for 39) and 235 (T. Kumar 100 not out, S.V. Bahutule 4 for 71, S.S. Patil 4 for 77)

Bombay 458 (S. More 112, Z. Bharuacha 101, S. Arfi 4 for 53, Avinash Kumar 4 for 131)

Bombay won by an innings and 41 runs

Madhya Pradesh became the first team to enter the quarter-finals when they had a thrilling win over Karnataka. Madhya's first innings of 406 was founded on an outstanding knock by Dwivedi, but Srinath's century kept Karnataka in touch. The bowling of the veteran Bhat and Ananth brought Karnataka right back into the game and left their side with a reasonable target of 238. At 150 for 7, the cause looked lost, but skipper Jeshwanth and wicket-keeper Vaidya added 75, only for the last three wickets to fall for seven runs.

In spite of Rajput's heroics, Tamil Nadu overwhelmed Assam. Ijaz Hussain and Rajinder Singh exploited some early zip in the pitch, and Tamil Nadu were 84 for 4, but scintillating centuries from Senthilnathan and the left-handed Sharath took them to 304 before the next wicket fell. Subramaniam and Sanjay then added 113 for the last wicket, and with Sunil Subramaniam bowling his left-arm spin on a nagging length, Assam were doomed.

Facing a total of 405, which had been boosted by Maharashtra's tail-enders, Railways seemed set to take a first-innings lead when Abhay Sharma made his highest Ranji Trophy score, hitting 170 off 227 balls with a six and 25 fours, but the tail-enders batted recklessly and the advantage was lost. It proved to be costly, for Kinikar and Jedhe, who had taken six wickets with his occasional off-spin, shared an unbroken stand of 242 and took Maharashtra into the quarter-finals.

The 32-year-old Abdul Azeem hit his 12th Ranji Trophy century and led Hyderabad to a good score, but Tushar Arothe's career best 171 gave Baroda an invaluable first-innings lead. Royapetha Swaroop's 125 kept Hyderabad's hopes alive, and Baroda were left to score 306 to win or to survive in order to move into the next round. With five minutes remaining, Mongia appeared to have saved the game for Baroda after Swaroop's career-best haul, but then he was caught at short-leg off Arshad Ayub. With only three balls of the match remaining, Sridhar trapped Rashid Patel leg before, and Hyderabad were the victors.

Punjab won a splendid victory over Bengal. Needing a daunting 341 to win, they were 25 for 2, and then Vikram Rathore hit a marvellous unbeaten 169, his fifth hundred in the national championship, to bring victory 25 minutes after tea on the final day.

A stand of 213 for the second wicket between Mudgal and Khandkar gave Uttar Pradesh dominance over Haryana whose flow of runs came too late, and, as expected, Bombay swamped Bihar who were encouraged by a century from Tarun Kumar, a young batsman who was playing in only his third Ranji Trophy match.

The mighty Bombay went out of the Trophy on the toss of a coin. Only 97 minutes' play was possible, and three days were totally washed out. At Bhusawal, Jedhe produced another outstanding all-round performance to steer Maharashtra into the semi-finals. For the second match in succession, he hit a century and took five wickets in an innings. He and Bhave added 213 for the second wicket.

Consistent batting took Madhya Pradesh to 347, but Delhi had to rely solely on the aggressive Bantoo Singh who, coming in at 10 for 1, did his utmost to take his side to a first-innings lead with a most responsible innings. He was let down by his colleagues, and Madhya Pradesh were content to hold what they had.

No play was possible on the first two days in Ludhiana, and when Gursharan Singh won the toss he asked Hyderabad to bat first. The visitors wilted against a varied attack. Their last five wickets went down for 14 runs and, even with seven penalty runs, they could muster only 82. Punjab, in contrast, showed great application and took a first-innings lead of 116. Hyderabad again faltered, with Punjab's medium-pacers doing most of the damage, and the home side won with ease.

QUARTER-FINALS

26, 27, 28 February, 1 and 2 March 1993 *at Green Park, Kanpur*

Bombay 133 for 2 dec. (S.S. Dighe 62 not out)
Uttar Pradesh 33 for 0

Match abandoned

Uttar Pradesh won on toss of a coin

at Railway Stadium, Bhusawal

Tamil Nadu 267 (D. Vasu 78, Ashish Kapoor 61, I. Siddiqi 6 for 59, S.V. Inamdar 4 for 71) and 215 (S. Sharath 55, S.V. Jedhe 5 for 72, I. Siddiqi 4 for 71)
Maharashtra 384 (S.V. Jedhe 168, S.S. Bhave 99, D. Vasu 5 for 81) and 102 for 0 (S.S. Bhave 64 not out)

Maharashtra won by 10 wickets

at BHEL Sports Ground, Bhopal

Madhya Pradesh 347 (Zuber Khan 72 not out) and 263 for 4 (K.K. Patel 100, M.S. Sahni 64)
Delhi 330 (Bantoo Singh 141 not out)

Match drawn

Madhya Pradesh won on first-innings lead

at Punjab Agricultural University, Ludhiana

Hyderabad 82 (Bhupinder Singh snr 4 for 37) and 180 (R.A. Swaroop 58, V. Jaisimha 56, A. Bedi 5 for 77, Bhupinder Singh snr 4 for 59)
Punjab 198 (Arshad Ayub 5 for 70) and 65 for 1

Punjab won by 9 wickets

SEMI-FINALS

12, 13, 14, 15 and 16 March 1993 *at Poona Club, Pune*

Maharashtra 378 (S.S. Bhave 72, S.V. Jedhe 61, A.W. Zaidi 5 for 115) and 317 (S.S. Sugwekar 143, S.V. Jedhe 62, O. Kamal 4 for 89, A.W. Zaidi 4 for 118)
Uttar Pradesh 314 (Rizwan Shamshad 145 not out, S.V. Jedhe 4 for 88) and 282 (Rizwan Shamshad 93, A. Gautam 62, I. Siddiqi 4 for 77, S.V. Jedhe 4 for 109)

Maharashtra won by 99 runs

13, 14, 15, 16 and 17 March 1993 *at Nehru Stadium, Indore*

Punjab 217 (Gursharan Singh 81, N.D. Hirwani 5 for 47) and 216 (N.D. Hirwani 4 for 75)
Madhya Pradesh 154 (A. Bedi 4 for 52) and 199 (B. Vij 4 for 63)

Punjab won by 80 runs

Obaid Kamal and Ashish Winston Zaidi kept a tight rein on Maharashtra on the opening day in Pune, and the young medium-pacers reduced Maharashtra from 168 for 1 to 290 for 6 at the close after Bhave and Jedhe had threatened massacre. The innings was ended 45 minutes before lunch on the second day, but neither side took much comfort from what followed. Uttar Pradesh closed on 171 for 4, but Rizwan had been dropped at short-leg and was generally troubled by the fast medium pace of Iqbal Siddiqi, who has had the benefit of coaching from Frank Tyson. Rizwan survived two more chances on the third day and added 97 for the eighth wicket with Obaid Kamal. Having ridden his luck, Rizwan ended with 145 and brought his side to within 64 runs of Maharashtra. Zaidi maintained the pressure for Uttar Pradesh by capturing three wickets before the close but, on the fourth day, Shantanu Sugwekar's century put Maharashtra firmly in control. They did not relax, and although Uttar Pradesh rallied on the last day after being 80 for 4 overnight, there was never any doubt that Maharashtra would enter the Ranji Trophy final for the first time in 22 years.

Some rather reckless batting against the leg-spin of Hirwani saw Punjab tumbled out for 217 on the opening day in Indore, but Punjab's varied attack saw them wrest the initiative on the second and claim a first-innings advantage of 63. The game continued to fluctuate as Punjab lost their first three second-innings wickets for 32, and their fourth at 80. The middle order showed admirable determination, but Hirwani still posed problems, and the last four wickets went down for 24 runs. Needing 280 to win, Madhya Pradesh lost two wickets for 51 before the end of the third day. Sodhi was out with only one run added on the fourth morning, and although Patil showed great application, it never looked as if the Punjab bowlers and fielders would be denied, and when D.K. Nilose was bowled by Bhupinder Singh snr, Punjab were in the Ranji Trophy final for the first time.

RANJI TROPHY FINAL
PUNJAB *v.* MAHARASHTRA, at Ludhiana

The excellent teamwork under the captaincy of Gursharan Singh which had taken Punjab into the Ranji Trophy final for the first time did not let them down on the big occasion. Winning the toss and batting first, they overcame an indifferent start through a brilliant innings from Amit Sharma who shared a stand of 100 for the sixth wicket with Mohan. It was the only century of the match, and Amit Sharma continued to dominate the play before being last out for an heroic 161.

Punjab relied on the three-pronged attack of medium-pacers Bhupinder Singh senior and Bedi, and left-arm spinner Vij. They whittled away at the Maharashtra batting and gained an invaluable first-innings lead of 106.

Jadhav and Jedhe, who had enjoyed a spectacularly successful tournament, maintained Maharashtra's interest in the match by bowling out Punjab for 146 and leaving their side with the attainable target of 253. They never looked likely to reach this score against Punjab's inspired tenacious attack supported by tigerish fielding, and Punjab won the Ranji Trophy on their first appearance in the final.

RANJI TROPHY FINAL – PUNJAB *v.* MAHARASHTRA
27, 28, 29 and 30 March 1993 at Punjab Agricultural University, Ludhiana

PUNJAB

	FIRST INNINGS			SECOND INNINGS		
A. Kalsi	c Kondhalkar, b Jedhe	16		c Kondhalkar, b Jadhav	29	
V. Rathore	c Sugwekar, b Kulkarni	24		(3) c Gunjal, b Jadhav	14	
N.S. Sidhu	c Gunjal, b Jedhe	9		(2) b Jedhe	15	
Gursharan Singh (capt)	run out	27		c Kinikar, b Jedhe	44	
Amit Sharma	c Kinikar, b Rai	161		c Bhave, b Jadhav	6	
P. Dharmani	c Bhave, b Jedhe	1		c Sugwekar, b Jedhe	1	
K. Mohan	b Jedhe	22		c and b Rai	10	
*Arun Sharma	run out	7		c and b Jadhav	5	
Bhupinder Singh snr	lbw, b Siddiqi	7		c Bhave, b Jadhav	6	
B. Vij	c Siddiqi, b Jadhav	23		b Jedhe	8	
A. Bedi	not out	0		not out	0	
Extras	b 5, lb 5, w 4, nb 7	21		b 4, lb 2, nb 2	8	
		318			**146**	

MAHARASHTRA

	FIRST INNINGS			SECOND INNINGS		
S.S. Bhave (capt)	c Gursharan, b Bedi	1		c Dharmani, b Mohan	19	
H.A. Kinikar	c Dharmani, b Vij	21		lbw, b Bedi	11	
S.V. Jedhe	st Arun Sharma, b Vij	42		b Bedi	25	
S.S. Sugwekar	c Amit, b Bhupinder	10		(5) c Dharmani, b Vij	14	
M.D. Gunjal	c Arun, b Bhupinder	15		(8) lbw, b Bhupinder	10	
J. Narse	c Arun, b Bhupinder	6		c Arun Sharma, b Vij	10	
P. Rai	c Gursharan, b Vij	29		(4) c Gursharan, b Bedi	11	
S.J. Jadhav	c Gursharan, b Vij	25		(7) c Arun, b Bhupinder	4	
*S. Kondhalkar	c Arun Sharma, b Vij	26		c Arun, b Bhupinder	7	
I. Siddiqi	c Gursharan, b Vij	1		c Bhupinder, b Vij	0	
M. Kulkarni	not out	17		not out	5	
Extras	b 4, lb 8, nb 7	19		b 6, lb 3, w 2, nb 1	12	
Penalty runs					4	
		212			**132**	

	O	M	R	W	O	M	R	W		O	M	R	W	O	M	R	W
Siddiqi	31	8	78	1	5	1	13	–	Bhupinder Singh snr	28	7	85	3	20.4	3	47	3
Kulkarni	16	4	53	1					Bedi	14	4	53	1	16	3	35	3
Jedhe	39	11	111	4	23	7	40	4	Vij	29.2	9	61	6	13	3	33	3
Jadhav	16	5	39	1	27.4	4	55	5	Mohan	4	3	1	–	3	1	4	1
Rai	17.4	7	27	1	12	3	27	1									
Sugwekar					3	1	5	–									

FALL OF WICKETS

1–39, 2–48, 3–58, 4–94, 5–95, 6–195, 7–227, 8–242, 9–318
1–34, 2–60, 3–61, 4–95, 5–100, 6–113, 7–122, 8–128, 9–144

FALL OF WICKETS

1–7, 2–61, 3–84, 4–86, 5–94, 6–111, 7–137, 8–175, 9–179
1–25, 2–46, 3–67, 4–72, 5–91, 6–96, 7–112, 8–112, 9–116

Umpires: A.L. Narasimhan & S. Purel

Punjab won by 120 runs

TEST MATCH

INDIA *v.* ZIMBABWE, at Delhi

It was unfortunate for Zimbabwe that their first venture in an overseas Test match should be against an Indian side which had never been so confident in itself nor so flushed with success. India made two changes from the team which had been triumphant against England: Yadav, making his Test debut, replaced More as wicket-keeper, and Maninder Singh completed his rehabilitation to the exclusion of Venkatapathy Raju. Zimbabwe gave first Test caps to Briant and Ranchod.

Azharuddin won the toss, India batted, and Zimbabwe claimed an early scalp when Prabhakar fell to Brain. This proved to be a false ray of hope for the visitors. Kambli joined Sidhu in a partnership of 107, and Tendulkar then shared a stand of 137 with his school companion. By the end of the day, India were in total control at 340 for 3, with Vinod Kambli having hit 176 off 220 balls.

There was to be no respite for Zimbabwe on a rain-curtailed second day. Azharuddin, to his chagrin, was run out when Kambli declined a second run to long-leg, but the young left-hander became only the third batsman

in Test history to score a second successive double century. India advanced to 411 for 4, Kambli to 207.

Kambli added 20 on the third morning before giving veteran off-spinner Traicos a return catch. It was a wicket that Traicos well deserved for he was by far the best of the Zimbabwe bowlers. India scored 125 in the morning session before declaring at lunch. Amre gave further indication of his smouldering talent but, inevitably, the honours had again gone to the left-handed Kambli.

Kapil Dev dismissed Arnott with the first ball of the Zimbabwe innings, and Campbell and Houghton fell to the spinners, but the Flower brothers remained until the close, 152 for 3, giving the visitors every hope of forcing a draw.

An hour after lunch on the fourth day that hope seemed sure to be realised. Grant and Andy Flower had added 192 and taken the score to 275 for 3 with some totally admirable batting. The left-handed Andy became Zimbabwe's third Test century-maker, but suddenly he charged at Maninder and was stumped. Maninder removed Grant six balls later, and the collapse gathered momentum. Seven wickets went down for 47 runs, and Zimbabwe followed-on 214 runs behind. Grant Flower was leg before to Prabhakar's fourth ball in the second innings, the first ball that the opener had faced, and

---

TEST MATCH – INDIA *v.* ZIMBABWE
13, 14, 15, 16 and 17 March 1993 at Ferozeshah Kotla Ground, Delhi

INDIA

FIRST INNINGS

M. Prabhakar	c A. Flower, b Brain	3
N.S. Sidhu	lbw, b Traicos	61
V.G. Kambli	c and b Traicos	227
S.R. Tendulkar	c Traicos, b Ranchod	62
M. Azharuddin (capt)	run out	42
P.K. Amre	not out	52
Kapil Dev	st A. Flower, b Traicos	16
*V. Yadav	b Brain	30
A.R. Kumble	not out	18
Maninder Singh		
R.K. Chauhan		
Extras	b 17, lb 6, w 2	25
	(for 7 wickets, dec.)	536

ZIMBABWE

	FIRST INNINGS		SECOND INNINGS	
K.J. Arnott	lbw, b Kapil Dev	0	b Maninder Singh	21
G.W. Flower	lbw, b Maninder	96	lbw, b Prabhakar	0
A.D.R. Campbell	b Chauhan	32	c Amre, b Kumble	61
D.L. Houghton (capt)	lbw, b Kumble	18	c Amre, b Kumble	1
*A. Flower	st Yadav, b Maninder	115	not out	62
G.A. Briant	st Yadav, b Kumble	1	c Kambli, b Maninder	16
A.H. Omarshah	run out	25	lbw, b Kumble	6
E.A. Brandes	c Sidhu, b Kumble	8	c Chauhan, b Maninder	1
D.H. Brain	c Kambli, b Maninder	0	lbw, b Kumble	0
U. Ranchod	b Chauhan	7	c Yadav, b Maninder	1
A.J. Traicos	not out	0	lbw, b Kumble	1
Extras	b 4, lb 10, w 1, nb 5	20	b 10, lb 16, w 2, nb 3	31
		322		201

	O	M	R	W
Brandes	26	4	93	–
Brain	34	1	146	2
Omarshah	10	3	43	–
Traicos	50	4	186	3
Ranchod	12	–	45	1

	O	M	R	W	O	M	R	W
Kapil Dev	13	4	37	1	4	1	4	–
Prabhakar	14	4	23	–	4	3	5	1
Chauhan	28.1	4	68	2	14	5	30	–
Kumble	43	12	90	3	38.5	16	70	5
Maninder Singh	32	4	79	3	35	8	66	4
Tendulkar	5	1	11	–				

FALL OF WICKETS

1–19, 2–126, 3–263, 4–370, 5–434, 6–464, 7–507

1–0, 2–53, 3–83, 4–275, 5–276, 6–276, 7–286, 8–287, 9–318
1–2, 2–53, 3–62, 4–126, 5–159, 6–167, 7–176, 8–177, 9–188

Umpires: S. Venkataraghavan & R.K. Bansal

India won by an innings and 13 runs

although Campbell and Arnott added 51, Arnott was bowled by Maninder, and Zimbabwe began the last day on an uneasy 62 for 2.

For the third successive time, India won a Test match by an innings when Kumble trapped Traicos leg before shortly before tea on the fifth day. Houghton had departed in the first over of the morning, and once Kumble had accounted for Campbell, who added 64 with Andy Flower, the combination of leg-spin and orthodox left-arm spin proved too much for the inexperienced Zimbabwe batsmen.

ONE-DAY INTERNATIONAL SERIES
INDIA v. ZIMBABWE

The Zimbabwe tour of India was restricted to a single Test match and three one-day internationals. The incomparable Kambli continued his purple patch with an innings of 80 off 70 balls in the first one-dayer after Prabhakar and Sidhu had given India a fine start with a

partnership of 114. The early loss of Andy Flower ended any chance Zimbabwe may have had of reaching a formidable target against a varied attack.

The second match was mutilated by rain. Grant Flower raised Zimbabwe's spirits with 57 off 67 balls and, well as India batted, they faced a demanding task. The pressure was eased when Azharuddin pulled the first ball of the penultimate over, bowled by Brain, for six, and his side went on to win with three balls to spare.

Batting first after winning the toss in the third match, Zimbabwe were given a blistering start by the Flower brothers who hit 58 in 11.4 overs. Andrew scored 32 off 36 balls before being run out at the non-striker's end by Azharuddin's brilliant throw. Grant Flower's 50 took 86 balls, but he and Campbell added 64 to put their side in a strong position. This was followed by a decline which saw nine wickets fall for 112 runs.

The Indian innings had a firm foundation with Sidhu and Raman scoring 114. Raman's return to the Indian side saw him hit 66 off 80 balls. He hit 9 fours and 2 sixes and was out in attempting to hit a third. Kambli and Ajay Sharma, who batted most impressively, took India to victory with 27 balls to spare.

FIRST ONE-DAY INTERNATIONAL – INDIA v. ZIMBABWE
19 March 1993 at Nahar Singh Stadium, Faridabad

INDIA			ZIMBABWE		
M. Prabhakar	c Houghton, b Traicos	56	*A. Flower	b Prabhakar	9
N.S. Sidhu	c Brain, b Crocker	56	G.W. Flower	c Kumble, b Venkatapathy Raju	42
V.G. Kambli	b Brain	80	A.D.R. Campbell	c Prabhakar, b Venkatapathy Raju	12
M. Azharuddin (capt)	c and b G.W. Flower	8	D.L. Houghton (capt)	run out	23
S.R. Tendulkar	c and b G.W. Flower	3	M.H. Dekker	c Azharuddin, b Srinath	22
P.K. Amre	c James, b Brandes	2	W.R. James	run out	0
*V. Yadav	not out	19	A.H. Omarshah	c Venkatapathy Raju, b Kumble	2
A.R. Kumble	c James, b Brain	0	E.A. Brandes	lbw, b Srinath	7
S.A. Ankola	not out	1	G.J. Crocker	c Yadav, b Srinath	2
J. Srinath			D.H. Brain	st Yadav, b Tendulkar	27
Venkatapathy Raju			A.J. Traicos	not out	7
Extras	b 7, lb 8, w 8, nb 1	24	Extras	b 8, lb 14, w 6, nb 1	29
		—			—
(48 overs)	(for 7 wickets)	249	(46.2 overs)		182

	O	M	R	W		O	M	R	W
Brandes	10	–	32	1	Prabhakar	9	1	33	1
Brain	9	–	36	2	Srinath	10	1	38	3
Omarshah	4	–	26	–	Ankola	7	1	20	–
Crocker	10	–	54	1	Venkatapathy Raju	10	–	26	2
Traicos	10	–	61	1	Kumble	10	–	37	1
G.W. Flower	5	–	25	2	Tendulkar	0.2	–	6	1

FALL OF WICKETS
1–114, 2–149, 3–183, 4–204, 5–207, 6–245, 7–245

FALL OF WICKETS
1–20, 2–71, 3–85, 4–105, 5–115, 6–126, 7–135, 8–141, 9–147

Man of the Match: V.G. Kambli

India won by 67 runs

SECOND ONE-DAY INTERNATIONAL – INDIA v. ZIMBABWE
22 March 1993 at Nehru Stadium, Guwahati

ZIMBABWE				INDIA			
*A. Flower	c Kumble, b Ankola		26	N.S. Sidhu	b Crocker		25
G.W. Flower	c Kambli, b Kumble		57	M. Prabhakar	c Houghton, b Brandes		51
A.D.R. Campbell	run out		29	V.G. Kambli	b G.W. Flower		32
D.L. Houghton (capt)	lbw, b Kumble		8	M. Azharuddin (capt)	not out		15
M.H. Dekker	b Prabhakar		2	S.R. Tendulkar	not out		8
K.J. Arnott	not out		1	P.K. Amre			
E.A. Brandes	b Srinath		2	Kapil Dev			
D.H. Brain	not out		6	*V. Yadav			
G.A. Briant				A.R. Kumble			
G.J. Crocker				S.A. Ankola			
A.J. Traicos				J. Srinath			
Extras	b 1, lb 12, w 3, nb 2		18	Extras	b 1, lb 6, w 10, nb 2		19
(28 overs)	(for 6 wickets)		149	(27.3 overs)	(for 3 wickets)		150

	O	M	R	W		O	M	R	W
Kapil Dev	6	–	21		Brain	6	–	39	–
Prabhakar	5	–	31	1	Brandes	6	–	14	1
Srinath	5	–	19	1	Traicos	6	–	32	–
Ankola	6	–	33	1	Crocker	6	–	35	1
Kumble	6	–	32	2	G.W. Flower	3.3	–	23	1

FALL OF WICKETS

1–56, 2–112, 3–137, 4–137, 5–145, 6–148

FALL OF WICKETS

1–67, 2–122, 3–128

Man of the Match: G.W. Flower   *India won by 7 wickets*

THIRD ONE-DAY INTERNATIONAL – INDIA v. ZIMBABWE
25 March 1993 at Nehru Stadium, Pune

ZIMBABWE				INDIA			
*A. Flower	run out		32	N.S. Sidhu	run out		45
G.W. Flower	c Yadav, b Kumble		50	W.V. Raman	c G.W. Flower, b Traicos		66
A.D.R. Campbell	st Yadav, b Kumble		22	A.K. Sharma	not out		59
D.L. Houghton (capt)	b Kapil Dev		46	V.G. Kambli	not out		47
M.H. Dekker	run out		8	M. Azharuddin (capt)			
G.A. Briant	run out		16	S.R. Tendulkar			
A.H. Omarshah	c Yadav, b Kapil Dev		1	Kapil Dev			
E.A. Brandes	c Kumble, b Srinath		5	*V. Yadav			
G.J. Crocker	b Kapil Dev		1	A.R. Kumble			
D.H. Brain	not out		12	S.A. Ankola			
A.J. Traicos	c Ankola, b Srinath		4	J. Srinath			
Extras	b 2, lb 14, w 17, nb 4		37	Extras	lb 8, w 10, nb 3		21
(49.5 overs)			234	(45.3 overs)	(for 2 wickets)		238

	O	M	R	W		O	M	R	W
Kapil Dev	10	1	54	3	Brandes	10	–	31	–
Srinath	9.5	1	34	2	Briant	9.3	–	47	–
Ankola	6	–	32	–	G.W. Flower	5	–	39	–
Tendulkar	4	–	30	–	Crocker	8	1	39	–
A.K. Sharma	10	–	34	–	Omarshah	3	–	24	–
Kumble	10	–	34	2	Traicos	10	–	50	1

FALL OF WICKETS

1–58, 2–122, 3–129, 4–154, 5–196, 6–199, 7–212, 8–215, 9–217

FALL OF WICKETS

1–114, 2–134

Man of the Match: A.K. Sharma   *India won by 8 wickets*

BATTING

	M	Inns	NO	Runs	HS	Av	100s	50s
M. Sanjay	7	7	6	118	51*	118.00	–	1
V.G. Kambli	11	16	5	1237	227	112.45	4	4
A.O. Malhotra	5	7	2	494	109	98.80	3	2
W.V. Raman	3	4	–	384	184	96.00	1	2
S. Kotak	2	3	1	170	76	85.00	–	2
Abakash Khatua	4	5	2	237	93*	79.00	–	2
N.R. Mongia	5	8	2	459	111*	76.50	1	4
T. Kumar	2	3	1	150	100*	75.00	1	1
R. Shamshad	7	12	2	732	145*	73.20	3	5
S.J. Kalyani	5	7	–	485	143	69.28	2	2
J.V. Paranjpe	8	11	2	611	218	67.88	1	4
S.S. Karim	6	10	2	538	180	67.25	2	1
J.J. Martin	5	9	3	402	86*	67.00	–	4
S.V. Jedhe	8	15	2	867	168	66.69	4	3
L.S. Rajput	5	8	1	463	125	66.14	2	3
V. Yadav	6	8	–	528	191	66.00	1	4
I.B. Roy	2	3	–	197	119	65.66	1	1
K. Srinath	6	8	1	447	144*	63.85	2	2
S.R. Tendulkar	6	8	1	446	165	63.71	1	4
Bantoo Singh	7	11	2	559	141*	62.11	2	4
R.S. Dravid	9	14	3	670	200*	60.90	1	5
P.K. Amre	7	8	1	426	86	60.85	–	5
T.B. Arothe	5	9	–	544	171	60.44	2	3
S.V. Manjrekar	3	4	1	179	96	59.66	–	1
M.H. Parmar	6	10	1	534	127*	59.33	2	4
Z. Bharuacha	6	8	–	470	101	58.75	2	2
N.R. Goel	5	9	2	404	102	57.71	1	3
S.V. Bahutule	7	7	2	286	123*	57.20	1	–
Amit Sharma	2	4	–	228	161	57.00	1	–
A. Roy	4	6	1	285	107	57.00	1	2
A.K. Sharma	8	14	2	684	150	57.00	2	5
S. More	5	5	–	284	112	56.80	1	2
Maninder Singh	9	9	4	284	102*	56.80	1	1
M. Azharuddin	6	8	–	451	182	56.37	2	2
Abdul Azeem	7	11	2	507	158	56.33	2	2
G. Vadhera	2	2	–	111	95	55.50	–	1
A.R. Khurasia	8	12	–	661	238	55.08	3	1
S.S. Bhave	8	16	1	821	220	54.73	1	5
H.A. Kinikar	8	16	2	754	205*	53.85	3	1
Robin Singh	9	14	3	590	108	53.63	2	3
K.S.V.D. Kamaraju	5	6	–	320	112	53.33	1	1
R.A. Swaroop	7	11	1	519	140	51.90	2	2
V.M. Jaisimha	7	9	1	412	73	51.50	–	5
A.C. Bedade	5	9	1	402	111*	50.25	2	2
K.A. Jeshwanth	6	8	–	396	101	49.50	1	3
P.V. Shashikanth	6	9	1	396	102*	49.50	1	2
S.S. Dighe	6	10	3	346	100	49.42	1	2
K. Mohan	8	13	5	393	129*	49.12	1	1
P.K. Dwivedi	7	12	–	588	174	49.00	1	2
Abhay Sharma	7	11	–	530	170	48.18	3	1
A. Kaypee	7	12	1	528	122	48.00	3	1
Parminder Singh	2	4	–	191	108	47.75	1	–
Iqbal Khan	4	3	–	139	69	46.33	1	2
Gursharan Singh	8	13	1	553	101	46.08	1	3
N.S. Sidhu	11	17	1	736	147	46.00	2	4
S.S. Sugwekar	7	12	–	547	143	45.58	2	1
V. Pratap	7	9	1	355	122*	44.37	1	2
B. Dutta	2	4	1	133	107	44.33	1	–
R.V. Sapru	7	11	1	439	144	43.90	1	2
K. Veerbrahman	5	6	1	219	90*	43.80	–	2
Yusuf Ali Khan	7	12	–	522	203	43.50	2	2
D. Vasu	8	11	1	431	78	43.10	–	4
V. Rathore	8	14	1	560	169*	43.07	1	2
S.M. Patil	6	10	–	430	95	43.00	–	3
P. Patel	2	4	–	168	123	42.00	1	–
S. Sawant	3	5	2	126	62	42.00	–	2
S.M.H. Kirmani	6	9	–	373	81	41.44	–	4
A.R. Kapoor	8	10	2	325	73*	40.62	–	3
R. Feroze	5	8	3	203	50*	40.60	–	1
Y.T. Ghare	3	6	–	243	124	40.50	1	1
S.S. Tanna	4	7	–	276	161	39.42	1	–
B.D. Mohanty	4	6	2	157	100*	39.25	1	–
Manvinder Singh	5	9	2	269	53	38.42	–	2
R.C. Thakkar	5	7	2	192	92	38.40	–	1
M. Senthilnathan	8	12	1	419	189	38.09	1	1

	M	Inns	NO	Runs	HS	Av	100s	50s
Bhupinder Singh jnr	7	11	3	304	116	38.00	1	1
M.S. Sahni	7	13	2	417	75*	37.90	–	3
M.V. Sridhar	7	10	1	341	176	37.88	1	–
U.I. Ghani	4	8	2	226	94	37.66	–	2
M. Karanjkar	5	4	–	150	84	37.50	–	1
I. Bose	2	4	1	112	80	37.33	–	1
M. Prabhakar	7	11	2	336	62	37.33	–	2
A. Pathak	5	7	1	223	145	37.16	1	–
Javed Khan	3	5	1	148	73	37.00	–	1
S.S. Khandkar	7	11	–	398	137	36.18	2	–
V.Z. Yadav	4	8	–	289	62	36.12	–	3
R. Nayyar	4	7	–	251	78	35.85	–	2
R.B. Biswal	5	9	1	282	97	35.25	–	2
K. Srikkanth	9	14	–	489	104	34.92	2	–
M. Mudgal	7	12	2	341	107	34.10	1	1
R. Manohar	4	7	2	170	48*	34.00	–	1
Sanjay Sharma	5	7	1	204	103	34.00	1	–
Kapil Dev	5	5	1	135	66*	33.75	–	1
M. Roy	4	7	–	235	112	33.57	1	–
R. Puri	7	11	1	335	150	33.50	1	–
G.K. Pandey	9	13	2	368	152	33.45	1	1
S.K. Kulkarni	4	8	–	267	91	33.37	–	2
Hitesh Sharma	2	3	–	100	88	33.33	–	1
M.F. Rehman	5	6	–	200	79	33.33	–	1
J. Arun Lal	6	9	–	300	169	33.33	1	1
K. Bharatan	5	8	–	266	107	33.25	1	1
K.K. Sharma	5	8	1	224	83	32.00	–	2
Zuber Khan	5	10	3	223	72*	31.85	–	1
Suni Subramaniam	7	8	2	190	68	31.66	–	3
K.K. Patel	9	16	–	499	101	31.18	2	2
M. Sawkar	4	8	–	249	77	31.12	–	1
K.P. Bhaskar	7	11	1	311	101*	31.10	1	1
S. Chopra	7	11	–	339	114	30.81	1	1
V. Narayan Kutty	5	9	–	277	125	30.77	1	–
A.N. Pandya	4	8	2	181	75	30.16	–	2
B. Ramprakash	5	9	1	238	71*	29.75	–	2
R.B. Parikh	5	9	–	267	101	29.66	1	–
M. Nayyar	7	11	–	326	88	29.63	–	2
A.V. Vijayvirgiya	6	10	–	296	142	29.50	1	–
P.R. Mohapatra	4	7	–	200	72	28.57	–	2
I.P. Prakash	4	6	2	114	57*	28.50	–	1
C. Saldanha	6	9	–	255	71	28.33	–	2
B.M. Radia	5	6	2	113	52*	28.25	–	1
B.S. Gossain	4	6	1	141	59*	28.20	–	1
Maqbul Malam	4	8	–	225	87	28.12	–	2
A.D. Jadeja	4	8	–	223	63	27.87	–	1
A.D. Sinha	4	8	–	222	100	27.75	1	–
M.G. Gogte	4	8	–	221	88	27.62	–	1
M.D. Gunjal	8	13	1	331	81*	27.58	–	2
A. Gautam	9	15	2	358	87	27.53	–	4
R. Bittoo	4	7	–	192	45	27.42	–	–
Sukhdev Singh	4	6	–	162	60	27.00	–	1
V. Vinay Kumar	3	5	–	135	62	27.00	–	1
S.J. Jadhav	5	8	2	134	74*	26.80	–	1
S. Sharath	7	8	–	214	102	26.75	1	1
B.M. Jadeja	4	8	1	187	65	26.71	–	2
S. Bhatnagar	4	7	–	187	48	26.71	–	–
Rajinder Singh	5	7	–	187	91	26.71	–	1
V.B. Chandrasekhar	7	10	–	266	58	26.60	–	2
S. Mahadevan	5	10	–	265	69	26.50	–	1
Snehashi Ganguly	6	9	1	212	69*	26.50	–	1
P. Sheppard	4	8	1	185	50	26.42	–	1
K.M. Roshan	4	7	–	185	71	26.42	–	1
N.R. Odedra	4	8	–	210	104	26.25	1	–
S.D. Lande	4	5	–	131	58	26.20	–	1
S.G. Gujar	4	8	–	209	87	26.12	–	1
S.R. Sinha	5	7	–	181	51	25.85	–	2
U. Chatterjee	6	9	1	204	54	25.50	–	1
S. Chatterjee	5	7	2	126	38	25.20	–	–
D.K. Nilose	7	12	1	274	91	24.90	–	2
M.V. Ramanamurthy	7	9	–	224	64	24.88	–	2
R. Naik	3	5	–	123	87	24.60	–	1
D. Chakraborty	5	8	1	171	47	24.42	–	–
R. Kalsi	5	9	1	191	38	23.87	–	–
Raj Kumar	4	7	1	143	32	23.83	–	–
R. Deb Burman	3	6	–	142	72	23.66	–	1
G.S. Thapa	4	7	–	165	48	23.57	–	–
M.S. Narula	5	8	1	164	58*	23.42	–	1

FIRST-CLASS AVERAGES

BATTING Continued

	M	Inns	NO	Runs	HS	Av	100s	50s
H.R. Wasu	4	7	–	164	79	23.42	–	1
A. Sheikh	5	8	2	140	67*	23.33	–	1
A. Vaidya	8	12	3	209	65	23.22	–	1
B.H. Mistry	4	8	–	185	55	23.12	–	2
P.B. Hingnikar	4	8	–	183	52	22.87	–	1
C.S. Pandit	5	8	–	183	58	22.87	–	2
K.S. Chavan	5	9	–	203	65	22.55	–	1
Saurav Ganguly	7	10	–	224	80	22.40	–	2
S. Shukla	4	6	1	111	39	22.20	–	–
N. Mody	3	6	–	132	56	22.00	–	1
S. Kumar	5	10	1	198	90	22.00	–	1
Dhanraj Singh	5	9	1	175	86	21.87	–	1
S. Das Gupta	4	8	–	171	48	21.37	–	–
J. Narse	3	6	–	127	57	21.16	–	1
P.T. Subramaniam	5	9	1	169	48	21.12	–	–
S.P. Mukherjee	4	5	–	105	56	21.00	–	1
Y.S. Bhandari	5	7	1	125	48	20.83	–	–
S.S. Patil	6	5	–	103	38	20.60	–	–
K.A. Thakkar	4	8	–	164	60	20.50	–	1
Kirti Azad	7	10	1	184	50	20.44	–	1
Rajesh Singh	4	6	–	121	45	20.16	–	–
O. Kamal	7	10	1	180	41*	20.00	–	–
A.S. Shetty	5	10	–	194	60	19.40	–	1
N.R. Yadav	7	9	–	173	61	19.22	–	2
R. Jaswant	4	7	1	115	37	19.16	–	–
M.M. More	5	8	2	113	30	18.83	–	–
N. Gautam	5	7	–	131	30	18.71	–	–
A.R. Kumble	7	8	1	127	67	18.14	–	1
V. Joshi	3	6	–	108	86	18.00	–	1
N. Parikh	4	8	1	124	47*	17.71	–	–
Shakti Singh	4	7	1	106	36	17.66	–	–
H. Bhaskar	3	6	–	106	34	17.66	–	–
K.N.A. Padmanabhan	6	7	1	106	39	17.66	–	–
A. Mishra	5	10	–	172	55	17.20	–	1
P.G. Sunder	4	7	1	101	25	16.83	–	–
J. Cardozo	3	6	–	100	41	16.66	–	–
M. Venkataramana	7	8	–	133	46	16.52	–	–
K. Arun Sharma	8	9	–	147	80	16.33	–	1
Deepak Sharma	5	8	–	129	31	16.12	–	–
Arshad Ayub	9	13	1	185	63	15.41	–	1
P.V. Gandhe	7	11	2	136	46	15.11	–	–
Bhupinder Singh snr	8	9	–	133	53	14.77	–	1
Shambhu Sharma	4	7	–	102	39	14.57	–	–
V. Razdan	7	9	1	112	48	14.00	–	–
I. Cherian	5	9	–	123	44	13.66	–	–
P. Rivonkar	4	8	–	100	57	12.50	–	1
S.S. Lahore	7	11	2	110	36	12.22	–	–
H.S. Sodhi	7	12	3	101	23	11.22	–	–

(Qualification – 100 runs, average 10.00)
(Played in one match – R. Lamba 89 & 39)

BOWLING

	Overs	Mds	Runs	Wkts	Av	Best	10/m	5/inn
A.R. Bhat	181.5	70	304	24	12.66	5-27	–	1
Suni Subramaniam	235.2	71	520	39	13.33	7-57	2	4
U. Chatterjee	273.5	75	621	42	14.78	7-63	1	4
A. Bedi	206.3	52	514	32	16.06	5-53	–	2
K.A. Jeshwanth	78.3	18	226	14	16.14	6-24	–	1
F. Ghayas	114	23	359	22	16.31	7-53	1	2
B. Vij	377.2	106	856	49	17.46	7-67	–	2
R.S.P. Rathore	144.4	31	440	25	17.60	7-110	–	3
P. Vaidya	93.2	20	247	14	17.64	4-31	–	–
Rajinder Singh	119	26	310	17	18.23	5-81	–	1
A.R. Kumble	380.2	112	834	45	18.53	7-64	1	4
Sanjeev Sharma	70.3	8	187	10	18.70	5-66	–	1
Maninder Singh	396	111	880	47	18.72	7-54	1	3
C.M. Sharma	110.5	27	337	18	18.72	5-87	–	2
Kapil Dev	78.2	24	189	10	18.90	3-35	–	–
M. Venkataramana	238.1	59	682	35	19.48	6-73	–	1
A. Saha	102.2	23	297	15	19.80	5-69	–	1
O. Kamal	308.4	80	854	43	19.86	6-21	–	3
Bhupinder Singh snr	325.4	98	723	36	20.08	5-47	–	1
Shakti Singh	133.5	26	385	19	20.26	6-30	–	2
Abinash Kumar	375.5	110	872	43	20.27	7-43	2	5
H.S. Sodhi	157.1	30	428	21	20.38	6-24	–	1

	Overs	Mds	Runs	Wkts	Av	Best	10/m	5/inn
P. Jain	269.5	68	592	28	21.14	7-119	1	3
Mohammad Aslam	75.2	12	215	10	21.50	5-94	–	1
N.D. Hirwani	452.3	110	1113	51	21.82	6-34	1	6
M. Karanjkar	117.3	41	241	11	21.90	4-39	–	–
H.R. Wasu	123.1	24	380	17	22.35	4-72	–	–
B. Ramprakash	173.3	38	385	17	22.64	5-96	–	1
S. Sen Sharma	133.4	17	386	17	22.70	5-38	–	1
D.T. Patel	115.2	24	319	14	22.78	4-83	–	–
T.N. Varsania	64.4	6	251	11	22.81	6-96	–	1
Venkatapathy Raju	334	98	756	33	22.90	6-46	1	2
I. Siddiqi	153.4	28	439	19	23.10	6-59	1	1
T.B. Arothe	196.5	28	581	25	23.24	6-75	1	3
S.V. Jedhe	330.1	91	861	37	23.27	6-119	–	2
S.A. Ankola	207.2	44	592	25	23.68	5-67	–	1
M.V. Ramanamurthy	152.1	33	389	16	24.31	4-62	–	–
S.J. Jadhav	202.1	50	489	20	24.45	5-55	–	2
R.C. Thakkar	204.5	57	499	20	24.95	4-35	–	–
S.S. Patil	276.4	99	650	26	25.00	5-94	–	1
Arshad Ayub	521	171	1206	48	25.12	6-90	–	3
P.V. Gandhe	268	56	773	30	25.76	6-65	–	2
S.P. Mukherjee	118.1	27	362	14	25.85	6-77	–	1
R. Ananth	234.2	68	596	23	25.91	5-53	–	1
K. Mohan	189.3	59	416	16	26.00	6-39	–	1
Kirti Azad	144.1	29	420	16	26.25	6-30	–	1
T. Gonsalves	78	6	342	13	26.30	4-67	–	–
D.K. Nilose	121.5	19	553	21	26.33	5-101	–	1
M.S. Narula	157.2	30	532	20	26.60	6-92	–	1
K. Bharatan	253.3	77	706	26	27.15	7-39	1	2
R.B. Biswal	150.1	28	490	18	27.22	5-76	–	2
A.S. Shetty	175	42	422	15	28.13	4-81	–	–
R.K. Chauhan	404	126	876	31	28.25	6-62	–	1
R. Sridhar	211.2	52	509	18	28.27	3-40	–	–
Pratap Singh	125.1	28	340	12	28.33	3-60	–	–
Deepak Sharma	238.5	66	494	17	29.05	5-54	–	1
V. Razdan	143	28	408	14	29.14	3-28	–	–
P. Kumar	121.4	24	321	11	29.18	4-63	–	–
M. Prabhakar	155	37	439	15	29.26	3-28	–	–
R.A. Swaroop	138.1	28	355	12	29.58	5-91	–	1
M. Majithia	228.3	59	711	24	29.62	6-57	–	1
S.V. Inamdar	99.2	18	300	10	30.00	4-71	–	–
K.N.A. Padmanabhan	202.4	47	517	17	30.41	5-120	–	1
N.R. Yadav	169	39	523	17	30.76	4-43	–	–
S. Kumar	138.2	38	379	12	31.58	5-98	–	1
I.P. Prakash	110.2	20	389	12	32.41	5-170	–	1
K.D. Amin	93.5	11	327	10	32.70	3-51	–	–
D. Chudasama	147.3	23	437	13	33.61	6-125	–	1
S. Mohapatra	135.2	21	454	13	34.92	6-38	–	1
M. Kulkarni	179	35	699	20	34.95	5-85	–	1
A.W. Zaidi	320	51	979	28	34.96	5-92	–	1
N. Kambli	112.3	10	386	11	35.09	4-88	–	–
D. Vasu	168.5	41	504	14	36.00	5-81	–	1
P. Venkatesh	209	51	612	17	36.00	3-28	–	–
S.S. Lahore	310	82	740	20	37.00	6-95	–	1
A. Kapoor	168	34	489	13	37.61	3-83	–	–
G.V.V. Gopala Raju	155.1	33	494	13	38.00	4-45	–	–
K.V.P. Rao	122.3	27	383	10	38.30	5-52	–	1
B.M. Radia	230	22	705	17	41.47	4-73	–	–
A.S. Wassan	141	23	440	10	44.00	3-70	–	–
K.K. Sharma	159.1	26	516	11	46.90	3-104	–	–
S.C. Kesarvani	205.4	41	661	14	47.21	4-76	–	–
S.V. Bahutule	235.3	69	639	13	49.15	4-71	–	–
A. Kuruvilla	216	23	765	15	51.00	6-61	–	1

(Qualification – 10 wickets)

LEADING FIELDERS

30 – M. Mudgal (ct 27/st 3); 26 – Arun Sharma (ct 21/st 5); 24 – S.S. Dighe (ct 22/st 2), Abhay Sharma (ct 14/st 10) and A. Vaidya (ct 16/st 8); 22 – K.K. Patel (ct 16/st 6); 19 – M. Sanjay (ct 14/st 5); 18 – A. Sheikh (ct 10/st 8) and V. Yadav (ct 15/st 3); 17 – M.G. Chaturvedi (ct 16/st 1) and K.S. More (ct 11/st 6); 16 – M.D. Gunjal and N.R. Mongia (ct 11/st 5); 15 – M.M. More; 14 – Gursharan Singh and C.S. Pandit (ct 11/st 3); 13 – Abdul Azeem, K. Srikkanth, V.M. Jaisimha and V. Rathore; 12 – A. Gautam, Yuvraj Singh, V.G. Kambli, S.S. Karim (ct 9/st 3) and S. Kondhalkar (ct 11/st 1); 11 – S.S. Bhave, H.A. Kinikar, S.K. Kulkarni (ct 8/st 3), G.K. Pandey and Raj Kumar (ct 9/st 2); 10 – P.K. Amre, K.P. Bhaskar, P.K. Dwivedi, Snehashi Ganguly and M. Senthilnathan

SECTION B
Sri Lanka
Australia tour, Test and one-day international series
New Zealand tour, Test and one-day international series
England tour, Test and one-day international series

The culmination of Sri Lanka's most successful season in their international history – Jayasuriya grabs a stump, having just hit Tufnell for six to complete Sri Lanka's first Test victory over England. (Richard Saker/Allsport)

One of the most welcome aspects of world cricket in 1992–3 was that Test cricket returned to Sri Lanka after an absence of five years. In April 1987, the series between Sri Lanka and New Zealand was abandoned after the first Test because of the intensive political unrest in the country and, in the years since, Sri Lanka has been forced to play in exile, and the opportunities afforded them have been grudgingly few. With a more stable position now established within Sri Lanka, Test series were arranged against both Australia and New Zealand, while England were to play one Test match and two one-day internationals following their tour of India.

Before the arrival of the Australians Arjuna Ranatunga was restored to the captaincy, replacing Aravinda de Silva. It was felt that the cares of leadership had affected de Silva's batting form, and he had failed to do himself justice in the World Cup.

AUSTRALIA TOUR

11, 12 and **13** August **1992** *at Asgiriya Stadium, Kandy*

Australians 278 for 9 dec. (M.E. Waugh 74, C.J. McDermott 58 not out)

Sri Lanka Board President's XI 293 for 6 (R.S. Mahanama 82, M.S. Atapattu 64 not out, S.T. Jayasuriya 51)

Match drawn

The Australia tour began at the height of the 1992 season in England so that Jones, Waugh and Moody were plucked from county cricket. Mark Waugh performed well enough on the opening day at Kandy, but it was left to Healy and McDermott to save Australian blushes with a ninth-wicket stand of 79. Only 29 overs were possible on the second day, and the Sri Lankan batsmen dominated the final day with some impressive stroke-play.

FIRST ONE-DAY INTERNATIONAL
SRI LANKA *v.* AUSTRALIA, at Colombo

Reinstated as captain of Sri Lanka, Arjuna Ranatunga accomplished the first of his tasks successfully when he won the toss, but his decision to ask Australia to bat first appeared unwise as Moody and Taylor began with a partnership of 109. The Australians continued to score freely and reached a commendable 247, with Mark Taylor hitting his highest score in a limited-over international.

Sri Lanka began badly, losing both openers for 12, but Aravinda de Silva was at his most brilliant. He dominated a third-wicket stand of 147 with Gurusinha and made his highest score in a limited-over international. It was his second century in this form of cricket, and the first by a Sri Lankan batsman against Australia. Aravinda de Silva hit 2

Arjuna Ranatunga restored to the captaincy of Sri Lanka. (David Munden/Sports-Line)

sixes and 12 fours and seemed to have put Sri Lanka in reach of victory. The quick loss of Atapattu and Kaluwitharana placed the pressure on Ranatunga, for 34 were needed from the last three overs. The Sri Lankan skipper responded by hitting McDermott for 20 in the 48th over, including 2 sixes, and his 45 off 49 balls won the game for his side in the last over.

Not surprisingly, de Silva was named Man of the Match for his 102-ball innings.

FIRST TEST MATCH
SRI LANKA *v.* AUSTRALIA, at Colombo

Sri Lanka gave a first Test cap to Romesh Kaluwitharana, a 23-year-old batsman who keeps wicket and is a professional coach in Bangladesh. He was to prove one of the stars of an extraordinary match.

Ranatunga won the toss and asked Australia to bat first on a pitch which offered some encouragement to the seam bowlers. Sri Lanka had immediate success when Moody fell to Ramanayake, but it was the gentle medium pace of Hathurusinghe which gave the home side their grip on the match. He claimed the wickets of Boon, Jones, Waugh and Border in the space of five overs, and, at 124 for 7, Australia were in despair.

It was at this point that Sri Lanka, and Ranatunga, showed a lack of conviction and self-belief. A dearth of penetrative bowling and some strangely defensive field-placings allowed Healy and McDermott to halt the col-

FIRST ONE-DAY INTERNATIONAL – SRI LANKA *v.* AUSTRALIA
15 August 1992 at P. Saravanamuttu Stadium, Colombo

AUSTRALIA

T.M. Moody	c and b Kalpage	54
M.A. Taylor	c Tillekeratne, b Kalpage	94
D.M. Jones	st Kaluwitharana, b Anurasiri	30
D.C. Boon	lbw, b Ramanayake	0
M.E. Waugh	b Wickramasinghe	31
A.R. Border (capt)	not out	19
G.R.J. Matthews	not out	1
*I.A. Healy		
A.I.C. Dodemaide		
C.J. McDermott		
M.R. Whitney		
Extras	b 2, lb 8, w 4, nb 4	18
(50 overs)	(for 5 wickets)	247

SRI LANKA

R.S. Mahanama	b Whitney	0
H.P. Tillekeratne	c Healy, b McDermott	7
A.P. Gurusinha	c Waugh, b Matthews	53
P.A. de Silva	run out	105
A. Ranatunga (capt)	not out	45
M.S. Atapattu	c Waugh, b Whitney	4
*R.S. Kaluwitharana	b Dodemaide	1
R.S. Kalpage	not out	11
C.P.H. Ramanayake		
S.D. Anurasiri		
G.P. Wickramasinghe		
Extras	b 4, lb 10, w 8, nb 3	25
(49.2 overs)	(for 6 wickets)	251

	O	M	R	W
Wickramasinghe	9	1	35	1
Ramanayake	10	–	54	1
Gurusinha	8	–	31	–
Ranatunga	3	–	22	–
Anurasiri	10	–	43	1
Kalpage	10	–	52	2

	O	M	R	W
McDermott	9.2	1	64	1
Whitney	10	1	33	2
Dodemaide	10	–	50	1
Moody	7	1	36	–
Matthews	10	–	34	1
Border	3	–	20	–

FALL OF WICKETS
1–109, 2–175, 3–176, 4–216, 5–244

FALL OF WICKETS
1–3, 2–12, 3–159, 4–202, 5–212, 6–214

Man of the Match: P.A. de Silva

Sri Lanka won by 4 wickets

Relieved of the captaincy, Aravinda de Silva played some spectacular innings for Sri Lanka. (David Munden/Sports-Line)

lapse. McDermott hit 22 off 28 balls, and Healy batted for more than three hours, hitting 8 fours in his unbeaten 66 and cajoling 132 runs from the last three wickets. Sri Lanka ended the day with nine runs without loss.

Hathurusinghe added 15 to his overnight score before falling to the medium pace of Mark Waugh, but Mahanama and Gurusinha engaged in a partnership which was attractive and productive. Mahanama played with elegance and aggression. He batted for three hours, hit 13 boundaries and seemed destined for the Test century which has eluded him since his debut in 1984, when he was brilliantly caught at the wicket by Healy. Aravinda de Silva went cheaply, but Ranatunga was again in belligerent mood. He took 29 off three overs from the leg-spinner Warne, including 3 sixes, to move to 69 by the close of play. Gurusinha was on 87, and Sri Lanka, 265 for 3, were in a commanding position.

Both Gurusinha, who reached a thousand runs in Test cricket, and Ranatunga completed centuries on the third morning. Their partnership realised 230, only 10 runs short of their record fourth-wicket stand against Pakistan, 1985–6, and the second highest stand in Sri Lanka's Test history. Gurusinha, his confidence and concentration enhanced by his new contact lenses, made the highest of his four Test centuries and batted for nearly

A highest Test score of 137 for Asanka Gurusinha in the first Test match against Australia. (David Munden/Sports-Line)

Romesh Kaluwitharana who hit 132 off 158 balls on the occasion of his Test debut. (Chris Cole/Allsport)

nine hours. His fellow left-hander Ranatunga hit his third Test hundred and played an innings full of blistering strokes. He batted for $4\frac{1}{2}$ hours and was out to a tired shot on the stroke of lunch. This brought in Atapattu who, having been padded up for the 266 minutes of the Gurusinha–Ranatunga stand, was out first ball. It was his third nought in his first three Test innings. So Romesh Kaluwitharana came to the wicket to play his first Test innings on a hat-trick.

With vicious cuts and hooks he hit seven boundaries in his first 30 runs. In all, he hit 26 boundaries and was unbeaten on 132 when Ranatunga declared, Sri Lanka having passed 500 in a Test innings for the first time. Kaluwitharana's runs came off only 158 balls. It was an astonishing Test debut.

With a first-innings deficit of 291, Australia were 26 for 0 when the game entered its rest day.

The rest day was good for Australia, for it gave them time to reflect and regather. However honest, the Sri Lankan attack was far from lethal. Without Ratnayake and Labrooy it lacked pace, and the gentle seamers of Hathurusinghe were hardly likely to cause havoc for a second time. Nevertheless, Sri Lanka worked hard on the fourth day against batsmen who were determined to survive. The Sri Lankan cause was not helped by a plethora of no-balls, and the number of extras they conceded in the match – 90 – was to prove significant in deciding the outcome of the match.

Moody went early in the day when he played over a ball from Ramanayake. Boon and Taylor added 66 before Taylor skied a ball from Anurasiri, the left-arm spinner,

who also accounted for Boon after he had added 88 with Jones. Boon batted for 174 minutes and hit 10 fours. Sri Lankan joy continued when Jones, called for a quick single by Waugh, was run out by Gurusinha's direct hit from square-leg.

At tea, Australia were 253 for 4, but almost immediately after the break Border fell to a bat-pad catch to give Anurasiri his third wicket. Matthews showed real grit, and he gained able support from McDermott after Healy had fallen to Hathurusinghe. Australia ended on 393 for 7, and Sri Lanka seemed to be in sight of a famous victory.

The Australian resistance continued on the final morning, and Sri Lanka were left the task of scoring 181 runs in 58 overs to win the match. It was more than may have been anticipated, but it was not a difficult task. Mahanama and Hathurusinghe provided a solid start and although both fell in quick succession, Sri Lanka reached 127 for 2 – victory, it seemed, a formality. Aravinda de Silva had begun with effortless grace. He hit 7 fours and scored 37 from 32 balls before he hooked rashly at McDermott and was well caught at mid-on by Border who ran some 30 yards to take the catch. Sri Lanka had no need of such wildness, and de Silva's shot heralded a sensational collapse. In 17.4 overs, they lost eight wickets for 37 runs, and Australia claimed a remarkable victory by 16 runs.

The main destroyer of the Sri Lankans was Greg Matthews, the combative off-spinner who does not believe in defeat, although Warne eased his difficult entry into Test cricket by taking the last three wickets. Border's imaginative and positive captaincy also did much to bring about Australia's first Test victory in Asia for nine years, but, in

FIRST TEST MATCH – SRI LANKA v. AUSTRALIA
17, 18, 19, 21 and 22 August 1992 at Sinhalese Sports Club, Colombo

AUSTRALIA

	FIRST INNINGS			SECOND INNINGS	
M.A. Taylor	lbw, b Wickramasinghe	42	(2) c Gurusinha, b Anurasiri		43
T.M. Moody	lbw, b Ramanayake	1	(1) b Ramanayake		13
D.C. Boon	c Ramanayake, b Hathurusinghe	32	c Ranatunga, b Anurasiri		68
D.M. Jones	lbw, b Hathurusinghe	10	run out		57
M.E. Waugh	c Kaluwitharana, b Hathurusinghe	5	c Kaluwitharana, b Wickramasinghe		56
A.R. Border (capt)	b Hathurusinghe	3	c Gurusinha, b Anurasiri		15
G.R.J. Matthews	lbw, b Ramanayake	6	c Kaluwitharana, b Ramanayake		64
*I.A. Healy	not out	66	lbw, b Hathurusinghe		12
C.J. McDermott	c Ranatunga, b Ramanayake	22	lbw, b Ramanayake		40
S.K. Warne	c and b Anurasiri	24	b Anurasiri		35
M.R. Whitney	c and b Wickramasinghe	13	not out		10
Extras	lb 10, w 3, nb 19	32	lb 23, w 1, nb 34		58
		256			**471**

SRI LANKA

	FIRST INNINGS		SECOND INNINGS	
R.S. Mahanama	c Healy, b Waugh	78	c Boon, b Matthews	39
U.C. Hathurusinghe	c Taylor, b Waugh	18	run out	36
A.P. Gurusinha	c Jones, b Whitney	137	not out	31
P.A. de Silva	lbw, b Matthews	6	c Border, b McDermott	37
A. Ranatunga (capt)	c Warne, b Matthews	127	c Border, b McDermott	0
M.S. Atapattu	b Matthews	0	b Matthews	1
*R.S. Kaluwitharana	not out	132	b Matthews	4
C.P.H. Ramanayake	c Healy, b McDermott	0	lbw, b Matthews	6
G.P. Wickramasinghe	c Matthews, b McDermott	21	c Waugh, b Warne	2
A.W.R. Madurasinghe	not out	5	(11) c Matthews, b Warne	0
S.D. Anurasiri			(10) c Waugh, b Warne	1
Extras	b 2, lb 7, w 1, nb 13	23	b 2, lb 3, nb 2	7
	(for 8 wickets, dec.)	**547**		**164**

	O	M	R	W	O	M	R	W
Ramanayake	20	4	51	3	37	10	113	3
Wickramasinghe	18	4	69	2	19	–	79	1
Hathurusinghe	22	5	66	4	27	7	79	1
Madurasinghe	10	1	21	–	14	1	50	–
Gurusinha	2	–	17	–				
Anurasiri	12	2	22	1	35	3	127	4

	O	M	R	W	O	M	R	W
McDermott	40	9	125	2	14	4	43	2
Whitney	32	10	84	1	5	2	13	–
Moody	17	3	44	–	5	–	10	–
Waugh	17	3	77	2	2	–	6	–
Warne	22	2	107	–	5.1	3	11	3
Matthews	38	11	93	3	20	2	76	4
Border	4	1	8	–				

FALL OF WICKETS

1–8, 2–84, 3–94, 4–96, 5–109, 6–118, 7–124, 8–162, 9–207
1–41, 2–107, 3–195, 4–233, 5–269, 6–319, 7–361, 8–417, 9–431

FALL OF WICKETS

1–36, 2–128, 3–137, 4–367, 5–367, 6–463, 7–472, 8–503
1–76, 2–79, 3–127, 4–132, 5–133, 6–137, 7–147, 8–150, 9–156

Umpires: K.T. Francis & T. M. Samarasinghe

Australia won by 16 runs

The destroyer of Sri Lanka on the final day of the first Test against Australia – off-spinner Greg Matthews. (Adrian Murrell/Allsport)

truth, Sri Lanka's pitiful batting was a major factor in deciding the match. Ranatunga could provide no example, and only Gurusinha offered the necessary determination. The golden opportunity of a famous victory was thrown away by loss of nerve. Not for the first time had Sri Lanka revealed their inability to maintain their challenge for the full five days.

Greg Matthews' all-round performance earned him the individual award.

24, 25 and 26 August 1992 *at Uyanwatte, Matara*

Australians 312 for 9 dec. (M.E. Waugh 118, I.A. Healy 78 not out, D.R. Martyn 61, K.I.W. Wijegunawardene 4 for 58) and 204 (D.C. Boon 57, E.A.R. de Silva 4 for 42)
Southern Province 164 (M.R. Whitney 4 for 34) and 34 for 2

Match drawn

An inconsistent batting display on the opening day was brightened by Waugh's 36th first-class century and by good innings from Martyn, who batted for 2½ hours, and from the ever-improving Healy. It was surprising that young Martyn was not offered some international experience on the tour. Dodemaide and Whitney bowled well for the tourists, and, on the last day, leg-spinner Asoka de Silva was most impressive.

SECOND TEST MATCH
SRI LANKA *v.* AUSTRALIA, at Colombo

Sri Lanka introduced two players to Test cricket, pace bowler Dulip Liyanage and off-spinner Muttiah Muralitharan. Liyanage had a splendid Test debut and quickly made his mark.

Play began 50 minutes late because of rain, and Ranatunga won the toss once more and asked Australia to bat first. With his third ball in Test cricket, Liyanage had

Moody caught behind. The young pace man bowled with fire and enthusiasm and also captured the wickets of Boon and Border. Jayasuriya, recalled to the side, held three bat-pad catches, but the Sri Lankan slip catching and wicket-keeping were quite dreadful. Jones, dropped on 1, finished the first day on 77 when Australia were 177 for 5, and although he was dismissed early on the second day, Sri Lanka had thrown away the chance of putting the visitors in a humiliating position.

Another gritty fifty from Greg Matthews took Australia to 247 on a day when only 123 minutes' play were possible. On the third day, Sri Lanka had every opportunity to take a firm hold on the match. Aravinda de Silva batted with controlled aggression and good sense, and he and Hathurusinghe added 107 in 41 overs for the third wicket. At 240 for 4, Sri Lanka were in sight of a substantial lead, but some characteristically reckless batting and a fine spell from McDermott – 4 for 11 in seven overs – saw them slip to 258 for 9.

Ranatunga attempted to compensate for lost time by declaring on the fourth morning. Once more, Sri Lanka

SECOND TEST MATCH – SRI LANKA *v.* AUSTRALIA
28, 29, 30 August, 1 and 2 September 1992 at Khetterama Stadium, Colombo

AUSTRALIA

	FIRST INNINGS		SECOND INNINGS	
T.M. Moody	c Kaluwitharana, b Liyanage	1	(2) b Muralitharan	54
M.A. Taylor	c Jayasuriya, b Hathurusinghe	15	(1) lbw, b Hathurusinghe	26
D.C. Boon	c Jayasuriya, b Liyanage	28	c Mahanama, b Anurasiri	15
D.M. Jones	lbw, b Gurusinha	77	not out	100
M.E. Waugh	c Jayasuriya, b Ramanayake	0	lbw, b Muralitharan	0
A.R. Border (capt)	b Liyanage	13	lbw, b Anurasiri	28
G.R.J. Matthews	c Muralitharan, b Ramanayake	55	c Mahanama, b Anurasiri	51
*I.A. Healy	lbw, b Gurusinha	0	not out	4
C.J. McDermott	lbw, b Muralitharan	9		
A.I.C. Dodemaide	not out	16		
M.R. Whitney	lbw, b Ramanayake	1		
Extras	b 10, lb 14, w 2, nb 6	32	b 4, lb 9, nb 5	18
		247	(for 6 wickets, dec.)	296

SRI LANKA

	FIRST INNINGS		SECOND INNINGS	
R.S. Mahanama	c Moody, b Dodemaide	14	lbw, b McDermott	69
U.C. Hathurusinghe	b Moody	67	c Moody, b McDermott	49
A.P. Gurusinha	c Healy, b Whitney	29	not out	8
P.A. de Silva	c Healy, b McDermott	85		
A. Ranatunga (capt)	c sub (Martyn), b Dodemaide	18		
S.T. Jayasuriya	c Healy, b McDermott	19	(4) not out	1
*R.S. Kaluwitharana	c sub (Martyn), b Border	1		
C.P.H. Ramanayake	b McDermott	8		
D.K. Liyanage	c Healy, b McDermott	4		
S.D. Anurasiri	not out	2		
M. Muralitharan	not out	0		
Extras	lb 6, nb 5	11	lb 6, nb 3	9
	(for 9 wickets, dec.)	258	(for 2 wickets)	136

	O	M	R	W	O	M	R	W
Ramanayake	23.3	7	64	3	12	–	49	–
Liyanage	30	10	66	3	13	1	47	–
Hathurusinghe	9	1	26	1	12	4	12	1
Gurusinha	9	2	18	2				
Anurasiri	8	–	17	–	44	11	66	3
Muralitharan	17	2	32	1	34	7	109	2

	O	M	R	W	O	M	R	W
McDermott	20	4	53	4	19	7	32	2
Whitney	16	1	49	1	5	2	13	–
Dodemaide	25	4	74	2	5	2	11	–
Matthews	10	2	20	–	21	5	59	–
Waugh	4	–	11	–				
Moody	6	1	17	1				
Border	11	3	28	1	4	–	15	–

FALL OF WICKETS

1–1, 2–34, 3–69, 4–72, 5–109, 6–181, 7–183, 8–200, 9–239
1–61, 2–102, 3–104, 4–104, 5–149, 6–280

FALL OF WICKETS

1–26, 2–67, 3–174, 4–211, 5–240, 6–243, 7–243, 8–255, 9–258
1–110, 2–129

Umpires: I. Anandappa & W.A.U. Wickremasinghe

Match drawn

The spearhead of Sri Lanka's attack, Ramanayake took 17 wickets in the series against Australia. (David Munden/Sports-Line)

had the opportunity to take a commanding position; once more they wasted that opportunity through bad fielding and captaincy that lacked confidence. Jones should have been stumped off Anurasiri before he had scored and was dropped at second slip when on 41. Like Anurasiri, debutant Muralitharan bowled admirably, but he was poorly supported by the field-placings, and Australia ended the fourth day on 206 for 5.

Dean Jones was missed four times on the way to his 11th Test century, and he and Matthews added 131 for the sixth wicket to make Australia safe. Border's declaration left Sri Lanka 62 overs in which to score 286 to win. To the consternation of the crowd, they made no attempt to score the runs. Aravinda de Silva, who might have set the game alight, did not bat, nor did skipper Ranatunga who had a most introverted match.

SECOND ONE-DAY INTERNATIONAL
SRI LANKA *v.* AUSTRALIA, at Colombo

Whatever their shortcomings in the Test series, Sri Lanka displayed their superiority in the one-day game and

clinched the series. Ranatunga won the toss and asked Australia to bat first on an excellent pitch. Moody and Taylor put on 56 in 14 overs, but Taylor and Boon were both run out, and although Jones hit 59 off 89 balls, Australia could never get on top of the bowling. They finished with a disappointing 216 from their 50 overs.

Rain reduced the match by six overs, and Sri Lanka were faced with a readjusted target of 191 in 44 overs. Hathurusinghe and Mahanama gave them a fine start, and de Silva punished the attack with an innings of great flair, 63 off 61 balls. Hathurusinghe was forced to retire hurt on 48, but he came back to reach his fifty and score the winning runs with seven balls to spare.

THIRD ONE-DAY INTERNATIONAL
SRI LANKA *v.* AUSTRALIA, at Colombo

The first floodlit match in Sri Lanka attracted a capacity crowd of 30,000. The Sri Lankan batting did not reach the heights of the earlier matches, and Australia were left with a comparatively easy target. They stumbled to 58 for 3, but Boon and Waugh added 84 in 18.2 overs, and Australia won with 2.1 overs to spare. It was a disappointment that Australia gave the promising Martyn only one match on the tour, especially as the form of Moody was generally poor.

THIRD TEST MATCH
SRI LANKA *v.* AUSTRALIA, at Moratuwa

Winning the toss for the first time in the series, Allan Border chose to bat first, but the uncertainty of Australia's top order was again all too apparent as five wickets went down for 58 runs. It was Border himself who rescued his side with a pugnacious century, his first in Test cricket for four years. He was dropped on 44 by Tillekeratne, who had been recalled as wicket-keeper but was as prone to error as his predecessor, but Border hit 16 boundaries and shared a sixth-wicket stand of 127 with Greg Matthews, an outstanding success on the tour. When these two were dismissed Healy took command, and Australia closed on 287 for 8.

On the second day, an hour was lost to rain at this new Test centre, and Australia were finally dismissed for 337, with Healy making his highest Test score. Sri Lanka had again bowled well. Ramanayake was particularly impressive. The fault once more lay in the catching.

McDermott soon accounted for Hathurusinghe and Gurusinha, but Mahanama and de Silva added 107 and, after strange stoppages for light which was allegedly bad, Sri Lanka closed on 143 for 4. There was no play until after tea on the third day when Ranatunga and Tillekeratne advanced the score to 215 for 4. Sri Lanka refused to play on the scheduled rest day so that a draw was inevitable.

This inevitability was not apparent on the fourth day when, after Ranatunga had declared 63 runs in arrears,

SECOND ONE-DAY INTERNATIONAL – SRI LANKA *v.* AUSTRALIA
4 September 1992 at Khetterama Stadium, Colombo

AUSTRALIA			SRI LANKA		
T.M. Moody	c Tillekeratne, b Gurusinha	17	R.S. Mahanama	run out	33
M.A. Taylor	run out	30	U.C. Hathurusinghe	not out	52
D.M. Jones	not out	59	A.P. Gurusinha	lbw, b Dodemaide	4
D.C. Boon	run out	35	P.A. de Silva	c Whitney, b Matthews	63
M.E. Waugh	lbw, b Ramanayake	10	A. Ranatunga (capt)	c Dodemaide, b Matthews	22
A.R. Border (capt)	c Kalpage, b Ramanayake	30	S.T. Jayasuriya	b McDermott	2
G.R.J. Matthews	c Tillekeratne, b Wickramasinghe	1	*H.P. Tillekeratne	not out	2
*I.A. Healy	run out	6	R.S. Kalpage		
C.J. McDermott	not out	1	C.P.H. Ramanayake		
A.I.C. Dodemaide			G.P. Wickramasinghe		
M.R. Whitney			S.D. Anurasiri		
Extras	b 1, lb 15, w 3, nb 8	27	Extras	b 2, lb 7, w 4, nb 3	16
(50 overs)	(for 7 wickets)	216	(42.5 overs)	(for 5 wickets)	194

	O	M	R	W		O	M	R	W
Ramanayake	10	2	43	2	McDermott	9	–	44	1
Wickramasinghe	10	–	40	1	Whitney	7	–	27	–
Hathurusinghe	10	1	34	–	Dodemaide	10	1	39	1
Gurusinha	4	1	21	1	Moody	9	–	35	–
Ranatunga	3	1	11	–	Matthews	6.5	–	34	2
Anurasiri	5	–	20	–	Waugh	1	–	6	–
Kalpage	8	–	31	–					

FALL OF WICKETS
1–56, 2–65, 3–127, 4–149, 5–194, 6–197, 7–207

FALL OF WICKETS
1–71, 2–77, 3–172, 4–176, 5–190

Man of the Match: U.C. Hathurusinghe   *Sri Lanka won on faster scoring rate*

THIRD ONE-DAY INTERNATIONAL – SRI LANKA *v.* AUSTRALIA
5 September 1992 at Khetterama Stadium, Colombo

SRI LANKA			AUSTRALIA		
R.S. Mahanama	c Taylor, b McDermott	0	M.A. Taylor	c Gurusinha, b Hathurusinghe	14
U.C. Hathurusinghe	c Boon, b Matthews	46	T.M. Moody	c Mahanama, b Ramanayake	13
A.P. Gurusinha	lbw, b Matthews	49	D.M. Jones	st Tillekeratne, b E.A.R. de Silva	17
P.A. de Silva	c Matthews, b Dodemaide	39	D.C. Boon	not out	69
A. Ranatunga (capt)	b Whitney	15	M.E. Waugh	run out	52
S.T. Jayasuriya	b Whitney	7	A.R. Border (capt)	c Gurusinha, b Ramanayake	14
*H.P. Tillekeratne	not out	35	G.R.J. Matthews	not out	10
R.S. Kalpage	not out	1	*I.A. Healy		
C.P.H. Ramanayake			C.J. McDermott		
E.A.R. de Silva			A.I.C. Dodemaide		
G.P. Wickramasinghe			M.R. Whitney		
Extras	b 1, lb 5, w 9	15	Extras	b 7, lb 4, w 4, nb 4	19
(50 overs)	(for 6 wickets)	207	(47.5 overs)	(for 5 wickets)	208

	O	M	R	W		O	M	R	W
McDermott	10	1	30	1	Ramanayake	8.5	–	34	2
Dodemaide	10	1	44	1	Wickramasinghe	9	–	32	–
Whitney	10	1	40	2	Gurusinha	2	–	8	–
Matthews	10	1	33	2	Hathurusinghe	10	–	38	1
Moody	7	–	38	–	E.A.R. de Silva	10	–	47	1
Border	3	–	16	–	Kalpage	6	–	28	–
					Jayasuriya	2	–	10	–

FALL OF WICKETS
1–0, 2–101, 3–112, 4–137, 5–145, 6–197

FALL OF WICKETS
1–28, 2–39, 3–58, 4–142, 5–186

Man of the Match: D.C. Boon   *Australia won by 5 wickets*

Australia's leading batsman in the series was Dean Jones, but in the months ahead he was to have an unhappy time at the top level.
(Adrian Murrell/Allsport)

Liyanage produced a blistering spell which sent back Taylor, Boon and Waugh in 10 deliveries. Ramanayake had Moody caught behind, and the tourists were 9 for 4. Waugh's 'duck' was his second of the match, and he became the sixth batsman to be dismissed for a 'pair' in successive Test matches.

Once more it was Border and Matthews to the rescue as they put on 72. Once more Border was reprieved by wicket-keeper Tillekeratne, and he was also dropped by Jayasuriya at short-leg. Anurasiri was the unlucky bowler, and his figures for the series did him scant justice.

Australia ended the day on 147 for 6, and the loss of three hours on the last day because of a damp outfield took away any remaining chance of a result. Matthews reached his fifth fifty in six Test innings in the series and came close to his second Test century.

THIRD TEST MATCH – SRI LANKA v. AUSTRALIA
8, 9, 10, 12 and 13 September 1992 at Tyronne Fernando Stadium, Moratuwa

AUSTRALIA

	FIRST INNINGS		SECOND INNINGS	
T.M. Moody	b Ramanayake	0	(2) c Tillekeratne, b Ramanayake	2
M.A. Taylor	c Ranatunga, b Anurasiri	19	(1) c Mahanama, b Liyanage	3
D.C. Boon	c de Silva, b Ramanayake	18	lbw, b Liyanage	0
D.M. Jones	lbw, b Liyanage	11	b Anurasiri	21
M.E. Waugh	b Ramanayake	0	c Tillekeratne, b Liyanage	0
A.R. Border (capt)	b Ramanayake	106	lbw, b Ramanayake	78
G.R.J. Matthews	run out	57	b Ramanayake	96
*I.A. Healy	c Jayasuriya, b Muralitharan	71	c Jayasuriya, b Liyanage	49
C.J. McDermott	c Tillekeratne, b Hathurusinghe	10		
S.K. Warne	c Gurusinha, b Ramanayake	7		
A.I.C. Dodemaide	not out	13	(9) not out	2
Extras	b 3, lb 9, w 3, nb 10	25	lb 4, w 1, nb 15	20
		337	(for 8 wickets)	271

SRI LANKA

	FIRST INNINGS	
R.S. Mahanama	lbw, b Matthews	50
U.C. Hathurusinghe	c Boon, b McDermott	2
A.P. Gurusinha	c Healy, b McDermott	0
P.A. de Silva	b Dodemaide	58
*H.P. Tillekeratne	c Waugh, b Dodemaide	82
A. Ranatunga (capt)	c Jones, b McDermott	48
S.T. Jayasuriya	c Boon, b McDermott	2
C.P.H. Ramanayake	not out	15
D.K. Liyanage	c Moody, b Dodemaide	1
S.D. Anurasiri	b Dodemaide	0
M. Muralitharan		
Extras	lb 8, w 3, nb 5	16
	(for 9 wickets, dec.)	274

	O	M	R	W	O	M	R	W
Ramanayake	31	3	82	5	22.1	4	75	3
Liyanage	17	–	54	1	16	3	56	4
Hathurusinghe	21	8	50	1	4	2	3	–
Anurasiri	22	2	57	1	29	5	49	1
Muralitharan	15.1	2	58	1	7	1	26	–
Jayasuriya	2	–	9	–	7	1	17	–
Gurusinha	3	–	15	–	1	–	5	–
Ranatunga					1	–	9	–
Mahanama					5	–	27	–

	O	M	R	W
McDermott	31	6	89	4
Dodemaide	23.5	9	65	4
Moody	3	–	8	–
Matthews	31	8	64	1
Warne	11	3	40	–

FALL OF WICKETS

1–0, 2–42, 3–46, 4–57, 5–58, 6–185, 7–252, 8–283, 9–302
1–6, 2–6, 3–6, 4–9, 5–60, 6–132, 7–261, 8–271

FALL OF WICKETS

1–4, 2–4, 3–111, 4–116, 5–232, 6–234, 7–262, 8–274, 9–274

Umpires: K.T. Francis & B.C. Cooray

Match drawn

TEST MATCH AVERAGES – SRI LANKA v. AUSTRALIA

SRI LANKA BATTING

	M	Inns	NO	Runs	HS	Av	100s	50s
R.S. Kaluwitharana	2	3	1	137	132*	68.50	1	–
A.P. Gurusinha	3	5	2	205	137	68.33	1	–
R.S. Mahanama	3	5	–	250	78	50.00	–	3
A. Ranatunga	3	4	–	193	127	48.25	1	–
P.A. de Silva	3	4	–	186	85	46.50	–	2
U.C. Hathurusinghe	3	5	–	172	67	34.40	–	1
S.T. Jayasuriya	2	3	1	22	19	11.00	–	–
C.P.H. Ramanayake	3	4	1	29	15*	9.66	–	–
D.K. Liyanage	2	2	–	5	4	2.50	–	–
S.D. Anurasiri	3	3	1	3	2*	1.50	–	–

Played in two Tests: M. Muralitharan 0*
Played in one Test: M.S. Atapattu 0 & 1; G.P. Wickramasinghe 21 & 2; A.W.R. Madurasinghe 5* & 0; H.P. Tillekeratne 82

AUSTRALIA BATTING

	M	Inns	NO	Runs	HS	Av	100s	50s
D.M. Jones	3	6	1	276	100*	55.20	1	2
G.R.J. Matthews	3	6	–	329	96	54.83	–	5
I.A. Healy	3	6	2	202	71	50.50	–	2
A.R. Border	3	6	–	243	106	40.50	1	1
D.C. Boon	3	6	–	161	68	26.83	–	1
M.A. Taylor	3	6	–	148	43	24.66	–	–
S.K. Warne	2	3	–	66	35	22.00	–	–
C.J. McDermott	3	4	–	81	40	20.25	–	–
M.R. Whitney	2	3	1	24	13	12.00	–	–
T.M. Moody	3	6	–	71	54	11.83	–	1
M.E. Waugh	3	6	–	61	56	10.16	–	1

Played in two Tests: A.I.C. Dodemaide 16*, 13* & 2*

SRI LANKA BOWLING

	Overs	Mds	Runs	Wkts	Av	Best	10/m	5/inn
C.P.H. Ramanayake	145.4	28	434	17	25.52	5-82	–	1
A.P. Gurusinha	15	2	55	2	27.50	2-18	–	–
D.K. Liyanage	76	14	223	8	27.87	4-56	–	–
U.C. Hathurusinghe	92	27	236	8	29.50	4-66	–	–
S.D. Anurasiri	150	23	338	10	33.80	4-127	–	–
G.P. Wickramasinghe	37	4	148	3	49.33	2-69	–	–
M. Muralitharan	73.1	12	225	4	56.25	2-109	–	–
S.T. Jayasuriya	9	1	26	0	–	–	–	–
A.W.R. Madurasinghe	24	2	71	0	–	–	–	–

Bowled in one innings: A. Ranatunga 1–0–9–0; R.S. Mahanama 5–0–27–0

AUSTRALIA BOWLING

	Overs	Mds	Runs	Wkts	Av	Best	10/m	5/inn
C.J. McDermott	124	30	342	14	24.42	4-53	–	–
A.I.C. Dodemaide	53.5	15	150	6	25.00	4-65	–	–
G.R.J. Matthews	120	28	312	8	39.00	4-76	–	–
M.E. Waugh	23	3	94	2	47.00	2-77	–	–
A.R. Border	19	4	51	1	51.00	1-28	–	–
S.K. Warne	38.1	8	158	3	52.66	3-11	–	–
T.M. Moody	31	4	79	1	79.00	1-17	–	–
M.R. Whitney	58	15	159	2	79.50	1-49	–	–

SRI LANKA FIELDING FIGURES

5 – S.T. Jayasuriya; 4 – R.S. Kaluwitharana; 3 – H.P. Tillekeratne, R.S. Mahanama, A.P. Gurusinha and A. Ranatunga; 1 – P.A. de Silva, C.P.H. Ramanayake, S.D. Anurasiri, G.P. Wickramasinghe and M. Muralitharan.

AUSTRALIA FIELDING FIGURES

7 – I.A. Healy; 3 – T.M. Moody, D.C. Boon and M.E. Waugh; 2 – D.M. Jones, A.R. Border, G.R.J. Matthews and sub (D.R. Martyn); 1 – M.A. Taylor and S.K. Warne

So Australia took the series, but theirs was not a totally satisfactory performance. Their top batting was very disappointing, and had Sri Lanka held on to their catches, played a specialist keeper and shown more self-belief, the result might have been different.

NEW ZEALAND TOUR

From Zimbabwe, the New Zealand cricket team flew straight to Sri Lanka where the host country eagerly anticipated a three-Test series and a tour that would last a month. It was in April 1987 that, following political unrest and terrorist atrocities, the New Zealand tour of Sri Lanka had been abandoned and, as mentioned earlier, no Test matches had been played in Sri Lanka in the five years since then until the Australians arrived in August. Tragically, it seemed that history would be repeated when, shortly after the New Zealanders arrived, a suicide bomber of the Tamil separatist movement killed four leading naval officers as well as himself.

By a narrow majority, the New Zealand party voted to abandon the tour but Peter McDermott, the Chairman of the New Zealand Cricket Board, flew to Colombo and asked the players to continue. He spoke to each player individually and, as a result of his intervention, the tour went ahead with, however, a reduced number of matches. Coach Warren Lees and five players – Great-

batch, Larsen, Latham, Patel and Watson – declined to remain in Sri Lanka and returned home. John Wright, the veteran opener, Grant Bradburn, the promising off-spinner, and uncapped pace bowler Michael Owens and all-rounder Justin Vaughan flew to Sri Lanka as replacements. The New Zealand party had already been weakened by the loss of Doull. The rescheduled programme began with two one-day matches.

23 November 1992 *at Uyanwatta, Matara*

Sri Lankan Board XI 181 for 7
New Zealanders 164 for 7

Sri Lankan Board XI won by 17 runs

24 November 1992 *at Uyanwatta, Matara*

New Zealanders 149 for 8
Sri Lankan Board XI 152 for 9 (C. Pringle 4 for 20)

Sri Lankan Board XI won by 1 wicket

FIRST TEST MATCH
SRI LANKA v. NEW ZEALAND, at Moratuwa

Heartened by their display against Australia, Sri Lanka made only two changes from the side which drew the final Test. Although Tillekeratne held his place as a

FIRST TEST MATCH – SRI LANKA v. NEW ZEALAND
27, 28 and 29 November, 1 and 2 December 1992 at Tyronne Fernando Stadium, Moratuwa

NEW ZEALAND

Batsman	FIRST INNINGS		SECOND INNINGS	
J.G. Wright	c Gurusinha, b Ramanayake	11	(2) st Wickremasinghe, b Anurasiri	42
B.R. Hartland	c de Silva, b Liyanage	3	(1) lbw, b Ramanayake	52
A.H. Jones	c Mahanama, b Liyanage	35	c Wickremasinghe, b Ramanayake	14
M.D. Crowe (capt)	c Ranatunga, b Warnaweera	19	c Tillekeratne, b Anurasiri	11
K.R. Rutherford	c Wickremasinghe, b Hathurusinghe	105	lbw, b Warnaweera	53
C.Z. Harris	b Warnaweera	56	not out	0
J.T.C. Vaughan	b Liyanage	17	not out	0
*A.C. Parore	c Wickremasinghe, b Anurasiri	3		
D.J. Nash	c Wickremasinghe, b Liyanage	4		
M.L. Su'a	b Anurasiri	0		
M.B. Owens	not out	0		
Extras	b 5, lb 12, w 2, nb 16	35	lb 8, w 1, nb 14	23
		288	(for 5 wickets)	**195**

SRI LANKA

Batsman	FIRST INNINGS	
R.S. Mahanama	run out	153
U.C. Hathurusinghe	c Jones, b Nash	10
A.P. Gurusinha	c Vaughan, b Su'a	43
P.A. de Silva	c Nash, b Su'a	62
H.P. Tillekeratne	b Owens	1
A. Ranatunga (capt)	c Parore, b Owens	3
*A.G.D. Wickremasinghe	not out	13
C.P.H. Ramanayake	not out	10
D.K. Liyanage		
S.D. Anurasiri		
K.P.J. Warnaweera		
Extras	lb 7, w 9, nb 16	32
	(for 6 wickets, dec.)	**327**

	O	M	R	W	O	M	R	W
Ramanayake	23	2	57	1	17	6	27	2
Liyanage	26.5	6	82	4	17	4	48	–
Hathurusinghe	8	4	12	1	10	6	22	–
Anurasiri	34	11	55	2	26	11	32	2
Warnaweera	34	15	46	2	25	15	31	1
De Silva	4	2	8	–				
Gurusinha	1	–	6	–				
Ranatunga	3	2	5	–	7	2	26	–
Tillekeratne					1	–	1	–

	O	M	R	W
Su'a	25	6	62	2
Owens	17	3	63	2
Nash	18	2	62	1
Vaughan	14	–	56	–
Harris	15	5	64	–
Jones	1	–	3	–
Crowe	2	–	10	–

FALL OF WICKETS
1–6, 2–44, 3–77, 4–87, 5–238, 6–265, 7–273, 8–283, 9–286
1–110, 2–122, 3–136, 4–160, 5–194

FALL OF WICKETS
1–27, 2–164, 3–297, 4–299, 5–300, 6–309

Umpires: K.T. Francis & T.M. Samarasinghe

Match drawn

batsman, specialist wicket-keeper Gamini Wickremasinghe was brought into the side and medium-pace off-break bowler Warnaweera returned. Jayasuriya and Muralitharan stood down. New Zealand gave first Test caps to Harris, Vaughan and Owens, and surprisingly left out Pringle who had impressed in the one-day warm-up games, in which New Zealand had been generally inept.

Put in to bat, New Zealand struggled through a reduced first day in which 61 overs were bowled and 139 runs were scored for the loss of four wickets. It was grim stuff, but for New Zealand it could have been worse, for their first four wickets had gone down for 87 runs, and it was left to Rutherford and debutant Harris to restore some order in the last 84 minutes of the day. They continued their partnership into the second day, adding 151. In his 33rd Test, Rutherford hit his second Test hundred, a worthy defensive effort, all the more significant as New Zealand's last five wickets fell for 50 runs.

Having scored 10 before the end of the second day, Sri Lanka batted with great spirit on the third, reaching New Zealand's score in 53 fewer overs. They shamed the New Zealanders and batted quite superbly, none more so than Roshan Mahanama. He and Gurusinha gave the innings substance with a second-wicket stand of 137, and Mahanama went on to reach his maiden century in Test cricket, a feat which he had often promised before. He enjoyed two missed chances, but this could not detract from a six-hour innings in which he timed the ball superbly and played some delightful shots. He hit 18 fours and faced 297 balls. With Aravinda de Silva, he added a spectacular 133 in 112 minutes. Both batsmen fell in quick succession just before the close. Having hit Su'a's second delivery with the second new ball out of the ground, de Silva then sliced to third man where Dion Nash took a splendid diving catch. Two runs later, Harris hit the stumps to run out Mahanama.

After the rest day, play again started late, and Sri Lanka batted for half an hour, losing two wickets and adding 28 runs, before declaring. Again scoring at little more than two runs an over, New Zealand moved to 104 without

Roshan Mahanama realised his full potential with centuries in both Test matches against New Zealand. (David Munden/Sports-Line)

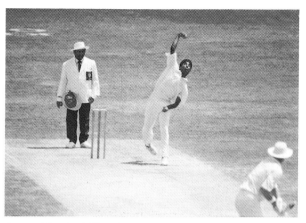

Seven wickets in the Test victory over New Zealand for Muralitharan. (Ben Radford/Allsport)

loss before the close, and the match seemed set to be drawn. Sri Lanka did not help their cause by dropping catches, Hartland surviving to hit his first fifty in Test cricket, and John Wright became the first New Zealand batsman to reach 5,000 runs in Test cricket.

Rain and bad light persisted into the final day when the game moved to its inevitable conclusion. The New Zealand innings was lightened only by Rutherford who hit 2 sixes and 9 fours as he made 53 off 62 balls. He hit Ranatunga for 4 fours in one over and reached his fifty with a six. This contrasted sharply with the rest of the New Zealand innings. In 54 overs on the last day, 91 runs were scored.

FIRST ONE-DAY INTERNATIONAL
SRI LANKA *v.* NEW ZEALAND, at Colombo

The first one-day (day/night) international between Sri Lanka and New Zealand was ruined by rain. New Zealand pace bowler Owens was hit in the face by a ball during practice and was unable to play. Against accurate bowling, supported by excellent ground fielding, New Zealand struggled to score runs. Only a partnership of 60 between Jones and Rutherford gave the innings any substance.

Pringle had Hathurusinghe caught behind and, two balls later, Gurusinha was out to a spectacular running catch at extra cover by Harris. Mahanama and de Silva

had begun to repair the damage when there was a heavy downpour. When the rain stopped, Sri Lanka were faced with a revised target of 67 in 20 overs, but Crowe refused to continue, saying that the outfield was not playable.

One felt that Crowe was not trying to hide his unhappiness at having to continue the tour without some of his leading players. He had been persuaded to remain in Sri Lanka, but was obviously most reluctant to do so. In the first Test, he had complained about the bowling of Warnaweera, who has escaped censure in any of the countries in which he has played, and he had also publicly criticised his bowlers, although he himself had dropped a vital chance offered by Mahanama. He was, perhaps, losing too many opportunities for keeping quiet.

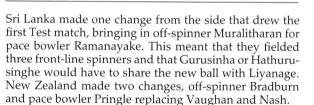

SECOND TEST MATCH
SRI LANKA *v.* NEW ZEALAND, at Colombo

Sri Lanka made one change from the side that drew the first Test match, bringing in off-spinner Muralitharan for pace bowler Ramanayake. This meant that they fielded three front-line spinners and that Gurusinha or Hathurusinghe would have to share the new ball with Liyanage. New Zealand made two changes, off-spinner Bradburn and pace bowler Pringle replacing Vaughan and Nash.

Ranatunga won the toss. Sri Lanka batted and showed refreshing enterprise. In the period before lunch, Mahanama and Hathurusinghe scored 102, and their stand was broken only on the stroke of the interval when Hathurusinghe fell to a full toss from Owens. Mahanama was again in brilliant form and reached his second hundred in successive Tests. He dominated the bowling, and his century came off 128 balls. In an innings which lasted 217 minutes, he hit 14 fours before being caught at midwicket off Owens.

Three wickets fell for 22 runs in the space of 42 balls, and there were fears of a Sri Lankan collapse. Ranatunga, in aggressive mood, and Tillekeratne added 92 in 33 overs to stop the rot. Two wickets, including that of Ranatunga,

FIRST ONE-DAY INTERNATIONAL – SRI LANKA *v.* NEW ZEALAND
4 December 1992 at Khetterama Stadium, Colombo

NEW ZEALAND

*A.C. Parore	run out	20
J.G. Wright	b Wickramasinghe	7
A.H. Jones	st Wickremasinghe, b Gurusinha	24
M.D. Crowe (capt)	c Wickremasinghe, b Wickramasinghe	1
K.R. Rutherford	c Liyanage, b Kalpage	36
C.Z. Harris	not out	32
J.T.C. Vaughan	b Kalpage	6
G.E. Bradburn	b Kalpage	6
D.J. Nash	run out	9
M.L. Su'a	lbw, b Gurusinha	1
C. Pringle	not out	3
Extras	lb 8, w 13	21
(50 overs)	(for 9 wickets)	166

SRI LANKA

R.S. Mahanama	not out	11
U.C. Hathurusinghe	c Parore, b Pringle	5
A.P. Gurusinha	c Harris, b Pringle	0
P.A de Silva	not out	13
A. Ranatunga (capt)		
H.P. Tillekeratne		
*A.G.D. Wickremasinghe		
D.K. Liyanage		
R.S. Kalpage		
S.D. Anurasiri		
G.P. Wickramasinghe		
Extras	lb 2, w 10	12
(10.2 overs)	(for 2 wickets)	41

	O	M	R	W
Liyanage	10	–	39	–
Wickramasinghe	6	–	24	2
Hathurusinghe	10	2	20	–
Anurasiri	5	–	21	–
Kalpage	10	–	29	3
Gurusinha	9	1	25	2

	O	M	R	W
Pringle	5.2	–	15	2
Su'a	4	–	13	–
Nash	1	–	11	–

FALL OF WICKETS
1–23, 2–37, 3–39, 4–99, 5–108, 6–124, 7–136, 8–148, 9–155

FALL OF WICKETS
1–20, 2–20

Match abandoned

---

fell to the second new ball, but Sri Lanka closed on a comfortable 303 for 6.

The second day saw Sri Lanka take total command. Tillekeratne punished the New Zealand attack to reach his highest score in Test cricket and was unlucky not to complete a century so intelligently and positively did he bat. Sri Lanka's last four wickets added 108 and gave the home side extra confidence in the field.

Hartland and Wright began solidly enough for New Zealand, but both fell to Warnaweera who took 4 for 24 in 14 overs to leave the visitors' innings in shreds. His medium-pace off-spinners zipped off the pitch, and he was most ably supported by the more orthodox Muralitharan who bowled quite beautifully. He beat Crowe's forward stroke to clip the leg stump and trapped Parore leg before. Harris was narrowly run out, and New Zealand, 100 for 7, faced the indignity of having to follow-on.

That indignity became a reality on the third morning when the New Zealand innings was terminated within 19 balls for the addition of just two runs. Both Warnaweera and Muralitharan finished with their best figures in Test cricket. There was little improvement when New Zealand batted again, 292 runs behind. The occasional right-arm medium pace of Gurusinha accounted for Hartland while Jones became Warnaweera's fifth victim of the match. At 30 for 2, Martin Crowe strode to the wicket. He had had a far from happy tour, which he had not tried to disguise, and he seemed out of form and out of step with the world.

Suddenly, he threw care aside to play one of the great Test innings of modern times. He lashed the ball to all parts of the ground and reached his hundred off 108 balls. It was his 15th century in Test cricket. He and Wright added 159 before Crowe was out in the last over before tea. He had batted for 159 minutes, faced 121 balls and hit 4 sixes and 10 fours. With justification, Crowe said later that he felt that it was the best innings he had played in a Test match.

Wright batted 231 minutes for his 22nd Test fifty, but New Zealand ended the day still 15 runs away from saving an innings defeat, and with just four wickets standing.

Adam Parore hit his highest score in Test cricket and cajoled the tail into adding a defiant 84 runs before the innings was brought to a close six overs after lunch on the fourth day. The most promising young off-spinner Muralitharan finished with the best figures of his embryo Test career. Sri Lanka had yet another star in Tillekeratne, one-time wicket-keeper, who held seven catches in the match to equal the record for a fielder in a Test match. He gained the individual award for that feat and his innings of 93.

Mahanama hit 6 fours in his 29 before being caught by Parore, but Hathurusinghe and Gurusinha took Sri Lanka to their third victory in 42 Tests. The win, of course, gave Sri Lanka the two-match series. It was a win well deserved, and they looked forward to England's visit with confidence.

SECOND TEST MATCH – SRI LANKA v. NEW ZEALAND
6, 7, 8 and 9 December 1992 at Sinhalese Sports Club, Colombo

SRI LANKA

Batsman	First innings		Second innings	
R.S. Mahanama	c Bradburn, b Owens	109	c Parore, b Owens	29
U.C. Hathurusinghe	c Harris, b Owens	27	not out	23
A.P. Gurusinha	st Parore, b Bradburn	22	not out	14
P.A. de Silva	c Parore, b Pringle	3		
A. Ranatunga (capt)	c Parore, b Su'a	76		
H.P. Tillekeratne	c Parore, b Bradburn	93		
*A.G.D. Wickremasinghe	c Rutherford, b Owens	2		
D.K. Liyanage	c Parore, b Su'a	16		
S.D. Anurasiri	c Su'a, b Owens	24		
M. Muralitharan	not out	4		
K.P.J. Warnaweera	c Crowe, b Bradburn	5		
Extras	b 3, lb 4, w 3, nb 3	13	lb 2, nb 2	4
		394	(for 1 wicket)	70

NEW ZEALAND

Batsman	First innings		Second innings	
B.R. Hartland	c Gurusinha, b Warnaweera	21	c Muralitharan, b Gurusinha	21
J.G. Wright	c Wickremasinghe, b Warnaweera	30	c Mahanama, b Muralitharan	50
A.H. Jones	c Tillekeratne, b Warnaweera	20	c Tillekeratne, b Warnaweera	5
M.D. Crowe (capt)	b Muralitharan	0	c Tillekeratne, b Muralitharan	107
K.R. Rutherford	c Tillekeratne, b Warnaweera	0	c sub (Jayasuriya), b Warnaweera	38
C.Z. Harris	run out	9	lbw, b Anurasiri	19
*A.C. Parore	lbw, b Muralitharan	5	c Tillekeratne, b Muralitharan	60
G.E. Bradburn	c Tillekeratne, b Liyanage	1	c Wickremasinghe, b Anurasiri	7
M.L. Su'a	not out	2	b Muralitharan	0
C. Pringle	b Liyanage	0	c Tillekeratne, b Liyanage	23
M.B. Owens	c Anurasiri, b Muralitharan	0	not out	8
Extras	lb 4, w 1, nb 9	14	b 2, lb 8, nb 13	23
		102		361

New Zealand bowling

	O	M	R	W	O	M	R	W
Su'a	26	7	50	2	2	–	14	–
Owens	30	7	101	4	6	1	36	1
Pringle	32	7	85	1	2	1	5	–
Bradburn	37.4	4	134	3	3	1	8	–
Harris	3	–	17	–				
Jones					1.5	1	5	–

Sri Lanka bowling

	O	M	R	W	O	M	R	W
Liyanage	9	3	9	2	12	3	35	1
Gurusinha	4	1	15	–	8	1	19	1
Anurasiri	6	1	13	–	22	4	54	2
Hathurusinghe	7	3	14	–	3	2	2	–
Warnaweera	14	3	25	4	34	4	107	2
Muralitharan	12.1	3	22	3	40	5	134	4

FALL OF WICKETS
1–102, 2–160, 3–167, 4–182, 5–274, 6–286, 7–316, 8–385, 9–385
1–36

FALL OF WICKETS
1–58, 2–61, 3–64, 4–65, 5–89, 6–98, 7–100, 8–101, 9–101
1–23, 2–30, 3–189, 4–196, 5–240, 6–261, 7–285, 8–286, 9–317

Umpires: T.M. Samarasinghe & I. Anandappa

Sri Lanka won by 9 wickets

SECOND ONE-DAY INTERNATIONAL
SRI LANKA v. NEW ZEALAND, at Colombo

Following his century in the second Test match, Martin Crowe announced that he would not be able to play in the remaining two one-day internationals due to a hamstring injury. New Zealand began well enough with Hartland and skipper Jones taking them to 96 for 1, but four wickets then fell for 12 runs. The second-wicket partnership had realised 79 in 21 overs, but New Zealand never regained the initiative against the Sri Lankan spinners. The bowlers were well supported in the field where Mahanama held three catches, two of them brilliant.

Mahanama continued his outstanding form with the bat, dominating an opening stand of 46 with Hathurusinghe and then adding 74 in 13 overs with Gurusinha. Having hit Harris for six, Gurusinha was out when he tried to repeat the shot, caught at deep mid-wicket. Aravinda de Silva joined Mahanama to bring Sri Lanka victory with 12.2 overs to spare. De Silva emphasised the majesty of Sri Lanka's victory when he ended the match by driving Pringle straight for six.

THIRD ONE-DAY INTERNATIONAL
SRI LANKA v. NEW ZEALAND, at Colombo

Put in to bat, Sri Lanka gave a dazzling display, scoring at more than five runs an over. Roshan Mahanama added a maiden limited-over international century to his two Test centuries and shared a glittering second-wicket partnership of 166 with Gurusinha.

New Zealand were never in touch with the required rate. Harris hit well towards the end, but the last six wickets went down for 66 runs.

Sri Lanka's dominance over the weakened New Zealand side was total in all forms of cricket, and they were justifiably heartened by their performance. New Zealand did not come out of the tour with much credit. They had not been the best of ambassadors in Zimbabwe, and Martin Crowe's attitude had brought them few friends in Sri Lanka, a sad lapse by these, usually the most popular of cricketers.

SECOND ONE-DAY INTERNATIONAL – SRI LANKA v. NEW ZEALAND
12 December 1992 at P. Saravanamuttu Stadium, Colombo

NEW ZEALAND

B.R. Hartland	st Wickremasinghe, b Jayasuriya	54
J.G. Wright	run out	1
A.H. Jones (capt)	c Kalpage, b Anurasiri	37
K.R. Rutherford	c Mahanama, b Kalpage	2
C.Z. Harris	c Mahanama, b Kalpage	2
*A.C. Parore	c Gurusinha, b Jayasuriya	17
D.J. Nash	not out	40
J.T.C. Vaughan	c Mahanama, b Jayasuriya	12
G.E. Bradburn	not out	11
C. Pringle		
M.L. Su'a		
Extras	b 4, lb 9, nb 1	14
(50 overs)	(for 7 wickets)	190

SRI LANKA

R.S. Mahanama	not out	84
U.C. Hathurusinghe	c Rutherford, b Su'a	14
A.P. Gurusinha	c Nash, b Harris	37
P.A. de Silva	not out	43
A. Ranatunga (capt)		
H.P. Tillekeratne		
S.T. Jayasuriya		
*A.G.D. Wickremasinghe		
R.S. Kalpage		
G.P. Wickremasinghe		
S.D. Anurasiri		
Extras	b 5, lb 3, w 4, nb 2	14
(37.4 overs)	(for 2 wickets)	192

	O	M	R	W
Wickramasinghe	7	1	29	–
Gurusinha	7	1	11	–
Hathurusinghe	3	–	16	–
Anurasiri	10	–	34	1
Ranatunga	5	–	20	–
Kalpage	10	2	34	2
Jayasuriya	8	–	33	3

	O	M	R	W
Pringle	9.4	1	45	–
Nash	6	2	15	–
Su'a	5	–	28	1
Vaughan	4	–	26	–
Harris	5	–	34	1
Bradburn	8	–	36	–

FALL OF WICKETS

1–17, 2–96, 3–100, 4–100, 5–108, 6–134, 7–150

FALL OF WICKETS

1–46, 2–120

Man of the Match: R.S. Mahanama   *Sri Lanka won by 8 wickets*

THIRD ONE-DAY INTERNATIONAL – SRI LANKA v. NEW ZEALAND
13 December 1992 at Khetterama Stadium, Colombo

SRI LANKA

R.S. Mahanama	c Jones, b Harris	107
U.C. Hathurusinghe	b Pringle	5
A.P. Gurusinha	b Haslam	76
P.A. de Silva	c and b Pringle	20
A. Ranatunga (capt)	c Jones, b Pringle	16
S.T. Jayasuriya	run out	26
R.S. Kalpage	not out	3
H.P. Tillekeratne		
*A.G.D. Wickremasinghe		
S.D. Anurasiri		
G.P. Wickremasinghe		
Extras	lb 2, w 5, nb 2	9
(49 overs)	(for 6 wickets)	262

NEW ZEALAND

B.R. Hartland	c Wickremasinghe, b Gurusinha	14
*A.C. Parore	b Gurusinha	13
A.H. Jones (capt)	c Jayasuriya, b Kalpage	32
K.R. Rutherford	c and b Kalpage	30
J.T.C. Vaughan	st Wickremasinghe, b Kalpage	33
C.Z. Harris	not out	68
D.J. Nash	run out	8
C. Pringle	c Gurusinha, b Anurasiri	3
G.E. Bradburn	run out	2
M.B. Owens	st Wickremasinghe, b Anurasiri	0
M.J. Haslam	c Ranatunga, b Tillekeratne	9
Extras	lb 14, w 4, nb 1	19
(48.5 overs)		231

	O	M	R	W
Owens	8	–	37	–
Pringle	8	–	59	3
Nash	6	–	44	–
Vaughan	10	1	27	–
Harris	10	–	48	1
Bradburn	2	–	17	–
Haslam	5	–	28	1

	O	M	R	W
Wickramasinghe	6	2	13	–
Gurusinha	7	1	29	2
Hathurusinghe	2	–	16	–
Anurasiri	10	–	45	2
Kalpage	10	–	46	3
Ranatunga	5	1	26	–
De Silva	6	–	31	–
Jayasuriya	2	1	8	–
Tillekeratne	0.5	–	3	1

FALL OF WICKETS

1–9, 2–175, 3–203, 4–218, 5–246, 6–262

FALL OF WICKETS

1–29, 2–35, 3–88, 4–108, 5–165, 6–187, 7–194, 8–199, 9–203

Man of the Match: R.S. Mahanama   *Sri Lanka won by 31 runs*

ENGLAND TOUR

The happy cricketers of Sri Lanka welcomed the less happy cricketers of England. Gooch had returned home, and England, battered and beaten in India, arrived in Sri Lanka under the captaincy of Alec Stewart who was also due to open the batting and to keep wicket – two things, as has been noted before, which he does not do for his county. For the opening game of this very brief tour, England brought in Emburey for Gooch, in an effort to give more variety to the bowling. Sri Lanka recalled wicket-keeper Ashley de Silva after an absence of eight years.

FIRST ONE-DAY INTERNATIONAL
SRI LANKA v. ENGLAND, at Colombo

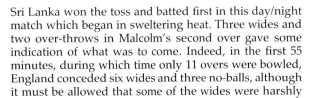

Sri Lanka won the toss and batted first in this day/night match which began in sweltering heat. Three wides and two over-throws in Malcolm's second over gave some indication of what was to come. Indeed, in the first 55 minutes, during which time only 11 overs were bowled, England conceded six wides and three no-balls, although it must be allowed that some of the wides were harshly judged. England had had their successes, however. Mahanama steered a steeply rising ball high to slip, and Gurusinha pulled another lifting delivery comfortably into the hands of long-leg. DeFreitas must have been comforted by this simple catch, for he received no comfort from Aravinda de Silva who pulled him into the crowd for six. After three overs from which 25 runs came, DeFreitas was withdrawn from the firing line.

De Silva fell to Reeve's slower ball, and Hathurusinghe was leg before to the steady Emburey. In the 29th over, Sri Lanka were 109 for 4, and England, not looking impressive in the field, could derive some satisfaction from the score. Their satisfaction quickly passed. Ranatunga managed only 1 four, but he took 36 off 41 balls in intelligent one-day style, and he and Tillekeratne added 71 in 13 overs.

The England bowling was wayward; the fielding was shoddy and petulant. Tillekeratne and Jayasuriya slaughtered the attack. From 35 balls, they plundered 70 runs. Lewis flung down his cap in disgust at one misfield, and the last ball of the innings saw the batsmen take three byes from a ball that went through to the keeper. Stewart rolled at the stumps and missed, as did the bowler, Jarvis, who was following through. It epitomised the farcical nature of England's out-cricket.

Stewart and Smith were out by the sixth over. Hick and Fairbrother added 58 before Hick swung a simple catch to deep square-leg. A light shower reduced England's target to 203 in 38 overs, but that was well beyond their capabilities, and they whimpered to defeat.

FIRST ONE-DAY INTERNATIONAL – SRI LANKA v. ENGLAND
10 March 1993 at Khetterama Stadium, Colombo

SRI LANKA

R.S. Mahanama	c Hick, **b** Malcolm	7
U.C. Hathurusinghe	lbw, **b** Emburey	43
A.P. Gurusinha	c DeFreitas, **b** Jarvis	5
P.A. de Silva	c and **b** Reeve	34
A. Ranatunga (capt)	c Stewart, **b** Lewis	36
H.P. Tillekeratne	not out	66
S.T. Jayasuriya	not out	34
*A.M. de Silva		
C.P.H. Ramanayake		
R.S. Kalpage		
G.P. Wickramasinghe		
Extras	b 3, lb 4, w 10, nb 8	25
		—
(47 overs)	(for 5 wickets)	250

ENGLAND

R.A. Smith	c and **b** Wickramasinghe	3
*A.J. Stewart (capt)	lbw, **b** Ramanayake	5
G.A. Hick	c Mahanama, **b** Hathurusinghe	31
N.H. Fairbrother	lbw, **b** Jayasuriya	34
M.W. Gatting	**b** Kalpage	1
C.C. Lewis	**b** Kalpage	16
D.A. Reeve	c Ranatunga, **b** Kalpage	16
P.A.J. DeFreitas	c Ranatunga, **b** Wickramasinghe	21
J.E. Emburey	st A.M. de Silva, **b** Jayasuriya	10
P.W. Jarvis	not out	16
D.E. Malcolm	run out	2
Extras	lb 10, w 4, nb 1	15
		—
(36.1 overs)		170

	O	M	R	W
Malcolm	7	1	32	1
Lewis	9	–	40	1
Jarvis	9	–	57	1
DeFreitas	3	–	25	–
Emburey	10	1	42	1
Reeve	9	1	47	1

	O	M	R	W
Ramanayake	7	–	25	1
Wickramasinghe	6.1	1	21	2
Hathurusinghe	6	–	28	1
Gurusinha	2	–	7	–
Kalpage	8	–	34	3
Jayasuriya	7	–	45	2

FALL OF WICKETS

1–16, 2–33, 3–101, 4–109, 5–180

FALL OF WICKETS

1–7, 2–9, 3–67, 4–70, 5–99, 6–103, 7–120, 8–137, 9–152

Umpires: K.T. Francis & S. Ponnadui   *Man of the Match:* H.P. Tillekeratne   *Sri Lanka won on faster scoring rate*

Robin Smith is bowled by Muralitharan after completing his first Test century for England overseas. (Richard Saker/Allsport)

Alec Stewart stumps Gurusinha off Tufnell in Sri Lanka's first innings. Stewart claimed six victims in the match. (Richard Saker/Allsport)

TEST MATCH
SRI LANKA *v.* ENGLAND, at Colombo

Having experimented for some years with the idea of asking a player who was primarily a batsman to keep wicket, Sri Lanka reverted to the now unfashionable practice of naming a specialist wicket-keeper in their Test side, and Ashley de Silva was given a first Test cap. Of the team that had beaten New Zealand, Liyanage and Anurasiri were omitted, and Ramanayake and Jayasuriya were brought into the side. It seemed a pity that the hostile Liyanage could not be found a place alongside Ramanayake.

Stewart won an important toss and England batted. They had an early mishap when Atherton, happily restored to the side, was rather harshly adjudged lbw. Smith, new in the coveted role of opener, was solidity itself, his concentration bordering on passivity, but he indicated from the start that he was intent on surviving a day of high temperature and humidity. At lunch, England were 63 for 1, not too adventurous a score against an attack which, with Gurusinha as a make-shift new-ball bowler, looked moderate.

Gatting was dropped by Ranatunga immediately after lunch, but the miss was not a costly one, for the former England captain, who had not enjoyed a happy tour, was caught at silly point, bat/pad, off the young spinner Muralitharan. Thanks to Hick, England arrived at tea with the score on 171 for 2, but Hick was taken at short-leg after adding only 11 runs in the final session and Smith, who finished the day on 91, could never change gear. England were 245 for 3, a seemingly strong position, but the innings now needed an infusion of energy.

That infusion did not come. Smith duly reached his eighth Test century – his first for England overseas – and, in all, he faced 338 balls and batted for 448 minutes. He waited for the bad ball and hit 20 fours, but the longer he waited, the fewer bad balls came his way. The situation was crying out for him to take command, but this he never did. He was fourth out when he tried to pull the admirable Muralitharan, and Stewart, who had shown some urgency, fell seven runs later. Fairbrother and Lewis, run out attempting a third run to third man, lost their wickets in trying to force the pace. England had been contemplating a declaration, but they lost their last five wickets for 22 runs in 55 balls, and 12 of those runs were provided by Malcolm's 2 sixes. England's 380 was barely satisfactory, but full credit should go to Muralitharan, who flighted the ball well, and to Warnaweera and his fierce off-cutters. They were well supported in the field where Sri Lanka's enthusiasm never lapsed.

Mahanama and Hathurusinghe quickly put the England innings into perspective with an opening partnership of 99 in 102 minutes. Emburey and Tufnell were somewhat belatedly introduced into the attack, and Tufnell, in particular, was soon being savaged as he sent down six no-balls and lost his rhythm. Emburey did capture the wicket of Mahanama, who hit 64 off 83 balls before mistiming a big hit, but Sri Lanka reached 140 for 1

Hashan Tillekeratne, Man of the Match, during his brilliant innings of 93 not out against England. (Richard Saker/Allsport)

by the close and, in contrast to England, runs had come at 3.5 an over.

The Sri Lankan top-order batsmen threatened to take the game out of England's reach on the third day, but the visitors worked hard and Lewis, in particular, bowled well, achieving the early breakthrough when he had Hathurusinghe caught in front of first slip by Stewart, who had a very good day behind the stumps and did all that could be expected of him as captain. Gurusinha also fell before lunch when he missed the ball as he swung against Tufnell's spin and was well stumped by Stewart.

The England spinners were put to the sword in the afternoon as Aravinda de Silva and Ranatunga scored 111 in less than 28 overs. The carnage was halted by the seamers as de Silva, whose excitement seems to increase with every thrilling shot he plays, glanced a ball from Jarvis for Stewart to take a good leg-side catch. This was on the stroke of tea, and nine runs after the break, Ranatunga was the victim of an excellent delivery which he edged to the keeper. Jayasuriya was splendidly caught at backward point, Ashley de Silva was taken at short-leg and Ramanayake was held in the gully off a sharp edge. Suddenly, the Sri Lankan innings had fallen apart, and with eight wickets down they were still four short of England's total.

Tillekeratne, however, had played some splendid shots, and he shielded Muralitharan to reach his fifty and to take Sri Lanka into the rest day 28 runs ahead of England.

It seemed that the game would be drawn, or that England might snatch victory if Emburey and Tufnell could exploit a wearing wicket on the final day. These conjectures were proved highly premature when Tillekeratne and Muralitharan, who was aided by some lapses in the field and by some unintelligent bowling, refused to surrender on the fourth morning. Muralitharan showed great resolve, and Tillekeratne was magnificent. England bowled poorly and missed two relatively easy chances, but nothing could detract from the splendour of Tillekeratne's innings. He drove with majesty, and his nine boundaries were all struck with a regal air. He nursed an invaluable 83-run stand out of Muralitharan, and Sri Lanka took a first-innings lead of 89, which was far beyond what had looked possible.

The Sri Lankan innings ended on the stroke of lunch and, four overs into the afternoon, England were in trouble. Atherton cut at Gurusinha and was caught in the gully. Gatting looked more positive than of late before being adjudged caught at short-leg, a decision which did not please England. Smith again looked solid but he rashly swept at the left-arm Jayasuriya and was bowled round his legs, his pad having been placed outside the line of the ball. This was Jayasuriya's first wicket in Test cricket.

Worse was to follow as Hick hit high to square-leg where Ramanayake took the catch, and Stewart deflected a ball from Warnaweera to slip off the pad and handle of his bat. Stewart questioned the decision, but he had questioned too many decisions on the tour to win sympathy. In four overs, England had lost three wickets and, effectively, they were 7 for 5.

Lewis and Fairbrother attempted to restore sanity. Lewis played the aggressive role and hit seven thundering fours in his 45 off 51 balls, but shortly after tea he lost Fairbrother. The Lancashire left-hander was sent back when an unlikely single was being debated. Fairbrother was stranded, but the wicket had been broken by Warnaweera who then smote the middle stump out of the ground with the ball. Fairbrother, and others, protested that he was not out as the stump should have been pulled from the ground. The Laws of Cricket (28.1.C) proved that the umpire's decision was the correct one.

TEST MATCH – SRI LANKA v. ENGLAND
13, 14, 15, 17 and 18 March 1993 at Sinhalese Sports Club, Colombo

ENGLAND

Batsman	FIRST INNINGS		SECOND INNINGS	
R.A. Smith	b Muralitharan	128	b Jayasuriya	35
M.A. Atherton	lbw, b Ramanayake	13	c Tillekeratne, b Gurusinha	2
M.W. Gatting	c Jayasuriya, b Muralitharan	29	c Tillekeratne, b Warnaweera	18
G.A. Hick	c Tillekeratne, b Muralitharan	68	c Ramanayake, b Warnaweera	26
*A.J. Stewart (capt)	c Tillekeratne, b Warnaweera	63	c Mahanama, b Warnaweera	3
N.H. Fairbrother	b Warnaweera	18	run out	3
C.C. Lewis	run out	22	c Jayasuriya, b Muralitharan	45
J.E. Emburey	not out	1	b Gurusinha	59
P.W. Jarvis	lbw, b Warnaweera	0	st A.M. de Silva, b Jayasuriya	3
P.C.R. Tufnell	lbw, b Muralitharan	1	c A.M. de Silva, b Warnaweera	1
D.E. Malcolm	c Gurusinha, b Warnaweera	13	not out	8
Extras	b 5, lb 3, w 1, nb 15	24	b 4, lb 2, w 1, nb 18	25
		380		**228**

SRI LANKA

Batsman	FIRST INNINGS		SECOND INNINGS	
U.C. Hathurusinghe	c Stewart, b Lewis	59	(2) c Stewart, b Tufnell	14
R.S. Mahanama	c Smith, b Emburey	64	(1) c Stewart, b Lewis	6
A.P. Gurusinha	st Stewart, b Tufnell	43	b Emburey	29
P.A. de Silva	c Stewart, b Jarvis	80	c Jarvis, b Emburey	7
A. Ranatunga (capt)	c Stewart, b Lewis	64	c Gatting, b Tufnell	35
H.P. Tillekeratne	not out	93	not out	36
S.T. Jayasuriya	c Atherton, b Lewis	4	not out	6
*A.M. de Silva	c Gatting, b Emburey	9		
C.P.H. Ramanayake	c Lewis, b Jarvis	1		
M. Muralitharan	b Lewis	19		
K.P.J. Warnaweera	b Jarvis	1		
Extras	b 2, lb 13, w 2, nb 15	32	b 1, lb 2, nb 6	9
		469	(for 5 wickets)	**142**

	O	M	R	W	O	M	R	W
Ramanayake	17	2	66	1	3	–	16	–
Gurusinha	5	1	12	–	6	3	7	2
Warnaweera	40.1	11	90	4	25	4	98	4
Hathurusinghe	8	2	22	–				
Muralitharan	45	12	118	4	16	3	55	1
Jayasuriya	12	1	53	–	16	3	46	2
Ranatunga	3	–	11	–				

	O	M	R	W	O	M	R	W
Malcolm	25	7	60	–	3	1	11	–
Jarvis	25.5	1	76	3	8	2	14	–
Lewis	31	5	66	4	8	1	21	1
Tufnell	33	5	108	1	7.4	1	34	2
Emburey	34	6	117	2	14	2	48	2
Hick	8	–	27	–	2	–	11	–

FALL OF WICKETS

1–40, 2–82, 3–194, 4–316, 5–323, 6–358, 7–366, 8–366, 9–367
1–16, 2–38, 3–83, 4–91, 5–96, 6–130, 7–153, 8–173, 9–188

FALL OF WICKETS

1–99, 2–153, 3–203, 4–330, 5–339, 6–349, 7–371, 8–376, 9–459
1–8, 2–48, 3–61, 4–61, 5–136

Umpires: K.T. Francis & T.M. Samarasinghe

Sri Lanka won by 5 wickets

The running out of Neil Fairbrother in England's second innings. (Ben Radford/Allsport)

Eight wickets for medium-pace off-cutter Warnaweera – a vital contribution to Sri Lanka's victory. (Richard Saker/Allsport)

Lewis was taken at short-leg, and it was apparent that the Sri Lankan spinners were making the ball lift and turn in a way that had eluded Emburey and Tufnell. Jarvis played well forward and missed, and Tufnell, to his obvious disgust, was given out caught down the leg side. In 39 minutes at the end of a day which had seen England at their worst, Emburey and Malcolm added 38. There was still the hope that, if set somewhere between 160 and 170, Sri Lanka might falter through nerves and anxiety as they had done against Australia.

This proved to be a vain wish. Emburey, who had batted with that ugly defiance which does encourage respect, and Malcolm added only two in six overs on the last morning before Emburey went back to Gurusinha and was bowled. Needing 140 to win, and with almost a day in which to get the runs, Sri Lanka lost Mahanama in Lewis' second over. He was well caught down the leg side by Stewart. Atherton made a brilliant attempt to catch Hathurusinghe in the gully, but Sri Lanka lunched at 43 for 1 in some confidence.

Emburey and, to a lesser extent, Tufnell bowled better than they had done at any time on the tour of India. Gurusinha had looked very positive, but he selected the wrong ball from Emburey to try to cut and chopped the ball into his stumps. Aravinda de Silva hit a boundary, but he looked too excitable and clouted a long hop from Emburey into the hands of backward square-leg. Without addition, Hathurusinghe was splendidly caught by Stew-art who dived to gather a ball that popped up on the leg side. In seven overs, Sri Lanka had lost three wickets for 13 runs, and the spectre of their defeat at the hands of Australia loomed large.

Ranatunga and Tillekeratne quickly dispelled any such fears. They were aggressive in attack, sound in defence, and there no longer remained even a flicker of hope for England. Ranatunga's positive approach gained just rewards, but the captain was not there at the finish to steer his side to their historic victory. In the first over after tea, with just four runs needed, he was superbly caught by Gatting at short-leg. Jayasuriya came in and hit the first ball he received over mid-wicket for six. It was a shot that summed up England's tour of the Indian subcontinent.

The inadequacies of the England side have been much emphasised as have the disastrous selections that were made at the outset and on the tour itself. However, what should be emphasised from this match is the quality of Sri Lanka's performance. They batted in the classical mould, technically proficient, regal in stroke-play. Tillekeratne, Man of the Match, revealed himself as a cricketer of exceptional talent, temperamentally sound and glorious to watch. The fielding was good and, if limited in resources, the bowling fulfilled its potential and, perhaps, did even better than could have been expected. In short, England were second best in every department of the game.

SECOND ONE-DAY INTERNATIONAL
SRI LANKA v. ENGLAND, at Moratuwa

England promoted Lewis to opener and brought in Taylor and Salisbury for Malcolm and DeFreitas. Sri Lanka won the toss and asked England to bat on a cloudy day. Lewis was not happy in his opening role and was often beaten by Ramanayake. He hit 2 fours before hooking Wickramasinghe into the hands of long-leg. Hick and Smith batted with assurance and took the score to 77 in the 17th over. The introduction of the spinners changed the course of the match.

Smith went forward to Jayasuriya and was stumped; Hick attempted to pull Kalpage and missed. Fairbrother edged a defensive shot to the keeper, Stewart played across the line, as did Gatting, and Emburey hit high to mid-on. Reeve hoicked across the line, Jarvis skied to the keeper and Taylor was bowled as he tried to swing the ball to leg. England had lost nine wickets for 103 runs. Even by their standards, this was a wretched performance. Jayasuriya returned the best performance by a Sri Lankan bowler in a one-day international, taking six of the last nine wickets with left-arm spin which was always

SECOND ONE-DAY INTERNATIONAL – SRI LANKA v. ENGLAND
20 March 1993 at Tyronne Fernando Stadium, Moratuwa

ENGLAND			SRI LANKA		
C.C. Lewis	c Ramanayake, b Wickramasinghe	8	R.S. Mahanama	c Stewart, b Salisbury	29
R.A. Smith	st A.M. de Silva, b Jayasuriya	31	U.C. Hathurusinghe	c and b Salisbury	33
G.A. Hick	lbw, b Kalpage	36	A.P. Gurusinha	not out	35
N.A. Fairbrother	c A.M. de Silva, b Jayasuriya	21	P.A. de Silva	not out	75
*A.J. Stewart (capt)	lbw, b Tillekeratne	14	A. Ranatunga (capt)		
M.W. Gatting	lbw, b P.A. de Silva	2	H.P. Tillekeratne		
D.A. Reeve	b Jayasuriya	20	S.T. Jayasuriya		
J.E. Emburey	c Ramanayake, b Jayasuriya	21	*A.M. de Silva		
I.D.K. Salisbury	not out	2	C.P.H. Ramanayake		
P.W. Jarvis	c A.M. de Silva, b Jayasuriya	4	R.S. Kalpage		
J.P. Taylor	b Jayasuriya	1	G.P. Wickramasinghe		
Extras	b 2, lb 9, w 3, nb 6	20	Extras	b 1, lb 2, w 2, nb 6	11
(48.5 overs)		180	(35.2 overs)	(for 2 wickets)	183

	O	M	R	W		O	M	R	W
Ramanayake	4	–	20	–	Lewis	7	1	13	–
Wickramasinghe	8	–	23	1	Jarvis	4	–	22	–
Gurusinha	4	–	21	–	Taylor	3	–	20	–
Hathurusinghe	2	–	13	–	Emburey	6	–	29	–
Kalpage	10	–	27	1	Salisbury	4	–	36	2
P.A. de Silva	7	1	22	1	Hick	6.2	1	36	–
Jayasuriya	9.5	–	29	6	Reeve	5	–	24	–
Tillekeratne	4	–	14	1					

FALL OF WICKETS
1–23, 2–77, 3–85, 4–111, 5–114, 6–126, 7–168, 8–172, 9–177

FALL OF WICKETS
1–66, 2–68

Umpires: B.C. Cooray & T.M. Samarasinghe   Man of the Match: S.T. Jayasuriya   Sri Lanka won by 8 wickets

accurate in length and direction. He bowled with intelligence, always pitched on the stumps, and the batsmen did the rest.

Mahanama and Hathurusinghe began at six runs an over, but slowed to four. The one ray of hope for England came when, belatedly, Salisbury was brought into the attack. Hathurusinghe drove too soon and was caught and bowled. Mahanama played back to a leg-break which turned and bounced. At the end of Salisbury's first over, Sri Lanka were 68 for 2.

Aravinda de Silva drove at the first ball of Salisbury's second over. It went high back over the bowler's head and Smith, running from mid-on, called for the catch. He missed it and damaged his knee in the process so that he had to be carried from the field. The batsmen ran two. De Silva hit the next two deliveries out of the ground and followed these with a four. He went on to make 75 off 68 balls, finishing the match with his fourth six. He also hit 7 fours. Sri Lanka had eight wickets and 14.4 overs in hand.

Sri Lanka have been shabbily treated since being granted Test status. They are a most entertaining side, and, as this brief visit by England proved, they deserve a three-Test series and a proper tour of England and Australia. Those who profess to be concerned about the welfare of cricket throughout the world need to match their words with actions.

For England, this was the ultimate humiliation.

More renowned as a batsman, Jayasuriya set a record for Sri Lanka by taking 6 for 29 in the second one-day international against England. (David Munden/Sports-Line)

SECTION C
Australia

Mercantile Mutual Cup

Sheffield Shield

Benson and Hedges World Series – Australia, West Indies and Pakistan

West Indies tour, Test series

Form charts

First-class averages

Merv Hughes hits out in the fourth Test match against West Indies. (Joe Mann/Allsport)

For three or four years, Australia had looked dominant in world cricket, but the failure of the national side to reach the final stages of the World Cup competition on their own soil, coupled with a tour of Sri Lanka which had served only to expose alarming weaknesses in the top-order batting, had brought about a sense of misgiving. Inevitably, there were calls for changes in the composition of the Test side, and there were several young players eager to press their claims: Martyn, Hayden, Lehmann, Bevan and Freedman among them. The opposition provided in the 1992–3 season was the strongest in the world: West Indies in a five-Test series, and West Indies and Pakistan in the Benson and Hedges one-day international series.

Few cricketers in the world play more one-day cricket than the Australian national side, and there was an increase in the number of limited-over matches in the Australian domestic season for 1992–3. The one-day interstate competition welcomed a new sponsor in Mercantile Mutual, an insurance and investment group, and the new format meant that each team would play all the other sides in the competition. These 15 preliminary matches would produce a league winner, and the sides finishing second and third would play each other for the right to meet the league winners in the final. The majority of the preliminary matches were scheduled for the start of the season.

There were the inevitable pre-season interstate movements and retirements. Terry Alderman succeeded Daryl Foster as coach of reigning Shield-holders Western Australia. Alderman announced that he would continue to play for the state side. Western Australia lost Brayshaw to South Australia, but Mark O'Neill returned from New South Wales to take up a coaching appointment in Perth. Both MacLeay and McCague announced their retirements from the Western Australian side. McCague, of course, had made his mark with Kent in 1992, but MacLeay had not been retained by Somerset.

Mark Taylor succeeded Geoff Lawson as captain of New South Wales; and Ian Healy became Queensland's fifth captain in as many seasons. Queensland added Greg Campbell from Tasmania and Paul Jackson from Victoria to their squad, but they lost Peter Taylor, Greg Ritchie and Dirk Wellham, who retired. In fact, three matches into the season, Wellham was to return to first-class cricket and take óver the captaincy, as international calls made Healy unavailable for much of the time and Carl Rackemann, vice-captain, was unfit. In being appointed captain of Queensland, Wellham became the first man to lead three state sides in the Sheffield Shield. (He had previously led both New South Wales and Tasmania.) Queensland were handicapped when left-arm spinner Jackson broke an arm and could not play in the first half of the season.

Victoria lost McIntyre as well as Jackson. McIntyre moved to South Australia, who were hit by the retirements of both Hookes and Hilditch. Tasmania suffered an even greater loss in the departure of both opening bowlers, Campbell and Gilbert.

MERCANTILE MUTUAL CUP

9 October 1992 *at WACA Ground, Perth*

Victoria 132
Western Australia 135 for 0 (M.R.J. Veletta 72 not out, G.R. Marsh 51 not out)

Western Australia won by 10 wickets

10 October 1992 *at Woolloongabba, Brisbane*

South Australia 158 for 8 (G.A. Bishop 63)
Queensland 159 for 2 (M.L. Hayden 73 not out, P.J.T. Goggin 60)

Queensland won by 8 wickets

11 October 1992 *at WACA Ground, Perth*

New South Wales 206 for 8 (M.A. Taylor 84)
Western Australia 207 for 2 (M.R.J. Veletta 58, T.M. Moody 52 not out)

Western Australia won by 8 wickets

17 October 1992 *at WACA Ground, Perth*

Western Australia 218 for 8 (T.M. Moody 65, M.P. Lavender 51)
Tasmania 219 for 3 (D.C. Boon 80, D.F. Hills 77)

Tasmania won by 7 wickets

18 October 1992 *at Adelaide Oval*

New South Wales 298 for 3 (S.R. Waugh 85 not out, S.M. Small 80, M.A. Taylor 67, M.E. Waugh 55)
South Australia 187

New South Wales won by 111 runs

24 October 1992 *at Adelaide Oval*

South Australia 249 for 6 (J.A. Brayshaw 101 not out)
Tasmania 213 for 7

South Australia won by 36 runs

25 October 1992 *at Woolloongabba, Brisbane*

Western Australia 221 for 7 (J.L. Langer 87, W.S. Andrews 56)
Queensland 222 for 4 (M.L. Hayden 121 not out, T.J. Barsby 76)

Queensland won by 6 wickets

31 October 1992 *at Adelaide Oval*

South Australia 173 for 9
Western Australia 176 for 4 (J.L. Langer 55 not out)

Western Australia won by 6 wickets

1 November 1992 *at Woolloongabba, Brisbane*

New South Wales 252 for 8 (S.R. Waugh 131)
Queensland 241 for 9

New South Wales won by 11 runs

4 November 1992 *at SCG, Sydney*

New South Wales 286 for 5 (M.G. Bevan 77 not out, M.A. Taylor 71)
Victoria 40 for 1

Match abandoned

15 November 1992 *at Princes Park, Melbourne*

Queensland 210 for 8 (T.J. Barsby 67)
Victoria 211 for 7 (P.C. Nobes 86)

Victoria won by 3 wickets

13 December 1992 *at Devonport Oval*

Victoria 222 (D.S. Lehmann 76, P.C. Nobes 52)
Tasmania 164

Victoria won by 58 runs

Western Australia's rising star, Justin Langer. (Joe Mann/Allsport)

The first dozen matches in the Mercantile Mutual Cup were played before Christmas and saw Western Australia complete their programme with three victories and two defeats. In the opening match, Victoria lost their last seven wickets for 16 runs, with Martyn taking 3 for 3. Man of the Match Veletta and skipper Geoff Marsh hit 135 in 32.4 overs. McDermott's 2 for 12 in 10 overs gave him the individual award as Queensland beat South Australia, while Bruce Reid's 3 for 19 won him the accolade in Western Australia's second victory. Peter McPhee became the third bowler to claim the Man-of-the-Match award when he took the wickets of Veletta, Moody and Martyn for 19 runs as Tasmania gained a surprise win over Western Australia. Hills and Boon added 132 for Tasmania's second wicket. Steve Waugh's all-round cricket led New South Wales to a comfortable win over South Australia, who recovered to beat Tasmania by means of Brayshaw's 101 not out off 111 balls. Matthew Hayden was the next century-maker as Queensland inflicted a second defeat on Western Australia. Hayden and Barsby put on 187 for Queensland's first wicket. Earlier, Langer and Andrews had effected a recovery for Western Australia by taking the score from 17 for 4 to 146 before they were separated. Reid's economical bowling again won him the individual award as Western Australia beat South Australia in their final match, and Steve Waugh's outstanding all-round cricket was again in evidence as New South Wales beat Queensland in a thrilling, high-scoring encounter. Victoria kept alive their hopes of qualifying for the final stages of the tournament when, having been thwarted by rain at Sydney, they beat Queensland with only two balls to spare. Nobes was their hero, and he followed his 86 with 52 against Tasmania, but it was Dodemaide's 3 for 11 which clinched this match. Victoria and New South Wales were one point behind Western Australia with one game each to play.

 SHEFFIELD SHIELD

21, 22, 23 and **24** October 1992 *at Woolloongabba, Brisbane*

Western Australia 370 (D.R. Martyn 133, G.R. Marsh 121) and 184 (D.R. Martyn 112, S.C. Storey 5 for 55)
Queensland 221 (B.A. Reid 4 for 58) and 283 (M.L. Hayden 63, A.R. Border 53, T.M. Alderman 4 for 55)

Western Australia won by 50 runs
Western Australia 6 pts., Queensland 0 pts.

The Sheffield Shield programme opened with holders Western Australia bowling out Queensland on the last afternoon to win by 50 runs. This was the first game to be played in Australia under the three-umpire system. Queensland gave a first-class debut to Bichel and recalled Tazelaar and Storey whose left-arm spin brought him the first five-wicket haul of his career on the third afternoon. Geoff Marsh asserted his right to be recalled to the Test side with a century on the opening day, but the outstanding feature of the match was the batting of Damien Martyn, the 21 year-old. He became the first player for 18 years to hit a century in each innings at Brisbane.

2 November 1992 *at Lilac Hill, Perth*

ACB Chairman's XI 209 for 9 (G.R. Marsh 72)
West Indians 210 for 3 (B.C. Lara 106, R.B. Richardson 53)

West Indians won by 7 wickets

A century in each innings in the first Sheffield Shield match of the season for Damien Martyn, Western Australia v. Queensland. (Joe Mann/Allsport)

4 November 1992 *at WACA Ground, Perth*

West Indians 199 (J. Angel 4 for 38)
Western Australia 171 (D.R. Martyn 52)

West Indians won by 28 runs

6, 7, 8 and 9 November 1992 *at WACA Ground, Perth*

West Indians 280 (B.C. Lara 55, D.L. Haynes 52, J.C. Adams 52, J. Angel 5 for 59, B.P. Julian 5 for 72) and 326 for 4 dec. (K.L.T. Arthurton 104 not out, D.L. Haynes 66, C.L. Hooper 60)
Western Australia 239 for 7 dec. (M.R.J. Veletta 51, W.S. Andrews 51, C.L. Hooper 4 for 61) and 131

West Indians won by 236 runs

The West Indian tourists began most encouragingly in Perth where they won all three matches, meeting virtually the same opposition in each match. Veterans Yardley and Lillee played in the first 50-over match. All of the West Indian batsmen showed good form, and off-spinner Carl Hooper was particularly successful with the ball.

6, 7, 8 and 9 November 1992 *at SCG, Sydney*

New South Wales 377 for 8 dec. (M.A. Taylor 102, M.E. Waugh 88, M.G. Bevan 68, T.H. Bayliss 64, M.G. Hughes 6 for 83) and 179 for 7 (G.R.J. Matthews 54)

Victoria 547 for 9 dec. (W.N. Phillips 205, S.P. O'Donnell 67, A.I.C. Dodemaide 53 not out, S.K. Warne 52, M.R. Whitney 4 for 122)

Match drawn

Victoria 2 pts., New South Wales 0 pts.

at Woolloongabba, Brisbane

South Australia 178 (D. Tazelaar 4 for 39, C.J. McDermott 4 for 48) and 246 (G.R. Blewett 50, C.J. McDermott 4 for 64)
Queensland 485 for 7 dec. (P.J.T. Goggin 120, M.L. Hayden 77, S.G. Law 69, I.A. Healy 53 not out, D.J. Hickey 4 for 120)

Queensland won by an innings and 61 runs

Queensland 6 pts., South Australia 0 pts.

Rain on the first day at Sydney reduced the chance of a result between the experienced sides of New South Wales and Victoria, and the conditions on the last day helped New South Wales to save the game. The main feature of the match was Wayne Phillips' career best 205. He hit 24 fours and batted for 582 minutes before he reached his double century, the slowest double hundred recorded for Victoria. He was eventually stumped off Steve Waugh.

South Australia introduced opening batsman Noel Fielke to Shield cricket, but the visitors collapsed on the first day at Brisbane as Dirk Tazelaar took 4 for 2 in 19 deliveries. Peter Goggin hit a maiden first-class hundred for Queensland, and South Australia were bowled out before lunch on the last day to give Queensland an innings victory.

12 November 1992 *at Manuka Oval, Canberra*

Prime Minister's XI 233 for 7 (D.M. Jones 76, M.G. Bevan 58)
West Indians 230 for 9 (D. Williams 57, P.R. Reiffel 4 for 44)

Prime Minister's XI won by 3 runs

14, 15, 16 and 17 November 1992 *at Bellerive Oval, Hobart*

Australian XI 341 (S.R. Waugh 95, C.L. Hooper 5 for 72) and 293 for 4 dec. (S.R. Waugh 100 not out, D.S. Lehmann 54 not out, M.L. Hayden 53)
West Indians 382 (P.V. Simmons 106, K.L.T. Arthurton 76, S.K. Warne 4 for 104) and 213 for 5 (D.L. Haynes 79)

Match drawn

The West Indian tourists suffered their first defeat when they were narrowly beaten in the 50-over match in Canberra. There was much interest in the match at Hobart where the Australian XI included several young men jockeying for a place in the Test side – Phillips, Hayden, Martyn, Lehmann, Freedman and Warne. The more experienced Steve Waugh also saw this as an important opportunity to reclaim his place in the national side, and he responded to the challenge with innings of 95 and 100 not out. All the young batsmen acquitted themselves well, with Martyn and Hayden being particularly impressive. Simmons and Arthurton again batted encouragingly for the West Indians who made a valiant attempt to win the match when set to score 253 in 53 overs.

14, 15, 16 and 17 November 1992 *at WACA Ground, Perth*

Western Australia 159 (T.J. Zoehrer 61, J.L. Langer 58, M.R. Whitney 5 for 43, P.J.S. Alley 5 for 43) and 286

New South Wales 220 (T.H. Bayliss 52, B.P. Julian 4 for 50) and 229 for 5 (G.R.J. Matthews 65 not out)

New South Wales won by 5 wickets

New South Wales 6 pts., Western Australia 0 pts.

The two left-arm pace bowlers, Alley and Whitney, routed Western Australia on the opening day. The pair returned identical figures and, astonishingly, the Western Australian innings was boosted by a stand of 100 for the sixth wicket between Langer and Zoehrer. The last five wickets fell for seven runs. New South Wales fared only marginally better when they batted, but they won the match early on the last day. Wayne Holdsworth was warned for intimidatory bowling after twice hitting Western Australian number nine Joe Angel, and Terry Alderman was warned and fined for a show of dissent in New South Wales' second innings.

20, 21, 22 and 23 November 1992 *at SCG, Sydney*

New South Wales 473 for 5 dec. (M.E. Waugh 200 not out, M.A. Taylor 101) and 34 for 1

West Indians 183 (C.L. Hooper 81 not out) and 507 for 9 dec. (C.L. Hooper 124, P.V. Simmons 109, A.L. Logie 99, R.B. Richardson 75, G.R.J. Matthews 4 for 148)

Match drawn

at Junction Oval, St Kilda

Queensland 222 for 9 dec. (A.R. Border 71, M.L. Hayden 51) and 144 for 9 dec.

Victoria 195 (P.C. Nobes 70, A.R. Border 5 for 46) and 95 for 9 (G.J. Rowell 5 for 31, M.S. Kasprowicz 4 for 42)

Match drawn

Queensland 2 pts., Victoria 0 pts.

at Adelaide Oval

South Australia 368 for 7 dec. (T.J. Nielsen 109, J.C. Scuderi 100 not out, G.A. Bishop 50) and 268 for 2 dec. (N.R. Fielke 74, J.A. Brayshaw 73 not out, J.C. Siddons 69 not out)

Tasmania 298 for 6 dec. (D.C. Boon 60, R. Ponting 56) and 123 (T.B.A. May 5 for 42)

South Australia won by 215 runs

South Australia 6 pts., Tasmania 0 pts.

Savaged by Mark Waugh and Mark Taylor who added 132 for New South Wales' third wicket, the West Indian tourists were forced to follow-on in Sydney, but they recovered well to force an honourable draw. Carl Hooper again batted with elegance and confidence while Phil Simmons established himself as a worthy successor to Gordon Greenidge, batting with great panache and certainty.

With drainage improvements being carried out at the MCG, Victoria were forced to play their home matches elsewhere in the early part of the season, and the game against Queensland at Junction Oval proved something of a nightmare for batsmen. Only 27 minutes' play was possible on the second day, after which the home side collapsed against Border, whose left-arm spin brought him his best return in Shield cricket. Healy eventually asked Victoria to make 172 in 32 overs on a difficult pitch, and only the defiance of Warne and Hughes who batted for 35 minutes and withstood 52 deliveries saved the home state from defeat. Kasprowicz produced his best figures in first-class cricket.

In the game at Adelaide, Tasmania included medium-pace bowler Colin Miller, formerly of Victoria and South Australia, and Ricky Ponting, an outstanding graduate of the Australian Cricket Academy. Tim Nielsen hit a maiden first-class century as he and Scuderi shared a sixth-wicket stand of 159. Boon and Ponting added 127 in 142 minutes for Tasmania's third wicket, and Boon declared 70 runs in arrears. South Australia's Tim May, having offended with 10 no-balls in the first innings, found his rhythm in the second and took 5 for 42. Tasmania collapsed, losing their last five wickets for 18 runs.

27, 28, 29 and 30 November 1992 *at Bellerive Oval, Hobart*

Tasmania 403 (R.J. Tucker 104, N.C.P. Courtney 60, M.G. Farrell 53 not out, W.J. Holdsworth 4 for 108) and 211 for 6 dec. (D.F. Hills 87, J. Cox 73)

New South Wales 272 (M.J. Slater 138, C.D. Matthews 4 for 75, C.R. Miller 4 for 93) and 287 for 7 (S.M. Small 88, P.A. Emery 62 not out)

Match drawn

Tasmania 2 pts., New South Wales 0 pts.

29 November 1992 *at Northam*

Pakistanis 167

Invitation XI 166 for 6

Pakistanis won by 1 run

1 December 1992 *at WACA Ground, Perth*

Pakistanis 270 for 3 (Ramiz Raja 98, Javed Miandad 69 not out)

Western Australia 243 (T.J. Zoehrer 83)

Pakistanis won by 27 runs

Tasmania took their first points of the season with Rodney Tucker leading them to a big first-innings score against a depleted New South Wales side. Slater's maiden first-class hundred helped the visitors to avoid the follow-on, but eventually it was a seventh-wicket stand of 97 between Emery and Alley which saved New South Wales from defeat.

Pakistan prepared for the World Series with victories in two one-day games.

FIRST TEST MATCH
AUSTRALIA *v.* WEST INDIES, at Brisbane

Australia omitted Dean Jones and gave a first Test cap to Damien Martyn. Border won the toss, and Australia batted, but they enjoyed only a moderate first day. Taylor was soon caught behind off Bishop, the pace man's first Test wicket for two years, most of which he has spent recovering from back injury. There was further disaster for Australia at 21 when Steve Waugh was adjudged caught behind down the leg side. The batsman had been subjected to a searching examination by the pace bowlers, but he seemed a little unfortunate to be given out. There were no more problems for Australia before lunch as Mark Waugh and David Boon repaired the innings in a positive manner.

Indeed, the problems were with West Indies. Walsh bowled only five balls before limping off the field with a strained hamstring, and Patterson was wildly inaccurate. Carl Hooper's off-breaks were used much earlier than had been anticipated, and with his fifth ball after the interval he caught and bowled Mark Waugh off a fierce drive. At 125, he claimed a second victim when he had Boon taken at short-leg. Martyn batted solidly before swinging at a wide ball from Ambrose and offering a catch in the slips.

Border and Matthews took Australia out of extreme danger with a partnership of 72 which ended when Border was run out by Hooper five minutes before the close, which came at 259 for 6.

Hooper made more significant contributions on the second morning, capturing the wickets of Healy and Hughes and taking a fine diving catch at slip to account for McDermott. Hooper's 4 for 75 was his best return in a Test match.

There was early success for Australia as Reid and Hughes reduced West Indies to 58 for 3, but Lara and Arthurton made a spirited riposte as they added 112 in 153 minutes. Both batsmen produced some exquisite drives, and the stand was ended in controversial manner when Lara went down the pitch to Matthews, missed and was given out stumped, although there was debate as to whether or not Healy had broken the wicket without the ball in his grasp. West Indies closed the day on 195 for 4.

Keith Arthurton was lucky to escape an appeal for a catch behind when he was 78, but this could not detract from a splendidly patient innings which saw him reach his first hundred in Test cricket. He hit a six and 16 fours

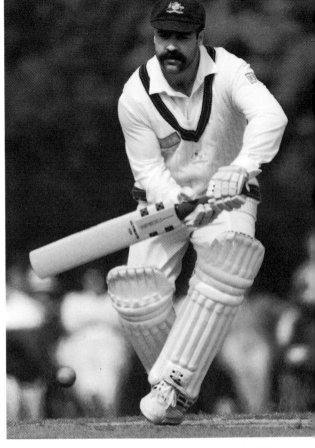

David Boon's second-innings century brought Australia back into contention in the first Test match at Brisbane. (Alan Cozzi)

and faced 343 balls in a knock which lasted for 447 minutes. His 157 was the highest score by a West Indian in a Brisbane Test, and it helped take his side to a first-innings lead of 78, which Boon and Taylor reduced by 21 before the end of the third day. The batting of Arthurton tended to overshadow another fine bowling performance by the tall, lean Bruce Reid.

Australia appeared to be moving to a position of dominance on the fourth day when they reached 250 for 3 in their second innings, but Ambrose restored the balance when he sent back Mark Waugh, Martyn and Matthews within the space of 11 balls at a personal cost of three runs. Australia closed on 266 for 6, and Ambrose's performance tended to obscure the achievement of David Boon. Dropped at slip by Hooper before he had added to his overnight score of 6, Boon scored 111 off 259 balls and hit 13 fours. It was his 14th Test hundred and his fourth in successive Tests in Australia. He and Mark Waugh put on 110 in even time for the third wicket.

Border ended the fourth day limping with an injured hamstring, but he battled on during the last morning when Australia added 42 more runs. West Indies, for whom Ambrose took five wickets and Williams held five catches behind the stumps, were left 65 overs in which to score 231 to win the match, a task well within their capabilities – or so it seemed, until, in the brief session before lunch, Australia emerged as the only probable winner.

In 4.5 overs, West Indies lost Haynes, Simmons and Lara for three runs, and McDermott, in an inspired, aggressive spell, bowled Arthurton shortly after the break. In the rest of the afternoon session, Richardson and Hooper restored the West Indian innings and even gave a hint of victory, taking the score to 93 for 4. One of the least happy features of the afternoon's play was an angry exchange between Hughes and Border on the one hand and umpire Randell on the other when the official rejected a confident appeal for leg before against Richardson. Hughes and Border were later censured and fined by match referee Subba Row for their show of dissent.

West Indies' last chance of victory disappeared immediately after tea when Hooper and Williams were out as only three more runs were added. At 123, Richardson's valiant and vital knock was ended when he edged Hughes to Healy. Australia needed three wickets in the last six overs, and they had Ambrose caught off Reid, but Bishop, who had batted for over an hour, and Walsh stood firm, although not without alarms.

David Boon took the individual award, but it could have gone to one of half a dozen players on either side without too much complaint.

4, 5, 6 and 7 December 1992 *at Junction Oval, St Kilda*

Western Australia 212 (J.L. Langer 70, D.R. Martyn 51) and 337 for 3 (D.R. Martyn 116 not out, G.R. Marsh 101)

Victoria 352 (S.K. Warne 69, D.S. Lehmann 60, A.I.C. Dodemaide 50, B.P. Julian 5 for 84)

Match drawn

Victoria 2 pts., Western Australia 0 pts.

6 December 1992 *at Alice Springs*

Pakistanis 273 for 6 (Saeed Anwar 135 not out, Wasim Akram 50)

Northern Territory 179 (Wasim Akram 5 for 33)

Pakistanis won by 94 runs

In a rather grim struggle at St Kilda, Damien Martyn hit his third Shield century of the season and Warne again showed competent batting form. In Pakistan's last one-day venture outside the World Series, Wasim Akram performed the hat-trick and Saeed Anwar hit 135 at a run a minute.

FIRST TEST MATCH – AUSTRALIA v. WEST INDIES
27, 28, 29, 30 November and 1 December 1992 at Woolloongabba, Brisbane

AUSTRALIA

	FIRST INNINGS		SECOND INNINGS	
M.A. Taylor	c Williams, b Bishop	7	c Williams, b Walsh	34
D.C. Boon	c Simmons, b Hooper	48	c Arthurton, b Bishop	111
S.R. Waugh	c Williams, b Ambrose	10	c Williams, b Ambrose	20
M.E. Waugh	c and b Hooper	39	c Haynes, b Ambrose	60
D.R. Martyn	c Lara, b Ambrose	36	lbw, b Ambrose	15
A.R. Border (capt)	run out	73	c Williams, b Walsh	17
G.R.J. Matthews	c Arthurton, b Bishop	30	lbw, b Ambrose	0
*I.A. Healy	c Lara, b Hooper	17	c Williams, b Bishop	18
M.G. Hughes	c Bishop, b Hooper	10	c Williams, b Ambrose	1
C.J. McDermott	c Hooper, b Patterson	3	not out	16
B.A. Reid	not out	1	c Richardson, b Hooper	1
Extras	b 4, lb 3, nb 12	19	b 4, lb 2, nb 9	15
		293		**308**

WEST INDIES

	FIRST INNINGS		SECOND INNINGS	
D.L. Haynes	c Taylor, b Reid	8	c Healy, b McDermott	1
P.V. Simmons	b Reid	27	c Healy, b Reid	1
R.B. Richardson (capt)	c Matthews, b Hughes	17	c Healy, b Hughes	66
B.C. Lara	st Healy, b Matthews	58	c Taylor, b McDermott	0
K.L.T. Arthurton	not out	157	b McDermott	0
C.L. Hooper	b S.R. Waugh	47	c Boon, b Matthews	32
*D. Williams	c Hughes, b Reid	15	lbw, b McDermott	0
I.R. Bishop	b McDermott	5	not out	16
C.E.L. Ambrose	lbw, b Reid	4	c Hughes, b Reid	4
B.P. Patterson	c M.E. Waugh, b Reid	0		
C.A. Walsh	b Hughes	17	(10) not out	0
Extras	lb 6, nb 10	16	lb 7, nb 6	13
		371	(for 8 wickets)	**133**

	O	M	R	W	O	M	R	W		O	M	R	W	O	M	R	W
Ambrose	29.1	12	53	2	32	8	66	5	McDermott	25	4	93	1	18	7	35	4
Bishop	23	3	51	2	27	6	58	2	Reid	37	2	112	5	16	7	39	2
Patterson	19	–	83	1	7	–	44	–	Hughes	18.3	3	58	2	13	4	28	1
Walsh	0.5	–	2	–	24	3	64	2	Matthews	27	12	41	1	13	4	18	1
Hooper	30.1	4	75	4	28.2	8	63	1	Border	1	–	7	–				
Simmons	7	2	16	–	1	–	5	–	S.R. Waugh	14	2	46	1	5	1	6	–
Arthurton	3	–	6	–	1	–	2	–	M.E. Waugh	2	–	8	–				

FALL OF WICKETS

1–8, 2–21, 3–88, 4–125, 5–180, 6–252, 7–264, 8–285, 9–288
1–64, 2–114, 3–224, 4–250, 5–255, 6–255, 7–280, 8–287, 9–295

FALL OF WICKETS

1–25, 2–50, 3–58, 4–170, 5–265, 6–293, 7–307, 8–321, 9–331
1–2, 2–2, 3–3, 4–9, 5–95, 6–96, 7–123, 8–128

Umpires: T.C. Prue & S.G. Randell

Match drawn

BENSON AND HEDGES WORLD SERIES
Phase One – Matches One to Eight

The first eight qualifying matches in the Benson and Hedges World Series were played in December. The series began with Pakistan beating West Indies in Perth. West Indies were never at home against Waqar and Wasim, and Javed's 82-ball innings, which included 45 singles, complemented Wasim's fire to ensure victory. Both Hooper and Aamir Sohail sustained minor injuries.

Allan Border's troubles continued. Having been fined a record £850 for dissent in the first Test, he suffered further damage to his hamstring and saw his side overwhelmed by West Indies, for whom Phil Simmons had an outstanding all-round match. Simmons and Haynes shared a stand of 111, and Haynes hit 81 off 121 balls.

The third match began three hours late due to heavy rain and was reduced to 30 overs. In the absence of the injured Border, Taylor led Australia for the first time, and he and Boon gave Australia a reasonable start with 31 in seven overs. Again they were undermined by the bowling of Simmons who took 3 for 2 in 12 balls with his gentle medium pace. Jones and Mark Waugh hit well, but the rest contributed little. Taylor led Australia intelligently and used his bowlers well. He himself established a record for Australia in a one-day international by holding four catches at first slip, and his bowlers responded magnificently to snatch victory by 14 runs.

The fourth match was the most sensational of the series. Consistent scoring took Australia to 228 in 50 overs – an adequate rather than commanding score – but, in

Mark Taylor led Australia in the early stages of the one-day series and won high praise. (Alan Cozzi)

spite of Salim Malik's 64, Pakistan were struggling at 129 for 6 by the 38th over. Asif Mujtaba and Rashid Latif added 68 to keep the game alive, but the last over arrived with Pakistan needing 17 to win. From the last ball Asif Mujtaba, who made 56 off 51 balls, had to hit a six to tie the match. Steve Waugh, who had dismissed Mushtaq Ahmed with the first ball of this final over, attempted to bowl a yorker, but it turned into a full toss and Asif clouted it over mid-wicket for six.

Rain reduced the fifth match to 42 overs, and once again Pakistan featured in a close finish. A stand of 52 in 43 minutes between Richardson, who hit 76 off 122 balls, and Hooper gave the West Indian innings its only substance, and when Aamir and Ramiz began Pakistan's challenge with a partnership of 63 the world champions

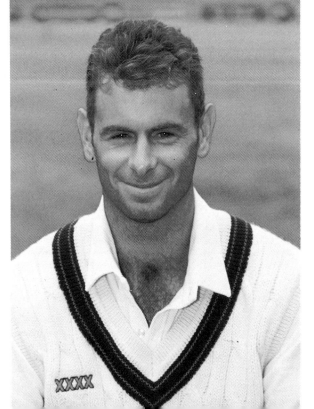

Impressive bowling in the Benson and Hedges World Series from Paul Reiffel. (Joe Mann/Allsport)

BENSON AND HEDGES WORLD SERIES – MATCH ONE – PAKISTAN v. WEST INDIES
4 December 1992 at WACA Ground, Perth

WEST INDIES		
D.L. Haynes	c Rashid Latif, b Waqar Younis	1
P.V. Simmons	c Rashid Latif, b Wasim Akram	6
R.B. Richardson (capt)	c Wasim Akram, b Aamir Sohail	23
B.C. Lara	c sub (Naved Anjum), b Mushtaq Ahmed	59
C.L. Hooper	c Inzamam-ul-Haq, b Mushtaq Ahmed	24
K.L.T. Arthurton	c Rashid Latif, b Wasim Akram	9
*J.R. Murray	b Waqar Younis	22
I.R. Bishop	c Rashid Latif, b Wasim Akram	6
C.E.L. Ambrose	not out	15
A.C. Cummins	c Javed Miandad, b Wasim Akram	0
K.C.G. Benjamin	not out	13
Extras	b 4, lb 3, w 8, nb 4	19
(50 overs)	(for 9 wickets)	197

PAKISTAN		
Aamir Sohail	c Haynes, b Bishop	2
Ramiz Raja	c Murray, b Benjamin	34
Salim Malik	c Murray, b Benjamin	35
Javed Miandad (capt)	not out	59
Inzamam-ul-Haq	c Lara, b Hooper	28
Asif Mujtaba	run out	3
Wasim Akram	not out	21
*Rashid Latif		
Mushtaq Ahmed		
Waqar Younis		
Ata-ur-Rehman		
Extras	lb 4, w 3, nb 10	17
(49.2 overs)	(for 5 wickets)	199

	O	M	R	W
Wasim Akram	9	1	46	4
Waqar Younis	7	2	26	2
Ata-ur-Rehman	10	–	29	–
Aamir Sohail	8	–	36	1
Mushtaq Ahmed	10	1	22	2
Asif Mujtaba	6	–	31	–

	O	M	R	W
Ambrose	9.2	2	30	–
Bishop	10	1	34	1
Cummins	10	–	41	–
Benjamin	10	–	46	2
Hooper	10	–	44	1

FALL OF WICKETS

1–1, 2–12, 3–64, 4–119, 5–138, 6–140, 7–153, 8–176, 9–177

FALL OF WICKETS

1–6, 2–62, 3–102, 4–157, 5–163

Umpires: R.J. Evans & L.J. King *Man of the Match:* Wasim Akram *Pakistan won by 5 wickets*

BENSON AND HEDGES WORLD SERIES – MATCH TWO – AUSTRALIA v. WEST INDIES
6 December 1992 at WACA Ground, Perth

AUSTRALIA		
M.A. Taylor	run out	0
D.C. Boon	c Murray, b Bishop	6
D.M. Jones	c Cummins, b Simmons	14
S.R. Waugh	c Hooper, b Simmons	4
M.E. Waugh	st Murray, b Hooper	36
A.R. Border (capt)	run out	15
G.R.J. Matthews	c Richardson, b Hooper	32
*I.A. Healy	not out	21
P.R. Reiffel	not out	9
C.J. McDermott		
M.R. Whitney		
Extras	lb 9, w 11, nb 3	23
(50 overs)	(for 7 wickets)	160

WEST INDIES		
D.L. Haynes	not out	81
B.C. Lara	c Border, b Reiffel	29
P.V. Simmons	not out	43
R.B. Richardson (capt)		
C.L. Hooper		
K.L.T. Arthurton		
A.L. Logie		
*J.R. Murray		
I.R. Bishop		
C.E.L. Ambrose		
A.C. Cummins		
Extras	lb 6, w 1, nb 4	11
(38.3 overs)	(for 1 wicket)	164

	O	M	R	W
Bishop	10	1	20	1
Cummins	10	1	35	–
Simmons	10	2	22	2
Ambrose	10	1	37	–
Hooper	10	–	37	2

	O	M	R	W
McDermott	7	2	32	–
Whitney	5	–	30	–
Reiffel	6	1	12	1
S.R. Waugh	8	2	31	–
Matthews	9	–	32	–
M.E. Waugh	3.3	–	21	–

FALL OF WICKETS

1–4, 2–15, 3–32, 4–35, 5–64, 6–122, 7–137

FALL OF WICKET

1–53

Umpires: T.A. Prue & S.G. Randell *Man of the Match:* P.V. Simmons *West Indies won by 9 wickets*

BENSON AND HEDGES WORLD SERIES – MATCH THREE – AUSTRALIA v. WEST INDIES
8 December 1992 at SCG, Sydney

AUSTRALIA			WEST INDIES		
M.A. Taylor (capt)	b Simmons	9	D.L. Haynes	c S.R. Waugh, b Reiffel	5
D.C. Boon	c Lara, b Simmons	8	B.C. Lara	b Whitney	4
D.M. Jones	c Murray, b Ambrose	21	P.V. Simmons	lbw, b McDermott	0
S.R. Waugh	c Murray, b Simmons	1	R.B. Richardson (capt)	c Healy, b Whitney	6
M.E. Waugh	st Murray, b Hooper	17	A.L. Logie	c Taylor, b Reiffel	20
D.R. Martyn	b Ambrose	0	K.L.T. Arthurton	c Taylor, b S.R. Waugh	3
G.R.J. Matthews	c Ambrose, b Cummins	11	C.L. Hooper	c Taylor, b Reiffel	6
*I.A. Healy	c Cummins, b Ambrose	3	*J.R. Murray	c Taylor, b S.R. Waugh	2
P.R. Reiffel	not out	9	I.R. Bishop	c Healy, b M.E. Waugh	11
C.J. McDermott	lbw, b Hooper	2	C.E.L. Ambrose	not out	13
M.R. Whitney	not out	1	A.C. Cummins	run out	2
Extras	lb 11, w 8	19	Extras	lb 13, w 2	15
(30 overs)	(for 9 wickets)	101	(29.3 overs)		87

	O	M	R	W		O	M	R	W
Bishop	6	–	20	–	McDermott	6	1	11	1
Simmons	6	2	11	3	Whitney	6	1	11	2
Ambrose	6	–	18	3	Reiffel	6	1	14	3
Cummins	6	1	16	1	S.R. Waugh	5.3	–	25	2
Hooper	6	–	25	2	M.E. Waugh	6	–	13	1

FALL OF WICKETS
1–31, 2–32, 3–34, 4–61, 5–62, 6–79, 7–85, 8–90, 9–98

FALL OF WICKETS
1–6, 2–7, 3–18, 4–22, 5–31, 6–49, 7–55, 8–65, 9–75

Umpires: D.B. Hair & S.G. Randell   *Man of the Match:* M.A. Taylor   *Australia won by 14 runs*

BENSON AND HEDGES WORLD SERIES – MATCH FOUR – AUSTRALIA v. PAKISTAN
10 December 1992 at Bellerive Oval, Hobart

AUSTRALIA			PAKISTAN		
M.A. Taylor (capt)	c Rashid Latif, b Aqib Javed	46	Aamir Sohail	c Martyn, b McDermott	6
D.C. Boon	lbw, b Aqib Javed	14	Ramiz Raja	c S.R. Waugh, b Whitney	4
D.M. Jones	run out	53	Salim Malik	c Healy, b McDermott	64
S.R. Waugh	run out	26	Javed Miandad (capt)	lbw, b Reiffel	14
M.E. Waugh	b Mushtaq Ahmed	13	Inzamam-ul-Haq	c Martyn, b M.E. Waugh	22
D.R. Martyn	run out	5	Asif Mujtaba	not out	56
*I.A. Healy	c Javed Miandad, b Wasim Akram	24	Wasim Akram	c Healy, b McDermott	3
P.R. Reiffel	not out	23	*Rashid Latif	run out	39
C.J. McDermott	not out	2	Waqar Younis	b McDermott	8
T.B.A. May			Mushtaq Ahmed	c Reiffel, b S.R. Waugh	0
M.R. Whitney			Aqib Javed	not out	5
Extras	b 3, lb 15, w 1, nb 3	22	Extras	lb 6, w 1	7
(50 overs)	(for 7 wickets)	228	(50 overs)	(for 9 wickets)	228

	O	M	R	W		O	M	R	W
Wasim Akram	10	3	34	1	McDermott	10	2	42	4
Waqar Younis	9	1	43	–	Whitney	10	3	29	1
Aqib Javed	10	–	35	2	Reiffel	8	2	29	1
Aamir Sohail	10	–	37	–	S.R. Waugh	10	–	56	1
Mushtaq Ahmed	10	–	52	1	May	5	–	29	–
Asif Mujtaba	1	–	9	–	M.E. Waugh	7	–	37	1

FALL OF WICKETS
1–32, 2–124, 3–138, 4–164, 5–172, 6–179, 7–217

FALL OF WICKETS
1–6, 2–10, 3–41, 4–91, 5–123, 6–129, 7–197, 8–207, 9–212

Umpires: S.G. Randell & C.D. Timmins   *Man of the Match:* Asif Mujtaba   *Match tied*

BENSON AND HEDGES WORLD SERIES – MATCH FIVE – PAKISTAN *v.* WEST INDIES
12 December 1992 at Adelaide Oval

WEST INDIES			PAKISTAN		
D.L. Haynes	**b** Wasim Akram	6	Aamir Sohail	**c** Bishop, **b** Simmons	41
B.C. Lara	**b** Aqib Javed	15	Ramiz Raja	run out	52
P.V. Simmons	**c** Aamir Sohail, **b** Wasim Akram	5	Salim Malik	**c** Simmons, **b** Ambrose	22
R.B. Richardson (capt)	not out	76	Javed Miandad (capt)	**c** Simmons, **b** Hooper	11
A.L. Logie	**c** Ramiz Raja, **b** Aamir Sohail	1	Inzamam-ul-Haq	run out	18
K.L.T. Arthurton	**c** Inzamam-ul-Haq, **b** Aamir Sohail	3	Asif Mujtaba	run out	0
C.L. Hooper	**c** Rashid Latif, **b** Wasim Akram	24	Wasim Akram	**b** Hooper	2
I.R. Bishop	**c** Asif Mujtaba, **b** Mushtaq Ahmed	17	*Rashid Latif	run out	1
A.C. Cummins	not out	4	Waqar Younis	**b** Hooper	5
*J.R. Murray			Mushtaq Ahmed	run out	3
C.E.L. Ambrose			Aqib Javed	not out	7
Extras	b **1**, lb **13**, w **8**, nb **4**	26	Extras	lb **3**, w **4**, nb **4**	11
(42 overs)	(for 7 wickets)	177	(41.5 overs)		173

	O	M	R	W		O	M	R	W
Wasim Akram	9	1	38	3	Bishop	8	–	38	–
Waqar Younis	8	–	38	–	Ambrose	9	–	41	1
Aamir Sohail	10	1	26	2	Cummins	9	1	31	–
Aqib Javed	5	2	30	1	Simmons	8	–	29	1
Mushtaq Ahmed	8	1	23	1	Hooper	7.5	–	31	3
Asif Mujtaba	2	–	8	–					

FALL OF WICKETS

1–16, **2**–27, **3**–56, **4**–61, **5**–81, **6**–133, **7**–172

FALL OF WICKETS

1–63, **2**–117, **3**–128, **4**–148, **5**–148, **6**–151, **7**–153, **8**–162, **9**–162

Umpires: S. Davis & T.A. Prue   *Man of the Match:* C.L. Hooper   *West Indies won by 4 runs*

BENSON AND HEDGES WORLD SERIES – MATCH SIX – AUSTRALIA *v.* PAKISTAN
13 December 1992 at Adelaide Oval

PAKISTAN			AUSTRALIA		
Aamir Sohail	run out	8	M.A. Taylor (capt)	run out	78
Ramiz Raja	**b** May	28	D.C. Boon	**b** Aamir Sohail	40
Asif Mujtaba	**b** S.R. Waugh	45	D.M. Jones	not out	48
Javed Miandad (capt)	**b** May	6	S.R. Waugh	not out	15
Inzamam-ul-Haq	not out	60	M.E. Waugh		
Saeed Anwar	run out	6	D.R. Martyn		
Wasim Akram	**c** Taylor, **b** McDermott	36	*I.A. Healy		
*Rashid Latif	not out	0	P.R. Reiffel		
Waqar Younis			C.J. McDermott		
Mushtaq Ahmed			M.R. Whitney		
Aqib Javed			T.B.A. May		
Extras	lb **4**, w **1**, nb **1**	6	Extras	lb **6**, w **5**, nb **4**	15
(47 overs)	(for 6 wickets)	195	(45 overs)	(for 2 wickets)	196

	O	M	R	W		O	M	R	W
McDermott	9	–	56	1	Wasim Akram	9	–	39	–
Whitney	10	3	22	–	Waqar Younis	10	2	32	–
Reiffel	9	–	36	–	Aqib Javed	9	–	36	–
S.R. Waugh	9	–	50	1	Aamir Sohail	9	–	36	1
May	10	–	27	2	Mushtaq Ahmed	7	–	36	–
					Asif Mujtaba	1	–	11	–

FALL OF WICKETS

1–10, **2**–60, **3**–68, **4**–120, **5**–137, **6**–194

FALL OF WICKETS

1–70, **2**–171

Umpires: C.D. Timmins & I.S. Thomas   *Man of the Match:* M.A. Taylor   *Australia won by 8 wickets*

BENSON AND HEDGES WORLD SERIES – MATCH SEVEN – AUSTRALIA *v.* WEST INDIES
15 December 1992 at MCG, Melbourne

AUSTRALIA

M.A. Taylor (capt)	c Hooper, b Simmons	10
D.C. Boon	c Haynes, b Ambrose	4
D.M. Jones	c Arthurton, b Cummins	22
S.R. Waugh	run out	34
M.E. Waugh	c Hooper, b Ambrose	57
D.R. Martyn	c Murray, b Ambrose	40
*I.A. Healy	c Haynes, b Hooper	13
G.R.J. Matthews	not out	6
P.R. Reiffel	run out	0
C.J. McDermott	not out	0
M.R. Whitney		
Extras	lb 5, w 6, nb 1	12
(50 overs)	(for 8 wickets)	198

WEST INDIES

D.L. Haynes	c Taylor, b Whitney	4
B.C. Lara	b M.E. Waugh	74
P.V. Simmons	c Healy, b Reiffel	24
R.B. Richardson (capt)	c Taylor, b M.E. Waugh	61
C.L. Hooper	c Martyn, b S.R. Waugh	6
A.L. Logie	run out	0
K.L.T. Arthurton	c Jones, b M.E. Waugh	9
*J.R. Murray	c and b M.E. Waugh	5
C.E.L. Ambrose	run out	0
A.C. Cummins	c McDermott, b M.E. Waugh	2
C.A. Walsh	not out	0
Extras	lb 9	9
(50 overs)		194

	O	M	R	W
Ambrose	10	3	25	3
Simmons	10	3	31	1
Walsh	10	1	42	–
Cummins	10	–	45	1
Hooper	10	–	50	1

	O	M	R	W
McDermott	7	1	27	–
Whitney	10	1	27	1
Reiffel	10	1	45	1
Matthews	7	–	24	–
S.R. Waugh	10	–	38	1
M.E. Waugh	6	–	24	5

FALL OF WICKETS

1–13, 2–17, 3–63, 4–86, 5–160, 6–186, 7–192, 8–197

FALL OF WICKETS

1–18, 2–66, 3–158, 4–173, 5–178, 6–178, 7–187, 8–192, 9–192

Umpires: L.J. King & T.A. Prue   *Man of the Match:* M.E. Waugh   *Australia won by 4 runs*

BENSON AND HEDGES WORLD SERIES – MATCH EIGHT – PAKISTAN *v.* WEST INDIES
17 December 1992 at SCG, Sydney

WEST INDIES

B.C. Lara	run out	3
D.L. Haynes	b Wasim Akram	96
P.V. Simmons	c Salim Malik, b Aamir Sohail	10
R.B. Richardson (capt)	c Wasim Akram, b Mushtaq Ahmed	33
C.L. Hooper	run out	17
A.L. Logie	b Waqar Younis	0
J.C. Adams	lbw, b Waqar Younis	17
K.C.G. Benjamin	not out	9
*J.R. Murray	run out	0
C.E.L. Ambrose	b Waqar Younis	0
B.P. Patterson	not out	0
Extras	b 4, lb 9, w 12, nb 4	29
(50 overs)	(for 9 wickets)	214

PAKISTAN

Aamir Sohail	c Benjamin, b Simmons	6
Ramiz Raja	c Lara, b Patterson	0
Asif Mujtaba	b Simmons	1
Salim Malik	c Hooper, b Simmons	0
Javed Miandad (capt)	c Murray, b Simmons	2
Inzamam-ul-Haq	c Hooper, b Benjamin	17
Wasim Akram	c Richardson, b Benjamin	7
*Rashid Latif	c Murray, b Patterson	8
Waqar Younis	lbw, b Hooper	17
Mushtaq Ahmed	c Benjamin, b Adams	15
Ata-ur-Rehman	not out	0
Extras	w 1, nb 7	8
(48 overs)		81

	O	M	R	W
Aamir Sohail	10	1	38	1
Ata-ur-Rehman	10	–	47	–
Waqar Younis	10	1	29	3
Mushtaq Ahmed	10	–	50	1
Wasim Akram	10	–	37	1

	O	M	R	W
Ambrose	10	4	19	–
Simmons	10	8	3	4
Patterson	9	2	19	2
Benjamin	9	1	28	2
Hooper	6	2	10	1
Adams	4	2	2	1

FALL OF WICKETS

1–10, 2–40, 3–107, 4–151, 5–156, 6–195, 7–209, 8–210, 9–213

FALL OF WICKETS

1–2, 2–4, 3–9, 4–9, 5–14, 6–35, 7–35, 8–54, 9–78

Umpires: I.S. Thomas & D.B. Hair   *Man of the Match:* P.V. Simmons   *West Indies won by 133 runs*

looked certain winners. This was emphasised by the fact that West Indies dropped five catches, none of them difficult, in the first 28 overs. With 6.1 overs remaining, Pakistan were 148 for 3, but, amid mass panic, they lost their last seven wickets for 25 runs in 30 balls.

Mark Taylor led Australia to a huge win in the sixth game. He shared stands of 70 with Boon and 101 with Jones as Pakistan struggled for most of the match. Taylor's unbeaten record as a captain of Australia continued in the next match when the West Indian batting collapsed with victory in sight. Lara and Richardson, who reached 5,000 runs in limited-over international cricket, added 92 off 115 balls and, needing 199 to win, West Indies were 158 for 2. The introduction of Mark Waugh into the attack changed the complexion of the game. He took 5 for 16 in 29 balls. He bowled the last over when West Indies needed seven to win and dismissed both Arthurton and Cummins.

The first phase of matches ended disastrously for Pakistan whose batting had suddenly become most suspect. Desmond Haynes hit 96 off 152 balls to lead West Indies to a total of 214 from their 50 overs. Phil Simmons opened the West Indian bowling and destroyed Pakistan. In 10 overs, there were only two scoring shots off his bowling and he finished with 4 for 3, a record for a one-day international.

Pakistan's defeat meant that they needed to win their last three matches to have a chance of reaching the final.

A fine all-round performance from Mark Waugh in the seventh match of the World Series. (Alan Cozzi)

11, 12, 13 and 14 December 1992 *at SCG, Sydney*

Queensland 447 (S.C. Storey 103, S.G. Law 79, P.J.T. Goggin 68, B.E. McNamara 4 for 68) and 256 for 9 dec. (T.J. Barsby 123, G. Robertson 6 for 104)

New South Wales 382 (T.H. Bayliss 107, B.E. McNamara 98 not out, M.J. Slater 61) and 247 for 6 (M.J. Slater 72, B.E. McNamara 55 not out, B. Oxenford 4 for 70)

Match drawn

Queensland 2 pts., New South Wales 0 pts.

at WACA Ground, Perth

South Australia 409 (J.A. Brayshaw 77, J.D. Siddons 67, N.R. Fielke 55, T.M. Alderman 4 for 99) and 284 for 6 dec. (J.D. Siddons 189 not out)

Western Australia 304 for 6 dec. (J.L. Langer 96, M.R.J. Veletta 68, P.R. Sleep 4 for 59) and 392 for 7 (G.R. Marsh 138, J.L. Langer 110, T.M. Moody 71)

Western Australia won by 3 wickets

Western Australia 6 pts., South Australia 2 pts.

A maiden first-class century by Stephen Storey and best performances with both bat and ball by Brad McNamara were the features of the game in Sydney where a closely fought contest ended in a draw.

In Perth, Western Australia breathed life into their Shield challenge with a sensational victory. Consistent batting took South Australia to 409, a last-wicket stand of

71 between Ritossa and Hickey adding to the home state's woes. In an effort to keep the game alive, Geoff Marsh declared 105 runs in arrears on the first innings. South Australia were 14 for 2 in their second innings before skipper Jamie Siddons blasted 189 at a run a minute. He and Peter Sleep shared an unbroken seventh-wicket stand of 148, runs coming at the rate of five an over. Siddons asked Western Australia to score 390 in 76 overs if they were to win the match. A second-wicket partnership of 203 between Langer and Marsh and some fierce hitting from Moody made this daunting task possible. Four batsmen were run out in the dash for runs, but Julian hit the winning boundary with four balls to spare.

18, 19, 20 and 21 December 1992 *at Adelaide Oval*

New South Wales 399 for 5 dec. (M.E. Waugh 164, M.A. Taylor 63, G.R.J. Matthews 53) and 204 for 7 (M.J. Slater 82, T.B.A. May 4 for 66)

South Australia 215 (G.R.J. Matthews 4 for 25) and 379 (T.J. Nielsen 84, G.R. Blewett 71, J.C. Scuderi 50)

New South Wales won by 9 runs

New South Wales 6 pts., South Australia 0 pts.

at WACA Ground, Perth

Western Australia 417 (D.R. Martyn 139, T.J. Zoehrer 52, P.T. McPhee 4 for 94) and 268 for 9 (M.P. Atkinson 52 not out, B.P. Julian 51, S. Young 5 for 88)

Five centuries in the season for Western Australia's captain Geoff Marsh, but no recall to the Test side. (George Herringshaw/ASP)

Tasmania 457 for 9 dec. (D.F. Hills 138, D.J. Buckingham 60, N.C.P. Courtney 58)

Match drawn

Tasmania 2 pts., Western Australia 0 pts.

19, 20, 21 and 22 December 1992 *at Bendigo*

Victoria v. West Indians

Match abandoned

at Woolloongabba, Brisbane

Queensland 260 (M.L. Hayden 79, T.J. Barsby 53, Mushtaq Ahmed 4 for 70) and 396 for 7 dec. (A.R. Border 116 not out, T.J. Barsby 116, Mushtaq Ahmed 4 for 136)

Pakistanis 368 for 6 dec. (Asif Mujtaba 102 not out, Shahid Saeed 83, Inzamam-ul-Haq 83, Aamir Sohail 65) and 291 for 5 (Asif Mujtaba 125 not out, Saeed Anwar 72)

Pakistanis won by 5 wickets

New South Wales and South Australia produced a match in Adelaide which was described as 'worthy of commemorating the centenary of the Sheffield Shield'. Another massive innings from Mark Waugh and some miserly bowling from Greg Matthews gave the visitors the early advantage, and Mark Taylor set South Australia the task of scoring 389 to win in 112 overs. Blewett and Fielke gave the home state a good start with a partnership of 83, and Blewett and Brayshaw put on 76 in 91 minutes before Blewett hit a full toss from Freedman into the hands of mid-wicket. This precipitated a minor collapse.

Three wickets fell for 37 runs, and South Australia were 214 for 4 at tea. The dangerous Siddons was one of the three wickets to fall in the collapse and when Darren Webber was caught and bowled by Matthews immediately after tea, South Australia seemed beaten. Nielsen and Scuderi revived hopes with 86 in 74 minutes before Scuderi was caught off Whitney. Nielsen was caught at silly point off Matthews after hitting 84 off 114 balls. From the last eight overs 39 were needed, but Sleep fell to Freedman and May was run out. When Matthews began the last over, 12 runs were needed with the last pair, Hickey and Reeves, together. Reeves hit the first ball, but the batsmen attempted to turn a comfortable two into three, and Reeves was run out at the bowler's end.

This win took New South Wales to the top of the Shield as Western Australia, without the injured Reid, surrendered the first-innings points to Tasmania. Martyn hit his fourth hundred of the season, and Hills hit the highest score of his career.

New South Wales led the table by virtue of the fact that Western Australia had lost 0.4 points for a slow over rate. Queensland were in third place with 10 points.

West Indies, needing practice before the second Test, were thwarted by rain at Bendigo, but Asif Mujtaba took the Pakistanis to victory in the only first-class match of their tour with an unbeaten century in each innings. There were centuries also for Allan Border and Trevor Barsby as Queensland fought back well.

SECOND TEST MATCH
AUSTRALIA v. WEST INDIES, at Melbourne

Australia made changes in their attack for the second Test match, bringing in Whitney for the injured Reid and Warne, the leg-spinner, for off-spinner Matthews. Allan Border dropped down to number six to strengthen the late middle order. West Indies included all-rounder Adams in place of Patterson who had had a poor tour. Border won the toss and Australia batted.

Taylor was out when he tried to cut Walsh and was caught at first slip. Thereafter, Boon and Steve Waugh took the score carefully to 100. To the chagrin of an appreciative crowd of nearly 50,000 Boon, Steve Waugh and Martyn all fell to slashes outside the off stump, and suddenly Australia were in trouble at 115 for 4. Recovery came in the shape of Mark Waugh and Allan Border. They nudged the score along, adding 112 in just under three hours to the close, by which time Mark Waugh was 63 and Border, having hit Hooper for a glorious six, was 51.

The match tilted most firmly in Australia's favour early on the second day when wicket-keeper Williams dived in front of Lara at first slip and dropped the simplest of chances offered by Mark Waugh, who was on 71 at the time. This was the only blemish on Waugh's elegant innings. His timing was perfection, and he and Border offered a thrilling and eloquent blend in a partnership which was worth 204 and which moved Australia to an impregnable position. Border's 25th Test century came when he swept Hooper for three, and he ran down the wicket, arms on high, to a mighty reception from another good-sized crowd. It was the Australian captain's first Test hundred in his own country for five years, and it re-established him in public favour after a few weeks of uncertainty and criticism. Border and Waugh, spectacularly, were both caught by Williams, after which the last five wickets went down for 33 runs.

The fine batting of Mark Waugh and his skipper was now complemented by the fiery bowling of Merv Hughes. In eight overs he took West Indies' first three wickets at a personal cost of 18 runs. In his first over, he saw Haynes edge the ball into his stumps. Simmons then offered a simple catch to short-leg, and Richardson edged to the keeper. It was left to Lara and Arthurton to stop the rot, but West Indies closed uneasily on 62 for 3.

The same pair appeared to be taking West Indies to safety on the third morning until Lara was leg before to a ball that kept low. In the last over before lunch, Hooper was caught and bowled by Steve Waugh, and West Indies were back in trouble at 144 for 5. Adams hung on grittily

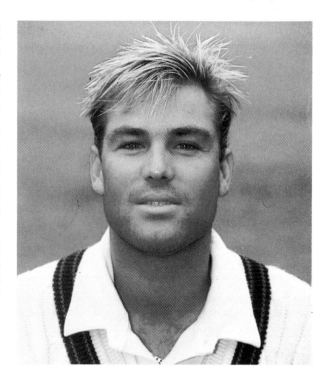

Leg-spinner Shane Warne bowled Australia to victory in the second Test match at Melbourne with an inspired 7 for 52. (Joe Mann/ Allsport)

SECOND TEST MATCH – AUSTRALIA v. WEST INDIES
26, 27, 28, 29 and 30 December 1992 at MCG, Melbourne

AUSTRALIA

	FIRST INNINGS		SECOND INNINGS	
M.A. Taylor	c Lara, b Walsh	13	b Bishop	42
D.C. Boon	c Williams, b Walsh	46	b Simmons	11
S.R. Waugh	c Lara, b Ambrose	38	(4) c Simmons, b Bishop	1
M.E. Waugh	c Williams, b Ambrose	112	(5) c Adams, b Walsh	16
D.R. Martyn	c Simmons, b Ambrose	7	(6) not out	67
A.R. Border (capt)	c Williams, b Bishop	110	(7) b Bishop	4
*I.A. Healy	c Hooper, b Walsh	24	(8) c and b Walsh	8
S.K. Warne	c Adams, b Bishop	1	(3) c Arthurton, b Ambrose	5
M.G. Hughes	not out	9	c Williams, b Ambrose	15
C.J. McDermott	b Walsh	17	c Arthurton, b Simmons	4
M.R. Whitney	lbw, b Bishop	0	run out	13
Extras	lb 14, w 1, nb 3	18	b 1, lb 8, nb 1	10
		395		**196**

WEST INDIES

	FIRST INNINGS		SECOND INNINGS	
D.L. Haynes	b Hughes	7	c Healy, b Hughes	5
P.V. Simmons	c Boon, b Hughes	6	c Boon, b Warne	110
R.B. Richardson (capt)	c Healy, b Hughes	15	b Warne	52
B.C. Lara	lbw, b Whitney	52	c Boon, b Whitney	4
K.L.T. Arthurton	c Healy, b McDermott	71	st Healy, b Warne	13
C.L. Hooper	c and b S.R. Waugh	3	c Whitney, b Warne	0
J.C. Adams	c Boon, b McDermott	47	c Taylor, b McDermott	16
*D. Williams	c Healy, b McDermott	0	c M.E. Waugh, b Warne	0
I.R. Bishop	b McDermott	9	c Taylor, b Warne	7
C.E.L. Ambrose	c McDermott, b Warne	7	not out	6
C.A. Walsh	not out	0	c Hughes, b Warne	0
Extras	lb 10, nb 6	16	b 3, lb 2, nb 1	6
		233		**219**

AUSTRALIA bowling

	O	M	R	W	O	M	R	W
Ambrose	35	10	70	3	30	9	57	2
Bishop	29	2	84	3	20	5	45	3
Walsh	39	10	91	4	21	7	42	2
Simmons	10	2	23	–	18	6	34	2
Hooper	36	3	95	–	2.4	1	9	–
Adams	4	–	18	–				

WEST INDIES bowling

	O	M	R	W	O	M	R	W
McDermott	25.1	8	66	4	17	6	66	1
Hughes	19	5	51	3	18	7	41	1
Whitney	13	4	27	1	10	2	32	1
Warne	24	7	65	1	23.2	8	52	7
S.R. Waugh	4	1	14	1				
M.E. Waugh					3	–	23	–

FALL OF WICKETS

1–38, 2–100, 3–104, 4–115, 5–319, 6–362, 7–366, 8–369, 9–394
1–22, 2–40, 3–41, 4–73, 5–90, 6–102, 7–121, 8–154, 9–167

FALL OF WICKETS

1–11, 2–28, 3–33, 4–139, 5–144, 6–192, 7–192, 8–206, 9–233
1–9, 2–143, 3–148, 4–165, 5–177, 6–198, 7–206, 8–206, 9–219

Umpires: S.G. Randell & C.D. Timmins

Australia won by 139 runs

but, at 192, McDermott had Arthurton and Williams caught behind with successive deliveries. The Queensland pace bowler then claimed Adams and Bishop, and West Indies' last five wickets went down for 41 runs. The sturdy Boon was bowled by Simmons, but Australia, 26 for 1, ended the third day 188 runs ahead with nine second-innings wickets in hand.

The batting of Mark Waugh and Allan Border and the bowling of Hughes and McDermott had put Australia in a position of great authority, but that authority became somewhat lessened on the fourth day by some determined, accurate and hostile West Indian bowling. Had the bowlers been better supported in the field, Australia could well have been dismissed for a score close to 100. Crucially, Taylor was dropped at slip by Hooper off the excellent Ambrose early in the day. Taylor was to bat for over four hours for his 42, an innings of grit and value. More significant, perhaps, was Martyn's 202-minute innings of 67 not out. The young man showed supreme confidence in only his second Test, and he cajoled 94 invaluable runs from Australia's last five wickets. He and Hughes added 33 in 55 minutes for the eighth wicket, and Whitney joined Martyn in a last-wicket stand of 29.

West Indies were faced with the task of scoring 395 to win or, more realistically, a day and half a session to survive on a wearing pitch and draw the match. Hughes soon had Haynes caught behind. The day ended with West Indies 32 for 1, defeat looming.

In the first session of the final day, West Indies appeared to have swept aside all thoughts of defeat. Richardson and Simmons batted with confidence and aggression, and they had taken their partnership to 134 when, 12 minutes before lunch, Richardson was bowled by Warne's 'flipper', the ball turning from middle and leg stumps through the batsman's guard to hit the off stump.

Richardson's dismissal heralded an astonishing collapse as eight wickets fell in the afternoon session and Australia claimed victory by tea-time. Six of the wickets fell to the leg-spinner Shane Warne, superbly supported in the field, whose figures of 7 for 52 were the best of his first-class career. While Warne received a little help from the pitch, nothing could justify the total surrender of the West Indian batsmen. The innings of Phil Simmons had even given them a slight chance of victory.

In just under three hours, Phil Simmons reached his maiden Test century. His 110 runs came off 178 balls and included 2 sixes and 8 fours. It was an inspiring innings, but West Indies' middle order failed to profit from it. The tourists' batting, with vice-captain Logie out of form and favour, was looking very fragile.

So Australia went one up in the series, and Shane Warne took the Man-of-the-Match award, but the batting of Mark Waugh and Allan Border had also played a vital part in the victory. This was a most positive team performance.

THIRD TEST MATCH
AUSTRALIA *v.* WEST INDIES, at Sydney

The third Test match was a delight for batsmen and statisticians. Matthews returned to the Australian side in place of Whitney, and West Indies preferred Murray to Williams as wicket-keeper. Again Border won the toss and Australia batted.

Runs came freely for most of the first day. Boon and Steve Waugh added 118 for the second wicket, and the Waugh brothers shared a stand of 94 at a run a minute for the third wicket. The running out of Mark Waugh, who hesitated over a short single to Carl Hooper at midwicket, instigated a collapse, three wickets falling for 16 runs. One of them was that of Steve Waugh who hit a flawless century. He batted for 4½ hours and hit 5 fours.

Neither Border nor Matthews had scored when Australia started the second day on 272 for 5, but they were to share a stand of 155 and make the game safe for their side. In his 136th Test match, Allan Border became only the second batsman to reach 10,000 runs in Test cricket. He was out when he touched a low catch to Junior Murray, who held four catches on his Test debut. Border declared when his side reached 500, and McDermott, bowling a lively pace, had Simmons caught at slip before the close when West Indies were 24 for 1.

Two hours were lost to rain on the third day, but Matthews struck quickly when he forced Haynes to play on at 31. It proved to be a false alarm. The pitch did not assist the spinners as had been expected, and Richardson and Lara celebrated, taking their side to 248 by the end of the day, by which time Lara had completed his first Test century.

Richardson moved to his 15th Test century on the fourth morning, and he and Lara took their partnership to 293 in 303 minutes after play had been delayed for an hour and a half because of rain. The stand was a third-wicket record for West Indies against Australia in Australia. Richardson hit 11 fours, and when he departed Lara and Arthurton added 124 in 140 minutes.

Brian Lara during his outstanding innings of 277 in the third Test at Sydney. (Joe Mann/Allsport)

THIRD TEST MATCH – AUSTRALIA v. WEST INDIES
2, 3, 4, 5 and 6 January 1993 at SCG, Sydney

AUSTRALIA

	FIRST INNINGS			SECOND INNINGS	
M.A. Taylor	c Murray, b Bishop	20	not out		46
D.C. Boon	c Murray, b Adams	76	not out		63
S.R. Waugh	c Simmons, b Ambrose	100			
M.E. Waugh	run out	57			
D.R. Martyn	b Ambrose	0			
A.R. Border (capt)	c Murray, b Hooper	74			
G.R.J. Matthews	c Murray, b Hooper	79			
*I.A. Healy	not out	36			
M.G. Hughes	c Haynes, b Bishop	17			
S.K. Warne	c Simmons, b Hooper	14			
C.J. McDermott					
Extras	b 2, lb 23, nb 5	30	b 1, lb 2, nb 5		8
	(for 9 wickets, dec.)	503	(for no wicket)		117

WEST INDIES

	FIRST INNINGS	
D.L. Haynes	b Matthews	22
P.V. Simmons	c Taylor, b McDermott	3
R.B. Richardson (capt)	c Warne, b Hughes	109
B.C. Lara	run out	277
K.L.T. Arthurton	c Healy, b Matthews	47
C.L. Hooper	b Warne	21
J.C. Adams	not out	77
*J.R. Murray	c Healy, b Hughes	11
I.R. Bishop	run out	1
C.E.L. Ambrose	c Martyn, b M.E. Waugh	16
C.A. Walsh	c Healy, b Hughes	0
Extras	b 4, lb 9, w 1, nb 8	22
		606

	O	M	R	W	O	M	R	W
Ambrose	35	8	87	2	6	2	10	–
Bishop	36	6	87	2	4	1	9	–
Walsh	30	8	86	–	8	3	13	–
Hooper	45.4	6	137	3	10	2	22	–
Adams	15	2	56	1	8	1	29	–
Simmons	10	2	25	–	3	2	9	–
Arthurton					5	1	14	–
Lara					2	–	4	–
Richardson					1	–	4	–

	O	M	R	W
McDermott	33	3	119	1
Hughes	16.4	1	76	3
Matthews	59	12	169	2
S.R. Waugh	11	1	43	–
Warne	41	6	116	1
Border	14	1	41	–
M.E. Waugh	10	1	29	1

FALL OF WICKETS

1–42, 2–160, 3–254, 4–261, 5–270, 6–425, 7–440, 8–469, 9–503

FALL OF WICKETS

1–13, 2–31, 3–324, 4–448, 5–481, 6–537, 7–573, 8–577, 9–606

Umpires: D.B. Hair & T.A. Prue

Match drawn

Lara reached his 200 off 266 balls, and the left-hander went on to score 277 off 372 balls in nearly eight hours before being run out when he scrambled back after changing his mind about a single. He hit 38 fours, and he batted with total majesty to record the fourth highest score made for West Indies in a Test match. This was an epic innings but, with West Indies 488 for 5 at the close, a draw was inevitable.

Jimmy Adams led his side to 606 on the last day, and there was time for just one more record before the game was given up. Taylor and Boon shared an opening stand of 117 without being parted, and Boon passed 5,000 runs in Test cricket.

To the surprise of no one, Brian Lara was named Man of the Match.

31 December 1992, 1, 2 and 3 January 1993 *at Bellerive Oval, Hobart*

Victoria 417 for 7 dec. (P.C. Nobes 145, G.J. Allardice 116, S.P. O'Donnell 59, D.M. Jones 56) and 196 for 3 dec. (D.M. Jones 72 not out, D.S. Lehmann 52)

Tasmania 204 (N.D. Maxwell 5 for 46) and 332 for 8 (N.C.P. Courtney 88, J. Cox 64, R.J. Tucker 50, N.D. Maxwell 4 for 107)

Match drawn

Victoria 2 pts., Tasmania 0 pts.

This match coincided with the Sydney Test so that both sides were deprived of key players. Victoria batted into the second day, with Paul Nobes making his highest score for the state, and Geoff Allardice reaching a maiden first-class century. Neil Maxwell took five wickets in an innings for the first time and produced one spell in which he took four wickets for one run in 25 balls as Tasmania slumped to 87 for 7. Atkinson and Matthews revived spirits with some hard hitting, and McPhee, last man out, disputed that he was caught in the gully. O'Donnell, surprisingly, did not enforce the follow-on, but his declaration left Tasmania some four sessions in which to survive. In fact, they came close to winning as Nick Courtney hit a career best, but the loss of wickets saw them give up the chase on the last evening.

Matthew Hayden hit the highest score of his career, 161 not out, for Queensland against South Australia at Adelaide, 10 January 1993, scored a thousand runs in the season and won a place in the party to tour England. (Alan Cozzi)

and Neil Maxwell added 160 in 213 minutes for the seventh wicket. Skipper Simon O'Donnell enjoyed a fine all-round match.

South Australia included former Victorian leg-spinner Peter McIntyre and pace bowler Brad Wigney in their side against Queensland, for whom Carl Rackemann returned after illness. Darren Webber dominated South Australia's first innings with 135 in what was only his third first-class innings. Matthew Hayden batted throughout the 138.2 overs of the Queensland innings to reach the highest score of his career, but the visitors were unable to force victory as South Australia batted stubbornly in their second innings.

13 January 1993 *at Cahill Oval, Newcastle*

West Indians 294 (K.L.T. Arthurton 94)
Australian Country XI 243 (B. Spanner 68, B. Irvine 56)

West Indians won by 51 runs

 BENSON AND HEDGES WORLD SERIES
Phase Two – Matches Nine to Twelve
The Finals

The Benson and Hedges World Series resumed with Pakistan having only the faintest of hopes of qualifying for the final. Within 24 hours, these hopes had been almost totally extinguished when Pakistan were humiliated by West Indies. Pakistan were bowled out in 23.4 overs for 71, their lowest total in a one-day international. Javed elected to bat when he won the toss, but his side were quickly reduced to 12 for 5, Bishop taking three of the wickets. There was no effective recovery, and the game was extended by one over into the scheduled lunch interval so that it could be completed in one session.

The following day West Indies qualified for the final when they narrowly beat Australia. Simmons had been injured while fielding in the match against Pakistan and was unable to play, and West Indies suffered more discomfort when Haynes was caught behind off a Reiffel out-swinger. Haynes questioned the decision and refused to walk for several minutes. He was later fined approximately £235 for dissent. Reiffel moved the ball appreciably, but Hooper showed a return of confidence with an impressive 56. Logie and Williams made valuable contributions, and West Indies reached 197.

Australia never recovered from the early loss of Boon and Jones and, as they fell behind the required run rate, batsmen squandered their wickets in an attempt to score quickly. There were four run outs in the final stages.

Australia ended Pakistan's hopes in the penultimate qualifying match. The home side were without Whitney

8, 9, 10 and **11** January 1993 *at WACA Ground, Perth*

Western Australia 440 (G.R. Marsh 129, M.P. Lavender 103, T.M. Moody 54, S.P. O'Donnell 4 for 102)
Victoria 265 (S.P. O'Donnell 62, D.S. Berry 57, J. Angel 6 for 71) and 457 for 7 (A.I.C. Dodemaide 123, S.P. O'Donnell 99, N.D. Maxwell 64 not out, L. Harper 58)

Match drawn

Western Australia 2 pts., Victoria 0 pts.

at Adelaide Oval

South Australia 333 (D.S. Webber 135, J.D. Siddons 75, D. Tazelaar 4 for 89) and 310 for 9 dec. (D.S. Webber 77, N.R. Fielke 57, J.D. Siddons 53)
Queensland 335 for 7 dec. (M.L. Hayden 161 not out, D.M. Wellham 56, P.R. Sleep 4 for 80) and 43 for 1

Match drawn

Queensland 2 pts., South Australia 0 pts.

An opening stand of 223 between Geoff Marsh and Mark Lavender put Western Australia in a commanding position against Victoria who were forced to follow-on, Angel furthering his Test claims with a six-wicket haul. Victoria ended the third day just 19 runs ahead with five wickets standing, but Laurie Harper gave consolation with 58 on his debut. Only two wickets fell on the last day, which saw Dodemaide save the game with a career best 123. He

BENSON AND HEDGES WORLD SERIES – MATCH NINE – PAKISTAN *v.* WEST INDIES
9 January 1993 at Woolloongabba, Brisbane

PAKISTAN

Saeed Anwar	c Lara, b Bishop	2
Shahid Saeed	c Lara, b Bishop	1
Inzamam-ul-Haq	c Simmons, b Benjamin	0
Javed Miandad (capt)	c Murray, b Bishop	0
Salim Malik	b Ambrose	8
Asif Mujtaba	b Benjamin	1
Wasim Akram	c Simmons, b Ambrose	19
*Rashid Latif	not out	22
Waqar Younis	c Lara, b Ambrose	0
Mushtaq Ahmed	c Richardson, b Bishop	2
Aqib Javed	c Benjamin, b Bishop	4
Extras	lb 3, w 8, nb 1	12
(23.4 overs)		71

WEST INDIES

B.C. Lara	c Waqar Younis, b Wasim Akram	10
D.L. Haynes	not out	25
R.B. Richardson (capt)	not out	22
P.V. Simmons		
K.L.T. Arthurton		
J.C. Adams		
C.L. Hooper		
*J.R. Murray		
I.R. Bishop		
C.E.L. Ambrose		
K.C.G. Benjamin		
Extras	w 6, nb 9	15
(19.2 overs)	(for 1 wicket)	72

	O	M	R	W
Bishop	8.4	–	25	5
Benjamin	6	2	16	2
Ambrose	6	1	13	3
Hooper	3	–	14	–

	O	M	R	W
Wasim Akram	9	–	33	1
Waqar Younis	7	3	13	–
Aqib Javed	2	–	16	–
Mushtaq Ahmed	1.2	–	10	–

FALL OF WICKETS

1–2, 2–7, 3–7, 4–11, 5–12, 6–32, 7–54, 8–55, 9–58

FALL OF WICKET

1–22

Umpires: L.J. King & S. Davis   *Man of the Match:* I.R. Bishop   *West Indies won by 9 wickets*

BENSON AND HEDGES WORLD SERIES – MATCH TEN – AUSTRALIA *v.* WEST INDIES
10 January 1993 at Woolloongabba, Brisbane

WEST INDIES

D.L. Haynes	c Healy, b Reiffel	36
B.C. Lara	c Healy, b Whitney	10
R.B. Richardson (capt)	c S.R. Waugh, b Reiffel	1
C.L. Hooper	c Reiffel, b M.E. Waugh	56
K.L.T. Arthurton	c Taylor, b Reiffel	2
A.L. Logie	c Reiffel, b McDermott	26
*D. Williams	not out	25
A.C. Cummins	run out	1
K.C.G. Benjamin	c S.R. Waugh, b May	17
C.A. Walsh	b S.R. Waugh	12
B.P. Patterson	not out	1
Extras	lb 8, w 2	10
(50 overs)	(for 9 wickets)	197

AUSTRALIA

M.A. Taylor	c Richardson, b Cummins	20
D.C. Boon	c Williams, b Patterson	3
D.M. Jones	c Williams, b Patterson	0
S.R. Waugh	c Logie, b Walsh	24
M.E. Waugh	run out	54
A.R. Border (capt)	b Hooper	11
*I.A. Healy	lbw, b Walsh	41
P.R. Reiffel	run out	4
C.J. McDermott	run out	7
T.B.A. May	not out	3
M.R. Whitney	run out	2
Extras	b 2, lb 6, w 9, nb 4	21
(49 overs)		190

	O	M	R	W
McDermott	10	2	25	1
Whitney	10	1	30	1
Reiffel	10	1	33	3
S.R. Waugh	7	1	30	1
May	8	–	48	1
M.E. Waugh	5	–	23	1

	O	M	R	W
Patterson	10	–	31	2
Benjamin	10	1	32	–
Cummins	10	1	27	1
Walsh	10	–	49	2
Hooper	9	–	43	1

FALL OF WICKETS

1–26, 2–38, 3–65, 4–72, 5–129, 6–149, 7–152, 8–175, 9–196

FALL OF WICKETS

1–5, 2–10, 3–51, 4–61, 5–81, 6–158, 7–173, 8–176, 9–187

Umpires: I.S. Thomas & C.D. Timmins   *Man of the Match:* C.L. Hooper   *West Indies won by 7 runs*

BENSON AND HEDGES WORLD SERIES – MATCH ELEVEN – AUSTRALIA *v.* PAKISTAN
12 January 1993 at MCG, Melbourne

AUSTRALIA				PAKISTAN			
M.A. Taylor	c Rashid Latif, **b** Aqib Javed		4	Aamir Sohail	c Healy, **b** McDermott		3
D.C. Boon	c Shahid Saeed, **b** Asif Mujtaba		64	Ramiz Raja	c Healy, **b** S.R. Waugh		40
D.M. Jones	**b** Waqar Younis		84	Shahid Saeed	**b** Dodemaide		3
S.R. Waugh	c and **b** Asif Mujtaba		5	Salim Malik	**b** McDermott		37
M.E. Waugh	**b** Waqar Younis		12	Javed Miandad (capt)	c Border, **b** M.E. Waugh		40
A.R. Border (capt)	not out		14	Inzamam-ul-Haq	not out		39
*I.A. Healy	run out		3	Wasim Akram	c M.E. Waugh, **b** Reiffel		3
A.I.C. Dodemaide	not out		15	*Rashid Latif	c Healy, **b** Reiffel		5
P.R. Reiffel				Asif Mujtaba	not out		5
C.J. McDermott				Waqar Younis			
T.B.A. May				Aqib Javed			
Extras	b **3**, lb **2**, w **3**, nb **3**		11	Extras	b **1**, lb **4**		5
(50 overs)	(for 6 wickets)		212	(50 overs)	(for 7 wickets)		180

	O	M	R	W		O	M	R	W
Wasim Akram	10	1	28	–	McDermott	10	2	26	2
Aqib Javed	8	–	39	1	Reiffel	10	1	37	2
Waqar Younis	10	–	39	2	S.R. Waugh	8	–	22	1
Aamir Sohail	5	–	27	–	May	10	–	41	–
Shahid Saeed	8	–	36	–	M.E. Waugh	4	–	24	1
Asif Mujtaba	9	–	38	2	Dodemaide	8	–	25	1

FALL OF WICKETS

1–9, **2**–133, **3**–153, **4**–180, **5**–181, **6**–187

FALL OF WICKETS

1–10, **2**–28, **3**–69, **4**–97, **5**–142, **6**–154, **7**–171

Umpires: D.B. Hair & C.D. Timmins   *Man of the Match:* D.M. Jones   *Australia won by 32 runs*

BENSON AND HEDGES WORLD SERIES – MATCH TWELVE – AUSTRALIA *v.* PAKISTAN
14 January 1993 at SCG, Sydney

AUSTRALIA				PAKISTAN			
D.C. Boon	c sub, **b** Asif Mujtaba		50	Aamir Sohail	**b** Dodemaide		7
M.A. Taylor	**b** Asif Mujtaba		58	Salim Malik	c Healy, **b** Dodemaide		6
D.M. Jones	**b** Mushtaq Ahmed		13	Ramiz Raja	c Border, **b** Matthews		67
S.R. Waugh	c Asif Mujtaba, **b** Waqar Younis		64	Javed Miandad (capt)	c M.E. Waugh, **b** Border		41
M.E. Waugh	run out		11	Inzamam-ul-Haq	**b** McDermott		40
*I.A. Healy	lbw, **b** Waqar Younis		0	Wasim Akram	**b** Matthews		0
A.R. Border (capt)	**b** Waqar Younis		28	Asif Mujtaba	not out		47
G.R.J. Matthews	not out		10	Waqar Younis	not out		18
A.I.C. Dodemaide	run out		5	*Rashid Latif			
P.R. Reiffel	not out		2	Mushtaq Ahmed			
C.J. McDermott				Aqib Javed			
Extras	b **6**, lb **5**, w **4**, nb **4**		19	Extras	b **1**, lb **6**, w **4**		11
(50 overs)	(for 8 wickets)		260	(50 overs)	(for 6 wickets)		237

	O	M	R	W		O	M	R	W
Wasim Akram	10	–	39	–	McDermott	9	3	27	1
Aqib Javed	9	–	52	–	Dodemaide	8	2	30	2
Waqar Younis	9	1	55	3	Reiffel	10	–	53	–
Mushtaq Ahmed	10	–	39	1	S.R. Waugh	5	–	26	–
Asif Mujtaba	9	–	47	2	Matthews	10	–	54	2
Aamir Sohail	3	–	17	–	Border	8	–	40	1

FALL OF WICKETS

1–112, **2**–124, **3**–144, **4**–167, **5**–230, **6**–230, **7**–245, **8**–257

FALL OF WICKETS

1–24, **2**–46, **3**–130, **4**–132, **5**–133, **6**–204

Umpires: S.G. Randell & T.A. Prue   *Man of the Match:* S.R. Waugh   *Australia won by 23 runs*

whose season had been brought to an end through injury. Dodemaide returned to the international scene.

Boon and Jones shared a second-wicket stand of 124, and Dean Jones was the hero as he scored 84 in 2½ hours in spite of batting with an injured thumb. Pakistan could not mount a real challenge for the 213 needed for victory.

Pakistan suffered their sixth successive defeat in the competition in the final match at Sydney. Australia batted consistently, and although Pakistan's batting showed some improvement, it was once again well below the expected standard. This had been a miserable tournament for the world champions.

Dean Jones has his middle stump knocked back by Waqar Younis after making 84 in the 11th match in the World Series. Jones lost his place in the Test side and, controversially, was not selected for the tour of England. (Joe Mann/Allsport)

BENSON AND HEDGES WORLD SERIES – FINAL TABLE

	P	W	L	Tie	Pts.
Australia	8	5	2	1	11
West Indies	8	5	3	–	10
Pakistan	8	1	6	1	3

An opening partnership of 90 in 19 overs between Haynes and Lara provided West Indies with a splendid platform in the first of the World Series finals. Lara hit 67 off 82 balls to take his side to a strong position. The Australian innings was undermined by Ambrose. Upset at having to remove his white wristband at the insistence of Jones, Ambrose topped and tailed the Australian innings and took his side to a 25-run victory. He dismissed both openers and had Jones dropped in an opening spell which brought him figures of 2 for 18 in seven overs. In his second spell, he took three wickets in 15 deliveries after Healy had offered some resistance.

West Indies won the Benson and Hedges World Series for the sixth time in 14 seasons when they beat Australia in a low-scoring game in Melbourne. Australia began well enough, but the accurate off-spin of Hooper, coupled

---

BENSON AND HEDGES WORLD SERIES – FIRST FINAL – AUSTRALIA v. WEST INDIES
16 January 1993 at SCG, Sydney

WEST INDIES

Batsman	Dismissal	Runs
B.C. Lara	c Dodemaide, b Border	67
D.L. Haynes	c and b Matthews	38
P.V. Simmons	c M.E. Waugh, b Matthews	5
R.B. Richardson (capt)	c Dodemaide, b Border	28
C.L. Hooper	b S.R. Waugh	45
A.L. Logie	b S.R. Waugh	38
K.C.G. Benjamin	run out	0
I.R. Bishop	b McDermott	1
C.E.L. Ambrose	not out	5
*J.R. Murray		
A.C. Cummins		
Extras	b 2, lb 8, nb 2	12
(50 overs)	(for 8 wickets)	239

AUSTRALIA

Batsman	Dismissal	Runs
D.C. Boon	c Murray, b Ambrose	16
M.A. Taylor	c Simmons, b Ambrose	28
D.M. Jones	c Simmons, b Benjamin	13
S.R. Waugh	c and b Hooper	15
M.E. Waugh	run out	51
A.R. Border (capt)	c Ambrose, b Hooper	27
*I.A. Healy	b Ambrose	33
G.R.J. Matthews	c Lara, b Benjamin	11
A.I.C. Dodemaide	c Lara, b Ambrose	3
P.R. Reiffel	not out	12
C.J. McDermott	c Simmons, b Ambrose	0
Extras	lb 3, w 1, nb 1	5
(49.3 overs)		214

Bowler	O	M	R	W
McDermott	8	–	40	1
Dodemaide	7	–	23	–
Reiffel	5	1	30	–
Matthews	10	–	45	2
Border	10	–	46	2
S.R. Waugh	10	–	45	2

Bowler	O	M	R	W
Bishop	10	–	45	–
Ambrose	9.3	2	32	5
Simmons	2	–	14	–
Benjamin	10	–	35	2
Cummins	8	–	39	–
Hooper	10	–	46	2

FALL OF WICKETS

1–90, 2–96, 3–128, 4–159, 5–216, 6–217, 7–220, 8–239

FALL OF WICKETS

1–41, 2–48, 3–69, 4–91, 5–147, 6–161, 7–179, 8–187, 9–214

Umpires: S.G. Randell & T.A. Prue   *Man of the Match: C.E.L. Ambrose*   *West Indies won by 25 runs*

BENSON AND HEDGES WORLD SERIES – SECOND FINAL – AUSTRALIA *v.* WEST INDIES
18 January 1993 at MCG, Melbourne

AUSTRALIA

M.A. Taylor	c Ambrose, **b** Bishop	33
D.C. Boon	run out	19
D.M. Jones	c Murray, **b** Bishop	5
S.R. Waugh	run out	25
M.E. Waugh	run out	8
A.R. Border (capt)	c and **b** Hooper	8
*I.A. Healy	c and **b** Ambrose	16
G.R.J. Matthews	c Logie, **b** Ambrose	15
A.I.C. Dodemaide	c Murray, **b** Ambrose	1
P.R. Reiffel	not out	7
C.J. McDermott	**b** Hooper	0
Extras	lb 3, nb 7	10
(47.3 overs)		147

WEST INDIES

D.L. Haynes	run out	0
B.C. Lara	c M.E. Waugh, **b** McDermott	60
P.V. Simmons	c M.E. Waugh, **b** Dodemaide	0
R.B. Richardson (capt)	c Reiffel, **b** McDermott	5
C.L. Hooper	not out	59
A.L. Logie	c Healy, **b** Reiffel	7
*J.R. Murray	c Healy, **b** Dodemaide	1
I.R. Bishop	not out	4
K.C.G. Benjamin		
C.E.L. Ambrose		
A.C. Cummins		
Extras	lb 7, w 2, nb 3	12
(47 overs)	(for 6 wickets)	148

	O	M	R	W
Bishop	9	2	33	2
Benjamin	10	–	33	–
Ambrose	10	–	26	3
Cummins	10	1	24	–
Hooper	8.3	1	28	2

	O	M	R	W
McDermott	10	–	35	2
Dodemaide	10	4	19	2
Reiffel	10	1	21	1
S.R. Waugh	10	1	30	–
M.E. Waugh	4	–	17	–
Matthews	3	–	19	–

FALL OF WICKETS
1–54, 2–63, 3–65, 4–74, 5–94, 6–113, 7–133, 8–137, 9–146

FALL OF WICKETS
1–7, 2–8, 3–23, 4–109, 5–125, 6–126

Umpires: D.B. Hair & C.D. Timmins   *Man of the Finals:* C.E.L. Ambrose   *West Indies won by 4 wickets*

with some bizarre running, blunted their progress. The aggression of Ambrose ended thoughts of recovery.

It still seemed that Australia could win when Haynes and Simmons went without scoring, but Lara and Hooper added 86 for the fourth wicket. Hooper crowned a fine individual performance when he took his side to victory with four wickets and three overs to spare.

This low-scoring match was typical of a tournament in which the ball had generally dominated and in which no century had been scored.

Ambrose was named Man of the Finals, and he had enjoyed an outstanding competition.

15, 16, 17 and 18 January 1993 *at Bellerive Oval, Hobart*

Tasmania 454 for 7 dec. (D.J. Buckingham 161 not out, M.G. Farrell 74, S. Young 60, D.F. Hills 55, R.T. Ponting 50)

South Australia 271 and 314 for 6 (D.S. Webber 89, G.A. Bishop 56, J.D. Siddons 56)

Match drawn

Tasmania 2 pts., South Australia 0 pts.

Inspired bowling for Queensland in the second half of the season from Mike Kasprowicz. (David Munden/Sports-Line)

Having lost two wickets for five runs, Tasmania recovered mainly because of Danny Buckingham, who batted for 7½ hours and shared a seventh-wicket stand of 131 with Farrell in even time. South Australia were without the promising Fielke who, it was stated, would miss the rest of the season through injury. Cooley returned to the Tasmanian side and took three wickets, but he sent down 19 no-balls. In spite of 54 extras, South Australia were forced to follow-on. Darren Webber again batted well as South Australia, helped by another 14 no-balls from Cooley, saved the game.

21, 22 and **23** January 1993 *at Woolloongabba, Brisbane*

Queensland 168 (T.J. Cooley 4 for 49) and 162 (P.T. McPhee 5 for 48)

Tasmania 335 (J. Cox 137 not out, D.J. Buckingham 51, M.S. Kasprowicz 6 for 59)

Tasmania won by an innings and 5 runs

Tasmania 6 pts., Queensland 0 pts.

Put in to bat on a green wicket, Queensland collapsed against Cooley and Matthews. Tasmania took a grip on the game when Jamie Cox, batting for 459 minutes and

---

BENSON AND HEDGES WORLD SERIES AVERAGES

AUSTRALIA BATTING

	M	Inns	NO	Runs	HS	Av	50s
P.R. Reiffel	10	8	6	66	23*	33.00	–
D.M. Jones	10	10	1	273	84	30.33	2
M.E. Waugh	10	9	–	259	57	28.77	3
M.A. Taylor	10	10	–	286	78	28.60	2
S.R. Waugh	10	10	1	213	64	23.66	1
D.C. Boon	10	10	–	224	64	22.40	2
G.R.J. Matthews	6	6	2	85	32	21.25	–
A.R. Border	6	6	1	103	28	20.66	–
I.A. Healy	10	9	1	154	41	19.25	–
D.R. Martyn	4	3	–	45	40	15.00	–
A.I.C. Dodemaide	4	4	1	24	15*	8.00	–
M.R. Whitney	6	2	1	3	2	3.00	–
C.J. McDermott	10	6	2	11	7	2.75	–

Played in four matches: T.B.A. May 3*

AUSTRALIA BOWLING

	Overs	Mds	Runs	Wkts	Av	Best	4/inn
M.E. Waugh	35.3	–	159	9	17.66	5-24	1
A.I.C. Dodemaide	33	6	97	5	19.40	2-19	–
C.J. McDermott	86	13	321	13	24.69	4-42	1
P.R. Reiffel	84	9	310	12	25.83	3-14	–
A.R. Border	18	–	86	3	28.66	2-46	–
M.R. Whitney	51	9	149	5	29.80	2-11	–
S.R. Waugh	82.3	4	353	9	39.22	2-25	–
G.R.J. Matthews	39	–	174	4	43.50	2-45	–
T.B.A. May	33	–	145	3	48.33	2-27	–

AUSTRALIA FIELDING FIGURES

13 – I.A. Healy; 8 – M.A. Taylor; 6 – M.E. Waugh; 4 – S.R. Waugh and P.R. Reiffel; 3 – A.R. Border and D.R. Martyn; 2 – A.I.C. Dodemaide; 1 – D.M. Jones, G.R.J. Matthews and C.J. McDermott.

WEST INDIES BATTING

	M	Inns	NO	Runs	HS	Av	50s
D.L. Haynes	10	10	2	292	96	36.50	2
R.B. Richardson	10	9	2	255	76*	36.42	2
C.L. Hooper	10	8	1	237	59*	33.85	2
B.C. Lara	10	10	–	331	74	33.10	4
K.C.G. Benjamin	6	4	2	39	17	19.50	–
C.E.L. Ambrose	9	5	3	33	15*	16.50	–
P.V. Simmons	9	8	1	93	43*	13.28	–
A.L. Logie	8	7	–	92	38	13.14	–
I.R. Bishop	7	5	1	39	17	9.75	–
J.R. Murray	9	5	–	30	22	6.00	–
K.L.T. Arthurton	7	5	–	26	9	5.20	–
A.C. Cummins	8	5	1	9	4*	2.25	–

Played in two matches: C.A. Walsh 0* & 12; J.C. Adams 17; B.P. Patterson 0* & 1*
Played in one match: D. Williams 25*

WEST INDIES BOWLING

	Overs	Mds	Runs	Wkts	Av	Best	4/inn
P.V. Simmons	46	15	110	11	10.00	4-3	1
B.P. Patterson	19	2	50	4	12.50	2-19	–
C.E.L. Ambrose	79.5	13	241	18	13.38	5-32	1
C.L. Hooper	80.2	3	328	15	21.86	3-31	–
K.C.G. Benjamin	55	4	190	8	23.75	2-16	–
I.R. Bishop	61.4	4	215	9	23.88	5-25	1
C.A. Walsh	20	1	91	2	45.50	2-49	–
A.C. Cummins	73	5	258	3	86.00	1-16	–

Bowled in one innings: J.C. Adams 4–2–2–1

WEST INDIES FIELDING FIGURES

14 – J.R. Murray (ct 12/st 2); 8 – B.C. Lara; 7 – P.V. Simmons and C.L. Hooper; 4 – R.B. Richardson and C.E.L. Ambrose; 3 – D.L. Haynes and K.C.G. Benjamin; 2 – A.C. Cummins, A.L. Logie and D. Williams; 1 – K.L.T. Arthurton

PAKISTAN BATTING

	M	Inns	NO	Runs	HS	Av	50s
Inzamam-ul-Haq	8	8	2	224	60*	37.33	1
Ramiz Raja	7	7	–	225	67	32.14	2
Asif Mujtaba	8	8	3	158	56*	31.60	1
Javed Miandad	8	8	1	173	59*	24.71	1
Salim Malik	7	7	–	172	64	24.57	1
Rashid Latif	8	6	2	75	39	18.75	–
Wasim Akram	8	8	1	91	36	13.00	–
Waqar Younis	8	5	1	48	18*	12.00	–
Aamir Sohail	7	7	–	73	41	10.42	–
Aqib Javed	6	3	2	16	7*	8.00	–
Mushtaq Ahmed	7	4	–	20	15	5.00	–

Played in two matches: Ata-ur-Rehman 0*; Saeed Anwar 6 & 2; Shahid Saeed 1 & 3

PAKISTAN BOWLING

	Overs	Mds	Runs	Wkts	Av	Best	4/inn
Waqar Younis	70	10	275	10	27.50	3-29	–
Wasim Akram	76	6	294	10	29.40	4-46	1
Asif Mujtaba	28	–	144	4	36.00	2-38	–
Mushtaq Ahmed	56.2	2	232	6	38.66	2-22	–
Aamir Sohail	55	2	217	5	43.40	2-26	–
Aqib Javed	43	2	208	4	52.00	2-35	–
Ata-ur-Rehman	20	–	76	–	–	–	–

Bowled in one innings: Shahid Saeed 8–0–36–0

PAKISTAN FIELDING FIGURES

7 – Rashid Latif; 3 – Asif Mujtaba; 2 – Javed Miandad, Inzamam-ul-Haq and Wasim Akram; 1 – Waqar Younis, Shahid Saeed, Aamir Sohail, Ramiz Raja and Salim Malik

facing 355 balls, hit his first century for two seasons. Mike Kasprowicz, strongly tipped to win a place in the side to tour England, returned his best figures in Shield cricket. Batting a second time, Queensland again collapsed, losing their last six wickets for 30 runs – four of them to McPhee – and the game was over inside three days. The win gave Tasmania a good chance of reaching the Shield final.

FOURTH TEST MATCH
AUSTRALIA v. WEST INDIES, at Adelaide

An injury to Damien Martyn in training allowed Justin Langer to play in a Test match for the first time. He was to acquit himself nobly in one of the very best of matches.

Richardson won the toss, and West Indies batted. In the pre-lunch period, they scored 100 in 31 overs for the loss of Simmons and Richardson. The game moved dramatically in favour of Australia in the afternoon session when three wickets fell for five runs at one point. Two of the wickets went to Tim May who had been brought into the Australian side in place of Greg Matthews. It was May's first Test match for four years, and he first had Haynes stumped and then tempted Arthurton to drive uppishly to mid-on. Hooper, wretchedly out of form, edged Hughes to Healy behind the stumps, and West Indies were 134 for 5. The impressively correct and forceful Lara was joined by Murray who gave joyful support in a stand of 55, but Hughes returned to capture three more wickets, and Australia were jubilant at having bowled out West Indies on the first day for 252.

There was less joy when, in poor light, Mark Taylor was taken at slip in the second over. Langer was hit on the helmet, but he fought bravely through the last 10 minutes to see Australia to 2 for 1. The left-handed Langer was playing his first innings since being struck while fielding, and now he had his helmet split in his first few minutes as a Test batsman.

The bombardment continued on the second morning when, with the score at 16 for 1, David Boon was hit on the left forearm by a ball from Ambrose and was forced to retire hurt for the first time in his long Test career. Unfortunately, Mark Waugh, his replacement, having survived a confident appeal for leg before first ball, was caught at slip second ball.

There was an interruption for rain after which Langer, who had been bruised and battered and had resisted bravely for 98 minutes, was caught off his glove as he attempted to hook. Steve Waugh and Allan Border took the score to 100 before rain brought an early close.

On the third morning, Ambrose dismissed Border, Healy and Steve Waugh in the space of nine balls to reduce Australia to 112 for 6. Boon resumed his innings at the fall of the fifth wicket and, with Hughes adopting effective agricultural clouts, 69 runs were added for the seventh wicket. The partnership was broken by Hooper who immediately accounted for Warne before the irrepressible Ambrose brought the innings to a close.

West Indies led by 39 runs on the first innings, and the

Heroic deeds by Tim May in the fourth Test at Adelaide failed to give Australia victory. (Joe Mann/Allsport)

gap between the two sides began to grow large, as Richardson threatened to dominate after McDermott had claimed both openers and Hughes had dismissed the dangerous Lara. At 124 for 4, West Indies were moving to an unassailable position. May was brought into the attack and, in his second over, Hooper swept him into the hands of deep square-leg. Richardson hit Warne for two leg-side sixes before, astonishingly, the last five West Indian wickets went down for nine runs.

Again, it was spin that proved to be the undoing of the men from the Caribbean. Four of the wickets fell to offbreak bowler Tim May who, the day before his 31st birthday, took 5 for 9 and virtually assured himself a trip to England. Praise, too, must go to Warne who stuck at his task when he was being attacked and found the outside edge of Richardson's bat as he came down the wicket. Seventeen wickets had fallen in one day, on a wicket which had life and some turn but which was always true in bounce – an excellent pitch. Australia had two days in which to score 186 runs to win the match and the rubber.

Australia Day dawned with expectations high, but where spin had been the undoing of West Indies, speed was to take its toll of Australia. The day was five overs old when Ambrose was denied a confident leg before appeal against Taylor, but two balls later there was no reprieve for Boon. This was a great blow to Australia, for Boon is the rock on which so much is founded. Taylor had looked uncomfortable all series, and now he jabbed once too often at Benjamin and was caught behind.

Mark Waugh suggested that he would counter the West Indian pace when he took 10 off an over from

Courtney Walsh celebrates as McDermott is caught by Murray and West Indies win the fourth Test by one run. (Joe Mann/Allsport)

Bishop, but Walsh found some extra bounce, and the first of the twins was caught at slip. The first ball of the afternoon session saw Steve Waugh hit to cover where Arthurton took a juggling catch. Border gloved a ball from Ambrose to short-leg, and Healy and Hughes were quickly accounted for. In seven overs, four Australian wickets had gone down for 10 runs, and the 112 runs needed for victory now looked to be an unattainable goal.

The fates gradually seemed to smile more kindly on Australia as Warne escaped some half-chances. He and Langer, a giant in his first Test, added 28. Then Langer and May added 42, 34 runs coming in six overs after tea before Langer attempted to pull and was caught behind. Langer had batted for 253 minutes, faced 146 balls and hit 4 fours. This was a massive contribution from a young man in his first Test, played at a time of great tension and drama when more experienced players were falling about him. Moreover, and perhaps more significantly for Australia, Langer looks to be the most technically correct and accomplished of their younger batsmen.

So McDermott joined May with 42 runs needed for victory from the last wicket. McDermott had once seemed a capable late-order batsman, but his nerve had become suspect against the pace men. Now he played with great resolve, getting into line and batting with courage and determination. For 88 minutes, the last-wicket pair defied the West Indians, and the score edged closer and closer to 186. The batsmen were tested by some short-pitched deliveries, but the bowlers were tiring and the ball was older.

FOURTH TEST MATCH – AUSTRALIA v. WEST INDIES
23, 24, 25 and 26 January 1993 at Adelaide Oval

WEST INDIES

	FIRST INNINGS		SECOND INNINGS	
D.L. Haynes	st Healy, b May	45	c Healy, b McDermott	11
P.V. Simmons	c Hughes, b S.R. Waugh	46	b McDermott	10
R.B. Richardson (capt)	lbw, b Hughes	2	c Healy, b Warne	72
B.C. Lara	c Healy, b McDermott	52	c S.R. Waugh, b Hughes	7
K.L.T. Arthurton	c S.R. Waugh, b May	0	c Healy, b McDermott	0
C.L. Hooper	c Healy, b Hughes	2	c Hughes, b May	25
*J.R. Murray	not out	49	c M.E. Waugh, b May	0
I.R. Bishop	c M.E. Waugh, b Hughes	13	c M.E. Waugh, b May	6
C.E.L. Ambrose	c Healy, b Hughes	0	st Healy, b May	1
K.C.G. Benjamin	b M.E. Waugh	15	c Warne, b May	0
C.A. Walsh	lbw, b Hughes	5	not out	0
Extras	lb 11, nb 12	23	lb 2, nb 12	14
		252		146

AUSTRALIA

	FIRST INNINGS		SECOND INNINGS	
M.A. Taylor	c Hooper, b Bishop	1	(2) c Murray, b Benjamin	7
D.C. Boon	not out	39	(1) lbw, b Ambrose	0
J.L. Langer	c Murray, b Benjamin	20	c Murray, b Bishop	54
M.E. Waugh	c Simmons, b Ambrose	0	c Hooper, b Walsh	26
S.R. Waugh	c Murray, b Ambrose	42	c Arthurton, b Ambrose	4
A.R. Border (capt)	c Hooper, b Ambrose	19	c Haynes, b Ambrose	1
*I.A. Healy	c Hooper, b Ambrose	0	b Walsh	0
M.G. Hughes	c Murray, b Hooper	43	lbw, b Ambrose	1
S.K. Warne	lbw, b Hooper	0	lbw, b Bishop	9
T.B.A. May	c Murray, b Ambrose	6	not out	42
C.J. McDermott	b Ambrose	14	c Murray, b Walsh	18
Extras	b 7, lb 3, nb 19	29	b 1, lb 8, nb 13	22
		213		184

	O	M	R	W	O	M	R	W
McDermott	16	1	85	1	11	–	66	3
Hughes	21.3	3	64	5	13	1	43	1
S.R. Waugh	13	4	37	1	5	1	8	–
May	14	1	41	2	6.5	3	9	5
M.E. Waugh	1	–	3	1				
Warne	2	–	11	–	6	2	18	1

	O	M	R	W	O	M	R	W
Ambrose	28.2	6	74	6	26	5	46	4
Bishop	18	3	48	1	17	3	41	2
Benjamin	6	–	22	1	12	2	32	1
Walsh	10	3	34	–	19	4	44	3
Hooper	13	4	25	2	5	1	12	–

FALL OF WICKETS

1–84, 2–99, 3–129, 4–130, 5–134, 6–189, 7–205, 8–206, 9–247
1–14, 2–49, 3–63, 4–65, 5–124, 6–137, 7–145, 8–146, 9–146

FALL OF WICKETS

1–1, 2–16, 3–46, 4–108, 5–108, 6–112, 7–181, 8–181, 9–197
1–5, 2–16, 3–54, 4–64, 5–72, 6–73, 7–74, 8–102, 9–144

Umpires: D.B. Hair & L.J. King

West Indies won by 1 run

The fifth ball of Walsh's 19th over arrived with Australia only two short of victory. Walsh delivered a long hop but McDermott, perhaps over-eager to make the winning hit, only laid the toe of his bat on the ball. The next delivery lifted viciously. McDermott attempted to sway out of the way, but the ball touched his glove, the peak of his helmet and then ended in the gloves of the jubilant Murray. West Indies had won by one run, the closest victory in the history of Test cricket.

Curtly Ambrose was named Man of the Match for his 10 for 120, but this was a game of many heroes – Langer, May, Walsh and Hughes among them. Cricket was the real victor, but Australia could reflect ruefully that they went into the final Test level at one game apiece when they had had the chances to have established a 3–0 lead.

FIFTH TEST MATCH
AUSTRALIA *v.* WEST INDIES, at Perth

Australia lost the services of Tim May, who was injured, and brought in Western Australian pace bowler Joe Angel

for his first Test. Damien Martyn returned and, somewhat surprisingly, Mark Taylor was dropped. Taylor had had a poor series, but to ask Langer to open – not his natural position – in only his second Test seemed rather absurd. West Indies chose Adams ahead of the out-of-form Hooper and gave Cummins a first Test cap in place of the injured Benjamin.

Border won the toss, and Australia batted first on a well-grassed pitch which, to no one's surprise, gave much encouragement to the pace bowlers, a fact which was to cost the curator his job some weeks later. Boon and Langer began cautiously, and the score had reached 27 after 69 minutes before Langer was caught behind off Bishop. Steve Waugh suffered the same fate before lunch, but there were few other alarms.

Boon and Mark Waugh took the score to 85 at which point Waugh was caught behind off Ambrose. The tall pace bowler's first spell had been uncertain in length and direction, but now he settled into the rhythm which had made him the man of the series. In one of the most remarkable displays of bowling to be seen in Test cricket, he took seven wickets for one run in the space of 32 deliveries, and Australia were left shattered, 119 all out, their last seven wickets having fallen for 29 runs. Border –

FIFTH TEST MATCH – AUSTRALIA *v.* WEST INDIES
30, 31 January and 1 February 1993 at WACA Ground, Perth

AUSTRALIA

	FIRST INNINGS		SECOND INNINGS	
J.L. Langer	c Murray, b Bishop	10	(2) c sub (Logie), b Ambrose	1
D.C. Boon	c Richardson, b Ambrose	44	(1) b Bishop	52
S.R. Waugh	c Murray, b Bishop	13	c sub (Logie), b Bishop	0
M.E. Waugh	c Murray, b Ambrose	9	c Richardson, b Bishop	21
D.R. Martyn	c Simmons, b Ambrose	13	(6) c Ambrose, b Cummins	31
A.R. Border (capt)	c Murray, b Ambrose	0	(7) b Bishop	0
*I.A. Healy	c Lara, b Ambrose	0	(8) c Murray, b Bishop	27
M.G. Hughes	c Arthurton, b Ambrose	0	(9) c Murray, b Walsh	22
S.K. Warne	run out	13	(5) c Murray, b Ambrose	0
J. Angel	c Murray, b Ambrose	0	not out	4
C.J. McDermott	not out	2	c Lara, b Bishop	8
Extras	lb 8, w 1, nb 6	15	b 1, lb 6, nb 5	12
		119		**178**

WEST INDIES

	FIRST INNINGS	
D.L. Haynes	c Healy, b Hughes	24
P.V. Simmons	c S.R. Waugh, b Angel	80
R.B. Richardson (capt)	c Langer, b McDermott	47
B.C. Lara	c Warne, b McDermott	16
K.L.T. Arthurton	c S.R. Waugh, b McDermott	77
J.C. Adams	b Hughes	8
*J.R. Murray	c Healy, b M.E. Waugh	37
I.R. Bishop	c Healy, b M.E. Waugh	0
A.C. Cummins	c M.E. Waugh, b Hughes	3
C.E.L. Ambrose	not out	9
C.A. Walsh	b Hughes	1
Extras	b 4, lb 10, nb 6	20
		322

	O	M	R	W	O	M	R	W
Ambrose	18	9	25	7	21	8	54	2
Bishop	11	6	17	2	16	4	40	6
Walsh	11.2	2	45	–	12	2	46	1
Cummins	7	–	24	–	8	3	31	1

	O	M	R	W
McDermott	22	4	85	3
Hughes	25.4	6	71	4
Angel	19	4	72	1
Warne	12	–	51	–
S.R. Waugh	6	3	8	–
M.E. Waugh	6	1	21	2

FALL OF WICKETS

1–27, 2–58, 3–85, 4–90, 5–90, 6–100, 7–102, 8–104, 9–104
1–13, 2–14, 3–66, 4–67, 5–95, 6–95, 7–130, 8–162, 9–170

FALL OF WICKETS

1–111, 2–136, 3–184, 4–195, 5–205, 6–280, 7–286, 8–301, 9–319

Umpires: C.D. Timmins & S.G. Randell

West Indies won by an innings and 25 runs

International Cricketer of the Year and destroyer of Australia in the fifth Test – Curtly Ambrose. (Ben Radford/Allsport)

out first ball – Healy, Hughes and Angel all failed to score. By the end of the day, West Indies, having lost Haynes, who had to retire hurt on 34, and Richardson, caught on the boundary off a bouncer at 111, were 135 for 1 and in total command.

Australia were encouraged when Lara was out to the third ball of the second day, but Simmons, who hit a six and 11 fours in his 147-ball innings, continued quite merrily until he provided Angel, who had come in for considerable punishment, with his first Test wicket. Adams went cheaply, and Haynes returned but added only three to his overnight score before edging Hughes to the keeper.

Junior Murray, who kept wicket splendidly and equalled the West Indies record with five catches in an innings against Australia, should have been caught at slip by Border off Hughes before he had scored, but he survived and, with Arthurton, added 75. The last five West Indian wickets went down for 42 runs in nine overs, but a lead of 203 was a formidable one on this wicket. Keith Arthurton had provided the substance with 77 off 154 balls in 224 minutes. Like Lara, he had come of age in this series.

TEST MATCH AVERAGES – AUSTRALIA v. WEST INDIES

AUSTRALIA BATTING

	M	Inns	NO	Runs	HS	Av	100s	50s
D.C. Boon	5	10	2	490	111	61.25	1	3
M.E. Waugh	5	9	–	340	112	37.77	1	2
G.R.J. Matthews	2	3	–	109	79	36.33	–	1
A.R. Border	5	9	–	298	110	33.11	1	2
D.R. Martyn	4	7	1	169	67*	28.16	–	1
S.R. Waugh	5	9	–	228	100	25.33	1	–
M.A. Taylor	4	8	1	170	46*	24.28	–	1
J.L. Langer	2	4	–	85	54	21.25	–	1
I.A. Healy	5	9	1	130	36*	16.25	–	–
M.G. Hughes	5	9	1	118	43	14.75	–	–
C.J. McDermott	5	8	2	82	18	13.66	–	–
S.K. Warne	4	7	–	42	14	6.00	–	–

Played in one Test: B.A. Reid 1* & 1; M.R. Whitney 0 & 13; T.B.A. May 6 & 42*; J. Angel 0 & 4*

AUSTRALIA BOWLING

	Overs	Mds	Runs	Wkts	Av	Best	10/m	5/inn
T.B.A. May	20.5	4	50	7	7.14	5-9	–	1
M.E. Waugh	22	2	84	4	21.00	2-21	–	–
B.A. Reid	53	9	151	7	21.57	5-112	–	1
M.G. Hughes	145.2	30	432	20	21.60	5-64	–	1
M.R. Whitney	23	6	59	2	29.50	1-27	–	–
S.K. Warne	108.2	23	313	10	31.30	7-52	–	1
C.J. McDermott	185.1	33	615	18	34.16	4-35	–	–
S.R. Waugh	58	13	162	3	54.00	1-14	–	–
G.R.J. Matthews	99	28	228	4	57.00	2-169	–	–

Bowled in one innings: J. Angel 19–4–72–1

AUSTRALIA FIELDING FIGURES

23 – I.A. Healy (ct 19/st 4); 6 – M.E. Waugh; 5 – D.C. Boon, M.A. Taylor, S.R. Waugh and M.G. Hughes; 3 – S.K. Warne; 1 – D.R. Martyn, G.R.J. Matthews, C.J. McDermott, M.R. Whitney and J.L. Langer

WEST INDIES BATTING

	M	Inns	NO	Runs	HS	Av	100s	50s
B.C. Lara	5	8	–	466	277	58.25	1	3
K.L.T. Arthurton	5	8	1	365	157*	52.14	1	2
J.C. Adams	3	4	1	148	77*	49.33	–	1
R.B. Richardson	5	8	–	380	109	47.50	1	3
P.V. Simmons	5	8	–	283	110	35.37	1	1
J.R. Murray	3	4	1	97	49*	32.33	–	–
C.L. Hooper	4	7	–	130	47	18.57	–	–
D.L. Haynes	5	8	–	123	45	15.37	–	–
I.R. Bishop	5	8	1	57	16*	8.14	–	–
C.E.L. Ambrose	5	8	2	47	16	7.83	–	–
C.A. Walsh	5	8	3	23	17	4.60	–	–
D. Williams	2	4	–	15	15	3.75	–	–

Played in one Test: B.P. Patterson 0; K.C.G. Benjamin 15 & 0; A.C. Cummins 3

WEST INDIES BOWLING

	Overs	Mds	Runs	Wkts	Av	Best	10/m	5/inn
C.E.L. Ambrose	260.3	77	542	33	16.42	7-25	1	3
I.R. Bishop	201	39	480	23	20.86	6-40	–	1
K.C.G. Benjamin	18	3	54	2	27.00	1-22	–	–
C.A. Walsh	175.1	42	467	12	38.91	4-91	–	–
C.L. Hooper	170.5	29	438	10	43.80	4-75	–	–
A.C. Cummins	15	3	55	1	55.00	1-31	–	–
P.V. Simmons	49	14	112	2	56.00	2-34	–	–
J.C. Adams	27	3	103	1	103.00	1-56	–	–
B.P. Patterson	26	–	127	1	127.00	1-83	–	–
K.L.T. Arthurton	9	1	22	–	–	–	–	–

Bowled in one innings: B.C. Lara 2–0–4–0; R.B. Richardson 1–0–4–0

WEST INDIES FIELDING FIGURES

19 – J.R. Murray; 11 – D. Williams; 7 – P.V. Simmons and C.L. Hooper; 6 – B.C. Lara and K.L.T. Arthurton; 3 – R. B. Richardson and D.L. Haynes; 2 – J.C. Adams and sub (A.L. Logie); 1 – I.R. Bishop, C.A. Walsh and C.E.L. Ambrose

Australia began their second innings after tea. Langer was dropped at slip by Simmons before he had scored and given out caught at short-leg when he had made one. Steve Waugh fell in the same manner. Mark Waugh and Boon suggested permanence until Waugh was the victim of a Bishop in-swinger. Night-watchman Warne was then caught behind off Ambrose. This was the Antiguan's 33rd wicket of the series, and it brought him alongside Grimmett and Davidson as record-holder for matches between the two countries.

Australia resumed on the third morning at 75 for 4, and all hope of salvation disappeared when Boon, having completed a splendid fifty in just under three hours, was bowled by Bishop. Border went back to his first ball and was bowled to complete his first 'pair' in 138 Test matches.

Martyn was dropped at slip before he became Cummins' first Test victim, taken low down at fine-leg, and all that remained were some bravely defiant clouts from Hughes and Healy. The match was over by lunch-time on the third day.

Ambrose was named Man of the Match and International Cricketer of the Year, most deservedly so. This had been a fine series and had produced some memorable cricket. It is worth giving credit for the atmosphere in which the cricket was played to West Indian skipper Richie Richardson. Ken Piesse, editor of Australia's *Cricketer*, the country's major magazine, described Richardson as 'a breath of fresh air, after the acrimony of Viv Richards' last troubled days as leader in 1991. Richie Richardson was assertive, constructive and inspired confidence. A great ambassador.'

27, 28, 29 and 30 January 1993 *at SCG, Sydney*

Tasmania 292 (R.T. Ponting 125, G. McGrath 5 for 79) and 295 for 9 (D.F. Hills 101, R.T. Ponting 69, G.R.J. Matthews 5 for 61)

New South Wales 338 for 9 dec. (M.J. Slater 79, M.G. Bevan 76, B.E. McNamara 51, C.D. Matthews 4 for 80)

Match drawn

New South Wales 2 pts., Tasmania 0 pts.

28, 29, 30 and 31 January 1993 *at Woolloongabba, Brisbane*

Queensland 201 and 321 for 7 dec. (M.L. Hayden 112, T.J. Barsby 81)

Victoria 155 (C.G. Rackemann 4 for 24) and 156 (M.S. Kasprowicz 5 for 61)

Queensland won by 211 runs

Queensland 6 pts., Victoria 0 pts.

With most interest centred on the fifth Test match, New South Wales and Queensland pressed their claims for a place in the Shield final. New South Wales included Glenn McGrath and Adam Gilchrist in their side for the first time, but the honours went to Ricky Ponting who reached 98 on a restricted first day and, on the second, became the youngest player to score a first-class hundred

for Tasmania. He was 41 days past his 18th birthday. McGrath took the last three wickets to complete an impressive debut. New South Wales took first-innings points on a tedious third day, and the tedium continued into the last day. Hills hit his second first-class hundred, and Greg Matthews sent down 54 overs for 61 runs.

Put in to bat, Queensland struggled to 201 against a Victorian attack which included newcomers Simon Cook and Peter Anderson, but Victoria collapsed on the second day, with Rackemann and part-time medium-pacer Stuart Law doing most of the damage. Law's 3 for 25 was the best return of his career. Barsby and Hayden began Queensland's second innings with a partnership of 198, Hayden hitting his fifth century of the season and batting for 226 minutes. Set to score 368 to win, Victoria collapsed before Rackemann and Kasprowicz, who claimed his second five-wicket haul within a week.

31 January 1993 *at Bradman Oval, Bowral*

New South Wales XI 193 for 9 (R. Chee Quee 50)

England 'A' 165 (P.J. Prichard 50)

New South Wales XI won by 28 runs

Such's 2 for 11 in 10 overs and Prichard's 50 off 70 balls were the only redeeming features as England 'A' embarrassingly lost their opening game, a 50-over contest.

2, 3 and 4 February 1993 *at Canberra*

England 'A' 379 for 7 dec. (M.D. Moxon 123, R.C. Russell 67)

ACT 65 (M.C. Ilott 4 for 12, A.R. Caddick 4 for 14) and 361 for 7 (N.J. Speak 120, P. Solway 104)

Match drawn

3, 4, 5 and 6 February 1993 *at MCG, Melbourne*

Victoria 406 for 8 dec. (D.S. Lehmann 112, W.N. Phillips 91, S.P. O'Donnell 58) and 201 for 6 dec. (M.T. Elliott 66)

South Australia 278 for 7 dec. (J.D. Siddons 100, T.J. Nielsen 63 not out) and 306 for 8 (G.R. Blewett 69, J.A. Brayshaw 65, J.D. Siddons 58)

Match drawn

Victoria 2 pts., South Australia 0 pts.

at SCG, Sydney

Western Australia 467 (T.M. Moody 78, B.P. Julian 75, S. Herzberg 57 not out, J. Stewart 51, T.H. Bayliss 4 for 64) and 168 (G.R.J. Matthews 8 for 52)

New South Wales 452 (M.J. Slater 124, M.G. Bevan 103, A.C. Gilchrist 75, S.M. Small 64, B.P. Julian 4 for 132) and 186 for 3

New South Wales won by 7 wickets

New South Wales 6 pts., Western Australia 2 pts.

Michael Slater hit a thousand runs in the season for New South Wales and emerged as an opening batsman of Test quality. (Alan Cozzi)

Put in to bat, England 'A' were held together by the batting of captain and vice-captain. Moxon batted for five hours, and he and Russell added 128 for the fifth wicket. The Capital Territory were routed by the pace of Ilott and Caddick but, following-on, they survived with ease on a pitch that had lost its bite. Solway and Speak, whom many believed should have been in the England side (although his team-mate Lloyd was also supported by some), added 213 for the third wicket in $4\frac{1}{2}$ hours.

Victoria introduced two new men to first-class cricket, left-handed opener Matthew Elliott and leg-spinner Craig Howard. Lehmann hit his first century of the season as Victoria reached a big score. South Australian captain Siddons kept his side in the match and passed 6,000 runs in Shield cricket. Victoria scored briskly on the third day and left the visitors the last day in which to score 330 to win. South Australia batted solidly and for a time looked likely to win but, in the end, they had to be content with a draw.

There were debutants at Sydney as the home side included Shane Lee, and Western Australia brought in batsman Robert Kelly and spinner Jamie Stewart. The first three days were dominated by the bat. Batting at number nine, Brendon Julian hit the highest score of his career, and Herzberg and Stewart both hit fifties as the last wicket added 82. Slater hit his second century of the summer, and Bevan his first hundred for two summers, but Western Australia took first-innings points. The visitors then collapsed against Greg Matthews whose 8 for 52 was the best performance of his career and of the season as a whole. New South Wales swept to victory and to the top of the table.

MERCANTILE MUTUAL CUP

31 January 1993 *at SCG, Sydney*

Tasmania 219 (D.F. Hills 81, R.J. Tucker 50)
New South Wales 221 for 8 (B.E. McNamara 65 not out)

New South Wales won by 2 wickets

6 February 1993 *at Bellerive Oval, Hobart*

Queensland 217 for 6 (M.L. Hayden 52, P.J.T. Goggin 51)
Tasmania 194

Queensland won by 23 runs

7 February 1993 *at MCG, Melbourne*

South Australia 135 for 9
Victoria 136 for 3 (M.T. Elliott 60)

Victoria won by 7 wickets

New South Wales clinched a place in the final on the resumption of the Mercantile Mutual Cup with a dramatic last-over win against Tasmania. New South Wales, needing 220 to win, were 117 for 7 before Emery and McNamara added 90. McNamara claimed the individual honours as he took his side to victory with four balls to spare.

QUALIFYING TABLE

	P	W	L	Ab	Pts.
New South Wales	5	3	1	1	7
Victoria	5	3	1	1	7
Western Australia	5	3	2	–	6
Queensland	5	3	2	–	6
Tasmania	5	1	4	–	2
South Australia	5	1	4	–	2

Western Australia qualified to meet Victoria in the qualifying final on faster run rate.

QUALIFYING FINAL

13 February 1993 *at MCG, Melbourne*

Victoria 187 for 9 (D.M. Jones 90 not out)
Western Australia 109 (N.D. Maxwell 4 for 13)

Victoria won by 78 runs

Maxwell took the last four Western Australian wickets which went down for nine runs. Jones was Man of the Match.

New South Wales pace bowler Wayne Holdsworth finished the season in storming fashion. His 53 wickets made him leading wicket-taker in the Australian season. (Alan Cozzi)

MERCANTILE MUTUAL CUP FINAL
NEW SOUTH WALES v. VICTORIA, at Sydney

Simon O'Donnell was under much pressure when he led Victoria into the final of the one-day competition. His captaincy had come under ever-increasing criticism, and the voice of approval from those in authority had not been forthcoming. O'Donnell's decision to bat first when he won the toss could not be censured, for Elliott and Nobes began with a stand of 71. Thereafter, things began to go badly for Victoria. Three wickets went down with the score on 82, two of them – top batsmen Jones and Lehmann – to Man of the Match Brad McNamara. O'Donnell helped to revive his side's fortunes in company with Herman, and there was later spirit from Maxwell and Berry to take Victoria to 186.

Small began belligerently for New South Wales, but Slater was less aggressive. He and Matthews were out on the same score, but McNamara helped Bevan to add 58.

MERCANTILE MUTUAL CUP FINAL – NEW SOUTH WALES v. VICTORIA
20 February 1993 at SCG, Sydney

VICTORIA			NEW SOUTH WALES		
M.T. Elliott	st Emery, b Robertson	29	M.J. Slater	c Berry, b Lehmann	54
P.C. Nobes	c Emery, b Robertson	41	S.M. Small	c Elliott, b Sutherland	31
D.M. Jones	c Emery, b McNamara	4	T.H. Bayliss	c Lehmann, b O'Donnell	4
D.S. Lehmann	lbw, b McNamara	0	M.G. Bevan	not out	64
R.J. Herman	c Robertson, b Bayliss	20	G.R.J. Matthews	run out	0
S.P. O'Donnell (capt)	lbw, b Bayliss	13	B.E. McNamara	run out	26
A.I.C. Dodemaide	c Emery, b Stobo	13	A.C. Gilchrist	b Fleming	0
N.D. Maxwell	b McNamara	34	G.R. Robertson	not out	2
*D.S. Berry	not out	21	*P.A. Emery (capt)		
J.A. Sutherland	run out	0	G.D. McGrath		
D.W. Fleming	run out	1	R.M. Stobo		
Extras	b 2, lb 6, w 1, nb 1	10	Extras	b 1, lb 3, w 2	6
(50 overs)		186	(49.4 overs)	(for 6 wickets)	187

	O	M	R	W		O	M	R	W
McGrath	7	1	21	–	Dodemaide	10	2	38	–
Stobo	10	2	49	1	Fleming	9.4	1	36	1
McNamara	10	1	27	3	Sutherland	10	4	27	1
Robertson	10	3	35	2	O'Donnell	7	2	28	1
Matthews	9	1	26	–	Lehmann	8	1	26	1
Bayliss	4	–	20	2	Maxwell	5	–	28	–

FALL OF WICKETS

1–71, 2–82, 3–82, 4–82, 5–114, 6–115, 7–146, 8–180, 9–181

FALL OF WICKETS

1–39, 2–56, 3–120, 4–120, 5–178, 6–183

Umpires: D.J. Hair & C.D. Timmins   Man of the Match: B.E. McNamara   New South Wales won by 4 wickets

Gilchrist fell for a 'duck' before Bevan brought the game to a nerve-racking finish with two balls of New South Wales' quota remaining.

A crowd of 11,070 watched the game. New South Wales took the trophy and $20,000 while Victoria took half that amount. The sponsors promised further bonuses and innovations in the future.

7 February 1993 *at NTCA Ground, Launceston*

Tasmania 224 for 3 (R.T. Ponting 59 not out, J. Cox 57)
England 'A' 200 (G.P. Thorpe 78, D.G. Cork 54)

Tasmania won by 24 runs

8, 9 and 10 February 1993 *at NTCA Ground, Launceston*

England 'A' 420 for 9 dec. (M.N. Lathwell 175, G.P. Thorpe 96, C.D. Matthews 4 for 110) and 92 for 1 dec.
Tasmania 159 for 0 dec. (D.F. Hills 77 not out, N.C.P. Courtney 73 not out) and 288 for 5 (J. Cox 115, D.F. Hills 109)

Match drawn

Having been beaten in the 50-over match, England 'A' gave a better account of themselves in the first-class match against Tasmania which was marred by rain. Thorpe and Lathwell added 184 for the tourists' fourth wicket, the young Somerset player hitting his second, and higher, career century. Hills and Courtney shared an unbroken opening partnership of 159, and when Tasmania batted again Hills shared a second-wicket stand of 202 with Cox.

13, 14, 15 and 16 February 1993 *at MCG, Melbourne*

England 'A' 220 (P.J. Prichard 77) and 286 (G.D. Lloyd 124, G.P. Thorpe 63, S.H. Cook 4 for 43)
Australian Institute of Sport XI 231 (D.F. Hills 66, P.M. Such 7 for 82) and 194 (M.G. Bevan 53, A.R. Caddick 4 for 46, P.M. Such 4 for 62)

England 'A' won by 81 runs

Some fine off-spin bowling by Peter Such and an excellent century from Lloyd gave England 'A' a good win over a team of most promising cricketers, 10 of whom had experience with state sides. The match was not recognised as first-class, however.

19, 20, 21 and 22 February 1993 *at Henzell Park, Caloundra*

England 'A' 287 for 9 dec. (D.J. Capel 80 not out, M.D. Moxon 57) and 104 for 3 dec.
Queensland 296 for 7 dec. (T.J. Barsby 78, M.L. Hayden 66)

Match drawn

In their second first-class game, the England batsmen could not score quickly enough to suggest that a result might be achieved. Barsby and Hayden began Queensland's innings with a stand of 139.

26, 27, 28 February and 1 March 1993 *at Adelaide Oval*

England 'A' 152 (D. Reeves 4 for 56) and 225 (M.D. Moxon 62, P.E. McIntyre 6 for 43)
South Australia 308 for 8 dec. (J.D. Siddons 74, D.S. Webber 55, D.J. Capel 4 for 71) and 70 for 3

South Australia won by 7 wickets

at Woolloongabba, Brisbane

Queensland 172 and 349 for 7 dec. (D.M. Wellham 111 not out, S.G. Law 84, M.L. Hayden 67, W.J. Holdsworth 4 for 127)
New South Wales 174 (S.M. Small 51, C.G. Rackemann 5 for 75) and 147 (G.J. Rowell 5 for 39)

Queensland won by 200 runs

Queensland 6 pts., New South Wales 2 pts.

at MCG, Melbourne

Victoria 225 (D.S. Lehmann 69, S. Young 5 for 56, P.T. McPhee 4 for 71) and 292 for 8 dec. (P.C. Nobes 146 not out)
Tasmania 297 (R.J. Tucker 120, S. Young 76, D.W. Fleming 4 for 47) and 217 for 9 (R.T. Ponting 64, J. Cox 51, C. Howard 4 for 53)

Match drawn

Tasmania 2 pts., Victoria 0 pts.

The England 'A' team continued to struggle through Australia. Against one of the weaker attacks in the Sheffield Shield, they stumbled their way to 152 and conceded a first-innings lead of 156. They lost seven wickets before clearing the arrears as they crumbled before leg-spinner Peter McIntyre who returned the best figures of his career, and South Australia ran out easy winners.

Queensland enhanced their chances of competing in the Shield final when they recovered from a poor first day to beat main rivals New South Wales. Put in to bat and hampered by an injury to Peter Goggin, Queensland were always struggling on the opening day, by the close of which New South Wales were 79 for 1. Rackemann and Kasprowicz brought the home state back into contention on the second morning, and skipper Dirk Wellham hit his first century of the summer after Hayden and Law had shared a third-wicket stand of 104. Queensland did not relax their grip on the game and won early on the last day, with spinner Paul Jackson, playing in his first Shield game for Queensland, supporting Rowell in the execution of New South Wales.

Shaun Young, who had a career-best bowling performance, and Peter McPhee dismissed Victoria on the opening day in Melbourne. Tasmania were 72 for 5 in reply before Tucker and Young added 162. Young, enjoying a fine all-round match, hit the highest score of his career. Paul Nobes hit his second century of the summer, and Jones, leading Victoria in the absence of O'Donnell, set Tasmania to score 221 to win in 66 overs. In an exciting finish, Tasmania finished four short of their target with the last pair together.

4, 5, 6 and 7 March 1993 *at SCG, Sydney*

England 'A' 238 (M.N. Lathwell 103, G.D. Lloyd 60, D.A. Freedman 6 for 89, G.R.J. Matthews 4 for 40) and 208 (R.C. Russell 51 not out, W.J. Holdsworth 5 for 47, D.A. Freedman 4 for 59)

New South Wales 421 for 6 dec. (M.G. Bevan 170, R. Chee Quee 90, T.H. Bayliss 52) and 26 for 0

New South Wales won by 10 wickets

5, 6, 7 and 8 March 1993 *at Adelaide Oval*

South Australia 362 (G.R. Blewett 119, J.A. Brayshaw 91, T.J. Nielsen 64) and 274 (J.A. Brayshaw 110, D.W. Fleming 7 for 90)

Victoria 365 for 8 dec. (W.N. Phillips 122, S.P. O'Donnell 86, D.M. Jones 67, B.N. Wigney 4 for 73) and 261 for 7 (P.C. Nobes 102 not out, W.N. Phillips 65)

Match drawn

Victoria 2 pts., South Australia 0 pts.

at WACA Ground, Perth

Queensland 381 (S.G. Law 116, P.W. Anderson 63, B.P. Julian 5 for 103) and 233 (D.R. Kingdon 59, B.P. Julian 4 for 82)

Western Australia 298 (M.W. McPhee 59, M.R.J. Veletta 55, M.S. Kasprowicz 5 for 64, C.G. Rackemann 4 for 75) and 318 for 3 (T.M. Moody 124, G.R. Marsh 107)

Western Australia won by 7 wickets

Western Australia 6 pts., Queensland 2 pts.

Even a weakened New South Wales side was far too strong for England 'A' who were without injured skipper Martyn Moxon. In spite of Lathwell's admirable second century of the tour, England were perplexed by the combined spin of Matthews and Freedman, who returned the best figures of his career. There followed another career best when Bevan hit 170. On his debut, Richard Chee Quee, the first player of Chinese extraction to play for New South Wales, hit 90 before becoming one of Caddick's three victims. Pace bowler Holdsworth wrecked England's early batting in the second innings and only acting-captain Russell offered significant resistance to Freedman's spin.

Blewett and Brayshaw shared a second-wicket stand of 198 for South Australia against Victoria, Blewett hitting 16 fours in what was his maiden first-class century. Wayne

Phillips' hundred put Victoria in contention, and O'Donnell hit 86 off 142 balls to give his side first-innings points. Brayshaw completed his highest score for South Australia in the second innings, but he was somewhat overshadowed by fast bowler Damien Fleming who, after a rather inconsistent season, returned the best figures of his career, 7 for 90. Needing 272 to win in 47 overs, Victoria were given a fine start by Phillips, and Nobes hit his third century of the summer, but they fell 11 runs short of their target.

Western Australia maintained their challenge for the Shield when they overcame a first-innings deficit of 83 to beat co-challengers Queensland. Stuart Law hit 19 fours in the fifth hundred of his career, and keeper Peter Anderson made a career best 63. Kasprowicz and Rackemann continued their excellent form to bowl Queensland to first-innings points, and eventually the home state were left 88 overs in which to make 317 to win. They lost McPhee through injury, but Geoff Marsh and Tom Moody virtually won the match with a second-wicket stand of 231 in 221 minutes. Marsh hit his fifth century of the season, and Moody his first, and Western Australia won with 10 overs to spare. They were helped in no small measure by Queensland conceding 108 extras in the two innings, 74 of the runs coming from no-balls.

10 March 1993 *at Alice Springs*

Northern Territory 147

England 'A' 148 for 2 (M.A. Roseberry 67 not out)

England 'A' won by 8 wickets

12 March 1993 *at WACA Ground, Perth*

Western Australian Invitation XI 213 for 6 (W.S. Andrews 82, D. Virgo 55)

England 'A' 214 for 5

England 'A' won by 5 wickets

11, 12, 13 and 14 March 1993 *at SCG, Sydney*

South Australia 317 (J.D. Siddons 197, W.J. Holdsworth 7 for 81) and 163 (J.C. Scuderi 57 not out, G.D. McGrath 5 for 36)

New South Wales 393 for 9 dec. (M.G. Bevan 130, G.R.J. Matthews 75, G.R. Blewett 4 for 45) and 88 for 1

New South Wales won by 9 wickets

New South Wales 6 pts., South Australia 0 pts.

at Bellerive Oval, Hobart

Western Australia 321 (T.J. Zoehrer 136, B.P. Julian 87, C.D. Matthews 4 for 77) and 299 (M.R.J. Veletta 104, T.M. Moody 71, T.J. Zoehrer 52)

Tasmania 370 for 7 dec. (R.T. Ponting 107, D.F. Hills 57, N.C.P. Courtney 56, S. Young 50 not out) and 190 for 6 (R.T. Ponting 100 not out)

Match drawn

Tasmania 2 pts., Western Australia 0 pts.

By beating South Australia most convincingly, New South Wales confirmed that they would be playing in the Sheffield Shield final. The South Australian first innings revolved around two heroes, one for each side: Siddons who carried his side on his shoulders with an outstanding knock of 197, and Holdsworth who took 10 wickets in the match in a storming finish to the season. Bevan's second century in succession gave New South Wales a first-innings lead, after which South Australia fell away to leave their opponents with an easy task.

Western Australia's failure in Hobart left them only a slim chance of qualifying to meet New South Wales in the final. They were 75 for 6 before Julian joined Zoehrer in a stand of 196. Zoehrer hit his first century of the season, and Julian bettered the career-best score he had established only a few weeks earlier. They were overshadowed by the exciting young batsman Ricky Ponting who hit a century in each innings.

14, 15, 16 and **17** March 1993 *at WACA Ground, Perth*

England 'A' 293 (G.P. Thorpe 97, C. McDonald 6 for 36) and 300 for 5 dec. (G.D. Lloyd 105, G.P. Thorpe 67, R.C. Russell 58 not out)

Western Australian Invitation XI 192 (M. Goodwin 59) and 141 (A.R. Caddick 5 for 38)

England 'A' won by 260 runs

England 'A' ended their tour with a comfortable win over a weak Western Australian side. The match was not first-class. This had been a low-key and rather disappointing tour for the English party.

18, 19, 20 and **21** March 1993 *at MCG, Melbourne*

New South Wales 182 (M.J. Slater 53, C. Howard 4 for 43) and 351 for 8 dec. (M.J. Slater 143, M.G. Bevan 65, P.A. Emery 58, N.D. Maxwell 4 for 79)

Victoria 258 (S.P. O'Donnell 58, L.D. Harper 53, M.T. Elliott 52, G.R.J. Matthews 6 for 76) and 217 (S.P. O'Donnell 86, D.S. Lehmann 84, W.J. Holdsworth 7 for 52)

New South Wales won by 58 runs

New South Wales 6 pts., Victoria 2 pts.

at Adelaide Oval

Western Australia 323 for 5 dec. (M.R.J. Veletta 104 not out, M.W. McPhee 59, T.J. Zoehrer 51 not out) and 235 for 9 dec. (G.R. Marsh 50, P.R. Sleep 7 for 79)

South Australia 334 for 8 dec. (J.D. Siddons 108, J.A. Brayshaw 82, G.R. Blewett 80, T.M. Moody 4 for 44) and 226 for 1 (G.R. Blewett 112 not out, M.P. Faull 56)

South Australia won by 9 wickets

South Australia 6 pts., Western Australia 0 pts.

at Bellerive Oval, Hobart

Queensland 290 (T.J. Barsby 100, M.L. Hayden 82, P.T. McPhee 4 for 77) and 210 (D.M. Wellham 74, C.D. Matthews 5 for 72)

Tasmania 339 (D.F. Hills 110, D.J. Buckingham 61, S. Young 53, G.J. Rowell 4 for 95) and 162 for 4 (D.F. Hills 50)

Tasmania won by 6 wickets

Tasmania 6 pts., Queensland 0 pts.

At the end of the second day in Melbourne, Victoria looked as if they might avoid the wooden spoon. They had taken a first-innings lead of 76 over New South Wales, who were 86 for 2 in their second innings, but on the third morning, Slater and Emery extended their partnership to 129. Slater reached his third century of the season, hitting 11 fours in his 143 which occupied 367 minutes, and sealed his place on the forthcoming tour of England. Bevan hit fiercely, and Holdsworth produced another outstanding fast-bowling performance to take New South Wales to victory. O'Donnell and Lehmann added 145 for Victoria's fifth wicket, but Fleming, with 10, was the only other batsman to reach double figures.

Where Victoria failed, South Australia succeeded. Mike Veletta dropped down the order to number four and hit his second century of the season in a match which Western Australia had to win to have a hope of retaining the Sheffield Shield. Those hopes were dashed when Siddons and Brayshaw put on 195 for South Australia's third wicket. Siddons' fourth century of the campaign confirmed him as Sheffield Shield Player of the Season. Marsh made every attempt to keep Western Australia in the match, but South Australia raced to victory, scoring 226 in 233 minutes. Blewett hit 112 off 189 balls, his second century of the summer.

Had Western Australia beaten South Australia, they would have won a place in the final, for Tasmania ended their best season in the Sheffield Shield with victory over Queensland in Hobart. Put in to bat, Queensland was given a fine start by Barsby and Hayden who hit 178 in 167 minutes. Thereafter, Queensland fell apart. Hills' patient century, and some excellent work by the late order, took Tasmania to a first-innings lead. Matthews and Miller blunted Queensland's revival, and Tasmania claimed third spot in the Shield table.

SHEFFIELD SHIELD – FINAL TABLE

	P	W	L	D	Pts.
New South Wales	10	5	1	4	34
Queensland	10	3	4	3	26
Tasmania	10	2	1	7	22
Western Australia	10	3	3	4	21
South Australia	10	2	4	4	14
Victoria	10	–	2	8	12

Western Australia deducted one point for slow over rate in two matches.

SHEFFIELD SHIELD FINAL
NEW SOUTH WALES *v.* QUEENSLAND, at Sydney

Queensland did not enter the final on a note of confidence, for they had been beaten in their last two matches. This may have been one reason why Emery asked them to bat when he won the toss. He soon had his reward as Holdsworth sent back Hayden and Wellham with the score on 13. Law and Barsby stopped the slide with a stand of 92, and Law held the innings together, finishing the day on 124 as Queensland reached 226 for 4.

Law was finally caught behind off Matthews, once again the most successful all-rounder in Shield cricket, but his innings, which occupied 223 balls and included a six and 13 fours, had put Queensland in a good position. He was fifth out at 259, but the tail failed to wag hard enough, and when Small and Slater began New South Wales' innings with a partnership of 119, Queensland's hopes began to fade. By the end of the second day, New South Wales were 133 for 2 and beginning to look as if they would take control of the game.

The third day produced batting of great tedium. It was a day of attrition and angry exchanges. In six hours, New South Wales scored 158 runs while four wickets went down. Matthews ended the day with 64 to his credit after batting for 338 minutes; Emery batted 97 minutes for 9. Matthews was finally out for 78 made off 284 balls in 434 minutes, and Emery's 17 came off 147 balls in 197 minutes. Yet both could justify their innings, for New South Wales took a lead of 30, and in 166 minutes, Holdsworth and McGrath had bowled out Queensland for 75. Holdsworth returned the best figures of his career, finished the season as leading wicket-taker and assured himself of a place in the party to tour England.

New South Wales lost Small to his first ball of their second innings, closed on 9 for 1, and won after just half an hour on the fifth day.

SHEFFIELD SHIELD FINAL – NEW SOUTH WALES *v.* QUEENSLAND
26, 27, 28, 29 and 30 March 1993 at SCG, Sydney

QUEENSLAND

	FIRST INNINGS		SECOND INNINGS	
T.J. Barsby	c Emery, b Whitney	51	(2) lbw, b Holdsworth	19
M.L. Hayden	c Bevan, b Holdsworth	4	(1) c Matthews, b Holdsworth	4
D.M. Wellham (capt)	c and b Holdsworth	0	c Emery, b Holdsworth	1
S.G. Law	c Emery, b Matthews	142	c Holdsworth, b McGrath	13
P.J.T. Goggin	lbw, b McGrath	19	c Emery, b Holdsworth	0
M.L. Love	c Emery, b McGrath	42	c Emery, b McGrath	9
*P.W. Anderson	c Whitney, b Matthews	2	b Holdsworth	9
M.S. Kasprowicz	c Slater, b McGrath	7	c Gilchrist, b McGrath	0
G.J. Rowell	b Matthews	26	not out	6
P.W. Jackson	not out	0	c McNamara, b Holdsworth	2
C.G. Rackemann	b McGrath	0	b Holdsworth	4
Extras	lb 5, w 1, nb 12	18	b 4, lb 2, nb 2	8
		311		75

NEW SOUTH WALES

	FIRST INNINGS		SECOND INNINGS	
M.J. Slater	st Anderson, b Jackson	69	c Rackemann, b Kasprowicz	18
S.M. Small	c Rackemann, b Rowell	40	c Hayden, b Kasprowicz	0
A.C. Gilchrist	c Anderson, b Rowell	6	not out	20
M.G. Bevan	b Jackson	10	not out	1
B.E. McNamara	lbw, b Rackemann	29		
G.R.J. Matthews	c Hayden, b Jackson	78		
T.H. Bayliss	run out	26		
*P.A. Emery (capt)	c Barsby, b Rackemann	17		
W.J. Holdsworth	not out	10		
M.R. Whitney	b Kasprowicz	7		
G.D. McGrath	c Anderson, b Kasprowicz	0		
Extras	b 5, lb 12, nb 32	49	w 3, nb 4	7
		341	(for 2 wickets)	46

	O	M	R	W	O	M	R	W
Holdsworth	18	5	43	2	19	8	41	7
McGrath	24.5	5	64	4	18	5	28	3
Whitney	22	7	55	1				
Matthews	19	4	89	3				
McNamara	11	1	55	–				

	O	M	R	W	O	M	R	W
Rackemann	37	5	92	2	6.2	1	23	–
Rowell	38	11	65	2				
Kasprowicz	30.5	9	67	2	6	1	23	2
Jackson	69	34	91	3				
Law	9	3	9	–				

FALL OF WICKETS

1–13, 2–13, 3–105, 4–184, 5–259, 6–269, 7–277, 8–298, 9–310
1–12, 2–18, 3–39, 4–39, 5–42, 6–50, 7–58, 8–58, 9–67

FALL OF WICKETS

1–119, 2–124, 3–134, 4–146, 5–195, 6–261, 7–320, 8–322, 9–341
1–0, 2–45

Umpires: D.B. Hair, T.A. Prue & S.G. Randell

New South Wales won by 8 wickets

Stuart Law – a century for Queensland in the Sheffield Shield final, but still the trophy eludes them. (David Munden/Sports-Line)

NEW SOUTH WALES
FIRST-CLASS MATCHES 1992–3
BATTING

	v. Victoria (Sydney) 6–9 November 1992	v. Western Australia (Perth) 14–17 December 1992	v. West Indians (Sydney) 20–3 November 1992	v. Tasmania (Hobart) 27–30 November 1992	v. Queensland (Sydney) 11–14 December 1992	v. South Australia (Adelaide) 18–21 December 1992	v. Tasmania (Sydney) 27–30 January 1993	v. Western Australia (Sydney) 3–6 February 1993	v. Queensland (Brisbane) 26 Feb.–1 March 1993	v. England 'A' (Sydney) 4–7 March 1993
S.M. Small	12 1	0 10	23 8	1 88	0 45		0 —	64 41	51 47	
M.A. Taylor	102 42	12 2	101 —			63 38				
S.R. Waugh	0 36		22 —			38 4				
M.E. Waugh	88 2	46 35	200* —			164 8*	76 —	103 44*	3 10	170
M.G. Bevan	68 7*	11 25	40 17*	21 33	8 19		18 —	7 28*	23 1	6*
G.R.J. Matthews	6 54	18 65*	20 —			53 33				
P.A. Emery	7 22	5 —	29* 4*	0 62*	23 36*	— 7	47* —	0 —	26* 19*	15 —
M.R. Whitney		6 —		1* —						
W.J. Holdsworth		4* —		8 —	0 —		17 —	4 —	0 4	
P.J.S. Alley		1 —		35 35	1 3					
D.A. Freedman	11* 5*			3 0*	5 —		12 —	32* —		
T.H. Bayliss	64 3	52 21		22 14	107 3	37* 16	0 —	11 29	10 1	52 —
B.E. McNamara		35 45*		1 9	98* 55*	23* 8	51 —	4 —	2 13	22* —
M.J. Slater				138 24	61 72	0 82	79 —	124 38	22 33	2 12*
M.T. Haywood				34 4	0 5					
G.R. Robertson					48 —					
A.C. Gilchrist							16 —	75 —	19 1	47 —
G.D. McGrath							—	— —	0 8	— —
S. Lee								4 —		
R.M. Stobo									6 0	
R. Chee Quee										90 10*
Byes	5		1	1	2		4	3	1	
Leg-byes	8 3	2 10	20 2	7 12	5 3	4 1	8	2 4	3 9	10 4
Wides			1	1 1		1 1	4	1	1	1
No-balls	6 4	28 16	16 3	4	26 4	16 6	6	18 2	8	6
Total	377 179	220 229	473 34	272 287	382 247	399 204	338	452 186	174 147	421 26
Wickets	8 7	10 5	5 1	10 7	10 6	5 7	9	10 3	10 10	6 0
Result	D	W	D	D	D	W	D	W	L	W
Points	0	6	—	0	0	6	2	6	2	—

BOWLING

	W.J. Holdsworth	M.R. Whitney	P.J.S. Alley	G.R.J. Matthews	D.A. Freedman	S.R. Waugh	M.G. Bevan	M.E. Waugh
v. Victoria (Sydney) 6–9 November 1992	26–3–101–0	37–5–122–4		40–11–116–1	32–8–81–1	27–6–90–3		8–0–17–0
v. Western Australia (Perth) 14–17 November 1992	5–1–16–0, 16–2–55–2	19–3–43–5, 27–9–72–3	17.4–4–43–5, 17–4–47–2	10–0–44–0, 15–6–34–1				5–0–30–0
v. West Indians (Sydney) 20–3 November 1992	11–1–53–2, 11–0–80–1	14–4–40–1, 14–2–55–0	10–4–11–2, 10–0–58–1	11.1–2–49–2, 49.3–12–148–4	5–1–26–3	19–4–64–1	6–0–40–0	
v. Tasmania (Hobart) 27–30 November 1992	23–2–108–4	30–5–96–2	24–6–64–1	3–0–20–0	25–3–82–1		1–1–0–0	
v. Queensland (Sydney) 11–14 December 1992	9–1–41–1, 22–3–106–2	19–4–55–3	3–0–20–0, 2–0–6–0	21–5–74–1	16–1–69–1, 27–5–72–3		1–0–10–0, 8–1–32–0	
v. South Australia (Adelaide) 18–21 December 1992			22–8–46–0, 24–5–76–1	19–4–68–3, 17–1–68–3	32.5–19–25–4, 39.1–5–113–2	15.5–4–21–1, 17–4–67–2	6–2–11–0, 8–3–30–0	
v. Tasmania (Sydney) 27–30 January 1993	23–5–74–2			46–15–78–3	14–3–41–0	22–3–80–1	9–1–25–0	
v. Western Australia (Sydney) 3–6 February 1993	17–4–41–0, 22–4–80–0			54–31–61–5	15–4–62–1	23–3–73–1	4–2–17–0	
v. Queensland (Brisbane) 26 February–1 March 1993	5–0–24–0, 17.2–5–41–2			38–14–77–1, 26.2–10–52–8	16–3–42–1			
v. England 'A' (Sydney) 4–7 March 1993	25.5–2–127–4, 14–4–44–0			17–5–40–4, 25–9–61–1	28.2–6–89–6	7–1–48–0	1–1–0–0	
v. South Australia (Sydney) 11–14 March 1993	16–1–47–5, 25.2–3–81–7			17–0–64–0, 10–4–33–0	7–1–48–0			
v. Victoria (Melbourne) 18–21 March 1993	16–0–62–3, 12–1–48–2	15–4–58–0		31–11–76–6, 19–4–45–1				
v. Queensland (Sydney) 26–30 March 1993	17.4–2–52–7, 18–5–43–2, 19–8–41–7	15–4–41–1, 22–7–55–1		19–4–89–3				
Bowler's average	374.1–57–1376–53 25.96	258–60–759–21 36.14	140.4–28–459–18 26.06	516–165–1247–47 26.53	297.2–62–955–26 36.73	57–14–174–3 58.00	30–6–124–0 —	13–0–47–0 —

		(Sydney) 11–14 March 1993	v. Victoria (Melbourne) 18–21 March 1993	v. Queensland (Sydney) 26–30 March 1993	M	Inns	NO	Runs	HS	Av
26	21	9	40	0	11	21	–	499	88	23.76
					4	7	–	360	102	51.42
					3	5	–	100	38	20.00
					4	7	2	543	200*	108.60
–	14	65	10	1*	12	21	4	875	170	51.47
–	22	9	78	–	11	17	3	516	78	36.85
	0	58	17	–	13	19	7	406	62*	33.83
	9	0*	7	–	7	5	2	23	9	7.66
	6	0	10*	–	12	11	3	57	17	7.12
					5	5	–	75	35	15.00
–					9	8	4	77	32*	19.25
			26	–	10	17	1	468	107	29.25
–	18	15*	29	–	11	17	6	477	98*	43.36
48*	53	143	69	18	10	19	2	1019	143	59.94
					2	4	–	43	34	10.75
					1	1	–	48	48	48.00
13*	13	28	6	20*	7	11	2	274	75	30.44
–	6*		0	–	6	4	1	274	75	30.44
					1	1	–	14	8	4.66
					1	1	–	4	4	4.00
–	20	18			1	2	–	6	6	3.00
		1	5							
1		1	12							
		2		3						
		2	32	4						
88	182	351	341	46						
1	10	8	10	2						
W	W	W								
6	6			–						

FIELDING FIGURES

54 – P.A. Emery (ct 52/st 2)
14 – S.M. Small and G.R.J. Matthews
10 – B.E. McNamara
9 – T.H. Bayliss, M.J. Slater and A.C. Gilchrist
8 – M.G. Bevan
6 – W.J. Holdsworth
4 – S.R. Waugh, D.A. Freedman and P.J.S. Alley
3 – M.A. Taylor, M.R. Whitney and R. Chee Quee
2 – M.E. Waugh, R.M. Stobo and subs

M.A. Taylor	B.E. McNamara	T.H. Bayliss	G.R. Robertson	G.D. McGrath	S. Lee	R.M. Stobo	Byes	Leg-byes	Wides	No-balls	Total	Wkts
-0-9-0							1	10		22	547	9
	1-0-8-0							5		4	159	10
	14-5-43-2							5		27	286	10
								4	2		183	10
17-4-43-1		3-1-2-0					2	17	1	4	507	9
22-4-80-2		11-5-10-0					3	5	2	14	403	10
22.5-4-68-4		8-2-25-1	21-4-72-1					5		12	211	6
2-0-5-0		4-0-17-0	38-7-104-6				5	18		14	447	10
	8-4-14-2						7	2		8	256	9
5-0-19-0		1-0-4-0					1	8	1	24	215	10
9-3-14-0				29.1-9-79-5				2		22	379	10
13.3-4-23-2		10-4-29-0		13.3-6-29-0			1	5	1	8	292	10
31-7-91-3		22-7-64-4			15-3-66-1			7	1	2	295	9
					2-0-8-0		3	7	1	22	467	10
21-9-46-3				19-6-50-2		13-5-28-1	6	5	1	2	168	10
12-1-33-1		4-0-9-0		19-3-82-1		16-3-49-0	4	3		12	172	10
6-3-10-0				16-4-47-0			4	3		16	349	7
		3-1-11-0		5-0-12-0				8		6	238	10
17-2-58-0				23-5-62-3			9	9	1	2	208	10
9-1-29-2				17.3-4-36-5				4		10	317	10
12.2-3-21-1				15-4-50-1			2	1		2	163	10
4-2-13-0				16-3-59-1			2	3		2	258	10
11-1-55-0				24.5-5-64-4				7		2	217	10
								5	1	12	311	10
				18-5-28-3			4	2		2	75	10
237.4-57-		66-20-	59-11-	216-54-	17-3-	29-8-						
673-23		171-5	176-7	598-25	74-1	77-1						
29.26		34.20	25.14	23.92	74.00	77.00						

QUEENSLAND FIRST-CLASS MATCHES 1992–3

BATTING

Batting	v. Western Australia (Brisbane) 21–4 October 1992		v. South Australia (Brisbane) 6–9 November 1992		v. Victoria (St Kilda) 20–3 November 1992		v. New South Wales (Sydney) 1–14 December 1992		v. Pakistanis (Brisbane) 19–22 December 1992		v. South Australia (Adelaide) 8–11 January 1993		v. Tasmania (Brisbane) 21–3 January 1993		v. Victoria (Brisbane) 28–31 January 1993		v. England 'A' (Caloundra) 22–2 February 1993		v. New South Wales (Brisbane) 26 Feb.–1 March 1993	
T.J. Barsby	1	7	49	–	35	0	34	123	53	116	26	1	8	39	20	81	78	–	14	0
M.L. Hayden	8	63	77	–	51	28	25	30	79	34	161*	35*	46	46	15	112	66	–	4	67
P.J.T. Goggin	46	15	120	–	25	45	68	2	6	2	34	4*	6	0	24	30	33	–	11*	7
S.G. Law	28	41	69	–	0	2	79	10	21	15	13	–			37	36	35	–	9	84
A.R. Border	23	53	12	–	71	21			22	116*										
S.C. Storey	7	23	21	–	0	20	103	8	29*	26	0	–	6	19	10	12				
I.A. Healy	49	39	53*	–	3	16			15	14	9	2*								
C.J. McDermott	4	5	25	–	26	10			9	2*										
M.S. Kasprowicz	35	3	20*	–	2	0	27*	22	2	–	18*	–	39	0	4	–	3	–	2	13
A.J. Bichel	0	9															13*	–		
D. Tazelaar	3*	3*	–	–	0*	–	37	3*			–	–	5	8*	1	–				
G.J. Rowell			–	–	2*	0*	0	4*	4	–			8	10					40	–
D.M. Wellham							12	0	16	49	56	–	9	4	28	2	42*	–	7	111*
P.W. Anderson							2	0			2	–	16	3	24	17			6	40
B.N.J. Oxenford							23	37			3	–								
C.G. Rackemann											–	–	4*	1					0	–
D.R. Kingdon													0	1	27*	12*	4	–	47	4
W.A. Seccombe																	5	–		
P.W. Jackson																	–	–	13	–
M.L. Love																				
Byes		4					5	7		8	7					1			4	4
Leg-byes	7	10	11		5	2	18	2	3	5	7	1	3	3	7	15	15		3	3
Wides			4							1	3		2	1	2					
No-balls	10	8	24			2	14	8	1	10	5	2	16	26	2	4	2		12	16
Total	221	283	485		222	144	447	256	260	398	335	43	168	162	201	321	296		172	349
Wickets	10	10	7		9	9	10	9	10	7	7	1	10	10	10	7	7		10	7
Result	L		W		D		D		L		D		L		W		D		W	
Points	0		6		2		2		–		2		0		6		–		6	

BOWLING

Bowling	C.J. McDermott	D. Tazelaar	M.S. Kasprowicz	A.J. Bichel	S.C. Storey	G.J. Rowell	A.R. Border	B.N.J. Oxenford
v. Western Australia (Brisbane) 21–4 October 1992	34–6–115–1 / 23–7–54–2	29–8–78–3 / 7–2–23–2	21.5–3–50–2 / 8–1–27–0	18–3–67–2 / 3–0–19–0	16–5–53–0 / 22.5–6–55–5			
v. South Australia (Brisbane) 6–9 November 1992	18.4–4–48–4 / 31–9–64–4	19–7–39–4 / 23–6–49–1	7–1–29–0 / 17–7–40–2		10–3–24–0 / 17–5–30–1	14–6–28–2 / 18–4–46–2		
v. Victoria (St Kilda) 20–3 November 1992	15–3–46–1 / 8–3–15–0	6–1–33–0 / 3–1–2–0			27.3–13–35–2	12–6–28–2 / 10–1–31–5	21–6–46–5	
v. New South Wales (Sydney) 11–14 December 1992		22.4–7–63–3 / 8–2–33–1	30–9–70–3 / 8–0–59–0		24–6–65–1 / 16–5–38–1	30–3–101–3 / 7–0–31–0		20–5–78–0 / 16–2–70–4
v. Pakistanis (Brisbane) 19–22 December 1992	26–4–95–1 / 17–5–50–1		24–6–70–2 / 17.2–4–60–3		21–1–105–1 / 15–1–67–1	26–6–68–0 / 8–1–37–0	3–0–16–0 / 11–2–45–0	
v. South Australia (Adelaide) 8–11 January 1993		31.4–7–89–4 / 14–5–35–2	31–7–76–3 / 20–7–44–1		19–2–77–1 / 35–16–72–2			5–0–32–0 / 18–1–72–4
v. Tasmania (Brisbane) 21–3 January 1993		29–12–62–0	25.3–6–59–6		16–1–59–0	23–6–47–1		
v. Victoria (Brisbane) 28–31 January 1993		21–8–40–1 / 11–3–18–1	21–6–41–2 / 20–5–61–5		6–1–17–0 / 7–2–12–1			
v. England 'A' (Caloundra) 20–2 February 1993			26–5–64–3 / 5–0–28–0	16–2–64–1 / 6–0–29–1				
v. New South Wales (Brisbane) 26 February–1 March 1993			17–3–41–3 / 13–3–40–1			13–3–39–1 / 17–6–39–5		
v. Western Australia (Perth) 5–8 March 1993			24–7–64–5 / 17–3–63–1			18–5–61–0 / 14.1–2–66–0		
v. Tasmania (Hobart) 18–21 March 1993			30.4–6–91–1 / 4–1–22–0			27–7–95–4 / 8.4–2–37–1		
v. New South Wales (Sydney) 26–30 March 1993			30.5–9–67–2 / 6–1–23–2			38–11–65–2 / 6.2–1–23–0		
Totals	172.4–41–487–14	224.2–69–564–22	435.1–100–1231–51	43–5–179–4	252.2–67–709–16	290.1–70–842–28	35–8–107–5	59–8–252–4
Bowler's average	34.78	25.63	24.13	44.75	44.31	30.07	21.40	63.00

					M	Inns	NO	Runs	HS	Av
			(Western Australia) (Perth) 5–8 March 1993	v. Tasmania (Hobart) 18–21 March	v. New South Wales (Sydney) 26–30 March 1993					
3	28	100	12	51	19	13	24	–	908	123	37.83
9	30	82	34	4	4	13	24	2	1150	161*	52.70
4	32	14	5	19	0	13	24	2	572	120	26.00
5	15	21	37	142	13	12	21	–	823	142	39.19
						4	7	1	318	116*	53.00
						8	14	1	284	103	21.84
						4	7	1	189	53*	31.50
						4	7	1	81	26	13.50
)	0	5	21	7	0	13	21	3	233	39	12.94
						2	3	1	22	13*	11.00
						7	8	5	60	37	20.00
3	30	0	6	26	6*	9	14	4	139	40	13.90
5	14	4	74	0	1	10	18	2	465	111*	29.06
3	0	35	6	2	9	8	15	–	225	63	15.00
						2	3	–	63	37	21.00
5	6*	3*	3	0	4	8	10	3	27	6*	3.85
9	59	5	1			6	11	2	169	59	18.77
						1	1	–	5	5	5.00
5*	5	5	3*	0*	2	5	7	3	33	13	8.25
				42	9	1	2	–	51	42	25.50
2	2				4						
8		7	6	5	2						
5		1	2	1							
2	12	8		12	2						
1	233	290	210	311	75						
0	10	10	10	10	10						
L		L		L							
2		0		–							

FIELDING FIGURES

29 – P.W. Anderson (ct 26/st 3)
20 – M.L. Hayden
15 – P.J.T. Goggin
14 – I.A. Healy (ct 13/st 1)
10 – S.G. Law
9 – D.M. Wellham
6 – T.J. Barsby, M.S. Kasprowicz, G.J. Rowell and D.R. Kingdon
4 – B.N.J. Oxenford, C.G. Rackemann and W.A. Seccombe (ct 3/st 1)
3 – S.C. Storey and D. Tazelaar
2 – P.W. Jackson
1 – C.J. McDermott and A.J. Bichel

S.G. Law	C.G. Rackemann	M.L. Hayden	P.W. Jackson	D.M. Wellham	Byes	Leg-byes	Wides	No-balls	Total	Wkts
						7		2	370	10
						6		6	184	10
					4	6			178	10
					5	12		4	246	10
					3	4		12	195	10
					3	2	4	8	95	9
						5		13	382	10
2–0–11–0					2	3		4	247	6
8–4–12–1						2		1	368	6
4–0–23–0					5	4		3	291	5
	19–5–55–2					4		31	333	10
5–1–16–1	21–1–60–2				6	5		18	310	9
	23–4–82–3				10	16	1	28	335	10
16–4–25–3	20–8–24–4	2–1–1–0			1	6		6	155	10
6–1–14–0	19.5–6–50–3					1		23	156	10
21–10–45–3	11.1–1–25–1		25–4–67–1	1–0–8–0	4	10	1	30	287	9
	5–0–26–0		7–1–19–1			2	2	12	104	3
4–1–7–1	15.3–0–75–5		8–3–9–0			3	1	8	174	10
	12–4–31–1		21.3–13–27–3		1	9			147	10
16–9–35–0	21–3–75–4		16–3–49–1		4	10	2	40	298	10
14–2–56–0	17–2–61–2		15–1–55–0		7	10	1	34	318	3
5–0–14–0	26–5–67–1		32–12–60–2			12		12	339	10
	10–1–51–3		13–1–50–0			2	1	4	162	4
9–3–9–0	37–5–92–2		69–34–91–3		5	12		32	341	10
							3	4	46	2
111–35–	257.3–45–	2–1–	206.3–72–	1–0–						
267–9	774–33	1–0	427–11	8–0						
29.66	23.45	–	38.81	–						

SOUTH AUSTRALIA
FIRST-CLASS MATCHES 1992–3
BATTING

Player	v. Queensland (Brisbane) 6–9 Nov 1992		v. Tasmania (Adelaide) 20–3 Nov 1992		v. Western Australia (Perth) 11–14 Dec 1992		v. New South Wales (Adelaide) 18–21 Dec 1992		v. Queensland (Adelaide) 8–11 Jan 1993		v. Tasmania (Hobart) 15–18 Jan 1993		v. Victoria (Melbourne) 3–6 Feb 1993		v. England 'A' (Adelaide) 26 Feb–1 Mar 1993		v. Victoria (Adelaide) 5–8 Mar 1993		v. New South Wales (Sydney) 11–14 Mar 1993	
G.R. Blewett	17	50	23	43	17	25	39	71	30	1	19	0	47	69	14	23	119	19	6	10
N.R. Fielke	21	23	6	74	55	0	12	48	19	57										
J.A. Brayshaw	49	32	23	73*			17	38	7	23	42	36	4	65	49	7	91	110	19	15
J.D. Siddons	30	15	25	69*	67	189*	3	21	75	53	16	56	100	58	74	–	28	6	197	0
G.A. Bishop	7	27	50	–	20	2					41	56	2	10					11	7
T.J. Nielsen	2	30	109	–	28	8	1	84	10	0	36	15	63*	34	20	15*	64	20	0	0
P.R. Sleep	18*	11	13	–	47	44*	6	23	17	38	6	3*	17	6	11	–	4	41	27	36
T.B.A. May	0	18*	3*	–			11	3			9	–								
P. Hutchison	5	2																		
P.W. Gladigau	15	5																		
D.J. Hickey	4	12	–		34	–	0	1*							–	–	0*	2		
J.C. Scuderi			100*	–	0	0	44	50	4	31	0	14*	19	24*					6	57*
D.A. Reeves			–	–	10	–	12*	14	0	1	2*	–	10*	3	12*	–	29	1	24	0
D.J. Ritossa					37*	–														
D.S. Webber							36	2	135	77	43	89	7	17	55	12*	12	29	9	30
B.N. Wigney									1	0*	3	–	–	2*	17	–	1	4	4	0
P.E. McIntyre									0*	–							1	2*	0*	3
A.J. Hammond															23	6	2	31		
M.P. Faull																				
G.J. Wright																				
S.P. George																				
Byes	4	5	1	1		9	1			6	1				2		3	1		2
Leg-byes	6	12	9	5	9	4	8	2	4	5	7	12	5	7	5	1	8	2	4	1
Wides				1		1	1				8	1	2	1						
No-balls		4	6	2	8		24	22	31	18	38	32	2	10	26	6		6	10	2
Total	178	246	368	268	409	284	215	379	333	310	271	314	278	306	308	70	362	274	317	163
Wickets	10	10	7	2	10	6	10	10	10	9	10	6	7	8	8	3	10	10	10	10
Result	L		W		L		L		D		D		D		W		D		L	
Points	0		6		2		0		0		0		0		—		0		0	

BOWLING

Match	D.J. Hickey	P. Hutchison	T.B.A. May	P.W. Gladigau	P.R. Sleep	G.R. Blewett	D. Reeves	J.C. Scuderi
v. Queensland (Brisbane) 6–9 November 1992	27-4-120-4	11-3-40-1	33-7-106-1	33-9-116-0	21-2-86-1	1-0-6-0		
v. Tasmania (Adelaide) 20–3 November 1992	18-4-75-3		35-9-80-2		10-0-33-0	1-1-0-0	15-1-60-1	10-0-44-0
	14-1-37-1		32.4-15-42-5		8-5-3-1		13-5-27-2	9-5-11-1
v. Western Australia (Perth) 11–14 December 1992	26-6-68-0				32-13-59-4	10-2-28-1	19-2-73-0	18-6-54-0
	25-0-134-2				14-1-62-0	8-1-38-0	6-1-28-1	17.2-0-99-0
v. New South Wales (Adelaide) 18–21 December 1992	8-1-60-0		23-3-99-1		23-1-84-0	5-2-6-0	12-2-70-2	21-4-76-2
	5-0-25-0		24-5-66-4		16.4-1-64-2		8-0-36-0	5-2-12-0
v. Queensland (Adelaide) 8–11 January 1993					40-10-80-4		8-0-38-0	21-4-59-1
							7-1-30-1	
v. Tasmania (Hobart) 15–18 January 1993			56-20-101-3		29-5-83-0	9-1-35-0	26-10-66-3	24-4-79-0
v. Victoria (Melbourne) 3–6 February 1993					24-7-60-0	4-0-8-0	22-4-72-1	18-2-83-2
						8-0-52-2	7.4-0-60-3	9-0-44-0
v. England 'A' (Adelaide) 26 February–1 March 1993	13-4-34-3				14-7-11-2		13.4-2-56-4	
	16-2-38-1				37-13-61-1		18-2-54-0	
v. Victoria (Adelaide) 5–8 March 1993	12-0-67-1				14-1-45-0		17-1-75-2	
	4-0-23-0						4-0-21-0	
v. New South Wales (Sydney) 11–14 March 1993					2-0-22-0	15.2-2-45-4	14-1-83-2	21-4-60-1
					10-2-24-0	2-1-3-0	5-1-27-0	
v. Western Australia (Adelaide) 18–21 March 1993					11-2-37-0	16-5-42-1		18-5-34-1
					22-5-79-7	7-4-17-0		7-0-23-1
Bowler's average	168-22-681-15 45.40	11-3-40-1 40.00	203.4-59-494-16 30.87	33-9-116-0 –	327.4-75-893-22 40.59	86.2-19-280-8 35.00	215.2-33-876-22 39.81	198.2-36-678-9 75.33

v. Western Australia (Adelaide) 18–21 March 1993		M	Inns	NO	Runs	HS	Av
80	112*	11	22	1	834	119	39.71
		5	10	–	315	74	31.50
82	47*	11	22	2	908	110	45.40
108	–	11	20	2	1190	197	66.11
		6	11	–	233	56	21.18
2	–	11	20	2	541	109	30.05
3	–	11	19	3	371	47	23.18
		4	6	2	44	18*	11.00
		1	2	–	7	5	3.50
		1	2	–	20	15	10.00
		6	7	2	53	34	10.60
0	–	8	14	4	349	100*	34.90
		9	13	4	118	29	13.11
		1	1	1	37	37*	–
0	–	8	15	1	553	135	39.50
0*	–	7	10	3	32	17	4.57
		5	5	3	6	3	3.00
		2	4	–	62	31	15.50
31	56	1	2	–	87	56	43.50
10*	–	1	1	1	10	10*	–
–	–	1					

3	
5	11
4	
6	
334	226
8	1
W	
6	

D. Ritossa	B.N. Wigney	P.E. McIntyre	D. Webber	T.J. Nielsen	J.A. Brayshaw	S.P. George	Byes	Leg-byes	Wides	No-balls	Total	Wkts
							11	4		24	485	7
							6	10		45	298	6
							3	3		6	123	10
5–1–14–0							8	1		20	304	6
5–0–18–0							13	1		10	392	7
							4	1		16	399	5
							1	1		6	204	7
	22–4–68–0	47.2–17–76–2					7	7	3	5	335	7
	6–3–7–0		1–0–2–0	1–0–3–0				1		2	43	1
	27–4–77–1						3	10		12	454	7
	22–2–78–1	36–10–100–3						5	3	14	406	8
	10–0–43–1							2	6	2	201	7
	16–4–29–0	8–4–16–0						6	1	6	152	10
	17–7–21–1	29–13–43–6			1–1–0–1			8	1	4	225	10
	27–7–73–4	39.3–10–92–1			1–0–1–0		7	5	3	12	365	8
	23–2–113–3	16–0–102–3					1	1	1		261	7
	30–1–96–2	26–6–74–0			4–1–8–0			5	3	8	393	9
	7–2–12–0	10.1–3–21–1						1			88	1
	29–4–98–1				11–5–26–0	30–6–76–1	1	9	5	4	323	5
	21–8–44–1					20–3–63–0	2	7		2	235	9
10–1–32–0 / –	257–48–759–15 / 50.60	212–63–524–16 / 32.75	1–0–2–0 / –	1–0–3–0 / –	17–7–35–1 / 35.00	50–9–139–1 / 139.00						

TASMANIA FIRST-CLASS MATCHES 1992–3

BATTING

	v. South Australia (Adelaide) 20–3 Nov 1992		v. New South Wales (Hobart) 27–30 Nov 1992		v. Western Australia (Perth) 18–21 Dec 1992		v. Victoria (Hobart) 31 Dec. 1992–3 Jan. 1993		v. South Australia (Hobart) 15–18 Jan 1993		v. Queensland (Brisbane) 21–3 Jan 1993		v. New South Wales (Sydney) 27–30 Jan 1993		v. England 'A' (Launceston) 8–10 Feb 1993		v. Victoria (Melbourne) 26 Feb.–1 Mar 1993		v. Western Australia (Hobart) 11–14 Mar 1993	
D.F. Hills	16	20	48	87	138	–	5	1	55	–	6	–	3	101	77*	109	8	12	57	0
N.C.P. Courtney	16	43	60	2	58	–	32	88	4	–	3	–	20	8	73*	27	10	14	56	12
D.C. Boon	60	8			38	–														
R.T. Ponting	56	4	32	18	25	–	6	41	50	–	11	–	125	69	–	1	34	64	107	100*
J. Cox	11	18	0	73			19	64	0	–	137*	–	33	1	–	115	6	51	45	22
R.J. Tucker	49*	6	104	2*	32	–	0	50	2	–	27	–	3	3	–	2	120	9	16	21
S. Young	0	7	43	–	29*	–	0	9	60	–	20	–	23	18			76	11	50*	0
C.D. Matthews	29*	4	20	4	3	–	29*	1*	–	–	0	–	0	18*	–	–	19*	3	–	–
M.N. Atkinson	–	1	1	–	28	–	45	15*	23*	–	9	–	23	46	–	12*	6	7*	2*	7*
C.R. Miller	–	0*	11	3	0	–													3	–
P.T. McPhee	–	0					4	–			15	–	1*	0*			0	0*		
B.A. Cruse			7	5*																
M.G. Farrell			53*	–			4	26	74	–			17	3			0	8		
D.J. Buckingham					60	–	41	6	161*	–	51	–	29	18	–	6*	2	6	15	18
T.J. Cooley											1	–			–	–				
D.J. Castle															–	–				
Byes			3		3		6	3	10				1		1	1	2	11	3	
Leg-byes	6	3	5	5	23		5	11	10		16		5	7	4	8	11	6	11	2
Wides	10	3	2		2				1				1	1	1		1	1	2	1
No-balls	45	6	14	12	18		14	14	12		28		8	2	4	6	2	14	6	4
Total	298	123	403	211	457		204	332	454		385		292	295	159	288	297	217	370	190
Wickets	6	10	10	6	10		10	8	7		10		10	9	0	5	10	9	7	6
Result	L		D		D		D		D		W		D		D		D		D	
Points	0		2		2		0		2		6		0		–		2		2	

BOWLING

	D.J. Hickey	P. Hutchison	T.B.A. May	P.W. Gladigau	P.R. Sleep	G.R. Blewett	D. Reeves	J.C. Scuderi
v. Queensland (Brisbane) 6–9 November 1992	27–4–120–4	11–3–40–1	33–7–106–1	33–9–116–0	21–2–86–1	1–0–6–0		
v. Tasmania (Adelaide) 20–3 November 1992	18–4–75–3		35–9–80–2		10–0–33–0	1–1–0–0	15–1–60–1	10–0–44–0
	14–1–37–1		32.4–15–42–5		8–5–3–1		13–5–27–2	9–5–11–1
v. Western Australia (Perth) 11–14 December 1992	26–6–68–0				32–13–59–4	10–2–28–1	19–2–73–0	18–6–54–0
	25–0–134–2				14–1–62–0	8–1–38–0	6–1–28–1	17.2–0–99–0
v. New South Wales (Adelaide) 18–21 December 1992	8–1–60–0		23–3–99–1		23–1–84–0	5–2–6–0	12–2–70–2	21–4–76–2
	5–0–25–0		24–5–66–4		16.4–1–64–2		8–0–36–0	5–2–12–0
v. Queensland (Adelaide) 8–11 January 1993					40–10–80–4		8–0–38–0	21–4–59–1
							7–1–30–1	
v. Tasmania (Hobart) 15–18 January 1993			56–20–101–3		29–5–83–0	9–1–35–0	26–10–66–3	24–4–79–0
v. Victoria (Melbourne) 3–6 February 1993					24–7–60–0	4–0–8–0	22–4–72–1	18–2–83–2
						8–0–52–2	7.4–0–60–3	9–0–44–0
v. England 'A' (Adelaide) 26 February–1 March 1993	13–4–34–3				14–7–11–2		13.4–2–56–4	
	16–2–38–1				37–13–61–1		18–2–54–0	
v. Victoria (Adelaide) 5–8 March 1993	12–0–67–1				14–1–45–0		17–1–75–2	
	4–0–23–0						4–0–21–0	
v. New South Wales (Sydney) 11–14 March 1993					2–0–22–0	15.2–2–45–4	14–1–83–2	21–4–60–1
					10–2–24–0	2–1–3–0	5–1–27–0	
v. Western Australia (Adelaide) 18–21 March 1993					11–2–37–0	16–5–42–1		18–5–34–1
					22–5–79–7	7–4–17–0		7–0–23–1
Bowler's average	168–22–681–15 45.40	11–3–40–1 40.00	203.4–59–494–16 30.87	33–9–116–0 –	327.4–75–893–22 40.59	86.2–19–280–8 35.00	215.2–33–876–22 39.81	198.2–36–678–9 75.33

v. Queensland (Hobart) 18–21 March 1993		M	Inns	NO	Runs	HS	Av
110	50	11	19	1	903	138	50.16
5	37	11	19	1	568	88	31.55
		2	3	–	106	60	35.33
12	27	11	18	1	782	125	46.00
0	11	10	17	1	606	137*	37.87
14	3*	11	18	3	463	120	30.86
53	–	10	15	2	399	76	30.69
35	–	11	13	5	165	35	20.62
16	–	11	15	6	241	46	26.77
9*	–	5	6	2	26	11	6.50
0	–	8	8	3	20	15	4.00
		1	2	1	12	7	12.00
		5	8	1	185	74	26.42
61	27*	9	14	3	501	161*	45.54
		3	1	–	1	1	1.00
		1					–
12	2						
	1						
12	4						
339	162						
10	4						
W							
6							

FIELDING FIGURES

32 – M.N. Atkinson (ct 31/st 1)
12 – R.J. Tucker
10 – D.J. Buckingham
9 – R.T. Ponting and N.C.P. Courtney
7 – J. Cox
6 – D.F. Hills
5 – S. Young
4 – M.G. Farrell and subs
3 – P.T. McPhee
2 – B.A. Cruse and C.D. Matthews
1 – D.C. Boon and D.J. Castle

D. Ritossa	B.N. Wigney	P.E. McIntyre	D. Webber	T.J. Nielsen	J.A. Brayshaw	S.P. George	Byes	Leg-byes	Wides	No-balls	Total	Wkts
							11	4		24	485	7
							6	10		45	298	6
							3	3		6	123	10
5–1–14–0							8	1		20	304	6
5–0–18–0							13	1		10	392	7
							4	1		16	399	5
							1	1		6	204	7
	22–4–68–0	47.2–17–76–2					7	7	3	5	335	7
	6–3–7–0		1–0–2–0	1–0–3–0				1		2	43	1
	27–4–77–1						3	10		12	454	7
	22–2–78–1	36–10–100–3						5	3	14	406	8
	10–0–43–1							2	6	2	201	7
	16–4–29–0	8–4–16–0						6	1	6	152	10
	17–7–21–1	29–13–43–6			1–1–0–1			8	1	4	225	10
	27–7–73–4	39.3–10–92–1			1–0–1–0		7	5	3	12	365	8
	23–2–113–3	16–0–102–3					1	1	1		261	7
	30–1–96–2	26–6–74–0			4–1–8–0			5	3	8	393	9
	7–2–12–0	10.1–3–21–1									88	1
	29–4–98–1				11–5–26–0	30–6–76–1	1	9	5	4	323	5
	21–8–44–1					20–3–63–0	2	7		2	235	9
10–1–	257–48–	212–63–	1–0–	1–0–	17–7–	50–9–						
32–0	759–15	524–16	2–0	3–0	35–1	139–1						
–	50.60	32.75	–	–	35.00	139.0–						

VICTORIA
FIRST-CLASS MATCHES 1992–3

BATTING

	v. New South Wales (Sydney) 6–9 November 1992		v. Queensland (St Kilda) 20–3 November 1992		v. Western Australia (St Kilda) 4–7 December 1992		v. West Indians (Bendigo) 19–22 December 1992		v. Tasmania (Hobart) 31 Dec. 1992–3 Jan. 1993		v. Western Australia (Perth) 8–11 January 1993		v. Queensland (Brisbane) 28–31 January 1993		v. South Australia (Melbourne) 3–6 February 1993		v. Tasmania (Melbourne) 26 Feb.–1 March 1993		v. South Australia (Adelaide) 5–8 March 1993	
W.N. Phillips	205	–	28	6	27	–			2	31	9	42	9	27	91	4	8	5	122	65
P.C. Nobes	42	–	70	4	8	–			145	35	9	0	24	0	45	35	4	146*	13	102*
S.K. Warne	52	–	0	3*	69	–					0	–								
D.M. Jones	9	–	14	1					56	72*			12	30	4	26	37	9	67	46
D.S. Lehmann	49	–	10	3	60	–			1	52	13	28	16	6	112	25	69	46	4	19
W.G. Ayres	16	–	13	10	22	–														
S.P. O'Donnell	67	–	7	28	34	–			59	–	62	99	0	5	58	5			86	1
A.I.C. Dodemaide	53*	–	8	0	50	–			14	–	31*	123			24	20	35	3	19	0
P.R. Reiffel	18	–	22	14					1*	–					6*	–				
D.S. Berry	1	–	4	2	16	–			–	–	57	15*	1	3	15*	–	13	35	3*	3*
M.G. Hughes	2*	–	0*	7*	1	–					24	–								
G.J. Allardice					31	–			116	0*	5	3	11	4						
D.W. Fleming					3*	–			–	–							1	14*	0*	–
N.D. Maxwell									–	–	6	64*	12	36	5	10*	6	1	2	3
L.D. Harper											2	58								
P.M. Anderson													19*	4						
S.H. Cook													2	7*						
M.T. Elliott															24	66	0	12	22	19
C. Howard															–	–	7	–	–	–
J.A. Sutherland															18*	0				
A.J. Amalfi																				
Byes	1		3	3	1				2			4	1				2	1	7	1
Leg-byes	10		4	2	11				14	6	12	9	6	1	5	2	4	6	5	1
Wides				4		1			3			1	2		3	6	1	2	3	1
No-balls	22		12		8	18			4		34	10	6	23	14	2	20	12	12	
Total	547		195	95	352				417	196	265	457	155	156	406	201	225	292	365	261
Wickets	9		10	9	10				7	3	10	7	10	10	8	7	10	8	8	7
Result	D		D		D		Ab.		D		D		L		D		D		D	
Points	2		0		2		–		2		0		0		2		0		2	

BOWLING

	M.G. Hughes	A.I.C. Dodemaide	P.R. Reiffel	S.K. Warne	S.P. O'Donnell	D.M. Jones	D.W. Fleming	D.S. Lehmann
v. New South Wales (Sydney) 6–9 November 1992	36.1–13–83–6	35–9–85–0	25–5–71–1	18–1–94–1	10–2–31–0			
v. Queensland (St Kilda) 20–3 November 1992	17.3–6–42–1	12–5–23–1	14–5–23–2	26–7–73–2	1–0–4–0	3–0–11–0		
v. Western Australia (St Kilda) 4–7 December 1992	22.2–4–51–3	23–9–44–2	15–3–55–1	21–3–59–1	8–4–8–2			
	12–6–18–2	14.5–3–41–3	15–5–24–0		13–0–48–1	5–1–11–1		
v. West Indians (Bendigo) 19–22 December 1992	20–3–52–2	16–3–45–0		17.3–4–49–5	4–1–12–0		18–4–45–3	
	13–2–44–0	24–2–80–1		27–4–74–2	14–3–34–0		21–1–77–0	1–0–1–0
v. Tasmania (Hobart) 31 December 1992–3 January 1993		21.5–8–51–3	19–7–44–0		4–1–17–0		21–10–41–1	
		34–12–58–2	24–7–71–0		11–3–19–0		18–3–52–1	9–5–8–1
v. Western Australia (Perth) 8–11 January 1993	38–6–112–3	30.2–9–81–2		29–5–89–0	28–3–102–4			6–3–6–1
v. Queensland (Brisbane) 28–31 January 1993			22–7–46–3		13–3–36–2			3–0–11–0
			25–8–68–2		9.2–3–23–1	7–3–24–0		15–2–38–1
v. South Australia (Melbourne) 3–6 February 1993		36–9–72–1	32–12–59–2		11–2–29–1			
		23–8–53–3	25–7–67–2		19–4–68–1			7–0–25–0
v. Tasmania (Melbourne) 26 February–1 March 1993		38–11–80–3					23.4–6–47–4	4–1–10–0
		13–4–21–0					22–4–80–3	
v. South Australia (Adelaide) 5–8 March 1993		27–12–67–1			8–0–27–0	2–0–9–0	28–10–72–2	3–0–24–0
		22–6–50–0			6–1–16–0		33.4–8–90–7	2–1–4–0
v. New South Wales (Melbourne) 18–21 March 1993					6–1–14–1		16–3–39–1	
					6–3–6–0		31–4–100–3	10–5–11–1
Bowler's average	159–40–402–17 23.64	370–110–851–22 38.68	216–66–528–13 40.61	151.3–24–486–12 40.50	163.2–35–457–13 35.15	12–3–44–0 –	232.2–53–643–25 25.72	60–17–138–4 34.50

v. New South Wales (Melbourne) 18–21 March 1993

		M	Inns	NO	Runs	HS	Av
23	7	10	18	–	711	205	39.50
		9	16	2	682	146*	48.71
		4	5	1	124	69	31.00
		7	13	1	383	72*	31.91
37	84	10	18	–	634	112	35.22
		3	4	–	61	22	15.25
58	86	9	15	–	655	99	43.66
		8	13	2	380	123	34.54
		5	7	2	107	36	21.40
4	10	10	15	4	182	57	16.54
		4	5	3	34	24	17.00
		4	7	1	170	116	28.33
6	7	5	6	3	31	14*	10.33
14	1	7	12	2	160	64*	16.00
53	2	2	4	–	115	58	28.75
		1	2	1	23	19*	23.00
0*	0	2	4	2	9	7*	4.50
52	3	4	8	–	198	66	24.75
0	2*	4	3	1	9	7	4.50
		1	2	1	18	18*	18.00
4	6	1	2	–	10	6	5.00
2							
3	7						
2	2						
258	217						
10	10						
L							
2							

FIELDING FIGURES

35 – D.S. Berry (ct 31/st 4)
17 – N.D. Maxwell
7 – D.M. Jones
6 – D.S. Lehmann
5 – S.P. O'Donnell
4 – W.N. Phillips, P.R. Reiffel and M.T. Elliott
3 – W.G. Ayres and A.I.C. Dodemaide
2 – S.K. Warne, D.W. Fleming, S.H. Cook and P.M. Anderson
1 – P.C. Nobes, M.G. Hughes, L.D. Harper, G.J. Allardice, C. Howard, J.A. Sutherland, A.J. Amalfi and sub

W.G. Ayres	P.C. Nobes	N.D. Maxwell	S.H. Cook	P.M. Anderson	C. Howard	J.A. Sutherland	M.T. Elliott	Byes	Leg-byes	Wides	No-balls	Total	Wkts
								5	8		6	377	8
									3		4	179	7
									5		2	222	9
									2			144	9
								4	5	1	24	212	10
2–0–11–0	2–0–7–0							4	5		12	337	3 Ab.
		23–7–46–5							5		14	204	10
		32–4–107–4						6	11		14	332	8
		13–2–41–0						8	1		32	440	10
		18–8–31–3	10.5–4–25–1	10–1–45–1					7	2	2	201	10
		22–4–73–2	12–1–50–1	7–0–30–0					15		4	321	7
		26–6–65–1			19–7–48–2				5	2	2	278	7
		14–0–51–1			8–1–35–0				7	1	10	306	8
		24–8–57–2			13–2–40–0	17–3–50–1		2	11	1	2	297	10
		8–0–34–1			17–2–53–4	6–2–12–0		11	6	1	14	217	9
		29–7–81–3			29.3–8–71–3			3	8			362	10
		21–9–47–2			19–5–48–0		1–0–16–0	1	2		6	274	10
		15–4–44–2	13.3–3–42–2		14–4–43–4							182	10
		27–9–79–4	21–1–71–0		21–2–82–0			1	1	2	2	351	8
2–0– 11–0 –	2–0– 7–0 –	272–68– 756–30 25.20	57.2–9– 188–4 47.00	17–1– 75–1 75.00	140.3–31– 420–13 32.30	23–5– 62–1 62.00	1–0– 16–0 –						

WESTERN AUSTRALIA
FIRST-CLASS MATCHES 1992–3
BATTING

	v. Queensland (Brisbane) 21–4 October 1992		v. West Indians (Perth) 6–9 November 1992		v. New South Wales (Perth) 14–17 November 1992		v. Victoria (St Kilda) 4–7 December 1992		v. South Australia (Perth) 11–14 December 1992		v. Tasmania (Perth) 18–21 December 1992		v. Victoria (Perth) 8–11 January 1993		v. New South Wales (Sydney) 3–6 February 1993		v. Queensland (Perth) 5–8 March 1993		v. Tasmania (Hobart) 11–14 March 1993	
G.R. Marsh	121	1	7	7	0	47	26	101	49	138	1	40	129	–	31	13	8	107	6	0
M.R.J. Veletta	26	1	51	2	12	28	3	20	68	10	23	26	6	–	45	5	55	20*	25	104
J.L. Langer	40	45	40	15	58	14	70	44	96	110	43	8	11	–						
T.M. Moody	4	0	15	0	0	34	2	35*	37	71	41	2	54		78	30	45	124	8	71
D.R. Martyn	133*	112	9	40			51	116*			139	40	29	–						
W.S. Andrews	3	8	51	19*	6	40	18	–	0	3	18	29	18	–	18	9				
T.J. Zoehrer	0	0	9	31	61	33	0	–	1	1	52	3	48	–	3	0	35	–	136	52
B.P. Julian	4	4	32*	0	0	35	3	–	4*	11*	16	51	3	–	75	18	7	–	87	4
J. Angel	16	0	5*	0	2	5*	0	–	–	–			11	–	2	5	2	–	8	5*
T.M. Alderman	11	1*	–	0	2*	7	1*	–			9*	–	0	–						
B.A. Reid	3	0	–	0	0	7	4	–												
M.P. Lavender					9	4			20*	24			103	–	40	46	11	4	0	0
M.P. Atkinson									–	0*	43	52*	5*	–			14	–	4	7
P.A. Capes											10	1								
R.C. Kelly															34	15	4	0*	7	34
S. Herzberg															57*	12*				
J. Stewart															51	1	2*	–	0*	5
M.W. McPhee																	59	11*	14	12
Byes							4	4	4				8		3	6	4	7	5	
Leg-byes	7	6	3	5	5	5	5	5	8	13	10	14	1		7	5	10	10	13	2
Wides							1		1	1	2	2			1	1	2	1	2	1
No-balls	2	6	17	12	4	27	24	12	20	10	6		32		22	2	40	34	6	2
Total	370	184	239	131	159	286	212	337	304	392	417	268	440		467	168	298	318	321	299
Wickets	10	10	7	10	10	10	10	3	6	7	10	9	10		10	10	10	3	10	10
Result	W		L		L		D		W		D		D		L		W		D	
Points	6		–		0		0		6		0		2		2		6		0	

BOWLING

BOWLING	B.A. Reid	T.M. Alderman	J. Angel	B.P. Julian	D.R. Martyn	T.J. Zoehrer	W.S. Andrews	M.P. Atkinson
v. Queensland (Brisbane) 21–4 October 1992	16-3-58-4	17-5-40-1	13-1-42-2	16-4-65-2	1-0-9-0			
	25-8-70-2	22.2-6-55-4	21-4-58-2	20-4-64-2		7-1-22-0		
v. West Indians (Perth) 6–9 November 1992	18-4-62-0	18-3-52-0	20.4-6-59-5	20-3-72-5			10-0-34-0	
	7-1-27-0	21-4-68-2	14-4-37-1			16-2-66-0	14-1-74-0	
v. New South Wales (Perth) 14–17 November 1992	19-1-89-3	15-4-46-1	9-3-33-1	12.3-1-50-4				
	22-3-58-2	26-10-40-1	18.3-8-63-0	13-1-58-2				
v. Victoria (St Kilda) 4–7 December 1992	17-5-31-1	21-4-67-0	14-3-53-0	25.2-5-84-5	4-0-18-0	24-4-66-3	7-0-21-1	
v. South Australia (Perth) 11–14 December 1992		28-6-99-4	26-11-60-2	28-4-85-1		9-4-34-0	6-0-25-0	25-1-97-3
		14-4-61-2	16-4-38-0	9-3-28-2		13-0-83-0	2-0-16-0	10-2-45-2
v. Tasmania (Perth) 18–21 December 1992		43.1-14-95-3		31-7-107-2	6-2-24-0		9-4-22-0	24-7-78-1
v. Victoria (Perth) 8–11 January 1993		10-0-40-1	19.5-6-71-6	13-0-76-1	3-1-4-0			19-2-62-2
		22-6-64-1	25-6-77-2	24-6-69-1	18-2-47-0	48-8-112-1		24-8-75-1
v. New South Wales (Sydney) 3–6 February 1993			15-1-72-0	33-7-132-4		8-0-21-0		
			2-0-12-0	7.2-1-23-0		10-0-39-1		
v. Queensland (Perth) 5–8 March 1993			17-3-71-1	29-6-103-5				28-11-71-2
								18-3-73-2
v. Tasmania (Hobart) 11–14 March 1993			19-5-53-3	24-4-82-4				21-1-86-3
			25-5-97-3	26-6-69-2				7-0-38-0
			6-1-35-1	10-0-32-0				
v. South Australia (Adelaide) 18–21 March 1993	16-1-62-0		22-6-70-2	17-4-61-0		5-1-25-0		
	10-4-39-0		16-5-39-0	8-2-36-0		11-2-35-1		
	150–30–	257.3–66–	319–82–	382.1–72–	32–5–	151–22–	48–5–	176–35–
	496–12	727–20	1040–31	1342–43	102–0	503–6	192–1	625–14
Bowler's average	41.33	36.35	33.54	31.20	–	83.83	192.00	44.64

v. South Australia (Adelaide) 18–21 March 1993		M	Inns	NO	Runs	HS	Av
23	50	11	21	–	905	138	43.09
104*	37	11	21	2	671	104*	35.31
38	40	8	15	–	672	110	44.80
29	17	11	21	1	697	124	34.85
		5	9	2	669	139	95.57
		7	13	1	222	51	18.50
51*	8	11	19	1	524	136	29.11
–	22	11	18	3	376	87	25.06
–	2*	10	14	4	63	16	6.30
		7	8	4	31	11	7.75
–	10*	5	7	1	24	10*	4.00
0	22	7	13	1	283	103	23.58
		5	7	3	125	52*	31.25
		1	2	–	11	10	5.50
		3	6	1	94	34	18.80
		1	2	2	69	57*	–
–	9	4	6	2	68	51	17.00
59	7	3	6	1	162	59	32.40

1	2
9	7
5	
4	2
323	235
5	9
L	
0	

FIELDING FIGURES

32 – T.J. Zoehrer (ct 31/st 1)
15 – M.R.J. Veletta (ct 14/st1)
14 – T.M. Moody
13 – J.L. Langer
5 – D.R. Martyn and M.P. Lavender
3 – G.R. Marsh, B.P. Julian, J. Angel and M.P. Atkinson
2 – W.S. Andrews and R.C. Kelly
1 – T.M. Alderman, S. Herzberg, J. Stewart and M.W. McPhee

P.A. Capes	T.M. Moody	J. Stewart	S. Herzberg	G.R. Marsh	Byes	Leg-byes	Wides	No-balls	Total	Wkts
						7		10	221	10
					4	10		8	283	10
						1		6	280	10
					4	4		4	326	4
						2		28	220	10
						10		16	229	5
					1	11	1	18	352	10
						9		8	409	10
					9	4	1		284	6
36–5–105–3					3	23	2	18	457	9
	6–2–16–0	29.4–6–109–3	26–5–97–2			12	1	34	265	10
	1–0–5–0	19–4–79–2	6–1–24–0		4	9	2	10	457	7
	23–8–66–2	12–2–40–0			3	2	1	18	452	10
	14–10–18–1	6–4–5–0				4		2	186	3
	19–5–45–0	18.1–4–62–1			12	18	5	12	381	10
	10–1–40–1	13–2–39–1		1–0–1–0	2			12	233	10
	19–6–44–4	14–4–64–1				11	2	6	370	7
	4–0–18–0	14–3–48–0			3	2	1	4	190	6
					3	5	4	6	334	8
						11			226	1

P.A. Capes	T.M. Moody	J. Stewart	S. Herzberg	G.R. Marsh
36–5– 105–3	96–32– 252–8	125.5–29– 446–8	32–6– 121–2	1–0– 1–0
35.00	31.50	55.75	60.50	–

AUSTRALIA: THE SUMMER OF CONTENT

By Ashley Mallett
(former Australian Test cricketer)

Australian cricket is on a roll: the Tests against the West Indies breathed new life into the traditional part of the game and the one-dayers are playing to packed houses.

The summer that was 1992–3 saw Australia almost topple the Windies in the Tests, finally going down 2–1, after an inglorious batting debacle in Perth, the Mecca of pace. Only Curtly Ambrose stood in Allan Border's way, and he proved too tough an obstacle, although it was significant that when Australia used a wise mix of pace and spin, the Windies looked decidedly vulnerable. Shane Warne's seven wickets on the MCG proved what we all knew: West Indians cannot fathom good-quality leg-spin.

Australia ignored the batting efforts of Matthew Hayden, who stood tall and erect like a Roman centurion, carving up attacks throughout the country with all the power and grace of a Graeme Pollock reincarnated. Australia stuck with Mark Taylor, with David Boon – the nation's best batsman by far – opening, instead of launching his skill from the vital number three batting spot. Steve Waugh was tried at that spot and was obviously out of sorts there. Waugh is a down-the-list striker, blessed with great talent but shaky early on, if up against a top-class spinner (especially a good 'offie') or one quick with the ability to move the ball either way. Waugh takes his time to get into stride – more than most, and this is why he is vulnerable at the top of the order.

Despite continual calls on its strength, NSW began well early. Greg Matthews was slow off the mark, but gradually began to turn in match-winning performances. He lost his Test spot to Tim May, a bowler with the classical upright action and ability to match. May's 5 for 9 to spin out the Windies in Adelaide was remarkable in that he had struggled to take a wicket the season before, claiming just 17 wickets at more than 70 runs apiece. While there were claims that May had changed his action, his reward came because Matthews failed to grab Test wickets and May, armed with a seemingly more aggressive strategy, was the only spinner who could possibly have been picked to replace him, given that ex-Victorian left-armer Paul Jackson had a horror of a time in his adopted state, Queensland, where he moved from Victoria. In Victoria there were Warne, Test incumbent, and Peter McIntyre, a leg-spinner with skill.

The three-way battle was never to develop, for McIntyre headed for Adelaide, as Clarrie Grimmett had done nearly 70 years before him, and Jackson flew to Brisbane. On the eve of the Sheffield Shield season, Jackson broke his bowling arm while batting against a fast-medium bowler. Steve Storey, a left-hand bat and similar type of trundler to Jackson – except that Storey bowls almost round arm and undercuts the ball – complicated Jack-

son's chance of a return to first-class cricket when his arm healed, by hitting a hurricane century against his old state, NSW, then following up with 5 for 53 to rout WA in Brisbane. Then Jackson broke his ring finger, finally getting his state team chance when the selectors realised he was easily the best spin bet.

NSW and Queensland fought out the final, with NSW again denying the poor old Queenslanders their first Sheffield Shield. For more than 60 years Queensland has had to endure taunts from southerners about its quest for the 'Holy Grail'. NSW batted at snail's pace to thwart Queensland. It was a disappointing end to an otherwise good Shield summer during which lots of good youngsters emerged. Tasmania unearthed an exciting 17-year-old batsman, Ricky Ponting, who has the poise of a young Greg Chappell, with an even greater array of strokes than Chappell had at 19. Ponting hit twin centuries against WA, another century against NSW in Sydney and was even given an outside chance of touring England. His time will come. Hayden starred and looked every inch a Test player of the not-too-distant future. He must 'work' the ball more and part of his education in England will have been trying to do just that, with Bob Simpson urging this strategy all the way. NSW opener Michael Slater played some heroic innings. It was some comeback for the youngster, given that he had been involved in a car accident and sustained nasty injuries to his hip only 18 months before his epic 1,000-run summer. NSW teammate Michael Bevan did too little too early to win a tour place, but this man has the touch of a Garry Sobers. We old stagers are willing him success in huge dollops, because the man is so gifted. So too is Victoria's Darren Lehmann (now lured back to his native SA). Lehmann averaged 40-odd for Victoria, but his talent is such he should be doing a lot more.

Victoria had internal strife, with skipper Simon O'Donnell reportedly at odds with cricket manager Bill Lawry. The side languished and finished last in the table. Dean Jones, inexplicably axed from the Test side, simply couldn't get going and missed the boat to England, despite going to New Zealand for the one-dayers. Neil Maxwell proved ever-reliable as an all-rounder, while Paul Nobes thrashed his way to a number of top-notch innings. Nobes is as good as Keith Stackpole was in his day, yet the current batting talent at the top of the order might mean Nobes never gets a Test match. His Victorian opening partner Wayne Phillips batted steadily, but generally the side lacked consistency. Young leg-spinner Craig Howard chimed in with two good hauls of four wickets when he played in place of Warne, who was on Test duty. Opening bowler Damien Fleming deserved success. Paul Reiffel made the England tour, although Fleming did more for Victoria on the first-class stage.

South Australia relied heavily on skipper Jamie Siddons, as exciting a batsman as Australia has had in recent times. Again he thrashed all comers, belting WA to an unconquered 189 in Perth, hitting a fabulous 197 against NSW in Sydney, plus taking some of the most extraordinary catches (at slip, or short cover, or silly point) imaginable. A few county attacks will never know how close they may have come to being smashed into oblivion by Siddons in 1993. James Brayshaw at number three batted with skill; however, he threw his wicket away too often when well set. Peter Sleep finished his lengthy first-class career with a haul of 7 for 79 against WA, while Ashley Hammond, a left-hand opening bat, proved his mettle by hitting 32 invaluable runs against England 'A' with a broken left hand. McIntyre spun well after his belated inclusion, but the attack lacked a spearhead. Dennis Hickey couldn't find much other than the bat's middle, and medium-fast men Reeves and Wigney struggled for direction. Shane George looks the best of the young fast men, but he needs to build his fitness and mental toughness. Opener Greg Blewett played a number of fabulous hands, two of which helped SA to a grand win over WA in the last match of the summer. Blewett, if he can curb his odd 'rush of blood', will one day wear a Test cap. Lots of rebuilding is needed for SA, who have finished second to last in the table for three years running.

Tasmania did better than one expected, for the side continually turned out with an imbalanced attack. Shaun Young bowled his medium-pacers well, as did the beefy left-hander Chris Matthews. However, the Apple Islanders should have won more games. With a balanced attack (at least one spinner to complement the pace men) Tasmania could well have played off in the final. There was much joy at Tasmania's efforts: there should have been lots of soul-searching, for while the effort was good, it should have been far better. Opener Dean Hills played well, as did the richly gifted Danny Buckingham (whose biggest drawback must be his bulk) and Ponting, upon whom so much rests, while Jamie Cox, who dines lavishly on pace and bad spin but flounders like a man with leaden boots in a bog against a class spinner, is also one to watch. A balanced attack and Tassie might start to really frighten the mainlanders. There's also room for a mention of the keeper, Mark Aitkinson. I think he'll be a top keeper, destined to play Test cricket. There's a touch of Alan Knott in Aitkinson.

Western Australia appears to be coming to the end of an era: Terry Alderman is set to retire; big Bruce Reid's injuries plagued him to the point that his confidence and form fell away when most needed for his chance to tour England; Geoff Marsh batted with grit, but his day is done on the Test stage; Tom Moody struggled and Mike Veletta did his usual top-notch job. Brendon Julian did well, as did Damien Martyn, although little, tough Justin Langer played well, but not well enough to overcome the psychological and physical barrage of the Windies pace men and some 'interesting' umpiring decisions. Langer's a black-belt in judo: he'll bounce back! Spinners Steve Herzberg (off-breaks) and Jamie Stewart (left-arm ortho-dox) did enough to show that WA is not completely dedicated to pace.

Queensland did well under the captaincy of Dirk Well-ham, who stepped in when the Test hands were away. Men such as Allan Border, Ian Healy and Craig McDer-mott were either on Test or one-day international duty or touring New Zealand. This gave Michael Kasprowicz and Greg Rowell the chance to show their skill. This they did. Often. But again Queensland fell in a hole. The batting

Terry Alderman – reprimanded, injured and finally dismissed from his post as coach to Western Australia in a sad season. (Adrian Murrell/ Allsport)

was a little brittle and the bowling good, but it lacked balance until Jackson was belatedly brought into the side. Carl Rackemann bowled well, but a spring virus prevented him playing in the early matches. Stuart Law regained a bit of batting form and began to show out with leg-spin.

NSW deservedly won the Shield. Greg Matthews finished the summer on a great note: he demolished WA in a late-summer match at the SCG, taking eight wickets in a dramatic ending. Slater thrashed all comers and Wayne Holdsworth bowled like the wind, when he got his rhythm right. He's like a pocket-sized Jeff Thomson: quick, mean and often explosive, a fairly volatile mix for any batsman to combat.

Australia has the batting depth, but the bowling does look a little thin. Lots more overs in the Sheffield Shield on any one day must come into the scheme of things. Mark Taylor showed just what sort of match could be had when a captain is prepared to gamble. NSW won the centenary match against SA on the Adelaide Oval by seven runs. It was a great game, full of incident, although the nostalgia of the Walking Wisden present during the game tended to overshadow all else. Taylor looks to be the man to take over from Border. I hope that means he will also score enough runs to stay there.

FIRST-CLASS AVERAGES

BATTING

	M	Inns	NO	Runs	HS	Av	100s	50s
J.D. Siddons	11	20	2	1190	197	66.11	4	7
M.E. Waugh	9	16	2	883	200*	63.07	3	3
D.R. Martyn	10	18	3	921	139	61.40	4	2
M.J. Slater	10	19	2	1019	143	59.94	3	6
M.L. Hayden	14	26	2	1249	161*	52.04	2	8
M.G. Bevan	12	21	4	875	170	51.47	3	3
D.F. Hills	11	19	1	903	138	50.16	4	5
D.C. Boon	8	15	2	635	111	48.84	1	4
P.C. Nobes	9	16	2	682	146*	48.71	3	1
R.T. Ponting	11	18	1	782	125	46.00	3	4
D.J. Buckingham	9	14	3	501	161*	45.54	1	3
J.A. Brayshaw	11	22	2	908	110	45.40	1	5
S.P. O'Donnell	9	15	–	655	99	43.66	–	8
B.E. McNamara	11	17	6	477	98*	43.36	–	3
G.R. Marsh	11	21	–	905	138	43.09	5	1
R. Chee Quee	3	5	1	170	90	42.50	–	1
A.R. Border	9	16	1	616	116*	41.06	2	4
J.L. Langer	10	19	–	757	110	39.84	1	4
G.R. Blewett	11	22	1	834	119	39.71	2	4
D.S. Webber	8	15	1	553	135	39.50	1	3
S.G. Law	12	21	–	823	142	39.19	2	3
J. Cox	10	17	1	606	137*	37.87	2	3
M.A. Taylor	8	15	1	530	102	37.85	2	1
T.J. Barsby	13	24	–	908	123	37.83	3	4
W.N. Phillips	11	20	–	752	205	37.60	2	2
D.S. Lehmann	11	20	1	704	112	37.05	1	5
G.R.J. Matthews	13	20	3	625	79	36.76	–	6
M.R.J. Veletta	11	21	2	671	104*	35.31	2	3
J.C. Scuderi	8	14	4	349	100*	34.90	1	2
S.R. Waugh	9	16	1	523	100*	34.86	2	1
T.M. Moody	11	21	1	697	124	34.85	1	4
A.I.C. Dodemaide	8	13	2	380	123	34.54	1	2
P.A. Emery	13	19	7	406	62*	33.83	–	2
M.W. McPhee	3	6	1	162	59	32.40	–	2
D.M. Jones	7	13	1	383	72*	31.91	–	3
N.C.P. Courtney	11	19	1	568	88	31.55	–	5
N.R. Fielke	5	10	–	315	74	31.50	–	3
M.P. Atkinson	5	7	3	125	52*	31.25	–	1
R.J. Tucker	11	18	3	463	120	30.86	2	1
S. Young	10	15	2	399	76	30.69	–	4
A.C. Gilchrist	7	11	2	274	75	30.44	–	1
T.J. Nielsen	11	20	2	541	109	30.05	1	3
T.H. Bayliss	10	17	1	468	107	29.25	1	3
T.J. Zoehrer	11	19	1	524	136	29.11	1	4
D.M. Wellham	10	18	2	465	111*	29.06	1	2
L.D. Harper	2	4	–	115	58	28.75	–	2
G.J. Allardice	4	7	1	170	116	28.33	1	–
M.N. Atkinson	11	15	6	241	46	26.77	–	–
M.G. Farrell	5	8	1	185	74	26.42	–	2
P.J.T. Goggin	12	24	2	572	120	26.00	1	1
B.P. Julian	11	18	3	376	87	25.46	–	3
M.T. Elliott	4	8	–	198	66	24.75	–	2
C.D. Matthews	12	14	6	191	35	23.87	–	–
S.M. Small	11	21	–	499	88	23.76	–	3
M.P. Lavender	7	13	1	283	103	23.58	1	–
P.R. Sleep	11	19	3	371	47	23.18	–	–
I.A. Healy	10	17	2	340	53*	22.66	–	1
S.C. Storey	8	14	1	284	103	21.84	1	–
P.R. Reiffel	5	7	2	107	36	21.40	–	–
G.A. Bishop	6	11	–	233	56	21.18	–	2
D.R. Kingdon	6	11	2	169	59	18.77	–	1
W.S. Andrews	7	13	1	222	51	18.50	–	1
D.S. Berry	10	15	4	182	57	16.54	–	1

	M	Inns	NO	Runs	HS	Av	100s	50s
N.D. Maxwell	7	12	2	160	64*	16.00	–	1
M.G. Hughes	10	15	4	166	43	15.09	–	–
P.W. Anderson	8	15	–	225	63	15.00	–	1
S.K. Warne	9	13	1	172	69	14.33	–	2
G.J. Rowell	9	14	4	139	40	13.90	–	–
C.J. McDermott	9	15	3	163	26	13.58	–	–
D.A. Reeves	9	13	4	118	29	13.11	–	–
M.S. Kasprowicz	13	21	3	233	39	12.94	–	–

(Qualification – 100 runs, average 10.00)

BOWLING

	Overs	Mds	Runs	Wkts	Av	Best	10/m	5/inn
M.G. Hughes	347.2	77	954	43	22.18	6-83	–	2
C.G. Rackemann	257.3	45	774	33	23.45	5-75	–	1
T.B.A. May	224.3	63	544	23	23.65	5-9	–	2
G.D. McGrath	216	54	598	25	23.92	5-36	–	2
M.S. Kasprowicz	435.1	100	1231	51	24.13	6-59	–	3
N.D. Maxwell	272	68	756	30	25.20	5-46	–	1
P.J.S. Alley	140.4	28	459	18	25.50	5-43	–	1
D. Tazelaar	224.2	68	564	22	25.63	4-39	–	–
D.W. Fleming	232.2	53	643	25	25.72	7-90	–	1
W.J. Holdsworth	374.1	57	1376	53	25.96	7-41	1	4
G.R.J. Matthews	615	193	1475	51	28.92	8-52	–	3
S. Young	341.3	98	984	34	28.94	5-56	–	2
B.E. McNamara	237.4	57	673	23	29.26	4-68	–	–
C.D. Matthews	478.1	97	1456	49	29.71	5-72	–	1
G.J. Rowell	290.1	70	842	28	30.07	5-31	–	2
B.P. Julian	382.1	72	1342	43	31.20	5-72	–	3
C. Howard	140.3	31	420	13	32.30	4-43	–	–
P.E. McIntyre	212	63	524	16	32.75	6-43	–	1
B.A. Reid	203	39	647	19	34.05	5-112	–	1
C.J. McDermott	339.5	74	1102	32	34.43	4-35	–	–
J. Angel	338	86	1112	32	34.75	6-71	–	2
S.P. O'Donnell	163.2	35	457	13	35.15	4-102	–	–
M.R. Whitney	281	66	818	23	35.56	5-43	–	1
T.J. Cooley	99	20	393	11	35.72	4-49	–	–
T.M. Alderman	257.3	66	727	20	36.35	4-55	–	–
S.K. Warne	309.5	56	983	27	36.40	7-52	–	2
P.T. McPhee	368.4	97	1020	28	36.42	5-48	–	1
A.I.C. Dodemaide	370	110	851	22	38.68	3-41	–	–
P.W. Jackson	206.3	72	427	11	38.81	3-91	–	–
D.A. Freedman	322.2	66	1068	27	39.55	6-89	1	1
C.R. Miller	171.2	36	556	14	39.71	4-93	–	–
D.A. Reeves	215.2	33	876	22	39.81	4-56	–	–
P.R. Sleep	327.4	75	893	22	40.59	7-79	–	1
P.R. Reiffel	216	66	528	13	40.61	3-46	–	–
S.C. Storey	252.2	67	709	16	44.31	5-55	–	1
M.P. Atkinson	176	35	625	14	44.64	3-97	–	–
D.J. Hickey	168	22	681	15	45.40	4-120	–	–
B.N. Wigney	257	48	759	15	50.60	4-73	–	–
R.J. Tucker	201.5	42	628	10	62.80	2-16	–	–

(Qualification – 10 wickets)

LEADING FIELDERS

54 – P.A. Emery (ct 52/st 2); 38 – I.A. Healy (ct 33/st 5); 35 – D.S. Berry (ct 31/st 4); 32 – M.N. Atkinson (ct 31/st 1) and T.J. Zoehrer (ct 31/st 1); 29 – P.W. Anderson (ct 26/st 3); 24 – T.J. Nielsen (ct 19/st 5); 20 – M.L. Hayden; 17 – N.D. Maxwell; 15 – P.J.T. Goggin, G.R.J. Matthews, J.D. Siddons and M.R.J. Veletta (ct 14/st 1); 14 – J.L. Langer, T.M. Moody and S.M. Small; 12 – R.J. Tucker; 11 – S.R. Waugh; 10 – D.J. Buckingham, S.G. Law and B.E. McNamara.

SECTION D
Zimbabwe
Inaugural Test match –
Zimbabwe *v.* India, plus one-day international
New Zealand tour, Tests and one-day internationals
One-day international, Zimbabwe *v.* Pakistan
Kent tour

Test cricket in Zimbabwe. Zimbabwe v. *India at the Harare Sports Club. (David Munden/Sports-Line)*

After several years of energetic striving and enthusiastic lobbying Zimbabwe were granted Test status in 1992. Their elevation to the highest level was not received with unanimous joy. There were those – England among them – who believed that Zimbabwe's cricket was not of a high enough standard to be accorded Test status, and there were those in Zimbabwe who believed that Test status should have come earlier before the defections of Hick, Penney, Rawson and Curran. In the years of waiting, much of the country's cricketing strength had been eroded, and the better players were at the veteran stage.

Zimbabwe's move towards Test status had been led wisely by David Ellman-Brown, the retiring President of the Zimbabwe Cricket Union, and their introduction was handled with equal sense. Zimbabwe were to play hosts to India who were on their way to a series in South Africa, and there were to be two Test matches against New Zealand who were then to go on to Sri Lanka.

Zimbabwe skipper Dave Houghton on his way to a magnificent century in the inaugural Test match. (David Munden/Sports-Line)

15 **October 1992** *at Harare Sports Club*

Indians 203 for 9 (R.J. Shastri 73)
Zimbabwe President's XI 187 for 9 (G. Briant 51 not out)

Indians won by 16 runs

INAUGURAL TEST MATCH
ZIMBABWE v. INDIA, at Harare

Of the Zimbabwe side, only Traicos, the off-spinner, had previously appeared in a Test match. In February and March 1970, he had played in South Africa's last three Test matches before their expulsion from international cricket. Twenty-two years later, at the age of 45, Traicos restarted his Test career. The match was umpired by three officials: Dickie Bird supervising, with Robinson and Kanjee of Zimbabwe alternating.

Houghton won the toss, and Zimbabwe batted. The chief quality of the opening day was the unrelenting concentration of the batting. In 34 overs before lunch, Grant Flower and Kevin Arnott scored 57, and only 15 runs were scored in the first 16 overs after the interval. Nevertheless, Zimbabwe became the first country to register a three-figure opening stand in their inaugural Test match. Arnott and Grant Flower had scored exactly 100 in 61 overs before Arnott was caught off a pull shot. The left-handed Campbell played some entertaining shots before falling to Kapil Dev with the second new ball. Grant Flower was caught behind in the last over of the day after a six-hour innings in which he had 7 fours. Zimbabwe's highly satisfactory, if slow, first day in Test cricket ended with them 188 for 3.

If the first day had been satisfactory for Zimbabwe, the second was a triumph. Night-watchman Burmester was

taken at slip off Prabhakar early in the day, and the resolute Pycroft was caught when he tried to steer the ball to third man shortly after lunch. That was India's last success of the day as Andy Flower joined Houghton in a stand which was to realise 165 runs for the sixth wicket. Houghton became the first man since Bannerman in 1877 to make a century in his country's inaugural Test match. Usually a gleeful stroke-maker, Houghton adopted a cautious approach and took 52 overs to reach his fifty and 81 to complete his hundred. He reached three figures with his 11th four in just over five hours of batting, and only in the final session when he and Flower added 89 did the batsmen really attack the bowling. The Indians' task was difficult – the pitch offered nothing but hard labour. Zimbabwe closed on 406 for 5, the highest score made by a side in its first Test match.

Houghton was out after batting six hours 54 minutes, facing 322 balls and hitting 15 fours, and the last three wickets then fell rapidly. There was early success for Zimbabwe when Shastri was caught high at first slip off a loose shot, but there was also disaster for the home side

Houghton and Burmester rush to congratulate Traicos as he captures one of his five wickets in his first Test match for 22 years. (David Munden/Sports-Line)

when leading bowler Brandes was forced to retire when he turned his ankle, after bowling just two overs.

Raman had seemed in control, but he was bowled by Crocker in the 51st over. Crocker had not been in the original Zimbabwe eleven, but he was called up as a late replacement when Ali Omarshah was injured in practice on the eve of the match. With only one run added Tendulkar gave Traicos a return catch and, five minutes before the close, the veteran off-spinner had Azharuddin taken at slip. India ended on 93 for 4, and a sensational result seemed possible.

Zimbabwe's dreams of heroism died on the fourth day when Sanjay Manjrekar reached 100 not out off 397 balls in 500 minutes. It was only with his seventh partner, More, that Manjrekar took India past the point where they would have been forced to follow-on, although Kapil Dev's 60 off 73 balls with 8 fours had earlier done much to relieve pressure. India closed on 278 for 7, and all three wickets in the day had gone to Traicos to give the bowler his first five-wicket haul in Test cricket.

The final day became of academic interest only, although Kapil Dev dismissed Grant Flower and Campbell with successive deliveries. Houghton was named Man of the Match, and Zimbabwe could look back with pride on their entry to Test cricket.

*Grant Flower pulls off a fine catch at slip to dismiss Azharuddin.
(David Munden/Sports-Line)*

INAUGURAL TEST MATCH – ZIMBABWE v. INDIA
18, 19, 20, 21 and 22 October 1992 at Harare Sports Club

ZIMBABWE

	FIRST INNINGS			SECOND INNINGS	
K.J. Arnott	c Raman, b Kumble	40	b Prabhakar		32
G.W. Flower	c More, b Srinath	82	c More, b Kapil Dev		6
A.D.R. Campbell	lbw, b Kapil Dev	45	b Kapil Dev		0
A.J. Pycroft	c Azharuddin, b Prabhakar	39	lbw, b Shastri		46
M.G. Burmester	c Azharuddin, b Prabhakar	7			
D.L. Houghton (capt)	c More, b Srinath	121	(5) not out		41
*A. Flower	b Prabhakar	59	(6) not out		1
G.J. Crocker	not out	23			
E.A. Brandes	lbw, b Srinath	0			
A.J. Traicos	b Kumble	5			
M.P. Jarvis	c Raman, b Kumble	0			
Extras	b 1, lb 19, nb 15	35	b 11, lb 4, nb 5		20
		456	(for 4 wickets)		146

INDIA

	FIRST INNINGS	
R.J. Shastri	c Pycroft, b Burmester	11
W.V. Raman	b Crocker	43
S.V. Manjrekar	c sub (Davis), b Jarvis	104
S.R. Tendulkar	c and b Traicos	0
M. Azharuddin (capt)	c G.W. Flower, b Traicos	9
S.L. Venkatapathy Raju	c Arnott, b Traicos	7
Kapil Dev	b Traicos	60
M. Prabhakar	c Arnott, b Traicos	14
*K.S. More	c Traicos, b Burmester	41
A.R. Kumble	c A. Flower, b Burmester	0
J. Srinath	not out	6
Extras	b 2, lb 9, nb 1	12
		307

	O	M	R	W	O	M	R	W
Kapil Dev	39	13	71	1	15	4	22	2
Prabhakar	45	15	66	3	14	4	22	1
Srinath	39	12	89	3	5	1	15	–
Venkatapathy Raju	39	15	79	–	7	2	15	–
Kumble	35.2	11	79	3	9	1	17	–
Shastri	17	3	52	–	12	4	32	1
Tendulkar					4	3	8	–

	O	M	R	W
Brandes	2	–	3	–
Burmester	39.4	18	78	3
Jarvis	38	17	73	1
Crocker	35	18	41	1
Traicos	50	16	86	5
G.W. Flower	5	–	15	–

FALL OF WICKETS

1–100, 2–175, 3–186, 4–199, 5–252, 6–417, 7–445, 8–445, 9–454
1–16, 2–16, 3–93, 4–119

FALL OF WICKETS

1–29, 2–77, 3–78, 4–93, 5–101, 6–197, 7–219, 8–287, 9–294

Umpires: H.D. Bird & I.D. Robinson/K. Kanjee

Match drawn

ONE-DAY INTERNATIONAL
ZIMBABWE v. INDIA, at Harare

Zimbabwe introduced four players to one-day international cricket: Brain, Crocker, Evans and Grant Flower. Crocker's meteoric rise to the national side culminated in his taking the individual award. He took 4 for 26 as India, put in to bat on an excellent pitch, batted wildly. Manjrekar hit 70 off 75 balls to restore some sanity in a stand of 73 with Amre.

Zimbabwe could never quite come to terms with the required run rate in spite of Andy Flower's 62. Crocker hit 50 off 55 balls, but they needed 10 an over off the last five overs and saw their last five wickets go down for 28 runs to the experienced Indian pace attack.

A match-saving 104 for India from Sanjay Manjrekar. (David Munden/Sports-Line)

ONE-DAY INTERNATIONAL – ZIMBABWE v. INDIA
25 October 1992 at Harare Sports Club

INDIA

Batsman	Dismissal	Runs
R.J. Shastri	c G.W. Flower, b Burmester	1
A.D. Jadeja	b Brain	0
M. Azharuddin (capt)	c Brain, b Crocker	29
S.R. Tendulkar	c Brain, b Crocker	39
S.V. Manjrekar	c A. Flower, b Crocker	70
P.K. Amre	lbw, b Traicos	36
Kapil Dev	c Evans, b G.W. Flower	5
M. Prabhakar	c sub (Peal), b Crocker	19
*K.S. More	run out	22
J. Srinath	not out	1
A.R. Kumble	run out	1
Extras	b 5, lb 4, w 7	16
(49.4 overs)		239

ZIMBABWE

Batsman	Dismissal	Runs
*A. Flower	run out	62
G.W. Flower	b Srinath	34
A.H. Omarshah	run out	16
D.L. Houghton (capt)	c Amre, b Jadeja	4
A.C. Waller	c Kumble, b Prabhakar	9
C.N. Evans	c Azharuddin, b Kumble	1
G.J. Crocker	b Kapil Dev	50
D. Brain	b Srinath	8
A.D.R. Campbell	b Srinath	0
M.G. Burmester	b Prabhakar	11
A.J. Traicos	not out	0
Extras	b 1, lb 6, w 4, nb 3	14
(49.1 overs)		209

	O	M	R	W
Brain	10	–	52	1
Burmester	6	–	38	1
Omarshah	10	1	23	–
Crocker	7.4	–	26	4
Traicos	10	–	48	1
G.W. Flower	6	–	43	1

	O	M	R	W
Kapil Dev	8.1	1	27	1
Prabhakar	10	–	43	2
Tendulkar	3	–	16	–
Srinath	10	1	35	3
Shastri	5	–	22	–
Jadeja	5	–	24	1
Kumble	8	1	35	1

FALL OF WICKETS
1–1, 2–1, 3–75, 4–78, 5–151, 6–168, 7–211, 8–223, 9–238

FALL OF WICKETS
1–63, 2–88, 3–98, 4–120, 5–123, 6–181, 7–196, 8–196, 9–209

Umpires: I.D. Robinson & R. Tiffin   *Man of the Match:* G.J. Crocker   *India won by 30 runs*

NEW ZEALAND TOUR

The Indians were engaged in the final stages of their brief visit to Zimbabwe when the New Zealanders arrived for their five-week tour. The New Zealand party had been badly hit, for, apart from the non-availability of players like John Wright, both Chris Cairns and Daniel Morrison had been forced to withdraw because of injury. They were replaced by pace bowler Simon Doull and left-arm spinner Mark Haslam, both of whom are in their early twenties. To add to the New Zealanders' troubles, Martin Crowe was unable to play in the first two matches of the tour as he was recovering from illness.

24 October 1992 *at Harare Sports Club*

Zimbabwe Country Districts 207 for 9 (R. Bentley 53, M.H. Dekker 50, M.L. Su'a 4 for 20)
New Zealanders 208 for 4 (M.J. Greatbatch 59, A.H. Jones 56 not out)

New Zealanders won by 6 wickets

26, 27 and 28 October 1992 *at Harare Sports Club*

Zimbabwe 'B' 246 for 8 dec. (C.N. Evans 66, W.R. James 63, D.N. Patel 5 for 54) and 194 (C.N. Evans 56, S.B. Doull 6 for 37)
New Zealanders 234 for 7 dec. (A.H. Jones 81 not out) and 208 for 2 (M.J. Greatbatch 126 not out)

New Zealanders won by 8 wickets

Simon Doull returned the best figures of his career, beating his previous best 6 for 38, and generated a good pace as the tourists won their first first-class match of the tour.

FIRST ONE-DAY INTERNATIONAL
ZIMBABWE *v.* NEW ZEALAND, at Bulawayo

Put in to bat, New Zealand got off to a spirited start. Greatbatch hit 21 out of 23, and Latham and Jones added 87 for the second wicket. Martin Crowe, in his first innings of the tour, kept up the momentum, and after 30 overs, New Zealand were 142 for 2. A huge total seemed

FIRST ONE-DAY INTERNATIONAL – ZIMBABWE *v.* NEW ZEALAND
31 October 1992 at Bulawayo Athletic Club

NEW ZEALAND

M.J. Greatbatch	c A. Flower, b Brain	21
R.T. Latham	run out	45
A.H. Jones	st A. Flower, b G.W. Flower	68
M.D. Crowe (capt)	c Dekker, b G.W. Flower	40
K.R. Rutherford	not out	35
D.N. Patel	c Crocker, b G.W. Flower	4
*A.C. Parore	c Houghton, b Omarshah	11
D.J. Nash	run out	3
S.B. Doull	not out	2
G.R. Larsen		
W. Watson		
Extras	b 5, lb 4, w 4, nb 2	15
(50 overs)	(for 7 wickets)	244

ZIMBABWE

G.W. Flower	c Greatbatch, b Watson	0
*A. Flower	b Patel	10
D.L. Houghton (capt)	c Watson, b Patel	19
M.H. Dekker	lbw, b Doull	79
A.C. Waller	st Parore, b Patel	23
C.N. Evans	st Parore, b Latham	22
A.H. Omarshah	run out	25
G.J. Crocker	c Crowe, b Doull	9
S.G. Peall	b Watson	1
D. Brain	not out	16
A.J. Traicos	not out	7
Extras	lb 8, w 3	11
(50 overs)	(for 9 wickets)	222

	O	M	R	W
Brain	8	1	46	1
Peall	10	1	32	–
Crocker	3	–	17	–
Omarshah	9	–	57	1
Traicos	10	–	44	–
G.W. Flower	10	1	39	3

	O	M	R	W
Doull	10	2	42	2
Watson	8	–	45	2
Patel	10	2	26	3
Larsen	6	–	33	–
Latham	5	–	27	1
Jones	10	–	36	–
Nash	1	–	5	–

FALL OF WICKETS
1–23, 2–110, 3–175, 4–192, 5–200, 6–233, 7–236

FALL OF WICKETS
1–4, 2–29, 3–34, 4–75, 5–126, 6–162, 7–195, 8–198, 9–200

Umpires: I.D. Robinson & K. Kanjee   *Man of the Match:* D.N. Patel   *New Zealand won by 22 runs*

possible, but left-arm spinner Grant Flower took the wickets of Jones, Crowe and Patel to help restrain the visitors.

Zimbabwe began badly and were soon 34 for 3. They were given every hope by Mark Dekker who, in his first international, batted with regal splendour for two hours, but the loss of big-hitters Houghton and Waller really put the game out of Zimbabwe's reach.

FIRST TEST MATCH
ZIMBABWE *v.* NEW ZEALAND, at Bulawayo

Omarshah replaced the injured Brandes for Zimbabwe's first Test in Bulawayo while New Zealand introduced Doull and Haslam to Test cricket.

Two hours were lost to a damp outfield at the start, but Greatbatch tried to make up the lost time by hitting 87 off 79 balls in an opening stand of 116. From the 60 overs that were bowled on the first day, New Zealand made 205 for 1. Only 2½ hours' play was possible on the second day, but

the rain was certainly welcome to the drought-stricken country if not to the cricketers. Zimbabwe suffered another hard day in the field as Latham and Jones extended their partnership to 127 before Latham was run out in a bad misunderstanding with his partner. Latham, who was playing in his second Test, reached his first Test century – a chanceless innings – and, in all, faced 232 balls and hit a six and 14 fours. It was a most impressive, determined innings. Crowe hit 42 off 44 balls, and Jones was his relentless self as New Zealand ended on 325 for 3.

Only 140 minutes of cricket were possible on the third day. Crowe declared, and he opened the New Zealand bowling with his spinner Patel, who claimed Grant Flower before the close when Zimbabwe were a rather grim 54 for 1. Patel excelled on the fourth day when he achieved a best return in Test cricket of 6 for 113. At 64 for 5, Zimbabwe were in danger of defeat, but Andy Flower batted most sensibly to help stage a recovery. New Zealand still pressed for victory and, in 35 overs before the close, hit 163 for the loss of Latham who had shared a second century opening partnership with Greatbatch.

Greatbatch added only eight to his overnight score,

FIRST TEST MATCH – ZIMBABWE *v.* NEW ZEALAND
1, 2, 3, 4 and 5 November 1992 at Bulawayo Athletic Club

NEW ZEALAND

	FIRST INNINGS			SECOND INNINGS	
M.J. Greatbatch	c Campbell, b Omarshah	87		c Houghton, b Jarvis	88
R.T. Latham	run out	119		c Houghton, b G. Flower	48
A.H. Jones	not out	67		retired hurt	39
M.D. Crowe (capt)	c Jarvis, b Traicos	42		(5) c A. Flower, b Jarvis	6
K.R. Rutherford	not out	7		(7) not out	11
*A.C. Parore				(4) c Houghton, b Jarvis	12
S.B. Doull				(6) b Traicos	2
D.N. Patel				not out	11
W. Watson					
M.J. Haslam					
M.L. Su'a					
Extras	lb 3	3		b 1, lb 3, nb 1	5
	(for 3 wickets, dec.)	325		(for 5 wickets, dec.)	222

ZIMBABWE

	FIRST INNINGS			SECOND INNINGS	
K.J. Arnott	c Haslam, b Patel	30		not out	101
G.W. Flower	c Latham, b Patel	29		c Latham, b Patel	45
M.G. Burmester	c Haslam, b Patel	0			
A.D.R. Campbell	run out	0		(3) not out	48
A.J. Pycroft	b Doull	2			
D.L. Houghton (capt)	b Patel	36			
*A. Flower	c Haslam, b Su'a	81			
A.H. Omarshah	c Parore, b Su'a	28			
G.J. Crocker	b Patel	1			
A.J. Traicos	b Patel	4			
M.P. Jarvis	not out	2			
Extras	lb 4, nb 2	6		lb 2, w 1	3
		219		(for 1 wicket)	197

	O	M	R	W	O	M	R	W
Jarvis	26.1	4	87	–	11	–	38	3
Burmester	14	1	71	–				
Omarshah	14	6	46	1	7	–	36	–
Traicos	23.1	4	56	1	17	1	82	1
Crocker	14	1	57	–	5	–	30	–
Houghton	0.5	–	0	–				
G.W. Flower	4	2	5	–	8	–	32	1

	O	M	R	W	O	M	R	W
Su'a	9	3	18	2	6.1	2	9	–
Patel	40.4	12	113	6	28	7	60	1
Doull	15	6	29	1	4	1	8	–
Watson	7	3	10	–	7	2	21	–
Haslam	21	8	44	–	19	4	76	–
Jones	1	–	1	–				
Latham					3	2	6	–
Crowe					4	–	15	–

FALL OF WICKETS

1–116, **2**–243, **3**–314
1–102, **2**–181, 3–193, **4**–196, **5**–204

FALL OF WICKETS

1–54, **2**–56, 3–59, 4–62, **5**–64, 6–134, 7–194, **8**–213, 9–213
1–92

Umpires: H.D. Bird & I.D. Robinson/K. Kanjee

Match drawn

ABOVE: *Adam Parore unsuccessfully attempts to stump Grant Flower in the first Test match between Zimbabwe and New Zealand. (Mike Hewitt/Allsport)*

LEFT: *One-day hero Gary Crocker. (David Munden/Sports-Line)*

The Flower brothers gave Zimbabwe a fine start, scoring 124 in 26 overs, but Grant Flower was warned six times by the bowlers and the umpires for his over-eagerness in backing up and, eventually and rightly, he was run out by Patel. Houghton and the impressive left-hander Dekker maintained the momentum, and Zimbabwe reached a formidable 271 in their 50 overs.

Once again, Greatbatch and Latham gave New Zealand a splendid start with 98 from 16 overs, but three wickets then fell for 16 runs. If Zimbabwe sensed victory, they were to be disappointed, for Martin Crowe and Ken Rutherford added 130 and swung the game most positively in New Zealand's favour. Crowe hit 8 fours and a six in his 94 off 87 balls but, exhausted, he was out on the brink of victory. It mattered not, for his side won with 19 balls and four wickets to spare.

and Jones was forced to retire hurt, but Crowe was able to declare and ask Zimbabwe to score 329 in 73 overs. They had no real chance of reaching this target, but two good stands between Arnott and Grant Flower, and Arnott and Campbell took them to a most respectable 197 for 1 before bad light ended play 50 minutes early. Kevin Arnott batted for four hours and hit 12 fours to become the second centurion for cricket's newest Test-playing country.

 ## SECOND ONE-DAY INTERNATIONAL
ZIMBABWE *v.* NEW ZEALAND, at Harare

For the first time, a Test match was punctuated by a one-day international. The second Test match began on the Saturday, and the second one-day international was played on the Sunday, a somewhat dangerous precedent. Zimbabwe gave first international appearances to Essop-Adam and Ranchod.

Zimbabwe's second centurion in Test cricket – Kevin Arnott. (Mike Hewitt/Allsport)

SECOND ONE-DAY INTERNATIONAL – ZIMBABWE v. NEW ZEALAND
8 November 1992 at Harare Sports Club

ZIMBABWE				NEW ZEALAND		
*A. Flower	c Parore, b Patel	56		M.J. Greatbatch	c A. Flower, b Brandes	55
G.W. Flower	run out	63		R.T. Latham	c Essop-Adam, b Ranchod	40
D.L. Houghton (capt)	c Greatbatch, b Harris	50		B.R. Hartland	c A. Flower, b Brandes	5
M.H. Dekker	c Parore, b Su'a	55		M.D. Crowe (capt)	b Brandes	94
C.N. Evans	c Latham, b Watson	12		K.R. Rutherford	c Essop-Adam, b G.W. Flower	37
E.A. Brandes	b Harris	2		C.Z. Harris	b Brain	16
E.A. Essop-Adam	not out	14		D.N. Patel	not out	1
A.H. Omarshah	not out	4		*A.C. Parore	not out	3
D. Brain				G.R. Larsen		
A.J. Traicos				W. Watson		
U. Ranchod				M.L. Su'a		
Extras	lb 7, w 3, nb 5	15		Extras	lb 8, w 10, nb 3	21
(50 overs)	(for 6 wickets)	271		(46.5 overs)	(for 6 wickets)	272

	O	M	R	W		O	M	R	W
Su'a	10	–	36	1	Brain	5	1	27	1
Patel	10	–	48	1	Ranchod	10	1	43	1
Watson	9	–	61	1	Omarshah	6	–	31	–
Larsen	10	–	45	–	Brandes	8.5	–	75	3
Harris	10	–	60	2	Traicos	10	1	50	1
Latham	1	–	14	–	G.W. Flower	7	–	38	1

FALL OF WICKETS

1–124, 2–130, 3–199, 4–221, 5–232, 6–261

1–98, 2–113, 3–114, 4–244, 5–266, 6–267

Umpires: K. Kanjee & I.D. Robinson   *Man of the Match:* M.D. Crowe   *New Zealand won by 4 wickets*

SECOND TEST MATCH – ZIMBABWE v. NEW ZEALAND
7, 9, 10, 11 and 12 November 1992 at Harare Sports Club

NEW ZEALAND

	FIRST INNINGS		SECOND INNINGS	
M.J. Greatbatch	c A. Flower, b Brain	55	c Brandes, b Brain	13
R.T. Latham	c A. Flower, b Crocker	15	c Houghton, b Brandes	10
A.H. Jones	c Pycroft, b Brandes	8	st A. Flower, b Traicos	28
M.D. Crowe (capt)	c Burmester, b Crocker	140	lbw, b Traicos	61
K.R. Rutherford	c A. Flower, b Traicos	74	c Arnott, b Brandes	89
D.N. Patel	c Campbell, b Traicos	6	not out	58
*A.C. Parore	run out	2		
D.J. Nash	not out	11		
M.L. Su'a	c Arnott, b Brandes	1		
W. Watson	b Brain	3		
M.J. Haslam	c A. Flower, b Brain	3		
Extras	lb 11, nb 6	17	lb 2, w 1	3
		335	(for 5 wickets, dec.)	262

ZIMBABWE

	FIRST INNINGS		SECOND INNINGS	
K.J. Arnott	b Watson	68	c Watson, b Nash	10
G.W. Flower	lbw, b Su'a	5	c Latham, b Su'a	4
A.D.R. Campbell	c Su'a, b Patel	52	c Greatbatch, b Patel	35
A.J. Pycroft	b Su'a	60	c Latham, b Watson	5
D.L. Houghton (capt)	c Parore, b Su'a	21	c Nash, b Patel	2
*A. Flower	c Patel, b Nash	14	c Parore, b Patel	9
E.A. Brandes	c Parore, b Su'a	0	c and b Patel	6
G.J. Crocker	b Su'a	12	c Greatbatch, b Haslam	33
D. Brain	c Su'a, b Patel	11	c Su'a, b Patel	17
M.G. Burmester	not out	30	not out	17
A.J. Traicos	not out	1	lbw, b Patel	0
Extras	lb 7, nb 2	9	lb 2	2
	(for 9 wickets, dec.)	283		137

	O	M	R	W	O	M	R	W		O	M	R	W	O	M	R	W
Brandes	22	6	49	2	19.4	3	59	2	Su'a	37	7	85	5	12	3	30	1
Brain	18	5	49	3	16	2	52	1	Nash	28	10	59	1	8	3	19	1
Crocker	15	1	65	2	7	–	24	–	Watson	25	6	51	1	3	2	3	1
Burmester	10	2	34	–	9	1	44	–	Patel	33	5	81	2	17.3	5	50	6
Traicos	23	1	82	2	27	8	70	2	Haslam					10	2	33	1
G.W. Flower	6	–	45	–	4	–	11	–									

FALL OF WICKETS

1–44, 2–73, 3–131, 4–299, 5–306, 6–313, 7–321, 8–327, 9–330

1–21, 2–27, 3–77, 4–132, 5–262

1–7, 2–114, 3–136, 4–210, 5–211, 6–211, 7–239, 8–239, 9–275

1–3, 2–15, 3–28, 4–34, 5–56, 6–62, 7–71, 8–91, 9–137

Umpires: H.D. Bird & I.D. Robinson/K. Kanjee   *New Zealand won by 177 runs*

SECOND TEST MATCH
ZIMBABWE v. NEW ZEALAND, at Harare

ONE-DAY INTERNATIONAL
ZIMBABWE v. PAKISTAN, at Harare

New Zealand were handicapped by the loss of Doull who was forced to return home with a stress fracture. He was replaced by Dion Nash, the 21-year-old Auckland medium-pace bowler, who was making his Test debut. Zimbabwe welcomed back Brandes, and they gave a first Test cap to Brain. Jarvis and Omarshah were omitted.

There were early successes for both Brandes and Brain, and New Zealand were 73 for 2 when Crowe came to the wicket. Greatbatch left at 131, but Rutherford joined Crowe in a partnership of 168 in 36 overs which devastated the Zimbabwe attack. Crowe was magnificent and completed his century just before tea. In the afternoon session, he hit 96 off 108 balls. His 140 was his 14th Test hundred, and he faced 163 balls, hitting 3 sixes and 17 fours. Zimbabwe looked doomed, but they fought back to claim three wickets for 14 runs so that New Zealand closed on 314 for 6.

The Zimbabwe resurgence continued on the Monday morning when they captured the last four New Zealand wickets – including that of Rutherford who added only two to his overnight score – for a mere 21 runs. Grant Flower became an early victim of Su'a, but Arnott was again rock-like, and he and Campbell added 107. Zimbabwe closed on 173 for 3, very much back in contention.

The thunder and rain returned to haunt New Zealand, and only 150 minutes' play was possible on the third day. Grittily, Zimbabwe advanced to 228 for 6. It was a spell of three wickets in seven balls from Murphy Su'a which tilted the game back in New Zealand's favour. Su'a finished with his best return in Test cricket, but Burmester led a minor recovery on the fourth morning, and Houghton declared 52 runs in arrears.

New Zealand had an uneasy start to their second innings, and once again it was Crowe and Rutherford who revived them. Crowe, nursing a strained Achilles tendon, did not achieve the fluency of the first innings, but the pair added 55, and Patel and Rutherford took New Zealand to 187 for 4 by the close.

They took their partnership to 130 on the last morning, batting with great spirit, and, on Rutherford's dismissal, Crowe declared, leaving Zimbabwe 71 overs in which to score 315 to record their first Test victory.

In the nine overs before lunch, they lost both openers for 15, and victory looked remote. Watson dismissed Pycroft soon after lunch, and Houghton fell to a rash shot, hitting against Patel's spin. At 34 for 4, it was now time to bat for survival, but Patel was deceptive in flight and in changes of pace and was extracting a little turn from the pitch. Above all, he was bowling with supreme confidence, and the New Zealand fielding and catching was at its best. By tea, Zimbabwe were 94 for 8. Crocker and Burmester added a stubborn 46 for the ninth wicket, but a vital first Test wicket for Haslam ended the partnership, and Patel had Traicos leg before to give him his best return in Test cricket and New Zealand victory by 177 runs.

Following their successful tour of England in 1992, Pakistan seemingly played cricket everywhere except in their own country. They visited Australia, New Zealand, Sharjah, South Africa and the West Indies and, prior to their trip to the Caribbean, they became the third national side to play in a one-day international in Zimbabwe.

The home side included Briant in a limited-over international for the first time, and he had to take over the wicket-keeping duties when Andy Flower was injured. The match was badly threatened by the weather, and a heavy downpour the night before meant that when Pakistan won the toss and asked Zimbabwe to bat first they gained an advantage, for the outfield was damp and run-getting difficult. There was added woe for Zimbabwe when, with the score on 17, Andy Flower was struck on the finger by a ball from Aqib Javed and was forced to retire hurt and have the wound stitched. He returned when Arnott was out at 55, but he was caught and bowled by Mushtaq Ahmed five runs later. The leg-spinner troubled all the Zimbabwe batsmen and, in spite of Houghton's 51 off 74 balls, the home side were restricted to 164.

Andy Flower did not field, but his brother Grant caught Ramiz at slip in Brandes' first over. At 27, Aamir Sohail fell to Omarshah, but the patient Shoaib joined Javed in a stand of 115 which virtually won the match. Javed's 86 came off 132 balls and included 2 sixes and 4 fours.

A crowd of 5,000 watched the match.

Zimbabwe joined with 11 South African provincial teams in a three-day and one-day tournament for under-24 sides. The three-day matches were not recognised as first-class. Zimbabwe won one of their three-day games, led on the first innings in three drawn matches and were beaten by Natal. They did not qualify for the final of this competition but they won the one-day tournament, beating Western Province in Harare.

Eddo Brandes. (David Munden/Sports-Line)

ONE-DAY INTERNATIONAL – ZIMBABWE *v.* PAKISTAN
2 March 1993 at Harare Sports Club

ZIMBABWE

A. Flower	c and b Mushtaq Ahmed	10
G.W. Flower	c Aamir Sohail, b Mushtaq Ahmed	35
K.J. Arnott	run out	17
D.L. Houghton (capt)	lbw, b Waqar Younis	51
*G.A. Briant	c Rashid Latif, b Mushtaq Ahmed	0
M.H. Dekker	c Rashid Latif, b Aqib Javed	16
A.H. Omarshah	c Shoaib Mohammad, b Wasim Akram	0
S.G. Peall	c Rashid Latif, b Waqar Younis	3
E.A. Brandes	b Waqar Younis	5
D.H. Brain	b Wasim Akram	1
A.J. Traicos	not out	0
Extras	b 2, lb 7, w 13, nb 4	26
		—
(49.1 overs)		164

PAKISTAN

Aamir Sohail	c Brandes, b Omarshah	15
Ramiz Raja	c G.W. Flower, b Brandes	0
Shoaib Mohammad	c Traicos, b Brain	43
Javed Miandad	not out	86
Zahid Fazal	not out	8
Asif Mujtaba		
Wasim Akram (capt)		
*Rashid Latif		
Waqar Younis		
Mushtaq Ahmed		
Aqib Javed		
Extras	b 2, lb 3, w 8	13
		—
(47.2 overs)	(for 3 wickets)	165

	O	M	R	W
Wasim Akram	10	–	35	2
Aqib Javed	10	1	32	1
Waqar Younis	8.1	1	31	3
Mushtaq Ahmed	10	2	22	3
Aamir Sohail	10	–	30	–
Asif Mujtaba	1	–	5	–

	O	M	R	W
Brandes	8.2	1	33	1
Brain	10	3	29	1
Omarshah	10	–	26	1
Traicos	10	1	29	–
Peall	9	–	43	–

FALL OF WICKETS

1–55, 2–60, 3–92, 4–92, 5–139, 6–140, 7–152, 8–159, 9–164

FALL OF WICKETS

1–1, 2–27, 3–142

Umpires: K. Kanjee & I.D. Robinson   *Man of the Match:* Javed Miandad   *Pakistan won by 7 wickets*

Zimbabwe also competed in the Sharjah Cup and undertook a brief tour of India. Off-spinner Steven Peall was dropped from the touring party at the last moment for disciplinary reasons and his place was taken by another off-spinner, Ujesh Ranchod, who was to make his first-class debut in a Test match. On the way back from India, Zimbabwe were beaten by Kenya in Nairobi where they were guilty of serious underestimation of the opposition.

As the side were returning from India, Kent arrived for a brief tour. Kent played six matches, but none of them had first-class status.

25, 26 and 27 March 1993 *at Mutare Sports Club*

Manicaland Select XI 204 for 8 dec. and 199 (S.P. Davis 6 for 64)

Kent 238 for 6 dec. (J.I. Longley 80 not out, T.R. Ward 65) and 166 for 3 (T.R. Ward 83)

Kent won by 7 wickets

28 March 1993 *at Mutare Sports Club*

Kent 239 for 7 (N.J. Llong 80, M.V. Fleming 72)

Manicaland Select XI 141

Kent won by 98 runs

30, 31 March and 1 April 1993 *at Old Hararians Sports Club*

Kent 323 for 5 dec. (J.I. Longley 94, N.J. Llong 72, T.R. Ward 62) and 151 for 8 dec. (G.J. Martin 4 for 38)

Zimbabwe 'B' 194 (C.B. Wishart 65, M.G. Burmester 50, A.P. Igglesden 7 for 37) and 101 for 5

Match drawn

3 April 1993 *at Harare South Country Club*

Zimbabwe Country Districts 78 (C. Penn 4 for 14)

Kent 79 for 3

Kent won by 7 wickets

4 April 1993 *at Harare Sports Club*

Kent 110 (S.G. Peall 5 for 6)

Zimbabwe Invitation XI 111 for 2

Zimbabwe Invitation XI won by 8 wickets

5 April 1993 *at St George's College*

Kent 200 for 8 (M.J. Walker 76)

Zimbabwe Under-19 XI 167

Kent won by 33 runs

SECTION E
New Zealand

New Zealand celebrate the fall of David Boon's wicket in the first Test match against Australia. (Joe Mann/Allsport)

In 1992–3, New Zealand engaged in the busiest pro-gramme in its cricket history. Tours to Zimbabwe and Sri Lanka were followed immediately by a home Test match and three one-day internationals against Pakistan.

The domestic season in New Zealand began on 26 November 1992 and lasted until 28 March 1993. The first five rounds of the Shell Trophy were completed by the second week in January, and the first-class competition then gave way to the one-day tournament – the Shell Cup – which was condensed into 22 days in January.

The last three rounds of the Shell Trophy were sched-uled as four-day matches, and the Trophy was due to be decided by 15 February. Australia's tour of New Zealand began the following day, including three Test matches and five one-day internationals.

This intensive fixture list inevitably put much pressure on the associations. Dipak Patel was appointed captain of Auckland in succession to Jeff Crowe, who had retired, while Ian Smith, who had also retired, became coach. Patel, however, was to be engaged in international matches for much of his time. There was a similar situ-ation in Central Districts where Mark Greatbatch had taken over from Scott Briasco.

Otago had taken the precaution of appointing Neil Mallender as vice-captain to Ken Rutherford who, sur-prisingly, was to lead New Zealand in the absence of Martin Crowe. Mallender, exceptionally popular in Otago and in New Zealand, was returning to Shell cricket for the 10th season in succession. He has been an exem-plary professional, and his achievements have been out-standing. There was much joy in New Zealand when he won two Test caps for England in 1992.

Otago were strengthened by the arrival of spinner Mark Richardson from Auckland and, particularly, by the acquisition of Dion Nash from Northern Districts. A student at Otago University, Nash, an inexperienced quick bowler who was a surprise choice for the tours of Zimbabwe and Sri Lanka, had decided to remain in Dunedin to play his cricket.

In contrast, Canterbury were handicapped by the early-season absence of Chris Cairns, who was conva-lescing after an operation, and by the loss of Peter Ken-nedy. Like Cairns, Kennedy had been playing cricket in England and had been involved in a car crash. He suf-fered injuries which restricted his cricket in New Zealand to minor matches in 1992–3.

Wellington had engaged Bob Carter as coach and were hoping that he could help realise the full potential of Heath Davis, believed by many to be the fastest bowler in New Zealand. Like Burnett and Williams before him, Davis had spent a season with Sussex 2nd XI.

PAKISTAN TOUR

The Pakistan tour of New Zealand lasted barely a fort-night and consisted of three one-day internationals and a Test match. New Zealand were at full strength again after the traumas of Sri Lanka, and Morrison declared himself fit again.

Javed Miandad scored 92 and led Pakistan to a memorable victory over New Zealand in Hamilton, and then found himself replaced as Pakistan's captain. (David Munden/Sports-Line)

ONE-DAY INTERNATIONAL SERIES
NEW ZEALAND v. PAKISTAN

The first game in the three-match series saw Wasim Akram and the Pakistan pace bowlers at their devastating best. However, the visitors batted tentatively. Ramiz Raja faced 100 balls for his fifty, and Javed Miandad 94 balls for his 46 after rain had reduced the match by one over per innings. Faced with a moderate target of 159, New Zea-land collapsed after the departure of Crowe. Wasim Akram's figures were his best in a one-day international.

New Zealand drew level by winning the second match, which became infamous for the behaviour of Aqib Javed. He verbally abused umpire Brian Aldridge and was later banned for one game. Pakistan's suspect batting seemed totally bemused by off-spinner Dipak Patel's opening spell, after the start of the game had been delayed for 90 minutes by rain. Salim Malik apart, Pakistan batted lamely, and, having overcome the early loss of Great-batch, New Zealand won with ease. Rutherford and Crowe shared a decisive fourth-wicket partnership of 62.

Another poor batting performance by Pakistan allowed New Zealand to take the series. Once again a stand between Crowe and Rutherford – this time worth 60 runs – was the substance of the New Zealand innings, but the

FIRST ONE-DAY INTERNATIONAL – NEW ZEALAND v. PAKISTAN
26 December 1992 at Basin Reserve, Wellington

PAKISTAN			NEW ZEALAND		
Aamir Sohail	b Morrison	8	M.J. Greatbatch	c Waqar Younis, b Wasim Akram	7
Ramiz Raja	b Harris	50	R.T. Latham	b Wasim Akram	1
Salim Malik	run out	25	A.H. Jones	c Rashid Latif, b Wasim Akram	0
Javed Miandad (capt)	c and b Morrison	46	M.D. Crowe (capt)	c Aamir Sohail, b Aqib Javed	28
Inzamam-ul-Haq	c Jones, b Watson	0	K.R. Rutherford	b Aqib Javed	18
Asif Mujtaba	c Patel, b Harris	0	C.Z. Harris	b Aqib Javed	7
Wasim Akram	c Morrison, b Harris	1	D.N. Patel	c Inzamam-ul-Haq, b Mushtaq Ahmed	1
*Rashid Latif	c Latham, b Watson	12	*A.C. Parore	c Salim Malik, b Wasim Akram	14
Waqar Younis	not out	4	G.R. Larsen	c Rashid Latif, b Wasim Akram	11
Mushtaq Ahmed	not out	1	D.K. Morrison	run out	3
Aqib Javed			W. Watson	not out	1
Extras	b 4, lb 3, w 3, nb 1	11	Extras	lb 8, w 6, nb 3	17
(49 overs)	(for 8 wickets)	158	(39.3 overs)		108

	O	M	R	W		O	M	R	W
Morrison	7	1	19	2	Wasim Akram	9	1	19	5
Watson	10	–	37	2	Waqar Younis	8	2	14	–
Patel	10	–	37	–	Aqib Javed	10	1	27	3
Larsen	10	–	30	–	Mustaq Ahmed	8	1	20	1
Harris	10	1	24	3	Aamir Sohail	4.3	–	20	–
Latham	2	–	4	–					

FALL OF WICKETS

1–14, 2–57, 3–116, 4–117, 5–119, 6–123, 7–152, 8–153

FALL OF WICKETS

1–10, 2–11, 3–19, 4–60, 5–73, 6–74, 7–77, 8–97, 9–106

Umpires: R.S. Dunne & C.E. King   *Man of the Match:* Wasim Akram   *Pakistan won by 50 runs*

SECOND ONE-DAY INTERNATIONAL – NEW ZEALAND v. PAKISTAN
28 December 1992 at McLean Park, Napier

PAKISTAN			NEW ZEALAND		
Aamir Sohail	b Patel	9	M.J. Greatbatch	c Rashid Latif, b Wasim Akram	0
Ramiz Raja	c Parore, b Patel	1	R.T. Latham	b Shahid Saeed	21
Salim Malik	c Parore, b Watson	39	A.H. Jones	c Rashid Latif, b Waqar Younis	17
Javed Miandad (capt)	b Larsen	19	M.D. Crowe (capt)	not out	47
Inzamam-ul-Haq	c Parore, b Larsen	2	K.R. Rutherford	c Inzamam-ul-Haq, b Shahid Saeed	34
Shahid Saeed	run out	14	C.Z. Harris	not out	3
*Rashid Latif	c Jones, b Morrison	20	D.N. Patel		
Wasim Akram	c Parore, b Watson	12	*A.C. Parore		
Waqar Younis	not out	0	G.R. Larsen		
Mushtaq Ahmed	not out	0	D.K. Morrison		
Aqib Javed			W. Watson		
Extras	b 3, lb 9, w 8	20	Extras	b 1, lb 1, w 5, nb 8	15
(42 overs)	(for 8 wickets)	136	(37.4 overs)	(for 4 wickets)	137

	O	M	R	W		O	M	R	W
Morrison	8	1	30	1	Wasim Akram	9	2	22	1
Patel	9	2	16	2	Waqar Younis	9	–	36	1
Watson	8	–	39	2	Aqib Javed	8	1	39	–
Larsen	9	2	15	2	Shahid Saeed	7	–	20	2
Harris	8	1	24	–	Mushtaq Ahmed	4	–	16	–
					Salim Malik	0.4	–	2	–

FALL OF WICKETS

1–9, 2–14, 3–67, 4–69, 5–92, 6–113, 7–128, 8–135

FALL OF WICKETS

1–0, 2–30, 3–71, 4–133

Umpires: B.L. Aldridge & D.M. Quested   *Man of the Match:* M.D. Crowe   *New Zealand won by 6 wickets*

THIRD ONE-DAY INTERNATIONAL – NEW ZEALAND v. PAKISTAN
30 December 1992 at Eden Park, Auckland

PAKISTAN

Ramiz Raja	b Watson	23
Shahid Saeed	run out	17
Salim Malik	c Crowe, b Larsen	23
Saeed Anwar	c Parore, b Watson	0
Javed Miandad (capt)	c Parore, b Watson	30
Inzamam-ul-Haq	run out	2
Wasim Akram	c Harris, b Morrison	21
Naved Anjum	st Parore, b Harris	0
*Rashid Latif	not out	9
Waqar Younis	c Crowe, b Morrison	0
Mushtaq Ahmed	c Greatbatch, b Watson	6
Extras	lb 5, nb 3	8
(47.4 overs)		139

NEW ZEALAND

M.J. Greatbatch	c Mushtaq Ahmed, b Wasim Akram	24
R.T. Latham	c Inzamam-ul-Haq, b Waqar Younis	0
A.H. Jones	lbw, b Naved Anjum	9
M.D. Crowe (capt)	not out	57
K.R. Rutherford	b Mushtaq Ahmed	28
C.Z. Harris	not out	11
D.N. Patel		
*A.C. Parore		
G.R. Larsen		
D.K. Morrison		
W. Watson		
Extras	lb 3, w 5, nb 3	11
(42.4 overs)	(for 4 wickets)	140

	O	M	R	W
Morrison	10	1	27	2
Patel	10	2	25	–
Watson	8.4	1	27	4
Larsen	10	2	20	1
Harris	6	1	22	1
Jones	2	–	6	–
Latham	1	–	7	–

	O	M	R	W
Wasim Akram	9	2	28	1
Waqar Younis	10	2	27	1
Naved Anjum	10	1	30	1
Mushtaq Ahmed	9.4	1	34	1
Salim Malik	1	–	4	–
Shahid Saeed	3	–	14	–

FALL OF WICKETS

1–35, 2–43, 3–47, 4–75, 5–77, 6–123, 7–123, 8–127, 9–128

FALL OF WICKETS

1–10, 2–34, 3–45, 4–105

Umpires: B.L. Aldridge & D.B. Cowie   *Man of the Match:* M.D. Crowe   *New Zealand won by 6 wickets*

real hero was Willie Watson. He returned his best figures in a one-day international, 4 for 27, dismissing Ramiz Raja and Saeed Anwar with consecutive deliveries and accounting for Javed Miandad when the Pakistan skipper was looking threatening.

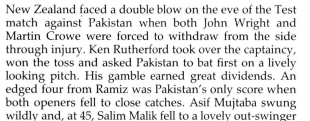

TEST MATCH
NEW ZEALAND v. PAKISTAN, at Hamilton

New Zealand faced a double blow on the eve of the Test match against Pakistan when both John Wright and Martin Crowe were forced to withdraw from the side through injury. Ken Rutherford took over the captaincy, won the toss and asked Pakistan to bat first on a lively looking pitch. His gamble earned great dividends. An edged four from Ramiz was Pakistan's only score when both openers fell to close catches. Asif Mujtaba swung wildly and, at 45, Salim Malik fell to a lovely out-swinger from Morrison.

Whether or not the pitch lost its early sting could not be determined, for Javed played with such total assurance as to tame any bowler on any wicket. He and Inzamam-ul-Haq added 42, and Wasim Akram helped take the score to 158. With the intelligent and impressive Rashid as his partner, it seemed that Javed would reach his century and

take Pakistan further out of trouble, but he suddenly played rashly at Su'a. He narrowly escaped being out, but the next ball he played on. The left-arm Su'a claimed five wickets, and Pakistan were out for 216. In 15 fiery overs before the close, New Zealand made 23 without loss and ended the day most happily.

Wickets continued to tumble on the second day, during which New Zealand reached 256 for 8. Had Pakistan accepted half the chances offered to them, New Zealand would not have reached 200, but catches at slip went untaken with alarming regularity. Hartland was one of the beneficiaries, but he stuck to his task well and shared an opening partnership of 108 with Mark Greatbatch, which offered New Zealand a firm base. The burly, left-handed Greatbatch was superb. He batted for just over seven hours and faced 317 balls to withstand the Pakistan pace attack virtually single-handed. The merit of the innings was that the runs were made against bowling of the highest quality. Wasim Akram accounted for Jones and Latham within the space of three balls with lethal yorkers, and when Waqar or Wasim were rested there was always the telling and taxing leg-spin of Mushtaq Ahmed.

Mushtaq it was who had Hartland stumped, and he also claimed the wickets of Rutherford and Patel. Harris led a charmed life for nearly 40 minutes before falling leg before to Waqar, and Greatbatch's heroic innings came to

Waqar Younis, match figures of 9 for 81 and the main reason for Pakistan's sensational win at Hamilton. (Alan Cozzi)

Mark Greatbatch hit a magnificent century against Pakistan and finished on the losing side. (David Munden/Sports-Line)

an end in the same manner three overs before the close. The unhappy part of the day lay in the acrimony that appeared to exist on the field between the two sides.

The atmosphere seemed to grow worse on the third day, which ended with match referee Peter Burge issuing a general warning to both sides about the amount of 'sledging' that had occurred. The centre of the problem seemed to be remarks made by Dipak Patel, fielding at short-leg, to batsman Rashid Latif, who complained to the umpires and had to be restrained when he threatened to react to Patel's comments. In spite of all this, the cricket was fascinating.

Waqar and Wasim brought the New Zealand innings to a close for the addition of only eight more runs, but the home side seemed set for victory when Pakistan lost five wickets before clearing the first-innings arrears of 48. It was Morrison who ripped apart the top order. Aamir Sohail was bowled by the first ball of the innings, and Morrison claimed the wickets of Ramiz Raja, Asif Mujtaba, and the vital one of Salim Malik for 0. With Su'a accounting for Javed, New Zealand had reduced Pakistan to 39 for 5.

Inzamam-ul-Haq and Rashid Latif added 80 to keep the game alive, and Inzamam played a number of high-class strokes before falling to Owens who was, perhaps, under-bowled while Patel was over-bowled. Following the dismissal of Inzamam, the end came quickly, Morri-

son finishing with 5 for 41, his best figures in Test cricket. New Zealand had bowled well; Pakistan had batted badly. Throughout the match the quality of the bowling on both sides was far superior to that of the batting.

New Zealand needed 127 runs to win, and they had two days and 20 overs in which to get them. The 20 overs at the end of the third day cost them dear. Wasim Akram bowled with pace and fury. Hartland was struck on the helmet, and, having been subjected to a withering attack, Greatbatch jabbed at Wasim and edged to Aamir Sohail at slip. Hartland was bowled and, for the addition of one no-ball, Morrison was palpably leg before. Jones and Parore remained, and New Zealand closed on 39 for 3.

Wasim and Waqar did all the bowling that was necessary on the fourth day and brought the match to a premature close with a memorable display of fast bowling which left the New Zealanders shattered and forlorn. At first, there was little indication of what was to come. Jones and Parore took the score to 65, at which point Jones was brilliantly caught at short-leg. Two runs later, Parore was caught behind, and, at 71, Waqar Younis blasted Latham's middle stump out of the ground.

At the first drinks interval, New Zealand were 76 for 6, but the break served only to refresh the Pakistan pace men. Three wickets fell at 88, and the psychological advantage had long since passed to the visitors who duly claimed a remarkable victory by 33 runs. This was a

Consistently hostile bowling by Willie Watson saw him regain his place in the Test side. (Adrian Murrell/Allsport)

deceptively small margin, for, in truth, on the fourth day, the result was never really in doubt.

Waqar Younis and Wasim Akram shared 17 wickets in the match, and Waqar took the individual award for his 9 for 81, which took him past 100 Test wickets. They confirmed that they are the best pair of fast bowlers in world cricket. Ironically, Pakistan were fined 10 per cent of their match fee for failing to maintain the required over rate of 15 overs an hour, which seemed rather harsh when they had finished a match in under 3½ days.

SHELL CUP

1 January 1993 *at Molyneux Park, Alexandra*

Otago 214 (R.N. Hoskin 70, R.P. de Groen 4 for 33)
Northern Districts 152

Otago (2 pts.) won by 62 runs

TEST MATCH – NEW ZEALAND *v.* PAKISTAN

2, 3, 4 and 5 January 1993 at Trust Bank Park, Hamilton

PAKISTAN

	FIRST INNINGS		SECOND INNINGS	
Ramiz Raja	c Rutherford, b Su'a	4	(2) c Parore, b Morrison	8
Aamir Sohail	c Owens, b Morrison	0	(1) b Morrison	0
Asif Mujtaba	c Owens, b Su'a	0	lbw, b Morrison	11
Javed Miandad (capt)	b Su'a	92	lbw, b Su'a	12
Salim Malik	c Parore, b Morrison	14	c Su'a, b Morrison	0
Inzamam-ul-Haq	c Morrison, b Su'a	23	lbw, b Owens	75
Wasim Akram	c Greatbatch, b Patel	27	(8) b Patel	15
*Rashid Latif	not out	32	(7) c Rutherford, b Su'a	33
Waqar Younis	run out	13	not out	4
Mushtaq Ahmed	lbw, b Su'a	2	c Rutherford, b Morrison	10
Aqib Javed	c Greatbatch, b Morrison	1	c Hartland, b Patel	2
Extras	w 4, nb 4	8	lb 2, nb 2	4
		216		174

NEW ZEALAND

	FIRST INNINGS		SECOND INNINGS	
M.J. Greatbatch	lbw, b Waqar Younis	133	(2) c Sohail, b Wasim	8
B.R. Hartland	st Rashid, b Mushtaq	43	(1) b Wasim Akram	9
A.H. Jones	lbw, b Wasim Akram	2	c Asif Mujtaba, b Waqar	19
R.T. Latham	lbw, b Wasim Akram	2	(6) b Waqar Younis	0
K.R. Rutherford (capt)	c Rashid, b Mushtaq	14	(7) c Sohail, b Wasim	9
C.Z. Harris	lbw, b Waqar Younis	6	(8) b Waqar Younis	9
D.N. Patel	lbw, b Mushtaq	12	(9) b Waqar Younis	4
*A.C. Parore	lbw, b Wasim Akram	16	(5) c Rashid, b Wasim	13
M.L. Su'a	c Rashid, b Waqar	0	(10) lbw, b Waqar	0
D.K. Morrison	not out	3	(4) lbw, b Wasim	0
M.B. Owens	b Waqar Younis	0	not out	0
Extras	b 1, lb 15, w 1, nb 16	33	b 1, lb 11, nb 10	22
		264		93

	O	M	R	W	O	M	R	W
Morrison	19.3	4	42	3	15	2	41	5
Su'a	24	2	73	5	13	1	47	2
Owens	12	3	48	–	7	–	19	1
Patel	14	2	53	1	20.1	5	65	2

	O	M	R	W	O	M	R	W
Wasim Akram	31	9	66	3	22	4	45	5
Aqib Javed	7	2	24	–	8	2	14	–
Waqar Younis	28	11	59	4	13.3	4	22	5
Mushtaq Ahmed	38	10	87	3				
Aamir Sohail	5	2	12	–				

FALL OF WICKETS (Pakistan)

1–4,, 2–4, 3–12, 4–45, 5–87, 6–158, 7–176, 8–202, 9–208
1–0, 2–20, 3–25, 4–25, 5–39, 6–119, 7–158, 8–158, 9–171

FALL OF WICKETS (New Zealand)

1–108, 2–111, 3–117, 4–147, 5–164, 6–193, 7–254, 8–256, 9–257
1–19, 2–31, 3–32, 4–65, 5–67, 6–71, 7–88, 8–88, 9–88

Umpires: B.L. Aldridge & R.S. Dunne

Pakistan won by 33 runs

at Lancaster Park, Christchurch

Canterbury 142 (A.J. Hunt 4 for 22)
Auckland 145 for 6

Auckland (2 pts.) won by 4 wickets

at Basin Reserve, Wellington

Wellington 174 for 9 (M.P. Speight 70, D.N. Askew 4 for 27)
Central Districts 108

Wellington (2 pts.) won by 66 runs

One of the features of New Zealand's domestic season was the bowling of Northern Districts' pace man Richard de Groen, but he finished on the losing side in Alexandra. Sussex's Martin Speight came to the wicket when Wellington were 23 for 3 and dominated a stand of 113 with Larsen.

3 January 1993 *at Levin Domain, Levin*

Canterbury 179 for 9 (D.J. Murray 57, C.L. Cairns 50, R.G. Twose 4 for 33)
Central Districts 89 for 7

Canterbury (2 pts.) won on faster run rate

at Molyneux Park, Alexandra

Otago 136
Wellington 137 for 9 (N.A. Mallender 4 for 16)

Wellington (2 pts.) won by 1 wicket

at Eden Park, Auckland

Auckland 210 for 8
Northern Districts 198 (B.A. Pocock 65, C. Pringle 4 for 34)

Auckland (2 pts.) won by 12 runs

It seemed that Otago were destined for victory over Wellington when Neil Mallender produced an inspired spell of bowling, but Williams and O'Rourke added 12 for the last wicket to steal the match for the visitors.

9 January 1993 *at Eden Park, Auckland*

Auckland 199 for 8 (M.J. Horne 67)
Otago 126

Auckland (2 pts.) won by 73 runs

at Lancaster Park, Christchurch

Canterbury 239 for 7 (C.L. Cairns 115, L.K. Germon 71)
Wellington 240 for 4 (M.D. Crowe 110, M.P. Speight 96)

Wellington (2 pts.) won by 6 wickets

at Smallbone Park, Rotorua

Northern Districts 158 (R.G. Twose 4 for 36)
Central Districts 164 for 3

Central Districts (2 pts.) won by 7 wickets

When Lee Germon joined Chris Cairns Canterbury were 27 for 4. In just over two hours, the pair added 198. Cairns hit 115 off as many deliveries – his first century in the competition – while Germon passed 50 in the one-day tournament for the first time. Martin Crowe responded with his fifth Shell Cup hundred and, with Martin Speight, added 174 in 115 minutes to set up a remarkable Wellington victory with two overs to spare. Like Wellington, Auckland maintained their 100 per cent record.

11 January 1993 *at Dannervirke Domain, Dannervirke*

Otago 258 for 6 (J.W. Wilson 99)
Central Districts 242 (R.G. Twose 68)

Otago (2 pts.) won by 16 runs

at Basin Reserve, Wellington

Wellington 202 for 8 (M.D. Crowe 79, A.H. Jones 55, W. Watson 4 for 41)
Auckland 152 (A.J. Hunt 68)

Wellington (2 pts.) won by 50 runs

at Blake Park, Mt Maunganui

Northern Districts 158 for 9 (M.N. Hart 62 not out, R.G. Petrie 4 for 32)
Canterbury 161 for 6

Canterbury (2 pts.) won by 4 wickets.

Back to New Zealand for a 10th season, Somerset's Neil Mallender enjoyed another year of spectacular success, topping the first-class averages with 26 wickets at 10.76 runs apiece. (David Munden/ Sports-Line)

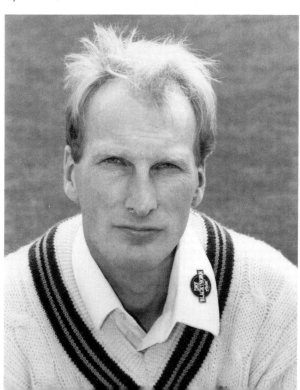

A splendid all-round performance by Jeff Wilson, who made his highest Shell Cup score, led to Otago's victory over Central Districts. With one round of matches remaining, only Northern Districts were out of contention for a place in the semi-finals.

13 January 1993 *at Lancaster Park, Christchurch*

Otago 223 for 8 (K.R. Rutherford 62, P.W. Dobbs 58)
Canterbury 214 for 8 (C.Z. Harris 74)

Otago (2 pts.) won by 9 runs

at Trust Bank Park, Hamilton

Wellington 212 for 6 (G.P. Burnett 102 not out)
Northern Districts 195 (M. Parlane 70)

Wellington (2 pts.) won by 17 runs

at Pukekura Park, New Plymouth

Auckland 133
Central Districts 137 for 5

Central Districts (2 pts.) won by 5 wickets

Although beaten by Otago, Canterbury qualified for the semi-finals ahead of Central Districts by virtue of a faster run rate. Had Central reached their target of 134 against Auckland five balls earlier, they would have qualified, as they would have done had Canterbury scored five runs

fewer. Graham Burnett hit his first century in the competition as Wellington completed their fifth victory in five matches. The one consolation for pointless Northern Districts was a fine innings from Parlane, a graduate from the under-20 side.

SHELL CUP FINAL TABLE

	P	W	L	Pts.	RR
Wellington	5	5	–	10	3.86
Otago	5	3	2	6	3.82
Auckland	5	3	2	6	3.40
Canterbury	5	2	3	4	3.80
Central Districts	5	2	3	4	3.68
Northern Districts	5	–	5	0	3.44

SEMI-FINALS

17 January 1993 *at Carisbrook, Dunedin*

Otago 191 for 7 (K.R. Rutherford 53)
Auckland 143

Otago won by 48 runs

at Basin Reserve, Wellington

Wellington 181 (M.B. Owens 4 for 31)
Canterbury 183 for 3 (R.T. Latham 73)

Canterbury won by 7 wickets

It was no surprise that Otago beat Auckland, who had fallen away in the later stages of the competition, but Canterbury routed the hitherto unbeaten Wellington to reach the final and astonish all. New international Michael Owens gave Canterbury a tremendous boost when he had Martin Crowe caught for seven, and another New Zealand national player, Rod Latham, hit a spectacular 73 and dominated an opening stand of 111 with Blair Hartland. Canterbury won with nearly 10 overs to spare.

 SHELL CUP FINAL
OTAGO *v.* CANTERBURY, at Dunedin

A crowd of 13,000 provided further evidence of the ever-increasing popularity of the one-day game in New Zealand. They were treated to a highly competitive match on a somewhat sluggish pitch. Against a tight attack in which Dion Nash was particularly impressive, Canterbury scored consistently without ever suggesting dominance. The innings had no real impetus until Astle hit 28 off 15 balls towards the close.

*John Wright provided the backbone to the New Zealand side, hit 118 for Auckland against Canterbury at the end of 1992, reached 5,000 runs in Test cricket and, at the end of the summer, announced that he was retiring from international cricket. He will be sadly missed.
(Joe Mann/Allsport)*

SHELL CUP FINAL – OTAGO v. CANTERBURY
23 January 1993 at Carisbrook, Dunedin

CANTERBURY				OTAGO		
B.R. Hartland	run out	23		P.W. Dobbs	lbw, b Astle	36
R.T. Latham	c Robinson, b Gale	12		J.W. Wilson	c Germon, b Owens	5
L.G. Howell	lbw, b Smith	29		K.R. Rutherford (capt)	c Priest, b Cairns	6
C.Z. Harris	b Gale	40		D.J. Nash	b Cairns	15
C.L. Cairns	c Robinson, b Mallender	5		R.N. Hoskin	c Harris, b Owens	45
*L.K. Germon (capt)	c Mallender, b Nash	12		*S.A. Robinson	run out	27
S.P. Fleming	run out	10		D.S. McHardy	c Priest, b Cairns	19
N.J. Astle	not out	28		R. Smith	b Owens	3
M.W. Priest	b Gale	8		N.A. Mallender	not out	4
M.A. Hastings	not out	0		E.J. Marshall	c Harris, b Cairns	3
M.B. Owens				A.J. Gale		
Extras	lb 9, w 6, nb 1	16		Extras	b 1, lb 4, w 1	6
(50 overs)	(for 8 wickets)	183		(50 overs)	(for 9 wickets)	169

	O	M	R	W		O	M	R	W
Mallender	10	2	34	1	Owens	10	1	30	3
Gale	9	1	38	3	Hastings	10	2	33	–
Nash	10	2	25	1	Cairns	10	1	41	4
Wilson	8	–	31	–	Astle	10	1	21	1
Marshall	5	–	18	–	Priest	4	1	16	–
Smith	8	1	28	1	Harris	6	–	23	–

FALL OF WICKETS

1–19, 2–57, 3–98, 4–103, 5–128, 6–147, 7–150, 8–183

FALL OF WICKETS

1–15, 2–23, 3–44, 4–96, 5–122, 6–153, 7–162, 8–163, 9–168

Umpires: B.L. Aldridge & R.S. Dunne   *Man of the Match:* N.J. Astle   *Canterbury won by 14 runs*

Otago began disappointingly, losing the highly promising 19-year-old Wilson and skipper Rutherford for 23. Nash and Dobbs suggested a revival, but Cairns knocked back Nash's off stump, and Dobbs fell to the accurate Astle. Hoskin and Robinson offered positive defiance, but Cairns returned to cut down the tail. Otago had fallen behind the required run rate, and, scurrying to stay in touch, they lost four wickets at the end for 16 runs.

SHELL TROPHY

26, 27 and **28** November 1992 *at Sunnyvale Park, Dunedin*

Otago 193 (I.S. Billcliff 51, D.K. Morrison 4 for 62) and 35 for 0

Auckland 105 (N.A. Mallender 4 for 21)

Match drawn

Otago 4 pts., Auckland 0 pts.

at Smallbone Park, Rotorua

Central Districts 177 (R.G. Twose 85, M.N. Hart 4 for 20) and 152 for 5 (R.K. Brown 51 not out)

Northern Districts 256 for 8 dec. (D.J. White 110, B.S. Oxenham 50)

Match drawn

Northern Districts 4 pts., Central Districts 0 pts.

at Basin Reserve, Wellington

Canterbury 288 for 6 dec. (R.T. Latham 134) and 52 for 0 dec.

Wellington 78 for 3 dec. and 261 for 9 (M.H. Austen 85, G.P. Burnett 79)

Match drawn

Canterbury 4 pts., Wellington 0 pts.

Rain massacred the first round of matches, the game at Dunedin being particularly affected. Otago moved the contest to Sunnyvale Park because Carisbrook was not ready after the wet winter and spring. The best feature of the match was the return to fitness of Morrison.

Central Districts collapsed from 170 for 4 to 177 all out at Rotorua, where Northern's skipper David White hit 110 with 11 fours. Roger Brown and Tony Blain saved Central in their second innings after they had slipped to 56 for 5.

Greatest excitement came at Wellington where Latham hit 3 sixes and 15 fours in his 134. Declarations compensated for a barren first day. Set to score 263 to win,

Wellington reached 251 for 5 with 21 balls remaining, but a lack of coolness, the captaincy of Germon and the bowling of Astle denied them.

3, 4 and 5 December 1992 at Queen Elizabeth Park, Masterton

Otago 106 (D.N. Askew 4 for 40) and 86 for 8
Central Districts 125 (N.A. Mallender 5 for 41)

Match drawn

Central Districts 4 pts., Otago 0 pts.

at Lancaster Park, Christchurch

Northern Districts 250 (B.A. Pocock 130, B.A. Young 58, S.J. Roberts 4 for 62, R.M. Ford 4 for 65) and 155 (S.A. Thomson 80 not out, S.J. Roberts 4 for 30)
Canterbury 249 (R.T. Latham 88, R.P. de Groen 4 for 51) and 132 for 7 (R.T. Latham 52)

Match drawn

Northern Districts 4 pts., Canterbury 0 pts.

4, 5 and 6 December 1992 at Eden Park, Auckland

Auckland 136 and 247 for 6 dec. (M.J. Clarke 64)
Wellington 153 (W. Watson 5 for 40) and 145 for 6

Match drawn

Wellington 4 pts., Auckland 0 pts.

A wretched wicket at Masterton brought Otago to the brink of defeat, but no play was possible on the last day. Blair Pocock hit the highest score of his career for Northern Districts against Canterbury, but his side lost their last seven wickets for 21 runs. In spite of another fine knock by Latham, Northern claimed first-innings points. The third day belonged to Shane Thomson who hit 80 out of 155 and then, bowling off-spinners, took three wickets in one over to halt Canterbury's challenge. Rain was the only winner in Auckland. Lee Germon, the Canterbury captain and wicket-keeper, equalled the New Zealand first-class record with nine catches in the match in Christchurch.

10, 11 and 12 December 1992 at Eden Park, Auckland

Central Districts 177 (D.K. Morrison 5 for 40) and 113 for 6
Auckland 168 (A.P. O'Dowd 85, D.J. Leonard 6 for 68)

Match drawn

Central Districts 4 pts., Auckland 0 pts.

at Trust Bank Park, Hamilton

Wellington 296 (G.P. Burnett 53, J.D. Wells 52)
Northern Districts 72 for 1

Match abandoned

Northern Districts 2 pts., Wellington 2 pts.

11, 12 and 13 December 1992 at Lancaster Park, Christchurch

Otago 131 (S.J. Roberts 4 for 51) and 318 for 9 (J.W. Wilson 78, R.N. Hoskin 65, N.A. Mallender 62 not out, S.J. Roberts 5 for 75)
Canterbury 319 (S.P. Fleming 94, D.J. Murray 80, E.J. Marshall 4 for 80)

Match drawn

Canterbury 4 pts., Otago 0 pts.

The matches at Auckland and Hamilton were ruined by rain. With the 19-year-old left-hander Stephen Fleming hitting the highest score of his career and the revitalised Roberts continuing his excellent form with the ball, Canterbury seemed set for victory over Otago who were 180 for 8 in the second innings. Neil Mallender joined Jeff Wilson in a stand of 134 to save the game, Wilson making the highest score of his career.

29, 30 and 31 December 1992 at Lancaster Park, Christchurch

Canterbury 300 for 7 dec. (B.Z. Harris 82, L.K. Germon 60, B.R. Hartland 54)
Auckland 293 (J.G. Wright 118)

Match drawn

Canterbury 4 pts., Auckland 0 pts.

at Basin Reserve, Wellington

Central Districts 143 (P.W. O'Rourke 4 for 26) and 275 (D.J. Leonard 61)
Wellington 219 for 6 dec. (M.H. Austen 79) and 127 for 6

Match drawn

Wellington 4 pts., Central Districts 0 pts.

at Molyneux Park, Alexandra

Otago 124 (R.P. de Groen 7 for 50) and 205 (P.W. Dobbs 77, R.P. de Groen 6 for 49)
Northern Districts 139 (A.J. Gale 4 for 12) and 105 (N.A. Mallender 5 for 30)

Otago won by 85 runs

Otago 12 pts., Northern Districts 4 pts.

A spectacular thunderstorm ended play at Christchurch after John Wright had completed a fine 118, which gave him a century against every Shell Trophy side. Wellington had every chance of victory against Central Districts, who trailed by 76 on the first innings and were 140 for 7 in their second innings. They were revived by Leonard, Alcock and Duff, and, eventually, it was Wellington who were struggling to avoid defeat.

Otago achieved the first outright win of the season in the Shell Trophy in spite of surrendering first-innings points to Northern Districts. The hero of the game was medium-pacer Richard de Groen who had a career-best bowling performance for both an innings and a match

Brian Young relinquished wicket-keeping duties for Northern Districts but continued to hold catches and score runs – 138 not out as Auckland were beaten by an innings, 5–7 January. (Adrian Murrell/Allsport)

and yet finished on the losing side. On a demanding pitch, Peter Dobbs played an innings of great concentration. His 77 came off 269 balls in 301 minutes, and it made Otago's victory possible. Northern found the task of making 191 against Mallender and Gale beyond them.

5, 6 and **7** January 1993 *at Horton Park, Blenheim*

Central Districts 277 (S.W. Duff 62, R.G. Twose 56) and 237 for 3 dec. (M.W. Douglas 102 not out, T.E. Blain 63 not out)

Canterbury 236 (C.L. Cairns 79) and 209 for 8 (B.Z. Harris 65)

Match drawn

Central Districts 4 pts., Canterbury 0 pts.

at Carisbrook, Dunedin

Wellington 283 (G.R. Larsen 93 not out, E.B. McSweeney 84, N.A. Mallender 4 for 22, J.W. Wilson 4 for 60) and 66 for 2 dec.

Otago 114 for 8 dec. (H.T. Davis 4 for 45) and 152 for 8 (P.W. Dobbs 59)

Match drawn

Wellington 4 pts., Otago 0 pts.

at Eden Park, Auckland

Northern Districts 367 for 7 dec. (D.J. White 155, B.A. Young 138 not out)

Auckland 170 (R.P. de Groen 5 for 39) and 178 (T.J. Franklin 56, M.N. Hart 5 for 37, G.E. Bradburn 4 for 59)

Northern Districts won by an innings and 19 runs

Northern Districts 16 pts., Auckland 0 pts.

Left-hander Mark Douglas returned to form with the fourth century of his career as he and Tony Blain shared an unbroken stand of 127 in 188 minutes for Central against Canterbury. Needing 279 in 68 overs, Canterbury fell well short and were fortunate to escape defeat.

Larsen and McSweeney added 164 for Wellington's sixth wicket against Otago, but rain plagued the match, and, in spite of challenging declarations, it was drawn.

As the Trophy began its mid-term break Northern Districts moved clear at the top of the table with a convincing win over Auckland. David White and Bryan Young shared a fourth-wicket stand of 211. Both men hit centuries, Young reaching the highest score of his career. Auckland collapsed twice, with de Groen doing the damage in the first innings and Hart and Bradburn bowling them out on the last day. The Auckland second innings was the only occasion in the season when de Groen failed to take a wicket in Trophy matches.

A century for Adam Parore for Auckland against Wellington, 25–8 January. (George Herringshaw/ASP)

25, 26, 27 and **28** January 1993 *at Trust Bank Park, Hamilton*

Northern Districts 318 (G.E. Bradburn 80, B.A. Pocock 74) and 230 for 9 dec. (S.A. Thomson 101, M.N. Hart 83, S.J. Roberts 5 for 59)

Canterbury 233 (D.J. Murray 106 not out, L.K. Germon 57, M.N. Hart 4 for 42) and 246 (S.P. Fleming 73, S.J. Roberts 55)

Northern Districts won by 69 runs

Northern Districts 16 pts., Canterbury 0 pts.

at Fitzherbert Park, Palmerston North

Central Districts 327 (R.G. Twose 154, J.W. Wilson 5 for 71) and 243 for 6 dec. (T.E. Blain 111)

Otago 328 for 8 dec. (D.S. McHardy 66, R.A. Lawson 55, R.P. Wixon 4 for 83) and 202 (P.D. Unwin 4 for 47)

Central Districts won by 40 runs

Central Districts 12 pts., Otago 4 pts.

at Basin Reserve, Wellington

Auckland 423 for 7 dec. (A.C. Parore 102 not out, J.T.C. Vaughan 95, T.J. Franklin 81, M.J. Sears 4 for 88) and 180 for 5 dec. (S.W. Brown 65 not out)

Wellington 256 (A.H. Jones 104, G.R. Larsen 91, C. Pringle 5 for 52) and 307 for 9 (M.D. Crowe 95, E.B. McSweeney 56)

Match drawn

Auckland 4 pts., Wellington 0 pts.

The Shell Trophy resumed with the first of its three rounds of four-day matches. Northern Districts consolidated their place at the top with another outright win, but the victory over Canterbury was not without alarms. In spite of Murray carrying his bat through the 364 minutes of the Canterbury innings, Northern led by 85 on the first innings, but they slipped to 16 for 5 when they batted again. Shane Thomson and Matthew Hart, who hit a career best 83, then added 180, and Canterbury were set to score 316 to win. With Hart adding three wickets to the four he had taken in the first innings, Canterbury were always facing defeat. Stu Roberts hit 55 off 50 balls in a late, defiant gesture.

Warwickshire's Roger Twose provided the backbone to Central's innings against Otago, but consistent batting gave Otago the first-innings points. Central were 51 for 4 in their second innings before Tony Blain hit 3 sixes and 9 fours in his 111 which occupied less than three hours. Otago floundered against Central's spinners, with leg-break bowler Unwin taking four wickets to give his side victory by 40 runs.

Parore hit a delightful century and Justin Vaughan made an accomplished 95 for Auckland against Wellington. The home side relied entirely upon a fifth-wicket stand of 165 between Jones and Larsen, but they could not prevent Wellington from falling 167 in arrears on the first innings. Surprisingly, Patel chose not to enforce the

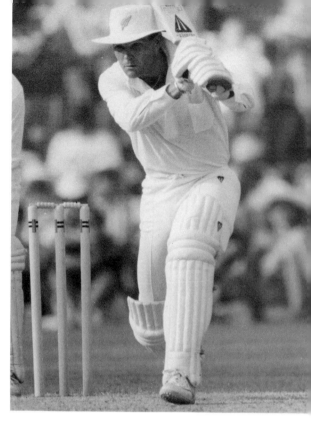

Martin Crowe hit a century in each innings for Wellington against Canterbury at Christchurch and overcame criticism and abuse to lead New Zealand with distinction against Australia. (Alan Cozzi)

follow-on, and he paid the price. Martin Crowe batted defiantly for 196 minutes, and Auckland did not capture Wellington's ninth wicket until the penultimate over of the match, with the result that number eleven Davis did not have to face a single ball.

30, 31 January, 1 and **2** February 1993 *at Eden Park, Auckland*

Auckland 155 (A.J. Gale 4 for 44) and 201 (J.T.C. Vaughan 50, E.J. Marshall 4 for 46, J.W. Wilson 4 for 71)

Otago 181 (P.W. Dobbs 72, M.L. Su'a 5 for 35) and 135 (D.N. Patel 4 for 52)

Auckland won by 40 runs

Auckland 12 pts., Otago 4 pts.

at McLean Park, Napier

Northern Districts 498 for 6 dec. (S.A. Thomson 167, D.J. White 91, B.A. Pocock 75, B.A. Young 69)

Central Districts 194 (M.N. Hart 4 for 44) and 141 (S.B. Doull 4 for 15)

Northern Districts won by an innings and 163 runs

Northern Districts 16 pts., Central Districts 0 pts.

at Lancaster Park, Christchurch

Wellington 381 (M.D. Crowe 152, A.H. Jones 77) and 284 for 1 dec. (M.D. Crowe 137 not out, A.H. Jones 86 not out)

Canterbury 342 for 5 dec. (S.P. Fleming 118, R.T. Latham 102 not out, H.T. Davis 4 for 79) and 187 for 4 (L.G. Howell 63)

Match drawn

Wellington 4 pts., Canterbury 0 pts.

Auckland won their first game of the season despite another miserable batting display on the opening day. Otago were 153 for 2 and looked set for a huge lead, but Murphy Su'a returned to take five wickets and restrict the difference between the two sides to 26 runs. Vaughan again batted well and, with Patel finding form with his off-breaks, Auckland ran out narrow winners.

Northern Districts sailed into the final with an innings win over Central Districts. There were another seven wickets for Matthew Hart, and Central lost their last six wickets in their second innings for seven runs. The first two days had seen Northern put the match out of Central's reach by hitting the highest score of the season. Shane Thomson – now, it seems, an out-and-out batsman – made the highest score of his career, hitting 28 fours in an innings which lasted 355 minutes. He faced 299 deliveries.

There were runs galore at Christchurch where the match was drawn. Martin Crowe hit a century in each innings, his second-innings 137 coming off 134 balls in 133 minutes. This innings contained 3 sixes and 20 fours. Fleming and Latham hit centuries for Canterbury. It was the first time Fleming had reached three figures.

4, 5, 6 and 7 February 1993 *at Trust Bank Park, Hamilton*

Northern Districts 102 (M.L. Su'a 4 for 35) and 147 (W. Watson 4 for 14)

Auckland 166 (J.G. Wright 84, R.P. de Groen 4 for 49) and 85 for 3

Auckland won by 7 wickets

Auckland 16 pts., Northern Districts 0 pts.

at Carisbrook, Dunedin

Canterbury 42 (J.W. Wilson 4 for 15, A.J. Gale 4 for 17) and 153 (C.L. Cairns 58, A.J. Gale 4 for 50)

Otago 104 (M.A. Hastings 4 for 30) and 95 for 7

Otago won by 3 wickets

Otago 16 pts., Canterbury 0 pts.

at Basin Reserve, Wellington

Central Districts 117 (M.W. Douglas 62, G.J. Mackenzie 5 for 41) and 162 (H.T. Davis 4 for 40)

Wellington 122 (R.G. Twose 4 for 42) and 160 for 7 (D.N. Askew 4 for 54)

Wellington won by 3 wickets

Wellington 16 pts., Central Districts 0 pts.

The final round of Shell Trophy matches epitomised why the four-day experiment had been something of a fiasco – the weather was poor and the pitches were dreadful. At Hamilton, Northern twice failed to make 200 as Su'a and Watson each took seven wickets. John Wright, the one batsman able to cope with the vagaries of the pitch, hit 84 and 37 and took the Man-of-the-Match award.

Put in to bat at Carisbrook, Canterbury were bowled out for their lowest total for 67 years. When they batted a second time, 62 runs in arrears, they were wrecked by a hat-trick from Aaron Gale. Needing 92 runs to win the match and a place in the final, Otago were 40 for 1, but they lost six wickets for 30 runs before Richardson threw caution to the wind and saw them home.

Wellington, too, squeezed home. They needed 158 to beat Central Districts, and were 122 for 7 before Lincoln Doull and Heath Davis steadied their nerves.

SHELL TROPHY FINAL TABLE

	P	W	L	D	Ab	1st inns lead	Pts.
Northern Districts	8	3	2	2	1	6	62
Otago	8	2	2	4	–	4	40
Wellington	8	1	–	6	1	5	34
Auckland	8	2	1	5	–	2	32
Central Districts	8	1	2	5	–	3	24
Canterbury	8	–	2	6	–	3	12

SHELL TROPHY FINAL
NORTHERN DISTRICTS *v.* OTAGO
at Hamilton

The Shell Trophy was decided by a final between the two top teams in 1993. This was the first occasion that a final had been played and, under the rules, the leading side, Northern Districts, had home advantage. It was also ruled that Otago must achieve an outright win if they were to deprive Northern Districts of the title.

To Northern's credit, they had reached the premier spot with a squad of local players. Aided in the past by professionals from England like Hick and Maynard, they had benefited from the influence of these players and, in 1993, they gathered their harvest. White, who was enjoying a benefit year, won the toss and asked Otago to bat. The incomparable de Groen quickly sent back Dobbs, and with Simon Doull taking five wickets, the home side were in total command by the end of the first day. Otago had laboured to 139, and Northern Districts were 90 for the loss of Pocock.

They failed to build a substantial lead on the firm base that the openers had given them, and the Otago medium-pace attack made scoring difficult. Northern led by 76 on the first innings, but Otago were 91 for 2 at the end of the second day.

Grant Bradburn, New Zealand's forgotten off-spinner, bowled admirably on the third day, but the hero was Aaron Gale. He had come to the wicket on the second evening when Hoskin fell to de Groen shortly before the close. Gale extended his night-watchman role long into the third day. He cemented one end while his colleagues prospered at the other. In all, he batted for seven minutes under five hours and faced 253 balls for his 37 which, incidentally, was his highest first-class score. Through his efforts, Otago had a lead of 233 and a fascinating final day was in prospect.

It was not to be. Persistent drizzle, which had plagued much of the New Zealand season, prevented any play before two o'clock. The umpires decreed that 80 overs were possible, and Otago declared, but it was soon apparent that the match would be drawn and that, deservedly, Northern Districts would take the title.

Simon Doull was named Man of the Match for the spell of bowling which shattered the middle of the Otago innings on the opening day, when they lost four wickets with the score on 88.

AUSTRALIA TOUR

16, 17 and **18** February 1993 *at Pukekura Park, New Plymouth*

New Zealand Board XI 264 for 9 dec. (M.D. Crowe 163, P.R. Reiffel 5 for 78) and 150 (M.G. Hughes 4 for 21)

Australian XI 348 (J.L. Langer 89, I.A. Healy 87 not out, M.J. Haslam 4 for 101) and 69 for 1

Australian XI won by 9 wickets

The Australians opened their tour with a convincing win. Crowe elected to bat first, and it was he who dominated the New Zealand innings with a magnificent 163. Chris Harris contributed 29 in a fourth-wicket stand of 137. Taylor and Langer began the Australian reply with a partnership of 119, but the visitors slipped from 182 for 1 to 217 for 7. Healy and Reiffel, who had bowled well, then added 98 and took the Australians to a comfortable lead. The home side batted limply against a varied attack in their second innings, and the Australians ran to an easy victory.

SHELL TROPHY FINAL – NORTHERN DISTRICTS *v.* OTAGO
12, 13, 14 and 15 February 1993 at Trust Bank Park, Hamilton

OTAGO

	FIRST INNINGS		SECOND INNINGS	
P.W. Dobbs	lbw, b de Groen	2	c Oxenham, b Bradburn	52
D.S. McHardy	c de Groen, b Bradburn	50	lbw, b de Groen	27
R.N. Hoskin	lbw, b Doull	12	lbw, b de Groen	6
K.R. Rutherford (capt)	c R.G. Hart, b Doull	5	(5) c Oxenham, b Bradburn	60
R.A. Lawson	c and b Bradburn	20	(6) c Doull, b Hayes	18
D.J. Nash	lbw, b Doull	0	(7) b Bradburn	42
*S.A. Robinson	c Bradburn, b Doull	0	(8) b Bradburn	24
M.H. Richardson	b Doull	0	(10) c Oxenham, b Bradburn	8
J.W. Wilson	lbw, b de Groen	10	not out	18
J.M. Paul	c Young, b Hayes	12	(11) not out	0
A.J. Gale	not out	21	(4) b Hayes	37
Extras	b 2, lb 4, nb 1	7	b 3, lb 13, w 1	17
		139	(for 9 wickets, dec.)	309

NORTHERN DISTRICTS

	FIRST INNINGS		SECOND INNINGS	
B.A. Pocock	lbw, b Paul	36	(2) not out	40
B.S. Oxenham	lbw, b Wilson	49	(1) lbw, b Nash	30
D.J. White (capt)	b Nash	23	not out	6
S.A. Thomson	b Nash	26		
B.A. Young	lbw, b Wilson	27		
G.E. Bradburn	lbw, b Nash	0		
M.N. Hart	lbw, b Gale	11		
S.B. Doull	lbw, b Gale	2		
*R.G. Hart	not out	10		
R.L. Hayes	b Gale	0		
R.P. de Groen	c Gale, b Wilson	14		
Extras	b 1, lb 12, nb 4	17	b 4, nb 1	5
		215	(for 1 wicket)	81

	O	M	R	W	O	M	R	W
De Groen	18	7	33	2	43.1	10	100	2
Hayes	10.3	6	15	1	24	7	67	2
Doull	16	3	46	5	18	6	41	–
M.N. Hart	12	3	20	–	21	12	29	–
Bradburn	18	11	19	2	39	16	56	5

	O	M	R	W	O	M	R	W
Wilson	26.2	12	46	3	10	5	20	–
Gale	25	8	42	3	8	3	14	–
Nash	17	6	31	3	10	4	10	1
Paul	12	2	50	1	14	9	14	–
Richardson	20	8	33	–	12	8	6	–
McHardy					4	–	13	–
Hoskin					1	1	0	–

FALL OF WICKETS

1–6, 2–31, 3–39, 4–88, 5–88, 6–88, 7–88, 8–104, 9–104
1–80, 2–86, 3–92, 4–176, 5–212, 6–216, 7–280, 8–291, 9–309

FALL OF WICKETS

1–57, 2–111, 3–131, 4–157, 5–157, 6–184, 7–186, 8–190, 9–195
1–73

Umpires: B.L. Aldridge & R.S. Dunne

Match drawn

22 February 1993 *at Trafalgar Park, Nelson*

Australians 222 for 8 (D.C. Boon 75, M.E. Waugh 56)
New Zealand President's XI 223 for 7 (K.R. Rutherford 97,
  B.A. Young 57)

New Zealand President's XI won by 3 wickets

This match was a double disappointment for the Australians. The original three-day game had to be scrapped because of rain, and a 50-over match was played on what would have been the last day of the first-class game. The home side won this one-day match with eight balls to spare. Rutherford and Young turned the match with a fifth-wicket stand of 141.

FIRST TEST MATCH
NEW ZEALAND *v.* AUSTRALIA
at Christchurch

Martin Crowe won the toss and asked Australia to bat first on a wicket which promised rewards for the quicker bowlers. Unfortunately, the New Zealand pace men were wayward in length and direction, and their only early success was in capturing the wicket of Boon, who edged Owens to the keeper. Taylor and Langer resisted with great determination to add 116. After 255 minutes of utmost concentration Taylor played an uncharacteristically careless hook shot at Morrison and was caught by Crowe, who dropped a straightforward slip chance offered by Langer from Patel's bowling. Patel had some consolation when Mark Waugh was caught behind off a poor shot, but Langer, showing exceptional maturity, stuck resolutely to his task and had batted for 255 minutes when Australia closed on 217 for 3.

However, Langer was leg before without addition on the second morning, but the rest of the day belonged to Australia, and to Allan Border. The Australian captain scored only 28 in the period before lunch, but in the afternoon he began to cut loose and when he clipped Patel off his legs to reach his fifty, he had also become the leading run-scorer in Test cricket, eclipsing Gavaskar's record of 10,122 Test runs. He looked certain to reach his 26th Test century but, 12 runs short, he was caught behind off Morrison. Steve Waugh, Healy and Hughes had all batted positively, and Australia had put the match out of New Zealand's reach by making 485. The visitors' grip on the game tightened as McDermott had Greatbatch caught in the first over and Jones leg before in the seventh. Wright and Crowe survived, and New Zealand ended a hard day on 30 for 2.

The third day was a disaster for New Zealand. At 124 for 3, they nursed hopes of matching Australia, but leg-

The historic moment – Border sweeps Patel for four and becomes the highest run-scorer in Test cricket. (Joe Mann/Allsport)

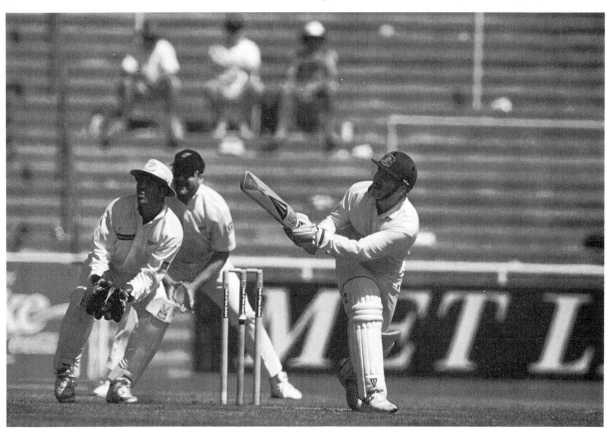

AUSTRALIA

	FIRST INNINGS	
D.C. Boon	c Parore, b Owens	15
M.A. Taylor	c Crowe, b Morrison	82
J.L. Langer	lbw, b Morrison	63
M.E. Waugh	c Parore, b Patel	13
S.R. Waugh	lbw, b Owens	62
A.R. Border (capt)	c Parore, b Morrison	88
*I.A. Healy	c Morrison, b Owens	54
M.G. Hughes	c Cairns, b Patel	45
P.R. Reiffel	c Greatbatch, b Su'a	18
S.K. Warne	not out	22
C.J. McDermott	c Jones, b Cairns	4
Extras	b 2, lb 6, w 5, nb 6	19
		485

NEW ZEALAND

	FIRST INNINGS		SECOND INNINGS	
M.J. Greatbatch	c Healy, b McDermott	4	c Reiffel, b Hughes	0
J.G. Wright	lbw, b Warne	39	b McDermott	14
A.H. Jones	lbw, b McDermott	8	c Border, b McDermott	10
M.D. Crowe (capt)	c Taylor, b Hughes	15	lbw, b Hughes	14
K.R. Rutherford	b Warne	57	c Healy, b Warne	102
C.L. Cairns	c Boon, b McDermott	0	c Taylor, b Warne	21
*A.C. Parore	c Boon, b Reiffel	6	c Boon, b Warne	5
D.N. Patel	c McDermott, b Hughes	35	b Warne	8
M.L. Su'a	c Healy, b Reiffel	0	b Hughes	44
D.K. Morrison	not out	4	c Healy, b Hughes	19
M.B. Owens	lbw, b Warne	0	not out	0
Extras	b 2, lb 4, w 4, nb 4	14	lb 2, nb 4	6
		182		**243**

	O	M	R	W
Morrison	36	11	81	3
Su'a	33	5	106	1
Cairns	31.3	9	87	1
Owens	26	9	58	3
Patel	31	3	145	2

	O	M	R	W	O	M	R	W
McDermott	21	4	73	3	19	6	45	2
Hughes	21	10	44	2	24.5	6	62	4
Reiffel	18	8	27	2	18	3	59	–
S.R. Waugh	4	2	9	–	2	2	0	–
Warne	22	12	23	3	26	7	63	4
M.E. Waugh					5	1	12	–

FALL OF WICKETS

1–33, 2–149, 3–170, 4–217, 5–264, 6–363, 7–435, 8–441, 9–480

FALL OF WICKETS

1–4, 2–18, 3–53, 4–124, 5–128, 6–138, 7–150, 8–152, 9–181

1–0, 2–19, 3–24, 4–51, 5–92, 6–110, 7–144, 8–190, 9–242

Umpires: B.L. Aldridge & C.E. King

Australia won by an innings and 60 runs

spinner Warne ended Wright's brave 4½-hour vigil and bowled Rutherford round his legs. Rutherford had hit 57 off 81 balls, and his innings included 2 sixes and 8 fours.

There was some lusty hitting from Patel, but Hughes, Reiffel and Warne, who had begun with six maidens, quickly accounted for the tail, and New Zealand followed-on 303 runs in arrears.

There was no respite as Greatbatch and Jones fell to fine catches and Wright played on to McDermott. New Zealand faced defeat at 37 for 3 at the end of the day.

The match was duly completed in four days, with Shane Warne taking the main honours for his beautifully controlled leg-spin which brought him match figures of 7 for 86 in 48 overs. For New Zealand, Rutherford again batted splendidly. He hit a six and 9 fours in completing his third Test century inside four hours.

Langer is leg before to Morrison at the start of the second day of the first Test. (Joe Mann/Allsport)

SECOND TEST MATCH
NEW ZEALAND v. AUSTRALIA, at Wellington

New Zealand brought in Watson for Su'a, and Tony Blain replaced Parore behind the stumps. Parore had been injured in net practice, and Blain was making his first international appearance for five years. His recall was something of a surprise, but he was to perform admirably. Australia were unchanged. Border won the toss and New Zealand batted, but persistent rain and drizzle allowed only 12 overs in which Wright and Greatbatch scored 28.

There was a full complement of 90 overs on the second day, and New Zealand advanced to 237 for 3. Greatbatch and Wright had given the innings the best of foundations with a partnership of 111, a record for New Zealand against Australia. Wright was caught behind off Hughes, and Greatbatch, having batted for 222 minutes, fell to a wild shot. Crowe looked in fine form and reached his fifty off 91 balls.

Crowe went on to reach 98 with some scintillating shots, and he may well have scored more had not an umpiring error made him run three and lose the strike when it was later deemed that Boon had gathered the ball beyond the boundary. Crowe was obviously distressed when Rutherford was adjudged caught behind, and for a while he was becalmed. The late middle order failed to prosper, and New Zealand were out for a disappointing 329. Boon and Taylor hit 92 for Australia's first wicket, and Taylor, in particular, looked in fine form until run out by substitute Su'a. Australia ended the day on 107 for 2.

Langer and Mark Waugh caused few problems on the fourth morning, but Border and Steve Waugh began to hit the ball hard and often, and it seemed that Australia would take command of the game. Crowe took the

New Zealand's batsman of the year – Ken Rutherford during his century in the first Test against Australia. (Joe Mann/Allsport)

SECOND TEST MATCH – NEW ZEALAND v. AUSTRALIA
4, 5, 6, 7 and 8 March 1993 at Basin Reserve, Wellington

NEW ZEALAND

	FIRST INNINGS		SECOND INNINGS	
M.J. Greatbatch	c Taylor, b Reiffel	61	(2) b McDermott	0
J.G. Wright	c Healy, b Hughes	72	(6) not out	46
A.H. Jones	b Reiffel	4	(1) lbw, b Warne	42
M.D. Crowe (capt)	b McDermott	98	(3) lbw, b McDermott	3
K.R. Rutherford	c Healy, b Hughes	32	(4) c Healy, b Reiffel	11
*T.E. Blain	b Hughes	1	(5) c Healy, b Warne	51
C.L. Cairns	c Border, b McDermott	13	lbw, b McDermott	14
D.N. Patel	not out	13	c Healy, b M.E. Waugh	25
D.K. Morrison	c Warne, b McDermott	2	not out	0
W. Watson	c Taylor, b Warne	3		
M.B. Owens	b Warne	0		
Extras	b 7, lb 11, w 2, nb 10	30	b 8, lb 8, w 1, nb 1	18
		329	(for 7 wickets)	**210**

AUSTRALIA

	FIRST INNINGS	
D.C. Boon	c and b Morrison	37
M.A. Taylor	run out	50
J.L. Langer	c Blain, b Watson	24
M.E. Waugh	c and b Owens	12
S.R. Waugh	c Blain, b Morrison	75
A.R. Border (capt)	lbw, b Morrison	30
*I.A. Healy	c Rutherford, b Morrison	8
M.G. Hughes	c Wright, b Morrison	8
P.R. Reiffel	lbw, b Morrison	7
S.K. Warne	c Greatbatch, b Morrison	22
C.J. McDermott	not out	7
Extras	lb 14, nb 4	18
		298

	O	M	R	W	O	M	R	W
McDermott	31	8	66	3	23	9	54	3
Hughes	35	9	100	3	11	5	22	–
Reiffel	23	8	55	2	16	7	27	1
S.R. Waugh	15	7	28	–				
Warne	29	9	59	2	40	25	49	2
M.E. Waugh	2	1	3	–	8	3	12	1
Border					12	5	15	–
Taylor					4	2	15	–
Boon					1	1	0	–

	O	M	R	W
Morrison	26.4	5	89	7
Cairns	24	3	77	–
Watson	29	12	60	1
Owens	21	3	54	1
Patel	1	–	4	–

FALL OF WICKETS

1–111, 2–120, 3–191, 4–287, 5–289, 6–307, 7–308, 8–314, 9–314
1–4, 2–9, 3–30, 4–101, 5–131, 6–154, 7–202

FALL OF WICKETS

1–92, 2–105, 3–128, 4–153, 5–229, 6–237, 7–251, 8–258, 9–271

Umpires: B.L. Aldridge & R.S. Dunne

Match drawn

second new ball and asked Morrison to bowl into the wind. What followed was sensational. A late in-swinger accounted for Border, and Reiffel fell to a similar delivery. Healy was taken at slip, and Steve Waugh's fine innings came to an end when Morrison made the ball rear off a length for Blain to take a leaping catch above his head. Hughes clouted high in the air, and, although Warne dominated a pugnacious last-wicket stand, he fell to a brilliant catch by Greatbatch after Rutherford had knocked the ball up at second slip. Greatbatch covered much ground to take the ball left-handed as he dived somewhere in the position of fourth slip. In an hour, Morrison, bowling fast and swinging the ball late, had taken six wickets to finish with the best figures of his Test career and the second best in New Zealand Test history.

New Zealand led by 31 on the first innings, but Morrison's marvellous work was soon threatened as McDermott sent back Greatbatch and Crowe in his first four overs, and Reiffel took the highly valuable wicket of Rutherford when he was introduced into the attack in the 18th over. New Zealand closed on a precarious 40 for 3.

Jones and Blain blighted Australia's hopes on the last morning, and Wright, batting at number six because of an injured ankle, occupied 217 minutes for his 46 to ensure that the game would be drawn.

THIRD TEST MATCH
NEW ZEALAND *v.* AUSTRALIA, at Auckland

New Zealand were heartened by the draw at Wellington, but they made two changes for the final Test, Su'a and Harris replacing Owens and the out-of-form Cairns. Blain, rightly, retained his place as wicket-keeper. Australia dropped Mark Waugh and brought in Martyn. There was much sympathy for Martin Crowe, who had offered to relinquish the captaincy after the first Test but had been given a vote of confidence by the selectors, only to be pilloried by a section of the press who had descended to the lowest forms of personal abuse. Crowe was to put aside these tribulations and lead New Zealand to a fine victory to square the series.

Once again Daniel Morrison was the New Zealand hero. Border elected to bat first when he won the toss. The wicket looked deceptively flat, but once more Morrison was able to move the ball appreciably. In the first hour, Boon and Taylor gave no indication of the Australian agonies that were to come. They scored 38 before Watson had Boon leg before, and Morrison, who had changed ends, dismissed Taylor in the same manner on

THIRD TEST MATCH – NEW ZEALAND *v.* AUSTRALIA
12, 13, 14, 15 and 16 March at Eden Park, Auckland

AUSTRALIA

	FIRST INNINGS		SECOND INNINGS	
D.C. Boon	lbw, b Watson	20	lbw, b Su'a	53
M.A. Taylor	lbw, b Morrison	13	st Blain, b Patel	3
J.L. Langer	c Blain, b Morrison	0	lbw, b Patel	0
D.R. Martyn	c Blain, b Watson	1	c Greatbatch, b Patel	74
S.R. Waugh	c Jones, b Watson	41	lbw, b Patel	0
A.R. Border (capt)	c Blain, b Morrison	0	c Harris, b Watson	71
*I.A. Healy	c Jones, b Morrison	0	c Blain, b Patel	24
M.G. Hughes	c Morrison, b Patel	33	not out	31
P.R. Reiffel	c Blain, b Morrison	9	b Watson	1
S.K. Warne	not out	3	c Jones, b Morrison	2
C.J. McDermott	b Morrison	6	c Wright, b Watson	10
Extras	lb 7, nb 6	13	b 1, lb 7, nb 8	16
		——		——
		139		285

NEW ZEALAND

	FIRST INNINGS		SECOND INNINGS	
J.G. Wright	c Taylor, b McDermott	33	run out	33
M.J. Greatbatch	c Border, b Hughes	32	b Hughes	29
A.H. Jones	c Healy, b Hughes	20	b Warne	26
M.D. Crowe (capt)	c Taylor, b Waugh	31	c Langer, b Warne	25
K.R. Rutherford	st Healy, b Warne	43	not out	53
C.Z. Harris	c Taylor, b Warne	13	lbw, b Waugh	0
*T.E. Blain	c Healy, b McDermott	15	not out	24
D.N. Patel	c Healy, b Warne	2		
M.L. Su'a	c Waugh, b Warne	3		
D.K. Morrison	not out	10		
W. Watson	lbw, b Hughes	0		
Extras	b 7, lb 10, nb 5	22	lb 10, nb 1	11
		——		——
		224	(for 5 wickets)	201

	O	M	R	W	O	M	R	W		O	M	R	W	O	M	R	W
Morrison	18.4	5	37	6	33	8	81	1	McDermott	19	6	50	2	12	3	38	
Su'a	14	3	27	–	18	4	56	1	Hughes	24.5	6	67	3	15.4	2	54	1
Watson	19	9	47	3	18	5	43	3	Reiffel	22	6	63	–	6	1	19	–
Patel	4	–	21	1	34	9	93	5	Warne	15	12	8	4	27	8	54	2
Harris					2	1	4	–	Waugh	14	6	19	1	6	1	15	1
									Martyn	1	1	0	–				
									Border					6	1	11	–

FALL OF WICKETS

1–38, 2–38, 3–39, 4–39, 5–43, 6–48, 7–101, 8–121, 9–133
1–5, 2–8, 3–115, 4–119, 5–160, 6–226, 7–261, 8–271, 9–274

FALL OF WICKETS

1–60, 2–91, 3–97, 4–144, 5–178, 6–200, 7–205, 8–206, 9–224
1–44, 2–65, 3–109, 4–129, 5–134

Umpires: S.J. Woodward & C.E. King

New Zealand won by 5 wickets

the same score. One run later, Langer and Martyn both fell to catches at the wicket.

Border was out in controversial circumstances. Television replays later revealed that a ball from Morrison had clipped his off stump without removing the bail, but he was given out caught behind. Healy also fell for nought, and it was only some hitting by Steve Waugh and Merv Hughes that enabled Australia to end a rain-shortened day on 139 for 9.

Morrison brought the innings to an abrupt close with the 10th ball of the second morning. He bowled McDermott to finish with a most impressive 6 for 37. The New Zealand batting offered more consistency than Australia's had shown, and John Wright, having completed 1,000 runs in Tests at Wellington, reached 1,000 runs in Tests at Auckland. He became the first New Zealander to score 1,000 runs at two Test venues, and later announced that he was retiring from Test cricket. No man has served his country better.

Australia came back into the game through the bowling of Shane Warne. New Zealand, at 200 for 5, were well in control before Warne bowled 10 overs, eight of them maidens, and took the wickets of Rutherford, Harris and Patel at a cost of five runs.

New Zealand added another 18 runs on the third morning as Warne captured another wicket in what was a golden series for him. Noticing the success of Warne's spin, Crowe chose Patel to open the New Zealand attack with Morrison when Australia batted a second time. His decision was justified as the off-spinner dismissed both Taylor and Langer, who 'bagged a pair'. Boon and Mar-

tyn added 107 before Patel grabbed two more wickets. He also had Healy caught behind by the ebullient Blain, and Australia closed on 226 for 6, with Border, 61 not out, holding the key to the likely outcome of the match.

It was Willie Watson who ended Border's innings on the fourth morning, and the same bowler took the wickets of Reiffel and McDermott as Australia added 59 to their overnight score, leaving New Zealand a target of 201 to win and plenty of time in which to score the runs.

Wright and Greatbatch began positively, scoring 44 in 49 minutes to put their side in good heart. Greatbatch missed a straight ball from Hughes, and Wright was run out by Steve Waugh. Jones and Crowe took New Zealand into three figures, but Crowe nudged a simple catch to short-leg when he played defensively at Warne. The leg-spinner bowled Jones with a ball that turned sharply, and Harris was rather harshly judged leg before to bring New Zealand to 134 for 5 and a state of uncertainty.

Rutherford and Blain, whose return to Test cricket had been a triumph, restored confidence with some determined batting, and New Zealand were 168 at the end of the day. On the last morning, the same pair adopted a positive approach. In 29 minutes, off 52 balls, they scored the remaining 33 runs that New Zealand needed for victory.

This was a fine win by a New Zealand side that showed great character. Rutherford and Morrison, in particular, had performed magnificently, and their advance boded well for the immediate future. For Australia, Warne had confirmed his immense talent, but the doubts as to the batting remained.

TEST MATCH AVERAGES – NEW ZEALAND v. AUSTRALIA

NEW ZEALAND BATTING

	M	Inns	NO	Runs	HS	Av	100s	50s
K.R. Rutherford	3	6	1	298	102	59.60	1	2
J.G. Wright	3	6	1	237	72	47.40	–	1
M.D. Crowe	3	6	–	186	98	31.00	–	1
T.E. Blain	2	4	1	91	51	30.33	–	1
M.J. Greatbatch	3	6	–	126	61	21.00	–	1
D.N. Patel	3	5	1	83	35	20.75	–	–
A.H. Jones	3	6	–	110	42	18.33	–	–
D.K. Morrison	3	5	3	35	19	17.50	–	–
M.L. Su'a	2	3	–	47	44	15.66	–	–
C.L. Cairns	2	4	–	48	21	12.00	–	–
W. Watson	2	2	–	3	1	1.50	–	–
M.B. Owens	2	3	1	0	0*	0.00	–	–

Played in one Test: A.C. Parore 6 & 5; C.Z. Harris 13 & 0

NEW ZEALAND BOWLING

	Overs	Mds	Runs	Wkts	Av	Best	10/m	5/inn
D.K. Morrison	114.2	29	288	17	16.94	7-89	–	2
W. Watson	66	26	150	7	21.42	3-43	–	–
M.B. Owens	47	12	112	4	28.00	3-58	–	–
D.N. Patel	70	12	263	8	32.87	5-93	–	1
M.L. Su'a	65	12	189	2	94.50	1-56	–	–
C.L. Cairns	55.3	12	164	1	164.00	1-87	–	–

Bowled in one innings: C.Z. Harris 2–1–4–0

NEW ZEALAND FIELDING FIGURES

8 – T.E. Blain (ct 7/st 1); 4 – A.H. Jones; 3 – M.J. Greatbatch, A.C. Parore and D.K. Morrison; 2 – J.G. Wright; 1– M.D. Crowe, K.R. Rutherford, M.B. Owens and C.Z. Harris

AUSTRALIA BATTING

	M	Inns	NO	Runs	HS	Av	100s	50s
A.R. Border	3	4	–	189	88	47.25	–	2
S.R. Waugh	3	4	–	178	75	44.50	–	2
M.G. Hughes	3	4	1	117	45	39.00	–	–
M.A. Taylor	3	4	–	148	82	37.00	–	2
D.C. Boon	3	4	–	125	53	31.25	–	1
S.K. Warne	3	4	2	49	22*	24.50	–	–
J.L. Langer	3	4	–	87	63	21.75	–	1
I.A. Healy	3	4	–	86	54	21.50	–	1
M.E. Waugh	2	2	–	25	13	12.50	–	–
C.J. McDermott	3	4	1	27	10	9.00	–	–
P.R. Reiffel	3	4	–	35	18	8.75	–	–

Played in one Test: D.R. Martyn 1 & 74

AUSTRALIA BOWLING

	Overs	Mds	Runs	Wkts	Av	Best	10/m	5/inn
S.K. Warne	159	73	256	17	15.05	4-8	–	–
C.J. McDermott	125	36	326	13	25.07	3-54	–	–
M.G. Hughes	132.2	38	349	13	26.84	4-62	–	–
M.E. Waugh	15	5	27	1	27.00	1-12	–	–
S.R. Waugh	41	18	71	2	35.50	1-15	–	–
P.R. Reiffel	103	33	250	5	50.00	2-27	–	–
A.R. Border	18	6	26	–	–	–	–	–

Bowled in one innings: M.A. Taylor 4–2–15–0; D.C. Boon 1–1–0–0; D.R. Martyn 1–1–0–0

AUSTRALIA FIELDING FIGURES

13 – I.A. Healy (ct 12/st 1); 7 – M.A. Taylor; 3 – A.R. Border and D.C. Boon; 1 – J.L. Langer, S.R. Waugh, P.R. Reiffel, S.K. Warne and C.J. McDermott

New Zealand's bowler of the year – Daniel Morrison, who took 7 for 89 at Wellington and 17 wickets in the three-match series. (David Munden/Sports-Line)

LIMITED-OVER SERIES
NEW ZEALAND v. AUSTRALIA

The opening encounter of the five-match series saw Australia win comfortably. Mark Waugh was reinstated in the Australian side and promoted to open the innings. He responded with a stylish 60, and with Taylor and Jones – also reinstated in the side – in good form Australia reached an impressive 258 in their 50 overs. Quickly reduced to 10 for 3, New Zealand lost all hope when Crowe walked after umpire King had turned down a confident appeal for caught behind. It was a chivalrous gesture and one in keeping with the attitudes of the two captains.

At Christchurch, in miserably cold and damp weather, New Zealand began promisingly before Paul Reiffel removed Greatbatch, Jones, Crowe and Harris for three runs within the space of nine balls. Blain and Rutherford led the counter-attack to take New Zealand to a commendable 196 in 45 overs. Australia were 51 for 2 from 13.3 overs and much depended on Mark Waugh when the game restarted on the Monday. He and Boon took the

FIRST ONE-DAY INTERNATIONAL – NEW ZEALAND v. AUSTRALIA
19 March 1993 at Carisbrook, Dunedin

AUSTRALIA				NEW ZEALAND		
M.E. Waugh	c Crowe, **b** Watson	60		M.J. Greatbatch	c Jones, **b** Hughes	0
M.A. Taylor	run out	78		R.T. Latham	c Healy, **b** Dodemaide	1
D.M. Jones	c Greatbatch, **b** Larsen	52		A.H. Jones	**b** Reiffel	24
S.R. Waugh	not out	23		M.D. Crowe (capt)	c Healy, **b** Dodemaide	1
D.R. Martyn	**b** Wilson	22		K.R. Rutherford	**b** Dodemaide	21
A.R. Border (capt)	not out	14		*T.E. Blain	**b** Dodemaide	0
*I.A. Healy				J.W. Wilson	**b** Reiffel	0
A.I.C. Dodemaide				D.N. Patel	c Martyn, **b** May	11
M.G. Hughes				G.R. Larsen	st Healy, **b** May	22
T.B.A. May				D.K. Morrison	not out	20
P. R. Reiffel				W. Watson	c Martyn, **b** May	21
Extras	lb 7, nb 2	9		Extras	lb 4, w 2, nb 2	8
(50 overs)	(for 4 wickets)	258		(42.2 overs)		129

	O	M	R	W		O	M	R	W
Morrison	10	–	36	–	Hughes	7	–	23	1
Wilson	10	–	58	1	Dodemaide	10	4	20	4
Patel	8	–	40	–	Reiffel	9	2	17	2
Watson	10	–	58	1	S.R. Waugh	7	–	14	–
Larsen	10	–	44	1	May	9.2	–	51	3
Latham	2	–	15	–					

FALL OF WICKETS
1–95, 2–199, 3–200, 4–236

FALL OF WICKETS
1–0, 2–2, 3–10, 4–46, 5–46, 6–49, 7–52, 8–72, 9–97

Umpires: C.E. King & R.S. Dunne   *Man of the Match:* A.I.C. Dodemaide   *Australia won by 129 runs*

SECOND ONE-DAY INTERNATIONAL – NEW ZEALAND v. AUSTRALIA
21 and 22 March 1993 at Lancaster Park, Christchurch

NEW ZEALAND				AUSTRALIA		
R.T. Latham	c S.R. Waugh, b Hughes		13	M.A. Taylor (capt)	c Crowe, b Patel	3
M.J. Greatbatch	c Jones, b Reiffel		32	M.E. Waugh	st Blain, b Harris	57
A.H. Jones	c Healy, b Reiffel		22	D.M. Jones	b Morrison	6
M.D. Crowe (capt)	b Reiffel		1	D.C. Boon	run out	55
K.R. Rutherford	b S.R. Waugh		35	S.R. Waugh	b Morrison	30
C.Z. Harris	b Reiffel		0	D.R. Martyn	c Jones, b Harris	1
*T.E. Blain	c Jones, b M.E. Waugh		41	*I.A. Healy	run out	15
D.N. Patel	run out		13	M.G. Hughes	c and b Pringle	0
G.R. Larsen	not out		23	A.I.C. Dodemaide	run out	8
C. Pringle	not out		2	P.R. Reiffel	not out	1
D.K. Morrison				T.B.A. May	not out	0
Extras	b 5, lb 7, w 1, nb 1		14	Extras	b 1, lb 13, w 4, nb 3	21
(45 overs)	(for 8 wickets)		196	(44.3 overs)	(for 9 wickets)	197

	O	M	R	W		O	M	R	W
Hughes	9	3	27	1	Morrison	9	–	45	2
Dodemaide	10	4	27	–	Patel	9	–	33	1
Reiffel	10	2	38	4	Larsen	9	2	28	–
May	9	–	52	–	Pringle	8.3	–	41	1
S.R. Waugh	6	–	35	1	Harris	9	1	36	2
M.E. Waugh	1	–	5	1					

FALL OF WICKETS
1–22, 2–65, 3–74, 4–75, 5–75, 6–139, 7–163, 8–191

FALL OF WICKETS
1–7, 2–19, 3–122, 4–130, 5–142, 6–179, 7–179, 8–196, 9–196

Umpires: R.S. Dunne & D.M. Quested *Man of the Match:* P.R. Reiffel *Australia won by 1 wicket*

THIRD ONE-DAY INTERNATIONAL – NEW ZEALAND v. AUSTRALIA
24 March 1993 at Basin Reserve, Wellington

NEW ZEALAND			AUSTRALIA		
M.J. Greatbatch	c S.R. Waugh, b Dodemaide	8	M.E. Waugh	b Morrison	0
R.T. Latham	lbw, b Reiffel	21	M.A. Taylor	c Latham, b Patel	50
A.H. Jones	st Healy, b Warne	29	D.M. Jones	c Blain, b Larsen	25
M.D. Crowe (capt)	not out	91	D.C. Boon	b Wilson	2
C.Z. Harris	run out	18	S.R. Waugh	b Harris	9
*T.E. Blain	c and b Border	9	A.R. Border (capt)	run out	0
J.W. Wilson	c S.R. Waugh, b Warne	15	*I.A. Healy	c Wilson, b Larsen	1
D.N. Patel	c M.E. Waugh, b Border	7	M.G. Hughes	b Larsen	2
G.R. Larsen	run out	4	A.I.C. Dodemaide	c Greatbatch, b Patel	7
C. Pringle	run out	1	P.R. Reiffel	not out	8
D.K. Morrison	c Boon, b Dodemaide	0	S.K. Warne	b Wilson	3
Extras	lb 3, w 8	11	Extras	b 4, lb 5, w 7, nb 3	19
(50 overs)		214	(37.2 overs)		126

	O	M	R	W		O	M	R	W
Hughes	4	–	21	–	Morrison	4	1	21	1
Dodemaide	9	1	38	2	Pringle	5	1	11	–
Reiffel	10	1	21	1	Wilson	5.2	–	21	2
Warne	10	–	40	2	Larsen	10	3	17	3
S.R. Waugh	7	–	37	–	Harris	8	1	33	1
Border	10	–	54	2	Patel	5	–	14	2

FALL OF WICKETS
1–26, 2–49, 3–95, 4–127, 5–140, 6–168, 7–178, 8–205, 9–213

FALL OF WICKETS
1–0, 2–42, 3–55, 4–71, 5–71, 6–77, 7–93, 8–108, 9–122

Umpires: C.E. King & D.M. Quested *Man of the Match:* G.R. Larsen *New Zealand won by 88 runs*

FOURTH ONE-DAY INTERNATIONAL – NEW ZEALAND v. AUSTRALIA
27 March 1993 at Trust Bank Park, Hamilton

AUSTRALIA

M.A. Taylor (capt)	c Blain, b Morrison	13
M.E. Waugh	b Morrison	108
D.M. Jones	run out	64
D.C. Boon	c Morrison, b Harris	2
S.R. Waugh	b Pringle	19
D.R. Martyn	c Blain, b Morrison	17
*I.A. Healy	lbw, b Pringle	1
A.I.C. Dodemaide	not out	1
M.G. Hughes	not out	10
P.R. Reiffel		
T.B.A. May		
Extras	b 1, lb 6, w 5	12
(50 overs)	(for 7 wickets)	247

NEW ZEALAND

M.J. Greatbatch	c Healy, b Hughes	13
A.H. Jones	run out	18
M.D. Crowe (capt)	run out	91
K.R. Rutherford	c Healy, b Reiffel	9
C.Z. Harris	c Healy, b Reiffel	0
*T.E. Blain	b Dodemaide	41
J.W. Wilson	not out	44
D.N. Patel	run out	4
G.R. Larsen	not out	12
C. Pringle		
D.K. Morrison		
Extras	b 2, lb 11, w 5	18
(49.4 overs)	(for 7 wickets)	250

	O	M	R	W
Morrison	9	–	35	3
Pringle	8	1	41	2
Larsen	10	–	42	–
Wilson	3	–	20	–
Patel	10	–	47	–
Harris	7	–	37	1
Jones	3	–	18	–

	O	M	R	W
Hughes	10	3	28	1
Dodemaide	10	1	39	1
Reiffel	10	2	46	2
May	10	–	45	–
S.R. Waugh	7.4	–	59	–
M.E. Waugh	2	–	20	–

FALL OF WICKETS

1–29, 2–172, 3–178, 4–215, 5–217, 6–227, 7–235

FALL OF WICKETS

1–24, 2–59, 3–88, 4–94, 5–172, 6–196, 7–210

Umpires: B.L. Aldridge & D.B. Cowie   *Man of the Match:* M.D. Crowe   *New Zealand won by 3 wickets*

FIFTH ONE-DAY INTERNATIONAL – NEW ZEALAND v. AUSTRALIA
28 March 1993 at Eden Park, Auckland

AUSTRALIA

M.E. Waugh	c Greatbatch, b Latham	83
M.A. Taylor	c and b Morrison	1
D.M. Jones	run out	25
D.C. Boon	c Patel, b Latham	40
S.R. Waugh	b Latham	39
A.R. Border (capt)	c Patel, b Latham	1
*I.A. Healy	c Crowe, b Pringle	17
A.I.C. Dodemaide	c Crowe, b Latham	0
M.G. Hughes	not out	12
P.R. Reiffel	not out	2
T.B.A. May		
Extras	b 1, lb 5, w 5, nb 1	12
(50 overs)	(for 8 wickets)	232

NEW ZEALAND

R.T. Latham	c M.E. Waugh, b Hughes	22
M.J. Greatbatch	c Border, b S.R. Waugh	68
A.H. Jones	st Healy, b May	2
M.D. Crowe (capt)	lbw, b May	11
K.R. Rutherford	run out	6
*T.E. Blain	run out	8
J.W. Wilson	c Border, b Dodemaide	21
D.N. Patel	c M.E. Waugh, b S.R. Waugh	8
G.R. Larsen	not out	33
C. Pringle	not out	22
D.K. Morrison		
Extras	lb 19, w 8, nb 1	28
(50 overs)	(for 8 wickets)	229

	O	M	R	W
Morrison	8	–	41	1
Wilson	7	–	36	–
Pringle	9	–	52	1
Larsen	10	1	32	–
Patel	6	–	33	–
Latham	10	1	32	5

	O	M	R	W
Hughes	10	–	46	1
Dodemaide	10	1	39	1
Reiffel	10	–	49	–
May	10	–	40	2
S.R. Waugh	8	1	27	2
M.E. Waugh	2	–	9	–

FALL OF WICKETS

1–7, 2–71, 3–145, 4–178, 5–183, 6–213, 7–213, 8–215

FALL OF WICKETS

1–50, 2–67, 3–97, 4–114, 5–136, 6–139, 7–166, 8–175

Umpires: B.L. Aldridge & D.B. Cowie   *Man of the Match:* M.E. Waugh   *Australia won by 3 runs*

score to 103, and both batsmen were given out after resort to the off-field umpire and his television monitor. Healy suffered the same fate, and Dodemaide was another to be given out by the off-field arbitrator. This happened with the scores level and one over remaining. Reiffel, having already done so much with the ball, won the match when he hit the third ball of the last over to leg for a single.

New Zealand kept the series alive by winning the third match in most convincing fashion. They were given a position of strength by Martin Crowe who, in spite of an injured knee which restricted his movement, hit 91 off 104 balls. Initially kept quiet by the spinners, he lashed 19 off Border's last over, including 2 sixes. Morrison bowled Mark Waugh without a run scored, and the gentle medium pace of Larsen troubed the Australian middle order, which could never give Taylor the support he needed.

At Hamilton Mark Waugh hit his first century in a one-day international, and Dean Jones showed excellent form with 64 in a second-wicket stand of 143 with the result that, even if Australia's 247 looked short of what had at one time seemed likely, it still promised to be a winning total. This certainly appeared to be the case when New Zealand slipped to 94 for 4. Martin Crowe then played another magnificent innings, hitting 91 off 101 balls with 8 fours and a six. He was most ably supported by Tony Blain in a stand of 78, but New Zealand still needed 76 from the last 10 overs. From the last five overs 37 runs were needed, and Larsen and Wilson hit 40 to win the match in spectacular style. The 19-year-old Jeff Wilson, new to international cricket in the series, was the hero as he thrashed 44 from 28 balls, batting with muscular disdain and earning from the clamorous fans the title of the 'new Botham'.

New Zealand could not quite repeat this success in the final match of a marvellous series. Mark Waugh was again on top form with a scintillating 83, his fourth fifty in five matches, but the Australian innings was curbed by Rod Latham's occasional medium pace which brought him five wickets for 32 runs. He then joined Greatbatch in

Tony Blain was recalled to the New Zealand side when Parore was injured and performed admirably to hold his place in the final Test and throughout the one-day series. (Adrian Murrell/Allsport)

an opening stand of 50, but the New Zealand innings lacked sufficient momentum. The injection of energy was provided by Larsen and Pringle who added an heroic 54 for the ninth wicket. They reached the last over needing 14 to win and had to hit six from the last ball to snatch the match and the series, but they could manage only two.

A large crowd applauded enthusiastically. In spite of some miserable weather, New Zealand cricket had shown healthy signs of recovery, and there was hope and joy in the air.

A common sight – leg-spinner Shane Warne is congratulated on taking a wicket. Like Morrison, he captured 17 in the series. (Joe Mann/Allsport)

FIRST-CLASS AVERAGES

BATTING

	M	Inns	NO	Runs	HS	Av	100s	50s
M.D. Crowe	7	14	1	803	163	61.76	3	2
J.G. Wright	7	13	1	580	118	48.33	1	2
S.A. Thomson	9	13	2	515	167	46.81	2	1
B.A. Young	9	12	2	406	138*	40.60	1	2
D.J. Murray	8	14	2	483	106*	40.25	1	1
R.T. Latham	7	12	1	440	134	40.00	2	2
G.R. Larsen	7	11	2	352	93*	39.11	–	2
S.P. Fleming	8	13	2	425	118	38.63	1	2
S.W. Brown	4	8	2	231	65*	38.50	–	1
D.J. White	9	14	2	459	155	38.25	2	1
B.A. Pocock	8	12	1	414	130	37.64	1	2
A.H. Jones	8	16	1	542	104	36.13	1	2
M.H. Austen	6	10	–	352	85	35.20	–	2
M.P. Speight	2	4	–	136	49	34.00	–	–
S.B. Doull	3	4	1	100	48*	33.33	–	–
K.R. Rutherford	8	16	1	492	102	32.80	1	3
T.E. Blain	10	19	3	522	111	32.62	1	2
B.Z. Harris	5	8	1	220	82	31.42	–	2
L.K. Germon	8	12	1	334	60	30.36	–	2
R.G. Twose	8	15	–	436	154	29.06	1	2
G.P. Burnett	8	15	3	348	79	29.00	–	2
E.B. McSweeney	8	12	1	317	84	28.81	–	2
J.T.C. Vaughan	5	8	–	211	95	26.37	–	2
C.D. Ingham	6	12	1	285	42*	25.90	–	–
A.J. Gale	9	15	9	154	37	25.66	–	–
P.W. Dobbs	9	18	1	431	77	25.35	–	4
G.E. Bradburn	6	9	1	199	80	24.87	–	1
M.J. Greatbatch	8	15	–	372	133	24.80	1	1
S.W. Duff	8	13	1	288	62	24.00	–	1
T.J. Franklin	8	13	–	310	81	23.84	–	2
A.P. O'Dowd	6	9	–	213	85	23.66	–	1
R.K. Brown	5	8	2	138	51*	23.00	–	1
M.W. Priest	6	9	3	132	22*	22.00	–	–
S.W.J. Wilson	7	13	–	283	45	21.76	–	–
M.N. Hart	10	13	–	279	83	21.46	–	1
N.A. Mallender	6	11	3	169	62*	21.12	–	1
M.W. Douglas	8	15	1	293	102*	20.92	1	1
R.T. Hart	7	13	–	258	49	19.84	–	1
C.L. Cairns	8	14	1	256	79	19.69	–	2
D.S. McHardy	9	17	–	333	66	19.58	–	2
J.D. Wells	8	14	3	215	52	19.54	–	1
A.C. Parore	6	11	2	174	102*	19.33	1	–
D.J. Nash	7	14	1	250	45	19.23	–	–
B.S. Oxenham	9	14	1	252	50	18.61	–	1
N.J. Astle	7	9	2	125	34	17.85	–	–
M.H. Richardson	6	11	4	125	26*	17.85	–	–
R.A. Lawson	8	16	–	267	55	16.68	–	1
J.W. Wilson	9	17	1	255	78	15.93	–	1
R.N. Hoskin	6	12	1	172	65	15.63	–	1
D.N. Patel	10	17	1	241	38	15.06	–	–
A.J. Hunt	8	11	–	165	34	15.00	–	–
B.R. Hartland	5	9	–	127	54	14.11	–	1
L.G. Howell	7	11	–	150	63	13.63	–	1
P.D. Unwin	7	12	3	113	38	12.55	–	–
E.J. Marshall	7	12	3	110	32	12.22	–	–
S.A. Robinson	9	17	1	183	39	11.43	–	–
D.J. Leonard	8	11	–	119	61	10.81	–	1

(Qualification – 100 runs, average 10.00)

BOWLING

	Overs	Mds	Runs	Wkts	Av	Best	10/m	5/inns
N.A. Mallender	156.4	49	280	26	10.76	5-30	–	2
A.J. Gale	216.5	79	408	30	13.60	4-12	–	–
S.B. Doull	88.1	31	186	12	15.50	5-46	–	1
D.K. Morrison	263.2	66	598	38	15.73	7-89	–	4
R.P. de Groen	380.4	139	775	46	16.84	7-50	1	3
W. Watson	288.3	99	579	34	17.02	5-40	–	1
R.G. Twose	123.4	35	284	16	17.75	4-42	–	–
J.W. Wilson	270	84	587	33	17.78	5-71	–	1
M.N. Hart	310	89	622	34	18.29	5-37	–	1
G.E. Bradburn	199	70	383	20	19.15	5-56	–	1
D.N. Askew	189.3	42	529	27	19.59	4-40	–	–
D.J. Nash	146.5	43	302	15	20.13	3-31	–	–
C. Pringle	173	50	406	20	20.30	5-52	–	1
E.J. Marshall	122.1	29	335	16	20.93	4-46	–	–
H.T. Davis	170.5	40	493	23	21.43	4-40	–	–
S.J. Roberts	216.2	44	597	27	22.11	5-59	–	2
M.B. Owens	140	35	385	16	24.06	3-18	–	–
M.F. Sharpe	123.1	32	268	11	24.36	3-27	–	–
M.J. Sears	187	40	488	20	24.40	4-88	–	–
G.R. Larsen	172.1	60	325	13	25.00	3-23	–	–
M.L. Su'a	219.4	51	600	24	25.00	5-35	–	2
R.J. Drown	132	42	307	12	25.58	3-33	–	–
A.J. Alcock	127.5	38	286	11	26.00	3-43	–	–
P.W. O'Rourke	205.3	61	419	16	26.18	4-26	–	–
D.J. Leonard	194	55	477	18	26.50	6-68	–	1
R.L. Hayes	245.3	94	504	19	26.52	3-25	–	–
C.L. Cairns	247	73	540	20	27.00	3-34	–	–
S.W. Duff	148.2	45	356	12	29.66	3-46	–	–
D.N. Patel	276.5	72	743	23	32.30	5-93	–	1
P.D. Unwin	159.3	49	414	12	34.50	4-47	–	–
M.W. Priest	248.3	78	556	16	34.75	3-8	–	–

(Qualification – 10 wickets)

LEADING FIELDERS

30 – L.K. Germon (ct 27/st 3); 29 – S.A. Robinson; 28 – T.E. Blain (ct 24/st 4); 24 – E.B. McSweeney (ct 23/st 1); 22 – B.A. Young; 20 – A.C. Parore; 17 – R.G. Hart (ct 15/st 2); 16 – J.M. Mills; 13 – M.N. Hart; 11 – B.S. Oxenham; 10 – A.J. Hunt

SECTION F
South Africa
India tour, Test and one-day international series
Total Power Shield
Castle Currie Cup
UCBSA Bowl
Triangular one-day tournament – South Africa, Pakistan and West Indies
Benson and Hedges Night Series
First-class averages

Hudson and McMillan, the bowler, appeal, Shastri looks enquiringly and, eventually, cricket history is made when Sachin Tendulkar is given out by the third umpire after consulting the television monitor. (Patrick Eagar)

1992 saw the return of Test cricket to South Africa after an absence of 22 years. The occasion of *The Friendship Tour*, as it was named, was given further lustre in that it was undertaken by the first side from India ever to visit the Republic. In this tour, lasting just over two months, India were to play four Test matches and seven one-day internationals, all of them day/night games.

With regard to domestic cricket, the President's Cup was abolished, leaving South Africa with two first-class competitions and, to the relief of many, no first-class tournament in which second-team players were permitted to play. The season began with a string of friendly matches.

PRE-SEASON FRIENDLY MATCHES

14, 15 and **16 September 1992** at Kingsmead, Durban

Western Province 249 (T.N. Lazard 57, P.W.E. Rawson 4 for 57) and 106 for 3
Natal 333 (J.N. Rhodes 77, N.E. Wright 69)

Match drawn

at Bredasdorp Sports Complex, Bredasdorp

Boland 261 for 7 dec. (W. van As 109) and 138
Border 214 (K. Brown 59, M. Krug 50, H. Williams 5 for 33) and 160 (G.C. Victor 53, A.G. Elgar 5 for 50)

Boland won by 25 runs

18, 19 and **20 September 1992** at Pretoria Technikon Oval, Pretoria

Transvaal 394 for 3 dec. (S.J. Cook 228, L. Seeff 87) and 173 for 4 dec.
Northern Transvaal 303 (L.P. Vorster 129 not out, M.D. Haysman 55, C.E. Eksteen 5 for 73) and 189 (V.F. du Preez 51, S.D. Jack 5 for 48)

Transvaal won by 75 runs

at De Beers Country Club, Kimberley

Griqualand West 269 (D. Jordaan 123, F.J.C. Cronje 59, E.A.E. Baptiste 4 for 43) and 168 (P. Kirsten 73, E.A.E. Baptiste 4 for 29)
Eastern Province 272 for 4 dec. (P.G. Amm 114, K.C. Wessels 63) and 166 for 7 (K.C. Wessels 74 not out)

Eastern Province won by 3 wickets

10, 11 and **12 October 1992** at De Beers Country Club, Kimberley

Griqualand West 210 (M.J. Cann 69, F.J.C. Cronje 55, C.F. Craven 4 for 21)
Orange Free State 261 for 8 (B.T. Player 100 not out, J.M. Arthur 67)

Match drawn

The friendly matches were significant for several individual performances of note. On his debut for Boland, Williams took 8 for 64 in the match against Border, while Jimmy Cook celebrated his recall to the South African squad for the matches against India with his highest score in South Africa. Bradley Player hit a maiden first-class century in the match between Orange Free State and Griqualand West. There was no play on the second day in this game.

THE FRIENDSHIP TOUR

29 October 1992 at Halfway House, Randjesfontein

Indians 207 for 6 (S.R. Tendulkar 100 not out, A.D. Jadeja 50, A.J. Kourie 4 for 50)
Nicky Oppenheimer's XI 127 (S.L. Venkatapathy Raju 4 for 11)

Indians won by 80 runs

The Indians were given a rapturous reception when they arrived in South Africa. They opened their tour with what was, in effect, a country-house match. Tendulkar hit 100 off 92 balls, with a six and 17 fours, and Chetan Sharma performed the hat-trick.

31 October, 1, 2 and **3 November 1992** at PAM Brink Stadium, Springs

Combined Bowl XI 230 (M.J. Cann 94, C.M. Sharma 4 for 56) and 85 (S.T. Banerjee 5 for 29)
Indians 556 for 3 dec. (A.D. Jadeja 254 not out, S.V. Manjrekar 186, S.R. Tendulkar 65)

Indians won by an innings and 241 runs

In their initial first-class match of the tour, the Indians completely overwhelmed the Bowl XI led by Michael Cann, the former Glamorgan player. Cann himself batted for five hours on the opening day to hold the Bowl XI innings together, but the feature of the match was a second-wicket stand of 415 in 114 overs between Jadeja and Manjrekar. This was the second highest stand ever recorded in South Africa and the highest by two Indian batsmen outside India. Manjrekar faced 338 balls and hit 21 fours while Jadeja hit a six and 36 fours in his 437-ball innings. A dispirited Bowl XI wilted against the impressive pace bowling of Banerjee.

6, 7, 8 and **9 November 1992** at Centurion Park, Verwoerdburg

President's XI 268 (W.J. Cronje 73) and 200 (W.J. Cronje 53, T.N. Lazard 52, J. Srinath 4 for 49)
Indians 164 (B.N. Schultz 5 for 35) and 9 for 0

Match drawn

No play was possible on the final day of the match at Centurion Park, but the South African side had enjoyed marginally the better of the encounter. Hansie Cronje captained the select eleven well and hit two half-centuries, but he could find a place only as 12th man in the Test side. The left-arm pace bowler Brett Schultz troubled the Indians greatly and was named in the South African side for the first Test, having narrowly missed selection for the sides that went to India, the World Cup and the West Indies.

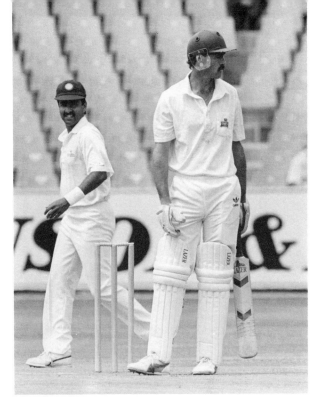

FIRST TEST MATCH
SOUTH AFRICA v. INDIA, at Durban

The return of Test cricket to South Africa was not greeted with quite the enthusiasm that had been anticipated and the attendances were poor. Still unable to find a place for Clive Rice, South Africa gave first Test caps to Cook, Rhodes, Henry, McMillan and Schultz. India brought in Jadeja and Amre for the first time. Azharuddin won the toss and asked South Africa to bat first, a debatable decision.

The game began sensationally. Kapil Dev's first ball was on a good length and moved away appreciably to take the outside edge of Cook's bat. Diving forward at third slip, Tendulkar took a fine catch. Cook waited for some time before leaving the wicket. His hesitation was brought about either by doubt as to the legality of the catch (of which there could be none) or by despair that this was how the dream had ended.

A mixture of despair and bewilderment as Jimmy Cook is caught at slip off Kapil Dev on the first ball of the first Test match. (Patrick Eagar)

Shastri falls leg before to Pringle for 14 in the first Test match. (Patrick Eagar)

Wessels lightened his side's gloom by steering his first ball through the gully for four. He played with determination and concentration, in contrast to Hudson who lasted only 11 overs before driving loosely at Kapil Dev to be bowled off an inside edge. Kirsten shared a stand of 60 with Wessels without ever looking convincing and, obsessed by defence, he fell to a ball which bounced sharply and took the outside shoulder. Rhodes was far more positive and matched Wessels in his resolve to hit the ball as well as to survive, but he was bemused by Kumble and taken bat/pad.

During his partnership with Rhodes, Wessels moved from 90 to 102 with three successive fours off Srinath, one of which was nearly caught by Jadeja. He soon lost McMillan, and he himself was sixth out when he was very well caught at slip. He batted for 82 overs, faced 264 balls and hit 18 fours. It was his fifth Test century, and he became the first man to score a century in a Test match for two countries. Henry fell in the last over of the day, and South Africa finished on a precarious 215 for 7.

Thanks to Pringle, the South African tail wagged to some effect, and the mood of the game changed on the second day as the home side's pace men bowled with fire and enthusiasm. Schultz celebrated his Test debut with the wicket of Jadeja, brilliantly caught at slip by McMillan who then had Manjrekar leg before. Tendulkar looked to be mounting a counter-attack, but he pushed a ball behind Rhodes at backward point and set off on a run. Wisely, Shastri sent him back. Rhodes threw to Hudson who broke the wicket, and Tendulkar became the first batsman in a Test match to be given out by the off-field umpire with recourse to a television monitor. Three balls later, Shastri fell to the often wayward Pringle, and India were 38 for 4. Azharuddin, who never looked at ease, and Amre added 87 in 26 overs before the former was run out by Donald, and Kapil Dev was then out second ball. Bad light brought relief to India, on 128 for 6.

After half an hour on the third day, India lost Prabhakar, caught at second slip, but that was to be South Africa's last success for 57 overs, during which time More and Amre scored 101 runs. Immediately after tea, Amre cut the ball into the hands of backward point. He batted for 378 minutes, faced 298 balls, hit 11 fours and joined the band of players who have scored a century on their Test debut. He had come to the wicket with his side at 38 for 4 and had batted with exceptional maturity and impressive technique.

South Africa had now lost their grip on the game. They

FIRST TEST MATCH – SOUTH AFRICA v. INDIA
13, 14, 15, 16 and 17 November 1992 at Kingsmead, Durban

SOUTH AFRICA

	FIRST INNINGS		SECOND INNINGS	
S.J. Cook	c Tendulkar, b Kapil Dev	0	c and b Kumble	43
A.C. Hudson	b Kapil Dev	14	c More, b Srinath	55
K.C. Wessels (capt)	c Azharuddin, b Kumble	118	c More, b Srinath	32
P.N. Kirsten	c More, b Srinath	13	not out	11
J.N. Rhodes	c Azharuddin, b Kumble	41	not out	26
B.M. McMillan	c Prabhakar, b Shastri	3		
*D.J. Richardson	lbw, b Prabhakar	15		
O. Henry	c Tendulkar, b Shastri	3		
M.W. Pringle	lbw, b Kapil Dev	33		
A.A. Donald	lbw, b Prabhakar	1		
B.N. Schultz	not out	0		
Extras	lb 6, nb 7	13	b 1, lb 2, nb 6	9
		254	(for 3 wickets)	176

INDIA

	FIRST INNINGS	
R.J. Shastri	lbw, b Pringle	14
A.D. Jadeja	c McMillan, b Schultz	3
S.V. Manjrekar	lbw, b McMillan	0
S.R. Tendulkar	run out	11
M. Azharuddin (capt)	run out	36
P.K. Amre	c Rhodes, b McMillan	103
Kapil Dev	c Richardson, b McMillan	2
M. Prabhakar	c McMillan, b Donald	13
*K.S. More	lbw, b Henry	55
A.R. Kumble	b Henry	8
J. Srinath	not out	1
Extras	b 1, lb 7, w 4, nb 19	31
		277

	O	M	R	W	O	M	R	W
Kapil Dev	22	6	43	3	19	11	19	–
Prabhakar	24.4	7	47	2	14	3	47	–
Srinath	18	3	69	1	16	3	42	2
Kumble	28	8	51	2	16	4	36	1
Shastri	11	1	38	2	14	2	22	–
Tendulkar					2	1	3	–
Manjrekar					1	–	4	–

	O	M	R	W
Donald	29	6	69	1
Schultz	14.5	7	25	1
McMillan	37	18	52	3
Pringle	34	10	67	1
Henry	19.1	3	56	2

FALL OF WICKETS

1–0, 2–41, 3–101, 4–183, 5–194, 6–206, 7–215, 8–251, 9–253
1–68, 2–129, 3–138

1–18, 2–22, 3–38, 4–38, 5–125, 6–127, 7–146, 8–247, 9–274

Umpires: S.U. Bucknor, K.C. Liebenberg & C.J. Mitchley

Match drawn

Pravin Amre on his way to a century on his Test debut. (Patrick Eagar)

had been deprived of the services of Schultz, who had pulled a hamstring, and they were blunted by the straight bat of More and the defiance of Kumble who stayed for 72 minutes. Eventually, India took a lead of 23, but gloom and threatening rain ended play for the day.

There was no play on the fourth day and, on a meaningless fifth, the match was drawn. To no one's surprise, Pravin Amre took the individual award.

20, 21, 22 and **23** November 1992 *at Springbok Park, Bloemfontein*

Indians 250 (P.K. Amre 101, S.V. Manjrekar 53) and 312 for 8 dec. (S.V. Manjrekar 102 not out, A.D. Jadeja 68, R.J. Shastri 63)

South African Invitation XI 219 (M.W. Rushmere 75, M. Prabhakar 4 for 41) and 129 for 1 (M. Yachad 64 not out, M.W. Rushmere 54 not out)

Match drawn

Some careless batting saw the tourists slip to 21 for 3 on the first morning, but Manjrekar and Amre added 113, Amre hitting his second century in succession. Wicket-keeper Yadav helped him in a sixth-wicket stand of 83 in 25 overs. When the Invitation XI batted, Rushmere, who had lost his Test place to Cook, was the only one to show conviction against the pace of Prabhakar. Shastri and Jadeja began the Indians' second innings with a stand of 130, and Manjrekar hit a patient century before the game moved to a draw on a bland pitch.

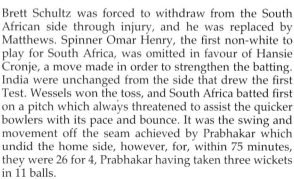

SECOND TEST MATCH
SOUTH AFRICA *v.* INDIA, at Johannesburg

Brett Schultz was forced to withdraw from the South African side through injury, and he was replaced by Matthews. Spinner Omar Henry, the first non-white to play for South Africa, was omitted in favour of Hansie Cronje, a move made in order to strengthen the batting. India were unchanged from the side that drew the first Test. Wessels won the toss, and South Africa batted first on a pitch which always threatened to assist the quicker bowlers with its pace and bounce. It was the swing and movement off the seam achieved by Prabhakar which undid the home side, however, for, within 75 minutes, they were 26 for 4, Prabhakar having taken three wickets in 11 balls.

Hudson and Wessels were taken at second slip off groping shots, and a similar tentative approach led to Cook being caught behind. Rhodes, coming in at 11 for 3, might have been caught behind first ball, but More failed to accept the difficult chance. He went on to rescue the South African innings, sharing a sixth-wicket stand of 85 with McMillan. Rhodes hit 10 fours and faced 189 balls, but his innings was marked by the most controversial of incidents. He had scored 28 when he attempted a quick single to Srinath at mid-off. The fielder's throw hit the stumps, and the Indians were unanimous in their appeal. Umpire Bucknor ruled 'not out', and, despite the decision being a close one, he refused to turn to the third umpire and the television monitor, although the fielding side requested him to do so. Had he acquiesced, he would

India's fine start to the second Test match – Wessels is caught at slip off Srinath. (Mike Hewitt/Allsport)

South Africa's saviour Jonty Rhodes in belligerent mood. (Mike Hewitt/Allsport)

have seen that Rhodes was some six inches short of his ground when the wicket was broken.

Rhodes eventually fell to Kumble against whom he was always uncertain, and South Africa closed on 226 for 7, a much healthier score than the early disasters had foretold. Brian McMillan, 69 not out overnight, continued the revival on the second morning when he and Matthews extended their eighth-wicket stand to 65. In trying to pull a short ball from Srinath, Pringle edged the ball into his face and sustained a fractured eye socket. He was to take no further part in the match. McMillan looked sure to reach a maiden Test century before he swung at a bouncer from Srinath and was splendidly caught, low down at long leg by Manjrekar.

Facing an unexpectedly comfortable score, India's start was almost as bad as South Africa's had been. Shastri, playing an airy shot, was caught at slip, and Jadeja went next ball. Manjrekar dragged a ball from the accurate McMillan into his stumps. By the end of the day, Azharuddin, Amre and Prabhakar were also out, and India were 128 for 6. Of these runs, Sachin Tendulkar had made 75. He had weathered a fearsome display of pace bowling from Donald and had played with great resolve, but India had their backs against the wall.

Tendulkar reached his fourth Test century on the third morning. He batted with great patience but punished the loose ball, hitting 19 fours. Kapil Dev batted with

An early strike for South Africa in the second Test as Matthews has Shastri taken at slip. (Mike Hewitt/Allsport)

customary belligerence, and the tail showed resolve, helping Tendulkar to edge the score nearer to that of the home side and giving him support while he reached his century – which he did when, after being marooned for 10 minutes on 99, he drove Matthews for successive boundaries.

Leading by 65 on the first innings, South Africa began their second innings too cautiously. Cook was caught down the leg side just before the close, at 75 for 1. This caution extended into the fourth day, and India gained the upper hand when Kumble changed ends and tantalised with his leg-spin. He took 3 for 17 in the afternoon, and he finished with his best figures in Test cricket, a just reward for fine bowling. South Africa's lack of a positive approach had cost them the initiative. India, needing 318 to win, ended the day on 15 for 0.

The last day was abysmal. The match had been watched by a good crowd, but they were subjected now to some dire batting. In 30 overs before lunch, Shastri and Jadeja scored only 41. Shastri was to bat for 3¼ hours, face 139 balls, hit 4 fours and score 23 runs. Any hope of an Indian victory soon evaporated, and, in fact, the quick dismissal of Azharuddin and Tendulkar gave hint of a South African triumph – but only a hint as Amre and Manjrekar batted out time.

The paying customer deserves better than this, but with two captains who seemed to lack both the imagination and the will and courage to win, the prospects for the last two Tests were not joyful.

Brian McMillan's all-round performance won him the individual award.

4 December 1992 *at Pietermaritzburg*

President's XI 196 for 8 (G. Kirsten 100)
Indians 199 for 6 (M. Azharuddin 69 not out)

Indians won by 4 wickets

The Indians began a series of eight one-day matches with a friendly encounter which ended in near riot as crowds invaded the pitch. An arranged four byes gave the match a hasty close, and the players sped from the field. Azharuddin hit his first fifty of the tour. Left-hander Gary Kirsten hit a century off 183 balls.

SECOND TEST MATCH – SOUTH AFRICA v. INDIA
26, 27, 28, 29 and 30 November 1992 at Wanderers, Johannesburg

SOUTH AFRICA

	FIRST INNINGS			SECOND INNINGS	
S. J. Cook	c More, b Prabhakar	2		c More, b Srinath	31
A.C. Hudson	c Azharuddin, b Prabhakar	8		b Kumble	53
K.C. Wessels (capt)	c Azharuddin, b Srinath	5		(4) run out	11
P.N. Kirsten	lbw, b Prabhakar	0		(5) b Kumble	26
J.N. Rhodes	lbw, b Kumble	91		(6) b Kumble	13
W.J. Cronje	c and b Kapil Dev	8		(7) b Kumble	15
B.M. McMillan	c Manjrekar, b Srinath	98		(8) c Prabhakar, b Kumble	5
*D.J. Richardson	lbw, b Kumble	9		(3) b Kumble	50
C.R. Matthews	b Prabhakar	31		c Tendulkar, b Prabhakar	18
M.W. Pringle	retired hurt	3		absent hurt	–
A.A. Donald	not out	14		(10) not out	7
Extras	lb 10, w 4, nb 9	23		b 1, lb 14, w 1, nb 7	23
		292			**252**

INDIA

	FIRST INNINGS			SECOND INNINGS	
R.J. Shastri	c Wessels, b Matthews	7		b Matthews	23
A.D. Jadeja	lbw, b McMillan	14		c Wessels, b Donald	43
S.V. Manjrekar	b McMillan	7		(5) not out	32
S.R. Tendulkar	c Hudson, b Cronje	111		lbw, b Donald	1
M. Azharuddin (capt)	c Wessels, b Matthews	9		(3) c Richardson, b Matthews	1
P.K. Amre	lbw, b McMillan	7		not out	35
M. Prabhakar	c Richardson, b Donald	2			
Kapil Dev	c McMillan, b Donald	25			
*K.S. More	c Richardson, b McMillan	10			
A.R. Kumble	not out	21			
J. Srinath	c Richardson, b Donald	5			
Extras	lb 4, w 4, nb 1	9		b 2, lb 2, nb 2	6
		227		(for 4 wickets)	**141**

	O	M	R	W	O	M	R	W
Kapil Dev	25	4	62	1	24	6	50	–
Prabhakar	29	3	90	4	23.2	3	74	1
Srinath	26.5	6	60	2	26	2	58	1
Kumble	26	8	60	2	44	22	53	6
Shastri	4	–	10	–				
Tendulkar					1	–	2	–

	O	M	R	W	O	M	R	W
Donald	31	9	78	3	20	6	43	2
McMillan	29	11	74	4	21	6	34	–
Matthews	29	13	41	2	20	10	23	2
Cronje	17	10	22	1	18	7	32	–
Kirsten	2	–	8	–	3	1	5	–

FALL OF WICKETS

1–10, 2–11, 3–11, 4–26, 5–73, 6–158, 7–186, 8–251, 9–292
1–73, 2–108, 3–138, 4–170, 5–194, 6–199, 7–209, 8–239, 9–252

FALL OF WICKETS

1–27, 2–27, 3–44, 4–77, 5–124, 6–127, 7–155, 8–174, 9–212
1–68, 2–70, 3–71, 4–73

Umpires: S.U. Bucknor, C.J. Mitchley & S.B. Lambson

Match drawn

FIRST ONE-DAY INTERNATIONAL — SOUTH AFRICA *v.* INDIA
7 December 1992 at Newlands, Cape Town

INDIA			SOUTH AFRICA		
A.D. Jadeja	c Kirsten, b Cronje	48	K.C. Wessels (capt)	run out	43
W.V. Raman	b Cronje	47	A.C. Hudson	c Prabhakar, b Tendulkar	33
M. Azharuddin (capt)	c Richardson, b Donald	9	P.N. Kirsten	c Raman, b Prabhakar	56
S.R. Tendulkar	b McMillan	15	J.N. Rhodes	c Tendulkar, b Srinath	13
S.V. Manjrekar	c Matthews, b Cronje	13	D.J. Callaghan	not out	17
P.K. Amre	c Hudson, b Cronje	4	W.J. Cronje	not out	12
Kapil Dev	c Cronje, b McMillan	27	B.M. McMillan		
M. Prabhakar	c Wessels, b Cronje	8	*D.J. Richardson		
*K.S. More	c Kirsten, b Donald	4	C.R. Matthews		
A.R. Kumble	not out	3	A.A. Donald		
J. Srinath	run out	0	P.S. de Villiers		
Extras	lb 5, nb 1	6	Extras	b 4, lb 5, w 1, nb 1	11
		—			—
(50 overs)		184	(49.3 overs)	(for 4 wickets)	185

	O	M	R	W		O	M	R	W
Donald	10	2	32	2	Kapil Dev	10	1	43	–
De Villiers	7	2	24	–	Prabhakar	9.3	1	36	1
Matthews	10	–	38	–	Tendulkar	10	1	25	1
McMillan	10	–	42	2	Srinath	10	2	34	1
Callaghan	3	–	11	–	Kumble	10	–	38	–
Cronje	10	–	32	5					

FALL OF WICKETS

1–92, 2–103, 3–109, 4–133, 5–140, 6–140, 7–153, 8–158, 9–184

FALL OF WICKETS

1–56, 2–108, 3–140, 4–168

Umpires: K.C. Liebenberg & S.B. Lambson   *Man of the Match:* W.J. Cronje   *South Africa won by 6 wickets*

SECOND ONE-DAY INTERNATIONAL — SOUTH AFRICA *v.* INDIA
9 December 1992 at St George's Park, Port Elizabeth

INDIA			SOUTH AFRICA		
A.D. Jadeja	c McMillan, b Schultz	5	A.C. Hudson	b Kapil Dev	5
W.V. Raman	b Matthews	33	K.C. Wessels (capt)	c Jadeja, b Prabhakar	30
M. Azharuddin (capt)	run out	5	P.N. Kirsten	run out	5
S.R. Tendulkar	c Richardson, b Callaghan	10	J.N. Rhodes	lbw, b Srinath	13
S.V. Manjrekar	run out	17	D.J. Callaghan	not out	45
P.K. Amre	run out	30	W.J. Cronje	not out	38
Kapil Dev	c Rhodes, b McMillan	1	B.M. McMillan		
M. Prabhakar	c Richardson, b McMillan	1	*D.J. Richardson		
*K.S. More	b McMillan	32	C.R. Matthews		
A.R. Kumble	b McMillan	7	A.A. Donald		
J. Srinath	not out	1	B.N. Schultz		
Extras	lb 3, nb 2	5	Extras	b 2, lb 4, w 3, nb 3	12
		—			—
(49.4 overs)		147	(46.4 overs)	(for 4 wickets)	148

	O	M	R	W		O	M	R	W
Donald	10	4	26	–	Kapil Dev	9	2	19	1
Schultz	9	1	35	1	Prabhakar	8	–	30	1
Matthews	10	4	20	1	Kumble	10	1	22	–
McMillan	9.4	–	32	4	Srinath	10	1	31	1
Cronje	6	–	18	–	Tendulkar	5	1	18	–
Callaghan	5	–	13	1	Jadeja	4.4	1	22	–

FALL OF WICKETS

1–8, 2–40, 3–48, 4–65, 5–81, 6–82, 7–84, 8–118, 9–144

FALL OF WICKETS

1–8, 2–20, 3–46, 4–70

Umpires: R.E. Koertzen, C.J. Mitchley & W. Diedricks   *Man of the Match:* B.M. McMillan   *South Africa won by 6 wickets*

ONE-DAY INTERNATIONAL SERIES
SOUTH AFRICA v. INDIA

Kepler Wessels needed several stitches in a cut on the forehead after he collided with Fanie de Villiers during fielding practice. De Villiers also needed stitches, but both men were deemed fit to play in the first match of the seven-game series. Callaghan made a happy return to the South African side after a year in which he had fought against serious illness.

Jadeja and Raman began India's innings with a partnership of 92, but both were dismissed by Cronje who then ate away at the rest of the visitors' batting. Wessels, dropped by Azharuddin, became the first player in a limited-over international to be given out with the aid of a television replay, and Peter Kirsten hit 56 off 90 balls. South Africa's hero, however, was Hansie Cronje. His side needed 17 from 13 balls, and eight off the last over. Cronje took two off the first ball, missed the second and hit the third for six.

The second match ended even more convincingly in victory for South Africa, but the image of the 'friendship' tour became rather tarnished. The Indians gave another miserable batting display and were 84 for 7 in the 36th over, having lost three men run out. More gathered runs with the tail, but a target of 148 posed no problems for South Africa.

The trouble erupted when Kapil Dev ran out Kirsten for backing up prematurely. The batsman, insisting he had received no warning, stood his ground and there were angry exchanges before he left. Wessels was then accused of hitting Kapil Dev on the shins with his bat while taking a second run. The South African captain pleaded that it was an accident and escaped punishment. Kirsten was fined for his show of dissent. As for the cricket, Callaghan and Cronje gradually gained command in an unbroken stand of 78 which gave South Africa victory with 20 balls to spare.

The one-day series was in danger of losing its appeal, and it was just as well that India at last found form and won the third encounter. Shastri returned to the exclusion of Manjrekar, and Azharuddin, winning the toss, asked South Africa to bat first. The home side were well served by Wessels and Hudson who scored 92 in 24 overs, but it was the advent of the spinners Kumble and Shastri that changed the balance of the game. Wessels swung at Kumble and was bowled, and the run rate slowed against the spin pair. Hudson looked by far the best of the South African batsmen and was out only when he responded to Callaghan's call for an improbable single. Callaghan responded a little by hitting out in the closing stages, but a target of 215 on a hard, bouncy pitch offered the Indian batsmen the chance to display their strokes.

The opportunity was grasped by Wookeri Raman who faced 149 balls and hit a six and 6 fours in a stylish innings

THIRD ONE-DAY INTERNATIONAL — SOUTH AFRICA v. INDIA
11 December 1992 at Centurion Park, Verwoerdburg

SOUTH AFRICA			INDIA		
K.C. Wessels (capt)	b Kumble	34	A.D. Jadeja	c Richardson, b Matthews	20
A.C. Hudson	run out	87	W.V. Raman	c McMillan, b Donald	113
P.N. Kirsten	b Shastri	19	P.K. Amre	c Donald, b Cronje	1
J.N. Rhodes	run out	18	M. Azharuddin (capt)	b Matthews	18
D.J. Callaghan	not out	32	S.R. Tendulkar	c Richardson, b Matthews	22
W.J. Cronje	b Kumble	0	Kapil Dev	b De Villiers	1
B.M. McMillan	not out	10	R.J. Shastri	not out	27
*D.J. Richardson			*K.S. More	not out	5
C.R. Matthews			M. Prabhakar		
A.A. Donald			A.R. Kumble		
P.S. de Villiers			J. Srinath		
Extras	lb 7, w 1, nb 6	14	Extras	lb 1, w 4, nb 3	8
(50 overs)	(for 5 wickets)	214	(49.1 overs)	(for 6 wickets)	215

	O	M	R	W		O	M	R	W
Kapil Dev	5	1	19	–	Donald	10	1	45	1
Prabhakar	9	1	31	–	De Villiers	10	1	33	1
Srinath	9	–	38	–	Matthews	10	–	56	3
Tendulkar	2	–	16	–	McMillan	9.1	–	36	–
Jadeja	8	–	38	–	Callaghan	3	–	13	–
Kumble	10	–	29	2	Cronje	7	–	31	1
Shastri	7	1	36	1					

FALL OF WICKETS

1–92, 2–124, 3–163, 4–180, 5–181

FALL OF WICKETS

1–56, 2–72, 3–123, 4–168, 5–171, 6–194

Umpires: W. Diedricks & S.B. Lambson   *Man of the Match:* W.V. Raman   *India won by 4 wickets*

FOURTH ONE-DAY INTERNATIONAL — SOUTH AFRICA v. INDIA
13 December 1992 at Wanderers, Johannesburg

INDIA

A.D. Jadeja	lbw, b Callaghan	18
W.V. Raman	b Donald	0
P.K. Amre	lbw, b Donald	2
M. Azharuddin (capt)	c Richardson, b Matthews	49
S.R. Tendulkar	c McMillan, b Donald	21
R.J. Shastri	c McMillan, b De Villiers	17
Kapil Dev	c Richardson, b Matthews	18
J. Srinath	c Rhodes, b McMillan	3
*K.S. More	run out	2
M. Prabhakar	not out	5
A.R. Kumble	not out	7
Extras	b 1, lb 5, w 11, nb 2	19
(50 overs)	(for 9 wickets)	161

SOUTH AFRICA

A.C. Hudson	c Azharuddin, b Kumble	22
K.C. Wessels (capt)	c Jadeja, b Srinath	45
P.N. Kirsten	lbw, b Srinath	21
J.N. Rhodes	not out	42
D.J. Callaghan	run out	12
W.J. Cronje	not out	11
B.M. McMillan		
*D.J. Richardson		
C.R. Matthews		
P.S. de Villiers		
A.A. Donald		
Extras	lb 9, w 2, nb 1	12
(48.3 overs)	(for 4 wickets)	165

	O	M	R	W
Donald	10	–	27	3
De Villiers	10	2	24	1
McMillan	10	–	39	1
Matthews	10	1	33	2
Callaghan	5	–	17	1
Cronje	5	–	15	–

	O	M	R	W
Kapil Dev	9	–	23	–
Prabhakar	8	1	24	–
Tendulkar	3	–	4	–
Kumble	9	1	33	1
Shastri	10	1	33	–
Srinath	9.3	1	39	2

FALL OF WICKETS
1–9, 2–12, 3–61, 4–107, 5–108, 6–136, 7–143, 8–149, 9–149

FALL OF WICKETS
1–47, 2–88, 3–95, 4–133

Umpires: C.J. Mitchley & K.E. Liebenberg   *Man of the Match:* J.N. Rhodes   *South Africa won by 6 wickets*

FIFTH ONE-DAY INTERNATIONAL — SOUTH AFRICA v. INDIA
15 December 1992 at Springbok Park, Bloemfontein

INDIA

A.D. Jadeja	c McMillan, b Donald	9
W.V. Raman	c McMillan, b Matthews	16
M. Prabhakar	run out	36
M. Azharuddin (capt)	not out	86
S.R. Tendulkar	b De Villiers	32
R.J. Shastri	not out	21
P.K. Amre		
Kapil Dev		
*V. Yadav		
A.R. Kumble		
J. Srinath		
Extras	b 1, lb 3, w 1, nb 2	7
(50 overs)	(for 4 wickets)	207

SOUTH AFRICA

K.C. Wessels (capt)	c and b Kumble	55
A.C. Hudson	c Azharuddin, b Srinath	108
P.N. Kirsten	not out	35
J.N. Rhodes	not out	0
W.J. Cronje		
D.J. Callaghan		
B.M. McMillan		
*D.J. Richardson		
C.R. Matthews		
A.A. Donald		
P.S. de Villiers		
Extras	lb 5, w 2, nb 3	10
(47.2 overs)	(for 2 wickets)	208

	O	M	R	W
Donald	10	2	36	1
De Villiers	10	–	29	1
Matthews	10	1	37	1
McMillan	10	–	59	–
Cronje	6	–	20	–
Callaghan	4	–	22	–

	O	M	R	W
Kapil Dev	9	1	35	–
Prabhakar	10	–	35	–
Srinath	9	–	43	1
Kumble	10	–	34	1
Shastri	5	–	25	–
Tendulkar	4	–	27	–
Amre	0.2	–	4	–

FALL OF WICKETS
1–17, 2–47, 3–88, 4–156

FALL OF WICKETS
1–125, 2–204

Umpires: R.E. Koertzen & S.B. Lambson   *Man of the Match:* A.C. Hudson   *South Africa won by 8 wickets*

SIXTH ONE-DAY INTERNATIONAL — SOUTH AFRICA v. INDIA
17 December 1992 at Kingsmead, Durban

SOUTH AFRICA				INDIA		
A.C. Hudson	c Yadav, b Kapil Dev	15		A.D. Jadeja	c Richardson, b Pringle	12
K.C. Wessels (capt)	c Manjrekar, b Prabhakar	78		M. Prabhakar	c Richardson, b Matthews	21
P.N. Kirsten	c Manjrekar, b Shastri	44		S.V. Manjrekar	run out	10
J.N. Rhodes	c Shastri, b Kapil Dev	16		M. Azharuddin (capt)	c De Villiers, b Cronje	41
D.J. Callaghan	st Yadav, b Kumble	8		S.R. Tendulkar	c Cronje, b Pringle	23
W.J. Cronje	b Kapil Dev	25		Kapil Dev	c Richardson, b Donald	30
*D.J. Richardson	run out	12		R.J. Shastri	c Kirsten, b Pringle	5
M.W. Pringle	run out	9		*V. Yadav	b Matthews	3
C.R. Matthews	not out	1		C.M. Sharma	c Rhodes, b De Villiers	15
P.S. de Villiers				A.R. Kumble	run out	0
A.A. Donald				Venkatapathy Raju	not out	3
Extras	b 2, lb 5, nb 1	8		Extras	b 1, lb 4, w 2, nb 7	14
(50 overs)	(for 8 wickets)	216		(47.5 overs)		177

	O	M	R	W		O	M	R	W
Prabhakar	10	1	54	1	Donald	9	3	18	1
Kapil Dev	10	4	23	3	De Villiers	8.5	2	22	1
Venkatapathy Raju	10	1	45	–	Matthews	10	–	40	2
Sharma	4	–	18	–	Pringle	10	–	51	3
Kumble	10	1	33	1	Cronje	6	1	20	1
Shastri	6	–	36	1	Callaghan	4	–	21	–

FALL OF WICKETS
1–28, 2–121, 3–157, 4–162, 5–173, 6–198, 7–215, 8–216

FALL OF WICKETS
1–40, 2–42, 3–65, 4–110, 5–127, 6–144, 7–153, 8–172, 9–173

Umpires: K.E. Liebenberg & W. Diedricks   *Man of the Match:* Kapil Dev   *South Africa won by 39 runs*

SEVENTH ONE-DAY INTERNATIONAL — SOUTH AFRICA v. INDIA
19 December 1992 at Buffalo Park, East London

SOUTH AFRICA				INDIA		
K.C. Wessels (capt)	c Tendulkar, b Venkatapathy Raju	57		M. Prabhakar	b Donald	12
A.C. Hudson	lbw, b Prabhakar	8		S.V. Manjrekar	lbw, b McMillan	6
P.N. Kirsten	c Banerjee, b Venkatapathy Raju	30		S.R. Tendulkar	c Richardson, b Matthews	21
J.N. Rhodes	c Kumble, b Prabhakar	37		M. Azharuddin (capt)	run out	24
D.J. Callaghan	c Yadav, b Venkatapathy Raju	0		P.K. Amre	not out	84
W.J. Cronje	c Manjrekar, b Kapil Dev	55		Kapil Dev	lbw, b Matthews	17
B.M. McMillan	not out	3		*V. Yadav	not out	34
*D.J. Richardson	b Prabhakar	0		C.M. Sharma		
C.R. Matthews	run out	1		S.T. Banerjee		
P.S. de Villiers				A.R. Kumble		
A.A. Donald				Venkatapathy Raju		
Extras	lb 9, w 1, nb 2	12		Extras	lb 4, w 1, nb 1	6
(50 overs)	(for 8 wickets)	203		(47.2 overs)	(for 5 wickets)	204

	O	M	R	W		O	M	R	W
Prabhakar	10	1	43	3	Donald	10	–	49	1
Kapil Dev	10	4	27	1	De Villiers	8.2	3	26	–
Sharma	8	–	34	–	McMillan	10	1	38	1
Banerjee	3	–	20	–	Matthews	10	2	44	2
Venkatapathy Raju	10	–	37	3	Callaghan	5	–	21	–
Kumble	9	–	33	–	Cronje	4	–	22	–

FALL OF WICKETS
1–21, 2–86, 3–108, 4–108, 5–199, 6–200, 7–201, 8–203

FALL OF WICKETS
1–16, 2–39, 3–43, 4–80, 5–130

Umpires: C.J. Mitchley, R.E. Koertzen & S.B. Lambson   *Man of the Match:* P.K. Amre   *India won by 5 wickets*

which took his side to the brink of victory. Raman, so prolific in domestic cricket, at last showed his true form at international level. He was aided by Azharuddin and Tendulkar after Jadeja and Amre had gone for 72, but when Raman was magnificently caught at mid-off by McMillan, India still wanted 21 from 19 balls. Shastri, justifying his recall with bat and ball, saw his side home with five balls to spare.

Rain caused the fourth one-day international to be put back for a day. Asked to bat first, India were at a disadvantage on a pitch that sweated after being long under the covers, with an outfield that was slow. Raman edged a wide delivery into his stumps, and just as Azharuddin and Tendulkar were suggesting revival they were out in the space of three deliveries. The necessary acceleration never came, and South Africa faced a meagre 161. Wessels, dropped on seven, gave his side a good start, and Rhodes and Callaghan made sure that there were no surprises in the middle-order.

The one-day series was decided in the fifth of the seven matches which South Africa won by the huge margin of eight wickets with 16 balls to spare. Once more India's circumspect batting contributed much to their downfall. They began tentatively and did not move above three runs an over until past the half-way stage. Prabhakar offered hope until run out by Azharuddin, who did not find his touch until late in his innings. Shastri hit 21 off 18

balls, but India's 207 was well short of the target anticipated on a firm pitch.

Wessels and Hudson soon confirmed this in an opening stand of 125 in 33 overs. Hudson hit 108 off 147 balls. His innings included a six and 8 fours, and he registered South Africa's first century in a one-day international.

A record crowd of 26,000 at Durban saw India give another limp display. Kepler Wessels played his best innings of the series, 78 off 120 balls, and he and Kirsten added 93 in 23 overs for South Africa's second wicket. Kapil Dev bowled beautifully for India, taking 1 for 3 in his first six overs, but the home side were always on top, and India's batting was so lacking in confidence that the result was never in doubt.

Already assured of a hostile reception when they returned home, India restored some pride with victory in the final one-day international. Prabhakar reached 100 wickets in this form of cricket, and Wessels again gave his side a solid start, but the stars of the match were Amre and Yadav. Amre hit 84 off 98 balls while the wicket-keeper made 34 off 22 balls. The pair added 74 in nine overs to bring India to victory with 16 balls to spare.

21, 22 and 23 December 1992 *at Buffalo Park, East London*

Combined Universities XI 174 (N.C. Johnson 61, Venkatapathy Raju 4 for 63) and 207 for 9 (Venkatapathy Raju 5 for 68)

Indians 273 for 8 dec. (S.R. Tendulkar 131, M. Handman 4 for 59)

Match drawn

The left-arm spin bowling of Venkatapathy Raju and a century from Sachin Tendulkar were the encouraging features for the Indians in a match which was overshadowed by the strong criticisms of their captain and their performances emanating from their native country.

THIRD TEST MATCH
SOUTH AFRICA *v.* INDIA, at Port Elizabeth

The pitch at Port Elizabeth was predicted to help the spinners in the closing stages, but Wessels adopted a positive approach by asking India to bat first when he won the toss. His pace bowlers responded admirably to his decision and by the end of the first day, the Indian first innings was in shreds.

There were no early alarms as the South African attack failed to find control but, some 15 minutes before lunch, Shastri was taken at point when he fended off a lifting delivery from McMillan. Shortly after the break, Raman fell to Donald's out-swinger, and Tendulkar, his footwork all astray, chased a wide delivery to give the keeper

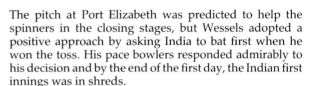

South Africa's first century in a one-day international was scored by Alan Hudson against India at Bloemfontein. (Patrick Eagar)

Fine all-round cricket in the one-day series and a brilliant century in the third Test match from Hansie Cronje. (Mike Hewitt/Allsport)

another catch. Manjrekar, too, was totally out of form and, having struggled painfully, he offered gully the simplest of chances.

Azharuddin showed some semblance of aggression before being caught off an inside edge by Richardson, who did have his share of misses as well as successes. Kapil Dev lunged wildly across the line and skied a catch to mid-off, and with Prabhakar falling to Matthews, India closed on a miserable 197 for 8.

Donald picked up his fifth wicket and India added only 15 on the second morning, but they received some early encouragement when Wessels played on to Prabhakar in the second over of the South African innings. Promoted to number three, Hansie Cronje now joined Hudson in a resolute stand of 117 in 56 overs. The batsmen never mastered the Indian spinners but they showed great determination, and South Africa moved slowly

THIRD TEST MATCH – SOUTH AFRICA *v.* INDIA
26, 27, 28 and 29 December 1992 at St George's Park, Port Elizabeth

INDIA

	FIRST INNINGS			SECOND INNINGS	
R.J. Shastri	c Henry, b McMillan	10	c Richardson, b McMillan	5
W.V. Raman	c Richardson, b Donald	21	b Donald	0
S.V. Manjrekar	c Henry, b McMillan	23	lbw, b Donald	6
S.R. Tendulkar	c Richardson, b Donald	6	c Richardson, b Schultz	0
M. Azharuddin (capt)	c Richardson, b Donald	60	c Wessels, b Donald	7
P.K. Amre	c McMillan, b Donald	11	c Richardson, b Schultz	7
Kapil Dev	c Kirsten, b McMillan	12	c McMillan, b Donald	129
M. Prabhakar	c McMillan, b Matthews	11	c Richardson, b Donald	17
*K.S. More	c Richardson, b Donald	20	b Donald	17
A.R. Kumble	c McMillan, b Schultz	14	c Richardson, b Donald	17
Venkatapathy Raju	not out	0	not out	2
Extras	lb 13, w 4, nb 7	24	lb 4, w 1, nb 3	8
		212		215

SOUTH AFRICA

	FIRST INNINGS			SECOND INNINGS	
A.C. Hudson	b Raju	52	(2) c Azharuddin, b Tendulkar	33
K.C. Wessels (capt)	b Prabhakar	0	(1) not out	95
W.J. Cronje	b Kumble	135	not out	16
P.N. Kirsten	c More, b Raju	0		
B.M. McMillan	lbw, b Raju	25		
J.N. Rhodes	c Prabhakar, b Kumble	2		
*D.J. Richardson	run out	1		
O. Henry	lbw, b Kapil Dev	16		
C.R. Matthews	c Azharuddin, b Kapil	17		
A.A. Donald	b Kumble	6		
B.N. Schultz	not out	0		
Extras	b 2, lb 13, nb 6	21	b 8, lb 3	11
		275	(for 1 wicket)	155

	O	M	R	W	O	M	R	W
Donald	27	11	55	5	28	4	84	7
Schultz	20.5	4	39	1	16	5	37	2
McMillan	20	9	41	3	12	2	30	1
Matthews	17	7	34	1	9	1	43	–
Henry	11	2	30	–	8	2	17	–

	O	M	R	W	O	M	R	W
Kapil Dev	24	6	45	2	5	1	9	–
Prabhakar	15	3	57	1	5	2	7	–
Kumble	50.3	16	81	3	20	5	65	–
Venkatapathy Raju	46	15	73	3	18	5	50	–
Tendulkar	1	1	0	–	3	–	9	1
Shastri	2	1	4	–				
Azharuddin					0.1	–	4	–

FALL OF WICKETS

1–43, 2–49, 3–59, 4–98, 5–143, 6–152, 7–160, 8–185, 9–208
1–1, 2–10, 3–11, 4–20, 5–27, 6–31, 7–88, 8–120, 9–197

FALL OF WICKETS

1–0, 2–117, 3–117, 4–171, 5–182, 6–185, 7–215, 8–259, 9–274
1–98

Umpires: D.R. Shepherd, R.E. Koertzen & W. Diedricks

South Africa won by 9 wickets

towards a position of strength. They ended the day with 163 runs scored and three wickets down. Cronje was unbeaten on 75.

The third day produced some dramatic cricket and two displays of dissent which went unpunished. The first occurred when Cronje, on 87, survived an appeal for leg before against Venkatapathy Raju. More threw down his glove and the ball in disgust when the appeal was rejected. Cronje was eventually last out, having scored a maiden Test century of relentless application, 135 off 411 balls, with a six and 12 fours. The going was always slow, but Cronje's concentration never wavered, while Azharuddin's lack of imaginative captaincy was something of an ally. The Indian bowlers, not always well supported in the field, could be praised for restricting the South African lead to 63, but suddenly this modest sum took on immense proportions.

In the first 21 overs of their second innings, India were reduced to 31 for 6. One of the six victims was Tendulkar who was adjudged caught off what he claimed and what appeared to be his thigh pad. Shastri exchanged words with umpire Koertzen and threw his bat to the ground. However, neither Shastri nor More were reprimanded. Shastri later became another Richardson victim, caught down the leg side. Donald's pace had, by then, proved too much for Raman, Manjrekar and Azharuddin. Kapil Dev and Prabhakar alone stood firm, and India were barely alive at the end of the day on 71 for 6.

There were two heroes on the fourth and final day. The first was Kapil Dev who scored 96 out of the 144 runs that India added. He batted with power and grandeur, dominating the South African bowling as no other Indian batsman had done during the series. He hit a six and 14 fours and faced 180 balls. This was a mighty knock, and it included a stand of 77 in 18 overs with Kumble for the ninth wicket, but it proved to be in vain. Alan Donald finished with 7 for 84, 12 for 139 in the match, and his pace bowling earned him the individual award and virtually won the match for South Africa.

Hudson and Wessels began South Africa's second innings with a partnership of 98 which removed any fear of defeat. Wessels was there at the end, having hit 12 fours and having led South Africa to their first Test win for 22 years. Donald, Cronje and Wessels took the main honours for the home side, but this was essentially a fine team performance.

Twelve wickets in the third Test for match-winner Allan Donald. (Patrick Eagar)

FOURTH TEST MATCH
SOUTH AFRICA *v.* INDIA, at Cape Town

South Africa gave a first Test cap to Cullinan; India brought back Srinath and had a new opening pair in Jadeja and Prabhakar. Neither Shastri nor Raman was fully fit. Indeed, Shastri had struggled throughout the tour and underwent a knee operation as the tour ended.

Not for the first time in the series, the opening stages of the Test promised an excitement that was ultimately to be denied. Prabhakar bowled Wessels with an in-swinger on his third delivery of the match, and it was 25 minutes before South Africa scored a run. Srinath, who bowled well and at a lively pace, took a return catch low down to account for Hudson, and Kumble had Cronje taken bat and pad. Kirsten did nothing to improve on a miserable series when he edged Kapil Dev to the keeper, and it was left to Cullinan and Rhodes to restore order to the South African innings.

Rhodes struggled painfully against the spinners, but he survived to add 99 with the impressive Cullinan who was finally caught head high at mid-on. South Africa closed on 189 for 5 from 93 overs. A familiar pattern had begun to emerge.

The pattern became more deeply engraved on a second day which virtually killed the match. South Africa crawled to 360 for 9 before Wessels declared with 35 minutes of the day remaining. McMillan hit 52 in 69 overs and Rhodes, if uncertain, at least suggested entertainment with his 86 in 4¾ hours. India spilled their usual quota of catches, and the grimmest of days ended with the visitors on 13 for 0.

On the third day, India scored 148 runs in six hours. Prabhakar occupied 5¼ hours for his 62 as Azharuddin and his side obviously lost all interest in winning the match. Five wickets fell, and India were 161 from 97 overs. There was no greater urgency on the fourth day when the Indians took their score to 276, from 151 overs,

FOURTH TEST MATCH – SOUTH AFRICA v. INDIA
2, 3, 4, 5 and 6 January 1993 at Newlands, Cape Town

SOUTH AFRICA

	FIRST INNINGS		SECOND INNINGS	
A.C. Hudson	c and b Srinath	19	(2) c More, b Srinath	11
K.C. Wessels (capt)	b Prabhakar	0	(1) c and b Srinath	34
W.J. Cronje	c Manjrekar, b Kumble	33	c More, b Srinath	0
P.N. Kirsten	c More, b Kapil Dev	13	c Manjrekar, b Kapil	13
D.J. Cullinan	c Prabhakar, b Raju	46	c More, b Srinath	28
J.N. Rhodes	c More, b Srinath	86	c Srinath, b Kumble	16
B.M. McMillan	c sub, b Kumble	52	not out	11
*D.J. Richardson	c Tendulkar, b Kumble	21	not out	10
O. Henry	run out	34		
C.R. Matthews	not out	28		
A.A. Donald	not out	1		
Extras	b 2, lb 22, w 2, nb 1	27	lb 4, nb 3	7
	(for 9 wickets, dec.)	360	(for 6 wickets, dec.)	130

INDIA

	FIRST INNINGS		SECOND INNINGS	
A.D. Jadeja	c Kirsten, b McMillan	19	not out	20
M. Prabhakar	c Wessels, b Henry	62	c Richardson, b Matthews	7
S.V. Manjrekar	c Hudson, b Donald	46	not out	2
P.K. Amre	c McMillan, b Donald	6		
S.R. Tendulkar	c Hudson, b Cronje	73		
M. Azharuddin (capt)	c Richardson, b McMillan	7		
Venkatapathy Raju	c Cullinan, b Matthews	18		
Kapil Dev	c Hudson, b Cronje	34		
*K.S. More	lbw, b Matthews	0		
A.R. Kumble	c Hudson, b Matthews	0		
J. Srinath	not out	0		
Extras	lb 7, w 3, nb 1	11		
		276	(for 1 wicket)	29

	O	M	R	W	O	M	R	W
Kapil Dev	29	8	42	1	17	4	29	1
Prabhakar	23	6	48	1	10	4	19	–
Venkatapathy Raju	47	15	94	1	20	8	25	–
Srinath	25	6	51	2	27	10	33	4
Kumble	47	13	101	3	23	11	20	1

	O	M	R	W	O	M	R	W
Donald	36	13	58	2	4	–	7	–
McMillan	36	9	76	2				
Matthews	28	12	32	3	6	1	17	1
Cronje	18.4	8	17	2	3	3	0	–
Henry	33	8	86	1				
Rhodes					1	–	5	–

FALL OF WICKETS

1–0, 2–28, 3–57, 4–78, 5–177, 6–245, 7–282, 8–319, 9–345

1–20, 2–28, 3–61, 4–61, 5–96, 6–107

FALL OF WICKETS

1–44, 2–129, 3–138, 4–144, 5–153, 6–200, 7–275, 8–276, 9–276

1–21

Umpires: D.R. Shepherd, S.B. Lambson & K.E. Liebenberg

Match drawn

TEST MATCH AVERAGES – SOUTH AFRICA v. INDIA

SOUTH AFRICA BATTING

	M	Inns	NO	Runs	HS	Av	100s	50s
J.N. Rhodes	4	7	1	275	91	45.83	–	2
K.C. Wessels	4	8	1	295	118	42.14	1	1
W.J. Cronje	3	6	1	207	135	41.40	1	–
B.M. McMillan	4	6	1	194	98	38.80	–	2
M.W. Pringle	2	2	1	36	33	36.00	–	–
C.R. Matthews	3	4	1	94	31	31.33	–	–
A.C. Hudson	4	8	–	245	55	30.62	–	3
D.J. Richardson	4	6	1	106	50	21.20	–	1
S.J. Cook	2	4	–	76	43	19.00	–	–
O. Henry	3	3	–	53	34	17.66	–	–
A.A. Donald	4	5	3	29	14*	14.50	–	–
P.N. Kirsten	4	7	1	76	26	12.66	–	–

Played in one Test: D.J. Cullinan 46 & 28
Played in two Tests: B.N. Schultz 0* & 0*

INDIA BATTING

	M	Inns	NO	Runs	HS	Av	100s	50s
Kapil Dev	4	5	–	202	129	40.40	1	–
P.K. Amre	4	6	1	169	103	33.80	1	–
S.R. Tendulkar	4	6	–	202	111	33.66	1	1
A.D. Jadeja	3	5	1	99	43	24.75	–	–
S.V. Manjrekar	4	7	2	116	46	23.20	–	–
K.S. More	4	5	–	102	55	20.40	–	1
M. Azharuddin	4	6	–	120	60	20.00	–	1
Venkatapathy Raju	2	3	2	20	18	20.00	–	–
M. Prabhakar	4	6	–	112	62	18.66	–	1
A.R. Kumble	4	5	1	60	21*	15.00	–	–
R.J. Shastri	3	5	–	59	23	11.80	–	–
J. Srinath	3	3	2	6	5	6.00	–	–

Played in one Test: W.V. Raman 21 & 0

SOUTH AFRICA BOWLING

	Overs	Mds	Runs	Wkts	Av	Best	10/m	5/inn
A.A. Donald	175	49	394	20	19.70	7-84	1	2
C.R. Matthews	109	44	190	9	21.11	3-32	–	–
B.M. McMillan	155	55	307	13	23.61	4-74	–	–
W.J. Cronje	56.4	28	71	3	23.66	2-17	–	–
B.N. Schultz	51.4	16	101	4	25.25	2-37	–	–
O. Henry	71.1	15	189	3	63.00	2-56	–	–
P.N. Kirsten	5	1	13	–	–	–	–	–

Bowled in one innings: M.W. Pringle 34–10–67–1; J.N. Rhodes 1–0–5–0

INDIA BOWLING

	Overs	Mds	Runs	Wkts	Av	Best	10/m	5/inn
S.R. Tendulkar	7	2	14	1	14.00	1-9	–	–
A.R. Kumble	254.3	87	467	18	25.94	6-53	–	1
J. Srinath	138.5	30	313	12	26.08	4-33	–	–
R.J. Shastri	31	4	74	2	37.00	2-38	–	–
Kapil Dev	165	46	299	8	37.37	3-43	–	–
M. Prabhakar	144	31	389	9	43.22	4-90	–	–
Venkatapathy Raju	131	43	242	4	60.50	3-73	–	–

Bowled in one innings: S.V. Manjrekar 1–0–4–0; M. Azharuddin 0.1–0–4–0

SOUTH AFRICA FIELDING FIGURES

16 – D.J. Richardson; 8 – B.M. McMillan; 5 – A.C. Hudson and K.C. Wessels; 2 – P.N. Kirsten and O. Henry; 1 – J.N. Rhodes and D.J. Cullinan

INDIA FIELDING FIGURES

11 – K.S. More; 6 – M. Azharuddin; 4 – S.R. Tendulkar and M. Prabhakar; 3 – S.V. Manjrekar and J. Srinath; 1– Kapil Dev, A.R. Kumble and sub

and Srinath took two wickets in South Africa's second innings as 48 runs were scored. More held the catches to dismiss Hudson and Cronje, but he also dropped Wessels off Kapil Dev.

The agony meandered to its inevitable end. It was a game totally lacking in urgency and imaginative or positive leadership – a travesty of cricket, and a total condemnation of what passes for Test cricket. Srinath, a bowler of life and enthusiasm, earned the individual award.

So ended the friendship series. It was, in the main, a dreadful affair in which runs came at an average of less than two an over. South Africa won this historic series, but it was one which alienated thousands of South Africans from Test cricket and which turned them more and more towards the one-day game.

TOTAL POWER SHIELD

ROUND ONE

3 October 1992 *at Queenstown*

Western Province 276 for 4 (G. Kirsten 103, B.M. McMillan 58 not out)
Border Country Districts 150 (D. MacHelm 4 for 41)

Western Province won by 126 runs

at Brackenfell

Boland 230 for 7 (C.P. Dettmer 64, W.N. van As 59)
Eastern Transvaal 225 (S.E. Mitchley 63, W. Bird 4 for 62)

Boland won by 5 runs

at Landau Recreation Club, Witbank

Transvaal 309 for 5 (R.F. Pienaar 105, G.A. Pollock 77, M. Yachad 55)
Eastern Transvaal Country Districts 105

Transvaal won by 204 runs

at De Beers Country Club, Kimberley

Griqualand West 155 (D. Jordaan 53, O.D. Gibson 5 for 19)
Border 156 for 2 (A.G. Lawson 76 not out)

Border won by 8 wickets

at Addison Park, Empangeni

Orange Free State 270 for 8 (W.J. Cronje 117, G. Ecclestone 4 for 43)
Natal Country Districts 94 (A.A. Donald 4 for 8)

Orange Free State won by 176 runs

at Pietersburg CC, Pietersburg

Eastern Province 286 for 3 (K.C. Wessels 127 not out, L.J. Koen 65 not out, M.W. Rushmere 56)

Northern Transvaal Country Districts 60 (E.A.E. Baptiste 6 for 13)

Eastern Province won by 226 runs

at Harmony Ground, Virginia

Orange Free State Country Districts 171 for 6
Northern Transvaal 173 for 2 (P.H. Barnard 85, J.J. Strydom 73)

Northern Transvaal won by 8 wickets

at Witrand Cricket Field, Potchefstroom

Natal 307 for 5 (N.E. Wright 116 not out, E.L.R. Stewart 90)
Western Transvaal 108 (M.D. Marshall 4 for 21)

Natal won by 199 runs

South Africa's competitive domestic season began with the first round of the 55-over knock-out competition which was under new sponsorship. It was decided that only the semi-finals would be played on a two-leg basis.

The first round saw the elimination of all the minnows. Eastern and Western Transvaal and Griqualand West were all beaten, leaving Boland – victors over Eastern Transvaal – as the only Bowl side in the second round.

A most promising newcomer showing his bowling worth in the Total Power Shield – MacHelm of Western Province. (Mike Hewitt/ Allsport)

West Indian players appearing in South African cricket were particularly successful. Gibson, Marshall and Baptiste all returned impressive bowling figures. Gary Kirsten and Neville Wright hit their first centuries in the competition.

SECOND ROUND

16 January 1993 *at Buffalo Park, East London*

Western Province 228 for 5 (G. Kirsten 88)
Border 162 (E.O. Simons 4 for 22)

Western Province won by 66 runs

at Wanderers, Johannesburg

Transvaal 132 (D.R. Laing 51 not out)
Orange Free State 135 for 3 (W.J. Cronje 61)

Orange Free State won by 7 wickets

17 January 1993 *at St George's Park, Port Elizabeth*

Boland 172 for 9 (C.P. Dettmer 55)
Eastern Province 174 for 4

Eastern Province won by 6 wickets

at Kingsmead, Durban

Natal 228 (P.S. de Villiers 5 for 30)

Northern Transvaal 185 (J.J. Strydom 54, T.J. Packer 4 for 42)

Natal won by 43 runs

Gary Kirsten played another fine innings to take Western Province to a comfortable win over Border while Orange Free State trounced Transvaal. The home side were bowled out in 46.2 overs, and Orange Free State won with 17.3 overs to spare.

Boland laboured against Eastern Province, and Fanie de Villiers had his best bowling performance in the tournament, only to see his side well beaten by Natal.

SEMI-FINALS
FIRST LEG

23 January 1993 *at Newlands, Cape Town*

Orange Free State 153 for 7
Western Province 154 for 5

Western Province won by 5 wickets

24 January 1993 *at St George's Park, Port Elizabeth*

Natal 184 for 9 (C.E.B. Rice 76 not out, R.E. Bryson 4 for 29)
Eastern Province 187 for 4 (K.C. Wessels 101 not out)

Eastern Province won by 6 wickets

SECOND LEG

30 January 1993 *at Kingsmead, Durban*

Eastern Province 184 for 8
Natal 158

Eastern Province won by 26 runs

at Springbok Park, Bloemfontein

Orange Free State 224 for 9 (L.J. Wilkinson 52)
Western Province 223 for 8 (B.M. McMillan 56)

Orange Free State won by 1 run

THIRD LEG

31 January 1993 *at Springbok Park, Bloemfontein*

Western Province 224 for 8
Orange Free State 225 for 3 (W.J. Cronje 72, L.J. Wilkinson 57 not out, J.M. Arthur 56)

Orange Free State won by 7 wickets

With skipper Kepler Wessels in command, Eastern Province brushed aside Natal to enter the final. Orange Free State had to work much harder. Runs were hard to come by in Cape Town, and in the second leg at Bloemfontein, Simons and Matthews just failed to give Western Province victory and a place in the final. The following day,

Eldine Baptiste – an all-rounder of tremendous power for Eastern Province in all forms of cricket. (David Munden/Sports-Line)

Western Province scored quite consistently to reach 224, but the Free State were never in trouble and won with 17 balls to spare.

FINAL

6 February 1993 *at Springbok Park, Bloemfontein*

Eastern Province 202 for 6 (E.A.E. Baptiste 61 not out, D.J. Richardson 57)

Orange Free State 205 for 4 (W.J. Cronje 75, P.J.R. Steyn 70 not out)

Orange Free State won by 6 wickets

Middle-order hitting by Richardson and Baptiste revived Eastern Province's hopes, but their total of 202 never looked to be a winning one. Steyn provided the stability for Orange Free State, and Cronje, the leading scorer in the competition, added the fireworks as the home side took the shield with 7.1 of their 55 overs unused. This was Orange Free State's second triumph in the tournament, having won the shield for the first time in 1992.

CASTLE CURRIE CUP

23, 24, 25 and **26** October 1992 *at St George's Park, Port Elizabeth*

Eastern Province 119 (P.W.E. Rawson 4 for 27) and 312 (K.C. Wessels 108, D.J. Richardson 77, C.E.B. Rice 6 for 35)

Natal 418 (A.C. Hudson 100, N.E. Wright 88, J.N. Rhodes 85, P.L. Symcox 50, E.A.E. Baptiste 5 for 86) and 14 for 0

Natal won by 10 wickets

Natal 6 pts., Eastern Province 0 pts.

at Centurion Park, Verwoerdburg

Northern Transvaal 126 (S.D. Jack 5 for 36) and 205 (S.D. Jack 5 for 78)

Transvaal 219 (M. Yachad 91, D.J. Cullinan 61, P.S. de Villiers 4 for 49) and 116 for 2

Transvaal won by 8 wickets

Transvaal 6 pts., Northern Transvaal 0 pts.

at Buffalo Park, East London

Orange Free State 422 for 9 dec. (L.J. Wilkinson 115, W.J. Cronje 88, C.J.P.G. van Zyl 81) and 83 for 3

Border 263 (I.L. Howell 67, A.G. Lawson 57, O. Henry 4 for 73) and 239 (B.M. Osborne 92)

Orange Free State won by 7 wickets

Orange Free State 6 pts., Border 0 pts.

South Africa's premier competition began with a very surprising result as reigning champions Eastern Province

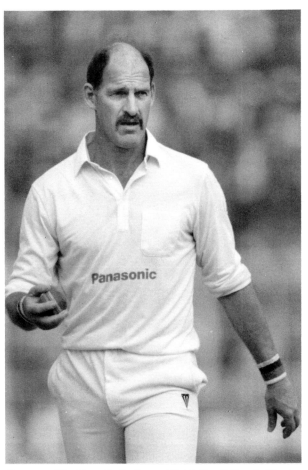

Evergreen Clive Rice – the backbone of Natal. (David Munden/Sports-Line)

were beaten in three days by Natal. Electing to bat first, Eastern Province were bowled out in 38.5 overs. Natal took the lead for the loss of only one wicket, and Hudson and Wright added 145 for the second wicket. Skipper Rhodes hit merrily, and there was a late flourish from Symcox who hit 50 of the last 71 runs. Only the tenacity of Wessels and Richardson saved Eastern from an innings defeat, but veteran Clive Rice was in splendid form and bowled Natal to an easy victory.

It was pace bowler Steven Jack who set up Transvaal's victory in three days over Northern Transvaal. Jimmy Cook won the toss and asked the home side to bat first, and when Transvaal looked likely to collapse before de Villiers, they were held together by Yachad and Cullinan who added 88 for the third wicket.

A third-wicket stand of 114 between Cronje and Wilkinson put Orange Free State on the path to success against Border, but there was a mid-order collapse, and it was left to Van Zyl's late hitting to restore supremacy. In spite of Howell's defiance, Border were forced to follow-on and they never looked like avoiding defeat, although Osborne made sure that at least an innings thrashing was avoided.

30, 31 October, **1** and **2** November 1992 *at Newlands, Cape Town*

Western Province 248 (E.O. Simons 55 not out, P.S. de Villiers 5 for 83) and 341 for 5 dec. (A.J. Lamb 206 not out, A.P. Kuiper 79, P.S. de Villiers 4 for 64)
Northern Transvaal 133 and 273 (M.J.R. Rindel 79)

Western Province won by 183 runs

Western Province 6 pts., Northern Transvaal 0 pts.

at Kingsmead, Durban

Orange Free State 280 (F.D. Stephenson 141, T.J. Packer 4 for 58) and 321 (J.M. Arthur 81, W.J. Cronje 80)
Natal 184 (N.E. Wright 65, A.C. Hudson 55, O. Henry 6 for 72) and 288 for 8 (A.C. Hudson 159 not out)

Match drawn

Orange Free State 2 pts., Natal 0 pts.

at Buffalo Park, East London

Border 322 (P.N. Kirsten 158) and 150 (T.G. Shaw 5 for 49)
Eastern Province 514 (M.W. Rushmere 110, K.C. Wessels 93, R.E. Bryson 57, T.G. Shaw 55, L.J. Koen 54, D.J. Callaghan 50, R.J. McCurdy 4 for 119)

Eastern Province won by an innings and 42 runs

Eastern Province 6 pts., Border 0 pts.

Having chosen to bat, Western Province struggled to 168 for 9 before Simons and Pringle added 80 for the last wicket. The varied home attack then caused Northern Transvaal much embarrassment, and Western began their second innings with a lead of 115. They lost four wickets for 51 runs, but Allan Lamb and Brian McMillan added 267. Lamb's 347-minute innings included a six and 27 fours.

Franklyn Stephenson hit 141 off 142 balls with 3 sixes and 21 fours to lift Orange Free State from their plight of 79 for 5. Omar Henry then bowled Free State into a strong position which was consolidated by Arthur and Cronje, but Hudson carried his bat through 134 overs and 455 minutes to save the game for Natal.

With Peter Kirsten hitting 158 to take Border from 18 for 4 to a total of 322, the home side must have felt reasonably happy, but a century from Rushmere and powerful scoring by Eastern Province's middle-order put the visitors in command. Border collapsed in their second innings, with Shaw taking five wickets and Baptiste 3 for 23 from 20 overs.

6, 7, 8 and **9** November 1992 *at Jan Smuts Ground, Pietermaritzburg*

Border 199 (O.D. Gibson 79 not out, M.D. Marshall 4 for 36) and 281 (P.N. Kirsten 66, M.D. Marshall 4 for 61)

Allan Lamb, 206 not out for Western Province against Northern Transvaal, 1 November 1992, and top of the first-class batting averages. (USPA)

Natal 210 (J.N. Rhodes 67, R.J. McCurdy 5 for 54) and 272 for 3 (J.N. Rhodes 135 not out, C.E.B. Rice 59 not out)

Natal won by 7 wickets

Natal 6 pts., Border 0 pts.

at Wanderers, Johannesburg

Western Province 410 for 8 dec. (A.J. Lamb 134, G. Kirsten 109, E.O. Simons 50) and 46 for 3
Transvaal 333 (S.J. Cook 123, D.J. Cullinan 72, C.R. Matthews 6 for 50)

Match drawn

Western Province 2 pts., Transvaal 0 pts.

at Springbok Park, Bloemfontein

Eastern Province 337 (E.A.E. Baptiste 86, M.W. Rushmere 85) and 199 for 6 dec. (E.A.E. Baptiste 68 not out, K.C. Wessels 54)
Orange Free State 230 (O. Henry 79, E.A.E. Baptiste 5 for 51) and 54 for 7

Match drawn

Eastern Province 2 pts., Orange Free State 0 pts.

Dave Callaghan hit 124 for Eastern Province against Transvaal, 20 November 1992. (Anne Laing)

Border suffered their third defeat in as many matches as Malcolm Marshall took eight wickets and Jonty Rhodes hit a career best 135 not out to take Natal to a fine win in Pietermaritzburg. Rice and Rhodes finished the match with an unbroken stand of 144.

In a high-scoring match at the Wanderers, Allan Lamb hit his second century in succession and shared a third-wicket stand of 180 with Gary Kirsten. Lamb's 134 came off 179 balls and included a six and 21 fours. In spite of Jimmy Cook's century, Western Province claimed first-innings points.

Eldine Baptiste's spectacular hitting and fast medium-pace bowling brought Eastern Province first-innings points against Orange Free State. The visitors came close to winning the game when they reduced the Free State to 54 for 7 in 39.2 overs in the second innings before rain ended the contest. Baptiste finished with match figures of 8 for 70 in 40 overs.

20, 21, 22 and **23** November 1992 *at Newlands, Cape Town*

Natal 102 (B.M. McMillan 5 for 35) and 294 (M.W. Pringle 5 for 92)

Western Province 219 (A.J. Lamb 87, P.W.E. Rawson 5 for 43) and 178 for 5 (G. Kirsten 66)

Western Province won by 5 wickets

Western Province 6 pts., Natal 0 pts.

at St George's Park, Port Elizabeth

Eastern Province 466 for 9 dec. (D.J. Callaghan 124, M.C. Venter 112)

Transvaal 202 (L. Seeff 72, E.A.E. Baptiste 5 for 47) and 292 for 4 (S.J. Cook 107, B.M. White 98)

Match drawn

Eastern Province 2 pts., Transvaal 0 pts.

at Centurion Park, Verwoerdburg

Border 317 (P.N. Kirsten 92, D.O. Nosworthy 68, P.C. Strydom 60) and 305 (S.J. Palframan 73 not out, P.J. Botha 65, B.M. Osborne 64)

Northern Transvaal 247 (V.F. du Preez 82) and 210 (V.F. du Preez 117, O.D. Gibson 4 for 59)

Border won by 165 runs

Border 6 pts., Northern Transvaal 0 pts.

Western Province moved to the top of the Castle Currie Cup table with a resounding victory over Natal who, put in to bat, were bowled out for 102 in 48.5 overs. Lamb led the home side to a comfortable first-innings lead, and it seemed as though Western Province would win easily, but the last two Natal second-innings wickets realised 104 runs.

Callaghan and Venter hit centuries as Eastern Province piled up a big score against Transvaal. The bowling of Baptiste and Bryson ensured that Transvaal would have to follow-on, but Cook and White began their second innings with a partnership of 208 and saved the game. White's 98 was the highest score of his career.

Veteran Peter Kirsten led Border to their first win of the season and left Northern Transvaal at the bottom of the table. Border led by 70 on the first innings, but they slipped to 194 for 7 in their second before wicket-keeper Palframan hit his maiden first-class fifty and helped cajole 111 from the last three wickets. Vernon du Preez hit the ninth century of his career, but only Haysman offered any sort of aid, and Border won comfortably.

19, 20, 21 and **22** December 1992 *at Wanderers, Johannesburg*

Transvaal 299 (S. Jacobs 83 not out, M. Yachad 61, O.D. Gibson 4 for 93) and 234 for 6 dec. (S.J. Cook 97 not out)

Border 160 (O.D. Gibson 83 not out, R.P. Snell 6 for 33) and 177 (M.P. Stonier 64, S.D. Jack 4 for 47, R.P. Snell 4 for 54)

Transvaal won by 196 runs

Transvaal 6 pts., Border 0 pts.

at Newlands, Cape Town

Western Province 278 (A.J. Lamb 121, G. Kirsten 65, R.E. Bryson 5 for 66) and 202 (E.O. Simons 57, R.E. Bryson 5 for 55)

Eastern Province 350 (M. Michau 86, L.J. Koen 54) and 134 for 2 (P.G. Amm 52 not out, M.W. Rushmere 50 not out)

Eastern Province won by 8 wickets

Eastern Province 6 pts., Western Province 0 pts.

at Centurion Park, Verwoerdburg

Northern Transvaal 388 (J.J. Strydom 105, M.D. Haysman 82, M.J.R. Rindel 79, N.W. Pretorius 4 for 102) and 100

Orange Free State 246 (O. Henry 75 not out, S. Elworthy 4 for 42) and 243 for 6 (P.J.R. Steyn 82 not out, L.J. Wilkinson 50, P.J. Newport 5 for 79)

Orange Free State won by 4 wickets

Orange Free State 6 pts., Northern Transvaal 2 pts.

Transvaal claimed their second win of the season as they built a reasonable score and then reduced Border to 48 for 7. At this point, West Indian Otis Gibson came to the wicket and hit 83 off 57 deliveries. His innings included 6 sixes and 8 fours, and he helped Border avoid the follow-on. He could not prevent the inevitable, however, and,

after Jimmy Cook had declared when three runs short of a century, Jack and Snell bowled Transvaal to victory.

Reigning champions Eastern Province moved to the top of the table with a fine win over Western Province. Allan Lamb hit his third century of the season, taking only 197 balls for his 121, but consistent batting gave Eastern Province a 72-run lead. Bryson then took five wickets for the second time in the match to earn match figures of 10 for 121, and the visitors strolled to victory.

Orange Free State overcame a first-innings deficit of 142 to beat Northern Transvaal whose two points were their first of the season. A second-wicket stand of 140 between Strydom and skipper Haysman put the home side in a strong position, which became stronger still when Free State were struggling at 151 for 8. Omar Henry hit 75 and shared a ninth-wicket stand of 95 with wicket-keeper Radley, and then Free State's varied attack bowled out Northern Transvaal for 100. Needing 243 to win in 61 overs, Free State were inspired by the batting of Phil Steyn and Louis Wilkinson, winning with five balls to spare.

1, 2, 3 and **4** January 1993 *at Springbok Park, Bloemfontein*

Orange Free State 262 (C.F. Craven 71, C.J.P.G. van Zyl 67, C.E. Eksteen 4 for 78) and 374 (F.D. Stephenson 108, L.J. Wilkinson 94, C.E. Eksteen 5 for 134, S.D. Jack 4 for 87)

Transvaal 517 for 4 dec. (M. Yachad 200, S.J. Cook 128 not out, L. Seeff 71, R.F. Pienaar 57) and 120 for 3

Transvaal won by 7 wickets

Transvaal 6 pts., Orange Free State 0 pts.

at Kingsmead, Durban

Northern Transvaal 209 (M.J.R. Rindel 106) and 337 for 8 dec. (V.F. du Preez 161, M.J.R. Rindel 111)

Natal 137 (P.S. de Villiers 6 for 62) and 285 (M.B. Logan 100, P.W.E. Rawson 60)

Northern Transvaal won by 124 runs

Northern Transvaal 6 pts., Natal 0 pts.

at Buffalo Park, East London

Western Province 171 (A.P. Kuiper 55) and 328 (E.O. Simons 93, O.D. Gibson 7 for 104)

Border 245 (D.B. Rundle 5 for 70) and 257 for 9 (G.C. Victor 62, D.B. Rundle 6 for 74)

Border won by 1 wicket

Border 6 pts., Western Province 0 pts.

Rudi Bryson took 10 wickets in the match to set up Eastern Province's win over Western Province, 19–22 December 1992. (David Munden/Sports-Line)

The first double century of his career for Mandy Yachad as Transvaal beat Orange Free State at the start of 1993. (David Munden/Sports-Line)

Orange Free State's cup hopes suffered a blow when they were humbled by Transvaal. The home side recovered well after being 90 for 5 in their first innings, but Transvaal took a commanding lead due to the efforts of Mandy Yachad, who hit the first double century of his career, and Jimmy Cook, who batted at number five. The pair added 222 for the fourth wicket. Yachad hit 22 fours and Cook 17. Wilkinson and Stephenson replied bravely for Orange Free State. They added 173 for the fourth wicket when the home side batted a second time, with Franklyn Stephenson again in violent mood, hitting 18 fours in his 105-ball innings. It proved to be of no avail, however, and Transvaal kept their title hopes alive with their third win of the season.

Northern Transvaal's first win owed a great debt to left-hander Michael Rindel who hit a century in each innings. Opener Vernon du Preez also batted splendidly in the second innings after Fanie de Villiers, who had match figures of 9 for 145, had bowled Northern Transvaal into a strong position. Logan and Rawson, batting at number eight, were the only batsmen to delay Northern's march to victory.

Border finished their season on a thrilling note. They bowled out Western Province for 171 and took a first-innings lead of 74. In spite of Gibson's pace bowling – he had match figures of 10 for 151 – Western Province's late order offered stern resistance in the second innings. Simons and Rundle added 113 for the seventh wicket, and off-spinner David Rundle almost won the game single-handed. He followed his first-innings 5 for 70 with 6 for 74, and the ninth Border wicket fell when the home side were still 27 runs short of victory, but McCurdy joined skipper Ian Howell in a resolute stand which gave their side an exciting win.

9, 10, 11 and 12 January 1993 *at Springbok Park, Bloemfontein*

Orange Free State 266 (O. Henry 104 not out, M.W. Pringle 6 for 60) and 303 for 1 dec. (W.J. Cronje 161 not out, J.M. Arthur 71, P.J.R. Steyn 56 not out)

Western Province 165 and 290 (G. Kirsten 105, E.O. Simons 50, O. Henry 5 for 68)

Orange Free State won by 114 runs

Orange Free State 6 pts., Western Province 0 pts.

at Wanderers, Johannesburg

Natal 279 (N.E. Wright 65, E.L.R. Stewart 60, C.E. Eksteen 5 for 48) and 71 (C.E. Eksteen 4 for 16)

Transvaal 154 (D.J. Cullinan 76 not out, M.D. Marshall 6 for 45) and 147 (M. Yachad 53, P.L. Symcox 4 for 40)

Natal won by 49 runs

Natal 6 pts., Transvaal 0 pts.

at St George's Park, Port Elizabeth

Northern Transvaal 236 (S. Elworthy 52) and 92 for 3

Eastern Province 286 for 7 dec. (K.C. Wessels 80, P.G. Amm 50, S. Elworthy 4 for 60)

Match drawn

Eastern Province 2 pts., Northern Transvaal 0 pts.

Orange Free State won the Castle Currie Cup for the first time in their history when they beat Western Province by 114 runs at Springbok Park. Cronje won the toss and chose to bat, but he saw his side lose seven wickets for 113 runs. They were saved by Omar Henry, batting at number eight, who hit the fifth century of his career and saw the last three wickets add 153. Against a balanced attack, Western Province were always struggling and conceded a first-innings lead of 101. Cronje then opened with Arthur, and the pair put on 166. Steyn joined Cronje in an unbroken partnership of 137. The Free State captain made the highest score of his career and hit 15 fours as runs came at four an over. Survival was all that Western could hope for, and Gary Kirsten led the fight with the eighth century of his career. Western Province held out for almost 122 overs, but the left-arm spin of Man of the Match Omar Henry finally won the day and the cup.

Had Transvaal beaten Natal as they were expected to do, they would have taken the title, but they were beaten by 49 runs. Cook won the toss and asked Natal to bat, but Transvaal were frustrated by the visitors' lower order. On a wicket that was now giving considerable assistance to

Brilliant all-round cricket by Omar Henry as Orange Free State beat Western Province to win the Castle Currie Cup for the first time. (Patrick Eagar)

the bowlers, Transvaal slumped to 66 for 9 before Jack helped Cullinan in a last-wicket stand of 88. Cullinan batted for 258 minutes for his 76. The pace of Snell and Jack and the left-arm spin of Eksteen routed Natal and left Transvaal with a target of 197 to win the match and the cup. At 101 for 3, victory looked probable, but Rawson brought about a middle-order collapse, and Transvaal's hopes perished.

Eastern Province's expectations were blighted by the weather and, initially, by the batting of Elworthy, De Villiers and Van Noordwyk who lifted Northern Transvaal from 93 for 7 to 236 all out. Eastern Province took first-innings points, but rain prevented them from taking more.

CASTLE CURRIE CUP FINAL TABLE

	P	W	L	D	Pts.
Orange Free State (2)	6	3	1	2	20
Eastern Province (1)	6	2	1	3	18
Natal (7)	6	3	2	1	18
Transvaal (5)	6	3	1	2	18
Western Province (4)	6	2	3	1	14
Border (6)	6	2	4	–	12
Northern Transvaal (3)	6	1	4	1	8

(1992 positions in brackets)

UNITED CRICKET BOARD OF SOUTH AFRICA BOWL

13, 14 and **15** November 1992 *at Kimberley Country Club, Kimberley*

Griqualand West 201 (D. Jordaan 76, F.J.C. Cronje 50, A.P. Igglesden 5 for 38) and 78 (A.P. Igglesden 7 for 28)

Boland 228 (R.I. Dalrymple 73) and 52 for 0

Boland won by 10 wickets

Boland 6 pts., Griqualand West 0 pts.

at PAM Brink Stadium, Springs

Western Transvaal 272 (J.D. Nel 104, L.C.R. Jordaan 4 for 74) and 183 (A.J. van Deventer 64, L.D. Botha 5 for 22, P.D. de Vaal 4 for 49)

Eastern Transvaal 244 (T.A. Marsh 87, B. Randall 70, A. Cilliers 4 for 61) and 120 for 5

Match drawn

Western Transvaal 2 pts., Eastern Transvaal 0 pts.

Boland indicated early superiority in the Bowl competition by trouncing Griqualand West. Star of the match was Kent pace bowler Alan Igglesden whose second-innings figures of 7 for 28 were the best of his career.

26, 27 and **28** November 1992 *at Witrand Cricket Field, Potchefstroom*

Griqualand West 262 (F.J.C. Cronje 138, A. Cilliers 5 for 38) and 261 for 3 dec. (F.J.C. Cronje 121 not out, M.J. Cann 90)

Western Transvaal 177 (M.N. Angel 5 for 44) and 220 (M.J. Cann 4 for 61)

Griqualand West won by 126 runs

Griqualand West 6 pts., Western Transvaal 0 pts.

27, 28 and **29** November 1992 *at Brackenfell Sports Field, Brackenfell*

Eastern Transvaal 244 (C.R. Norris 71, A.G. Elgar 6 for 44) and 64 (A.P. Igglesden 6 for 11, H. Williams 4 for 21)

Boland 215 (C.P. Dettmer 67, L.D. Botha 6 for 70) and 97 for 1

Boland won by 9 wickets

Boland 6 pts., Eastern Transvaal 2 pts.

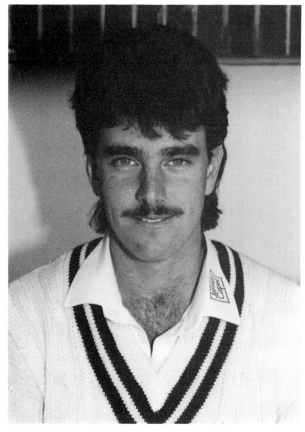

The dominant bowler of the UCBSA Bowl competition, Kent and Boland's Alan Igglesden. (Tom Morris)

After two rounds of matches the dominance of the two more experienced associations was obvious. Frans Cronje hit a century in each innings for the first time in his career and shared a third-wicket stand of 133 with skipper Michael Cann, the former Glamorgan player, who had the best bowling performance of his career with his occasional off-breaks. Another devastating bowling spell from Alan Igglesden brought Boland an easy win after they had surprisingly conceded first-innings points.

11, 12 and **13** December 1992 *at Brackenfell Sports Field, Brackenfell*

Western Transvaal 148 and 213 (H.G. Prinsloo 70, C.W. Henderson 4 for 62, A.P. Igglesden 4 for 67)

Boland 257 for 8 dec. (W.S. Truter 107, N.N. Snyman 54, A. Cilliers 4 for 88) and 105 for 2 (R.I. Dalrymple 59 not out)

Boland won by 8 wickets

Boland 6 pts., Western Transvaal 0 pts.

at PAM Brink Stadium, Springs

Eastern Transvaal 225 for 6 dec. (I.A. Hoffman 92) and 0 for 0 dec.

Griqualand West 0 for 0 dec. and 226 for 8 (M.J. Cann 76, L.D. Botha 4 for 50)

Griqualand West won by 2 wickets

Griqualand West 6 pts., Eastern Transvaal 2 pts.

Boland placed one hand on the trophy with their third win in as many matches. Wayne Truter hit the third century of his career, and there was further impressive bowling from the young left-arm medium-pace bowler Alex Cilliers of Western Transvaal. In an attempt to beat the rain and produce a result, the captains forfeited an innings each in the match at Springs.

7, 8 and **9** January 1993 *at Witrand Cricket Field, Potchefstroom*

Western Transvaal 167 and 193

Boland 310 for 8 dec. (W.S. Truter 134, J.S. Roos 56) and 53 for 0

Boland won by 10 wickets

Boland 6 pts., Western Transvaal 0 pts.

8, 9 and **10** January 1993 *at Kimberley Country Club, Kimberley*

Eastern Transvaal 260 (P.J. Grobler 61) and 210 for 7 dec. (I.A. Hoffman 125 not out, M.J. Cann 4 for 44)

Griqualand West 232 for 8 dec. (P. Kirsten 50, L.C.R. Jordaan 5 for 72) and 192 (D. Jordaan 112, P.D. de Vaal 6 for 41)

Eastern Transvaal won by 46 runs

Eastern Transvaal 6 pts., Griqualand West 0 pts.

A second century in successive matches from Truter saw Boland to their fourth victory in succession and confirmed them as winners of the Bowl, while at Kimberley Griqualand West suffered a surprise defeat at the hands of Eastern Transvaal. Ian Hoffman hit a maiden first-class hundred, and Deon Jordaan's century could not save the home side for whom Cann bettered his recently established best bowling figures.

29, 30 and **31** January 1993 *at Kimberley Country Club, Kimberley*

Griqualand West 320 for 7 dec. (F.J.C. Cronje 123, P. Kirsten 60 not out) and 156 for 6 dec.

Western Transvaal 188 (M.N. Angel 4 for 48) and 201

Griqualand West won by 87 runs

Griqualand West 6 pts., Western Transvaal 0 pts.

at PAM Brink Stadium, Springs

Eastern Transvaal 155 (H. Williams 4 for 32) and 194 (C.W. Henderson 7 for 82)

Boland 223 (R.I. Dalrymple 65, P.D. de Vaal 4 for 45) and 130 for 7 (L.C.R. Johnson 4 for 50)

Boland won by 3 wickets

Boland 6 pts., Eastern Transvaal 0 pts.

Frans Cronje's third century of the season set up Griqualand West's victory over Western Transvaal, and on a difficult pitch at Springs, Boland claimed their fifth victory. Twenty-year-old leg-spinner Claude Henderson returned a career best 7 for 82.

19, 20 and 21 February 1993 *at Witrand Cricket Field, Potchefstroom*

Western Transvaal 259 for 7 dec. (A.J. van Deventer 117 not out) and 279 for 7 (H.G. Prinsloo 87, A.J. van Deventer 68)

Eastern Transvaal 339 for 5 dec. (K.A. Moxham 117, H.M. Human 114, P.J. Grobler 53 not out)

Match drawn

Eastern Transvaal 2 pts., Western Transvaal 0 pts.

at Brackenfell CC, Brackenfell

Boland 295 (C.P. Dettmer 107) and 191 for 6 dec. (W.S. Truter 74)

Griqualand West 224 (M.N. Angel 52 not out) and 92 for 3

Match drawn

Boland 2 pts., Griqualand West 0 pts.

Andre van Deventer hit a maiden first-class century for Western Transvaal as did Henry Human in what was only his third first-class match for Eastern Transvaal. Human and Kevin Moxham put on 234 for Eastern Transvaal's first wicket, a record stand for any wicket for Eastern. Colin Dettmer of Boland was another to hit a maiden first-class hundred.

UCBSA BOWL FINAL TABLE

	P	W	L	D	Pts.
Boland (2)	6	5	–	1	32
Griqualand West (3)	6	3	2	1	18
Eastern Transvaal (1)	6	1	3	2	12
Western Transvaal (4)	6	–	4	2	2
(1992 positions in brackets)					

TOTAL INTERNATIONAL TROPHY TRIANGULAR TOURNAMENT

South Africa's insatiable appetite for one-day cricket gave birth to a triangular tournament between Pakistan, West Indies and the home country, with each side playing the other three times, and the competition condensed into 18 days. As Pakistan and West Indies were then to go to the Caribbean for five more one-day internationals and three Tests, one could be forgiven for believing that we are surfeiting the appetite, and it may sicken and so die.

The opening match in the Total Trophy produced some sensational cricket. Pakistan struggled for runs and, facing a target of 209, South Africa seemed set for victory at 159 for 1. Hudson and Wessels had put on 101 for the first wicket, and Hudson reached 93 off 124 balls before being bowled by Waqar Younis. This heralded a sensational collapse. Waqar took 5 for 10 in five overs, and South Africa lost nine wickets for 39 runs to suffer defeat by 10 runs.

South Africa gained compensation in the second match when they beat West Indies in a low-scoring match on a slow wicket. Kirsten and Rhodes shared an unbroken partnership of 85. West Indies did not help their cause by conceding six wides and 20 no-balls in a total of 150. The third match was marred by rain and, after a two-hour delay, West Indies easily reached their revised target of 106 in 27 overs. Shoaib Mohammad had been the only Pakistan batsman to show enterprise, hitting 49 off 67 balls.

Rain interrupted the fourth match of the competition, but Wasim Akram's fine bowling denied South Africa

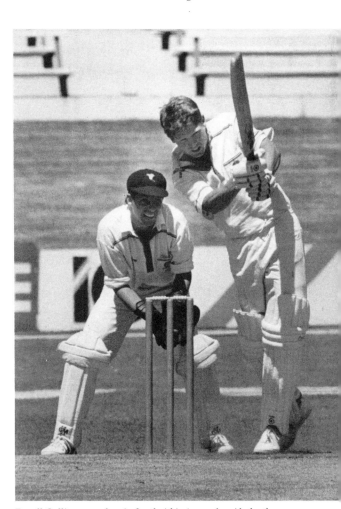

Daryll Cullinan – a place in South Africa's one-day side for the Triangular Tournament. (The Argus)

FIRST ONE-DAY INTERNATIONAL — SOUTH AFRICA *v.* PAKISTAN
9 February 1993 at Kingsmead, Durban

PAKISTAN			**SOUTH AFRICA**		
Saeed Anwar	b Donald	0	A.C. Hudson	b Waqar Younis	93
Ramiz Raja	c Richardson, b Matthews	29	K.C. Wessels (capt)	lbw, b Wasim Akram	42
Inzamam-ul-Haq	run out	47	P.N. Kirsten	b Asif Mujtaba	18
Javed Miandad	c Richardson, b McMillan	22	W.J. Cronje	b Waqar Younis	11
Salim Malik	c McMillan, b Cronje	14	D.J. Cullinan	b Waqar Younis	0
Asif Mujtaba	not out	49	J.N. Rhodes	run out	5
*Rashid Latif	c Richardson, b McMillan	15	B.M. McMillan	run out	2
Wasim Akram (capt)	not out	20	*D.J. Richardson	run out	11
Waqar Younis			C.R. Matthews	b Waqar Younis	3
Mushtaq Ahmed			P.S. de Villiers	b Waqar Younis	1
Aqib Javed			A.A. Donald	not out	1
Extras	lb 10, w 2	12	Extras	lb 7, w 1, nb 3	11
(50 overs)	(for 6 wickets)	208	(50 overs)		198

	O	M	R	W		O	M	R	W
Donald	10	2	32	1	Wasim Akram	10	1	36	1
De Villiers	10	–	41	–	Aqib Javed	10	1	38	–
Matthews	10	–	54	1	Mushtaq Ahmed	10	–	46	–
McMillan	10	1	35	2	Waqar Younis	10	–	25	5
Cronje	10	–	36	1	Asif Mujtaba	10	1	46	1

FALL OF WICKETS

1–0, 2–46, 3–93, 4–107, 5–132, 6–166

FALL OF WICKETS

1–101, 2–159, 3–165, 4–165, 5–180, 6–181, 7–182, 8–195, 9–197

Man of the Match: Waqar Younis   *Pakistan won by 10 runs*

SECOND ONE-DAY INTERNATIONAL — SOUTH AFRICA *v.* WEST INDIES
11 February 1993 at St George's Park, Port Elizabeth

WEST INDIES			**SOUTH AFRICA**		
D.L. Haynes	b De Villiers	43	K.C. Wessels (capt)	c Murray, b Patterson	8
B.C. Lara	lbw, b Pringle	13	A.C. Hudson	c Murray, b Patterson	10
P.V. Simmons	lbw, b Pringle	0	W.J. Cronje	c Simmons, b Walsh	1
R.B. Richardson (capt)	b McMillan	3	P.N. Kirsten	not out	45
C.L. Hooper	c Richardson, b Callaghan	17	D.J. Callaghan	c Hooper, b Bishop	10
A.L. Logie	c Richardson, b Donald	8	J.N. Rhodes	not out	46
*J.R. Murray	not out	30	B.M. McMillan		
I.R. Bishop	lbw, b De Villiers	7	*D.J. Richardson		
C.E.L. Ambrose	c Wessels, b McMillan	9	M.W. Pringle		
C.A. Walsh	c Cronje, b Donald	12	P.S. de Villiers		
B.P. Patterson	b Donald	1	A.A. Donald		
Extras	lb 4, nb 2	6	Extras	lb 4, w 6, nb 20	30
(49 overs)		149	(46.5 overs)	(for 4 wickets)	150

	O	M	R	W		O	M	R	W
Donald	10	1	27	3	Ambrose	10	3	17	–
De Villiers	9	2	21	2	Bishop	9	1	23	1
Pringle	10	1	25	2	Patterson	8.5	–	46	2
McMillan	10	–	32	2	Walsh	10	1	32	1
Cronje	7	–	23	–	Hooper	7	1	21	–
Callaghan	3	–	17	1	Simmons	2	–	7	–

FALL OF WICKETS

1–27, 2–27, 3–42, 4–77, 5–89, 6–91, 7–103, 8–125, 9–144

FALL OF WICKETS

1–29, 2–32, 3–33, 4–65

Man of the Match: J.N. Rhodes   *South Africa won by 6 wickets*

Fanie de Villiers – four wickets for South Africa in the fourth match of the Triangular Tournament. (Tom Morris)

victory after Wessels and Cronje had given them its scent with a stand of 72 in 12 overs. Rhodes, 35 off 34 balls, and Cronje added 69 in nine overs, but Wasim and Waqar proved irresistible in the final four overs. Javed Miandad's splendid 107 off 144 balls won the individual ward.

South Africa kept alive their hopes of reaching the final with a narrow victory over West Indies in another low-scoring game in Cape Town. Wessels and Hudson were out with only five scored, and only Daryll Cullinan, with 40 off 56 balls, came to terms with the sluggish pitch. A fifth-wicket stand of 41 between Logie and Hooper seemed to have set up a West Indian victory, but Meyrick Pringle denied the visitors at the close.

A second-wicket stand of 197 between Lara and Simmons demolished Pakistan in Durban. Lara struck 20 boundaries in a chanceless innings which saw him hit 128 off 126 balls. Pakistan were never in contention, but they completed a hat-trick of wins over South Africa two days later when Ramiz Raja, 53 off 79 balls, and Aamir Sohail, 62 off 92 balls, gave them a vigorous start with a stand of 121. They faltered in mid-innings, but late hitting from Wasim and Waqar lifted them to 220. The South African batting, looking distinctly long in the tail without the

THIRD ONE-DAY INTERNATIONAL — PAKISTAN *v.* WEST INDIES
13 February 1993 at Wanderers, Johannesburg

PAKISTAN

Ramiz Raja	c Logie, b Patterson	13
Shoaib Mohammad	c Lara, b Bishop	49
Inzamam-ul-Haq	c and b Simmons	23
Javed Miandad	c Hooper, b Ambrose	13
Salim Malik	lbw, b Walsh	1
Asif Mujtaba	c Richardson, b Ambrose	5
*Rashid Latif	b Patterson	9
Wasim Akram (capt)	c Logie, b Bishop	11
Waqar Younis	not out	3
Mushtaq Ahmed	lbw, b Bishop	5
Aqib Javed	c Hooper, b Bishop	0
Extras	lb 4, w 7, nb 7	18
(41.4 overs)		150

WEST INDIES

D.L. Haynes	not out	50
P.V. Simmons	lbw, b Waqar Younis	17
B.C. Lara	b Waqar Younis	0
C.L. Hooper	not out	22
R.B. Richardson (capt)		
*J.R. Murray		
I.R. Bishop		
A.L. Logie		
C.E.L. Ambrose		
C.A. Walsh		
B.P. Patterson		
Extras	lb 8, w 5, nb 7	20
(25.1 overs)	(for 2 wickets)	109

	O	M	R	W
Bishop	9.4	–	25	4
Patterson	8	1	33	2
Ambrose	8	–	31	2
Simmons	7	–	35	1
Walsh	9	2	22	1

	O	M	R	W
Wasim Akram	6	–	24	–
Aqib Javed	6	–	16	–
Waqar Younis	5	–	19	2
Mushtaq Ahmed	5	–	25	–
Salim Malik	1	–	8	–
Shoaib Mohammad	1.1	–	6	–
Asif Mujtaba	1	–	3	–

FALL OF WICKETS
1–21, **2**–72, **3**–100, **4**–103, **5**–111, **6**–127, **7**–135, **8**–143, **9**–150

FALL OF WICKETS
1–62, **2**–62

Umpires: C.J. Mitchley & S.B. Lambson   *Man of the Match:* D.L. Haynes   *West Indies won on faster scoring rate*

FOURTH ONE-DAY INTERNATIONAL — SOUTH AFRICA v. PAKISTAN
15 February 1993 at Buffalo Park, East London

PAKISTAN				SOUTH AFRICA		
Ramiz Raja	c Callaghan, b De Villiers	5		A.C. Hudson	b Wasim Akram	4
Shoaib Mohammad	b De Villiers	0		K.C. Wessels (capt)	run out	27
Salim Malik	c Callaghan, b Pringle	13		W.J. Cronje	run out	81
Javed Miandad	run out	107		P.N. Kirsten	c Shoaib Mohammad, b Salim Malik	1
Asif Mujtaba	c Wessels, b De Villiers	74		J.N. Rhodes	b Wasim Akram	35
Wasim Akram (capt)	c Stewart, b De Villiers	2		D.J. Callaghan	b Waqar Younis	0
Saeed Anwar	not out	1		*E.L.R. Stewart	c Rashid Latif, b Wasim Akram	1
*Rashid Latif				B.M. McMillan	lbw, b Wasim Akram	1
Mushtaq Ahmed				M.W. Pringle	run out	2
Waqar Younis				P.S. de Villiers	not out	0
Aqib Javed				A.A. Donald	b Wasim Akram	0
Extras	lb 4, w 6, nb 2	12		Extras	b 3, lb 6, nb 1	10
(50 overs)	(for 6 wickets)	214		(30.1 overs)		162

	O	M	R	W		O	M	R	W
Donald	10	2	38	–	Wasim Akram	6.1	–	16	5
De Villiers	10	2	27	4	Aqib Javed	6	–	29	–
Pringle	10	1	41	1	Mushtaq Ahmed	6	–	37	–
McMillan	10	–	62	–	Waqar Younis	6	–	30	1
Cronje	8	–	30	–	Shoaib Mohammad	1	–	11	–
Callaghan	2	–	12	–	Salim Malik	5	–	30	1

FALL OF WICKETS

1–0, 2–7, 3–29, 4–194, 5–206, 6–214

FALL OF WICKETS

1–8, 2–80, 3–82, 4–151, 5–154, 6–154, 7–155, 8–160, 9–162

Umpires: W. Diedricks & K.E. Liebenberg   *Man of the Match:* Javed Miandad   *Pakistan won by 9 runs on revised rate*

FIFTH ONE-DAY INTERNATIONAL — SOUTH AFRICA v. WEST INDIES
17 February 1993 at Newlands, Cape Town

SOUTH AFRICA				WEST INDIES		
A.C. Hudson	c Simmons, b Patterson	0		D.L. Haynes	run out	0
K.C. Wessels (capt)	b Patterson	1		P.V. Simmons	c Cronje, b Pringle	20
W.J. Cronje	c Murray, b Simmons	31		R.B. Richardson (capt)	c De Villiers, b Donald	2
P.N. Kirsten	c Logie, b Walsh	30		B.C. Lara	run out	14
D.J. Cullinan	c Haynes, b Simmons	40		C.L. Hooper	lbw, b Cronje	34
J.N. Rhodes	b Walsh	0		A.L. Logie	c Hudson, b Cronje	15
*E.L.R. Stewart	c and b Bishop	1		*J.R. Murray	run out	1
C.R. Matthews	c sub, b Hooper	9		I.R. Bishop	c Rhodes, b Pringle	6
M.W. Pringle	not out	8		C.E.L. Ambrose	not out	19
P.S. de Villiers	c and b Hooper	0		C.A. Walsh	c Stewart, b Cronje	10
A.A. Donald	not out	0		B.P. Patterson	lbw, b Pringle	1
Extras	lb 5, w 6, nb 9	20		Extras	lb 9, w 4, nb 1	14
(50 overs)	(for 9 wickets)	140		(47 overs)		136

	O	M	R	W		O	M	R	W
Patterson	9	–	20	2	Donald	10	2	20	1
Walsh	10	2	24	2	De Villiers	10	3	28	–
Ambrose	10	3	23	–	Pringle	9	–	27	3
Bishop	10	1	31	1	Matthews	10	1	25	–
Simmons	10	–	36	2	Cronje	8	–	27	3
Hooper	1	–	1	2					

FALL OF WICKETS

1–2, 2–5, 3–66, 4–99, 5–100, 6–110, 7–130, 8–139, 9–140

FALL OF WICKETS

1–15, 2–17, 3–30, 4–47, 5–88, 6–91, 7–99, 8–113, 9–134

Umpires: C.J. Mitchley & R.E. Koertzen   *Man of the Match:* W.J. Cronje   *South Africa won by 4 runs*

SIXTH ONE-DAY INTERNATIONAL — WEST INDIES v. PAKISTAN
19 February 1993 at Kingsmead, Durban

WEST INDIES

D.L. Haynes	lbw, b Wasim Akram	6
B.C. Lara	c Shoaib Mohammad, b Waqar Younis	128
P.V. Simmons	c Ramiz Raja, b Aamir Sohail	70
R.B. Richardson (capt)	c Rashid Latif, b Waqar Younis	7
C.L. Hooper	not out	20
A.L. Logie	c Rashid Latif, b Waqar Younis	5
J.C. Adams	not out	12
*J.R. Murray		
I.R. Bishop		
C.E.L. Ambrose		
C.A. Walsh		
Extras	lb 8, w 6, nb 6	20
(50 overs)	(for 5 wickets)	268

PAKISTAN

Aamir Sohail	c Hooper, b Bishop	14
Ramiz Raja	run out	34
Shoaib Mohammad	c Hooper, b Bishop	0
Javed Miandad	c and b Hooper	67
Zahid Fazal	c Haynes, b Ambrose	8
Asif Mujtaba	b Hooper	3
*Rashid Latif	c Hooper, b Bishop	0
Wasim Akram (capt)	c Ambrose, b Bishop	6
Waqar Younis	c Simmons, b Hooper	2
Ata-ur-Rehman	c Murray, b Walsh	0
Aqib Javed	not out	3
Extras	lb 3, nb 4	7
(46.5 overs)		144

	O	M	R	W
Wasim Akram	10	–	41	1
Aqib Javed	10	2	40	–
Ata-ur-Rehman	10	1	57	–
Waqar Younis	10	–	53	3
Aamir Sohail	4	–	27	1
Shoaib Mohammad	3	–	23	–
Asif Mujtaba	3	–	19	–

	O	M	R	W
Ambrose	8	2	18	1
Walsh	10	1	21	1
Simmons	9	–	43	–
Bishop	10	1	32	4
Hooper	9.5	1	27	3

FALL OF WICKETS

1–12, 2–209, 3–229, 4–230, 5–238

FALL OF WICKETS

1–20, 2–20, 3–95, 4–108, 5–113, 6–114, 7–125, 8–133, 9–133

Umpires: W. Diedricks & S.B. Lambson   *Man of the Match:* B.C. Lara   *West Indies won by 124 runs*

SEVENTH ONE-DAY INTERNATIONAL — SOUTH AFRICA v. PAKISTAN
21 February 1993 at Centurion Park, Verwoerdburg

PAKISTAN

Aamir Sohail	c Wessels, b Donald	62
Ramiz Raja	c Wessels, b De Villiers	53
Javed Miandad	c Richardson, b Pringle	16
Zahid Fazal	c Kirsten, b Pringle	16
Salim Malik	run out	9
Asif Mujtaba	c Wessels, b Pringle	8
*Rashid Latif	c Richardson, b Donald	3
Wasim Akram (capt)	run out	16
Waqar Younis	not out	20
Mushtaq Ahmed	not out	1
Ata-ur-Rehman		
Extras	lb 5, w 9, nb 2	16
(50 overs)	(for 8 wickets)	220

SOUTH AFRICA

A.C. Hudson	c Rashid Latif, b Aqib Javed	7
K.C. Wessels (capt)	run out	39
W.J. Cronje	c Waqar Younis, b Mushtaq Ahmed	17
P.N. Kirsten	st Rashid Latif, b Mushtaq Ahmed	35
D.J. Cullinan	run out	15
J.N. Rhodes	c Javed Miandad, b Wasim Akram	25
R.P. Snell	lbw, b Waqar Younis	19
*D.J. Richardson	run out	10
M.W. Pringle	b Waqar Younis	10
P.S. de Villiers	not out	5
A.A. Donald	not out	6
Extras	lb 2, w 2, nb 6	10
(50 overs)	(for 9 wickets)	198

	O	M	R	W
Donald	10	–	61	2
De Villiers	10	2	27	1
Pringle	10	–	52	3
Snell	10	–	31	–
Cronje	10	–	44	–

	O	M	R	W
Wasim Akram	10	–	34	1
Aqib Javed	10	–	31	1
Waqar Younis	10	–	50	2
Mushtaq Ahmed	10	–	29	2
Aamir Sohail	7	–	32	–
Asif Mujtaba	3	–	20	–

FALL OF WICKETS

1–121, 2–131, 3–147, 4–167, 5–169, 6–174, 7–192, 8–218

FALL OF WICKETS

1–18, 2–52, 3–84, 4–117, 5–130, 6–163, 7–167, 8–185, 9–188

Umpires: C.J. Mitchley & R.E. Koertzen   *Man of the Match:* Ramiz Raja   *Pakistan won by 22 runs*

EIGHTH ONE-DAY INTERNATIONAL — SOUTH AFRICA v. WEST INDIES
23 February 1993 at Springbok Park, Bloemfontein

SOUTH AFRICA

K.C. Wessels (capt)	b Simmons	49
A.C. Hudson	lbw, b Simmons	17
W.J. Cronje	b Bishop	5
P.N. Kirsten	b Ambrose	10
D.J. Cullinan	c Richardson, b Bishop	45
J.N. Rhodes	run out	22
*E.L.R. Stewart	not out	23
R.P. Snell	not out	0
M.W. Pringle		
P.S. de Villiers		
A.A. Donald		
Extras	b 4, lb 5, w 2, nb 3	14
(50 overs)	(for 6 wickets)	185

WEST INDIES

D.L. Haynes	c Stewart, b Snell	57
B.C. Lara	not out	111
P.V. Simmons	not out	6
R.B. Richardson (capt)		
C.L. Hooper		
A.L. Logie		
J.C. Adams		
*J.R. Murray		
I.R. Bishop		
C.E.L. Ambrose		
C.A. Walsh		
Extras	b 2, lb 9, w 2, nb 1	14
(44.3 overs)	(for 1 wicket)	188

	O	M	R	W
Ambrose	10	1	31	1
Walsh	10	2	26	–
Simmons	10	–	36	2
Bishop	10	–	52	2
Hooper	10	–	31	–

	O	M	R	W
Donald	10	1	24	–
De Villiers	10	–	38	–
Pringle	10	–	50	–
Snell	10	1	36	1
Cronje	4	–	25	–
Kirsten	0.3	–	4	–

FALL OF WICKETS

1–52, 2–60, 3–84, 4–92, 5–138, 6–183

FALL OF WICKET

1–152

Umpires: S.B. Lambson & K.E. Liebenberg *Man of the Match:* B.C. Lara *West Indies won by 9 wickets*

NINTH ONE-DAY INTERNATIONAL — PAKISTAN v. WEST INDIES
25 February 1993 at Newlands, Cape Town

PAKISTAN

Ramiz Raja	c Lara, b Patterson	0
Ghulam Ali	c Hooper, b Patterson	2
Saeed Anwar	c Murray, b Walsh	5
Zahid Fazal	c Lara, b Simmons	21
Salim Malik	c Haynes, b Walsh	1
Asif Mujtaba	c Lara, b Walsh	0
Wasim Akram (capt)	c Hooper, b Walsh	0
*Rashid Latif	c Logie, b Cummins	0
Waqar Younis	b Cummins	0
Mushtaq Ahmed	c Simmons, b Cummins	0
Aqib Javed	not out	4
Extras	b 1, lb 1, w 2, nb 6	10
(19.5 overs)		43

WEST INDIES

D.L. Haynes	lbw, b Waqar Younis	0
B.C. Lara	not out	26
P.V. Simmons	c Salim Malik, b Wasim Akram	2
C.L. Hooper	c Mushtaq Ahmed, b Wasim Akram	1
R.B. Richardson (capt)	not out	7
A.L. Logie		
J.C. Adams		
*J.R. Murray		
A.C. Cummins		
C.A. Walsh		
B.P. Patterson		
Extras	lb 7, nb 2	9
(12.3 overs)	(for 3 wickets)	45

	O	M	R	W
Patterson	6	–	14	2
Walsh	9	2	17	4
Cummins	4	–	10	3
Simmons	0.5	–	0	1

	O	M	R	W
Waqar Younis	5	1	7	1
Wasim Akram	6	–	22	2
Aqib Javed	1.3	–	9	–

FALL OF WICKETS

1–0, 2–10, 3–11, 4–14, 5–14, 6–14, 7–25, 8–25, 9–26

FALL OF WICKETS

1–0, 2–9, 3–11

Umpires: K.E. Liebenberg & W. Diedricks *Man of the Match:* C.A. Walsh *West Indies won by 7 wickets*

injured McMillan, never came to terms with the required run rate nor looked like approaching the target.

At Bloemfontein, West Indies reached the final and eliminated South Africa from the competition with a crushing nine-wicket victory. Restricted to 185 in their 50 overs, the home side could not contain Haynes and Lara who began West Indies' reply with a stand of 152. Lara played another devastating innings, hitting 111 off 140 balls with a six and 12 fours.

The final match in the qualifying competition had no significance as both West Indies and Pakistan had qualified for the final, but it did produce an element of farce. On a dreadful pitch of dangerously uncertain bounce, Pakistan were bowled out for 43, the lowest score in a one-day international. Put in to bat, Pakistan lost Ramiz Raja to the first ball of the innings, and there was no respite as they slipped to 26 for 9.

FINAL POSITIONS

	P	W	L	Pts.
West Indies	6	4	2	12
Pakistan	6	3	3	6
South Africa	6	2	4	4

FINAL

West Indies maintained their dominance over Pakistan by winning the Total International Trophy with 10.2 overs and five wickets to spare. Put in to bat, Pakistan fell apart after Aamir Sohail and Ramiz Raja had given them a sound start. They were rescued to some extent by the late hitting of Wasim Akram and Waqar Younis, but their 187 was never likely to trouble West Indies unduly. So it proved when Haynes and Lara put on 112 for West Indies' first wicket. Haynes became the first batsman to pass 8,000 runs in limited-over international cricket, and he received a standing ovation from the capacity crowd of 30,000.

Waqar Younis was measured as being the fastest bowler in the competition.

 BENSON AND HEDGES NIGHT SERIES

3 October 1992 *at Buffalo Park, East London*

Natal 183 for 9 (O.D. Gibson 4 for 35)
Border 164

Natal (2 pts.) won by 19 runs

TOTAL INTERNATIONAL TROPHY — FINAL — PAKISTAN *v.* WEST INDIES
27 February 1993 at Wanderers, Johannesburg

PAKISTAN

Aamir Sohail	c Hooper, b Ambrose	57
Ramiz Raja	b Simmons	11
Shoaib Mohammad	b Bishop	0
Javed Miandad	lbw, b Bishop	0
Zahid Fazal	c Murray, b Simmons	7
Asif Mujtaba	run out	25
Wasim Akram (capt)	run out	34
*Rashid Latif	run out	1
Waqar Younis	b Ambrose	37
Mushtaq Ahmed	not out	0
Aqib Javed	b Ambrose	0
Extras	lb 7, w 5, nb 3	15
		—
(50 overs)		187

WEST INDIES

D.L. Haynes	b Waqar Younis	59
B.C. Lara	b Aamir Sohail	49
P.V. Simmons	b Waqar Younis	5
C.L. Hooper	b Aqib Javed	12
R.B. Richardson (capt)	c Ramiz Raja, b Aamir Sohail	11
A.L. Logie	not out	41
J.C. Adams	not out	5
*J.R. Murray		
I.R. Bishop		
C.E.L. Ambrose		
C.A. Walsh		
Extras	lb 4, w 1, nb 3	8
		—
(39.4 overs)	(for 5 wickets)	190

	O	M	R	W
Ambrose	10	2	33	3
Walsh	10	3	28	–
Simmons	10	2	23	2
Bishop	10	–	46	2
Hooper	10	–	50	–

	O	M	R	W
Wasim Akram	8	–	32	–
Aqib Javed	7	–	32	1
Mushtaq Ahmed	5	–	27	–
Waqar Younis	9.4	1	63	2
Aamir Sohail	10	–	32	2

FALL OF WICKETS
1–46, 2–48, 3–55, 4–73, 5–87, 6–141, 7–142, 8–187, 9–187

FALL OF WICKETS
1–112, 2–114, 3–124, 4–142, 5–158

Umpires: S.B. Lambson & K.E. Liebenberg   *Man of the Match:* D.L. Haynes   *Man of the Series:* B.C. Lara   *West Indies won by 5 wickets*

8 October 1992 *at PAM Brink Stadium, Springs*

Western Province 173 for 3
Impalas 117 for 9 (C.R. Matthews 4 for 24)

Western Province (2 pts.) won by 56 runs

9 October 1992 *at Centurion Park, Verwoerdburg*

Eastern Province 131 for 2 (K.C. Wessels 67 not out)
Northern Transvaal 108 for 5

Northern Transvaal (2 pts.) won on faster scoring rate

14 October 1992 *at Centurion Park, Verwoerdburg*

Transvaal 225 for 7 (M. Yachad 81, S.J. Cook 74)
Northern Transvaal 160 for 8

Transvaal (2 pts.) won by 65 runs

16 October 1992 *at Springbok Park, Bloemfontein*

Orange Free State 198 for 7 (W.J. Cronje 59)
Northern Transvaal 183 (P.H. Barnard 65, M.J.R. Rindel 56,
   F.D. Stephenson 4 for 26)

Orange Free State (2 pts.) won by 15 runs

at Wanderers, Johannesburg

Transvaal 201 for 5 (D.J. Cullinan 63 not out, S.J. Cook 63)
Natal 203 for 5 (J.N. Rhodes 60 not out)

Natal (2 pts.) won by 5 wickets

20 October 1992 *at PAM Brink Stadium, Springs*

Eastern Province 192 for 5 (M.W. Rushmere 68)
Impalas 105 for 9 (T.A. Marsh 51 not out, R.E. Bryson
   4 for 27)

Eastern Province (2 pts.) won by 87 runs

21 October 1992 *at Kingsmead, Durban*

Western Province 186 for 5 (A.P. Kuiper 62 not out)
Natal 188 for 6

Natal (2 pts.) won by 4 wickets

At the break in the Benson and Hedges 45-over night
series, Impalas, the surprise team of the previous season,
shared the bottom of the table with Border. Eagerly led by
Jonty Rhodes, Natal won their first three matches to
suggest that they would be early qualifiers for the semi-
finals.

3 March 1993 *at St George's Park, Port Elizabeth*

Orange Free State 155 for 5
Eastern Province 156 for 4 (K.C. Wessels 82 not out)

Eastern Province (2 pts.) won by 6 wickets

at PAM Brink Stadium, Springs

Impalas 192 for 7 (B.C. Fourie 4 for 40)
Border 176 for 3 (M.P. Stonier 52)

Border (2 pts.) won on faster scoring rate

*Fearsome form from Malcolm Marshall for Natal in the Benson and
Hedges Night Series. (David Munden/Sports-Line)*

at Newlands, Cape Town

Northern Transvaal 187 for 8
Western Province 191 for 7 (E.O. Simons 59 not out)

Western Province (2 pts.) won by 3 wickets

5 March 1993 *at Springbok Park, Bloemfontein*

Orange Free State 265 for 6 (P.J.R. Steyn 117, J.M. Arthur
   50)
Impalas 125 for 6 (D. Jordaan 50)

Orange Free State (2 pts.) won by 140 runs

at Centurion Park, Verwoerdburg

Border 158
Northern Transvaal 162 for 4 (J.J. Strydom 55, K.J. Rule 50
   not out)

Northern Transvaal (2 pts.) won by 6 wickets

10 March 1993 *at Newlands, Cape Town*

Border 149
Western Province 151 for 5 (A.J. Lamb 51)

Western Province (2 pts.) won by 5 wickets

at PAM Brink Stadium, Springs

Impalas 140 for 7
Transvaal 141 for 1

Transvaal (2 pts.) won by 9 wickets

at Kingsmead, Durban

Northern Transvaal 178 for 9
Natal 181 for 8 (M.J.R. Rindel 4 for 28)

Natal (2 pts.) won by 2 wickets

12 March 1993 *at Kingsmead, Durban*

Natal 204 for 8 (M.B. Logan 55)
Impalas 49 for 6 (M.D. Marshall 4 for 15)

Natal (2 pts.) won on faster scoring rate

at Wanderers, Johannesburg

Transvaal 204 for 2 (D.J. Cullinan 78 not out, S.J. Cook 65)
Eastern Province 136 for 7

Transvaal (2 pts.) won by 68 runs

at Buffalo Park, East London

Border 145
Orange Free State 146 for 1 (P.J.R. Steyn 63 not out, W.J. Cronje 51 not out)

Orange Free State (2 pts.) won by 9 wickets

17 March 1993 *at Springbok Park, Bloemfontein*

Orange Free State 195 for 8 (F.D. Stephenson 68 not out)
Natal 196 for 9 (C.J.P.G. van Zyl 4 for 35)

Natal (2 pts.) won by 1 wicket

at St George's Park, Port Elizabeth

Eastern Province 226 for 4 (K.C. Wessels 98, P.G. Amm 74)
Border 186 for 5 (P.C. Strydom 52 not out)

Eastern Province (2 pts.) won on faster scoring rate

at Wanderers, Johannesburg

Transvaal 188 for 5 (S.J. Cook 53)
Western Province 184 for 6 (F.B. Touzel 66)

Transvaal (2 pts.) won by 4 runs

19 March 1993 *at Centurion Park, Verwoerdburg*

Impalas 148 for 6 (A.J. van Deventer 63)
Northern Transvaal 149 for 1 (P.H. Barnard 59 not out, M.J. Mitchley 50 not out)

Northern Transvaal (2 pts.) won by 9 wickets

at St George's Park, Port Elizabeth

Western Province 207 for 7 (A.J. Lamb 62)
Eastern Province 211 for 4 (D.J. Callaghan 82 not out)

Eastern Province (2 pts.) won by 6 wickets

24 March 1993 *at Buffalo Park, East London*

Transvaal 217 for 8
Border 191 for 7

Transvaal (2 pts.) won by 26 runs

at Newlands, Cape Town

Western Province 107 (F.D. Stephenson 4 for 10)
Orange Free State 87

Western Province (2 pts.) won by 20 runs

26 March 1993 *at Springbok Park, Bloemfontein*

Transvaal 224 for 4 (S.J. Cook 105 not out)
Orange Free State 227 for 2 (P.J.R. Steyn 114 not out, L.J. Wilkinson 56)

Orange Free State (2 pts.) won by 8 wickets

at Kingsmead, Durban

Eastern Province 133
Natal 104

Eastern Province (2 pts.) won by 29 runs

Semi-finalists in 1992, Impalas lost all seven matches in 1992–3 to finish bottom of the table. By winning their last match, against Transvaal, in such resounding fashion – they hit 227 for 2 in 41.5 overs – Orange Free State drew level on points with Western Province, but their inferior run rate during the competition kept them out of the semi-finals for the second year in succession. The wicket at Newlands came in for more criticism on the 24th of March when Orange Free State bowled out Western Province for 107 in 41.2 overs, and then were bowled out themselves for 87 in 42.1 overs. In the rain-affected match in Durban on the 12th, Impalas' target was reduced to 129 in 20 overs, but Malcolm Marshall took 4 for 15 in 7.5 overs to send them crashing to 49 for 6. Marshall, with 17 wickets, was to finish the leading wicket-taker in the competition. Baptiste and Jack had 15 apiece.

BENSON AND HEDGES NIGHT SERIES – QUALIFYING TABLE

	P	W	L	Pts.
Natal	7	6	1	12
Transvaal	7	5	2	10
Eastern Province	7	5	2	10
Western Province	7	4	3	8
Orange Free State	7	4	3	8
Northern Transvaal	7	3	4	6
Border	7	1	6	2
Impalas	7	–	7	0

SEMI-FINALS
FIRST LEG

30 March 1993 *at Newlands, Cape Town*

Natal 173 for 5
Western Province 135 (M.D. Marshall 4 for 15)

Natal won by 38 runs

31 March 1993 *at St George's Park, Port Elizabeth*

Eastern Province 165 (D.J. Callaghan 60)
Transvaal 167 for 2

Transvaal won by 8 wickets

SECOND LEG

2 April 1993 *at Kingsmead, Durban*

Western Province 164 for 9 (D.N. Crookes 4 for 37)
Natal 165 for 6

Natal won by 4 wickets

at Wanderers, Johannesburg

Transvaal 173 for 8
Eastern Province 176 for 2 (K.C. Wessels 56)

Eastern Province won by 8 wickets

THIRD LEG

3 April 1993 *at Wanderers, Johannesburg*

Transvaal 218 for 8 (M. Yachad 63)
Eastern Province 213 for 8 (K.C. Wessels 122 not out)

Transvaal won by 5 runs

Natal had suffered some close contests in the qualifying matches, but they won both legs of their semi-final with ease. The tie between Transvaal and Eastern Province had to go to a decider and, facing a target of 219, Eastern Province were well served by skipper Kepler Wessels who hit his highest score in the competition. He failed to find any support, however, with Rushmere, 39, and Callaghan, 13, being the only other batsmen to reach double figures, and Transvaal won by five runs.

FINAL

7 April 1993 *at Kingsmead, Durban*

Transvaal 193 for 7 (M. Yachad 86, S.J. Cook 50)
Natal 192 for 8 (A.C. Hudson 85, N.E. Wright 65)

Transvaal won by 1 run

Transvaal won the trophy by an even closer margin. They were given a fine start by Cook and Yachad, but their final total was disappointing. However, it proved too much for Natal who had been put in sight of victory by Hudson

and Wright after Logan had gone for 0. The only other batsman to reach double figures was Crookes who was unbeaten on 11 as he and Rawson failed by two runs to bring Natal victory.

 LATE-SEASON FRIENDLY MATCHES

2, 3 and 4 February 1993 *at Centurion Park, Verwoerdburg*

South Africa Under-24 XI 219 (M. Muralitharan 4 for 60) and 158 (M. Muralitharan 6 for 62)
Sri Lanka Under-24 XI 228 (D.K. Liyanage 56, S. Ranatunga 51 not out) and 113

South Africa Under-24 XI won by 36 runs

26, 27 and 28 March 1993 *at Newlands, Cape Town*

Western Province 258 for 5 dec. (T.N. Lazard 63 not out) and 131 for 6 dec. (J.D. Batty 4 for 54)
Yorkshire 110 (M.W. Pringle 5 for 31) and 172 for 5 (M.D. Moxon 97)

Match drawn

2, 3 and 4 April 1993 *at Brackenfell Sports Field, Brackenfell*

Boland 226 (N.M. Snyman 86, Asif Din 5 for 61) and 163 for 5 (B.H. Richards 50 not out, W.N. van As 50)
Warwickshire 393 for 6 dec. (T.L. Penney 117 not out, R.G. Twose 60, A.J. Moles 59, D.P. Ostler 56)

Match drawn

Sri Lanka's under-24 side, including five players with Test experience, made a short tour of South Africa and engaged in one first-class match. Several English club sides made tours of the Republic, and Yorkshire and Warwickshire both played pre-English season matches as part of their preparations for the 1993 campaign. The Zimbabwe cricketer Trevor Penney hit the fourth century of his first-class career.

At the end of the season, the party to tour Sri Lanka in August and September was chosen: K.C. Wessels (capt); W.J. Cronje (vice-capt); S.J. Cook; A.C. Hudson; J.N. Rhodes; D.J. Richardson; S.J. Palframan; P.L. Symcox; D.J. Cullinan; C.E. Eksteen; R.P. Snell; A.A. Donald; P.S. de Villiers; B.N. Schultz; B.M. McMillan (or D.J. Callaghan).

FIRST-CLASS AVERAGES

BATTING

	M	Inns	NO	Runs	HS	Av	100s	50s
A.J. Lamb	5	10	1	636	206*	70.66	3	1
S.J. Cook	9	16	3	864	228	66.46	4	1
H.M. Human	2	3	–	174	114	58.00	1	–
K.C. Wessels	10	17	2	832	118	55.46	2	6
W.J. Cronje	9	17	3	744	161*	53.14	2	4
P.G. Amm	5	8	2	311	114*	51.83	1	2
M. Yachad	7	13	1	618	200	51.50	1	4
M.W. Rushmere	7	12	2	511	110	51.10	1	4
J.N. Rhodes	10	17	2	761	135*	50.73	1	5
K.J. Bridgens	7	10	5	244	41	48.80	–	–
E.O. Simons	6	10	2	380	93	47.50	–	5
A.J. van Deventer	6	12	1	502	117*	45.63	1	2
D.J. Callaghan	5	6	–	267	124	44.50	1	1
I.A. Hoffman	6	10	1	394	125*	43.77	1	1
A.C. Hudson	8	16	2	609	159*	43.50	2	4
B.T. Player	6	8	3	213	100*	42.60	1	–
F.J.C. Cronje	9	16	1	635	138	42.33	3	3
M.J.R. Rindel	7	14	1	549	111	42.23	2	2
O. Henry	9	11	2	376	104*	41.77	1	2
D.J. Cullinan	7	13	3	416	76*	41.60	–	3
W.S. Truter	8	14	2	494	134	41.16	2	1
P.D. de Vaal	7	11	6	195	37*	39.00	–	–
G. Kirsten	8	15	1	545	109	38.92	2	2
H.G. Prinsloo	5	10	–	381	87	38.10	–	2
L. Seeff	7	12	2	379	87	37.90	–	3
F.D. Stephenson	6	10	–	377	141	37.70	2	–
V.F. du Preez	7	14	1	486	161*	37.38	2	2
S. Jacobs	6	8	4	148	83*	37.00	–	1
D. Jordaan	9	16	–	581	123	36.31	2	1
M.J. Cann	9	16	1	530	94	35.33	–	4
B.M. McMillan	8	14	3	373	98	33.90	–	2
E.A.E. Baptiste	7	9	1	261	86	32.62	–	2
P.N. Kirsten	9	17	1	516	158	32.25	1	2
O.D. Gibson	6	12	2	320	83*	32.00	–	2
C.P. Dettmer	7	14	3	352	107	32.00	1	1
L.J. Wilkinson	7	12	–	378	115	31.50	1	2
M.P. Stonier	2	4	–	123	64	30.75	–	1
M.D. Haysman	7	14	1	391	82	30.07	–	2
P. Kirsten	7	10	1	267	73	29.66	–	3
R.F. Pienaar	6	10	3	207	57	29.57	–	1
K.A. Moxham	5	8	–	236	117	29.50	1	–
L.P. Vorster	3	6	1	147	129*	29.40	1	–
P.C. Strydom	6	12	–	350	60	29.16	–	1
P.J.R. Steyn	7	13	2	319	82*	29.00	–	2
P.J.L. Radley	4	5	1	116	29	29.00	–	–
P.J. Grobler	5	8	1	203	61	29.00	–	2
N.E. Wright	7	12	–	344	88	28.66	–	4
J.S. Roos	7	11	1	286	56	28.60	–	1
L.J. Koen	7	11	2	256	54	28.44	–	2
R.I. Dalrymple	7	11	1	284	73	28.40	–	3
B.H. Richards	3	5	1	113	50*	28.25	–	1
P.L. Symcox	4	7	1	169	50	28.16	–	1
C.R. Norris	6	9	–	251	71	27.88	–	1
B.M. White	5	9	–	246	98	27.33	–	1
W.N. van As	5	9	–	243	109	27.00	1	1
B.M. Osborne	5	10	–	268	92	26.80	–	2
S.J. Palframan	6	12	4	211	73*	26.37	–	1
A.P. Kuiper	6	10	–	263	79	26.30	–	2
I.L. Howell	6	12	3	235	67	26.11	–	1
F. Davids	4	6	–	152	38	25.33	–	–
R.E. Bryson	6	7	1	152	57	25.33	–	1
M.B. Logan	7	13	1	303	100	25.25	1	–
C.F. Craven	3	4	–	101	71	25.25	–	1
G.C. Victor	5	10	–	251	62	25.10	–	2
N.M. Snyman	6	12	1	271	86	24.63	–	2
J.M. Arthur	7	13	–	318	81	24.46	–	3
A. Cilliers	6	12	4	195	42*	24.37	–	–
S. Elworthy	6	11	4	166	52	23.71	–	1
B.A.S. Chedburn	5	6	1	118	34	23.60	–	–
D.B. Rundle	8	14	5	210	47	23.33	–	–
C.J.P.G. van Zyl	8	12	–	279	81	23.25	–	2
T.N. Lazard	8	16	2	320	63*	22.85	–	3
T.G. Shaw	7	9	3	136	55	22.66	–	1
P.H. Barnard	8	15	–	339	56	22.60	–	1
D.J. Richardson	9	13	2	243	77	22.09	–	2
C.E.B. Rice	6	11	1	217	59*	21.70	–	1
D.O. Nosworthy	4	8	–	173	68	21.62	–	1
J.J. Strydom	3	6	–	128	105	21.33	1	–
M.W. Pringle	8	8	2	127	43	21.16	–	–
J.D. Nel	4	8	–	169	104	21.12	1	–
R.E. Veenstra	5	7	–	147	49	21.00	–	–
F.C. Brooker	7	11	1	203	45	20.30	–	–
D.P. le Roux	4	8	1	142	47*	20.28	–	–
P.W.E. Rawson	7	11	–	220	60	20.00	–	1
H.M. de Vos	7	14	–	280	43	20.00	–	–
C.R. Matthews	9	9	1	156	31	19.50	–	–
R.J. Ryall	8	10	3	134	45*	19.14	–	–
E.L.R. Stewart	9	16	–	304	60	19.00	–	1
D.R. Laing	6	9	1	149	33	18.62	–	–
W.E. Schonegevel	6	11	1	183	39	18.30	–	–
M.N. Angel	8	11	5	106	52*	17.66	–	1
T.A. Marsh	6	9	2	120	87	17.14	–	1
J.E. Johnson	6	8	1	120	37	17.14	–	–
M.J. Mitchley	3	6	–	102	47	17.00	–	–
M.C. Venter	7	12	–	200	112	16.66	1	–
G.F.J. Liebenberg	6	10	2	130	44	16.25	–	–
J.F. Venter	4	7	–	112	33	16.00	–	–
M. Erasmus	5	8	1	112	38	16.00	–	–
B. Randall	7	12	–	186	70	15.50	–	1
H.M. Smith	4	8	–	112	34	14.00	–	–
A.G. Lawson	6	12	–	165	57	13.75	–	1
P.J. Botha	7	14	–	192	65	13.71	–	1
J.P.B. Mulder	5	10	1	120	41	13.33	–	–
C.P.J. Pienaar	5	10	–	123	48	12.30	–	–
R.V. Jennings	7	14	1	131	47	10.07	–	–

(Qualification – 100 runs, average 10.00)

BOWLING

	Overs	Mds	Runs	Wkts	Av	Best	10/m	5/inn
A.P. Igglesden	209.2	50	460	39	11.79	7-28	1	3
A.G. Elgar	68.2	20	159	13	12.23	4-48	–	2
H. Williams	257.4	64	515	32	16.09	5-33	–	1
M.D. Marshall	202.4	47	451	28	16.10	6-45	–	1
E.A.E. Baptiste	293.1	92	534	33	16.18	5-47	–	3
M.W. Pringle	256.1	66	534	30	17.80	6-60	–	3
P.W.E. Rawson	217.3	70	498	27	18.44	5-43	–	1
S.D. Jack	260.2	62	770	41	18.78	5-36	1	3
L.D. Botha	148.1	32	459	24	19.12	6-70	–	2
L.C.R. Jordaan	156.3	45	386	20	19.30	5-72	–	1
P.D. de Vaal	187.1	52	465	24	19.37	6-41	–	1
R.E. Bryson	193.2	34	582	29	20.06	5-55	1	2
B.C. Fourie	142.3	37	325	16	20.31	3-25	–	–
R.P. Snell	254.5	61	657	31	21.19	6-53	1	1
C.R. Matthews	262.4	79	555	26	21.34	6-50	–	1
C.W. Henderson	275.4	82	666	31	21.48	7-82	–	1
C.E. Eksteen	334.4	118	774	36	21.50	5-48	–	3
T.J. Packer	64	10	218	10	21.80	4-58	–	–
P.S. de Villiers	225.3	47	665	30	22.16	6-62	–	2
C.J.P.G. van Zyl	276.5	98	515	23	22.39	3-28	–	–
C.E.B. Rice	142.3	45	315	14	22.50	6-35	–	1
M.N. Angel	283.3	78	713	31	23.00	5-44	–	1
P.L. Symcox	105	32	232	10	23.20	3-24	–	–
A.J. Swanepoel	175.4	38	478	20	23.90	3-24	–	–
O.D. Gibson	257.5	39	796	33	24.12	7-104	1	1
B.T. Player	172.5	45	394	16	24.62	3-35	–	–
B.N. Schultz	297.4	70	760	30	25.33	5-35	–	1
A.A. Donald	307.1	89	696	26	26.76	7-84	1	2
B.M. McMillan	246	72	588	21	28.00	5-35	–	1
J.E. Johnson	124.1	33	340	12	28.33	3-60	–	–

FIRST-CLASS AVERAGES

BOWLING *continued*

	Overs	Mds	Runs	Wkts	Av	Best	10/m	5/inn
O. Henry	355.5	95	865	30	28.83	6-72	–	2
A. Cilliers	201.4	40	583	20	29.15	5-38	–	1
M.J. Cann	240.1	71	558	19	29.36	4-44	–	–
R.A. Lyle	197.4	35	650	22	29.54	3-36	–	–
P.J. Newport	108	16	365	12	30.41	5-79	–	1
A. Martyn	141.2	27	396	13	30.46	3-22	–	–
D. MacHelm	168	40	413	13	31.76	3-58	–	–
S. Elworthy	180.3	34	550	17	32.35	4-42	–	–
F.D. Stephenson	239.4	60	574	17	33.76	3-24	–	–
R.J. McCurdy	207.4	53	513	15	34.20	5-54	–	1
D.B. Rundle	319.5	80	746	21	35.52	6-74	1	2
N.W. Pretorius	114	18	357	10	35.70	4-102	–	–

	Overs	Mds	Runs	Wkts	Av	Best	10/m	5/inn
T.G. Shaw	289.2	118	537	15	35.80	5-49	–	1
T. Bosch	123.3	13	464	10	46.40	2-40	–	–

(Qualification – 10 wickets)

LEADING FIELDERS

35 — E.L.R. Stewart (ct 34/st 1); 34 – D.J. Richardson (ct 33/st 1); 28 – R.J. Ryall (ct 24/st 4) and K.J. Bridgens (ct 26/st 2); 26 – S.J. Palframan (ct 24/st 2); 24 – B. Randall (ct 19/st 5); 23 – R.V. Jennings (ct 20/st 3); 19 – P.J.L. Radley (ct 18/st 1); 13 – B.M. McMillan, D.B. Rundle and J.A. Teegar (ct 11/st 2); 11 – B. McBride (ct 10/st 1) and K.C. Wessels; 10 – R.A. Brown, D.J. Callaghan and D. Jordaan

SECTION G
Sharjah
The Sharjah Trophy: Pakistan, Sri Lanka and Zimbabwe

The stadium at Sharjah. (David Munden/Sports-Line)

Sharjah offers glittering cash prizes but, with the increase in international cricket throughout the world, the Gulf region is finding it difficult to arrange tournaments and attract national sides. The Wills International Trophy was hastily scheduled for the beginning of February and, as with the last tournament in Sharjah 16 months earlier, it was restricted to three teams. India, of course, have declined to play in future tournaments in Sharjah after their accusation that the rules were made exclusively to suit Pakistan.

Pakistan started the Trophy as overwhelming favourites, and it proved to be that neither Sri Lanka nor Zimbabwe – competing in Sharjah for the first time – could offer serious resistance. In the opening match, Pakistan, led for the first time by Wasim Akram who had deposed Javed Miandad and who had Waqar Younis as his lieutenant, introduced a virtually unknown spinner, Arshad Khan, to international cricket. The favourites were in some trouble at 88 for 4, having been put in to bat, but Inzamam-ul-Haq played a hard-hitting innings, and there was some sparkling batting from Wasim and Waqar. The Flower brothers began Zimbabwe's challenge with a stand of 121 in 32 overs, but thereafter the batting fell apart.

In the second match, Sri Lanka were put in to bat. Hathurusinghe and Gurusinha provided them with an excellent base, adding 96 for the second wicket, but

A match-winning innings for Pakistan from Inzamam-ul-Haq in the opening game of the tournament. (Alan Cozzi)

WILLS INTERNATIONAL TROPHY – MATCH ONE – PAKISTAN v. ZIMBABWE
1 February 1993 at Sharjah Cricket Association Stadium

PAKISTAN			ZIMBABWE		
Saeed Anwar	c and b Omarshah	26	*A. Flower	run out	49
Ramiz Raja	c A. Flower, b Brandes	5	G.W. Flower	c Waqar Younis, b Mushtaq Ahmed	57
Inzamam-ul-Haq	c Ranchod, b Brandes	90	K.J. Arnott	c Rashid Latif, b Salim Malik	7
Javed Miandad	c A. Flower, b Omarshah	14	D.L. Houghton (capt)	b Waqar Younis	36
Salim Malik	c A. Flower, b Omarshah	0	M.H. Dekker	run out	7
*Rashid Latif	c Dekker, b Brain	39	G.A. Briant	not out	14
Wasim Akram (capt)	c Omarshah, b Brain	38	A.H. Omarshah	b Waqar Younis	0
Waqar Younis	c G.W. Flower, b Brain	26	S.G. Peall	not out	12
Mushtaq Ahmed	not out	4	E.A. Brandes		
Arshad Khan	not out	0	D. H. Brain		
Aqib Javed			U. Ranchod		
Extras	b 4, lb 6, w 10	20	Extras	lb 16, w 13, nb 2	31
(50 overs)	(for 8 wickets)	262	(50 overs)	(for 6 wickets)	213

	O	M	R	W		O	M	R	W
Brandes	10	–	66	2	Wasim Akram	10	–	34	–
Brain	10	–	51	3	Aqib Javed	7	1	11	–
Ranchod	10	1	40	–	Arshad Khan	6	–	43	–
Peall	10	–	62	–	Waqar Younis	10	3	26	2
Omarshah	10	2	33	3	Mushtaq Ahmed	10	–	42	1
					Salim Malik	7	–	41	1

FALL OF WICKETS

1–18, 2–47, 3–88, 4–88, 5–163, 6–199, 7–252, 8–258

FALL OF WICKETS

1–121, 2–127, 3–138, 4–178, 5–188, 6–189

Man of the Match: Inzamam-ul-Haq

Pakistan won by 49 runs

WILLS INTERNATIONAL TROPHY – MATCH TWO – PAKISTAN *v.* SRI LANKA
2 February 1993 at Sharjah Cricket Association Stadium

SRI LANKA

R.S. Mahanama	lbw, b Wasim Akram	1
U.C. Hathurusinghe	c Saeed Anwar, b Salim Malik	36
A.P. Gurusinha	c sub (Zahid Fazal), b Wasim Akram	90
P.A. de Silva	c Asif Mujtaba, b Waqar Younis	7
A. Ranatunga (capt)	c Rashid Latif, b Aqib Javed	· 8
H.P. Tillekeratne	lbw, b Aqib Javed	2
R.S. Kalpage	c Asif Mujtaba, b Wasim Akram	6
*A.G.D. Wickremasinghe	b Wasim Akram	2
C.P.H. Ramanayake	b Waqar Younis	15
G.P. Wickremasinghe	not out	1
S.D. Anurasiri		
Extras	lb 7, w 3, nb 2	12
(46 overs)	(for 9 wickets)	180

PAKISTAN

Saeed Anwar	c Tillekeratne, b de Silva	55
Ramiz Raja	c Gurusinha, b de Silva	73
Inzamam-ul-Haq	not out	27
Asif Mujtaba	not out	15
Javed Miandad		
Salim Malik		
*Rashid Latif		
Wasim Akram (capt)		
Mushtaq Ahmed		
Waqar Younis		
Aqib Javed		
Extras	b 2, lb 1, w 7, nb 1	11
(40.2 overs)	(for 2 wickets)	181

	O	M	R	W
Wasim Akram	10	1	24	4
Aqib Javed	10	1	31	2
Waqar Younis	10	–	37	2
Mushtaq Ahmed	10	1	41	–
Asif Mujtaba	2	–	16	–
Salim Malik	4	–	24	1

	O	M	R	W
Ramanayake	8.2	1	19	–
G.P. Wickremasinghe	7	–	30	–
Kalpage	7	–	29	–
Hathurusinghe	3	–	19	–
Anurasiri	7	–	39	–
de Silva	5	–	24	2
Ranatunga	3	–	18	–

FALL OF WICKETS

1–2, 2–98, 3–119, 4–141, 5–147, 6–160, 7–160, 8–164, 9–180

FALL OF WICKETS

1–132, 2–137

Man of the Match: Wasim Akram

Pakistan won by 8 wickets

WILLS INTERNATIONAL TROPHY – MATCH THREE – SRI LANKA *v.* ZIMBABWE
3 February 1993 at Sharjah Cricket Association Stadium

SRI LANKA

R.S. Mahanama	c Arnott, b Crocker	62
U.C. Hathurusinghe	lbw, b Brandes	66
P.A. de Silva	b Brain	46
A.P. Gurusinha	run out	20
A. Ranatunga (capt)	c Campbell, b Brandes	39
*H.P. Tillekeratne	not out	13
R.S. Kalpage	not out	8
N. Ranatunga		
C.P.H. Ramanayake		
G.P. Wickremasinghe		
S.D. Anurasiri		
Extras	lb 3, w 8, nb 1	12
(43 overs)	(for 5 wickets)	266

ZIMBABWE

*A. Flower	b Gurusinha	26
G.W. Flower	c Tillekeratne, b Ramanayake	0
K.J. Arnott	c Kalpage, b Ramanayake	7
D.L. Houghton (capt)	run out	31
G.A. Briant	run out	3
E.A. Brandes	c A. Ranatunga, b Ramanayake	55
A.D.R. Campbell	c Mahanama, b N. Ranatunga	8
A.H. Omarshah	b Wickremasinghe	25
G.J. Crocker	not out	36
D.H. Brain	b Wickremasinghe	12
U. Ranchod	not out	3
Extras	lb 18, w 11, nb 1	30
(43 overs)	(for 9 wickets)	236

	O	M	R	W
Brandes	9	1	57	2
Brain	7	–	41	1
Ranchod	9	1	46	–
Omarshah	6	–	37	–
G.W. Flower	7	–	45	–
Crocker	5	–	37	1

	O	M	R	W
Ramanayake	9	–	28	3
G.P. Wickremasinghe	9	–	50	2
de Silva	3	–	26	–
Gurusinha	8	1	34	1
Anurasiri	2	–	24	–
N. Ranatunga	9	–	33	1
A. Ranatunga	3	–	23	–

FALL OF WICKETS

1–112, 2–154, 3–165, 4–243, 5–246

FALL OF WICKETS

1–2, 2–20, 3–54, 4–65, 5–85, 6–85, 7–154, 8–194, 9–219

Man of the Match: E.A. Brandes

Sri Lanka won by 30 runs

WILLS INTERNATIONAL TROPHY – FINAL – PAKISTAN *v.* SRI LANKA
4 February 1993 at Sharjah Cricket Association Stadium

PAKISTAN

Saeed Anwar	c Ramanayake, b Gurusinha	110
Ramiz Raja	not out	109
Inzamam-ul-Haq	c Wickremasinghe, b Ramanayake	20
Wasim Akram (capt)	b Gurusinha	22
Javed Miandad	not out	12
Salim Malik		
Asif Mujtaba		
*Rashid Latif		
Waqar Younis		
Mushtaq Ahmed		
Aqib Javed		
Extras	lb 6, w 2	8
(41 overs)	(for 3 wickets)	281

SRI LANKA

R.S. Mahanama	lbw, b Wasim Akram	0
U.C. Hathurusinghe	c Mushtaq Ahmed, b Aqib Javed	42
P.A. de Silva	lbw, b Aqib Javed	9
A.P. Gurusinha	run out	36
A. Ranatunga (capt)	lbw, b Wasim Akram	25
*H.P. Tillekeratne	lbw, b Wasim Akram	11
R.S. Kalpage	not out	19
N. Ranatunga	lbw, b Wasim Akram	0
C.P.H. Ramanayake	not out	1
G.P. Wickremasinghe		
K.P.J. Warnaweera		
Extras	b 4, lb 6, w 11, nb 3	24
(41 overs)	(for 7 wickets)	167

	O	M	R	W
Ramanayake	10	1	62	1
G.P. Wickremasinghe	5	–	38	–
Gurusinha	7	–	63	2
N. Ranatunga	8	–	49	–
Warnaweera	7	–	39	–
Kalpage	4	–	24	–

	O	M	R	W
Wasim Akram	10	3	24	4
Aqib Javed	10	2	30	2
Mushtaq Ahmed	10	–	59	–
Waqar Younis	10	–	36	–
Salim Malik	1	–	8	–

FALL OF WICKETS

1–204, 2–231, 3–267

FALL OF WICKETS

1–4, 2–15, 3–105, 4–105, 5–139, 6–162, 7–162

Man of the Match: Saeed Anwar

Pakistan won by 114 runs

usually rich stroke-players like Arjuna Ranatunga, Aravinda de Silva and Tillekeratne failed to take advantage of the position. Gurusinha played a lone hand with his splendid 90, and Pakistan strolled to victory and into the final after Saeed Anwar and Ramiz Raja had survived a hesitant start to score 132 for the first wicket.

There was another first-wicket century partnership the following day when Mahanama and Hathurusinghe began Sri Lanka's innings against Zimbabwe with a stand of 112. This was followed by some spectacular stroke-play from the middle order as Sri Lanka averaged more than six runs an over. Sri Lanka had introduced Nishantha Ranatunga – brother of the newly restored captain, Arjuna – to international cricket, but it was Ramanayake, the tireless medium-pacer, who set them on the path to victory with two early wickets. In spite of Brandes' vigorous fifty, Zimbabwe never looked like reaching their target.

The final was disappointingly one-sided. Put in to bat, Pakistan thrived through a record opening stand of 204 between Saeed Anwar and Ramiz Raja. Then came some violence from Inzamam-ul-Haq and Wasim Akram, and Pakistan put the game out of Sri Lanka's reach by totalling 281 at seven an over. Mahanama and de Silva went for 15, and the contest was over. Wasim Akram finished with four wickets for the second time in the tournament and was named Man of the Series. Used to exciting finishes, the Sharjah crowd must have been a little disappointed, but Sikhander Bakht and Ramiz Raja benefited to the sum of US$35,000 each.

Man of the Series Wasim Akram who led Pakistan to victory in his first tournament as captain. (David Munden/Sports-Line)

SECTION H
Pakistan
Patron's Trophy
Quaid-e-Azam Trophy
First-class averages

*Forceful cricket from Ijaz Ahmed who led Habib Bank in the Patron's Trophy
and played a major part in their success. (Adrian Murrell/Allsport)*

Although the national side played in as many as six different countries in 1992–3, there were no Tests or one-day internationals in Pakistan itself during that time. Again, few of the top players appeared in domestic cricket and, even when there were no national matches scheduled, the lucrative lure of such events as the six-hit competition in Hong Kong led Javed Miandad and Wasim Akram to forsake Pakistan's one-day competition, the Wills Cup, at the semi-final stage. Javed did return to lead Habib Bank in the final, in which they lost to National Bank.

It would have been strange had the Pakistan Board not changed the rules of the first-class competitions once again. The limitation of first innings to 85 overs was abolished, although bonus points could be gained only in the first 85 overs, and there were to be no points for a first-innings lead. Twelve points were awarded for an outright win.

BCCP PATRON'S TROPHY

17, 18, 19 and **20** October 1992 *at Multan CC Stadium, Multan*

PIA 228 (Asif Mohammad 55, Waqar Younis 5 for 52) and 225 (Waqar Younis 4 for 51, Mushtaq Ahmed 4 for 91)
United Bank 392 (Basit Ali 124 not out, Raees Ahmed 83, Amir Bashir 57, Asif Mohammad 5 for 86) and 63 for 2

United Bank won by 8 wickets

at Montgomery Biscuit Factory, Sahiwal

PNSC 402 (Sohail Miandad 91, Zafar Iqbal 87, Sajjad Akbar 63, Mohammad Zahid 6 for 152)
PACO 146 (Amin Lakhani 8 for 60) and 389 for 8 (Umar Rasheed 90, Mujahid Jamshed 75, Shahid Saeed 74, Aamir Hanif 52, Amin Lakhani 4 for 116)

Match drawn

at Sargodha Stadium, Sargodha

HBFC 187 and 266 (Aamir Khurshid 100, Rifat Alam 59)
Habib Bank 420 for 7 dec. (Shakeel Ahmed 142, Ijaz Ahmed 134, Zulfiqar Butt 4 for 105) and 34 for 0

Habib Bank won by 10 wickets

at Arbab Niaz Stadium, Peshawar

National Bank 348 for 8 dec. (Sajid Ali 121, Shahid Anwar 101) and 310 for 8 (Hafeez-ur-Rehman 76, Naeem Ashraf 62 not out, Mohammad Asif 4 for 72)
ADBP 390 (Saeed Anwar 101, Mansoor Rana 95, Atif Rauf 75)

Match drawn

With the Patron's Trophy (the competition between business houses) preceding the Quaid-e-Azam Trophy in

1992–3, Waqar Younis was able to lead United Bank in the first two matches, and his bowling blasted aside PIA in the first round. The impressive batting of Basit Ali was also a feature of the United Bank side, and Basit was later to win international recognition. Habib Bank, the reigning champions, also started on a winning note, although House Building Finance Corporation were short of two men, absent ill, in their second innings.

24, 25, 26 and **27** October 1992 *at Multan CC Stadium, Multan*

PNSC 275 (Mahmood Hamid 89, Mohammad Javed 50, Wasim Akram 4 for 90) and 245 (Sohail Miandad 80, Wasim Akram 6 for 53)
PIA 290 (Zahid Fazal 117, Sohail Farooqi 4 for 72) and 183 for 8 (Amin Lakhani 4 for 69)

Match drawn

at Montgomery Biscuit Factory, Sahiwal

PACO 274 (Aamir Hanif 85, Umar Rasheed 68, Raees Ahmed 4 for 37) and 227 for 9 (Zulqarnain 52 not out, Mushtaq Ahmed 5 for 118)
United Bank 428 (Iqbal Imam 113, Rashid Latif 66, Mohammad Zahid 7 for 198)

Match drawn

Thirty-eight wickets in the Patron's Trophy for Zakir Khan of ADBP. (Bob Martin/Allsport)

at Rawalpindi Stadium, Rawalpindi

ADBP 253 (Bilal Ahmed 71, Javed Hayat 60, Shezad Alyas 6 for 69) and 342 for 5 dec. (Saeed Anwar 100, Zahoor Elahi 58, Manzoor Elahi 53 not out)

HBFC 269 (Munir-ul-Haq 53, Tariq Alam 52, Zakir Khan 4 for 84) and 138 (Zakir Khan 4 for 49, Ghayyur Qureshi 4 for 50)

ADBP won by 188 runs

at Arbab Niaz Stadium, Peshawar

Habib Bank 276 (Tahir Rashid 55, Shaukat Mirza 52, Shakeel Ahmed 50, Nadeem A. Khan 7 for 84) and 366 for 4 (Shahid Javed 111 not out, Ijaz Ahmed 109 not out, Hafeez-ur-Rehman 4 for 72)

National Bank 448 for 9 dec. (Saeed Azad 133, Shahid Anwar 117, Wasim Arif 53, Nadeem Ghauri 4 for 89)

Match drawn

Wasim Akram took 10 wickets in the match against PNSC, but he could not lead his side to victory. Indeed, PIA narrowly avoided defeat, as PNSC skipper Amin Lakhani brought his total of wickets to 19 in two matches with his left-arm spin. ADBP reversed a first-innings deficit to beat HBFC and become the only winners of the round, while Ijaz Ahmed and Shahid Javed shared an unbroken fifth-wicket stand of 213 for Habib Bank against National Bank.

31 October, **1**, **2** and **3** November 1992 *at Multan CC Stadium, Multan*

PACO 224 (Ghulam Ali 135 not out, Zahid Ahmed 5 for 74, Iqbal Sikander 4 for 93) and 264 for 8 dec. (Shahid Nawaz 110, Ghulam Ali 68, Umar Rasheed 56)

PIA 163 (Mohammad Zahid 5 for 52) and 183 (Mohammad Zahid 4 for 56)

PACO won by 142 runs

at Montgomery Biscuit Factory, Sahiwal

PNSC 277 (Farrukh Bari 54, Waqar Younis 7 for 76) and 222 (Mahmood Hamid 81, Waqar Younis 5 for 29)

United Bank 518 (Inzamam-ul-Haq 178, Mansoor Akhtar 90, Basit Ali 73)

United Bank won by an innings and 19 runs

at Rawalpindi Stadium, Rawalpindi

HBFC 156 (Maqsood Rana 7 for 70) and 405 (Munir-ul-Haq 120, Wasim Ali 119)

National Bank 270 (Ameer Akbar Babar 73, Sohail Khan 5 for 100) and 41 for 1

Match drawn

at Arbab Niaz Stadium, Peshawar

ADBP 152 (Naved Anjum 5 for 59) and 457 (Saeed Anwar 151, Mansoor Rana 66, Ghaffar Kazmi 58, Akram Raza 4 for 149)

Habib Bank 123 (Zakir Khan 9 for 45) and 127 (Manzoor Elahi 5 for 39, Mohammad Asif 4 for 33)

ADBP won by 359 runs

Ghulam Ali carried his bat throughout the first innings for PACO to set up victory over PIA, while Waqar Younis and Inzamam-ul-Haq played their last games of the season in Pakistan before setting forth on tour and were dominant in United Bank's rout of PNSC. Waqar finished with 21 wickets at 9.90 runs each from the two matches in which he appeared. He was almost upstaged by Zakir Khan whose 9 for 45 in ADBP's annihilation of Habib Bank was the best bowling performance of the season and of Zakir's career.

7, 8, 9 and **10** November 1992 *at LCCA Ground, Lahore*

Habib Bank 213 (Mohammad Hasnain 120, Sajjad Akbar 7 for 44) and 171 (Shahid Javed 57, Sajjad Akbar 4 for 30)

PNSC 270 (Mahmood Hamid 78, Sohail Jaffer 78, Akram Raza 5 for 64) and 115 for 4 (Zafar Iqbal 59)

PNSC won by 6 wickets

at Sargodha Stadium, Sargodha

United Bank 362 (Raees Ahmed 108, Pervez Shah 75 not out) and 182 for 3 (Basit Ali 76, Pervez Shah 56)

ADBP 310 (Mansoor Rana 92 not out, Zahoor Elahi 83, Tauseef Ahmed 7 for 83)

Match drawn

at Bagh-i-Jinnah Ground, Lahore

National Bank 467 (Shahid Tanvir 113, Shahid Anwar 110, Sajid Ali 107, Tahir Shah 64 not out, Mohammad Zahid 5 for 158) and 290 for 7 (Shahid Tanvir 142, Shahid Anwar 68)

PACO 353 (Mujahid Jamshed 119, Shahid Nawaz 92)

Match drawn

at Rawalpindi Stadium, Rawalpindi

PIA 202 (Kabir Khan 5 for 92, Ali Ahmed 4 for 64) and 204 (Babar Zaman 74, Ali Ahmed 5 for 76, Shahzad Ilyas 4 for 93)

HBFC 272 (Wasim Ali 62, Wasim Yousufi 54, Rashid Khan 5 for 93) and 135 for 3 (Munir-ul-Haq 51 not out)

HBFC won by 7 wickets

PNSC gained their first win of the season against Habib Bank who were still searching for consistent form. Sajjad Akbar's 11 for 74 with his off-breaks was the decisive factor. There were six centuries but no result in Lahore, and HBFC won their first match at the higher level with bowlers dominating.

Former Test bowler Azeem Hafeez in good form for PIA. (Adrian Murrell/Allsport)

14, 15, 16 and **17** November 1992 *at Iqbal Stadium, Faisalabad*

HBFC 267 (Aamir Khurshid 82, Amin Lakhani 5 for 104, Sajjad Akbar 4 for 90) and 204 for 6 (Aamir Khurshid 74, Wasim Yousufi 50)

PNSC 300 (Mahmood Hamid 107, Zulfiqar Butt 5 for 90)

Match drawn

at Sargodha Stadium, Sargodha

PACO 233 (Kamran Khan 67) and 232 for 6 (Kamran Khan 65, Ghulam Ali 52, Mohammad Asif 4 for 58)

ADBP 238 (Mohammad Zahid 5 for 107)

Match drawn

15, 16, 17 and **18** November 1992 *at National Stadium, Karachi*

PIA 435 (Zahid Fazal 109, Rizwan-uz-Zaman 58, Aamir Malik 55, Ijaz Ahmed 5 for 95)

Habib Bank 576 (Tahir Rasheed 182, Shahid Javed 107, Akram Raza 79, Shakeel Ahmed 60, Mohammad Hasnain 50)

Match drawn

at Rawalpindi Stadium, Rawalpindi

United Bank 168 (Ameer Akbar Babar 4 for 34) and 284 (Mansoor Akhtar 60)

National Bank 271 (Naeem Ashraf 114, Shahid Tanvir 68) and 130 (Tanvir Mehdi 4 for 22)

United Bank won by 51 runs

With a saturation of runs and slow batting condemning the other matches to be drawn, United Bank moved to the top of the table with their third win in five matches. The outstanding performance of the round was by Tahir Rasheed, the Habib Bank wicket-keeper, who, batting at number seven, hit a career best 182 and shared a seventh-wicket stand of 217 with Akram Raza.

21, 22, 23 and **24** November 1992 *at Qaddafi Stadium, Lahore*

National Bank 296 (Ameer Akbar Babar 121, Azeem Hafeez 6 for 114) and 216 (Sajid Ali 66, Azeem Hafeez 5 for 77)

PIA 325 for 7 dec. (Moin Khan 100 not out, Rizwan-uz-Zaman 52, Naeem Ashraf 4 for 117) and 158 for 5

Match drawn

at Iqbal Stadium, Faisalabad

PNSC 110 (Manzoor Elahi 6 for 60) and 263 (Mahmood Hamid 107, Mohammad Javed 71, Manzoor Elahi 4 for 48)

ADBP 254 (Mohammad Asif 70, Mansoor Rana 50, Zafar Iqbal 5 for 64) and 120 for 4 (Zahoor Elahi 59, Nadeem Afzal 4 for 35)

ADBP won by 6 wickets

at National Stadium, Karachi

United Bank 216 (Saifullah 59, Ijaz Ahmed 4 for 61) and 223 (Basit Ali 121 not out, Asadullah Butt 7 for 93)

Habib Bank 439 for 6 dec. (Ijaz Ahmed 143, Anwar Miandad 77, Shahid Javed 74) and 1 for 0

Habib Bank won by 10 wickets

at Bagh-i-Jinnah Ground, Lahore

HBFC 308 (Faisal Qureshi 96, Shazad Ilyas 78, Munir-ul-Haq 62, Mohammad Zahid 5 for 143)

PACO 506 for 7 (Aamir Hanif 129, Shahid Nawaz 127 not out, Mujahid Jamshed 116, Umar Rasheed 65 not out)

Match drawn

Veteran left-arm medium-pace bowler Azeem Hafeez enjoyed a fine match for Pakistan International Airlines against National Bank for whom Ameer Akbar Babar continued to bat well. The match also saw a maiden first-class century from Moin Khan who had lost his place in the national side to Rashid Latif. Another former Test player, Manzoor Elahi, returned the best bowling figures of his career as ADBP beat PNSC. There was also a career-best bowling performance from the young medium-pacer Asadullah Butt of Habib Bank who demolished United Bank in their second innings. Skipper Ijaz Ahmed was the real hero of this match with four first-innings wickets and a most impressive hundred. Ijaz is still fighting to reclaim a place in the Pakistan side. There was no play on the first day of the game between HBFC and PACO and a run feast on the following days.

28, 29, 30 November and 1 December 1992 *at National Stadium, Karachi*

HBFC 318 (Salim Taj 72, Masood Anwar 6 for 98) and 197 for 1 (Aamir Khurshid 101 not out)

United Bank 507 (Raees Ahmed 131, Iqbal Amam 95, Zulfiqar Butt 4 for 150)

Match drawn

at Montgomery Biscuit Factory, Sahiwal

PNSC 501 (Sohail Jaffer 160) and 156 for 2 (Sohail Jaffer 102 not out)

National Bank 314 (Sajid Ali 73, Wasim Arif 65, Amin Lakhani 4 for 77)

Match drawn

at Municipal Stadium, Gujranwala

PACO 376 (Shahid Nawaz 139, Umar Rasheed 54, Abdullah Khan 50, Asadullah Butt 6 for 107)

Habib Bank 302 for 6 (Shakeel Ahmed 125, Shaukat Mirza 53)

Match drawn

at LCCA Ground, Lahore

ADBP 182 (Zahoor Elahi 54, Rashid Khan 5 for 76) and 112 (Azeem Hafeez 7 for 54)

PIA 210 (Aamir Malik 103, Shoaib Mohammad 57, Manzoor Elahi 5 for 90) and 89 for 5 (Zakir Khan 4 for 38)

PIA won by 5 wickets

Runs abounded in the stalemate in Karachi, and in Sahiwal where Sohail Jaffer hit the first century of his career in the first innings and followed it with another century in the second innings. Sohail's performance was overshadowed, however, by the events at Gujranwala. Tahir Rasheed, the Habib Bank wicket-keeper, held eight catches and stumped the last batsman to establish a world record with nine dismissals in an innings. Thirty-two years old, Tahir made his first-class debut in 1979,

and five of his six brothers have appeared in first-class cricket.

Pakistan International Airlines ended the season with their first win in seven matches. Four former Test players – Rashid Khan, Azeem Hafeez, Aamir Malik and Shoaib Mohammad – played significant parts in their victory.

SEMI-FINALS

4, 5, 6 and 7 December 1992 *at Qaddafi Stadium, Lahore*

ADBP 106 (Nadeem Afzal 7 for 51) and 262 for 8 dec. (Ghaffar Kazmi 100 not out, Mansoor Rana 57, Mohsin Kamal 4 for 111)

PNSC 176 (Aamir Ishaq 52, Manzoor Elahi 6 for 94) and 122 (Manzoor Elahi 6 for 71, Zakir Khan 4 for 43)

ADBP won by 70 runs

at National Stadium, Karachi

United Bank 203 (Mansoor Akhtar 54) and 188 (Mansoor Akhtar 52, Asadullah Butt 5 for 31, Akram Raza 4 for 60)

Habib Bank 170 (Masood Anwar 6 for 60) and 224 for 6 (Agha Zahid 82, Shaukat Mirza 72, Tauseef Ahmed 4 for 113)

Habib Bank won by 4 wickets

Routed on the opening day by the medium pace of Nadeem Afzal, who returned the best bowling figures of his career, ADBP made a remarkable recovery through the bowling of Zakir Khan and Manzoor Elahi, the batting of Ghaffar Kazmi, and the intelligent captaincy of Mansoor Rana to beat PNSC by 70 runs. Seventy runs behind on the first innings, ADBP were 75 for 4 in their second before Ghaffar and Mansoor added 104. Ghaffar Kazmi also had valuable help from Raja Afaq in an unbroken ninth-wicket stand of 50. Mansoor Rana declared after his side had scored at five runs an over, and Manzoor Elahi and Zakir Khan demolished PNSC in 35.5 overs, the last nine wickets going down for 50 runs. Manzoor Elahi's match figures of 12 for 165 were the best of his career.

Habib Bank also came from behind to beat United Bank. Their heroes were Agha Zahid and Shaukat Mirza who virtually won the match with a fourth-wicket stand of 120 in the second innings.

PATRON'S TROPHY FINAL TABLE

	P	W	L	D	Pts.
United Bank	7	3	1	3	82
ADBP	7	3	1	3	80
Habib Bank	7	2	2	3	68
PNSC	7	1	2	4	59
PACO	7	1	–	6	57
HBFC	7	1	2	4	55
PIA	7	1	3	3	54
National Bank	7	–	1	6	44

(National Bank were deducted two points for slow over rate)

FINAL

12, 13, 14, 15, 16 and 17 December 1992 *at Qaddafi Stadium, Lahore*

Habib Bank 683 (Shakeel Ahmed 161, Mohammad Hasnain 118, Shaukat Mirza 114, Ijaz Ahmed 94, Akram Raza 71, Zakir Khan 5 for 146)

ADBP 367 (Atif Rauf 119 not out, Javed Hayat 108, Bilal Ahmed 86, Qasim Jamal 4 for 106, Asadullah Butt 4 for 114)

Match drawn

Habib Bank retained the Patron's Trophy by virtue of their first-innings lead in a match which, although extended to six days, could not produce a result. There was no play on the first day due to rain, and there was a delayed start on the second day. Ijaz Ahmed had no hesitation in batting when he won the toss, and the nature of the wicket may be seen from the fact that Habib Bank's innings lasted into the fourth day, and that play was extended into a sixth day for 45 minutes in order to get a decision on the first innings. There were five centuries in the match, and Shakeel Ahmed's 161 off 376 balls was the highest score of his career. He and Mohammad Hasnain, who also batted well, added 203 for the second wicket. Shaukat Mirza joined in the batting spree, but the most joyful innings came from Ijaz Ahmed who hit 94 off 97 balls with 2 sixes and 12 fours. When Mansoor Rana took the third new ball on the fourth day five wickets fell for 76 runs, but by then the match was beyond the reach of ADBP.

QUAID-E-AZAM TROPHY

An outstanding all-round season for Manzoor Elahi who took 55 wickets for ADBP and Multan and played some splendidly aggressive innings. (David Munden/Sports-Line)

26, 27, 28 and **29** December 1992 *at National Stadium, Karachi*

Faisalabad 260 for 9 (Ijaz Ahmed 53, Saadat Gul 51 not out) and 193 (Humayun F. Hussain 4 for 54)

Karachi Whites 136 (Wasim Haider 4 for 37, Nadeem Afzal 4 for 41) and 50 (Nadeem Afzal 5 for 22, Naseer Shaukat 5 for 27)

Faisalabad won by 267 runs

at Bahawal Stadium, Bahawalpur

Sargodha 210 (Mohammad Nawaz 54) and 127 (Murtaza Hussain 4 for 40)

Bahawalpur 215 for 8 (Saifullah 51, Sajjad Akbar 5 for 62) and 123 for 4

Bahawalpur won by 6 wickets

at Montgomery Biscuit Factory, Sahiwal

Multan 286 (Zahoor Elahi 81, Tariq Mahboob 69, Mohammad Shafiq 51, Mohammad Riaz 5 for 86, Syed Zahir Shah 4 for 100) and 206 (Naeem Akhtar 7 for 98)

Rawalpindi 217 (Asif Siddique 5 for 50, Manzoor Elahi 4 for 62) and 139 for 8

Match drawn

at LCCA Ground, Lahore

Lahore 215 (Rafaqat Ali 66, Asadullah Butt 4 for 53, Arshad Khan 4 for 59) and 267 (Tariq Javed 71, Shahid Anwar 52, Asadullah Butt 5 for 126)

Islamabad 184 (Shakeel Ahmed 51, Shahid A. Khan 5 for 67, Tanvir Mehdi 5 for 81) and 242 (Atif Rauf 74, Tanvir Mehdi 5 for 81)

Lahore won by 56 runs

Karachi Whites, looking for their third Quaid-e-Azam Trophy championship in succession, began their campaign disastrously, being routed by Faisalabad. Pakistan's premier competition maintained the 85-over limit on the first innings. As in 1991–2, only regional teams were allowed to compete in the Quaid-e-Azam, and the tournament welcomed Islamabad for the first time. For this, Islamabad owed much to former Test cricketer Majid Khan who championed their cause. Originally part of the Rawalpindi Division, the Federal Cricket Association had come into being in 1982 and, having been granted associate membership by the BCCP in 1988, they took the name of Islamabad. They showed spirit in their opening match, but were beaten by Lahore City.

2, 3, 4 and 5 January 1993 *at Sargodha Stadium, Sargodha*

Sargodha 233 for 8 (Pervez Shah 108) and 97 (Arshad Pervez 50 not out, Humayun F. Hussain 6 for 44)

Karachi Whites 286 for 8 (Aamir Hanif 127 not out, Munir-ul-Haq 57) and 46 for 0

Karachi Whites won by 10 wickets

at Bahawal Stadium, Bahawalpur

Faisalabad 145 (Murtaza Hussain 4 for 45) and 155 (Bilal Rana 5 for 35, Murtaza Hussain 5 for 48)
Bahawalpur 288 for 7 (Sher Ali 101, Aamir Sohail 51, Ijaz Ahmed 4 for 63) and 14 for 1

Bahawalpur won by 9 wickets

at Marghazar, Islamabad

Islamabad 300 for 7 dec. (Atif Rauf 85, Ijaz Ahmed 69, Nadeem Iqbal 4 for 77)
Multan 156 for 3 (Zahoor Elahi 60 not out)

Match drawn

at KRL Ground, Rawalpindi

Lahore 226 (Mujahid Jamshed 106 not out, Raja Afaq 5 for 89)
Rawalpindi 229 for 9 (Shahid Javed 61, Sabih Azhar 57)

Match drawn

Karachi Whites regained form against Sargodha, and Bahawalpur, expected to be their strongest challengers, won easily against Faisalabad. The other two matches were badly affected by rain. No play was possible on the first day in Islamabad and only 20 overs on the second.

9, 10, 11 and 12 January 1993 *at LCCA Ground, Lahore*

Lahore 32 for 1
***v.* Karachi Whites**

Match drawn

at Sargodha Stadium, Sargodha

Multan 248 (Zahoor Elahi 53, Akram Raza 6 for 80) and 141 (Manzoor Elahi 61, Akram Raza 4 for 47)
Sargodha 223 (Mohammad Nawaz 69, Zameer-ul-Hasan 56, Asif Siddique 4 for 63) and 167 for 5 (Mohammad Nawaz 70)

Sargodha won by 5 wickets

at Iqbal Stadium, Faisalabad

Rawalpindi 217 and 191 for 5 (Salim Taj 80 not out, Rashid Wali 4 for 40)
Faisalabad 258 (Shahid Nawaz 108, Sabih Azhar 5 for 72)

Match drawn

at Marghazar, Islamabad

Bahawalpur 361 for 6 (Sher Ali 201 not out)
Islamabad 247 (Atif Rauf 77, Mufeez Murtaza 52, Mohammad Zahid 4 for 63)

Match drawn

Bad weather again disrupted matches, with only 10 overs of the first day possible in Lahore. Sargodha overcame the loss of most of the second day's play to beat Multan,

but restrictions proved too much elsewhere. Sher Ali hit the first double century of his career, and the first of the season, in Islamabad.

16, 17, 18 and 19 January 1993 *at Montgomery Biscuit Factory, Sahiwal*

Multan 335 for 6 (Tariq Mahboob 150 not out, Manzoor Elahi 87, Aamir Bashir 51)
Karachi Whites 338 (Ghulam Ali 123, Aamir Hanif 60, Mahmood Hamid 52, Nadeem Nazir 5 for 108)

Match drawn

at LCCA Ground, Lahore

Lahore 246 for 9 (Tariq Javed 65)
Faisalabad 218 (Mohammad Ramzan 96, Shahid A. Khan 6 for 72)

Match drawn

at Sargodha Stadium, Sargodha

Islamabad 240 for 6 (Mufeez Murtaza 89, Atif Rauf 56, Akram Raza 4 for 89)
Sargodha 223 (Akram Raza 80 not out, Zameer-ul-Hasan 50)

Match drawn

at KRL Ground, Rawalpindi

Bahawalpur 107
Rawalpindi 111 for 1 (Nadeem Younis 53 not out)

Match drawn

Rain prevented play on the first day in all matches, and only one innings a side was possible.

23, 24, 25 and 26 January 1993 *at Bahawal Stadium, Bahawalpur*

Bahawalpur 317 for 9 (Sher Ali 84, Shahzad Arshad 51) and 265 (Tanvir Razzaq 72, Iqbal Zahoor 4 for 57)
Lahore 197 (Shahid Anwar 55, Mohammad Zahid 5 for 50, Murtaza Hussain 5 for 55) and 119 (Murtaza Hussain 5 for 27)

Bahawalpur won by 266 runs

at Iqbal Stadium, Faisalabad

Faisalabad 292 (Shahid Nawaz 75, Sami-ul-Haq 58, Zahoor Elahi 5 for 55, Asif Siddique 4 for 99) and 330 for 9 (Mohammad Ramzan 58, Naseer Shaukat 57, Bilal Ahmed 54, Mohammad Afzal 4 for 81)
Multan 331 (Zahoor Elahi 110, Aamir Bashir 67, Naved Nazir 5 for 85)

Match drawn

at KRL Ground, Rawalpindi

Sargodha 191 (Mohammad Nawaz 71, Mohammad Riaz 5 for 53) and 122 (Mohammad Riaz 5 for 48)

Rawalpindi 275 (Nadeem Younis 87, Salim Taj 71, Akram Raza 7 for 91) and 39 for 0

Rawalpindi won by 10 wickets

at Marghazar, Islamabad

Islamabad 202 (Nadeem Khan 4 for 60, Haaris A. Khan 4 for 67) and 248 (Sahid Hussain 90, Haaris A. Khan 5 for 101, Nadeem Khan 4 for 88)

Karachi Whites 277 (Aamir Hanif 104) and 175 for 8 (Ghulam Ali 51)

Karachi Whites won by 2 wickets

Bahawalpur and Karachi Whites virtually assured themselves of places in the semi-finals although Karachi were hard-pressed by newcomers Islamabad. The veteran left-arm spinner Mohammad Riaz bowled Rawalpindi to their first win of the season, but, in spite of Zahoor Elahi's fine all-round cricket – which included a best bowling performance – Multan could not force victory against Faisalabad.

30, 31 January, **1** and **2 February 1993** *at Bahawal Stadium, Bahawalpur*

Multan 117 (Mohammad Altaf 7 for 30) and 179

Bahawalpur 137 (Asif Siddique 4 for 30) and 163 for 5 (Saifullah 53 not out)

Bahawalpur won by 5 wickets

at Sargodha Stadium, Sargodha

Lahore 170 (Sajjad Akbar 6 for 57) and 138 (Sajjad Akbar 4 for 22, Akram Raza 4 for 29)

Sargodha 226 (Zameer-ul-Hasan 79, Tariq Rashid 4 for 21) and 85 for 1 (Mohammad Hasnain 52 not out)

Sargodha won by 9 wickets

at National Stadium, Karachi

Karachi Whites 348 for 6 (Sajid Ali 130, Aamir Hanif 96) and 323 for 7 dec. (Sajid Ali 83, Azam Khan 60, Aamir Hanif 54, Zahir Shah 4 for 92)

Rawalpindi 300 for 9 (Salim Taj 105 not out, Shahid Javed 88) and 216 (Nadeem Khan 5 for 60)

Karachi Whites won by 155 runs

at Marghazar, Islamabad

Islamabad 352 for 7 (Shakeel Ahmed 184, Ijaz Ahmed 5 for 80) and 274 for 6 dec. (Kashif Khan 91 not out, Shakeel Ahmed 51)

Faisalabad 281 (Mohammad Ramzan 84, Sami-ul-Haq 52, Shahid Hussain 5 for 103) and 222 for 4 (Sami-ul-Haq 86, Mohammad Ashraf 51 not out)

Match drawn

Bahawalpur moved to the top of the table with victory over Multan on a wicket which always aided the bowlers, to the extent that the match was over in three days. Left-arm spinner Mohammad Altaf returned the best bowling figures of his career, 7 for 30. Sajjad Akbar helped Sargodha to their second win of the season, his off-breaks bringing him match figures of 10 for 79. Opener Sajid Ali played two fine innings in Karachi's big win in the high-scoring game with Rawalpindi, while Shakeel Ahmed hit 184 off 208 balls in the drawn match in Islamabad.

6, 7, 8 and **9 February 1993** *at National Stadium, Karachi*

Bahawalpur 222 (Saifullah 50, Nadeem Khan 5 for 96) and 196 (Athar Laeeq 4 for 55)

Karachi Whites 248 for 7 (Sajid Ali 55, Munir-ul-Haq 50) and 174 for 2 (Aamir Hanif 80 not out, Azam Khan 57 not out)

Karachi Whites won by 8 wickets

at Montgomery Biscuit Factory, Sahiwal

Multan 220 (Manzoor Elahi 75) and 283 (Mohammad Siddique 64, Manzoor Elahi 53, Aamir Bashir 51)

Lahore 251 (Mansoor Rana 74, Shahid Anwar 57) and 253 for 2 (Shahid Anwar 75 not out, Mansoor Rana 74 not out, Tahir Ghulzar 55)

Lahore won by 8 wickets

at Iqbal Stadium, Faisalabad

Sargodha 276 (Mohammad Nawaz 61, Pervez Shah 54, Ijaz Ahmed 6 for 62) and 267 (Aziz-ur-Rehman 98 not out, Nadeem Afzal 4 for 76, Rashid Wali 4 for 90)

Faisalabad 203 for 9 (Mohammad Ramzan 75, Sami-ul-Haq 54, Akram Raza 6 for 71) and 211 for 7 (Shahid Nawaz 65, Sajjad Akbar 5 for 64)

Match drawn

at KRL Ground, Rawalpindi

Islamabad 296 for 7 (Shakeel Ahmed 120) and 274 (Aamir Nazir 73, Atif Rauf 69, Mohammad Riaz 7 for 115)

Rawalpindi 313 for 8 (Shahid Javed 79, Mohammad Riaz 65, Shahid Hussain 4 for 129) and 116 for 6

Match drawn

Karachi Whites' win put them level with Bahawalpur at the top of the table, and Lahore's victory over Multan gave them a place in the semi-finals. Sargodha had the better of the draw with Faisalabad, and Rawalpindi's failure to beat Islamabad left Sargodha in fourth spot, and Rawalpindi out of the semi-finals. Islamabad finished without a win, but Shakeel Ahmed brought his total of runs for them to 565 and so completed 1,000 runs for the season.

A maiden first-class century for Moin Khan who led Karachi Whites to triumph in the Quaid-e-Azam Trophy and had a fine season behind the stumps for both Karachi and PIA. (David Munden/Sports-Line)

QUAID-E-AZAM TROPHY FINAL TABLE

	P	W	L	D	Pts.
Karachi Whites	7	4	1	2	44
Bahawalpur	7	4	1	2	44
Lahore	7	2	2	3	24
Sargodha	7	2	3	2	24
Rawalpindi	7	1	1	5	22
Faisalabad	7	1	1	5	14
Islamabad	7	–	2	5	8
Multan	7	–	3	4	8

SEMI-FINALS

13, 14, 15 and **16** February 1993 *at National Stadium, Karachi*

Karachi Whites 322 for 4 (Basit Ali 121, Aamir Hanif 82 not out, Sajid Ali 67) and 371 for 3 dec. (Sajid Ali 203 not out, Azam Khan 80, Mahmood Hamid 62)

Lahore 225 for 8 (Mansoor Rana 58, Nadeem Khan 5 for 103) and 157 for 7 (Haaris A. Khan 6 for 52)

Match drawn

at Qaddafi Stadium, Lahore

Sargodha 224 (Mohammad Nawaz 92, Aziz-ur-Rehman 64, Mohammad Altaf 4 for 48) and 366 for 5 dec. (Mohammad Nawaz 146, Anis-ur-Rehman 70, Aziz-ur-Rehman 51)

Bahawalpur 104 (Amanullah 5 for 32, Naeem A. Khan 5 for 49) and 101 for 4 (Sher Ali 50 not out)

Match drawn

Both Karachi Whites and Sargodha entered the final by virtue of a lead on the first innings although both sides dominated the drawn matches in which they were engaged. The highly talented Basit Ali struck a century on the opening day for Karachi Whites who led by 97 on the first innings. There followed Sajid Ali's 203 off 362 balls, the highest score of the season, and the highest score of his career. Off-spinner Haaris A. Khan might well have won the match for Karachi, but skipper Moin Khan opted to bat into the last day and to settle for the first-innings advantage to give his side a place in the final.

Aziz-ur-Rehman and Mohammad Nawaz began Sargodha's innings with a partnership of 159, and once Bahawalpur were bowled out on the second day, Sargodha's place in the final was virtually assured. Mohammad Nawaz ended all doubts when he hit 146 off 323 balls in 426 minutes.

FINAL

19, 20, 21, 22 and **23** February 1993 *at National Stadium, Karachi*

Karachi Whites 593 (Basit Ali 145, Munir-ul-Haq 135, Sajid Ali 131, Moin Khan 61, Akram Raza 6 for 164)

Sargodha 209 (Mohammad Hasnain 54) and 210 (Aziz-ur-Rehman 67, Haaris A. Khan 5 for 67, Nadeem Khan 4 for 68)

Karachi Whites won by an innings and 174 runs

Karachi Whites completed a hat-trick of championship successes in the Quaid-e-Azam Trophy, and they beat Sargodha in grand style, winning by an innings with a day to spare. Karachi had reached their peak at the right time and their batting was formidable. Sajid Ali, in top form, hit 18 fours in his 131 which came off 170 balls. He and the majestic Basit Ali put on 189 in 40.2 overs for the second wicket, and by the end of the first day Karachi were 342 for 3 from 85 overs. They had increased to 560 for 8 by the end of the second day, with Munir-ul-Haq becoming the third centurion of the innings. After more than two days in the field Sargodha struggled with the bat. They crashed to 49 for 4, and closed the third day on 198 for 9. On the fourth day, the game was over – Haaris turned his off-breaks sharply and finished with match figures of 8 for 103 while the left-arm spinner Nadeem Khan had 5 for 84 in the two innings.

FIRST-CLASS AVERAGES

BATTING

	M	Inns	NO	Runs	HS	Av	100s	50s
Saeed Anwar (ADBP)	3	5	–	387	151	77.40	3	–
Sajid Ali (K/NB)	11	19	1	1232	203*	68.44	5	5
Aamir Hanif (K/PACO)	14	22	3	1042	129	54.84	3	7
Shahid Tanvir (NB)	4	7	–	382	142	54.57	2	1
Shakeel Ahmed (I/HB)	15	24	2	1198	184	54.45	5	4
Raees Ahmed (UB)	7	10	1	490	131	54.44	2	1
Umar Rasheed (PACO)	7	11	3	426	90	53.25	–	5
Basit Ali (K/UB)	14	19	2	865	145	50.88	4	2
Ijaz Ahmed (I/HB)	10	13	–	655	133	50.38	3	2
Shahid Javed (R/HB)	14	20	1	884	111*	46.52	2	6
Mansoor Akhtar (UB)	6	9	–	411	90	45.66	–	4
Aamir Khurshid (HBFC)	6	11	1	436	101*	45.60	2	2
Mahmood Hamid (K/PNSC)	16	23	4	863	107	45.42	2	5
Tariq Mahboob (M)	7	11	2	406	150*	45.11	1	2
Mohammad Ramzan (F)	7	12	1	493	84	44.81	–	5
Mansoor Rana (L/ADBP)	15	21	2	837	92*	44.05	–	8
Shahid Nawaz (F/PACO)	14	23	1	957	139	43.50	4	3
Shahid Anwar (L/NB)	14	24	3	905	117	43.09	3	5
Atif Rauf (I/ADBP)	15	23	1	919	119*	41.77	1	7
Sher Ali (B)	8	16	2	557	201*	39.78	2	2
Ghulam Ali (K/PACO)	11	16	1	594	135	39.60	2	3
Sohail Jaffer (PNSC)	8	14	1	514	160	39.53	2	1
Iqbal Imam (UB)	7	11	1	394	113	39.40	1	1
Tahir Rasheed (HB)	9	12	1	433	182	39.36	1	1
Mujahid Jamshed (L/PACO)	14	20	1	747	119	39.31	3	1
Salim Taj (R/HBFC)	11	19	3	604	105*	37.75	1	3
Naeem Ashraf (NB)	6	10	1	337	114	37.44	1	1
Wasim Ali (HBFC)	7	12	1	359	119	35.90	1	1
Mufeez Murtaza (I)	6	10	–	357	89	35.70	–	2
Aamir Malik (PIA)	6	10	–	352	103	35.20	1	1
Moin Khan (K/PIA)	12	17	5	422	100*	35.16	1	1
Zahid Fazal (L/PIA)	6	10	–	351	117	35.10	2	–
Munir-ul-Haq (K/HBFC)	15	21	1	694	135	34.70	2	5
Aamir Bashir (M/UB)	12	17	–	583	67	34.29	–	5
Mohammad Nawaz (S)	9	17	–	579	146	34.05	1	6
Nadeem Younis (R)	6	11	2	306	87	34.00	–	2
Mohammad Hasnain (S/HB)	15	26	2	812	120	33.83	2	3
Faisal Qureshi (HBFC)	6	11	1	335	96	33.50	–	1
Sami-ul-Haq (F)	7	12	–	401	86	33.41	–	4
Aamir Akbar (NB)	7	11	–	358	121	32.54	1	1
Zahoor Elahi (M/ADBP)	16	25	1	779	110	32.45	1	7
Shaukat Ahmed (S)	9	13	–	412	114	31.69	1	3
Ghaffar Kazmi (L/ADBP)	11	17	2	427	100*	28.46	1	1
Akram Raza (S/HB)	17	23	5	508	80*	28.22	–	3
Sohail Miandad (PNSC)	8	14	–	394	91	28.14	–	2
Saifullah (B/UB)	16	26	3	637	59	27.69	–	4
Ijaz Ahmed (F)	7	12	–	303	59	27.54	–	2
Aziz-ur-Rehman (S)	8	15	2	349	67	26.84	–	3
Manzoor Elahi (M/ADBP)	15	22	1	559	87	26.61	–	5
Tariq Javed (L)	7	12	–	307	71	25.58	–	2
Aamir Ishaq (PNSC)	8	14	–	358	52	25.57	–	1
Pervez Shah (S/UB)	13	24	1	588	108	25.56	1	3
Rizwan-uz-Zaman (PIA)	7	13	–	330	58	25.38	–	2
Murtaza Hussain (B/PACO)	15	20	7	308	47*	23.69	–	–
Zameer-ul-Hasan (S)	8	14	–	321	79	22.92	–	3
Raja Arshad (M/UB)	9	14	–	308	49	22.00	–	–
Sajjad Akbar (S/PNSC)	15	23	3	406	63	20.30	–	2
Bilal Ahmed (F/ADBP)	13	20	2	347	86	19.27	–	3

(Qualification – 300 runs)

BOWLING

	Overs	Mds	Runs	Wkts	Av	Best	10/m	5/inn
Waqar Younis (UB)	75.5	16	208	21	9.90	7-76	1	3
Mohammad Altaf (B/PACO)	135.4	30	342	22	15.54	7-30	–	1
Arshad Khan (I)	105	15	320	18	17.77	4-59	–	–
Haaris A. Khan (K)	328.1	78	776	42	18.47	6-52	–	3
Ijaz Ahmed (F)	180.1	35	459	23	19.95	6-62	–	2
Mohammad Zahid (B/PACO)	486.1	105	1333	64	20.82	7-198	–	7
Zakir Khan (ADBP)	301.3	72	799	38	21.02	9-45	1	2
Asadullah Butt (I/HB)	276.4	47	972	45	21.60	7-93	–	4
Tauseef Ahmed (UB)	141.4	44	346	16	21.62	7-83	–	1
Mohammad Riaz (R)	246.3	46	633	29	21.82	7-115	1	4
Asif Siddique (M)	263.4	35	710	32	22.18	5-50	–	1
Manzoor Elahi (M/ADBP)	427.5	80	1230	55	22.36	6-60	2	5
Amin Lakhani (PNSC)	370.1	103	855	38	22.50	8-60	1	2
Iqbal Zahoor (L)	125.3	18	348	15	23.20	4-57	–	–
Humayun F. Hussain (K)	176	24	630	26	24.23	6-44	–	1
Nadeem Afzal (F/PNSC)	225	24	801	33	24.27	7-51	–	2
Akram Raza (S/HB)	615.2	123	1724	71	24.28	6-71	1	5
Masood Anwar (UB)	252.1	74	644	27	24.59	6-60	–	2
Shahid A. Khan (L)	159.2	35	444	18	24.66	6-72	–	2
Nadeem Khan (K/NB)	487	105	1283	51	25.15	7-84	–	4
Sajjad Akbar (S/PNSC)	565.3	128	1351	53	25.49	7-44	2	4
Rashid Khan (PIA)	196.3	39	596	23	25.91	5-76	–	2
Athar Laeeq (K)	172	22	630	24	26.25	4-55	–	–
Murtaza Hussain (B/PACO)	505.5	92	1350	50	27.00	5-27	1	3
Azeem Hafeez (PIA)	193.3	37	706	26	27.15	7-54	1	3
Naeem Akhtar (R)	106.4	20	408	15	27.20	7-98	–	1
Shahid Hussain (I)	233.2	46	726	24	30.25	5-103	–	1
Naeem A. Khan (S/HB)	174.5	34	582	19	30.63	5-49	–	1
Tanvir Mehdi (L/UB)	225.2	31	840	27	31.11	5-81	1	2
Nadeem Ghauri (HB)	274	69	671	20	33.55	4-89	–	–
Mohammad Asif (L/ADBP)	334.5	54	923	27	34.18	4-33	–	–
Raja Afaq (R/ADBP)	319.3	64	871	25	34.84	5-89	–	1
Iqbal Sikander (PIA)	156.5	29	538	15	35.86	4-93	–	–
Zahid Ahmed (PIA)	230.2	50	612	17	36.00	5-74	–	1
Maqsood Rana (NB)	125	20	542	15	36.13	7-70	–	1
Shahzad Ilyas (HB)	143.4	24	555	15	37.00	6-69	–	1
Naveed Nazir (F)	201	36	627	15	41.80	5-85	–	1
Zulfiqar Butt (HBFC)	218.4	40	681	16	42.56	5-90	–	1
Nadeem Nazir (M/HB)	188.3	15	739	17	43.47	5-108	–	1

(Qualification – 15 wickets)

LEADING FIELDERS

40 – Tahir Rashid (HB) (ct 38/st 2); 33 – Moin Khan (K/PIA) (ct 30/st 3) and Saifullah (B/UB) (ct 29/st 4); 31 – Bilal Ahmed (F/ADBP) (ct 26/st 5); 25 – Pervez-ul-Hassan (PNSC) (ct 20/st 5); 16 – Nadeem Abbasi (R) (ct 14/st 2); 15 – Mohammad Shafiq (M) (ct 10/st 5) and Zulqarnain (PACO) (ct 10/st 5); 14 – Wasim Yousafi (HB) (ct 10/st 4), Shahid Javed (R/HB) and Mohammad Ashraf (F); 13 – Mohammad Ashraf (F), Sajid Ali (K/NB), Mohammad Zahid (B/PACO) and Akram Raza (S/HB); 12 – Abdul Shakoor (S) (ct 6/st 6), Zameer-ul-Hasan (S), Manzoor Elahi (M/ADBP) and Mahmood Hamid (K/PNSC); 11 – Aamir Nazir (I) (ct 8/st 3) and Atif Rauf (I/ADBP); 10 – Haider Nisar (PIA), Faisal Qureshi (HBFC), Naseer Ahmed (R) (ct 9/st 1) and Sajjad Akbar (S/PNSC).

ABBREVIATIONS USED FOR TEAM NAMES

ADBP – Agricultural Development Bank of Pakistan; B – Bahawalpur; F – Faisalabad; HB – Habib Bank; HBFC – House Building Finance Corporation; I – Islamabad; K – Karachi Whites; L – Lahore City; M – Multan; NB – National Bank; PACO – Pakistan Automobile Corporation; PIA – Pakistan International Airlines; PNSC – Pakistan National Shipping Corporation; R – Rawalpindi; S – Sargodha; UB – United Bank

SECTION I
West Indies
Geddes Grant Shield
Red Stripe Cup
Pakistan tour, one-day international and Test series
First-class averages

Queen's Park Oval, Port of Spain, Trinidad, West Indies v. Pakistan. (Ben Radford/Allsport)

Once more West Indian domestic cricket was bereft of its leading players who, following their arduous tour of Australia, were engaged in a lengthy one-day series in South Africa which involved the host nation and Pakistan. By the time Pakistan arrived in the Caribbean for a three-Test series and five one-day internationals and the West Indian Test players had returned from their travels, the Red Stripe Cup and the Geddes Grant Shield had been completed.

GEDDES GRANT SHIELD

27 January 1993 *at Guaracara Park, Pointe-à-Pierre, Trinidad*

Trinidad & Tobago 154 for 9 (R.A.M. Smith 77)
Windward Islands 147 for 2 (D.A. Joseph 83)

Windward Islands (2 pts.) won on faster scoring rate

3 February 1993 *at Queen's Park Oval, Port of Spain, Trinidad*

Leeward Islands 144
Trinidad & Tobago 148 for 5 (K.A. Williams 62 not out)

Trinidad & Tobago (2 pts.) won by 5 wickets

at Sabina Park, Kingston, Jamaica

Barbados 191 for 6
Jamaica 111

Barbados (2 pts.) won by 80 runs

at Albion Sports Complex, Berbice, Guyana

Windward Islands 186 for 6 (D.A. Joseph 71)
Guyana 186 for 9 (D.A. Joseph 4 for 55)

Windward Islands (2 pts.) won on losing fewer wickets with the scores level

10 February 1993 *at Queen's Park, St George's, Grenada*

Barbados 133
Windward Islands 137 for 4

Windward Islands (2 pts.) won by 6 wickets

at Warner Park, Basseterre, St Kitts

Guyana 195
Leeward Islands 197 for 6 (R.D. Jacobs 52)

Leeward Islands (2 pts.) won by 4 wickets

at Sabina Park, Kingston, Jamaica

Jamaica 181 for 9 (F.R. Redwood 70)
Trinidad & Tobago 185 for 6

Trinidad & Tobago (2 pts.) won by 4 wickets

17 February 1993 *at Kensington Oval, Bridgetown, Barbados*

Barbados 201 for 6 (H.R. Waldron 54 not out)
Guyana 204 for 4 (K.F. Semple 58 not out)

Guyana (2 pts.) won by 6 wickets

18 February 1993 *at Recreation Ground, Antigua*

Leeward Islands 238 for 7 (S.C. Williams 105)
Jamaica 241 for 9 (T.O. Powell 76, D.S. Morgan 65)

Jamaica (2 pts.) won by 1 wicket

24 February 1993 *at Sturge Park, Montserrat*

Barbados 155 (M.J. Lavine 53, W.K.M. Benjamin 4 for 21)
Leeward Islands 159 for 9 (O.D. Gibson 4 for 32)

Leeward Islands (2 pts.) won by 1 wicket

at Enmore, Demerara, Guyana

Trinidad & Tobago 176 (R.A. Harper 5 for 37)
Guyana 180 for 4 (C.B. Lambert 67)

Guyana (2 pts.) won by 6 wickets

at Arnos Vale, St Vincent

Jamaica 256 for 9 (R.G. Samuels 75)
Windward Islands 150

Jamaica (2 pts.) won by 106 runs

3 March 1993 *at Mindoo Phillip Park, St Lucia*

Windward Islands 194 (U. Pope 54)
Leeward Islands 151 for 2 (S.C. Williams 68 not out, R.D. Jacobs 67 not out)

Leeward Islands (2 pts.) won on faster scoring rate

at Bourda, Georgetown, Guyana

Guyana 144 for 9
Jamaica 115 for 9 (R.A. Harper 4 for 27)

Guyana (2 pts.) won by 29 runs

at Kensington Oval, Bridgetown, Barbados

Trinidad & Tobago 183
Barbados 185 for 3 (R.I.C. Holder 79 not out, P.A. Wallace 63)

Barbados (2 pts.) won by 7 wickets

The 50-over Geddes Grant Shield tournament was expanded in 1993, with the six regions meeting each other on a league basis and the top two teams qualifying for the final. The competition proved to be somewhat low-key, played in the shadow of the Red Stripe Cup. Windward Islands set the early pace and, having won their first three games, they seemed assured of a place in the final, but they were ousted by Leeward Islands who scored at six runs an over in the last round of matches to beat Windwards and claim first position in the table.

Stuart Williams of Leeward Islands hit the only century of the tournament but still finished on the losing side against Jamaica, while the leading scorer of the season was Windwards' skipper Dawnley Joseph who also bowled his medium pace to good effect. Roger Harper and Ottis Gibson were the leading wicket-takers, and Harper, a shrewd captain, bowled with great economy.

Inspired all-round cricket and leadership for Guyana from Roger Harper in both the Geddes Grant Shield and the Red Stripe Cup. (Alan Cozzi)

RED STRIPE CUP

29, 30, 31 January and 1 February 1993 *at Guaracara, Pointe-à-Pierre, Trinidad*

Trinidad & Tobago 220 (K.A. Williams 113, R.A. Marshall 6 for 41) and 193 (H. Gangapersad 50, C.A. Davis 4 for 71)

Windward Islands 315 (R.A. Marshall 79, U. Pope 62, D.A. Joseph 56, A.H. Gray 4 for 78) and 99 for 1 (D.A. Joseph 52 not out)

Windward Islands won by 9 wickets

Windward Islands 16 pts., Trinidad & Tobago 0 pts.

On the opening day of the season, Ken Williams hit the second century of his career and left-arm spinner Roy Marshall took six wickets for the first time in his career. Marshall followed his best bowling performance with the highest score of his career to put Windwards well on top. The visitors did not relax their hold on the match. Trinidad lost six wickets before clearing the first-innings arrears, and Windwards won with ease.

5, 6, 7 and 8 February 1993 *at Skeldon, Berbice, Guyana*

Windward Islands 128 and 117 (C.G. Butts 6 for 31)

Guyana 471 for 4 dec. (C.B. Lambert 263 not out, Sudesh Dhaniram 74, K.F. Semple 50 not out)

Guyana won by an innings and 226 runs

Guyana 16 pts., Windward Islands 0 pts.

GEDDES GRANT SHIELD – FINAL POSITIONS

	P	W	L	Pts.	Net RR
Leeward Islands	5	3	2	6	+.35
Guyana	5	3	2	6	+.15
Windward Islands	5	3	2	6	−.38
Jamaica	5	2	3	4	+.21
Barbados	5	2	3	4	+.02
Trinidad & Tobago	5	2	3	4	−.13

The final was due to be played at Albion, Berbice on 13 and 14 March 1993, but was abandoned because of rain. Leeward Islands and Guyana shared the title.

Red Stripe Cup record score of 263 not out by Clayton Lambert, Guyana v. Windward Islands, 5–8 February. (David Munden/Sports-Line)

at Queen's Park Oval, Port of Spain, Trinidad

Leeward Islands 285 (L.L. Lawrence 74, R. Mahabir 4 for 52) and 237 for 8 dec. (R.D. Jacobs 119 not out)

Trinidad & Tobago 200 (W.D. Phillip 5 for 54) and 232 (A.H. Gray 69, W.D. Phillip 5 for 81)

Leeward Islands won by 90 runs

Leeward Islands 16 pts., Trinidad & Tobago 0 pts.

at Sabina Park, Kingston, Jamaica

Barbados 456 for 9 dec. (R.I.C. Holder 162 not out, P.A. Wallace 96, H.R. Waldron 62)

Jamaica 287 for 9 (P.J.L. Dujon 107)

Match abandoned

Jamaica 4 pts., Barbados 4 pts.

Windward Islands' elation was short-lived as, having been put in, they were crushed in three days by Guyana. Veteran off-spinner Clyde Butts posed the greatest problems for Windwards, but Man of the Match was the left-handed opener Clayton Lambert who shared an opening stand of 195 with Sudesh Dhaniram and went on to score 263 not out, the highest score recorded in regional competition since sponsorship started in 1966.

Wicket-keeper Ridley Jacobs, who bats left-handed, hit the first century of his career as Leewards mastered a rather limp Trinidad side. The chief honours went to left-arm spinner Warrington Phillip who, in his third first-class match, took 10 wickets for 135 runs. In his two previous games he had taken one wicket for 164 runs.

Jeff Dujon postponed his retirement and captained and kept wicket for Cup-holders Jamaica. The game in Kingston was ruined by rain, but both captains hit centuries. Roland Holder made the highest score of his career, and Dujon's 107 was his 20th first-class hundred.

12, 13, 14 and **15 February 1993** *at Queen's Park, St George's, Grenada*

Barbados 193 and 170 for 5 (P.A. Wallace 67)

Windward Islands 183 (D.A. Joseph 98, O.D. Gibson 4 for 50, V.C. Drakes 4 for 60)

Match drawn

Barbados 8 pts., Windward Islands 4 pts.

at Sabina Park, Kingston, Jamaica

Jamaica 400 (P.J.L. Dujon 163 not out, R.G. Samuels 57) and 187 for 4 (D.S. Morgan 85, R.G. Samuels 60)

Trinidad & Tobago 331 (K.A. Williams 103, R.A.M. Smith 58, F.A. Rose 5 for 65)

Match drawn

Jamaica 8 pts., Trinidad & Tobago 4 pts.

at Warner Park, Basseterre, St Kitts

Guyana 380 (Sudesh Dhaniram 131, R.A. Harper 73)

Sudesh Dhaniram hit 131 for Guyana in the drawn match with Leeward Islands. (David Munden/Sports-Line)

Leeward Islands 156 (S. Chanderpaul 4 for 48) and 375 (S.C. Williams 91, A.C.H. Walsh 88, L.L. Lawrence 70, C.G. Butts 4 for 106)

Match drawn

Guyana 8 pts., Leeward Islands 4 pts.

Barbados, who had lost Best to an injury sustained in the 50-over competition, took first-innings points in the rain-affected game with Windward Islands, and Jamaica had to be content with eight points against Trinidad. Jeff Dujon produced the highest score of his career in his final season, and Ken Williams replied with his second century of the season. The man to catch the eye, however, was Jamaican fast bowler Franklyn Rose, 20 years old and playing his début first-class season, who took 5 for 65 and looked quick and dangerous.

Sudesh Dhaniram confirmed his return to form when he equalled his career-best score as Guyana dominated the early stages of the match against Leewards. The home side, forced to follow-on, saved the game with some solid batting in a consistent second-innings display.

19, 20, 21 and **22 February 1993** *at Kensington Oval, Bridgetown, Barbados*

Barbados 117 (R.A. Harper 6 for 24) and 213 (P.A. Wallace 85, B.S. Browne 4 for 46)

Guyana 113 (S.M. Skeete 4 for 19) and 218 for 6 (S. Chanderpaul 56)

Guyana won by 4 wickets

Guyana 16 pts., Barbados 5 pts.

at Recreation Ground, Antigua

Leeward Islands 159 (N.O. Perry 5 for 54) and 359 (R.D. Jacobs 115, S.C. Williams 99, L.A. Harrigan 57, N.O. Perry 4 for 90)

Jamaica 228 (D.S. Morgan 70, W.K.M. Benjamin 7 for 64) and 196 for 3 (P.J.L. Dujon 77 not out, C.A. Davidson 62)

Match drawn

Jamaica 8 pts., Leeward Islands 4 pts.

Guyana placed one hand on the Red Stripe Cup when they recovered from trailing narrowly on the first innings to beat Barbados in the vital match at Bridgetown. Put in to bat, the home side were routed by Roger Harper who was leading Guyana with skill and intelligence. Guyana failed to take advantage of their skipper's bowling and conceded a first-innings lead of four runs, but Barrington Browne, an experienced pace bowler who enjoyed his best season in his five years in the Red Stripe Cup, kept his side in the game. Needing 218 to win, Guyana batted with great good sense to clinch victory.

In the match in Antigua, Winston Benjamin returned his best figures in Caribbean domestic cricket and left-hander Ridley Jacobs hit his second century of the season.

26, 27, 28 February and 1 March 1993 *at Arnos Vale, St Vincent*

Windward Islands 159 (F.A. Rose 4 for 31) and 145 (R.C. Haynes 4 for 33)

Jamaica 302 (N.O. Perry 75, L.R. Williams 64, C.A. Davis 4 for 76) and 5 for 0

Jamaica won by 10 wickets

Jamaica 16 pts., Windward Islands 0 pts.

at Bourda, Georgetown, Guyana

Guyana 362 (R.A. Harper 94, C.B. Lambert 56)

Trinidad & Tobago 132 (B.S. Browne 6 for 51) and 85 (C.G. Butts 7 for 40)

Guyana won by an innings and 145 runs

Guyana 16 pts., Trinidad & Tobago 0 pts.

at Grove Park, Nevis

Leeward Islands 341 (A.C.H. Walsh 92, R.D. Jacobs 65) and 345 for 7 (A.C.H. Walsh 59, R.D. Jacobs 56, L.A. Harrigan 51, L.L. Harris 51)

A resounding finish to an outstanding career from Jeff Dujon of Jamaica. (Adrian Murrell/Allsport)

Barbados 445 (R.I.C. Holder 125, C.O. Browne 71, A.F.G. Griffith 63, L.C. Lake 4 for 99)

Match drawn

Barbados 8 pts., Leeward Islands 4 pts.

Jamaica's convincing victory over Windward Islands could not stop Guyana from claiming the Red Stripe Cup with one round of matches still to be played. The new champions completely outplayed Trinidad, whose form

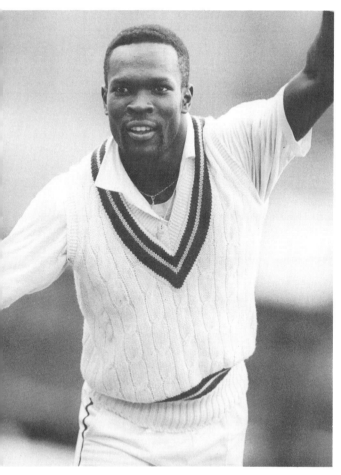

Superb form in the Red Stripe Cup took Winston Benjamin back into the West Indies side. (Alan Cozzi)

throughout the season had been less than impressive. Put in to bat, Guyana batted with consistent application, but they owed much to Roger Harper. The all-rounder had once seemed destined to captain West Indies, but that honour had passed him by. Nevertheless, he had shown excellent qualities of leadership with Guyana and played a major part in their success. He was aided by the fact that Guyana were able to field the most experienced side in the competition, and it was veteran Clyde Butts who returned the best figures of the season as Guyana moved to a crushing innings victory inside three days.

Thanks to a century from skipper Roland Holder, Barbados led Leeward Islands by 104 runs on the first innings, but the home side fought a determined rearguard action to save the game.

5, 6, 7 and **8 March 1993** *at Kensington Oval, Bridgetown, Barbados*

Barbados 79 (R. Dhanraj 4 for 19) and 418 for 8 dec. (R.I.C. Holder 124, S.L. Campbell 113, H.R. Waldron 67, E.C. Antoine 5 for 85)

Trinidad & Tobago 178 (C.G. Yorke 51, O.D. Gibson 5 for 48) and 122

Barbados won by 197 runs

Barbados 16 pts., Trinidad & Tobago 5 pts.

at Bourda, Georgetown, Guyana

Jamaica 181 (C.A. Davidson 51, B.S. Browne 4 for 33) and 165 (B.S. Browne 5 for 44)

Guyana 159 (C.B. Lambert 61, N.O. Perry 4 for 20, F.A. Rose 4 for 35) and 188 for 4

Guyana won by 6 wickets

Guyana 16 pts., Jamaica 5 pts.

at Mindoo Phillip Park, St Lucia

Windward Islands 131 (W.K.M. Benjamin 4 for 30) and 116 (H.A.G. Anthony 6 for 22)

Leeward Islands 137 (C.E. Cuffy 5 for 35) and 111 for 3 (A.C.H. Walsh 62 not out)

Leeward Islands won by 7 wickets

Leeward Islands 16 pts., Windward Islands 0 pts.

Barbados staged a remarkable recovery to overcome Trinidad in the last round of matches. Trailing by 99 on the first innings, Barbados were 16 for 2 in their second when Holder joined Sherwin Campbell, who was making his first appearance of the season. The pair added 209, with Campbell hitting a maiden century and Holder his third hundred of the season. The promising Waldron also batted well, and Barbados swept to victory when Trinidad collapsed in their second innings.

The bowling of Barrington Browne gave Guyana victory in their final match. Pace man Browne finished the season with 26 wickets, the most by a quick bowler. He nearly doubled the number of wickets he had taken in 13 previous matches.

The quick bowlers dominated in St Lucia where Hamish Anthony turned the game in Leewards' favour with a career-best bowling performance.

Clyde Butts, the 35-year-old off-spinner from Guyana, took 34 Red Stripe wickets to bring his total to 252, only four short of Nanan's record.

RED STRIPE CUP – FINAL TABLE

	P	W	L	D	Pts.
Guyana (4)	5	4	–	1	72
Leeward Islands (2)	5	2	–	3	44
Barbados (3)	5	1	1	3*	41
Jamaica (1)	5	1	1	3*	41
Windward Islands (6)	5	1	3	1	20
Trinidad & Tobago (5)	5	–	4	1	9

*Includes one no-result
(1992 positions in brackets)

PAKISTAN TOUR

18, 19, 20 and **21** March 1993 *at Sabina Park, Kingston, Jamaica*

Pakistanis 319 for 4 dec. (Inzamam-ul-Haq 106, Zahid Fazal 62, Basit Ali 51 not out) and 263 for 8 dec. (Basit Ali 84 not out, Asif Mujtaba 79, L.R. Williams 4 for 66)

Jamaica 283 (C.A. Davidson 86, L.R. Williams 65, Mushtaq Ahmed 5 for 86) and 155

Pakistanis won by 144 runs

Selection of national sides has never been a strong point with Pakistan, but the omission of Salim Malik and Shoaib Mohammad from the party to tour West Indies surprised even the most cynical followers of the game. In England in 1992, Pakistan had seemed on the verge of greatness. They lacked only a little substance in batting, and Shoaib had provided that at The Oval. Since then, an unending diet of one-day internationals had done much to undermine the quality of the side. In an incomprehensible move, Javed had been replaced as captain by Wasim Akram, with Waqar Younis as his vice-captain. Imran Khan, now an adviser to the selectors, seemed to have an influence in this decision, as he did in the 'resting' of

Salim Malik from the side to fly to the Caribbean. Rarely has a selection committee been guilty of such a stupid act, and one fears that political manoeuvring behind the scenes may have taken its effect.

Aamir Nazir, a young fast bowler of whom little was known, and Basit Ali, a 22-year-old batsman with an impressive record in domestic cricket and for Pakistan 'B', were the newcomers to the Pakistan side. Basit Ali performed most impressively against Jamaica in the opening match of the tour.

Inzamam-ul-Haq hit a century on the first day and Basit Ali reached his fifty before the declaration on the second day, after which Jamaica fared badly against Mushtaq Ahmed's leg-spin. The last six Jamaican wickets went down for 34 runs, and Asif Mujtaba and Basit Ali pillaged runs in Pakistan's second innings. A varied attack destroyed Jamaica for the second time, and the tourists began their ventures with a comprehensive and morale-boosting victory.

ONE-DAY INTERNATIONAL SERIES
WEST INDIES *v.* PAKISTAN

The one-day series in the Caribbean began as the series in South Africa had finished – with Brian Lara rampant. Put in to bat in the first match of the series, Pakistan made

FIRST ONE-DAY INTERNATIONAL – WEST INDIES *v.* PAKISTAN
23 March 1993 at Sabina Park, Kingston, Jamaica

PAKISTAN			WEST INDIES		
Aamir Sohail	c sub (Arthurton), b Ambrose	88	B.C. Lara	b Aamir Sohail	114
Ramiz Raja	b Simmons	22	D.L. Haynes	c Ramiz Raja, b Wasim Akram	7
Inzamam-ul-Haq	lbw, b Bishop	49	P.V. Simmons	b Mushtaq Ahmed	28
Wasim Akram (capt)	c Hooper, b Bishop	0	R.B. Richardson (capt)	b Wasim Akram	17
Javed Miandad	c Simmons, b Hooper	16	C.L. Hooper	c and b Aamir Sohail	21
Basit Ali	st Murray, b Hooper	17	A.L. Logie	c Mushtaq Ahmed, b Aamir Sohail	7
*Rashid Latif	not out	1	J.C. Adams	not out	11
Asif Mujtaba			*J.R. Murray	not out	1
Waqar Younis			C.E.L. Ambrose		
Mushtaq Ahmed			I.R. Bishop		
Aqib Javed			C.A. Walsh		
Extras	b 4, lb 7, w 11, nb 8	30	Extras	lb 6, w 5, nb 7	18
(50 overs)	(for 6 wickets)	223	(44 overs)	(for 6 wickets)	224

	O	M	R	W		O	M	R	W
Ambrose	10	1	31	1	Wasim Akram	9	–	47	2
Walsh	10	2	40	–	Aqib Javed	6	1	18	–
Simmons	10	2	26	1	Waqar Younis	10	1	46	–
Bishop	9	1	54	2	Mushtaq Ahmed	10	–	64	1
Hooper	8	–	28	2	Aamir Sohail	9	–	43	3
Adams	3	–	33	–					

FALL OF WICKETS

1–67, 2–185, 3–185, 4–187, 5–221, 6–223

FALL OF WICKETS

1–21, 2–101, 3–180, 4–184, 5–197, 6–223

Umpires: S.U. Bucknor & L.H. Barker   *Man of the Match:* B.C. Lara   *West Indies won by 4 wickets*

SECOND ONE-DAY INTERNATIONAL – WEST INDIES *v.* PAKISTAN
26 March 1993 at Queen's Park Oval, Port of Spain, Trinidad

PAKISTAN			WEST INDIES		
Aamir Sohail	c Richardson, b Simmons	47	B.C. Lara	not out	95
Ramiz Raja	c Richardson, b Bishop	15	D.L. Haynes	c sub, b Aamir Nazir	11
Inzamam-ul-Haq	run out	11	P.V. Simmons	c Rashid Latif, b Waqar Younis	13
Javed Miandad	c Simmons, b Hooper	41	R.B. Richardson (capt)	b Aamir Nazir	32
Basit Ali	c Haynes, b Walsh	34	C.L. Hooper	lbw, b Aamir Nazir	0
Wasim Akram (capt)	run out	0	A.L. Logie	c Rashid Latif, b Wasim Akram	1
*Rashid Latif	run out	10	J.C. Adams	not out	15
Waqar Younis	not out	4	*J.R. Murray		
Mushtaq Ahmed	not out	0	C.E.L. Ambrose		
Ata-ur-Rehman			C.A. Walsh		
Aamir Nazir			I.R. Bishop		
Extras	b 1, lb 6, w 20, nb 5	32	Extras	lb 11, w 9, nb 9	29
		—			—
(45 overs)	(for 7 wickets)	194	(41 overs)	(for 5 wickets)	196

	O	M	R	W		O	M	R	W
Ambrose	10	–	40	–	Wasim Akram	9	–	36	1
Walsh	8	2	30	1	Waqar Younis	8	1	39	1
Bishop	7	–	42	1	Aamir Nazir	9	–	43	3
Simmons	10	1	34	1	Ata-ur-Rehman	10	–	42	–
Hooper	10	–	41	1	Mushtaq Ahmed	5	–	25	–

FALL OF WICKETS
1–56, 2–85, 3–108, 4–170, 5–170, 6–187, 7–188

FALL OF WICKETS
1–35, 2–69, 3–133, 4–133, 5–137

Umpires: S.U. Bucknor & C.E. Cumberbatch   Man of the Match: B.C. Lara   *West Indies won by 5 wickets*

THIRD ONE-DAY INTERNATIONAL – WEST INDIES *v.* PAKISTAN
27 March 1993 at Queen's Park Oval, Port of Spain, Trinidad

WEST INDIES			PAKISTAN		
D.L. Haynes	c Basit Ali, b Aamir Nazir	68	Aamir Sohail	c Ambrose, b Bishop	42
B.C. Lara	c Rashid Latif, b Aamir Nazir	5	Ramiz Raja	run out	43
P.V. Simmons	not out	80	Inzamam-ul-Haq	not out	90
R.B. Richardson (capt)	c Inzamam-ul-Haq, b Aamir Sohail	46	Basit Ali	run out	17
C.L. Hooper	c Wasim Akram, b Waqar Younis	34	Asif Mujtaba	not out	45
A.L. Logie	not out	1	Wasim Akram (capt)		
J.C. Adams			*Rashid Latif		
*J.R. Murray			Waqar Younis		
C.E.L. Ambrose			Nadim Khan		
I.R. Bishop			Ata-ur-Rehman		
C.A. Walsh			Aamir Nazir		
Extras	lb 15, w 4, nb 6	25	Extras	lb 11, w 10, nb 3	24
		—			—
(45 overs)	(for 4 wickets)	259	(43.1 overs)	(for 3 wickets)	261

	O	M	R	W		O	M	R	W
Wasim Akram	10	–	62	–	Ambrose	9	1	49	–
Waqar Younis	10	3	50	1	Walsh	10	–	63	–
Aamir Nazir	8	–	52	2	Bishop	10	–	49	1
Ata-ur-Rehman	10	–	31	–	Simmons	7	–	44	–
Nadim Khan	6	–	39	–	Hooper	7.1	–	45	–
Aamir Sohail	1	–	10	1					

FALL OF WICKETS
1–32, 2–115, 3–182, 4–249

FALL OF WICKETS
1–71, 2–100, 3–130

Umpires: S.U. Bucknor & C.E. Cumberbatch   Man of the Match: Inzamam-ul-Haq   *Pakistan won by 7 wickets*

PAKISTAN

Aamir Sohail	c Richardson, b Simmons	29
Ramiz Raja	lbw, b Bishop	2
Inzamam-ul-Haq	c Murray, b Hooper	17
Javed Miandad	b Ambrose	19
Basit Ali	b Walsh	60
Asif Mujtaba	c and b Hooper	23
Wasim Akram (capt)	b Walsh	1
*Rashid Latif	not out	17
Waqar Younis	run out	2
Ata-ur-Rehman	run out	2
Aamir Nazir	not out	1
Extras	lb 3, w 5, nb 5	13
(50 overs)	(for 9 wickets)	186

WEST INDIES

B.C. Lara	c Rashid Latif, b Waqar Younis	5
D.L. Haynes	lbw, b Wasim Akram	6
P.V. Simmons	c Rashid Latif, b Ata-ur-Rehman	20
R.B. Richardson (capt)	c Rashid Latif, b Ata-ur-Rehman	2
C.L. Hooper	b Aamir Sohail	16
J.C. Adams	c Javed Miandad, b Wasim Akram	27
A.L. Logie	c Wasim Akram, b Asif Mujtaba	8
*J.R. Murray	b Waqar Younis	14
I.R. Bishop	not out	18
C.E.L. Ambrose	b Wasim Akram	4
C.A. Walsh	lbw, b Wasim Akram	3
Extras	b 3, lb 3, w 9, nb 10	25
(44.3 overs)		148

	O	M	R	W
Bishop	10	–	44	1
Walsh	10	–	34	2
Ambrose	10	2	32	1
Hooper	10	1	34	2
Simmons	10	–	39	1

	O	M	R	W
Wasim Akram	7.3	2	18	4
Waqar Younis	8	2	27	2
Ata-ur-Rehman	10	–	38	2
Aamir Nazir	6	1	17	–
Aamir Sohail	6	1	23	1
Asif Mujtaba	7	–	19	1

FALL OF WICKETS
1–9, 2–52, 3–54, 4–111, 5–159, 6–161, 7–166, 8–169, 9–180

FALL OF WICKETS
1–14, 2–14, 3–19, 4–48, 5–75, 6–87, 7–108, 8–125, 9–134

Umpires: L.H. Barker & C.T. Johnson   *Man of the Match:* Basit Ali   *Pakistan won by 38 runs*

their highest total in nine one-day internationals against West Indies. They owed much to an admirable innings of 88 by Aamir Sohail, who batted until the 45th over. With Inzamam, Aamir added 118 in 21 overs for the second wicket, Inzamam hitting 49 off 48 balls. Once more it must be said that the Pakistanis were indebted to a liberal sprinkling of wides and no-balls to keep their score moving. Pakistan's 223 was soon proved inadequate by Lara's blistering 114 off 116 balls. He hit a six and 11 fours, and although he was twice missed off Mushtaq Ahmed, he played a full range of shots before being bowled round his legs in the 34th over. Another 44 runs were still required when he was out, but Hooper steered West Indies to the brink of victory before tapping a return catch to Aamir Sohail with the scores level.

The second match revolved around a dropped catch. Put in to bat, Pakistan had their innings interrupted by a shower which cost them five overs. They were given a good start by Ramiz and Aamir, and Basit Ali and Javed Miandad added 62 for the fourth wicket, so that the Pakistan score was, at least, satisfactory. Lara hit the first ball of the West Indian innings past cover for four. The second, bowled by Wasim Akram, he edged to first slip where Inzamam dropped the easiest of chances. Lara hit nine more fours and proceeded to 95 off 106 balls to win the match for West Indies.

Richardson won the toss in the third match as he had done in the first two, but this time he chose to bat first. The early dismissal of Lara was a bonus to Pakistan, but Haynes and Simmons added 83. Richardson hit 46 off 28

balls, and Hooper 34 off 28, as 122 runs came from the last 15 overs, during which the Pakistan fielding fell apart. Wasim Akram, carrying the unnecessary burden of captaincy, seemed to lose all control. Ramiz Raja helped restore faith along with Aamir Sohail, but it was Inzamam and Asif Mujtaba who brought about a sensational victory by adding 131 off 95 balls. Pakistan had played at their very best with the bat, and at their very worst in the field.

In St Vincent, Richardson won the toss for the fourth time and asked Pakistan to bat, but the pitch was uneven in bounce and increasingly offered help to spin. Pakistan scored only 59 for 3 in their first 20 overs, but Basit Ali rallied the side in two stands, the first with Javed and the second with Asif Mujtaba. The last five wickets fell for 21 runs, and West Indies had a seemingly easy task, but Lara and Haynes fell to successive deliveries and Richardson three overs later. They never recovered from these early losses.

At Bourda, Wasim Akram won the toss for the first time in the series and his side raced to 50 in seven overs. In the next 23 overs, however, they advanced by only another 53 runs. Inzamam and Basit Ali consolidated with a stand of 103 in 20.3 overs, and Wasim Akram hit 39 in 27 balls. West Indies began slowly, but Richardson hit fiercely for 41 off 37 balls as he and Haynes added 63 in under 10 overs. Hooper and Haynes put on 106 in 19.2 overs, but Waqar Younis put a brake on the scoring, and the last over arrived with 12 needed. Ten came from Wasim Akram's first five balls, and Bishop was left to hit two off

FIFTH ONE-DAY INTERNATIONAL – WEST INDIES v. PAKISTAN
3 April 1993 at Bourda, Georgetown, Guyana

PAKISTAN				WEST INDIES		
Aamir Sohail	c and b Ambrose	33		D.L. Haynes	lbw, b Waqar Younis	82
Ramiz Raja	c and b Hooper	26		B.C. Lara	b Aamir Nazir	15
Inzamam-ul-Haq	lbw, b Walsh	53		P.V. Simmons	run out	12
Javed Miandad	lbw, b Cummins	2		R.B. Richardson (capt)	st Rashid Latif, b Aamir Sohail	41
Basit Ali	c Murray, b Walsh	57		C.L. Hooper	not out	69
Wasim Akram (capt)	not out	39		A.L. Logie	b Wasim Akram	1
*Rashid Latif	c sub (Arthurton), b Bishop	15		I.R. Bishop	not out	3
Asif Mujtaba				*J.R. Murray		
Waqar Younis				C.E.L. Ambrose		
Ata-ur-Rehman				A.C. Cummins		
Aamir Nazir				C.A. Walsh		
Extras	b 1, lb 6, w 6, nb 6	19		Extras	lb 13, w 5, nb 3	21
(50 overs)	(for 6 wickets)	244		(50 overs)	(for 5 wickets)	244

	O	M	R	W		O	M	R	W
Bishop	10	–	62	1	Wasim Akram	10	1	50	1
Simmons	2	–	20	–	Waqar Younis	10	–	54	1
Walsh	10	–	46	2	Ata-ur-Rehman	8	–	39	–
Ambrose	10	1	44	1	Aamir Nazir	8	–	28	1
Hooper	10	–	28	1	Aamir Sohail	10	1	42	1
Cummins	8	–	37	1	Asif Mujtaba	4	–	18	–

FALL OF WICKETS
1–66, 2–75, 3–85, 4–188, 5–189, 6–244

FALL OF WICKETS
1–24, 2–54, 3–117, 4–223, 5–228

Umpires: L.H. Barker & C. Duncan   *Man of the Match:* C.L. Hooper   *Match tied*

---

the last delivery to tie the scores and so win the match for West Indies who had lost fewer wickets. Bishop on-drove to substitute Fazal who gathered cleanly and returned to Wasim with Bishop still short of his ground. The Pakistan captain dropped the ball, and West Indies seemingly had won. However, the crowd had invaded the pitch as soon as Bishop had hit the ball, and Pakistan complained that their fieldsmen had been impeded. Referee Raman Subba Row upheld their complaint, and he declared the match a tie and the series drawn, which is probably the most sensible decision regarding cricket made for some years.

Capacity crowds watched all the matches, so throwing more questions of doubt on the future of Test cricket.

5, 6 and 7 April 1993 at Bourda, Georgetown, Guyana

Pakistanis 255 for 8 dec. (Inzamam-ul-Haq 84, Ramiz Raja 75, S. Chanderpaul 4 for 68) and 146 for 1 (Asif Mujtaba 67 not out, Shakeel Ahmed 52 not out)

West Indies Board President's XI 508 for 5 dec. (R.I.C. Holder 144, S. Chanderpaul 140 not out, R.D. Jacobs 100 not out, K.L.T. Arthurton 74)

Match drawn

Pakistan had come out of the one-day series better than had been expected, and a stand of 113 between Basit Ali and Inzamam-ul-Haq, after Ramiz Raja had made an attractive 75, gave further cause for encouragement. The home side lost two wickets for 23 runs before the end of

the first day, and Pakistan's joy was complete. There the elation ended. Aqib developed a back problem which forced him to leave the tour, and Roland Holder hit his fourth century of the season in a manner which suggested that he could well claim Logie's place in the West Indian side, now that the little batsman from Trinidad had announced his retirement from international cricket. Others to stake a claim were leg-spinner Chanderpaul who took four wickets on a flat surface and hit a maiden first-class century, while wicket-keeper Jacobs added to his growing reputation with an innings of 100 in a 224-run stand with fellow left-hander Chanderpaul.

10, 11 and 12 April 1993 at Queen's Park, St George's, Grenada

Pakistanis 284 for 2 dec. (Shakeel Ahmed 132 not out, Asif Mujtaba 102) and 221 for 7 dec. (Zahid Fazal 80)

West Indies Under-23 XI 184 (Nadim Khan 4 for 21) and 210 (Aamir Sohail 5 for 50)

Pakistanis won by 111 runs

Pakistan's troubles multiplied. Four of their players, including captain and vice-captain, were charged with drug offences which, from the evidence presented, were subsequently quite rightly dropped. It was a most unfortunate incident which could have been avoided had the local authorities shown more sense. At first it seemed that the match in Grenada would not be completed and even that the tour would be abandoned, but sensitive diplo-

macy helped to placate the Pakistanis, although the beginning of the first Test match was put back a day.

Shakeel Ahmed and Asif Mujtaba shared a second-wicket stand of 208, and left-arm spinner Nadim Khan and Mushtaq Ahmed routed the home side. Aamir Sohail bowled well in the second innings.

FIRST TEST MATCH
WEST INDIES *v.* PAKISTAN, at Port of Spain

Rashid Latif became the latest of Pakistan's walking wounded and was unable to play in the first Test. Moin Khan returned, and Basit Ali made his Test debut as expected. Richardson won the toss and, defying tradition at Queen's Park Oval, he decided to bat first. Initially, there was nothing to suggest that the West Indian captain had erred. Haynes and Simmons went off with a flourish. Wasim bowled a succession of no-balls, and Waqar looked positively tame. Pakistan had already begun to droop when Simmons chased a wide long-hop and was caught behind. Mushtaq came into the attack as early as the 11th over and made the vital contribution of bowling Richardson behind his legs.

In the first over after lunch, Haynes was caught behind off an out-swinger and, in the second, Lara was brilliantly

Chaos as Keith Arthurton is run out in the first Test. This was one of the 17 wickets to fall on the opening day. (Ben Radford/Allsport)

caught low down at second slip by Aamir Sohail off Waqar, and the floodgates were open. Two overs later, Waqar claimed both Hooper and Murray leg before and, in his next over, he had Arthurton dropped at third slip by Asif Mujtaba, only for Aamir Sohail to run the batsman out off the same ball. In the following over, Bishop was taken at slip, and West Indies had gone from 63 for 0 to 102 for 8 in 15 overs. Cummins and Ambrose added 25,

FIRST TEST MATCH – WEST INDIES *v.* PAKISTAN
16, 17 and 18 April 1993 at Queen's Park Oval, Port of Spain, Trinidad

WEST INDIES

	FIRST INNINGS		SECOND INNINGS	
D.L. Haynes	c Moin, **b** Rehman	31	not out	143
P.V. Simmons	c Moin, **b** Rehman	27	c Asif, **b** Aamir Sohail	22
R.B. Richardson (capt)	**b** Mushtaq Ahmed	7	c Wasim, **b** Waqar	68
B.C. Lara	c Sohail, **b** Younis	6	**b** Asif Mujtaba	96
K.L.T. Arthurton	run out	3	(6) lbw, **b** Wasim	1
C.L. Hooper	lbw, **b** Waqar Younis	9	(7) lbw, **b** Waqar	0
*J.R. Murray	lbw, **b** Waqar Younis	0	(8) lbw, **b** Waqar	0
I.R. Bishop	c Inzamam, **b** Rehman	4	(5) c Moin, **b** Wasim	3
C.E.L. Ambrose	lbw, **b** Wasim Akram	4	lbw, **b** Wasim Akram	5
A.C. Cummins	not out	14	lbw, **b** Wasim Akram	0
C.A. Walsh	**b** Wasim Akram	0	run out	6
Extras	b 6, lb 3, w 2, nb 11	22	b 1, lb 18, w 2, nb 17	38
		127		**382**

PAKISTAN

	FIRST INNINGS		SECOND INNINGS	
Aamir Sohail	c Hooper, **b** Bishop	55	lbw, **b** Walsh	15
Ramiz Raja	lbw, **b** Bishop	9	lbw, **b** Ambrose	11
Inzamam-ul-Haq	lbw, **b** Walsh	10	lbw, **b** Walsh	6
Javed Miandad	lbw, **b** Ambrose	20	c Murray, **b** Bishop	4
Basit Ali	**b** Bishop	0	c Richardson, **b** Hooper	37
Asif Mujtaba	c Lara, **b** Bishop	10	lbw, **b** Hooper	20
Wasim Akram (capt)	c Richardson, **b** Ambrose	2	st Murray, **b** Hooper	4
*Moin Khan	c Murray, **b** Ambrose	0	c Bishop, **b** Hooper	18
Waqar Younis	c Lara, **b** Ambrose	16	lbw, **b** Walsh	1
Mushtaq Ahmed	c Hooper, **b** Bishop	3	not out	12
Ata-ur-Rehman	not out	3	c Ambrose, **b** Hooper	19
Extras	lb 6, nb 6	12	lb 10, nb 8	18
		140		**165**

	O	M	R	W	O	M	R	W		O	M	R	W	O	M	R	W
Wasim Akram	10.2	2	32	2	27	3	75	4	Ambrose	17	6	34	4	13	3	37	1
Waqar Younis	11	3	37	3	23	2	88	3	Bishop	15.5	6	43	5	11	2	28	1
Mushtaq Ahmed	8	1	21	1	13	1	45	–	Walsh	7	4	13	1	12	3	29	3
Ata-ur-Rehman	9	1	28	3	19	–	82	–	Cummins	5	–	19	–	5	1	16	–
Aamir Sohail					5	1	30	1	Hooper	4	–	25	–	11.5	3	40	5
Asif Mujtaba					10	1	43	1	Simmons					1	–	5	–

FALL OF WICKETS
1–63, 2–76, 3–85, 4–85, 5–95, 6–95, 7–102, 8–102, 9–127
1–57, 2–160, 3–329, 4–342, 5–356, 6–358, 7–358, 8–371, 9–371

FALL OF WICKETS
1–17, 2–52, 3–100, 4–100, 5–102, 6–104, 7–108, 8–120, 9–136
1–17, 2–34, 3–41, 4–42, 5–109, 6–111, 7–114, 8–127, 9–134

Umpires: H.D. Bird & S.U. Bucknor

West Indies won by 204 runs

but the innings was soon over. The weather was mostly cloudy, the pitch was one of uneven bounce without ever being malicious, and, in contrast to the one-day internationals, the ground was half-full.

Aamir Sohail played by far the best innings of the day and, with 14 overs of the day remaining, Pakistan were 100 for 2 and, seemingly, in an excellent position. At this point, Aamir was out, and, in quick succession, the heart of the Pakistani batting followed him. They closed on 113 for 7, Asif Mujtaba on 8, Waqar Younis on 1. In 14 overs, Pakistan had lost their way and, as it proved, the match.

West Indies brought the Pakistan innings to an end within 50 minutes of the start of the second day. There was some smart slip catching to aid Ambrose and Bishop, and only some positive hitting by Waqar Younis gave Pakistan a lead of 13, well short of what had at one time seemed possible. Haynes and Simmons soon showed that Pakistan had missed their chance and scored 57 before Simmons was caught at cover on the stroke of lunch.

For the rest of the day, with Wasim bowling too short and with Waqar and Mushtaq well below par, West Indies put the Pakistani attack to the sword. Richardson hit 8 fours and a six as he raced to his fifty off 57 balls before being brilliantly caught by Wasim at mid-off. The fortunate bowler was Waqar Younis, who had been hit for three consecutive fours by Richardson. In 19 overs, the West Indian captain and Desmond Haynes added 103.

Inevitably, Lara continued the assault, and he and Haynes put on 169. By the end of the day, 333 runs had come in 76 overs for the loss of three wickets.

Haynes had reached his 17th century in Test cricket and, as wickets tumbled on the third morning, with Waqar and Wasim bowling a fuller length, he carried his bat through a completed Test innings for the third time in his career. He batted for 459 minutes and hit 20 fours.

Five of the last seven West Indian batsmen dismissed were leg-before decisions, as were the first three in the Pakistani innings, so establishing a new Test record of 16 lbws. The early dismissal of Javed brought Pakistan to 42 for 4, and this was the point of no return. Batsmen had played back when they would have done better to go forward, and the West Indian pace men had broken the back of the innings. Basit Ali and Asif Mujtaba offered sensible resistance, but both fell victim to Hooper's gentle off-spin. Hooper claimed five of the last six wickets, and the match came to an end with 6.1 overs and two days still unused.

SECOND TEST MATCH – WEST INDIES v. PAKISTAN
23, 24, 25 and 27 April 1993 at Kensington Oval, Bridgetown, Barbados

WEST INDIES

	FIRST INNINGS			SECOND INNINGS	
D.L. Haynes	b Aamir Nazir	125	not out		16
P.V. Simmons	c Moin, b Rehman	87	not out		8
R.B. Richardson (capt)	lbw, b Waqar Younis	31			
B.C. Lara	c Moin, b Rehman	51			
K.L.T. Arthurton	b Wasim Akram	56			
C.L. Hooper	c Moin, b Waqar	15			
*J.R. Murray	st Moin, b Sohail	35			
I.R. Bishop	c Moin, b Nazir	11			
C.E.L. Ambrose	not out	12			
W.K.M. Benjamin	b Waqar Younis	0			
C.A. Walsh	c and b Waqar Younis	3			
Extras	b 1, lb 1, nb 27	29	w 3, nb 2		5
		455	(for no wicket)		29

PAKISTAN

	FIRST INNINGS			SECOND INNINGS	
Aamir Sohail	c Murray, b Ambrose	10	c Benjamin, b Ambrose		4
Ramiz Raja	c Haynes, b Ambrose	37	lbw, b Walsh		25
Asif Mujtaba	c Richardson, b Walsh	13	lbw, b Benjamin		41
Javed Miandad	c Richardson, b Benjamin	22	c Arthurton, b Hooper		43
Inzamam-ul-Haq	lbw, b Bishop	7	(7) lbw, b Benjamin		26
Basit Ali	not out	92	b Walsh		37
Wasim Akram (capt)	c Simmons, b Hooper	29	(8) b Benjamin		0
*Moin Khan	c Murray, b Walsh	0	(5) c Murray, b Hooper		17
Waqar Younis	c Murray, b Walsh	0	c Lara, b Hooper		29
Ata-ur-Rehman	c Benjamin, b Walsh	0	c Simmons, b Walsh		13
Aamir Nazir	c Arthurton, b Benjamin	1	not out		6
Extras	lb 3, nb 7	10	b 12, lb 5, nb 4		21
		221			262

	O	M	R	W	O	M	R	W
Wasim Akram	32	2	95	1	2.3	–	18	–
Waqar Younis	25.5	2	132	4				
Aamir Nazir	21	1	79	2	2	–	11	–
Ata-ur-Rehman	21	1	103	2				
Asif Mujtaba	3	–	30	–				
Aamir Sohail	4	1	14	1				

	O	M	R	W	O	M	R	W
Ambrose	16	5	42	2	26	10	55	1
Bishop	16	5	43	1	4	1	13	–
Walsh	18	2	56	4	24	7	51	3
Benjamin	19	5	55	2	17	7	30	3
Hooper	7	–	22	1	32.3	6	96	3

FALL OF WICKETS

1–122, 2–200, 3–303, 4–337, 5–363, 6–426, 7–440, 8–440, 9–445

FALL OF WICKETS

1–12, 2–31, 3–62, 4–79, 5–109, 6–189, 7–190, 8–190, 9–200
1–4, 2–47, 3–113, 4–133, 5–141, 6–207, 7–207, 8–215, 9–238

Umpires: H.D. Bird & L.H. Barker

West Indies won by 10 wickets

SECOND TEST MATCH
WEST INDIES *v.* PAKISTAN, at Bridgetown

Mushtaq Ahmed became the second member of the Pakistan squad to leave the Caribbean and head for England for medical treatment. His place in the Test side was taken by Aamir Nazir who, while he captured the wickets of Haynes and Bishop, seemed hardly ready for Test cricket. Winston Benjamin replaced Cummins in the West Indian side.

Wasim Akram won the toss and asked West Indies to bat. Had Simmons not been dropped twice behind the wicket – straightforward chances – in Waqar's second over of the day, Wasim might have been able to claim success for his decision. As it was, Simmons went on to score 87 off 90 balls in an opening stand of 122. Once again the Pakistan attack was savaged, and once again Wasim produced a plethora of no-balls. The loss of Simmons did not slow the West Indian scoring rate. Desmond Haynes, who had disappointed in Australia and had been deemed close to the end of his career, hit his second century in succession and moved from 90 to 102 with successive pulls for six off Asif Mujtaba. Lara made a brisk 51, and West Indies ended the day on 351 for 4, a highly satisfactory position.

There was quick success on the second morning for the Pakistanis when Waqar had Hooper caught behind, but Arthurton and Murray added 63 at a run a minute and, although the last four wickets went down for only 15 runs, Pakistan faced a formidable 455. Their task of saving the game became more difficult from the first as Aamir fell to a ball from Ambrose which was slanted across him and compelled a stroke. Asif Mujtaba was caught at gully off the shoulder of the bat in the last over before tea, and Pakistan were 31 for 2. They added 100 in the final session, but in the process they lost Ramiz, Javed and Inzamam, and that they would be forced to follow-on seemed inevitable.

Basit Ali and Wasim Akram suggested otherwise on the third morning, extending their partnership to 80. The introduction of Hooper into the attack half an hour before lunch broke the stand, Wasim being caught at short-leg off bat and pad. Two more wickets fell before lunch, Moin and Waqar groping at successive deliveries from Walsh to give catches to the wicket-keeper. When Ata-ur-Rehman steered Walsh to square-leg Pakistan were 200 for 9, and Basit Ali was on 72. In only his second Test, Basit Ali played a selfless innings, shielding Aamir Nazir from the bowling as 21 runs were added. He batted for 228 chanceless minutes, faced 174 balls, hit 11 fours and a six and deserved a century. Sadly, when Basit was on 92, Aamir was caught at silly mid-off. Pakistan followed-on 234 runs in arrears.

Aamir Sohail, limping with a variety of strains, was

ABOVE: *The discovery of the tour for Pakistan – Basit Ali hits out during his splendid 92 not out in the second Test match in Barbados. (Ben Radford/Allsport)*

RIGHT: *Night-watchman Moin Khan is caught by Murray off Hooper in the second innings of the second Test. Junior Murray established himself as West Indies' first-choice wicket-keeper and performed admirably. (Ben Radford/Allsport)*

soon gone. Ramiz batted for 90 minutes before being leg before, and Javed, on whom so much depended, perished rashly. He survived a stumping chance off Hooper on 19, and in the last over pulled the same bowler for six. He tried to repeat the stroke and was easily caught at mid-wicket. Pakistan were 113 for 3.

West Indies put down three chances on the fourth day's play, but none of them proved to be costly. Moin had added only one when he was caught off an inside edge, but Basit Ali was dropped in the same over and survived for another 115 minutes to score an accomplished 37. Asif Mujtaba batted for 250 minutes and faced 196 balls for his 41 before being adjudged leg before, a bad decision by umpire Barker. The decision against Inzamam-ul-Haq by the more experienced Dickie Bird seemed almost as harsh, but these mishaps could not detract from West Indies' superiority, and it was only Waqar's brave hitting at the end of the innings that forced West Indies to bat again to win the match and the series.

THIRD TEST MATCH
WEST INDIES *v.* PAKISTAN, at Antigua

Pakistan had entered the series as the best side in the world. Results had proved otherwise. They had been handicapped by a selection policy distorted by internal politics, and Wasim Akram, while doing much to main-

tain the spirits of his side, was straining to carry the twin burdens of captaincy and world-class all-rounder. To add to Pakistan's miseries, Aamir Sohail became the third player to depart from the tour, returning home with a groin injury. One compensation was that Rashid Latif was able to take his place in the Test eleven, having recovered from a back strain. Shakeel Ahmed and Nadim Khan came in for Aamir Sohail and Aamir Nazir. Cummins returned for West Indies in place of Bishop who was injured in the second Test.

West Indies won the toss and batted, but although Simmons went off with a flourish once more and no batsman failed, they arrived at tea with 213 for 4 on the board, and Pakistan hinting that they could gain control. The left-arm spinner Nadim Khan had claimed two wickets in his first Test and had bowled intelligently. Waqar was the main destroyer after tea as West Indies, pressing too quickly for runs, lost five more wickets and reached 344. Sixty of these had come in an eighth-wicket stand between Hooper and Cummins.

It seemed that Pakistan would soon wrap up the West Indies innings on the second morning, but they endured an horrendous 25 overs during which Hooper and Walsh extended their last-wicket partnership to 106, a West Indies record against all opposition, and then lost their opening pair for four.

Hooper, whose hold on a Test place has been somewhat tenuous and who has never fully realised his enormous potential at international level, was all eloquence and grace in a masterly innings. He hit 2 sixes and 19 fours as he faced 248 balls in under five hours and gave not the semblance of a chance in his 178. His partnership with Walsh, who batted with much confidence, occupied only 18 overs on the second day when 97 of their runs were scored. Walsh was out when he was unable to avoid a bouncer in the first over after lunch.

Ramiz edged the first ball he received to the keeper, and Shakeel, in his first Test, was leg before to the first ball of Ambrose's second over. After this, to close on 85 for 3 on a day curtailed by rain was something of a recovery. Javed, unluckily, was the 27th batsman to be adjudged leg before in the series.

Asif Mujtaba batted well for his 59 and, increasingly, he looks a very sound player who was too long denied a regular place in the Pakistan side, but the honours of the third day went to the two 22-year-old batsmen, Basit Ali and Inzamam-ul-Haq. It was not simply that they added 88 for the fifth wicket, but that they did so in a manner which was at once regal and assured. Nadim Khan also gave Inzamam good support, and the follow-on was avoided as Inzamam began to attack the bowling. He was badly dropped at long-leg by Benjamin off Ambrose when he was on 51, but he batted for 5¼ hours and hit 11 fours and a six in his 123 before being caught at extra cover. He had restored much-needed pride to Pakistan.

Rain prevented play starting until two hours and 44 minutes after the scheduled time on the fourth day.

Carl Hooper enjoyed a splendid series, claiming 10 wickets and hitting his highest Test score, 178 not out, at Antigua. (David Munden/ Sports-Line)

THIRD TEST MATCH – WEST INDIES *v.* PAKISTAN
1, 2, 4, 5 and 6 May 1993 at Recreation Ground, Antigua

WEST INDIES

	FIRST INNINGS			SECOND INNINGS	
D.L. Haynes	c Rashid, b Nadim	23	not out		64
P.V. Simmons	c Wasim, b Rehman	28	b Waqar Younis		17
R.B. Richardson (capt)	c Wasim, b Waqar	52	lbw, b Waqar Younis		0
B.C. Lara	st Rashid, b Nadim	44	lbw, b Waqar Younis		19
K.L.T. Arthurton	lbw, b Waqar Younis	30	lbw, b Waqar Younis		0
C.L. Hooper	not out	178	not out		29
*J.R. Murray	lbw, b Waqar Younis	4			
C.E.L. Ambrose	lbw, b Wasim Akram	1			
A.C. Cummins	lbw, b Waqar Younis	14			
W.K.M. Benjamin	c Wasim, b Waqar	12			
C.A. Walsh	c Asif Mujtaba, b Wasim	30			
Extras	lb 6, nb 16	22	b 8, lb 5, nb 11		24
		—			—
		438	(for 4 wickets)		153

PAKISTAN

	FIRST INNINGS	
Ramiz Raja	c Murray, b Walsh	0
Shakeel Ahmed	lbw, b Ambrose	0
Asif Mujtaba	c Haynes, b Hooper	59
Javed Miandad	lbw, b Benjamin	31
Basit Ali	b Cummins	56
Inzamam-ul-Haq	c Haynes, b Cummins	123
*Rashid Latif	lbw, b Cummins	2
Wasim Akram (capt)	c Hooper, b Benjamin	9
Waqar Younis	c Hooper, b Benjamin	4
Nadim Khan	c Murray, b Cummins	25
Ata-ur-Rehman	not out	1
Extras	lb 6, nb 10	16
		—
		326

	O	M	R	W	O	M	R	W
Wasim Akram	26.2	5	108	2	10	2	30	–
Waqar Younis	28	4	104	5	11	1	23	4
Ata-ur-Rehman	17	3	66	1	9	1	24	–
Nadim Khan	38	5	147	2	14	–	48	–
Asif Mujtaba	1	–	7	–	4	1	9	–
Basit Ali					1	–	6	–

	O	M	R	W
Ambrose	23	9	40	1
Walsh	19	5	58	1
Benjamin	20	4	53	3
Cummins	20	4	54	4
Hooper	28	2	98	1
Simmons	5	–	17	–

FALL OF WICKETS
1–35, 2–77, 3–153, 4–159, 5–218, 6–241, 7–252, 8–312, 9–332
1–36, 2–36, 3–68, 4–68

FALL OF WICKETS
1–0, 2–4, 3–85, 4–108, 5–196, 6–206, 7–221, 8–227, 9–323

Umpires: S.U. Bucknor & H.D. Bird (sub – C. Mack)

Match drawn

Man of the Series – Desmond Haynes, 402 runs, average 134, on his way to another century in Barbados. (Ben Radford/Allsport)

Simmons and Haynes took the score to 36, at which point Waqar Younis joined the attack and dismissed Simmons and Richardson with successive deliveries. He later accounted for Lara and Arthurton with successive deliveries and finished with 4 for 20 in an eight-over spell. This was the Waqar who had tormented England and New Zealand (and everybody else), rather than the shadow who had performed in the first two Tests in the Caribbean.

Rain ended play and, it transpired, the match, for umpire Bird and the captains decreed the pitch too wet for any play to commence on the fifth day.

Inzamam-ul-Haq and Waqar Younis had lifted Pakistan's spirits towards the end but, in truth, West Indies had commanded the series from start to finish, with the visitors looking a rank bad side on occasions. Captaincy had seemed to deprive Wasim Akram of his rhythm, and one felt that the men mainly responsible for Pakistan's poor showing were those back in Pakistan itself.

West Indies had begun the year feeling their way: they ended it supreme again among cricket-playing nations.

TEST MATCH AVERAGES – WEST INDIES v. PAKISTAN

WEST INDIES BATTING

	M	Inns	NO	Runs	HS	Av	100s	50s
D.L. Haynes	3	6	3	402	143*	134.00	2	1
C.L. Hooper	3	5	2	231	178*	77.00	1	–
B.C. Lara	3	5	–	216	96	43.20	–	2
P.V. Simmons	3	6	1	189	87	37.80	–	1
R.B. Richardson	3	5	–	158	68	31.60	–	2
K.L.T. Arthurton	3	5	–	90	56	18.00	–	1
A.C. Cummins	2	3	1	28	14*	14.00	–	–
J.R. Murray	3	4	–	39	35	9.75	–	–
C.A. Walsh	3	4	–	39	30	9.75	–	–
C.E.L. Ambrose	3	4	1	22	12*	7.33	–	–
I.R. Bishop	2	3	–	18	11	6.00	–	–
W.K.M. Benjamin	2	2	–	12	12	6.00	–	–

WEST INDIES BOWLING

	Overs	Mds	Runs	Wkts	Av	Best	10/m	5/inn
C.A. Walsh	80	19	207	12	17.25	4-56	–	–
W.K.M. Benjamin	56	16	138	8	17.25	3-30	–	–
I.R. Bishop	46.5	14	127	7	18.14	5-43	–	1
A.C. Cummins	30	5	89	4	22.25	4-54	–	–
C.E.L. Ambrose	95	33	208	9	23.11	4-34	–	–
C.L. Hooper	83.2	11	281	10	28.10	5-40	–	1
P.V. Simmons	6	–	22	–	–	–	–	–

WEST INDIES FIELDING FIGURES
9 – J.R. Murray (ct 8/st 1); 4 – R.B. Richardson and C.L. Hooper; 3 – D.L. Haynes and B.C. Lara; 2 – P.V. Simmons, K.L.T. Arthurton and W.K.M. Benjamin; 1 – I.R. Bishop and C.E.L. Ambrose

PAKISTAN BATTING

	M	Inns	NO	Runs	HS	Av	100s	50s
Basit Ali	3	5	1	222	92*	55.50	–	2
Inzamam-ul-Haq	3	5	–	172	123	34.40	1	–
Asif Mujtaba	3	5	–	143	59	28.60	–	1
Javed Miandad	3	5	–	120	43	24.00	–	–
Aamir Sohail	2	4	–	84	55	21.00	–	1
Ramiz Raja	3	5	–	82	37	16.40	–	–
Ata-ur-Rehman	3	5	2	36	19	12.00	–	–
Waqar Younis	3	5	–	50	29	10.00	–	–
Wasim Akram	3	5	–	44	28	8.80	–	–
Moin Khan	2	4	–	35	18	8.75	–	–

Played in one Test: Mushtaq Ahmed 3 & 12*; Aamir Nazir 1 & 6*; Shakeel Ahmed 0; Rashid Latif 2; Nadim Khan 25

PAKISTAN BOWLING

	Overs	Mds	Runs	Wkts	Av	Best	10/m	5/inn
Waqar Younis	98.5	12	384	19	20.31	5-104	–	1
Aamir Sohail	9	2	44	2	22.00	1-14	–	–
Wasim Akram	108.1	14	358	9	39.77	4-75	–	–
Aamir Nazir	23	1	90	2	45.00	2-79	–	–
Ata-ur-Rehman	75	6	303	6	50.50	3-28	–	–
Mushtaq Ahmed	21	2	66	1	66.00	1-21	–	–
Asif Mujtaba	18	2	89	1	89.00	1-43	–	–
Nadim Khan	52	5	195	2	97.50	2-147	–	–

Bowled in one innings – Basit Ali 1-0-6-0

PAKISTAN FIELDING FIGURES
8 – Moin Khan (ct 7/st 1); 4 – Wasim Akram; 2 – Rashid Latif (ct 1/st 1) and Asif Mujtaba; 1 – Aamir Sohail, Inzamam-ul-Haq and Waqar Younis

---

FIRST-CLASS AVERAGES

BATTING

	M	Inns	NO	Runs	HS	Av	100s	50s
D.L. Haynes	3	6	3	402	143*	134.00	2	1
R.I.C. Holder	6	9	1	654	162*	81.75	4	–
C.L. Hooper	3	5	2	231	178*	77.00	1	–
P.J.L. Dujon	6	9	3	454	163*	75.66	2	1
C.B. Lambert	5	7	1	441	263*	73.50	1	2
R.D. Jacobs	6	11	3	523	119*	65.37	3	2
A.C.H. Walsh	5	10	1	408	92	45.33	–	4
S. Chanderpaul	7	10	2	356	140*	44.50	1	2
L.L. Lawrence	5	9	1	348	74	43.50	–	2
Sudesh Dhaniram	5	7	–	304	131	43.42	1	1
B.C. Lara	3	5	–	216	96	43.20	–	2
R.A. Harper	5	7	1	257	94	42.83	–	2
P.A. Wallace	6	10	–	428	96	42.80	–	3
P.V. Simmons	3	6	1	189	87	37.80	–	1
D.A. Joseph	6	10	1	317	98	35.22	–	3
C.A. Davidson	4	7	–	242	86	34.57	–	3
S.C. Williams	6	11	–	370	99	33.63	–	2
A.F.G. Griffith	4	7	1	200	63	33.33	–	1
R.G. Samuels	7	13	1	399	60	33.25	–	2
R.B. Richardson	3	5	–	158	68	31.60	–	2
K.A. Williams	5	9	–	276	113	30.66	2	–
A.H. Gray	4	7	1	183	69	30.50	–	1
D.S. Morgan	6	11	1	291	85	29.10	–	2
L.R. Williams	5	9	2	196	65	28.00	–	2
K.L.T. Arthurton	4	6	–	164	74	27.33	–	1
H.R. Waldron	6	10	–	256	67	25.60	–	2
K.F. Semple	5	6	1	128	50*	25.60	–	1
Sunil Dhaniram	5	5	1	101	43	25.25	–	–
U. Pope	5	8	1	172	62	24.57	–	1
C.O. Browne	6	10	–	214	71	23.77	–	1
L.A. Harrigan	5	10	–	232	57	23.20	–	2
N.O. Perry	4	6	1	112	76	22.40	–	1
R.A. Marshall	5	8	–	170	79	21.25	–	1
R.A.M. Smith	5	9	–	187	58	20.77	–	1
V.C. Drakes	4	6	–	123	49	20.50	–	–
W.K.M. Benjamin	7	11	1	204	37*	20.40	–	–
K. Mason	5	9	–	182	43	20.22	–	–
D. Williams	3	5	–	100	36	20.00	–	–
R. Mahabir	4	7	–	124	40	17.71	–	–
S.L. Mahon	5	8	–	136	42	17.00	–	–
J. Eugene	6	11	1	160	44*	16.00	–	–
R.C. Haynes	6	8	1	110	32	15.71	–	–
H.A.G. Anthony	6	11	–	136	32	12.36	–	–
L.L. Harris	5	10	–	115	51	11.50	–	1

(S.L. Campbell: one match – 113 & 4)
(Qualification – 100 runs, average 10.00)

BOWLING

	Overs	Mds	Runs	Wkts	Av	Best	10/m	5/inn
R.A. Harper	144.2	39	243	18	13.50	6-24	–	1
B. St A. Browne	135.4	40	360	26	13.84	6-51	–	2
C.G. Belgrave	62	11	166	11	15.09	3-23	–	–
N.O. Perry	146.3	49	262	17	15.41	5-54	–	1
C.G. Butts	228	61	525	34	15.44	7-40	–	2
C.A. Walsh	80	19	207	12	17.25	4-56	–	–
W.K.M. Benjamin	209.2	55	494	28	17.64	7-64	–	1
V.C. Drakes	81	14	229	11	20.81	4-60	–	–
S.M. Skeete	79.4	20	220	10	22.00	4-19	–	–
F.A. Rose	198.3	39	632	27	23.40	5-65	–	1
W.D. Phillip	176.2	51	402	17	23.64	5-54	1	2
L.R. Williams	137.4	26	410	17	24.11	4-66	–	–
V.D. Walcott	136.5	36	368	15	24.53	3-35	–	–
O.D. Gibson	120.4	18	384	15	24.60	5-48	–	1
H.A.G. Anthony	166.1	37	448	17	26.35	6-22	–	1
R.A. Marshall	189.2	44	372	14	26.57	6-41	–	1
C.E. Cuffy	160.4	30	467	17	27.47	5-35	–	1
C.L. Hooper	83.2	11	281	10	28.10	5-40	–	1
E.C. Antoine	180.1	26	554	19	29.15	5-85	–	1
A.H. Gray	142.5	29	382	13	29.38	4-78	–	–
R.N. Lewis	113.4	22	296	10	29.60	3-42	–	–
C.A. Davis	137.5	23	460	15	30.66	4-71	–	–
V.A. Walsh	163.3	30	469	15	31.26	3-31	–	–
S. Chanderpaul	119.5	22	411	11	37.36	4-48	–	–
R. Dhanraj	267.2	51	648	17	38.11	4-19	–	–
R.C. Haynes	228.2	48	508	12	42.33	4-33	–	–

(Qualification – 10 wickets)

LEADING FIELDERS
28 – C.O. Browne (ct 24/st 4); 20 – R.D. Jacobs (ct 18/st 2); 16 – P.J.L. Dujon (ct 13/st 3); 15 – K.A. Wong (ct 11/st 4); 13 – U. Pope (ct 10/st 3); 9 – R.A. Harper and J.R. Murray (ct 8/st 1); 8 – S. Chanderpaul, C.B. Lambert and K.F. Semple

SECTION J
England
Benson and Hedges Cup
Britannic Assurance County Championship
AXA Equity & Law Sunday League
Australia tour, Tetley Bitter Challenge, Texaco Trophy
England *v.* Australia, the Ashes Test series, sponsored by Cornhill Insurance
NatWest Trophy
Limited-over form charts
First-class form charts
First-class averages

The Australians eager in the field in the opening first-class match of their tour, at Worcester. They were to prove to be too strong a combination for England. (Adrian Murrell/Allsport)

Having been bewitched, bothered and bewildered by spin in India and Sri Lanka, the England side returned home to a barrage of criticism concerning ability, attitude, temperament and – mainly, it seemed – dress and facial hair. It was refreshing for the present writer, speaking alongside Bob Bennett at a dinner in Manchester, to hear the England manager say that India had outplayed England in every department of the game, that England had played well below their potential, and that the Indian side was, he believed, the best that that nation had put into the Test arena. Would that there were always such honest appraisal.

Some players had returned from the tour with their reputations in tatters; others, Hick and Lewis among them, had given glimpses of future Test glory. All returned to an England season which offered a new structure of four-day championship cricket, a knock-out Benson and Hedges Cup and a 50-over coloured-clothing knock-about on Sundays.

The close season had seen its usual quota of transfers. Among them were Lefebvre's movement from Somerset to Glamorgan; Headley leaving Middlesex for Kent and Feltham leaving Surrey for Middlesex; Broad returning from Nottinghamshire to Gloucestershire; and Sussex signing Athey from Gloucestershire and Hemmings from Nottinghamshire.

Gloucestershire seemed particularly hard hit. They had not wanted to lose Athey and, on the eve of the season, they suffered a great blow when David Lawrence, working hard to regain full fitness, suffered another serious knee injury.

Viv Richards had stated that this would be his last season and, as the players gathered for pre-season training, Ian Botham announced that he, too, would be retiring from first-class cricket at the end of the year, but he still hoped to be considered for England against Australia.

The old enemy arrived and met the media at a delightful reception arranged by their sponsors, Castlemaine XXXX. There was a balance of youth and experience. All looked frighteningly fit and eager. The traumas of India and Sri Lanka began to fade in the memory, and we were ready to take on the Aussies and try the new format of cricket in England.

John Morris hit the season's first century, 136 for Derbyshire against Cambridge University. Morris enjoyed a fine season, helping Derbyshire to win the Benson and Hedges Cup and hitting the first double century of his career. (Alan Cozzi)

Under the Murray report, the Universities of Oxford and Cambridge had retained their first-class status and, as is usual, they hosted the opening matches. At Fenner's, John Morris hit the first century of the season, and he was quickly followed by Tim O'Gorman. In a match which was little more than batting practice, John Crawley gave more evidence of his immense talent.

Oxford University flattered to deceive. A varied attack bowled out Durham for 191 in 83 overs, but jubilation was short-lived as Oxford were reduced to 34 for 5 by the close of the first day. Durham showed more confidence in their second innings, Fowler making his first fifty for his new county. Set 357 to win in just under five hours, Oxford finished on a commendable 226 for 6, Keey and Mac-Millan adding 127 for the fourth wicket.

14, 15 and 16 April *at Cambridge*

Derbyshire 380 for 5 dec. (J.E. Morris 136, T.J.G. O'Gorman 130 not out, D. G. Cork 56) and 137 for 2 dec. (P.D. Bowler 73 not out)

Cambridge University 140 (J.P. Crawley 73) and 98 for 3

Match drawn

at Oxford

Durham 191 and 251 for 7 dec. (G. Fowler 50, M. Jeh 4 for 46)

Oxford University 86 and 226 for 6 (C.L. Keey 70, G.I. MacMillan 51)

Match drawn

17, 18 and 19 April *at Cambridge*

Yorkshire 270 for 3 dec. (A.A. Metcalfe 133 not out, S.A. Kellett 53) and 181 for 4 dec. (D. Byas 90)

Cambridge University 137 (J.D. Batty 5 for 36) and 62 for 0

Match drawn

17, 19 and 20 April *at Oxford*

Lancashire 309 for 4 dec. (M.A. Atherton 107, N.J. Speak 87) and 194 for 6 dec. (G.D. Lloyd 100 not out)

Oxford University 194 (R.R. Montgomerie 65, P.J. Martin 4 for 42) and 164 for 3 (R.R. Montgomerie 75 not out)

Match drawn

At Fenner's, Ashley Metcalfe scored his first century for two years. Byas also enjoyed a lengthy stay at the wicket, and Batty, the young off-spinner, indicated an increasing maturity. Oxford University gained another honourable draw in spite of their captain, Gallian, suffering a damaged thumb and being unable to bat. Atherton, Lloyd and Speak – all England contenders – made their mark for Lancashire.

21, 22 and 23 April *at Cambridge*

Kent 300 for 6 dec. (N.J. Llong 116 not out, S.A. Marsh 57)
Cambridge University 142 (C. Penn 4 for 12) and 124 (R.P. Davis 5 for 26)

Kent won by an innings and 34 runs

at Oxford

Glamorgan 463 for 2 dec. (M.P. Maynard 110 not out, I.V.A. Richards 109 not out, H. Morris 109 retired hurt, A. Dale 67) and 115 for 3 (P.A. Cottey 60)
Oxford University 99

Match drawn

22, 23, 24 and 25 April *at Chelmsford*

Essex 394 (N. Hussain 118, G.A. Gooch 88, J.P. Taylor 4 for 99) and 75 for 1
England 'A' 174 (D.G. Cork 52, P.M. Such 5 for 26) and 294 (G.D. Lloyd 95, M.N. Lathwell 84, P.M. Such 6 for 98)

Essex won by 9 wickets

Kent, fresh from a successful tour of Zimbabwe, began badly at Cambridge and lost five wickets for 107, but they were rallied by the left-hander Nigel Llong who hit a maiden first-class century. Marsh gave him able support and led the Kent side to a competent victory.

Glamorgan ravaged Oxford on the opening day in The Parks. Morris and Dale added 142 in 40 overs for the second wicket, but Morris, the Glamorgan captain, having hit a most accomplished century, retired with a knee injury after the tea interval. This allowed Viv Richards to add 233 in 33 overs of spectacular stroke-play with Matthew Maynard. Oxford were skittled out on the second day, but rain prevented play on the third.

The match between the County Champions and the England 'A' side was played at Chelmsford rather than at Lord's, as had been the tradition. There was a prize of £1,500 for the winners of the match, and the Tetley Bitter Shield. Moxon asked Essex to bat first when he won the toss, but Gooch and Stephenson began with a stand of 89, and Gooch dominated a second-wicket stand of 69 with Lewis. By the end of the day, Essex were 306 for 7. Nasser Hussain completed an excellent century on the second day and reminded the England selectors that he was seen as a key batsman in future Test sides only a few years ago. The last four Essex wickets produced 159 runs, and Ilott, Such and Childs – all England contenders – embarrassed the young pretenders to the extent that they closed on 137 for 8. An aggressive and impressive innings from Lath-

A maiden century for Nigel Llong of Kent. Llong followed his 116 not out against Cambridge University with a sparkling hundred against Middlesex at Lord's. (Tom Morris)

well and a rather fortunate knock by Lloyd helped restore some pride after England 'A' had been forced to follow-on, but there was no escape from defeat. Rain delayed the start until after lunch on the Sunday, but Essex still won with 21 overs to spare after Peter Such had claimed a 10-wicket haul in a match for the first time.

 BENSON AND HEDGES CUP

PRELIMINARY ROUND

27 April *at Bristol*

Gloucestershire 198 for 7 (B.C. Broad 58)
Derbyshire 198 for 5 (P.D. Bowler 92)

Derbyshire won on losing fewer wickets with scores equal
(Gold Award – P.D. Bowler)

at Canterbury

Glamorgan 236 for 7 (M.P. Maynard 89)
Kent 132 (S.R. Barwick 4 for 15)

Glamorgan won by 104 runs
(Gold Award – M.P. Maynard)

at Forfar

Scotland 106 for 8 (M.C. Ilott 5 for 21)
Essex 107 for 1 (J.P. Stephenson 50 not out)

Essex won by 9 wickets
(Gold Award – M.C. Ilott)

at Southampton

Combined Universities 177 for 7 (J.N. Snape 52)

Hampshire 178 for 1 (T.C. Middleton 91 not out)

Hampshire won by 9 wickets

(Gold Award – T.C. Middleton)

28 April *at Hartlepool*

Minor Counties 156 for 8

Durham 157 for 4

Durham won by 6 wickets

(Gold Award – A.R. Fothergill)

With the Benson and Hedges Cup transformed into a straight knock-out competition, seven first-class counties found themselves faced with the possibility of being ousted from a major and most lucrative tournament before the end of April, before the main season had, in fact, begun. It transpired that the counties so threatened were the first seven of the 18 in alphabetical order.

At Bristol, Chris Broad returned to the county he had left 10 years earlier and hit 58 as he and Scott, 44, added 94 for the second wicket, but both were out in quick succession and the initiative was lost. Gloucestershire had little hope of defending their total of 198 when Barnett and Bowler began the Derbyshire reply with a stand of 101 in 29 overs. Kevin Cooper, the former Nottinghamshire medium-pacer, bowled frugally and dismissed Morris as three Derbyshire wickets went down for 16 runs. Gloucestershire never appeared to be in contention, but when O'Gorman was run out for 34, 13 were needed from 11 balls. Eventually, it came down to one off the last delivery, and Krikken drove the ball through the on-side to level the scores and win the match.

Glamorgan were put in to bat at Canterbury and they were forced to defend doggedly in the opening stages as Igglesden and McCague exploited early movement. James mis-hooked in the fourth over and was caught and bowled, and the first boundary did not come until the 17th over. To the first ball of the next over – Fleming's first – Dale was leg before, and Glamorgan were 44 for 2. It was now that the match changed course. Morris batted with intelligence and patience, and in 20 overs he and Maynard added 91. If Maynard offered the spectacular with his exciting 89 on a difficult wicket, Morris played the innings of 44, spread over 38 overs, without which none of the successes later in the match would have been possible. Glamorgan's 236 was a highly creditable performance on a pitch which had offered batsmen no encouragement. If their batting had been commendable, Glamorgan's out-cricket was exhilarating. Ward was splendidly caught at slip by Maynard in the third over with only one scored, the bowler being the economic Lefebvre. Kent found runs very hard to score against Watkin's medium pace, Croft's admirable off-breaks and the off-cutters of Steve Barwick who bowled Taylor, had Llong caught and Fleming brilliantly stumped by Metson off a leg-side wide, a wicket which virtually ended the contest.

Scotland batted for 55 painful overs to score 106 against Essex for whom Mark Ilott took five wickets in a Benson and Hedges match for the first time and won his first Gold Award. Essex scored the winning runs off the third ball of the 29th over.

It took Hampshire 50 overs to beat Combined Universities whose two practice matches had been washed out. Snape of Durham University and Northamptonshire batted extremely well before being caught by Robin Smith, who then tumbled into advertising boards and gashed his forehead. The injury needed 20 stitches. Middleton won his first Gold Award.

No play was possible on the Tuesday at Hartlepool, and Durham scrambled home with seven balls to spare when Botham hit Arnold over square-leg for six. The Gold Award went to wicket-keeper Andy Fothergill who made four catches and a stumping.

So ended the *preliminary* round of the Benson and Hedges Cup, but surely no side should exit from such an important competition so early in the season.

29, 30 April, 1 and 2 May *at Cardiff*

Glamorgan 331 (S.P. James 78, R.D.B. Croft 60, E.E. Hemmings 4 for 69) and 362 for 5 dec. (A. Dale 81, P.A. Cottey 68 not out, S.P. James 61, M.P. Maynard 52)

Sussex 309 (A.P. Wells 120, S.L. Watkin 5 for 87) and 110 (R.D.B. Croft 4 for 55)

Glamorgan won by 274 runs

Glamorgan 20 pts., Sussex 5 pts.

at Bristol

Gloucestershire 299 (B.C. Broad 58, A.R.C. Fraser 4 for 76) and 95 (J.E. Emburey 4 for 15, P.C.R. Tufnell 4 for 33)

Middlesex 180 (K.E. Cooper 4 for 33, M.J. Gerrard 4 for 50) and 216 for 6 (M.R. Ramprakash 75)

Middlesex won by 4 wickets

Middlesex 20 pts., Gloucestershire 6 pts.

at Southampton

Somerset 500 for 6 dec. (N.D. Burns 102 not out, M.N. Lathwell 99, R.J. Harden 97, N.A. Folland 81, G.D. Rose 64)

Hampshire 156 (M.C.J. Nicholas 76, A.R. Caddick 6 for 48) and 196 (A.R. Caddick 4 for 44)

Somerset won by an innings and 148 runs

Somerset 24 pts., Hampshire 2 pts.

at Leicester

Surrey 245 (D.J. Bicknell 50, A.R.K. Pierson 4 for 57) and 315 (A.J. Stewart 109, A.R.K. Pierson 5 for 124)

Leicestershire 255 (N.E. Briers 79) and 216 (T.J. Boon 91, M.P. Bicknell 4 for 53)

Surrey won by 89 runs

Surrey 21 pts., Leicestershire 6 pts.

Steve Barwick took 4 for 15 in an outstanding spell of bowling as Glamorgan beat Kent in the preliminary round of the Benson and Hedges Cup. (Tom Morris)

at Trent Bridge

Worcestershire 203 and 325 for 8 dec. (T.S. Curtis 113, G.W. Mike 5 for 65)

Nottinghamshire 233 and 295 (D.W. Randall 98, C.L. Cairns 68, P.J. Newport 6 for 63)

Match tied

Nottinghamshire 13 pts., Worcestershire 13 pts.

at Edgbaston

Warwickshire 345 (T.L. Penney 68, K.M. Curran 4 for 64) and 263 for 5 dec. (D.A. Reeve 87 not out, T.L. Penney 65, N.M.K. Smith 51 not out)

Northamptonshire 240 (N.A. Felton 93) and 171 (M.B. Loye 63, A. Fordham 55, N.M.K. Smith 5 for 81)

Warwickshire won by 197 runs

Warwickshire 22 pts., Northamptonshire 5 pts.

29, 30 April, 1 and 3 May *at Leeds*

Yorkshire 319 (R.J. Blakey 95, S.A. Kellett 62, A.A. Barnett 5 for 83) and 258 (M.D. Moxon 91, P.J. Martin 5 for 35)

Lancashire 200 (G.D. Lloyd 116) and 261 (G.D. Lloyd 88, R.D. Stemp 6 for 92)

Yorkshire won by 116 runs

30 April *at Radlett*

Australians 292 for 3 (M.L. Hayden 151, M.A. Taylor 53)
England Amateur XI 198

Australians won by 94 runs

The Britannic Assurance County Championship began in kindly weather, and each of the six matches produced a result. If this offered a positive recommendation for four-day cricket, the rate of scoring in some matches did not. An exception was at Cardiff where James and Morris began with a partnership of 110, but then the home side lost their way against the combined spin of Hemmings and Salisbury, and it was left to Croft to rally the later order and claim the third batting point. In spite of Alan Wells' century, Sussex could not match Glamorgan's scoring rate. They scored only 262 on the second day, and finally surrendered 22 runs in arrears on the first innings. Steve Watkin captured five of the last six wickets. Glamorgan's positive and fresh approach to the game was exemplified by their second-innings batting. They scored at nearly four runs an over, and four batsmen hit fifties. Morris was able to declare and set Sussex a target of 385 while leaving his bowlers a day in which to bowl out the visitors. On a wearing pitch, Sussex lost Lenham in the opening over and struggled against a lively and varied attack. Steve Barwick took 2 for 7 in 21 overs, 16 of them maidens; Croft claimed four wickets to add to his 44 not out; and Watkin destroyed the middle order with three wickets in seven balls. Glamorgan looked a very exciting side.

At Bristol, Angus Fraser returned his best figures for two years, but Kevin Cooper, giving further signs of his rejuvenation, and Martin Gerrard, with his best performance in a championship match, bowled Gloucestershire to a 119-run lead over Middlesex. The combined spin of Emburey and Tufnell brought about a familar Gloucestershire story in the second innings, however, and in spite of the efforts of Cooper who helped reduce Middlesex to 156 for 6, Brown and Feltham steered the visitors to victory.

There were sensations at Southampton. Batting first, Somerset reached 343 for 5 on the first day. Both Lathwell and Harden had fallen within touching distance of their centuries, but on the second day, wicket-keeper Neil Burns hit the first championship hundred of the season, and Tavaré declared when his side reached 500. This was followed by a total change in the balance of bat over ball as, with an opening spell of four wickets for three runs in the half-hour after lunch, Andrew Caddick reduced Hampshire to 5 for 5. Nicholas and Aymes saved greater embarrassment with a stand of 61, and Hampshire ended the day on 140 for 8. There was to be no reprieve, however. Forced to follow-on on the Saturday, Hampshire lost their last four second-innings wickets for six runs, Caddick finished with match figures of 10 for 92, and the game was over in three days.

Surrey had a rather gruelling first day at Grace Road where Adrian Pierson, the Leicestershire off-spinner formerly with Warwickshire, sent down 32 overs to take 4 for 57. The home county lost Boon before the close, and slipped to 98 for 5 on the second day before Briers found

Four catches, a stumping and the Gold Award for Andy Fothergill as Durham beat Minor Counties in the Benson and Hedges Cup. (David Munden/Sports-Line)

defensive bowling of Illingworth curbed Randall and Crawley, but Cairns hit 68 off 92 balls and shared a stand of 56 with Lewis. The last over arrived with five needed and the last pair together. Afford, not noted for his batting, hit two off the first ball and one off the fifth. Pick then hit Newport to deep square-leg and was run out by Seymour's fine throw as he attempted what would have been the winning run.

Warwickshire began the season looking short of a top-class batsman, and Northamptonshire began it without Curtly Ambrose. There was competence and dedication in Warwickshire's first innings rather than flare, but Northamptonshire's more illustrious batsmen could not match them. Felton finished the second day on 90 not out, but added only three the following morning, and Warwickshire took a lead of 105 on the first innings. Reeve inspired his side to capitalise on this advantage, and he was able to set Northamptonshire a target of 369. Their interest in this challenge ended quickly when Donald and Small humbled them to 11 for 3. Loye hit his maiden first-class fifty, but Neil Smith's off-spin took the home side to a surprisingly easy win.

In a first-class friendly match, Lancashire enjoyed some excellent individual performances from Martin, who took five wickets in an innings for the first time, and from Lloyd, who continued his fine early-season form, but Stemp had an equally good match for Yorkshire who won comfortably. The Australians, too, won comfortably, with Hayden hitting 151 off 189 balls at the lovely setting in Radlett.

an able partner in Potter. Wells and Parsons also displayed determination and, with the aid of 41 extras, Leicestershire took a first-innings lead of 10. Alec Stewart reached a century in 4½ hours on the Saturday, but the batting was again rather grim, with Pierson producing another long, economic spell. His 5 for 124 in the second innings came from 50 overs. Needing 306 to win, Leicestershire reached 138 before losing their second wicket, and Kendrick, the left-arm spinner, could not produce the form that Pierson and Potter had shown. At tea, with eight wickets standing, Leicestershire needed 136 off 33 overs, but the dismissal of Boon brought about a collapse, and Surrey won with 6.5 overs to spare when Martin Bicknell, who had bowled with fire and passion, held a high catch at slip to account for Mullally.

The dourest of contests at Trent Bridge came to an unexpectedly exciting climax on the final day. The beginning suggested no joy as Worcestershire made 203 in 104 overs on the first day and, on the second, Nottinghamshire showed no more enterprise in scoring 233 off 98.3 overs. In the first 90 minutes of the third day, Curtis and Philip Weston added 39 at a rate of 1.39 runs an over, but the opening stand was eventually worth 104. Greg Mike then took three wickets in 27 balls, but Worcestershire recovered, scored more freely, and Curtis was finally out having hit 113 off 314 balls. His declaration on the Sunday left the home county a target of 296 in 87 overs. Randall and Pollard began with 63 off 60 balls, but Newport then dismissed Pollard and Robinson in the same over. The

A very great cricketer in the last weeks of his career. Ian Botham leaves the field at Arundel after batting for Lavinia, Duchess of Norfolk's XI against the Australians. (David Munden/Sports-Line)

1, 2 and **3 May** *at Cambridge*

Essex 323 (N. Hussain 111, G.A. Gooch 105 retired) and 228 for 4 dec. (N.V. Knight 94, P.J. Prichard 54)
Cambridge University 105 (J.P. Crawley 63) and 145 for 3 (J.P. Crawley 60)

Match drawn

2 May *at Arundel*

Australians 203 for 9 (S.R. Waugh 59, D.W. Headley 5 for 51)
Duchess of Norfolk's XI 196 (P.W.G. Parker 77, M.E. Waugh 5 for 32)

Australians won by 7 runs

3 May *at Lord's*

Australians 243 for 5 (M.L. Hayden 122, D.R. Martyn 66)
Middlesex 174

Australians won by 69 runs

Essex's visit to Fenner's would not usually be deserving of comment but, in 1993, it was the scene of Graham Gooch's *official* 100th hundred. Many – Gooch included – felt that he had reached the landmark in India, but the ICC's incomprehensible decision to rob him of a century scored in South Africa – a political, not a cricketing decision – left him on 99 at the start of the England season. Gooch made his point against Cambridge, hitting a six to reach his century then tucking his bat under his arm and walking off immediately, mission accomplished. Hussain also hit a century, his second of the season, and John Crawley impressed.

The Australians won the annual party match at Arundel and also beat Middlesex in a 55-over game the following day. Hayden hit his second century in four days to establish an early claim for a Test place, but most interest centred on Gatting who audibly vented his rage at Fraser after the bowler had conceded 35 runs in his first four overs and then, having been run out, put his arm through a pane of glass and sustained an injury which necessitated several stitches and kept him out of the game for nearly three weeks.

5, 6 and **7 May** *at Worcester*

Australians 262 (D.C. Boon 108) and 287 for 5 (D.C. Boon 106, M.L. Hayden 96)
Worcestershire 90 and 458 for 4 dec. (G.A. Hick 187, S.R. Lampitt 68 not out, T.S. Curtis 67, A.C.H. Seymour 54 not out)

Australians won by 5 wickets

at Cambridge

Glamorgan 298 for 8 dec. (R.D.B. Croft 107, H. Morris 51) and 187 for 5 dec.
Cambridge University 172 (R. Cake 57 not out, S.L. Watkin 4 for 36) and 153 for 5

Match drawn

at Oxford

Hampshire 169 (M.C.J. Nicholas 62, M. Jeh 5 for 63) and 236 for 2 dec. (V.P. Terry 117 retired, T.C. Middleton 63)
Oxford University 230 for 9 dec. (J.E.R. Gallian 83) and 166 for 8 (H. Malik 64 not out)

Match drawn

The Australians began their first-class matches of the 1993 tour in the traditional manner, at Worcester. Taylor led the side, won the toss and, on a pitch where the ball darted and seamed, the visitors were bowled out for 262 on the opening day. That they reached this total was due entirely to a fine century from the ever-reliable David Boon. Worcestershire lost Curtis before the close and, on the second day, they were bowled out for 90 by an attack that was never below medium pace. Following-on 172 runs behind, the county were 21 for 1 at lunch, and an early end looked most probable. By the close, however, Graeme Hick had completely changed the mood of the game. He reached a hundred off 136 balls and was unbeaten on 161 by the end of the day, having hit 2 sixes and 24 fours. He added two more sixes on the last morning before falling to Holdsworth, and Curtis' declaration left the Australians 55 overs in which to score 287 runs. Again it was Boon who gave the Australian innings its backbone and impetus. He hit 2 sixes and 11 fours in a flawless hundred off 97 balls, and with the aggressive Hayden he added 181 for the second wicket. Newport's economic bowling made the Australian task more difficult, and the last over arrived with 12 runs needed. The fifth ball of Illingworth's over was hit over long-off for six by Steve Waugh, and the Australians had won their first £2,000 from the Tetley Bitter Challenge.

Robert Croft, the best off-spinner in England in the opinion of many, hit a maiden first-class century in the drawn match at Cambridge while Hampshire endured another batting nightmare at Oxford. They were bowled out for 169, having been 27 for 4 at one time. Pace bowler Michael Jeh, having arrived at the University via Sri Lanka and Queensland, returned a career best 5 for 63. Terry put matters to rights in the second innings and, with Nicholas injured, he set Oxford a target of 176 in 43 overs. In spite of Malik's highest score, they fell short, a lack of experience helping to produce four run outs.

6, 7, 8 and **10 May** *at Chelmsford*

Yorkshire 397 (D. Byas 156, S.A. Kellett 52, M.C. Ilott 4 for 79) and 307 (R.J. Blakey 74, A.P. Grayson 55, D. Byas 50)
Essex 250 (M.A. Garnham 53) and 215 (M.A. Garnham 58, G.A. Gooch 50, P.W. Jarvis 4 for 76)

Yorkshire won by 239 runs
Yorkshire 24 pts., Essex 6 pts.

at Old Trafford

Durham 515 for 9 dec. (P.W.G. Parker 123, P. Bainbridge 79, W. Larkins 76, J.A. Daley 50) and 83 (M. Watkinson 5 for 12, A.A. Barnett 5 for 36)

Lancashire 442 (M.A. Atherton 137, J. Wood 4 for 106, D.A. Graveney 4 for 131) and 157 for 4

Lancashire won by 6 wickets

Lancashire 21 pts., Durham 8 pts.

at Leicester

Leicestershire 219 (N.E. Briers 53) and 203 (J.J. Whitaker 93)

Nottinghamshire 280 (R.T. Robinson 70, B.N. French 54, L. Potter 5 for 45) and 143 for 2 (P.R. Pollard 51 not out)

Nottinghamshire won by 8 wickets

Nottinghamshire 22 pts., Leicestershire 5 pts.

at Lord's

Kent 265 (M.R. Benson 57, M.V. Fleming 57, P.C.R. Tufnell 4 for 64) and 392 for 8 dec. (N.J. Llong 108, M.R. Benson 107, M.V. Fleming 62)

Middlesex 311 (J.D. Carr 108 not out, A.P. Igglesden 5 for 81) and 231 for 5 (J.D. Carr 70 not out, M.R. Ramprakash 55)

Match drawn

Middlesex 7 pts., Kent 6 pts.

at Northampton

Gloucestershire 107 (K.M. Curran 5 for 38) and 295 (A.J. Wright 75, R.J. Scott 51)

Northamptonshire 293 (M.B. Loye 105, A. Fordham 54, K.M. Curran 53, M. Davies 5 for 84) and 110 for 5 (M. Davies 5 for 57)

Northamptonshire won by 5 wickets

Northamptonshire 22 pts., Gloucestershire 3 pts.

at Hove

Sussex 213 (M.P. Bicknell 6 for 43) and 243 (D.M. Smith 74, M.P. Bicknell 5 for 65)

Surrey 456 (D.J. Bicknell 190, A.J. Stewart 127, E.E. Hemmings 4 for 87) and 1 for 0

Surrey won by 10 wickets

Surrey 24 pts., Sussex 5 pts.

at Edgbaston

Warwickshire 192 (D.P. Ostler 57, A.E. Warner 4 for 54) and 115 (J.D. Ratcliffe 64)

Derbyshire 379 (J.E. Morris 95, T.J.G. O'Gorman 86, C.J. Adams 65)

Derbyshire won by an innings and 72 runs

Derbyshire 24 pts., Warwickshire 3 pts.

8, 9 and 10 May *at Taunton*

Australians 431 (M.J. Slater 122, M.E. Waugh 68, A.R. Border 54, A.P. van Troost 4 for 89) and 40 for 0 dec.

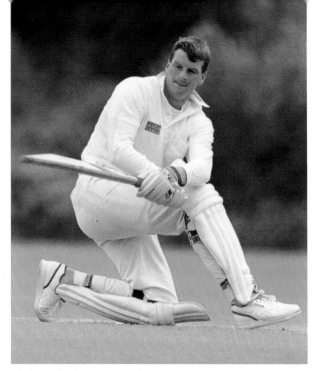

The hero of Yorkshire's triumph over Essex at Chelmsford, 6–10 May – David Byas, a career best 156. (Alan Cozzi)

Somerset 151 for 4 dec. (C.J. Tavaré 62) and 285 (A.N. Hayhurst 89, T.B.A. May 4 for 75, S.K. Warne 4 for 77)

Australians won by 35 runs

Firmly believed to be favourites to win the Britannic Assurance County Championship for the third year in succession, Essex had a disastrous start to their campaign. Yorkshire, without Moxon and Richardson, were led by Jarvis who won the toss, elected to bat and saw Byas and Kellett add 126 for the second wicket after the early loss of Metcalfe. Byas batted exceptionally well, exuding confidence with a wide range of elegant off-side shots. He hit 3 sixes and 23 fours in his highest first-class score. Essex clawed their way back into the game by capturing four wickets for 11 runs at the end of the first day, but they themselves moved from 94 for 1 to 98 for 4 on the second day. They batted poorly and only narrowly avoided having to follow-on. Again it was the final half-hour of the day which saw Essex make their strongest challenge as Mark Ilott, by far their best bowler, took three wickets to leave Yorkshire staggering at 11 for 3 at the close. The Essex surge was not maintained, however. Nightwatchman Stemp proved obdurate, and the Yorkshire middle-order was resolute. Essex were left to score a massive 455 if they were to win the match. Gooch and Stephenson batted on the Saturday evening as if they were totally confident of reaching this target and scored 91 briskly before Stephenson fell to Robinson. On the Monday, wickets tumbled regularly, and Yorkshire claimed the victory that they deserved. They had outplayed the champions in every department of the game.

There was an extraordinary match at Old Trafford. Durham hit 330 for 2 on the opening day, with Fowler and Larkins scoring 143 for the first wicket. Parker hit his third championship century for the county, and Durham, having scored 515, seemed in an impregnable position. Lancashire matched them bravely on the third day, with Atherton batting six hours 21 minutes for his 137, and Chapple and Barnett not only saving the follow-on but adding 82 for the last wicket. On the last morning, Durham inexplicably collapsed against the spin of Barnett and Watkinson, losing their last nine wickets for 31 runs, and Lancashire ran out astonishingly easy winners.

There was another dour struggle at Leicester. The home side occupied the first day scoring 219, but Notts made better progress on the second day, hitting 280 from 112 overs. With Randall and Crawley failing to score, Nottinghamshire owed much to a consistent middle-order. On the Saturday, only Whitaker and Smith offered resistance to the spin of Field-Buss and Afford, and Nottinghamshire won comfortably on the Monday.

Electing to bat first at Lord's, Kent promised more than they achieved. They suffered two minor collapses, going from 109 for 1 to 121 for 4, and from 186 for 4 to 207 for 7. Middlesex relied entirely upon acting captain Carr who reached his century in 62 overs to take them into a lead. The third day saw a shift in power, with Kent gaining the advantage through a second-wicket stand of 203 between Benson and Llong. The Kent skipper scored a most valuable century, but the main honours went to the young left-hander Nigel Llong who hit a glorious first hundred in the championship. He played some exquisite shots, lifting Emburey into the top tier of the pavilion and hitting 15 fours in his 108 which came off 175 balls. This was a most impressive and attractive innings. Eventually, Middlesex were set a target of 347, but their main purpose became saving the match, which they did through another accomplished unbeaten knock from Carr.

The frailty of the Gloucestershire batting was cruelly exposed by the Northamptonshire seamers. By the end of the first day, the visitors were already in a desperate position, having been bowled out for 107 and with Northamptonshire having come within two runs of that score with four wickets down. The home county emphasised their strength on the second day when Malachy Loye, 20 years old, six feet two inches, repaid the trust shown in him with his maiden first-class century, an innings of nimble footwork and assured timing. Leading by 186, Northamptonshire captured the wickets of Broad and Hinks before the close, but Gloucestershire lost only five wickets on the third day as they added 225 at barely two runs an over. Only 14 runs were added on the last morning, however, and Northamptonshire duly completed a comfortable victory. Gloucestershire were not without a hero, though. Left-arm spinner Mark Davies took five wickets in an innings for the first time and bettered his career-best bowling figures twice in the match, claiming his first 10-wicket haul.

Surrey moved to the top of the embryo championship with their second win of the season, overwhelming Sussex inside three days. The home county had no answer to the bowling of Martin Bicknell on the opening day, nor to

Lord's, Sunday, 9 May 1993, Middlesex v. Kent, and coloured clothing arrives at headquarters. (Adrian Murrell/Allsport)

the batting of his brother Darren on the second. The elder Bicknell shared a third-wicket stand of 240 with Alec Stewart who hit his second century of the season. Stewart's hundred came off 165 balls, and the stand with Darren Bicknell occupied 68 overs. On the third morning, the left-handed opener reached the highest score of his career, after which his brother routed Sussex for the second time. It remains one of the mysteries of English cricket as to why the England selectors do not look in the direction of the Surrey fast medium-pace bowler.

Derbyshire, too, won in three days. A mainly medium-pace attack accounted for Warwickshire in $4\frac{1}{2}$ hours while Derbyshire, in contrast, batted with tremendous zest. By the end of the day, with Morris and Adams roaring away, they were 143 for 2 after 37 overs. O'Gorman and the middle-order continued the assault on the second morning and, with Malcolm dismissing Moles and Twose in the last session, a Derbyshire victory on the Saturday became inevitable.

The Australians hit 431 at nearly five runs an over on the opening day at Taunton. Michael Slater hit a century on his first-class debut in England, hitting 20 fours in his 149-ball innings, which saw Caddick put to the sword. The least experienced of the Australian side, Slater had made an early claim for Test recognition. Rain sliced away much of the second day, but a fiery opening spell by McDermott accounted for Lathwell and Harden. Hayhurst and Tavaré added 117, and Tavaré kept the game alive by declaring at the overnight score. Set to make 321 in 81 overs, Somerset were encouraged by Hayhurst, but they eventually succumbed to the contrasting spin of May and Warne.

AXA EQUITY & LAW LEAGUE

9 May *at Chelmsford*

Essex 192 (D.R. Pringle 72)
Yorkshire 170 (P.M. Such 5 for 32)

Essex (4 pts.) won by 22 runs

at Old Trafford

Lancashire 229 for 7 (M.A. Atherton 96)
Durham 217 for 6 (P. Bainbridge 69 not out)

Lancashire (4 pts.) won by 12 runs

at Leicester

Leicestershire 216 for 7 (J.J. Whitaker 50)
Nottinghamshire 126 (L. Potter 5 for 28)

Leicestershire (4 pts.) won by 90 runs

at Lord's

Middlesex 104
Kent 105 for 1

Kent (4 pts.) won by 9 wickets

at Northampton

Northamptonshire 185 for 5 (A. Fordham 66)
Gloucestershire 123 (A.L. Penberthy 5 for 36)

Northamptonshire (4 pts.) won by 62 runs

at Hove

Sussex 310 for 9 (F.D. Stephenson 103, M.P. Speight 55, D.M. Smith 52)
Surrey 245 (D.M. Ward 73, M.A. Lynch 54, I.D.K. Salisbury 4 for 49)

Sussex (4 pts.) won by 65 runs

at Edgbaston

Derbyshire 173 for 9 (P.D. Bowler 77)
Warwickshire 174 for 7 (R.G. Twose 65)

Warwickshire (4 pts.) won by 3 wickets

New sponsors, 50 overs and garish coloured clothing – the Sunday League opened in less than friendly weather. Peter Such took five wickets in a Sunday League match for the first time to give Essex victory at Chelmsford, Tony Penberthy did exactly the same for Northamptonshire and so did Laurie Potter for Leicestershire. Mike Atherton made his highest league score as Lancashire beat Durham, and Warwickshire won a rather tedious game against Derbyshire with one ball to spare. Haynes and Hooper returned from the West Indies in time to play in the match at Lord's, where Kent routed the reigning champions. In a match reduced to 44 overs, Kent won with 17.2 overs to spare. The high jinks were at Hove where Smith and Stephenson hit 162 in 25 overs for Sussex's first wicket. Stephenson hit 103, his first Sunday League century, off 79 balls with 15 fours. Surrey died bravely, but they could never quite come to terms with being asked to score 311 to win.

BENSON AND HEDGES CUP

ROUND ONE

11 May *at Derby*

Derbyshire 253 for 8 (C.J. Adams 58, J.E. Morris 57)
Middlesex 239 for 9 (D.L. Haynes 60, M.A. Roseberry 58)

Derbyshire won by 14 runs

(Gold Award – C.J. Adams)

at Cardiff

Sussex 263 for 7 (D.M. Smith 55, A.P. Wells 53)
Glamorgan 230 (M.P. Maynard 57)

Sussex won by 33 runs

(Gold Award – I.D.K. Salisbury)

at Leeds

Northamptonshire 211 for 9 (N.A. Felton 62, A.J. Lamb 54)
Yorkshire 177 (M.D. Moxon 52, R.B. Richardson 52)

Northamptonshire won by 34 runs

(Gold Award – N.A. Felton)

at Leicester

Leicestershire 206 for 8 (P.E. Robinson 70)
Warwickshire 206 (A.J. Moles 63)

Matthew Hayden is stumped by Moores, bowled by Salisbury for 66 in the Australians' match against Sussex at Hove. (Patrick Eagar)

Leicestershire won on losing fewer wickets with scores level

(Gold Award – P.E. Robinson)

at Stockton

Durham 196 for 5 (W. Larkins 110 not out)
Hampshire 197 for 7 (V.P. Terry 79)

Hampshire won by 3 wickets

(Gold Award – W. Larkins)

at The Oval

Lancashire 236 (N.H. Fairbrother 87)
Surrey 230 (G.P. Thorpe 103, A.J. Stewart 95)

Lancashire won by 6 runs

(Gold Award – N.H. Fairbrother)

at Trent Bridge

Nottinghamshire 279 for 6 (P.R. Pollard 80, P. Johnson 59)
Somerset 283 for 9 (N.A. Folland 83, M.N. Lathwell 77, G.W. Mike 4 for 44)

Somerset won by 1 wicket

(Gold Award – M.N. Lathwell)

at Worcester

Essex 115
Worcestershire 117 for 1 (G.A. Hick 62 not out)

Worcestershire won by 9 wickets

(Gold Award – G.A. Hick)

Fine weather greeted the first round of the Benson and Hedges Cup, but, for a time, things looked far from fine for Derbyshire. Put in to bat, they were much indebted to a third-wicket stand of 97 between Morris and Adams who was to win his first Gold Award. A middle-order collapse followed before late hitting from Cork and Bishop took them to 253. This seemed totally insufficient as Haynes and Roseberry reached 100 in 22 overs for Middlesex's first wicket. Two wickets then fell at this score, and two more fell with the score on 161. Warner's 11 nagging overs cost only 29 runs, and Bishop and Malcolm gave away nothing at the death as wickets fell, and Derbyshire won with unexpected comfort.

Sussex followed their fierce scoring of the Sunday with another aggressive batting performance, Stephenson and Smith beginning with a stand of 96. There were contributions throughout the order, and Glamorgan faced a formidable 263. They maintained a serious challenge until Ian Salisbury's mid-innings spell of 11 overs for 28 runs and the wicket of Croft halted their charge and virtually decided the match.

Yorkshire's attack gave their batsmen every chance of success against Northamptonshire. Felton and Lamb added 118 for the third wicket but, in the last 12 overs, seven wickets fell as only 53 runs were scored. Richie Richardson, in his first innings for Yorkshire, and Moxon added 104 for the second wicket. The West Indies captain

batted immaculately, and victory seemed assured, but Moxon was run out and, three overs later, Richardson was splendidly caught by Cook at mid-off. The rest of the batting fell apart, and Northamptonshire won with ease.

Batting first on a pitch which was never easy for run-scoring, Leicestershire slipped to 34 for 3 before Phil Robinson rallied them in a 95-run stand with Ben Smith. Even so, Leicestershire's final score of 206 did not look as if it should pose many problems for Warwickshire, but the visitors lost their way after a comfortable start. Reserve keeper Burns looked a likely saviour but, with nine needed from two overs, he heaved at Wells and missed. A single was needed from the last ball, but bowler Winston Benjamin threw down Donald's wicket with the batsman short of his ground, and Leicestershire snatched a thrilling victory.

Wayne Larkins hit his sixth century in the Benson and Hedges Cup, gained his seventh Gold Award, and still finished on the losing side as Aymes and Udal took Hampshire to victory with five balls to spare.

The most incredible events took place at The Oval where the third umpire was employed, equipped with a television monitor. Stewart won the toss and invited Lancashire to bat, and his decision was vindicated when Martin Bicknell produced another magnificent spell with the new ball. After 16 overs, Lancashire were 34 for 2. Soon they were 50 for 3 as Mark Butcher, an impressive fifth bowler, had Mendis caught in the gully. Lloyd now joined Fairbrother in a stand which took Lancashire to 146 at lunch. Nothing daunted Fairbrother. He pulled Boiling for six, and hit the last ball before the interval over mid-wicket for another six, the bowler this time being Butcher. Lloyd touched the first ball after lunch to the keeper, and the bowler, Waqar Younis, also had Fairbrother caught well at slip by Lynch. The Lancashire captain had hit a spectacular 87 off 91 balls, shrugging off any sensation of crisis. Wasim Akram struck some fine blows, Martin supported ably in a last-wicket stand of 33, and Lancashire's 236 looked far in excess of what had seemed possible earlier in the day. It seemed greater still when Darren Bicknell played a dreadful shot to drag the fourth ball of the Surrey innings onto his stumps. Stewart survived a strong appeal for leg before first ball, but thereafter he played with confidence and maturity. In 49 overs, he and Thorpe added 212 and took their side to the point where victory looked inevitable. It was in the 50th over that Stewart was bowled by Martin, and, in the next over, Lynch touched a leg-side catch to the keeper. Thorpe, having completed a highly impressive first century in the competition, was caught at mid-on. Austin, maintaining a steady line, frustrated Surrey batsmen into suicide, and he accounted for Ward, Brown and Butcher in quick succession. Suddenly 14 runs were needed from the last over, and Boiling was run out off the final ball with seven runs still needed. The Surrey supporters found it hard to believe, and even harder to accept.

Somerset came close to emulating Surrey. They faced a formidable 279, but once Lathwell and Folland had scored 137 in 22 overs for the first wicket, the task looked simple. Harden and Tavaré kept up the momentum, but Gregory Mike produced a four-wicket burst, one of his victims being the injured Hayhurst. Three more wickets fell, and the last ball arrived with the scores level. Andre van Troost slogged Pick's delivery to the cover boundary, and Somerset had won.

There were no breath-taking events at New Road where Worcestershire won the toss, asked Essex, the favourites, to bat, and bowled them out in 53.3 overs for a feeble 115. Worcestershire reached their target with 22.5 overs and nine wickets to spare. It had been a miserable week for Essex.

13, 14 and 15 May *at Hove*

Sussex 353 (A.P. Wells 93, I.D.K. Salisbury 59, K. Greenfield 55, B.P. Julian 5 for 63) and 92 for 4

Australians 490 for 5 dec. (D.R. Martyn 136, S.R. Waugh 124, M.J. Slater 73, M.L. Hayden 66)

Match drawn

13, 14, 15 and 17 May *at Derby*

Glamorgan 320 (I.V.A. Richards 86, S.J. Base 4 for 53) and 368 for 8 dec. (M.P. Maynard 145, H. Morris 100)

Derbyshire 283 (P.D. Bowler 96, J.E. Morris 51) and 214 (K.J. Barnett 108 not out, S.L. Watkin 5 for 71)

Glamorgan won by 191 runs

Glamorgan 23 pts., Derbyshire 6 pts.

at Stockton-on-Tees

Hampshire 289 for 3 (V.P. Terry 111, T.C. Middleton 65, D.I. Gower 64)

v. Durham

Match drawn

Hampshire 2 pts., Durham 1 pt.

at Canterbury

Warwickshire 305 (A.J. Moles 65, T.L. Penney 57) and 213 (D.A. Reeve 72 not out, A.J. Moles 50)

Kent 177 (C.L. Hooper 75, T.A. Munton 7 for 41) and 231 (M.R. Benson 107, N.M.K. Smith 6 for 122)

Warwickshire won by 110 runs

Warwickshire 22 pts., Kent 3 pts.

at Lord's

Middlesex 281 (M.A. Roseberry 79 not out, M.A. Feltham 73, C.L. Cairns 5 for 68) and 266 for 9 dec. (D.L. Haynes 98, J.E. Emburey 54, J.A. Afford 4 for 59)

Nottinghamshire 266 (R.T. Robinson 112, P.R. Pollard 70, P.C.R. Tufnell 5 for 77) and 247 for 6 (R.T. Robinson 69, P. Johnson 52)

Match drawn

Nottinghamshire 6 pts., Middlesex 5 pts.

at Taunton

Somerset 195 (M.N. Lathwell 71, P.A.J. DeFreitas 7 for 76) and 114 (P.A.J. DeFreitas 5 for 55, Wasim Akram 4 for 42)

Lancashire 222 (N.J. Speak 58, Mushtaq Ahmed 4 for 40) and 72 (A.R. Caddick 9 for 32)

Somerset won by 15 runs

Somerset 20 pts., Lancashire 5 pts.

at The Oval

Essex 418 (G.A. Gooch 79, J.J.B. Lewis 56, D.R. Pringle 52) and 153 (N. Hussain 52)

Surrey 330 (G.P. Thorpe 89, M.C. Ilott 7 for 85) and 178 for 4 (D.M. Ward 52)

Match drawn

Essex 8 pts., Surrey 6 pts.

at Bradford

Worcestershire 192 (M.A. Robinson 7 for 47)

Yorkshire 196 for 4 (A.A. Metcalfe 76, M.D. Moxon 51)

Match drawn

Yorkshire 4 pts., Worcestershire 1 pt.

Six wickets and the award of his county cap for Warwickshire's Neil Smith at Canterbury, 17 May. (David Munden/Sports-Line)

With rain eliminating the final session of the second day, the Australians had to settle for a draw at Hove. Athey was in the Sussex side which displayed good application on the opening day, but the Australians gave further indication of their batting strength as Damien Martyn hit his first century of the tour, and shared a fourth-wicket stand of 205 with another centurion, Steve Waugh.

Glamorgan again proved the county of enterprising batting. They hit 320 and captured the wicket of Barnett on the first day at Derby. Viv Richards lashed 86 off 117 balls, and Devon Malcolm was the main sufferer. His 23 overs cost 101 runs, although he did finally have Richards caught. Rain interrupted the second day, and the backbone of the Derbyshire innings was provided by Bowler and Morris, who shared a second-wicket stand of 116. Glamorgan were constantly positive in their approach to the game. They scored at four runs an over on the Saturday when Morris and Maynard both hit centuries and shared a third-wicket stand of 155. Morris' declaration left his bowlers more than a day in which to win the match and, in spite of Kim Barnett carrying his bat for the bravest of hundreds, they did not let him down. Barnett must have regretted his decision to ask Glamorgan to bat first.

Play was possible only on the first and third days at Stockton-on-Tees where Terry and Middleton started Hampshire's innings with a partnership of 134.

Warwickshire batted consistently, if rather grimly, to reach 305 on the second morning at Canterbury. Their caution was proved to be the right policy when Kent – Carl Hooper apart – succumbed to the fast medium pace of Tim Munton who moved the ball appreciably. The visitors took a firm grip on the game with another batting performance which relied more on sheer application than flair or style. Kent were left to make 342 on the last day on a pitch which was slow and on which the ball kept low and offered some turn to the spinners. Off-spinner Neil Smith was brought into the Warwickshire attack in the 12th over, and he then bowled 46.1 overs in a row. It was a dour day, with Mark Benson offering a captain's defiance, but once he, Ward and Hooper had gone – all victims of Smith – Kent looked a beaten side. Warwickshire still needed three wickets in the last hour, and they won with 6.5 overs to spare when Smith had Igglesden taken at silly mid-off. This was Neil Smith's sixth wicket, a career best, and when he returned to the dressing room he was awarded his county cap.

Middlesex drew with Nottinghamshire at Lord's and suffered injuries to Feltham and Roseberry in the process. Robinson and Pollard shared a second-wicket stand of 170 for Nottinghamshire on a rain-interrupted second day, but the last five Notts wickets went down for 28 runs on the Saturday. Carr set Nottinghamshire a target of 282 in 81 overs, and a third-wicket stand of 116 between Robinson and Johnson put them in sight of victory, but thereafter they played with incomprehensible timidity.

It was at Taunton that the sensational took place. Batting first, Somerset were wrecked for 195 in 55.3 overs. Only Mark Lathwell, named in England's Texaco Cup squad, offered serious and aggressive resistance to the Lancashire pace attack. Phillip DeFreitas took 7 for 76, his

The best bowling figures of the season – 9 for 32 – for Andrew Caddick, and Somerset snatch a remarkable victory over Lancashire at Taunton, 17 May. (Alan Cozzi)

best performance for four years, and looked sharper than he had done for some time. By the end of the day, Lancashire, with Speak and Wasim Akram together, were 142 for 4 and in command. They were handicapped by an injury to Fairbrother, and they failed to press home their advantage on the second morning, losing their last four wickets for 18 runs. It appeared to matter little as DeFreitas and Wasim Akram again cut swathes through the Somerset batting. The home side were out for 114 in 36.2 overs. Lancashire needed just 88 to win, and a four-day match was certain to finish inside two days. It did – but not as we had anticipated. Tavaré entrusted his bowling to Caddick from one end, and to Mushtaq Ahmed from the other, a blend of pace and leg-spin. Mushtaq accounted for Speak, Caddick for Mendis, Atherton, Lloyd and Hegg, and Lancashire were 8 for 5. Fairbrother and Wasim Akram doubled the score before the former was caught behind off Caddick. Wasim and Watkinson added 23 and seemed to have restored sanity when Wasim was caught and bowled by Caddick off a fierce drive. DeFreitas fell without adding to the score. When Caddick bowled Watkinson the impossible had happened. Somerset won an extraordinary game by 15 runs. Lancashire had been bowled out for 72 and Andrew Caddick, the hero of the hour, had taken a magnificent career best 9 for 32 in 67 deliveries. There was, moreover, another hero who is likely to be overlooked in years to come: Somerset were 72 for 9 in their second innings when Andre van Troost came to the wicket and lashed 35 out of a last-wicket stand of 42, the biggest partnership of the innings. Only later was it realised how important those runs were.

Essex regained some pride at The Oval where they batted into the second day with consistency to claim four batting points. Mark Ilott then produced a career-best bowling performance to take Essex to a first-innings lead of 88. From that point on, the game belonged to Surrey. The Essex second innings was painful in the extreme. In 85.2 overs, they scored 153. This was gruesome stuff. Surrey needed to score 242 off 34 overs to win the match and, to their credit, they made the bravest of efforts before rain ended play. From 21.3 overs, they had scored 178 for 4. Such's six overs had cost 66 runs.

Worcestershire made 185 for 7 on the first day at Bradford, but there was no play on the second day, and only limited play on the third and fourth days. Mark Robinson had cause to celebrate with the best bowling performance of his career.

15, 16 and 17 May *at Cambridge*

Cambridge University 179 (M.E.D. Jarrett 51, J. Dakin 4 for 45) and 256 for 6 dec. (J.P. Crawley 86, R. Cake 83)
Leicestershire 282 (L. Potter 103 not out, G.J. Parsons 59)

Match drawn

15, 17 and 18 May *at Oxford*

Northamptonshire 334 for 5 dec. (R.J. Bailey 91, D. Ripley 62 not out, M.B. Loye 57 not out) and 89 for 3 dec. (D. Ripley 50 not out)
Oxford University 180 (C.L. Keey 111) and 147 for 6

Match drawn

Pace bowler Dakin took four wickets on his first-class debut for Leicestershire at Fenner's while Chris Keey hit a maiden first-class century for Oxford University against Northamptonshire.

16 May *at Northampton*

Northamptonshire 273 for 2 (A. Fordham 101, R.J. Bailey 82 not out)
Australians 183 for 2 (M.A. Taylor 89 not out, M.E. Waugh 74)

Northamptonshire won on faster scoring rate

Scheduled as a 55-over match, the game at Northampton was ended by rain when the Australian innings was only 39 overs old. This gave victory to the county by virtue of their run rate – 4.96 compared to 4.69 – but the Australians, who thus suffered their first defeat of the tour, were well paced and placed for a win.

 AXA EQUITY & LAW LEAGUE

16 May *at Derby*

Derbyshire 215 (P.D. Bowler 96, C.J. Adams 52, S.R. Barwick 6 for 28)
Glamorgan 212 for 8 (H. Morris 70, M.P. Maynard 69, F.A. Griffith 4 for 48)

Derbyshire (4 pts.) won by 3 runs

at Stockton-on-Tees

Hampshire 127 for 6 (R.A. Smith 53 not out, A.C. Cummins 4 for 24)
Durham 48 for 0

Match abandoned

Durham 2 pts., Hampshire 2 pts.

at Canterbury

Kent 289 for 8 (T.R. Ward 99, N.R. Taylor 50 not out)
Warwickshire 223 (T.L. Penney 83 not out)

Kent (4 pts.) won by 66 runs

at Lord's

Middlesex 257 for 6 (J.D. Carr 92, M.R. Ramprakash 88, C.C. Lewis 4 for 45)
Nottinghamshire 252 for 8 (G.W. Mike 51 not out)

Middlesex (4 pts.) won by 5 runs

at Taunton

Lancashire 210 for 8
***v.* Somerset**

Match abandoned

Somerset 2 pts., Lancashire 2 pts.

at The Oval

Essex 207 for 9 (G.A. Gooch 65)
Surrey 208 for 8 (A.J. Stewart 53, A.D. Brown 52)

Surrey (4 pts.) won by 2 wickets

at Leeds

Yorkshire 187 for 7
Worcestershire 55 for 1

Match abandoned

Yorkshire 2 pts., Worcestershire 2 pts.

Steve Barwick, proving to be the master limited-over bowler, returned his best figures in the Sunday League as Derbyshire went from 209 for 2 to 215 all out in an astonishing collapse. Glamorgan lost James without scoring, but they seemed set for victory while Morris and the hobbling Maynard were together. Cork and Griffith brought restraint, however, and Metson, needing to hit the last ball for four, was caught on the square-leg boundary instead.

The pitch at Canterbury proved more amiable to batsmen than the four-day track had done. Trevor Ward hit 99 off 93 balls to set up Kent's match-winning 289.

Ramprakash and Carr added 165 in 29 overs for Middlesex's third wicket, although Nottinghamshire nearly won the match through Gregory Mike but he failed to hit the last ball for six which would have given the visitors victory.

Essex omitted Nasser Hussain with no explanation and their batting was never good enough to pose problems for Surrey who, nevertheless, did their best to lose the game as they had done in the Benson and Hedges Cup. Elsewhere it was rain and gloom.

18 May at Shenley Park

MCC 231 for 3 dec. (C.W.J. Athey 70, M.J. Roberts 60)

Hertfordshire 212 for 8 (N. Ilott 104, K.T. Medlycott 4 for 78)

Match drawn

19, 20 and 21 May at Cambridge

Lancashire 342 for 3 (G.D. Mendis 106, M.A. Atherton 91
retired hurt)

v. Cambridge University

Match drawn

at Oxford

Middlesex 236 (M.W. Gatting 60, R.H. MacDonald 5 for 20)
and 31 for 0 dec.

Oxford University 37 for 1 dec. and 177 for 6 (C.M. Gupte
61)

Match drawn

Although it is not customary to draw attention to any of the numerous MCC matches that are played every season, one must point to the opening of the Shenley Cricket Centre by Sir Colin Cowdrey. A strong MCC side met Hertfordshire to mark the occasion. This surely is one of the most beautiful grounds in England and has been reclaimed as part of a project that aims at making facilities available for all, from the handicapped to the county player and the England under-19 squad. Along with the lovely ground, there is a six-lane indoor cricket school, a luxurious pavilion and accommodation. Under the guidance of Eric Russell, the former Middlesex and England opener, this should indeed become a centre of excellence of which this country will be proud. Ignore it at your peril.

There was no play after the first day at Fenner's, and no play on the second day at Oxford where Mike Gatting made his return after injury and the South African Rob MacDonald returned his best figures in first-class cricket with his medium-pacers.

Sir Colin Cowdrey at the opening of the cricket centre at Shenley Park, Hertfordshire.

 TEXACO TROPHY
ENGLAND *v.* AUSTRALIA

The England selectors showed enterprise in their choices, but less enterprise in the final elevens that they put into the field. Fairbrother reported fit to play at Old Trafford, and Lathwell and Cork were those omitted from the 13 selected. This meant first matches at international level for Caddick and Thorpe. Australia gave an international debut to Hayden.

Gooch won the toss and asked Australia to bat. Caddick and Pringle began tidily enough but Australia were soon into their stride, with Hayden and Taylor pulling and clipping with ease. Hayden fell to a poor shot, chasing a wide ball from Lewis, but Mark Waugh and Taylor plundered easy runs from some poor bowling by Jarvis and Illingworth, and the fielding threatened to disintegrate. Suddenly, and without any apparent reason, it all changed. Four wickets went down in seven overs for 18 runs, and from being 161 for 1 in 36 overs at lunch, Australia plunged to 186 for 5 by early afternoon. Having added 108 in 21 overs with Taylor, Mark Waugh top-edged a hook. Boon then cut the ball into the hands of backward point, and Taylor mistimed a sweep. On each occasion, the catcher was Fairbrother. Border pulled to square-leg, and England were on top.

ABOVE: *Craig McDermott takes a brilliant one-handed catch off his own bowling to account for Robin Smith in the first Texaco Trophy match. (Ben Radford/Allsport)*

BELOW: *Mark Waugh responds for Australia, and he and Border take their side to a remarkably comfortable victory. (Adrian Murrell/ Allsport)*

TOP: *Robin Smith slashes another boundary during his breathtaking 167 not out in the second Texaco Trophy match at Edgbaston. (Adrian Murrell/Allsport)*

ABOVE: *Ian Healy congratulates Man of the Match Brendon Julian, who took three wickets and turned the course of the match at Lord's. (Ben Radford/Allsport)*

Healy batted busily and sensibly to hit 20 off 21 balls, and Steve Waugh was looking totally commanding when he was brilliantly caught and bowled low down by Lewis. Hughes hit a six and a four as he took 20 off 13 balls, and Australia went past 250, but their 258 looked well within England's reach.

McDermott corrected this notion in his opening spell in which he had Gooch caught at second slip and held Smith off his own bowling in a manner to rival Lewis' dismissal of Steve Waugh. An excited Stewart had been bowled by Hughes, and England were 44 for 3. The gloom was quickly dismissed by Hick and Fairbrother who, in 17 overs, added 127 runs. Reiffel, in particular, was savagely treated, but it was he who broke the stand by taking a well-judged catch to account for Fairbrother. A greater prize was to come when he bowled Hick 23 runs later.

By then, Thorpe had started an impressive first innings in international cricket. At 211, he was unlucky to lose Lewis, run out when Steve Waugh deflected a drive onto the stumps. The run rate was becoming a problem, and Pringle skied to third man. When Thorpe was well taken at mid-off, 19 runs were needed from 18 balls with two wickets standing. Jarvis was caught off a towering hit to deep mid-on, and seven runs were needed from the last over. Off the penultimate ball, Illingworth foolishly refused a reasonable call for a second run, and England were beaten. If there was disappointment in the manner of defeat, worse was to come.

Cork replaced Illingworth for the match at Edgbaston while Australia were unchanged. Australia won the toss and asked England to bat. Again it was McDermott who put England in jeopardy. He beat Stewart for pace, had Gooch groping before being caught behind, and bowled with the utmost economy on a pitch which was a batsman's paradise. Hick drove at Reiffel and got an outside edge, and England were 55 for 3.

Fairbrother dominated a stand of 50 with Smith before falling to a leaping catch at extra cover. Thorpe now joined Smith in a stand of 142 in 21 overs. If his contribution of 36 to that partnership looks meagre, that is far from the truth. He gave invaluable and unselfish support to a man who suddenly found the richest vein of form that a batsman could dream of.

Robin Smith had reached a commendable hundred, but his next fifty came off 20 balls, and the last 30 balls he faced produced 76 runs. In all, he faced 163 deliveries, hit 3 sixes and 17 fours and finished on 167 not out, the highest score made by an England batsman in a one-day international. He was an irrepressible force. Rarely has one seen batting to compare with this.

Smith, one presumed, had set up an England victory, and nothing in the early stages of the Australian innings suggested otherwise. Hayden was bowled through the gap between bat and pad, and Taylor played on. A measured start had seen Australia reach 55 for 2. Boon was out on the stroke of tea when he tried to run the ball

---

TEXACO TROPHY – FIRST ONE-DAY INTERNATIONAL – ENGLAND v. AUSTRALIA
19 May at Old Trafford, Manchester

AUSTRALIA				ENGLAND		
M.L. Hayden	c Stewart, b Lewis	29		G.A. Gooch (capt)	c M.E. Waugh, b McDermott	4
M.A. Taylor	c Fairbrother, b Illingworth	79		*A.J. Stewart	b Hughes	22
M.E. Waugh	c Fairbrother, b Jarvis	56		R.A. Smith	c and b McDermott	9
D.C. Boon	c Fairbrother, b Illingworth	2		G.A. Hick	b Reiffel	85
A.R. Border (capt)	c Lewis, b Illingworth	4		N.H. Fairbrother	c Reiffel, b S.R. Waugh	59
S.R. Waugh	c and b Lewis	27		G.P. Thorpe	c Taylor, b McDermott	31
*I.A. Healy	c Thorpe, b Caddick	20		C.C. Lewis	run out	4
M.G. Hughes	b Lewis	20		D.R. Pringle	c Taylor, b S.R. Waugh	6
P.R. Reiffel	run out	2		R.K. Illingworth	run out	12
C.J. McDermott	not out	3		P.W. Jarvis	c Reiffel, b S.R. Waugh	2
T.B.A. May	not out	1		A.R. Caddick	not out	1
Extras	b 1, lb 8, w 2, nb 4	15		Extras	lb 8, w 9, nb 2	19
(55 overs)	(for 9 wickets)	258		(54.5 overs)		254

	O	M	R	W		O	M	R	W
Caddick	11	1	50	1	McDermott	11	2	38	3
Pringle	10	3	36	–	Hughes	9.5	1	40	1
Lewis	11	1	54	3	May	11	2	40	–
Jarvis	11	–	55	1	Reiffel	11	–	63	1
Illingworth	11	–	48	3	M.E. Waugh	2	–	12	–
Hick	1	–	6	–	S.R. Waugh	10	–	53	3

FALL OF WICKETS

1–60, 2–168, 3–171, 4–178, 5–186, 6–219, 7–237, 8–254, 9–255

FALL OF WICKETS

1–11, 2–38, 3–44, 4–171, 5–194, 6–211, 7–227, 8–240, 9–247

Umpires: B.J. Meyer & D.R. Shepherd   *Man of the Match:* C.J. McDermott   *Australia won by 4 runs*

TEXACO TROPHY – SECOND ONE-DAY INTERNATIONAL – ENGLAND v. AUSTRALIA
21 May at Edgbaston, Birmingham

ENGLAND				AUSTRALIA			
G.A. Gooch (capt)	c Healy, b McDermott		17	M.A. Taylor	b Lewis		26
*A.J. Stewart	b McDermott		0	M.L. Hayden	b Jarvis		14
R.A. Smith	not out		167	M.E. Waugh	c Fairbrother, b Lewis		113
G.A. Hick	c Healy, b Reiffel		2	D.C. Boon	c Stewart, b Pringle		21
N.H. Fairbrother	c Taylor, b S.R. Waugh		23	A.R. Border (capt)	not out		86
G.P. Thorpe	c Border, b McDermott		36	S.R. Waugh	not out		6
C.C. Lewis	not out		13	*I.A. Healy			
D.R. Pringle				M.G. Hughes			
D.G. Cork				C.J. McDermott			
P.W. Jarvis				P.R. Reiffel			
A.R. Caddick				T.B.A. May			
Extras	b 2, lb 4, w 2, nb 11		19	Extras	lb 5, w 3, nb 6		14
(55 overs)	(for 5 wickets)		277	(53.3 overs)	(for 4 wickets)		280

	O	M	R	W		O	M	R	W
McDermott	11	1	29	3	Caddick	11	1	43	–
Hughes	11	2	51	–	Jarvis	10	1	51	1
Reiffel	11	1	70	1	Lewis	10.3	–	61	2
May	11	–	45	–	Pringle	11	–	63	1
S.R. Waugh	8	–	55	1	Cork	11	1	57	–
M.E. Waugh	3	–	21	–					

FALL OF WICKETS

1–3, 2–40, 3–55, 4–105, 5–247

FALL OF WICKETS

1–28, 2–55, 3–95, 4–263

Umpires: M.J. Kitchen & K.E. Palmer   *Man of the Match:* R.A. Smith   *Australia won by 6 wickets*

TEXACO TROPHY – THIRD ONE-DAY INTERNATIONAL – ENGLAND v. AUSTRALIA
23 May at Lord's

AUSTRALIA				ENGLAND			
M.L. Hayden	c Stewart, b Caddick		4	G.A. Gooch (capt)	c Hughes, b May		42
M.A. Taylor (capt)	c Stewart, b Reeve		57	*A.J. Stewart	c M.E. Waugh, b Julian		74
M.E. Waugh	c Stewart, b Caddick		14	R.A. Smith	st Healy, b May		6
D.C. Boon	b Illingworth		73	G.A. Hick	b Julian		7
D.R. Martyn	not out		51	N.H. Fairbrother	c Boon, b Julian		18
S.R. Waugh	c Gooch, b Caddick		8	G.P. Thorpe	c Healy, b S.R. Waugh		22
*I.A. Healy	not out		12	D.A. Reeve	run out		2
B.P. Julian				D.G. Cork	b Hughes		11
M.G. Hughes				R.K. Illingworth	c Healy, b Hughes		9
C.J. McDermott				P.W. Jarvis	c Hayden, b McDermott		3
T.B.A. May				A.R. Caddick	not out		2
Extras	lb 3, w 6, nb 2		11	Extras	lb 6, w 8, nb 1		15
(55 overs)	(for 5 wickets)		230	(53.1 overs)			211

	O	M	R	W		O	M	R	W
Jarvis	11	1	51	–	McDermott	10	1	35	1
Caddick	11	3	39	3	Hughes	10.1	–	41	2
Cork	9	2	24	–	Julian	11	1	50	3
Illingworth	10	–	46	1	May	11	1	36	2
Reeve	11	1	50	1	S.R. Waugh	11	–	43	1
Hick	3	–	17	–					

FALL OF WICKETS

1–12, 2–31, 3–139, 4–193, 5–208

FALL OF WICKETS

1–96, 2–115, 3–129, 4–159, 5–160, 6–169, 7–195, 8–201, 9–208

Umpires: H.D. Bird & R. Palmer   *Man of the Match:* B.P. Julian   *Australia won by 19 runs*

down to third man, and Australia were 95 for 3, needing more than a run a ball to win the match from that far distant point – a formidable task.

If the innings that followed were different in character from that of Smith, they were no less worthy of praise. Only once in their fourth-wicket stand of 168, scored at better than one a ball, did Mark Waugh hint at slogging, but a quick reprimand from Allan Border restored him to orthodox placing of the ball and off-drives and pulls of a vintage nature. It all looked so easy, and although Mark Waugh played a rash shot which had him caught by the diving Fairbrother at mid-wicket, the result never seemed in doubt.

This was cricket of style and judgement. Mark Waugh's 113 came off 122 balls and contained 8 fours; Border's 86, an innings of infinite wisdom, came off 97 balls and contained 9 fours. England were shattered.

With the Texaco Trophy gone, England had the chance to restore pride and blood young Lathwell. They failed to do either. Illingworth returned to the exclusion of Lewis and, with Pringle unfit, Dermot Reeve was called into the side, a strange and unwise selection. Border stood down to give Martyn a game in the Australian side, and Julian came in for his first international match at the expense of Reiffel. Gooch won the toss; Australia batted.

Runs were not easy to score in the early stages, and in the sixth over, Hayden was adjudged caught behind off Caddick. Mark Waugh was dropped by Stewart off Cork in the 13th over, but he was caught by the same player in the next over off Caddick, whose impressive opening spell gave him 2 for 11 from seven overs. A stand of 108 in 28 overs between the old warriors Taylor and Boon revived Australia, and there was a most encouraging 51 not out off 43 balls from Martyn, who looked a batsman of high calibre. Boon's 73 came off 125 balls, but he was twice put down by Thorpe who otherwise fielded well.

Facing a target of 231, England seemingly had no problems. Gooch and Stewart moved serenely towards tea until, with the cups clattering, Gooch swept May to square-leg. At 96 for 1 from 25 overs, it appeared that we were set for a mundane finish to the match, but Smith, having hit his first ball for four, stretched forward to a ball that, incomprehensibly, was called wide and was stumped. By now, Stewart, so fluent before tea, had almost ceased to hit the ball.

In the press box before the start of the England innings, the Australian contingent were running a sweep on how many wides Brendon Julian would bowl. His three overs from the Pavilion end had cost him 27 runs, and he had bowled three wides. It seemed unlikely that he would bowl again, but Taylor brought him back at the Nursery end from where he was to take 3 for 23 in eight overs. Hick played round a straight ball, and Fairbrother hit to cover. Stewart was taken at backward point, and England were 160 for 5. Reeve ran when Thorpe stood after an appeal for leg before and was needlessly run out and, with pressure mounting, Cork heaved at a straight ball. Thorpe was splendidly taken low down by Healy, and the end was nigh. Hayden pulled off a marvellous one-handed catch above his head to get rid of Jarvis, and the end came when Healy dived to catch Illingworth. Austra-

lia had snatched an improbable victory and won the series 3–0, but, as Taylor said with sense and caution, it is the Ashes that matter.

20, 21, 22 and 24 May *at Chelmsford*

Essex 471 for 7 dec. (N. Hussain 152, Salim Malik 132)

Derbyshire 203 (C.J. Adams 54, F.A. Griffith 53) and 253 for 1 (K.J. Barnett 130 not out, P.D. Bowler 71 not out)

Match drawn

Essex 8 pts., Derbyshire 3 pts.

at Swansea

Glamorgan 165 (I.V.A. Richards 64, A.L. Penberthy 5 for 37) and 212 (H. Morris 61, C.E.L. Ambrose 4 for 61)

Northamptonshire 217 (A.L. Penberthy 54 not out, S.L. Watkin 4 for 79) and 103 for 1 (A. Fordham 56 not out)

Match drawn

Northamptonshire 5 pts., Glamorgan 4 pts.

at Bristol

Durham 320 (C.W. Scott 64, A.C. Cummins 62) and 174 for 7 dec. (I.T. Botham 73)

Gloucestershire 227 for 6 dec. (M.W. Alleyne 104) and 168 for 4

Match drawn

Durham 5 pts., Gloucestershire 5 pts.

at Southampton

Hampshire 307 for 8 dec. (A.N. Aymes 50 not out) and 162 for 9 dec. (K.D. James 51, D. Gough 5 for 50)

Yorkshire 248 (M.D. Moxon 75, K.D. James 4 for 33) and 224 for 4 (M.D. Moxon 61, D. Byas 53 not out)

Yorkshire won by 6 wickets

Yorkshire 20 pts., Hampshire 7 pts.

at Trent Bridge

Kent 394 (M.V. Fleming 76, M.R. Benson 73, R.M. Ellison 68, J.A. Afford 5 for 79) and 104 (M.G. Field-Buss 6 for 42, J.A. Afford 4 for 35)

Nottinghamshire 242 (C.L. Cairns 93, M.A. Crawley 81) and 330 (D.W. Randall 73, P. Johnson 54, P.R. Pollard 50, R.P. Davis 7 for 127)

Nottinghamshire won by 74 runs

Nottinghamshire 20 pts., Kent 8 pts.

at Horsham

Sussex 271 (A.P. Wells 78)

Leicestershire 97 (E.E. Hemmings 5 for 27, F.D. Stephenson 4 for 45) and 72 (E.E. Hemmings 7 for 31)

Sussex won by an innings and 102 runs

Sussex 22 pts., Leicestershire 4 pts.

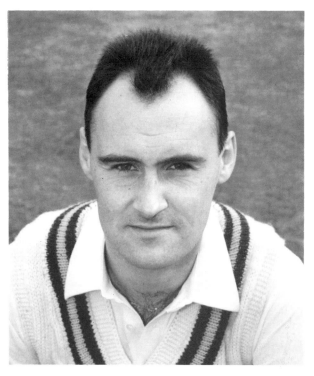

Michael Field-Buss helped bowl Nottinghamshire to victory over Kent with a career best 6 for 42. (David Munden/Sports-Line)

Veteran Eddie Hemmings took 12 for 58 for his new county Sussex and bowled them to victory over Leicestershire at Horsham. (David Munden/Sports-Line)

at Worcester

Somerset 236 (K.C.G. Benjamin 6 for 70) and 151 (R.J. Harden 72 not out, P.J. Newport 4 for 31)
Worcestershire 142 (Mushtaq Ahmed 5 for 51) and 246 for 8 (S.J. Rhodes 54 not out, Mushtaq Ahmed 5 for 94)

Worcestershire won by 2 wickets
Worcestershire 20 pts., Somerset 5 pts.

Only at Trent Bridge and Swansea was play possible on the first day, and just 43 overs were bowled at Trent Bridge. When play did begin at Chelmsford it seemed that the reigning champions had refound their form. They batted into the Saturday and hit 471 at nearly four runs an over. Salim Malik and Nasser Hussain both hit centuries – for Hussain his third of the season – and added 290 for the fourth wicket. There was some spectacular stroke-play in this partnership. A varied attack bowled out Derbyshire who were forced to go into bat for a second time on the Saturday evening, but Essex's first championship victory of the season did not materialise. They captured the lone wicket of nightwatchman Sladdin on the Monday, but Barnett batted through the day to save his side. The sad news for Derbyshire after this worthy draw was that fast bowler Ian Bishop was deemed unfit for the remainder of the season because of his back injury.

Put in to bat at Swansea, Glamorgan lost four middle-innings wickets for 13 runs and became victims of Tony Penberthy's career-best bowling performance. The medium-pacer wobbled the ball to such an extent as to disconcert all and clean bowl four. By the end of the day, having lost four wickets, Northamptonshire were within 32 runs of the Glamorgan score. Watkin and Croft managed to keep the visitors' lead within bounds, but the Glamorgan batsmen again found things difficult, and it was left to rain to save the game for the Welsh county.

Rain also blighted the game at Bristol where Durham were revived by an eighth-wicket stand of 93 between Scott and Cummins. Alleyne, batting with a sense of responsibility, hit an impressive 104 for Gloucestershire who declared on the Saturday evening, but later found the task of scoring 268 in 50 overs not to their liking.

In contrast, Yorkshire won excitingly and gloriously at Southampton. A generally consistent, if uninspired, batting performance took Hampshire to 307 on the Saturday morning. Yorkshire, perhaps batting with too great a sense of urgency, conceded a first-innings lead of 59 runs to their hosts. Hampshire lost three wickets in seven balls on the last morning, with Darren Gough in particularly fine form. Nevertheless, Yorkshire were left the challenging task of scoring 222 in 42 overs if they were to win the match. Moxon hit 61 from 70 balls, Richardson 33 off 35, and Yorkshire were off to the flying start they needed. Byas, impressing with every innings, and Blakey increased the momentum with 63 in seven overs, and Yorkshire won with 7.4 overs in hand. The left-handed Byas hit 2 sixes and 6 fours in his undefeated 53. Optimism ran high in Yorkshire.

Optimism was running high in Kent. Consistent batting took them to a commanding 394 by the end of the second day and, on the Saturday, in spite of a fifth-wicket stand of 190 between Crawley and Cairns, Nottinghamshire were forced to follow-on. Confronted mostly by the spin attack of Hooper and Davis, who sent down 77 overs between them and captured all nine wickets to fall, the Nottinghamshire batsmen showed a determination in their second innings which had not been prevalent in their first. Robinson adopted a positive approach, and asked Kent to make 179 in 36 overs. The wicket was now offering the spinners considerable help, but Ward began with a frenzy which suggested that this would present little problem. Then three wickets, including those of Ward and Hooper, fell for one run, and from that point Field-Buss and Afford were in command. Field-Buss returned the best figures of his career, and Nottinghamshire, thanks to the combination of off-spin and slow left-arm spin, won a remarkable victory.

The off-spinner they had released in order to give more opportunity to Field-Buss – Eddie Hemmings – won a two-day victory for his new county at Horsham. Sussex made 271 on the Friday, with everybody contributing a few, and Leicestershire finished on 57 for 3. The next day they lost 17 wickets while scoring 112 runs, displaying the greatest ineptitude against the wily off-spin of the veteran Hemmings who took 11 of the wickets to fall on the Saturday and finished with match figures of 12 for 58.

Put in to bat at Worcester, Somerset struggled through the Friday on which only 65 overs could be bowled. The game came alight on the Saturday when Mushtaq Ahmed encouraged Somerset's tail to wag, and then bowled his side to a first-innings lead of 94, a lead which looked mighty in the context of the match. It was to prove otherwise. Somerset quickly lost three wickets on the last morning and, eventually, Worcestershire needed 246 in 73 overs to win the match. With Mushtaq Ahmed again turning the ball and teasing the batsmen, it seemed unlikely that the home county would reach the target, and six men were out for 160. Rhodes and Newport added 77, but with two overs left Newport was caught at cover. With eight balls remaining, Tolley was caught at mid-on. Rhodes, who had hit the ball cleanly and crisply in a fine innings, remained firm and saw his side to their first win of the season with four balls to spare.

AXA EQUITY & LAW LEAGUE

22 May *at Chelmsford*

Essex 142 for 9 (N.V. Knight 54)
Derbyshire 145 for 8
Derbyshire (4 pts.) won by 2 wickets

at Pentrych

Glamorgan 169 for 9 (N.G.B. Cook 4 for 22)
Northamptonshire 170 for 7
Northamptonshire (4 pts.) won by 3 wickets

at Bristol

Durham 215 (G. Fowler 91, P.W.G. Parker 53)
Gloucestershire 216 for 5 (G.D. Hodgson 104 not out, A.J. Wright 61)
Gloucestershire (4 pts.) won by 5 wickets

at Southampton

Yorkshire 200 for 8 (R.B. Richardson 81)
Hampshire 170 (D. Gough 4 for 25)
Yorkshire (4 pts.) won by 30 runs

at Trent Bridge

Kent 264 for 9 (T.R. Ward 131, C.L. Hooper 94, C.L. Cairns 6 for 52)
Nottinghamshire 265 for 1 (P. Johnson 167 not out, R.T. Robinson 63 not out)
Nottinghamshire (4 pts.) won by 9 wickets

at Horsham

Sussex 283 for 8 (D.M. Smith 75, M.P. Speight 52)
Leicestershire 220 for 7
Sussex (4 pts.) won by 63 runs

Paul Johnson hit 167 off 106 balls as Nottinghamshire beat Kent at Trent Bridge, 22 May. Johnson hit 7 sixes and 20 fours. (Alan Cozzi)

at Worcester

Somerset 99
Worcestershire 100 for 6

Worcestershire (4 pts.) won by 4 wickets

An injury to Hussain and another limp batting performance by Essex allowed Derbyshire to win at Chelmsford with four balls to spare and to go joint top of the league on a Sunday sparkling with outstanding individual performances: Nick Cook had a Sunday best as Northamptonshire beat Glamorgan; Fowler and Parker put on 130 for Durham's second wicket against Gloucestershire, who won thanks to Dean Hodgson's first Sunday century; and Richie Richardson made his first significant contribution for Yorkshire in their victory over Hampshire. The real sensations were at Trent Bridge, however, where Trevor Ward and Carl Hooper both hit Sunday bests and put on 218 in 41 overs for Kent's second wicket. Chris Cairns took six wickets in a Sunday League game for the first time, but Notts faced the seemingly impossible task of scoring 265 to win. That they won with 14.4 overs to spare was due to an astonishing innings by Paul Johnson whose 167 not out was the highest score by a Nottinghamshire batsman in any one-day competition. He hit 7 sixes and 20 fours and faced only 106 balls. He and Robinson shared an unbroken second-wicket stand of 213 in 28 overs. This was dazzling stuff.

BENSON AND HEDGES CUP

QUARTER-FINALS

25 May *at Leicester*

Leicestershire 205 for 9 (N.E. Briers 58)
Worcestershire 150 (G.A. Hick 82, V.J. Wells 4 for 37)

Leicestershire won by 55 runs

(Gold Award – W.K.M. Benjamin)

at Hove

Sussex 178 for 7 (C.W.J. Athey 61 not out)
Lancashire 182 for 5

Lancashire won by 5 wickets

(Gold Award – Wasim Akram)

25 and 26 May *at Southampton*

Hampshire 223 for 7 (V.P. Terry 76)
Northamptonshire 227 for 3 (N.A. Felton 73)

Northamptonshire won by 7 wickets

(Gold Award – N.A. Felton)

at Taunton

Derbyshire 69 for 0
v. Somerset

Match abandoned

Derbyshire won 6–3 on bowl-out

Uncertain weather welcomed the Benson and Hedges Cup quarter-finals, and after 20.3 overs on the first day, the match at Taunton had to be abandoned. In the bowl-out – the only method available to decide the match in the time allowed – Derbyshire triumphed over Somerset. Derbyshire themselves had been beaten in a bowl-out against Hertfordshire in the NatWest Bank Trophy in 1991. Meanwhile, in more traditional manner, Leicestershire won comfortably against Worcestershire.

Choosing to bat first, Leicestershire found difficulty in coming to terms with a slow pitch and were in some trouble at 51 for 3. Nigel Briers stood firm, and he and Smith added 76, but it was the last five overs of the Leicestershire innings that were to prove decisive. Nixon and Benjamin improvised excitingly, and 58 runs were scored. Worcestershire lost both openers with three scored and, in spite of Hick's 82 off 122 balls, they blundered against some tight bowling. Winston Benjamin took the wickets of both openers, conceded only 13 runs in nine overs, held two catches and ran out Rhodes to gain the Gold Award.

Put in to bat, Sussex were denied the chance of aggression by Lancashire's pace bowlers, particularly Wasim Akram, and it was the Pakistani captain who lifted the visitors when it seemed they might stumble in their task of scoring 179 to win. He dominated a stand of 79 from 17 overs with Lloyd which brought Lancashire to the brink of victory.

Hampshire had to play in unfavourable conditions when they were put in to bat at Southampton, and rain caused two interruptions to play with 70 minutes lost. In the event, the Hampshire innings was a stuttering affair, played in murky light in the early stages. After the loss of Middleton at 7, Smith and Terry added 86, but by the halfway stage, Hampshire were a mere 72 for 1. They never really gained a grip on the game. Fordham and Felton began the Northamptonshire innings with a stand of 74, and Felton and Bailey added 83. Both were out within the space of six balls before bad light brought an early closure, but Lamb and Loye took Northamptonshire into the semi-finals with eight balls to spare the following morning.

25, 26 and 27 May *at The Oval*

Australians 378 for 9 dec. (M.E. Waugh 178, D.R. Martyn 84, G.P. Thorpe 4 for 40) and 171 for 4 dec. (M.A. Taylor 80, M.J. Slater 50)
Surrey 231 and 144 (S.K. Warne 4 for 38)

Australians won by 174 runs

There was some glorious batting on the opening day of the match. Following his impressively controlled century in the Texaco Trophy, Mark Waugh hit a breathtaking 178 off 174 balls with 8 sixes and 15 fours. He and Martyn added 237 in two hours, 26 minutes for the fourth wicket. Without Martin Bicknell and Waqar Younis, the Surrey attack looked thin, but Graham Thorpe claimed a career best 4 for 40. By the end of the second day, having taken a first-innings lead of 147, the tourists were 152 for 2 in their second innings, with Mark Taylor in bustling form. There were more sensations on the last day when Surrey capitulated to a varied attack, and Tim Zoehrer dismissed eight batsmen – six catches and two stumpings. Zoehrer's eight victims in an innings was only the third occasion the feat had been accomplished in England, David East of Essex having claimed eight at Taunton in 1985, and Steve Marsh eight for Kent at Lord's in 1991.

27, 28, 29 and **31** May *at Derby*

Hampshire 243 (T.C. Middleton 90, A.E. Warner 4 for 52) and 290 for 4 (R.A. Smith 101, V.P. Terry 96, D.I. Gower 52)

Derbyshire 389 for 7 dec. (P.D. Bowler 79, C.J. Adams 65, J.E. Morris 61, K.J. Barnett 58, T.J.G. O'Gorman 55)

Match drawn

Derbyshire 8 pts., Hampshire 4 pts.

Jason Gallian led Oxford University to victory over Nottinghamshire, 1 June. (David Munden/Sports-Line)

at Darlington

Durham 160 (W. Larkins 54, A.P. Igglesden 6 for 58) and 135 (M.J. McCague 5 for 33, A.P. Igglesden 4 for 67)

Kent 317 (M.V. Fleming 70)

Kent won by an innings and 22 runs

Kent 23 pts., Durham 4 pts.

at Gloucester (King's School)

Gloucestershire 101 (R.K. Illingworth 6 for 28) and 116 (K.C.G. Benjamin 4 for 35)

Worcestershire 222 (T.S. Curtis 68, G.A. Hick 68, C.A. Walsh 5 for 62)

Worcestershire won by an innings and 5 runs

Worcestershire 21 pts., Gloucestershire 4 pts.

at Liverpool

Lancashire 279 for 7 dec. (W.K. Hegg 69 not out) and 0 for 0 dec.

Warwickshire 0 for 0 dec. and 171 for 7

Match drawn

Lancashire 5 pts., Warwickshire 3 pts.

at Lord's

Sussex 161 (F.D. Stephenson 60, N.F. Williams 6 for 61) and 143 (C.W.J. Athey 55, P.C.R. Tufnell 5 for 47, J.E. Emburey 4 for 46)

Middlesex 339 (D.L. Haynes 73, M.W. Gatting 70, K.R. Brown 66, J.E. Emburey 62 not out, I.D.K. Salisbury 4 for 104)

Middlesex won by an innings and 35 runs

Middlesex 23 pts., Sussex 2 pts.

at Taunton

Somerset 185 (M.N. Lathwell 84, S.L. Watkin 4 for 45) and 366 for 7 dec. (C.J. Tavaré 141 not out)

Glamorgan 252 (I.V.A. Richards 56, H. Morris 53, A.R. Caddick 4 for 63) and 215 (A.R. Caddick 6 for 66)

Somerset won by 84 runs

Somerset 20 pts., Glamorgan 6 pts.

29, 30 and **31** May *at Leicester*

Australians 323 for 3 dec. (D.C. Boon 123, M.J. Slater 91) and 88 for 4 dec. (M.J. Slater 50 not out)

Leicestershire 168 for 7 dec. and 146

Australians won by 97 runs

29, 31 May and **1** June *at Oxford*

Nottinghamshire 249 for 7 dec. (R.T. Robinson 60, M. Saxelby 56) and 158 for 4 dec. (P.R. Pollard 64 not out, C.C. Lewis 51)

Oxford University 151 (C.C. Lewis 4 for 51) and 257 for 3 (J.E.R. Gallian 141 not out, G.I. MacMillan 51)

Oxford University won by 7 wickets

Australian reserve keeper Tim Zoehrer held six catches and made two stumpings in Surrey's second innings at The Oval, 27 May. In dismissing eight batsmen, he equalled the record for a first-class match in England held jointly by David East and Steve Marsh. (Alan Cozzi)

No play on the first day at Derby and a limited second day condemned the match between Derbyshire and Hampshire to a draw. Derbyshire's first five scored very briskly in an attempt to force a result, but Robin Smith and Paul Terry added 177 on the last afternoon, Smith's 101 being his first significant first-class score of the season.

Kent gained their first championship win of the season, beating a Durham side that was looking old and frail. Igglesden clinched a recall to the England side with 10 for 125 in the match, and although Kent made only 317 through consistent rather than spectacular batting, they won by an innings early on the third day.

There was no play on the first two days at Liverpool and, in spite of contrivances and gifts, Warwickshire and Lancashire could not produce a result.

Like Durham, Gloucestershire were patently a weak side, and although there was no play on the first day of their match against Worcestershire, the visitors won in just over two days. Put in to bat, Gloucestershire quickly succumbed to Illingworth's left-arm spin and were bowled out in 52.4 overs. Worcestershire lost their last nine wickets for 85 runs, but by the close on Saturday, Gloucestershire were 50 for 5, and they were soon put out of their misery on the last morning.

Sussex chose to bat first at Lord's but the loss of six middle-innings wickets for 27 runs put paid to any advantage they may have gained from doing so. Middlesex began well with Haynes and Gatting adding 115 for the second wicket, but it was a sixth-wicket stand of 107 between Brown and Emburey that gave the innings its substance when it seemed likely to sag. Sussex batted

poorly in their second innings, and they ended the third day on 120 for 5. They scored only another 23 runs on the Monday morning, collapsing before the combined spin of Tufnell and Emburey.

Somerset moved to the top of the table with victory over Glamorgan. Put in to bat, Somerset were bowled out for 185 by the Glamorgan seam attack, with only Mark Lathwell meeting the problems posed by the conditions and the bowlers with confidence and aggression. At 134 for 2 at the end of the first day, Glamorgan were in a commanding position but, in spite of a gem of an innings from Viv Richards – 56 off 89 balls in his last appearance in a championship match at Taunton where he once gave so much excitement and pleasure – they failed to press home their advantage. Nevertheless, at the end of the second day, Somerset were 124 for 3, and Glamorgan still had the upper hand. Rain brought play to a close at tea-time on Saturday, but by that time, Chris Tavaré had reached the 48th hundred of his career, and Somerset had a lead of 222 with five wickets in hand. They batted for an hour on the last morning, and by the time Tavaré effected the closure of the innings he had batted for close on seven hours. It was a knock which changed the course of the match. James was out to the last ball before lunch, and from that point on, Glamorgan were struggling. Dale, Richards and Croft all suggested big innings which did not materialise. Caddick finished with six wickets – 10 in the match – and Somerset were top.

Slater and Boon shared a second-wicket stand of 214 for the Australians at Leicester, but rain disrupted the second day. It made little difference to the tourists who demolished the county side on the last afternoon, May and Warne sharing the honours. Slater's two belligerent innings enhanced his prospects of opening the Australian innings in the first Test, for Hayden seemed out of luck and out of form.

Border is stumped by Stewart off Such for 17. (USPA)

Oxford University gained a spectacular and most worthy victory over Nottinghamshire in The Parks. Set a target of 257 in the last two sessions of the match, the University were given a good start by Gallian and Gupte who put on 87. Gallian was then joined by MacMillan, and the pair added 105. MacMillan was caught on the boundary immediately after completing his half-century, and Gallian reached the second century of his career in the same over. He eventually led his side to a memorable victory, reaching the highest score of his career, facing 214 balls and hitting 15 fours.

AXA EQUITY & LAW LEAGUE

30 May *at Checkley*

Derbyshire *v.* Hampshire

Match abandoned

Derbyshire 2 pts., Hampshire 2 pts.

at Darlington

Kent 300 for 7 (C.L. Hooper 85)
Durham 91 for 0

Match abandoned

Kent 2 pts., Durham 2 pts.

at Gloucester

Worcestershire 108 for 3 (G.A. Hick 59)
Gloucestershire 93 for 3

Worcestershire (4 pts.) won by 15 runs

at Old Trafford

Lancashire 174 for 7 (N.M.K. Smith 5 for 26)
***v.* Warwickshire**

Match abandoned

Lancashire 2 pts., Warwickshire 2 pts.

at Lord's

Middlesex 247 for 7 (M.W. Gatting 91)
Sussex 247 for 8 (C.W.J. Athey 85)

Match tied

Middlesex 2 pts., Sussex 2 pts.

at Taunton

Somerset *v.* Glamorgan

Match abandoned

Somerset 2 pts., Glamorgan 2 pts.

The rain was particularly cruel on Durham, for Botham and Larkins had hit 91 off 12.3 overs when the game at Darlington was brought to a halt. Ten overs an innings

The turning point: Mike Gatting is bowled by Shane Warne's first ball in a Test match in England. This delivery was to have a profound effect on the rest of the series. (USPA)

was the fare at Gloucester where Hick reached 50 off 31 balls, and Neil Smith's best bowling performance in limited-over cricket mattered little when rain descended on Manchester.

Wind kept the rain away at Lord's and didn't help Sussex in their attempts to catch Mike Gatting who added 81 with Carr and 93 for the fifth wicket with Brown at 7.15 an over. Sussex, with Athey and Alan Wells in good form, looked set for victory, but Wells and Greenfield were out in quick succession, and Moores and Athey were out within the space of eight balls. Ten were needed from the last over. Lenham was caught off Emburey's second ball, but Colin Wells and Pigott took eight off the next four to tie the match, Pigott hitting three off the final delivery.

 FIRST TEST MATCH
ENGLAND *v.* AUSTRALIA, at Old Trafford

The England selectors showed some bravery in their initial choices, naming Such, Ilott and Igglesden in the attack. Then Igglesden, whose one and only Test cap had

A first Test wicket for Peter Such – Boon is caught at slip by Lewis.
(Patrick Eagar)

been won in 1989, was forced to withdraw through injury the day before the match. He was replaced by DeFreitas who played and opened the bowling, although he was not in the original selection. The selectors' courage had by now failed them, and Ilott was omitted. Like Such, Caddick earned his first Test cap, and New Zealand – where he was born and played his first cricket – lamented.

In their choice of batsmen, the selectors were far from brave. The retention of Gatting was as inexplicable as had been his recall for the tour of India, and the omission of a specialist wicket-keeper was again a cause for concern, not least because Russell, Metson, Marsh, Burns and others were being sacrificed due to the failings of specialist batsmen and all-rounders.

Australia gave first Test caps to Slater, whose experience in first-class cricket was far less than Lathwell's, and to Julian. Martyn and May were those who were unlucky not to be selected.

Gooch won the toss and asked Australia to bat. The start was delayed by an hour when it was discovered that the bowlers' run-ups were damp, although this did seem ultra-cautious. Gooch's decision to field first was based on the assumption that the ball would seam appreciably at the start of the match and that the wicket would get better. Only the first assumption proved to be correct.

Caddick began his Test career with a tidy maiden and was warned for running on the pitch. DeFreitas began with a ball which swung wildly down the leg side, and he did not concede a run until his fourth over, but neither did he force the batsmen to play.

Taylor looked solid and met the ball with the middle of the bat, and Slater was wristy, compact and impressively eager and alert. At lunch, Australia were 58 without loss, and they were well satisfied with a morning which had demanded less of them than had been expected.

Such and Tufnell both bowled before lunch, but they promised more than they achieved in the early stages. Slater became more eager, showing an obvious relish for Test cricket. He hit Such for an all-run four, an off-drive, and then straight-drove him powerfully to the boundary next ball. Taylor played an exquisite cover drive off Tufnell, and both batsmen used their feet with a nimbleness that would have delighted Fred Astaire.

The hundred came up in the 36th over, and fifties for Taylor and Slater quickly followed. The bowling was changed by rotation rather than from tactics, but in the 44th over England obtained the breakthrough that had looked unlikely. DeFreitas bowled a ball to Slater that was well wide of the off stump, and short. The batsman could have cut it for four but chose to pull. It was a wretched shot, and he edged to Stewart – so unworthy an end to a fine Test debut. At tea, Australia were 148 for 1 from 53 overs, but they should have been in a worse position, for Taylor was dropped at second slip by Hick – a straightforward chance – when 64, with the score on 135.

Boon never suggested that he would approach the fluency of Taylor, but he did not look as if he would get out either, and it came as some surprise when, in the 69th over, he steered a straight ball from Such to Lewis at slip, and the fielder caught the ball at the second attempt. It was Such's first Test wicket, and in the next hour he was to become an instant hero. But first, Taylor swept him for a single to reach his century out of 193 in 73 overs. Then Taylor straight-drove Tufnell for a magnificent six, and the next over he put Such over long-on for another six. The Australian vice-captain was threatening to run riot.

The Australian advance was halted when Mark Waugh went to drive Tufnell, did not get to the pitch of the ball and was caught and bowled. Worse was to follow. Border hit the second ball he received high over mid-wicket for three, a strange shot at this stage of the game, and then Taylor, attempting to whip Such through the leg side, was deceived in the flight and caught and bowled. Steve Waugh went to drive Such and was bowled between bat and pad by a ball which turned expansively.

Australia ended an intriguing first day on 242 for 5. Such's three wickets had brought England back into the game after Taylor's splendid 124 off 234 balls – an innings which included 12 fours as well as his 2 sixes – had threatened to put Australia in an unassailable position.

Such's success continued on the second morning. Border pushed forward and lifted his heel for Stewart to pull off a smart stumping. The wicket-keeper missed an easier one the same over, allowing Julian to escape, but it was not a costly miss, for Julian was soon taken at short-leg off the Essex off-spinner. Hughes could not resist the challenge of spin and hit Such high to square-leg where DeFreitas held the ball as he ran forward. This was Such's sixth wicket, and he was to complete a memorable debut when he held a head-high catch to get rid of Healy.

England must have been heartened to be facing a total of 289 rather than the one of over 400 which had seemed likely at one time, and Gooch and Atherton raised spirits higher with a purposeful opening stand of 71 in 99 minutes, a stand which was ended only when Atherton failed to get his bat out of the way of a lifting ball from Hughes.

Now came the turning point of the match in every respect: Shane Warne was introduced into the attack. His first ball in Test cricket in England was bowled to Gatting. It pitched outside leg stump and hit Gatting's off stump, a delivery of immense psychological impact. In Warne's next over, Smith pushed forward and was caught low at slip.

By the time that Gatting had been dismissed, Gooch had already reached a highly commendable fifty, but even now much rested upon him as Warne, operating from the Warwick Road end, threatened to control the match. Gooch attempted to wrest control and, if he did not always read the leg-spinner aright, he reacted positively at all times, and the last ball before tea – a googly – he hit high to the long-on boundary.

He had been solid for three hours, but he was beaten by both the leg-break and the googly before he clouted a full toss to mid-on. England had lost her rudder, and the ship began to drift. Hick was dropped at gully off McDermott before slashing Hughes to cover. Lewis nudged the same bowler to short-leg, and DeFreitas became Julian's first Test victim when he was beaten by a delivery of full length. Stewart had looked ill at ease at number six, and he became Julian's second victim when he played outside an in-swinger. England were 202 for 8 at the close, and Such's great performance was already fading into the past.

Healy claimed two catches on the third morning, Warne and Hughes finished with four wickets apiece, and England added just eight more runs, but Such was still to be reckoned with. In his first over, the ninth of the innings, he had Taylor leg before when the left-hander missed an attempted sweep. Eight overs later, Slater was taken at mid-on. But this was false dawn. In the next 136 minutes, Boon and Mark Waugh added 109. Boon was rugged, rock-like, blending high-quality drives on the off side with nudges and deflections. Waugh was majestic. He hooked the ineffective Lewis for six, and his 107-ball innings included 5 fours. He was out when a ball from Tufnell, pitched well outside leg stump, was diverted into the stumps by his pads. Border and Boon moved to 231 for 3 at stumps.

There was really no hope for England at that point, but

Gooch's very fine innings is at an end as, with his hand, he instinctively brushes away a ball that was dropping on the stumps. (Patrick Eagar)

An ecstatic Ian Healy waves his bat to the crowd to acknowledge the applause for his maiden first-class century, made in the first Test match. (David Munden/Sports-Line)

there were flickers early on the fourth morning. Hick put down another catch, but almost immediately Border was caught in two minds against Caddick and lofted a gentle catch to give the bowler his first Test wicket. Steve Waugh started uncertainly, but it was Boon who fell, driving DeFreitas to cover. If this was a bonus for England, there were no more to come. Steve Waugh was now settled, and Ian Healy batted with jubilance. The bowling, for the

Stewart, caught Healy, bowled Warne, 11. (Ben Radford/Allsport)

most part, degenerated into the pedestrian, and the fielders lost heart.

Healy and Steve Waugh added 180 in 164 minutes. Healy was a revelation. In each Test he has played, his batting has shown improvement so that he entered this, his 48th Test, with an average of 21.72 from 71 innings. He had hit seven fifties, and now he reached his first century in first-class cricket. It came from 133 balls and included 12 fours, and was a joyful effort, worthy of high praise. Border declared, and England needed 512 to win or, more realistically, they had to survive for 8½ hours.

Atherton did not breathe confidence against Warne, but he survived for more than an hour and a half and had hit 25 when he pushed forward to a leg-break and was taken at slip. There was under an hour left until the end of play, but Gatting and the dominant Gooch scored quite freely. England were gaining in strength – and then came disaster. With the last ball of the day, Merv Hughes yorked Gatting via his pads, and England were 133 for 2. As in the first innings, Gatting's dismissal could be seen as crucial.

Still there was Gooch and, for a time on the last morning, there was Robin Smith. How he survived two

FIRST CORNHILL TEST MATCH – ENGLAND v. AUSTRALIA
3, 4, 5, 6 and 7 June 1993 at Old Trafford, Manchester

AUSTRALIA

	FIRST INNINGS			SECOND INNINGS		
M.A. Taylor	c and b Such	124	(2) lbw, b Such		9
M.J. Slater	c Stewart, b DeFreitas	58	(1) c Caddick, b Such		27
D.C. Boon	c Lewis, b Such	21	c Gatting, b DeFreitas		93
M.E. Waugh	c and b Tufnell	6	b Tufnell		64
A.R. Border (capt)	st Stewart, b Such	17	c and b Caddick		31
S.R. Waugh	b Such	3	not out		78
*I.A. Healy	c Such, b Tufnell	12	not out		102
B.P. Julian	c Gatting, b Such	0		
M.G. Hughes	c DeFreitas, b Such	2		
S.K. Warne	not out	15		
C.J. McDermott	run out	8		
Extras	b 8, lb 8, nb 7	23	b 6, lb 14, w 8		28
		289	(for 5 wickets, dec.)		**432**

ENGLAND

	FIRST INNINGS			SECOND INNINGS		
G.A. Gooch (capt)	c Julian, b Warne	65	handled ball		133
M.A. Atherton	c Healy, b Hughes	19	c Taylor, b Warne		25
M.W. Gatting	b Warne	4	b Hughes		23
R.A. Smith	c Taylor, b Warne	4	b Warne		18
G.A. Hick	c Border, b Hughes	34	c Healy, b Hughes		22
*A.J. Stewart	b Julian	27	c Healy, b Warne		11
C.C. Lewis	c Boon, b Hughes	9	c Taylor, b Warne		43
P.A.J. DeFreitas	lbw, b Julian	5	lbw, b Hughes		7
A.R. Caddick	c Healy, b Warne	7	c Warne, b Hughes		25
P.M. Such	not out	14	c Border, b Hughes		9
P.C.R. Tufnell	c Healy, b Hughes	1	not out		0
Extras	b 6, lb 10, nb 5	21	lb 11, w 1, nb 4		16
		210			**332**

	O	M	R	W	O	M	R	W		O	M	R	W	O	M	R	W
Caddick	15	4	38	–	20	3	79	1	McDermott	18	2	50	–	30	9	76	–
DeFreitas	23	8	46	1	24	1	80	1	Hughes	20.5	5	59	4	27.2	4	92	4
Lewis	13	2	44	–	9	–	43	–	Julian	11	2	30	2	14	1	67	1
Such	33	9	67	6	31	6	78	2	Warne	24	10	51	4	49	26	86	4
Tufnell	28	5	78	2	37	4	112	1	Border	1	–	4	–				
Hick					9	1	20	–									

FALL OF WICKETS

1–128, 2–183, 3–221, 4–225, 5–232, 6–260, 7–264, 8–266, 9–289
1–23, 2–46, 3–155, 4–234, 5–252

FALL OF WICKETS

1–71, 2–80, 3–84, 4–123, 5–148, 6–168, 7–178, 8–183, 9–203
1–73, 2–133, 3–171, 4–223, 5–230, 6–238, 7–260, 8–299, 9–331

Umpires: H.D. Bird & K.E. Palmer

Australia won by 179 runs

Robin Smith looks back in dismay as a delivery from Shane Warne spins back onto his stumps. (Ben Radford/Allsport)

appeals for leg before against Warne, only umpire Palmer will know, but survive he did until Gooch had reached a marvellous century. Gooch had been dropped at short-leg by Boon, but there was no escape for Smith when he pushed forward at Warne and met the ball with the bat, only to see it spin viciously back onto his stumps. There were no more alarms, however, and England were 197 for 3 at lunch, with hopes growing that they could yet save the game.

Those hopes began to disappear after the bizarre dismissal of Gooch. He had batted for 314 minutes, and had hit 21 fours and 2 sixes in his 133 off 217 balls. He had given strength to his team with the quality and character of his performance. This was indeed a captain's innings, and thus the end was sad. He played a ball from Hughes defensively on the back foot, but the ball leapt back and seemed that it would drop on the stumps. Instinctively, Gooch brushed it away with his hand, and he knew immediately what he had done. A moment of bathos after the heroics.

Hick, never impressive and twice close to being out, was caught behind two overs later. Stewart's stay was brief, the victim of a Warne leg-break which turned less than expected. Four vital wickets had fallen in the afternoon session, and England had an uncomfortable tea at 273 for 7, for DeFreitas had fallen just as he had done in the first innings, beaten on the back foot by a ball of full length from Julian.

Warne was back in the attack after tea, and if Lewis was able to benefit from the close field which offered him runs, he could not delay the inevitable and edged a leg-break to slip. Now came unexpected resistance from Such and Caddick, and even at this late stage it seemed the game could be saved. Caddick's great effort was ended when Warne took a splendid catch off a leg-glance, and when Border held a diving catch at silly point to claim Such, Australia had won with 9.4 overs remaining.

Warne was named Man of this memorable Test match which had so many heroes – Such, Gooch, Taylor, Boon, Healy and the unflagging Merv Hughes who, with McDermott ailing, gave a mighty effort with the ball. Australia celebrated; and England mused on their sixth Test match defeat in succession.

Such is caught by Border off Hughes, and Australia win the first Test. (Patrick Eagar)

A century of heroic proportions from Mark Lathwell failed to save Somerset from defeat by Essex at Chelmsford, 6 June. (Alan Cozzi)

3, 4, 5 and 6 June *at Chelmsford*

Somerset 202 (Mushtaq Ahmed 71) and 197 (M.N. Lathwell 132, N.A. Foster 5 for 58)

Essex 265 (P.J. Prichard 123, D.R. Pringle 54) and 136 for 3 (J.J.B. Lewis 50)

Essex won by 7 wickets

Essex 22 pts., Somerset 5 pts.

at Tunbridge Wells

Gloucestershire 243 (G.D. Hodgson 75, B.C. Broad 64, D.W. Headley 7 for 79) and 162 (M.V. Fleming 4 for 31)

Kent 474 (M.R. Benson 103, C.L. Hooper 96, M.A. Ealham 55, S.A. Marsh 54, K.E. Cooper 4 for 108)

Kent won by an innings and 69 runs

Kent 22 pts., Gloucestershire 3 pts.

at Leicester

Durham 160 (L. Potter 4 for 46) and 206 (I.T. Botham 65, P.W.G. Parker 58)

Leicestershire 371 (T.J. Boon 105, W.K.M. Benjamin 83)

Leicestershire won by an innings and 5 runs

Leicestershire 23 pts., Durham 3 pts.

at Lord's

Derbyshire 168 (C.J. Adams 53, M.A. Feltham 4 for 48) and 89 (N.F. Williams 4 for 36)

Middlesex 193 and 68 for 0

Middlesex won by 10 wickets

Middlesex 20 pts., Derbyshire 4 pts.

at Northampton

Northamptonshire 494 for 6 dec. (A. Fordham 193, A.J. Lamb 64, N.A. Felton 59, D.J. Capel 54) and 110 for 4

Worcestershire 231 (P.J. Newport 79 not out, C.M. Tolley 60, J.P. Taylor 4 for 64) and 370 (T.S. Curtis 74, S.J. Rhodes 72, G.R. Haynes 70, R.J. Bailey 4 for 50)

Northamptonshire won by 6 wickets

Northamptonshire 23 pts., Worcestershire 1 pt.

at Trent Bridge

Hampshire 355 (D.I. Gower 153, A.N. Aymes 62, M.G. Field-Buss 4 for 66) and 256 for 9 dec. (V.P. Terry 94)

Nottinghamshire 288 (P. Johnson 100, C.L. Cairns 81, S.D. Udal 5 for 97) and 154 (C.L. Cairns 64, S.D. Udal 5 for 74)

Hampshire won by 169 runs

Hampshire 23 pts., Nottinghamshire 5 pts.

at The Oval

Lancashire 392 (M. Watkinson 107, G.D. Lloyd 79, N.J. Speak 73, Wasim Akram 60, J.E. Benjamin 4 for 96) and 266 (N.J. Speak 69, G.D. Mendis 68, Waqar Younis 5 for 52)

Surrey 260 (M.P. Bicknell 57, P.J. Martin 4 for 63) and 302 (M.A. Lynch 63, D.J. Bicknell 58, G.P. Thorpe 51, Wasim Akram 6 for 49)

Lancashire won by 96 runs

Lancashire 24 pts., Surrey 6 pts.

at Edgbaston

Sussex 414 (A.P. Wells 130, D.M. Smith 80) and 207 for 3 dec. (D.M. Smith 71, C.W.J. Athey 69)

Warwickshire 301 for 7 dec. (J.D. Ratcliffe 101, A.J. Moles 77) and 199 for 5 (E.E. Hemmings 4 for 70)

Match drawn

Sussex 6 pts., Warwickshire 5 pts.

at Middlesbrough

Glamorgan 323 (A. Dale 100, S.P. James 76) and 304 for 3 dec. (H. Morris 134 not out, M.P. Maynard 58)

Yorkshire 314 (R.B. Richardson 81, C. White 67, M.D. Moxon 51, R.J. Blakey 50, S.L. Watkin 4 for 59) and 192 (A.A. Metcalfe 56, S.L. Watkin 4 for 59)

Glamorgan won by 121 runs

Glamorgan 21 pts., Yorkshire 5 pts.

Essex, the reigning champions, beat Somerset and so gained their first championship win of the season and knocked Somerset off the top of the table. Put in to bat, Somerset struggled against a varied attack and, in spite of Lathwell's glistening 48, slipped to 98 for 7. They were revived by Mushtaq who hit 11 fours and a six in his 71 off 100 balls after being dropped at slip on four. Essex bowled well, and Garnham held five catches behind the stumps. Stephenson and Prichard began brightly, and Essex were 73 for 1 at the end of the first day. Somerset's medium-pace attack, aided by Tavaré's excellent slip catching, accounted for four wickets on the second morning, but Pringle helped Prichard to add 118, and acting captain Prichard reached a stylish century. Essex had some fortune at the start of Somerset's second innings when Hayhurst was run out backing up. Foster, working up a good pace, then took four wickets, one of them an incredible one-handed catch by Hussain on the long-leg boundary to dismiss Folland, and Topley had Tavaré taken at slip so that Somerset ended the second day in disarray at 88 for 6, defeat imminent. That the game was not over early on the third morning was due entirely to Mark Lathwell. In an astonishing innings, which included 2 sixes and 13 fours, he hit 132 out of Somerset's 197, with extras (15) and Mallender (13) being the only ones to contribute double figures to the score. He delayed the inevitable in heroic and belligerent manner, but Essex moved to victory shortly after tea.

Gloucestershire's limp batting was again in evidence. Broad and Hodgson gave them a good start with a partnership of 117, but the Gloucestershire batsmen failed to maintain even two runs an over on the first day. Dean Headley finished the innings on the second morning and produced by far the best bowling figures of his brief career. Thanks to a second-wicket stand of 206 between Benson and Hooper, Kent were ahead by the end of the day, and on a sleepy third day at the most beautiful ground in England, they moved sedately to a big score. Broad and Hodgson again began brightly, but three wickets fell for 11 runs – two of them to Hooper – and Kent were easy winners on the last morning.

Like Gloucestershire, their neighbours at the bottom of the table, Durham found runs hard to score. Bowled out for a tedious 160 on the first day at Grace Road, they were then ground down by Tim Boon's five-hour century. Winston Benjamin hit fiercely at the close, and Leicestershire claimed an innings victory on the Saturday even though Botham and Parker had begun Durham's second innings with a partnership of 95.

In an extraordinary match at Lord's, neither Middlesex nor Derbyshire reached 200, and the match was over in two days with Middlesex winning by 10 wickets. Both medium pace and spin captured wickets, and the exciting Chris Adams was the only batsman to reach 50. Middlesex's early victory sent them to the top of the table.

Northamptonshire were given a fine start against Worcestershire when Fordham and Felton put on 152. Fordham's 193 was the highest score of the season, and a quick finish seemed likely when Worcestershire plummeted to 68 for 8. Newport and Tolley, who hit a career best 60, added 108, and Newport and Benjamin put on 55

for the last wicket, but the follow-on was not avoided. Batting a second time, Worcestershire again found their strength in their tail, and it was Bailey who finally ousted them with a career best four wickets. Needing to score 108 in 24 overs to win, Northamptonshire found the task difficult, but Bailey hit Illingworth for six to bring victory with three balls to spare.

David Gower chose the first day of the first Test to hit his first century of the season and, in spite of a fifth-wicket stand of 150 between Johnson and Cairns, Nottinghamshire trailed Hampshire by 67 runs on the first innings. Terry, leading Hampshire in the absence of the injured Nicholas, gave substance to their second innings and was able to leave his bowlers the last day on which to win the match. Cairns was again Nottinghamshire's resistance fighter, but Udal and Turner spun Hampshire to victory, their first of the season.

There was some bright batting on the first day at The Oval where Lancashire recovered from 44 for 3 to score at nearly four runs an over. There were fast runs from Speak, Lloyd and Wasim, and Mike Watkinson hit 107 off 165 balls with 12 boundaries. Lynch's decision to field had paid early dividends, but his bowlers had suffered once Lancashire decided to attack. Surrey could not match such belligerence, and they were rescued from the depths of 123 for 6 only by the positivity of Martin Bicknell and Waqar Younis. Asked to score 399 to win, Surrey were given a splendid start by Darren Bicknell and Lynch who hit 114 before the close of play on the Saturday. They added only 10 runs more on the Monday, however, but Thorpe, Brown and Andrew Smith maintained the challenge until Wasim Akram brought about a collapse, and the last five wickets went down for six runs.

A shortened first day at Edgbaston was followed by Alan Wells' 130 in 258 minutes for Sussex on the second. Jason Ratcliffe hit a maiden championship century on the Saturday and shared an opening stand of 153 with Andy Moles. Reeve declared 113 runs in arrears but, challenged to score 321 in 60 overs to win the match, Warwickshire were blunted by the accuracy of Eddie Hemmings who was returning to the ground where he began his first-class career 27 years earlier.

A second-wicket partnership of 149 between James and Dale gave Glamorgan a fine start at Middlesbrough. Dale reached his fifth first-class hundred, but Glamorgan lost their last five wickets for 46 runs. Yorkshire built their innings with ever-increasing momentum. Richardson hit a spirited maiden fifty in the championship, and they ended the second day on 265 for 4, with White and Blakey unbeaten and having already added 100. They added 23 more on the third morning, but six wickets then fell for 30 runs. Glamorgan seized their chance. Morris and Dale batted solidly, and Maynard and Richards provided the dash. Morris' declaration allowed Yorkshire 83 overs in which to score 314 runs. They began well enough and were 137 for 2 before Watkin and Richards brought about the collapse which gave Glamorgan a comfortable win and took them near to the top of the table, just below Middlesex.

Bank on NatWest for a First Class Performance

We at NatWest are extremely proud of our long-standing involvement in the community.

Our aim is to promote financial effectiveness and enterprise through projects linked to the environment, education and equal opportunities as well as supporting the arts and sport.

We are active supporters of grass roots cricket, sponsoring the NatWest Under 13s Championships for the Ken Barrington Cup, NatWest Old England XI, NCA Proficiency Awards and Cricket Society Coaching scholarships.

National Westminster Bank
Investing in the Community

National Westminster Bank Plc
Registered Number 929027 England Registered Office 41 Lothbury London EC2P 2BP

AXA EQUITY & LAW LEAGUE

6 June *at Chelmsford*

Somerset 201 for 9 (R.J. Harden 89)
Essex 179

Somerset (4 pts.) won by 22 runs

at Tunbridge Wells

Gloucestershire 204 (M.W. Alleyne 78, B.C. Broad 52)
Kent 207 for 3 (N.R. Taylor 80, C.L. Hooper 70 not out)

Kent (4 pts.) won by 7 wickets

at Leicester

Leicestershire 217 for 7 (B.F. Smith 51 not out)
Durham 214 for 9 (P. Bainbridge 61)

Leicestershire (4 pts.) won by 3 runs

at Lord's

Derbyshire 240 for 2 (P.D. Bowler 104 not out, C.J. Adams 80)
Middlesex 241 for 8 (M.R. Ramprakash 84, D.E. Malcolm 4 for 36)

Middlesex (4 pts.) won by 2 wickets

at Northampton

Northamptonshire 168 for 9
Worcestershire 168 for 9 (D.B. D'Oliveira 83)

Match tied

Northamptonshire 2 pts., Worcestershire 2 pts.

at Trent Bridge

Nottinghamshire 204 for 9 (R.T. Robinson 66)
Hampshire 208 for 2 (D.I. Gower 59)

Hampshire (4 pts.) won by 8 wickets

at The Oval

Surrey 259 for 9 (A.D. Brown 103, D.M. Ward 55, Wasim Akram 4 for 32)
Lancashire 94 (A.J. Hollioake 4 for 33)

Surrey (4 pts.) won by 165 runs

at Edgbaston

Warwickshire 133 (A.N. Jones 4 for 24)
Sussex 134 for 8

Sussex (4 pts.) won by 2 wickets

at Middlesbrough

Glamorgan 208 for 9 (S.P. James 51)
Yorkshire 183 (S.R. Barwick 4 for 27)

Glamorgan (4 pts.) won by 25 runs

With the perversity that is characteristic of the fixture list, there was a full complement of matches on the Sunday of the first Test match although there had been only six the previous weekend – a bank holiday weekend, to boot – when there had been no Test in progress. Essex played poorly against Somerset, who had their first Sunday win of the season, while Kent regained composure and the top spot of the table by beating Gloucestershire at Tunbridge Wells. Taylor and Hooper scored 147 for Kent's third wicket, after Gloucestershire had lost their last five wickets for 10 runs in 15 balls.

Durham still found it impossible to win after being in a good position, and they could not manage 11 in the last over against Leicestershire. Bowler and the exuberant Adams hit 141 for Derbyshire's first wicket, but their scoring rate over the last 20 overs was not sufficient to take them to a commanding total against Middlesex. Ramprakash batted well for the home side, but a fine second spell by Malcolm put Derbyshire back on top. Then Johnson and Keech added 38 off 23 balls, and Middlesex won with seven deliveries to spare.

On a dull pitch at Northampton, Worcestershire needed only 27 from the last 38 balls with six wickets standing, but a collapse followed, and three were needed from the last four balls. Even this proved too much. Tolley

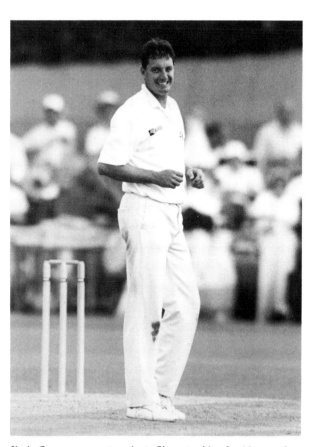

Kevin Cooper gave great service to Gloucestershire after 16 years of endeavour for Nottinghamshire. (Tom Morris)

was bowled, Benjamin run out, and Illingworth managed just one from the last ball when two were needed.

There was no such closeness at Trent Bridge where Hampshire beat Nottinghamshire with 14 balls to spare, nor at The Oval where Surrey, a model of inconsistency, overwhelmed Lancashire. Alistair Brown's brilliant century came off only 60 balls and included a six and 15 fours. Lancashire were left shattered, and Adam Hollioake returned his best bowling figures in any of his three matches for the county.

On another sluggish pitch, at Edgbaston, Sussex laboured to reach a target of 134. They won with an over to spare thanks to Donelan and Jones who scored an unbeaten and vital 12 for the ninth wicket. The win put Sussex to the top alongside Kent. Glamorgan gained their first Sunday success, with Steve Barwick's relentless accuracy proving too much for Yorkshire.

BENSON AND HEDGES CUP

SEMI-FINALS

8 June *at Derby*

Northamptonshire 210 (A.J. Lamb 60, R.J. Bailey 51)
Derbyshire 214 for 2 (K.J. Barnett 61, C.J. Adams 53 not out)

Derbyshire won by 8 wickets

(Gold Award – J.E. Morris)

at Leicester

Lancashire 218 for 6 (N.H. Fairbrother 64 not out)
Leicestershire 108 (Wasim Akram 5 for 10)

Lancashire won by 110 runs

(Gold Award – N.H. Fairbrother)

Derbyshire overcame financial worries and the absence of Bishop and Mortensen to beat Northamptonshire, the favourites, in most convincing fashion and enter the Benson and Hedges Cup final for the third time. Asked to bat first, Northamptonshire were soon in trouble as Devon Malcolm, in a fast and accurate opening spell, claimed both openers for a personal cost of 12 runs in eight overs. Bailey and Lamb added 99, but Bailey laboured for 101 balls for his 51, never able to find his touch. Lamb's 60 came off 69 balls, but the Derbyshire bowling was always demanding and the fielding was outstanding. Krikken dived to scoop up a catch to dismiss Lamb, and to give Cork revenge for the two successive boundaries struck off him by the Northamptonshire captain. No other batsman could lift the tempo.

In contrast, Barnett was dropped behind the wicket when 10, and Bowler also escaped. Well as Ambrose and the rest bowled, Northamptonshire could not break the opening partnership which was worth 102 in 36 overs. It

ended when Barnett swung rashly at Taylor, and 17 runs later, Bowler was run out by Ripley. Derbyshire needed to score at more than six runs an over in the last 15 overs, but Morris attacked from the start, and Adams was blistering. He hit Curran and Taylor for sixes on the leg side before driving Taylor for four to win the match and complete his fifty off 36 balls.

Lancashire elected to bat first on a sluggish wicket at Grace Road. Mendis and Atherton did not find runs easy to score, and both fell in the same manner, clipping catches to square-leg. Gordon Parsons bowled admirably for Leicestershire, but Fairbrother found gaps either side of the wicket in his customary one-day manner. Lancashire seemed short of a winning total when Wells bowled Watkinson with the first ball of the last over, but DeFreitas hoisted the next ball for six, and 17 runs came from the over, a crucial psychological blow. There was a further blow when Briers, on whom so much depends, was well caught behind off DeFreitas. At 47, Boon was splendidly stumped off Barnett, who took two wickets in his first three overs and bowled very tidily and with menace. Whitaker took root, but he was unable to play a shot of note. The return of Wasim Akram ended the match. He yorked Whitaker, who had batted 28 overs for his 32, and trapped Nixon leg before first ball. Benjamin was also adjudged leg before, and Parsons and Mullally had their stumps sent flying with successive balls. Leicestershire's last six wickets had gone for 22 runs, and Wasim Akram, with his best bowling performance in the competition, had taken 5 for 2 in nine balls.

9, 10 and **11 June** *at Edgbaston*

Australians 317 for 7 dec. (D.R. Martyn 116, A.R. Border 66, M.J. Slater 64)
Warwickshire 184 for 8

Match drawn

No play was possible on the last day, but Martyn gave further indication of the Australians' wealth of talent, and Neil Smith again bowled his off-spin well for Warwickshire.

10, 11, 12 and **14 June** *at Chesterfield*

Yorkshire 154 for 6 (D.E. Malcolm 4 for 57)
***v.* Derbyshire**

Match drawn

Derbyshire 2 pts., Yorkshire 0 pts.

at Gateshead Fell

Durham 234 (P.W.G. Parker 109, N.F. Williams 4 for 73) and 11 for 0
Middlesex 0 for 0 dec.

Match drawn

Middlesex 4 pts., Durham 1 pt.

Kent 275 (C.L. Hooper 69, N.R. Taylor 57, S.D. Udal 4 for 43)

Hampshire 232 for 7 (M.C.J. Nicholas 73)

Match drawn

Hampshire 5 pts., Kent 5 pts.

at Old Trafford

Lancashire 321 (N.J. Speak 99, N.H. Fairbrother 63, S.J.W. Andrew 7 for 47) and 129 for 3

Essex 304 for 6 dec. (G.A. Gooch 66, D.R. Pringle 65 not out)

Match drawn

Essex 7 pts., Lancashire 5 pts.

at The Oval

Surrey 282 (G.P. Thorpe 104, A.J. Stewart 75, R.P. Lefebvre 4 for 70) and 310 for 6 dec. (D.J. Bicknell 87, A.W. Smith 57 not out, M.P. Bicknell 53 not out, A.J. Stewart 52)

Glamorgan 166 (P.A. Cottey 70, Waqar Younis 5 for 60) and 93 for 4

Match drawn

Surrey 6 pts., Glamorgan 4 pts.

at Hove

Northamptonshire 447 for 6 (R.J. Bailey 200, N.A. Felton 109, A.J. Lamb 60)

***v.* Sussex**

Match drawn

Northamptonshire 4 pts., Sussex 2 pts.

at Worcester

Worcestershire 207 for 6 (G.A. Hick 104 not out, W.K.M. Benjamin 5 for 67)

***v.* Leicestershire**

Match drawn

Leicestershire 2 pts., Worcestershire 1 pt.

12, 13 and 14 June *at Bristol*

Gloucestershire 211 (B.C. Broad 80, S.K. Warne 5 for 61, M.G. Hughes 4 for 27)

Australians 400 (D.C. Boon 70, M.E. Waugh 66, M.L. Hayden 57, D.R. Martyn 51, J.M. De La Pena 4 for 77)

Match drawn

at Cambridge

Nottinghamshire 200 for 5 dec. (P.R. Pollard 104 not out)

Cambridge University 51 for 2

Match drawn

Alec Stewart held nine catches in the rain-affected match between Surrey and Glamorgan at The Oval, 10–14 June. (Alan Cozzi)

at Eglinton

Ireland 327 for 9 dec. (M.P. Rae 115, D.A. Lewis 56 not out, G.M. Hamilton 5 for 65) and 168 for 5 dec. (D.A. Lewis 73, J.D. Govan 4 for 34)

Scotland 216 (J.D. Govan 50) and 130 for 3

Match drawn

12, 14 and 15 June *at Oxford*

Warwickshire 177 for 3 dec. (A.J. Moles 79)

Oxford University 118 for 6

Match drawn

Rain totally ruined the first-class programme for the second week of June. There was no play after the first day at Chesterfield, and, in spite of Middlesex forfeiting their first innings, there was no result at Gateshead Fell where very little play was possible after the first day's 74 overs. There were nearly two days' play at Basingstoke after which the match was abandoned, and only 110 overs on the first two days at Hove. Northamptonshire began in ferocious mood. They lost Fordham at 17, but Felton and Bailey then added 281 in 65 overs. Bailey hit the first double century of the season, his runs coming off 209 balls, and he hit 2 sixes and 28 fours. Felton reached his century just before the close, and he was out just before the rain ended the game on the second day.

Rain ruined an interesting encounter at Old Trafford. Lancashire hit 321 on the first day, which ended with Essex on 37 for 1. Speak and Fairbrother put on 141 for Lancashire's third wicket, but the highlight of the day was the bowling of Steve Andrew who had a career best 7 for 47. The erratic Andrew has not really developed since his Hampshire days, but he can be fierce and lively and, in the words of his two captains, Gooch and Nicholas, 'bowl the wicket ball'. Also in the news at Old Trafford was Neil Foster who bowled well, but with no luck nor support in the field, and kicked down the stumps in frustration, for which he was fined. Gooch and Pringle batted with sparkle, and Gooch declared as soon as a third batting point was won. Such and Salim Malik captured wickets, but rain ended the contest.

Championship front-runners Glamorgan asked Surrey to bat first at The Oval, but they were thwarted by a third-wicket stand of 136 between Thorpe and Stewart. Thorpe completed his century on the second morning and emphasised that he could be the left-handed batsman of which England were in sore need. Without Maynard, who was injured in the field, Glamorgan were routed in 50.5 overs by the Surrey pace attack led by Waqar Younis. At one time, Glamorgan were 24 for 5, and they were lifted only by the brave Tony Cottey. Alec Stewart took six catches behind the stumps, and then helped as his side went on the run rampage before declaring and setting Glamorgan a target of 427 to win. They lost their first three wickets for 11, but rain saved them on the Monday. Stewart took three more catches in Glamorgan's shortened second innings.

Graeme Hick reached 20,000 runs in first-class cricket and hit a century in a match in which only 75 overs were possible and during which Winston Benjamin troubled all other Worcestershire batsmen.

Chris Broad stood alone against the pace of Merv Hughes and the leg-spin of Shane Warne as Gloucestershire took on the Australians, who batted consistently. Ian Healy was unable to bat, however, for he sustained an injured thumb. Jason De La Pena took a career best four wickets for the county side.

In the matches involving the universities, both games lost two days' play, but the weather was better in Ireland where the home side had the better of the match against Scotland but could not force victory.

AXA EQUITY & LAW LEAGUE

13 June *at Chesterfield*

Derbyshire 207 for 7 (C.J. Adams 56, P.D. Bowler 55)
Yorkshire 208 for 1 (D. Byas 106 not out, M.D. Moxon 80)

Yorkshire (4 pts.) won by 9 wickets

at Gateshead Fell

Middlesex 158 for 7
Durham 159 for 4 (P. Bainbridge 53 not out)

Durham (4 pts.) won by 6 wickets

at Basingstoke

Hampshire 198 (M.A. Ealham 6 for 53)
Kent 202 for 3 (T.R. Ward 112, M.V. Fleming 58)

Kent (4 pts.) won by 7 wickets

at Old Trafford

Essex 222 (J.P. Stephenson 93, G.A. Gooch 67)
Lancashire 162 (P.M. Such 4 for 38)

Essex (4 pts.) won by 60 runs

at The Oval

Surrey 168 (G.P. Thorpe 75)
Glamorgan 169 for 0 (H. Morris 98 not out, S.P. James 65 not out)

Glamorgan (4 pts.) won by 10 wickets

at Hove

Northamptonshire 214 (A.J. Lamb 60, F.D. Stephenson 4 for 27)
Sussex 217 for 5 (A.P. Wells 92 not out, D.M. Smith 52)

Sussex (4 pts.) won by 5 wickets

at Worcester

Leicestershire 178 (T.J. Boon 66, N.V. Radford 4 for 26)
Worcestershire 174 for 9

Leicestershire (4 pts.) won by 4 runs

Kent and Sussex moved six points clear at the top of the Sunday League. The programme was not interrupted by bad weather. Trevor Ward of Kent, one of the very best of one-day batsmen, hit 112 off 91 balls while Sussex captain Alan Wells steered his side to victory with two overs to spare against Northamptonshire. Durham won their first Sunday League match of the season as Middlesex had to leave Lord's for the first time, and Yorkshire and Glamorgan achieved overwhelming victories. David Byas hit his first century in limited-over cricket, and Mark Ealham gave a career-best bowling performance in the Sunday League for Kent.

Essex won only their second Sunday game of the season, and Leicestershire kept in touch with the leaders with a narrow win over Worcestershire.

SECOND TEST MATCH
ENGLAND *v.* AUSTRALIA, at Lord's

England made only one change from the twelve that had formed the final party at Old Trafford, Neil Foster replacing DeFreitas, but once again it was Mark Ilott whose fate it was to be omitted on the morning of the match. May replaced Julian in the Australian side. The selection of Foster was hard to justify. The Essex pace bowler had struggled through the first few weeks of the season, suggesting neither form nor fitness, and his recall to the England side was bewildering. Sadly, this was to prove not only his last Test match but his last appearance in first-class cricket as his unrelenting knee problems were to force him to announce his retirement from the first-class game at the end of July.

ABOVE: *Mark Taylor pulls . . . (Adrian Murrell/Allsport)*

ABOVE RIGHT: *Mike Slater drives . . . (Adrian Murrell/Allsport)*

RIGHT: *David Boon plays the ball through mid-wicket. Australia's three centurions. (Adrian Murrell/Allsport)*

Border won the toss, and Taylor faced the bowling of Caddick. Foster's return to Test cricket was greeted with a four through mid-on by Slater. The young Australian opener was not at his best in the early stages, and an inside edge off Caddick narrowly missed the leg stump before shooting to the fine-leg boundary. In truth, however, neither batsman looked like losing his wicket, and Taylor hooked and drove Caddick for four and three in the 15th over to bring up the fifty. The spinners failed to halt the flow of runs. The hundred came in the 30th over, and at lunch, from 33 overs, Australia were 101 for 0: Taylor, 36; Slater, 63.

Taylor pulled Gooch for six to reach his fifty in the 43rd over, and in the next over Slater hit two magnificent boundaries off Such – an off-drive and a straight drive – and one felt that one had not seen better driving than Slater's in 50 years of watching cricket.

He reached his century off the last ball of the 52nd over, out of 163 runs, a record first-wicket stand for Australia against England at Lord's. If Taylor was less extravagant in his stroke-play, he was none the less assured in his batting, and his driving square of the wicket was a wonder to behold.

Mid-way through the afternoon, Foster beat Slater's outside edge to earn some applause. This, along with an 'Ooh' in the morning session, was all that came England's way. In the 63rd over, Taylor was beaten by Tufnell's turn and was stranded, but Stewart failed to accept the stumping chance. Taylor was on 86 at the time, and this remained his score at the tea interval when Australia were 212, with Slater on 120.

One ran out of superlatives for Slater. His straight driving was of a standard rarely seen even at Test level. Generally, a crowd is excited only by big hitting and falling wickets, but this was a day when the quality of batting was such that one whispered to oneself 'Let this last for ever'. Of course, it did not. Taylor reached his

hundred in the 77th over, and Slater went to 150 in the same over. Two overs and three runs later, Slater held back a drive through mid-wicket and was caught by Ben Smith, fielding for Gatting. Slater had batted for 293 minutes, faced 263 balls and hit 18 fours. The statistics tell nothing of the glory. The opening partnership was worth 260, a record for any wicket by either side for a Test match between the two countries at Lord's.

Six overs later, Taylor played down the wrong line to Tufnell's arm-ball and was stumped. His 111 included a six and 10 fours and came off 245 balls in 323 minutes. It was his second century in successive Test matches. He serves as a mighty foundation for the Australian innings.

The cricket now lost its urgency and glamour as Boon and Mark Waugh batted to the end of the day which came with Australia on 292 for 2: Boon, 11; Waugh, 6.

If there was hesitancy in Mark Waugh's play at the start of the second day, it soon vanished. In the first hour, 51 runs came, and by the 18th over of the day, the field was spread far and wide. In the morning session, Boon and Mark Waugh took the score to 397, and Waugh, 66, had overtaken Boon, 55, whom he had trailed by some margin at one time.

In the afternoon, the Australians did not have to work for their runs, for they came with awesome ease. Boon was, as ever, the rock; Mark Waugh has the lazy air of

Smith is stumped Healy, bowled May. (Patrick Eagar)

contemptuous mastery. It seemed that he must move effortlessly to his century, until, on 93, he swept falsely at Tufnell, having already hit Such for six – but Caddick failed to respond to the chance. On 99, however, Waugh tried to play Tufnell through the leg side and was bowled off his pads. He had faced 162 balls and batted for 222 minutes.

Border announced himself with a magnificent off-drive, and Boon reached his century in the 64th over of the day, having been 88 not out at tea. He showed no signs of surrendering his wicket, but he was dropped at gully by Lewis off Foster on 131.

The last 20 minutes of the day were played with four lights showing by the scoreboard, but the batsmen had scorned the offer to leave the field. The afternoon session had produced 95 runs; the evening session realised exactly 100. As on the first day, only two wickets fell. The second was that of Border who, in a cameo of regal splendour, hit 77 off 121 balls with 12 fours. He was out when he got an inside edge to a ball from Lewis that was wide of the off stump. Boon finished the day on 138; Steve Waugh had faced four balls without scoring. Throughout, the England bowling had been massacred. Foster

SECOND CORNHILL TEST MATCH – ENGLAND v. AUSTRALIA
17, 18, 19, 20 and 21 June 1993 at Lord's

AUSTRALIA

	FIRST INNINGS	
M.A. Taylor	st Stewart, b Tufnell	111
M.J. Slater	c sub (Smith), b Lewis	152
D.C. Boon	not out	164
M.E. Waugh	b Tufnell	99
A.R. Border (capt)	b Lewis	77
S.R. Waugh	not out	13
*I.A. Healy		
T.B.A. May		
M.G. Hughes		
S.K. Warne		
C.J. McDermott		
Extras	lb 1, w 1, nb 14	16
	(for 4 wickets, dec.)	632

ENGLAND

	FIRST INNINGS		SECOND INNINGS	
G.A. Gooch (capt)	c May, b Hughes	12	c Healy, b Warne	29
M.A. Atherton	b Warne	80	run out	99
M.W. Gatting	b May	5	lbw, b Warne	59
R.A. Smith	st Healy, b May	22	c sub (Hayden), b May	5
G.A. Hick	c Healy, b Hughes	20	c Taylor, b May	64
*A.J. Stewart	lbw, b Hughes	3	lbw, b May	62
C.C. Lewis	lbw, b Warne	0	st Healy, b May	0
N.A. Foster	c Border, b Warne	16	c M.E. Waugh, b Border	20
A.R. Caddick	c Healy, b Hughes	21	not out	0
P.M. Such	c Taylor, b Warne	7	b Warne	4
P.C.R. Tufnell	not out	2	b Warne	0
Extras	lb 8, nb 9	17	b 10, lb 13	23
		205		365

	O	M	R	W
Caddick	38	5	120	–
Foster	30	4	94	–
Such	36	6	90	–
Tufnell	39	3	129	2
Lewis	36	5	151	2
Gooch	9	1	26	–
Hick	8	3	21	–

	O	M	R	W	O	M	R	W
Hughes	20	5	52	4	31	9	75	–
M.E. Waugh	6	1	16	–	17	4	55	–
S.R. Waugh	4	1	5	–	2	–	13	–
May	31	12	64	2	51	23	81	4
Warne	35	12	57	4	48.5	17	102	4
Border	3	1	3	–	16	9	16	1

FALL OF WICKETS

1–260, 2–277, 3–452, 4–591

FALL OF WICKETS

1–33, 2–50, 3–84, 4–123, 5–131, 6–132, 7–167, 8–174, 9–189

1–71, 2–175, 3–180, 4–244, 5–304, 6–312, 7–361, 8–361, 9–365

Umpires: M.J. Kitchen & D.R. Shepherd

Australia won by an innings and 62 runs

was a pale carbon copy of a once-fine bowler. Caddick, hostile and quick with Somerset, had sunk into medium pace of no subtlety. Tufnell bowled far too many bad balls. Lewis remained the enigmatic cricketer of talent whose destiny seemed likely to be that of a nearly man.

Australia were not without their problems. Craig McDermott, their main strike bowler, had been rushed to hospital where a twisted bowel was later diagnosed. He was to take no further part in the match, nor in the tour.

On the third morning, Australia added 40 runs in nine overs before Border declared. Boon finished with 164, made in 471 minutes with 15 fours off the 378 balls that he faced. On firm foundations like this greatness is built.

Gooch and Atherton began England's innings with 33 in 10 overs, and they looked mostly positive and secure. Merv Hughes then bowled a bouncer to Gooch. It was an excellent delivery, more off than leg side and inviting the instinctive hook. Gooch responded, hit mainly with the top edge, and May sprinted some 20 yards at long-leg to take a very fine tumbling catch.

After lunch, Gatting's 35-minute agony came to an end when he drove outside a full-length ball from May and was bowled. Smith became the first batsman in a Test match in England to be given out by the third umpire and the television monitor. He had batted for 42 minutes without suggesting that he had mastered spin before he charged down the pitch at May and was beaten down the leg side. Healy whipped off the bails, but umpire Kitchen called for Balderstone's response to the television replay. It seemed – as does the entire system – an abnegation of responsibility, and there was a seemingly interminable interval before Balderstone, having studied the picture from three angles, gave the decision that Smith was out.

Hick drove Warne for four, and then swept the same bowler for another four, but Hughes posed greater problems. He tested Hick with the bouncer, and then the

Warne turns a ball from well outside leg stump to bowl Such, and Australia are one ball away from victory. (Patrick Eagar)

Atherton's mighty innings comes to the saddest of ends. (Patrick Eagar)

Worcestershire batsman succumbed, stepping away to try to cut a ball too close to him and edging wretchedly to the keeper. Stewart was beaten by a ball on middle and leg as he erred across the line, and Lewis played back fatally to a quicker ball from Warne to find himself as clearly leg before as it is possible for a batsman to be.

Foster joined Atherton in a stand that raised spirits if not hope, but he was rather unlucky to be adjudged caught at silly point off a ball that seemed to hit his boot rather than his bat. Earlier, he had been saved by the television monitor when he had charged down the wicket and been 'stumped'.

Atherton's 255-minute innings ended when he went to drive Warne and edged the ball onto his pads, from where it rolled back onto his stumps. Had all the England batsmen shown Atherton's resolve and technical application, the day would not be remembered as one of the most miserable and disastrous in the country's recent cricket history. Such also fell before the close, caught at slip. England closed a wretched day on 193 for 9, Caddick having already resisted for an hour.

He lasted another half-hour on the Sunday morning before a rising ball found the outside edge. England followed-on 427 runs behind. Gooch and Atherton took them to lunch with just one alarm, Atherton escaping an appeal for leg before that could only have been turned down because the batsman got the faintest of edges to the ball. In the third over of the afternoon, however, Gooch was beaten by Warne's leg-break on the off stump and Healy, an inspiration behind the stumps, took the catch.

Gatting endured torture from May and Warne, but he was to survive the remaining four hours of the day, a triumph of character rather than technique or ability, and a resistance worthy of praise. The chief honours went to Mike Atherton, however, who had never quite looked as if this woeful England side were the right environment for him. He played with admirable correctness, smiled disconcertingly at Hughes' verbals, and drove and

Lord's in mid-summer, and England crash to an innings defeat against Australia. (David Munden/Sports-Line)

Smith's second innings ends with a brilliant catch at short-leg by substitute Hayden. (Adrian Murrell/Allsport)

clipped with a purpose that was as commanding as it was heartening. If he had resisted in the first innings, he now carried the attack to the enemy, hitting 13 fours in an innings lasting 242 minutes. He was in sight of a most well-deserved century when he was called for a third run off a shot to the Grand Stand boundary. The run would have given him his hundred, but Hughes gathered the ball on the ropes and hurled it to Healy. Gatting sent

Atherton back, but the Lancastrian slipped and was unable to make his ground as Healy did remarkably well to gather a wide and high return and dive to break the wicket.

Three overs later, Smith prodded at May and Hayden, substituting for Boon, took a splendid diving catch at short-leg. Hick remained with Gatting for the last 71 minutes of the day, and, at 237 for 3, England still nursed hopes of drawing the match.

Those hopes suffered a set-back 25 minutes into the last day when Gatting went back in an attempt to cut Warne's top-spinner. He missed and was leg before on the back foot. It was an ill-judged shot. Hick had looked like salvaging a sinking Test career when he went back to May, who was bowling round the wicket. The ball was slanted across the batsman who touched it to slip. Worse followed as, having batted for 13 minutes without scoring, Lewis went down the pitch to May and was beaten as he pushed forward. The stumping needed no third-umpire confirmation.

Stewart hit firmly and often, but in the afternoon he played half-forward to May, missed and was palpably leg before. Foster again perished to a close catch, this time at silly mid-on, but again there seemed to be more boot than bat involved.

The end was nigh, and it came very quickly. Such was bowled by a ball which pitched more than a foot outside his leg stump and turned sharply, and Tufnell suffered exactly the same fate next ball. At 3.25 p.m., Australia were two up in the series, and they had won the second Test by an innings without a ball being delivered by their main strike bowler, who was recovering in hospital from an emergency operation. It was England's seventh defeat in a row.

17, 18, 19 and **21** June *at Colwyn Bay*

Glamorgan 300 (A. Dale 60, H. Morris 52, I.T. Botham 4 for 11) and 363 for 7 dec. (M.P. Maynard 98, A. Dale 85, I.V.A. Richards 62)

Durham 263 (W. Larkins 77, P. Bainbridge 71, R.D.B. Croft 4 for 70) and 287 (P. Bainbridge 62, A.C. Cummins 56, I.T. Botham 50, S.L. Watkin 4 for 93)

Glamorgan won by 113 runs

Glamorgan 22 pts., Durham 6 pts.

at Canterbury

Derbyshire 135 (J.E. Morris 57, M.J. McCague 5 for 34, A.P. Igglesden 4 for 26) and 229 (A.E. Warner 95 not out, A.P. Igglesden 4 for 51)

Kent 341 (N.J. Llong 84, N.R. Taylor 73, M.V. Fleming 53, S.A. Marsh 51, S.J. Base 5 for 93) and 25 for 1

Kent won by 9 wickets

Kent 23 pts., Derbyshire 4 pts.

at Old Trafford

Sussex 402 (C.W.J. Athey 101, P. Moores 85 not out, J.W. Hall 53, G. Yates 5 for 108, Wasim Akram 4 for 55) and 202 (K. Greenfield 60 not out, A.P. Wells 53, A.A. Barnett 5 for 65)

Lancashire 280 (G.D. Mendis 63, S.P. Titchard 57, B.T.P. Donelan 5 for 112, E.E. Hemmings 4 for 86) and 326 for 6 (S.P. Titchard 87, G.D. Mendis 85, N.J. Speak 59, B.T.P. Donelan 4 for 157)

Lancashire won by 4 wickets

Lancashire 21 pts., Sussex 7 pts.

at Northampton

Northamptonshire 125 (R.J. Bailey 59, K.J. Shine 6 for 62) and 303 (A. Fordham 109, K.M. Curran 71, N.A. Felton 64)

Hampshire 247 (C.E.L. Ambrose 5 for 76) and 182 for 3 (K.D. James 71, V.P. Terry 58 not out)

Hampshire won by 7 wickets

Hampshire 21 pts., Northamptonshire 4 pts.

at Trent Bridge

Essex 450 for 8 dec. (Salim Malik 121, J.P. Stephenson 97, P.J. Prichard 58, M.C. Ilott 50 not out, C.L. Cairns 4 for 88) and 260 for 1 dec. (J.J.B. Lewis 136 not out, J.P. Stephenson 113 not out)

Nottinghamshire 379 for 6 dec. (C.L. Cairns 80, G.F. Archer 59 not out, R.T. Robinson 59, M. Saxelby 57) and 197 for 8 (D.R. Pringle 4 for 33)

Match drawn

Nottinghamshire 5 pts., Essex 5 pts.

Steve Watkin – the leading wicket-taker in the country, and the first bowler to 50 first-class wickets. A main factor in Glamorgan's highly successful season. (Alan Cozzi)

at Bath

Somerset 318 (I. Fletcher 65 retired hurt, N.A. Folland 54, N.F. Williams 4 for 71) and 240 for 8 dec. (N.D. Burns 79, J.D. Carr 4 for 73)

Middlesex 301 for 8 dec. (M.R. Ramprakash 70) and 258 for 5 (D.L. Haynes 115)

Middlesex won by 5 wickets

Middlesex 22 pts., Somerset 5 pts.

at Edgbaston

Warwickshire 88 (Waqar Younis 6 for 43) and 157 (M.P. Bicknell 6 for 50)

Surrey 175 (G.C. Small 4 for 39) and 71 for 2

Surrey won by 8 wickets

Surrey 20 pts., Warwickshire 4 pts.

at Sheffield

Yorkshire 445 (P.J. Hartley 102, P.W. Jarvis 76, A.A. Metcalfe 63, R.B. Richardson 54, C. White 53, K.E. Cooper 5 for 83)

Gloucestershire 241 (M.W. Alleyne 62, G.D. Hodgson 57,

J.D. Batty 4 for 27) and 235 for 3 dec. (B.C. Broad 87, M.W. Alleyne 78)

Match drawn

Yorkshire 6 pts., Gloucestershire 3 pts.

18, 19 and 20 June *at Worcester*

Worcestershire 351 for 7 dec. (W.P.C. Weston 113, D.A. Leatherdale 51 not out) and 185 for 0 dec. (T.S. Curtis 100 not out, W.P.C. Weston 81 not out)

Oxford University 229 for 8 dec. (J.E.R. Gallian 81) and 249 for 6 (R.R. Montgomerie 109, G.B.T. Lovell 71)

Match drawn

Glamorgan remained level with Middlesex at the top of the Britannic Assurance County Championship table, both sides taking 22 points from victories at Colwyn Bay and Bath respectively. Glamorgan seemed in a strong position as they reached 223 for 3, but the advent of Botham and Berry in the Durham attack changed the course of the innings. Seven wickets fell for 77 runs, and Botham finished with 4 for 11 in 6.5 overs, his best figures for Durham. The Durham innings followed the usual uneven pattern. It was boosted by a fourth-wicket stand of 129 between Larkins and Bainbridge, and then by a useful knock from Berry. Glamorgan took a grip on the game on the Saturday when they scored at four runs an over. Maynard hit 98 off 109 balls, and Dale and Richards gave

admirable support. Morris declared, and two wickets were captured before the close, while only Bainbridge and Cummins offered real resistance on the Monday.

The two pace bowlers being spoken of as England contenders, Igglesden and McCague, routed Derbyshire on the opening day at Canterbury. Kent lost both openers for nought, but Taylor and Llong added 141 for the fourth wicket to put the home side in a strong position. Batting again 206 runs in arrears, Derbyshire lost eight wickets before clearing the deficit, and that the game went into a third day was due entirely to the heroic batting of Warner who hit the highest score of his career after coming to the wicket at 74 for 6.

There was a remarkable game at Old Trafford where Lancashire beat Sussex in spite of being 122 runs behind on the first innings. Bill Athey overcame cramped fingers to hit his first century for Sussex. He and Hall began the match with a stand of 147, and, although three middle-order wickets fell for six runs, Moores rallied the tail. By Friday evening, Sussex were batting for a second time after the off-spin pair of Hemmings and Donelan had bowled out Lancashire for 280. Mendis and Titchard had scored 127 for the home side's first wicket. Eventually, Lancashire had more than a day in which to score 325 to win and again it was Mendis and Titchard who were to star with an opening partnership of 179. Speak and Fairbrother maintained the consistent scoring, and Lancashire won with surprising ease.

There was disaster for the home side at Northampton where Hampshire won the toss, asked Northampton-

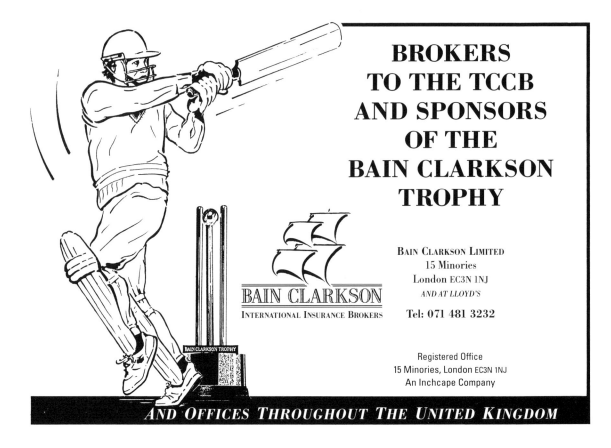

shire to bat and then bowled them out for 125, besides which, in the process, Marshall struck Capel with a lifting delivery which broke the batsman's forearm. Marshall took three wickets, and Shine six. Hampshire subsequently took a first-innings lead of 122, but this was wiped out by Felton and Fordham in an opening stand of 141. Fordham went on to reach his century, and there was positive batting by Curran, but the wicket had now eased and Hampshire moved comfortably to victory on the last morning.

Essex scored freely on the first day at Trent Bridge where Prichard and Stephenson hit 146 for the first wicket. Mark Ilott drove up the M1 from Lord's in time to be night-watchman, and he helped Salim Malik add 52, saw the Pakistani reach his century and then completed his own maiden first-class fifty. Nottinghamshire could not match Essex's pace of scoring, but they batted consistently. Stephenson and Lewis, who hit a career best 136 not out, both hit centuries and shared a second-wicket stand of 242 when Essex batted a second time, but both batsmen were aided by some generous offerings on the final morning. Needing to score 332 in 73 overs to win, Nottinghamshire were never in touch against the movement of Pringle and the spin of Childs, and only Robinson saved them from defeat.

Middlesex's challenge for the title was maintained at Bath, but not without recourse to farce. Carr won the toss and asked Somerset to bat, but Folland and Fletcher, in his second county match, put on 120 for the first wicket. Fletcher was forced to retire after having a finger broken by a ball from Williams. The wicket was slow, and Somerset batted into the second day which saw Middlesex reach 24 for 2 by lunch, after which rain ended play. They eventually approached parity on the first innings and scored at a brisker rate than had Somerset. The latter were without both Fletcher and Hayhurst, also injured, in their second innings, but the farce commenced in the form of Carr bowling long-hops as he and Haynes offered 134 runs in 17 overs. This enabled Tavaré to set a target of 257 in the last two sessions. That the target was reached on a pitch that was never easy was due mainly to Desmond Haynes who gave an exemplary display in reaching his first hundred of the season. He was capably supported by Ramprakash who showed great technical skill and application in scoring 48 in 106 minutes as he and Haynes added 95.

The game at Edgbaston was over in two days. Warwickshire were twice routed, first by Waqar Younis and then by Martin Bicknell who was also Surrey's top scorer in the first innings with 37. It seemed that Surrey might struggle to win, losing Lynch and Thorpe without scoring, but Brown hit 42 not out and led them to victory. Nineteen wickets fell on the first day.

A second-wicket stand of 106 between Metcalfe and Richardson helped Yorkshire to a score of 282 for 6 at the end of the first day at Sheffield. Overnight batsmen Jarvis and Hartley extended their partnership to 111, and Peter Hartley, playing his first innings of the season following a back strain, hit the second century of his career as 138 runs came in the morning session of the second day. Facing a total of 445, Gloucestershire ended on a grim 105

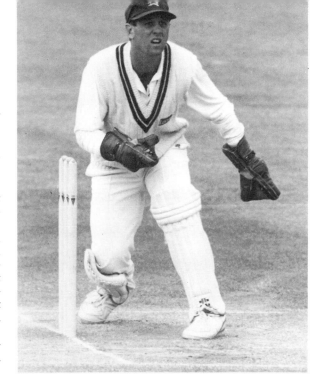

As middle-order batsman and wicket-keeper, Keith Brown was an integral part of Middlesex's success. (Tom Morris)

for 1, scored at less than two runs an over. The rate did not improve on the Saturday. Batty took 4 for 27 in 31 overs, and Gloucestershire's innings occupied 144 overs. Following-on, they showed more enterprise when saving the game.

Left-hander Philip Weston hit a maiden first-class hundred for Worcestershire against Oxford University, and there was a second – and higher – century for Richard Montgomerie. Curtis and Weston began Worcestershire's second innings with an unbroken stand of 185.

 AXA EQUITY & LAW LEAGUE

20 June *at Colwyn Bay*

Glamorgan 271 for 6 (M.P. Maynard 79, H. Morris 59, S.P. James 58)
Durham 105 (A. Dale 6 for 22)
Glamorgan (4 pts.) won by 166 runs

at Canterbury

Derbyshire 248 for 8 (C.J. Adams 92)
Kent 245 for 8 (C.L. Hooper 72, G.R. Cowdrey 57)
Derbyshire (4 pts.) won by 3 runs

at Old Trafford

Sussex 118 (Wasim Akram 4 for 20)
Lancashire 122 for 4

Lancashire (4 pts.) won by 6 wickets

at Northampton

Hampshire 226 for 2 (J.R. Wood 92 not out, T.C. Middleton 69)
Northamptonshire 229 for 6 (A.J. Lamb 96 not out)

Northamptonshire (4 pts.) won by 4 wickets

at Trent Bridge

Essex 261 for 8 (P.J. Prichard 107)
Nottinghamshire 186 (R.T. Robinson 52, J.H. Childs 4 for 38)

Essex (4 pts.) won by 75 runs

at Bath

Somerset 144
Middlesex 145 for 2 (M.R. Ramprakash 73 not out, J.D. Carr 57 not out)

Middlesex (4 pts.) won by 8 wickets

at Edgbaston

Surrey 194 (N.M.K. Smith 4 for 21)
Warwickshire 176 (M.P. Bicknell 4 for 19)

Surrey (4 pts.) won by 18 runs

at Sheffield

Yorkshire 166 for 8 (D. Byas 50)
Gloucestershire 167 for 3 (B.C. Broad 75 not out, A.J. Wright 73 not out)

Gloucestershire (4 pts.) won by 7 wickets

Leaders Kent and Sussex were both beaten, so allowing a gathering pack to close to within four points of them. Among the pack were Glamorgan who scored with their customary vigour and then were indebted to Adrian Dale who returned his best Sunday performance with the ball and did the hat-trick. At Canterbury, Kent fell victims to Chris Adams' thrilling batting, 92 off 85 balls, and brilliant fielding – the first three Kent wickets all fell to spectacular catches by Adams. Wood's Sunday League best score was not sufficient to deny Allan Lamb and Northamptonshire, but Paul Prichard's highest Sunday League century was enough to help Essex to victory at Trent Bridge. There was a welcome win for Gloucestershire at Sheffield where Broad and Wright shared an unbroken fourth-wicket partnership of 123.

NATWEST TROPHY

ROUND ONE

22 June *at Marlow*

Leicestershire 289 for 9 (T.J. Boon 117)
Buckinghamshire 214 for 8 (S. Burrow 57 not out, M.J. Roberts 54)

Leicestershire won by 75 runs

(Man of the Match – T.J. Boon)

at Warrington

Nottinghamshire 208 for 9 (C.L. Cairns 64)
Cheshire 146 (I. Cockbain 57, C.L. Cairns 4 for 18)

Nottinghamshire won by 62 runs

(Man of the Match – C.L. Cairns)

at Exmouth

Derbyshire 266 for 7 (T.J.G. O'Gorman 68 not out, K.J. Barnett 60, P.D. Bowler 58)
Devon 133 (D.G. Cork 4 for 18)

Derbyshire won by 133 runs

(Man of the Match – D.G. Cork)

at Swansea

Glamorgan 322 for 5 (I.V.A. Richards 162 not out, M.P. Maynard 67)
Oxfordshire 191 for 5 (D.A.J. Wise 68)

Glamorgan won by 131 runs

(Man of the Match – I.V.A. Richards)

at Bristol

Gloucestershire 274 for 9 (M.W. Alleyne 73, M. Jahangir 4 for 57)
Hertfordshire 164 (M.R. Gouldstone 68 not out)

Gloucestershire won by 110 runs

(Man of the Match – M.W. Alleyne)

at Canterbury

Kent 282 for 7 (C.L. Hooper 62, M.R. Benson 60, N.R. Taylor 57)
Middlesex 116 (M.J. McCague 5 for 26)

Kent won by 166 runs

(Man of the Match – M.J. McCague)

at Lakenham

Warwickshire 285 for 9 (D.P. Ostler 104)
Norfolk 142 (N.M.K. Smith 5 for 17)

Warwickshire won by 143 runs

(*Man of the Match – D.P. Ostler*)

at Northampton

Lancashire 178 for 7 (M. Watkinson 60 not out)
Northamptonshire 181 for 4 (R.J. Bailey 96 not out)

Northamptonshire won by 6 wickets

(*Man of the Match – R.J. Bailey*)

at Edinburgh (Myreside)

Worcestershire 238 for 8 (G.A. Hick 51)
Scotland 162 for 7

Worcestershire won by 76 runs

(*Man of the Match – G.A. Hick*)

at Telford (St George's)

Somerset 301 for 4 (M.N. Lathwell 103, R.J. Harden 65,
    C.J. Tavaré 56 not out, G.D. Rose 52)
Shropshire 185 (J.B.R. Jones 66)

Somerset won by 116 runs

(*Man of the Match – M.N. Lathwell*)

at Stone

Staffordshire 165
Hampshire 166 for 3 (R.A. Smith 105 not out)

Hampshire won by 7 wickets

(*Man of the Match – R.A. Smith*)

at Bury St Edmunds

Essex 251 for 9 (J.P. Stephenson 84, Salim Malik 74,
    I.D. Graham 4 for 66)
Suffolk 130 (P.J. Caley 54 not out, Salim Malik 4 for 25)

Essex won by 121 runs

(*Man of the Match – Salim Malik*)

at The Oval

Dorset 163 (J.J.E. Hardy 73)
Surrey 164 for 0 (A.J. Stewart 104 not out, D.J. Bicknell 54
    not out)

Surrey won by 10 wickets

(*Man of the Match – A.J. Stewart*)

at Hove

Sussex 257 for 7 (K. Greenfield 96 not out, C.W.J. Athey
    92)
Wales Minor Counties 143 for 6

Sussex won by 114 runs

(*Man of the Match – K. Greenfield*)

Hugh Morris – a century in each innings for Glamorgan against Nottinghamshire, 24–8 June. An inspiring captain and the first batsman to 1,000 runs. (Alan Cozzi)

at Trowbridge

Durham 320 for 5 (S. Hutton 95, P. Bainbridge 82,
    I.T. Botham 55)
Wiltshire 217 for 8 (L.K. Smith 73)

Durham won by 103 runs

(*Man of the Match – S. Hutton*)

at Leeds

Yorkshire 272 for 4 (A.A. Metcalfe 77, M.D. Moxon 63,
    R.B. Richardson 54, D. Byas 54)
Ireland 187 for 5 (S.J.S. Warke 64)

Yorkshire won by 85 runs

(*Man of the Match – A.A. Metcalfe*)

There were no surprises in the first round of the NatWest Trophy, and those first-class counties playing against minor counties suffered only minor tremors. Nottinghamshire were 87 for 4 against Cheshire but the all-round cricket of Chris Cairns revived them, while Glamorgan trembled at 40 for 3 against Oxfordshire. What followed was slaughter. Maynard and Richards added 105, and Richards went on to score 162 not out, his highest score in the competition and the highest by a Glamorgan batsman in one-day cricket. His hundred came off 144 balls, and his last 58 runs came from 19 deliveries. He hit 6 sixes and 15 fours.

Russell Cake of Cambridge, a late replacement for John Crawley, hitting a maiden first-class century. On the final day, the Australian attack proved too much for the students; Tim Zoehrer took three wickets with his leg-spin.

24, 25, 26 and 28 June *at Derby*

Lancashire 477 (M.A. Atherton 137, Wasim Akram 117, N.J. Speak 74, D.E. Malcolm 5 for 98) and 327 for 8 dec. (G.D. Lloyd 80, N.H. Fairbrother 59)

Derbyshire 426 (K.J. Barnett 161, C.J. Adams 74, P.A.J. DeFreitas 5 for 109) and 267 (J.E. Morris 151, Wasim Akram 6 for 45, M. Watkinson 4 for 72)

Lancashire won by 111 runs

Lancashire 21 pts., Derbyshire 8 pts.

at Stockton

Durham 187 (P. Bainbridge 69, K.C.G. Benjamin 5 for 65) and 355 (I.T. Botham 101, A.C. Cummins 70, P.W.G. Parker 63)

Worcestershire 277 (G.A. Hick 69, S.R. Lampitt 58) and 268 for 7 (T.S. Curtis 116 not out)

Worcestershire won by 3 wickets

Worcestershire 22 pts., Durham 4 pts.

at Ilford

Warwickshire 448 (D.P. Ostler 174, J.D. Ratcliffe 80, T.L. Penney 50) and 206 (A.J. Moles 55, J.P. Stephenson 5 for 31, Salim Malik 5 for 67)

Essex 384 for 4 dec. (N. Hussain 107 not out, Salim Malik 90, G.A. Gooch 71, P.J. Prichard 68) and 273 for 7 (J.P. Stephenson 64, G.A. Gooch 63)

Essex won by 3 wickets

Essex 22 pts., Warwickshire 5 pts.

at Swansea

Glamorgan 329 (H. Morris 102, A. Dale 92, C.L. Cairns 4 for 66) and 352 for 5 dec. (H. Morris 133, P.A. Cottey 100 not out, A. Dale 51)

Nottinghamshire 346 (R.T. Robinson 119, P. Johnson 70, R.D.B. Croft 5 for 112) and 338 for 2 (R.T. Robinson 139 not out, P. Johnson 112 not out, P.R. Pollard 72)

Nottinghamshire won by 8 wickets

Nottinghamshire 23 pts., Glamorgan 7 pts.

at Leicester

Gloucestershire 245 (G.D. Hodgson 79, R.M. Wight 54, A.D. Mullally 7 for 72) and 376 (G.D. Hodgson 89, R.C. Russell 64, B.C. Broad 56, A.R.K. Pierson 5 for 72)

Kent disposed of Middlesex with surprising ease. They scored consistently and then routed the visitors who lost their last eight wickets for 36 runs. In the other match between two first-class counties, Northamptonshire won the toss, asked Lancashire to bat and reduced them to 70 for 6 with their medium-pace attack. Watkinson and Austin gave a hint of respectability in the closing overs, but with Bailey in total command after the early loss of Felton, Northamptonshire were never troubled.

Dominic Ostler hit his first NatWest century and Neil Smith returned his best bowling figures in the competition as Warwickshire overcame Norfolk, and Mark Lathwell hit a century before lunch as Somerset beat Shropshire. Essex beat a Suffolk side that included five Essex 'old boys', and Darren Bicknell and Alec Stewart hit 164 in 28.4 overs as Surrey beat Dorset. Greenfield and Hutton hit their highest scores in the competition.

23, 24 and 25 June *at Oxford*

Australians 388 for 5 dec. (D.R. Martyn 138 not out, M.J. Slater 111, M.L. Hayden 98) and 233 for 6 dec. (M.E. Waugh 84, M.A. Taylor 57, R.H. MacDonald 4 for 80)

Combined Universities 298 for 7 dec. (R. Cake 108, R.R. Montgomerie 52) and 157

Australians won by 166 runs

The tourists plundered runs on the first day, but the undergraduates responded well on the second day with

Leicestershire 454 (J.D.R. Benson 153, T.J. Boon 85, L. Potter 62, C.A. Walsh 4 for 70) and 168 for 5

Leicestershire won by 5 wickets

Leicestershire 24 pts., Gloucestershire 3 pts.

at Lord's

Surrey 322 (D.J. Bicknell 72, A.D. Brown 67) and 225 (D.J. Bicknell 77, A.J. Stewart 58, N.F. Williams 4 for 73)

Middlesex 330 (D.L. Haynes 112, K.R. Brown 80, J.E. Emburey 65 not out, J. Boiling 5 for 100) and 219 for 6 (K.R. Brown 79 not out)

Middlesex won by 4 wickets

Middlesex 23 pts., Surrey 7 pts.

at Luton

Northamptonshire 383 (A.J. Lamb 172, K.M. Curran 91, G.D. Rose 5 for 96, A.R. Caddick 4 for 91)

Somerset 161 and 216 (C.E.L. Ambrose 4 for 36)

Northamptonshire won by an innings and 6 runs

Northamptonshire 24 pts., Somerset 2 pts.

at Leeds

Yorkshire 209 (P.J. Hartley 54, A.P. Igglesden 5 for 66) and 410 for 6 dec. (M.D. Moxon 171 not out, R.J. Blakey 71, R.B. Richardson 51)

Kent 298 (C.L. Hooper 99, T.R. Ward 68, P.W. Jarvis 4 for 51) and 167 for 6

Match drawn

Kent 6 pts., Yorkshire 5 pts.

26, 27 and **28 June** *at Southampton*

Australians 393 for 7 dec. (D.C. Boon 146, M.L. Hayden 85) and 271 for 7 dec. (M.L. Hayden 115, M.G. Hughes 61 not out, C.A. Connor 4 for 77)

Hampshire 374 for 5 dec. (R.A. Smith 191, T.C. Middleton 53) and 220 for 6 (V.P. Terry 82, T.C. Middleton 78)

Match drawn

at Hove

Sussex 350 for 3 dec. (C.M. Wells 185, J.W. Hall 114) and 223 for 4 dec. (C.W.J. Athey 107, J.A. North 70 not out)

Cambridge University 300 for 4 dec. (J.P. Crawley 187 not out, R. Cake 57) and 115 for 5

Match drawn

There was a feast of runs and some fine individual performances in the match at Derby where the home side suffered defeat at the hands of their opponents in the Benson and Hedges Cup final. Barnett's decision to ask Lancashire to bat first proved to be disastrous as Michael Atherton reached a hundred off 176 balls and hit 19 fours in his 137. With Wasim Akram reaching 91, Lancashire totalled 433 for 7 on the first day, and Derbyshire lost Dominic Cork from their attack, banished by umpire Sharp for persistently running onto the pitch. Wasim duly completed his century on the second morning, but Derbyshire responded vigorously with Barnett and Adams adding 167 for the third wicket. There was an unfortunate incident when Morris trapped a delivery from Watkinson between glove and pad. He tipped the ball obligingly to the wicket-keeper at which Watkinson appealed. Sharp had no option but to give the batsman out, but it was hardly within the spirit of the game. Morris took vengeance on Lancashire on the last day. Derbyshire needed 379 in 86 overs, and Morris hit a brilliant 151 off 176 balls with 23 fours and a six. His side reached 243 for 2, but Wasim Akram then produced a devastating spell of 6 for 11 in 49 balls, and eight wickets went down for 24 runs. There was some acrimony between the sides, for Derbyshire later sent the ball used by Wasim to the TCCB for scrutiny.

Fifteen wickets fell on the first day at Stockton, and on the second, it looked as if Durham would take a first-innings lead until Newport and Lampitt added 104 for the eighth wicket for Worcestershire. The highlight of Saturday's play was a stand of 152 for Durham's sixth wicket, a county record, between Botham and Cummins, who made a career-best score. Botham's 101 came off 151 balls with 18 fours. It was the 38th first-class hundred of his career, and it was to prove to be this great player's last first-class century. Tim Curtis, the Worcestershire captain, overcame a blow on the head and batted for 7½ hours to take his side to victory on the last day when only 57 runs were scored in 36 overs before lunch and 59 in 30 overs in the afternoon. David Graveney bowled 53 overs to take 1 for 53.

Essex recorded their second championship win of the season when they beat Warwickshire with 19 overs to spare at Ilford. Ratcliffe and Ostler added 127 for Warwickshire's second wicket, and the visitors' innings continued into the second day. Ostler's 174 included 21 fours. Essex replied in an attacking manner, and Hussain and Salim Malik put on 163 for the fourth wicket. Salim then produced his best bowling performance for Essex as he and Stephenson bowled out Warwickshire after the front-line bowlers had failed to penetrate. The last nine Warwickshire wickets went down for 95 runs. Gooch and Stephenson began Essex's challenge with a partnership of 114 and, although Essex stumbled in mid-innings, they always looked likely winners.

Glamorgan's championship hopes suffered a severe set-back at Swansea where they seemed to be in charge of the match against Nottinghamshire for much of the time, only to be crushed on the last afternoon. A second-wicket stand of 162 between Morris and Dale gave Glamorgan a fine basis on the opening day, but Robinson and Johnson countered with a third-wicket stand of 94 for Nottinghamshire, and Robinson went on to bring his side to parity with a century which included 21 fours. Steve Watkin became the first bowler to reach 50 wickets in the season, and Morris hit his second century of the match on the Saturday. Cottey reached a hundred off as many balls on the last morning, and Morris' declaration set

Nottinghamshire a target of 336 in 91 overs. Pollard hit 72, but victory was brought about by the spectacular batting of Robinson, who hit his second hundred of the match, and Johnson. They were unseparated in a stand of 198 which brought victory with 8.4 overs to spare. Johnson's hundred came off 73 balls and was the fastest of the season at the time.

With Mullally recording his career-best bowling figures and taking 10 wickets in a match for the first time, Leicestershire beat a Gloucestershire who seemed unable to find any batting form in any match until the second innings. Justin Benson, out of the side for much of the season, hit the highest score of his career. His innings included a six and 16 fours.

Glamorgan's defeat allowed Middlesex to move clear at the top of the table when they beat Surrey. The Surrey tail took them to 322, while the Middlesex first innings, in contrast, was a most inconsistent affair. Brown and Haynes added 109 after four wickets had fallen for 74, and Emburey dominated the closing stages of the innings. Surrey lost their way on the third day, their last six wickets going down for 33 runs, and Brown and Emburey steered Middlesex to victory on the last day after six wickets had fallen for 120.

Northamptonshire beat Somerset inside three days at Luton. Lamb and Curran added 212 in 60 overs for the home side's sixth wicket. Lamb hit 3 sixes and 23 fours in his 50th first-class hundred for Northamptonshire, and Somerset twice surrendered meekly.

At Headingley, Yorkshire were revived by their last three wickets which realised 99. Kent owed much to Hooper and looked set for a big lead until Jarvis ended the innings with three wickets in six balls. Moxon faced 426 balls for his 171, but Kent found his challenge – 322 in 75 overs – too daunting.

At Southampton, Robin Smith saved his immediate Test future with a fighting innings against the Australians, while at Hove, Colin Wells and James Hall shared a second-wicket partnership of 313. More importantly, perhaps, the immensely talented John Crawley hit the highest score of his career, his first hundred for Cambridge against a first-class county.

AXA EQUITY & LAW LEAGUE

27 June *at Derby*

Lancashire 234 for 6 (M.A. Atherton 105)
Derbyshire 73 (P.A.J. DeFreitas 4 for 16)

Lancashire (4 pts.) won by 161 runs

at Stockton

Durham 232 for 7 (P.W.G. Parker 72, G. Fowler 52, P.J. Newport 4 for 46)
Worcestershire 227 for 9 (N.V. Radford 70)

Durham (4 pts.) won by 5 runs

at Ilford

Warwickshire 253 for 9 (D.P. Ostler 69, A.J. Moles 66)
Essex 207 (J.P. Stephenson 90)

Warwickshire (4 pts.) won by 46 runs

at Swansea

Nottinghamshire 210 (C.L. Cairns 53)
Glamorgan 211 for 7 (M.P. Maynard 72 not out)

Glamorgan (4 pts.) won by 3 wickets

at Leicester

Leicestershire 214 for 8 (W.K.M. Benjamin 55)
Gloucestershire 183 (A.J. Wright 51, J.D.R. Benson 4 for 27, W.K.M. Benjamin 4 for 35)

Leicestershire (4 pts.) won by 31 runs

at Lord's

Middlesex 172 for 6 (P.N. Weekes 66 not out)
Surrey 173 for 3 (D.J. Bicknell 65 not out, A.D. Brown 64)

Surrey (4 pts.) won by 7 wickets

at Luton

Northamptonshire 263 for 7 (M.B. Loye 122, R.J. Bailey 72)
Somerset 246 (N.A. Folland 69)

Northamptonshire (4 pts.) won by 17 runs

at Leeds

Kent 200 for 9
Yorkshire 192 for 7

Kent (4 pts.) won by 8 runs

With Sussex idle, Kent moved four points clear at the top of the Sunday League table with a narrow victory at Headingley. Glamorgan, for whom Metson caught four and stumped two, moved into equal second place alongside Sussex and Northamptonshire. Loye hit his first one-day century in the match at Luton. Benson returned the best limited-over bowling figures of his career at Leicester where Winston Benjamin hit his first limited-over fifty.

30 June, 1 and 2 July *at Lord's*

Oxford University 400 for 6 dec. (J.E.R. Gallian 115, G.B.T. Lovell 114, G.I. MacMillan 63) and 100 for 1 (J.E.R. Gallian 53 not out)
Cambridge University 241 (J.P. Crawley 63, M. Jeh 4 for 61) and 255

Oxford University won by 9 wickets

Oxford's form throughout the season had established them as firm favourites for the Varsity match, and they did not disappoint their supporters. Crawley won the toss and asked Oxford to bat, the reasoning being that Cambridge's best, or only, chance of winning was to chase a target. The dark blues suffered an early set-back when Montgomerie was run out for one, but MacMillan then joined skipper Gallian in a stand of 167. Both batsmen were to perish on the temptingly short square-leg boundary. MacMillan had batted with patience; Gallian with mastery. Lovell, captain in 1992, arrived to play some fluent and delightful strokes and, benefiting from being twice dropped, he reached an admirable century on the second day. Crawley and Jones put on 95 for Cambridge's first wicket, but once Crawley was leg before to Jeh, the innings began to fall apart, and Cambridge followed-on 159 runs in arrears. Crawley looked as if he might save the game, but he played across the line to Gallian and was leg before. Whittall and Pitcher added 70 in 15 overs for Cambridge's last wicket, but Gallian and Oxford were not to be denied.

THIRD TEST MATCH
ENGLAND v. AUSTRALIA, at Trent Bridge

The humiliation of the crushing defeat at Lord's caused the England selectors to make sweeping changes for the third Test match. Gatting, Hick, Lewis, Foster and Tufnell were dropped in favour of Thorpe, Hussain, Lathwell, McCague and Martin Bicknell. Thorpe, Lathwell and McCague gained their first Test caps but, sadly and wrongfully, Martin Bicknell was omitted from the side on the morning of the match. Julian replaced McDermott in the Australian eleven.

There was considerable controversy regarding the selection of McCague who had learned and played his cricket in Australia before joining Kent. England now had a pair of opening bowlers who, by right, should have been playing for other countries. Having missed out on the first two Tests, Mark Ilott won his first Test cap so that England had four debutants.

Gooch won the toss, and England batted. Lathwell hit 3 fours and seemed eager to play his shots but, after half an hour, Hughes found the edge of his bat with an out-swinger. Smith was positive from the outset, and when Warne came into the attack Atherton took the spinner for the first three overs to shield Smith. Unfortunately, the policy was shattered when Atherton was given out caught at silly mid-off, bat and pad.

Julian had bowled too much down the leg side, but he was convinced that he had Smith leg before with a straight ball. He did not get the verdict, and Smith punched his way to 50 by lunch. England were going well, and Smith and Stewart had added 90 in pugnacious manner when Stewart reached too far for a long-hop and hit it into the hands of cover. Six runs later, Smith drove hard at Julian who took a magnificent one-handed catch low to his left. Thorpe lasted only 13 balls before being deceived by Hughes' pace and lift and looping the ball to gully off his glove. In the afternoon session, England had scored 103 runs, but they stood at 209 for 5, having lost three vital wickets in the space of eight overs.

Gooch had dropped himself down to number five to accommodate Lathwell and, with his county colleague Hussain, the England captain now had the task of restoring the England innings. In 19 overs, they added 46, but Hughes was always testing with his variations in pace and in his exploitation of the use of the ball short of a length. Eventually, Gooch aimed to play the ball through mid-wicket and was caught at cover off a leading edge. Caddick stayed with Hussain for the last 104 minutes. The Essex man reached his fifty, and England were 276 for 6.

Caddick lasted another 20 minutes on the second morning before being deceived by a straight ball from Hughes. McCague gloved to second slip, and Hussain, having batted for 254 minutes, faced 197 balls and hit 9 fours, was taken off pad and glove at short-leg. If he failed

ABOVE: *Gooch in glory, 120 in the third Test. (Adrian Murrell/Allsport)*

LEFT: *England's young heroes of the third Test match, Thorpe and Hussain. (Adrian Murrell/Allsport)*

to assert himself in the final stages of the innings as he might have done, Hussain had nevertheless played with admirable technical correctness and shown a determination and spirit that was most welcome to England.

Ilott edged limply to slip, and Australia began their first innings at 12.30. By lunch, they were 11 for 0. Eleven overs into the afternoon, Taylor edged McCague to the wicket-keeper, and after eight overs more, Slater was hit on the knee roll by a ball which moved back at him. Boon and Mark Waugh halted any further England progress, and in the remaining 10 overs before tea, they added 50.

They were so much in control of the attack that total slaughter looked probable. They added 123 in a mere 23 overs, and Mark Waugh was driving with supreme elegance and power. He had hit 70 off 67 balls, but on the 68th, he wasted his wicket. He chose to try to hit Such over the top and McCague took a running catch at mid-on. It was a profligate shot, and it was to prove to be the moment when Australia lost their hold on the match. Steve Waugh edged to the keeper off a tentative push, and Ilott's first Test wicket came when Healy was taken at first slip. Australia closed on 262 for 5, Boon 88, and the advantage that was theirs in the mid-afternoon had gone.

Stewart took a diving catch off Ilott's bowling to

England's hopes are raised as Such bowls Slater. (Patrick Eagar)

THIRD CORNHILL TEST MATCH – ENGLAND v. AUSTRALIA
1, 2, 3, 5 and 6 July 1993 at Trent Bridge, Nottingham

ENGLAND

	FIRST INNINGS		SECOND INNINGS	
M.N. Lathwell	c Healy, b Hughes	20	lbw, b Warne	33
M.A. Atherton	c Border, b Warne	11	c Healy, b Hughes	9
R.A. Smith	c and b Julian	86	c Healy, b Warne	50
*A.J. Stewart	c M.E. Waugh, b Warne	25	lbw, b Hughes	6
G.A. Gooch (capt)	c Border, b Hughes	38	c Taylor, b Warne	120
G.P. Thorpe	c S.R. Waugh, b Hughes	6	(7) not out	114
N. Hussain	c Boon, b Warne	71	(8) not out	47
A.R. Caddick	lbw, b Hughes	15	(6) c Boon, b Julian	12
M.J. McCague	c M.E. Waugh, b Hughes	9		
M.C. Ilott	c Taylor, b May	6		
P.M. Such	not out	0		
Extras	b 5, lb 23, w 4, nb 2	34	b 11, lb 11, nb 9	31
		321	(for 6 wickets, dec.)	422

AUSTRALIA

	FIRST INNINGS		SECOND INNINGS	
M.J. Slater	lbw, b Caddick	40	(2) b Such	26
M.A. Taylor	c Stewart, b McCague	28	(1) c Atherton, b Such	28
D.C. Boon	b McCague	101	c Stewart, b Caddick	18
M.E. Waugh	c McCague, b Such	70	b Caddick	1
S.R. Waugh	c Stewart, b McCague	13	(6) not out	47
*I.A. Healy	c Thorpe, b Ilott	9	(7) lbw, b Ilott	5
B.P. Julian	c Stewart, b Ilott	5	(8) not out	56
A.R. Border (capt)	c Smith, b Such	38	(5) c Thorpe, b Caddick	2
M.G. Hughes	b Ilott	17		
S.K. Warne	not out	35		
T.B.A. May	lbw, b McCague	1		
Extras	b 4, lb 8, w 4	16	b 5, lb 5, w 4, nb 5	19
		373	(for 6 wickets)	202

	O	M	R	W	O	M	R	W
Hughes	31	7	92	5	22	8	41	2
Julian	24	3	84	1	33	10	110	1
Warne	40	17	74	3	50	21	108	3
May	14.4	7	31	1	38	6	112	–
S.R. Waugh	8	4	12	–	1	–	3	–
M.E. Waugh	1	1	0	–	6	3	15	–
Border					5	–	11	–

	O	M	R	W	O	M	R	W
McCague	32.3	5	121	4	19	6	58	–
Ilott	34	8	108	3	18	5	44	1
Such	20	7	51	2	23	6	58	2
Caddick	22	5	81	1	16	6	32	3

FALL OF WICKETS

1–28, 2–63, 3–153, 4–159, 5–174, 6–220, 7–290, 8–304, 9–321
1–11, 2–100, 3–109, 4–117, 5–159, 6–309

FALL OF WICKETS

1–55, 2–74, 3–197, 4–239, 5–250, 6–262, 7–284, 8–311, 9–356
1–46, 2–74, 3–75, 4–81, 5–93, 6–115

Umpires: R. Palmer & B.J. Meyer

Match drawn

Joy for Caddick as Mark Waugh is bowled for 1. (Patrick Eagar)

account for Julian without addition on the Saturday morning, which brought in Border at number eight. The Australian skipper had dropped down the order because he was feeling unwell, and his batting suggested that he was very much below his best. Boon reached his fifth hundred against England, with 17 fours, but almost immediately he played on to McCague. Hughes hit a couple of fours before swinging across the line at Ilott, and Border, who hit 7 fours, drove Such into the hands of mid-on. Warne had proved an obdurate number ten, and when May was finally given out leg before to McCague to give the Irish-Australian-Kent bowler four wickets on his Test debut, Australia led by 52.

Before the arrears were wiped out, Atherton was caught behind low down as he gloved the ball from an attempted hook. At tea, England were 12 for 1, with Smith not off the mark.

The session after tea revealed something that England followers found disquieting. Lathwell, a choice for the side by most of the media, was shown to be totally bewildered by top-class spin bowling, particularly the leg-spin of Warne. He might well have been given out when he offered no shot to a googly; he was out when he offered no shot to a leg-break. Four overs earlier, England had lost the belligerent Smith who was once more undone by the leg-spinner, caught behind as he pushed forward to a leg-break. When Stewart was leg before as he aimed to hit the ball to the on side, England had lost three top batsmen in nine overs for 17 runs. Gooch and night-watchman Caddick took the score to 122 at the close.

England took control on the Monday. They lost Caddick before lunch, and Gooch in the final session of the day, but they advanced their score to 362. In fairness to the Australians, they lost the services of Merv Hughes who limped off with a groin strain.

The first praise must go to Gooch. If he has shown liabilities in selection and tactics, he has ever led by example, and his 120 off 265 balls in 324 minutes was a

Healy leg before to Ilott for 5. (Patrick Eagar)

model of concentration, technical proficiency and, above all, character. He judged to a nicety which balls must be hit, and his innings included a six and 18 fours. This was a massive achievement, revitalising England and keeping the Ashes alive. He had added 150 in 61 overs with Thorpe when he was caught at slip off a leg-break that turned sharply and greatly. Thorpe and Hussain thereafter moved serenely to the close.

They extended their partnership to 113 in as many minutes before Gooch declared at 11.40. Graham Thorpe hit a century in his first Test match. In all, he batted for 334 minutes and faced 280 balls, hitting 11 fours. There was much hope for the future in the batting of Hussain and Thorpe.

Slater went off to his usual brisk start, and 46 runs had come in under the hour when he was bowled between bat and pad while playing a poor shot towards leg off Such. In the afternoon five wickets fell, and we dared to dream of an England victory. First Taylor edged to gully, bat and pad, off Such. In the next over, Mark Waugh attempted to drive Caddick, who looked more lively than he had done in previous Tests, and played on. Four overs more and Border guided Caddick to first slip. Then the redoubtable Boon was caught behind as he unwisely tried to square-cut. Healy pushed forward at Ilott without playing a shot, and Australia were 115 for 6 on the stroke of tea.

There the dream ended. After tea England did not really look like taking a wicket. Steve Waugh batted most sensibly; Julian reached a maiden Test fifty. McCague's bowling became wild and woolly, and Caddick reverted to the pedestrian, but England had recaptured some pride and honour and had at least matched the opposition.

Thorpe was named Man of the Match as Slater had been at Lord's, but Gooch's monumental innings will live long in the memory.

Unfortunately, the match was sullied by two things. Referee Clive Lloyd cautioned the Australians regarding their verbal abuse and behaviour on the field. Off the field, we were subjected to the 'rent-a-mob' imported from Nottingham Forest with their constant moronic chants.

ABOVE: *Glamorgan's Viv Richards . . . (David Munden/Sports-Line)*

ABOVE LEFT: *. . . and Adrian Dale shared a record stand of 425 against Middlesex. Both batsmen hit double centuries and finished on the losing side. (Alan Cozzi)*

1, 2, 3 and 5 July *at Cardiff*

Glamorgan 562 for 3 dec. (I.V.A. Richards 224 not out, A. Dale 214 not out) and 109 (P.C.R. Tufnell 8 for 29)

Middlesex 584 (M.W. Gatting 173, J.E. Emburey 123, K.R. Brown 88 not out, D.L. Haynes 73, M.A. Roseberry 58, S.L. Watkin 4 for 87) and 88 for 0 (D.L. Haynes 50 not out)

Middlesex won by 10 wickets

Middlesex 20 pts., Glamorgan 3 pts.

at Bristol

Gloucestershire 501 for 7 dec. (G.D. Hodgson 166, B.C. Broad 131) and 102 (D.P.J. Flint 5 for 32)

Hampshire 393 for 6 dec. (R.S.M. Morris 92, M.C.J. Nicholas 83, K.D. James 69 not out, D.I. Gower 63) and 213 for 9 (M. Davies 4 for 82)

Hampshire won by 1 wicket

Hampshire 20 pts., Gloucestershire 6 pts.

at Maidstone

Kent 445 for 9 dec. (M.V. Fleming 100, M.R. Benson 96, N.J. Llong 89, J.P. Stephenson 5 for 111) and 335 for 4 dec. (C.L. Hooper 142, M.R. Benson 71, N.J. Llong 52 not out)

Essex 440 for 9 dec. (P.J. Prichard 104, D.R. Pringle 76, J.J.B. Lewis 67, M.A. Garnham 66, N. Shahid 60) and 311 for 9 (P.J. Prichard 106, J.P. Stephenson 83)

Match drawn

Kent 6 pts., Essex 6 pts.

at Leicester

Leicestershire 455 (P.A. Nixon 113 not out, T.J. Boon 85, N.E. Briers 58, A.R.K. Pierson 58)

Lancashire 204 (N.J. Speak 64, W.K.M. Benjamin 7 for 83) and 193 (G.D. Lloyd 75, A.R.K. Pierson 6 for 87)

Leicestershire won by an innings and 58 runs

Leicestershire 23 pts., Lancashire 4 pts.

at Northampton

Northamptonshire 212 (R.J. Bailey 63, C.C. Lewis 4 for 58) and 364 (K.M. Curran 68, N.A. Felton 65, M.B. Loye 58, C.L. Cairns 5 for 54)

Nottinghamshire 172 (R.T. Robinson 51, K.M. Curran 5 for 32) and 233 (M. Saxelby 77, R.J. Bailey 5 for 54)

Northamptonshire won by 171 runs

Northamptonshire 21 pts., Nottinghamshire 4 pts.

at Taunton

Somerset 558 (G.D. Rose 138, N.A. Folland 101, Mushtaq Ahmed 90, N.D. Burns 73, K.A. Parsons 63, E.S.H. Giddins 5 for 120) and 226 for 6 dec. (N.A. Folland 108 not out, C.J. Tavaré 57, E.E. Hemmings 4 for 67)

Sussex 435 (A.P. Wells 144, C.W.J. Athey 137, Mushtaq Ahmed 5 for 84) and 229 (C.W.J. Athey 93, Mushtaq Ahmed 7 for 91)

Somerset won by 120 runs

Somerset 21 pts., Sussex 5 pts.

at The Oval

Surrey 473 for 9 dec. (A.D. Brown 150 not out, D.M. Ward 86, D.J. Bicknell 71, P.D. Atkins 62, P. Bainbridge 5 for 90)

Durham 148 (M.P. Bicknell 4 for 44) and 120 (C.W. Scott 58 not out, Waqar Younis 4 for 21, M.P. Bicknell 4 for 26)

Surrey won by an innings and 205 runs

Surrey 24 pts., Durham 4 pts.

at Edgbaston

Warwickshire 346 (A.J. Moles 113, D.A. Reeve 53) and 115 for 4

Yorkshire 178 and 282 (R.B. Richardson 112, M.D. Moxon 72, A.A. Donald 7 for 98)

Warwickshire won by 6 wickets

Warwickshire 23 pts., Yorkshire 3 pts.

at Kidderminster

Derbyshire 251 (P.D. Bowler 65) and 358 (K.J. Barnett 168, D.G. Cork 57, P.D. Bowler 56, K.C.G. Benjamin 4 for 81)

Worcestershire 560 (G.A. Hick 173, W.P.C. Weston 109, T.S. Curtis 81, S.J. Base 5 for 82) and 50 for 1

Worcestershire won by 9 wickets

Worcestershire 24 pts., Derbyshire 2 pts.

The third Test match could not overshadow the events at Cardiff where the two top counties met in an astonishing match. Batting first, Glamorgan reached 319 for 3 on the first day and Hugh Morris became the first batsman to score 1,000 runs in the season. Dale also reached 1,000 runs as he hit the first double century of his career and shared an unbroken fourth-wicket stand of 425 with Viv Richards. This is a record stand for any Glamorgan wicket. Dale faced 455 balls and hit 22 fours while Richards faced 357 balls and hit 4 sixes and 28 fours in what was his highest score for Glamorgan. The partnership occupied 417 minutes. Undaunted, Middlesex replied with a first-wicket stand of 122, and Emburey, who had come in at number three as night-watchman, shared a third-wicket stand of 262 with Gatting. Gatting was severely criticised for batting into the last day, but then the game took a remarkable turn. Glamorgan lost their last five wickets for nine runs. Phil Tufnell took 8 for 29 in 23 overs, the best bowling performance of his career. Gleefully, Middlesex hit the 88 runs they needed to win inside 19 overs.

Poor Gloucestershire, without a win in the championship all season, suffered a shock as big as Glamorgan's. Broad and Hodgson both scored centuries and put on 279

for the first wicket. Hampshire kept in touch through Morris, who hit his highest first-class score, and Nicholas and James who added 131 for the sixth wicket. On the last day, Gloucestershire were bowled out by the spinners, Udal and Flint. Flint, a slow left-arm bowler, took five wickets in an innings on his first-class debut. He was to gain further honours as Hampshire chased a target of 211 in 64 overs and found batting difficult against Wight and Davies. Aymes was run out on the third ball of the last over – a wide – but Flint kept his nerve, hit a single, and Connor hit the penultimate ball of the match for six.

There were some strange faces at Maidstone where Kent had Bobby Parks and Spencer in their eleven, and Essex, deprived of six first-team players through injury and Test calls, gave first-class debuts to Cousins and Robinson and a championship debut to Robert Rollins, whose brother Adrian was making his championship debut for Derbyshire at Kidderminster on the same day. Benson and Llong added 158 for Kent's fourth wicket, and Fleming hit a brisk and attractive century on the second morning. Essex responded positively with Prichard hitting 104 off 105 balls. The Essex captain was to hit two centuries in a match for the first time when, after Hooper's graceful 142, Essex were asked to score 341 in 81 overs to win the match. Prichard and Stephenson gave their side a fine start with a partnership of 185, and Essex reached 298 for 5, only to fall apart against Hooper and Davis. Garnham and Childs survived the last five overs to save the match.

Phil Tufnell took a career best 8 for 29 to snatch a sensational victory for Middlesex against Glamorgan, 5 July. (Alan Cozzi)

Leicestershire swept aside Lancashire in three days. Boon and Briers started with a stand of 132, but Leicestershire lost four wickets for one run in mid-innings. Nixon and Pierson both made career-best scores in sharing a ninth-wicket partnership of 119. Winston Benjamin then tore Lancashire apart with his best performance in the championship, and in their second innings, they fell to pieces against the off-spin of Pierson who returned his best figures for Leicestershire.

Seventeen wickets fell on the first day at Northampton, and the match was over in three. The pitch was reported as poor and inspected by Harry Brind, but Robert Bailey had some joy in claiming five wickets in an innings for the first time with his off-breaks.

Nicholas Folland, once of Devon, hit his maiden first-class century, for Somerset against Sussex, and hit his second in the second innings. Folland and Keith Parsons, who hit his first fifty in first-class cricket, put on 112 after Somerset had lost three wickets for 92, and Rose shared century stands with Burns and Mushtaq. Athey hit his highest score for Sussex, and skipper Alan Wells also batted splendidly, but when, following Folland's second hundred, Sussex were left to make 350 in 86 overs, only Athey could cope with the leg-spin of Mushtaq Ahmed. The Pakistani Test cricketer bowled unchanged for 40.5 overs and took 7 for 91, his best performance for Somerset.

Surrey were put in to bat at The Oval. Atkins, in his first innings of the season, and Darren Bicknell scored 165 for the first wicket. David Ward and Alistair Brown added 176 for the fourth wicket and, although Bainbridge had his best bowling performance for Durham, Surrey totalled 473 for 9 on the first day. Brown reached his 100 off 108 balls. Durham surrendered feebly on the second day. Neither Glendenen nor Graveney could bat when they followed-on, and, at one time, Durham were 29 for 7. The game was over shortly after tea on the second day. Durham looked a dreadful side.

Moles and Ratcliffe put on 140 for Warwickshire's first wicket against Yorkshire, and Moles' patient century took the home side to a reasonable score on a slow pitch. Yorkshire gave a poor performance and were forced to follow-on. Moxon and Richardson, who hit his first century for Yorkshire, added 174 for the fourth wicket in the second innings, but Donald proved too quick for the remaining batsmen, and Warwickshire moved to victory on the last morning.

At Kidderminster Philip Weston hit his first championship century and shared stands of 175 for the first wicket and 135 for the second with Curtis and Hick respectively. Hick's 173 came off 176 balls and included 4 sixes and 27 fours. Derbyshire had been bowled out in 57.3 overs on the first day, and they batted a second time 309 runs in arrears. An heroic innings by Kim Barnett who batted for 409 minutes nearly saved the game for the visitors, but Benjamin ended the innings with four wickets in 15 balls, three of them in four balls.

AXA EQUITY & LAW LEAGUE

4 July *at Cardiff*

Glamorgan 287 for 8 (S.P. James 94, A. Dale 61, P.N. Weekes 4 for 61)
Middlesex 166

Glamorgan (4 pts.) won by 121 runs

at Bristol

Gloucestershire 240 for 7 (S.G. Hinks 74)
Hampshire 216 (D.I. Gower 60, T.C. Middleton 54)

Gloucestershire (4 pts.) won by 24 runs

at Maidstone

Kent 309 for 7 (C.L. Hooper 103, T.R. Ward 86)
Essex 152 (P.J. Prichard 67, C.L. Hooper 5 for 41)

Kent (4 pts.) won by 157 runs

at Leicester

Lancashire 300 for 7 (S.P. Titchard 84)
Leicestershire 217

Lancashire (4 pts.) won by 83 runs

at Northampton

Northamptonshire 227 for 7 (M.B. Loye 85, K.M. Curran 65 not out)
Nottinghamshire 164

Northamptonshire (4 pts.) won by 63 runs

at Taunton

Sussex 302 for 8 (M.P. Speight 126)
Somerset 197 (A.N. Jones 4 for 26)

Sussex (4 pts.) won by 105 runs

at The Oval

Surrey 205 for 9 (M.A. Lynch 78, G.J. Kersey 50)
Durham 169

Surrey (4 pts.) won by 36 runs

at Edgbaston

Yorkshire 131 for 9 (P.A. Smith 4 for 33)
Warwickshire 135 for 2 (D.P. Ostler 81 not out)

Warwickshire (4 pts.) won by 8 wickets

at Worcester

Worcestershire 190 for 9
Derbyshire 194 for 5 (C.J. Adams 63)

Derbyshire (4 pts.) won by 5 wickets

Kent maintained their lead at the top of the Sunday League table by crushing Essex at Maidstone. Carl

Hooper hit his first hundred in the league and followed it with his best bowling performance. He and Trevor Ward scored 126 in 21 overs for the second wicket. Glamorgan kept up their challenge with victory over Middlesex. James and Dale set up a Glamorgan one-day record with a second-wicket stand of 172. Martin Speight hit his highest score in one-day cricket as Sussex crushed Somerset. He retired hurt on 93, but he returned with a runner to reach 100 off 47 balls. In all, he hit 4 sixes and 20 fours. Surrey recovered from 63 for 5 to beat Durham and stay six points behind Kent with two games in hand.

NATWEST TROPHY

ROUND TWO

7 July *at Chelmsford*

Essex 286 for 5 (P.J. Prichard 92, J.P. Stephenson 90, N. Hussain 50)

Northamptonshire 290 for 5 (A.J. Lamb 124 not out, M.B. Loye 65)

Northamptonshire won by 5 wickets

(Man of the Match – A.J. Lamb)

at Cardiff

Durham 245 for 5 (W. Larkins 75, P.W.G. Parker 73 not out)

Glamorgan 248 for 3 (M.P. Maynard 101)

Glamorgan won by 7 wickets

(Man of the Match – M.P. Maynard)

at Bristol

Gloucestershire 241 for 3 (B.C. Broad 114 not out, G.D. Hodgson 62)

Yorkshire 243 for 8 (R.B. Richardson 90)

Yorkshire won by 2 wickets

(Man of the Match – B.C. Broad)

at Leicester

Leicestershire 129

Surrey 131 for 3 (A.J. Stewart 56)

Surrey won by 7 wickets

(Man of the Match – A.W. Smith)

at Trent Bridge

Nottinghamshire 203 (C.L. Cairns 71)

Somerset 204 for 7 (N.A. Folland 63)

Somerset won by 3 wickets

(Man of the Match – C.L. Cairns)

at Hove

Hampshire 248 for 4 (R.A. Smith 104 not out, V.P. Terry 71)

Sussex 252 for 1 (D.M. Smith 123, C.W.J. Athey 107 not out)

Sussex won by 9 wickets

(Man of the Match – D.M. Smith)

at Edgbaston

Kent 262 for 9 (M.A. Ealham 58 not out, T.R. Ward 50, A.A. Donald 4 for 69)

Warwickshire 265 for 5 (D.A. Reeve 72 not out, P.A. Smith 61)

Warwickshire won by 5 wickets

(Man of the Match – D.A. Reeve)

at Worcester

Derbyshire 244 for 9 (C.J. Adams 93, J.E. Morris 71)

Worcestershire 245 for 6 (T.S. Curtis 82)

Worcestershire won by 4 wickets

(Man of the Match – T.S. Curtis)

The remarkable thing about the second round of the NatWest Trophy was that the eight captains who won the toss all chose to bat first, and the eight sides who batted second won. Essex seemed to be cruising to victory at Chelmsford. At lunch, Stephenson and Prichard had scored 160 from 40 overs, but the off-spin of Bailey had proved to be something of a curb on the scoring rate

Dermot Reeve, an astute captain, steered Warwickshire to victory over Kent. (Alan Cozzi)

Brilliant batting from Matthew Maynard took Glamorgan to victory over Durham in the second round of the NatWest Trophy. (David Munden/Sports-Line)

immediately before lunch just as the openers were looking to accelerate. Bailey continued to frustrate immediately after lunch, but it was Ambrose who broke the partnership when he had Prichard leg before at 187. Two runs later, Bailey had his reward when he bowled Stephenson who should have been stumped off his bowling some overs earlier. Hussain hit 50 off 43 balls, and there was some brisk scoring from Salim and from Gooch and Pringle, but Essex seemed some 25 runs short of what had looked possible at one time. The score seemed ample, however, when Pringle had Fordham leg before in his first over, and when Felton was caught at mid-off by Gooch and Bailey run out, Northamptonshire were 46 for 3, and Essex were winning. Lamb then joined the impressive Loye – a tall, commanding young batsman – in a partnership of 137 which breathed new life into the Northamptonshire challenge. Curran did not stay long, but Penberthy showed the utmost confidence in supporting his skipper as the last 94 runs were scored with remarkable ease. Lamb, missed by Ilott off his own bowling on 24, was in total authority against an attack which often failed to bowl to its field, and his 124 came from 127 balls. Northamptonshire won with 13 balls to spare.

Glamorgan won with 17 balls to spare. On a sluggish pitch, Durham made only 37 from the first 20 overs, but Larkins and Parker added 107 in 24 overs, and Botham hit 33 off 27 balls. This ensured that the visitors would reach a respectable score which was, however, unlikely to be a winning one. So it proved. James and Morris provided a steady start, and Maynard's mature century gave the innings the necessary impetus. He and Richards added 85 in 15 overs, and he and James put on 100 for the second wicket.

Chris Broad and Dean Hodgson began Gloucestershire's innings against Yorkshire with a record stand of 165, and Broad carried his bat through the 60 overs for 114, but Yorkshire snatched victory in the last two overs. Richie Richardson hit 90 off 111 balls to give the Yorkshire innings both backbone and urgency, and with six overs and six wickets remaining, the White Rose county needed 42 runs and looked set for a comfortable win, but Richardson and White fell in the same over. Jarvis and Gough followed, and 23 were needed from two overs.

Mike Smith conceded 15 in the penultimate over, and Hartley's bold hitting took the visitors to victory with two balls to spare.

Off-break bowler Andrew Smith took three wickets and won the individual award as Surrey brushed aside Leicestershire. Stewart hit 56 off 38 balls.

Nottinghamshire reached 162 for 3 by the 42nd over, and then lost their last seven wickets for 41 runs against Somerset. Somerset themselves lost four wickets in three overs, and Mushtaq was dropped when four runs were still needed for victory, but the target was reached with 13 balls to spare.

Robin Smith hit his fourth hundred in the competition, but finished on the losing side at Hove. Needing 249 to win, Sussex benefited from Hampshire missing chances, the most crucial being Aymes' failure twice to catch Bill Athey. The misses helped Athey and David Smith to establish a first-wicket record for the competition, Smith being yorked when the scores were level. Both batsmen batted magnificently: Smith reached his hundred off 158 balls, and Athey his off 159 balls. Speight hit the winning four with seven balls to spare. Hampshire's miserable day was compounded when Kevin Shine withdrew from the attack with hamstring problems, but by that time he had conceded 61 runs in 9.3 overs.

Hooper and Ward promised more than they achieved at Edgbaston, and Kent slipped to 172 for 7. It was Mark Ealham's hitting at the close which lifted them. He hit 3 sixes in his 58 off 44 balls, and 22 runs came from the final over. Paul Smith was the sufferer, but after Warwickshire had lost Ratcliffe and Ostler for 58, he shared stands with Moles and Reeve to put his side on course for victory. Twose and Reeve added 78 for the fifth wicket before Twose was run out, and Reeve steered Warwickshire into the quarter-finals with three balls to spare.

Derbyshire began disastrously, losing both openers for 13, but Adams and Morris added 162 in 40 overs. Morris was out with 12 overs remaining, and the late order failed to capitalise on the situation, managing only 69 runs in the closing stages of the innings as eight wickets went down. Curtis, with 82 off 151 balls, steered Worcestershire into the last eight in his customary solid manner and without too many alarms.

8 July *at Stone*

Australians 230 (M.A. Taylor 53, P.R. Reiffel 50 not out)
Minor Counties 172 (I. Cockbain 70, P.R. Reiffel 5 for 28)

Australians won by 58 runs

9 July *at Haarlem*

England XI 238 for 5 (M.R. Benson 61, T.R. Ward 53, N. Hussain 52)
Holland 110 for 7

England XI won by 128 runs

10 July *at Haarlem*

England XI 188 for 7 (M.R. Benson 58)
Holland 189 for 3 (R. Bradley 88 not out, P. Cantrell 64)

Holland won by 7 wickets

at Dublin (Clontarf)

Australians 361 for 3 (M.L. Hayden 133 not out, A.R. Border 111, M.J. Slater 56)
Ireland 89

Australians won by 272 runs

An England XI under the captaincy of Mark Benson played two one-day international matches against Holland on the weekend of the Benson and Hedges Cup final and were embarrassingly beaten in the second match. In Ireland, Allan Border hit five consecutive sixes off off-spinner Angus Dunlop and reached 111 in 45 minutes of a slaughter of the innocents.

BENSON AND HEDGES CUP FINAL
LANCASHIRE *v.* DERBYSHIRE, at Lord's

Rarely in a major final has a county started as such total underdogs as Derbyshire. They had lost their overseas player with injury for the entire season, were deep in debt and had sacked leading executives as part of their economy drive. Their opponents were noted as limited-over experts and appeared to be able to win as they pleased. Moreover, nothing in the early stages of the game contradicted this opinion. Lancashire won the toss, asked Derbyshire to bat and trapped Bowler leg before in the second over of the match. If Derbyshire were to have any chance of success, it was believed, everything depended upon their top four, prolific and quick scorers. One of them had gone offering no shot to DeFreitas, and 10 overs later, skipper Barnett dragged a ball from Wasim Akram onto his stumps.

Morris played two magnificent shots – one, a straight

drive off Wasim Akram, has rarely been bettered at headquarters. There was a spirit of belligerence and adventure in the air. Runs had come at four an over. Adams had been greeted by an appeal for leg before, and then by a beamer, apparently deliberate, which struck him on the left shoulder and brought the physio from the pavilion to administer first aid. The bowler was Wasim. There was obviously no love lost between the two sides.

Morris and Adams are the hopes of Derbyshire cricket. They are exciting and entertaining, and they breathe youth and enthusiasm. They added 29 in four overs, and then came disaster. Watkinson came on at the Nursery End. Morris attempted an extravagant square drive at his first delivery and was caught behind. Adams followed in the same over, pushing forward and getting an inside edge onto the stumps. Sixteen overs into the match, at 66 for 4, with the main batsmen all gone, an early and embarrassing finish beckoned.

Cork began with a splendid cover-drive off Wasim who was to lose all control as he searched for aggression, and aggression that was ill-disciplined. This was where Lancashire lost the game. Their fielding had been ragged from the start; it now became awful. One cannot remember witnessing such a dreadful display in a match of this status. At lunch, Derbyshire were 133 for 4 off 35 overs, and it is no exaggeration to say that some 30 of those runs had been gifted to them in the field. O'Gorman had flicked one majestic six into the Grand Stand, but generally he was playing the supporting role to Cork who had found his touch from the moment he walked to the wicket.

In 28 overs, the pair added 109 and turned a lost cause into a contest. They ran well in spite of Cork's limp, and they went on the offensive at every conceivable opportunity. O'Gorman was finally caught behind when he tried to steer DeFreitas to third man, and Griffith went first ball when he was over-ambitious with a square-drive. Eleven overs remained, and it seemed that Derbyshire might have suddenly lost their way. Cork and Krikken had other ideas, though, and from those last

Chris Adams is felled by Wasim Akram's beamer. (David Munden/Sports-Line)

Derbyshire's saviour and Gold Award winner Dominic Cork on his way to 92. (David Munden/Sports-Line)

*Despair for Derbyshire as Kim Barnett is bowled by Wasim Akram.
(Patrick Eagar)*

exhausting overs they chased and harried 77 runs. Cork moved outside the off stump and flicked Wasim's penultimate delivery to fine leg for four. It confirmed the victors of the battle, if not the war. Wasim had 1 for 65 from his 11 overs.

Cork finished on 92 from 124 deliveries. He hit 7 fours, and a Lancastrian would have to play a mighty innings to rob him of the Gold Award. Krikken, it should be noted, hit 37 off 35 balls, and he had missed much of the season through injury.

Like Lancashire, Derbyshire had an early success. Warner found the edge of Titchard's bat in his first over and Adams held a splendid catch, low at second slip. There were no more alarms before tea. Atherton played with good sense after this set-back, allowing Speak to bat with more freedom. Tea came with the favourites on 78 for 1 from 25 overs.

The first over after tea saw Speak play on as he pushed forward to Mortensen, but Atherton and Fairbrother, the master one-day batsman, showed calm and authority. They took the score to 141 for 2 in 38 overs when rain stopped play shortly after six. It seemed that once more the Benson and Hedges final would be forced into a second day, but the skies cleared, and play began again shortly before 7.15.

Atherton's important stabilising innings came to an end almost immediately as he gave a return catch to Griffith in the 41st over just after Lancashire had posted the 150. Lloyd went three overs later when he unwisely attempted to swing Warner to leg. Wasim completed a miserable match by heaving 12 off 13 balls before giving the admirable Warner a return catch. The Lancashire captain did not seem pleased with Wasim's shot, but while he remained his side were still well capable of scoring the 69 they needed from just over seven overs.

As Watkinson gave sound support, the target was reduced to 55 from six overs, at which point Cork bowled a bad over and conceded 12. He made amends in his next over when he bowled the dangerous Watkinson, and 32 runs were needed from the last three overs.

DeFreitas hoisted the young and inexperienced Griffith for six, and it was the same bowler who had to bowl the last over with Lancashire just 11 short of victory. Barnett set his field carefully and encouraged Griffith. The first two deliveries were right in the batsman's block hole, and Fairbrother could only squeeze a single as the tension mounted. The third ball was low and overpitched. DeFreitas went for a mighty – and hideous – heave, and Krikken took a catch off a ball that hung long and high in the air. Two runs after a desperate dive by Fairbrother were all that came from the fourth ball, and a single was all Griffith offered from the next. Fairbrother finished with 87 off 85 balls, but the glory went to Derbyshire whose eagerness, discipline and team spirit had won them a deserved victory in an epic final.

AXA EQUITY & LAW LEAGUE

11 July *at Llanelli*

Glamorgan 269 for 8 (S.P. James 107, H. Morris 67)
Sussex 219 (P. Moores 56, A.P. Wells 51)
Glamorgan (4 pts.) won by 50 runs

at Moreton-in-Marsh

Gloucestershire 243 (P.C.R. Tufnell 4 for 44)
v. Middlesex
Match abandoned
Gloucestershire 2 pts., Middlesex 2 pts.

at Southampton

Somerset 214 (N.A. Folland 60)
Hampshire 215 for 3 (M.C.J. Nicholas 84 not out, V.P. Terry 83 not out)
Hampshire (4 pts.) won by 7 wickets

at Leicester

Leicestershire 26 for 1
v. Surrey

Match abandoned

Leicestershire 2 pts., Surrey 2 pts.

at Trent Bridge

Worcestershire 155
Nottinghamshire 158 for 6

Nottinghamshire (4 pts.) won by 4 wickets

at Edgbaston

Northamptonshire 196 for 7 (R.J. Bailey 69)
Warwickshire 183 for 2 (D.P. Ostler 68 not out, P.A. Smith 63 not out)

Warwickshire (4 pts.) won on faster scoring rate

James and Morris set Glamorgan on the road to victory with an opening stand of 120 against Sussex. James hit his first Sunday League century, and Glamorgan went to the top of the table to join Kent. Rain caused the game at Moreton-in-Marsh to be abandoned, but Courtney Walsh led Gloucestershire for the first time, Wright having resigned following bad form and poor results. The match at Leicester was abandoned because umpires and captains considered the pitch too dangerous. An inquiry followed. In his last season, Derek Randall became the third batsman after Amiss and Gooch to reach 7,000 runs in the Sunday League. He was 30 not out as Nottinghamshire won their second match of the season.

The Harrogate Festival, once sponsored by Tilcon, had its final ruined by rain. The previous day, Byas, who had been dropped from the NatWest Trophy game after a run of poor form, starred in the win over Durham. Yorkshire had had a full meeting to discuss recent poor showings on the field.

JESMOND FESTIVAL

13 July

Rest of the World XI 309 for 5 (P.V. Simmons 104, A.D. Jadeja 87, C.G. Greenidge 59)
England XI 272 for 9 (M.W. Gatting 90, R.A. Harper 4 for 67)

Rest of the World XI won by 37 runs

14 July

Rest of the World XI 149 for 4 (P.V. Simmons 58)
***v.* England XI**

Match abandoned

TETLEY BITTER TROPHY
at Harrogate

12 July

Nottinghamshire 299 for 8 (M.A. Crawley 113, C.C. Lewis 55, V.J. Wells 5 for 57)
Leicestershire 286 for 9 (T.J. Boon 84, J.J. Whitaker 69, C.L. Cairns 4 for 48)

Nottinghamshire won by 13 runs

13 July

Durham 235 for 7 (G. Fowler 51)
Yorkshire 238 for 4 (D. Byas 80, R.B. Richardson 77)

Yorkshire won by 6 wickets

FINAL

14 July

Nottinghamshire 159 for 9 (J.D. Batty 4 for 20)
Yorkshire 43 for 5

Nottinghamshire won on faster scoring rate

Steve James is now among the most reliable of openers and a significant reason for Glamorgan's success in 1993. (Alan Cozzi)

PRIZE STRUCTURE

£93,445 of the £614,032 Benson and Hedges sponsorship of this event will go in prize money for teams or individuals.

The breakdown is as follows:

- The Champions will win £30,000 (and hold, for one year only, the Benson and Hedges Cup)
- For the Runners-up £15,000
- For the losing Semi-finalists £7,500
- For the losing Quarter-finalists £3,750
- For the First round winners £1,200
- For the Preliminary round winners £900.

INDIVIDUAL GOLD AWARDS

There will be a Benson and Hedges Gold Award for the outstanding individual performance at all matches throughout the Cup.

These will be:

• In the Preliminary round	£135
• In the First round	£165
• In the Quarter-finals	£275
• In the Semi-finals	£325
• In the Final	£600

The playing conditions and Cup records are on the reverse.

HOLDERS:
HAMPSHIRE COUNTY CRICKET CLUB

BENSON and HEDGES CUP 1993

MARYLEBONE CRICKET CLUB

50p   50p

FINAL

DERBYSHIRE v. LANCASHIRE
at Lord's Ground, Saturday, July 10th 1993

Any alterations to teams will be announced over the public address system

DERBYSHIRE

†1 K. J. Barnett	b Wasim Akram	19
2 P. D. Bowler	l b w b DeFreitas	4
3 J. E. Morris	c Hegg b Watkinson	22
4 C. J. Adams	b Watkinson	11
5 T. J. G. O'Gorman	c Hegg b DeFreitas	49
6 D. G. Cork	not out	92
7 F. A. Griffith	c Hegg b DeFreitas	0
*8 K. M. Krikken	not out	37
9 A. E. Warner		
10 D. E. Malcolm		
11 O. H. Mortensen		

B , 1 b **12**, w **1**, n-b **5**, ... **18**

Total . **252**

FALL OF THE WICKETS
1...7 2...32 3...61 4...66 5...175 6...175 7... 8... 9... 10...

Bowling Analysis	O.	M.	R.	W.	Wd.	N-b
Austin	11	2	47	0	...	...
DeFreitas	11	2	39	3	1	...
Wasim Akram	11	0	65	1	...	5
Watkinson	11	2	44	2	...	...
Barnett	11	0	45	0	...	...

LANCASHIRE

1 M. A. Atherton	c and b Griffith	54
2 S. P. Titchard	c Adams b Warner	0
3 N. J. Speak	b Mortensen	42
†4 N. H. Fairbrother	not out	87
5 G. D. Lloyd	l b w b Warner	5
6 Wasim Akram	c and b Warner	12
7 M. Watkinson	b Cork	10
8 P. A. J. DeFreitas	c Krikken b Griffith	16
9 I. D. Austin	not out	0
*10 W. K. Hegg		
11 A. A. Barnett		

B , 1-b **11**, w **3**, n-b **6**, ... **20**

Total... **246**

FALL OF THE WICKETS
1...9 2...80 3...150 4...159 5...184 6...218 7...243 8... 9... 10...

Bowling Analysis	O.	M.	R.	W.	Wd.	N-b
Malcolm	11	0	53	0	1	4
Warner	11	1	31	3	1	...
Cork	11	1	50	1	1	2
Mortensen	11	0	41	1	...	...
Griffith	11	0	60	2	...	...

† Captain   * Wicket-keeper
Umpires—B. J. Meyer & D. R. Shepherd
Scorers—S. W. Tacey, W. Davies & J. Dickson

Toss won by—Lancashire who elected to field
RESULT—Derbyshire won by 6 runs

The playing conditions for the Benson & Hedges Cup Competition are printed on the back of this score card.

Total runs scored at end of each over :—

Derbyshire	1	2	3	4	5	6	7	8	9	10	11	12	13	14	15	16	17	18	19	20
	21	22	23	24	25	26	27	28	29	30	31	32	33	34	35	36	37	38	39	40
	41	42	43	44	45	46	47	48	49	50	51	52	53	54	55					

Lancashire	1	2	3	4	5	6	7	8	9	10	11	12	13	14	15	16	17	18	19	20
	21	22	23	24	25	26	27	28	29	30	31	32	33	34	35	36	37	38	39	40
	41	42	43	44	45	46	47	48	49	50	51	52	53	54	55					

Reproduced by kind permission of MCC.

A splendid catch at slip by Chris Adams to dismiss Titchard and give Derbyshire their first wicket. (David Munden/Sports-Line)

Contrasting moods – joy for Kim Barnett and Derbyshire; gloom for Neil Fairbrother and Lancashire. (David Munden/Sports-Line)

13, 14 and 15 July *at Derby*

Derbyshire 305 (K.J. Barnett 114, D.G. Cork 58, W.J. Holdsworth 5 for 117, P.R. Reiffel 4 for 82)
Australians 268 for 1 (M.J. Slater 133 not out, M.E. Waugh 60 not out)
Match drawn

No play was possible on the last day at Derby. Earlier, Kim Barnett had hit a worthy century, and Dominic Cork had given further evidence of his all-round worth. Holdsworth, the fastest of the Australian bowlers, who had failed to find a consistent length on the tour, performed the hat-trick. Slater and Mark Waugh savaged the Derbyshire attack, and runs came at more than six an over.

SEEBOARD TROPHY

14 July *at Canterbury*

Kent 209 for 8 (S.A. Marsh 50)
Surrey 213 for 5 (A.J. Stewart 53)
Surrey won by 5 wickets

15, 16, 17 and 19 July *at Southend*

Leicestershire 321 (P.E. Robinson 71, T.J. Boon 70, P.A. Nixon 56, P.M. Such 5 for 66) and 199 (J.H. Childs 5 for 64, P.M. Such 5 for 80)
Essex 233 (N. Hussain 103, G.A. Gooch 51, A.D. Mullally 4 for 62) and 210 (P.J. Prichard 60, D.R. Pringle 57 not out, A.R.K. Pierson 5 for 78)
Leicestershire won by 77 runs
Leicestershire 23 pts., Essex 4 pts.

at Portsmouth

Hampshire 355 for 9 dec. (R.A. Smith 91, S.D. Udal 66, A.N. Aymes 50 not out, K.C.G. Benjamin 4 for 99)
Worcestershire 206 for 5 (D.B. D'Oliveira 94, G.A. Hick 52)
Match drawn
Hampshire 6 pts., Worcestershire 5 pts.

at Old Trafford

Lancashire 310 (M.A. Atherton 63) and 235 for 1 dec. (G. Chapple 109 not out, G. Yates 94 not out)
Glamorgan 303 for 5 dec. (S.P. James 138 not out, P.A. Cottey 67) and 244 for 3 (A. Dale 95, M.P. Maynard 55)
Glamorgan won by 7 wickets
Glamorgan 23 pts., Lancashire 5 pts.

at Trent Bridge

Somerset 241 (N.A. Folland 57, Mushtaq Ahmed 50, R.A. Pick 4 for 43) and 195 for 6 (R.J. Harden 99 not out, C.C. Lewis 4 for 54)
Nottinghamshire 200 for 3 dec. (P.R. Pollard 91, M. Saxelby 71)
Match drawn
Nottinghamshire 5 pts., Somerset 2 pts.

at Guildford

Gloucestershire 153 (Waqar Younis 6 for 42) and 162 (G.D. Hodgson 60, M.P. Bicknell 5 for 41)
Surrey 381 (M.A. Lynch 90, G.P. Thorpe 57)
Surrey won by an innings and 66 runs
Surrey 24 pts., Gloucestershire 4 pts.

at Arundel

Sussex 168 (M.J. McCague 4 for 55) and 59 for 1
Kent 200 for 5 dec. (N.R. Taylor 74 not out, C.L. Hooper 65)

Match drawn

Kent 5 pts., Sussex 2 pts.

at Edgbaston

Warwickshire 237 (J.D. Ratcliffe 82, P.C.R. Tufnell 4 for 71)
  and 206 (J.E. Emburey 6 for 61)
Middlesex 387 (J.D. Carr 192 not out, J.E. Emburey 55,
  N.M.K. Smith 4 for 133) and 60 for 1

Middlesex won by 9 wickets

Middlesex 23 pts., Warwickshire 4 pts.

at Harrogate

Northamptonshire 97 (M.A. Robinson 9 for 37) and 305
  (R.J. Bailey 68, N.A. Felton 66, P.J. Hartley 5 for 51)
Yorkshire 168 (R.B. Richardson 58, D. Byas 54,
  K.M. Curran 7 for 47) and 238 for 6 (R.J. Blakey 74,
  D. Byas 71)

Yorkshire won by 4 wickets

Yorkshire 20 pts., Northamptonshire 4 pts.

17, 18 and 19 July *at Durham University*

Durham 385 for 8 dec. (W. Larkins 151, A.C. Cummins 69)
Australians 221 (I.A. Healy 70 not out, S.J.E. Brown
  7 for 70) and 295 for 3 dec. (M.L. Hayden 151 not out,
  D.C. Boon 112)

Match drawn

Rain marred all the matches in the Britannic Assurance
County Championship, and the games at Portsmouth
and Arundel were completely ruined, no play being
possible at either venue on the last day.

At Southend, where the match between Essex and
Leicestershire was the only one to start on time, Gooch
won the toss and, surprisingly, asked the visitors to bat.
He had no reward as, in spite of interruptions, Boon and
Briers scored 109 for the first wicket. The Essex spinners
brought about a collapse as five wickets went down for 56
runs, but Robinson, in his first innings of any substance
in the season, and Nixon added 97. Benjamin also hit
well, and Leicestershire could be well satisfied with their
effort. When Essex batted the pitch revealed previously
unknown demons which Mullally and Benjamin
exploited. In spite of Gooch's 51, Essex slumped to 159 for
8. Hussain alone stood firm and drove with majesty.
Eventually, he found an able partner in John Childs. Fifty
runs were added for the last wicket, and Hussain reached
a well-deserved hundred. Such and Childs combined to
bowl out Leicestershire on the Saturday and to leave their
side with every chance of victory. Needing 288 to win,
Essex lost Gooch and Stephenson before the close of
play and surrendered rather meekly to Pierson on the
Monday.

*Jason Ratcliffe enjoyed a good season and established a regular place as
Warwickshire's opening batsman. (David Munden/Sports-Line)*

Glamorgan beat Lancashire and kept alive their championship hopes, but not without resorting to tactics
which had more than an element of farce about them.
There was no play on the first day, while Lancashire's
innings occupied the second day and Glamorgan's the
third. Steve James hit his first century of the summer in
under four hours. On the last morning, Morris declared
and offered Lancashire runs in an attempt to give his side
a target to chase in the afternoon. Accordingly, Maynard
and Cottey bowled six overs each: the 12 overs occupied
half an hour during which time Lancashire scored 235.
Nineteen-year-old Glen Chapple hit a maiden first-class
century. It took him 21 minutes and came off 27 balls; he
hit 34 off Cottey's second over and 32 off the third. His
century included 10 sixes and 9 fours, and it was the
fastest on record. Play had not been possible until 1.40 so
that Glamorgan's eventual target was 243 off 52 overs, a
task they accomplished with the utmost ease. Dale and
Maynard scored 131 for the second wicket to set up the
victory.

The captains at Trent Bridge did their best to keep the
game alive, but rain was the eventual winner, with
Richard Harden left marooned on 99 when the final
deluge came.

Surrey won in two days at Guildford. Waqar Younis
and Martin Bicknell twice demolished Gloucestershire,
and Surrey scored with a capable consistency to make
their win automatic.

Middlesex staged another fine recovery to beat Warwickshire at Edgbaston. Warwickshire laboured on a
shortened first day, but the balance of the game tilted
somewhat on the second when Middlesex lost their first
six wickets for 90 runs. Carr and Emburey stopped the
rot, batting into the third day and adding 150. Carr then

had admirable support from Williams, Fraser and Tufnell, and the last three wickets realised 147. Carr – not otherwise a model on which a young batsman should base his style – was enjoying a splendid season, a triumph of character and determination. His unbeaten 192 was a career-best performance and occupied seven hours during which there was barely a false stroke or an alarm. That Middlesex remained firmly at the top of the table was due in no small measure to Carr's consistency throughout the season and, in particular, to his ability to respond positively to any crisis. By the close of play on Saturday, Warwickshire had been reduced to 142 for 8. Most damage had been inflicted by John Emburey, but although Reeve opened with his spinners when Middlesex went in search of 57, he was rewarded only with the wicket of Haynes and the leaders cantered to victory.

The Yorkshire meeting to discuss the county's poor showing in recent matches brought dramatic results at Harrogate. There was no play on the first day, and, on the second, Northamptonshire were put in to bat and bowled out in 34.2 overs for 97. The Yorkshire hero was Mark Robinson who took a career best nine wickets against his former county. Robinson had been dropped for the previous championship match. Richardson and Byas added 84 for Yorkshire's third wicket, but then the last seven wickets went down for 53 runs. Hartley proceeded to capture five wickets and Robinson three – to bring his match figures to 12 for 124 – but the visitors batted with some determination, and Yorkshire were asked to make 235 on the last day. This task was accomplished mainly because of a fourth-wicket stand of 145 between Byas and Blakey, who scored the runs in 22 overs after rain had delayed the start until 2.40. This meant that, after a further interruption, Yorkshire had only 41 overs in which to reach their target. Eventually, five runs were needed from the last over. Four came from the first three balls, but then came a bouncer and another ball from which no runs were scored. Curran's last delivery came and White lashed it to the mid-wicket boundary to win the match.

Wayne Larkins hit 18 fours and 2 sixes in a spectacular 151 for Durham against the Australians. On the Sunday, the tourists fell apart against left-arm pace bowler Simon Brown, who returned the best bowling figures of his career, and the Australians had to endure the indignity of being forced to follow-on. Normal service was then resumed as Hayden and Boon shared a second-wicket stand of 221. Meanwhile, Ian Botham hit 32 and failed to take a wicket. One mentions this only because the great all-rounder had announced that this was to be his last match and that he was to retire from first-class cricket. The game was suddenly deprived of not only one of the greatest cricketers that it has known but also a man whose achievements – epic in stature – and personality have drawn men and women to watch the game who previously would have shown, at best, a passing interest. Like W.G. Grace, he bestrode the narrow world of cricket like a Colossus; like W.G. Grace, he enriched the sport and gladdened the hearts of those who were lucky enough to watch him. Both men as a result became part of the vocabulary of everyday life.

AXA EQUITY & LAW LEAGUE

18 July *at Southend*

Essex 192
Leicestershire 166

Essex (4 pts.) won by 26 runs

at Portsmouth

Hampshire 203 for 5 (R.A. Smith 79, C.M. Tolley 4 for 50)
***v.* Worcestershire**

Match abandoned

Hampshire 2 pts., Worcestershire 2 pts.

at Old Trafford

Lancashire 167 for 9 (M.A. Atherton 64)
Glamorgan 168 for 2 (H. Morris 87 not out, M.P. Maynard 72)

Glamorgan (4 pts.) won by 8 wickets

at Trent Bridge

Somerset 200 for 9 (G.D. Rose 50 not out)
Nottinghamshire 203 for 6 (C.L. Cairns 73)

Nottinghamshire (4 pts.) won by 4 wickets

Mark Robinson, a career best 9 for 37 against his former county Northamptonshire as Yorkshire win at Harrogate. (David Munden/ Sports-Line)

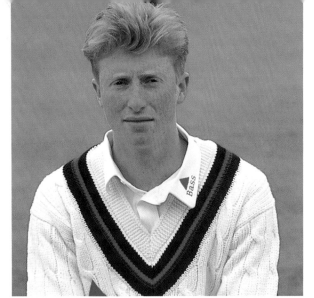

A century in 21 minutes for Glen Chapple, Lancashire v. Glamorgan, 19 July. (Mike Cooper/Allsport)

at Guildford

Gloucestershire 155
Surrey 110 for 1

Surrey (4 pts.) won on faster scoring rate

at Hove

Sussex 177 (N.J. Llong 4 for 24)
Kent 3 for 0

Match abandoned

Sussex 2 pts., Kent 2 pts.

at Edgbaston

Middlesex 261 for 2 (D.L. Haynes 142 not out, M.A. Rose-berry 66)
Warwickshire 253 for 8 (Asif Din 94, D.P. Ostler 83, P.N. Weekes 4 for 49)

Middlesex (4 pts.) won on faster scoring rate

at Leeds

Northamptonshire 172 for 9 (M.A. Robinson 4 for 23)
Yorkshire 175 for 1 (D. Byas 88 not out, M.D. Moxon 70)

Yorkshire (4 pts.) won by 9 wickets

Rain affected several matches and helped Glamorgan to take a lead over Kent at the top of the table. Morris and Maynard added 145 for Glamorgan's second wicket, and the Welshmen beat Lancashire with 16.2 overs to spare. Moxon and Byas put on 165 for Yorkshire's first wicket against Northamptonshire, and Haynes and Roseberry began the Middlesex innings against Warwickshire with a partnership of 176. Haynes hit his highest Sunday League score. Ostler and Asif Din, in reply, scored 161 after Moles had gone for 0, but Warwickshire were deprived of one over by rain and so lost by 0.06 on run rate.

FOURTH TEST MATCH
ENGLAND *v.* AUSTRALIA, at Leeds

Before the start of play in the fourth Test match Ladbrokes made England 5–2 to win, Australia 2–1, with the draw as the evens favourite. By close of play on the first day, Australia were 4–6 favourites and England were 50–1.

England's selectors must take much of the blame for seeing their side disappear from the contest on the first day. Believing in past history rather than present realities, they omitted Such from their twelve and went into the match without a spinner. With Julian unfit, Australia included Reiffel in his place. Border won the toss, and the visitors batted. Gooch shook hands with Martin Bicknell who was winning his first Test cap as England took the field – a nice gesture. McCague's first ball to Slater was steered majestically to the third-man boundary – a prophetic gesture.

Headingley has much changed in character. The facilities have improved impressively, and the wicket is no longer a seamer's paradise, or so it proved for England. Ilott began with a wide to slip, and McCague was all over the place so that the field Gooch set had the merits of neither defence nor attack. From the start, England were in no man's land. Caddick's first ball was overpitched and went for four. McCague returned from the Football Ground end and continued to bowl dreadfully. The fifty was raised in 58 minutes during the 14th over.

At 12.17, from the Kirkstall Lane end, Martin Bicknell bowled his first over in Test cricket. It cost him eight runs, but he steadied. Slater reached 50 out of 85 in the 22nd over, and in the next over, Bicknell moved a ball in to Taylor and trapped him leg before, umpire Plews giving the decision after some deliberation. Slater escaped when an inside edge from a good delivery by Bicknell just

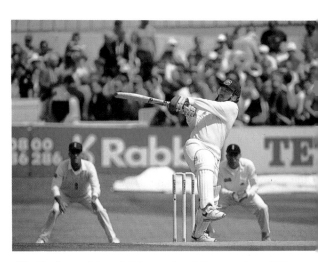

Allan Border, a mixture of violence and majesty, moves toward his first double century against England and the Man-of-the-Match award. (Ben Radford/Allsport)

Steve Waugh, Border's partner in a stand worth 332 runs. (Adrian Murrell/Allsport)

missed the leg stump and went for four, but generally he was in total control, and by lunch he had scored 64 out of 103, from 28 overs.

Four overs into the afternoon, Slater, such a fine batsman, played all round a ball of full length from Ilott and was bowled. Boon had looked far from composed initially, but now two successive overpitched deliveries from Ilott were dispatched through mid-wicket for fours. Only Martin Bicknell seemed capable of presenting the slightest problem to the Australian batsmen, although Mark Waugh should possibly have been run out by Smith when Boon sent him back following a hit to mid-wicket. McCague and Caddick were picked off at will, and it was Gooch who temporarily halted the flow of runs. At tea, after 57 overs, Australia were 209 for 2: Boon 57, Mark Waugh 45.

Waugh's is an exceptional talent. One effortless on-drive for four off Gooch had the kiss of genius about it. So great is his ability that his dismissals often appear feckless, and so it was at Headingley. He shouldered arms to a ball from Ilott which held its line and hit the top of the off stump – a bad error of judgement and a dreadful waste.

The dismissal of Mark Waugh heralded a period of entrenchment. Runs dried up as Ilott posed some problems and Caddick offered steadiness. But the Headingley pitch has been rendered harmless. Where once there was the excitement of the unpredictable, there is now the correctness demanded by authority. Will all pitches soon be the same, offering no local character or deviation from the approved norm? Initially, Border could not find his timing. The crowd, several in fancy dress, became restless, and there were endless rounds of the Mexican wave, complete with rubbish.

Ilott began to drop short, fatally; McCague was still all over the place; Border found his timing. Runs flowed. Boon square-cut the second new ball for four – his 17th –

Healy stumps Atherton off May. (Adrian Murrell/Allsport)

to reach the 50th century of his career off 199 balls. The rock on which Australian innings are founded remained as firm as ever. At the close, Boon was 102, Border 38, and Australia 307 for 3.

There was early joy for England on the second morning for, in the sixth over, Boon played across the line at Ilott and was leg before. His third Test century in succession had taken him to 500 runs for the series and 1,000 runs in Tests in England. If his dismissal gave England joy, there was no more to come. At lunch, Border was 75, Steve Waugh 37, and Australia 393 for 4 from 118 overs.

Half an hour after lunch, McCague left the field injured, and it was later diagnosed that he had a back problem and that his season was over. The England attack was slaughtered, and there was relief when rain stopped play at 3.27, with Border 115, Steve Waugh 93, Australia 492. The relief was short-lived. An early tea was taken, and 121 runs then came in the final session, by the end of which Border was on 175 and Steve Waugh on 144. One chance only had been offered, by Waugh to Atherton at slip off Thorpe, but by then the *elder* twin had already made 136. Border's 16th Test century was chanceless. It brought him level with Sobers' number of Test centuries, and, like Bradman, he had made 14 of them while captain of Australia.

England's agony was extended for another 13 overs on the third morning. Border completed his double century, his first against England, and 40 runs were added.

A rare success for England – Boon is leg before to Ilott for 107. (Patrick Eagar)

Australia's 653 for 4 was the highest score ever made in a first-class match at Headingley. The stand of 332 off 589 balls between Border and Waugh was the seventh highest partnership for Australia in all Test matches.

Border hit 26 fours in his 565-minute innings, and he faced 399 balls. Steve Waugh's 157 came from 305 balls, included 19 fours and spanned 405 minutes. They had routed England totally and utterly in a masterly display of batting, but the contest was always grotesquely one-sided.

It seemed almost inevitable that England would lose an early wicket, and indeed Lathwell touched Hughes' third delivery low to the admirable Healy. At lunch, England were 38 for 1.

Smith added only three to his interval score when he mistimed a drive and gave Tim May a return catch. Seven runs later, Stewart tried to whip the ball through the leg side but simply edged it onto his pad from where it looped to silly-point. Following this mishap, England seemed to settle down in the persons of Atherton and Gooch who batted with sense and technical application. Gooch passed Sobers' aggregate of Test runs, reached his fifty, and at tea, England were 134 for 3.

Nothing immediately after tea suggested that Gooch and Atherton would be separated. They were cautious, but they looked secure. The turning point came in the 63rd over, and it was brought about by the medium pace of Reiffel who bowled a full length and moved the ball late. He totally deceived Atherton, who offered no shot at a ball which came back and hit his off stump. Three balls later, Thorpe edged low to the keeper. Worse followed for, in the 67th over, Gooch went back to a ball from

FOURTH CORNHILL TEST MATCH – ENGLAND v. AUSTRALIA
22, 23, 24, 25 and 26 July 1993 at Headingley, Leeds

AUSTRALIA

	FIRST INNINGS	
M.J. Slater	b Ilott	67
M.A. Taylor	lbw, b Bicknell	27
D.C. Boon	lbw, b Ilott	107
M.E. Waugh	b Ilott	52
A.R. Border (capt)	not out	200
S.R. Waugh	not out	157
*I.A. Healy		
P.R. Reiffel		
M.G. Hughes		
S.K. Warne		
T.B.A. May		
Extras	b 8, lb 22, w 4, nb 9	43
	(for 4 wickets, dec.)	653

ENGLAND

	FIRST INNINGS		SECOND INNINGS	
M.N. Lathwell	c Healy, b Hughes	0	b May	25
M.A. Atherton	b Reiffel	55	st Healy, b May	63
R.A. Smith	c and b May	23	lbw, b Reiffel	35
*A.J. Stewart	c Slater, b Reiffel	5	c M.E. Waugh, b Reiffel	78
G.A. Gooch (capt)	lbw, b Reiffel	59	st Healy, b May	26
G.P. Thorpe	c Healy, b Reiffel	0	c Taylor, b Reiffel	13
N. Hussain	b Reiffel	15	not out	18
A.R. Caddick	c M.E. Waugh, b Hughes	9	lbw, b Hughes	12
M.P. Bicknell	c Border, b Hughes	12	lbw, b Hughes	0
M.J. McCague	c Taylor, b Warne	0	b Hughes	11
M.C. Ilott	not out	0	c Border, b May	4
Extras	b 2, lb 3, nb 17	22	b 5, lb 3, w 1, nb 11	20
		200		305

	O	M	R	W
McCague	28	2	115	–
Ilott	51	11	161	3
Caddick	42	5	138	–
Bicknell	50	8	155	1
Gooch	16	5	40	–
Thorpe	6	1	14	–

	O	M	R	W	O	M	R	W
Hughes	15.5	3	47	3	30	10	79	3
Reiffel	26	6	65	5	28	8	87	3
May	15	3	33	1	27	6	65	4
Warne	23	9	43	1	40	16	63	–
M.E. Waugh	3	–	7	–	2	1	3	–

FALL OF WICKETS

1–86, 2–110, 3–216, 4–321

FALL OF WICKETS

1–0, 2–43, 3–50, 4–158, 5–158, 6–169, 7–184, 8–195, 9–200

1–60, 2–131, 3–149, 4–202, 5–256, 6–263, 7–279, 8–279, 9–295

Umpires: H.D. Bird & N.T. Plews

Australia won by an innings and 148 runs

Merv Hughes becomes the seventh Australian to take 200 Test wickets. Caddick is leg before. (Patrick Eagar)

Brief stoppages for rain were to do nothing to aid England's cause on the last day. Thorpe added just three to his overnight score before he edged to second slip. This was a disappointment, for Stewart had begun the day with a fierce attack on the Australian bowling which included 4 fours in succession off Merv Hughes. Reiffel exacted revenge for Hughes when Stewart cut wildly at a ball outside off stump and Mark Waugh took a spectacular catch at second slip.

Hughes then took his own revenge on England. Caddick tried to cut a ball which moved back at him and kept low. He was palpably leg before, and Hughes had become the seventh Australian to take 200 wickets in Test cricket. To celebrate, he had Bicknell leg before first ball, and shortly after lunch McCague had his off stump knocked back by the Victorian with the prominent moustache. When Ilott skied May to Border at cover, Australia had retained the Ashes in emphatic manner.

Border was named Man of the Match, and – in stark contrast – Graham Gooch announced that he was resigning the England captaincy. He had endured a terrible year, but the blame was not all his, and no man has led more bravely from the front. The unhappy truth was that England were much lacking in talent.

Reiffel which moved into him and kept low, and he was clearly leg before. Four overs after this disaster, Hussain, having hit 2 fours, tried to cut a ball from Reiffel that was too close to him for such a shot and played on. At the close, the score was 195 for 7, and it seemed that England would be batting in their second innings before lunch on the fourth day.

So it proved. Inside 20 minutes, Australia captured England's last three wickets for five runs. Caddick was taken at slip in the first over of the morning. McCague provided Warne with his only wicket of the innings when he pushed forward to a leg-break and was caught at slip, and Bicknell was caught at backward short-leg off an uppish shot. England followed-on 453 runs in arrears.

There were two brief stoppages for rain before an early lunch was taken with the score on 37. Where England had omitted a spinner, Australia had included two, and it was May who broke the opening partnership when Lathwell pushed forward and saw an inside edge spin back onto his stumps. This was the only wicket to fall in the afternoon session, however. Atherton looked secure, and if Smith was still tremulous against spin, he looked more positive than of late.

This time it was to be the medium pace of Reiffel, who had a splendid match, which was to bring about the downfall of Smith. The batsman offered no shot to a ball which nipped back sharply from just outside the off stump. Atherton was the next to go when he went down the pitch to May and was beaten on the outside edge, for Healy to pull off an excellent stumping. Gooch suffered the same fate. He had faced only 40 balls but had hit 5 fours and was determined to take the battle to the enemy, before being beaten by May whose inclusion in the Australian side could be seen to have been totally justified. Stewart, too, was most positive, and he and Thorpe remained until the close, 237 for 4, with Stewart on 59.

22, 23, 24 and 26 July *at Derby*

Derbyshire 183 (K.J. Barnett 73 not out) and 379 (J.E. Morris 104, C.J. Adams 96, P.D. Bowler 87, E.E. Hemmings 4 for 65)

Sussex 193 (F.D. Stephenson 57 not out, S.J. Base 5 for 59) and 174 (C.W.J. Athey 72 not out, D.E. Malcolm 6 for 57)

Derbyshire won by 195 runs

Derbyshire 20 pts., Sussex 4 pts.

at Chelmsford

Durham 483 (P. Bainbridge 150 not out, W. Larkins 80, J.H. Childs 5 for 99) and 199 for 8 dec. (J.H. Childs 4 for 55, P.M. Such 4 for 61)

Essex 382 (M.A. Garnham 106, P.J. Prichard 67, D.R. Pringle 57, S.J.E. Brown 5 for 111) and 154 (A.C. Cummins 5 for 32)

Durham won by 146 runs

Durham 24 pts., Essex 7 pts.

at Old Trafford

Lancashire 295 (M. Watkinson 102, C.L. Cairns 6 for 70) and 262 (M. Watkinson 64, J.P. Crawley 56, J.A. Afford 4 for 84)

Nottinghamshire 560 (P. Johnson 187, C.C. Lewis 83, P.R. Pollard 65, C.L. Cairns 51, M. Watkinson 4 for 117)

Nottinghamshire won by an innings and 3 runs

Nottinghamshire 24 pts., Lancashire 4 pts.

at Leicester

Warwickshire 284 (K.J. Piper 52, D.P. Ostler 51) and 11 for 1

Leicestershire 188 (P.A. Nixon 64 not out, A.A. Donald 6 for 57)

Match drawn

Warwickshire 6 pts., Leicestershire 4 pts.

at Lord's

Hampshire 280 (D.I. Gower 91, R.S.M. Morris 54, J.E. Emburey 4 for 75) and 88 (J.E. Emburey 8 for 40)

Middlesex 310 (M.W. Gatting 84, M.J. Thursfield 4 for 78) and 59 for 1

Middlesex won by 9 wickets

Middlesex 23 pts., Hampshire 6 pts.

at Northampton

Northamptonshire 238 (N.A. Felton 66) and 363 (A.J. Lamb 88, A. Fordham 87, R.J. Bailey 86)

Surrey 189 (C.E.L. Ambrose 4 for 40, J.P. Taylor 4 for 51) and 108 (J.P. Taylor 5 for 45, K.M. Curran 4 for 11)

Northamptonshire won by 304 runs

Northamptonshire 21 pts., Surrey 4 pts.

at Taunton

Kent 144 (N.J. Llong 56 not out, Mushtaq Ahmed 4 for 55) and 201 (T.R. Ward 95, Mushtaq Ahmed 6 for 40, N.A. Mallender 4 for 33)

Somerset 211 (R.J. Harden 121, D.W. Headley 5 for 70) and 135 for 3 (N.A. Folland 58)

Somerset won by 7 wickets

Somerset 21 pts., Kent 4 pts.

at Worcester

Worcestershire 267 (D.B. D'Oliveira 73, S.D. Thomas 4 for 84) and 247 (P.J. Newport 54, S.D. Thomas 5 for 76)

Glamorgan 184 (R.P. Lefebvre 50, C.M. Tolley 4 for 67) and 334 for 9 (A. Dale 124, D.L. Hemp 52)

Glamorgan won by 1 wicket

Glamorgan 20 pts., Worcestershire 6 pts.

Put in to bat, Derbyshire were bowled out on the first day by the Sussex pace attack. Kim Barnett alone stood firm for the home county, carrying his bat through the 53.2 overs of the innings. Nine more wickets fell on the opening day when the Derbyshire seamers got to work, and it was only the late aggression of Stephenson which enabled Sussex to take a slender lead. This was quickly wiped out by Morris, opening in place of Barnett, and Bowler who hit 177 for the first wicket of Derbyshire's second innings. Adams maintained the attack on the Sussex bowling, but Derbyshire's last six second-innings wickets went down for 57 runs. Needing 370 to win, Sussex were reduced to 66 for 5, and, although Moores joined Athey in a stand of 93, Malcolm returned to claim the last five wickets and to give Derbyshire a comfortable win in three days. Bill Athey emulated Barnett in carrying his bat through the innings.

Given a brisk start by Larkins, Durham scored freely against an Essex attack devoid of teeth in the pace department. From 114 overs, Durham scored 364 for 8 on the first day, with only John Childs posing any threat to the batsmen. The position worsened for Essex on the second morning. Graveney partnered Bainbridge in a ninth-wicket stand of 61, and Brown helped to add 60 for the last wicket. Bainbridge reached his first century for Durham and raced on to 150 in dashing style. Garnham's first century of the season and his sixth-wicket stand of 146 with Pringle saw Essex save the follow-on, but much of their batting was far from convincing. Childs and Such kept hopes alive for the home side, but Graveney was still able to declare at lunch on the last day, and Essex folded limply against Cummins and Brown on the last afternoon. Their last six wickets fell for 16 runs, emphasising the length of their tail and the lack of balance in the side. So Durham celebrated their first win for over a year, and Essex reached the depths of their miserable season: the defeat by Durham had coincided with the day that Gooch announced that he was to relinquish the England captaincy, and Foster announced his retirement due to injury.

Lancashire, another side who did not seem to be in the best of spirits, were trounced by Nottinghamshire. Batting first, Lancashire lost six wickets for 132, but they were revived by a century from acting captain Mike Watkinson. Chris Cairns was the pick of the Nottinghamshire bowlers, and he also added weight with the bat, sharing a stand of 91 with Paul Johnson. Johnson played an outstanding innings, a career best 187 which occupied 306 balls and was structured throughout to meet the needs of the moment. With Chris Lewis, he added 178 in 37 overs for the sixth wicket. Batting a second time 265 runs in arrears, Lancashire succumbed to the Nottinghamshire spinners on the last day.

Warwickshire were bowled out on the first day at Leicester, but thereafter rain restricted play. In his last championship match for Warwickshire before joining the South African side for training, Alan Donald took 6 for 57.

At Lord's, Gower and Morris scored 139 for Hampshire's second wicket, after which there was something of a collapse as the visitors plodded to 216 for 8. Thursfield and Connor added 59, with Thursfield finishing on 36 not out in his maiden first-class innings. Like Hampshire, Middlesex found the going hard, and the obduracy of Gatting and Brown was the only reason that they reached 231 for 8 by the close of the second day. Williams, Fraser and Tufnell all gave the innings a boost on the third morning, the last two wickets realising 94 runs. The mundane cricket of the first two days was suddenly transformed into fierce activity on the third afternoon as John Emburey, a month short of his 41st birthday, took a career best 8 for 40. Tufnell took the other two wickets, and the spinners bowled all but five overs as Hampshire

ABOVE: *The heir apparent Michael Atherton surveys the scene at Lord's. (Ben Radford/Allsport)*

BELOW LEFT: *Phil Bainbridge hit his first century for Durham as they beat Essex to gain their first victory of the season. (David Munden/ Sports-Line)*

were shot out for 88. Middlesex's grip on the title now seemed fixed, particularly as one of their main challengers, Surrey, were heavily beaten at Northampton.

All seemed well for Surrey at the start when they won the toss and asked the home county to bat. Felton, Curran and Penberthy offered resistance to an all-seam attack, but Northamptonshire were bowled out in 74 overs. Surrey fared even worse, however, losing their first four wickets for 45 before Ward and Smith stopped the rot. Butcher also batted defiantly, but Surrey trailed by 49 on the first innings. Northamptonshire showed great resilience when they batted for the second time. Fordham and Bailey put on 133 for the second wicket; Fordham and an aggressive Lamb, who hit Murphy for 4 fours in one over, added 124 for the third. Loye also batted sensibly, and Surrey were left with the task of scoring 413 to win. Darren Bicknell and Ward were out on the Saturday evening, and the rest followed early on the Monday as the last eight wickets fell for 48 runs.

Put in to bat at Taunton, Kent were quickly dismissed by a mixture of pace and leg-spin. Somerset lost five wickets for 34 runs in reply, but Harden batted for four hours to reach his first hundred of the season and take his side to an important lead. He was well supported by Van Troost in a vital last-wicket stand of 64. Again the combination of medium pace and leg-spin accounted for Kent in spite of Ward's belligerent 95, and Somerset moved to a comfortable victory early on the third day.

Darren Thomas, so successful in his debut year of 1992, played his first game of the season for Glamorgan, having completed his academic studies for the year. He combined with Steve Watkin to bowl out Worcestershire on the first day as Glamorgan gave another impressive display of out-cricket. Colin Metson held six catches behind the stumps. Glamorgan's batting did not measure up to their bowling, and six middle-order wickets went down for 13 runs. Lefebvre saved the visitors with an innings of 50, but Glamorgan trailed by 83 on the first innings. On the third day, Thomas and Watkin again combined to bowl out Worcestershire, with Thomas claiming his third five-wicket haul in his seventh first-class match. The Worcestershire tail had proved particularly defiant, the last three wickets adding 96. Metson took three catches in the innings to establish a Glamorgan record with nine in the match. The visitors had the last day in which to score 331 to win and so keep alive their championship challenge. When four wickets fell before lunch for 92 they seemed to have little hope of success. With Hemp, however, Dale added 88, and with Croft he put on 89. Adrian Dale batted for five hours 40 minutes and hit 16 fours in his 124, an innings of tremendous character. Having opened the innings, he was seventh out at 293, and it seemed that Glamorgan would still fail in spite of his magnificent effort. Metson was run out and Watkin leg before so that when the 18-year-old Thomas joined Lefebvre 10 runs were still needed. The left-handed Thomas hit nine of them, sweeping Illingworth for the winning boundary.

AXA EQUITY & LAW LEAGUE

25 July *at Derby*

Derbyshire 199 for 6 (T.J.G. O'Gorman 60, P.D. Bowler 57)
Sussex 118 (D.E. Malcolm 4 for 42)

Derbyshire (4 pts.) won by 81 runs

at Chelmsford

Durham 136
Essex 137 for 4 (Salim Malik 71 not out)

Essex (4 pts.) won by 6 wickets

at Old Trafford

Lancashire 122 for 7
Nottinghamshire 96 for 9

Lancashire (4 pts.) won by 26 runs

at Leicester

Leicestershire 170 for 7 (J.J. Whitaker 83, P.A. Smith 5 for 54)
Warwickshire 124 for 6

Warwickshire (4 pts.) won on faster scoring rate

at Lord's

Middlesex 246 for 3 (M.W. Gatting 104 not out, M.R. Ramprakash 69)
Hampshire 165 (A.R.C. Fraser 4 for 17, P.C.R. Tufnell 4 for 50)

Middlesex (4 pts.) won by 81 runs

at Northampton

Northamptonshire 193 for 9 (M.B. Loye 64, D. Ripley 52 not out, Waqar Younis 4 for 38)
***v.* Surrey**

Match abandoned

Northamptonshire 2 pts., Surrey 2 pts.

at Taunton

Somerset 193 for 6 (G.D. Rose 78 not out, A. Payne 55 not out)
Kent 196 for 7 (G.D. Rose 4 for 26)

Kent (4 pts.) won by 3 wickets

at Worcester

Glamorgan 259 for 7 (H. Morris 87, I.V.A. Richards 63, A. Dale 57)
Worcestershire 232 (T.S. Curtis 62)

Glamorgan (4 pts.) won by 27 runs

Glamorgan and Kent both won and so drew clear of Surrey whose match was abandoned. Rose had an outstanding match for Somerset against Kent while Gatting reached his century off 95 balls as Middlesex routed Hampshire. The match at Old Trafford was reduced to 15 overs, and there was also an interruption at Leicester.

NATWEST TROPHY

QUARTER-FINALS

27 and 28 July *at Swansea*

Glamorgan 279 for 9 (M.P. Maynard 84, S.P. James 68)
Worcestershire 175

Glamorgan won by 104 runs

(Man of the Match – M.P. Maynard)

at Northampton

Sussex 230 for 9
Northamptonshire 190 (A.J. Lamb 71, N.A. Felton 53)

Sussex won by 40 runs

(Man of the Match – F.D. Stephenson)

John Emburey, a career-best bowling performance for Middlesex against Hampshire and a surprise return to the England side. (David Munden/Sports-Line)

at Taunton

Somerset 230 for 9 (M.P. Bicknell 4 for 35)
Surrey 187 (G.P. Thorpe 58, A.R. Caddick 5 for 30)

Somerset won by 43 runs

(*Man of the Match – Mushtaq Ahmed*)

at Leeds

Warwickshire 245 (J.D. Ratcliffe 105, D.A. Reeve 50)
Yorkshire 224 (R.J. Blakey 75, P.A. Smith 4 for 37)

Warwickshire won by 21 runs

(*Man of the Match – J.D. Ratcliffe*)

Put in to bat at Swansea, Glamorgan took a grip on the game against Worcestershire which they never relinquished. Play could not begin until after lunch, but Morris and James, nursing a broken thumb, gave Glamorgan a solid start with a partnership of 66. James hit 68 off 143 balls, and the fireworks were provided by Maynard who hit 84 from 65 balls. He batted through 24 overs, and Glamorgan scored freely at the death to reach a formidable 279. Lefebvre was relentlessly accurate, and Worcestershire began the second day on 40 for 2 from 23 overs. Barwick, Dale and Watkin maintained the pressure, and Glamorgan strolled into the semi-finals.

Sussex, too, were asked to bat first and batted solidly to reach 230. This did not look to be a winning score when Northamptonshire made 146 for 3 in 40 overs before play ended on the first day. Lamb had been run out just before the close, but Felton remained undefeated on 40. Incredibly, Northamptonshire fell apart on the following morning. They lost their last seven wickets for 43 runs against some accurate seam bowling and a few overs of leg-spin from Salisbury.

Asked to bat first, Somerset saw several batsmen establish themselves but none go on to play the big innings that would have taken the home side to a score of match-winning proportions. Mushtaq Ahmed was top scorer with 35 and helped raise the total from 134 for 6 to 230 for 9. Surrey lost Stewart before the close, but they reached 144 for 3 on the second day before fading against Mushtaq and Mallender. Caddick kept up the pressure.

Warwickshire were the one side to bat first when they won the toss, but Reeve must have had doubts when three wickets fell for 31 runs. The captain then joined Ratcliffe in a partnership worth 136, and Ratcliffe's 105 off 142 balls, an innings of quality, was his first hundred in one-day cricket. Twose also batted well against an attack which showed too many weaknesses. The game seemed over by the close on the first day when Yorkshire were 69 for 5 with Byas needlessly run out off the last ball. White and Blakey equalled the competition's sixth-wicket record when they added 105 on the second morning, but Yorkshire never looked likely to avoid defeat.

28, 29 and **30** July *at Old Trafford*

Australians 282 for 3 dec. (M.A. Taylor 122, D.R. Martyn 70 not out, M.L. Hayden 61) and 194 for 8 dec. (M.L. Hayden 79, A.A. Barnett 4 for 83)
Lancashire 250 for 7 dec. and 228 for 5 (J.P. Crawley 109)

Lancashire won by 5 wickets

Helping to keep a rain-affected match alive with declarations, the Australians lost their first Tetley Bitter Challenge game of the tour. The significant aspect of the match was a splendid century on the last afternoon by John Crawley who faced 180 balls, hit 11 fours and virtually won the game for Lancashire. Greatly admired by many good judges, Crawley furthered his claims for a place in the party to tour West Indies in 1994.

29, 30, 31 July and **2** August *at Chelmsford*

Worcestershire 379 (D.A. Leatherdale 119 not out, T.S. Curtis 65, R.K. Illingworth 58, P.M. Such 4 for 92) and 208 (T.S. Curtis 82, J.H. Childs 6 for 37)
Essex 305 (N. Hussain 65, P.M. Such 54) and 286 for 6 (G.A. Gooch 159 not out, P.J. Prichard 64)

Essex won by 4 wickets

Essex 22 pts., Worcestershire 7 pts.

at Durham University

Sussex 440 (F.D. Stephenson 90, N.J. Lenham 88, A.C.S. Pigott 52, M.P. Speight 51, A.C. Cummins 6 for 115) and 362 for 2 dec. (C.W.J. Athey 118 not out, N.J. Lenham 78, A.P. Wells 67 not out, M.P. Speight 66)
Durham 325 (W. Larkins 106, P.W.G. Parker 65, N.J. Lenham 4 for 13) and 210 (F.D. Stephenson 5 for 55, I.D.K. Salisbury 4 for 63)

Sussex won by 267 runs

Sussex 24 pts., Durham 6 pts.

at Cheltenham

Derbyshire 521 (J.E. Morris 229, D.G. Cork 104, M.J. Vandrau 57, C.A. Walsh 4 for 95) and 139 for 3 (J.E. Morris 71 not out)

Gloucestershire 139 (A.E. Warner 5 for 27, D.E. Malcolm 4 for 77) and 520 (B.C. Broad 120, R.C. Russell 99 not out, G.D. Hodgson 64, T.H.C. Hancock 56, A.E. Warner 5 for 93)

Derbyshire won by 7 wickets

Derbyshire 24 pts., Gloucestershire 4 pts.

at Southampton

Warwickshire 190 (S.D. Udal 4 for 51) and 392 (T.L. Penney 135 not out, D.P. Ostler 55, S.D. Udal 6 for 141, D.P.J. Flint 4 for 131)

Hampshire 294 (R.A. Smith 131, A.N. Aymes 74) and 208 (M.C.J. Nicholas 63, M.A.V. Bell 5 for 43, N.M.K. Smith 4 for 93)

Warwickshire won by 80 runs

Warwickshire 20 pts., Hampshire 6 pts.

at Canterbury

Leicestershire 249 (V.J. Wells 81, T.J. Boon 72, M.A. Ealham 4 for 40) and 266 (J.J. Whitaker 69, P.E. Robinson 53, C.L. Hooper 4 for 55)

Kent 291 (N.R. Taylor 86, M.A. Ealham 59, W.K.M. Benjamin 5 for 46) and 225 for 7 (M.R. Benson 71 not out)

Kent won by 3 wickets

Kent 22 pts., Leicestershire 5 pts.

at Taunton

Yorkshire 244 (C. White 74 not out, G.D. Rose 4 for 33) and 209 (R.B. Richardson 68, Mushtaq Ahmed 6 for 86)

Somerset 235 (J.D. Batty 4 for 80) and 170 (D.G. Gough 7 for 42)

Yorkshire won by 48 runs

Yorkshire 21 pts., Somerset 5 pts.

at The Oval

Surrey 228 (A.D. Brown 60, J.A. Afford 5 for 64, K.P. Evans 4 for 51) and 147 for 7 (C.C. Lewis 4 for 34)

Nottinghamshire 68 (J.E. Benjamin 6 for 19) and 306 (P.R. Pollard 97, C.L. Cairns 56, K.P. Evans 56, N.M. Kendrick 7 for 115)

Surrey won by 3 wickets

Surrey 21 pts., Nottinghamshire 4 pts.

31 July, 1 and 2 August *at Neath*

Australians 414 for 4 dec. (M.E. Waugh 152 not out, D.C. Boon 120, M.J. Slater 72) and 235 for 7 dec. (M.G. Hughes 71, P.R. Reiffel 52)

Glamorgan 363 for 8 dec. (M.P. Maynard 132, P.A. Cottey 68, S.K. Warne 4 for 67) and 169 for 6

Match drawn

In spite of some good catching and some steady bowling by Peter Such, Essex again found it difficult to remove the opposition's tail. Following a typically gritty 65 from Tim Curtis, Steve Andrew took three mid-innings wickets to reduce Worcestershire to 187 for 7. Leatherdale, out of form and favour for most of the season, offered resistance and shared a ninth-wicket stand of 142 with Illingworth which stretched into the second day and helped him to gather a pugnacious hundred. Essex struggled in reply, and when Hussain was out for 65, with the score on 187, it seemed that they would be forced to follow-on. On the third morning, however, Peter Such hit a brave and worthy maiden fifty, and he was ably supported by Andrew and Childs so that Essex finished only 74 behind on the first innings. Left-arm spin bowling of the highest quality by John Childs put Essex back in the match. At one time he took three middle-order wickets in 10 balls. Rhodes and Curtis, whose innings was necessary but painfully slow, temporarily halted the decline. Childs quickly ended the innings on the Monday morning, and Essex were left to score 283 to win. Gooch and Prichard put on 164 for the second wicket to set the reigning champions on the right path. D'Oliveira took three quick wickets but Gooch steered his side to victory with his first championship century of the season.

Sussex tore Durham apart during the opening day on the University ground, and the only significant resistance from the home county came in a second-wicket stand of 173 between Larkins and Parker. Lenham broke the partnership and finished with a career best 4 for 13. He then joined in the Sussex run spree. Athey passed 1,000 runs for the season, hitting the second century of the match, but one which could not quite equal Larkins' spectacular effort for Durham. Stephenson captured two wickets before the close, and Sussex claimed their second win of the season on the last day.

Derbyshire won their third championship victory of the season, beating Gloucestershire at Cheltenham. They hit 408 off 80 overs on a shortened first day, with Dominic Cork reaching an admirable maiden first-class century, batting with a runner in the later stages, and John Morris hitting a truly spectacular maiden double century. His second hundred came off only 70 balls and he hit 3 sixes and 32 fours. Vandrau hit the highest score of his career on the second day, after which Warner and Malcolm wrecked Gloucestershire, and the home side had to follow-on. Gloucestershire showed great resilience when they batted again. Six of the first seven batsmen scored 46 or more, with Chris Broad hitting a defiant century at number four. Russell was left unbeaten on 99 when Gerrard fell to the occasional off-breaks of Chris Adams. Allan Warner, one of the very best and most improved of county professionals, claimed 10 wickets in a match for the first time, although he joined Barnett, Cork and Vandrau on the injured list. Morris bustled Derbyshire to victory early on the last day.

Warwickshire came from behind to beat Hampshire at Southampton. They fell to the combined spin of Udal and Flint on the first day and surrendered a first-innings lead of 104 when Smith and Aymes added 158 after five wickets had fallen for 106. Warwickshire batted with increasing determination until the last morning, inspired by Penney's first century of the season. Udal and Flint again monopolised the wickets for Hampshire and sent down 89.4 overs between them. Left to score 289 in 81 overs to win, Hampshire made a brave effort, particularly through Nicholas, but lost their last four wickets in six overs as Michael Bell took a career best 5 for 43.

On a pitch that was never easy, Kent gained a narrow win over Leicestershire at Canterbury. Neither side was able to gain an advantage, and Kent faced a hard task in their second innings even though they had more than a day in which to score 225 to win. Benson held one end firm, but not until Taylor arrived, batting at number seven because of a bruised foot, did Kent look capable of winning. He and Benson took the score from 74 for 5 to 154, and Marsh and Ealham gave further valuable support to the Kent captain to bring victory with 16 overs remaining.

Yorkshire's win at Taunton came as something of a surprise. They chose to bat and were bowled out in 85 overs. They would have fared worse had it not been for White's unbeaten 74 and for the support he received from Hartley and the tail. But Somerset could do no better and finished nine runs behind on the first innings as Batty's off-spin began to take advantage of the pitch, which offered all bowlers some assistance. Certainly Mushtaq Ahmed exploited the conditions and gave his side every chance of victory. Eventually, however, it was the fast medium pace of Darren Gough which proved to be the match-winner. Somerset added 26 runs on the last morning to take them within 51 runs of victory with four wickets standing, but with the score on 168, Gough took three wickets in five balls and ended resistance, Hartley taking the final wicket two runs later. Gough's 7 for 42 was the best performance of his career, and he took 10 wickets in a match for the first time.

There was also a career-best bowling performance by Surrey's Joey Benjamin. Bowled out for 228 on the first day, Surrey could scarcely have expected to be asking Nottinghamshire to follow-on before lunch on the second. That they were able to do so was due to Benjamin's inspired aggression which included a spell of 5 for 12 in 24 deliveries. Nottinghamshire's second innings was a different matter, however. Pollard dropped anchor for a solid 97, and there was some flair from Cairns which was ended early on the third day by Kendrick, who was to finish with a career best 7 for 115. Lewis, finding one of those flashes of form which too often elude, bowled with great hostility when Surrey went in search of the modest target of 147, and he almost bowled Nottinghamshire to an improbable victory.

Surrey's victory moved them to second in the table, for Glamorgan were engaged in a jolly exhibition with the Australians who hit 414 at four an over on the first day at Neath. Slater and Boon began with a partnership of 158. Boon made 120 off 199 balls with 20 fours – yet another

impressive century – but the main honours went to Mark Waugh. In spectacular fashion, he hit 152 off 151 balls with 16 fours and 8 sixes, four of them off successive deliveries from debutant slow left-armer Phelps. Maynard took revenge on the Sunday by hitting 132 from 115 balls with a five and 25 fours. His century came before lunch. Things quietened down after that, and the match was eventually drawn.

AXA EQUITY & LAW LEAGUE

1 August *at Durham University*

Durham 194 for 9 (N.J. Lenham 5 for 28)
Sussex 195 for 8 (A.P. Wells 69 not out)
Sussex (4 pts.) won by 2 wickets

at Chelmsford

Essex 248 for 4 (J.P. Stephenson 103 not out)
Worcestershire 250 for 6 (G.A. Hick 120 not out)
Worcestershire (4 pts.) won by 4 wickets

at Cheltenham

Gloucestershire 99 (S.J. Base 4 for 14)
Derbyshire 100 for 2 (C.J. Adams 58)
Derbyshire (4 pts.) won by 8 wickets

at Southampton

Warwickshire 232 for 6 (Asif Din 132 not out)
Hampshire 233 for 1 (R.A. Smith 118 not out, V.P. Terry 74 not out)
Hampshire (4 pts.) won by 9 wickets

The most joyful moment in the England season. Victory in the Women's World Cup final over New Zealand at Lord's, 1 August. (David Munden/Sports-Line)

at Canterbury

Kent 327 for 6 (M.V. Fleming 67 not out, C.L. Hooper 64, N.R. Taylor 57)

Leicestershire 264 for 5 (T.J. Boon 135 not out, N.E. Briers 63)

Kent (4 pts.) won by 63 runs

at Taunton

Somerset 202 for 6 (A.N. Hayhurst 80)

Yorkshire 203 for 6 (R.B. Richardson 58 not out)

Yorkshire (4 pts.) won by 4 wickets

at The Oval

Nottinghamshire 314 for 7 (C.L. Cairns 126 not out, P.R. Pollard 74, P. Johnson 55)

Surrey 317 for 6 (D.M. Ward 101, G.P. Thorpe 94)

Surrey (4 pts.) won by 4 wickets

Kent moved back to the top of the Sunday League table on a day of huge scoring. Even Tim Boon's maiden league century could not rob Kent of victory after they had scored consistently and very quickly. There was also a Sunday League best for Graeme Hick at Chelmsford where John Stephenson hit a century for the home side. Asif Din hit a massive 132 not out – a Sunday best – but Robin Smith's century led Hampshire to a nine-wicket victory. Neil Lenham had a league-best bowling performance in Sussex's win at Durham while, in an astonishing match at The Oval, Nottinghamshire hit 314, with Cairns making a maiden Sunday century – 126 off 111 balls – but Surrey won with four overs to spare as Ward hit 101 off 91 balls.

The real enjoyment, though, came at Lord's where England's women beat New Zealand to win the Women's World Cup. It was a magnificent effort. At last, England had something to cheer about.

Border is magnificently caught at slip by Hussain off Such, and Australia are 80 for 4. (David Munden/Sports-Line)

4 August *at Hove*

Sussex 233 for 9 (A.P. Wells 52, A.J. Hollioake 4 for 46)

Surrey 153 for 3 (P.D. Atkins 56 not out, A.D. Brown 53 not out)

Surrey won on faster scoring rate

(*Man of the Match – A.J. Hollioake*)

 FIFTH TEST MATCH
ENGLAND *v.* AUSTRALIA, at Edgbaston

Michael Atherton was named as England's captain in succession to Graham Gooch. This was a wise and welcome choice, but it made the selection of Emburey as second spinner in the England side all the more bewildering. Emburey had not been in the original twelve which had seen Malcolm, Watkin and Maynard replace Lathwell, Caddick and McCague. On looking at the Edgbaston pitch, the selectors had felt that another spinner was necessary, but, instead of opting for Tufnell or Salisbury – who would have offered a contrast to Such – they brought in another off-spinner, the 41-year-old John Emburey. This was in every way a most unwise choice: it was both retrograde and tactically unsound. It compounded a summer of blunders. Russell was also asked to attend, for there were doubts as to Stewart's fitness. Sadly, Russell did not play. After alarms as to the fitness of May, the Australians were unchanged. Atherton performed his first job as captain well. He won the toss, and England batted.

The first ball was rather ominous as Merv Hughes, bowling from the Pavilion end, beat Gooch's forward push. Atherton was more successful. Reiffel's first delivery was a no-ball; Atherton steered the second to the third-man boundary. Reiffel was quick to retaliate: he had Gooch reaching for the fourth ball of his third over, and Taylor took the catch low at slip.

Smith, ever looking to turn the ball square on the leg side, hit 2 fours and was at one time confronted by the Waugh twins bowling in tandem. Of the two, it was Mark Waugh who dismissed him. He had batted for 67 minutes but had never looked totally secure, when he tried to drive indecisively off the back foot and was bowled between bat and pad. Maynard fished dangerously at the first ball he received, and Tim May was immediately introduced into the attack. His first ball turned prodigiously and Maynard offered no shot. To the fifth ball of the same over, Maynard pushed forward and was caught off his glove at silly-point. Atherton, meanwhile, had batted with authority. He hit two successive fours off Reiffel whom he also straight-drove majestically to the boundary.

Stewart began with 3 fours – the first was an edge off Mark Waugh, but the second was an off-drive off May and the third an on-drive off Mark Waugh. England lunched at 93 for 3 from 33 overs, Atherton 43, Stewart 12.

The hundred came up in the 37th over, and in the next over, Atherton reached a most worthy fifty to rapturous applause. Stewart was as positive after lunch as he had been before the break, and England breathed the hope of youth. Shane Warne joined the attack, and Stewart pulled him over mid-wicket for six. Next over, the 50th, the 150 arrived.

Warne was bowling more loose deliveries than we had seen all summer from him, but with the last ball of the 53rd over Stewart tried to turn a leg-break to leg, succeeded only in getting a leading edge and was easily caught and bowled. Two balls later, Atherton went back to a ball which kept low and shot through, and was bowled. Eight minutes later, Hussain pushed forward and was bowled by a splendid delivery which moved off the pitch. England had lost three major batsmen in 16 balls for four runs. Joy had quickly turned to despair.

Emburey and Thorpe revived spirits. Emburey cut at Warne and should have been caught at slip, but Taylor missed the chance and the ball went for four. Thorpe played some excellent shots; Emburey played his dangerous paddle and survived. At tea, England were 194 for 6.

Thorpe's innings ended when he drove wildly at May and got an inside edge to the keeper. Warne, like Hughes, was bowling too short, and Emburey pulled him for six. Emburey's stance brought memories of Peter Willey, and he played some weird and inadvisable shots against both spinners. He dabbed and missed, but when Hughes returned he hooked him twice for four.

Reiffel was a different proposition. He maintained a full length and was always dangerous, moving the ball late, using the pitch well. He had Bicknell taken at second slip off an ambitious drive, and four balls later he comprehensively bowled Such. Emburey reached a brave fifty off 141 balls, an innings of character and determination rather than of style, and eminently valuable. England closed on 276 for 9.

Any hopes they had of adding to that score were ended in the first over of the second morning when Reiffel found the edge of Ilott's bat. Reiffel's 6 for 71 was a just reward for some excellent bowling. He earned his ovation, and once again he was the surprise ace up the Australian sleeve.

Slater gave Australia their customary bright start, hitting 4 fours, but the introduction of Such brought about an abrupt change. In his fourth over, he accounted for Slater, who went back to a ball that turned quite sharply and was caught at short-leg off bat and pad. Atherton immediately brought Emburey into the attack, and Boon played back fatally to an off-break and missed. Having captured two wickets before lunch, England now captured two more shortly after the break. The first was gifted to them by Taylor who swept Emburey fine but most unwisely went for a second run against Maynard's clean pick-up-and-throw. Mark Waugh might have been caught when he drove hard into, and out of, Smith's midriff at short-leg but, in fairness, it would have been a

sensational catch. Border was out to a magnificent catch when he pushed forward at Such and edged the ball low and fast to Hussain's right at slip. Australia were 80 for 4 in the 36th over, and they should have been 80 for 5 two balls later when Steve Waugh went down the wicket to Such and was beaten in the flight. But Stewart, who did not have the best of days, missed the stumping. That proved to be the end of the party for England.

Neither Bicknell nor Ilott had learned from Reiffel's success and bowled too short. Bicknell, by far the best of the quicker bowlers to have played for England in the series, had moments of great promise before becoming obsessed with bowling short at Mark Waugh and thereby involved in some private feud. Ilott had neither control of length nor line and looked almost as bad as McCague had done at Headingley. Emburey's better years were clearly behind him at this level, and only Such was consistently reliable. While Steve Waugh concentrated mainly on defence, Mark began to drive, pull and cut to all parts of the field. By tea, he had scored 84 – 75 of them in the afternoon session at a time of crisis – Steve was on 21, and Australia were 153 for 4.

To his credit, Atherton changed his bowlers intelligently, and the fielding was generally very good. Mark Waugh raced to his century shortly after tea, but he finally fell to the second new ball, although it was error rather than Ilott's bowling which brought about the dismissal. The batsman flicked the ball rather lazily off his toes, and was caught at square-leg. Mark Waugh's was an innings of the very highest quality. His 137 included 18 fours and had come off 219 balls in 239 minutes at a time when Australia were in trouble. His timing had been perfect, and he made batting look so easy. There is greatness here.

Steve Waugh, 47 when his brother was dismissed 25 minutes before the close, reached 57 by the end of the day. Ian Healy had already shown his intentions by hitting 12 off 19 balls but, with Australia 258 for 5, England still breathed and hoped.

There was success for England in the fourth over of the third day when Steve Waugh was adjudged caught behind. The last specialist batsman had gone, but Australia's tail is made of firmer stuff than England's. Hughes, usually a hit-or-miss man, elected to defend and support Healy, and what followed was a stand of 107 in 25 overs that began to take the game further and further out of England's reach.

Keith Fletcher, the England manager, had made the incredible statement at the end of the second day that Stewart was at least the equal of Healy as a wicket-keeper. One hopes that this was said simply in public defence of one of his team, for if it was his true opinion, he should not be selecting sides for England. Healy had proved his superiority as a wicket-keeper throughout the series, and if doubts remained as to his batting ability – in spite of a century in the first Test – he now dismissed them totally. He hit 80 off 107 balls with 11 fours. He was ever on the attack, batted thrillingly and seemed set for his second hundred of the series when he tried to square-drive a ball from Bicknell that lifted and swung more than expected, and was caught behind. England underrate this man at

The decisive ball: Gooch is bowled round his legs by Warne for 48. (Adrian Murrell/Allsport)

their peril. He is the only wicket-keeper in the world to have maintained his form and held his place in a Test side over the past five years, and he can bat.

Healy's going produced anti-climax. Hughes had 2 fours and a six to his credit before losing patience and pulling at Bicknell, only to drag the ball onto his stumps. Warne swept and looped the ball to the keeper, and Reiffel played inside a ball of full length. On a pitch which had been deemed 'difficult' in a match seen as low-scoring, Australia had made 408 and now led by 132 runs. England pulled back 89 of those before the close, but they lost Atherton in the process, caught at silly mid-off after pushing forward.

Warne and May bowled from the start on the fourth day, and as the ball nipped and turned, one wondered if they were bowling on the same pitch that the England spinners had operated on. In his 10th innings of the series, Robin Smith looked no closer to solving the mysteries of spin than he had been at Old Trafford. He was lucky to escape being leg before when he played no shot to a googly and was all but bowled when he tried to cut May. The agony ended when he was hit on the back pad in front of the wicket by Warne's flipper. Maynard lasted for a frenzied 15 balls before edging May's arm-ball to the keeper. Worse followed, for in the next over Warne, bowling round the wicket, pitched a ball some two feet

FIFTH CORNHILL TEST MATCH – ENGLAND *v.* AUSTRALIA
5, 6, 7, 8 and 9 August 1993 at Edgbaston, Birmingham

ENGLAND

	FIRST INNINGS		SECOND INNINGS	
G.A. Gooch	c Taylor, b Reiffel	8	b Warne	48
M.A. Atherton (capt)	b Reiffel	72	c Border, b Warne	28
R.A. Smith	b M.E. Waugh	21	lbw, b Warne	19
M.P. Maynard	c S.R. Waugh, b May	0	c Healy, b May	10
*A.J. Stewart	c and b Warne	45	lbw, b Warne	5
G.P. Thorpe	c Healy, b May	37	st Healy, b Warne	60
N. Hussain	b Reiffel	3	c S.R. Waugh, b May	0
J.E. Emburey	not out	55	c Healy, b May	37
M.P. Bicknell	c M.E. Waugh, b Reiffel	14	c S.R. Waugh, b May	0
P.M. Such	b Reiffel	1	not out	7
M.C. Ilott	c Healy, b Reiffel	3	b May	15
Extras	b 4, lb 6, nb 7	17	b 11, lb 9, nb 2	22
		276		**251**

AUSTRALIA

	FIRST INNINGS		SECOND INNINGS	
M.A. Taylor	run out	19	(2) c Thorpe, b Such	4
M.J. Slater	c Smith, b Such	22	(1) c Thorpe, b Emburey	8
D.C. Boon	lbw, b Emburey	0	not out	38
M.E. Waugh	c Thorpe, b Ilott	137	not out	62
A.R. Border (capt)	c Hussain, b Such	3		
S.R. Waugh	c Stewart, b Bicknell	59		
*I.A. Healy	c Stewart, b Bicknell	80		
M.G. Hughes	b Bicknell	38		
P.R. Reiffel	b Such	20		
S.K. Warne	c Stewart, b Emburey	10		
T.B.A. May	not out	3		
Extras	b 7, lb 8, nb 2	17	b 3, lb 5	8
		408	(for 2 wickets)	**120**

	O	M	R	W	O	M	R	W		O	M	R	W	O	M	R	W
Hughes	19	4	53	–	18	7	24	–	Bicknell	34	9	99	3	3	–	9	–
Reiffel	22.5	3	71	6	11	2	30	–	Ilott	24	4	85	1	2	–	14	–
M.E. Waugh	15	5	43	1	5	2	5	–	Such	52.5	18	90	3	20.3	4	58	1
S.R. Waugh	5	2	4	–					Emburey	39	9	119	2	18	4	31	1
May	19	9	32	2	48.2	15	89	5									
Warne	21	7	63	1	49	23	82	5									
Border					2	1	1	–									

FALL OF WICKETS

1–17, 2–71, 3–76, 4–156, 5–156, 6–160, 7–215, 8–262, 9–264
1–60, 2–104, 3–115, 4–115, 5–124, 6–125, 7–229, 8–229, 9–229

FALL OF WICKETS

1–34, 2–39, 3–69, 4–80, 5–233, 6–263, 7–370, 8–379, 9–398
1–12, 2–12

Umpires: J.H. Hampshire & D.R. Shepherd

Australia won by 8 wickets

outside Gooch's leg stump. Gooch thrust out his pad – as had been his custom – but the ball spun round it to hit middle and leg. This was wizardry, and England were shattered.

Nine runs later, Stewart pushed forward at a ball on middle and leg which held its line, and was clearly leg before. When Hussain pushed the ball into the hands of silly-point, England were 125 for 6 or, in effect, −7 for 6. Hussain stood his ground, and umpire Shepherd angrily waved his finger at him. England had several players whose attitudes were not of the best. They had claimed catches against Mark Waugh and Merv Hughes, and television had proved their claims invalid. Their reactions had been poor, and their attempts to intimidate the umpires unsavoury. Since the worst decision in the match appeared to be umpire Hampshire's ruling that Steve Waugh was caught behind, England had little to complain about. Sadly, Test cricketers of all nations now seem to believe that umpire harassment is an accepted part of the game.

Thorpe and Emburey came together in the 58th over of the England innings. By lunch, they had added 28, and England were ahead. By tea, the score was 216 for 6, and England even nursed dreams of an improbable victory.

Having batted for 200 minutes with total dedication and unorthodox application, and having demonstrated to *batsmen* how spinners can be played on a turning wicket, Emburey was caught behind as he tried to steer May's first ball from the Pavilion end through the slips. England's tightening grip had been loosened, and it relaxed completely when Bicknell pushed to silly-point second ball, and when Thorpe, in trying to assert himself, jumped out to drive Warne and was clearly stumped. This gave Warne 29 wickets in five Tests and brought him equal to the great Bill O'Reilly's record for a leg-spinner in a five-Test series. Thorpe's 60 came off 192 balls and occupied 234 minutes, and, most importantly, it had shown that he has the temperament and the growing maturity to become a Test batsman. England are in need of him.

Ilott and Such added 22 merry runs for the last wicket before May deservedly claimed his fifth victim. The South Australian off-break bowler had come of age as a Test player during the series. Australia needed 120 to win, and Slater and Taylor scored nine in six overs before the close.

Both openers were quickly out when, following overnight rain, play began 15 minutes late on the last day. Both were taken at silly-point, but the England off-spinners never looked like emulating May and Warne. Mark Waugh escaped one close call for leg before, but he was again in majestic form, and with Boon emphasising that his first-innings nought was a temporary aberration, Australia won just before two o'clock. To no one's surprise, Mark Waugh was named Man of the Match.

At the same time, it was announced that Ted Dexter was to stand down as chairman of the England Committee. Nine defeats in the last 10 matches – it had been a long year for England.

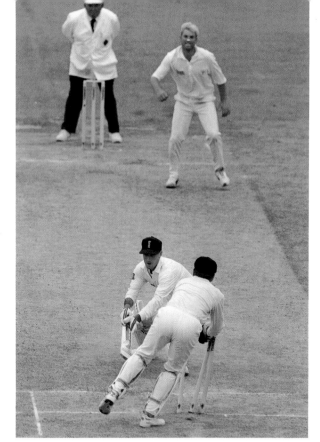

Another stumping for Ian Healy: Thorpe falls to Shane Warne for a brave 60. (David Munden/Sports-Line)

5, 6, 7 and 9 August *at Durham University*

Derbyshire 322 (F.A. Griffith 56, A.S. Rollins 52, R.W. Sladdin 51 not out, S.J.E. Brown 4 for 68) and 182 for 5 (J.E. Morris 83)

Durham 299 (P. Bainbridge 78, S. Hutton 57, G. Fowler 54, O.H. Mortensen 5 for 55)

Match drawn

Derbyshire 7 pts., Durham 6 pts.

at Cardiff

Warwickshire 125 (A. Dale 6 for 18, S.D. Thomas 4 for 49) and 248 (J.D. Ratcliffe 68, Asif Din 66, D.A. Reeve 57)

Glamorgan 236 (R.D.B. Croft 54, M.A.V. Bell 5 for 86) and 138 for 8 (H. Morris 54, P.A. Smith 4 for 35)

Glamorgan won by 2 wickets

Glamorgan 21 pts., Warwickshire 4 pts.

at Cheltenham

Lancashire 294 (G.D. Mendis 81, W.K. Hegg 59) and 213 (C.A. Walsh 5 for 83)

Gloucestershire 450 (M.W. Alleyne 142 not out, S.G. Hinks 64, T.H.C. Hancock 59, K.E. Cooper 52, P.A.J. De-Freitas 5 for 104) and 58 for 1

Gloucestershire won by 9 wickets

Gloucestershire 24 pts., Lancashire 5 pts.

at Canterbury

Surrey 464 (A.D. Brown 141, D.J. Bicknell 119, D.M. Ward 61, M.A. Ealham 4 for 100, C. Penn 4 for 121) and 305 for 3 dec. (D.M. Ward 151 not out, D.J. Bicknell 81)

Kent 467 (T.R. Ward 141, C.L. Hooper 81, M.R. Benson 61, M.A. Ealham 54, J.E. Benjamin 5 for 114)

Match drawn

Surrey 8 pts., Kent 6 pts.

at Lord's

Middlesex 551 for 5 dec. (M.A. Roseberry 185, M.W. Gatting 121, M.R. Ramprakash 83, J.D. Carr 74 not out)

Leicestershire 114 (A.R.C. Fraser 7 for 40) and 253 (W.K.M. Benjamin 63)

Middlesex won by an innings and 184 runs

Middlesex 24 pts., Leicestershire 1 pt.

at Northampton

Essex 286 (J.P. Stephenson 95, P.J. Prichard 61, C.E.L. Ambrose 4 for 35) and 146 (N. Shahid 69 not out)

Northamptonshire 370 (A. Fordham 160, A.J. Lamb 52) and 64 for 2

Northamptonshire won by 8 wickets

Northamptonshire 24 pts., Essex 6 pts.

at Trent Bridge

Nottinghamshire 316 (C.L. Cairns 92, W.A. Dessaur 62) and 259 (P. Johnson 101, R.D. Stemp 5 for 89)

Yorkshire 240 (K.P. Evans 6 for 67) and 220 (C. White 74 not out, J.D. Batty 50, J.A. Afford 5 for 77)

Nottinghamshire won by 115 runs

Nottinghamshire 23 pts., Yorkshire 5 pts.

at Hove

Worcestershire 253 (T.S. Curtis 107, M.J. Weston 51) and 337 (P.J. Newport 65, M.J. Weston 59)

Sussex 424 (A.P. Wells 133, C.W.J. Athey 81, M.P. Speight 72, D.M. Smith 58, C.M. Tolley 4 for 90) and 167 for 1 (M.P. Speight 71 not out, N.J. Lenham 55)

Sussex won by 9 wickets

Sussex 24 pts., Worcestershire 4 pts.

There was no play on the first day at Durham where Rollins and Sladdin made the highest scores of their careers for Derbyshire. A fourth-wicket stand of 126 between Hutton and Bainbridge for Durham was ended

The snap returns to Angus Fraser's bowling – 7 for 40 – as Middlesex trounce Leicestershire, 5–9 August. (USPA)

by Mortensen who then brought about a middle-order collapse. Further rain on the Monday ended any chance of a result.

Glamorgan were engaged in yet another close finish as they beat Warwickshire in three days on a doubtful Cardiff pitch to maintain some pressure on Middlesex. Put in to bat, Warwickshire were shot out on the first day by Adrian Dale, who returned the best bowling figures of his career, and by young Darren Thomas who claimed 7 for 106 in the match. Glamorgan slipped to 111 for 6 in reply before Croft and Lefebvre, a most valuable cricketer, added 83. Eventually, they took a first-innings lead of 111 in spite of Hemp being forced to retire unwell. Left-arm seamer Bell claimed his second five-wicket haul in successive matches for Warwickshire. The visitors showed more resilience when they batted a second time, and Glamorgan had to score 138 to win. That they reached the target was due mainly to an heroic innings by skipper Morris, who was hit on the helmet and on the body, and to Lefebvre and Thomas who hit the last 15 runs together.

There were celebrations at Cheltenham where Gloucestershire won their first championship match of the season. Lancashire hit 294 on the opening day, and the home side took a narrow lead for the loss of seven wickets on the second, Alleyne ending unbeaten on 69. The following morning he hit 73 out of 135 in 105 minutes and was most ably supported by Kevin Cooper who hit his first fifty in 18 years of first-class cricket. Heartened by his team's batting performance and revitalised, it seems, by being given the captaincy, Walsh sent Lancashire reeling to 17 for 3. Babington gave good support, Cooper dismissed Speak, and a poor-looking Lancashire side were beaten in three days.

Surrey lost ground on the leaders in the drawn match on a placid pitch at Canterbury. Darren Bicknell and Alistair Brown put on 188 for Surrey's fourth wicket, but Kent responded in positive fashion. Trevor Ward hit his first championship century of the season and shared century stands with Benson and Hooper. David Ward became a welcome fourth centurion of the match on the Monday, but rain prevented Kent from taking up the challenge. David Ward's first first-class hundred of the season was full of his usual vigour, his 151 coming off 238 balls.

The Middlesex surge on the title looked unstoppable as they swept to their sixth championship win in succession in three days. It was their eighth win in nine matches. On the opening day, Roseberry and Gatting shared a second-wicket stand of 230. Roseberry made the highest score of his career, and poor David Millns, playing his first game of the season for Leicestershire after injury, had to be content with Roseberry's wicket at a cost of 108 runs. Middlesex batted until after lunch on the second day, but when Leicestershire batted, a pitch which had been docile suddenly revealed demons. Angus Fraser, once the front man in England's attack, returned the best bowling figures of his career, and the country held its breath in hope that he had returned to full form and fitness after so long in the wilderness through injury. When Leicestershire followed-on, their misery deepened as skipper Nigel Briers retired hurt with an Achilles tendon injury which threatened to keep him out for the rest of the season. At this stage Middlesex led Glamorgan by 39 points with five matches remaining.

Northamptonshire moved into fourth place as they demolished Essex. On a pitch favouring seam bowling, Prichard and Stephenson added 135 for Essex's second wicket, and a score of 286 looked reasonable. A patient innings from Fordham deemed otherwise, and there were useful contributions from most in the order, as only Childs presented a real threat. Essex lost their first five second-innings wickets for 41 runs, and Stephenson was forced to retire hurt. Shahid battled bravely, but Northamptonshire won with ease inside three days.

Yorkshire suffered a second-innings collapse as embarrassing as that of Essex. Cairns and Wayne Dessaur revived Nottinghamshire on the first day with a 101-run partnership for the fifth wicket, and there was some late vigour from French. Yorkshire conceded a first-innings lead of 76 in spite of the fact that Nottinghamshire were short of off-break bowler Field-Buss, who broke his forearm while batting. Medium-pacer Kevin Evans had the best bowling figures of his career, and Nottinghamshire built on their lead through young Dessaur, who shared a century partnership for the second time in the match. He and Johnson added 145 after three wickets had gone for 20. Johnson reached his fourth hundred of the summer and reminded the England manager that he had once been deemed the outstanding success of an 'A' tour. Any hope Yorkshire had of victory disappeared when they sank to 48 for 5 and 101 for 8. White and Batty added 105, but the cause had long since been lost.

Tim Curtis and Martin Weston began the Worcestershire innings at Hove with a stand of 104, but thereafter, in spite of Curtis' unusual aggression – he hit 16 fours – the side fell apart. In contrast, Sussex batted with early consistency and dash as soon as Speight joined Alan Wells in a partnership which raised 112 in 33 overs. Wells hit his fourth century of the summer and reached 1,000 runs. The last four Sussex wickets went down for 12 runs on the Saturday. Nevertheless, they led by 171 runs, and Worcestershire lost six wickets just in clearing these arrears. Newport breathed life into the tail, but he added only one run on the Monday, and Sussex romped to victory.

AXA EQUITY & LAW LEAGUE

8 August *at Durham University*

Durham 281 for 2 (G. Fowler 124, P.W.G. Parker 92)
Derbyshire 169

Durham (4 pts.) won by 112 runs

at Neath

Warwickshire 163 for 8
Glamorgan 164 for 6 (A. Dale 54)

Glamorgan (4 pts.) won by 4 wickets

at Cheltenham

Gloucestershire 202 (S.G. Hinks 92)
Lancashire 202 (N.H. Fairbrother 81)

Match tied

Gloucestershire 2 pts., Lancashire 2 pts.

at Canterbury

Kent 248 for 8 (C.L. Hooper 61)
Surrey 194 (A.J. Hollioake 58)

Kent (4 pts.) won by 54 runs

at Lord's

Leicestershire 179 (J.J. Whitaker 78, P.C.R. Tufnell 5 for 28, M.R. Ramprakash 5 for 38)
Middlesex 183 for 2 (M.R. Ramprakash 89 not out)

Middlesex (4 pts.) won by 8 wickets

at Northampton

Northamptonshire 241 for 4 (R.J. Bailey 58 not out, A. Fordham 50)
Essex 107

Northamptonshire (4 pts.) won by 134 runs

at Trent Bridge

Nottinghamshire 261 for 8 (R.T. Robinson 83, C.C. Lewis 65, P. Johnson 55, P.J. Hartley 4 for 54)

Yorkshire 264 for 4 (R.B. Richardson 103, R.J. Blakey 57 not out)

Yorkshire (4 pts.) won by 6 wickets

at Hove

Sussex 261 (A.P. Wells 86, C.W.J. Athey 64, R.K. Illingworth 4 for 37)

Worcestershire 232 (G.A. Hick 66)

Sussex (4 pts.) won by 29 runs

In the vital match at Canterbury, Kent beat Surrey comfortably, and, with Glamorgan winning against Warwickshire, the Sunday League developed into a straight contest between Kent and the Welsh county. Fowler hit his Sunday best and shared a stand of 184 with Parker for Durham. Gloucestershire lost eight wickets for 33 runs in 11 overs, but they fought back to take three wickets in the last over and force a tie with Lancashire. Spinners bowled out Leicestershire at Lord's as Mark Ramprakash took five wickets in an innings for the first time in any county match. Richardson reached a century off 86 balls to steer Yorkshire to victory over Nottinghamshire, and Richard Illingworth closed the Sussex innings with a hat-trick but still finished on the losing side.

 NATWEST TROPHY

SEMI-FINALS

10 August *at Taunton*

Warwickshire 252 for 8 (D.P. Ostler 58)

Somerset 200 (N.A. Folland 61)

Warwickshire won by 52 runs

(Man of the Match – D.P. Ostler)

at Hove

Glamorgan 220 (M.P. Maynard 84)

Sussex 224 for 7 (A.P. Wells 106 not out)

Sussex won by 3 wickets

(Man of the Match – A.P. Wells)

Warwickshire entered the NatWest final by beating Somerset thanks to a fine team performance. Reeve won the toss, elected to bat and found his openers deeply uncomfortable against the pace of Van Troost. Ratcliffe was well caught at slip, and Asif Din, frustrated, flashed wildly and was caught behind. Fifteen overs had elapsed, and Warwickshire were 27 for 2. Ostler and Paul Smith reshaped the innings with a stand of 62, Ostler making an excellent 58 off 90 balls. Paul Smith was deeply troubled by Mushtaq Ahmed and was eventually stumped off him, but he had shown great determination amid his bemused

state, and his 33 was invaluable. So, too, was Twose's excellent innings of 41. He had endured a miserable season but, like Paul Smith, he is a resilient cricketer. Meanwhile, resilience was what Dermot Reeve needed. He was on 11 when he collided with Somerset keeper Neil Burns while taking a run. Both men were hurt; Reeve was so dazed that he was forced to retire hurt. He returned later and finished unbeaten on 28 as Warwickshire made 252 for 8. On the uncertain Taunton pitch, this looked a good score. Van Troost had bowled well initially, but had ended up as one of the walking wounded. Mallender bowled splendidly, but Rose and Mushtaq were disappointing.

Somerset got off to a poor start. Lathwell was beaten by a ball that nipped back at him and was leg before to Small, who also had Hayhurst brilliantly caught at slip by Ostler in his next over. There was reprieve for Somerset as Small became another of the injured, retiring after five overs. Folland and Harden added 53, but Harden, Tavare – run out as he hesitated – and Rose all went quickly. Mushtaq offered brief resistance, but Somerset's real hope and joy came in the innings of Burns. He gave the innings urgency, clouting 31 out of a stand of 60 with Folland, who battled bravely through 51 overs. Burns was caught off a long-hop, Caddick went first ball, and Somerset were doomed.

Glamorgan were happy to win the toss and bat first at Hove, and the early form of James and Morris gave hints of a big score. It was the unexpected bowling of Neil Lenham which broke the 54-run partnership. He trapped James leg before with what was little more than a straight delivery. Morris chopped on as he tried to pull Pigott, who bowled with accuracy and aggression, and when Dale was well caught in the gully by Smith off the same bowler, the whole complexion of the game had changed. Maynard and Richards came together at 71 for 3. They began with care, although some of Maynard's attempts to lob the erratic Salisbury to leg did not inspire confidence. Richards could not find his timing on a pitch which grew increasingly slower, and he gave Greenfield a simple return catch off a leading edge when the score was 124. Greenfield bowled Cottey for 1, and Sussex were humming again. Maynard now hit cleanly and sweetly, and he found a good ally in Croft. They added 57 before the young off-spinner was bowled by Salisbury. Maynard's 84 off 112 balls kept Glamorgan alive, but when he was caught in the deep off Stephenson the Welsh county slipped to a quiet end. Their 220 looked some 40 runs short of a winning total.

The Glamorgan bowlers and fielders had other ideas, however. Watkin and Lefebvre, backed by ground fielding of the highest quality, strangled the Sussex openers, and neither Barwick nor Dale relaxed the grip. Smith played on to Watkin, and Speight hit the same bowler high to square-leg where Lefebvre took a fine running catch and displayed his excitement at doing so. After 17 overs, Sussex were 17 for 2. Athey was frustrated into submission, hitting Dale into Maynard's hands at mid-on. Greenfield was quickly run out in a misunderstanding with Alan Wells, and it was not until the 36th over, when Stephenson hit Dale over long-on – and was nearly caught in the process – that Sussex hit their third four. Watkin returned and Stephenson was coolly caught by Cottey on the mid-wicket boundary, and when Richards held Moores in the gully off Dale's last delivery Glamorgan's dream of Lord's seemed a reality. Unfortunately, while Morris had captained Glamorgan admirably throughout the season, here, surely, he erred. Croft had bowled seven very good and tidy overs, but the young man was replaced by Viv Richards who began with a no-ball, was unable to find his line and was hit for 25 runs in three overs. Croft had been put out of his rhythm and when he was brought back he, too, was savaged. Morris juggled his bowlers, but Alan Wells had paced his innings wonderfully. He and Lenham, a luxury at number eight, added 107 in 15 overs, and by the time Lenham was bowled by Lefebvre only four runs were needed and more than two overs remained. Wells was magnificent, and no batsman has more clearly been a Man of the Match. His 106 came from 131 balls, and it had turned what seemed total disaster into victory. This was, indeed, a captain's innings.

11, 12 and 13 August *at Canterbury*

Australians 391 for 4 dec. (S.R. Waugh 123, D.R. Martyn 105 not out, M.A. Taylor 78) and 34 for 0 dec.

Kent 114 for 2 dec. and 222 (T.R. Ward 69, G.R. Cowdrey 51)

Australians won by 89 runs

Matthew Hayden became the first Australian in history to reach 1,000 runs on a tour of England without playing in a Test match. Hayden had looked certain of a place until shortly before the first Test, but he had lost out to Slater. Nevertheless, he continued to score prolifically and must soon claim a place in the Test side. Damien Martyn also gave another indication of his quality, and the tourists were able to win a good contest after declarations had kept a rain-affected match alive.

Man of the Match as Warwickshire beat Somerset in the NatWest semi-final – Dominic Ostler. (Alan Cozzi)

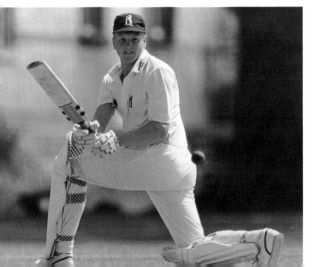

12, 13, 14 and 16 August *at Derby*

Derbyshire 135 (C.J. Adams 50, A.R. Caddick 5 for 49, N.A. Mallender 5 for 49) and 221 (A.S. Rollins 85, Mushtaq Ahmed 4 for 28)

Somerset 453 for 9 dec. (A.N. Hayhurst 169, M.N. Lathwell 109, D.G. Cork 4 for 90)

Somerset won by an innings and 97 runs
Somerset 23 pts., Derbyshire 2 pts.

at Southampton

Hampshire 384 (D.I. Gower 117, V.P. Terry 57, M. Watkinson 4 for 104) and 258 for 6 dec. (V.P. Terry 143 not out, P.A.J. DeFreitas 4 for 50)

Lancashire 386 (M. Watkinson 81, G.D. Mendis 58, M.A. Atherton 56, P.A.J. DeFreitas 51, S.D. Udal 5 for 131) and 138 for 3

Match drawn
Lancashire 7 pts., Hampshire 6 pts.

at Leicester

Glamorgan 351 for 8 dec. (P.A. Cottey 105, M.P. Maynard 82, D.L. Hemp 62)

Leicestershire 178 (J.J. Whitaker 75, S.L. Watkin 4 for 49) and 315 for 4 dec. (V.J. Wells 167, P.N. Hepworth 129)

Match drawn
Glamorgan 8 pts., Leicestershire 3 pts.

at Northampton

Durham 210 (P. Bainbridge 68, K.M. Curran 4 for 53) and 89 (C.E.L. Ambrose 4 for 24)

Northamptonshire 347 (M.B. Loye 80, A.J. Lamb 70, D.A. Graveney 5 for 78)

Northamptonshire won by an innings and 48 runs
Northamptonshire 23 pts., Durham 2 pts.

at Eastbourne

Sussex 424 (M.P. Speight 184, P. Moores 78, J.A. Afford 4 for 112) and 283 for 5 dec. (C.W.J. Athey 75, N.J. Lenham 71)

Nottinghamshire 278 (R.T. Robinson 69, G.W. Mike 50, A.C.S. Pigott 4 for 51) and 308 for 8 (P.R. Pollard 117, C.L. Cairns 57)

Match drawn
Sussex 8 pts., Nottinghamshire 4 pts.

at Edgbaston

Warwickshire 280 (A.J. Moles 117, Asif Din 53, C.A. Walsh 4 for 102) and 124 (C.A. Walsh 5 for 59)

Gloucestershire 145 (M.A.V. Bell 7 for 48) and 263 for 5 (G.D. Hodgson 85 not out)

Gloucestershire won by 5 wickets
Gloucestershire 20 pts., Warwickshire 6 pts.

at Worcester

Worcestershire 406 (G.A. Hick 182, P.J. Newport 52, M.P. Bicknell 6 for 86) and 313 for 9 dec. (C.M. Tolley 78, D.A. Leatherdale 53, D.B. D'Oliveira 50, M.P. Bicknell 5 for 106)

Surrey 427 (G.P. Thorpe 171, D.J. Bicknell 130, P.J. Newport 4 for 86) and 227 (A.J. Stewart 54)

Worcestershire won by 65 runs

Worcestershire 21 pts., Surrey 8 pts.

at Scarborough

Yorkshire 256 (D. Byas 76, A.R.C. Fraser 4 for 25) and 184 for 9 (M.D. Moxon 93, A.R.C. Fraser 4 for 49)

Middlesex 439 for 5 dec. (M.W. Gatting 182, M.R. Ramprakash 140)

Match drawn

Middlesex 8 pts., Yorkshire 4 pts.

14, 15 and **16** August *at Chelmsford*

Australians 357 for 6 dec. (M.L. Hayden 111, M.E. Waugh 108, A.R. Border 57) and 218 (B.P. Julian 66, P.M. Such 4 for 52, D.R. Pringle 4 for 65)

Essex 268 (G.A. Gooch 61, N. Hussain 57) and 277 for 9 (N.V. Knight 87, G.A. Gooch 73)

Match drawn

Bowled out by the Somerset seamers Mallender and Caddick on the opening day, Derbyshire then suffered as Lathwell and Hayhurst scored 226 for the visitors' first wicket. In spite of Adrian Rollins' career best 85 off 110 balls, Derbyshire were beaten in three days as Mushtaq Ahmed quickly dismissed the late order.

Centuries from Gower and Terry and solid middle-order batting from the dependable Mike Watkinson could not beat the weather, and the match between Hampshire and Lancashire was inevitably drawn, as was the match at Leicester.

Only 11.1 overs were possible on the first day at Leicester, and Glamorgan lost both openers for 12, finishing on 28 for 2. They quickly made up for lost time on the second day, racing to maximum batting points. Maynard hit 82 off 87 balls, and Cottey and Hemp added 161 for the fifth wicket. Glamorgan seemed set for an innings victory when Watkin and Barwick were the prime destroyers in bowling Leicestershire out for 178 on the Saturday. Watkin also dismissed Boon before the close so that Glamorgan began the last day needing nine wickets for victory. They were thwarted by Vincent Wells and Peter Hepworth who shared a second-wicket stand of 278 which lasted until after tea. Wells hit the maiden first-class century of his career, and Hepworth, playing his first championship game of the season, hit the highest of his three centuries. Glamorgan's failure to win the match was a severe set-back to their title aspirations.

Durham suffered another three-day defeat when they were shot out for 89 on the Saturday by Ambrose, Taylor

and Bowen. A stand of 168 for the fourth wicket between Lamb and Loye was the backbone of the Northamptonshire innings, and the home side's win took them to a challenging place in the championship with a game in hand from the leaders.

A shortened first day at Eastbourne saw Sussex close on 170 for 5, but on the Friday, Speight and Moores extended their partnership to 241 in 66 overs. Speight hit an exciting career best 184, reaching his hundred with a straight six off Bates. Nottinghamshire looked doomed to follow-on but, with Gregory Mike hitting 50, the last two wickets realised 61, and Sussex were denied. Wells' declaration on Monday morning left Nottinghamshire 96 overs in which to score 430 runs. Pollard hit his first championship century of the season, and Sussex dropped several catches to draw a match they should have won.

Warwickshire seemed in total control against Gloucestershire when left-arm seamer Michael Bell, enjoying a wonderful run of form, took a career best 7 for 48 and bowled his side to a first-innings lead of 135. Walsh, Babington and Alleyne brought the visitors back into contention, and Hodgson steered them to victory after he and Broad had begun the second innings with a partnership of 92.

Scoring at four runs an over, and inspired by Hick – who passed 1,000 runs for the season – Worcestershire seemed in command against Surrey, but a second-wicket stand of 309 between Thorpe and Darren Bicknell put the championship hopefuls well in contention. Surrey even grabbed a first-innings lead, but Worcestershire gave a second-innings batting display of consistency which was aided by a plethora of no-balls and a total of 53 extras. Surrey, needing 293 in 64 overs, failed after the middle-order efforts of Stewart, Brown, Ward and Martin Bicknell had been brought to an end. Bicknell, in spite of an injured knee, batted well and took 11 wickets in a match for the second time in the season.

Middlesex could have virtually clinched the championship had they beaten Yorkshire, but they were frustrated by the weather and by Martyn Moxon. At the end of a rain-affected first day, Yorkshire were 89 for 5, but Byas and the last five wickets added 167 on the second day. Middlesex took total command on the Saturday, however. Gatting and Ramprakash shared a third-wicket stand of 321. Gatting hit a six and 28 fours, and Ramprakash a six and 15 fours, as the Yorkshire attack was demolished. Fraser then took three wickets in 10 balls, and Yorkshire ended on 110 for 4. Rain delayed the start until 3.45 on the last day. With White falling early on, Moxon stood fast as first Hartley, then Gough gave passive support. When Moxon was caught on the leg side by Brown off Embury, it seemed Middlesex must win. The last pair, Robinson and Batty, came together with 13 balls remaining, and Batty, badly missed, struck two belligerent blows to save the game.

In their last Tetley Bitter Challenge match, the Australians played an entertaining draw with Essex. Hayden, pressing strongly for the out-of-form Slater's place in the final Test, hit a hundred as did the effervescent Mark Waugh. Gooch and Hussain led the Essex response, and eventually the county needed 308 in 72 overs to win. Knight and Gooch began with 121, and Essex were always in the chase until the ninth wicket fell with eight balls remaining. They had looked likely winners before losing four wickets in three overs for two runs.

AXA EQUITY & LAW LEAGUE

15 August *at Derby*

Derbyshire 281 for 3 (P.D. Bowler 138 not out, C.J. Adams 93)

Somerset 168 (G.D. Rose 52)

Derbyshire (4 pts.) won by 113 runs

at Southampton

Hampshire 158 (M.C.J. Nicholas 64 not out, P.A.J. De-Freitas 5 for 26)

Lancashire 159 for 4 (M.A. Atherton 51)

Lancashire (4 pts.) won by 6 wickets

at Leicester

Glamorgan 228 for 7 (A. Dale 56, M.P. Maynard 54)

Leicestershire 220 for 7 (J.J. Whitaker 117, S.R. Barwick 4 for 46)

Glamorgan (4 pts.) won by 8 runs

at Northampton

Durham 246 for 7

Northamptonshire 198 (A.C. Cummins 4 for 27)

Durham (4 pts.) won by 48 runs

at Eastbourne

Sussex 262 (M.P. Speight 57)

Nottinghamshire 168 (R.T. Robinson 51)

Sussex (4 pts.) won by 94 runs

at Edgbaston

Gloucestershire 232 for 5 (M.W. Alleyne 52 not out)

Warwickshire 221 (N.M.K. Smith 54, P.A. Smith 50)

Gloucestershire (4 pts.) won by 11 runs

at Worcester

Worcestershire 194 (G.A. Hick 64)

Surrey 157

Worcestershire (4 pts.) won by 37 runs

at Scarborough

Yorkshire 245 for 2 (R.B. Richardson 88 not out, R.J. Blakey 69 not out, M.D. Moxon 50)

Middlesex 168 (D.L. Haynes 60)

Yorkshire (4 pts.) won by 77 runs

With Kent idle, Glamorgan's victory over Leicestershire took them to the top of the Sunday League. They led by two points, and both Glamorgan and Kent had three games remaining. As they were due to meet on the last Sunday of the season, it seemed that the finish to the competition would be an exciting one. The Glamorgan victory was close, for Leicestershire captain James Whitaker hit a fine century and was not dismissed until the last over. Sussex maintained their outside chance of winning the league with a comfortable win over Nottinghamshire, but Surrey's dreams ended at Worcester. Derbyshire, inconsistent as ever, thrashed Somerset. Adams and Bowler began with a partnership of 210.

SIXTH TEST MATCH
ENGLAND *v.* AUSTRALIA, at The Oval

Disaster haunted England until the end of the summer. Hick and Tufnell had been brought into the party, and Smith, Emburey and Ilott omitted. Martin Bicknell was then declared unfit for a five-day Test, and Angus Fraser returned to international cricket. This was the most joyful occurrence of the season, for there had been doubts as to whether Fraser, a bowler of the very highest quality, would ever regain full form and fitness after his hip injury. His performances in recent weeks had shown how complete was his recovery. On the morning of the match, Thorpe injured his left thumb in practice, and Mark Ramprakash was hastily summoned from Lord's. It is questionable whether he would have been the first-choice replacement had an emergency not occurred.

England left out Tufnell from the final twelve, and so took the field with four main bowlers, three of whom – Malcolm, Fraser and Watkin – had not played at Edgbaston.

Atherton won the toss; England batted. Hughes began with a maiden, but Atherton then turned Reiffel for four, and the boundaries began to stream. There were five in the first 25 runs, as Hughes and Reiffel bowled too short on a pitch which was, it seemed, a batsman's paradise.

At 11.35, there was chaos as spectators at the Vauxhall end had to be reseated because they were behind the bowler's arm. On the resumption, Atherton was given not out by umpire Barry Meyer when he offered no shot to a ball from Reiffel which struck him on the pad. Why the England captain survived, only the umpire can tell. This escape apart, Atherton and Gooch were batting with great freedom, and the fifty came in the 11th over. Six overs later, Gooch, who had hit 10 fours and faced 66 balls, cut Steve Waugh into the hands of Border, low at gully. Atherton was dropped at slip by Taylor off Reiffel, but England lunched happily at 115 for 1 from 25 overs.

Atherton is a calm, reassuring batsman who can only have a beneficial influence on those under him. He clipped Steve Waugh to leg for his ninth four and his fifty, but the very next ball he was leg before as he walked across his stumps trying to turn the ball to leg.

Warne was late into the attack, but his impact was quick. Maynard again looked over-eager. His 20 came off

One of Angus Fraser's eight victims on his return to Test cricket: Steve Waugh is bowled for 20. (Adrian Murrell/Allsport)

34 balls in half an hour and included 3 fours. Then he offered no shot at a top-spinner which went straight on and hit the off stump. Hussain square-cut Warne for four to bring up 200 in the 49th over, by which time Hick had already reached 50 off 77 balls with 10 fours. His batting was uninhibited without ever indicating permanence, but it was entertaining. Mark Waugh was brought on at the Pavilion end, and Hick hit him for four boundaries in succession. A single took him to face May whom he drove straight for six. Heady with success, he slashed into the hands of extra cover. England were 237 for 4 at tea.

Hussain was taken at slip off Warne shortly after tea, and Ramprakash, looking very ill at ease, was caught behind off Hughes. Two runs later, Stewart was clearly caught at slip off Warne, but he stayed his ground and umpire Kitchen did not raise the finger. This was an astonishing decision. Stewart was 21 at the time.

Graham Gooch drives Reiffel for four to become the highest-scoring English Test batsman. (Patrick Eagar)

Like Hick, Stewart played with a refreshing lack of inhibition, without ever suggesting security, and he offered some lavish strokes, mainly to leg. He pulled Warne over mid-wicket for six to reach his fifty, and finally fell to the first delivery with the second new ball. He essayed a hook at Hughes, and Healy jumped to take the ball high on the leg side. Again, it seemed clear that Stewart made no contact with the ball, which hit him high on the arm. Nevertheless, umpire Kitchen's finger was raised. This was a very bad series for the umpires, Bird and Shepherd apart. England closed on 353 for 7.

In the fourth over of the second morning, Watkin sliced to gully. Five overs later, Such ducked to a rising ball from Hughes, but left his bat in the air and the ball hit it and looped to gully. Fraser threw his bat at everything in the next over and missed the fifth ball as he tried to give himself room to hit on the off side. The England innings was over for the addition of 27 runs in 42 minutes.

Malcolm opened the bowling from the Vauxhall end and looked very quick. In his second over, he bowled a short ball to Slater who, justifiably, went to hook. The ball was on him quicker than expected and he skied it to leg where Gooch ran to take the catch. Boon opened his account by upper-cutting Malcolm over slips and third man for six. He also hit a four before being caught, bat and pad, at short-leg. How refreshing it was to see a batsman walk immediately. Australia were 42 for 2 at lunch; England were happy.

Mark Waugh never looked settled, and Watkin once all but bowled him. Fraser came on at the Pavilion end immediately after lunch and with his 17th delivery he dismissed Waugh, who tried to cut a ball that moved back at him. Taylor and Border now appeared to master the bowling and to give the bat the dominance one had always felt it should have on this pitch. They added 79 before Taylor slashed wildly at Malcolm, who was fierce and fast, and was caught at gully. Australia went to tea at 134 for 4.

Steve Waugh hit 3 fours off Malcolm when the pace man strayed down the leg side, but he was bowled by a superb ball from Fraser which held its line, and for the first time in the series, the Australians really had their backs to the wall. Border was caught behind when he cut at a ball too close to him. This was Fraser's 50th wicket in Test cricket, and the persevering Watkin next accounted for Hughes and Reiffel in the same over. Australia were 196 for 8.

Atherton's leadership had been exemplary. His field-placings were a necessary blend of attack and wise defence. He handled the attack intelligently, offering variety and freshness and ever maintaining the pressure through Malcolm and Fraser. Healy steered Australia to 239 by the close.

Warne added only two to his overnight score before being caught behind off Fraser, but the force of the previous day seemed to have left Malcolm, and Healy cut him for four to reach an excellent fifty. At 12.15, he hooked Watkin for four to put the 300 up, but almost immediately, May drove lavishly at Fraser and was caught behind. Healy remained unbeaten on 83 made off 117 balls and through him the last two Australian wickets

Allan Border congratulates Gooch on his great achievement. (Adrian Murrell/Allsport)

drove Reiffel to the mid-off boundary and so became England's highest run-scorer in Test cricket, overtaking the record which David Gower had established only last season. The crowd stood, and Border shook his hand. It was a moment to savour. Gooch's career is scarred with wounds – many of them self-inflicted – but his dedication to the game and to batting for England and Essex has never been in question. There is an immensity in the man.

Lifted by Malcolm and Fraser, and now elevated and joyful at Gooch's record, the crowd roared England on. Bathed in sunlight, The Oval is a complex stage, a hotch-potch of architectural styles with a stark backdrop of buildings – the Houses of Parliament, the Post Office Tower, the NatWest Tower all merging into a jagged pattern against which the play is enacted. England raced ahead, and by the time Warne joined the attack in the 19th over, the score was 73.

Atherton had been batting with a liberated exuberance, outpacing Gooch, but he cut once too often at Reiffel and was taken at point. Hick straight-drove a six and hit 5 fours, but he mistimed a pull and hit low to mid-on. Maynard fretted to hit to leg, was dropped by Border off a hard chance at short square-leg and then hooked poorly

had added 107 runs. He had been a mighty power in the series with bat and gloves.

Gooch launched England's second innings with a magnificent off-drive for four, and the first three overs realised 29 runs. In the last over before lunch, Gooch

---

SIXTH CORNHILL TEST MATCH – ENGLAND v. AUSTRALIA
19, 20, 21, 22 and 23 August 1993 at The Oval, Kennington

ENGLAND

	FIRST INNINGS		SECOND INNINGS	
G.A. Gooch	c Border, b S.R. Waugh	56	c Healy, b Warne	79
M.A. Atherton (capt)	lbw, b S.R. Waugh	50	c Warne, b Reiffel	42
G.A. Hick	c Warne, b May	80	c Boon, b May	36
M.P. Maynard	b Warne	20	c Reiffel, b Hughes	9
N. Hussain	c Taylor, b Warne	30	c M.E. Waugh, b Hughes	0
*A.J. Stewart	c Healy, b Hughes	76	c M.E. Waugh, b Reiffel	35
M.R. Ramprakash	c Healy, b Hughes	6	c Slater, b Hughes	64
A.R.C. Fraser	b Reiffel	28	c Healy, b Reiffel	13
S.L. Watkin	c S.R. Waugh, b Reiffel	13	lbw, b Warne	4
P.M. Such	c M.E. Waugh, b Hughes	4	lbw, b Warne	10
D.E. Malcolm	not out	0	not out	0
Extras	lb 7, w 1, nb 9	17	b 5, lb 12, w 1, nb 3	21
		380		**313**

AUSTRALIA

	FIRST INNINGS		SECOND INNINGS	
M.A. Taylor	c Hussain, b Malcolm	70	(2) b Watkin	8
M.J. Slater	c Gooch, b Malcolm	4	(1) c Stewart, b Watkin	12
D.C. Boon	c Gooch, b Malcolm	13	lbw, b Watkin	0
M.E. Waugh	c Stewart, b Fraser	10	c Ramprakash, b Malcolm	49
A.R. Border (capt)	c Stewart, b Fraser	48	c Stewart, b Malcolm	17
S.R. Waugh	b Fraser	20	lbw, b Malcolm	26
*I.A. Healy	not out	83	c Maynard, b Watkin	5
M.G. Hughes	c Ramprakash, b Watkin	7	c Watkin, b Fraser	12
P.R. Reiffel	c Maynard, b Watkin	0	c and b Fraser	42
S.K. Warne	c Stewart, b Fraser	16	lbw, b Fraser	37
T.B.A. May	c Stewart, b Fraser	15	not out	4
Extras	b 5, lb 6, w 2, nb 4	17	b 2, lb 6, w 2, nb 7	17
		303		**229**

	O	M	R	W	O	M	R	W
Hughes	30	7	121	3	31.2	9	110	3
Reiffel	28.5	4	88	2	24	8	55	3
S.R. Waugh	12	2	45	2				
Warne	20	5	70	2	40	15	78	3
M.E. Waugh	1	–	17	–				
May	10	3	32	1	24	6	53	1

	O	M	R	W	O	M	R	W
Malcolm	26	5	86	3	20	3	84	3
Watkin	28	4	87	2	25	9	65	4
Fraser	26.4	4	87	5	19.1	5	44	3
Such	14	4	32	–	9	4	17	–
Hick					8	3	11	–

FALL OF WICKETS

1–88, 2–143, 3–177, 4–231, 5–253, 6–272, 7–339, 8–363, 9–374
1–77, 2–157, 3–180, 4–180, 5–186, 6–254, 7–276, 8–283, 9–313

FALL OF WICKETS

1–9, 2–30, 3–53, 4–132, 5–164, 6–181, 7–196, 8–196, 9–248
1–23, 2–23, 3–30, 4–92, 5–95, 6–106, 7–142, 8–143, 9–217

Umpires: M.J. Kitchen & B.J. Meyer

England won by 161 runs

to square-leg. Hussain went first ball to a vicious lifter which he tried to fend off, and six runs later, Gooch became the victim of a beautiful leg-break. He had hit 13 fours and faced 183 balls in an innings which was an historic one.

England were now 186 for 5, and had Taylor caught Ramprakash at slip second ball as he should have done, Australia would have scented victory. The natives became restless and threw rubbish with their boring Mexican wave. There was much in the crowd in the Test series of 1993 that was less than pleasant, and The Oval managed a better discipline than one or two other grounds.

Ramprakash hit May through the covers for four, and he was then beaten by four balls in succession. England ended thankfully on 210 for 5.

Rain delayed the start of the fourth day and brought play to an early close. Stewart and Ramprakash subdued early nerves before Stewart edged to second slip. Fraser

edged to the keeper, and Watkin and Warne both fell leg before to balls of full length. Ramprakash was last out, driving Hughes to mid-off, but he had done an excellent job, remaining steadfast for four hours while 127 runs were scored and the game was put out of Australia's reach.

Australia had to endure four torrid overs before the premature close and managed a single. They began the last day needing 391 to win, and if they had any hope of victory, it soon disappeared. Sadly, it was an appalling decision by umpire Meyer which started the decline. A lifting delivery from Watkin hit Slater on the arm-guard as he raised his bat to let the ball go through. Stewart and the slips appealed without justification, but Meyer's finger went up. Next ball, Boon offered no shot and was leg before. When Taylor edged Watkin into his stumps Australia were 30 for 3, all three wickets having gone to the Glamorgan bowler, the season's leading wicket-taker.

Mark Waugh had surmounted early insecurity, and

TEST MATCH AVERAGES – ENGLAND v. AUSTRALIA

ENGLAND BATTING

	M	Inns	NO	Runs	HS	Av	100s	50s
G.A. Gooch	6	12	–	673	133	56.08	2	4
M.A. Atherton	6	12	–	553	99	46.08	–	6
G.P. Thorpe	3	6	1	230	114*	46.00	1	1
G.A. Hick	3	6	–	256	80	42.66	–	2
A.J. Stewart	6	12	–	378	78	31.50	–	3
N. Hussain	4	8	2	184	71	30.66	–	1
R.A. Smith	5	10	–	283	86	28.30	–	2
M.W. Gatting	2	4	–	91	59	22.75	–	1
M.N. Lathwell	2	4	–	78	33	19.50	–	–
A.R. Caddick	4	8	1	101	25	14.42	–	–
C.C. Lewis	2	4	–	52	43	13.00	–	–
M.P. Maynard	2	4	–	39	20	9.75	–	–
P.M. Such	5	9	3	56	14*	9.33	–	–
M.C. Ilott	3	5	1	28	15	7.00	–	–
M.J. McCague	2	3	–	20	11	6.66	–	–
M.P. Bicknell	2	4	–	26	14	6.50	–	–
P.C.R. Tufnell	2	4	2	3	2*	1.50	–	–

Played in one Test: J.E. Emburey 35* & 37; M.R. Ramprakash 6 & 64; A.R.C. Fraser 28 & 13; N.A. Foster 20 & 16; S.L. Watkin 13 & 4; P.A.J. DeFreitas 5 & 7; D.E. Malcolm 0* & 0*.

AUSTRALIA BATTING

	M	Inns	NO	Runs	HS	Av	100s	50s
S.R. Waugh	6	9	4	416	157*	83.20	1	2
D.C. Boon	6	10	2	555	164*	69.37	3	1
M.E. Waugh	6	10	1	550	137	61.11	1	5
I.A. Healy	6	7	2	296	102*	59.20	1	2
A.R. Border	6	9	1	433	200*	54.12	1	1
M.A. Taylor	6	10	–	428	124	42.80	2	1
M.J. Slater	6	10	–	416	152	41.60	1	2
S.K. Warne	6	5	2	113	37	37.66	–	–
B.P. Julian	2	3	1	61	56*	30.50	–	1
P.R. Reiffel	3	3	–	62	42	20.66	–	–
M.G. Hughes	6	5	–	76	38	15.20	–	–
T.B.A. May	5	4	2	23	15	11.50	–	–

Played in two Tests: C.J. McDermott 8

ENGLAND BOWLING

	Overs	Mds	Runs	Wkts	Av	Best	5/inn
A.R.C. Fraser	45.5	9	131	8	16.37	5-87	1
S.L. Watkin	53	13	152	6	25.33	4-65	–
D.E. Malcolm	46	8	170	6	28.33	3-84	–
P.M. Such	239.5	64	541	16	33.81	6-67	1
J.E. Emburey	57	13	150	3	50.00	2-119	–
M.C. Ilott	129	28	412	8	51.50	3-108	–
P.A.J. DeFreitas	47	9	126	2	63.00	1-46	–
P.C.R. Tufnell	104	12	319	5	63.80	2-78	–
M.P. Bicknell	87	17	263	4	65.75	3-99	–
M.J. McCague	79.3	13	294	4	73.50	4-121	–
A.R. Caddick	153	28	488	5	97.60	3-32	–
C.C. Lewis	58	7	238	2	119.00	2-151	–
G.A. Hick	25	7	52	–	–	–	–
G.A. Gooch	25	6	66	–	–	–	–
N.A. Foster	30	4	94	–	–	–	–

Bowled in one innings: G.P. Thorpe 6–1–14–0.

AUSTRALIA BOWLING

	Overs	Mds	Runs	Wkts	Av	Best	5/inn
P.R. Reiffel	140.4	31	396	19	20.84	6-71	2
S.K. Warne	439.5	178	877	34	25.79	5-82	1
M.G. Hughes	296.2	78	845	31	27.25	5-92	1
T.B.A. May	278	90	592	21	28.19	5-89	1
A.R. Border	27	11	35	1	35.00	1-16	–
S.R. Waugh	32	9	82	2	41.00	2-45	–
B.P. Julian	82	16	291	5	58.20	2-30	–
M.E. Waugh	56	17	161	1	161.00	1-43	–
C.J. McDermott	48	11	126	–	–	–	–

ENGLAND FIELDING FIGURES

16 – A.J. Stewart (ct 14/st 2); 5 – G.P. Thorpe; 2 – G.A. Gooch, N. Hussain, R.A. Smith, M.W. Gatting, M.N. Lathwell, A.R. Caddick, M.P. Maynard, P.M. Such and M.R. Ramprakash; 1 – M.A. Atherton, C.C. Lewis, M.J. McCague, P.C.R. Tufnell, P.A.J. DeFreitas, A.R.C. Fraser, S.L. Watkin and sub (B.F. Smith).

AUSTRALIA FIELDING FIGURES

26 – I.A. Healy (ct 21/st 5); 11 – M.A. Taylor; 9 – M.E. Waugh; 8 – A.R. Border; 5 – S.R. Waugh and D.C. Boon; 4 – S.K. Warne; 2 – M.J. Slater, B.P. Julian and T.B.A. May; 1 – P.R. Reiffel and sub (M.L. Hayden).

Border was as rock-like as ever. They took Australia to 92 for 3 at lunch, but in the first over of the afternoon Border was adjudged caught behind as Malcolm slanted the ball across him. Three runs later, Mark Waugh played a rash hook and skied to backward square-leg. Arguably, Mark Waugh was the best batsman on either side in the series; unquestionably, he is an infuriating batsman in the way in which so often he wastes his wicket. Healy played uncharacteristically and skied to behind the keeper as he, too, tried to hook. Steve Waugh and Hughes suggested solidity, but they went within the space of two overs – Waugh trapped on the back foot by an excellent, very fast delivery, and Hughes attempting to pull while off balance. At tea, the score was 148 for 8.

Reiffel and Warne offered the most sensible batting of the day, and they added 74 in 18 overs. They played some exciting shots, but suddenly Reiffel hit a full toss straight back to the bowler. Four overs later, Warne was beaten by Fraser's straight ball, and England had ended an horrendous run of Test misery and beaten Australia for the first time in seven years. It was some consolation for England after a depressing year, and Atherton deserves much credit.

The return of Man of the Match Angus Fraser and the pace of Devon Malcolm made much difference, as did Watkin's variations in pace and his accuracy. Gooch and Warne were named Men of the Series, and Australia won by four to one. They had been deprived of their main strike bowler after the first Test, yet they had played to their full potential in every aspect of the game. All their batsmen had scored runs, and quickly. Hughes had carried an immense burden manfully, and May had proved himself a Test bowler of quality. Reiffel had revealed unexpected talent, and Warne turned the ball more than one has ever seen a spinner do. And behind and in front of the stumps was Ian Healy.

Any side that can win a series so convincingly as Border's 1993 Australians did without calling on Hayden and Martyn must be a very good one.

19, 20, 21 and 23 August *at Ilkeston*

Surrey 205 (A.W. Smith 68, A.E. Warner 5 for 57) and 332 (A.J. HolLioake 123, M.A. Lynch 58)

Derbyshire 438 for 9 dec. (P.D. Bowler 143, J.E. Morris 127, Waqar Younis 4 for 97) and 100 for 4

Derbyshire won by 6 wickets

Derbyshire 24 pts., Surrey 4 pts.

at Darlington

Warwickshire 281 (P.A. Smith 55, S.J.E. Brown 5 for 78) and 327 (D.P. Ostler 85, A.C. Cummins 5 for 83)

Durham 369 (P.W.G. Parker 159, J.A. Daley 79, R.G. Twose 4 for 85) and 243 for 1 (W. Larkins 113 not out, G. Fowler 72)

Durham won by 9 wickets

Durham 23 pts., Warwickshire 5 pts.

at Swansea

Hampshire 417 (V.P. Terry 174, M.D. Marshall 75 not out, A.N. Aymes 55, R.D.B. Croft 5 for 157) and 196 for 4 dec. (D.I. Gower 56, R.D.B. Croft 4 for 74)

Glamorgan 288 (S.P. James 80, I.V.A. Richards 67, M.D. Marshall 5 for 62) and 227 (D.L. Hemp 63, H. Morris 60, S.D. Udal 5 for 75)

Hampshire won by 98 runs

Hampshire 23 pts., Glamorgan 4 pts.

at Bristol

Gloucestershire 320 (M.W. Alleyne 104, T.H.C. Hancock 52, D.R. Pringle 4 for 90) and 220 (R.C. Russell 65)

Essex 216 and 240 for 5 (D.D.J. Robinson 67, J.J.B. Lewis 56)

Match drawn

Gloucestershire 7 pts., Essex 5 pts.

at Old Trafford

Yorkshire 242 (M.P. Vaughan 64, A.P. Grayson 64, Wasim Akram 8 for 68) and 258 (D. Byas 73, R.B. Richardson 50, Wasim Akram 4 for 57)

Lancashire 167 (G.D. Mendis 55, D. Gough 4 for 46, P.J. Hartley 4 for 62) and 314 (J.P. Crawley 80, M.A. Robinson 6 for 62)

Yorkshire won by 19 runs

Yorkshire 21 pts., Lancashire 4 pts.

at Lord's

Middlesex 402 (J.E. Emburey 120, K.R. Brown 72, K.M. Curran 4 for 82) and 11 for 0

Northamptonshire 232 (R.J. Bailey 95 not out) and 180 (J.E. Emburey 4 for 38)

Middlesex won by 10 wickets

Middlesex 23 pts., Northamptonshire 3 pts.

at Weston-super-Mare

Somerset 112 and 193 (D.J. Millns 5 for 78, A.D. Mullally 4 for 63)

Leicestershire 320 (J.J. Whitaker 92, P.A. Nixon 61, G.D. Rose 6 for 83)

Leicestershire won by an innings and 15 runs

Leicestershire 23 pts., Somerset 4 pts.

at Worcester

Kent 189 (M.A. Ealham 54 not out, C.M. Tolley 5 for 55) and 249 (R.K. Illingworth 4 for 68)

Worcestershire 568 for 7 dec. (G.R. Haynes 158, T.S. Curtis 127, S.J. Rhodes 100 not out)

Worcestershire won by an innings and 130 runs

Worcestershire 24 pts., Kent 1 pt.

Wayne Larkins – a tower of strength for ailing Durham. (Tony Marshall/Sports-Line)

Hancock who added 102. Both were dropped, but they batted well, and Alleyne led his side past 300, hitting 14 boundaries in his 4½-hour innings. Prichard batted down the order for Essex due to a viral infection, and he helped to raise a sagging side from 148 for 7 to 216. Childs and Ilott then bowled Essex back into the game, but the batsmen never properly paced their challenge in spite of reaching 173 for 2, and the match limped to a draw.

In contrast, the Roses match produced a fine and close contest. Michael Vaughan made his first-class debut for Yorkshire and struck an impressive 64 after his side had been asked to bat first. The outstanding performance of the opening day, however, came from Wasim Akram who took a career best 8 for 68. He was halted, temporarily, only by the resilience of the Yorkshire tail. Surprisingly, Lancashire were to struggle more desperately than Yorkshire had done and trailed by 75 on the first innings. The White Rose county seemed set for a large score in the second innings, but their last six wickets went down for 42 runs, Wasim Akram finishing with his best match figures of 12 for 125. Needing 334 to win, Lancashire reached 137 for 2 by the close of play on Saturday. Crawley and Speak went early on the last morning. Watkinson, Hegg and Wasim all raised hopes of a Lancashire victory after Fairbrother had perished to a wild hoick, but Hartley and Robinson nibbled away accurately, and Gough produced the killer blow when he trapped Chapple leg before.

Middlesex effectively won the Britannic Assurance County Championship when they disposed of challengers Northamptonshire with the utmost ease. Middlesex slipped to 161 for 5 on the opening day but, in a stand which continued into the second morning, Emburey and Brown added 161. On his 41st birthday, Emburey hit his second century of the season, and then took three wickets as the visitors fell apart. Only Bailey offered serious resistance, and Northamptonshire never seemed to have a remote chance of avoiding the follow-on. Norman Cowans bowled well in both innings, and with batsmen like Curran – stumped first ball as he charged down the wicket – seemingly seeking a day off, the visitors' challenge ended in a whimper.

On the suspicious pitch at Weston-super-Mare, Somerset were twice routed by the Leicestershire seamers. Whitaker, thriving on captaincy, and Nixon showed admirable technique in the circumstances, adding 141 after five wickets had fallen for 76. This partnership made possible Leicestershire's victory in three days.

Meanwhile, Worcestershire overwhelmed Kent. Two young men gave them particular pleasure: Chris Tolley took a career best 5 for 55 on the opening day and, on the second, Gavin Haynes joined Tim Curtis in a second-wicket stand of 262. Both batsmen reached hundreds, and, in the case of the 23-year-old Haynes, it was a maiden first-class century. His was a patient, six-hour innings in which he struck 27 fours. Steve Rhodes joined in the fun with his first century of the season on the third day, and Kent were left to bat for survival. They lost four

Surrey's late-season decline continued with defeat in three days at Ilkeston. Put in to bat, they were rushed out by the Derbyshire seam attack, and Bowler and Morris then began the home county's innings with a partnership of 192. On the Saturday, Surrey slumped to 150 for 6. Adam Hollioake, making his championship debut, hit 123 off 138 balls with 2 sixes and 15 fours. He and Kersey added 138 in 44 overs, but they could not prevent Derbyshire from winning with ease.

Having reached the NatWest final, Warwickshire, too, seemed to be in a losing vein. They batted only moderately at Darlington, and Parker and Daley added 185 in 63 overs to put Durham in a strong position after four wickets had gone for 79. Warwickshire showed consistent resolution in their second innings, but Wayne Larkins and Graeme Fowler scored 202 for the first wicket as Durham went in search of their first home victory of the season. It came with 27 balls to spare, Larkins hitting a match-winning 113 off 135 balls. During the course of the match, Simon Brown became the first Durham bowler to capture 100 first-class wickets.

Glamorgan's championship challenge was effectively ended when they lost to Hampshire. Paul Terry occupied 125 overs in scoring 174 on the opening day, and with Marshall playing an enterprising innings on the second morning, Hampshire took a grip on the game which was never relaxed. Glamorgan lost their last five wickets for 63 runs, but they did avoid the follow-on. The collapse was even more marked in the second innings, the last seven wickets falling for 56 runs to Marshall and Udal. One of the heroes of the match was Glamorgan's Robert Croft who sent down 96 overs in the two Hampshire innings and took 9 for 231.

Seeking their third win in a row, Gloucestershire were lifted from the uncertainty of 91 for 4 – three of the wickets to Derek Pringle – by Mark Alleyne and Tim

wickets before the close, and although Fleming was defiant on the last morning, Worcestershire won shortly after lunch. Benson was unable to bat because of a knee injury.

AXA EQUITY & LAW LEAGUE

22 August *at Ilkeston*

Derbyshire 201 (P.D. Bowler 76 not out, C.J. Adams 66)
Surrey 203 for 5 (D.M. Ward 81 not out, A.W. Smith 58)

Surrey (4 pts.) won by 5 wickets

at Darlington

Warwickshire 195 (Asif Din 66, A.C. Cummins 4 for 29)
Durham 197 for 8

Durham (4 pts.) won by 2 wickets

at Swansea

Hampshire 207 for 8 (R.A. Smith 75)
Glamorgan 209 for 4 (H. Morris 81, P.A. Cottey 75 not out)

Glamorgan (4 pts.) won by 6 wickets

at Bristol

Gloucestershire 135
Essex 139 for 7

Essex (4 pts.) won by 3 wickets

at Old Trafford

Yorkshire 173 for 9
Lancashire 174 for 7 (Wasim Akram 51 not out)

Lancashire (4 pts.) won by 3 wickets

at Lord's

Middlesex 185 for 6 (D.L. Haynes 67)
Northamptonshire 173 for 6 (A.J. Lamb 65 not out)

Northamptonshire (4 pts.) won on faster scoring rate

at Weston-super-Mare

Somerset 240 for 8 (N.A. Folland 107 not out, M.N. Lathwell 75, G.J. Parsons 4 for 31)
Leicestershire 144

Somerset (4 pts.) won by 96 runs

at Worcester

Worcestershire 186 for 9 (A.P. Igglesden 5 for 29)
Kent 143 for 5

Kent (4 pts.) won on faster scoring rate

The race for the Sunday League title between Glamorgan and Kent moved into the final lap with both counties still separated by just two points. Both sides won comfortably. Morris and Cottey batted splendidly for Glamorgan,

and Igglesden's five wickets in 10 overs was a match-winning performance for Kent in the rain-affected game at Worcester. Elsewhere, Nick Folland hit a maiden Sunday League century as Somerset won their second match of the season, and Bowler and the bubbling Adams began Derbyshire's innings with a stand of 104, only to see Surrey win with 4.5 overs to spare.

26, 27, 28 and **30 August** *at Colchester*

Essex 148 (A.R.C. Fraser 4 for 19, N.G. Cowans 4 for 43) and 153 (N. Hussain 73)
Middlesex 167 (M.C. Ilott 6 for 42) and 135 for 3 (M.W. Gatting 76 not out)

Middlesex won by 7 wickets
Middlesex 20 pts., Essex 4 pts.

at Abergavenny

Glamorgan 292 (I.V.A. Richards 95, M.P. Maynard 93, C.A. Walsh 4 for 71) and 297 (M.P. Maynard 95, P.A. Cottey 63, D.L. Hemp 52)
Gloucestershire 158 (B.C. Broad 72) and 349 (G.D. Hodgson 126, C.A. Walsh 57, S.L. Watkin 4 for 106, R.D.B. Croft 4 for 115)

Glamorgan won by 82 runs
Glamorgan 22 pts., Gloucestershire 4 pts.

at Portsmouth

Sussex 439 (D.M. Smith 150, M.P. Speight 121, K.D. James 4 for 55) and 318 for 7 dec. (C.W.J. Athey 74, I.D.K. Salisbury 63 not out, A.P. Wells 57)
Hampshire 349 (D.I. Gower 113, A.N. Aymes 107 not out) and 351 (R.A. Smith 98, S.D. Udal 79 not out, I.D.K. Salisbury 5 for 95)

Sussex won by 57 runs
Sussex 24 pts., Hampshire 5 pts.

at Lytham

Kent 263 (M.A. Ealham 85, S.A. Marsh 63, Wasim Akram 5 for 69) and 427 for 8 dec. (C.L. Hooper 166 not out, M.A. Ealham 79)
Lancashire 328 (J.P. Crawley 78, N.H. Fairbrother 75, M.M. Patel 5 for 107) and 203 (G.D. Mendis 94, M.M. Patel 7 for 75)

Kent won by 159 runs
Kent 21 pts., Lancashire 6 pts.

at Northampton

Northamptonshire 467 (A.J. Lamb 162, N.A. Felton 105, R.J. Bailey 59, A.D. Mullally 4 for 111)
Leicestershire 307 (T.J. Boon 110, V.J. Wells 50) and 344 for 8 dec. (B.F. Smith 84, P.E. Robinson 54)

Match drawn
Northamptonshire 8 pts., Leicestershire 6 pts.

at Trent Bridge

Nottinghamshire 500 for 8 dec. (P.R. Pollard 180, W.A. Dessaur 104, R.T. Robinson 78) and 241 for 4 dec. (P.R. Pollard 91, W.A. Dessaur 82)

Derbyshire 403 for 6 dec. (C.J. Adams 175, P.D. Bowler 153 not out) and 129 for 3 (K.J. Barnett 55 not out)

Match drawn

Nottinghamshire 6 pts., Derbyshire 5 pts.

at The Oval

Somerset 275 for 9 dec. (I. Fletcher 63) and 344 for 7 dec. (R.J. Harden 132, R.J. Turner 70, J.E. Benjamin 4 for 79)

Surrey 199 (A.P. van Troost 5 for 47) and 139

Somerset won by 281 runs

Somerset 22 pts., Surrey 4 pts.

at Edgbaston

Warwickshire 206 (D.P. Ostler 56) and 201 (Asif Din 63, D.P. Ostler 50, P.J. Newport 4 for 38, R.K. Illingworth 4 for 55)

Worcestershire 397 (S.J. Rhodes 101, P.J. Newport 76, N.M.K. Smith 5 for 103) and 11 for 0

Worcestershire won by 10 wickets

Worcestershire 21 pts., Warwickshire 3 pts.

at Leeds

Yorkshire 400 (C. White 146, M.D. Moxon 77, P. Bainbridge 5 for 53) and 228 for 8 dec. (S.A. Kellett 85, P. Bainbridge 4 for 65)

Durham 332 (G. Fowler 138, S. Hutton 73, D. Gough 5 for 79) and 229 for 7 (P. Bainbridge 103 not out)

Match drawn

Yorkshire 7 pts., Durham 5 pts.

27 August *at Haslingden*

League Cricket Conference 231 for 8 (P.R. Sleep 71)

Zimbabwe 232 for 2 (A. Flower 75, D.L. Houghton 56 not out, G.W. Flower 51)

Zimbabwe won by 8 wickets

Middlesex won the Britannic Assurance County Championship when they beat Essex inside two days at Colchester and Northamptonshire failed to win against Leicestershire. Essex chose to bat first on a wicket which was quick and on which the seamers found help for movement. Twenty wickets fell on the first day, with Cowans and Fraser doing the damage for Middlesex, and Ilott and Stephenson for Essex. The home side were 60 for 4 in their second innings, but Hussain showed that the pitch held no devils. Only Garnham gave him adequate support, however, and the last five wickets fell for 30 runs. A third-wicket stand of 93 between Gatting and Ramprakash virtually assured Middlesex of victory and a

well-deserved title. It was fitting that the new champions should defeat the old to gain the prize, but it was a somewhat premature climax to the season.

Glamorgan maintained their spirited challenge to the last, but they had to work hard to beat Gloucestershire. Maynard and Richards added 187 for Glamorgan's second wicket in less than two hours of superb stroke-play. The stand was ended by the unlikely medium pace of Tim Hancock who took three wickets in nine balls. Gloucestershire crumbled against Glamorgan's varied attack, and with Maynard again just missing a century, the home side left Gloucestershire with an improbable target of 432. To their credit, the visitors made a brave fight of it, Hodgson batting six hours for his 126, but a middle-order collapse ended hopes of a sensational victory.

There was massive scoring at Portsmouth where Smith and Speight scored 214 for Sussex's third wicket. The runs came in 62 overs, and Speight's century was his second in three innings. Moores hit well at the close of the innings, but a cultured knock from Gower and a maiden first-class hundred from wicket-keeper Adrian Aymes kept Hampshire in contention. Eventually, Wells set the home side a target of 409. Hampshire made a spirited start and were 198 for 2, but Giddins and Stephenson wrecked the middle-order, and Salisbury mopped up the tail with only Udal showing defiance.

Kent achieved a remarkable victory over Lancashire at Lytham. Winning the toss, Kent slumped to 116 for 6 before Marsh and Ealham added 100. Solid batting by the home side took them to a first-innings lead of 65. Crawley again showed his class, and Fairbrother gave a welcome glimpse of form with his highest score of the season. Min Patel and Hooper bowled well, and the West Indian went on to play a magnificent innings of 166 which gave Kent a position of strength. Hooper and Ealham added 156 for the seventh wicket, and Marsh's declaration left Lancashire the daunting task of trying to score 363 in 91 overs. In spite of Mendis' heroic 94, Lancashire were beaten just after four o'clock on the last afternoon, their sixth defeat in seven championship matches. On a pitch offering only slow turn, Min Patel bowled with intelligence and variety to claim a career best 7 for 75, and best match figures of 12 for 182.

Centuries from Felton and Lamb gave Northamptonshire the advantage against Leicestershire, who were forced to follow-on in spite of Tim Boon's century. Smith, out of form and out of the side for much of the season, and Robinson defied Northants and determined that Middlesex would be champions. Smith held out for nearly 2½ hours, and it was he more than anyone who frustrated the home side.

The pitch at Trent Bridge was a paradise for batsmen and a source of fascination for the statistician. Pollard and Dessaur began with 291 for Nottinghamshire's first wicket. Pollard hit the highest score of his career, and Dessaur a maiden championship hundred. Bowler and the highly promising Adams, who hit a career best 175, shared a second-wicket stand of 275 for Derbyshire. Then Pollard and Dessaur began Nottinghamshire's second innings with a 180-run stand, and the match was drawn.

A limp Surrey side who lost Stewart through injury during the match surrendered meekly to Somerset at The Oval. Facing a total of 275, Surrey lost both openers for ducks, and only a ninth-wicket stand of 59 between Kendrick and Waqar Younis gave them any respectability. Acting captain Harden and Turner, who had deposed Burns as wicket-keeper for reasons not explained, added 151 for Somerset's third wicket when they batted again, and, following Harden's declaration, Surrey lost Darren Bicknell before the close. The game was all over before lunch on the last day, with Van Troost again bowling in a fast and hostile manner.

Steve Rhodes hit his second century in succession as Worcestershire routed Warwickshire, whose only thoughts were on the NatWest final, while White hit a maiden first-class century for Yorkshire against Durham. Fowler, who had seemed to be one of Durham's less wise acquisitions, restored pride with a century, but his side trailed on the first innings and, in the end, owed their salvation very much to the all-round cricket of Phil Bainbridge.

AXA EQUITY & LAW LEAGUE

---

29 **August** at Colchester

Middlesex 236 for 6 (D.L. Haynes 101, M.R. Ramprakash 53)

Essex 236 (Salim Malik 67, P.N. Weekes 4 for 46)

Match tied

Essex 2 pts., Middlesex 2 pts.

at Ebbw Vale

Glamorgan 242 for 9 (M.P. Maynard 69, A.M. Smith 4 for 56)

Gloucestershire 211 (S.G. Hinks 62)

Glamorgan (4 pts.) won by 31 runs

at Portsmouth

Sussex 312 for 8 (A.P. Wells 127, N.J. Lenham 69, F.D. Stephenson 59, C.A. Connor 4 for 69)

Hampshire 313 for 2 (R.A. Smith 129, V.P. Terry 124 not out)

Hampshire (4 pts.) won by 8 wickets

at Old Trafford

Lancashire 192 (G.D. Lloyd 53, M.V. Fleming 4 for 56)

Kent 193 for 4 (C.L. Hooper 87 not out)

Kent (4 pts.) won by 6 wickets

at Northampton

Leicestershire 196 for 6 (B.F. Smith 53 not out)

Northamptonshire 200 for 3 (R.J. Warren 71 not out)

Northamptonshire (4 pts.) won by 7 wickets

at Trent Bridge

Nottinghamshire 329 for 6 (P.R. Pollard 91, R.T. Robinson 78 not out, P. Johnson 75)

Derbyshire 187 (A.S. Rollins 57)

Nottinghamshire (4 pts.) won by 142 runs

at The Oval

Somerset 238 for 8 (M.N. Lathwell 85, Waqar Younis 4 for 25)

Surrey 241 for 5 (D.J. Bicknell 76, P.D. Atkins 55)

Surrey (4 pts.) won by 5 wickets

at Edgbaston

Warwickshire 188 for 7

Worcestershire 144 (P.A. Smith 5 for 36)

Warwickshire (4 pts.) won by 44 runs

at Leeds

Durham 230 for 9 (W. Larkins 114, P.W.G. Parker 54)

Yorkshire 217 for 9 (M.D. Moxon 64)

Durham (4 pts.) won by 13 runs

Glamorgan and Kent both negotiated hurdles comfortably to enter the last two matches in the Sunday League devoid of any challengers. In spite of Haynes' century, Essex were strolling to victory over Middlesex. They then contrived to lose four wickets for seven runs, and tied the match only with two off the last ball. Boden was run out in going for what would have been the winning run. Sussex scored a mighty 312 with another century from skipper Wells, only to lose by eight wickets with a ball to spare. Terry and Smith put on 235 for Hampshire's second wicket.

30 **August** at Scarborough

President's World XI 256 for 6 (D.M. Jones 101, K.L.T. Arthurton 52, E.A. Brandes 4 for 32)

Zimbabwe 256 for 6 (A.D.R. Campbell 102, A. Flower 101)

Zimbabwe won on faster scoring rate over first 15 overs

31 **August, 1, 2 and 3 September** at Chester-le-Street

Durham 308 (J. Wood 63 not out, W. Larkins 62) and 164 (D.B. Pennett 5 for 36, R.A. Pick 5 for 53)

Nottinghamshire 629 (C.C. Lewis 247, P. Johnson 130, B.N. French 123, A.C. Cummins 4 for 137)

Nottinghamshire won by an innings and 157 runs

Nottinghamshire 24 pts., Durham 5 pts.

at Canterbury

Kent 479 (G.R. Cowdrey 139, M.A. Ealham 76, D.P. Fulton 75, M.N. Bowen 4 for 124) and 165 for 3 dec. (N.J. Llong 54 not out, D.P. Fulton 52)

Northamptonshire 331 (M.B. Loye 153 not out, D. Ripley 54,

M.A. Ealham 5 for 66) and 140 for 7 (C.L. Hooper 4 for 35)

Match drawn
Kent 6 pts., Northamptonshire 4 pts.

at Leicester

Leicestershire 158 and 271 (J.J. Whitaker 126)
Yorkshire 202 (D. Byas 62, A.D. Mullally 5 for 67) and 153 (D.J. Millns 4 for 37, A.D. Mullally 4 for 41)

Leicestershire won by 74 runs
Leicestershire 20 pts., Yorkshire 5 pts.

at Taunton

Gloucestershire 256 (T.H.C. Hancock 76, R.C. Russell 65, Mushtaq Ahmed 5 for 81) and 263 (S.G. Hinks 68, B.C. Broad 58, H.R.J. Trump 4 for 74, Mushtaq Ahmed 4 for 109)
Somerset 382 (G.D. Rose 124, A.N. Hayhurst 117, R.J. Harden 70, M.C.J. Ball 6 for 123) and 115 (M.C.J. Ball 8 for 46)

Gloucestershire won by 22 runs
Gloucestershire 20 pts., Somerset 6 pts.

at The Oval

Surrey 380 (D.J. Bicknell 122, A.D. Brown 62, K.J. Shine 6 for 97) and 281 for 8 (A.J. Hollioake 70, A.D. Brown 54, D.J. Bicknell 50, D.P.J. Flint 4 for 64)
Hampshire 559 (R.A. Smith 127, M.C.J. Nicholas 95, V.P. Terry 91, R.M.F. Cox 63, C.A. Connor 59)

Match drawn
Hampshire 7 pts., Surrey 5 pts.

at Hove

Sussex 591 (J.A. North 114, K. Greenfield 107, A.P. Wells 106, M.P. Speight 95, N.J. Lenham 52, M.C. Ilott 4 for 119) and 312 for 3 dec. (N.J. Lenham 149, C.W.J. Athey 96, K. Greenfield 50 not out)
Essex 493 for 4 dec. (P.J. Prichard 225 not out, Salim Malik 73, N. Hussain 70 not out, M.C. Ilott 51) and 412 for 3 (J.P. Stephenson 122, N. Hussain 118, G.A. Gooch 74 not out, Salim Malik 63 not out)

Essex won by 7 wickets
Essex 21 pts., Sussex 5 pts.

at Worcester

Lancashire 320 (R.K. Illingworth 4 for 91) and 330 for 8 dec. (N.J. Speak 122, N.H. Fairbrother 62, M. Watkinson 52)
Worcestershire 322 (G.A. Hick 91, T.S. Curtis 52, G.R. Haynes 50, P.A.J. DeFreitas 4 for 48) and 329 for 9 (G.A. Hick 90, T.S. Curtis 65)

Worcestershire won by 1 wicket
Worcestershire 23 pts., Lancashire 7 pts.

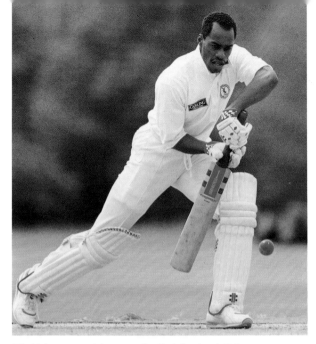

The highest score of the season for Chris Lewis – 247 for Nottinghamshire against Durham at the end of August. (Alan Cozzi)

1, 2 and **3** September *at Scarborough*

Zimbabwe 160 (G.W. Flower 53, R.A. Harper 6 for 71) and 279 for 2 (G.W. Flower 130, K.J. Arnott 111 not out)
President's World XI 460 for 7 dec. (P.R. Sleep 151, K.L.T. Arthurton 103, R.A. Harper 76 not out)

Match drawn

Durham were put in to bat at Chester-le-Street and were 191 for 7 against the Nottinghamshire seamers before John Wood hit a maiden first-class fifty and led them to three batting bonus points. In 110 overs on the second day, Nottinghamshire scored 508 for 6, and, in all, their innings occupied only 132.1 overs. Their total of 629 was boosted by 70 extras, but on the second day, Johnson passed 1,000 runs for the season as he and Lewis shared a stand of 178 after four wickets had fallen for 71. On a bowlers' burial ground, Lewis and French added a record 301 for the seventh wicket. Lewis batted for seven hours to record his first double century in county cricket. He faced 371 balls and hit 35 fours and 2 sixes. French also hit a career best, and Pennett became the third Nottinghamshire player to give a best performance when he took 5 for 36 and, with Pick, destroyed a limp Durham side in 49 overs in their second innings to give the Midlands county victory in three days.

Umpire Dicky Bird earned the wrath of the Northamptonshire side when he recalled Graham Cowdrey, reversing his decision after he had judged the Kent man caught behind off Ambrose. Cowdrey went on to make 139, and, with Ealham's lusty hitting, 153 were added for the seventh wicket from 26 overs. An obviously unhappy and deflated Northamptonshire side struggled to avoid the follow-on, and that they did so was due almost entirely to

Loye, who was supported by Ripley in a sixth-wicket stand of 123. Rain on the last day hampered the chance of a result, which was probably just in the circumstances.

Leicestershire struggled against the Yorkshire seam attack and were bowled out in 55.4 overs, but the visitors' batsmen failed to press home the advantage that their bowlers had given them. Reprieved, Leicestershire, inspired by skipper James Whitaker whose end-of-season form was joyous, batted their way back into the game. Needing 228 to win, and with the better part of two days in which to get the runs, Yorkshire began well enough before Millns took wickets late on the second day, the rock-like White falling to a brilliant catch by Hepworth at extra cover. Yorkshire ended the day on 139 for 7, and there was no recovery on the last morning.

At Taunton, Somerset took a first-innings lead of 126. This was due mainly to a second-wicket stand of 117 between Hayhurst and Harden, and to a robust century from Graham Rose. Off-break bowler Martyn Ball, out of favour for much of the season, gave Gloucestershire some hope with a career best six wickets, and Broad and Hinks then wiped off the arrears before being separated. The loss of four wickets for 19 runs slowed Gloucestershire's progress, and only some lively hitting from Babington, who added 37 for the last wicket with Davies, gave the visitors any cause for further joy. Needing 138 to win, Somerset were confronted immediately by off-spinner Ball who took two wickets. Cooper had Hayhurst caught by Ball, and Somerset ended the third day on 18 for 3. Ball gnawed away at them on the last morning and finished with career-best figures for both innings and match, giving his side victory by 22 runs.

There was less excitement at The Oval where a placid wicket produced the dullest of draws. Darren Bicknell made his century off 238 balls on the opening day when Surrey reached 327 for 5. Smith and Terry began Hampshire's innings with a partnership of 170. On the second day, Cardigan Connor hit a brisk career best, and Nicholas and Cox added 132 in 45 overs for the sixth wicket, but it was mostly dour stuff. Surrey emphasised the defensive qualities of the match when they batted throughout the last day.

There was a record at Hove where 1,808 runs were scored for the loss of 20 wickets in the four days. Seven batsmen made hundreds and two were out in the nineties. There were seven other scores of 50 or more. North's 114 was the first century of his career, and Prichard dominated with a century off 94 balls before racing on to 225 out of 493 in 104.4 overs. Eventually, Essex were set to make 411 in 84 overs. Stephenson and Hussain shared a second-wicket stand of 215 in 51 overs, and Salim Malik and Gooch took Essex to victory with an unbroken partnership of 143. Good for the averages, but is this really what the TCCB and, more importantly, the public want? Oh, for uncovered wickets and three-day matches, and a proper contest between bat and ball!

There were thrills of a different nature at Worcester where Lancashire batted with consistency to score 320. Curtis and Hick added 117 for Worcestershire's second wicket, and Haynes hit another promising fifty, but DeFreitas and Wasim restricted the home side's lead to

two. Fairbrother and Speak hit 119 for Lancashire's second-innings fourth wicket, with Speak – a star of 1992 – hitting his first championship hundred of 1993. Set to make 329 in 76 overs, Worcestershire were well served by Curtis and Hick who hit 124 in 21 overs, but then they lost their way a little as Martin took wickets in successive overs. Some fierce bowling from Wasim, splendid catches by DeFreitas and spirited batting from Newport set up a fine finish. Illingworth and Benjamin had to score 34 for the last wicket to win the match. They did so with the help of two byes and a wide in Wasim's last over.

Exciting centuries from Sleep and Arthurton were countered by Grant Flower and Kevin Arnott, who shared an opening stand of 207 in 252 minutes to give Zimbabwe a draw in the festival match at Scarborough.

NORTHERN ELECTRIC TROPHY

4 September *at Scarborough*

Durham 181 for 1 (W. Larkins 107 not out, G. Fowler 55)
Yorkshire 184 for 3 (M.P. Vaughan 57, D. Byas 53)

Yorkshire won by 7 wickets

NATWEST TROPHY FINAL
SUSSEX v. WARWICKSHIRE, at Lord's

A fine day, a capacity crowd and Lord's at its best – the perfect setting for an astonishing game of cricket which will long be remembered by those who saw it. Neither Sussex nor Warwickshire could claim to be among the strongest sides in the country. Sussex were short on bowling, and Warwickshire were short on batting, but, in

Martin Speight's glorious innings comes to an end as he skies an attempted hook. (Stephen Munday/Allsport)

such circumstances, it is the stronger bowling side that generally triumphs. So it proved here, but in no logical or foreseen manner.

Reeve won the toss and asked Sussex to bat: Lord's generally is at its best for bowlers in the early morning. His decision seemed justified when, in Munton's first over – the second of the day – Athey attempted a wild hook shot – totally out of character – and gloved a looping ball to the keeper. Athey was meant to be the rock on which Sussex were to found their innings and he was out, rashly, second ball.

Then the mood changed. Martin Speight immediately pulled 2 fours off the front foot. This was just a hint of the excitement to come as this highly talented and thrilling stroke-maker set about the Warwickshire bowling with joyful abandon. He was beaten by Small, but he was never downed, and he responded by driving him straight to the Nursery end boundary. He went down the wicket to hit Munton back over his head for four, and he repeated the shot in the 10th over but this time it went for six and brought up the fifty. Six overs later, the hundred was posted. This was heady stuff at any time. Before coffee break, it was stunning.

Speight's fifty came off as many balls, but next delivery he swept at Reeve and skied the ball over the keeper's head. Running back, Piper held the catch. Speight had set a pattern for the day, and there could only be disappointment at his going. It had been a spellbinding innings.

In comparison, the stand between Smith and Wells was sedate. Smith's fifty was delayed because he went for a quick single and umpire Bird asked for the television verdict – unnecessarily, it seemed – to determine whether he had been run out. He had not been, and he received his belated applause. He batted very well indeed, providing not simply a base but also a constant source of aggression. At lunch, Sussex were 172 for 2, and Warwickshire, surely, were out of contention. Wells was out almost straight after lunch when he swept at Neil Smith and was bowled. Stephenson was promoted to maintain the momentum which Neil Smith and Twose had lessened, but he soon hit to extra cover. Lenham did regain the initiative, immediately producing two majestic cover-drives off Twose which raced to the boundary. He then adopted less classical methods – but equally effective – and hit a most impressive 58 off 51 balls before moving across his stumps in an attempt to clout Reeve to leg. Lenham and Smith added 119 in 16 overs and, with Warwickshire in total disarray, 83 runs came from the last 10 overs of the innings.

David Smith – upright, ever watchful, ever on the offensive – hit 124 off 179 balls, hitting a six and 9 fours and playing an innings which, to all sane judges, had given Sussex the match. He led them to the highest score in a Lord's final and, surely, we believed, to victory. He was out off the last ball of the innings, sadly and stupidly. Greenfield tried a reverse sweep when he should have gone for the clout, and Smith was run out as they tried to take a bye to the keeper. It was a wicket which would have cost them the match, but for later events.

By the fifth over, Warwickshire were 18 for 2. Ratcliffe

NATWEST TROPHY FINAL – SUSSEX v. WARWICKSHIRE
4 September 1993 at Lord's

SUSSEX

D.M. Smith	run out	124
C.W.J. Athey	c Piper, **b** Munton	0
M.P. Speight	c Piper, **b** Reeve	50
A.P. Wells (capt)	**b** N.M.K. Smith	33
F.D. Stephenson	c N.M.K. Smith, **b** Twose	3
N.J. Lenham	lbw, **b** Reeve	58
K. Greenfield	not out	8
*P. Moores		
I.D.K. Salisbury		
A.C.S. Pigott		
E.S.H. Giddins		
Extras	lb **11**, w **18**, nb **16**	45
(60 overs)	(for 6 wickets)	321

WARWICKSHIRE

A.J. Moles	c Moores, **b** Pigott	2
J.D. Ratcliffe	**b** Stephenson	13
D.P. Ostler	c Smith, **b** Salisbury	25
P.A. Smith	c Moores, **b** Stephenson	60
Asif Din	c Speight, **b** Giddins	104
D.A. Reeve (capt)	not out	81
R.G. Twose	not out	2
N.M.K. Smith		
*K.J. Piper		
G.C. Small		
T.A. Munton		
Extras	b 3, lb 13, w 13, nb 6	35
(60 overs)	(for 5 wickets)	322

	O	M	R	W
Small	12	–	71	–
Munton	9	–	67	1
P.A. Smith	7	–	45	–
Reeve	12	1	60	2
N.M.K. Smith	12	1	37	1
Twose	8	1	30	1

	O	M	R	W
Giddins	12	–	57	1
Stephenson	12	2	51	2
Pigott	11	–	74	1
Salisbury	11	–	59	1
Greenfield	7	–	31	–
Lenham	7	–	34	–

FALL OF WICKETS
1–4, 2–107, 3–183, 4–190, 5–309, 6–321

FALL OF WICKETS
1–18, 2–18, 3–93, 4–164, 5–306

Umpires: H.D. Bird & M.J. Kitchen   *Man of the Match:* Asif Din   *Warwickshire won by 5 wickets*

was bowled through the gate, and Moles had reached and edged Pigott's first delivery to the keeper. Stephenson apart, the Sussex bowling looked no more demanding than had the Warwickshire bowling, and there were some lapses in the field which did not bode well. Salisbury failed to find any sort of length, but in his second over, he accounted for Ostler who hit a full toss into the hands of David Smith at mid-wicket. At tea, Warwickshire were 107 for 3 from 25 overs. Sussex sipped happily.

Paul Smith had batted with his usual positivity and, in company with Asif Din, he began to expose the limitations of the Sussex out-cricket. They added 71 in 15 overs, and Wells, sensing the danger, brought back Stephenson who had Smith caught behind, although clearly the batsman disagreed with the decision. Reeve could well have been caught first delivery when the ball popped up on the leg side – he *would* have fallen to a more agile fielding side. He certainly should have gone when he lobbed a leading edge back to the bowler, Stephenson, who turned and tried to catch the ball one-handed and thereby obstructed Wells, who might well have taken the catch. That was to be Sussex's last chance.

In 23 overs, Asif Din and Dermot Reeve added 142 runs. They clubbed the ball to all parts of the ground. At times, there appeared to be gaps everywhere, with Greenfield on the boundary in front of the Grand Stand performing lone heroics. Asif Din was wrist and subtlety; Reeve uninhibited clout. Warwickshire were further encouraged when Pigott proved temperamentally ill-suited to the occasion, bowling two beamers at Reeve, yielding no-balls and earning a reprimand. This was a dreadful lapse by a seasoned professional, and it cost his side dear. Salisbury was brought back at the Pavilion end, but he is now a sad imitation of the bowler who played for England only months previously.

In a match in which several men were in contention for the individual accolade, the honour was eventually to go to Asif Din whose 104 off 106 balls was a memorable and masterly innings, marked as much for the placing of the ball and the eagerness between the wickets as for a constant peppering of the boundary. With one over to go in the gathering gloom, he hit Giddins to cover, and Twose joined Reeve with 16 runs needed. Giddins bowled a splendid penultimate over, conceding just five runs and claiming that wicket of Asif Din, so that when Stephenson bowled the last over, 14 were wanted to tie the scores and so win the match. The West Indian offered Reeve too much room outside the off stump, and the first ball was hit back over his head for four. The second was clubbed to long-on, but Wells' throw to Moores would have had Reeve run out, had the wicket-keeper not missed the stumps with his little, excited flick of the ball. There were two more off the third ball, and a crashing boundary through extra cover from the fourth. The fifth ball brought only an edged single to short fine-leg, and so Roger Twose, having endured a season of almost relentless misery, was faced with the prospect of having to hit the last ball for a run to win the trophy. Wells' field was somewhat messy and ragged, with a heavy concentration on the left-hander's off side. Twose kept his nerve and hit the ball over gully. The batsmen ran two, even though the

Roger Twose hits the last ball of the match for two to win the NatWest Trophy for Warwickshire. (Patrick Eagar)

umpires had uprooted the stumps by the time the second was completed. Sussex's record score for a NatWest final had lasted just half a match, and Warwickshire had won an astonishing and truly wonderful victory.

There was sympathy for Sussex, and for David Smith and Martin Speight in particular. There were heaps of congratulations for Warwickshire and for the controversial captain Dermot Reeve whose 81 had come off 84 balls at a time when all seemed lost. The man does not know defeat.

5 September *at Brecon*

Glamorgan 221 for 8 (S.P. James 77)
Zimbabwe 168

Glamorgan won by 53 runs

 AXA EQUITY & LAW LEAGUE

5 September *at Chester-le-Street*

Nottinghamshire 260 for 6 (M. Saxelby 100 not out)
Durham 262 for 7 (W. Larkins 128, R.A. Pick 4 for 68)

Durham (4 pts.) won by 3 wickets

at Canterbury

Northamptonshire 165 for 8
Kent 166 for 7 (N.J. Llong 64 not out)

Kent (4 pts.) won by 3 wickets

at Leicester

Yorkshire 318 for 7 (M.J. Foster 118, R.J. Blakey 96)
Leicestershire 253 (P.E. Robinson 71)

Yorkshire (4 pts.) won by 65 runs

Alan Wells is bowled by Neil Smith for 33. (Adrian Murrell/Allsport)

at Taunton

Somerset 111
Gloucestershire 115 for 7

Gloucestershire (4 pts.) won by 3 wickets

at The Oval

Surrey 213 (A.J. Stewart 83)
Hampshire 136 (J. Boiling 4 for 26)

Surrey (4 pts.) won by 77 runs

at Worcester

Worcestershire 188 for 9
Lancashire 191 for 4 (N.H. Fairbrother 56 not out, N.J. Speak 55)

Lancashire (4 pts.) won by 6 wickets

Kent went to the top of the table by beating Northamptonshire while Glamorgan were engaged in a friendly match with the Zimbabwe touring side. This meant that the Sunday League would be decided on the last afternoon of the season. The Kent heroes were Nigel Llong and Duncan Spencer. They came together at 141 for 7, but kept calm to win the match. Llong hit his highest score in the competition, as did Mark Saxelby of Nottinghamshire whose hundred came off 133 balls. The outstanding performance of the day, however, came from Yorkshire's Michael Foster who hit 118 off 70 balls with 8 sixes and 7 fours. He and Blakey added 190 in 21 overs for the fifth wicket.

7 September *at Hove*

Sussex 290 for 7 (K. Greenfield 65 not out, D.M. Smith 51)
Essex 229 (N. Shahid 64, G.A. Gooch 58, F.D. Stephenson 5 for 23)

Sussex (4 pts.) won on faster scoring rate

Essex lost four wickets in an over as they slipped to defeat in the match postponed from the Sunday because of Sussex's commitment in the NatWest final.

7 September *at Edgbaston*

Zimbabwe 209 for 8 (G.W. Flower 54, G. Whitall 52 not out)
Warwickshire 109 for 2

Match abandoned

 JOSHUA TETLEY TROPHY at Scarborough

6 September

Derbyshire 198 for 7 (A.S. Rollins 91 not out, K.J. Barnett 59, P.J. Hartley 4 for 35)
Yorkshire 199 for 1 (M.D. Moxon 86 not out, D. Byas 78 not out)

Yorkshire won by 9 wickets

7 September

Gloucestershire 219 for 9 (A.J. Wright 59)
Durham 217 (A.C. Cummins 107, A.M. Babington 6 for 44)

Gloucestershire won by 2 runs

FINAL

8 September

Yorkshire 228 for 8 (A.P. Grayson 67 not out, C.A. Walsh 5 for 24)
Gloucestershire 168 (D. Gough 4 for 32)

Yorkshire won by 60 runs

The outstanding performance in the Joshua Tetley Trophy came in the match between Durham and Gloucestershire when Cummins hit an astonishing century after Durham had been 25 for 6.

8, 9 and **10** September *at The Oval*

Surrey 304 for 7 dec. (A.D. Brown 138, A.W. Smith 60) and 189 for 9 dec.
Zimbabwe 221 for 9 dec. (G. Briant 54, A.J. Murphy 5 for 58) and 196 for 6 (A. Flower 82, M.A. Butcher 4 for 51)

Match drawn

9, 10, 11 and **13** September *at Derby*

Derbyshire 127 (K.J. Barnett 53, K.M. Curran 4 for 35) and 195 (M.J. Vandrau 58, C.E.L. Ambrose 6 for 49)
Northamptonshire 368 for 5 dec. (R.J. Bailey 103, A. Fordham 71)

Northamptonshire won by an innings and 46 runs

Northamptonshire 24 pts., Derbyshire 2 pts.

at Cardiff

Glamorgan 169 (S.J.W. Andrew 7 for 69) and 217 for 5 dec. (D.L. Hemp 90 not out)

Essex 186 (N. Hussain 51, S. Bastien 6 for 52) and 178 (J.J.B. Lewis 54, S. Bastien 6 for 53)

Glamorgan won by 22 runs

Glamorgan 20 pts., Essex 4 pts.

at Bristol

Gloucestershire 277 for 9 dec. (R.C. Russell 69 not out) and 232 for 4 dec. (M.C.J. Ball 71, R.I. Dawson 58)

Nottinghamshire 251 for 8 dec. (M. Saxelby 59, C.A. Walsh 4 for 76) and 155 for 6

Match drawn

Nottinghamshire 6 pts., Gloucestershire 5 pts.

at Southampton

Hampshire 115 (D.J. Millns 5 for 21)

Leicestershire 85 for 1

Match drawn

Leicestershire 4 pts., Hampshire 0 pts.

at Lord's

Middlesex 328 for 7 (M.R. Ramprakash 117 not out, M.W. Gatting 73)

v. Lancashire

Match drawn

Middlesex 3 pts., Lancashire 3 pts.

at Edgbaston

Warwickshire 282 (A.J. Moles 75, J.D. Ratcliffe 67, D.A. Reeve 55 not out, Mushtaq Ahmed 6 for 55) and 118 for 1 dec. (J.D. Ratcliffe 58, A.J. Moles 52 not out)

Somerset 61 for 0 dec.

Match drawn

Somerset 4 pts., Warwickshire 2 pts.

at Scarborough

Sussex 397 for 8 dec. (A.P. Wells 123, C.W.J. Athey 112)

Yorkshire 224 (M.D. Moxon 63, I.D.K. Salisbury 4 for 53, E.E. Hemmings 4 for 89) and 97 for 1 (D. Byas 55)

Match drawn

Sussex 8 pts., Yorkshire 4 pts.

11, 12 and **13 September** *at Canterbury*

Kent 264 (S.A. Marsh 111, D.J. Spencer 75, D. Brain 6 for 48) and 68 for 1 dec.

Zimbabwe 53 for 1 dec. and 83 (M.A. Ealham 5 for 14, D.J. Spencer 4 for 46)

Kent won by 196 runs

Rain decimated the penultimate round of championship matches. Northamptonshire won their first away match of the season by beating Derbyshire in just over two rain-interrupted days. Bailey and Fordham shared a second-wicket stand of 136, and Derbyshire twice succumbed meekly to the Northamptonshire seamers.

There was no play on the first day at Cardiff and little on the second, but by the close of play on Saturday, both counties had completed an innings, and Glamorgan were 64 for 3 in their second. On a pitch that aided the seamers, Steve Andrew, out of the Essex side for long periods, took his second seven-wicket haul of the season; while Steve Bastien twice bettered his previous career-best bowling performance and finished with 12 wickets in a match for the first time in what was only his fourth match of the season. Occasional bowling gave Glamorgan runs on the last morning and led to a generous declaration, but the task of scoring 201 to win proved to be beyond Essex's capabilities.

Gloucestershire and Nottinghamshire did their best to overcome the rain at Bristol, but eventually the visitors were fortunate to escape defeat. Martyn Ball, who was having a sensational finish to his season, profited from some occasional bowling to hit the highest score of his career, and then took 3 for 56 as Nottinghamshire went in search of 259 in 46 overs, a task well beyond them.

There was no play after a very restricted second day at Southampton, nor after the third day at Lord's. Ramprakash and Gatting added 131 for Middlesex's third wicket. Gatting received the Britannic Assurance County Championship trophy, and Ramprakash hit a delightful century.

Rain ultimately defeated both Warwickshire and Somerset. Moles and Ratcliffe began Warwickshire's innings with partnerships of 162 and 109, and Mushtaq Ahmed brought his total of wickets for the season to 80. Reeve left Somerset the last day in which to score 340, but rain prevented any play.

A third-wicket partnership of 230 between Athey and Alan Wells put Sussex in a strong position against Yorkshire at Scarborough. Both batsmen scored centuries to confirm highly successful seasons. Yorkshire then fell to the combined and contrasting spin of Hemmings and Salisbury and were forced to follow-on, but rain prevented play on the last day.

Rain also affected the match at Canterbury where Marsh and Spencer, who hit the first fifty of his career, added 166 for Kent's seventh wicket. Declarations kept the game alive, but Zimbabwe collapsed on the last day, an unhappy end to a brief and unsuccessful tour which seemed to be of little benefit to them. Spencer added a career-best bowling performance to his best batting score.

 AXA EQUITY & LAW LEAGUE

12 September *at Derby*

Derbyshire 214 for 8 (K.J. Barnett 79)

v. Northamptonshire

Match abandoned

Derbyshire 2 pts., Northamptonshire 2 pts.

at Cardiff

Essex 7 for 2
***v.* Glamorgan**

Match abandoned

Glamorgan 2 pts., Essex 2 pts.

at Bristol

Gloucestershire 43 for 1
***v.* Nottinghamshire**

Match abandoned

Gloucestershire 2 pts., Nottinghamshire 2 pts.

at Southampton

Hampshire *v.* Leicestershire

Match abandoned

Hampshire 2 pts., Leicestershire 2 pts.

at Lord's

Middlesex 75 for 4
***v.* Lancashire**

Match abandoned

Middlesex 2 pts., Lancashire 2 pts.

at Edgbaston

Somerset 133 for 6
***v.* Warwickshire**

Match abandoned

Warwickshire 2 pts., Somerset 2 pts.

at Scarborough

Yorkshire 255 for 7 (R.B. Richardson 89, R.J. Blakey 61)
Sussex 234 (A.P. Wells 80, C.W.J. Athey 51, P.J. Hartley 5 for 36)

Yorkshire (4 pts.) won by 21 runs

Rain caused the abandonment of all matches save the one at Scarborough. Only five overs were possible at Cardiff where Glamorgan had captured the wickets of Prichard and Shahid. The abandonment of this game meant that Kent and Glamorgan would meet in the last match with identical records. A stand of 146 in 29 overs between Richardson and Blakey was the basis of the Yorkshire score against Sussex. Peter Hartley kept the home side on course for victory with a competition-best performance of 5 for 36.

AXA EQUITY & LAW LEAGUE

19 September *at Hartlepool*

Somerset 164 for 7

Durham 168 for 3 (W. Larkins 52)

Durham (4 pts.) won by 7 wickets

at Chelmsford

Essex 287 for 4 (J.P. Stephenson 102 not out, P.J. Prichard 71, N. Hussain 50)
Hampshire 188 (P.M. Such 5 for 33)

Essex (4 pts.) won by 99 runs

at Canterbury

Kent 200 for 9 (C.L. Hooper 60)
Glamorgan 201 for 4 (H. Morris 67)

Glamorgan (4 pts.) won by 6 wickets

at Old Trafford

Lancashire 246 for 7 (G.D. Lloyd 69, N.J. Speak 63 not out)
Northamptonshire 247 for 5 (R.J. Bailey 93, M.B. Loye 56, R.J. Warren 56)

Northamptonshire (4 pts.) won by 5 wickets

at Leicester

Leicestershire 246 for 6 (B.F. Smith 97 not out, V.J. Wells 50)
Derbyshire 232

Leicestershire (4 pts.) won by 14 runs

at Trent Bridge

Warwickshire 276 for 9 (Asif Din 60, D.P. Ostler 53)
Nottinghamshire 116 (M.A.V. Bell 5 for 21)

Warwickshire (4 pts.) won by 160 runs

at The Oval

Yorkshire 185 (A.J. Hollioake 4 for 42)
Surrey 188 for 5 (A.D. Brown 52)

Surrey (4 pts.) won by 5 wickets

at Hove ·

Sussex 224 (F.D. Stephenson 81)
Gloucestershire 192 (S.G. Hinks 60, E.S.H. Giddins 4 for 36)

Sussex (4 pts.) won by 32 runs

at Worcester

Worcestershire 197 (R.L. Johnson 4 for 66)
Middlesex 199 for 4 (M.R. Ramprakash 63)

Middlesex (4 pts.) won by 6 wickets

Glamorgan won a limited-over competition for the first time when they beat Kent in front of a capacity crowd at Canterbury. Kent batted first when they won the toss, and by the 20th over they were 72 for 1 and in control. Fleming had batted in cavalier fashion, but he drove once too often at the admirable Croft and was taken at cover by Morris. Hooper played patiently at first, but he had just begun to display his majestic authority when Dale plucked the ball out of the air as Hooper tried to hit over mid-wicket. Now, from 168 for 4 with nine overs remaining, Kent plunged to 182 for 9. Igglesden and Headley took the score to 200, which just about looked respectable.

Igglesden dismissed James in his third over and he restricted Morris, but suddenly he lost his line, and Morris hit him for 3 fours in an over. Morris and Dale added 78 in 21 overs before Dale chased a wide-ish delivery, and Maynard quickly fell to the very lively Duncan Spencer. This brought Viv Richards to the wicket, his last appearance before a big crowd in England. The ground stood to him and clapped and cheered him all the way to the middle. He was not to play a good innings, but it was a winning one. He came close to being run out, and he was caught off a no-ball, but he played some lovely, belligerent shots on the off side. Morris had held his side together, but with 12 overs remaining and 60 runs needed, he was caught at mid-wicket. Cottey should have suffered the same fate, but this time Fleming spilled the catch. There was no second chance and, after one wayward over from the generally immaculate Hooper, Glamorgan swept to victory with 14 balls to spare. Richards and Cottey ran excitedly from the field, and the celebrations could be heard in Cardiff long into the night.

A splendid end-of-season flourish for the Kent spinner Min Patel. (Tony Marshall/Sports-Line)

AXA EQUITY & LAW LEAGUE – FINAL TABLE

	P	W	L	Tie	Ab.	Pts.
Glamorgan (16)	17	13	2	–	2	56
Kent (5)	17	12	3	–	2	52
Surrey (4)	17	11	4	–	2	48
Sussex (11)	17	10	5	1	1	44
Northamptonshire (13)	17	9	5	1	2	42
Lancashire (11)	17	8	5	1	3	40
Durham (8)	17	8	7	–	2	36
Middlesex (1)	17	7	6	2	2	36
Yorkshire (15)	17	8	8	–	1	34
Derbyshire (13)	17	7	8	–	2	32
Essex (2)	17	7	8	1	1	32
Warwickshire (8)	17	7	8	–	2	32
Gloucestershire (8)	17	5	9	1	2	26
Leicestershire (18)	17	5	10	–	2	24
Hampshire (3)	17	4	9	–	4	24
Worcestershire (7)	17	4	10	1	2	22
Nottinghamshire (17)	17	4	12	–	1	18
Somerset (5)	17	2	12	–	3	14
(1992 positions in brackets)						

16, 17, 18 and 20 September *at Hartlepool*

Somerset 352 (R.J. Harden 100, G.D. Rose 83) and 101 for 5

Durham 194 (J.A. Daley 73, A.R. Caddick 6 for 73) and 258 (P. Bainbridge 51, G.D. Rose 5 for 46, Mushtaq Ahmed 4 for 63)

Somerset won by 5 wickets

Somerset 24 pts., Durham 4 pts.

at Chelmsford

Hampshire 347 (D.I. Gower 134, P.M. Such 5 for 89, J.H. Childs 4 for 89) and 240 for 8 dec. (V.P. Terry 87, K.D. James 54, P.M. Such 5 for 71)

Essex 268 (G.A. Gooch 109, N. Hussain 102, S.D. Udal 4 for 77) and 196 for 5 (G.A. Gooch 114)

Match drawn

Hampshire 7 pts., Essex 6 pts.

at Canterbury

Kent 524 for 6 dec. (C.L. Hooper 236 not out, T.R. Ward 137, N.J. Llong 62, M.A. Ealham 50) and 95 for 2 dec. (M.V. Fleming 81 not out)

Glamorgan 144 (P.A. Cottey 79) and 239 (I.V.A. Richards 83, P.A. Cottey 53, D.W. Headley 4 for 97)

Kent won by 236 runs

Kent 24 pts., Glamorgan 2 pts.

at Old Trafford

Lancashire 277 (N.H. Fairbrother 110, M. Watkinson 67, J.P. Taylor 6 for 82, C.E.L. Ambrose 4 for 86) and 392 for 8 dec. (G. Yates 134 not out, J.P. Crawley 103)

Northamptonshire 240 (A.J. Lamb 67, R.J. Bailey 55, Wasim Akram 5 for 63) and 161 for 2 (N.A. Felton 72 not out, R.J. Bailey 71 not out)

Match drawn

Lancashire 6 pts., Northamptonshire 5 pts.

at Leicester

Derbyshire 213 (I.G.S. Steer 67) and 175 for 1 dec. (K.J. Barnett 94 not out)

Leicestershire 128 for 4 dec. (P.N. Hepworth 50, S.J. Base 4 for 35) and 61 for 5

More honours for Middlesex and their captain Mike Gatting. (Alan Cozzi)

Match drawn

Leicestershire 4 pts., Derbyshire 2 pts.

at Trent Bridge

Warwickshire 172 for 2 (A.J. Moles 54 not out)

***v.* Nottinghamshire**

Match drawn

No points

at The Oval

Surrey 359 for 7 dec. (A.J. Hollioake 85, M.A. Butcher 66 not out, G.P. Thorpe 60, A.J. Stewart 58)

Yorkshire 30 for 0

Match drawn

Surrey 4 pts., Yorkshire 3 pts.

at Hove

Gloucestershire 304 (S.G. Hinks 66, I.D.K. Salisbury 5 for 81) and 177 (I.D.K. Salisbury 4 for 99)

Sussex 355 (M.P. Speight 114, N.J. Lenham 105, K.E. Cooper 4 for 93) and 128 for 0 (C.W.J. Athey 57 not out)

Sussex won by 10 wickets

Sussex 24 pts., Gloucestershire 7 pts.

at Worcester

Middlesex 68 (P.J. Newport 4 for 20) and 148 (J.D. Carr 67, N.V. Radford 6 for 49)

Worcestershire 252 (P.C.R. Tufnell 4 for 40)

Worcestershire won by an innings and 36 runs

Worcestershire 22 pts., Middlesex 4 pts.

The season ended in rain, and with Middlesex suffering their only defeat of the season, beaten in two days by Worcestershire who, in winning their fifth game in succession, claimed second spot in the table.

Gooch hit a century in each innings and became the only batsman to complete 2,000 runs in the season. Mushtaq Ahmed ended an outstanding first season for Somerset with 85 wickets, and Somerset's win over Durham condemned the northerners to bottom place in the championship for the second year in succession.

Carl Hooper hit the highest score of his career as Kent routed Glamorgan. Neil Fairbrother hit his first century of the season at Old Trafford where Yates made a career best. Most attention was focused off the field, however, where David Hughes resigned as manager.

Ian Steer hit his highest first-class score for Derbyshire at Leicester, and Ian Salisbury celebrated his selection for the tour of West Indies with nine wickets in Sussex's win over Gloucestershire. Rain denied Phil Carrick the six

runs he needed to complete 10,000 runs and 1,000 wickets for Yorkshire. Having been released by Yorkshire, Carrick is unlikely to have another opportunity of reaching the 'double'.

In truth, the season ended in a damp whimper.

BRITANNIC ASSURANCE COUNTY CHAMPIONSHIP – FINAL TABLE

	P	W	L	D	Bonus Pts. Bat.	Bonus Pts. Bowl.	Pts.
Middlesex (11)	17	11	1	5	37	59	272
Worcestershire (17)	17	9	4	3	32	52	236
Glamorgan (14)	17	9	5	3	32	55	231
Northamptonshire (3)	17	8	4	5	35	59	222
Somerset (9)	17	8	7	2	26	59	213
Surrey (13)	17	6	6	5	40	60	196
Nottinghamshire (4)	17	6	3	7	34	56	194
Kent (2)	17	6	4	7	40	54	190
Leicestershire (8)	17	6	5	6	23	61	180
Sussex (7)	17	5	7	5	42	54	176
Essex (1)	17	4	6	7	44	55	163
Yorkshire (16)	17	5	4	8	21	56	157
Hampshire (15)	17	4	5	8	39	47	150
Lancashire (12)	17	4	8	5	38	48	150
Derbyshire (5)	17	4	7	6	33	50	147
Warwickshire (6)	17	4	8	5	24	49	137
Gloucestershire (10)	17	3	10	4	24	56	128
Durham (18)	17	2	10	5	29	52	113

Match tied between Nottinghamshire and Worcestershire, 8 pts. each.

(1992 positions in brackets)

FIRST-CLASS AVERAGES

BATTING

	M	Inns	NO	Runs	HS	Av	100s	50s		M	Inns	NO	Runs	HS	Av	100s	50s
G. Yates	7	10	6	367	134*	91.75	1	1	R.R. Montgomerie	8	14	1	462	109	35.53	1	3
K.J. Barnett	16	24	5	1223	168	64.36	5	5	G.B.T. Lovell	8	13	2	389	114	35.36	1	1
C.W.J. Athey	17	30	5	1600	137	64.00	5	9	S.J. Rhodes	18	27	3	848	101	35.33	2	2
G.A. Gooch	19	35	3	2023	159*	63.21	6	14	J.D.R. Benson	6	7	–	243	153	34.71	1	–
C.L. Hooper	16	24	2	1304	236*	59.27	3	6	M.G.N. Windows	2	4	–	138	44	34.50	–	–
A.P. Wells	18	27	2	1432	144	57.28	6	5	R.B. Richardson	14	23	1	759	112	34.50	1	6
M.W. Gatting	16	24	4	1132	182	56.60	3	6	C. White	19	32	6	896	146	34.46	1	4
G.A. Hick	18	30	2	1522	187	54.35	4	7	M.V. Fleming	18	28	4	826	100	34.41	1	6
T.S. Curtis	19	32	3	1553	127	53.55	5	9	T.L. Penney	17	29	6	788	135*	34.26	1	4
N. Hussain	20	35	5	1604	152	53.46	7	7	J.J. Whitaker	18	28	1	925	126	34.25	1	4
J.E. Morris	18	29	1	1461	229	52.17	5	6	B.C. Broad	18	34	–	1161	131	34.14	2	7
J.E. Emburey	17	21	7	730	123	52.14	2	5	D.P. Ostler	19	34	3	1052	174	33.93	1	6
R.J. Bailey	18	30	5	1282	200	51.28	2	9	D.R. Pringle	14	22	4	610	76	33.88	–	6
M.A. Ealham	12	16	3	666	85	51.23	–	8	J.P. Stephenson	17	32	2	1011	122	33.70	2	4
P.R. Pollard	19	32	3	1463	180	50.44	3	9	M.N. Lathwell	17	31	1	1009	132	33.63	2	4
C.M. Wells	3	5	1	198	185	49.50	1	–	S.A. Kellett	5	9	–	301	85	33.44	–	4
M.P. Speight	13	22	1	1009	184	48.04	3	5	N.H. Fairbrother	18	31	4	901	110	33.37	1	4
J.P. Crawley	20	34	3	1474	187*	47.54	3	8	R.C. Russell	19	33	7	863	99*	33.19	–	5
I.V.A. Richards	17	32	6	1235	224*	47.50	2	7	T.J. Boon	18	29	1	921	110	32.89	2	5
V.P. Terry	19	33	2	1469	174	47.38	4	7	W.A. Dessaur	7	10	–	325	104	32.50	1	2
J.D. Carr	17	24	6	848	192*	47.11	2	3	Asif Din	6	9	–	291	66	32.33	–	3
R.A. Smith	17	29	2	1253	191	46.40	4	4	G.D. Mendis	18	34	–	1099	106	32.32	1	7
A.D. Brown	19	34	3	1382	150*	44.58	3	4	N.A. Folland	17	30	3	872	108*	32.29	2	4
M.P. Maynard	19	32	1	1378	145	44.45	3	7	K.M. Curran	16	23	4	612	91	32.21	–	5
R.T. Robinson	18	30	4	1152	139*	44.30	3	7	W.P.C. Weston	13	21	2	610	113	32.10	2	1
M.A. Atherton	19	32	1	1364	137	44.00	3	9	C.C. Lewis	15	24	2	705	247	32.04	1	2
J.E.R. Gallian	11	19	3	702	141*	43.87	2	3	G.D. Rose	17	29	2	865	138	32.03	2	2
C.L. Cairns	15	23	1	962	93	43.72	–	9	P.J. Newport	17	26	6	630	79*	31.50	–	6
A.S. Rollins	7	13	4	392	85	43.55	–	2	I.G.S. Steer	4	7	2	157	67	31.40	–	1
M.R. Benson	15	23	2	913	107	43.47	3	6	M.A. Roseberry	16	26	4	685	185	31.13	1	2
P.D. Bowler	17	29	3	1123	153*	43.19	2	7	T.R. Ward	19	30	1	903	141	31.13	2	3
G.D. Hodgson	14	27	2	1079	166	43.16	2	7	A.A. Metcalfe	10	16	1	467	133*	31.13	1	3
D.J. Bicknell	19	35	2	1418	190	42.96	4	8	M.W. Alleyne	18	34	2	994	142*	31.06	3	2
N.J. Llong	18	27	5	943	116*	42.86	2	4	M. Saxelby	12	18	–	558	77	31.00	–	5
G. Chapple	8	13	7	256	109*	42.66	1	–	C.M. Gupte	9	16	3	397	61	30.53	–	1
M.D. Moxon	19	33	2	1317	171*	42.48	1	9	A.N. Hayhurst	14	23	1	669	169	30.40	2	1
P. Johnson	16	27	1	1099	187	42.26	5	3	D.L. Hemp	10	19	2	508	90*	29.88	–	5
D.I. Gower	16	28	1	1136	153	42.07	4	5	P.W.G. Parker	19	32	1	924	159	29.80	3	3
A.J. Stewart	16	28	1	1094	127	40.51	2	8	G.F. Archer	6	9	2	208	59*	29.71	–	1
A.J. Lamb	18	28	1	1092	172	40.44	2	6	M.P. Vaughan	2	4	–	118	64	29.50	–	1
K.R. Brown	18	24	6	725	88*	40.27	–	5	G.R. Haynes	9	13	–	383	158	29.46	1	2
H. Morris	19	35	2	1326	134*	40.18	5	6	J.D. Ratcliffe	19	34	–	999	101	29.38	1	6
P.J. Prichard	19	36	3	1319	225*	39.96	4	7	V.J. Wells	15	23	2	602	167	28.66	1	2
A. Dale	20	38	1	1472	214*	39.78	3	7	R.J. Blakey	19	32	2	859	95	28.63	–	5
D.L. Haynes	15	24	4	793	115	39.65	2	4	J.A. North	7	11	3	228	114	28.50	1	1
A.J. Moles	19	34	3	1228	117	39.61	2	8	P.J. Martin	16	21	7	399	43	28.50	–	–
A.N. Aymes	19	29	11	709	107*	39.38	1	5	T.J.G. O'Gorman	14	21	3	511	130*	28.38	1	2
K. Greenfield	8	12	3	353	107	39.22	1	3	F.D. Stephenson	14	21	2	538	90	28.31	–	3
A.J. Hollioake	5	9	–	352	123	39.11	1	2	N.R. Taylor	16	26	2	679	86	28.29	–	4
M. Watkinson	19	30	4	1016	107	39.07	2	4	S.P. James	16	30	1	810	138*	28.24	1	4
R.J. Harden	18	32	3	1133	132	39.06	3	4	C.J. Adams	18	30	–	843	175	28.10	1	7
W. Larkins	17	30	3	1045	151	38.70	3	5	D.D.J. Robinson	2	4	–	112	67	28.00	–	1
M.R. Ramprakash	17	24	1	883	140	38.39	2	5	D.W. Randall	5	10	–	280	98	28.00	–	2
P. Bainbridge	19	32	2	1150	150*	38.33	2	7	K.D. James	17	29	4	694	71	27.76	–	4
M.B. Loye	18	28	3	956	153*	38.24	2	4	M.A. Garnham	17	29	4	694	106	27.76	1	3
N.J. Lenham	12	22	1	799	149	38.04	2	5	D.M. Ward	13	22	1	580	151*	27.61	1	3
G.D. Lloyd	18	31	2	1095	116	37.75	2	5	S. Hutton	10	17	–	469	73	27.58	–	2
A. Fordham	17	29	1	1052	193	37.57	3	5	D.G. Cork	16	24	2	606	104	27.54	1	4
P.N. Weekes	4	5	1	148	47	37.00	–	–	P.N. Hepworth	8	13	1	328	129	27.33	1	1
J.J.B. Lewis	13	24	4	736	136*	36.80	1	5	M.A. Butcher	6	11	3	218	66*	27.25	–	1
M.C.J. Nicholas	18	29	4	918	95	36.72	–	6	N.E. Briers	12	19	1	487	79	27.05	–	3
Salim Malik	15	27	2	917	132	36.68	2	3	L. Potter	12	17	2	404	103*	26.93	1	1
N.A. Felton	18	30	2	1026	109	36.64	2	7	T.H.C. Hancock	16	29	2	723	76	26.77	–	4
D.M. Smith	15	23	1	802	150	36.45	1	4	S.A. Marsh	19	27	2	667	111	26.68	1	4
D.A. Reeve	17	28	7	765	87*	36.42	–	5	P.J. Hartley	13	21	6	400	102	26.66	1	1
R. Cake	11	19	6	472	108	36.30	1	3	A.W. Smith	14	23	2	560	68	26.66	–	3
G.P. Thorpe	17	31	2	1043	171	35.96	3	5	R.D.B. Croft	20	34	7	718	107	26.59	1	2
N.J. Speak	21	35	2	1185	122	35.90	1	8	R.S.M. Morris	8	14	–	372	92	26.57	–	2
P.A. Cottey	19	34	5	1040	105	35.86	2	8	G. Fowler	14	24	–	633	138	26.37	1	3
D. Byas	19	33	3	1073	156	35.76	1	9	C.J. Tavaré	13	25	1	628	141*	26.16	1	2

FIRST-CLASS AVERAGES

BATTING *continued*

	M	Inns	NO	Runs	HS	Av	100s	50s
N.A. Foster	8	12	3	235	37	26.11	–	–
I.T. Botham	10	17	1	416	101	26.00	1	3
J.W. Hall	9	16	1	390	114	26.00	1	1
T.C. Middleton	12	22	–	571	90	25.95	–	5
G.I. MacMillan	9	14	1	336	63	25.84	–	3
J.A. Daley	13	22	–	563	79	25.59	–	3
D.P. Fulton	7	13	1	307	75	25.58	–	2
P. Moores	19	27	4	583	85*	25.34	–	2
G.J. Parsons	18	23	7	405	59	25.31	–	1
D.A. Leatherdale	11	16	2	354	119*	25.28	1	2
R.K. Illingworth	18	24	8	401	58	25.06	–	1
N.A. Mallender	13	16	6	250	46	25.00	–	–
I. Fletcher	7	10	1	223	65*	24.77	–	2
M.A. Lynch	15	28	1	666	90	24.66	–	3
Wasim Akram	13	21	–	516	117	24.57	1	1
S.P. Titchard	5	10	–	237	87	23.70	–	2
A.C.H. Seymour	7	11	1	237	54*	23.70	–	1
M.P. Bicknell	12	19	2	398	57	23.41	–	2
H. Malik	9	13	3	234	64*	23.40	–	1
P.J. Berry	9	14	4	232	46	23.20	–	–
K.P. Evans	10	14	4	231	56	23.10	–	1
M.J. Weston	7	13	1	277	59	23.08	–	2
M.E.D. Jarrett	8	13	1	277	51	23.08	–	1
N.D. Burns	13	23	2	479	102*	22.80	1	2
P.A. Nixon	19	28	6	501	113*	22.77	1	3
G.R. Cowdrey	12	21	–	478	139	22.76	1	1
C.L. Keey	10	16	1	341	111	22.73	1	1
A.P. Grayson	10	17	–	386	64	22.70	–	2
N.V. Knight	7	13	–	295	94	22.69	–	2
R.M.F. Cox	6	10	1	204	63	22.66	–	1
W.K. Hegg	21	34	9	566	69*	22.64	–	2
W.K.M. Benjamin	9	13	–	294	83	22.61	–	2
N. Shahid	7	13	1	270	69*	22.50	–	2
C.M. Tolley	18	24	7	381	78	22.41	–	2
D. Ripley	18	24	6	398	62*	22.11	–	3
R.I. Dawson	9	17	1	350	58	21.87	–	1
R.J. Turner	6	10	1	195	70	21.66	–	1
I.D.K. Salisbury	16	23	5	390	63*	21.66	–	2
D.W. Headley	14	20	7	281	36	21.61	–	–
D.B. D'Oliveira	15	24	–	513	94	21.37	–	3
S.G. Hinks	12	24	1	482	68	20.95	–	3
A.C. Cummins	16	26	2	502	70	20.91	–	4
G.M. Charlesworth	10	15	3	250	49	20.83	–	–
D.A. Graveney	19	28	14	289	32	20.64	–	–
S.D. Udal	19	27	2	509	79*	20.36	–	2
P.E. Robinson	18	29	3	526	71	20.23	–	3
B.N. French	17	24	3	420	123	20.00	1	1
G.W. Mike	8	13	1	240	50	20.00	–	1
C.A. Connor	10	11	1	200	59	20.00	–	1
Mushtaq Ahmed	16	25	–	498	90	19.92	–	3
R.P. Lefebvre	19	28	3	484	50	19.36	–	1
M.J. Vandrau	15	23	2	404	58	19.23	–	2
M.A. Feltham	16	19	4	288	73	19.20	–	1
M.A. Crawley	10	18	2	306	81	19.12	–	1
S.R. Lampitt	16	25	2	438	68*	19.04	–	2
P.D. Atkins	7	12	–	228	62	19.00	–	1
R.I. Alikhan	4	8	–	149	41	18.62	–	–
F.A. Griffith	11	14	–	257	56	18.35	–	2
A.E. Warner	12	14	1	238	95*	18.30	–	1
M. Keech	5	10	1	164	35	18.22	–	–
P.A. Booth	7	11	3	144	49*	18.00	–	–
R.J. Scott	5	10	–	179	51	17.90	–	1
M.D. Marshall	13	16	2	250	75*	17.85	–	1
J. Wood	9	17	3	250	63*	17.85	–	1
N.M.K. Smith	18	26	2	420	51*	17.50	–	1
D.J. Capel	5	8	2	102	54	17.00	–	1
A.J. Wright	11	21	2	322	75	16.94	–	1
P.A. Smith	10	15	–	253	55	16.86	–	1
K.A. Parsons	5	9	1	134	63	16.75	–	1
P.A.J. DeFreitas	21	31	3	465	51	16.60	–	1
R.W. Sladdin	9	11	3	131	51*	16.37	–	1
C.W. Scott	14	24	3	343	64	16.33	–	2
K.M. Krikken	13	18	4	227	40	16.21	–	–
G.W. Jones	10	16	1	241	45*	16.06	–	–
I. Smith	6	12	–	192	39	16.00	–	–
P.W. Jarvis	9	14	1	207	76	15.92	–	1
N.M. Kendrick	12	20	5	237	41	15.80	–	–
R.D. Stemp	16	23	6	265	37	15.58	–	–
R. Yeabsley	10	13	4	138	36	15.33	–	–
R.M. Wight	7	11	1	152	54	15.20	–	1
C.E.L. Ambrose	13	15	2	197	38	15.15	–	–
G.J. Kersey	12	20	2	272	38*	15.11	–	–
C.A. Walsh	14	21	3	266	57	14.77	–	1
C.P. Metson	20	31	8	338	25*	14.69	–	–
B.F. Smith	11	18	–	263	84	14.61	–	1
A.R. Caddick	16	26	4	318	35*	14.45	–	–
M.C.J. Ball	4	8	–	113	71	14.12	–	1
T.D. Topley	8	12	1	155	33	14.09	–	–
K.J. Piper	10	14	1	183	52	14.07	–	1
A.R.K. Pierson	18	23	6	238	58	14.00	–	1
M.C. Ilott	18	25	5	280	51	14.00	–	2
A.C.S. Pigott	12	13	2	153	52	13.90	–	1
A.L. Penberthy	9	14	2	164	54*	13.66	–	1
R.A. Pick	13	12	4	109	22	13.62	–	–
C.W.J. Lyons	9	12	4	108	28	13.50	–	–
N.F. Williams	14	12	1	146	44	13.27	–	–
J.D. Batty	15	19	2	221	50	13.00	–	1
S.L. Watkin	19	24	8	204	31	12.75	–	–
Waqar Younis	13	18	1	214	28	12.58	–	–
J. Boiling	9	13	5	100	28	12.50	–	–
R.G. Twose	11	18	–	224	37	12.44	–	–
M. Davies	14	23	5	220	44*	12.22	–	–
D. Gough	16	24	3	248	39	11.80	–	–
N.V. Radford	13	14	5	106	29	11.77	–	–
R.P. Davis	14	16	2	164	42	11.71	–	–
J.P. Arscott	10	12	3	105	22*	11.66	–	–
K.E. Cooper	14	25	6	218	52	11.47	–	1
A.R.C. Fraser	18	17	2	162	29	10.80	–	–
P.C.R. Tufnell	18	18	6	128	30*	10.66	–	–
P.M. Such	20	27	5	228	54	10.36	–	1

(Qualification – 100 runs, average 10.00)
(D.A. Lewis 73 & 56*; M.P. Rea 115 & 2)

BOWLING

	Overs	Mds	Runs	Wkts	Av	Best	10/m	5/inn
N.G. Cowans	81	16	234	16	14.62	4-43	–	–
Wasim Akram	409.2	93	1137	59	19.27	8-68	1	5
K.M. Curran	458	123	1293	67	19.29	7-47	–	3
J.E. Emburey	710.4	226	1401	71	19.73	8-40	1	2
A.P. Igglesden	438.5	111	1068	54	19.77	6-58	1	3
M.P. Bicknell	502.2	137	1341	67	20.01	6-43	2	6
C.E.L. Ambrose	543.4	150	1207	59	20.45	6-49	–	2
Mushtaq Ahmed	694.3	212	1773	85	20.85	7-91	3	8
D.J. Capel	117.4	37	252	12	21.00	3-15	–	–
C. White	132	36	328	15	21.86	3-9	–	–
W.K.M. Benjamin	281.3	81	702	32	21.93	7-83	–	3
A.E. Warner	322.5	76	900	41	21.95	5-27	1	3
Waqar Younis	449.4	89	1407	62	22.69	6-42	–	4
A.R.C. Fraser	533.4	132	1388	61	22.75	7-40	–	2
S.L. Watkin	766.4	173	2098	92	22.80	5-71	–	2
D.J. Millns	184.3	51	584	25	23.36	5-21	–	2
C.L. Cairns	411.5	74	1242	53	23.43	6-70	–	3
C.A. Walsh	528.1	119	1516	64	23.68	5-59	–	3
P.C.R. Tufnell	688.5	189	1529	64	23.89	8-29	–	3
D.A. Reeve	284.1	108	528	22	24.00	3-38	–	–
N.A. Mallender	329.5	102	772	32	24.12	4-45	–	1
P.J. Newport	546.5	135	1454	60	24.23	6-63	–	4
A.D. Mullally	528.1	141	1506	62	24.29	7-72	1	2
M.C.J. Ball	157.3	35	439	18	24.38	8-46	1	2

FIRST-CLASS AVERAGES

BOWLING *continued*

	Overs	Mds	Runs	Wkts	Av	Best	10/m	5/inn
E.E. Hemmings	638.2	208	1541	63	24.46	7-31	1	2
K.C.G. Benjamin	283.5	42	911	37	24.62	6-70	–	2
C. Penn	142	39	296	12	24.66	4-12	–	–
G.J. Parsons	490.1	151	1111	45	24.68	3-23	–	–
M.N. Bowen	147.5	30	554	22	25.18	4-124	–	–
G.D. Rose	324.3	62	1090	43	25.34	6-83	–	3
P. Bainbridge	333.1	76	1021	40	25.52	5-53	–	2
R.K. Illingworth	645	219	1404	55	25.52	6-28	–	1
J.P. Taylor	646.5	191	1789	69	25.92	6-82	–	2
M.A.V. Bell	212.1	52	649	25	25.96	7-48	–	3
K.D. James	327.2	83	942	36	26.16	4-33	–	–
K.E. Cooper	502.4	149	1233	47	26.23	5-83	–	1
K.P. Evans	265.3	69	660	25	26.40	6-67	–	1
D. Gough	507.3	115	1517	57	26.61	7-42	1	3
A.R. Caddick	541	115	1678	63	26.63	9-32	3	5
M.G. Field-Buss	307.3	104	748	28	26.71	6-42	–	1
J.I.D. Kerr	109.1	15	405	15	27.00	3-47	–	–
A.A. Donald	268.1	59	811	30	27.03	7-98	1	2
P.W. Jarvis	267.4	62	705	26	27.11	4-51	–	–
M.W. Alleyne	246.3	50	707	26	27.19	3-25	–	–
T.A. Munton	334.3	113	740	27	27.40	7-41	–	1
R.G. Twose	102.2	16	302	11	27.45	4-85	–	–
M.A. Robinson	514	134	1346	49	27.46	9-37	1	3
P.J. Hartley	351.4	91	1027	37	27.75	5-51	–	1
S.D. Thomas	141.3	21	556	20	27.80	5-76	–	1
J.E. Benjamin	624.2	153	1783	64	27.85	6-19	–	2
J.H. Childs	709	207	1729	62	27.88	6-27	–	3
F.D. Stephenson	397	77	1155	41	28.17	5-55	–	1
P.M. Such	812	197	2148	76	28.26	6-67	3	7
D.W. Headley	439.4	106	1191	42	28.35	7-79	–	2
C.M. Tolley	442.5	115	1194	42	28.52	5-55	–	1
M.J. McCague	298.1	67	888	31	28.64	5-33	–	2
A.L. Penberthy	171	43	522	18	29.00	5-37	–	1
N.F. Williams	372	65	1131	39	29.00	6-61	–	1
M.A. Butcher	134	24	436	15	29.06	4-51	–	–
J.A. Afford	719.5	225	1659	57	29.10	5-64	–	3
M.A. Ealham	281.2	56	917	31	29.58	5-46	–	2
D.G. Cork	396.5	85	1102	37	29.78	4-90	–	–
G.C. Small	251.4	71	629	21	29.95	4-39	–	–
S.J. Base	310.1	69	1080	36	30.00	5-59	–	3
S. Bastien	167.3	28	573	19	30.15	6-52	1	2
S.D. Udal	763.2	183	2232	74	30.16	6-141	2	5
R.D. Stemp	540	188	1207	40	30.17	6-92	–	2
J.P. Stephenson	265.5	52	908	30	30.26	5-31	–	2
A.C. Cummins	504.3	95	1614	53	30.45	6-115	–	3
D.B. Pennett	172	34	520	17	30.58	5-36	–	1
O.H. Mortensen	255	66	643	21	30.61	5-55	–	1
N.V. Radford	269.5	44	1012	33	30.66	6-49	–	1
M.D. Marshall	345.3	102	859	28	30.67	5-62	–	1
D.E. Malcolm	336.5	56	1262	41	30.78	6-57	–	2
R.P. Davis	479.4	141	1118	36	31.05	7-127	1	2
A.R.K. Pierson	528.5	141	1371	44	31.15	6-87	–	4
M.A. Feltham	327.3	88	905	29	31.20	4-48	–	–
S.R. Lampitt	332	62	1062	34	31.23	3-9	–	–
P.J. Martin	406.5	105	1188	38	31.26	5-35	–	1
R.P. Lefebvre	619.4	176	1379	44	31.34	4-70	–	–
M.M. Patel	199.5	52	533	17	31.35	7-75	1	2
L. Potter	352.1	118	758	24	31.58	5-45	–	1
M.V. Fleming	422	103	1086	34	31.94	4-31	–	–
A.J. Murphy	338.4	81	1043	32	32.59	5-58	–	1
P.A.J. DeFreitas	651.4	128	1971	60	32.85	7-76	1	4
Salim Malik	255.1	40	792	24	33.00	5-67	–	1
P.A. Booth	174.5	49	396	12	33.00	2-16	–	–
N.M. Kendrick	368	103	960	29	33.10	7-115	–	1
N.M.K. Smith	588.1	151	1593	48	33.18	6-122	–	3

	Overs	Mds	Runs	Wkts	Av	Best	10/m	5/inn
M.C. Ilott	640.4	130	1962	59	33.25	7-85	–	2
S.J.W. Andrew	281.4	55	934	28	33.35	7-47	–	2
A.P. van Troost	282	49	1036	31	33.41	5-47	–	1
A. Dale	393.1	81	1238	37	33.45	6-18	–	1
R.J. Bailey	244.3	69	612	18	34.00	5-54	–	1
J.D. Batty	383.2	97	1065	31	34.35	5-36	–	1
D.A. Graveney	579.1	187	1306	38	34.36	5-78	–	1
D.P.J. Flint	390.2	95	1066	31	34.38	5-32	–	1
R.D.B. Croft	850.5	265	2158	61	35.37	5-112	–	2
R.H. MacDonald	249	66	709	20	35.45	5-20	–	1
D.R. Pringle	378.5	93	1041	29	35.89	4-33	–	–
P.A. Smith	130.5	18	505	14	36.07	4-35	–	–
I.D.K. Salisbury	616.3	132	2007	54	37.16	5-81	–	2
R. Yeabsley	287.1	53	762	20	38.10	3-30	–	–
M. Davies	515.1	141	1412	37	38.16	5-57	1	2
M. Watkinson	662.5	146	1950	51	38.23	5-12	–	1
C.C. Lewis	561.1	122	1619	42	38.54	4-34	–	–
C.L. Hooper	545	126	1281	33	38.81	4-35	–	–
P. Trimby	143.2	31	469	12	39.08	3-72	–	–
V.J. Wells	241.4	66	705	18	39.16	2-5	–	–
H.R.J. Trump	237.4	79	589	15	39.26	4-74	–	–
S.J.E. Brown	521	77	1861	47	39.59	7-70	–	3
I.T. Botham	185.5	46	516	13	39.69	4-11	–	–
A.R. Roberts	289.5	75	760	19	40.00	3-51	–	–
G.W. Mike	205	42	708	17	41.64	5-65	–	1
T.D. Topley	181.5	41	627	15	41.80	3-15	–	–
F.A. Griffith	170.5	29	593	14	42.35	3-32	–	–
A.A. Barnett	713	177	2005	47	42.65	5-36	–	3
R.A. Pick	345.3	78	1070	25	42.80	5-13	–	1
P.J. Berry	200.1	33	648	15	43.20	3-39	–	–
G. Yates	233	46	692	16	43.25	5-108	–	1
R.W. Sladdin	326.5	96	1017	23	44.21	3-30	–	–
J. Wood	192	26	735	16	45.93	4-106	–	–
G. Chapple	155	34	507	11	46.09	3-50	–	–
M.P.W. Jeh	297	48	1141	24	47.54	5-63	–	1
A.C.S. Pigott	283.3	43	1001	21	47.66	4-51	–	–
S.R. Barwick	505.4	208	1016	21	48.38	3-26	–	–
R.M. Pearson	335.3	68	1020	21	48.57	3-61	–	–
A.M. Babington	220.2	49	634	13	48.76	3-51	–	–
K.J. Shine	296.1	57	1172	24	48.83	6-62	–	2
C.M. Pitcher	203.1	35	698	14	49.85	3-50	–	–
C.A. Connor	261.4	65	803	16	50.18	4-77	–	–
A.R. Whittall	309.3	63	969	19	51.00	3-79	–	–
E.S.H. Giddins	378.5	55	1490	29	51.37	5-120	–	1
J.E.R. Gallian	195	43	585	11	53.18	3-52	–	–
G.M. Charlesworth	229.5	52	645	12	53.75	3-33	–	–
A.M. Smith	205.2	36	672	12	56.00	3-59	–	–
M.J. Vandrau	284.4	62	937	16	58.56	2-8	–	–
N.A. Foster	250.3	60	723	12	60.25	5-58	–	1
G.A. Hick	203.4	58	603	10	60.30	2-15	–	–
J. Boiling	221.1	62	669	11	60.81	5-100	–	1
N.J. Haste	225	43	715	10	71.50	2-44	–	–

(Qualification – 10 wickets)

LEADING FIELDERS

64 – R.C. Russell (ct 57/st 7); 61 – S.A. Marsh (ct 57/st 4); 58 – W.K. Hegg (ct 50/st 8); 56 – D. Ripley (ct 52/st 4); 54 – C.P. Metson (ct 50/st 4); 47 – S.J. Rhodes (ct 40/st 7) and P.A. Nixon (ct 41/st 6); 46 – R.J. Blakey (ct 41/st 5) and B.N. French (ct 41/st 5); 44 – K.R. Brown (ct 38/st 6) and P. Moores (ct 39/st 5); 41 – N.D. Burns (ct 37/st 4); 39 – M.A. Garnham (ct 35/st 4) and A.N. Aymes (ct 34/st 5); 37 – G.J. Kersey (ct 34/st 3); 36 – A.J. Stewart (ct 34/st 2); 35 – J.D. Carr; 33 – R.J. Harden; 32 – C.W. Scott (ct 28/st 4); 28 – M.A. Lynch; 26 – P.R. Pollard and K.M. Krikken (ct 21/st 5); 24 – G.A. Hick, W. Larkins and C.W.J. Lyons (ct 22/st 2); 22 – M.P. Maynard, D.A. Reeve, C.L. Hooper and C.J. Tavaré; 21 – S.R. Lampitt, P.E. Robinson, J.P. Stephenson and D. Byas

English Counties Form Charts

The games covered are:

AXA Equity & Law Sunday League (AEL)
Tetley Trophy (TT)
Benson and Hedges Cup (B & H)
National Westminster Bank Trophy (NW)
Joshua Tetley Festival (JT)
Seeboard Trophy (SB)

Once again averages are not produced as it is felt that they have little relevance in limited-over cricket where batsmen often sacrifice wickets for quick runs and bowlers are ordered to contain rather than capture wickets.
In the batting tables a blank indicates that a batsman did not *play* in a game, a dash (–) that he did not *bat*.

FIELDING FIGURES

23 – K.M. Krikken (ct 22/st 1)
13 – C.J. Adams
10 – K.J. Barnett
7 – D.G. Cork
5 – P.D. Bowler and B.J.M. Maher
4 – F.A. Griffith, S.J. Base and A.E. Warner
3 – O.H. Mortensen
2 – T.J.G. O'Gorman and J.E. Morris
1 – R.W. Sladdin, D.E. Malcolm, A.S. Rollins and M.J. Vandrau

BEST BATSMEN & BOWLERS

Derbyshire won the Benson and Hedges Cup in 1993 for the first time. They were beaten finalists in 1978 and 1988.

Debutants in the season were A.S. Rollins and M.J. Vandrau.

The county were deprived of the services of their overseas player, I.R. Bishop, after the first match of the season because of injury.

C.J. Adams hit his first fifties in the Benson and Hedges Cup and eight innings of 50 or more in the Sunday League. In four previous seasons, he had scored seven fifties in the league. He also took his first wickets in the Sunday League.

P.D. Bowler's two centuries in the Sunday League were his first in the competition. He reached 1,000 runs in one-day cricket.

DERBYSHIRE CCC — BATTING (first half of season)

Batting	B&H 27 April (Bristol) v. Gloucestershire	AEL 9 May (Edgbaston) v. Warwickshire	B&H 11 May (Derby) v. Middlesex	AEL 16 May (Derby) v. Glamorgan	AEL 23 May (Chelmsford) v. Essex	B&H 25 & 26 May (Taunton) v. Somerset	AEL 30 May (Checkley) v. Hampshire	AEL 6 June (Lord's) v. Middlesex	B&H 8 June (Derby) v. Northamptonshire	AEL 13 June (Chesterfield) v. Yorkshire	AEL 20 June (Canterbury) v. Kent	NW 22 June (Exmouth) v. Devon	AEL 27 June (Derby) v. Lancashire	Runs
K.J. Barnett	40	0	29	32	42	35*		104*	61	5	6	60	2	574
P.D. Bowler	92	77	30	96	7	25*		4	45	55	18	58	0	1034
J.E. Morris	1		57	27	20	–		80	48*	1	12	21	4	378
C.J. Adams	34	0	58	52	9	–		38*	53*	56	92	13	4	883
T.J.G. O'Gorman	27	15	8	0	1	–		–	–	45	17	68*	34*	498
F.A. Griffith	13*	1	1	1	16	–		–	–		20	0	10	111
K.M. Krikken	4*	7	23						–	7		14	11	115
D.G. Cork	–	26			0				–			–		246
A.E. Warner	–	0		0					–		31	–		54
D.E. Malcolm	–	7*		0					–		2	0*		12
O.H. Mortensen	–		2*						–	2*	32*	21		12
A.S. Rollins		18		3*	14*					14*	5			219
S.J. Base		6*	12*	2	4					13				85
I.R. Bishop					23*									12
B.J.M. Maher														23
M.J. Vandrau	18											0*		140
R.W. Sladdin	6*													21
I.G.S. Steer														26
Byes	1	5	8			4		5	3	3	2	2	3	
Leg-byes	6	3	6		7	1		1	3		7	5		
Wides	6	4	7	2	2	4		8	1	6	4	4	1	
No-balls		4	1											
Total	198	173	253	215	145	69	Ab.	240	214	207	248	266	73	
Wickets	5	9	10	10	8	Ab.	2	2	2	7	8	7	10	
Result	W	L	W	W	W			L	W	L	W	W	L	
Points	–	0	4	4	4			0	2	0	4	W	0	

DERBYSHIRE CCC — BATTING (second half of season)

Batting	AEL 4 July (Worcester) v. Worcestershire	NW 7 July (Worcester) v. Worcestershire	B&H 10 July (Lord's) v. Lancashire	AEL 25 July (Derby) v. Sussex	AEL 1 August (Cheltenham) v. Gloucestershire	AEL 8 August (Durham) v. Durham	AEL 15 August (Derby) v. Somerset	AEL 22 August (Ilkeston) v. Surrey	AEL 29 August (Trent Bridge) v. Nottinghamshire	JT 6 September (Scarborough) v. Yorkshire	AEL 12 September (Derby) v. Northamptonshire	AEL 19 September (Leicester) v. Leicestershire	Runs
K.J. Barnett	34*	1	19	11*	3	32	138*	76*	28	59	79	31	574
P.D. Bowler	14	6	4	57	35*	17	14	14	5	6	40	46	1034
J.E. Morris	63	71	22	43	58	16	93	66	11	2	9		378
C.J. Adams	27	93	11	60	0*	31	1	8	5	0	17	39	883
T.J.G. O'Gorman	20	8	49	1*	–		–	3	16	–	14*	11*	498
F.A. Griffith	20*	9*	37*	8	–		–	–	4	14	2	2	111
K.M. Krikken	–	23	92*	1	–	1	–	6	15	7	4	21	115
D.G. Cork		2	–	–		5*		8		–	6	10	246
A.E. Warner	–	0	–	–		0		1	2*	91*	14*	2	54
D.E. Malcolm	–	4*	–	–		31	13*	0	57	2		3	12
O.H. Mortensen	–			–		4		0	23				12
A.S. Rollins					4	7						30	219
S.J. Base						16							85
I.R. Bishop													12
B.J.M. Maher										3		19	23
M.J. Vandrau		13	1	6		5	8	9	10	9	5	1	140
R.W. Sladdin		9	11	2		5	8	5	8	3	18	8	21
I.G.S. Steer	4	4	5	4	4		6	2	0	2	2	2	26
Byes	2		1										
Leg-byes	3	13	11	6		5	8	9	10	3	5	8	
Wides	3	9	9	2		5	8	5	8	9	18	7	
No-balls	4	4	5	4	4		6	2		2	2	2	
Total	194	244	252	199	100	170	281	201	187	198	214	232	
Wickets	W	9	W	W	W	10	3	10	10	7	8	10	
Result	W	L	W	W	W	L	W	L	L	L	Ab.	L	
Points	W	0	W	4	4	0	4	0	0	L	2	0	

DERBYSHIRE CCC

BOWLING

Opponent (venue)	Date		D.E. Malcolm	D.G. Cork	O.H. Mortensen	A.E. Warner	F.A. Griffith	S.J. Base	I.R. Bishop	M.J. Vandrau	C.J. Adams	R.W. Sladdin	K.J. Barnett	I.G.S. Steer	P.D. Bowler	Byes	Leg-byes	Wides	No-balls	Total	Wkts
v. Gloucestershire (Bristol)	27 April	B&H	11-1-42-1	11-2-39-2	11-2-30-1	11-2-33-0	11-2-48-2										6	6		198	7
v. Warwickshire (Edgbaston)	9 May	AEL	10-3-15-0	9.5-0-34-2		9-1-48-1	10-0-37-3	10-0-35-0									4	5	2	174	7
v. Middlesex (Derby)	11 May	B&H	11-1-62-3	11-0-56-0		11-2-29-0	11-0-49-2		11-1-37-2							1	6	14	6	239	9
v. Glamorgan (Derby)	16 May	AEL	10-1-35-2	10-1-30-2		10-1-41-0	10-0-48-4	10-0-53-0									5	1	8	212	8
v. Essex (Chelmsford)	23 May	AEL	10-0-31-1			10-5-11-3	10-1-31-0	10-0-29-2		5-0-20-0	4.4-0-15-2						5	5	8	142	9
v. Somerset (Taunton)	25 & 26 May	B&H																			Ab.
v. Hampshire (Checkley)	30 May	AEL																			Ab.
v. Middlesex (Lord's)	6 June	AEL	10-0-36-4			9.5-0-49-2		8-0-44-0		10-1-38-0		10-0-62-1	1-0-2-1				10	3		241	8
v. Northamptonshire (Derby)	8 June	B&H	10-3-23-3	11-0-46-3		9.2-3-19-1	9-0-49-1			11-1-46-1	3-0-18-0						9	9	8	210	10
v. Yorkshire (Chesterfield)	13 June	AEL			10-2-33-0	8-0-34-1		10-1-39-0		6.3-0-47-0		9-0-50-0					5	3	6	208	1
v. Kent (Canterbury)	20 June	AEL			10-1-36-1		10-0-72-1	10-0-60-3		10-1-39-2		10-1-37-1					1	5	4	245	8
v. Devon (Exmouth)	22 June	NW	7.4-1-29-3	8-1-18-4	7-0-30-1		6-3-18-1			7-4-9-1			8-0-30-0			1	3	6	2	133	10
v. Lancashire (Derby)	27 June	AEL	10-2-44-1	10-0-38-2	10-0-52-0		10-1-48-2	10-2-38-1								7	7	6		234	6
v. Worcestershire (Worcester)	4 July	AEL		10-0-53-0	10-2-24-2	10-2-23-2	10-0-39-1	10-0-30-2								9	12	4		190	9
v. Worcestershire (Worcester)	7 July	NW	11-1-77-1	12-2-55-1	12-2-31-1	12-1-33-1	10.2-0-46-1										3	3	12	245	6
v. Lancashire (Lord's)	10 July	B&H	11-0-53-0	11-1-50-1	11-0-41-1	11-1-31-3	11-0-60-2										11	3	6	246	7
v. Sussex (Derby)	25 July	AEL	8-1-42-4	7-0-24-2	6.2-0-20-2	8-1-29-2											3	3	4	118	10
v. Gloucestershire (Cheltenham)	1 August	AEL			10-2-20-2		8-1-33-1	10-3-14-4				8-1-26-2					6	4	2	99	10
v. Durham (Durham)	8 August	AEL	10-0-52-0		8-1-25-0			10-1-54-0		6-0-46-0	9-0-51-1	7-0-42-0				2	9	7	4	281	2
v. Somerset (Derby)	8 August	AEL	7.1-0-41-1	7-0-20-0	10-1-39-3			7-2-17-2		7-0-50-2						1	5	7	2	168	10
v. Surrey (Ilkeston)	15 August	AEL		10-1-48-1	10-2-21-1	9-1-40-0	6.1-0-53-0	10-0-34-3			7-0-28-0					1	6	13	8	203	5
v. Nottinghamshire (Trent Bridge)	22 August	AEL		8-0-96-1	10-0-53-1	8-0-52-1		10-0-62-2				9-0-49-0		7-0-33-1			5	3	18	329	6
v. Yorkshire (Scarborough)	29 August	JT		3-0-23-0	7-0-25-1	3-1-15-0		4-0-31-0							7.4-0-51-0	4	1	3	3	199	1
v. Northamptonshire (Derby)	6 September	AEL																			
v. Northamptonshire (Derby)	12 September	AEL																			Ab.
v. Leicestershire (Leicester)	19 September	AEL			10-1-20-2	10-0-59-1	10-0-67-0			10-1-46-2			6-0-27-1	4-1-21-0		1	5	18		246	6
Wickets			24	23	19	18	21	20	2	8	2	4	2	1	0						

FIELDING FIGURES

18 – A.R. Fothergill (ct 14/st 4)
10 – I. Smith and C.W. Scott (ct 9/st 1)
9 – W. Larkins, P.W.G. Parker and D.A. Graveney
8 – P. Bainbridge
7 – G. Fowler
6 – S. Hutton
5 – S.P. Hughes
4 – S.J.E. Brown
2 – A.C. Cummins, J.D. Glendenen and J. Wood
1 – I.T. Botham, J.A. Daley, M.P. Briers, P.J. Berry,
D.A. Blenkiron and sub

BEST BATSMEN & BOWLERS

A.C. Cummins and G. Fowler played their first season with Durham. Fowler had scored 4,853 runs in the Sunday League for Lancashire between 1978 and 1992.

The season marked the end of the career of Ian Botham. He first played in the Sunday League, for Somerset, in 1973, and he later played for Worcestershire before moving to Durham in 1992. He appeared in 204 Sunday League matches, scored 5,032 runs and took 256 wickets as well as holding 79 catches. In the Benson and Hedges Cup, he won 10 Gold Awards, and he was four times named Man of the Match in the NatWest Trophy.

DURHAM CCC — BATTING

	v. Minor Counties (Hartlepool) 28 April B&H	v. Lancashire (Old Trafford) 9 May AEL	v. Hampshire (Stockton) 11 May B&H	v. Hampshire (Stockton) 16 May AEL	v. Gloucestershire (Bristol) 23 May AEL	v. Kent (Darlington) 30 May AEL	v. Leicestershire (Leicester) 6 June AEL	v. Middlesex (Gateshead) 13 June AEL	v. Glamorgan (Colwyn Bay) 20 June AEL	v. Wiltshire (Trowbridge) 22 June NW	v. Worcestershire (Stockton) 27 June AEL	v. Surrey (The Oval) 4 July AEL	v. Glamorgan (Cardiff) 7 July NW	Runs
W. Larkins	42	28	110*	21*	1	38*	–	1	7	35	–	5	75	814
G. Fowler	0	19	7	23*	91	–	34*	–	–	–	52	21	24	554
I. Smith	34	36	15	–	8	–	61	53*	31	82	5	46	10	282
P. Bainbridge	34*	69*	5	–	4	45*	28	11	18	55	0	19	33	561
I.T. Botham	35*	13	36	–	7	–	2	31	–	4	72	8	73*	288
P.W.G. Parker	3*	–	0	–	53	–	0	–	0	–	13*	–	–	520
A.R. Fothergill	–	–	–	–	9	–	–	–	2	–	11*	9*	–	43
J. Wood	–	–	–	–	11	–	–	–	1	–	–	7	–	26
D.A. Graveney	–	–	–	–	2	–	10	1*	21	–	–	–	–	133
S.P. Hughes	–	–	–	–	1*	–	4*	–	9*	20*	22	–	–	43
S.J.E. Brown	–	–	–	–	–	–	–	–	–	5*	8	3	2	57
M.P. Briers	15*	–	3*	–	9	–	13	–	1	–	–	6	–	16
A.C. Cummins	–	5*	–	–	–	–	28	–	–	–	–	–	–	233
J.D. Glendenen	–	–	–	–	–	–	–	–	–	–	–	–	–	42
P.J. Berry	–	–	–	–	–	–	10	–	11	–	–	6	–	6
J.A. Daley	–	–	–	–	–	–	5	–	–	–	–	25	18*	10
S. Hutton	46	–	11	–	–	–	–	44	–	95	30	5	–	437
C.W. Scott	36*	–	–	–	–	–	–	–	–	–	–	–	–	94
D.A. Blenkiron	36	–	–	–	–	–	–	–	–	–	–	–	–	36
M.M. Betts	–	–	–	–	–	–	–	–	–	–	–	–	–	–
Byes	7	1	8	1	7	5	6	1	1	11	10	5	4	
Leg-byes	2	12	6	3	2	3	10	13	3	7	3	6	4	
Wides		10	6		11		1	2		6	6	4	2	
No-balls		8	6		10		2	2		6				
Total	157	217	196	48	215	91	214	159	105	320	232	169	245	
Wickets	4	6	5	0	10	0	9	4	10	5	7	10	5	
Result	W	L	L	Ab.	L	Ab.	L	W	L	W	W	L	L	
Points	–	0	0	2	–	2	–	4	0	–	4	0	–	

DURHAM CCC — BATTING (continued)

	v. Yorkshire (Harrogate) 13 July TT	v. Essex (Chelmsford) 25 July AEL	v. Sussex (Durham) 1 August AEL	v. Derbyshire (Durham) 8 August AEL	v. Northamptonshire (Northampton) 15 August AEL	v. Warwickshire (Darlington) 22 August AEL	v. Yorkshire (Leeds) 29 August AEL	v. Nottinghamshire (Chester-le-Street) 5 September AEL	v. Gloucestershire (Scarborough) 7 September TT	v. Somerset (Hartlepool) 19 September AEL	Runs
W. Larkins	10	9	44	1*	45	43	114	128	10	52	814
G. Fowler	51	20	6	124	45	38	15	22	0	15	554
I. Smith	0	37	1	34*	45	17	4	5*	0	25	282
P. Bainbridge	27	20	6		16	32	17	9	6		561
I.T. Botham		12	5	92	43	3	54	18	17	28*	288
P.W.G. Parker							1	1		–	520
A.R. Fothergill	1		2		1*	4*	4*	4*	18		26
J. Wood	17*	19*	33*			–	1*	–	43*	–	133
D.A. Graveney		5	14*			0*	0	–		–	43
S.P. Hughes	–	7									57
S.J.E. Brown											16
M.P. Briers		11	11		2	19	2	4	107	38*	233
A.C. Cummins	46	1	33	8*	23	9	3	48	0		42
J.D. Glendenen	36*	9	17	–	12*	15					42
P.J. Berry	36										10
J.A. Daley											437
S. Hutton											94
C.W. Scott											94
D.A. Blenkiron											36
M.M. Betts	–										–
Byes	6	4	6	2	1	2	1	10	8	3	
Leg-byes	1	5	12	9	7	9	13	7	2	1	
Wides	4	4	4	7	9	4	1	6	6	6	
No-balls				4		2		6			
Total	235	163	194	281	246	197	230	262	217	168	
Wickets	7	10	9	2	7	8	9	7	10	3	
Result	L	L	W	W	W	W	W	W	L	W	

DURHAM CCC — BOWLING

Opponent (venue)	Date	Comp	J. Wood	S.J.E. Brown	I.T. Botham	S.P. Hughes	D.A. Graveney	P. Bainbridge	A.C. Cummins	P.J. Berry	I. Smith	J.D. Glendenen	M.M. Betts	Byes	Leg-byes	Wides	No-balls	Total	Wkts
v. Minor Counties (Hartlepool)	28 April	B&H	8-2-19-1	9-2-32-2	6-0-21-0	10-2-35-2	11-2-17-0	11-1-24-3						1	7			156	8
v. Lancashire (Old Trafford)	9 May	AEL		10-0-64-1	10-0-41-3	10-1-41-1		10-1-40-2	10-1-35-0					1	7	5	15	229	7
v. Hampshire (Stockton)	11 May	B&H	6-0-23-0		11-1-36-1	11-2-33-1	5-0-24-0	10.1-1-41-1	11-1-36-3						4	4	2	197	7
v. Hampshire (Stockton)	16 May	AEL				8-0-38-1		7-0-29-1	10-3-24-4	9-0-31-0				2	3	6	6	127	6
v. Gloucestershire (Bristol)	23 May	AEL	5-1-17-1		10-0-31-0	9-1-31-0	9.5-0-63-1	6-0-29-0	9-1-40-2						5	4	2	216	5
v. Kent (Darlington)	30 May	AEL			10-0-45-1	9-0-61-1	8-0-37-1	9-1-38-2	10-1-78-1		4-0-27-1			4	10	5		300	7
v. Leicestershire (Leicester)	6 June	AEL			10-0-47-0	10-2-33-1	10-0-35-0	10-0-45-3	10-1-46-1					1	10	6	4	217	7
v. Middlesex (Gateshead Fell)	13 June	AEL	5-0-14-1		10-2-25-2	9-0-29-1	9-0-34-0	10-0-45-3	8-1-26-1					1	5	1	2	158	7
v. Glamorgan (Colwyn Bay)	20 June	AEL	8-0-39-2		10-0-39-0	10-0-53-2	7-0-49-0	5-0-34-1	10-1-47-1					1	9	3	2	271	6
v. Wiltshire (Trowbridge)	22 June	NW	12-3-35-1			11-3-29-3	12-0-40-1	12-1-65-2	12-3-38-1			1-0-6-0			4	1	14	217	8
v. Worcestershire (Stockton)	27 June	AEL	7-0-33-0		8-1-37-0	10-0-39-1	7-0-30-1	8-0-32-2	10-1-46-2					1	9	6	6	227	9
v. Surrey (The Oval)	4 July	AEL		5-0-30-2	10-4-22-3	10-1-41-3		9-1-29-0	8-2-33-1	8-0-43-0					7	4	2	205	9
v. Glamorgan (Cardiff)	7 July	NW			12-1-49-0	9-0-27-0	10.1-0-47-0	7-1-27-0	12-1-43-0	7-0-35-2				2	18	1	4	248	3
v. Yorkshire (Harrogate)	13 July	TT	5.2-0-46-1	8-0-43-1			11-0-36-0	5-1-14-1	9.5-2-34-0		11-3-31-2		6-0-39-0		17	3	8	238	4
v. Essex (Chelmsford)	25 July	AEL		10-2-35-1		10-4-26-1	5-0-22-1	10-3-21-3	10-1-37-3						6	4	2	137	4
v. Sussex (Durham)	1 August	AEL	9.3-1-59-0			10-2-44-2	10-1-33-0	10-0-36-3	7-0-26-2					1	1	6	16	195	8
v. Derbyshire (Durham)	8 August	AEL		10-1-35-2		7-0-30-0	10-1-35-3	10-2-32-2	9-3-27-4						6	2		169	10
v. Northamptonshire (Northampton)	15 August	AEL		10-1-46-0		8.5-2-28-2	9-0-53-2	10-2-49-2	10-2-29-4						12	11	2	198	10
v. Warwickshire (Darlington)	22 August	AEL		10-1-37-1		10-3-29-1	8-1-32-0	10-2-41-2	10-0-51-2		2-0-17-1				2	2		195	10
v. Yorkshire (Leeds)	29 August	AEL		6-0-33-0		10-0-39-0	10-0-32-2	10-0-47-0	10-1-62-1		4-0-17-1				4	1	4	217	9
v. Nottinghamshire (Chester-le-Street)	5 September	AEL		10-1-31-1		10-0-58-2	6-1-29-1	10-0-37-2	10-3-34-2		4-0-25-0			1	7	1	2	260	6
v. Gloucestershire (Scarborough)	7 September	JT		7-2-26-3		10-0-52-1	8-0-31-1		10-1-41-0		5-0-25-0			1	13	12		219	9
v. Somerset (Hartlepool)	19 September	AEL		10-2-25-2		10-1-31-1	10-2-25-1				10-0-39-3				3	4		164	7
Wickets			7	16	10	27	17	33	35	2	8	0	0						

FIELDING FIGURES

25 – M.A. Garnham (ct 16/st 9)
8 – G.A. Gooch
6 – J.P. Stephenson, P.J. Prichard and N.V. Knight
5 – Salim Malik
4 – R.J. Rollins (ct 3/st 1)
3 – N. Hussain, N. Shahid, T.D. Topley, D.R. Pringle, J.H. Childs and P.M. Such
2 – J.J.B. Lewis and D.J.P. Boden
1 – N.A. Foster

BEST BATSMEN & BOWLERS

Peter Such took five wickets in a Sunday League match for the first time: S.J.W. Andrew's 3 for 25 against Derbyshire was his best performance in the Sunday League. In 11 Sunday League matches prior to 1993, Salim Malik had taken only one wicket. His 4 for 25 in the NatWest Trophy was his best performance in limited-over cricket in England.

D.J.P. Boden, D.M. Cousins, D.D.J. Robinson and R.J. Rollins all made their Sunday League debuts in 1993.

ESSEX CCC — BATTING

BATTING	Runs	v. Scotland (Forfar) 27 April B&H	v. Yorkshire (Chelmsford) 9 May AEL	v. Worcestershire (Worcester) 11 May B&H	v. Surrey (The Oval) 16 May AEL	v. Derbyshire (Chelmsford) 23 May AEL	v. Somerset (Chelmsford) 9 June AEL	v. Lancashire (Old Trafford) 13 June AEL	v. Nottinghamshire (Trent Bridge) 20 June AEL	v. Suffolk (Bury St Edmunds) 22 June NW	v. Warwickshire (Ilford) 27 June AEL	v. Kent (Maidstone) 4 July AEL	v. Northamptonshire (Chelmsford) 7 July NW	v. Leicestershire (Southend) 18 July AEL
G.A. Gooch	406	41	29	13	65	5	23	67	30	14	21	16	12*	20
J.P. Stephenson	903	50*	37	16	37	3	16	93	107	84	90	67	90	26
P.J. Prichard	496	8*	18	6	16	13	22	5	23	24	16	8	92	32
Salim Malik	399	–	–	1	7	29*	17	5	20	74	5	8	19	22
N. Hussain	272	–	8	10	0	54	42*	3	20	17	4	8	50	21
N.V. Knight	218	–	9	5	6	14	18	2	37	6	1	0	–	19
M.A. Garnham	130	–	11	16*	16	7	1	17	7	2	20	14	13	6
D.R. Pringle	229	–	72	11	19	4	1	0	5	8	12	16*	–	20
T.D. Topley	85	–	1	14	11*	2	12	1	1	5	14*	6*	–	3
M.C. Ilott	92	–	1	3	6*	1	1	8	–	0*	0	2	–	7
P.M. Such	53	–	0*	9	7	0*	7	9*	–	1*	1*	1	–	1*
N.A. Foster	10	–	0	–	–	–	–	–	–	–	–	–	–	–
J.J.B. Lewis	50	–	–	–	–	–	–	–	–	–	–	–	–	–
S.J.W. Andrew	33	–	–	–	–	–	–	–	–	–	–	–	–	–
N. Shahid	183	–	–	–	–	–	–	–	–	–	–	–	–	–
J.H. Childs	13	–	–	–	–	–	–	–	–	–	–	–	–	–
D.D.J. Robinson	2	–	–	–	–	–	–	–	–	–	–	–	–	–
D.M. Cousins	1	–	–	–	–	–	–	–	–	–	–	–	–	–
D.J.P. Boden	4	–	–	–	–	–	–	–	–	–	–	–	–	–
R.J. Rollins	0	–	–	–	–	–	–	–	–	–	–	–	–	–
Byes		5	3	1	1	–	–	6	–	7	4	1	2	4
Leg-byes		5	1	4	8	5	11	4	4	3	9	–	6	2
Wides		3	2	6	8	5	4	4	5	6	2	2	2	7
No-balls		–	–	–	–	–	4	–	2	–	–	–	–	1
Total		107	192	115	207	142	179	222	261	251	207	162	286	192
Wickets		1	10	10	9	9	10	10	8	W	10	10	5	10
Result		W	W	L	L	L	L	L	W	W	L	L	L	W
Points		–	4	–	–	–	–	–	4	–	–	–	–	4

BATTING	Runs	v. Durham (Chelmsford) 25 July AEL	v. Worcestershire (Chelmsford) 1 August AEL	v. Northamptonshire (Northampton) 8 August AEL	v. Gloucestershire (Bristol) 22 August AEL	v. Middlesex (Colchester) 29 August AEL	v. Sussex (Hove) 7 September AEL	v. Glamorgan (Cardiff) 12 September AEL	v. Hampshire (Chelmsford) 19 September AEL
G.A. Gooch	406	4	19	–	35	10	58	–	37
J.P. Stephenson	903	13	103*	–	8	41	20	1*	102*
P.J. Prichard	496	71*	40*	–	12	23	18	3	71
Salim Malik	399	–	40	–	22	67	–	0*	–
N. Hussain	272	16	–	1	9	15	25*	–	50
N.V. Knight	218	–	–	9	20	12*	0	–	1*
M.A. Garnham	130	–	7	–	–	2	0	–	–
D.R. Pringle	229	1	–	–	–	3	19	–	–
T.D. Topley	85	–	15	15	13*	0	15	–	12
M.C. Ilott	92	–	9	9	–	–	–	–	–
P.M. Such	53	–	11	11	18	40	64	–	–
N.A. Foster	10	–	0*	0*	–	–	–	–	–
J.J.B. Lewis	50	–	–	–	–	–	–	–	–
S.J.W. Andrew	33	–	2	2	–	–	–	–	–
N. Shahid	183	20*	–	–	–	2	0	–	–
J.H. Childs	13	–	–	–	–	–	–	–	–
D.D.J. Robinson	2	–	–	–	–	–	–	–	–
D.M. Cousins	1	–	–	–	–	–	–	–	–
D.J.P. Boden	4	–	–	–	–	–	–	–	–
R.J. Rollins	0	–	–	–	–	–	–	–	–
Byes		6	4	3	3	8	1	–	5
Leg-byes		4	5	4	3	5	1	–	9
Wides		2	2	13	2	8	8	3	–
No-balls									
Total		137	248	107	139	236	229	–	287
Wickets		4	4	10	7	Tie	10	Ab.	4
Result		W	L	L	L	Tie	L	Ab.	W
Points		4	–	–	–	2	–	2	4

ESSEX CCC — BOWLING

Opponent		M.C. Ilott	D.R. Pringle	T.D. Topley	J.P. Stephenson	P.M. Such	G.A. Gooch	N.A. Foster	S.J.W. Andrew	J.H. Childs	Salim Malik	D.M. Cousins	D.J.P. Boden	N.V. Knight	Byes	Leg-byes	Wides	No-balls	Total	Wkts
v. Scotland (Forfar) 27 April	B&H	11-2-21-5	11-4-20-0	11-1-29-1	11-5-13-0	5-0-9-0	6-2-11-2									3	6		106	8
v. Yorkshire (Chelmsford) 9 May	AEL	9.5-0-38-1	9-1-27-1	5-0-18-1	5-0-22-0	10-1-32-5		8-1-28-1							2	3	5		170	10
v. Worcestershire (Worcester) 11 May	B&H	6-1-21-0	7-3-21-1		5.1-0-36-0	6-1-20-0		8-0-17-0								2	1		117	1
v. Surrey (The Oval) 16 May	AEL	9.5-0-53-2	9-1-37-1	10-1-41-2	8-0-42-2	10-2-27-1										8	6	2	208	8
v. Derbyshire (Chelmsford) 23 May	AEL	10-1-24-0		10-1-42-1	9.2-2-25-3	10-2-22-1			10-1-25-3							7		2	145	8
v. Somerset (Chelmsford) 6 June	AEL	10-1-37-0	10-3-36-2	10-0-22-2	10-2-31-3											15		2	201	9
v. Lancashire (Old Trafford) 13 June	AEL	6.5-2-8-2	6-1-16-0	5-0-29-0	6-0-23-2	10-2-38-4			10-0-46-1							2	2	3	162	10
v. Nottinghamshire (Trent Bridge) 20 June	AEL	6-2-30-1	6-1-17-1	10-0-38-2	7-0-31-1					10-0-60-0						4	2	4	186	10
v. Suffolk (Bury St Edmunds) 22 June	NW	6-2-7-1	6-2-8-0	11-2-34-3	7-1-26-0	7-3-15-1			6.3-0-28-1							3			130	10
v. Warwickshire (Ilford) 27 June	AEL	8-3-45-3	10-2-44-2	5-0-31-0	10-0-37-1				5-2-12-1	10-0-38-4	6.2-0-25-4					8	4	12	253	9
v. Kent (Maidstone) 4 July	AEL	10.5-0-59-0	10-2-42-1	10-1-61-2	8-0-46-1	10-0-47-1			5-0-59-0	7-0-41-0		7-0-31-1			3	9	5	6	309	7
v. Northamptonshire (Chelmsford) 7 July	NW	9-0-35-0	12-1-53-1	11-0-54-1	8-0-39-0	12-0-54-1			4-0-25-1	10-0-58-2						6	4	2	290	5
v. Leicestershire (Southend) 18 July	AEL		9.1-1-16-3	10-2-33-1	10-1-40-3	10-1-30-1									1	11	6	6	166	10
v. Durham (Chelmsford) 25 July	AEL		9.1-3-18-1	10-0-43-3	9-1-25-1	10-2-25-3							10-0-48-2			4	4		163	10
v. Worcestershire (Chelmsford) 1 August	AEL		9-0-48-1	10-2-24-3	8.3-0-47-0	8-0-45-1					10-0-56-0					8	5	4	250	6
v. Northamptonshire (Northampton) 8 August	AEL	3-0-22-0	10-2-40-0	10-1-68-1	9.1-1-24-3				10-1-39-0	10-1-35-1			10-0-54-1			5	6	10	241	4
v. Gloucestershire (Bristol) 22 August	AEL	10-2-16-1		10-3-40-2	7-0-30-1											5	2		135	10
v. Middlesex (Colchester) 29 August	AEL	10-1-37-2		5-0-31-0		10-0-41-1				10-1-19-1			10-1-31-1		1	1	2	6	236	6
v. Sussex (Hove) 7 September	AEL	10-0-72-1		10-1-54-0	10-0-58-1	10-1-35-1			10-0-56-3		9-0-36-3		4-1-29-0	5-0-30-0	1	15	8	16	290	7
v. Glamorgan (Cardiff) 12 September	AEL																			Ab.
v. Hampshire (Chelmsford) 19 September	AEL	6-1-15-2		10-1-32-1	10-1-33-0	10-0-33-5	3-0-15-1		7-0-36-0					3-0-14-1		10	7	12	188	10
Wickets		21	15	26	22	25	3	1	10	8	7	1	4	1						

FIELDING FIGURES

32 – C.P. Metson (ct 24/st 8)
22 – R.P. Lefebvre
13 – I.V.A. Richards
12 – P.A. Cottey
10 – A. Dale
9 – H. Morris
6 – S.R. Barwick
4 – M.P. Maynard, S.L. Watkin, D.L. Hemp and S.P. James
3 – R.D.B. Croft
1 – A.D. Shaw

BEST BATSMEN & BOWLERS

Glamorgan's previous best position in the Sunday League was fifth in 1988.

S.P. James hit his highest Sunday League score in the first match of the season, and I.V.A. Richards made his highest score in the NatWest Trophy.

R.P. Lefebvre's 33 wickets in the season's limited-over matches far outstripped his record in three seasons with Somerset.

Having lost their first two Sunday League matches of the season, Glamorgan were unbeaten in the next 15.

A. Dale's Sunday League best bowling performance, of 6 for 22 against Durham, included the hat-trick.

GLAMORGAN CCC — BATTING

	Kent (Canterbury) 27 Apr B&H	Sussex (Cardiff) 11 May B&H	Derbyshire (Derby) 16 May AEL	Northants (Prentych) 23 May AEL	Somerset (Taunton) 30 May AEL	Yorkshire (Middlesbrough) 6 Jun AEL	Surrey (The Oval) 13 Jun AEL	Durham (Colwyn Bay) 20 Jun AEL	Oxfordshire (Swansea) 22 Jun NW	Nottinghamshire (Swansea) 27 Jun AEL	Middlesex (Cardiff) 4 Jul AEL	Durham (Cardiff) 7 Jul NW	Sussex (Llanelli) 11 Jul AEL	Runs
S.P. James	3	21	0	26		51	65*	58	5	18	94	48	107	738
H. Morris	44	28	70	2	–	21	98*	59	6	30	3	–	67	882
A. Dale	19	23	12	43		39	–	7	9	3	61	29	2	569
M.P. Maynard	89	57	69	7		27	–	79	67	72*	43	2	31	1007
I.V.A. Richards	21	17	30	2		20		49*	162*	2	18	101	22	557
P.A. Cottey	14	23		14		24	–	2	41	9	13	45*	4	341
R.D.B. Croft	10*	23	13	9		0	–	1*	12*	24	8	0*	4	192
R.P. Lefebvre	8	19*	1*	36*		2		3		10	4*		12	161
C.P. Metson	1*	1		0		14*		–		24*	2*		13*	76
S.L. Watkin	–	0		1*									1*	7
S.R. Barwick	–	0											–	6
D.L. Hemp	–			–		1*								69
M. Frost														1
A.J. Jones														3
S. Bastien														–
A.D. Shaw														6
Byes	12	6	5	1		1		1		1	4	2	1	
Leg-byes	5	4	1	12		3	2	9	7	5	24	18	3	
Wides				10		3	4	2	13	7	9	1	2	
No-balls	10	8	8	4	2	2				6	2	4		
Total	236	230	212	169	Ab.	208	169	271	322	211	287	248	269	
Wickets	7	10	8	9		9	6	6	5	7	4	3	8	
Result	W	L	L	L		W	W	W	W	W	W	W	W	
Points	–	–	0	0		4	4	4	–	4	4	–	4	

BATTING

	Lancashire (Old Trafford) 18 Jul AEL	Worcestershire (Worcester) 25 Jul AEL	Worcestershire (Swansea) 27 & 28 Jul NW	Warwickshire (Neath) 8 Aug AEL	Sussex (Hove) 10 Aug NW	Leicestershire (Leicester) 15 Aug AEL	Hampshire (Swansea) 22 Aug AEL	Gloucestershire (Ebbw Vale) 29 Aug AEL	Zimbabwe (Brecon) 5 Sep	Essex (Cardiff) 12 Sep AEL	Kent (Canterbury) 19 Sep AEL	Runs
S.P. James	87*	87	68	14	31	7	4	38	77	–	3	738
H. Morris	–	57	39	46	21	14	81	5	7	–	67	882
A. Dale	72*	0	41	54	1	56	20	29	33	–	31	569
M.P. Maynard	5*	63	84		84	54		69	0	–		1007
I.V.A. Richards		5	12	2	22	27	5	14	12	–	46*	557
P.A. Cottey		16	11	14	1	7	75*	19	13	–	33*	341
R.D.B. Croft		4*	8*	6*	20	27*	6*	20	0	–	–	192
R.P. Lefebvre		0*	–	6*	8*	3*	–	1	–	–	–	161
C.P. Metson					8	–		–	–		–	76
S.L. Watkin					2		–	2*	–		–	7
S.R. Barwick	–				1			4*	–		–	6
D.L. Hemp		12		3		16		–				69
M. Frost									39			1
A.J. Jones												3
S. Bastien												–
A.D. Shaw									6*			6
Byes	1	–	1	3	–	4	3	6	8		7	
Leg-byes	–	4	7	7	15	5	1	2	12		1	
Wides	3	9	6	9	6	8	14	14	14		7	
No-balls		2	2								4	
Total	168	259	279	164	220	228	209	242	221	Ab.	201	
Wickets	2	7	9	6	10	7	4	9	8		4	
Result	W	W	W	W	L	W	W	W	W		W	
Points		W	W	W	L	W	W	W	W	2	4	

GLAMORGAN CCC
BOWLING

Opponent / Date		R.P. Lefebvre	S.L. Watkin	S.R. Barwick	R.D.B. Croft	A. Dale	I.V.A. Richards	M. Frost	S. Bastien	Byes	Leg-byes	Wides	No-balls	Total	Wkts
v. Kent (Canterbury) 27 April	B&H	9-2-15-1	11-2-35-2	9.4-3-15-4	11-3-27-1	4-0-19-0	5-1-18-2				3	4		132	10
v. Sussex (Cardiff) 11 May	B&H	8-1-33-1	10-0-47-1	11-0-62-1	8-0-44-0	11-1-37-3	7-0-30-0			1	9	13		263	7
v. Derbyshire (Derby) 16 May	AEL	10-1-43-0	10-0-38-1	9.3-1-28-6	10-0-28-1	6-0-48-0	4-0-28-0				2			215	10
v. Northamptonshire (Pentrych) 23 May	AEL	10-3-20-0	10-3-28-2	10-0-33-0	8-0-29-1	3-0-18-0	8.4-0-36-2				6	4		170	7
v. Somerset (Taunton) 30 May	AEL														Ab.
v. Yorkshire (Middlesbrough) 6 June	AEL	9.5-3-28-2		10-1-27-4	10-1-28-0	5-0-33-0	6-1-21-3	8-1-40-1			6	7		183	10
v. Surrey (The Oval) 13 June	AEL	9-0-21-1	10-2-38-3	10-1-22-2	4-0-21-0	8-0-31-1	8-1-34-0				1	3		168	10
v. Durham (Colwyn Bay) 20 June	AEL	9.1-3-22-2	7-2-16-1		9-1-19-0	10-1-22-6	5-0-22-1			1	3			105	10
v. Oxfordshire (Swansea) 22 June	NW	10-5-14-1	6-3-9-0	8-0-43-0	12-1-32-1	12-2-49-2	12-2-30-1			1	13	3		191	5
v. Nottinghamshire (Swansea) 27 June	AEL	10-2-31-3	10-0-57-1	10-0-36-1	10-2-29-2	5-0-40-1	5-1-12-2				5	2	2	210	10
v. Middlesex (Cardiff) 4 July	AEL	8-3-10-2	9-3-19-1	9-1-32-0	10-0-44-2	7-0-35-1	5.3-0-23-3			1	2	2		166	10
v. Durham (Cardiff) 7 July	NW	12-4-31-2	11-1-33-1	12-2-44-1	12-1-42-1	4-0-24-0	9-0-63-0			4	4	2		245	5
v. Sussex (Llanelli) 11 July	AEL	8-0-25-1	10-0-53-1	8-1-27-2	7-0-33-1	9.2-1-38-3	3-0-35-0				8	2	2	219	10
v. Lancashire (Old Trafford) 18 July	AEL	10-1-40-1	10-1-26-3	10-0-25-1	10-1-28-1	6-0-23-0	4-0-19-2				6	2		167	9
v. Worcestershire (Worcester) 25 July	AEL	9.1-0-38-3	10-1-33-2	10-1-43-0	5-0-27-1	9-0-54-0	6-0-27-2			2	8	7		232	10
v. Worcestershire (Swansea) 27 & 28 July	NW	11-5-13-2	9-2-31-0	10-0-39-2	5-1-16-1	12-0-54-3	3.5-0-13-0			1	8			175	10
v. Warwickshire (Neath) 8 August	AEL	10-3-22-2	8-1-28-0	10-2-30-1	10-1-38-3	9-1-30-1	3-0-13-1				2	2		163	8
v. Sussex (Hove) 10 August	NW	12-4-24-1	12-2-43-3	11.2-1-33-0	9-0-52-0	12-3-43-2	3-0-25-0				4	4	2	224	7
v. Leicestershire (Leicester) 15 August	AEL	10-4-20-1	10-0-41-0	10-0-46-4	10-0-42-0	10-0-68-2					3	5		220	7
v. Hampshire (Swansea) 22 August	AEL	10-2-22-2		9-1-49-2	8-0-46-0	6-0-25-3	7-0-15-1		10-1-33-0	2	15	11		207	8
v. Gloucestershire (Ebbw Vale) 29 August.	AEL	8.5-3-23-2	10-0-55-3	9-1-49-1	10-1-33-1	9-0-41-3	1-0-6-0				4	5	4	211	10
v. Zimbabwe (Brecon) 5 September		9-4-18-2	11-2-35-1	10-1-23-2	11-3-25-0	10.2-0-59-2					8	7		168	10
v. Essex (Cardiff) 12 September	AEL	2-2-0-0	3-0-7-2									3		7	2
v. Kent (Canterbury) 19 September	AEL	10-0-43-1	10-1-33-3	10-1-33-1	10-1-42-2	10-1-41-2					8		1	201	9
Wickets		33	31	35	19	35	20	1	0						

FIELDING FIGURES

26 – R.C. Russell (ct 23/st 3)
9 – A.J. Wright
8 – T.H.C. Hancock
7 – M.W. Alleyne
5 – S.G. Hinks
4 – M.C.J. Ball and A.M. Smith
3 – R.J. Scott, A.M. Babington and C.A. Walsh
2 – G.D. Hodgson, R.C. Williams and M.G.N. Windows
1 – B.C. Broad, R.J. Dawson and R.M. Wight
†A.M. Smith retired hurt

BEST BATSMEN & BOWLERS

B.C. Broad scored 1,333 runs and took 17 wickets in the Sunday League for Gloucestershire, 1979 to 1983. He played for Nottinghamshire, 1984-92, before returning to Gloucestershire in 1993.

M.G.N. Windows and R.M. Wight made their debuts in the Sunday League.

G.D. Hodgson made his first Sunday League century, 104 not out, against Durham.

R.J. Cunliffe made his county debut in the last Sunday League match of the season.

GLOUCESTERSHIRE CCC — BATTING

Player	v. Derbyshire (Bristol) 27 April B&H	v. Northamptonshire (Northampton) 9 May AEL	v. Durham (Bristol) 23 May AEL	v. Worcestershire (Gloucester) 30 May AEL	v. Kent (Tunbridge Wells) 6 June AEL	v. Yorkshire (Sheffield) 20 June AEL	v. Hertfordshire (Bristol) 22 June NW	v. Leicestershire (Leicester) 27 June AEL	v. Hampshire (Bristol) 4 July AEL	v. Yorkshire (Bristol) 7 July NW	v. Middlesex (Moreton-in-Marsh) 11 July AEL	v. Surrey (Guildford) 18 July AEL	v. Derbyshire (Cheltenham) 1 August AEL	Runs
B.C. Broad	58	22	2	—	52	75*	14	3	74	114*	47	39	2	511
S.G. Hinks	6	4	—	—	5	—	21	6	18	19*	26	14	—	429
R.J. Scott	44	25	0	5	78	6	73	41	36	—	42	3	5	267
M.W. Alleyne	30*	12	6	33*	16	73*	45	51	21	32	14	36	3	580
A.J. Wright	23	10	61	27	13	1	2	2	7	—	36	7	36	424
T.H.C. Hancock	—	5	4*	26	13*	—	—	41	—	—	31	22*	4	308
R.C. Russell	11	3	—	—	—	—	—	12*	7	—	—	9	—	285
M.C.J. Ball	6*	10*	27	—	—	—	8*	—	—	—	—	—	0	56
A.M. Smith	—	11	—	—	1	—	—	—	—	—	1	—	—	65
K.E. Cooper	—	—	—	—	—	—	—	—	—	—	—	—	—	1
M.J. Gerrard	—	4	—	—	—	—	—	—	—	—	—	—	—	4
G.D. Hodgson	—	10	104*	—	15	0	9	6	47	62	—	—	7	272
A.M. Babington	—	—	—	—	3	—	1*	0	—	—	—	—	10	36
R.C. Williams	—	—	—	—	—	—	—	—	—	—	—	—	—	33
C.A. Walsh	—	—	—	—	—	—	9	1	0	—	1	2	4	151
R.M. Wight	—	—	0*	—	1	—	37	1	—	—	24	4	5	35
R.J. Dawson	—	—	—	—	—	—	18	—	21*	—	11*	4	13*	36
M. Davies	—	—	—	—	—	—	—	—	—	—	—	—	—	26
M.G.N. Windows	—	—	—	6	—	—	—	—	—	—	—	—	—	104
R.J. Cunliffe	—	—	—	—	—	—	—	—	—	—	—	—	—	22
Byes	6	1	—	—	4	5	9	1	1	1	1	4	6	
Leg-byes	6	3	5	—	3	3	17	6	7	7	4	7	4	
Wides	6	3	5	2	—	4	6	12	7	2	4	—	4	
No-balls	—	3	2	0	10	—	—	—	2	—	Ab.	—	—	
Total	198	123	216	93	204	167	274	183	240	241	243	155	99	
Wickets	7	10	5	3	10	4	9	10	7	7	10	10	10	
Result	L	L	W	L	L	W	W	L	W	L	Ab.	L	L	
Points	—	0	4	0	0	4	—	0	4	—	2	0	0	

GLOUCESTERSHIRE CCC — BATTING

Player	v. Lancashire (Cheltenham) 8 August AEL	v. Warwickshire (Edgbaston) 15 August AEL	v. Essex (Bristol) 22 August AEL	v. Glamorgan (Ebbw Vale) 29 August AEL	v. Somerset (Taunton) 5 September AEL	v. Durham (Scarborough) 7 September TT	v. Yorkshire (Scarborough) 8 September TT	v. Nottinghamshire (Bristol) 12 September AEL	v. Sussex (Hove) 19 September AEL	Runs
B.C. Broad	44	36	3	62	7	15	4	0	60	511
S.G. Hinks	92	42	4	26	21*	35	49	—	—	429
R.J. Scott	16	2	45	28	14	59	0	14*	8	267
M.W. Alleyne	—	52*	4	11	—	18	17	—	2	580
A.J. Wright	3	—	10	23	7	0	9	14*	46	424
T.H.C. Hancock	0	28	27	22	7	4	6*	—	3	308
R.C. Russell	0*	34*	—	—	12	1*	0*	—	10*	285
M.C.J. Ball	—	—	0*	14*	15*	4	0*	—	3	56
A.M. Smith	—	—	—	—	—	—	—	—	—	65
K.E. Cooper	—	—	—	—	—	—	—	—	—	1
M.J. Gerrard	—	—	—	—	—	—	—	—	—	4
G.D. Hodgson	3	20	2	2	—	24	4	—	—	272
A.M. Babington	—	—	0	0	—	16	—	—	—	36
R.C. Williams	—	—	18	8	4	—	26	24*	4	33
C.A. Walsh	1	—	—	—	6	—	—	—	16	151
R.M. Wight	—	—	9	—	—	21	38	—	6	35
R.J. Dawson	—	—	—	—	—	—	—	—	—	36
M. Davies	4	—	—	—	—	—	—	—	—	26
M.G.N. Windows	6	—	9	9	9	1	8	4	22	104
R.J. Cunliffe	—	—	—	—	—	—	—	—	—	22
Byes	10	8	5	4	4	1	8	4	9	192
Leg-byes	10	6	2	5	5	13	7	1	1	10
Wides	4	4	6	—	10	12	—	Ab.	2	2
No-balls	4	6	—	—	—	—	—	—	—	
Total	202	232	135	211	115	219	168	43	192	
Wickets	10	5	10	10	7	9	9†	1	10	
Result	Tie	W	L	L	W	W	W	Ab.	L	

GLOUCESTERSHIRE CCC — BOWLING

Match	Date	Comp	K.E. Cooper	M.J. Gerrard	A.M. Smith	M.C.J. Ball	R.J. Scott	A.M. Babington	R.C. Williams	M.W. Alleyne	C.A. Walsh	R.M. Wight	T.H.C. Hancock	M. Davies	Byes	Leg-byes	Wides	No-balls	Total	Wkts
v. Derbyshire (Bristol)	27 April	B&H	11-3-20-1	11-1-44-0	11-1-43-1	11-1-32-1	11-0-52-0								1	6	6		198	5
v. Northamptonshire (Northampton)	9 May	AEL		10-1-42-1	7-0-51-1	2-0-15-0	8-1-41-2	10-2-34-1								2	2	2	185	5
v. Durham (Bristol)	23 May	AEL		8-2-36-0	9-0-33-2	3-0-28-0	10-1-35-2									7	2	10	215	10
v. Worcestershire (Gloucester)	30 May	AEL	2-0-14-1		2-0-30-1		1-0-12-1		10-0-46-3	10-0-30-2	2-0-14-0					1	1	7	108	3
v. Kent (Tunbridge Wells)	6 June	AEL	7-0-47-0				6.2-1-25-0		1-0-17-0	2-0-20-0	8-1-31-2	10-1-41-1				7	1	6	207	3
v. Yorkshire (Sheffield)	20 June	AEL			9-1-29-2		10-2-24-1			6-0-33-0	10-1-20-2	7-0-33-1				2	8	4	166	8
v. Hertfordshire (Bristol)	22 June	NW			12-6-17-2		10-0-37-1			4-0-20-0	9-1-27-2	12-0-34-1	1.5-0-7-2			4	3	16	164	10
v. Leicestershire (Leicester)	27 June	AEL			10-0-52-1		6-0-24-2			3-0-9-1	10-3-31-2	4-1-18-0			1	7	4		214	8
v. Hampshire (Bristol)	4 July	AEL			9-0-39-1		7-0-29-0			10-0-44-2	9.3-2-38-2			6-0-35-1		4	9	8	216	10
v. Yorkshire (Bristol)	7 July	NW	12-3-35-1		12-1-58-0		6-0-30-0			10-0-48-3	11.4-1-40-2	8-1-24-1				8	5	2	243	8
v. Middlesex (Moreton-in-Marsh)	11 July	AEL																	Ab.	Ab.
v. Surrey (Guildford)	18 July	AEL			4-0-17-1			8-0-40-1		4-0-16-0	7.3-1-34-1					3	1	6	110	1
v. Derbyshire (Cheltenham)	1 August	AEL			3.5-0-26-2			5-1-27-0			3-0-28-0			3-0-19-0				4	100	2
v. Lancashire (Cheltenham)	8 August	AEL			10-1-34-0		10-0-46-1	10-1-28-1		9-0-42-3	10-1-38-2			1-0-11-1		3	5	4	202	10
v. Warwickshire (Edgbaston)	15 August	AEL			10-0-54-2		5-0-17-0	10-0-33-2		10-0-55-1	9.4-4-21-2			5-0-38-1		2	2	2	221	10
v. Essex (Bristol)	22 August	AEL			9.1-3-33-2		10-3-17-0	10-0-53-1	10-3-29-2	6-0-15-2	10-1-25-0				1	3	3	2	139	7
v. Glamorgan (Ebbw Vale)	29 August	AEL			10-1-56-4		6-1-21-0	6-2-13-2	10-0-37-2	4-0-24-0	10-1-45-2			4-0-17-1		6	2	14	242	9
v. Somerset (Taunton)	5 September	AEL			6-2-19-0	9.5-0-24-3	5-0-14-0	10-1-44-6	8-0-30-1	7-2-8-3						3	5	4	111	10
v. Durham (Scarborough)	7 September	JT			8.5-1-54-2	8-2-27-0		10-1-46-2	10-1-28-0	3-0-23-0	10-2-33-1					8	2	6	217	10
v. Yorkshire (Scarborough)	8 September	JT			10-1-40-1	2-0-19-0			6-1-40-0	1-0-9-0	10-4-24-5				1	5	1	20	228	8
v. Nottinghamshire (Bristol)	12 September	AEL											6-0-45-0						Ab.	Ab.
v. Sussex (Hove)	19 September	AEL			10-1-52-1	10-0-30-2			10-0-51-0	8-0-46-0	9.3-1-33-3		2-0-7-0		1	4	2	14	224	10
Wickets			3	1	25	6	10	20	8	18	28	4	2	4						

FIELDING FIGURES

18 – A.N. Aymes (ct 14/st 4)
13 – V.P. Terry
8 – M.C.J. Nicholas
7 – S.D. Udal
4 – R.A. Smith
3 – M.D. Marshall and C.A. Connor
2 – R.F.M. Cox
1 – D.I. Gower, T.C. Middleton, J.R. Ayling, K.D. James, I.J. Turner and M.J. Thursfield

BEST BATSMEN & BOWLERS

M.D. Marshall's career with Hampshire, which began in 1979, ended in 1993. He took 150 wickets and scored 1,340 runs in the Sunday League.

J.R. Ayling was forced to retire through injury. M. Jean-Jacques and M.J. Thursfield both appeared for Hampshire in the Sunday League for the first time. Jean-Jacques previously played for Derbyshire; Thursfield was with Middlesex but did not appear in limited-over cricket.

J.N.B. Bovill previously played for Buckinghamshire and represented the Combined Universities in the Benson and Hedges Cup when he was up at Durham.

J.R. Wood hit his highest Sunday League score, 92 not out, against Northamptonshire.

J.S. Laney made his debut in the last game of the season.

HAMPSHIRE CCC — BATTING

BATTING	v. Comb. Universities (Southampton) 27 April B&H	v. Durham (Stockton) 11 May B&H	v. Durham (Stockton) 16 May AEL	v. Yorkshire (Southampton) 23 May AEL	v. Northamptonshire (Southampton) 25 & 26 May B&H	v. Derbyshire (Checkley) 30 May AEL	v. Nottinghamshire (Trent Bridge) 6 June AEL	v. Kent (Basingstoke) 13 June AEL	v. Northamptonshire (Northampton) 20 June AEL	v. Staffordshire (Stone) 22 June NW	v. Gloucestershire (Bristol) 4 July AEL	v. Sussex (Hove) 7 July NW	v. Somerset (Southampton) 11 July AEL	Runs
V.P. Terry	30	79	12	13	76		46*	23	49*	12	27	71	83*	816
T.C. Middleton	91*	8	12	10	3		48	16	69	34	54	9	9	396
D.I. Gower	41*	4	8	27	31		59			11	60	2	33	347
R.A. Smith		29	53*		30			15		105*		104*		768
M.C.J. Nicholas			13	59	27		46*	31		3*	9	12	0	400
M.D. Marshall		4		0	1*			27			0	31*	84*	147
J.R. Ayling			10	5	25			15			10*			66
A.N. Aymes		16	1*	1*	1*			0			0			129
S.D. Udal		23*			4*									120
I.J. Turner		9*		12				1*			1			3
C.A. Connor				6				0	7		9			47
K.D. James		13						17*			0			112
M. Jean-Jacques				20				33			25			4
J.R. Wood									92*					248
M.J. Thursfield														17
K.J. Shine														1
R.F.M. Cox														15
J.N.B. Bovill														7
J.S. Laney														12
Byes	1	4	2	4	5			6	5	1	4	7	2	
Leg-byes	7	6	3	9	2		5	4	2		9	6	4	
Wides		2	1	1			4	4	2		8	6		
No-balls	8		6		10									
Total	178	197	127	170	223		208	198	226	166	216	248	215	
Wickets	1	7	6	10	7		2	10	2	3	10	4	3	
Result	W	W	Ab.	L	L	Ab.	W	L	L	W	L	L	W	
Points	–		2	0		2	4	0		–	0	–	4	

BATTING	v. Worcestershire (Portsmouth) 18 July AEL	v. Middlesex (Lord's) 25 July AEL	v. Warwickshire (Southampton) 1 August AEL	v. Lancashire (Southampton) 15 August AEL	v. Glamorgan (Swansea) 22 August AEL	v. Sussex (Portsmouth) 29 August AEL	v. Surrey (The Oval) 5 September AEL	v. Leicestershire (Southampton) 12 September AEL	v. Essex (Chelmsford) 19 September AEL	Runs
V.P. Terry	29	9	74*	4	48	124*	5		2	816
T.C. Middleton	27		26	1		129			33	396
D.I. Gower	79	17	118*	64*	75		30			347
R.A. Smith	2			6	21	28*	28		18	768
M.C.J. Nicholas		14			8					400
M.D. Marshall										147
J.R. Ayling				1	7*			21	44	66
A.N. Aymes	17	17		44	0		21	15	16	129
S.D. Udal	3*	18*		0	6*		15	0	2	120
I.J. Turner		2						12		3
C.A. Connor	5*	25		1	4		0		11	47
K.D. James		32			8		12			112
M. Jean-Jacques										4
J.R. Wood				0	2		10	4		248
M.J. Thursfield	44	9		9		7		0		17
K.J. Shine		4					1*	9	10	1
R.F.M. Cox							3		7	15
J.N.B. Bovill							0		12	7
J.S. Laney									12	12
Byes	9	1	2	4	2	11	2	10	10	
Leg-byes	3	14	8	6	15	5	7	7	7	
Wides	3		1	5	9	9	2		12	
No-balls	2		4	12	11					
Total	203	165	233	158	207	313	136	188	188	
Wickets	10	10	1	10	2	2	7	10	10	

HAMPSHIRE CCC

BOWLING

Opponent	Date	Comp.	M.D. Marshall	C.A. Connor	J.J. Turner	J.R. Ayling	S.D. Udal	M. Jean-Jacques	K.D. James	M.J. Thursfield	K.J. Shine	M.C.J. Nicholas	J.N.B. Bovill	Byes	Leg-byes	Wides	No-balls	Total	Wkts
v. Combined Universities (Southampton)	27 April	B&H	11-4-24-2	11-2-36-1	11-0-41-1	11-0-29-1	11-1-39-2							1	7	3		177	7
v. Durham (Stockton)	11 May	B&H	11-1-29-2	11-2-34-1		11-4-39-1	11-1-27-0	11-0-59-1							8	6	6	196	5
v. Durham (Stockton)	11 May	AEL	5-1-12-0	2-0-11-0		1-0-6-0	3-0-15-0							1	3			48	0
v. Yorkshire (Southampton)	16 May	AEL	10-3-26-2	8-0-26-1	5-0-14-0	10-1-42-1	10-0-51-2		7-0-36-1						5	3		200	8
v. Northamptonshire (Southampton)	23 May	AEL	11-1-48-0	10.4-1-43-1	11-0-52-1	10-0-37-0	11-1-44-0								3	5	9	227	3
v. Derbyshire (Checkley)	25 & 26 May	B&H																	Ab.
v. Nottinghamshire (Trent Bridge)	30 May	AEL		10-3-23-3	7-0-29-1	10-0-38-1	10-0-45-3		7-0-23-1	6-0-38-0					8	6		204	9
v. Kent (Basingstoke)	6 June	AEL	5-0-35-0	6-1-53-0		6-0-45-1	10-0-33-0		7-0-33-1						3		2	202	3
v. Northamptonshire (Northampton)	13 June	AEL	9.4-0-46-1	10-4-25-1		8-0-42-1	10-0-47-1		7-0-45-0		5-0-15-2			2	7	9	2	229	6
v. Staffordshire (Stone)	20 June	NW	11.1-0-28-0	12-3-21-3		12-1-51-2	12-1-24-2		12-2-29-2						12	8		165	10
v. Gloucestershire (Bristol)	22 June	AEL	10-1-44-0	10-1-38-2			10-0-40-1	10-1-59-2	10-0-52-2						7	7	2	240	7
v. Sussex (Hove)	4 July	AEL	12-0-36-0	11.5-0-59-1			12-0-42-0		12-1-47-0						2	2	14	252	1
v. Somerset (Southampton)	7 July	NW	10-2-26-1	10-2-40-1	9.4-1-58-3		10-0-34-2		10-0-46-3		9.3-0-61-0	1.3-0-5-0		5	5	2	2	214	10
v. Worcestershire (Portsmouth)	11 July	AEL																	Ab.
v. Middlesex (Lord's)	18 July	AEL		10-1-24-0	10-0-47-1		9.1-1-60-0		10-0-48-1	10-0-44-1		0.5-0-8-0		4	11	6		246	3
v. Warwickshire (Southampton)	25 July	AEL	10-0-50-0	10-2-46-1	10-0-51-2		10-0-38-1			10-0-42-2					5	3		232	6
v. Lancashire (Southampton)	1 August	AEL	9-1-25-1	8.4-1-37-0	10-0-24-0		10-1-24-1			10-1-46-1					3	3		159	4
v. Glamorgan (Swansea)	15 August	AEL	9.3-2-32-0	10-0-53-0	10-0-41-1		8-0-33-0	10-0-47-1							3	1	14	209	4
v. Sussex (Portsmouth)	22 August	AEL		10-0-69-4	10-0-51-2		10-0-61-2		10-1-37-0		10-0-87-0			1	6	2	2	312	8
v. Surrey (The Oval)	29 August	AEL		10-2-33-3			10-0-34-2		10-0-47-0		10-0-54-1		10-0-40-3	1	4	5	4	213	10
v. Leicestershire (Southampton)	5 September	AEL																	Ab.
	12 September	AEL																	
v. Essex (Chelmsford)	19 September	AEL		10-2-37-0			9-0-66-0		10-1-50-1	10-0-50-2		4-0-24-0	7-0-55-0	5	5	9		287	4
Wickets			9	23	12	8	19	4	12	6	3	0	3						

FIELDING FIGURES

19 – S.A. Marsh (ct 18/st 1)
13 – C.L. Hooper and M.V. Fleming
9 – N.J. Llong
7 – G.R. Cowdrey
4 – M.J. McCague, A.P. Igglesden and M.R. Benson
3 – N.R. Taylor, T.R. Ward and D.W. Headley
2 – D.J. Spencer, D.P. Fulton and C. Penn
1 – J.I. Longley, M.A. Ealham and R.J. Parks (st 1)

BEST BATSMEN & BOWLERS

Kent won the Sunday League title in 1972, 1973 and 1976.

D.P. Fulton and D.J. Spencer made their debuts in the Sunday League. R.J. Parks and D.W. Headley previously appeared for Hampshire and Middlesex respectively.

T.R. Ward and C.L. Hooper hit their first Sunday League centuries. Hooper also had a best Sunday League bowling performance of 5 for 41 against Essex.

N.J. Llong, 4 for 24 against Sussex, and M.A. Ealham, 6 for 53 against Hampshire, also had Sunday League best bowling performances.

C.L. Hooper was Player of the Season in the Sunday League.

KENT CCC — BATTING

	v. Glamorgan, Canterbury, 27 April (B&H)	v. Middlesex, Lord's, 9 May (AEL)	v. Warwickshire, Canterbury, 16 May (AEL)	v. Nottinghamshire, Trent Bridge, 23 May (AEL)	v. Durham, Darlington, 30 May (AEL)	v. Gloucestershire, Tunbridge Wells, 6 June (AEL)	v. Hampshire, Basingstoke, 13 June (AEL)	v. Derbyshire, Canterbury, 20 June (AEL)	v. Middlesex, Canterbury, 22 June (NW)	v. Yorkshire, Leeds, 27 June (AEL)	v. Essex, Maidstone, 4 July (AEL)	v. Warwickshire, Edgbaston, 7 July (NW)	v. Surrey, Canterbury, 14 July (SB)	Runs
T.R. Ward	0	16	99	131	49	23	112	15	34	49	86	50	5	804
M.R. Benson	13	42*	40	3	18	80	–	8	60	20	19	16	40	271
N.R. Taylor	42	–	50*	6	22	11*	11*	6	57	35	15	25	47	535
N.J. Llong	5	–	17	2	20	–	16*	3	27*	4	16	1	30	365
G.R. Cowdrey	33	1	–	0	46	9	58	57	5	9	45*	5	14	248
M.V. Fleming	7	–	14	1	19	–	–	4	18	1	0	34	50	364
S.A. Marsh	6	–	4	–	–	–	–	28	–	17	–	6	10*	207
R.P. Davis	18*	–	–	–	–	–	–	–	–	–	–	–	–	28
C. Penn	0	–	–	–	–	–	–	–	–	–	–	–	–	0
M.J. McCague	0	–	–	4*	–	–	–	11*	–	1*	–	6*	2*	24
A.P. Igglesden	1	–	–	–	–	–	–	–	–	–	–	–	–	7
C.L. Hooper	–	37*	29	94	85	70*	0	72	62	32	103	38	–	954
D.J. Spencer	–	–	4	2	9*	–	–	31*	1*	6	8*	0	1	42
D.W. Headley	–	–	–	–	12*	–	–	–	0	18*	3	58*	4	41
M.A. Ealham	–	–	–	–	–	–	–	–	–	–	–	–	–	216
R.J. Parks	–	–	–	–	–	–	–	–	–	–	–	–	–	–
J.I. Longley	–	–	–	–	–	–	–	–	–	–	–	–	–	27
D.P. Fulton	–	–	–	–	–	–	–	–	–	–	–	–	–	35
Byes	3	3	3	2	4	7	3	1	1	1	3	4	5	
Leg-byes	4	1	15	13	10	1	–	5	4	5	9	6	1	
Wides	–	2	–	6	6	6	2	–	11	–	2	7	–	
No-balls	4	4	4	–	–	–	–	–	2	–	4	–	–	
Total	132	105	289	264	300	207	202	245	282	200	309	262	209	
Wickets	10	1	8	9	7	3	7	8	7	9	7	9	8	
Result	L	W	W	L	Ab.	W	W	L	W	W	W	L	L	
Points	–	4	4	0	2	4	4	0	–	4	4	–	1	

KENT CCC — BATTING (continued)

	v. Sussex, Hove, 18 July (AEL)	v. Somerset, Taunton, 25 July (AEL)	v. Leicestershire, Canterbury, 1 August (AEL)	v. Surrey, Canterbury, 8 August (AEL)	v. Worcestershire, Worcester, 22 August (AEL)	v. Lancashire, Old Trafford, 29 August (AEL)	v. Northamptonshire, Canterbury, 5 September (AEL)	v. Glamorgan, Canterbury, 19 September (AEL)	Runs
T.R. Ward	3*	4	18	43	27	12	22	11	804
M.R. Benson	–	4	30	3	9	–	22	–	271
N.R. Taylor	–	44	57	36	6	44*	64*	25	535
N.J. Llong	–	42	13	2	10*	8	–	10	365
G.R. Cowdrey	–	1	43	24	11*	13	8	44	248
M.V. Fleming	–	18	67*	15	–	–	13	6	364
S.A. Marsh	–	20*	4*	–	–	–	–	–	207
R.P. Davis	–	–	–	–	–	–	–	–	28
C. Penn	–	–	–	–	–	–	–	–	0
M.J. McCague	–	6	–	–	–	87*	–	6*	24
A.P. Igglesden	–	–	–	–	–	–	–	–	7
C.L. Hooper	–	6	64	51	47	–	17	60	954
D.J. Spencer	–	–	–	16*	–	–	17*	5	42
D.W. Headley	–	–	–	4*	–	–	7	10*	41
M.A. Ealham	32*	32*	–	32	20	6	7	13	216
R.J. Parks	–	–	–	–	–	–	–	–	–
J.I. Longley	–	–	–	–	–	–	–	1	27
D.P. Fulton	–	–	–	–	–	29	–	–	35
Byes		8	3	3	3	1	5	1	
Leg-byes		5	10	8	11	4	4	8	
Wides		12	6	11	2	3	8	1	
No-balls			12						
Total	3	196	327	248	143	193	166	200	
Wickets	0	7	6	8	5	4	7	9	
Result	Ab.	W	W	W	W	W	W	L	
Points	2	4	4	4	4	4	4	0	

KENT CCC BOWLING

Match		A.P. Igglesden	M.J. McCague	C. Penn	M.V. Fleming	R.P. Davis	D.J. Spencer	C.L. Hooper	D.W. Headley	N.J. Llong	M.A. Ealham	Byes	Leg-byes	Wides	No-balls	Total	Wkts
v. Glamorgan (Canterbury) 27 April	B&H	11-2-31-1	11-0-39-3	11-1-54-0	11-1-52-3	11-0-48-0							12	5	10	236	7
v. Middlesex (Lord's) 9 May	AEL	8-3-19-2	10-2-18-3		6.1-0-15-2								6	4	4	104	10
v. Warwickshire (Canterbury) 16 May	AEL	8-0-31-2			9.1-0-39-3		8-0-28-1	9-2-18-2	9-0-38-0	6-0-40-1			16	8	2	223	9 [A]
v. Nottinghamshire (Trent Bridge) 23 May	AEL	8-1-37-1	7-0-67-0		7.2-0-72-0		4-0-17-0	10-0-42-1	4-0-30-0				6	9	12	265	1
v. Durham (Darlington) 30 May	AEL	6-0-45-0	6-0-39-0					9-0-53-0					5	3		91	0
v. Gloucestershire (Tunbridge Wells) 6 June	AEL			9-0-58-2	9-0-50-1			0.3-0-2-0	8-0-15-0	3-0-13-0	9.4-4-41-3		4	3		204	10
v. Hampshire (Basingstoke) 13 June	AEL		10-0-35-1	10-1-27-1	10-2-45-0			10-2-23-2			10-1-53-6		6	4	2	198	10
v. Derbyshire (Canterbury) 20 June	AEL	10-0-50-1	10-1-45-2		10-0-52-2			10-1-32-2			10-1-55-2		2	7	4	248	8
v. Middlesex (Canterbury) 22 June	NW	7-1-20-0	12-3-26-5					10-0-44-0	11-1-45-3		3-0-10-0		3	10	4	116	10
v. Yorkshire (Leeds) 27 June	AEL		10-1-29-2		10-1-47-1			3-0-12-2	10-2-29-0		10-1-52-0		12	3		192	7
v. Essex (Maidstone) 4 July	AEL				5-0-27-0	7-0-25-1		10-1-23-2	8-0-35-1		7-0-22-1		1		2	152	10
v. Warwickshire (Edgbaston) 7 July	NW		12-1-54-1		12-1-55-1			10-0-41-5	12-2-48-1	1.2-0-1-1	12-1-38-1	1	20	2	2	265	5
v. Surrey (Canterbury) 14 July	SB	8-1-28-0	9-0-38-0		6-0-21-2	9.1-0-48-2		11.3-1-49-0	6-0-38-0		5-0-32-1	5	3	15	6	213	5
v. Sussex (Hove) 18 July	AEL		10-0-54-1	8-1-19-1	3.3-0-12-1				8-1-30-0	9-1-24-4	6-1-31-1		4	2	3	177	10
v. Somerset (Taunton) 25 July	AEL	10-1-36-0			8-0-57-2			10-2-22-2	10-3-30-1	4-0-27-0	10-2-44-1		8	2	2	193	6
v. Leicestershire (Canterbury) 1 August	AEL			10-0-49-1	10-0-66-1		4-1-29-2	10-5-8-1	9.1-0-32-3		10-0-45-2		8	1		264	5
v. Surrey (Canterbury) 8 August	AEL	10-2-47-1			8-0-32-2			10-0-60-1	10-0-47-3		8-2-27-1	2	2	8	8	194	10
v. Worcestershire (Worcester) 22 August	AEL	10-1-29-5			10-0-25-0			6-0-23-0	9.5-1-50-2		10-2-43-0	4	12	4	4	186	9
v. Lancashire (Old Trafford) 29 August	AEL	10-3-39-2			10-0-46-4			10-1-26-1	10-0-37-2		10-2-29-0		7	2		192	10
v. Northamptonshire (Canterbury) 5 September	AEL	10-0-30-0					7-0-21-0	10-1-21-0	10-0-43-1		7-3-21-2	7	4	5	4	165	8
v. Glamorgan (Canterbury) 19 September	AEL	10-1-43-1			6-0-26-2		8.4-1-43-1	9-0-44-0			10-3-20-1		1	7	4	201	4
Wickets		16	18	5	27	3	4	21	19	6	22						

A.A.A. Donald absent hurt

338 THE BENSON and HEDGES CRICKET YEAR

LANCASHIRE CCC

FIELDING FIGURES

29 – W.K. Hegg (ct 24/st 5)
6 – N.H. Fairbrother
4 – M. Watkinson, Wasim Akram, I.D. Austin and G.D. Lloyd
3 – A.A. Barnett, P.A.J. DeFreitas and M.A. Atherton
2 – P.J. Martin, S.P. Titchard, G. Yates, N.J. Speak and J.P. Crawley

BEST BATSMEN & BOWLERS

By their standards, Lancashire enjoyed a moderate season in limited-over cricket, although they reached the final of the Benson and Hedges Cup.

G. Chapple made his Sunday League debut.

S.P. Titchard made his highest score in the Sunday League, 84 against Leicestershire.

G. Yates' 3 for 27 against Worcestershire was his best bowling performance in the Sunday League.

BATTING (first part)

	Durham 9 May (Old Trafford) AEL	Surrey 11 May (The Oval) B&H	Somerset 16 May (Taunton) AEL	Sussex 25 May (Hove) B&H	Warwickshire 30 May (Old Trafford) AEL	Surrey 6 June (The Oval) AEL	Leicestershire 8 June (Leicester) B&H	Essex 13 June (Old Trafford) AEL	Sussex 20 June (Old Trafford) AEL	Northamptonshire 22 June (Northampton) NW	Derbyshire 27 June (Derby) AEL	Leicestershire 4 July (Leicester) AEL	Derbyshire 10 July (Lord's) B&H	Runs
M.A. Atherton	96	11	28	38	31		33	38	0	37	105	36	54	624
N.J. Speak	0*	0	40	20	17		27	12	9	0	21	25	42	421
N.H. Fairbrother	29	87	28	9	16	1	64*	15	1	22	26	15	87*	606
G.D. Lloyd	24	25	27	32*	3	11	34	24	9	1	6	22	5	386
M. Watkinson	6	15	14	8*	2	8	16	1		60*	4*	16	10	221
P.A.J. DeFreitas	2	38	9	46	21*		7	18	39*	8	15*	42*	16	185
Wasim Akram	14	0	1		24	11	5	23	0	0	33		12	423
W.G. Hegg	22*	0*	16*		2*	0		9*		38*				90
I.D. Austin	0*		13*			23		0	38*			0*	0*	178
P.J. Martin						6	9*		11*					38
A.A. Barnett						11*	0							21
G.D. Mendis		19	16	19	34		8							38
S.P. Titchard						2	11			4	10	84	0	286
G. Chapple						3						34		12
R.C. Irani														67
J.P. Crawley														125
G. Yates										27				9
Byes	1	4	10	6	2	4	13	2	1	1	7	4	11	
Leg-byes	7	15	6	6	6	4	2	2	2	2	7	11	3	
Wides	4	5	2	2	10	3	4	3	4	5		7	6	
No-balls	15	6		2	6		4					4		
Total	229	236	210	182	174	94	218	162	122	178	234	300	246	
Wickets	7	10	8	5	7	10	6	10	4	7	4	7	7	
Result	W	W	Ab.	W	Ab.	L	W	L	W	L	W	W	L	
Points	4	–	2	–	2	0	–	0	4	–	4	4	–	

BATTING (second part)

	Glamorgan 18 July (Old Trafford) AEL	Nottinghamshire 25 July (Old Trafford) AEL	Gloucestershire 8 August (Cheltenham) AEL	Hampshire 15 August (Southampton) AEL	Yorkshire 22 August (Old Trafford) AEL	Kent 29 August (Old Trafford) AEL	Worcestershire 5 September (Worcester) AEL	Middlesex 12 September (Lord's) AEL	Northamptonshire 19 September (Old Trafford) AEL	Runs
M.A. Atherton	64	0	30	51	14	1	25		12	624
N.J. Speak	9		81	10	32	24	55		63*	421
N.H. Fairbrother		8	12	25*		3	56*		69	606
G.D. Lloyd	0	0	11		1	53	35		15	386
M. Watkinson	7	28	34		3	20			5	221
P.A.J. DeFreitas	8	3	8	17*	51*	21	0*		10	185
Wasim Akram	18	16*	1		3*	29				423
W.G. Hegg	4	15			25	5*			20*	90
I.D. Austin						7				178
P.J. Martin	10*									38
A.A. Barnett										21
G.D. Mendis	24		5	31	18				29	38
S.P. Titchard	9*	44*	6	19	11	12				286
G. Chapple	6					8				12
R.C. Irani			1*							67
J.P. Crawley	6	1								125
G. Yates	2									9
Byes	6	6	3	3	4	7	1		2	
Leg-byes	2	1	5	3	3	2	4		4	
Wides			4		3		4		4	
No-balls					6		4		6	
Total	167	122	202	159	174	192	191		246	
Wickets	9	7	10	W	7	10	4		7	
Result	L	W	Tie	W	W	L	W	Ab.	L	
Points	0	4	2	4	4	0	4	2	0	

LANCASHIRE CCC
BOWLING

Opponent (venue)	Date	Comp	Wasim Akram	P.A.J. DeFreitas	I.D. Austin	P.J. Martin	M. Watkinson	A.A. Barnett	G. Chapple	R.C. Irani	G. Yates	Byes	Leg-byes	Wides	No-balls	Total	Wkts
v. Durham (Old Trafford)	9 May	AEL	10-0-47-1	10-2-26-0	9-0-38-1	8-0-32-2	10-1-38-1	3-0-23-0				1	12	10	8	217	6
v. Surrey (The Oval)	11 May	B&H	11-1-47-2	11-2-37-1	11-0-40-3	11-2-29-1	11-0-66-1					5	6	4	2	230	10
v. Somerset (Taunton)	16 May	AEL														Ab.	Ab.
v. Sussex (Hove)	25 May	B&H	11-2-27-2	11-1-31-0		11-0-50-2	11-1-19-1	11-0-41-0					10	3	8	178	7
v. Warwickshire (Old Trafford)	30 May	AEL														Ab.	Ab.
v. Surrey (The Oval)	6 June	AEL	10-0-32-4		10-1-43-2	5-0-48-1	10-1-49-1	10-1-43-1	5-0-38-0				6	7	4	259	9
v. Leicestershire (Leicester)	8 June	B&H	7-2-10-5	6-2-13-1	9-2-10-1		7-0-26-0	11-0-43-3					6	2		108	10
v. Essex (Old Trafford)	13 June	AEL	9.5-0-36-3	10-1-38-2	10-0-37-2	10-1-52-3		10-0-53-0					6	4	2	222	10
v. Sussex (Old Trafford)	20 June	AEL	10-4-20-4	8-3-10-1	10-3-19-1		9.1-3-17-1	10-1-33-1		2-0-13-1			6	6	4	118	10
v. Northamptonshire (Northampton)	22 June	NW	11-2-35-0	11-3-31-1	11.5-3-36-0		11-0-41-0	12-2-29-2				4	5	1	2	181	4
v. Derbyshire (Derby)	27 June	AEL	6-0-21-2	7-1-16-4	5-2-6-0		4-0-12-1	4.5-0-15-3					3	1		73	10
v. Leicestershire (Leicester)	4 July	AEL	10-1-26-2	6-1-21-2	10-1-44-1		8-0-39-2	10-0-58-2		3.2-0-17-1		4	8	5	8	217	10
v. Derbyshire (Lord's)	10 July	B&H	11-0-65-1	11-2-39-3	11-2-47-0		11-2-44-2	11-0-45-0				1	11	1	5	252	6
v. Glamorgan (Old Trafford)	18 July	AEL		6-0-40-0	6-1-29-0		5-0-22-0	4-0-27-0	8.4-0-42-1	4-1-7-1			1	3		168	2
v. Nottinghamshire (Old Trafford)	25 July	AEL	3-0-8-2	3-0-17-1	3-0-31-2	2-0-15-1	3-0-20-1		1-0-4-1		10-1-32-1		1	2	1	96	9
v. Gloucestershire (Cheltenham)	8 August	AEL	8.2-0-40-2	10-0-31-3	9-1-33-2		10-0-56-2				10-0-34-0		10	10	4	202	10
v. Hampshire (Southampton)	15 August	AEL	9-0-37-1	10-4-26-5	8-0-22-2		10-1-29-2					4	6	5	12	158	10
v. Yorkshire (Old Trafford)	22 August	AEL	9-0-30-1	8-0-31-3	5-3-7-0		9-2-26-0	5-0-35-2			9-0-35-2	2	7	7	2	173	9
v. Kent (Old Trafford)	29 August	AEL	7-0-28-0	10-0-42-1	8-0-37-0		8.3-0-47-0				9-2-34-0	1	4	3	10	193	4
v. Worcestershire (Worcester)	5 September	AEL	10-0-48-2	10-2-26-1	10-0-42-2		10-1-25-0				10-0-27-3	4	16	5	4	188	9
v. Middlesex (Lord's)	12 September	AEL	3-0-20-0	5-1-22-1	7-2-25-2	2-0-2-1	3-1-5-0						1	2		75	4
v. Northamptonshire (Old Trafford)	19 September	AEL	9.5-1-41-2	10-0-49-0	10-3-23-2		10-0-54-0				10-0-75-1	2	3	3	10	247	5
Wickets			36	30	23	11	15	14	2	3	7						

FIELDING FIGURES

21 – P.A. Nixon (ct 18/st 3)
9 – T.J. Boon
7 – J.J. Whitaker and J.D.R. Benson
5 – P.E. Robinson, N.E. Briers and B.F. Smith
4 – L. Potter, V.J. Wells and W.K.M. Benjamin
2 – J. Dakin, G.J. Parsons, A.R.K. Pierson and P.N. Hepworth
1 – A.D. Mullally, D.J. Millns, D.L. Maddy and sub

BEST BATSMEN & BOWLERS

T.J. Boon hit his first century in the Sunday League. B.F. Smith reached 50 for the first time in the same competition.

J. Dakin and A.R.K. Pierson appeared for Leicestershire in the Sunday League for the first time, although Pierson played for Warwickshire, 1985–91.

J.D.R. Benson returned his best bowling figures in the Sunday League, 4 for 27 against Gloucestershire.

M.T. Brimson, D.L. Maddy and A. Sheryar all made their debuts in the last game of the season.

LEICESTERSHIRE CCC — BATTING (first half of season)

	Runs	Notts 9 May AEL	War 11 May B&H	Sussex 23 May AEL	Worcs 25 May B&H	Durham 6 Jun AEL	Lancs 8 Jun B&H	Worcs 13 Jun AEL	Bucks 22 Jun NW	Glos 27 Jun AEL	Lancs 4 Jul AEL	Surrey 7 Jul NW	Surrey 11 Jul AEL	Notts 12 Jul TT
T.J. Boon	659	0	19	28	1	31	21	66	117	17	8	45	2	84
N.E. Briers	285	1	5	4	58	23	5	5	22	7	8	17	11*	18
J.J. Whitaker	651	50	7	13	5	51*	32	1	35	26	13	22	9*	69
P.E. Robinson	384	22	70	22	17	8	9		42	9	38			9*
B.F. Smith	512	30	43	25	34	51*	7	5		45	19	1*		39*
L. Potter	213	37	6		3	8	6	26	4		31	17*		6
V.J. Wells	335	17	15	37	10	17	15*		9	17*	19	4		0
P.A. Nixon	272	37*	21		27	23*	0	19	7	4	13	2		
G.J. Parsons	315	6*			10*			0	5*	19*	38*	1		10*
A.R.K. Pierson	24		1*								2	4		10*
A.D. Mullally	35				1*			2*		55	0	1		1
W.K.M. Benjamin	120	4*	3*	20*	20		0	16	2		22	10		
J. Dakin	78					42		31	13	3	22	2		
J.D.R. Benson	149	7												
W. Adlam	11													11
P. Whitticase	12													12*
D.J. Millns	17													
P.N. Hepworth	31													
D.L. Maddy	3													
M.T. Brimson	3													
A. Sheryar	–													
Byes		5	3	1	8	1	6	1	1	1	4	1		1
Leg-byes		4	6	21	5	10	2	7	6	7	8	2	4	14
Wides		3	5	8	5	1	2	4	3	4	5	1		6
No-balls		4	2		6	4	4	4	4	4	8			6
Total		216	206	220	205	217	108	178	289	214	217	129	26	286
Wickets		7	8	L	9	7	10	10	W	8	10	10	1	8
Result		W	W	L	W	W	L	W	–	W	L	L	Ab.	L
Points		4	–	0	–	4	–	4	–	–	0	–	2	–

LEICESTERSHIRE CCC — BATTING (second half of season)

	Runs	Essex 18 Jul AEL	War 25 Jul AEL	Kent 1 Aug AEL	Mid 8 Aug AEL	Glam 15 Aug AEL	Som 22 Aug AEL	Northants 29 Aug AEL	Yorks 5 Sep AEL	Hants 12 Sep AEL	Derbys 19 Sep AEL
T.J. Boon	659	32	4	135*	13	19	14	8	26		10
N.E. Briers	285	28	10	63	78	117	0	0	49		8
J.J. Whitaker	651	0	83	14	2	24	18	18	71		97*
P.E. Robinson	384	13	22	15	27	35	25	53*	4		8
B.F. Smith	512	25									50
L. Potter	213	18	2	24*	0	12*	0	35	0		3
V.J. Wells	335	18	23	1	6*	0*	7	35	28*		37*
P.A. Nixon	272	10			1		0*	24*	2		
G.J. Parsons	315	4*	6*				13		7		
A.R.K. Pierson	24										
A.D. Mullally	35	7		3					9		
W.K.M. Benjamin	120		10		27	7		16			14
J. Dakin	78					4	2		10		3
J.D.R. Benson	149					1			17		37*
W. Adlam	11										
P. Whitticase	12										
D.J. Millns	17										
P.N. Hepworth	31										14
D.L. Maddy	3										3
M.T. Brimson	3										
A. Sheryar	–										
Byes		1	1	8	5	3	8	1	2		1
Leg-byes		11	5	5	5	5	4	8	9		5
Wides		6	3	1	1	5	2	9	19		18
No-balls											
Total		166	170	264	179	220	144	196	253		246
Wickets		10	7	5	10	7	10	6	10		6
Result		L	L	L	L	L	L	L	L	Ab.	W

LEICESTERSHIRE CCC

BOWLING

Date	Opponent		A.D. Mullally	G.J. Parsons	A.R.K. Pierson	V.J. Wells	L. Potter	W.K.M. Benjamin	J. Dakin	J.D.R. Benson	W. Adlam	D.J. Millns	A. Sheryar	M.T. Brimson	P.N. Hepworth	Byes	Leg-byes	Wides	No-balls	Total	Wkts
9 May	v. Nottinghamshire (Leicester)	AEL	8-2-14-1	6.5-0-25-2	9-0-33-2	8-0-16-0	10-2-28-5									3	7	2		126	10
11 May	v. Nottinghamshire (Leicester)	B&H	11-1-43-1		11-1-42-3	11-1-37-1	11-1-37-2	11-0-43-1									4	2		206	10
23 May	v. Sussex (Horsham)	AEL	10-0-52-2	10-0-72-2		10-0-54-2	10-0-31-1		10-1-62-1							4	8	2	4	283	8
23 May	v. Worcestershire (Leicester)	B&H	8-2-21-1	10.2-0-25-1		10-0-37-4	11-1-41-1	9-3-13-2									13	2		150	10
25 May	v. Durham (Leicester)	AEL	10-0-50-1	10-0-32-2		10-1-29-2	10-0-37-0		10-1-50-2							6	10	1	2	214	9
6 June	v. Lancashire (Leicester)	B&H	11-1-44-1	11-4-21-3		11-1-59-2	11-2-35-0	11-0-46-0									13	4		218	6
8 June	v. Worcestershire (Worcester)	AEL	10-3-30-2	10-1-32-3		10-0-30-1	10-1-30-3	10-1-41-0								3	8	1	4	174	9
13 June	v. Buckinghamshire (Marlow)	NW	12-4-32-0	12-0-60-1		12-1-46-2	12-2-32-1	10-3-25-1		2-0-13-3							6	5	2	214	8
22 June	v. Gloucestershire (Leicester)	AEL	8-2-19-1	9-1-31-1		9-1-31-1	6-0-33-0	9.2-3-35-4		7-0-27-4						1	6	12		183	10
27 June	v. Lancashire (Leicester)	AEL	9-0-61-2	10-0-39-1		9-1-46-1	7-0-41-0	10-0-61-1		5-0-37-1							11	4	8	300	7
4 July	v. Surrey (Leicester)	AEL	4-2-15-0	0.1-0-4-0	12-1-38-1		12-0-40-2	4-0-33-0								4	1	2		131	3
7 July	v. Surrey (Leicester)	NW																		Ab.	Ab.
12 July	v. Nottinghamshire (Harrogate)	TT	11-2-43-1		11-0-61-0	11-0-57-5	11-0-57-0				11-0-69-1					4	8	5	7	299	8
18 July	v. Essex (Southend)	AEL	6.5-0-35-2	9-0-30-0	10-0-44-2		10-0-46-0	10-2-13-3		3-1-18-1						4	2	7	4	192	10
25 July	v. Warwickshire (Leicester)	AEL	3-0-19-1	8-1-38-2		5-0-24-2		6.5-1-41-0									2	2	6	124	6
1 August	v. Kent (Canterbury)	AEL	10-0-53-1	10-2-56-1		10-0-54-2	9-0-57-0		7-0-64-0							3	10	6	2	327	6
8 August	v. Middlesex (Lord's)	AEL		10-3-24-0	10-1-28-1	9-1-40-0			7-0-22-0	4-0-30-1						6	3	12	2	183	2
15 August	v. Glamorgan (Leicester)	AEL	10-2-42-1		10-0-39-0	10-1-47-0			10-2-45-3	2-0-15-0		8-0-45-1				4	5	8	12	228	7
22 August	v. Somerset (Weston-super-Mare)	AEL		10-1-31-4	10-0-55-2	10-0-51-0			6-0-38-0	6-0-35-1		4-0-14-1				7	3	5	2	240	8
29 August	v. Northamptonshire (Northampton)	AEL	8-0-37-1	10-0-32-0	10-0-48-1	4-0-14-0			5.4-0-30-0	4-0-13-0						2	2	13	8	200	3
5 September	v. Yorkshire (Leicester)	AEL	10-0-70-1	10-4-38-2	10-0-82-3							6-0-35-0					16	1	6	318	7
12 September	v. Hampshire (Southampton)	AEL																		Ab.	Ab.
19 September	v. Derbyshire (Leicester)	AEL		10-0-41-2	10-1-42-1	9.5-0-57-3			10-0-64-0			10-0-48-1	5-0-29-0	10-2-28-1	5-0-26-0	1	8	7	10	232	10
Wickets			20	27	16	28	15	12	6	11	1	3	0	1	0						

FIELDING FIGURES

24 – K.R. Brown (ct 19/st 5)
13 – J.D. Carr
9 – P.N. Weekes
8 – M.A. Roseberry
6 – J.E. Emburey
5 – A.R.C. Fraser and M.W. Gatting
4 – M.R. Ramprakash
2 – D.L. Haynes, N.F. Williams, M. Keech and sub
1 – N.G. Cowans, R.J. Sims, P.C.R. Tufnell and C.W. Taylor

BEST BATSMEN & BOWLERS

Aftab Habib, R.L. Johnson and M.A. Feltham all appeared in limited-over competitions for Middlesex for the first time. Feltham was with Surrey from 1983 to 1992.

D.L. Haynes hit his highest Sunday League score, against Warwickshire.

In the match against Leicestershire, P.C.R. Tufnell and M.R. Ramprakash both returned their best bowling figures in the Sunday League.

T.A. Radford made his debut in the last game of the season.

MIDDLESEX CCC — BATTING

	v. Australians 3 May (Lord's) AEL	v. Kent 9 May (Lord's) AEL	v. Derbyshire 11 May (Derby) B&H	v. Nottinghamshire 16 May (Lord's) AEL	v. Sussex 30 May (Lord's) AEL	v. Derbyshire 9 June (Lord's) AEL	v. Durham 13 June (Gateshead Fell) AEL	v. Somerset 20 June (Bath) AEL	v. Kent 22 June (Canterbury) NW	v. Surrey 27 June (Lord's) AEL	v. Glamorgan 4 July (Cardiff) AEL	v. Gloucestershire 11 July (Moreton-in-Marsh) AEL	v. Warwickshire 18 July (Edgbaston) AEL	Runs
M. Keech	0	0	7	0	14*	21*	23	–	3	2	34	–	66	108
M.A. Roseberry	47	20	58	88	28	84	14	73*	5	19	2	–	8	363
M.R. Ramprakash	0	0	0	92	43	41	26	57*	25	18	8	–	16*	590
J.D. Carr	32	25	41	5*	91	–	4	–	2	4	–	–	–	504
M.W. Gatting	12	5	0	26	0	40	36	–	2	66*	2	–	–	270
P.N. Weekes	24	16	24	7*	33	6	10	–	10	37	24	–	–	270
K.R. Brown	17	0	17	–	1	1	17*	–	2*	–	16	–	–	240
M.A. Feltham	10*	2	1*	17	–	15	–	–	2*	9*	25	–	–	65
J.E. Emburey	0*	3	–	–	10	0*	9	–	–	–	28	–	–	128
A.R.C. Fraser	0	8	–	–	0*	18	8*	–	–	0	14	–	–	29
N.G. Cowans	3	11*	0*	–	8*	2	–	0	–	–	2*	–	–	4
D.L. Haynes	–	–	60	–	–	–	–	3	41	–	6	–	142*	557
N.F. Williams	–	–	–	15	–	–	–	–	–	–	–	–	–	16
R.L. Johnson	–	–	–	–	–	–	–	–	–	–	–	–	–	42
R.J. Sims	–	–	–	–	–	–	–	–	5	–	–	–	–	18
J.C. Pooley	–	–	–	–	–	–	–	–	–	–	–	–	–	5
P.C.R. Tufnell	–	–	–	–	–	–	–	–	–	–	–	–	–	–
A. Habib	–	–	–	–	–	–	–	–	–	–	–	–	–	15
C.W. Taylor	–	–	–	–	–	–	–	–	–	–	–	–	–	–
T.A. Radford	–	–	–	–	–	–	–	–	–	–	–	–	–	38
Byes	6	6	6	2	1	10	1	8	3	2	1	–	8	
Leg-byes	9	4	6	3	12	3	5	1	10	13	2	–	7	
Wides	14	4	14	2	4	–	3	2	4	–	2	–	6	
No-balls	–	–	6	–	2	–	2	–	–	–	2	–	8	
Total	174	104	239	257	247	241	158	145	116	172	166	Ab.	261	
Wickets	10	10	9	6	7	8	7	W	10	6	10	–	W	
Result	L	L	L	W	Tie	W	L	4	L	L	L	2	4	
Points	–	0	–	4	2	4	2		–	0	0			

BATTING

	v. Hampshire 25 July (Lord's) AEL	v. Leicestershire 8 August (Lord's) AEL	v. Yorkshire 15 August (Scarborough) AEL	v. Northamptonshire 22 August (Lord's) AEL	v. Essex 29 August (Colchester) AEL	v. Lancashire 12 September (Lord's) AEL	v. Worcestershire 19 September (Worcester) AEL	Runs
M. Keech	31	–	2	2*	–	51	20	108
M.A. Roseberry	69*	47	2	32	53	8	63	363
M.R. Ramprakash	104*	89*	0	2	6	5*	38*	590
J.D. Carr	–	23*	13	36	15	0*	–	504
M.W. Gatting	–	–	14	10*	46	1	3	270
P.N. Weekes	–	–	13	–	3*	–	–	270
K.R. Brown	–	–	2	–	0	4	23*	240
M.A. Feltham	–	–	36*	–	–	–	–	65
J.E. Emburey	–	–	10	–	–	–	–	128
A.R.C. Fraser	–	–	–	–	–	–	–	29
N.G. Cowans	–	–	–	–	–	–	–	4
D.L. Haynes	21	–	60	67	101	–	–	557
N.F. Williams	–	1	–	3	0*	–	–	16
R.L. Johnson	–	–	–	–	–	–	–	42
R.J. Sims	–	–	–	3	–	–	–	18
J.C. Pooley	–	–	–	–	–	–	–	5
P.C.R. Tufnell	–	–	–	–	–	–	–	–
A. Habib	–	–	–	15	–	–	–	15
C.W. Taylor	–	–	–	–	–	–	–	–
T.A. Radford	–	–	–	–	–	–	38	38
Byes	4	6	5	2	1	1	2	
Leg-byes	11	3	5	6	1	2	5	
Wides	6	12	2	6	8	4	7	
No-balls	–	2	4	4	2	–	–	
Total	246	183	168	185	236	75	199	
Wickets	3	2	10	W	6	4	W	
Result	W	W	L	4	L	Ab.	4	
Points	4	4	0		0	2		

MIDDLESEX CCC
BOWLING

Match	Comp	M.A. Feltham	N.G. Cowans	J.E. Emburey	A.R.C. Fraser	P.N. Weekes	M. Keech	N.F. Williams	R.L. Johnson	P.C.R. Tufnell	M.R. Ramprakash	C.W. Taylor	Byes	Leg-byes	Wides	No-balls	Total	Wks
v. Australians (Lord's) 3 May		8-4-19-1	11-0-36-0	11-4-37-0	11-0-76-2	7-1-31-0	7-0-37-0							7	6		243	5
v. Kent (Lord's) 9 May	AEL	6-1-23-0		1.4-0-7-0	6-0-24-0		1-0-3-0						3	1	2	4	105	1
v. Derbyshire (Derby) 11 May	B&H	11-1-39-2		11-0-45-0	11-0-50-3		8-0-37-1	6-0-22-1					8	6	7	4	253	8
v. Nottinghamshire (Lord's) 16 May	AEL			10-1-38-0	10-1-50-1	4-0-18-0	9-2-34-2	10-2-50-1	6-0-22-0				5	25	14	2	252	8
v. Sussex (Lord's) 30 May	AEL			10-0-55-3	10-0-52-1	6-0-33-2	9-0-47-0	10-1-36-2	5-0-31-1					15	7	2	247	8
v. Derbyshire (Lord's) 6 June	AEL			10-1-52-0	9-1-54-0	9-0-39-3		10-3-43-1	10-1-43-0					5	1	8	240	2
v. Durham (Gateshead Fell) 13 June	AEL		10-3-15-1	7.5-0-35-0	8-0-30-1	8-0-44-2	10-1-31-0	7-1-18-0	7-3-20-0				1	13	2	2	159	4
v. Somerset (Bath) 20 June	AEL		10-4-12-1	10-5-10-1	10-1-36-2	3-0-19-1	4-0-13-1	8-3-15-1						4	7	6	144	10
v. Kent (Canterbury) 22 June	NW		11-0-47-1	12-0-59-3	11-1-53-1	6-0-27-1	9-0-38-0	10-1-42-2	10-0-44-0				1	4	11	2	282	7
v. Surrey (The Oval) 27 June	AEL		5-0-25-0	8-0-31-1	7-0-33-0	7-0-36-2	7-2-12-1		10-1-42-1					10	4	4	173	3
v. Glamorgan (Cardiff) 4 July	AEL	10-1-54-0	10-0-38-1	10-0-42-2	10-1-42-0	8-1-20-0	3-0-22-0						4	24	9	2	287	8
v. Gloucestershire (Moreton-in-Marsh) 11 July	AEL		10-0-49-3	10-1-34-0	7-0-43-1	7-0-61-4	3-1-21-0			10-0-44-4				4			243	10
v. Warwickshire (Edgbaston) 18 July	AEL		10-2-58-2	9-0-43-0	10-2-36-1	10-0-47-1			10-0-62-0				1	5	4	4	253	8
v. Hampshire (Lord's) 25 July	AEL		7-1-20-0	10-2-25-1	8.5-2-17-4	10-0-49-4				10-0-50-4			1	14	3		165	10
v. Leicestershire (Lord's) 8 August	AEL	7-1-24-0	10-0-45-0		7-2-17-0	9-1-38-1	7-0-22-0							5	5		179	10
v. Yorkshire (Scarborough) 15 August	AEL	7-0-57-0	8-0-52-0		8-1-39-0		3-0-16-0			10-3-28-5	8-1-38-5			1	9	6	245	2
v. Northamptonshire (Lord's) 22 August	AEL		7-3-30-0	7-1-50-1		8-1-28-1	4-0-22-2		7.2-1-46-0	10-0-47-1	4-0-30-1	8-0-33-2	7	7	10	6	173	6
v. Essex (Colchester) 29 August	AEL				8-0-40-0	10-0-46-4			7-0-35-3			5-0-20-1		8	5	8	236	10
v. Lancashire (Lord's) 12 September	AEL																Ab.	
v. Worcestershire (Worcester) 19 September	AEL			10-0-40-0	10-2-31-2	10-0-40-1			10-0-66-4	10-0-34-1		9.3-2-24-1	2	2	7	2	197	10
Wickets		3	9	12	19	27	7	8	10	15	6	4						

FIELDING FIGURES

21 – D. Ripley (ct 18/st 3)
11 – A.J. Lamb
7 – N.G.B. Cook and M.B. Loye
6 – A. Fordham
5 – R.J. Bailey
4 – K.M. Curran and N.A. Felton
3 – J.P. Taylor and C.E.L. Ambrose
2 – A.L. Penberthy, A. Walker and R.J. Warren

BEST BATSMEN & BOWLERS

Before 1993, M.B. Loye's appearances in limited-over cricket had been restricted to two Sunday League games. In 1993, he achieved career-best performances in all competitions, including a Sunday League century. M.N. Bowen had career-best performances in the Sunday League with bat and ball. A.L. Penberthy had a career-best bowling performance in the first Sunday League match of the season.

J.N. Snape took a career best 3 for 25 in his only Sunday League game of the season.

R.J. Warren and R.R. Montgomerie made their Sunday League debuts.

NORTHAMPTONSHIRE CCC — BATTING

	v. Gloucestershire (Northampton) 9 May AEL	v. Yorkshire (Leeds) 11 May B&H	v. Australians (Northampton) 16 May	v. Glamorgan (Pentyrch) 23 May AEL	v. Hampshire (Southampton) 25 & 26 May B&H	v. Worcestershire (Northampton) 6 June AEL	v. Derbyshire (Derby) 8 June B&H	v. Sussex (Hove) 13 June AEL	v. Hampshire (Northampton) 20 June AEL	v. Lancashire (Northampton) 22 June NW	v. Somerset (Luton) 27 June AEL	v. Nottinghamshire (Northampton) 4 July AEL	v. Essex (Chelmsford) 7 July NW	Runs
A. Fordham	66	23	101	19	30	4	10	1	18	39	10	17	0	552
N.A. Felton	4	62	32	4	73	3	8	0	7	3	16	0	10	346
M.B. Loye	36	9	37*	8	31*	19	60	60	24	4	122	85	65	625
A.J. Lamb	27	54	82*	49	31*	43	51	47	96*	4	72	14	124*	765
R.J. Bailey	18	3	–	47	45	17	12	20	14	96*	72	15	31	882
D.J. Capel	22*	3	–	19	–	2	15	43	4	–	9	65*	–	121
K.M. Curran	6*	–	–	7	–	6	2	22	35	23*	4	1	41*	273
A.L. Penberthy	–	–	–	–	–	24	6*	8	11*	–	7*	–	–	144
J.P. Taylor	–	0	–	5*	–	24	9	1*	–	–	–	–	–	42
D. Ripley	–	15	–	–	–	–	–	0	–	–	6*	0*	–	235
N.G.B. Cook	–	1*	–	2*	–	–	–	–	–	–	–	–	–	29
C.E.L. Ambrose	–	16*	–	–	–	8*	–	–	–	–	–	–	–	72
A. Walker	–	–	–	–	–	–	3	–	–	–	–	–	–	50
M.N. Bowen	–	–	–	–	–	–	–	1	–	–	2	–	–	21
N.A. Stanley	–	–	–	–	–	–	–	–	–	–	–	–	–	2
W.M. Noon	–	–	–	–	–	–	–	–	–	–	–	7	–	7
R.J. Warren	–	–	–	–	–	–	–	–	–	–	–	–	–	209
R.R. Montgomerie	–	–	–	–	–	–	–	–	–	–	–	–	–	0
J.G. Hughes	–	–	–	–	–	–	–	–	–	–	–	–	–	21
Byes	2	4	12	6	3	9	9	8	2	4	8	2	6	
Leg-byes	2	8	5		5	5	9	1	7	5	5	10		
Wides	2	5	4	4	9	4	8	2	9	1	2	2	4	
No-balls	2	2							2	2			6	
Total	185	211	273	170	227	168	210	214	229	181	263	227	290	
Wickets	5	9	2	7	3	9	10	10	6	4	7	7	5	
Result	W	W	W	W	W	Tie	L	L	W	W	W	W	W	
Points	4	–	–	4	–	2	0	0	4	–	4	4	–	

BATTING

	v. Warwickshire (Edgbaston) 11 July AEL	v. Yorkshire (Leeds) 18 July AEL	v. Surrey (Northampton) 25 July AEL	v. Sussex (Northampton) 27 & 28 July NW	v. Essex (Northampton) 8 August AEL	v. Durham (Northampton) 15 August AEL	v. Middlesex (Lord's) 22 August AEL	v. Leicestershire (Northampton) 29 August AEL	v. Kent (Canterbury) 5 September AEL	v. Derbyshire (Derby) 12 September AEL	v. Lancashire (Old Trafford) 19 September AEL	Runs
A. Fordham	33	17	21	16	50	3	36	10	19	–	12	552
N.A. Felton	32	12	–	53	44	5	–	37	22	–	–	346
M.B. Loye	1	32	64	8	24	48	11	42*	19	–	56	625
A.J. Lamb	0	5	0	71	58*	39	65*	11	1	–	–	765
R.J. Bailey	69	16	6	4	–	–	7	–	–	–	93	882
D.J. Capel	5	0	10	1	0	–	17	–	–	–	–	121
K.M. Curran	23	1	0	3	–	3*	–	–	–	–	9*	273
A.L. Penberthy	–	47*	6	1	–	9	–	–	–	–	–	144
J.P. Taylor	16*	20	52*	10*	–	5	0	–	19	–	3*	42
D. Ripley	–	3*	1*	1	–	26	1*	–	1*	–	–	235
N.G.B. Cook	2*	–	16	0	–	30	–	–	–	–	–	29
C.E.L. Ambrose	–	–	–	–	–	–	–	–	–	–	–	72
A. Walker	2*	–	–	–	–	–	–	–	9*	–	–	50
M.N. Bowen	–	–	–	–	–	–	–	–	20	–	–	21
N.A. Stanley	–	–	–	–	–	–	–	–	–	–	–	2
W.M. Noon	–	–	–	–	–	–	–	–	–	–	–	7
R.J. Warren	–	–	–	–	44*	5	12	71*	21	–	56	209
R.R. Montgomerie	–	–	–	–	–	0	–	–	–	–	–	0
J.G. Hughes	–	–	–	–	–	–	–	–	21	–	–	21
Byes	2	2	7	12	5	12	7	2	4	2	2	
Leg-byes	10	10	8	8	6	11	7	2	5	3	3	
Wides	4	1	2	2	10	2	10	13	4	3	10	
No-balls	4	6						12		10		
Total	196	172	193	190	241	198	173	200	165	–	247	
Wickets	7	9	9	10	3	10	6	3	8	–	5	
Result	–	–	W	W	W	L	W	W	W	Ab	W	

NORTHAMPTONSHIRE CCC
BOWLING

Opponent	Comp	J.P. Taylor	K.M. Curran	D.J. Capel	A.L. Penberthy	N.G.B. Cook	R.J. Bailey	C.E.L. Ambrose	A. Walker	M.N. Bowen	J.N. Snape	Byes	Leg-byes	Wides	No-balls	Total	Wkts
v. Gloucestershire (Northampton) 9 May	AEL	8-3-11-1	6-0-24-0	6-0-29-1	10-0-36-5	3.2-0-13-2	1-0-6-0					1	3	3		123	10
v. Yorkshire (Leeds) 11 May	B&H	10-2-26-2	11-0-25-1	10-0-54-3		8-0-27-0	4-0-19-0						5	3		177	10
v. Australians (Northampton) 16 May		7-0-26-0		5-0-35-0	6-0-32-0	8-0-34-1	8-1-35-1	9.1-2-21-1	5-0-17-0			3	1	1		183	2
v. Glamorgan (Pentrych) 23 May	AEL	9-1-32-3	7-0-43-1	9-0-28-0	5-0-11-0	10-3-22-4		10-1-20-0				1	12	10	4	169	9
v. Hampshire (Southampton) 25 & 26 May	B&H	11-2-34-2	11-3-38-1		11-0-53-0	5-0-33-1	6-0-28-0	11-3-30-2				5	2	10		223	7
v. Worcestershire (Northampton) 6 June	AEL	10-1-24-2	9-0-42-2	5-0-18-1	10-0-30-1	10-1-31-1	3-0-12-0	10-2-27-0	3-0-4-0			1	6	6		168	9
v. Derbyshire (Derby) 8 June	B&H	9.3-3-34-1	9-0-49-0	5-0-20-0	10-0-49-0		8-0-29-0					3	3	1		214	2
v. Sussex (Hove) 13 June	AEL	9-3-27-1	9-1-37-1	10-1-48-1	8-0-51-0	7-0-34-1	3-0-17-0			5-0-18-0			2	4	2	217	5
v. Hampshire (Northampton) 20 June	AEL	10-2-40-1	9-0-49-1		8-0-44-0	10-1-35-0		10-0-36-0					5	2	2	226	2
v. Lancashire (Northampton) 22 June	NW	12-4-35-1	12-3-39-2		12-3-33-2	12-1-34-0		12-3-34-1				1	2	5		178	7
v. Somerset (Luton) 27 June	AEL	9.4-1-40-3	10-2-43-1		8-0-65-1	3-0-23-0	9-0-39-0	10-2-30-3					6	2	8	246	10
v. Nottinghamshire (Northampton) 4 July	AEL	8-2-29-1	8-1-25-3		9-0-38-2	10-0-27-2	1-0-11-0	8-1-26-1				1	7	2		164	10
v. Essex (Chelmsford) 7 July	NW	11-2-45-1	11-2-54-0		9-1-47-0	7-0-42-0	10-0-49-2	12-0-47-2					2	6	2	286	5
v. Warwickshire (Edgbaston) 11 July	AEL	9-2-28-0	9.1-0-50-1		2-0-11-0		3-0-18-0	8-1-30-0				7	3	2		183	2
v. Yorkshire (Leeds) 18 July	AEL	9-2-33-1	5-0-28-0		3-0-31-0	5-1-21-0	3-0-21-0		9-1-39-1			5	5	5	2	175	1
v. Surrey (Northampton) 25 July	AEL								8.4-2-36-0								Ab.
v. Sussex (Northampton) 27 & 28 July	NW	12-2-44-1	12-1-38-1		6-0-35-0	12-1-53-3	6-1-27-0	12-4-25-1				1	7	5	4	230	9
v. Essex (Northampton) 8 August	AEL	4-1-25-1	6-1-23-1			10-0-17-3	1.2-0-2-1	6-3-8-1			7-2-25-3	3	4	13		107	10
v. Durham (Northampton) 15 August	AEL	10-0-45-2	10-1-39-1			10-0-37-1		10-0-50-2				1	7	9		246	7
v. Middlesex (Lord's) 22 August	AEL	8-0-37-2	8-0-46-1			4-0-26-0	3-0-12-1	8-1-18-2	7-1-38-0	6-0-24-0		2	6	6	4	185	6
v. Leicestershire (Northampton) 29 August	AEL	10-0-45-1	7-1-29-1			10-1-34-0	10-3-25-1		7-0-30-2			1	8	9		196	6
v. Kent (Canterbury) 5 September	AEL	8-0-38-1				10-1-30-1	10-0-44-1		9-1-38-1	10-4-12-2			4	8		166	7
v. Derbyshire (Derby) 12 September	AEL	10-0-60-0	10-2-23-0			10-0-56-2		10-1-35-2		10-2-35-3			5	18	2	214	8
v. Lancashire (Old Trafford) 19 September	AEL	10-0-54-1	10-1-38-1			10-0-43-3		10-0-48-0		10-1-57-2		2	4	2	6	246	7
Wickets		29	20	6	11	25	7	18	7	7	3						

FIELDING FIGURES

19 – B.N. French
13 – P.R. Pollard
9 – P. Johnson
6 – G.W. Mike
5 – M.A. Crawley and R.A. Pick
4 – C.L. Cairns
3 – M.G. Field-Buss and J.A. Afford
2 – R.T. Robinson, G.F. Archer, C.C. Lewis, R.T. Bates, W.A. Dessaur and L.N. Walker (ct 1/st 1)
1 – D.B. Pennett, K.P. Evans, M. Saxelby, D.W. Randall and S. Sylvester

BEST BATSMEN & BOWLERS

M.P. Dowman and R.T. Bates made their Sunday League debuts. C.L. Cairns hit his first Sunday League century and took a Sunday career best of 6 for 52 against Kent. D.W. Randall retired at the end of the season. He scored 7,059 runs in the Sunday League.

NOTTINGHAMSHIRE CCC — BATTING

BATTING	Leics 9 May AEL	Somerset 11 May B&H	Middlesex 16 May AEL	Kent 23 May AEL	Hants 6 June AEL	Essex 20 June AEL	Cheshire 22 June NW	Glamorgan 27 June AEL	Northants 4 July AEL	Somerset 7 July NW	Worcs 11 July AEL	Leics 12 July TT	Yorks 14 July TT	Runs
P.R. Pollard	1	80	8	–	17	24	17	37	4	22	30*	–	21	472
D.W. Randall	33	5	–	63*	–	–	–	–	–	5	22	–	7	110
R.T. Robinson	41	29	1	–	66	52	19	6	27	41	3	8	–	639
P. Johnson	15	59	42	167*	31	6	13	32	8	19	7	42	20	740
M.A. Crawley	5	26*	22	–	7*	11	64	53	47	8	47	113	8	292
C.L. Cairns	4	1	2	–	10	18	0	1	–	71	11*	34	–	590
G.W. Mike	1	25*	51*	–	0	12	14*	0	–	–	–	–	–	144
B.N. French	5	–	7	–	32	2	–	21*	12	2	–	7	13*	151
R.A. Pick	4	–	–	–	9	7	–	5	–	0	–	–	1*	84
M.G. Field-Buss	3*	–	–	–	0	–	–	–	1	5*	–	–	–	23
D.B. Pennett	–	–	–	–	1*	–	–	–	–	–	–	–	–	4
C.C. Lewis	–	25	19	–	–	–	0	26	6	7	12	55	8	276
J.A. Afford	–	–	–	–	–	–	0*	–	0*	1	–	–	–	2
M. Saxelby	–	–	37	8	–	11	17	–	39	–	–	3	3	283
K.P. Evans	–	–	17*	–	17	17	5	–	9	–	12	–	14	106
G.F. Archer	–	–	–	–	–	18	39	10	1	–	–	13	27	85
W.A. Dessaur	–	–	–	–	–	–	–	10	–	–	–	1*	–	40
L.N. Walker	–	–	–	–	–	–	–	–	–	–	–	–	20	21
S. Sylvester	–	–	–	–	–	–	–	–	–	–	–	–	–	1
M.P. Dowman	–	–	–	–	–	–	–	–	–	–	–	–	–	39
R.T. Bates	–	–	–	–	17	–	–	–	–	–	–	–	–	1
Byes	3	4	5	6	8	4	1	5	1	6	1	4	1	
Leg-byes	7	11	25	9	6	–	5	2	7	–	4	8	–	
Wides	2	10	14	12	–	–	14	2	2	8	6	5	8	
No-balls	–	4	2	–	–	4	–	–	–	8	4	6	6	
Total	126	279	252	265	204	186	208	210	164	203	158	299	159	
Wickets	10	6	8	1	9	10	9	10	10	10	6	8	9	
Result	L	L	L	W	L	L	W	L	L	L	W	W	W	
Points	0	–	0	4	0	0	–	0	0	–	4	–	2	

NOTTINGHAMSHIRE CCC — BATTING (continued)

BATTING	Somerset 18 July AEL	Lancs 25 July AEL	Surrey 1 Aug AEL	Yorks 8 Aug AEL	Sussex 15 Aug AEL	Derby 29 Aug AEL	Durham 5 Sept AEL	Gloucs 12 Sept AEL	Warwicks 19 Sept AEL	Runs
P.R. Pollard	19	12	74	12	2	91	40	–	12	472
D.W. Randall	22	11	1	–	–	–	–	–	3	110
R.T. Robinson	5	1	1	83	51	78*	14	–	–	639
P. Johnson	34	12	55	55	1	75	17	–	47	740
M.A. Crawley	73	16*	126*	28	22	16	17	–	–	292
C.L. Cairns	–	–	–	4	4	0	13	7	–	590
G.W. Mike	–	14	19*	6	9	6*	17*	0	7	144
B.N. French	–	4	–	0*	33	–	–	0	0	151
R.A. Pick	–	0	–	–	11*	–	–	–	2	84
M.G. Field-Buss	–	–	–	–	–	–	–	–	–	23
D.B. Pennett	–	–	–	–	–	–	–	–	–	4
C.C. Lewis	20*	8	5	65	14	30	100*	0	–	276
J.A. Afford	–	–	–	–	–	–	–	6*	–	2
M. Saxelby	–	–	–	–	–	–	–	–	23	283
K.P. Evans	12*	4	11	–	–	7	–	–	–	106
G.F. Archer	–	–	–	–	–	–	–	–	–	85
W.A. Dessaur	–	–	–	–	–	–	31	2	–	40
L.N. Walker	1*	–	–	6	–	–	–	–	–	21
S. Sylvester	–	–	–	–	–	–	–	–	–	1
M.P. Dowman	–	–	–	0*	1	–	–	1	2	39
R.T. Bates	–	–	–	–	–	–	–	–	1	1
Byes	1	4	5	4	12	5	1	7	7	
Leg-byes	2	1	6	12	7	3	7	2	2	
Wides	1	2	1	2	–	–	1	–	4	
No-balls	2	–	9	–	–	18	2	4	–	
Total	203	96	314	261	168	329	260	116		

NOTTINGHAMSHIRE CCC — BOWLING

Match	Comp	C.L. Cairns	D.B. Pennett	R.A. Pick	G.W. Mike	M.G. Field-Buss	C.C. Lewis	J.A. Afford	M.A. Crawley	K.P. Evans	M. Saxelby	P.R. Pollard	S. Sylvester	R.T. Bates	M.P. Dowman	Byes	Leg-byes	Wides	No-balls	Total	Wkts
v. Leicestershire (Leicester) 9 May	AEL	10-1-30-2	10-1-42-2	10-0-41-1	10-1-50-1	10-0-44-1										5	4	3		216	7
v. Somerset (Trent Bridge) 11 May	B&H	11-0-63-2		10-0-60-1	11-1-44-4		11-0-34-1									1	6	4	4	283	9
v. Middlesex (Lord's) 16 May	AEL	10-1-34-2			10-0-60-0	10-0-39-0		9-1-56-1	3-0-19-0							2	3		4	257	6
v. Kent (Trent Bridge) 23 May	AEL	10-0-52-6		10-0-48-1	8-0-39-0	9-0-50-0	10-3-45-4		3-0-17-0	7-0-57-0						2	13	6	2	264	9
v. Hampshire (Trent Bridge) 6 June	AEL	9.4-0-43-0	10-1-51-0	9-1-26-0	9-0-36-1	10-1-47-1			4-0-20-0	9-1-40-0							5	4		208	2
v. Essex (Trent Bridge) 20 June	AEL	10-0-50-1		10-0-55-2	10-1-53-1	10-0-45-2				10-0-54-0							4	5	2	261	8
v. Cheshire (Warrington) 22 June	NW	9.3-5-18-4		10-1-29-3				12-3-15-1		12-4-30-1	9-1-42-1	3-0-9-0					3	14		146	10
v. Glamorgan (Swansea) 27 June	AEL	10-0-31-2		8-1-30-1	4-0-17-0	10-0-45-1	10-0-60-1			6.5-1-22-2						1	5	7	6	211	7
v. Northamptonshire (Northampton) 4 July	AEL	10-0-48-0				10-0-42-1	10-2-32-1	10-2-33-3		10-1-60-2						2	10	9	2	227	7
v. Somerset (Trent Bridge) 7 July	NW	10.5-1-39-2		12-1-38-2		12-1-44-0	11-1-24-3	11-1-39-0	1-0-4-0								16	4	4	204	7
v. Worcestershire (Trent Bridge) 11 July	AEL	8-0-32-3		8-0-26-1	5-0-20-0	8-2-25-3	8.2-1-28-1		10-2-21-1							1	2	4	10	155	10
v. Leicestershire (Harrogate) 12 July	TT	11-0-48-4		8-0-49-0		9-1-46-1	11-0-55-2	9-1-45-2	7-0-28-0							1	14	6	6	286	9
v. Yorkshire (Harrogate) 14 July	TT	6-1-13-2		3-2-5-2			5-0-16-0			7-4-7-1							2	1	2	43	5
v. Somerset (Trent Bridge) 18 July	AEL	10-0-35-1		7-0-37-1	3-0-27-2	10-0-32-3	10-1-35-2		3-0-21-0	10-0-32-1							8	9		200	9
v. Lancashire (Old Trafford) 25 July	AEL					2-0-16-1	3-0-12-2		2-0-21-0	3-0-21-2			2-0-19-0				6	1		122	7
v. Surrey (The Oval) 1 August	AEL	10-0-61-2		9-1-59-0		4-0-40-0	10-0-42-3		4-0-37-0	9-0-70-0						1	7	8		317	6
v. Yorkshire (Trent Bridge) 8 August	AEL		4-0-26-1	10-0-49-0	9.4-0-65-2		10-2-29-0		10-0-50-2					10-0-48-0	6-0-42-1		5	5		264	4
v. Sussex (Eastbourne) 15 August	AEL			10-1-57-0	9-0-55-3									10-0-38-2			6	12	4	262	10
v. Derbyshire (Trent Bridge) 29 August	AEL		8-2-18-1	8-2-20-2	9.2-0-46-2		5.3-0-46-0	4-0-10-1	8-0-33-1	5.4-0-17-1				6.5-0-43-3			10	8		187	10
v. Durham (Chester-le-Street) 5 September	AEL		10-0-42-0	10-0-68-4	9-0-43-0				9.1-0-36-2					3-0-30-0	7-0-33-1		10	7	6	262	7
v. Gloucestershire (Bristol) 12 September	AEL			1.5-0-8-0	4-0-19-0		6-2-12-1										4	1		43	1
v. Warwickshire (Trent Bridge) 19 September	AEL	10-0-55-2	10-0-32-3	10-1-61-1			10-1-39-1							10-1-78-2		5	6	4	2	276	9
Wickets		35	7	22	16	14	22	8	7	10	1	0	0	7	2						

FIELDING FIGURES

24 – N.D. Burns (ct 21/st 3)
7 – C.J. Tavaré, N.A. Folland and R.J. Turner (ct 5/st 2)
6 – R.J. Harden and H.R.J. Trump
3 – G.D. Rose, N.A. Mallender and M.N. Lathwell
2 – Mushtaq Ahmed
1 – A.P. van Troost, J.I.D. Kerr, K.A. Parsons, M. Trescothick, A. Payne, G.W. White and sub

BEST BATSMEN & BOWLERS

A.C. Cottam's only appearance for Somerset during the season was in the Sunday League match against Kent. At the end of the season, he left Somerset to join Northamptonshire.

A.P. van Troost, Mushtaq Ahmed, K.A. Parsons, J.I.D. Kerr, M. Trescothick, G.W. White, I. Fletcher and R.J. Turner all appeared in the Sunday League for the first time.

N.A. Folland made his first century in the Sunday League. Folland played for Devon, 1981–92, and scored 100 not out for Minor Counties against Nottinghamshire in the Benson and Hedges Cup, 1991.

SOMERSET CCC — BATTING

Match columns:
1. v Nottinghamshire (Trent Bridge) 11 May — B&H
2. v Lancashire (Taunton) 16 May — AEL
3. v Worcestershire (Worcester) 23 May — AEL
4. v Derbyshire (Taunton) 25 & 26 May — B&H
5. v Glamorgan (Taunton) 30 May — AEL
6. v Essex (Chelmsford) 6 June — AEL
7. v Middlesex (Bath) 20 June — AEL
8. v Shropshire (Telford) 22 June — NW
9. v Northamptonshire (Luton) 27 June — AEL
10. v Sussex (Taunton) 4 July — AEL
11. v Nottinghamshire (Trent Bridge) 7 July — NW
12. v Hampshire (Southampton) 11 July — AEL
13. v Nottinghamshire (Trent Bridge) 18 July — AEL

Batsman	1	2	3	4	5	6	7	8	9	10	11	12	13	Runs
M.N. Lathwell	77		11			27	8	103	40	5	8	46	12	617
N.A. Folland	83					0	7	19	69	21	63	60	29	602
R.J. Harden	49		6			89	1	65	2	13	31	27	20	519
C.J. Tavaré	19		1			1	12	56*	39	5	30	7	37	264
N.D. Burns	2		4			22	4	52	11	5	2	12*		100
G.D. Rose	13		10			24	28		37		8	9		485
A.N. Hayhurst	5													110
A.R. Caddick	4					0	32		9			11		88
Mushtaq Ahmed	7		6								0*			150
A.P. van Troost	9*		8								5*			37
H.R.J. Trump	0*		7*			10*	6*		2*					31
J.I.D. Kerr			11*			4	0		17	13*	33		17	60
A. Payne						1	9	0*		15			16	110
K.A. Parsons						6*	20		3	34				116
N.A. Mallender									1	20		0		115
M. Trescothick										28		3		32
J.C. Hallett										26		14		26
G.W. White												13		41
K.J. Parsons														22
A.C. Cottam														–
I. Fletcher														57
R.J. Turner														71
Byes	1									6	16	5	8	
Leg-byes	6		5				4	1	6	4	4	5	9	
Wides	4		8			15	7	3	2		4			
No-balls	4		8			2	6	2	8	2	4	2		
Total	283	Ab.	99	Ab.	Ab.	201	144	301	246	197	204	214	200	
Wickets	9		10			9	10	4	10	10	7	10	9	
Result	W		L			W	L	W	L	L	W	L	L	
Points	–	2	0	–	2	4	0	–	0	0	–	0	0	

BATTING (continued)

Match columns:
1. v Kent (Taunton) 25 July — AEL
2. v Surrey (Taunton) 27 & 28 July — NW
3. v Yorkshire (Taunton) 1 August — AEL
4. v Warwickshire (Taunton) 10 August — NW
5. v Derbyshire (Derby) 15 August — AEL
6. v Leicestershire (Weston-super-Mare) 22 August — AEL
7. v Surrey (The Oval) 29 August — AEL
8. v Gloucestershire (Taunton) 5 September — AEL
9. v Warwickshire (Edgbaston) 12 September — AEL
10. v Durham (Hartlepool) 19 September — AEL

Batsman	1	2	3	4	5	6	7	8	9	10	Runs
M.N. Lathwell	15	34	13	12	4	75	85		32	5	617
N.A. Folland		17	38	61	0	107*	39	36	27	6	602
R.J. Harden		33	47*	29	16	3	31	20	41*	0	519
C.J. Tavaré		29	3*	1							264
N.D. Burns	78*	2		31							100
G.D. Rose	8	18	80	6	52	6	29	2	4	30	485
A.N. Hayhurst		8	2	2	17			2			110
A.R. Caddick	0	8		0	9			2			88
Mushtaq Ahmed		0		14	1	3		0	1	36*	150
A.P. van Troost					0					2	37
H.R.J. Trump		17*		3	0*	15*	1*	15			31
J.I.D. Kerr							14	0			60
A. Payne	55*		0	11*	0*	4		0	5*	31*	110
K.A. Parsons								11			116
N.A. Mallender					26	5					115
M. Trescothick					33	1					32
J.C. Hallett											26
G.W. White	1	8*					0	11		40	41
K.J. Parsons	22	1					15				22
A.C. Cottam	–										–
I. Fletcher		22				7*	5*	11*	14		57
R.J. Turner										7	71
Byes	8	12	2	1	1	7	4	3	4	3	
Leg-byes	2	10	6	9		3	5	5	1	4	
Wides	2		3	8	7	5	5	4	2		
No-balls	2	4	4	12	2	6	6	2	2		
Total	193	230	202	200	168	240	238	111	133	164	
Wickets	6	10	6	10	8	8	8	2	10	7	

SOMERSET CCC

BOWLING

		A.R. Caddick	A.P. van Troost	Mushtaq Ahmed	G.D. Rose	A.N. Hayhurst	H.R.J. Trump	M.N. Lathwell	J.I.D. Kerr	A. Payne	N.A. Mallender	K.A. Parsons	R.J. Harden	C.J. Tavaré	J.C. Hallett	A.C. Cottam	Byes	Leg-byes	Wides	No-balls	Total	Wks
v. Nottinghamshire (Trent Bridge) 11 May	B&H	11-2-36-2	10.4-0-38-2	11-0-50-0	11-1-45-2	1.2-0-17-0	6-0-29-0	4-0-49-0									4	11	10	4	279	6
v. Lancashire (Taunton) 16 May	AEL	9-0-44-2	5.1-0-33-0	9-1-37-2	8-2-22-1				5-0-21-1	8-0-43-2								10	6	2	210	8
v. Worcestershire (Worcester) 23 May	AEL		9.4-0-36-1	10-3-17-2	10-3-18-1				6-2-13-2	6-2-10-0								6	3	10	100	6
v. Derbyshire (Taunton) 25 & 26 May	B&H																	4	1	4	69	0
v. Glamorgan (Taunton) 30 May	AEL																					Ab.
v. Essex (Chelmsford) 6 June	AEL			10-1-16-2	9-1-31-2				10-1-34-3	9.5-1-52-1	10-2-35-2							11	4	4	179	10
v. Middlesex (Bath) 20 June	AEL			6-0-32-0	4.3-0-15-0		8-1-30-0		5-0-31-0	4-0-17-0	6-3-11-2						8	1	1	2	145	2
v. Shropshire (Telford) 22 June	NW			8.4-3-16-2	6-3-11-3												4	8	6	8	185	10
v. Northamptonshire (Luton) 27 June	AEL	6-2-21-1	6-2-16-1		10-0-61-2		10-0-46-0	11-4-23-1	10-0-63-2		6-1-10-0	12-0-47-2	3-0-23-0	1-0-6-0				8	5	2	263	7
v. Sussex (Taunton) 4 July	AEL	10-1-41-3			10-0-50-0		10-0-43-1		10-0-67-3		10-0-44-0	4-0-19-1			6-0-61-1			10	5	2	302	8
v. Nottinghamshire (Trent Bridge) 7 July	NW	10-2-34-2	11-1-45-3	12-1-44-0	12-0-41-3						10-1-52-2	5-0-30-0						6	8	8	203	10
v. Hampshire (Southampton) 11 July	AEL	9.5-4-38-0		10-1-48-1	9-1-43-2		6-0-36-0			10-0-34-1	10.4-2-33-3							2	4		215	3
v. Nottinghamshire (Trent Bridge) 18 July	AEL	8.4-0-50-0			10-2-36-3					4-1-17-0	9-2-32-0						1	2	1	2	203	6
v. Kent (Taunton) 25 July	AEL		9-0-45-1	6.3-0-38-0	10-2-26-4					7-1-31-0	10-0-49-2						1	8	5	12	196	7
v. Surrey (Taunton) 27 & 28 July	NW	10.5-1-30-5	10-0-45-0	12-2-36-2	12-1-42-1						10-1-24-1					6-0-24-0		6	7	2	187	10
v. Yorkshire (Taunton) 1 August	AEL	10-0-51-2	12-1-57-3	10-5-15-2			10-0-38-1	9-0-37-0		5-1-30-1	12-3-28-2						5	7	13	4	203	6
v. Warwickshire (Taunton) 10 August	NW	12-2-41-0		12-0-40-1	12-0-63-2						5-0-20-0						4	15	12	4	252	8
v. Derbyshire (Derby) 15 August	AEL		7.3-1-17-3	10-0-40-0	7-1-44-1				6-0-36-0	8-0-51-2	12-4-32-1							8	8	6	281	3
v. Leicestershire (Weston-super-Mare) 22 August	AEL	9-0-74-0		10-1-28-2	8-1-28-1			2-0-14-0	8-0-33-2	6-0-15-0	10-1-28-2						1	8	4	2	144	10
v. Surrey (The Oval) 29 August	AEL			10-2-37-3	9.3-2-33-0		10-0-56-1		10-1-57-0	9-0-55-1								3	1	2	241	5
v. Gloucestershire (Taunton) 5 September	AEL	8-0-31-2	8-1-43-2	10-4-17-3			9-4-20-0											4	5	10	115	7
v. Warwickshire (Edgbaston) 12 September	AEL																					Ab.
v. Durham (Hartlepool) 19 September	AEL	5-0-32-0	4-0-20-0	6-0-38-0	4-1-13-1		8-3-15-1	2-0-15-0			6-0-32-1				6-0-32-1			3	1	6	168	3
Wickets		19	15	22	29	0	4	1	13	6	18	3	0	0	1	0						

FIELDING FIGURES

17 – A.J. Stewart (ct 16/st 1), M.A. Lynch and G.J. Kersey (ct 14/st 3)
10 – A.W. Smith
9 – A.D. Brown
8 – G.P. Thorpe, M.A. Butcher and J. Boiling
6 – D.M. Ward
3 – Waqar Younis
2 – D.J. Bicknell, M.P. Bicknell, A.J. Hollioake, P. D. Atkins and J.E. Benjamin

BEST BATSMEN & BOWLERS

G.P. Thorpe hit his first century in the Benson and Hedges Cup. A.J. Hollioake, who had played in only two Sunday League games prior to 1993, had career-best performances in the competition with both bat and ball.

A.W. Smith made his Sunday League debut. He had played only in the Seeboard Trophy prior to 1993.

G.J. Kersey played one Sunday League for Kent in 1992 before joining Surrey in 1993 to share the wicket-keeping duties with A.J. Stewart.

SURREY CCC — BATTING

First half of season

Player	v. Sussex (Hove) 9 May AEL	v. Lancashire (The Oval) 11 May B&H	v. Essex (The Oval) 16 May AEL	v. Lancashire (The Oval) 6 June AEL	v. Glamorgan (The Oval) 13 June AEL	v. Warwickshire (Edgbaston) 20 June AEL	v. Dorset (The Oval) 22 June NW	v. Middlesex (Lord's) 27 June AEL	v. Durham (The Oval) 4 July AEL	v. Leicestershire (Leicester) 7 July NW	v. Leicestershire (Leicester) 11 July AEL	v. Kent (Canterbury) 14 July SB	v. Gloucestershire (Guildford) 18 July AEL	Runs
D.J. Bicknell	15	0	8	30	6	20	54*	65*	16	19	—	33	44*	482
A.D. Brown	15	1	52	103	12	26	—	54	5	14*	—	16	32	518
D.M. Ward	73	0	53	55	4	26	104*	9	25	56	—	53	24*	453
A.J. Stewart	17	95	27	15	39	30	—	21	78	10	—	47	—	608
G.P. Thorpe	18	2	14	5	15	2	—	6*	7*	25*	—	—	—	477
M.A. Lynch	8	1	27*	—	8	4	—	—	0	—	—	—	—	334
M.A. Butcher	10	3	—	3*	4	3*	—	—	1*	—	—	—	—	117
M.P. Bicknell	0	1	0	3*	3*	0	—	—	0*	—	—	—	—	55
J. Boiling	2*	4*	1*	1*	4	4*	—	—	—	—	—	4*	—	45
J.E. Benjamin	0	—	—	—	—	—	—	—	—	—	—	31	—	35
A.J. Murphy	—	—	—	—	—	—	—	—	—	—	—	0*	—	10
Waqar Younis	3	3	9	—	—	4*	—	—	8	1	—	—	—	99
A.J. Hollioake	—	—	—	5	5	14	—	8	50	2	—	—	3	164
G.J. Kersey	—	—	14	6	1	33	—	10	4	4	—	—	1	128
A.W. Smith	—	—	—	15	1	—	—	—	—	—	—	—	6	168
P.D. Atkins	—	—	—	—	—	—	—	—	—	—	—	—	—	142
I.J. Ward	—	—	—	—	—	—	—	—	—	—	—	—	—	0
Byes	17	5	8	6	1	9	4	10	7	1		5	—	
Leg-byes	10	6	6	7	3	9	2	4	1	2		3	3	
Wides	6	4	2			14		4	2	4		15	1	
No-balls	—	2										6	6	
Total	245	230	208	259	168	194	164	173	205	131	Ab.	213	110	
Wickets	10	10	W	W	10	10	W	3	9	3		5	1	
Result	L	L	W	W	L	W	W	W	W	W		W	W	
Points	0	—	4	4	0	4	4	4	4	—	2	4	4	

Second half of season

Player	v. Northamptonshire (Northampton) 25 July AEL	v. Somerset (Taunton) 27 & 28 July NW	v. Nottinghamshire (The Oval) 1 August AEL	v. Sussex (Hove) 4 August SB	v. Kent (Canterbury) 8 August AEL	v. Worcestershire (Worcester) 15 August AEL	v. Derbyshire (Ilkeston) 22 August AEL	v. Somerset (The Oval) 29 August AEL	v. Hampshire (The Oval) 5 September AEL	v. Yorkshire (The Oval) 19 September AEL	Runs
D.J. Bicknell	—	32	7	13	21	18	0	76	1	4	482
A.D. Brown	—	26	1	53*	0	19	5	26	6	52	518
D.M. Ward	—	3	101	0	26	3	81*	—	7	24	453
A.J. Stewart	—	15	42*	—	26	7	—	—	83	35	608
G.P. Thorpe	—	58	94	30	9	8	3	0	2	16	477
M.A. Lynch	—	5	35	—	—	4	27*	22*	16	—	334
M.A. Butcher	—	15	—	—	—	23*	—	—	—	—	117
M.P. Bicknell	—	12	7*	—	2*	12	9	—	8	8	55
J. Boiling	—	1*	—	—	1	9	—	1*	8	—	45
J.E. Benjamin	—	—	—	—	0	21	6	—	1*	—	35
A.J. Murphy	—	—	—	—	6	—	—	—	—	—	10
Waqar Younis	—	3	14	—	58	16	1	47*	39	21*	99
A.J. Hollioake	—	—	—	56*	2	—	58	9	28	30*	164
G.J. Kersey	—	—	—	—	49	—	—	55	—	—	128
A.W. Smith	—	—	—	—	—	—	—	—	—	—	168
P.D. Atkins	—	—	—	—	—	—	—	—	—	—	142
I.J. Ward	—	—	—	—	—	—	—	—	—	—	0
Byes		6	1		2	2	1	1	1	1	
Leg-byes		7	7		8	9	6	3	4	4	
Wides		2	8	1	8	8	13	1	5	1	
No-balls											
Total		187	316	153	194	157	203	241	213	188	
Wickets	Ab.	10	6	3	10	10	5	5	10	5	
Result		L	W	W	L	L	W	W	W	W	
Points	2	—	4	—	0	0	4	4	4	4	

SURREY CCC
BOWLING

Match	Comp	M.P. Bicknell	J.E. Benjamin	A.J. Murphy	M.A. Butcher	J. Boiling	Waqar Younis	G.P. Thorpe	A.J. Hollioake	M.A. Lynch	A.W. Smith	I.J. Ward	Byes	Leg-byes	Wides	No-balls	Total	Wkts
v. Sussex (Hove) 9 May	AEL	10-1-63-2	10-0-66-0	9-0-70-1	10-0-52-3	10-0-52-3								7	3	8	310	9
v. Lancashire (The Oval) 11 May	B&H	11-5-27-3	11-3-30-0	8-3-25-1	11-2-41-2	9-0-76-1	10.1-3-27-3	2-0-16-0					4	15	5	6	236	10
v. Essex (The Oval) 16 May	AEL	7-1-23-2	7-1-23-2		10-0-39-0	9-0-38-2		7-0-27-2					1	8	8		207	9
v. Lancashire (The Oval) 6 June	AEL	6-1-25-2	5-1-19-2			0.4-0-1	9-1-46-2		7-1-33-4					4	3		94	10
v. Glamorgan (The Oval) 13 June	AEL	10-3-28-0	10-2-40-0			10-0-29-0	7-0-32-0			3.2-0-14-0				2	4	2	169	0
v. Warwickshire (Edgbaston) 20 June	AEL	9.5-2-19-4	10-0-39-0			10-0-40-2	10-1-34-2	9-0-39-1	6-0-24-0					5	6		176	10
v. Dorset (The Oval) 22 June	NW	12-4-26-3	12-2-24-1	11-2-27-2		12-1-27-0	11.5-0-59-3						2	4			163	10
v. Middlesex (Lord's) 27 June	AEL	10-2-18-3	10-1-31-1		10-2-29-2	10-0-44-0	9-1-46-0							2	13		172	6
v. Durham (The Oval) 4 July	AEL	9-2-22-3	9.3-1-33-2		10-1-35-3	10-0-54-1	10-2-20-1							5	6	4	169	10
v. Leicestershire (Leicester) 7 July	NW	8-2-26-1	3-0-18-0			12-1-29-2	7.5-1-18-3			4-0-10-1	12-4-25-3		1	2	1		129	10
v. Leicestershire (Leicester) 11 July	AEL	6-1-9-0	5-2-13-1										4				26	1
v. Kent (Canterbury) 14 July	SB	10-2-32-3	10-1-40-2	8-2-28-0		10-1-39-2	10-0-37-0				8-0-37-0		5	4	1		209	8
v. Gloucestershire (Guildford) 18 July	AEL	9-2-23-2	10-1-34-3		10-0-29-1	10-1-28-3	10-1-38-4							7	7	4	155	10
v. Northamptonshire (Northampton) 25 July	AEL		7-0-38-0	10-1-44-2	10-0-46-0	10-0-21-2			8-0-37-1			4-0-28-0		12	8	2	193	9
v. Somerset (Taunton) 27 & 28 July	NW	12-2-35-4			12-2-57-2	12-1-22-1	12-1-44-1			5-1-22-1				6	10	4	230	9
v. Nottinghamshire (The Oval) 1 August	AEL	10-0-73-1	9-1-62-2	10-1-41-2		10-0-39-2	9-0-64-1		10-0-65-1				5	2	1	9	314	7
v. Sussex (Hove) 4 August	SB					10-0-44-1	10-1-43-1		10-1-46-4	4-0-24-0	6-0-40-0			8	3	4	233	9
v. Kent (Canterbury) 8 August	AEL		10-1-36-2	10-3-54-2		10-0-59-2	10-1-37-2		10-0-44-2				3	6	11		248	8
v. Worcestershire (Worcester) 15 August	AEL		10-2-37-1	9.4-0-27-1		10-1-47-1	10-1-33-3		10-2-37-2					9	7	2	194	10
v. Derbyshire (Ilkeston) 22 August	AEL		9.4-0-40-3		9-0-50-0	10-0-40-1	9-2-25-4		9-0-43-2					5	5	2	201	10
v. Somerset (The Oval) 29 August	AEL		7.4-1-26-1	10-2-48-1	10-0-71-2	10-0-41-0	8-0-29-3		10-2-44-1				4	2	3	6	238	8
v. Hampshire (The Oval) 5 September	AEL			8-3-12-2	7-0-23-0	10-1-26-4	10-0-34-1							7	7	2	136	10
v. Yorkshire (The Oval) 19 September	AEL		8-0-44-0	10-1-36-3	10-4-34-1	10-0-33-1			9.5-1-42-4				6	6	5		185	10
Wickets		31	23	17	16	32	35	3	22	2	3	0						

FIELDING FIGURES

31 – P. Moores
9 – M.P. Speight, K. Greenfield and A.P. Wells
7 – C.W.J. Athey
5 – N.J. Lenham and D.M. Smith
4 – E.S.H. Giddins and I.D.K. Salisbury
3 – C.M. Wells
2 – A.N. Jones and subs
1 – C.C. Remy, A.C.S. Pigott and E.E. Hemmings

BEST BATSMEN & BOWLERS

D.M. Smith's century in the NatWest final was his highest score in the competition.

F.D. Stephenson hit his first Sunday League century in the opening match of the season.

M.P. Speight (126 against Somerset) and A.P. Wells (127 against Hampshire) made their highest Sunday League scores.

K. Greenfield made his highest score in the NatWest Trophy.

C.W.J. Athey, previously with Yorkshire and Gloucestershire, and E.E. Hemmings, previously with Warwickshire and Nottinghamshire, were both playing for their third county in limited-over competitions.

N.J. Lenham's 5 for 28 in the Sunday League match against Durham was his best bowling performance in limited-over cricket.

SUSSEX CCC — BATTING

	v. Surrey (Hove) 9 May AEL	v. Glamorgan (Cardiff) 11 May B&H	v. Leicestershire (Horsham) 23 May AEL	v. Lancashire (Hove) 25 May B&H	v. Middlesex (Lord's) 30 May AEL	v. Warwickshire (Edgbaston) 6 June AEL	v. Northamptonshire (Hove) 13 June AEL	v. Lancashire (Old Trafford) 20 June AEL	v. Wales Minor Counties (Hove) 22 June NW	v. Somerset (Taunton) 4 July AEL	v. Hampshire (Hove) 7 July NW	v. Glamorgan (Llanelli) 11 July AEL	v. Kent (Hove) 18 July AEL	Runs
D.M. Smith	52	55	75	10	27	23	52	10		9	123	42	8	776
F.D. Stephenson	103	43	30	13	13	17	2			16		18	2	536
M.P. Speight	55	17	52	4	13	31	92*	1	8	126	4*	14	32	614
A.P. Wells	10	53	21	23	40					19		51	33	1036
C.M. Wells	31	23	30	2	15*	0	48	9	96*	35				143
K. Greenfield	18	10			6	3	5		9	15		0		384
P. Moores	3	8	10	22	19			5	0*	20		56	6	348
I.D.K. Salisbury	16	16*	8	2*		5*			0*	13*		17		131
A.N. Jones	2	–	–				–	1*	–			3		28
E.E. Hemmings	2	–						24				0*	0	10
E.S.H. Giddins	0*	–	24*	20	0		1	5			107*		42	11
N.J. Lenham		15*	19	61*	85	2		26	92	23		6	8	406
C.W.J. Athey					5*	6	9*		3	9*			17*	690
A.C.S. Pigott						10		19	20				20	66
J.W. Hall														13
B.T.P. Donelan														47
J.A. North	48	11		1		11*	9*	1*						135
D.R. Law														10
C.C. Remy														20
K. Newell														—
Byes	7	1	4	10	15	4	4	6	5	10	2	8	4	
Leg-byes	3	9	8	3	7	10	4	6	11	5	2	2	2	
Wides	3	13	2	8	2	4	2	4	2	2	14	2	3	
No-balls	8					4		4	8					
Total	310	263	283	178	247	134	217	118	257	302	252	219	177	
Wickets	W	7	W	7	Tie	8	5	8	7	8	1	10	10	
Result	W	W	W	L	Tie	W	W	L	W	W	W	L	Ab.	
Points	4	–	4	–	2	4	4	–	–	4	–	–	2	

BATTING (continued)

	v. Derbyshire (Derby) 25 July AEL	v. Northamptonshire (Northampton) 27 & 28 July NW	v. Durham (Durham) 1 August AEL	v. Surrey (Hove) 4 August SB	v. Worcestershire (Hove) 8 August AEL	v. Glamorgan (Hove) 10 August NW	v. Nottinghamshire (Eastbourne) 15 August AEL	v. Hampshire (Portsmouth) 29 August AEL	v. Warwickshire (Lord's) 4 September NW	v. Essex (Hove) 7 September AEL	v. Yorkshire (Scarborough) 12 September AEL	v. Gloucestershire (Hove) 19 September AEL	Runs
D.M. Smith	10	47	15	17	6	8	25	59	124	51	0	81	776
F.D. Stephenson	4	18	9	10	3	25	35	8	3	16	10	12	536
M.P. Speight	14	34	10	46	32	0	57	127	50	24	80	15	614
A.P. Wells	0	23	69*	52	86	106*	24	127	33	39	0		1036
C.M. Wells	11	7	3	6	14	1	35	9	8*	65*	40	18	143
K. Greenfield	18		6		34	8	19*	12		24	0	48	384
P. Moores		25*		3*	6*	2*	10	2				13	348
I.D.K. Salisbury		3						1*	9*			4*	131
A.N. Jones													28
E.E. Hemmings	0*	0*	–		0	47	1	1*	58		9*	0	10
E.S.H. Giddins	1		34	35	9	17	28	69	0	15	30	12	11
N.J. Lenham	42		13	39	64		6	0			51	0	406
C.W.J. Athey			2*	5	0								690
A.C.S. Pigott	2							14*	16				66
J.W. Hall													13
B.T.P. Donelan													47
J.A. North	48	11	11	1*			0			19	1		135
D.R. Law													10
C.C. Remy													20
K. Newell													—
Byes	3	1	1	2	4	4	6	1	11	15	6	1	
Leg-byes	3	7	1	3	4	4	12	6	18	6	3	4	
Wides	4	5	6	4	3	2	4	2	16	6	4	2	
No-balls	4	4	16					2	16	16		14	
Total	118	230	195	233	261	224	262	312	321	290	234	224	
Wickets	10	9	8	9	10	7	10	8	6	7	10	10	
Result	W	W	W	L	W	W	W	L	W	W	L	W	

SUSSEX CCC — BOWLING

Match	Date		F.D. Stephenson	E.S.H. Giddins	A.N. Jones	C.M. Wells	E.E. Hemmings	I.D.K. Salisbury	N.J. Lenham	A.C.S. Pigott	C.W.J. Athey	B.T.P. Donelan	J.A. North	K. Greenfield	D.R. Law	C.C. Remy	K. Newell	Byes	Leg-byes	Wides	No-balls	Total	Wkts
v. Surrey (Hove)	9 May	AEL	9-0-48-1	9-0-42-3	7-0-24-1	4-0-22-0	6-0-43-1	8.5-1-49-4											17	10	6	245	10
v. Glamorgan (Cardiff)	11 May	B&H	10-0-48-3	9.2-0-42-2	7-0-36-1	4-0-20-0		11-1-28-1											6	4	8	230	10
v. Leicestershire (Horsham)	23 May	AEL	10-1-29-3	10-4-32-0		10-0-34-3		10-0-34-0	11-0-50-1	10-0-69-0								1	21	8		220	7
v. Lancashire (Hove)	25 May	B&H	11-2-44-1	10-1-33-0		9-1-27-1	11-3-31-1	11-3-41-2											6	2	2	182	5
v. Middlesex (Lord's)	30 May	AEL	10-1-48-1	10-0-38-2		7-1-41-1			6-0-26-0		6-0-39-1							1	12	4	2	247	7
v. Warwickshire (Edgbaston)	6 June	AEL	9-2-18-1	7.1-1-19-1	10-2-24-4					10-0-42-2		8-1-25-1						2	10	3	4	133	10
v. Northamptonshire (Hove)	13 June	AEL	10-1-27-4	9.5-2-44-3	10-0-30-0					10-2-21-2	3-0-14-0		10-0-49-1						8	1	2	214	10
v. Lancashire (Old Trafford)	20 June	AEL	5-1-16-0	5-0-22-0	5-0-26-1					10-0-56-1		10-0-27-1	1-0-13-0						1	2	4	122	4
v. Wales Minor Counties (Hove)	22 June	NW	5-2-4-0	12-2-24-1	7-2-10-1	10-0-48-2	12-4-15-1	8-1-17-2		5-1-16-2	7-0-25-0		2-0-17-0	7-0-23-0				1	8	4		143	6
v. Somerset (Taunton)	4 July	AEL	6-1-21-0	5-0-19-1	8-2-26-4					5-0-16-0	4.3-0-24-2			10-0-37-1					6	4	2	197	10
v. Hampshire (Hove)	7 July	NW	12-3-52-2	12-3-41-0	12-1-60-1	6-0-23-0		12-3-41-1						6-0-24-0					7	6	6	248	4
v. Glamorgan (Llanelli)	11 July	AEL	10-3-32-2	10-0-59-2	10-0-68-1	10-0-58-0		10-0-48-1										1	3	2		269	8
v. Kent (Hove)	18 July	AEL	1-0-1-0	0.1-0-2-0																		3	0
v. Derbyshire (Derby)	25 July	AEL	10-0-44-3	10-0-65-1		12-0-43-0		7-0-40-0		10-0-36-0			1-0-8-1						6	2	4	199	6
v. Northamptonshire (Northampton)	27 & 28 July	NW	11-5-25-2	10-3-21-2				12-0-49-2		10.2-1-40-2									12	8	2	190	10
v. Durham (Durham)	1 August	AEL	10-2-30-0	10-2-40-1				10-0-34-1	10-0-28-5	8-0-40-1			2-0-16-0						6	12	4	194	9
v. Surrey (Hove)	4 August	SB	5-0-16-2				4-0-30-1	5-0-35-0	5-1-22-0	2.2-0-29-0					5-1-21-0					1		153	3
v. Worcestershire (Hove)	8 August	AEL	10-1-36-3	9.3-0-46-2				4-0-24-1	5-0-37-0	10-0-39-1				10-1-44-3				4	2	8		232	10
v. Glamorgan (Hove)	10 August	NW	12-1-25-3	12-2-46-0				11-1-45-1		9-1-23-3				9-1-35-2					15	6		220	10
v. Nottinghamshire (Eastbourne)	15 August	AEL	7-2-17-2	8-3-16-2				10-0-30-3	7-0-31-1				0.1-0-1-0	10-0-39-1					12	7		168	10
v. Hampshire (Portsmouth)	29 August	AEL	9.5-1-39-0	10-0-56-1			7.3-0-26-0	10-0-73-0	10-0-54-1				6-0-48-1	3.3-0-36-0				11	5	9		313	2
v. Warwickshire (Lord's)	4 September	NW	12-2-51-2	12-0-57-1				11-0-59-1	3-0-19-0	11-0-74-1				7-0-31-0				3	13	13	6	322	5
v. Essex (Hove)	7 September	AEL	9.3-1-23-5	8-0-53-1				6-0-44-1	7-0-34-0							10-1-44-1	6-0-44-0		1	1	8	229	10
v. Yorkshire (Scarborough)	12 September	AEL	10-2-39-3	10-0-44-1		10-0-51-0		4-0-27-0						1-0-20-0		10-0-48-2			5	2		255	7
v. Gloucestershire (Hove)	19 September	AEL	9-3-30-3	8.1-1-36-4			10-0-44-1	10-1-28-2	6-0-41-0					4-0-17-0		6-1-28-0			9	1	2	192	10
Wickets			46	31	14	7	5	23	8	15	3	2	6	7	0	3	0						

FIELDING FIGURES

14 – M. Burns (ct 9/st 5)
12 – T.L. Penney and N.M.K. Smith
10 – D.P. Ostler
10 – R.G. Twose and K.J. Piper
8 – D.A. Reeve
7 – A.J. Moles
5 – J.D. Ratcliffe and T.A. Munton
3 – G.C. Small, P.A. Smith, Asif Din and P.C.L. Holloway
2 – A.A. Donald
1 – P.A. Booth
†A.A. Donald absent hurt

BEST BATSMEN & BOWLERS

Warwickshire won the NatWest Trophy (previously the Gillette Cup) for the fourth time in their history. Reeve enjoyed success in his first season as captain. Wicket-keeper Burns had appeared in only one Sunday League game prior to 1993, while Bell and Giles made their debuts in the competition.

A.A. Donald was unable to play for Warwickshire after the NatWest Trophy quarter-final as he was required by South Africa for their tour of Sri Lanka.

T.L. Penney's 83 not out against Kent was his highest Sunday League score.

P.A. Smith took five wickets in a Sunday League match for the first time.

A. Dean made his debut in the last game of the season.

WARWICKSHIRE CCC — BATTING

	v. Derbyshire (Edgbaston) 9 May AEL	v. Leicestershire (Leicester) 11 May B&H	v. Kent (Canterbury) 16 May AEL	v. Lancashire (Old Trafford) 30 May AEL	v. Sussex (Edgbaston) 6 June AEL	v. Surrey (Edgbaston) 20 June AEL	v. Norfolk (Lakenham) 22 June NW	v. Essex (Ilford) 27 June AEL	v. Yorkshire (Edgbaston) 4 July AEL	v. Kent (Edgbaston) 7 July NW	v. Northamptonshire (Edgbaston) 11 July AEL	v. Middlesex (Edgbaston) 18 July AEL	v. Leicestershire (Leicester) 25 July AEL	Runs
A.J. Moles	28	63	14	—	7	10	44	66	7	37	21	0	8	396
R.G. Twose	65	12	1	—	5	14	25	42	38*	35	63*	0		369
P.A. Smith	7	3	7	—		49	104	7	81*	61	68*	7	25	552
D.P. Ostler	3	36	44	—	13	17	14	69		10		83	24	784
T.L. Penney	23	22	83*	—	2	41	17	18		7*		27*	5*	330
D.A. Reeve	3	8	4	—	38					72*	19	20	15*	422
M. Burns	22	22	23	—	0	4	1	0				7	18*	151
N.M.K. Smith	7	8		—	15	0	0	6	4	18				224
G.C. Small	4*	8		—	6	0	2*							37
A.A. Donald	2	5*	13	—	1	3*	1*					0*		12
T.A. Munton	0		4	—	2*									34
M.A.V. Bell														19
J.D. Ratcliffe					25	24	40	1						296
P.C.L. Holloway						1	16	20	0		19	94	23	18
Asif Din	105							5*				0*		583
P.A. Booth	1													15
K.J. Piper		14	132*											14
D.R. Brown														—
A.F. Giles														—
G. Welch														—
A. Dean														17
Byes	1	4	16		2	5	6	8	4	1	7	5	2	
Leg-byes	4	2	8		10	6	13	5	1	20	3	4	2	
Wides	5	4	2	Ab.	3	2	2	5	—	2	2	6	2	
No-balls	2		2		4	2	2	6		2				
Total	174	206	223		133	176	285	253	135	265	183	253	124	
Wickets	W	10	9†	2	10	10	9	9	2	5	2	8	4	
Result	W	L	L	—	L	L	W	W	W	W	W	L	W	
Points	4	—	0		0	0		4			4	0	4	

BATTING

	v. Yorkshire (Leeds) 27 & 28 July NW	v. Hampshire (Southampton) 1 August AEL	v. Glamorgan (Neath) 8 August AEL	v. Somerset (Taunton) 10 August NW	v. Gloucestershire (Edgbaston) 15 August AEL	v. Durham (Darlington) 22 August AEL	v. Worcestershire (Edgbaston) 29 August AEL	v. Sussex (Lord's) 4 September NW	v. Zimbabwe (Edgbaston) 7 September AEL	v. Somerset (Edgbaston) 12 September AEL	v. Nottinghamshire (Trent Bridge) 19 September AEL	Runs
A.J. Moles	2	9	12	41	26	4	6	2	39		0	396
R.G. Twose	36	21	34	33	10	25	32*	2*			46	369
P.A. Smith	6	4	27	58	50	39	11	60			53	552
D.P. Ostler	10	18	28	6	0	20	43	25	0*		17	784
T.L. Penney	50	3	22	28*	27						22	330
D.A. Reeve			23*	17	1	5*	21	81*	48*		26	422
M. Burns			6	11	54	17	0				12*	151
N.M.K. Smith	12*	23*			10	0						224
G.C. Small	2					3						37
A.A. Donald	0					6	5					12
T.A. Munton			6*		22							34
M.A.V. Bell			1	4	6	66		13	19		6	19
J.D. Ratcliffe	105	14		15			42	104				296
P.C.L. Holloway												18
Asif Din		132*	2		8*	6	10*				60	583
P.A. Booth	1			4*								15
K.J. Piper												14
D.R. Brown												—
A.F. Giles												—
G. Welch												—
A. Dean	5	5	2	4	1	2	8	3	2		17	17
Byes	5	5	2	4	1	2	8	3	2		5	
Leg-byes	2	5		15	2	2	8	13	1		6	
Wides	2	3		12	2			13			4	
No-balls	12			4	2			6				
Total	245	232	163	252	221	195	188	322	109		276	
Wickets	10	6	8	8	10	10	7	5	1	Ab.	9	
Result	L	L	L	W	L	L	W	W	L		W	

WARWICKSHIRE CCC
BOWLING

Opponent (Venue)	Date	Comp	T.A. Munton	D.A. Reeve	A.A. Donald	G.C. Small	N.M.K. Smith	P.A. Smith	R.G. Twose	M.A.V. Bell	J.D. Ratcliffe	D.P. Oster	P.A. Booth	Asif Din	D.R. Brown	G. Welch	A.F. Giles	Byes	Leg-byes	Wides	No-balls	Total	Wkts
v. Derbyshire (Edgbaston)	9 May	AEL	10-5-32-1	6.3-3-23-2	10-1-30-0	8.3-1-27-3	7-0-22-0	7-0-31-1										5	3	4	4	173	9
v. Leicestershire (Leicester)	11 May	B&H	11-1-40-1	9-2-20-0	10-0-47-2	11-1-27-2	4-1-20-0	7-0-33-3	3-0-10-0									3	6	5	2	206	8
v. Kent (Canterbury)	16 May	AEL	9-0-55-1	7-0-41-1	8.4-2-39-1	9.4-0-31-0	10-0-40-3	7-0-54-1	0.2-0-2-0	7-0-49-0								3	6	15	4	289	8
v. Lancashire (Old Trafford)	30 May	AEL	9-1-33-1	8-1-17-1	10-0-59-0	10-1-28-2	8-0-26-5											2	6	10	6	174	7
v. Sussex (Edgbaston)	6 June	AEL	10-6-11-3	10-3-26-1	10-2-33-0	10-1-27-2	9-2-22-1											4	10	8	4	134	8
v. Surrey (Edgbaston)	20 June	AEL	9-1-46-0		10-0-27-2		9.5-1-21-4	10-0-55-1										4	9	14		194	10
v. Norfolk (Lakenham)	22 June	NW	12-1-33-1				12-5-17-5											9	13	5	6	142	10
v. Essex (Ilford)	27 June	AEL	8.2-1-17-1				8-0-48-2				4-0-16-0	1.3-0-4-1							4	9	2	207	10
v. Yorkshire (Edgbaston)	4 July	AEL	10-2-24-0	5-1-16-1	7-2-13-0	6-0-18-1	8-0-22-1	6-1-12-0	4-0-26-1				3-0-19-0					5	5	6	2	131	9
v. Kent (Edgbaston)	7 July	AEL	12-3-25-2	9-1-50-1	10-2-27-2	6-0-11-2	7-0-40-0	8-0-32-2	7-2-11-1									4	6	7	6	262	9
v. Northamptonshire (Edgbaston)	11 July	NW	10-3-46-2	5-2-9-0	11-1-69-4		6-1-19-0	10-2-33-4	12-3-30-2									2	5	4	4	196	7
v. Middlesex (Edgbaston)	18 July	AEL		10-2-28-0	10-0-41-3		10-0-49-1	8-0-60-1	4-0-16-0				10-0-48-0					8	7	6	8	261	2
v. Leicestershire (Leicester)	25 July	AEL		10-3-41-2	10-1-46-0	7-2-11-1	2-0-21-0	7-0-26-0	4-0-20-0									1	5	3		170	7
v. Yorkshire (Leeds)	27 & 28 July	AEL		7-0-43-0	5-0-38-1	12-2-38-1	4-0-17-1	9-1-40-0	8-0-39-0									1	12	15	2	224	10
v. Hampshire (Southampton)	1 August	NW	8-0-37-0	10-2-40-0	12-3-38-2		9-0-53-0	10-1-54-5	4-0-20-0					3.5-0-31-0				2	8	1	4	233	1
v. Glamorgan (Neath)	8 August	AEL	8-0-28-0	12-3-42-1			10-0-27-1	11.2-1-37-4	7-1-25-1	10-0-40-1	5-0-11-2			1-0-3-0				3	7	9		164	6
v. Somerset (Taunton)	10 August	NW	10-3-23-0	7-1-31-0		7-1-21-1	11-1-51-1	6-0-30-0	5.3-0-26-1		1-0-4-0							1	9	8	12	200	10
v. Gloucestershire (Edgbaston)	15 August	NW	10-4-29-1	7-0-20-0		5-2-9-2		12-1-40-2	10-0-50-2						10-1-37-1				8	6	4	232	5
v. Durham (Darlington)	22 August	AEL	9.2-1-28-0	12-0-37-3			10-1-61-1	10-0-47-0	7-0-31-3	10-1-40-1					7-3-23-0			2	9	4	2	197	8
v. Worcestershire (Edgbaston)	29 August	AEL	8-3-11-1				10-1-28-3	6-0-36-0	10-1-35-3						8-1-23-0			2	4	3	10	144	10
v. Sussex (Lord's)	4 September	NW	9-0-67-1	5.3-1-12-1		12-0-71-0	5-1-21-0	10-0-36-5	8-1-30-1										11	18	16	321	6
v. Zimbabwe (Edgbaston)	7 September			12-1-60-2			12-1-37-1	7-0-45-0		8-0-43-2					10-0-57-1	11-1-28-3	11-3-16-1	11	11	6	2	209	8
v. Somerset (Edgbaston)	12 September	AEL	10-3-17-1				10-0-26-2	8-0-27-0	1-0-2-0	6-0-36-0					5-0-25-1				4	1	2	133	6
v. Nottinghamshire (Trent Bridge)	19 September	AEL	8-0-48-1	7-1-30-1			6-0-10-3	8-1-23-0		7-1-21-5								7	7	2	4	116	10
Wickets			**19**	**17**	**18**	**17**	**35**	**29**	**15**	**9**	**3**	**1**	**0**	**0**	**3**	**3**	**1**						

FIELDING FIGURES

32 – S.J. Rhodes (ct 27/st 5)
11 – D.A. Leatherdale
8 – R.K. Illingworth and D.B. D'Oliveira
7 – S.R. Lampitt
4 – T.S. Curtis and P.J. Newport
3 – M.J. Weston and G.A. Hick
2 – A.C.H. Seymour and G.R. Haynes
1 – W.P.C. Weston, K.C.G. Benjamin, N.V. Radford, C.M. Tolley and sub

BEST BATSMEN & BOWLERS

K.C.G. Benjamin, the West Indian pace bowler, and W.P.C. Weston made their debuts in limited-over competitions.

C.M. Tolley took a Sunday League best of 4 for 50 against Hampshire.

N.V. Radford opened the innings in the Sunday League match against Durham and hit 70, his highest score in the competition.

K.R. Spring and V.S. Solanki made their debuts in the last game of the season.

WORCESTERSHIRE CCC — BATTING

BATTING	v. Essex (Worcester) 11 May B&H	v. Yorkshire (Leeds) 16 May AEL	v. Somerset (Worcester) 23 May AEL	v. Leicestershire (Leicester) 25 May B&H	v. Gloucestershire (Gloucester) 30 May AEL	v. Northamptonshire (Northampton) 6 June AEL	v. Leicestershire (Worcester) 13 June AEL	v. Scotland (Edinburgh) 22 June NW	v. Durham (Stockton) 27 June AEL	v. Derbyshire (Worcester) 4 July AEL	v. Derbyshire (Worcester) 7 July NW	v. Nottinghamshire (Trent Bridge) 11 July AEL	v. Hampshire (Portsmouth) 18 July AEL	Runs
T.S. Curtis	20	31	12	0	6*	—	12	48	1	8	82	14	—	393
W.P.C. Weston	32*	15*	22	1	—	5	5	31	32	9	27	27	—	200
G.A. Hick	62*	0*	—	82	59	83*	11	51	25	30	48	15	—	737
D.B. D'Oliveira	—	—	5	9	—	—	30	32	—	27	15	—	—	363
A.C.H. Seymour	—	—	2	3	—	—	—	4	—	—	—	—	—	26
S.R. Lampitt	21	17	12	14	—	28	41*	4	29	17*	1	2	—	255
S.J. Rhodes	37	19	24*	11	—	23	20	18	40	8	—	2*	—	315
R.K. Illingworth	13*	18	—	8*	—	1*	30	2*	0*	14*	13*	6	—	151
P.J. Newport	3	2	—	2	20	5	2*	—	5*	7	—	14	—	103
K.C.G. Benjamin	—	—	—	2	—	0	1	9*	0*	—	—	19	—	37
C.M. Tolley	3	—	3	—	—	0	—	—	—	—	—	—	—	34
M.J. Weston	1	—	—	—	13	5	7	2	70	17	4*	28	—	152
N.V. Radford	6	1	1*	—	1*	4	1	22	0	28	36	9	—	192
D.A. Leatherdale	38	20	—	—	—	—	—	—	5	—	—	—	—	201
K.R. Spring	—	—	—	—	—	—	—	—	—	—	—	—	—	7
G.R. Haynes	—	—	—	—	—	—	—	—	—	—	—	—	—	195
V.S. Solanki	—	—	—	—	—	—	—	—	—	—	—	—	—	22
Byes	2	1	6	13	1	1	3	5	1	9	3	1	—	
Leg-byes	—	4	3	2	1	6	8	3	9	12	4	4	—	
Wides	1	4	10	—	7	6	1	11	4	4	12	10	—	
No-balls	—	—	—	—	—	—	—	—	6	—	—	—	—	
Total	117	55	100	150	108	168	174	238	227	190	245	155	Ab.	
Wickets	W	Ab.	W	10	3	9	9	8	9	9	6	10		
Result	—	—	—	L	W	Tie	L	W	L	L	W	L		
Points	—	2	4	—	4	2	0	—	0	0	—	0	2	

WORCESTERSHIRE CCC — BATTING (continued)

BATTING	v. Glamorgan (Worcester) 25 July AEL	v. Glamorgan (Swansea) 27 & 28 July NW	v. Essex (Chelmsford) 1 August AEL	v. Sussex (Hove) 8 August AEL	v. Surrey (Worcester) 15 August AEL	v. Kent (Worcester) 22 August AEL	v. Warwickshire (Edgbaston) 29 August AEL	v. Lancashire (Worcester) 5 September AEL	v. Middlesex (Worcester) 19 September AEL	Runs
T.S. Curtis	62	10	23	30	8	6	16	4	2	393
W.P.C. Weston	5	25	—	66	64	25	17	26	17	200
G.A. Hick	26	11	120*	11	9	20	5	35	—	737
D.B. D'Oliveira	—	24	22	—	—	—	—	0	5	363
A.C.H. Seymour	21	17	0	2	28	23*	19	3	15	26
S.R. Lampitt	37	19	31	24	8	35	4*	25	6	255
S.J. Rhodes	13*	18	—	22	26*	3*	9	0	0*	315
R.K. Illingworth	3	2	—	3	0	14	—	—	—	151
P.J. Newport	—	12*	10	5*	3	24	18	1*	42	103
K.C.G. Benjamin	—	—	—	35	1	6	0	—	22	37
C.M. Tolley	3	—	5	13	32	0	5	18	—	34
M.J. Weston	1	—	—	—	—	—	—	—	—	152
N.V. Radford	—	20	28*	7	—	6	28	41*	7	192
D.A. Leatherdale	38	—	—	—	—	—	—	—	48	201
K.R. Spring	—	—	—	—	—	—	—	—	22	7
G.R. Haynes	—	—	—	—	—	—	—	—	—	195
V.S. Solanki	—	—	—	—	—	—	—	—	—	22
Byes	2	1	8	4	6	4	2	4	2	
Leg-byes	8	8	3	2	7	12	4	16	7	
Wides	7	—	—	8	2	4	3	5	5	
No-balls	—	—	—	—	—	4	10	10	2	
Total	232	175	250	232	194	186	144	188	197	
Wickets	10	10	6	10	10	9	10	9	9	
Result	L	L	W	L	W	L	L	L	L	
Points	0	—	4	0	4	0	0	0	0	

WORCESTERSHIRE CCC
BOWLING

Match	Comp	K.C.G. Benjamin	C.M. Tolley	P.J. Newport	S.R. Lampitt	R.K. Illingworth	N.V. Radford	D.B. D'Oliveira	C.A. Hick	D.A. Leatherdale	G.R. Haynes	M.J. Weston	W.P.C. Weston	Byes	Leg-byes	Wides	No-balls	Total	Wkts
v. Essex (Worcester), 11 May	B&H	11-2-28-2	11-3-13-1	11-4-20-2	10-3-28-1	10-3-21-3								1	4			115	10
v. Yorkshire (Leeds), 16 May	AEL	10-3-29-2	10-0-50-2	10-0-38-2	10-1-48-0	10-3-14-1									8	6	4	187	7
v. Somerset (Worcester), 23 May	AEL	3.1-0-11-1		8-2-19-2	6-2-12-3										5	2	8	97	10
v. Leicestershire (Leicester), 25 May	B&H	11-4-37-2	11-2-48-1	11-0-24-1	9-0-50-2	11-0-30-1	10-2-25-3	8-0-27-1	2-0-8-0						8	8	8	205	9
v. Gloucestershire (Gloucester), 30 May	AEL	2-0-15-1	1-0-8-0	2-0-12-1	1-0-17-0	2-0-23-0	2-0-16-1								2	5	6	93	3
v. Northamptonshire (Northampton), 6 June	AEL	10-2-35-1	5-3-13-1	8-0-24-0	8-0-37-2	10-1-23-3	9-3-27-1								9	5		168	9
v. Leicestershire (Worcester), 13 June	AEL	8.1-2-15-2	10-0-61-0		9-0-36-0	10-1-39-1	9-0-26-4				3-0-18-0				1	2	4	178	10
v. Scotland (Edinburgh), 22 June	NW	4-1-11-0	10-3-15-1		12-2-23-3		7-0-26-1	1-0-4-0	12-3-32-1	2-0-8-0				4	7	12		162	7
v. Durham (Stockton), 27 June	AEL	10-3-35-0		10-0-46-4	9-0-25-0	9-0-48-1	9-0-50-0								10	3	4	232	7
v. Derbyshire (Worcester), 4 July	AEL		9.3-0-45-0	7-1-29-1	5-0-16-0	10-0-29-3	8-1-37-3		10-1-33-1					2	3	3	6	194	5
v. Derbyshire (Worcester), 7 July	AEL	12-3-38-2	9-1-25-3	11-0-72-3		12-1-22-0									13	9	4	244	9
v. Nottinghamshire (Trent Bridge), 11 July	NW	10-2-25-3	9-0-43-0	10-2-31-1		10-3-23-1	12-1-52-1		4-0-22-0						4	6	4	158	6
v. Hampshire (Portsmouth), 18 July	AEL	8-0-35-0	10-1-50-4	8-1-25-1		7-0-37-0	9-0-47-0		9.3-0-32-1						9	3	2	203	5
v. Glamorgan (Worcester), 25 July	AEL		8-0-41-0	10-1-37-1	4-0-25-2	10-0-51-0	5-0-38-0		10-0-49-2			3-0-14-1			4	9	2	259	7
v. Glamorgan (Swansea), 27 & 28 July	NW		10-0-40-0	12-1-41-2	12-2-56-2	11-1-64-1	12-1-55-3		3-0-15-0					1	7	6	2	279	9
v. Essex (Chelmsford), 1 August	AEL		5-0-34-1	10-0-56-1	10-0-49-0	10-0-44-0		5-0-19-0	10-0-41-0		10-1-42-1	10-0-49-1		4	1	5		248	4
v. Sussex (Hove), 8 August	AEL		8-0-55-2	9-0-39-1	6-0-35-0	5.4-0-37-4	10-1-39-3				10-1-39-1				4	3		261	10
v. Surrey (Worcester), 15 August	AEL		2-0-15-0	9-3-26-1	7-2-8-1	6.1-0-21-2	9-0-35-0				10-2-30-2				9	8		157	10
v. Kent (Worcester), 22 August	AEL			8-1-34-1	9-0-21-1	2-0-12-0	10-1-42-2				10-1-21-2				11	2		143	5
v. Warwickshire (Edgbaston), 29 August	AEL			10-5-24-0	10-1-48-0	10-0-45-1							1-0-2-1	1	8	8		188	7
v. Lancashire (Worcester), 5 September	AEL		4-1-17-0	10-2-35-0	9.2-3-18-1	10-1-41-0			8-0-26-2		7-0-47-0				4	7	2	191	4
v. Middlesex (Worcester), 19 September	AEL			10-1-35-0	5-0-29-0	10-0-26-2	7-0-36-0		4-0-17-1		10-2-32-1	3-0-17-0		2	5	7	4	199	4
Wickets		17	18	25	18	25	20	1	8	0	7	2	1						

FIELDING FIGURES

22 – R.J. Blakey (ct 18/st 4)
17 – C. White
10 – D. Byas
6 – A.P. Grayson
5 – M.D. Moxon and J.D. Batty
4 – P.W. Jarvis and R.B. Richardson
3 – P.J. Hartley and M.J. Foster
2 – D. Gough and A.A. Metcalfe
1 – C.E.W. Silverwood, R.D. Stemp, S.A. Kellett, M.A. Robinson, M.P. Vaughan and C.A. Chapman

BEST BATSMEN & BOWLERS

R.B. Richardson, the West Indies Test captain, C.E.W. Silverwood, B. Parker, M.P. Vaughan and R.D. Stemp played for Yorkshire in limited-over competitions for the first time. Stemp had previously assisted Worcestershire.

Also in his first season for Yorkshire was M.J. Foster who hit a remarkable 118 against Leicestershire in the Sunday League match.

D. Byas hit a maiden Sunday League century. D. Gough (4 for 25 against Hampshire), C. White (3 for 52 against Leicestershire) and P.J. Hartley (5 for 36 against Sussex) all recorded Sunday League best bowling figures.

YORKSHIRE CCC — BATTING

Player	Essex (Chelmsford) 9 May AEL	Northamptonshire (Leeds) 11 May B&H	Worcestershire (Leeds) 16 May AEL	Hampshire (Southampton) 23 May AEL	Glamorgan (Middlesbrough) 6 June AEL	Derbyshire (Chesterfield) 13 June AEL	Gloucestershire (Sheffield) 20 June AEL	Ireland (Leeds) 22 June NW	Kent (Leeds) 27 June AEL	Warwickshire (Edgbaston) 4 July AEL	Gloucestershire (Bristol) 7 July NW	Durham (Harrogate) 13 July TT	Nottinghamshire (Harrogate) 14 July TT	Runs
M.D. Moxon	47	52	20	38	6	80	0	63	40	18	29	0	0	785
S.A. Kellett	11	7	38	2	6	50	—	54	3	7	3	80	—	27
D. Byas	25	12	43	38	44	31	23	0*	41*	27	28	3*	0	726
R.J. Blakey	7	0	20	19*	8	106*	6	—	2	3	28	1*	10*	736
C. White	30	16	4	0	22	—	—	—	—	1	12	49	8	392
A.P. Grayson	11	20	7*	6	38*	—	4*	—	0*	2	13	—	3*	314
P.W. Jarvis	15	5	2*	3*	3	—	—	—	—	—	2	—	—	71
D. Gough	3	1	—	1	1	—	—	—	—	2*	—	—	—	111
J.D. Batty	6*	3*	—	—	—	—	—	—	—	—	—	—	—	21
M.A. Robinson	0	2	—	—	—	—	—	—	—	—	—	—	—	13
C.E.W. Silverwood	—	52	17	81	20	8*	24	54	20	23	90	77	1	2
R.B. Richardson	—	—	22	2	16	—	3	77	45	12	—	—	—	819
A.A. Metcalfe	5*	—	—	—	—	—	—	—	1	—	—	—	—	190
M.J. Foster	—	—	—	—	—	—	11	—	25	0	22*	—	6	214
P.J. Hartley	—	—	—	—	—	—	—	—	—	23*	1*	—	—	172
R.D. Stemp	—	—	—	—	—	—	—	—	—	—	—	—	—	36
M.P. Vaughan	—	—	—	—	—	—	—	—	—	—	—	—	—	55
B. Parker	—	—	—	—	—	—	—	—	—	—	—	—	—	5
C.A. Chapman	—	—	—	—	—	—	—	—	—	—	—	—	—	37
Byes	2	—	8	—	6	5	2	5	12	5	8	17	2	
Leg-byes	3	5	2	5	7	3	8	9	3	6	5	3	1	
Wides	5	3	—	3	—	—	4	10	—	2	2	8	2	
No-balls	—	—	4	—	—	6	4	—	—	—	—	—	—	
Total	170	177	187	200	183	208	166	272	192	131	243	238	43	
Wickets	L	L	Ab.	W	L	W	L	W	L	L	W	W	L	
Result	—	—	2	4	—	4	—	—	—	—	—	—	—	
Points														

YORKSHIRE CCC — BATTING (continued)

Player	Northamptonshire (Leeds) 18 July AEL	Warwickshire (Leeds) 27 & 28 July NW	Somerset (Taunton) 1 August AEL	Nottinghamshire (Trent Bridge) 8 August AEL	Middlesex (Scarborough) 15 August AEL	Lancashire (Old Trafford) 22 August AEL	Durham (Leeds) 29 August AEL	Leicestershire (Leicester) 5 September AEL	Derbyshire (Scarborough) 6 September TT	Gloucestershire (Scarborough) 8 September TT	Sussex (Scarborough) 12 September AEL	Surrey (The Oval) 19 September AEL	Runs
M.D. Moxon	70	7	21	14	50	35	64	15	86*	41	4	3	785
S.A. Kellett	88*	20	31	21	22	12	6	8	78*	0	24	—	27
D. Byas	—	75	5	57*	69*	38	28	96	—	14	61	41	726
R.J. Blakey	—	46	1	27*	—	24	28	15	—	1	41	41	736
C. White	—	5	12	32	—	3	21	—	—	67*	32*	36	392
A.P. Grayson	—	—	—	—	—	—	18*	—	—	—	2	—	314
P.W. Jarvis	—	—	—	—	—	15	3	3*	28	28	—	8	71
D. Gough	—	16	—	—	—	3	1	—	5*	5*	—	—	111
J.D. Batty	—	3	—	—	—	0*	1*	—	—	—	—	—	21
M.A. Robinson	5*	0*	—	—	—	—	—	—	—	—	—	0	13
C.E.W. Silverwood	—	8	58*	103	88*	—	—	—	—	—	89	1	2
R.B. Richardson	—	12	—	—	—	—	—	118	—	—	—	—	819
A.A. Metcalfe	—	—	—	—	—	7	17	10*	—	—	21	7	190
M.J. Foster	—	2	46*	—	—	12*	21	11	27	41	0	15	214
P.J. Hartley	—	—	—	—	—	6	—	5	—	5	—	—	172
R.D. Stemp	—	—	—	—	—	—	—	—	—	—	15*	22*	36
M.P. Vaughan	—	—	—	—	—	—	—	—	—	—	—	—	55
B. Parker	—	—	—	—	—	—	—	—	—	—	—	—	5
C.A. Chapman	—	—	—	—	—	—	—	—	—	—	—	—	37
Byes	5	1	5	5	1	2	4	16	4	5	5	6	
Leg-byes	5	12	7	5	9	7	4	11	1	1	2	5	
Wides	2	15	13	—	6	7	4	10	3	20	—	—	
No-balls	—	2	4	—	—	2	—	—	—	—	—	—	
Total	175	224	203	264	245	173	217	318	199	228	255	185	
Wickets	W	10	6	4	2	9	9	7	1	8	7	10	
Result		L	W	W	W	L	L	W	W	W	W	L	

YORKSHIRE CCC
BOWLING

Opponent	Comp	M.A. Robinson	P.W. Jarvis	C.E.W. Silverwood	D. Gough	J.D. Batty	A.P. Grayson	C. White	M.J. Foster	P.J. Hartley	R.D. Stemp	Byes	Leg-byes	Wides	No-balls	Total	Wkts
v. Essex (Chelmsford) 9 May	AEL	10-0-45-1	9-1-26-2	9-1-40-1	8.5-1-23-3	10-0-55-3						3		1	2	192	10
v. Northamptonshire (Leeds) 11 May	B&H	11-1-51-3	9-0-40-0	7-1-19-1	9-2-27-1		8-1-32-0					4	8	5	2	211	9
v. Worcestershire (Leeds) 16 May	AEL	4-1-16-1	5-1-9-0	3-1-11-0	5-1-14-0			11-0-30-2				1	4		4	55	1
v. Hampshire (Southampton) 23 May	AEL	6-1-10-0			7.4-0-25-4	10-0-34-2	7-0-30-1	10-0-24-1	7-0-34-0			4	9	1		170	10
v. Glamorgan (Middlesbrough) 6 June	AEL	10-1-36-2	10-1-28-2		9-1-53-2	10-0-41-3	4-0-17-0	7-0-29-0				1	3	3	2	208	9
v. Derbyshire (Chesterfield) 13 June	AEL	5-0-30-0	10-0-44-3			10-0-34-1	10-0-31-1	5-1-25-0		10-0-40-1					6	207	7
v. Gloucestershire (Sheffield) 20 June	AEL			4-1-19-0		10-1-40-0	4-0-13-0	10-1-21-2		10-2-30-0			3	3	4	167	3
v. Ireland (Leeds) 22 June	NW	12-1-26-0	11-1-25-1			5-2-17-0		11-0-41-1		9-1-25-2		1	5		6	187	5
v. Kent (Leeds) 27 June	AEL				10-2-38-1	10-1-29-3		9-0-30-1	1-0-13-0	10-1-44-1			18	5		200	9
v. Warwickshire (Edgbaston) 4 July	AEL	6-2-11-1	7-1-23-1		5-0-22-0			4-0-9-0		7.3-1-44-0	10-0-43-1	4	3	1	4	135	2
v. Gloucestershire (Bristol) 7 July	NW	12-2-31-1	12-1-57-0		10-3-31-2			4-1-12-0		12-0-60-0	3-0-22-0	1	7	2	4	241	3
v. Durham (Harrogate) 13 July	TT	10-3-52-1	11-2-42-2			11-1-32-0		6-0-38-0		11-3-33-3	10-0-42-0		6	1	4	235	7
v. Nottinghamshire (Harrogate) 14 July	TT	8-3-16-1	10-1-42-2		9-1-32-1	10-0-20-4	5-0-20-1		9-1-33-1	8-0-20-0	6-0-32-0	1	8	6	2	159	9
v. Northamptonshire (Leeds) 18 July	AEL	10-2-23-4			10-1-21-1	4-0-15-1	2-0-6-0	7-1-31-0		10-3-37-0		2	10	1	6	172	9
v. Warwickshire (Leeds) 27 & 28 July	NW	12-3-35-1			11.4-2-31-3	10-0-63-0		12-1-41-2		12-2-64-3			5	2	12	245	10
v. Somerset (Taunton) 1 August	AEL	8-3-26-1			10-2-39-1	10-1-41-1	3-0-9-0		9-1-39-0	10-0-40-3		2	6	3	4	202	6
v. Nottinghamshire (Trent Bridge) 8 August	AEL	10-1-47-1			8-1-59-2		8-0-36-0	4-0-21-0		10-0-54-4	10-0-40-0	4	5	2	2	261	8
v. Middlesex (Scarborough) 15 August	AEL	8-0-28-3			6-0-31-1	8-0-27-1	2-0-24-0	2.3-0-12-2			8-0-41-3	5	5	2	4	168	10
v. Lancashire (Old Trafford) 22 August	AEL	9-1-44-1			8.4-1-27-0	3-0-27-0		9-1-35-2	5-0-20-1	6-1-22-1	4-0-14-0	4	3	3	6	174	7
v. Durham (Leeds) 29 August	AEL	10-1-36-2			10-1-40-1		3-0-18-2	10-0-43-0	4-0-29-1	10-3-23-2		1	13	1		230	9
v. Leicestershire (Leicester) 5 September	AEL	10-2-38-2			9.5-0-67-2	10-0-25-0	10-0-44-1	8-0-52-3	5-1-14-0	10-0-41-1		2	9	19	2	253	10
v. Derbyshire (Scarborough) 6 September	JT			7-0-44-1	7.4-2-32-4	3-0-11-1		6-0-24-1	1-0-13-0	10-1-35-4		3	9	3		198	7
v. Gloucestershire (Scarborough) 8 September	JT	9-0-37-1					2-0-11-0	6-0-27-1			10-1-33-0		8	7		168	9 A
v. Sussex (Scarborough) 12 September	AEL	10-0-41-0			9-2-20-1		10-0-75-1	10-0-56-1		9.4-1-36-5	9-2-40-2		6	3	4	234	10
v. Surrey (The Oval) 19 September	AEL	10-1-35-0			10-2-27-1		6-0-23-1	7.3-1-37-0		9-2-41-1		1	4	1		188	5
Wickets		27	13	3	32	20	8	19	4	31	6						

A A.M. Smith retired hurt

English Counties Form Charts

The games covered are:

Britannic Assurance County Championship
Matches against touring and representative sides

In the batting table a blank indicates that a batsman did not play in a game, a dash (–) that he did not *bat*. A dash (–) is placed in the batting averages if a player had 2 innings or less, and in the bowling figures if no wicket was taken.

FIELDING FIGURES

53 – I.A. Healy (ct 42/st 11)
25 – M.A. Taylor
21 – T.J. Zoehrer (ct 17/st 4)
18 – M.E. Waugh
15 – A.R. Border
10 – D.C. Boon and D.R. Martyn (ct 9/st 1)
9 – M.L. Hayden
8 – S.K. Warne
7 – B.P. Julian and S.R. Waugh
6 – M.J. Slater
5 – T.B.A. May
3 – C.J. McDermott, M.G. Hughes, P.R. Reiffel and W.J. Holdsworth
2 – sub

AUSTRALIANS IN ENGLAND, 1993 — BATTING

Season batting summary

Batting	M	Inns	NO	Runs	HS	Av
M.L. Hayden	13	21	1	1150	151*	57.50
M.A. Taylor	15	25	2	972	124	42.26
D.C. Boon	14	23	4	1437	164*	75.63
M.E. Waugh	16	25	4	1361	178	71.63
D.R. Martyn	12	15	3	838	138*	69.83
S.R. Waugh	16	16	4	875	157*	67.30
I.A. Healy	16	20	7	499	102*	38.38
B.P. Julian	13	9	1	284	66	38.38
P.R. Reiffel	13	9	6	181	52	25.81
S.K. Warne	9	15	4	246	47	22.36
W.J. Holdsworth	9	5	1	17	12	5.66
M.J. Slater	17	28	4	1275	200*	53.12
A.R. Border	16	21	3	823	152	45.72
T.J. Zoehrer	8	9	1	115	38	14.37
M.G. Hughes	14	12	5	299	71	33.22
T.B.A. May	17	9	5	31	15	7.75
C.J. McDermott	6	3	–	42	23	14.00

First half of tour (12 matches)

Batting	v. Worcs (Worcester) 5–7 May	v. Somerset (Taunton) 8–10 May	v. Sussex (Hove) 13–15 May	v. Surrey (The Oval) 25–7 May	v. Leics (Leicester) 29–31 May	FIRST TEST (Manchester) 3–7 June	v. Warwicks (Birmingham) 9–11 June	v. Gloucs (Bristol) 12–14 June	SECOND TEST (Lord's) 17–21 June	v. Comb. Univs (Oxford) 23–5 June	v. Hants (Southampton) 26–8 June	THIRD TEST (Nottingham) 1–6 July
M.L. Hayden	3 96	0 18*		36 7	2 15		10	57		98	85 115	28 18
M.A. Taylor	39 40	27	66	80	123	124		12	111		49 146	101 70
D.C. Boon	108 106	68		178 84		21		70	164* 99		6	
M.E. Waugh	7 15		136	124 16*	44*	6	8	66	13*	29* 138*	6 13	13 9
D.R. Martyn	25 3	38	124 24*			3 0	116	51			26* 28	9 5
S.R. Waugh	49* 12*					15*	1*	21		1	8*	56*
I.A. Healy	6 1*		16*	27 0*	6		5		13*	5		35*
B.P. Julian	9			6*		58 17				111	41	40 38
P.R. Reiffel	5		73 33	5 50	91 42*	2	64	46* 11		4		17 1
S.K. Warne	5	11		28 1	50*	8	66		152	0		
W.J. Holdsworth	0						20		77			
M.J. Slater		122										
A.R. Border		54										
T.J. Zoehrer		22										
M.G. Hughes		36										
T.B.A. May		4*										
C.J. McDermott		23										
Byes	5	4	1	5	6	8 8	1 15	10	1	2	15 3	5 5
Leg-byes	4	8	7	4	3	8 8	15					4 8
Wides	1	1	2									5 4
No-balls	2	14	8			7	10	35	14		8 8	5
Total	**262**	**431**	**490**	**378 171**	**323 88**	**289 432**	**317**	**400**	**632**	**388 233**	**393 271**	**373 202**
Wickets	10	10	5	9 4	3 4	10 5	7	9	4	5 6	7 7	10 6
Result	W	W	D	W	W	W	D	D	W	W	D	D

BATTING (second half of tour, 9 matches)

Batting	v. Derbys (Derby) 13–15 July	v. Durham (Durham) 17–19 July	FOURTH TEST (Leeds) 22–6 July	v. Lancs (Manchester) 28–30 July	v. Glamorgan (Neath) 31 July–2 Aug	FIFTH TEST (Birmingham) 5–9 Aug	v. Kent (Canterbury) 11–13 Aug	v. Essex (Chelmsford) 14–16 Aug	SIXTH TEST (The Oval) 19–23 Aug	M	Inns	NO	Runs	HS	Av
M.L. Hayden	40	7 151*		61 122	120 2*	19 0	31 78	36	70 13	13	21	1	1150	151*	57.50
M.A. Taylor		10 1	27	79 7*	152* 18	4 38*			8 0	15	25	2	972	124	42.26
D.C. Boon	60*	27 112	107		38	137 62*		111 15	13 10	14	23	4	1437	164*	75.63
M.E. Waugh		0 0	52	4* 70*	5	59 80	105* 123	108 9	20 26	16	25	4	1361	178	71.63
D.R. Martyn		19 6*		38 17		20 10	33*	32 4	83*	12	15	3	838	138*	69.83
S.R. Waugh		70*	157*			22 3		1* 66		16	16	4	875	157*	67.30
I.A. Healy		6			52	38 3*		15	0 26	16	20	7	499	102*	38.38
B.P. Julian		39							16 42	13	9	1	284	66	38.38
P.R. Reiffel							17		37	13	9	6	181	52	25.81
S.K. Warne		5 12					17			9	15	4	246	47	22.36
W.J. Holdsworth								0 0		9	5	1	17	12	5.66
M.J. Slater		17	67 200*	20	72 43			57	4 48	17	28	4	1275	200*	53.12
A.R. Border	133*				14* 23			12 17*	16 17	16	21	3	823	152	45.72
T.J. Zoehrer				9					7 15	8	9	1	115	38	14.37
M.G. Hughes			157*	4 0*	38			0*	12 4*	14	12	5	299	71	33.22
T.B.A. May		0			3*					17	9	5	31	15	7.75
C.J. McDermott	60*									6	3	–	42	23	14.00
Byes	3	4	8	1	2	7	3	6	5 2						
Leg-byes	1	7 3	22	1	1	3 5	1	2	6 6						
Wides		3 4	4			5			2 2						
No-balls	31	4 9	9	12	4	2	10	10	4 7						
Total	**268**	**221 295**	**653**	**282 194**	**414 235**	**408 120**	**391 34**	**357 218**	**303 229**						
Wickets	1	10 3	4	3 8	4 7	10 2	4 1	6 10	10 10						
Result	D	D	W	L	D	W	W	D	L						

BOWLING

This table records the Australian first‑class bowling for 1993. It is a very wide matrix (match × bowler); figures are overs–maidens–runs–wickets. The two innings of a match are separated by a comma.

Match (venue), dates	W.J. Holdsworth	B.P. Julian	P.R. Reiffel	M.E. Waugh	S.K. Warne	D.R. Martyn	C.J. McDermott	M.G. Hughes	T.B.A. May	S.R. Waugh	A.R. Border	T.J. Zoehrer	M.A. Taylor	M.L. Hayden	Byes	Leg-byes	Wides	No-balls	Total	Wkts
v. Worcestershire (Worcester), 5–7 May	7.5-3-15-3, 23-3-96-2	13-6-31-3, 19-1-96-1	10-5-21-3, 26-7-68-0	3-0-17-0, 15.1-2-59-0	23-6-122-1, 6-3-5-1	2-1-7-0									1	5	3	12	90	10
				6-0-17-0, 1-0-3-0											—	10	1	28	458	4
v. Somerset (Taunton), 8–10 May			21-2-58-0, 5-1-9-1		28-6-77-4										17	7	—	18	151	4
v. Sussex (Hove), 13–15 May		22-5-63-5, 5-0-13-0			23.5-8-68-3, 19.1-6-38-4										4	9	3	18	285	4
v. Surrey (The Oval), 25–7 May	17-2-81-2, 10-2-43-1	15-4-31-1, 12-4-30-3, 10-2-19-1	10-3-22-2, 11-0-27-2	5-2-13-1	12-5-31-3, 13-3-27-3		10-2-36-2, 14-0-72-0	15-3-63-0, 11-2-32-1	10-2-23-1, 23-5-75-4						6	12	—	30	353	10
v. Leicestershire (Leicester), 29–31 May		6-0-21-1			24-10-51-4, 49-26-86-4		23-3-89-2, 5-1-16-0	16-3-58-2, 10-3-19-0	17-3-53-0, 14-6-19-3						2	10	8	18	92	4
FIRST TEST MATCH (Manchester), 3–7 June	9-0-34-1	11-2-30-2, 14-1-67-1			13-3-27-3		11-1-27-0, 14-4-38-2	9-2-19-0, 8-1-21-0	24-7-62-3, 13.3-4-39-3		1-0-4-0				2	4	4	4	231	10
							18-2-50-0, 30-9-76-0	20.5-5-59-4, 27.2-4-92-4							2	4	1	10	144	10
v. Warwickshire (Birmingham), 9–11 June		11-2-40-1	14-8-30-1	5-0-19-0	28-9-61-5		18-4-45-0	15-5-27-4	23-5-58-3			4.2-3-3-1			6	10	—	5	168	7
v. Gloucestershire (Bristol), 12–14 June									14-5-24-1	5-0-24-0					8	11	—	4	146	10
SECOND TEST MATCH (Lord's), 17–21 June	21-5-52-2, 6-0-19-0	16.5-4-67-1, 12-1-57-3	15-5-43-1, 9-1-30-1	6-1-16-0, 17-4-55-0	35-12-57-4, 48.5-17-102-4			20-5-52-4, 31-9-75-0	31-12-64-2, 51-23-81-4	4-1-5-0, 2-0-13-0	3-1-3-0, 16-9-16-1	17-4-53-0, 11.4-7-16-3			3	8	1	26	332	8
v. Combined Universities (Oxford), 23–5 June	19-1-95-0, 7-1-16-0		15-1-76-0, 10-1-45-0	9-2-19-0	22-7-45-3, 12-6-21-2				15-2-63-2, 18-4-57-2		7-0-45-0, 15-3-49-1		3-0-10-0		10	13	—	28	205	10 [A]
v. Hampshire (Southampton), 26–8 June		24-3-84-1, 33-10-110-1			40-17-74-3, 50-21-108-1			18-2-60-3, 14-3-47-2	14-4-7-31-1, 38-6-112-0	6-1-29-0, 8-4-12-0	5-0-11-0				4	2	2	45	298	7
THIRD TEST MATCH (Nottingham), 1–6 July	22-3-117-5	19-3-71-1	22.5-3-71-6, 11-2-30-0	1-1-0-0, 6-3-15-0	31-7-92-5, 22-8-41-2			31-7-92-5, 22-8-41-2	14.4-7-31-1, 38-6-112-0	1-0-3-0, 2-1-1-0					3	2	10	2	374	5
v. Derbyshire (Derby), 13–15 July			21-3-82-4	6-3-15-0	50-21-108-1, 15-5-20-0										5	23	4	9	220	6
v. Durham (Durham), 17–19 July	18-1-118-2	25-0-62-0	21-7-50-1	3-0-7-0, 2-1-3-0	23-9-43-1, 40-16-63-0	6-1-14-0		15.5-3-47-3, 30-10-79-3	16-4-63-1	14-3-50-1		7.4-1-24-1		7.4-1-24-1	11	14	1	30	422	6
FOURTH TEST MATCH (Leeds), 22–6 July			26-6-65-5, 28-8-87-3		32.4-12-54-3, 24-7-61-1			13-5-32-2	15-3-33-1, 27-8-65-4						4	4	1	6	385	8
v. Lancashire (Manchester), 28–30 July	12-0-58-1, 2-0-11-0		8-0-58-0, 10-1-34-0	2-0-13-0, 15-4-56-1	26.2-6-67-4, 17-3-44-2			6-1-20-0, 7-1-23-1	15-2-48-0, 25.2-3-99-2	1-0-5-0	5-1-13-0, 5-2-12-1	8-2-26-0	5-0-17-0		2	3	—	17	200	10
v. Glamorgan (Neath), 31 July–2 August	12-5-91-1, 12-2-43-2														5	3	4	11	305	10
FIFTH TEST MATCH (Birmingham), 5–9 August		9-2-41-0, 8-1-49-0	22.5-3-71-6, 11-2-30-0	15-5-43-1, 5-2-5-0	49-23-82-5, 9-1-30-1			19-4-53-0, 18-7-24-0	19-9-32-2, 48.2-15-89-5	5-2-4-0	2-1-1-0			1-0-4-1	14	4	1	6	250	7
v. Kent (Canterbury), 11–13 August	7-2-20-0, 16-4-35-1	8-2-40-1	14-5-32-2, 15-4-32-0		9-1-30-1			10-1-55-0, 9-1-32-0	14-2-39-2, 29-10-71-3	6-3-13-1, 5-2-9-2		9.2-1-24-2, 21.3-3-57-3	1-0-4-1		15	2	—	6	228	5
v. Essex (Chelmsford), 14–16 August		5-0-25-0	28.5-4-88-2, 24-8-55-3	8-1-26-3, 1-0-17-0	20-6-50-1			30-7-121-3, 31.2-9-110-3	13-3-44-2, 10-3-32-1	12-2-45-2	6-0-23-0	16-1-71-3			4	9	1	8	363	8
SIXTH TEST MATCH (The Oval), 19–23 August		5-0-25-0		8-1-26-3, 1-0-17-0	20-5-70-2, 40-15-78-3				10-3-32-1, 24-6-53-1						10	7	1	9	277	10
															5	12	—	3	313	10
Bowler's average	204.5-54-833-23 / 36.21	323.5-53-1158-29 / 39.93	375.4-85-1113-37 / 30.08	125.1-28-403-6 / 67.16	765.4-277-1698-75 / 22.64	8-2-21-0 / —	143-26-449-6 / 74.83	470.2-113-1420-48 / 29.58	562.5-156-1429-53 / 26.96	73.1-19-229-7 / 32.71	65-17-177-3 / 59.00	87.5-21-250-12 / 20.83	9-0-31-1 / 31.00	8.4-1-31-1 / 31.00						

A G.B.T. Lovell retired hurt

FIELDING FIGURES

13 – J.P. Arscott (ct 12/st 1)
6 – J.P. Crawley and C.M. Pitcher
5 – R. Cake and N.J. Haste
3 – M.E.D. Jarrett and G.M. Charlesworth
2 – A.R. Whittall and R.M. Pearson
1 – J.P. Carroll, G.W. Jones and sub

CAMBRIDGE UNIVERSITY — BATTING

Batsman	M	Inns	NO	Runs	HS	Av
J.P. Crawley	9	15	1	828	187*	69.00
G.W. Jones	10	16	1	241	45*	16.06
J.P. Carroll	8	12	1	69	21	6.27
G.M. Charlesworth	10	15	3	250	49	20.83
R. Cake	10	17	6	348	83	31.63
J. Leppard	5	6	0	55	20	9.16
J.P. Arscott	10	12	3	105	20	11.66
R.M. Pearson	9	9	1	93	31	11.62
A.R. Whittall	10	9	2	80	40	11.42
N.J. Haste	10	9	1	76	36	9.50
P.M.C. Millar	1	1	0	2	2*	2.00
C.M. Pitcher	9	8	2	61	27*	10.16
M.E.D. Jarrett	8	13	1	277	51	23.08
R.H.J. Jenkins	1	–	–	–	–	–

BOWLING — Bowler's average

Bowler	Overs–Maidens–Runs–Wkts	Average
G.M. Charlesworth	229.5–52–645–12	53.75
N.J. Haste	225–43–715–10	71.50
R.M. Pearson	310.3–67–876–20	43.80
P.M.C. Millar	20–4–61–0	–
A.R. Whittall	309.3–63–969–19	51.00
J. Leppard	11–0–40–0	–
C.M. Pitcher	203.1–35–698–14	49.85
R.H.J. Jenkins	16–1–77–0	–

Matches:
v. Derbyshire (Cambridge) 14–16 April
v. Yorkshire (Cambridge) 17–19 April
v. Kent (Cambridge) 21–3 April
v. Essex (Cambridge) 1–3 May
v. Glamorgan (Cambridge) 5–7 May
v. Leicestershire (Cambridge) 15–17 May
v. Lancashire (Cambridge) 19–21 May
v. Nottinghamshire (Cambridge) 12–14 June
v. Sussex (Hove) 26–8 June
v. Oxford University (Lord's) 30 June–2 July

FIELDING FIGURES

24 – C.W.J. Lyons (ct 22/st 2)
8 – G.B.T. Lovell
6 – H. Malik
5 – G.I. MacMillan and R. Yeabsley
4 – C.L. Keey and J.E.R. Gallian
3 – C.M. Gupte and M. Jeh
2 – C.J. Townsend, R.R. Montgomerie and P. Trimby
1 – sub
†J.E.R. Gallian absent hurt

OXFORD UNIVERSITY — BATTING

Batsman	M	Inns	NO	Runs	HS	Av
R.R. Montgomerie	6	11	1	371	109	37.10
J.E.R. Gallian	9	15	2	643	141*	49.46
G.I. MacMillan	9	14	1	336	63	25.84
G.B.T. Lovell	7	11	1	365	114	36.50
C.L. Keey	10	16	1	341	111	22.73
C.M. Gupte	9	16	3	397	61	30.53
H. Malik	9	13	3	234	64*	23.40
C.J. Townsend	1	1	0	0	0*	–
R. Yeabsley	10	13	4	138	36	15.33
M. Jeh	10	10	4	26	9	4.33
R.H. MacDonald	9	7	2	18	11	3.60
C.W.J. Lyons	9	12	4	108	28	13.50
R.D. Oliphant-Callum	2	3	1	20	13*	6.66
A. MacLay	1	1	1	0	0*	–
E. Fowler	2	3	1	19	9*	–
P. Trimby	2	3	1	–	6*	6.33
B. Ellison	1	2	2	3	2*	–

Matches: v. Durham (Oxford) 14–16 April (D); v. Lancashire (Oxford) 17–20 April (D); v. Glamorgan (Oxford) 21–3 April (D); v. Hampshire (Oxford) 5–7 May (D); v. Northamptonshire (Oxford) 15–18 May (D); v. Middlesex (Oxford) 19–21 May (D); v. Nottinghamshire 29 May–1 June (W); v. Warwickshire (Oxford) 12–15 June (D); v. Worcestershire (Worcester) 18–20 June (D); v. Cambridge University (Lord's) 30 June–2 July (W)

OXFORD UNIVERSITY — BOWLING

M. Jeh — v. Durham 19-3-47-2; v. Lancashire 28-8-46-4; v. Glamorgan 22-4-74-0; v. Hampshire 31-5-156-0; v. Northamptonshire 12-1-47-2; v. Middlesex 21-5-60-0; v. Nottinghamshire 9-1-56-0; v. Warwickshire 11-0-55-1; v. Worcestershire 23-0-93-2, 11-1-55-0; v. Cambridge 14-2-61-4; Average 297-48-1141-24, 47.54

J.E.R. Gallian — v. Durham 15-5-27-0; v. Lancashire 13-3-50-1; v. Glamorgan 9-2-20-0; v. Hampshire 16-5-42-2; v. Middlesex 11.4-16-1, 7-1-20-0; v. Nottinghamshire 14-4-42-1; v. Warwickshire 13-4-41-0; v. Worcestershire 13-5-29-0, 9-1-30-0; v. Cambridge 5-0-14-0, 8-2-52-3; Average 166-43-464-10, 46.40

R.H. MacDonald — v. Durham 17-7-27-3; v. Lancashire 19-6-48-0; v. Glamorgan 21-6-58-1; v. Hampshire 10-3-27-0, 22-6-66-0; v. Northamptonshire 15.1-3-36-3; v. Middlesex 11.4-3-26-0; v. Nottinghamshire 5-0-22-0; v. Warwickshire 16.1-7-20-5; v. Worcestershire 16-6-29-2; v. Cambridge 4-0-22-0, 10-2-22-0, 8-2-23-1; Average 216-63-561-16, 35.06

R. Yeabsley — v. Durham 20-6-46-1; v. Lancashire 11-3-37-0; v. Glamorgan 19-5-48-1; v. Hampshire 12-2-30-3; v. Northamptonshire 18-3-101-1; v. Middlesex 8-3-23-0; v. Nottinghamshire 14-4-21-0, 22-5-49-1; v. Warwickshire 18-4-52-2; v. Worcestershire 20.3-3-87-1, 4-0-31-0, 5-0-40-0, 1.4-1-0-1; v. Cambridge 6-3-12-2, 20.1-7-20-5, 13.3-3-36-2, 6-1-26-0; Average 237.1-53-762-20, 38.10

H. Malik — v. Durham 3-1-7-0; v. Lancashire 11-6-18-2; v. Glamorgan 19-3-50-1; v. Hampshire 7.5-2-30-1; v. Northamptonshire 15-1-71-1; v. Middlesex 7-3-32-0; v. Nottinghamshire 14-6-30-1, 7-1-32-0; v. Warwickshire 12-1-50-0, 2-1-3-0; v. Worcestershire 6-0-23-0; v. Cambridge 12-3-52-1, 2-0-16-0; Average 117.5-28-414-7, 59.14

G.I. MacMillan — v. Durham 9.2-1-21-3; v. Lancashire 10-1-44-0; v. Glamorgan 18-1-57-1; v. Hampshire 3-0-13-0, 9-4-20-0; v. Middlesex 6-0-33-0; v. Warwickshire 1-1-0-0; v. Worcestershire 9-5-13-3; v. Cambridge 2-1-10-0; Average 67.2-14-211-7, 30.14

A. MacLay — v. Worcestershire 9-0-40-0, 3-0-11-1; Average 12-0-51-0, 51.00

C.M. Gupte — v. Middlesex 1-0-7-0; Average 1-0-7-0, –

P. Trimby — v. Nottinghamshire 18-1-73-1, 6-1-17-0, 14-3-37-1; v. Worcestershire 17-2-53-1, 10-4-28-1, 18-6-33-1; v. Cambridge 16-5-48-1, 5-0-29-0, 24.2-8-79-3, 15-1-72-3; Average 143.2-31-469-12, 39.08

R.R. Montgomerie — v. Warwickshire 1-0-5-0; v. Cambridge 1-0-1-0; Average 2-0-6-0, –

B. Ellison — v. Worcestershire 11-1-40-2; Average 11-1-40-2, 20.00

Extras and totals per match (Byes, Leg-byes, Wides, No-balls, Total, Wkts):

Match	Byes	Leg-byes	Wides	No-balls	Total	Wks
v. Durham (Oxford) 14–16 April	10	6	5	2	191	10
v. Lancashire (Oxford) 17–20 April	2	6	1	2	251	7
v. Glamorgan (Oxford) 21–3 April	1	1	2	4	309	4
v. Hampshire (Oxford) 5–7 May	1			4	194	6
v. Northamptonshire (Oxford) 15–18 May	3	6		14	463	2
v. Middlesex (Oxford) 19–21 May		2	4	4	115	3
v. Nottinghamshire (Oxford) 29 May–1 June	2	3	3	14	169	10
v. Warwickshire (Oxford) 12–15 June	1	7	1	24	236	5
v. Worcestershire (Worcester) 18–20 June		4	1	12	334	10
					89	5
	4	2	1		236	10
					31	7
v. Cambridge University (Lord's) 30 June–2 July	6	4	3	8	249	7
		2			158	4
		8	1	10	177	3
	2	10	3	28	351	7
		2			185	0
	4	8	1	18	241	10
		8	5	16	255	10

FIELDING FIGURES

26 – K.M. Krikken (ct 21/st 5)
18 – C.J. Adams
13 – P.D. Bowler
11 – D.G. Cork
9 – B.J.M. Maher and T.J.G. O'Gorman
8 – S.J. Base and J.E. Morris
7 – M.J. Vandrau
6 – K.J. Barnett and A.S. Rollins (ct 5/st 1)
5 – F.A. Griffith
4 – A.E. Warner, O.H. Mortensen and subs
2 – R.W. Sladdin

DERBYSHIRE

I.G.S. Steer, A.S. Rollins and M.J. Vandrau made their first-class debuts.

J.E. Morris hit the first double century of his career.

C.J. Adams made the highest score of his career.

A.E. Warner also made his highest score and was one of the leading bowlers in the country.

J.E. Morris resigned as vice-captain and was re-placed by P.D. Bowler.

Derbyshire were without their overseas player I.R. Bishop for the whole of the first-class programme.

DERBYSHIRE CCC — BATTING (first half)

	v. Cambridge U. (Cambridge) 14-16 April	v. Warwickshire (Birmingham) 6-10 May	v. Glamorgan (Derby) 13-17 May	v. Essex (Chelmsford) 20-24 May	v. Hampshire (Derby) 27-31 May	v. Middlesex (Lord's) 3-7 June	v. Yorkshire (Chesterfield) 10-14 June	v. Kent (Canterbury) 17-21 June	v. Lancashire (Derby) 24-8 June	v. Worcestershire (Kidderminster) 1-5 July	v. Australians (Derby) 13-15 July	v. Sussex (Derby) 22-6 July	M	Inns	NO	Runs	SH	Av
P.D. Bowler	15 73*	8 –	96 6	5 71*	79	53	–	38	32 25	65 56	30	7 87	17	29	3	1123	153*	43.19
C.J. Adams	5 16	65 10	24 51	54	65	10	–	2 5	74 13	36	4	3 96	18	30	1	843	175	28.10
J.E. Morris	136	95 86	14	61	61	53 38	–	57 24	21 151	3 168	41	10 104	18	29	1	1461	229	52.17
T.J.G. O'Gorman	130*	20	14	17	55	10 0	–	5 12	27 27	4 7	56	10 5	14	21	3	511	130*	28.38
F.A. Griffith	25	4 10	38* 17	53	14	0	–	–	27	3	114	6 17	11	14	0	257	56	18.35
D.G. Cork	56	34	13 108*	2 130*	25*	38 33	–	4 17	0 161	36 168	56	5 73*	15	24	4	539	104	26.95
K.J. Barnett	–	8	6 24	–	–	3	–	1 95*	19 7	12 15	1	6	16	23	4	1223	168	64.36
K.M. Krikken	42	22	29	–	29	3	–	1* 8	12	4 42	–	20 16	13	18	4	227	40	16.21
A.E. Warner	–	5 8*	–	3 10	–	1 7*	–	8 7	19 12	–	7 0*	–	12	14	1	238	95*	18.30
R.W. Sladdin	–	5*	–	–	–	0 0	–	–	–	–	0*	–	9	11	3	131	51*	16.37
S.J. Base	–	1	0 22	21	10*	7 8	–	0 2	17 2*	4	0*	27 0	14	21	2	139	27	7.31
D.E. Malcolm	–	–	1 9	0	–	–	–	1 2	–	6 46*	–	0 10	10	12	5	69	19	9.85
M.J. Vandrau	0* 1*	1	–	130*	–	–	–	–	2*	–	–	–	15	25	4	404	58	19.23
O.H. Mortensen	–	–	–	–	–	–	–	–	–	3*	–	–	10	5	1	22	17	5.50
B.J.M. Maher	57	–	–	–	–	–	–	–	–	–	–	3 1*	7	13	3	70	29	7.00
A.S. Rollins	–	–	–	–	–	–	–	–	–	–	–	–	14	11	2	392	85	43.55
I.G.S. Steer	–	–	–	–	–	–	–	–	–	–	–	–	4	6	1	157	67	31.40
A.W. Richardson	–	–	–	–	–	–	–	–	–	–	–	–	1	2	0	9	9	4.50
Byes	4	11	7	4 7	2	3	–	10 4	8 4	6 5	14	1 1						
Leg-byes	7	10	6	7 1		2	2	4 7	4 2	5 10		17 4						
Wides				2								4						
No-balls		6		2	12			2 8	18 8	10 2	30	2						
Total	380 137	379	283 214	203 253	389	168		135 229	426 267	251 358	305	183 379						
Wickets	5	10	10	10 1	8	10	D	10 10	10 10	10 10	10	10 10						
Result	D	W	D	D	D	L	2	L	L	L	D	W						
Points	5	24	6	3	8	4		4	8	5	–	20						

DERBYSHIRE CCC — BATTING (second half)

	v. Gloucestershire (Cheltenham) 29 July-2 August	v. Durham (Durham) 5-9 August	v. Somerset (Derby) 12-16 August	v. Surrey (Ilkeston) 19-23 August	v. Nottinghamshire (Nottingham) 26-30 August	v. Northamptonshire (Derby) 6-13 September	v. Leicestershire (Leicester) 16-20 September	M	Inns	NO	Runs	SH	Av
P.D. Bowler	20 2	17 5	0 4	143 45	6 153*	0 26	45*	17	29	3	1123	153*	43.19
C.J. Adams	33 71*	50 0	50 11	42 15	175 13	1 22	5 5	18	30	1	843	175	28.10
J.E. Morris	229 22*	45 83	11 37	127 35	12	21 53	13 94*	18	29	1	1461	229	52.17
T.J.G. O'Gorman	0	–	–	–	27	27 2*	14	14	21	3	511	130*	28.38
F.A. Griffith	–	56	11 7	5	–	–	11 5	11	14	0	257	56	18.35
D.G. Cork	104	–	5 20*	13* 20*	55*	0 4	11	15	24	4	539	104	26.95
K.J. Barnett	18	10 4*	–	25	2*	22 5	14	16	23	4	1223	168	64.36
K.M. Krikken	40	51*	–	–	–	0 7	–	13	18	4	227	40	16.21
A.E. Warner	19	–	–	–	–	–	11	12	14	1	238	95*	18.30
R.W. Sladdin	–	–	11	–	–	0 58	–	9	11	3	131	51*	16.37
S.J. Base	–	8 11	3 4	2 0*	3	3* 19	18 29	14	21	2	139	27	7.31
D.E. Malcolm	–	–	30 41	18 0	–	44*	3* 37	10	12	5	69	19	9.85
M.J. Vandrau	57	29 –	0* 2	36 1*	5 46*	19	–	15	25	4	404	58	19.23
O.H. Mortensen	–	52 35	5 5	–	–	–	67	10	5	1	22	17	5.50
B.J.M. Maher	–	–	–	–	–	–	–	7	13	3	70	29	7.00
A.S. Rollins	–	0 37*	9	–	–	–	–	14	11	2	392	85	43.55
I.G.S. Steer	–	–	–	17	–	–	–	4	6	1	157	67	31.40
A.W. Richardson	–	–	–	–	–	3 1	–	1	2	0	9	9	4.50
Byes	6	5	5	17	1	2	2						
Leg-byes	5	1	3		12	13	13						
Wides	5	4	4	10	1	2	1						
No-balls	2	22	8		10	4	4						
Total	521 139	322 182	135 221	438 100	403	127 195	213 175						
Wickets	10	10 6	10 2	9 4	10 5	10 10	10						
Result	W	D	D	W	D	L	D						
Points	24	6	2	24	5	5	5						

BOWLING

The following table records the bowling figures (overs–maidens–runs–wickets) for each bowler in each first-class match, together with extras and innings totals. Values have been read from the rotated tabular layout.

Opponent (Dates)	D.G. Cork	A.E. Warner	F.A. Griffith	S.J. Base	R.W. Sladdin	C.J. Adams	P.D. Bowler	J.E. Morris	D.E. Malcolm	M.J. Vandrau	K.J. Barrett	O.H. Mortensen	A.W. Richardson	I.G.S. Steer	Byes	Leg-byes	Wides	No-balls	Total	Wks
v. Cambridge University (Cambridge) 14–16 April	15-4-21-3 & 10-4-17-0	16-11-9-0 & 8-4-16-0	15.4-6-31-2 & 8-1-16-0	12-3-20-2 & 2-1-3-0	30-11-56-3 & 24-15-20-2	8-2-10-0	2-0-8-0								2 / 1	3	3 / 4		140 / 98	10 / 3
v. Warwickshire (Birmingham) 6–10 May	12.1-2-32-2 & 14-3-24-3	21-3-54-4 & 6-1-23-1	9-1-32-3	21-5-42-0 & 13.2-3-36-3					14-4-28-1 & 12-4-28-2						4		1	2	192 / 115	10 / 9 A
v. Glamorgan (Derby) 13–17 May	17-3-50-1 & 17-4-53-3	19-4-27-2 & 16-3-55-2	17.4-5-76-2 & 13.5-1-46-1	15-4-53-4 & 12-2-51-1		11-0-53-1 & 12-1-66-0			23-4-101-1 & 22-3-98-0						5	7 / 8		8 / 8	320 / 368	10 / 8
v. Essex (Chelmsford) 20–24 May		20-4-81-2	13-2-43-1		34-11-121-2				19-4-63-1	24-9-79-1					10		1		471	7
v. Hampshire (Derby) 27–31 May	27-7-39-3 & 10-1-34-0	30-10-52-4 & 8-1-32-1	15-0-38-1 & 7-0-35-0	13-5-24-1 & 2-0-11-0		7-0-28-0			18-2-45-2 & 11-3-54-0	10-3-25-0 & 22-7-73-1					1 / 8	15 / 14	4	12 / 10	243 / 290	10 / 4
v. Middlesex (Lord's) 3–7 June	21-4-48-2		7-1-14-0						21-2-54-2 & 6-2-18-0	6-1-8-2 & 0.1-0-6-0	17-7-40-2				4	11		2	193 / 68	10 / 0
v. Yorkshire (Chesterfield) 10–14 June		16-4-38-0		17-8-32-1					24-8-57-4			15-6-22-1				8	1		154	6
v. Kent (Canterbury) 17–21 June	11.3-1-37-1 & 16-3-78-0	20-4-57-1		23.5-3-93-5	29-5-114-2	7-2-19-0 & 1.4-0-22-0 & 8-0-25-0			25.2-3-98-5 & 14-1-42-3	4-3-1-0 & 30.3-7-119-1		20-5-48-2 & 2-0-3-1			2	7		22	341 / 25	10 / 1
v. Lancashire (Derby) 24–28 June	28-5-102-1		22-2-102-2 & 9-2-48-1	31.2-7-82-5	39-5-185-1	7-0-36-1 & 2-0-21-0 & 3-0-13-0				18-3-78-1 & 28-6-72-1		25-6-82-1 & 31-10-59-1			5 / 13	9 / 10	5	4 / 2	477	10
v. Worcestershire (Kidderminster) 1–5 July	4-1-11-1			10-1-85-0	1.4-0-18-0				12-0-85-0	7-1-27-0					6	18		14	327 / 560	8
v. Australians (Derby) 13–15 July	12-0-55-1											8-0-23-0 & 17-10-19-0				3		6 / 31	50 / 268	1 / 1
v. Sussex (Derby) 22–26 July	13-3-31-3 & 11-4-16-2	9-2-26-1 & 15-7-39-2		19-5-59-5 & 11-3-30-0					8-1-47-1 & 16.3-3-57-6						7	7 / 13	2	2 / 8	193 / 174	10 / 10
v. Gloucestershire (Cheltenham) 29 July–2 August		7.3-1-27-5	7.4-3-16-0	8-2-30-1		6.4-0-44-1	7-5-2-0		15-0-77-4	29-7-91-1		18-2-55-5			18	5	1	24	139	10
v. Durham (Durham) 5–9 August		29-3-93-5		20-5-94-0		9-2-22-0			30-4-140-3	10-0-40-1	16-2-38-0					3		32	520	10
v. Somerset (Derby) 12–16 August	32.5-7-90-4			35-7-116-2		5-0-19-0				22-5-49-1		32-9-79-0	22-5-74-0		6	20	4	40 / 23	299 / 453	10 / 9
v. Surrey (Ilkeston) 19–23 August	16-6-27-1 & 27-4-80-2	21.4-5-57-5 & 22.4-5-73-2		24-6-77-2 & 8-2-24-0	12-7-30-0 & 22.5-66-1	2-1-6-0				8-0-34-2 & 11-1-41-1		14-6-34-2 & 13-3-42-1		3-1-11-0	2 / 1	4 / 6	1	8	205 / 332	10 / 8
v. Nottinghamshire (Nottingham) 26–30 August	27-5-97-1		20-5-60-1	19-2-63-0	39.2-15-126-2	6-1-20-0	11-3-35-0			30-6-81-2 & 26-2-104-1				6-1-23-3		4	3	20	500	4
v. Northamptonshire (Derby) 9–13 September	10-2-24-0 & 12-2-58-0	24-3-87-2			24-4-83-3	16-0-88-2		6-1-6-1		3-1-9-0		19-3-55-1			3	3	3		241 / 368	5 / 5
v. Leicestershire (Leicester) 16–20 September		5-0-19-0 & 9-1-35-2	6-0-36-0	12-2-35-4								11-4-38-0 & 9-1-26-3				8 / 13		17	128 / 61	4 / 5

Bowler's average

	D.G. Cork	A.E. Warner	F.A. Griffith	S.J. Base	R.W. Sladdin	C.J. Adams	P.D. Bowler	J.E. Morris	D.E. Malcolm	M.J. Vandrau	K.J. Barrett	O.H. Mortensen	A.W. Richardson	I.G.S. Steer
Overs–Maidens	363.3-75-	322.5-76-	170.5-29-	310.1-69-	326.5-96-	111.2-9-	20-8-	6-1-	290.5-48-	284.4-62-	33-9-	255-66-	22-5-	9-2-
Runs–Wkts	1024-34	900-41	593-14	1080-36	1017-23	492-5	45-0	6-1	1092-35	937-16	78-2	643-21	74-0	34-3
Average	30.11	21.95	42.35	30.00	44.21	98.40	—	6.00	31.20	58.56	39.00	30.61	—	11.33

A K.J. Piper absent hurt

FIELDING FIGURES

32 – C.W. Scott (ct 28/st 4)
24 – W. Larkins
13 – P.W.G. Parker
12 – D.A. Graveney
8 – I.T. Botham, S. Hutton and A.R. Fothergill (ct 6/st 2)
7 – P. Bainbridge, G. Fowler and J.A. Daley
6 – I. Smith
5 – S.J.E. Brown and A.C. Cummins
3 – P.J. Berry
1 – M.P. Briers, J.D. Glendenen, S.P. Hughes and sub
†W. Larkins retired hurt
‡J.D. Glendenen retired hurt, absent hurt
D.A. Graveney absent hurt

DURHAM

S. Lugsden and M.M. Betts made their first-class debuts.

G. Fowler, previously of Lancashire, made his debut for Durham.

A.C. Cummins replaced D.N. Jones as overseas player and has been retained for 1994.

J.D. Glendenen and M.P. Briers have left the county.

P.W.G. Parker has taken up a teaching post but may be available in the holidays.

I.T. Botham retired from first-class cricket. The greatest English all-rounder since W.G. Grace, he scored 19,399 runs, took 1,172 wickets and held 354 catches.

DURHAM CCC — BATTING (season averages)

	M	Inns	NO	Runs	HS	Av
G. Fowler	14	24	–	633	138	26.37
W. Larkins	17	30	3	1045	151	38.70
P.W.G. Parker	19	32	1	924	159	29.80
P. Bainbridge	19	32	2	1150	150*	38.33
J.A. Daley	13	22	3	563	79	25.59
I. Smith	6	12	–	192	39	16.00
C.W. Scott	14	24	3	343	64	16.33
P.J. Berry	9	14	4	232	46	23.20
J. Wood	9	17	1	250	63*	17.85
D.A. Graveney	19	28	14	289	32	20.64
S.J.E. Brown	16	24	5	152	31	8.00
I.T. Botham	10	17	1	416	101	26.00
M.P. Briers	1	2	–	2	1	1.00
A.C. Cummins	16	26	3	502	70	20.91
A.R. Fothergill	5	8	5	53	29	6.62
S.P. Hughes	6	8	2	37	30	6.16
J.D. Glendenen	6	11	1	41	18	8.20
S. Hutton	10	17	–	469	73	27.58
S. Lugsden	1	1	1	5	5*	–
M.M. Betts	1	2	1	4	4	4.00

BOWLING

Match	J. Wood	S.J.E. Brown	P.J. Berry	P. Bainbridge	I. Smith	D.A. Graveney	T.T. Botham	M.P. Briers	A.C. Cummins	S.P. Hughes	P.W.G. Parker	S. Lugsden	S. Hutton	W. Larkins	M.M. Betts	Byes	Leg-byes	Wides	No-balls	Total	Wkts
v. Oxford University (Oxford) 14–16 April	13-1-41-3	13-2-19-3	6-1-9-1	5.5-0-10-2		35-16-49-4											7	2	2	86	10
v. Lancashire (Manchester) 6–10 May	3-0-7-0	12-1-46-0	22-3-62-1	5-1-24-0		42-7-131-4										4	3	5	6	226	6
	35-7-106-4	39-8-104-1	14-5-18-1	5-1-13-0		16-1-66-3											11	2	8	442	10
v. Hampshire (Stockton) 13–17 May		10.4-0-36-1		3-1-2-0		16-5-24-1	18-4-32-1	13-3-41-0	15-2-48-0	28-10-64-0							2	3	4	157	4
				20-4-66-1	11-1-35-1		3.3-0-23-0	6-0-28-0								2	6			289	4
v. Gloucestershire (Bristol) 20–4 May	16-2-54-0		6-1-34-1	6.4-3-8-1		22-5-54-1	8-2-23-0		17-5-43-3							2	9	2	16	227	6
	4-1-18-0		15-0-44-1			19-3-57-2			9-2-45-1							2	2		12	168	4
v. Kent (Darlington) 27–31 May	17-2-75-2	29-9-71-1		5-1-15-2		2-0-9-0	19.3-3-52-3		29-9-76-2							5	14	3	19	317	10
v. Leicestershire (Leicester) 3–7 June		31.2-3-102-3	12-3-45-1	17-4-54-3		33-8-74-1	18-8-27-0		19-2-58-2							8	3		12	371	10
v. Middlesex (Gateshead) 10–14 June																		0	0		
v. Glamorgan (Colwyn Bay) 17–21 June	12-1-47-1	17-1-59-1	16-3-39-3	6-0-34-1		26-5-65-1	6.5-2-11-4		24-5-75-0							9	4	1	22	300	10
	7-1-37-1	6-1-25-0	29-3-112-1			20-5-64-1	4-0-27-0		17.2-6-48-3							10	7	5	18	363	7
v. Worcestershire (Stockton) 24–8 June		25-3-98-3	1-0-8-0	3.4-1-8-2		11-4-18-0	31-10-55-3		24-3-75-2							8	13		16	277	10
				5-1-23-1		53-31-53-1	20-6-44-2		29-4-80-3							5	10		8	266	7
v. Surrey (The Oval) 1–5 July	14-3-74-1	15-1-40-0	1-0-8-0	24-1-90-5		3-0-18-0	20-3-95-0		22-4-83-2	27-9-87-1						4	21	1	32	473	9
v. Australians (Durham) 15–19 July		22.4-1-70-7	4-0-12-0	5-0-27-0		10-6-18-1	6-2-21-0		18-4-62-1		5-0-32-0					5	7	3	10	221	10
		11-3-39-0	14-1-91-2	11-1-51-0		3-2-6-0	11-2-45-0		11-3-25-1								3		4	295	3
v. Essex (Chelmsford) 22–6 July		31-10-111-5		16-3-47-0		22-6-50-0			14.4-5-32-5	5-0-32-0						8	6	4	26	382	10
		15-5-40-3	14-2-47-0	8-2-11-0		13-7-23-2										7	4	2	18	154	10
v. Sussex (Durham) 29 July–2 August		25-4-101-1		19-1-80-1	6-1-19-0	24-7-48-2			36-9-115-6	29.3-6-91-1							12	8	12	440	10
		14-1-87-0			4-0-29-0	12-1-57-1			11-1-48-0	16-3-47-0		14-1-42-0					14	7	22	362	2
v. Derbyshire (Durham) 5–9 August		25-8-68-4	3.1-1-4-1	13-4-43-2		22-9-53-2			24-3-107-1		2-0-2-0	12-1-43-2					5	1		322	5
		11-3-40-1	15-7-26-0			7-1-24-0			17-5-44-2				2-1-1-0				2			182	10
v. Northamptonshire (Northampton) 12–16 August		14-2-74-0		18-7-37-1		43.1-18-78-5			28-7-89-1	24-10-48-3						13	8	4	14	347	10
v. Warwickshire (Darlington) 19–23 August		28-2-78-5		23-9-58-1		17-10-28-0		19-3-69-0	19-3-41-2	22-6-60-2						4	12	1		281	10
		28-2-102-3		12-3-29-0		26-9-49-2			29.4-6-83-5							2	16			327	10
v. Yorkshire (Leeds) 26–30 August	27-4-87-3	29-2-114-1			6-1-16-0	24-5-64-1			25-9-46-0	16-2-48-1						1	4	2	6	400	10
	18-3-41-1	12-2-31-1			8-4-10-1	9-3-20-0			24-6-61-0							1	12	2	14	228	8
v. Nottinghamshire (Chester-le-Street) 31 August–3 September	26-1-148-0	31-3-161-2		35-5-132-3		47-12-105-3			29.1-0-137-4		7-3-10-0			4-0-18-0	6-1-19-1	12	11	3	44	629	10
v. Somerset (Hartlepool) 16–20 September		28-1-120-0		9-4-10-2		2-1-1-0			22.3-3-58-3	7-3-10-0	7-0-26-0					6	8	1	12	352	10
		6-0-25-1		4.2-1-31-3					9-2-40-1												
Bowler's average	192-26-735-16 — 45.93	521-77-1861-47 — 39.59	200.1-33-648-15 — 43.20	333.1-76-1021-40 — 25.52	35-7-109-2 — 54.50	579.1-187-1306-38 — 34.36	185.5-46-516-13 — 39.69	19-3-69-0 —	504.3-95-1614-53 — 30.45	211.3-61-552-8 — 69.00	21-3-70-0 —	26-2-85-2 — 42.50	2-1-1-0 —	4-0-18-0 —	6-1-19-1 — 19.00						

ESSEX CCC

BATTING

	v. England 'A' (Chelmsford) 22–5 April		v. Cambridge University (Cambridge) 1–3 May		v. Yorkshire (Chelmsford) 6–10 May		v. Surrey (The Oval) 13–17 May		v. Derbyshire (Chelmsford) 20–4 May		v. Somerset (Chelmsford) 3–7 June		v. Lancashire (Manchester) 10–14 June		v. Nottinghamshire (Nottingham) 17–21 June		v. Warwickshire (Ilford) 24–8 June		v. Kent (Maidstone) 1–5 July		v. Leicestershire (Southend) 15–19 July		v. Durham (Chelmsford) 22–6 July		M	Inns	NO	Runs	HS	Av
G.A. Gooch	88	32*	105	–	38	50	79	5					66	–			71	63			51	25	0	13	13	23	3	1350	159*	67.50
J.P. Stephenson	38	29			32	40	16	0	43	–	32	17	4	–	97	113*	15	64	2	83	5	8	32	10	17	32	2	1011	122	33.70
J.J.B. Lewis	16	5*					56	24	8	–	10	50			35	136*			67	14					13	24	4	736	136*	36.80
N. Hussain	118	–	111	–	9	13	41	52	152	–	2	1*	36	–	30	–	107*	12			103	16			16	27	3	1420	152	59.16
N.V. Knight	0	–	11	94																			10	36	7	13	–	295	94	22.69
M.A. Garnham	0	–	10	18	53	58	33	12	40*	–	12	–	45	–	8	–	4*	11	66	14*	0	10	106	42	17	29	4	694	106	27.76
D.R. Pringle	25	–			52*	13	39	7			54	–	65*	–	17	–		14*	76	48	12	57*	57	0	14	22	4	610	76	33.88
T.D. Topley	10	–	25	19*					0	–	0	–											22	2	8	12	1	155	33	14.09
M.C. Ilott	32	–			11*	5	5	0							50*	–		0*			0	0			15	20	4	252	51	15.75
P.M. Such	26	–	0	–	6	1	25	0													5	2	1	0	15	18	2	172	54	10.75
J.H. Childs	1*	–	1*	–	0	12*					2*	–			–	–		1*	18*	6	0*	1*			17	19	11	89	23	11.12
P.J. Prichard			6	54	12	7	26	7	33	–	123	5	12	–	58	8	68	30	104	106	0	60	67	2	19	36	3	1319	225*	39.96
N. Shahid			4	8											8	–			60	13					7	13	1	270	69*	22.50
N.A. Foster			37	26*	18	0	19	10*	37	–	15	–	29*	–		8			12	0	2	0	6	0	7	10	3	199	37	28.42
S.J.W. Andrew			1	–							4	–									20	19			11	14	4	75	18	7.50
Salim Malik					4	0	41	16	132	–	0	49*	6	–	121	–	90	35					40	30	15	27	2	917	132	36.68
R.J. Rollins																			7	1					3	4	1	14	7	4.66
D.D.J. Robinson																			27	12					2	4	–	112	67	28.00
D.M. Cousins																			0*	0					1	2	1	0	0*	0.00
D.J.P. Boden																									2	2	–	5	5	2.50
B.J. Hyam																									1	2	–	1	1	0.50
Byes	14		4	2	4		1		10			2			4	1		5			1	2	5	8						
Leg-byes	11	1	5	5	10	10	8	12	8		7	8	10		9	2	13	14	17	13	9	3	6	4						
Wides	1		1			2					2		1		3				2		5		4	2						
No-balls	14	8	2	2	14	10	16	2	8		2	4	30		10		16	16			2	2	26	4						
Total	394	75	323	228	250	215	418	153	471		265	136	304		450	260	384	273	440	311	233	210	382	154						
Wickets	10	1	10	4	10	10	10	10	7		10	3	6		8	1	4	7	9	9	10	10	10	10						
Result	W		D		L		D		D		W		D		D		W		D		L		L							
Points	–		–				6		8		22		7		5		22		6		4		7							

BATTING

	v. Worcestershire (Chelmsford) 29 July–2 August		v. Northamptonshire (Northampton) 5–9 August		v. Australians (Chelmsford) 14–16 August		v. Gloucestershire (Bristol) 19–23 August		v. Middlesex (Colchester) 26–30 August		v. Sussex (Hove) 31 August–3 September		v. Glamorgan (Cardiff) 9–13 September		v. Hampshire (Chelmsford) 16–20 September		M	Inns	NO	Runs	HS	Av
G.A. Gooch	31	159*			61	73			15	4	–	74*	23	14	109	114	13	23	3	1350	159*	67.50
J.P. Stephenson	44	5	95	11*					4	10	9	122	12	0	5	43	17	32	2	1011	122	33.70
J.J.B. Lewis			6	7	8	1*	46	56			43	–	29	54	13	10*	13	24	4	736	136*	36.80
N. Hussain	64	4			57	32			40	73	70*	118	51	0	102	5	16	27	3	1420	152	59.16
N.V. Knight			2	10	1	87	0	30					0	14			7	13	–	295	94	22.69
M.A. Garnham	30	16	34	2	17	12	1	17*	0	23							17	29	4	694	106	27.76
D.R. Pringle	7	11	28	4	9	1	14	–									14	22	4	610	76	33.88
T.D. Topley			22	5			11	–	33	6							8	12	1	155	33	14.09
M.C. Ilott	11	0*			24	1	0	–	5	5	51	–	1	43	8	–	15	20	4	252	51	15.75
P.M. Such	54	–			15	0*			3	4*	–	–	7	19	4	–	15	18	2	172	54	10.75
J.H. Childs	4*	–	4	23	11*	0	4	–	0*	1	–	–			0	–	17	19	11	89	23	11.12
P.J. Prichard	28	64	61	0	21	1	46*	21*	0	5	225*	24	8	21	4	2	19	36	3	1319	225*	39.96
N. Shahid			5	69*			45	12					32	1	3	10	7	13	1	270	69*	22.50
N.A. Foster													16*	0*	5*	–	7	10	3	199	37	28.42
S.J.W. Andrew	18	–	6*	5			25	23	36	1	73	63*					11	14	4	75	18	7.50
Salim Malik	1	19	14	3	17	39											15	27	2	917	132	36.68
R.J. Rollins											–	–			0	6*	3	4	1	14	7	4.66
D.D.J. Robinson							6	67									2	4	–	112	67	28.00
D.M. Cousins									0	5	–	–					1	2	1	0	0*	0.00
D.J.P. Boden													1	0			2	2	–	5	5	2.50
B.J. Hyam																	1	2	–	1	1	0.50
Byes	1			2	4	10		7			4	3			4	2						
Leg-byes	11	7	7	3	9	14	6	3	6	12	4	3	2	7	6	2						
Wides			1			2					2	3		1	1	4						
No-balls			2		14	6	12	2	6	4	12	2	4		6							
Total	305	286	286	146	268	277	216	240	148	153	493	412	186	178	268	196						
Wickets	10	6	10	9†	10	9	10	5	10	10	4	3	10	10	10	5						
Result	W		L		L		D		L		W		L		D							

ESSEX

G.A. Gooch hit his 100th hundred during the season and was the only batsman in the country to reach 2,000 runs.

D.M. Cousins, D.D.J. Robinson and B. Hyam made their first-class debuts.

N.A. Foster was forced to retire through injury.

Salim Malik will not be returning to Essex in 1994.

J.J.B. Lewis made the highest score of his career.

M.C. Ilott and S.J.W. Andrew returned the best bowling figures of their careers.

BOWLING

(Figures given as inn.1; inn.2 where two innings were bowled. Analyses are Overs–Maidens–Runs–Wickets.)

Match	D.R. Pringle	M.C. Ilott	T.D. Topley	J.H. Childs	P.M. Such	J.P. Stephenson	N.A. Foster	S.J.W. Andrew	N. Shahid	Salim Malik	G.A. Gooch	D.M. Cousins	D.J.P. Boden	N. Hussain	P.J. Prichard	Byes	Leg-byes	Wides	No-balls	Total	Wkts
v. England 'A' (Chelmsford) 22–5 April	13-6-17-0; 21-3-48-1	19-2-59-2; 12-2-43-0	6-1-23-0; 5-0-17-0	16-3-47-3; 13.3-4-39-1	13.5-6-26-5; 8-1-42-2	–; 8-1-42-2										1; –	2; 6	–; 1	8; 2	174; 294	10; 10
v. Cambridge University (Cambridge) 1–3 May			12.4-8-15-3; 5-1-12-0	13-7-11-3; 18-8-28-2	1-0-1-0		12-4-30-1; 12-2-40-0		6-4-6-0		4-1-25-0					3; 4	11; 12			105; 145	10; 3
v. Yorkshire (Chelmsford) 6–10 May	18-8-32-1	25-6-79-4; 21.4-2-67-3		20-3-57-0; 21-4-76-2	17-4-44-1; 23.3-3-55-2	5-1-25-0	24-4-94-2; 13-8-21-0	20-4-47-3; 6-5-1-0		11-0-39-1; 5-0-25-1						4; –	20; 6	6; –	6; 4	397; 307	10; 10
v. Surrey (The Oval) 13–17 May	6-1-21-0; 14-2-59-0	31.4-8-85-7; 7-4-46-1		27-8-73-3; 29-8-57-1	27-8-73-3; 29-8-57-1		30-8-91-0; 6.3-1-46-0			4-2-7-1						–; 4	6; 7	–; 1	–; 2	330; 178	10; 4
v. Derbyshire (Chelmsford) 20–4 May	2-0-14-2	23-7-49-3; 11-5-37-0	5-0-17-1; 5-0-17-0	26-12-26-1; 28-19-24-0	6-0-66-1; 17-2-51-1	6-0-21-0; 3-1-22-0	13-6-16-2; 17-4-47-0	20-9-48-3; 12-3-31-0		16.4-5-33-2; 23-8-56-1	4-1-25-0					–; 4	7; –	2; –	2; 10	203; 253	10; 1
v. Somerset (Chelmsford) 3–7 June	20.1-8-29-2; 5-1-22-0	24-3-79-3; 7-0-41-0		6-1-13-1; 9-2-23-1	19-5-44-0		19-4-40-2; 29-8-58-5	15.1-2-47-7		1.5-0-6-1; 3-0-6-0						4; 3	3; 13	–; 2	–; –	202; 197	10; 10
v. Lancashire (Manchester) 10–14 June	16-3-55-0		14-3-46-2; 14-4-50-2		8-0-41-0; 17-10-20-2	14-3-43-2	19-2-77-0; 8-2-26-0			11-3-33-1; 12-1-39-0						4; 11	5; 1	–; 1	6; 18	321; 129	10; 3
v. Nottinghamshire (Nottingham) 17–21 June	18-3-50-0; 13.5-4-33-4	27-4-60-1; 20-3-54-1		37-9-90-2; 24-7-50-2	28-3-95-2; 13-1-44-0	16-5-44-2; 12.2-4-31-5		29-5-75-1; 11-5-39-0		8-3-15-1; 17-2-70-1						4; 2	2; 18	1; –	14; 14	379; 197	6; 8
v. Warwickshire (Ilford) 24–8 June	10-3-36-1	23-4-64-3; 4-0-19-0		37.1-9-82-1; 14-5-28-0	32.2-6-66-5; 27-7-80-5	38-4-111-5; 19-2-99-1	15-3-37-0; 3-0-6-0			26-5-67-5						18; 4	7; 8		14; 8	448; 206	10; 10
v. Kent (Maidstone) 1–5 July	33-7-102-1; 12-3-31-1			25-10-59-2; 4-0-36-0	17-2-69-1; 30.2-11-61-4	3-0-11-0		28-4-98-0; 25-3-114-1	2-0-7-0			19-4-58-0; 8-0-51-1				6; 4	4; 8	2; –	16; 8	445; 335	9; 4
v. Leicestershire (Southend) 15–19 July	15-3-24-1; 13-5-24-0	18-5-54-0; 4-0-19-0		43-8-106-3; 23.5-6-64-5	10-3-27-0; 36-9-92-4	13-6-33-0; 10-3-27-0		3-0-6-0		16-4-46-1; 3-0-7-0						2; 3	8; –	–; 2	8; –	321; 199	10; 10
v. Durham (Chelmsford) 22–6 July	25-7-88-1; 8-3-13-0	19-5-36-1; 14-3-44-1	19-4-100-0; 9-3-18-0	48-11-99-5; 23-9-53-0	33-12-58-3	8.3-2-34-1; 9-2-18-0		13-1-35-1		11.3-0-43-2						4; 15	12; 1		24; 4	483; 199	10; 8
v. Worcestershire (Chelmsford) 29 July–2 August	18-2-46-0	19-1-86-1; 14-3-44-1		18-3-53-2	16-2-102-0; 14.1-3-52-4	19-3-55-2		24-5-79-3; 2-0-22-0		12-1-34-1; 6-0-18-0						4; –	–; 9	1; –	14; 8	379; 208	10; 10
v. Northamptonshire (Northampton) 5–9 August	30.5-8-71-3	30-6-79-2; 29-10-38-3		23-4-86-3; 17-6-52-1	6-0-27-0; 5-0-27-0	11-0-42-3; 9-1-27-2		21-1-91-0; 1.3-1-6-1								8; –	9; –		28; 10	370; 64	10; 4
v. Australians (Chelmsford) 14–16 August	14-1-48-2	13-2-42-6; 6-0-36-0			26-4-87-0; 3-1-11-0											6; 3	6; 3	–; 3	4; 10	357; 218	6; 10
v. Gloucestershire (Bristol) 19–23 August	19-4-65-4; 26-6-90-4	9-1-47-1	24-4-92-2; 9-1-34-0	30-9-62-3				6-2-14-0		12-0-49-1	6-2-14-0					5; 6	–; 6	1; –	20; 14	320; 220	10; 10
v. Middlesex (Colchester) 26–30 August		38.3-11-119-4		5-0-23-0									5-0-36-1			1; –	2; 9		–; 8	135; 167	3; 10
v. Sussex (Hove) 31 August–3 September		7.5-0-23-1; 14-5-47-0	19.1-3-77-2; 23.5-6-71-2	34-12-104-2; 17-4-47-0	48-13-89-5; 27-5-71-5	33-8-111-2; 9-1-42-0				16-4-36-1; 15-1-38-1	1-0-5-0		25-3-118-2; 10-0-62-0	4.1-0-33-0		1	–	6	14	591	10
v. Glamorgan (Cardiff) 9–13 September		6-0-28-1				11-4-42-2; 3-0-6-1		18-3-69-7; 6-2-26-1		7-0-37-0; 18.1-1-88-2				6.2-0-75-2	6-0-77-1	6; 6	–; –	2; –	6; 20	312; 169	10; 3
v. Hampshire (Chelmsford) 16–20 September		19-1-86-1; 10-5-18-2	5.1-1-20-1	31.3-6-89-4; 21-5-79-1		5-1-13-0; 1-0-9-0		10-0-44-0; 17-2-56-0	5-1-15-0							–; –	5; 11	1; –	12; 12	217; 347	5; 10
Bowler's average	378.5-93- 1041-29 35.89	511.4-102- 1550-51 30.39	181.5-41- 627-15 41.80	709-207- 1729-62 27.88	572.1-133- 1607-60 26.78	265.5-52- 908-30 30.26	220.3-56- 629-12 52.41	281.4-55- 934-28 33.35	13-5- 28-0 –	255.1-40- 792-24 33.00	11-3- 44-0 –	27-4- 109-1 109.00	40-3- 216-3 72.00	10.3-0- 108-1 108.00	6-0- 77-1 77.00						

GLAMORGAN CCC

FIELDING FIGURES

54 – C.P. Metson (ct 50/st 4)
20 – M.P. Maynard
17 – I.V.A. Richards and S.P. James
16 – H. Morris
15 – P.A. Cottey
12 – A. Dale
11 – R.P. Lefebvre and R.D.B. Croft
9 – subs
6 – S.L. Watkin
4 – D.L. Hemp
3 – S.R. Barwick
2 – S.D. Thomas

† M.P. Maynard absent hurt
‡ D.L. Hemp retired ill
§ I.V.A. Richards absent hurt
¶ M.P. Maynard absent hurt

GLAMORGAN

S.L. Watkin was the leading wicket-taker in the country.

A. Dale hit the first double century of his career and returned the best bowling figures of his career.

R.D.B. Croft hit a maiden first-class hundred.

D.L. Hemp made his highest first-class score.

R.P. Lefebvre took 44 wickets in his first season with the county. He took 74 in three seasons with Somerset, 1990–2.

S. Bastien returned the best bowling figures of his career.

BATTING

	v. Oxford University (Oxford) 21–3 April	v. Sussex (Cardiff) 29 April–2 May	v. Cambridge University (Cambridge) 5–7 May	v. Derbyshire (Derby) 13–17 May	v. Northamptonshire (Swansea) 20–4 May	v. Somerset (Taunton) 27–31 May	v. Yorkshire (Middlesbrough) 3–7 June	v. Surrey (The Oval) 10–14 June	v. Durham (Colwyn Bay) 17–21 June	v. Nottinghamshire (Swansea) 24–8 June	v. Middlesex (Cardiff) 1–5 July	v. Lancashire (Manchester) 15–19 July	M	Inns	NO	Runs	HS	Av
S.P. James	41	78 / 45	31 / 6	34 / 24	28 / 8	35 / 12	76 / 30	2 / 7	32	9	42 / 27	138* / 24	16	30	1	819	138*	28.24
H. Morris	109*	18	51	37 / 100	7 / 61	53 / 20	29 / 134*	5 / 7	52 / 33	102 / 133	14 / 14	39 / 2	19	35	2	1326	134*	40.18
A. Dale	67	81	29 / 17	33 / 2	20	47 / 42	100 / 58	5 / 2	60 / 85	92 / 51	214*	2 / 95	20	38	1	1472	214*	39.78
M.P. Maynard	110*	37 / 52	20	15 / 145	64	25 / 8	27 / 43*	1	46 / 98	49 / 49	14 / 32	5 / 55	17	28	6	1339	145	49.59
I.V.A. Richards	109*	8 / 17		86 / 3		56 / 9	56	70	34 / 62*	11 / 0	224*	44* / 9*	17	32	5	1235	224*	47.50
P.A. Cottey		22 / 68*	107	15 / 25*	2	9 / 19	22 / 3	48	7 / 5	14 / 100*	0 / 15	67 / 9*	19	34	5	1040	105	35.86
R.D.B. Croft	60	27 / 44*	14 / 24*	25 / 0	12 / 15	6 / 28	3 / 1	25	36 / 5	14 / 17*			20	34	7	718	107	26.59
R.P. Lefebvre		9 / 7	14 / 35	14 / 25*	5	0 / 6	15 / 9*	2	12 / 1*	10	15	67 / 33*	19	28	8	484	50	19.36
C.P. Metson	9*	22*	2* / 1*	31	7 / 14*	0 / 12			13 / 10*	16*	0 / 0		20	31	8	338	25*	14.69
S.L. Watkin	1*	29*	19 / 33	14*	0 / 10	2* / 5*		0*	1* / 2	0	1		18	22	9	187	31	13.35
S.R. Barwick		23*								8*	0	9*	12	19	11	60	23*	7.50
D.L. Hemp													10	19	2	508	90*	29.88
S. Bastien		5 / 4		5 / 8	5 / 13	4 / 1	4 / 8		4 / 1	5 / 9	4 / 13	9 / 11	5	5	4	23	14*	19.00
M. Frost	6 / 2	4 / 8	3 / 1	8 / 7	1 / 2	3 / 1	8 / 8		1 / 1	9 / 2	1 / 1	6 / 6	5	4	1	19	7	—
S.D. Thomas									9 / 7	12 / 2			4	7	3	46	16*	15.33
J.R.A. Williams						2* / 5*		0*	22 / 18	2 / 2				2		6	6	3.00
B.S. Phelps								0*					1					
Byes	3	5 / 4	3 / 7	5 / 5	3 / 3	4 / 1	4 / 1	3	9 / 7	5 / 9	4 / 6	9 / 6						
Leg-byes	6	8	1	8 / 7		3 / 13	8 / 8		7	5 / 2	13 / 4	11						
Wides	4 / 1	4 / 1	1 / 1		3 / 3	3 / 1	2 / 2		4 / 1	2 / 2	1 / 1							
No-balls	14	8		14*		10	22	1	22 / 18	22	10	23						
Total	463 / 115	331 / 362	298 / 187	320 / 368	165 / 212	252 / 215	323 / 304	166 / 93	300 / 363	329 / 352	562 / 109	303 / 244						
Wickets	2 / 3	10 / 5	—	10 / 8	10 / 10	10 / 10	10 / 3	10 / 4	10 / 7	10 / 5	10 / 3	11 / 3						
Result	D	W	D	W	D	L	W	D	W	L	W	W						
Points		20	—	23		4	22		22	7	23	23						

BATTING

	v. Worcestershire (Worcester) 22–6 July	v. Australians (Neath) 31 July–2 August	v. Warwickshire (Cardiff) 5–9 August	v. Leicestershire (Leicester) 12–16 August	v. Hampshire (Swansea) 19–23 August	v. Gloucestershire (Abergavenny) 26–30 August	v. Essex (Cardiff) 9–13 September	v. Kent (Canterbury) 16–20 September	M	Inns	NO	Runs	HS	Av
S.P. James	13 / 15	18 / 54	0 / 10	8 / 3	80 / 19	0 / 1	30 / 4	9 / 6	16	30	1	819	138*	28.24
H. Morris	44 / 124	25 / 132	18 / 30	54 / 18	60 / 5		18 / 18		19	35	2	1326	134*	40.18
A. Dale	34 / 24	36	30	22 / 82	5 / 36	93 / 95	28 / 10	— / 0	20	38	1	1472	214*	39.78
M.P. Maynard	4 / 7		26 / 8	105	67 / 1	95 / 4	6 / 6	17 / 83	17	28	6	1339	145	49.59
I.V.A. Richards	4 / 3	38 / 11*	54 / 18	7	6 / 23	16 / 21	44*	79 / 53	17	32	5	1235	224*	47.50
P.A. Cottey	50 / 18*	17	40 / 15*	24 / 18*	4 / 7	25 / 1	16 / 4	7 / 0	19	34	5	1040	105	35.86
R.D.B. Croft	22	11*	0*	7	11 / 3	6* / 0	11 / 1	0 / 49	20	34	7	718	107	26.59
R.P. Lefebvre		22* / 7	2*		24 / 63	18		5 / 14	19	28	8	484	50	19.36
C.P. Metson	14	0	5 / 2*	62	11 / 24	52	2 / 90*	13 / 9	20	31	8	338	25*	14.69
S.L. Watkin	0	16			16*			5* / 3*	18	22	9	187	31	13.35
S.R. Barwick	5* / 9*		9 / 0				9*	6 / 2	12	19	11	60	23*	7.50
D.L. Hemp									10	19	2	508	90*	29.88
S. Bastien	1		1 / 1	1	7 / 12	4 / 5	6 / 5	1	5	5	4	23	14*	19.00
M. Frost	8	9 / 12	7 / 1	7	1 / 2	5 / 1	5 / 1	6	5	4	1	19	7	—
S.D. Thomas	2 / 12	20 / 8	36 / 14	4	18 / 14	16 / 6	20 / 12	6 / 2	4	7	3	46	16*	15.33
J.R.A. Williams										2		6	6	3.00
B.S. Phelps									1					
Byes	1	2 / 1	9 / 7	1	7 / 12	4 / 5	6 / 5	1						
Leg-byes	8	9 / 12	7 / 1	7	1 / 2	5 / 1	5 / 1	6						
Wides	2 / 12	20 / 8	36 / 14	4	18 / 14	16 / 6	20 / 12	6 / 2						
No-balls				8										
Total	184 / 334	363	236 / 138	351	288 / 227	292 / 297	169 / 217	144 / 239						
Wickets	10 / 9	8	9 / 6	8	10 / 10	10 / 10	10 / 5	10 / 10						
Result	W	D	D	D	L	W	W	L						
Points	20		21	8	4	22	20	10						

BOWLING	S.L. Watkin	R.P. Lefebvre	S.R. Barwick	R.D.B. Croft	A. Dale	S. Bastien	M. Frost	I.V.A. Richards	M.D. Maynard	P.A. Cottey	S.D. Thomas	B.S. Phelps	Byes	Leg-byes	Wides	No-balls	Total	Wkts
v. Oxford University (Oxford)	13–6–11–1	17–8–22–1	19.4–9–26–3	22–13–23–2	6–2–14–1								3				99	10
21–3 April																		
v. Sussex (Cardiff)	29–6–87–5	20–8–38–1	35–11–71–1	36–13–88–0	12–5–21–2									4			309	10
29 April–2 May	14–5–26–3	7–3–11–1	21–16–7–2	19.5–6–55–4	1–0–4–0								1	6		2	110	10
v. Cambridge University	21–8–36–4	16–4–31–2	22–5–39–2	25–13–39–2	5–1–16–0								4	7			172	10
(Cambridge) 5–7 May	10–2–33–0	8–5–22–0	10–2–31–1	20–11–32–2	12–5–30–2								2	3			153	5
v. Derbyshire (Derby)	22–8–87–2	20–3–59–3		2–0–6–1	18–2–63–3	16–1–61–1								7			283	10
13–17 May	20–2–71–5	19–4–47–2		17–7–33–1	4–1–17–0	13–4–40–2								6			214	10
v. Northamptonshire (Swansea)	27–4–79–4	18–3–47–1	22–15–26–0	17–9–22–2	5–2–13–0		14.1–4–25–3							5		2	217	10
20–4 May	8–0–32–0	6–1–9–0	9–4–15–0	6–1–17–1	4–0–11–0		5–1–15–0							4		4	103	1
v. Somerset (Taunton)	20.2–8–45–4	23–4–50–3		1–0–1–0	11–0–42–0		13–1–45–2							2			185	10
27–31 May	34–8–71–2	36–14–63–1		49.1–25–88–0	15–5–30–1		26–5–95–2	5–2–4–0					4	11			366	7
v. Yorkshire (Middlesbrough)	29.3–8–59–4	28–12–53–2	37–19–55–3	27–5–106–0	9–3–30–1								7	4		4	314	10
3–7 June	22–8–59–4	11–6–11–3	12–4–45–0	17–6–50–0				16–5–22–3					1	4			192	10
v. Surrey (The Oval)	27–10–60–2	30.5–7–70–4		11–3–26–1	12–1–52–2	18–2–68–1								6	2		282	10
10–14 June	21–3–63–3	18–6–50–0		33–5–94–3	11–1–36–0	16.4–2–53–0							5	9	1	2	310	6
v. Durham (Colwyn Bay)	24–7–54–1	24–7–55–3	28–12–54–0	42–11–70–4	10.5–3–14–2								2	14			263	10
17–21 June	23–4–93–4	22.2–7–50–3	22–12–28–1	21–7–40–2	10–1–52–0			4–1–18–0						6		8	287	10
v. Nottinghamshire (Swansea)	23.2–4–72–3	20–2–59–1	27–12–58–1	37–8–112–5	3–0–14–0			10–5–21–0					4	6		2	346	10
24–8 June	14–1–55–1	9–1–35–0	14–3–55–0	29–4–97–1	5.2–0–41–0			11–3–49–0						6			338	2
v. Middlesex (Cardiff)	31–4–87–4	30–8–72–1	44–14–131–0	54–9–174–3	22–6–55–2			13–1–51–0					9	5		2	584	10
1–5 July	2–0–7–0		3–0–9–0	8.4–2–45–0				6–0–20–0					4	3			88	0
v. Lancashire (Manchester)	23.5–5–69–3	22–9–38–1	21–8–53–2	33–9–101–3	5–0–13–0			12–1–30–1					3	3	1		310	9
15–19 July									6–0–110–1	6–0–121–0			4		4	20	235	1
v. Worcestershire (Worcester)	26–10–35–3	23.1–8–48–1		18–6–47–0	19–7–49–2						25–5–84–4			4	5	8	267	10
22–6 July	26–7–63–3	22–9–30–0		21–8–39–1	9–1–27–1						23.3–2–76–5		5	7	4	2	247	10
v. Australians (Neath)				21–2–71–0	20–3–66–1	17–0–70–1					20–2–93–1	23–3–105–1	2	7		4	414	4
31 July–2 August				12–2–46–1	9–0–41–2	10–0–31–0					18–2–95–3	3–0–17–0		5			235	7
v. Warwickshire (Cardiff)	8–0–26–0	13–3–30–0			13.3–3–18–6						16–5–49–4			2		6	125	10
5–9 August	25.4–1–64–3	24–8–52–2		4–1–11–0	25–5–59–2						17–2–57–3		1	4		4	248	10
v. Leicestershire (Leicester)	23–8–49–4	18–7–35–0	27–17–28–3	18.4–6–38–2	13–6–24–1								3	1		2	178	10
12–16 August	20–6–52–1	16–4–33–0	25–11–51–0	33–12–85–1	26.3–3–90–2					1–0–2–0				2			315	4
v. Hampshire (Swansea)		29.5–6–74–3	42–12–93–1	62–16–157–5				5–0–13–0			19–3–78–0		1	1			417	10
19–23 August		2–0–5–0	23–7–59–0	34–9–74–4	10–1–32–0						3–0–24–0			2	2		196	4
v. Gloucestershire (Abergavenny)	21–4–60–3	6–1–20–2	12–4–26–1	17.4–9–35–3	9–3–14–1									3			158	10
26–30 August	35.3–10–106–4		30–11–56–0	51–22–115–4	22–6–66–2									6	1		349	10
v. Essex (Cardiff)	22–5–49–3	17–5–37–1			13–3–46–0	25.5–8–52–6								2		4	186	10
9–13 September	21–2–60–1	8–0–17–0		8.5–3–15–2	5–1–22–0	17–5–53–6							4	7	1		178	10
v. Kent (Canterbury)	26.3–2–126–2	35–3–106–2		18–1–91–0	8–0–73–0	30–5–115–2								13	1	4	524	6
16–20 September				4–1–15–1	10–1–43–1	4–1–30–0		2–0–7–0									95	2
	713.4–160–	619.1–176–	505.4–208–	850.5–265–	393.1–81–	167.3–28–	58.1–11–	84–18–	6–0–	7–0–	141.3–21–	26–3–						
	1946–86	1379–44	1016–21	2158–61	1238–37	573–19	180–7	235–4	110–1	123–0	556–20	122–1						
Bowler's average	22.62	31.34	48.38	35.37	33.45	30.15	25.71	58.75	110.00	–	27.80	122.00						

FIELDING FIGURES

62 – R.C. Russell (ct 55/st 7)
13 – M.C.J. Ball
12 – R.I. Dawson
10 – S.G. Hinks
9 – M.W. Alleyne, A.J. Wright, R.M. Wight and G.D. Hodgson
6 – B.C. Broad and M. Davies
5 – K.E. Cooper and T.H.C. Hancock
4 – C.A. Walsh
1 – R.J. Scott, A.M. Smith, R.C. Williams, M.J. Gerrard and sub

GLOUCESTERSHIRE

R.M. Wight, the former Cambridge captain, made his first-class debut for Gloucestershire.

C.A. Walsh replaced A.J. Wright as captain. Wright resigned in mid-season.

B.C. Broad played for Gloucestershire, 1979–83, and returned to the county from Nottinghamshire last season. He was one of only two batsmen to reach 1,000 runs for the county.

G.D. Hodgson hit a career best 166.

M. Davies took 10 wickets in a match for the first time.

K.E. Cooper played for Nottinghamshire, 1976–92.

M.C.J. Ball had career-best performances with bat and ball.

GLOUCESTERSHIRE CCC

BATTING — Averages

Player	M	Inns	NO	Runs	HS	Av
B.C. Broad	18	34	–	1161	131	34.14
S.G. Hinks	12	24	1	482	68	20.95
R.J. Scott	5	10	2	179	51	17.90
M.W. Alleyne	18	34	2	994	142*	31.06
A.J. Wright	18	31	2	322	75	16.94
T.H.C. Hancock	16	29	2	723	76	26.77
R.C. Russell	16	31	7	852	99*	35.50
A.M. Smith	7	11	1	87	33	8.70
M. Davies	14	23	5	220	44*	12.22
K.E. Cooper	14	25	6	218	52	11.47
M.J. Gerrard	5	5	3	20	9	6.66
R.M. Wight	7	11	1	152	54	15.20
G.D. Hodgson	14	27	2	1079	166	43.16
C.A. Walsh	14	21	3	266	57	14.77
R.I. Dawson	9	17	1	350	58	21.87
R.C. Williams	4	7	3	92	38	23.00
J.M. De La Pena	4	7	3	7	7	7.00
A.M. Babington	7	9	3	40	23	6.66
M.C.J. Ball	7	8	1	113	71	14.12
M.G.N. Windows	1	2	–	58	37	29.00

Match results

First half of season:

Opponent	Venue	Date	Result
v. Middlesex	Bristol	29 April–2 May	L
v. Northamptonshire	Northampton	6–10 May	L
v. Durham	Bristol	20 May–4 May	D
v. Worcestershire	Gloucester	27–31 May	L
v. Kent	Tunbridge Wells	3–7 June	L
v. Australians	Bristol	12–14 June	D
v. Yorkshire	Sheffield	17–21 June	D
v. Leicestershire	Leicester	24–8 June	L
v. Hampshire	Bristol	1–5 July	L
v. Surrey	Guildford	15–19 July	L
v. Derbyshire	Cheltenham	29 July–2 August	L
v. Lancashire	Cheltenham	5–9 August	W

Second half of season:

Opponent	Venue	Date	Result
v. Warwickshire	Birmingham	12–16 August	L
v. Essex	Bristol	19–23 August	L
v. Glamorgan	Abergavenny	26–30 August	D
v. Somerset	Taunton	31 August–3 September	L
v. Nottinghamshire	Bristol	9–13 September	L
v. Sussex	Hove	16–20 September	L

BOWLING

	K.E. Cooper	M.J. Gerrard	A.M. Smith	M. Davies	R.J. Scott	T.H.C. Hancock	R.M. Wight	M.W. Alleyne	C.A. Walsh	J.M. De La Pena	R.C. Williams	A.M. Babington	M.C.J. Ball	B.C. Broad	S.G. Hinks	R.C. Russell	Byes	Leg-byes	Wides	No-balls	Total	Wkts
v. Middlesex (Bristol)	22-9-33-4	25-4-50-4	17-5-49-2	3-0-13-0	12-3-19-0	6-4-6-0												10	4	4	180	10
29 April–2 May	22-7-53-3	13.3-3-39-0	22-5-59-3	17-2-45-0	4-1-13-0													7	2	4	216	6
v. Northamptonshire	24.1-15-26-2		27-5-56-1	37-10-84-5	9-2-28-0													5	1		293	10
(Northampton) 6–10 May	16-6-23-0		11.2-5-30-0	19-2-57-5			39-13-85-1	5-1-9-1												6	110	5
v. Durham (Bristol)			28-4-109-2	24.1-8-32-2	12-4-25-0	3-0-15-0	10-2-32-0	20-3-48-2	20-7-54-3											20	320	10
20–4 May	24-11-26-2		14-1-45-2	7-0-30-1				3-1-7-0	16-2-43-2								4	4		10	174	7
v. Worcestershire (Gloucester)			19-4-42-1	32-7-74-2	12-3-48-2	2-0-7-0			31.3-10-62-5								2	9	2	6	222	10
27–31 May	39-10-108-4		27-6-71-1	32-7-109-3	11-1-24-0	2-0-7-0	27.4-6-71-3	15.5-0-59-1	31-7-87-0		24-2-115-1							9	3	8	474	10
v. Kent (Tunbridge Wells)						2-1-8-0		8.2-0-55-2	15-2-50-2	20-2-77-4								10		35	400	9
3–7 June	40-11-83-5		19-1-85-0	38-13-95-1				5-2-23-0	34-7-87-1	14-1-79-0							2	5	3	10	445	10
v. Australians (Bristol)							27.4-6-71-3	3-1-7-0	34-12-70-4		33-7-101-3	24-7-77-0					3	13	1	18	454	10
12–14 June	22.1-7-56-1			30-7-119-1			34-9-85-1		16.2-3-55-2		5-0-32-0	11-2-30-1					8	7		4	168	5
v. Yorkshire (Sheffield)				12-0-66-3			33.4-8-86-1	14-3-30-1			12-4-43-1						2	3	3	20	393	6
17–21 June	36-10-99-1			22.5-6-82-4			18-3-58-2	16.5-3-52-3	36-10-90-3		4-2-12-0						1	8	1	4	213	9
v. Leicestershire (Leicester)				8-3-42-0			9-3-29-1				12-0-59-1						8	2	2	27	381	10
24–8 June	28-4-119-2	19-0-125-1	18-0-108-0	29-9-85-3		4-0-13-1		11-2-55-2	30.1-10-95-4			23.3-5-67-2					1	6	5	22	521	10
v. Hampshire (Bristol)	8-1-40-0	3.4-0-26-0	3-0-18-0	7-3-24-0				8-0-30-0	14-1-52-3			14-1-52-3					2	2		6	139	3
1–5 July	25-8-41-2			38.1-15-62-2		2-1-8-0		6-2-22-1	24-4-68-2			15-4-51-3					3	3	10	12	294	10
v. Surrey (Guildford)	9-3-19-1			5-1-9-0			10-2-32-0	12-5-25-3	19.2-2-83-5			17-4-44-0					4	4	10	15	213	10
15–19 July								16-7-19-1	30-4-102-4			23-7-30-2					1	1	6	6	280	10 A
v. Derbyshire (Cheltenham)	22-8-30-3			8-5-21-0		2-1-12-0		12-0-27-0	24.2-5-59-5								6	6		12	124	10
29 July–2 August	20-5-48-2			23-9-34-1		4-0-10-3		14-3-54-0	21-6-57-3			18-2-70-0	17-5-43-1				7	3		16	216	5
v. Lancashire (Cheltenham)	14-1-51-1			11-2-54-1		8-1-35-1		8-3-14-1	24-7-51-2				8-1-28-0				4	14	2	5	240	10
5–9 August	25.2-8-66-3			17-3-57-1		6-4-3-1		19-5-41-1	14.1-3-71-4			16-5-42-0	54.1-14-123-6							5	292	10
v. Warwickshire (Birmingham)				36-13-90-0					25-6-83-3			10-2-17-0	25.2-8-46-8				6	6	1	2	297	9 B
12–16 August	29-8-77-2							15-0-50-1	28.5-5-76-4			16-2-47-0	8-2-15-0				2	4		3	382	10
v. Essex (Bristol)	12-2-34-1			5-0-12-1		2-0-6-0		9.3-2-33-3	11.3-4-26-1			6-0-28-1	13-0-56-3	1-0-1-0	1-0-2-0		2	5		4	115	10
19–23 August	23-7-50-3					2-0-11-0		5-1-9-0	21-1-72-2			16-4-42-1	23-3-96-0				1	8		2	251	8
v. Glamorgan (Abergavenny)	10-1-39-1					1-0-2-0			7-1-23-0			5-0-18-0	9-2-32-0		1-0-2-0			2	1		155	6
26–30 August	26-6-93-4																				355	10
v. Somerset (Taunton)	6-1-19-0													1-0-1-0		1.5-0-15-0					128	0 C
31 August–3 September																						
v. Nottinghamshire (Bristol)																						
9–13 September																						
v. Sussex (Hove)																						
16–20 September																						
Bowler's average	502.4-149-1233-47 26.23	89.1-16-298-8 37.25	205.2-36-672-12 56.00	515.1-141-1412-37 38.16	60-14-157-2 78.50	44-12-136-6 22.66	181.2-46-478-9 53.11	246.3-50-707-26 27.19	528.1-119-1516-64 23.68	34-3-156-4 39.00	90-15-362-6 60.33	220.2-49-634-13 48.76	157.3-35-439-18 24.38	1-0-1-0 –	1-0-2-0 –	1.5-0-15-0 –						

A D.A. Reeve retired hurt
B I.V.A. Richards absent hurt
C M.G.N. Windows 1-0-3-0
   R.J. Dawson 1-0-2-0

FIELDING FIGURES

39 – A.N. Aymes (ct 34/st 5)
16 – V.P. Terry
13 – T.C. Middleton and R.S.M. Morris
11 – D.I. Gower
8 – S.D. Udal and M.C.J. Nicholas
7 – D.P.J. Flint
6 – R.A. Smith
5 – K.D. James
4 – K.J. Shine, R.F.M. Cox and sub
3 – I.J. Turner, C.A. Connor, J.R. Ayling and M.D. Marshall
2 – R.J. Maru
1 – M. Jean-Jacques
†M.D. Marshall retired hurt

HAMPSHIRE

M.D. Marshall retired at the end of the season. I.J. Turner and J.R. Wood also left the county. J.R. Ayling was forced to retire through injury. M. Jean-Jacques previously played for Derbyshire. D.P.J. Flint and J.N.B. Bovill made their first-class debuts. M.J. Thursfield returned the best bowling figures of his career.

HAMPSHIRE CCC — BATTING

	v. Somerset (Southampton) 29 April–2 May	v. Oxford University (Oxford) 5–7 May	v. Durham (Stockton) 13–17 May	v. Yorkshire (Southampton) 20–4 May	v. Derbyshire (Derby) 27–31 May	v. Nottinghamshire (Nottingham) 3–7 June	v. Kent (Basingstoke) 10–14 June	v. Northamptonshire (Northampton) 17–21 June	v. Australians (Southampton) 26–8 June	v. Gloucestershire (Bristol) 1–5 July	v. Worcestershire (Portsmouth) 15–19 July	v. Middlesex (Lord's) 22–6 July	M	Inns	NO	Runs	HS	Av
V.P. Terry	2, 10	11, 117	111	24, 8	4, 96	26, 94	46	7, 58*	2, 82	17, 43	—	7, 13	19	33	2	1469	174	47.38
T.C. Middleton	0, 7	0*, 63	65	46, 11	9, 90	8, 23	10	9, 4	53, 78	12, 6	9	54, 5	12	22	—	571	90	25.95
R.S.M. Morris	0, 37	—	64	28, 1	15	0, 15	24	31, 41	8	92, 8	14	91, 8	8	14	1	372	92	26.57
D.I. Gower	3	62	31*	28*, 34	5, 15	153	73	24, 5*	19, 12	61, 83	14, 38	54, 91	16	28	4	1136	153	42.07
M.C.J. Nicholas	76, 47	—	64, 31*	50*, 39	0*	4*, 8	18*	8, 31	17*, 8*	17*, 16	50*, 66	0, 25	18	29	4	918	95	36.72
M.D. Marshall	0, 8	—	—	—	5, 15*	27, 23	—	—	—	16, 17	0	7, 7	18	16	11	250	75*	17.85
A.N. Aymes	33, 26	2	—	37	20	10, 10	0, 18*	44	0	16, 10	—	27	19	29	2	709	107*	39.38
S.D. Udal	16, 39	6	4*	—	9, 101	—	12	24	191	11*	91	27	19	27	1	509	79*	20.36
I.J. Turner	—	5	—	—	—	—	—	0*	—	1*	—	—	4	5	1	17	8	4.25
C.A. Connor	0, 0	7, 15*	—	2	20	4, 16	—	22, 71	31*	69*	—	13	10	11	5	200	59	20.00
K.J. Shine	12, 0	3, 0*	—	21, 21	9, 101	21, 25	11	25	1	6	—	0*	13	14	2	54	12	6.00
R.A. Smith	6*	—	—	37	9, 101	4*, 16	12	22	45	—	—	2, 6	12	19	1	970	191	57.05
J.R. Ayling	—	15*	4*	—	—	10*	—	—	—	—	—	18	4	6	5	89	27*	17.80
K.D. James	7	0, 27*	—	21, 0	37	4, 25	12	—	—	—	0	4, 17	17	29	4	694	71	27.76
M. Jean-Jacques	0	—	—	—	9, 101	10	11	25	—	—	—	36*	3	3	2	42	21*	42.00
R.J. Wood	12, 0	32*	4*	—	11*	—	—	—	—	1*	14*	0*	1	1	—	25	25	25.00
R.J. Maru	—	21*	—	—	—	10	—	—	—	—	—	—	—	—	—	—	—	—
D.P.J. Flint	—	—	—	—	—	—	—	—	—	—	—	4, 17	10	13	5	47	14*	5.87
R.F.M. Cox	—	—	—	—	—	—	—	—	—	—	—	36*	6	10	1	204	63	22.66
M.J. Thursfield	—	—	—	—	—	—	—	—	—	—	—	—	2	4	2	36	36*	18.00
J.N.B. Bovill	—	—	—	—	—	—	—	—	—	—	—	—	1	2	2	3	3*	—
Byes	4	3	2	2	8	10	4	2	4	2	4	2						
Leg-byes	4	7	6	6	15	8	3	16	3	1	5	6						
Wides	—	1	2	—	1	1	2	4	2	3	—	—						
No-balls	4	4	4	18	12	6	2	4	45	20	6	18						
Total	156	169	289	307	243	355	232	247	374	393	355	280						
Wickets	10	10	3	8	10	10	7	10	5	6	9	10						
Result	L	D	D	L	L	W	D	W	D	W	D	L						
Points	2	—	2	7	4	23	5	21	—	20	6	6						

BATTING (continued)

	v. Warwickshire (Southampton) 29 July–2 August	v. Lancashire (Southampton) 12–16 August	v. Glamorgan (Swansea) 19–23 August	v. Sussex (Portsmouth) 26–30 August	v. Surrey (The Oval) 31 August–3 September	v. Leicestershire (Southampton) 6–13 September	v. Essex (Chelmsford) 16–20 September	M	Inns	NO	Runs	HS	Av
V.P. Terry	36, 10	57, 143*	174	11, 20	91	4	17, 87	19	33	2	1469	174	47.38
T.C. Middleton	7, 3	28, 0	32	—	—	—	41, 16	12	22	—	571	90	25.95
R.S.M. Morris	37	117	6	113	13	—	134, 25	8	14	1	372	92	26.57
D.I. Gower	4, 63	21, 36	31, 75*	35, 11*	95	8	48, 11	16	28	4	1136	153	42.07
M.C.J. Nicholas	12, 32	6, 11*	75*, 55	107*, 12	9, 10	4, 23	4, 15*	18	29	4	918	95	36.72
M.D. Marshall	74, 7	33*, 8	0	12, 79*	10	12	17, 5	18	16	11	250	75*	17.85
A.N. Aymes								19	29	2	709	107*	39.38
S.D. Udal			59		59			19	27	1	509	79*	20.36
I.J. Turner					—			4	5	1	17	8	4.25
C.A. Connor	131	0	12	4, 0	0, 63	7	0	10	11	5	200	59	20.00
K.J. Shine		38, 34	29	12, 98	127	5	6	13	14	2	54	12	6.00
R.A. Smith	22		48	14, 45	44	22	54	12	19	1	970	191	57.05
J.R. Ayling	5, 13	21	7, 7*	7				4	6	5	89	27*	17.80
K.D. James								17	29	4	694	71	27.76
M. Jean-Jacques							41	3	3	2	42	21*	42.00
R.J. Wood	8	8		5	0*, 63	1, 21	0, 19	1	1	—	25	25	25.00
R.J. Maru	4		21	4, 6	—	—	0*	—	—	—	—	—	—
D.P.J. Flint	0*	—	—	10		—	3*, 0*	10	13	5	47	14*	5.87
R.F.M. Cox	6, 1	5, 12	1, 1	4, 6	1, 38	5	3, 4	6	10	1	204	63	22.66
M.J. Thursfield		16, 1	1, 2	10, 3	2		4	2	4	2	36	36*	18.00
J.N.B. Bovill	4	10, 8	2, 7	4	38	8	12, 12	1	2	2	3	3*	—
Byes	6	5	1	5	1	—	3						
Leg-byes	1	12	2	10	4	11	4						
Wides	4	8	—	3	2	—	12						
No-balls	4	2	16	4	38	4	12						
Total	294	364	417	349	559	115	347 / 240						
Wickets	10 / 208	10	6 / 10	9 / 10	10	10	10 / 10 / 8						

BOWLING

Match (dates)	M.D. Marshall	C.A. Connor	K.J. Shine	I.J. Turner	S.D. Udal	M.C.J. Nicholas	M. Jean-Jacques	J.R. Ayling	K.D. James	T.C. Middleton	R.J. Maru	D.P.J. Flint	M.J. Thursfield	R.S.M. Morris	R.A. Smith	J.N.B. Bovill	Byes	Leg-byes	Wides	No-balls	Total	Wkts
v. Somerset (Southampton) 29 April–2 May	30-8-67-1	36-12-81-3	20-1-101-0	30-6-120-0	34-6-118-2	1-0-4-0											1	8		8	500	6
v. Oxford University (Oxford) 5–7 May			16-6-41-1	25-11-43-2	28-7-62-3		21-6-45-1	15-7-13-0	13-5-20-1								1	5	1	2	230	9
			5-0-26-0	10-3-29-1	15.5-2-64-2		6-0-16-1		6-0-27-0									4			166	8 Ab
v. Durham (Stockton) 13–17 May																						
v. Yorkshire (Southampton) 20–4 May	18-8-35-2	15-5-37-1	12-3-41-0		3-0-17-0			17-2-68-3	12.4-3-33-4								1	16		6	248	10
	10-1-44-1	7-3-34-0	2-0-30-0		6-1-37-2			5-0-38-0	4-0-36-1									1	1	22	224	4
v. Derbyshire (Derby) 27–31 May	17-2-69-1	5-0-25-0			36-14-78-2		24-5-117-2		24-2-90-1	0.2-0-4-0							2	8		12	389	7
v. Nottinghamshire (Nottingham) 3–7 June			8-1-38-0	28-11-67-2	32-7-68-1		1.3-0-3-0		14-2-51-2								3	1	1		288	10
			11-6-17-2	15.4-3-51-3					19-4-69-2								1	7			154	10
v. Kent (Basingstoke) 10–14 June	21.3-5-67-3	7-3-13-0	17-3-63-0	3-0-27-0	24-4-123-2													6	2		275	10
v. Northamptonshire (Northampton) 17–21 June	13-5-29-3	17-1-51-1	14-1-62-6		2-0-7-0			7-2-28-0	8-5-9-0								5	5	1	10	125	9 A
	30-12-53-2	16-0-55-0	21.4-5-74-2		17-3-94-2			4-2-4-0	19-8-40-3								17	17		4	303	10
v. Australians (Southampton) 26–8 June	33-10-81-0	19-3-77-4	16-2-81-1		30-7-98-1				17-2-57-3		15-1-62-1						15	15		8	393	7
	8-3-19-1		2.4-0-8-0		12-4-25-3				11.2-3-32-1		15-3-57-0						3	3		8	271	7
v. Gloucestershire (Bristol) 1–5 July	21-8-37-3	44.1-13-143-2	19-5-64-2		16-1-58-1				25-7-60-2			39-9-112-2						3		30	501	7
		8-1-26-1	4-0-11-0		29-8-72-2				11-4-21-0			13-3-32-5					4	7		8	102	10
v. Worcestershire (Portsmouth) 15–19 July	19-4-57-1	10-4-35-0	9-2-35-1		27.4-8-51-4				19-7-25-1			16-2-42-1						9	1	4	206	5
v. Middlesex (Lord's) 22–6 July	25-7-50-0	25.3-8-70-2	9-2-35-0		48.4-9-141-6				7-0-17-1			22-5-47-1	25-10-78-4				1	17		2	310	10
		2-1-6-0	21-2-104-2		47.5-8-131-5				7-4-13-0			3-0-16-0									59	1
v. Warwickshire (Southampton) 29 July–2 August	14-2-44-0		15-3-74-0		21-3-68-3				3-0-20-0			12-4-34-3	10-3-27-1	0.4-0-1-0			3	4	1	2	190	10
													8-0-38-0				2	16	2	2	392	10
v. Lancashire (Southampton) 12–16 August	6-2-10-0		25.5-3-97-6		38-9-109-2				8-2-32-0			41-8-131-4			1-0-2-0		9	9		22	386	10
			20-9-49-1		24.1-6-75-5				16.3-3-55-4			51-17-116-3						4		2	138	3
v. Glamorgan (Swansea) 19–23 August	23-8-62-5		10-1-48-0		41-12-102-2				24-6-67-3			19-9-34-2						7	1	18	288	3
v. Sussex (Portsmouth) 26–30 August	15-6-31-3		12-1-41-0		30-4-96-1				20-8-49-2			20-9-43-2					4	12	2	14	227	9 B
					36-13-56-1				13-2-47-2			17-4-74-2						18		18	439	7
v. Surrey (The Oval) 31 August–3 September	33-10-73-1	36-6-121-1	6-1-32-0		2-1-1-0				3.5-1-3-0			20-3-87-0					4	4	2	16	318	10
					21.1-4-77-4							23-0-73-3					3	10	1	18	380	8
v. Leicestershire (Southampton) 9–13 September		14-5-29-1			17-3-70-3				18-5-53-3			12-1-44-0					5	3	2	16	281	1
									4-0-16-0			38-16-64-4						2	1	18	85	10
v. Essex (Chelmsford) 16–20 September	9-1-31-1		12-1-41-0		21.1-4-77-4							22-3-57-0				13-5-32-2	2	6	1	6	268	10
			6-1-32-0		17-3-70-3							22.2-2-60-1				7-3-16-1	2	2	4		196	5
Bowler's average	345.3-102-859-28 30.67	261.4-65-803-16 50.18	296.1-57-1172-24 48.83	111.4-34-337-8 42.12	763.2-183-2232-74 30.16	1-0-4-0 –	52.3-11-181-4 45.25	48-13-151-3 50.33	327.2-83-942-36 26.16	0.2-0-4-0 –	30-4-119-1 119.00	390.2-95-1066-31 34.38	43-13-143-5 28.60	0.4-0-10-0 –	1-0-2-0 –	20-8-48-3 16.00						

A D.J. Capel retired hurt, absent hurt
B A.C.S. Pigott absent hurt

FIELDING FIGURES

61 – S.A. Marsh (ct 57/st 4)
22 – C.L. Hooper
14 – R.P. Davis
13 – N.J. Llong
12 – D.P. Fulton
11 – T.R. Ward
9 – D.W. Headley
8 – M.V. Fleming
7 – G.R. Cowdrey
6 – M.R. Benson
4 – J.J. Longley, M.J. McCague, R.J. Parks and N.R. Taylor
3 – M.A. Ealham and M.M. Patel
2 – S. Willis and C. Penn
1 – D.J. Spencer, R.M. Ellison and sub
†M.R. Benson absent hurt

KENT

D.W. Headley was previously with Middlesex, and R.J. Parks with Hampshire.

D.J. Spencer, fast bowler, and S. Willis, wicket-keeper, made their first-class debuts.

N.J. Llong hit the first centuries of his first-class career.

C.L. Hooper made the highest score of his career in the final match of the season.

M.M. Patel returned the best bowling figures of his career in the match against Lancashire.

KENT CCC — BATTING (season aggregate)

Player	M	Inns	NO	Runs	HS	Av
T.R. Ward	19	30	1	903	141	31.13
J.J. Longley	2	3	–	52	47	17.33
N.R. Taylor	16	26	2	679	86	28.29
G.R. Cowdrey	12	21	–	478	139	22.76
N.J. Llong	18	27	5	943	116*	42.86
M.V. Fleming	18	28	4	826	100	34.41
S.A. Marsh	19	27	2	667	111	26.68
D.W. Headley	14	20	7	281	36	21.61
R.P. Davis	14	16	2	164	42	11.71
C. Penn	4	7	3	63	23	15.75
A.P. Igglesden	13	13	7	32	10	5.33
M.R. Benson	15	23	2	913	107	43.47
M.J. McCague	16	9	4	49	22*	9.80
C.L. Hooper	16	24	2	1304	236*	59.27
R.M. Ellison	3	7	4	92	68	30.66
M.A. Ealham	12	16	3	666	85	51.23
M.M. Patel	7	7	4	14	14	4.66
R.J. Parks	2	2	2	13	13*	–
D.J. Spencer	7	4	2	79	75	39.50
D.P. Fulton	7	13	1	307	75	25.58
S. Willis	1	1	1	0	0*	–

The batting details are recorded match-by-match against, in the first part of the season: Cambridge University (Cambridge) 21–3 April; Middlesex (Lord's) 6–10 May; Warwickshire (Canterbury) 13–17 May; Nottinghamshire (Nottingham) 20–4 May; Durham (Darlington) 27–31 May; Gloucestershire (Tunbridge Wells) 3–7 June; Hampshire (Basingstoke) 10–14 June; Derbyshire (Canterbury) 17–21 June; Yorkshire (Leeds) 24–8 June; Essex (Maidstone) 1–5 July; Sussex (Arundel) 15–19 July; Somerset (Taunton) 22–6 July.

And in the second part of the season: Leicestershire (Canterbury) 29 July–2 August; Surrey (Canterbury) 5–9 August; Australians (Canterbury) 11–13 August; Worcestershire (Worcester) 19–23 August; Lancashire (Lytham) 26–30 August; Northamptonshire (Canterbury) 31 August–3 September; Zimbabwe (Canterbury) 11–13 September; Glamorgan (Canterbury) 16–20 September.

BOWLING

	A.P. Igglesden	C. Penn	M.V. Fleming	D.W. Headley	R.P. Davis	N.J. Llong	M.J. McCague	C.L. Hooper	R.M. Ellison	M.A. Ealham	M.M. Patel	D.J. Spencer	Byes	Leg-byes	Wides	No-balls	Total	Wks
v. Cambridge University (Cambridge) 21–3 April	10-1-27-1	12-7-12-4	11-6-12-1	14-5-28-1	11-4-28-1	6-1-27-0							5	3			142	10
	13.5-5-14-2	13-3-21-0	5-2-7-0	4-0-17-0	24-11-26-5	23-10-29-3								10			124	10
v. Middlesex (Lord's) 6–10 May	29-7-81-5	24-9-45-2	15-3-45-0	22-8-50-1	28-8-67-2	5-0-8-0		18.2-2-49-2					7	3	1	14	311	10
	19-6-48-1	16-4-28-0	6-2-9-0		19-1-63-2	2-0-6-0		9-2-19-1					3	5		6	231	5
v. Warwickshire (Canterbury) 13–17 May	23-6-43-1		19-3-35-0	25-4-59-2	32-9-54-3		22-7-62-0	37-4-116-2						9		2	305	10
	20-8-35-2		20.2-5-44-3	16.2-4-32-2	28-10-71-3		25-7-65-2							2	5	2	213	10
v. Nottinghamshire (Nottingham) 20–4 May	14-4-49-3		5-0-15-0	10-4-20-0	40-8-127-7	3-1-4-0	25-5-62-3		10-4-30-2				6	12	1		232	9
	9-1-29-0		2-0-4-0	21-10-32-1		1-0-8-0	14.1-3-43-2		3-1-15-0				6	13	5	2	330	10
v. Durham (Darlington) 27–31 May	24-4-67-4		8-5-7-1	8-3-20-0	17-8-17-0		18-6-33-5	11.5-4-8-1		28-12-58-1				20	1		160	9
			5-3-3-1	39-11-79-7	23-8-47-1		3.1-0-9-0	21-9-27-2		6-2-12-0				12	1		135	10
v. Gloucestershire (Tunbridge Wells) 3–7 June	16-6-26-4		28.5-9-60-1	6-0-21-0	16-5-43-2	3-1-4-0	11.2-4-15-3	22-6-37-0	18-8-27-0		1-0-4-0		3	9	1	6	243	10
	19-4-51-4		11-2-31-4											5	3	2	162	10
v. Hampshire (Basingstoke) 10–14 June		22-9-32-1	28-8-82-3										4	3	2	2	232	6
v. Derbyshire (Canterbury) 17–21 June	25-5-66-5		6-0-27-0	23-8-43-1	9-3-14-1		13.4-3-34-5	2-0-4-0		9-1-30-1			10	4			135	10
	14-1-31-2		11-3-28-2	28-5-95-0	3.4-0-21-1		19.4-3-87-2	5-2-12-0		7-3-28-0			4	5	1	8	229	10
v. Yorkshire (Leeds) 24–8 June			7-1-19-0	22-3-61-3	53-18-94-1		25-6-46-1	4-2-7-1						7	5		209	10
			18-1-68-1	22-5-75-3	21-4-69-0		16.5-1-74-0	13.1-1-29-1					7	17	2	4	410	6
v. Essex (Maidstone) 1–5 July	23.4-11-41-2		21.2-4-63-3		14-1-51-2	1-0-8-0		25-3-81-1		24-5-76-2		17-2-62-0		13		22	440	9
	4-0-17-0		9-1-36-1		1-0-1-0	2-0-11-0		17-4-48-2		13-0-56-0		7-1-32-0		11		6	311	9
v. Sussex (Arundel) 15–19 July			15-7-32-3	21.2-3-70-5	12-5-8-1		21-6-55-4	10-2-21-1					7	1	2		168	10
				8-1-34-0			4-2-9-0	13-4-24-0		15-1-49-3				1			59	1
v. Somerset (Taunton) 22–6 July			5-1-9-0			5.2-3-6-1		22-3-51-0		3-0-26-0			4	4		2	211	10
								14-8-17-1		19-5-40-4			4	1		8	135	3
v. Leicestershire (Canterbury) 29 July–2 August			27.4-4-74-3	26-2-68-3	13-6-27-2			14-3-36-0		24-8-60-1			4	4		4	249	10
			26-7-48-3	12-3-31-1	15-3-44-1			34.4-13-55-4		30-3-100-4			4	5	1	4	266	10
v. Surrey (Canterbury) 5–9 August		43-7-121-4	34-8-81-0		11-2-29-0	5-1-18-0		33-7-73-2		5-0-33-0	19-3-63-0		4	10			464	10
	22-4-59-1	12-0-37-1	6-1-8-0		17-4-45-0	3-0-12-0		31-6-106-1		25-1-103-1	31-7-108-1		4	9		10	305	3
v. Australians (Canterbury) 11–13 August											4-1-10-0		4	3		8	391	4
														2			34	0
v. Worcestershire (Worcester) 19–23 August	32-10-67-1		41.5-10-128-2	35-6-108-2	35-12-96-0	6-1-19-0		37-6-117-1	30-6-97-2	27-4-103-1			4	22	1	14	568	7
v. Lancashire (Lytham) 26–30 August	19-5-58-2			17-4-54-1	5-0-22-0	1-0-4-0		45-13-93-2			52-15-107-5		6	10		2	328	10
	7-0-27-1		15-5-46-1	6-0-22-1				30-6-74-1			30-9-75-7						203	10
v. Northamptonshire (Canterbury) 31 August–3 September	29-7-69-1			7-2-25-1				40-13-89-2		25.4-6-66-5	27-11-44-0		5	12		6	331	10
	14-5-33-1							17-2-35-4		4-1-16-0	14.5-4-31-1					6	140	7
v. Zimbabwe (Canterbury) 11–13 September			2-0-10-0	8-2-15-0								7-4-20-0	4	4			53	1
			3-1-14-1	8-5-6-0						5.4-3-14-5		11-1-46-4		3			83	10
v. Glamorgan (Canterbury) 16–20 September	9-2-27-2		10-1-41-0	15-6-29-3				6-0-26-1		9-1-31-3	3-0-15-1		4	1	1		144	9
	12.2-3-45-3			15-2-97-4						2-0-16-0	8-1-43-2		6	6		2	239	10
Bowler's average	438.5-111-1068-54 19.77	142-39-296-12 24.66	422-103-1086-34 31.94	439.4-106-1191-42 28.35	479.4-141-1118-36 31.05	62.2-17-152-4 38.00	218.4-54-594-27 22.00	545-126-1281-33 38.81	61-19-169-4 42.25	281.2-56-917-31 29.58	199.5-33-533-17 31.35	42-8-160-4 40.00						

FIELDING FIGURES

58 – W.K. Hegg (ct 49/st 9)
15 – P.A.J. DeFreitas
13 – M.A. Atherton
12 – G.D. Lloyd
11 – N.J. Speak
10 – N.H. Fairbrother
9 – M. Watkinson
5 – G.D. Mendis and sub
5 – J.P. Crawley and A.A. Barnett
3 – Wasim Akram and G. Yates
2 – P.J. Martin
1 – S.P. Titchard and R.C. Irani

LANCASHIRE

G. Chapple hit a maiden first-class century which was the fastest in the history of the game.

G. Yates hit the highest score of his career.

Wasim Akram finished top of the first-class bowling averages of those that bowled regularly.

G.D. Mendis, who had a benefit in 1993, was not retained for 1994. S.D. Fletcher also left the staff.

D. P. Hughes resigned as manager, and D. Lloyd was appointed coach.

M. Watkinson completed the 'double' of 1,000 runs and 50 wickets.

LANCASHIRE CCC — BATTING

	M	Inns	NO	Runs	HS	Av
G.D. Mendis	18	34	—	1099	106	32.32
M.A. Atherton	13	20	1	811	137	42.68
N.J. Speak	21	35	2	1185	122	35.90
N.H. Fairbrother	18	31	4	901	110	33.37
G.D. Lloyd	17	29	2	994	116	36.81
W.K. Hegg	21	34	9	566	69*	22.64
M. Watkinson	19	30	4	1016	107	39.07
I.D. Austin	2	3	—	31	20	10.33
A.A. Barnett	9	23	7	157	38	9.81
P.A.J. DeFreitas	20	29	3	453	51	17.42
P.J. Martin	16	21	7	399	43	28.50
G. Chapple	8	13	7	256	109*	42.66
Wasim Akram	13	21	1	516	117	24.57
S.D. Fletcher	1	—	—	—	—	—
S.P. Titchard	5	10	1	237	87	23.70
G. Yates	7	5	—	367	134*	91.75
J.P. Crawley	10	17	6	631	109	37.11
J.E.R. Gallian	1	2	1	42	42*	42.00
R.C. Irani	2	4	—	44	44	11.00

Individual match scorecards (two-innings matches, April–July and July–September) accompany the above averages. Match totals, wickets, results and points are recorded beneath each match column.

BOWLING

Lancashire — first-class bowling, 1993

BOWLING	P.A.J. Defreitas	P.J. Martin	M. Watkinson	I.D. Austin	A.A. Barnett	M.A. Atherton	G. Chapple	Wasim Akram	C. Yates	J.E.R. Gallian	R.C. Irani	Byes	Leg-byes	Wides	No-balls	Total	Wks
v. Oxford University (Oxford) 17–20 April	19-3-57-2	17-7-42-4	17.4-5-29-2	4-1-18-0	12-2-31-0							11	6	5	6	194	9
	6-1-21-0	5-1-11-0	16-2-43-0	8-1-36-0	19-4-40-2							4	1	1	8	164	3
v. Yorkshire (Leeds) 29 April–3 May	18-6-49-2	18-8-35-0	33-8-89-3		40-12-83-5		16-4-47-0					3	13		2	319	10
v. Durham (Manchester) 6–10 May	19-3-52-3	20-8-35-5	24-3-72-1		30-12-63-0		12-5-15-1					2	19		12	258	10
v. Somerset (Taunton) 13–17 May	34-3-118-1	29-9-83-2	40-12-125-3		37-9-65-0		29-6-97-3					13	14		32	515	9
	11-4-18-0	4-1-13-0	10.1-5-12-5		19-7-36-5		2-2-0-0					4		2		83	10
v. Cambridge University (Cambridge) 19–21 May			4-1-13-0		8-3-17-0	5-0-8-1						1	8		10		Ab.
v. Warwickshire (Liverpool) 29 May–1 June	17.3-4-76-7	11-1-35-1						15-1-45-2				2	6		4	170	10
	17-2-55-5	1.2-0-15-1						18-5-42-4					5		20	260	10
v. Surrey (The Oval) 3–7 June	10-2-21-1	7-3-12-0	27-6-82-3		27.4-9-48-3		15.4-5-50-3	24-8-65-3				12	5		2	302	10
		24-7-63-4	24-7-54-1		10-3-23-0		14-6-40-0	28-10-49-6					5		30	304	6
v. Essex (Manchester) 10–14 June	16-0-75-1	18-4-54-0	21-4-58-1		30.4-7-84-3			15-2-46-0					10	1		403	10
		15-3-61-1	6.3-1-34-1		26-6-78-3							9	12		28	202	10
v. Sussex (Manchester) 17–21 June	23-8-67-0	18-7-41-0	37-7-75-2		34-6-111-0			27.1-8-55-4	40-8-108-5				10		12	426	10
	16-4-27-0	6-1-10-2			37.5-13-65-5				27-6-90-3			8	8		18	267	10
v. Derbyshire (Derby) 24–8 June	23-3-109-5	20.3-1-64-2			39-14-79-0		25.3-0-101-2	17-4-83-0				4	4	2	18	455	10
	15-2-49-0	6-0-34-0			41-11-98-3			18.1-5-45-6				17	3	3	8	303	5
v. Leicestershire (Leicester) 1–5 July	30-6-70-2		48-18-119-3		21-2-76-0			24-6-47-0				4	11		2	244	3
					14-2-57-1							9	6		2	560	10
v. Glamorgan (Manchester) 15–19 July	17-6-31-1		25-2-97-3				7-1-22-0		17-2-62-1			24	10	1	10	282	3
	16.1-2-66-2		12-0-54-0				1-0-13-0		9-0-39-0						4	194	8
v. Nottinghamshire (Manchester) 22–6 July	25-4-81-1	32-6-105-3	40-10-117-4		45-13-140-0		20.5-4-83-2						1			450	10
v. Gloucestershire (Cheltenham) 28–30 July	17-2-41-0	20-5-63-2	14-1-68-0	18-4-66-1	20-1-87-1							4	11	2	30	58	1
	14-4-46-2	12-2-36-1	8-1-28-1	1.2-0-13-0	24-5-83-4								3	1	4	364	10
v. Australians (Manchester) 5–9 August	33.3-7-104-5	21-1-75-0			29-4-98-2			32-6-92-2		9-0-22-0		5	12		10	258	6
	5-0-24-0	5-1-12-1						2-0-6-0				16	8		2	242	10
v. Hampshire (Southampton) 12–16 August	24-7-49-2	25-8-65-2	40.3-11-104-4		23-5-95-2		7-1-17-0	23-4-68-8	14-2-34-0			4	7	1	18	258	10
	16-2-50-4	23-2-74-1	19-4-74-1				5-0-22-0	29.4-8-57-4	15-3-36-0			1	3		8	263	8
v. Yorkshire (Manchester) 19–23 August	20-7-76-0	4-1-10-0			19-4-74-1			21.4-4-69-5	4-2-11-0		1-0-6-0	5	3		18	427	10
	22-4-55-3	20-6-71-1						21-5-55-3	37-5-108-2			4	1		10	332	10
v. Kent (Lytham) 26–30 August	23-7-46-1	31-7-89-2	18-3-40-2		24-8-54-3			28-4-80-2	14-5-40-0			8	6	3	18	329	9
	16-2-57-0	30-4-127-2	19-4-75-0					19.4-4-83-3	12-2-42-3			6	11	1	12	328	7
v. Worcestershire (Worcester) 31 August–3 September	18.3-4-48-4	30-9-82-3							14-5-40-0			3	6	7	18	240	10
	15-1-73-1	13-1-51-0							30-5-86-1								
v. Middlesex (Lord's) 9–13 September	24-5-74-1	17-3-49-2	24-8-54-3		16.2-2-63-2			18-5-56-0									
v. Northamptonshire (Manchester) 16–20 September	14-5-39-2	16-1-42-0	16-1-42-0		17.3-3-83-0			17-3-63-5	12-6-27-1			2	6		24	161	2
	10-4-21-0	8-2-10-0	8-2-10-0					11-1-31-2	2-0-9-0				5		2		
Bowler's average	604.4-124-1845-58 **31.81**	406.5-105-1188-38 **31.26**	662.5-146-1950-51 **38.23**	31.2-2-133-1 **133.00**	713-177-2005-47 **42.65**	5-0-8-1 **8.00**	155-34-507-11 **46.09**	409.2-93-1137-59 **19.27**	233-46-692-16 **43.25**	9-0-22-0 **—**	1-0-6-0 **—**						

FIELDING FIGURES

47 – P.A. Nixon (ct 41/st 6)
21 – P.E. Robinson
14 – W.K.M. Benjamin
13 – J.D.R. Benson
11 – V.J. Wells
10 – L. Potter and G.J. Parsons
9 – J.J. Whitaker
8 – T.J. Boon
5 – D.J. Millns
4 – A.D. Mullally
3 – A.R.K. Pierson
2 – N.E. Briers, B.F. Smith and P.N. Hepworth

LEICESTERSHIRE

J.M. Dakin and M.T. Brimson made their first-class debuts.

N.E. Briers was unable to play after being injured in the match at Lord's and J.J. Whitaker took over the captaincy.

V.J. Wells hit his maiden first-class hundred.

L. Potter announced his retirement at the end of the season.

W.K.M. Benjamin was not re-engaged as the county's overseas player. P.V. Simmons, the West Indian all-rounder, will replace him.

G.J. Parsons was named as the county's player of the year.

Veteran administrator Mike Turner announced his retirement.

LEICESTERSHIRE CCC — BATTING

Season averages

Player	M	Inns	NO	Runs	HS	Av
T.J. Boon	18	29	1	921	110	32.89
N.E. Briers	12	19	1	487	79	27.05
A.R.K. Pierson	18	23	6	238	58	14.00
J.J. Whitaker	18	28	3	925	126	34.25
P.E. Robinson	11	29	3	526	71	20.23
B.F. Smith	12	18	2	263	84	14.61
L. Potter	15	17	2	404	103*	26.93
V.J. Wells	19	23	2	602	167	28.66
P.A. Nixon	18	28	6	501	113*	22.77
G.J. Parsons	17	20	4	405	59	25.31
J.D.R. Benson	8	13	1	132	26	8.25
A.D. Mullally	6	7	–	243	153	34.71
P.N. Hepworth	8	13	1	328	129	27.33
J.M. Dakin	9	–	–	5	5	5.00
W.K.M. Benjamin	7	13	–	294	83	22.61
D.J. Millns	7	8	3	59	24	11.80
M.T. Brimson	2	1	1	0	0	0.00

Match list (first half)

- v. Surrey (Leicester) 29 April–2 May
- v. Nottinghamshire (Leicester) 6–10 May
- v. Cambridge University (Cambridge) 15–17 May
- v. Sussex (Horsham) 20–4 May
- v. Australians (Leicester) 29–31 May
- v. Durham (Leicester) 3–7 June
- v. Worcestershire (Worcester) 10–14 June
- v. Gloucestershire (Leicester) 24–8 June
- v. Lancashire (Leicester) 1–5 July
- v. Essex (Southend) 15–19 July
- v. Warwickshire (Leicester) 22–6 July
- v. Kent (Canterbury) 29 July–2 August

Match list (second half)

- v. Middlesex (Lord's) 5–9 August
- v. Glamorgan (Leicester) 12–16 August
- v. Somerset (Weston-super-Mare) 19–23 August
- v. Northamptonshire (Northampton) 26–30 August
- v. Yorkshire (Leicester) 31 August–3 September
- v. Hampshire (Southampton) 6–13 September
- v. Derbyshire (Leicester) 16–20 September

BOWLING

Opponent (venue) / date	A.D. Mullally	G.J. Parsons	V.J. Wells	A.R.K. Pierson	L. Potter	B.F. Smith	J.M. Dakin	P.N. Hepworth	P.E. Robinson	W.K.M. Benjamin	D.J. Millns	M.T. Brimson	T.J. Boon	Byes	Leg-byes	Wides	No-balls	Total	Wks
v. Surrey (Leicester) 29 April–2 May	25-8-70-2	12.2-4-37-2	13-5-19-0	32-7-57-4	26-10-60-2									2	11		6	245	10
	24-10-49-1	10-4-22-0	7-2-25-0	50-15-124-5	46-17-79-3									5	7	1	6	315	10
v. Nottinghamshire (Leicester) 6–10 May	24-5-65-2	24-7-61-3	7-2-32-0	25-9-60-0	32-17-45-5									10	8	1	6	280	10
v. Cambridge University (Cambridge) 15–17 May	6-1-8-0	9-3-17-0		22-4-61-1	11.4-4-17-2	2-0-3-0	22-9-45-4	9-1-26-1	1-0-13-1					7	5	1		143	4
	13-6-28-1	11-6-23-2	7-2-12-1	17-5-38-1	18-3-34-0	7-2-22-0	12-1-39-0							1	8	1	4	179	10
v. Sussex (Horsham) 20–4 May	16-7-42-1	10-2-36-2	16-4-52-2	16-2-49-2	14-3-34-0					20-10-46-3					15	4	2	256	6
	22-6-71-3													4	3			271	10
v. Australians (Leicester) 29–31 May	26-5-65-1	28-6-64-0	25-7-70-2	23-6-82-0				5-0-33-0						6	3	8	4	323	3
	18.4-10-25-3	9-3-12-1	5-0-28-1	7.5-0-45-2											3			88	4
v. Durham (Leicester) 3–7 June		16-6-29-1	7-2-25-1		23-7-46-4					19-13-24-1					4	1	2	160	9 A
	16-7-45-2	10-2-30-3	15-5-32-0		20-7-53-2					13-0-50-2				5	3		2	206	10
v. Worcestershire (Worcester) 10–14 June	24-6-73-0	14-5-27-1	9-4-25-0							28-11-67-5					10	10	2	207	6
v. Gloucestershire (Leicester) 24–8 June	23.4-6-72-7	20-5-59-3		6-0-21-0	10-4-32-0					16-1-49-0				10	12	2	2	245	10
	31-6-98-3	30.4-9-72-1		50-18-72-5	29-11-52-1					26-6-58-0				4	14	2	2	326	10
v. Lancashire (Leicester) 1–5 July	14-2-58-0	14-2-58-0		11-5-12-1						23.3-3-83-7				4	5			204	10
	5-4-14-0	10-2-33-2		19.3-3-87-6	21-10-35-2					5-3-10-0				1	10		2	193	10
v. Essex (Southend) 15–19 July	24-7-62-4	20-6-56-2		1.5-0-11-1	15-4-36-0					21-5-58-3				2	3	5	2	233	10
	9-2-38-0	8-2-18-2		22.4-4-78-5	5-2-17-0					22-3-54-3				6	3		2	210	10
v. Warwickshire (Leicester) 22–6 July	21-6-64-3	18-9-29-1		29-6-86-3	16.4-5-31-1					20-5-60-1				11	8	1	20	284	10
	1.4-0-5-0									2-1-4-1				11	2			11	1
v. Kent (Canterbury) 29 July–2 August	29.2-6-80-3	18-6-43-1	13-0-43-1	16-3-41-0	7-3-19-0					22-8-46-5					8	8	18	291	10
	14-1-56-2	19-9-20-2	6-1-16-1	18-6-55-1	7.4-1-18-0					22-6-45-1					4	10	10	225	7
v. Middlesex (Lord's) 5–9 August		32-6-79-1	26.4-5-113-1	27-5-82-1	30-4-111-1					22-6-48-0	26-6-108-1			1	10		2	551	5
v. Glamorgan (Leicester) 12–16 August	12-4-43-2	27-4-74-1	12-3-39-2	16-3-55-0		4-2-5-0		7-1-17-1			24-5-92-2	20-3-66-2		1	7	1	4	351	8
v. Somerset (Weston-super-Mare) 19–23 August		11.2-7-23-3	5-3-5-2	11-6-10-0							15-7-33-3			4	4	1	12	112	10
	20.4-5-63-4	11-4-17-1	7-5-7-0								25-9-78-5			17	1	1		193	10
v. Northamptonshire (Northampton) 26–30 August	29.2-5-111-4	31-11-62-2	26-4-70-1	33-8-94-2				2-0-14-0			27-4-104-1			3	9	1	10	467	10
v. Yorkshire (Leicester) 31 August–3 September	26-5-67-5	18.4-4-44-1	5-3-10-0	13-3-25-2				1-0-1-0			17-3-54-2				1		2	202	10
v. Hampshire (Southampton) 9–13 September	21.5-8-41-4	17-3-34-1		25-10-38-1							18-7-37-4				3	2		153	10
	12-4-31-2	13.1-8-13-1	14-4-36-2	4-0-14-0							16-8-21-5					2	4	115	4
v. Derbyshire (Leicester) 16–20 September	19-3-62-3	14-2-35-3	9-4-24-1	8-1-20-1				6-1-23-0	13.3-1-78-1		16.3-2-57-2			2	13	3	2	213	10
			7-2-22-0	10-7-8-0									8-1-38-0		1	2	4	175	1
Bowler's average	528.1-141-1506-62 24.29	490.1-151-1111-45 24.68	241.4-66-705-18 39.16	528.5-141-1371-44 31.15	352.1-118-758-24 31.58	13-4-30-0 –	34-10-84-4 21.00	30-3-114-2 57.00	14.3-1-91-1 91.00	281.3-81-702-32 21.93	184.3-51-584-25 23.36	20-3-66-2 33.00	8-1-38-0 –						

A W. Larkins retired hurt

FIELDING FIGURES

44 – K.R. Brown (ct 38/st 6)
35 – J.D. Carr
18 – J.E. Emburey
17 – M.R. Ramprakash
13 – M.W. Gatting
12 – M.A. Roseberry
8 – D.L. Haynes
6 – A.C.R. Fraser and P.C.R. Tufnell
5 – M. Keech
4 – M.A. Feltham
3 – N.F. Williams and sub
2 – R.J. Sims and K.P. Dutch
1 – N.G. Cowans

MIDDLESEX

Middlesex won the county championship for the 10th time. They did not suffer a defeat until the last game of the season.

K.P. Dutch made his debut in first-class cricket.

M.A. Feltham was previously with Surrey.

J.D. Carr and M.A. Roseberry made their highest scores in first-class cricket.

A.R.C. Fraser returned his best bowling figures, 7 for 40 against Leicestershire.

The success of Middlesex was due to balanced teamwork, but the all-round cricket of J.E. Emburey should be noted. He took 68 wickets at 18.39 runs each, scored 638 runs, at an average of 49.07 which was bettered only by Gatting, and held 18 catches.

MIDDLESEX CCC — BATTING

Batting averages

Player	M	Inns	NO	Runs	HS	Av
M. Keech	5	10	1	164	35	18.22
M.A. Roseberry	15	24	4	679	185	33.95
M.W. Gatting	14	20	4	1041	182	65.06
M.R. Ramprakash	16	22	1	813	140	38.71
J.D. Carr	17	24	6	848	192*	47.11
K.R. Brown	18	24	6	725	88*	40.27
M.A. Feltham	16	19	4	288	73	19.20
J.E. Emburey	16	15	2	638	123	49.07
A.R.C. Fraser	17	15	2	121	29	9.30
C.W. Taylor	2	3	1	28	28*	14.00
P.C.R. Tufnell	18	14	4	125	30*	12.50
J.C. Pooley	2	3	—	89	49	29.66
N.F. Williams	16	12	1	146	44	13.27
D.L. Haynes	14	24	4	793	115	39.65
R.J. Sims	3	3	1	28	28	14.00
P.N. Weekes	4	5	1	148	47	37.00
N.G. Cowans	6	6	2	23	14	5.75
K.P. Dutch	1	2	—	8	8	—
R.L. Johnson	1	2	—	8	4	4.00

Match results summary

Match	Totals	Result	Points
v. Gloucestershire (Bristol) 29 April–2 May	180 & 216	W	20
v. Kent (Lord's) 6–10 May	311 & 231	D	7
v. Nottinghamshire (Lord's) 13–17 May	281 & 266	W	23
v. Oxford University (Oxford) 19–21 May	236 & 31	D	—
v. Sussex (Lord's) 27–31 May	339	W	23
v. Derbyshire (Lord's) 3–7 June	193 & 68	W	23
v. Durham (Gateshead) 10–14 June	—	D	4
v. Somerset (Bath) 17–21 June	301 & 258	W	22
v. Surrey (Lord's) 24–8 June	330 & 219	W	23
v. Glamorgan (Cardiff) 1–5 July	584	W	20
v. Warwickshire (Birmingham) 15–19 July	387 & 60	W	23
v. Hampshire (Lord's) 22–6 July	310 & 59	W	23
v. Leicestershire (Lord's) 5–9 August	551	W	24
v. Yorkshire (Scarborough) 12–16 August	439	D	8
v. Northamptonshire (Lord's) 19–23 August	402	W	23
v. Essex (Colchester) 26–30 August	167 & 135	W	—
v. Lancashire (Lord's) 9–13 September	328	D	3
v. Worcestershire (Worcester) 16–20 September	68 & 148	L	6

BOWLING

Bowling figures are given as overs–maidens–runs–wickets. Two figures in a cell are the two innings. (Extras and opposition totals are read in innings order.)

Match	A.R.C. Fraser	C.W. Taylor	J.E. Emburey	M.A. Feltham	M. Keech	P.C.R. Tufnell	N.F. Williams	N.G. Cowans	P.N. Weekes	M.W. Gatting	J.D. Carr	D.L. Haynes	M.R. Ramprakash	K.P. Dutch	R.L. Johnson	B	l-b	w	n-b	Total	Wkts
v. Gloucestershire (Bristol) 29 April–2 May	30-10-76-4 / 10-2-30-1	30-7-93-1	10-4-9-0 / 13.2-6-15-4	34.4-13-68-3	16-7-28-2	10-6-15-0										3 / 2	7 / 7	9	12 / 8	299 / 95	10 / 10
v. Kent (Lord's) 6–10 May	15-5-24-0 / 25-5-76-1		30-9-60-1	10-6-8-1 / 16-5-49-2	6-1-20-0	20-10-33-4										2 / 3	12 / 15		2 / 3	265 / 392	10 / 8
v. Nottinghamshire (Lord's) 13–17 May	23-8-52-2 / 13-5-15-1		32.5-5-110-2 / 26-5-83-3	17-1-73-1	6-1-9-0 / 3-1-5-0	26.4-9-64-4 / 15-2-65-0 / 40.4-9-77-5	21-4-53-3 / 18-2-54-0									1	9	1	6	266 / 37	10 / 6
v. Oxford University (Oxford) 19–21 May		7-2-16-0 / 11-2-25-1			2-1-4-0	28-3-87-2 / 1-1-0-0	13-2-33-3 / 9-1-40-0	4-1-12-1 / 8-0-20-0	1-0-1-0 / 20-1-55-2							4	13		3	177 / 6	1 / 6
v. Sussex (Lord's) 27–31 May	14-1-38-3 / 13-1-40-0		23-9-37-2 / 37-17-46-4			1-0-4-0 / 29.2-12-47-5	5-3-5-0 / 6-1-29-0	7-1-17-2 / 3-2-1-0								4	3 / 2		8 / 10	161 / 143	10 / 10
v. Derbyshire (Lord's) 3–7 June	5-0-13-0 / 16.3-3-39-3		6-2-5-1	13-1-48-4 / 3-2-2-0			19-2-61-6	6-0-35-1								3	9 / 2		2	168 / 89	10 / 10
v. Durham (Gateshead) 10–14 June	14-1-33-3 / 24-5-69-2		14-6-14-3 / 8-1-28-0	16.2-6-31-3 / 1-0-1-0			14-1-38-1 / 13.1-2-36-4			4-0-10-0						2 / 2	3 / 4	3	18	234 / 11	0 / 9 [A]
v. Somerset (Bath) 17–21 June	1.2-0-5-0 / 33-5-93-2		21-5-45-0 / 11-8-11-0	28-7-48-2	12-5-17-1 / 7-1-30-2	15-7-17-1	23-2-73-4		9-2-29-0 / 14-2-32-1		10.5-0-73-4	7-1-61-1				3 / 4	12 / 5	1 / 3	9	318 / 240	8 / 10
v. Surrey (Lord's) 24–8 June	4-0-18-0 / 24-5-94-0		26.2-12-48-3 / 34.1-14-50-2	10.2-2-41-2 / 6-2-20-1		23-7-54-2 / 21-7-39-2	28.1-4-71-4 / 3-1-7-0									4	4		34 / 10	322 / 225	10 / 10
v. Glamorgan (Cardiff) 1–5 July	14-3-41-1 / 33-3-127-0		35-5-102-0 / 23.2-6-52-1	27-4-117-1		45-8-114-1	17-2-76-2 / 21-4-73-4									6 / 4	4 / 13		23	562 / 109	10 / 10
v. Warwickshire (Birmingham) 15–19 July	3-2-2-0 / 16.4-5-42-3		39-12-68-3	10-3-20-0		23-8-29-8 / 34-5-71-4	26-5-85-1 / 3-0-16-0						3-1-6-0			4 / 6	4 / 7		10 / 18	206 / 237	10 / 10
v. Hampshire (Lord's) 22–6 July	5.2-1-13-1 / 20-4-42-1		48-15-61-6 / 39.5-13-75-4	17-7-46-1 / 3-1-3-0		45-10-92-2 / 16-7-29-2	15-6-25-0 / 5-1-16-0									6 / 2	12 / 6		14	280 / 88	9 [B] / 10
v. Leicestershire (Lord's) 5–9 August	2-1-2-0 / 17-4-40-7		28.2-9-40-8	7.2-1-24-3		28-11-42-2	26-6-80-2									2	2		18	114	9
v. Yorkshire (Scarborough) 12–16 August	21-6-56-1 / 17-8-25-4		9-2-23-1	20-4-78-1 / 15.3-40-3		27-8-57-2 / 16-5-27-3	10-1-48-0 / 16-2-54-1						3.4-0-22-1 / 2-0-11-0	5-1-18-0		4 / 6	6 / 5	1	16 / 26	253 / 256	10 / 10
v. Northamptonshire (Lord's) 19–23 August	16-5-49-4		18-6-34-3 / 37-10-51-3	15-3-30-1		24-14-30-0 / 33-7-70-2	33-6-94-1	15.5-2-43-3 / 9-1-37-2	6-2-15-0 / 5-0-19-0							4 / 6	6 / 5	1	28	184 / 232	10 / 10
v. Essex (Colchester) 26–30 August	16-8-19-4		21.3-8-38-4 / 11-2-25-1	8-3-21-0		14-3-56-3 / 8-3-12-0	14.4-3-35-0 / 4-2-5-0	13.1-4-43-4 / 15-5-26-3								8	10 / 9		10 / 9	180 / 148	10 / Ab.
v. Lancashire (Lord's) 9–13 September	14.1-7-27-3		23-8-36-3	3-1-13-0		21-9-39-1											6		6	153	10
v. Worcestershire (Worcester) 16–20 September	27-8-57-2		11-3-30-3	21-7-58-0		20.1-6-40-4									16-5-58-1		12	2	24	252	10
Bowler's average	487-121-1257-53 — 23.71	48-11-134-2 — 67.00	668.4-213-1251-68 — 18.39	327.3-88-905-29 — 31.20	52-17-113-5 — 22.60	584.5-177-1210-59 — 20.50	372-65-1131-39 — 29.00	81-16-234-16 — 14.62	55-7-151-3 — 50.33	4-0-10-0 — —	10.5-0-73-4 — 18.25	7-1-61-1 — 61.00	8.4-1-39-1 — 39.00	5-1-18-0 — —	16-5-58-1 — 58.00						

A 1. Fletcher retired hurt, absent hurt; A.N. Hayhurst absent ill
B N.E. Briers retired hurt

FIELDING FIGURES

56 – D. Ripley (ct 53/st 3)
18 – M.B. Loye
16 – N.A. Felton
15 – R.J. Bailey
13 – A.J. Lamb
12 – A. Fordham
6 – K.M. Curran
5 – A.L. Penberthy and J.P. Taylor
4 – subs
3 – N.G.B. Cook, C.E.L. Ambrose and R.J. Warren
2 – A.R. Roberts
1 – D.J. Capel, A. Walker and M.N. Bowen
†D.J. Capel retired hurt, absent hurt

NORTHAMPTONSHIRE

M.B. Loye made his maiden first-class century.

D.J. Capel sustained a broken arm in the match against Hampshire and was unable to play again during the season.

A.L. Penberthy returned the best bowling figures of his career in the match against Glamorgan.

W.M. Noon, wicket-keeper, has moved to Nottinghamshire. A. Walker has retired.

NORTHAMPTONSHIRE CCC — BATTING

BATTING	v. Warwickshire (Birmingham) 29 April–2 May	v. Gloucestershire (Northampton) 6–10 May	v. Oxford University (Oxford) 15–18 May	v. Glamorgan (Swansea) 20–4 May	v. Worcestershire (Northampton) 3–7 June	v. Sussex (Hove) 10–14 June	v. Hampshire (Northampton) 17–21 June	v. Somerset (Luton) 24–8 June	v. Nottinghamshire (Northampton) 1–5 July	v. Yorkshire (Harrogate) 15–19 July	v. Surrey (Northampton) 22–6 July	v. Essex (Northampton) 5–9 August	M	Inns	NO	Runs	HS	Av
A. Fordham	20 55	54 17	28	6 56*	193	4	3 109	0 7	4 19	23 9	18 87	160	17	29	1	1052	193	37.57
N.A. Felton	93 7	16 45	16	6 27	59 11		10 64	0 7	20 65	10 66	66 3	7	18	30	2	1026	109	36.64
R.J. Bailey	3 1	0 10*	91	47 12*	40 35*	200	59 4	22	63 39	0 68	15 86	14	18	30	5	1282	200	51.28
A.J. Lamb	13 3	8 14	46	45	6 18	60	6 0	172	21 12	16 25	15 88	52	18	28	3	1092	172	40.44
M.B. Loye	44 63	105 8	57* 20*	2	38* 54*	35	18* 0	28	10 58	1 48	16 42	21	18	28	3	956	153*	38.24
D.J. Capel	1 0	16 9*		23			0 71						5	8	2	102	54	17.00
K.M. Curran	7 0	16 53		23 54*	64	6 11*	0	91 14	19 68	0 10	54	36	16	23	4	612	91	32.21
A.L. Penberthy	2	9	62*	54* 11	38*	3*	18*	12	3* 43	10* 0*	2*	0	9	14	2	164	54*	13.66
D. Ripley	11* 2	2 9		14			9* 0		9* 6	0 7	2*	22	18	24	6	398	62*	22.11
J.P. Taylor	12*	1*	0 50*	11 1			1 0		14* 1	38* 7	2* 2*	4*	18	20	10	79	14*	7.90
N.G.B. Cook	8 18	11		1					13	8 11	10	0	8	9	1	50	18	6.25
A.R. Roberts			3				2 19	6*	25	19 1	15	21* 0	10	16	1	109	19*	7.26
A. Walker													1	1	—			
C.E.L. Ambrose									5 5	4 6	5 1	9	13	15	2	197	38	15.15
M.N. Bowen									1 5	6 16	1 2	28	5	6	1	72	23*	18.00
R.R. Montgomerie													1	1	—	35	35	35.00
Byes	6	5	1	5	3	12	5	11	5	4	2	9						
Leg-byes	17		4		13		17		5	6	2							
Wides	1	4	24	2	6	5	10		2	2	2	28						
No-balls	8	6	12	4	16	2	4	16	12	16	14	4						
Total	240 171	293 110	334 89	217 103	494 110	447	125 303	382	212 364	97 305	238 363	370 64						
Wickets	10 10	10 5	5 3	10 1	6 4	6	9† 9	10	10 10	10 10	10 10	10 2						
Result	L	W	D	D	W	D	L	W	W	L	W	W						
Points	5	22		5	23	4	4	24	21	4	21	24						

BATTING	v. Durham (Northampton) 12–16 August	v. Middlesex (Lord's) 19–23 August	v. Leicestershire (Northampton) 26–30 August	v. Kent (Canterbury) 31 August–3 September	v. Derbyshire (Derby) 9–13 September	v. Lancashire (Manchester) 16–20 September	M	Inns	NO	Runs	HS	Av
A. Fordham	30	4 0	21	39 27	71 15	0 6	17	29	1	1052	193	37.57
N.A. Felton	18	0 105	10 15	27 7	7	46 72*	18	30	2	1026	109	36.64
R.J. Bailey	70	95* 29	59	8 4	15 103	55 71*	18	30	5	1282	200	51.28
A.J. Lamb	80	41 35	162 7	21	38	67	18	28	3	1092	172	40.44
M.B. Loye	4	0 0	47	153*	15	0 23	18	28	3	956	153*	38.24
K.M. Curran	27	10 8*	6 0*	54 7*	58*	1*	16	23	4	612	91	32.21
A.L. Penberthy	0	16 3	5	0		10	9	14	2	164	54*	13.66
D. Ripley		19 16	10 22	11	37*	10 3	18	24	6	398	62*	22.11
J.P. Taylor	18			38 3		1	18	20	10	79	14*	7.90
N.G.B. Cook	23*			5		6	8	9	1	50	18	6.25
A.R. Roberts	35						10	16	1	109	19*	7.26
C.E.L. Ambrose							13	15	2	197	38	15.15
M.N. Bowen							5	6	1	72	23*	18.00
R.R. Montgomerie							1	1	—	35	35	35.00
Byes	13	8	3	5	8	6						
Leg-byes	8	10	9	12	3	2						
Wides	4	9	1	6		5						
No-balls	14	10	10	6	20	24						
Total	347	232 180	467	331 140	368	240 161						
Wickets	10	10 10	10	10 7	5	10 10						
Result	W	L	D	D	W	D						
Points	22	3	8	4	24	5						

BOWLING

Match	J.P. Taylor	K.M. Curran	D.J. Capel	A.L. Penberthy	N.G.B. Cook	R.J. Bailey	A.R. Roberts	A. Walker	C.E.L. Ambrose	M.B. Loye	M.N. Bowen	Byes	Leg-byes	Wides	No-balls	Total	Wks
v. Warwickshire (Birmingham) 29 April–2 May	32-10-82-2	35-10-64-4	25-6-66-2	22-7-50-1	21.5-7-50-1	4-2-13-0			18-5-47-1			1	19	2	8	345	10
	22-6-76-2	16-6-51-0	14-5-30-0		19-5-51-3	13-1-42-0			27-7-61-4				13	2	6	263	5
v. Gloucestershire (Northampton) 6–10 May	14-8-22-2	15-6-38-5	11.3-5-15-3		7-3-16-0		2-0-11-0		21-8-38-1			3	5			107	10
	32-9-61-3	27-8-71-3	32.1-13-56-3				21-9-45-0		35-5-84-2			2	2	1	2	295	10
v. Oxford University (Oxford) 15–18 May	19-10-27-3	14.2-2-45-3		10-4-23-1	6-3-7-0	1-1-0-0	20-7-33-2	20.5-6-62-3					4	1	2	180	6
	11-2-32-1	20-7-44-3		10-1-37-1	18-5-34-3		11.1-4-22-1	4-0-16-0					5			147	10
v. Glamorgan (Swansea) 20–4 May	9-1-33-1	12-0-60-2		10-1-37-5	5-0-17-0							5	13	3	8	165	10
	20-7-36-1	23-5-59-1		18-3-53-2	34-20-33-0							15	7	2	2	212	10
v. Worcestershire (Northampton) 3–7 June	17.4-4-64-4		15-4-44-3			17.4-7-50-4							11			231	10
	31-7-77-2		20-4-41-1										16	1	10	370	10
v. Sussex (Hove) 10–14 June																	Ab.
v. Hampshire (Northampton) 17–21 June	21-7-49-2	27-8-62-2		12-3-22-3	21-7-33-0	9-6-9-1			33.5-7-76-5	0.1-0-1-0		2	3		4	247	10
	10-2-32-0	9-2-31-0		12-2-49-1	19-5-57-0	17-8-30-0			19-7-28-2				5			182	3
v. Somerset (Luton) 24–8 June	13-5-38-2	8.4-1-32-3		6-2-28-1					17-5-64-2				7			161	10
	16-6-46-1	12-5-32-2		5-1-16-0		1-0-1-0	10-3-44-1					1	7	2		216	10
v. Nottinghamshire (Northampton) 1–5 July	11-4-44-2	10-3-27-0		13-3-34-1		5-3-5-0	3-1-2-0		19-6-36-4				5	1	8	172	10
	12-3-32-1	19-4-47-7		2-0-15-0		27.5-9-54-5	27-5-70-3		17-3-53-2			5	4		6	233	10
v. Yorkshire (Harrogate) 15–19 July	12-3-35-0	14-1-80-1				2-0-11-0			16-6-24-1		14-3-37-2	1	8		12	168	6
	12-2-52-1	10-3-34-0									13-1-82-3	9	17			238	10
v. Surrey (Northampton) 22–6 July	23-9-51-4	12-7-11-4		14-6-22-0		2-0-6-1	7-3-10-1		26.3-12-40-4			1	1			189	10
	19.4-7-45-5	25-8-58-1		8-4-13-0		1-0-8-0	2-0-7-0		19-11-22-1			1	1			108	10
v. Essex (Northampton) 5–9 August	23-2-82-3	6.5-1-22-3		21-5-96-2		2-0-8-0			22.2-7-35-4			2	7	2		286	10
	18-4-53-3	15.2-3-53-4		8-1-27-0					20-8-39-3			1	3			146	9 A
v. Durham (Northampton) 12–16 August	19-4-60-2	4-1-13-0				4-1-7-1			21-8-43-1		12-2-34-2	2	12		6	210	10
	12-4-18-2	30-8-82-4				1-1-0-0			12.3-4-24-4		14-4-32-3	1	13	2	8	89	0
v. Middlesex (Lord's) 19–23 August	27-8-69-2				20-3-65-0	10-1-34-0	23-4-69-1		30-9-69-3			1		1		402	10
	1-0-9-0															11	0
v. Leicestershire (Northampton) 26–30 August	18-6-57-1	16-6-35-3				19-7-32-0	24-6-51-3		23.5-3-60-1		17-3-57-2	8	7	1	2	307	10
	28-12-40-1	16-5-48-1				27-8-46-1	44-15-83-3		26-5-57-0		16-6-43-1	13	14	1		344	10
v. Kent (Canterbury) 31 August–3 September	26.4-8-80-1					30-6-108-3	28-5-108-1		27-8-55-1		29-4-124-4		3		10	479	8
	10-6-12-1					18-2-49-1	8.4-0-25-1		15-3-31-0		13-6-45-0	1	2			165	3
v. Derbyshire (Derby) 9–13 September	8-1-32-1	10.2-2-35-4							7.4-3-9-2		9-1-48-3		3		2	127	10
	12-2-51-2	7-2-38-0							18-4-49-6			3	5	1	2	195	10
v. Lancashire (Manchester) 16–20 September	18.5-4-82-6	6-0-17-0				11-3-25-0	23-10-56-0		25-4-86-4		10.5-0-52-2	4	7	2	2	277	10
	25-8-70-1	24-7-72-2				14-1-44-1	36-3-124-2		27-2-77-1			2	3	1	6	392	8
Bowler's average	612.5-181-1649-65 25.36	458-123-1293-67 19.29	117.4-37-252-12 21.00	171-43-522-18 29.00	199.5-68-412-8 51.50	244.3-69-612-18 34.00	289.5-75-760-19 40.00	24.5-6-78-3 26.00	543.4-150-1207-59 20.45	0.1-0-1-0 –	147.5-30-554-22 25.18						

A J.P. Stephenson retired hurt

FIELDING FIGURES

46 – B.N. French (ct 41/st 5)
26 – P.R. Pollard
12 – R.T. Robinson
9 – C.C. Lewis and K.P. Evans
8 – M.A. Crawley and C.L. Cairns
7 – P. Johnson
6 – D.W. Randall and J.A. Afford
5 – M. Saxelby, M.G. Field-Buss and G.F. Archer
4 – subs and R.A. Pick
3 – G.W. Mike
2 – R.T. Bates and W.A. Dessaur
1 – S. Bramhall
†M.G. Field-Buss absent hurt

NOTTINGHAMSHIRE

D.W. Randall retired from first-class cricket. He scored 28,456 runs and gave delight to thousands.
C.C. Lewis made the highest score of the season, 247 against Durham.
R.T. Bates made his first-class debut.
P.R. Pollard made the highest score of his career.
W.A. Dessaur hit his first championship century.
D.G. Pennett and M.G. Field-Buss returned the best bowling figures of their careers.

NOTTINGHAMSHIRE CCC BATTING

Season averages

Batsman	M	Inns	NO	Runs	HS	Av
D.W. Randall	5	10	3	280	98	28.00
P.R. Pollard	19	32	3	1463	180	50.44
R.T. Robinson	18	30	4	1152	139*	44.30
M.A. Crawley	10	18	1	306	81	19.12
C.L. Cairns	15	23	1	962	93	43.72
C.C. Lewis	13	20	2	653	247	36.27
G.W. Mike	8	13	1	240	50	20.00
B.N. French	17	24	3	420	123	20.00
R.A. Pick	13	12	6	109	22	13.62
M.G. Field-Buss	10	14	6	99	20*	12.37
J.A. Afford	14	17	8	50	11	5.55
G.F. Archer	6	7	2	208	59*	29.71
D.B. Pennett	7	4	2	11	10*	5.50
P. Johnson	16	27	1	1099	187	42.26
M. Saxelby	12	18	0	558	77	31.00
R.T. Bates	5	5	3	70	33*	35.00
K.P. Evans	10	14	4	231	56	23.10
S. Bramhall						
W.A. Dessaur	7	10	0	325	104	32.50
J.E. Hindson	2	1	1	1	1	1.00

BOWLING	C.C. Lewis	R.A. Pick	J.A. Afford	C.L. Cairns	G.W. Mike	M.G. Field-Buss	M.A. Crawley	D.B. Pennett	K.P. Evans	R.T. Bates	P.R. Pollard	G.F. Archer	W.A. Dessaur	J.E. Hindson	Byes	Leg-byes	Wides	No-balls	Total	Wkts
v. Worcestershire (Nottingham)	22–7–27–2	16–8–28–3	26–11–43–3	17–3–53–2	16–5–25–0	7–4–8–0									6	13	6	11	203	10
29 April–2 May	34–13–69–1		36–10–67–1	15–2–49–0	24–5–65–5	22–6–60–1	2–0–2–0								7	6	2		325	8
v. Leicestershire (Leicester)		18–5–44–0	29–13–44–2	21.2–3–50–3		13–6–20–1		25–10–42–2								19		10	219	10
6–10 May		12–3–42–1	22.3–8–53–3	14–3–32–2		16–7–28–3		14–2–39–1							1	8		4	203	10
v. Middlesex (Lord's)	23–13–37–1	17–6–55–1	14–4–25–1	22.3–4–68–5	20–5–56–1		9–2–32–1								4	4		4	281	10
13–17 May	19–1–42–0	12.2–1–53–3	22–8–59–4	22–3–76–2	4–0–19–0										4	13		8	266	9
v. Kent (Nottingham)		21–3–79–1	30.2–8–79–5	18–4–61–0	20–5–71–2	33–12–85–2									2	17	2	4	394	10
20–4 May			14.3–3–35–4	2–0–27–0		14–5–42–6												2	104	10
v. Oxford University (Oxford)	19.5–4–51–4	13–3–27–0					10–3–13–2		23–11–31–3	16–11–15–1					3	11		4	151	10
29 May–1 June	16–1–50–0	15–2–69–0					24.3–5–86–3			14–2–48–0					2	2	2		257	3
v. Hampshire (Nottingham)		18–5–51–1	41.3–15–78–3	28–6–77–2	11–0–57–0	36–13–66–4	3–0–8–0								10	8	1		355	10
3–7 June		18.3–4–37–2	41.1–14–92–1	12–2–26–0	4–1–17–1	23.3–10–51–2	2–0–12–0								4	17	1	6	256	9
v. Cambridge University (Cambridge) 12–14 June		6–0–18–0	2–2–0–0		5–2–10–0	2–1–1–0		6–1–14–1	4–1–6–1						1	1		2	51	2
v. Essex (Nottingham)		22–2–95–0	31–11–72–0	30.2–4–88–4		18–3–80–1			36–7–102–3						4	9	3	10	450	8
17–21 June		12–1–30–0	19–8–42–0	8–2–19–1		6–4–5–0			14–4–33–0		8–0–56–0	6.3–0–72–0			1	2			260	1
v. Glamorgan (Swansea)		19–2–63–1	36–11–92–1	23.3–6–66–4		20–5–46–1			22–6–48–3						5	9	2	2	329	10
24–8 June		15.2–2–71–0	25–4–86–0	14–2–58–1		33–0–82–3			9–0–43–0							12		2	352	5
v. Northamptonshire	18.1–2–58–4			14–1–58–3				9–2–42–1	16–4–44–1						5	5	1	2	212	10
(Northampton) 1–5 July	21–2–82–2		33–11–84–1	19.1–2–54–5				14–2–74–1	19–5–48–1						9	13	1	12	364	10
v. Somerset (Nottingham)	27–5–79–2	19.2–5–43–4	5–1–12–1	17–2–63–2					15–4–42–1						1	1	7	4	241	10
15–19 July	18–4–54–4	9–0–42–0	10–2–21–0	17–3–53–2					12–0–24–0							1		12	195	6
v. Lancashire (Manchester)	29–5–105–1		33–13–65–2	27–9–70–6		8–2–22–1			6–1–23–0						9	1		18	295	10
22–6 July	6–3–11–0		38–10–84–4	11–2–18–3		38–18–105–3			7–2–23–0						14	7	2	10	262	10
v. Surrey (The Oval)	18–5–36–1		29.5–8–64–5	11–2–44–0		9–7–14–0			17–4–51–4						9	10		4	228	10
29 July–2 August	12–3–34–4		22–5–51–2	5–0–11–1		9–1–33–0			2–1–5–0						4	9		2	147	7
v. Yorkshire (Nottingham)	31–9–69–2		50–18–94–2	4–1–6–0					33–10–67–6							4		16	240	10
5–9 August	24–3–84–3		31.2–9–77–5						16–4–39–2				2–0–11–0		2	7		18	220	10
v. Sussex (Eastbourne)	30–6–114–1		48.4–14–112–4		26.3–3–105–1				14.3–5–31–0	17–6–43–2					4	15	1	38	424	10
12–16 August	19–2–67–0		29–4–128–3		12.3–4–47–2					8–0–29–0					6	6	1	10	283	5
v. Derbyshire (Nottingham)	27–5–91–3				23–6–87–2		11–4–18–0	14–1–57–0		24–7–70–1				15–2–67–0	1	12	1	10	403	6
26–30 August	11–1–43–0				4–2–2–0			13–3–29–3		14–7–28–0			4–2–3–0	14–6–23–0		1	4	4	129	3
v. Durham (Chester-le-Street)	26–9–44–2	23–8–66–1			21–3–90–3			24–3–73–3						10.5–2–24–1	3	8		20	308	10
31 August–3 September	2–0–7–0	17–5–53–5			14–1–57–0			16–5–36–5							2	9	3	8	164	10
v. Gloucestershire (Bristol)	31.1–6–87–3	30–11–67–2		23–6–47–3				23–5–55–0		5–2–8–1					5	8	1	22	277	9
9–13 September	6–0–18–0	3–1–6–0		5–1–10–1				3–0–18–0		10–3–19–1	6–0–79–2		11–0–80–0		1	1		8	232	4
v. Warwickshire (Nottingham) 16–20 September	14–6–22–0	9–1–31–0		11–1–58–1				11–0–41–0		5–2–18–0						2	1	24	172	2
Bowler's average	503.1–115– 1381–40 34.52	345.3–78– 1070–25 42.80	719.5–225– 1659–57 29.10	411.5–74– 1242–53 23.43	205–42– 708–17 41.64	307.3–104– 748–28 26.71	61.3–14– 171–6 28.50	172–34– 520–17 30.58	265.3–69– 660–25 26.40	113–40– 278–6 47.83	14–0– 135–2 67.50	6.3–0– 72–0 –	17–2– 94–0 –	39.5–10– 114–1 114.00						

FIELDING FIGURES

41 – N.D. Burns (ct 37/st 4)
33 – R.J. Harden
22 – C.J. Tavaré
18 – M.N. Lathwell and R.J. Turner (ct 15/st 3)
14 – Mushtaq Ahmed
13 – N.A. Folland
10 – G.D. Rose
7 – A.N. Hayhurst
5 – H.R.J. Trump
4 – M. Trescothick and subs
3 – K.A. Parsons and J.I.D. Kerr
2 – A. Payne, A.P. van Troost and A.R. Caddick
1 – N.A. Mallender and I. Fletcher
†1 Fletcher retired hurt, absent hurt
A.N. Hayhurst absent ill

SOMERSET

C.J. Tavaré retired at the end of the season. He scored 24,906 runs in his career. He formerly played for Kent. K.A. Parsons, J.I.D. Kerr and A.R. Caddick made their first-class debuts.

Pakistan leg-spinner Mushtaq Ahmed played his first season for the county and his 85 wickets placed him second only to S.L. Watkin among wicket-takers. A.R. Caddick returned career-best bowling figures, 9 for 32 against Lancashire, the best of the season. M.N. Lathwell was named as the Cricket Writers' Club Young Cricketer of the Year.

SOMERSET CCC — BATTING (season averages)

Player	M	Inns	NO	Runs	HS	Av
A.N. Hayhurst	14	23	1	669	169	30.40
M.N. Lathwell	14	25	1	817	132	34.04
R.J. Harden	18	32	3	1133	132	39.06
C.J. Tavaré	13	25	1	628	141*	26.16
N.A. Folland	17	30	3	872	108*	32.29
N.D. Burns	17	23	2	479	102*	22.80
G.D. Rose	17	29	2	865	138	32.03
A.R. Caddick	11	16	3	214	35*	16.46
N.A. Mallender	13	16	6	250	46	25.00
H.R.J. Trump	11	11	8	79	22*	26.33
A.P. van Troost	14	17	6	108	35	9.81
K.A. Parsons	5	11	3	134	63	16.75
J.I.D. Kerr	5	9	1	67	19*	8.37
M. Trescothick	7	7	1	14	6	2.33
Mushtaq Ahmed	16	25	0	498	90	19.92
R.J. Turner	6	10	1	195	70	21.66
A. Payne	6	2	1	39	22*	39.00
I. Fletcher	7	10	1	223	65*	24.77

Match-by-match batting (first half of season)

Player	v. Hampshire (Southampton) 29 April–2 May	v. Australians (Taunton) 8–10 May	v. Lancashire (Taunton) 13–17 May	v. Worcester (Worcester) 20–4 May	v. Glamorgan (Taunton) 27–31 May	v. Essex (Chelmsford) 3–7 June	v. Middlesex (Bath) 17–21 June	v. Northamptonshire (Luton) 24–8 June	v. Sussex (Taunton) 1–5 July	v. Nottinghamshire (Nottingham) 15–19 July	v. Kent (Taunton) 22–6 July	v. Yorkshire (Taunton) 29 July–2 August
A.N. Hayhurst	23	49*	71	20	0	6	17	4	24	29	5	30 & 27
M.N. Lathwell	99	0 & 15	5	10 & 72*	84 & 40	48 & 0	16 & 24	29 & 4	24 & 31	16 & 9	14 & 41*	31 & 5
R.J. Harden	97	7 & 34	3 & 3	46 & 0	2 & 35	10 & 5	47 & 43	48 & 39	101 & 57	17 & 29	121 & 8	13 & 13
C.J. Tavaré	15	62 & 31	26 & 13	24 & 4	21 & 141*	0 & 9	54 & 79	34 & 13	73 & 108*	57 & 2	0 & 58	0 & 29
N.A. Folland	81	1 & 32	10 & 9	24 & 1	21 & 22	8 & 0	30 & 38	23 & 14	138 & 9	16 & 19	8	11 & 27
N.D. Burns	102*	7*	6 & 13	44 & 7	7 & 33	7	30 & 30	25 & 12	—	2 & 8	36	41 & 43
G.D. Rose	64	—	—	—	35* & 30*	12	—	3 & 46	22* & 63	19 & 4*	4 & 7	20 & 0
A.R. Caddick	2*†	13	9 & 35	10*	9*	1	4	—	—	14	—	0*
N.A. Mallender	—	8	3*	2	3	19*	0	4	—	—	13* & 4*	8
H.R.J. Trump	—	8	22	6	8	8*	0	5 & 1*	22* & 0	4*	4 & 7	0*
A.P. van Troost	—	—	12	8	—	71	0	4	63	14	1	41
K.A. Parsons	—	—	—	36	24	—	18	19	90	50	—	—
J.I.D. Kerr	28	—	—	—	—	—	—	—	—	—	—	—
M. Trescothick	—	—	—	0	—	—	—	—	6	—	—	—
Mushtaq Ahmed	—	17	24	17	—	—	65*	43	6 & 90	—	1	14 & 41
R.J. Turner	22*	—	—	—	—	—	—	—	—	—	—	—
A. Payne	—	—	—	—	—	—	—	—	—	—	—	—
I. Fletcher	8	—	—	—	—	—	—	—	—	—	—	—
Byes	1	—	1	1	2	4	3	5	5	1	4	2
Leg-byes	8	7	2	11	11	3	12	7	15	1	4	7
Wides	—	—	10	2	—	2	1	—	6	7	1	8
No-balls	8	18	10	6	—	8	9	2	12	12	21	2
Total	500	151 & 285	195 & 114	236 & 151	185 & 366	202 & 197	318 & 240	161 & 216	558 & 226	241 & 195	211 & 135	235 & 170
Wickets	W	4 & 10	W & 10	W & 10	W & 10	10 & 10	W & 9†	10 & 10	W & 10	10 & 6	10 & 10	10 & 10
Result	W	L	W	W	W	L	W	L	W	D	W	L
Points	24	—	20	20	20	5	8	10	21	2	5	5

Match-by-match batting (second half of season)

Player	v. Derbyshire (Derby) 12–16 August	v. Leicestershire (Weston-super-Mare) 19–23 August	v. Surrey (The Oval) 26–30 August	v. Gloucestershire (Taunton) 31 August–3 September	v. Warwickshire (Birmingham) 9–13 September	v. Durham (Hartlepool) 16–20 September
A.N. Hayhurst	169	5 & 13	17 & 6	117	—	37
M.N. Lathwell	109	15 & —	6 & 6	7 & 12	9 & 29*	30 & 24
R.J. Harden	0	21 & 38	32 & 132	70 & 11	—	100 & 28
C.J. Tavaré	33	4 & 12	6*	11	32*	28
N.A. Folland	7	7 & 40	6 & 27	124	—	9
N.D. Burns	24	4 & 6	32* & 34*	—	6*	83 & 6*
G.D. Rose	0*	0* & 25*	19 & 15*	10* & 0*	—	5
A.R. Caddick	—	—	—	—	—	—
N.A. Mallender	—	4	23 & 30	16 & 10	—	—
H.R.J. Trump	28	11 & 1	—	0 & 34	—	0 & 0*
A.P. van Troost	22*	11	63	0 & 18	—	2 & 11
K.A. Parsons	—	9 & 24	—	—	—	—
J.I.D. Kerr	—	—	—	—	—	—
M. Trescothick	—	—	—	—	—	—
Mushtaq Ahmed	—	—	—	24	—	9
R.J. Turner	—	—	—	—	—	—
A. Payne	—	—	—	—	—	—
I. Fletcher	—	—	—	—	—	—
Byes	6	4	3	6	—	6
Leg-byes	20	1 & 1	1 & 12	1 & 4	4	4 & 1
Wides	—	2	8 & 16	1	—	1 & 12
No-balls	23	12 & 9	30 & 70	12 & 22	—	12 & 14
Total	453	112 & 193	275 & 344	382 & 115	61	352 & 101
Wickets	9	10 & 10	W & 22	10 & 6	D & 4	10 & 5
Result	L	L	W	L	D	W
Points	23	4	22	6	4	24

BOWLING

Match	N.A. Mallender	A.R. Caddick	A.P. van Troost	G.D. Rose	H.R.J. Trump	A.N. Hayhurst	M.N. Lathwell	J.I.D. Kerr	Mushtaq Ahmed	A. Payne	C.J. Tavaré	K.A. Parsons	R.J. Harden	Byes	Leg-byes	Wides	No-balls	Total	Wks
v. Hampshire (Southampton) 29 April–2 May	21-12-15-2	25-10-48-6	9.3-4-24-0	15.3-4-31-1	13-3-29-1	2-0-5-0	4-0-14-0								4		4	156	10
	8-4-17-0	22-5-44-4		16-1-37-2	30.3-13-59-3	13-7-21-1	2-0-12-0								4		2	196	10
v. Australians (Taunton) 8–10 May		22-1-90-1	18-2-89-4	13-2-60-3	22-3-101-2	14-4-50-0		12.4-2-77-3						4	8		14	431	10
		6-1-14-0	5-1-16-0					0.3-0-8-0						1	1	1	8	40	0
v. Lancashire (Taunton) 13–17 May	23.2-4-88-3	8-2-24-0	8-2-24-0						14-2-40-4						10		2	222	10
	11.1-2-32-9								11-3-39-1					1	1			72	10
v. Worcestershire (Worcester) 20–4 May			11-2-38-1	10-4-21-1				5-0-15-1	21.2-9-51-5	6-1-15-2					2	1	12	142	10
			11-1-44-0	11-1-57-2				9.2-3-34-0	33-7-94-5	6.2-2-13-1				1	3		4	246	8
v. Glamorgan (Taunton) 27–31 May		23-4-63-4	12-2-30-2	11-2-34-0				16-2-56-2	29.5-11-62-2					4	13	1	2	252	10
		22.4-6-66-6	4-1-12-0	4-0-13-0				7-2-21-1	29-9-89-2					1	7	2	2	215	10
v. Essex (Chelmsford) 3–7 June	15.1-4-36-3		5-1-12-0	19-4-55-2		8-3-22-0		17-2-47-3	25-6-60-2		1-0-2-0			2	8		4	265	10
	10-4-27-0			9-2-24-1		3-0-13-1		8-3-14-1	14-5-31-0						4	2	4	136	10
v. Middlesex (Bath) 17–21 June	19-2-48-1		21.3-8-50-1	18-4-48-2		3-0-21-0	4-2-3-0	16-1-51-3	26-7-70-1					2	23		16	301	8
	14-1-32-0			12-4-36-2				7-0-29-1	27-5-101-1					9	11		8	258	5
v. Northamptonshire (Luton) 24–8 June	21-9-41-1	32-12-91-4	9-2-37-1	24-2-96-5	28-9-68-0				23-5-75-0						4		16	382	10
v. Sussex (Taunton) 1–5 July	19-5-47-0		19-1-86-3	17-3-51-1	56-16-162-1				40-13-84-5					1	4	1	28	435	10
	8-3-20-1		18-1-73-2	6-0-27-0	15-7-25-0				40.5-16-91-7					2	18		36	229	10
v. Nottinghamshire (Nottingham) 15–19 July	19-5-49-0	13-2-39-0			15.5-4-35-2				14-1-44-1			1-0-14-0			6			200	3
v. Kent (Taunton) 22–6 July	15-4-42-3		12-4-14-1	9-2-26-2				6-1-28-0	17.2-7-55-4					4	3		10	144	10
	15-6-33-4		9-2-44-0	3-0-42-0			1-1-0-0		19-6-40-6						3		8	201	10
v. Yorkshire (Taunton) 29 July–2 August	11-3-29-0	19.4-6-65-2	10-2-45-2	14-5-33-4					31-12-68-2					1	7		18	244	10
	9-6-8-2	25-6-80-2		5-0-27-2					39.3-10-86-6					1	5		2	209	10
v. Derbyshire (Derby) 12–16 August	16-3-49-5	16-5-49-5		4-2-19-0					2-0-13-0						3		4	135	10
	11-0-46-2	15.5-3-57-3		10-0-53-0					11-2-28-4	6-1-34-1						1	8	221	10
v. Leicestershire (Weston-super-Mare) 19–23 August	28-10-78-1	2-0-8-0		26-4-83-6		12-5-20-1	2-2-0-0		49-14-115-2					4	12	2	12	320	10
v. Surrey (The Oval) 26–30 August	14.4-5-35-2		18-4-47-5	11-0-44-1		3-0-16-0			21-6-45-2					7	5	1	12	199	10
	12-4-27-2		14-6-40-3	10-6-18-1					10.2-1-36-3						18	1	12	139	9 A
v. Gloucestershire (Taunton) 31 August–3 September			15-1-68-2	13-4-29-1	17-6-36-2		1-0-4-0	5-0-25-0	24.2-5-81-5					10	7		12	256	10
			12-1-46-2	3-0-13-0	40.2-18-74-4				37-10-109-4					6	11		12	263	10
v. Warwickshire (Birmingham) 9–13 September	23-7-30-1	19.4-6-64-1	16-0-65-1	12-3-47-1			11-3-40-1		40-23-55-6				0.3-0-0-0	6	15	1	22	282	10
		7-0-38-0		4-0-20-0					5-2-16-0					4		1	2	118	1
v. Durham (Hartlepool) 16–20 September	11-4-24-2	19.2-4-73-6	6-0-58-1	13-1-46-5					14-5-32-1					2	5	1	36	194	10
	10-1-39-0	23-6-63-1	7-0-36-0						26-10-63-4					10	1	1	22	258	10
Bowler's average	329.5-102-772-32 / 24.12	347-81-1072-57 / 18.80	282-49-1036-31 / 33.41	324.3-62-1090-43 / 25.34	237.4-79-589-15 / 39.26	58-19-168-3 / 56.00	25-8-73-1 / 73.00	109.1-15-405-15 / 27.00	694.3-212-1773-85 / 20.85	18.2-4-62-4 / 15.50	1-0-2-0 / —	1-0-14-0 / —	0.3-0-0-0 / —						

A A.J. Stewart absent hurt

SURREY CCC

FIELDING FIGURES

37 – G.J. Kersey (ct 34/st 3)
28 – M.A. Lynch
20 – A.J. Stewart
18 – A.D. Brown
12 – G.P. Thorpe
11 – D.J. Bicknell
9 – M.P. Bicknell
7 – A.W. Smith
6 – D.M. Ward and N.M. Kendrick
4 – A.J. Murphy, A.J. Hollioake, P.D. Atkins and M.A. Butcher
3 – J.E. Benjamin, Waqar Younis and J. Boiling
2 – subs
1 – R.I. Alikhan
†A.J. Stewart absent hurt

SURREY

Wicket-keeper G.J. Kersey was previously with Kent. A.W. Smith and A.J. Hollioake made their first-class debuts.

A.D. Brown scored 1,000 runs in a season for the first time.

R.I. Alikhan announced his retirement at the end of the season. He also played for Sussex and in first-class cricket in Pakistan.

G.P. Thorpe returned his best bowling figures, 4 for 40 against the Australians.

BATTING — Season averages

	M	Inns	NO	Runs	HS	Av
D.J. Bicknell	19	35	2	1418	150*	42.96
A.J. Stewart	10	16	1	716	127	47.73
G.P. Thorpe	13	23	1	787	171	35.77
M.A. Lynch	15	28	1	666	90	24.66
D.M. Ward	13	28	3	580	151*	27.61
A.D. Brown	19	34	3	1382	150*	44.58
G.J. Kersey	10	15	2	272	57	15.11
M.P. Bicknell	12	19	5	372	38*	28.61
N.M. Kendrick	14	26	10	237	41	15.80
J.E. Benjamin	17	24	5	128	23*	6.73
A.J. Murphy	9	13	9	88	24*	22.00
J. Boiling	13	11	3	100	28	12.50
Waqar Younis	6	8	1	214	28	27.25
M.A. Butcher	4	11	1	218	66*	18.62
R.I. Alikhan	14	8	2	149	41	26.66
A.W. Smith	7	23	1	560	68	19.00
P.D. Atkins	5	9	–	228	62	19.00
A.J. Hollioake				352	123	39.11

(The match-by-match batting grid that accompanies these averages records the following fixtures:)

Top half:
v. Leicestershire (Leicester) 29 April–2 May; v. Sussex (Hove) 6–10 May; v. Essex (The Oval) 13–17 May; v. Australians (The Oval) 25–7 May; v. Lancashire (The Oval) 3–7 June; v. Glamorgan (The Oval) 10–14 June; v. Warwickshire (Birmingham) 17–21 June; v. Middlesex (Lord's) 24–8 June; v. Durham (The Oval) 1–5 July; v. Gloucestershire (Guildford) 15–19 July; v. Northamptonshire (Northampton) 22–6 July; v. Nottinghamshire (The Oval) 29 July–2 August.

Bottom half:
v. Kent (Canterbury) 5–9 August; v. Worcestershire (Worcester) 12–16 August; v. Derbyshire (Ilkeston) 19–23 August; v. Somerset (The Oval) 26–30 August; v. Hampshire (The Oval) 31 August–3 September; v. Zimbabwe (The Oval) 8–10 September; v. Yorkshire (The Oval) 16–20 September.

BOWLING

Opponent / Date	M.P. Bicknell	J.E. Benjamin	A.J. Murphy	G.P. Thorpe	N.M. Kendrick	J. Boiling	R.I. Alikhan	Waqar Younis	M.A. Butcher	A.W. Smith	A.J. Hollioake	M.A. Lynch	A.D. Brown	D.J. Bicknell	Byes	Leg-byes	Wides	No-balls	Total	Wkts
v. Leicestershire (Leicester) 29 April–2 May	19-4-46-1 / 26-9-53-4	30.5-4-86-3 / 21.1-3-63-3	26-10-55-5 / 25-10-56-3	10-3-29-1	20-11-28-2 / 15-4-40-0										1 / 1	10 / 3	1 / 1	29 / 6	255 / 216	10 / 10
v. Sussex (Hove) 6–10 May	25-11-43-6 / 16.5-2-66-5	22.1-7-64-3 / 16-6-52-1	20-5-53-3		15-5-33-1 / 13-3-24-0										4	6 / 14		6 / 16	213 / 243	10 / 10
v. Essex (The Oval) 13–17 May	38.3-10-98-2	35-5-111-2		13-1-53-2 / 7-3-8-0	19-13-30-1	9-8-2-0 / 12-6-34-1		34-9-117-3 / 25.2-7-43-2							1		1	2	418	10
v. Australians (The Oval) 25–7 May	25-11-46-2	24-10-33-3 / 9-4-19-2	20-1-66-0 / 17.4-0-48-3	13.3-4-40-4 / 8-1-41-0 / 10-1-47-0	4-2-11-2 / 25-6-90-2 / 19-4-60-1 / 12-3-49-0	12-1-85-0 / 4-1-18-0			16-2-73-1						6 / 1	12 / 5	3	2 / 4	153 / 378	9 / 4
v. Lancashire (The Oval) 3–7 June	30-3-92-3	26.1-5-96-4	10-3-49-0					22-4-85-2 / 23-6-52-5		3-0-13-1 / 11-1-44-1						4 / 4			171 / 392	10 / 10
v. Glamorgan (The Oval) 10–14 June	18-3-65-1 / 16-5-30-2	19-3-64-3 / 10.5-3-24-2		4-0-13-0				14-4-60-5 / 10-2-32-2		1-0-3-0					6 / 1	3 / 1			266 / 166	9 [A] / 4
v. Warwickshire (Birmingham) 17–21 June	13-3-44-2	9.4-5-16-3 / 20-8-36-2			11-2-31-0 / 23-4-66-2	28-3-100-5 / 14-2-39-1		15-3-43-6 / 15-5-32-2							1 / 9	7 / 16	1		93 / 88	4 / 10
v. Middlesex (Lord's) 24–8 June	14-7-27-1 / 22.4-5-50-6	19-4-43-3	10-4-15-0					22-4-68-0 / 24-3-70-3		4-0-11-0					6	5	4	6	157 / 330	6 / 9 [B]
v. Durham (The Oval) 1–5 July	21-10-28-0 / 11-4-33-1	16.4-4-40-1 / 11.5-2-44-4	5-2-23-2 / 9-2-23-0	1-0-4-0		13-4-24-2		11-4-41-3 / 5-0-21-4		5-2-20-0						12 / 4		4 / 6	219 / 148	10 / 10
v. Gloucestershire (Guildford) 15–19 July	11.5-2-44-4	9-1-27-0						18.3-5-42-6 / 16-4-44-3		1-1-0-0 / 5-2-7-2					1 / 2	4 / 2		4 / 10	120 / 153	10 / 10
v. Northamptonshire (Northampton) 22–6 July	20-7-54-3	11-0-51-0 / 17-3-55-1	19-4-63-2 / 26-7-94-1		7-2-11-2 / 39.1-11-115-7	4-3-4-0 / 29-13-44-0		20-4-58-1 / 21-4-74-2	13-4-51-3 / 18-5-73-3	10-0-56-1 / 2-0-7-0					4 / 1	7 / 1		14	162 / 238	10 / 9
v. Nottinghamshire (The Oval) 29 July–2 August	16.5-6-41-5	22-5-58-1 / 13-7-19-6	12-6-22-2 / 11-3-32-1		23.2-4-81-3	25-2-98-1				7-0-40-0 / 4-1-32-0					4 / 9	15	1	2 / 18	363 / 68	9 / 4
v. Kent (Canterbury) 5–9 August	31-9-86-6 / 31-7-106-5	31-13-73-1 / 31-9-114-5	40-9-118-1	3-1-11-0	18-6-71-0 / 7-2-12-0	14-4-46-0 / 17-4-45-0		20.5-4-75-2 / 26-3-69-2			23.3-3-75-2	1-1-0-0			9 / 5	12 / 14	1	28 / 34	306 / 467	9 / 7
v. Worcestershire (Worcester) 12–16 August		24-3-107-2 / 23-6-51-1						27-3-97-4		9-1-23-0			1-0-6-0		9	17		10	406 / 313	10 / ...
v. Derbyshire (Ilkeston) 19–23 August		40-10-111-1 / 10.5-1-30-1	23-1-115-1 / 8-1-38-3						18-3-45-1 / 14-1-35-0	5-1-23-0	24-4-49-1 / 18-3-63-1				3	4	3	12	438 / 100	...
v. Somerset (The Oval) 26–30 August		30-7-80-2 / 29-6-79-4			7-2-13-2 / 37-15-50-1			24-5-73-3 / 28-6-85-1	28-6-81-2	13-1-67-0	24-5-76-0				1	8 / 7	2	16 / 38	275 / 344	...
v. Hampshire (The Oval) 31 August–3 September		34-6-104-3			33.3-8-94-3	40.1-9-129-2	3-0-15-1		10-2-24-1 / 15-1-51-4 / 2-0-3-0	4-1-20-0 / 9-4-21-0	11-0-37-1 / 2-0-5-0		1-0-6-0	1-0-21-0	1				559	10
v. Zimbabwe (The Oval) 8–10 September			21-7-58-5 / 16-2-69-2			14-1-51-0 / 11-3-48-0									6	10 / 2	2	12	221 / 196	9 / 6
v. Yorkshire (The Oval) 16–20 September			2-2-0-0															8	30	0
Bowler's average	415.2-120-1078-63 / 17.11	624.2-153-1783-64 / 27.85	333.4-81-1043-32 / 32.59	69.3-14-246-7 / 35.14	368-103-960-29 / 33.10	221.1-62-669-11 / 60.81	3-0-15-1 / 15.00	449.4-89-1407-62 / 22.69	134-24-436-15 / 29.06	93-15-387-5 / 77.40	102.3-17-305-5 / 61.00	1-1-0-0 / —	1-0-6-0 / —	1-0-21-0 / —						

A M.P. Maynard retired hurt
B J.D. Glendenen retired hurt, absent hurt; D.A. Graveney absent hurt

FIELDING FIGURES

44 – P. Moores (ct39/st 5)
19 – A.P. Wells
16 – C.W.J. Athey
15 – D.M. Smith
11 – M.P. Speight, I.D.K. Salisbury and E.E. Hemmings
6 – J.W. Hall
5 – F.D. Stephenson, K. Greenfield and sub
4 – A.C.S. Pigott
3 – N.J. Lenham and E.S.H. Giddins
2 – J.A. North and S. Humphries
1 – C.M. Wells, B.T.P. Donelan and C.C. Remy
†A.C.S. Pigott absent ill

SUSSEX

E.E. Hemmings and C.W.J. Athey were the leading wicket-taker and leading run-scorer respectively. Both were in their first season with Sussex. Hemmings was previously with Warwickshire and Nottinghamshire, Athey with Yorkshire and Gloucestershire.

D.R. Law, S. Humphries and N.C. Phillips made their first-class debuts.

J.A. North hit his maiden first-class century.

M.P. Speight hit a career best 184.

B.T.P. Donelan and A.C.S. Pigott left the county at the end of the season. P.W. Jarvis was signed from Yorkshire.

SUSSEX CCC — BATTING (season averages)

	M	Inns	NO	Runs	HS	Av
N.J. Lenham	12	22	1	799	149	38.04
J.W. Hall	9	16	1	390	114	26.00
D.M. Smith	15	23	1	802	150	36.45
A.P. Wells	18	27	2	1432	144	57.28
M.P. Speight	13	22	1	1009	184	48.04
F.D. Stephenson	14	21	2	538	90	28.31
P. Moores	19	27	4	583	85*	25.34
I.D.K. Salisbury	15	21	4	372	63*	21.88
A.C.S. Pigott	13	20	13	153	52	13.90
E.E. Hemmings	15	19	5	79	17*	5.26
E.S.H. Giddins	20	15	8	12	4	1.09
C.W.J. Athey	17	30	5	1600	137	64.00
K. Greenfield	8	12	3	353	107	39.22
C.M. Wells	5	8	1	198	185	49.50
A.N. Jones	5	6	1	38	20	6.33
C.C. Remy	4	6	1	85	39	21.25
B.T.P. Donelan	3	3	3	79	41	39.50
J.A. North	7	3	1	228	114	28.50
D.R. Law	3	3	3	11	11	5.50
S. Humphries	3	2	—	11	11	—
N.C. Phillips	1	—	—	—	—	—

Matches (left table, in order): v. Glamorgan (Cardiff) 29 April–2 May; v. Surrey (Hove) 6–10 May; v. Australians (Hove) 13–15 May; v. Leicestershire (Horsham) 20–4 May; v. Middlesex (Lord's) 27–31 May; v. Warwickshire (Birmingham) 3–7 June; v. Northamptonshire (Hove) 10–14 June; v. Lancashire (Manchester) 17–21 June; v. Cambridge University (Hove) 26–8 June; v. Somerset (Taunton) 1–5 July; v. Kent (Arundel) 15–19 July; v. Derbyshire (Derby) 22–6 July.

Matches (right table, in order): v. Durham (Durham) 29 July–2 August; v. Worcestershire (Hove) 5–9 August; v. Nottinghamshire (Eastbourne) 12–16 August; v. Hampshire (Portsmouth) 26–30 August; v. Essex (Hove) 31 August–3 September; v. Yorkshire (Scarborough) 9–13 September; v. Gloucestershire (Hove) 16–20 September.

BOWLING

	F.D. Stephenson	E.S.H. Giddins	A.C.S. Pigott	E.E. Hemmings	I.D.K. Salisbury	N.J. Lenham	C.M. Wells	C.W.J. Athey	A.N. Jones	K. Greenfield	B.T.P. Donelan	J.A. North	D.R. Law	N.C. Phillips	C.C. Remy	P. Moores	Byes	Leg-byes	Wides	No-balls	Total	Wkts
v. Glamorgan (Cardiff) 29 April–2 May	16-1-63-2 / 17-7-27-2	16-2-75-0 / 12-2-70-0	6.1-1-18-1 / 10-1-36-0	30-6-69-4 / 24-4-91-1	32-7-93-2 / 28-6-93-2	1-0-4-1 / 5-0-33-0											5 / 4	4 / 8	– / 1	4 / 8	331 / 362	10 / 5
v. Surrey (Hove) 6–10 May	36-10-98-3	15-2-66-1 / 0.2-0-1-0	16-0-66-0	46.1-19-87-4	24-4-92-1	8-0-31-0											1	16		8	456 / 1	10 / 0
v. Australians (Hove) 13–15 May		21-3-95-1	25-4-73-0		33-1-116-1		18-0-67-2	8-0-41-0	18-1-90-0									7	2	8	490	5
v. Leicestershire (Horsham) 20–4 May	14-2-45-4 / 4-1-8-1	3-1-6-0 / 15-7-19-2		16.2-7-27-5 / 14.1-7-31-7	6-2-10-1 / 4-1-12-0		15-4-36-2		2-2-0-0								6 / 1	3 / 1		2	97 / 72	10 / 10
v. Middlesex (Lord's) 27–31 May	28.4-4-63-2	22-4-60-0		28-9-56-1	47-14-104-4	1-1-0-0											10	10	1	2	339	10
v. Warwickshire (Birmingham) 3–7 June	30-7-81-2 / 12-3-30-0	17-3-49-0 / 5-0-7-0	15-7-27-1 / 9-2-33-0	33.3-8-75-1 / 33-10-70-4				3-1-9-0 / 6-0-12-0	21-2-108-2	20-6-51-2 / 7-1-41-1	12-2-51-0						3 / 2	6 / 16			301 / 199	7 / 5
v. Northamptonshire (Hove) 10–14 June	29-3-91-1	19-0-96-2	23-2-77-1															12	5	2	447	6
v. Lancashire (Manchester) 17–21 June	9-1-26-1 / 13-2-35-0			23-4-86-4					7-0-35-0 / 5-0-19-0				13-3-41-0 / 7-2-20-1				5 / 13	1 / 2			280 / 326	10 / 6
v. Cambridge University (Hove) 26–8 June				38.2-10-100-2				1-0-3-0 / 2-0-2-0				16-3-56-0 / 3-0-15-0			13-5-37-2			5		4	300 / 115	10 / 4
v. Somerset (Taunton) 1–5 July	22-4-87-0	27.5-4-120-5 / 14-2-60-1	20-6-63-1 / 8-2-21-0	32-10-92-2 / 32.4-7-67-4	32.7-128-3 / 14-1-80-1			1-0-3-0	27-1-108-0 / 4-2-13-0		21.3-0-112-5 / 35-3-157-4			21-3-64-0 / 22-10-39-3		1-1-0-0	5	6 / 15	1	12	558 / 226	5 / 6
v. Kent (Arundel) 15–19 July		15-6-30-1	16-4-43-3	25-6-70-1	11-1-50-0												1	6			200	5
v. Derbyshire (Derby) 22–6 July	12-3-31-3 / 16-2-61-0	18.2-1-60-3 / 20-1-85-1	15-3-45-3 / 14-1-53-1	35.5-10-65-4 / 15-4-38-0	27-8-89-2 / 19.2-5-63-4	15-9-13-4 / 7-2-17-0						8-2-29-1 / 15-1-65-1					1 / 1	17 / 11	4 / 1	2	183 / 379	10 / 10
v. Durham (Durham) 29 July–2 August	11-0-48-0 / 18-5-55-5	14.4-2-71-3 / 14-1-66-0	5-0-10-0	14-4-23-2 / 43-15-61-3	12-5-6-3 / 26.2-6-88-2	23-7-50-2 / 10-1-26-0											2	8 / 3		10 / 8	325 / 210	10 / 10
v. Worcestershire (Hove) 5–9 August	17-7-43-2 / 9-1-18-1	13-0-69-2	18-2-51-4	20-6-58-1	23-5-86-1 / 36-6-127-3	3-0-15-1		10-1-40-2 / 5-1-14-0			10.4-2-38-2 / 14-3-38-0	11-1-46-1 / 17-7-32-3					14 / 4	9 / 6	4	2	253 / 337	10 / 10
v. Nottinghamshire (Eastbourne) 12–16 August	14-1-48-2 / 19-5-59-3	23-0-86-1	9.2-0-30-2	42.5-6-97-2 / 32-15-74-3	13-1-65-1 / 13-1-45-1	9-2-28-0		6-2-23-0				4-0-15-1 / 7-0-16-0					4 / 6	6 / 4		2 / 2	278 / 308	8 / 8
v. Hampshire (Portsmouth) 26–30 August		18-5-73-2	16-3-86-0		24.1-4-95-5 / 13-1-65-1	7-1-27-1		5-2-22-0 / 3-0-31-0		11-0-40-2 / 1-0-4-0	14-2-64-0 / 12-1-66-0						5 / 4	10 / 4		16	349 A / 351	9 A / 4
v. Essex (Hove) 31 August–3 September	19.5-3-56-3	21.4-2-99-1	23-0-127-1	38-15-89-4	24.1-4-102-0 / 30-13-53-4	4-0-11-0						10-0-52-0 / 13-0-87-0			4-1-16-0		4 / 2	4 / 3	3 / 3	4 / 12	493 / 412	10 / 3
v. Yorkshire (Scarborough) 9–13 September	14-2-41-1 / 9-1-27-1	10-0-37-1	12-2-43-0	6.3-0-17-0	2-0-6-0								15-1-72-1 / 4-1-7-1		2-0-28-0		5 / 4	10 / 3	3	4	224 / 97	3 / 1
v. Gloucestershire (Hove) 16–20 September	19.5-3-56-3 / 7.3-2-14-2	7-2-14-1 / 2-0-19-0		34-7-81-5 / 28-4-99-4	34-7-81-5 / 28-4-99-4										5-1-22-0		4 / 7	6 / 4	4	24 / 18	304 / 177	10 / 10
Bowler's average	397-77-1155-41 — 28.17	378.5-55-1490-29 — 51.37	283.3-43-1001-21 — 47.66	683.2-208-1541-63 — 24.46	580.5-122-1910-52 — 36.73	93-23-255-9 — 28.33	33-4-103-2 — 51.50	50-7-200-2 — 100.00	84-8-373-2 — 186.50	39-7-136-5 — 27.20	94.3-8-450-9 — 50.00	104-14-413-7 — 59.00	63.4-12-216-5 — 43.20	43-13-103-3 — 34.33	24-7-103-2 — 51.50	1-1-0-0 — –						

A M.D. Marshall retired hurt

FIELDING FIGURES

22 – D.A. Reeve
19 – D.P. Ostler
14 – K.J. Piper
13 – J.D. Ratcliffe
10 – T.L. Penney and M. Burns (ct 9/st 1)
8 – A.A. Donald
6 – P.C.L. Holloway
5 – G.C. Small
4 – R.G. Twose, P.A. Booth and Asif Din
3 – P.A. Smith
2 – N.M.K. Smith and M.A.V. Bell
1 – sub
†K.J. Piper absent hurt
‡D.A. Reeve retired hurt

WARWICKSHIRE

J.D. Ratcliffe, son of a former Warwickshire player, hit his first championship century.

N.M.K. Smith returned the best bowling figures of his career in the match against Kent. He, too, is the son of a former Warwickshire player.

M.A.V. Bell had taken only eight first-class wickets with a best of 3 for 78 before 1993.

Warwickshire used three wicket-keepers during the season: Piper, Burns and Holloway. Burns bowled in the match against Gloucestershire when the attack was depleted, and Asif Din went behind the stumps.

WARWICKSHIRE CCC — BATTING

	M	Inns	NO	Runs	HS	Av
A.J. Moles	19	34	3	1228	117	39.61
R.G. Twose	11	18	–	224	37	12.44
J.D. Ratcliffe	17	34	1	999	101	29.38
D.P. Ostler	19	34	3	1052	174	33.93
T.L. Penney	17	29	6	788	135*	34.26
D.A. Reeve	17	28	7	765	87*	36.42
N.M.K. Smith	18	26	2	420	51*	17.50
K.J. Piper	18	14	1	183	52	14.07
G.C. Small	10	12	4	147	39	9.80
A.A. Donald	10	13	4	68	19	8.50
T.A. Munton	10	13	5	51	18	6.37
M. Burns	6	10	1	96	22	9.60
A.F. Giles	4	4	–	53	23	17.66
P.A. Smith	10	15	1	253	55	16.86
P.C.L. Holloway	3	4	–	68	44	22.66
P.A. Booth	7	11	3	144	49*	18.00
M.A.V. Bell	9	12	5	60	22*	8.57
Asif Din	6	9	–	291	66	32.33

Match columns (first table):
- v. Northamptonshire (Birmingham) 29 April–2 May
- v. Derbyshire (Birmingham) 6–10 May
- v. Kent (Canterbury) 13–17 May
- v. Lancashire (Liverpool) 27–31 May
- v. Sussex (Birmingham) 3–7 June
- v. Australians (Birmingham) 9–11 June
- v. Oxford University (Oxford) 12–15 June
- v. Surrey (Birmingham) 17–21 June
- v. Essex (Ilford) 24–8 June
- v. Yorkshire (Birmingham) 1–5 July
- v. Middlesex (Birmingham) 15–19 July
- v. Leicestershire (Leicester) 22–6 July

BATTING (continued)

	M	Inns	NO	Runs	HS	Av
A.J. Moles	19	34	3	1228	117	39.61
R.G. Twose	11	18	–	224	37	12.44
J.D. Ratcliffe	17	34	1	999	101	29.38
D.P. Ostler	19	34	3	1052	174	33.93
T.L. Penney	17	29	6	788	135*	34.26
D.A. Reeve	17	28	7	765	87*	36.42
N.M.K. Smith	18	26	2	420	51*	17.50
K.J. Piper	18	14	1	183	52	14.07
G.C. Small	10	12	4	147	39	9.80
A.A. Donald	10	13	4	68	19	8.50
T.A. Munton	10	13	5	51	18	6.37
M. Burns	6	10	1	96	22	9.60
A.F. Giles	4	4	–	53	23	17.66
P.A. Smith	10	15	1	253	55	16.86
P.C.L. Holloway	3	4	–	68	44	22.66
P.A. Booth	7	11	3	144	49*	18.00
M.A.V. Bell	9	12	5	60	22*	8.57
Asif Din	6	9	–	291	66	32.33

Match columns (second table):
- v. Hampshire (Southampton) 29 April–2 May
- v. Glamorgan (Cardiff) 5–9 August
- v. Gloucestershire (Birmingham) 12–16 August
- v. Durham (Darlington) 19–23 August
- v. Worcestershire (Birmingham) 26–30 August
- v. Somerset (Birmingham) 9–13 September
- v. Nottinghamshire (Nottingham) 16–20 September

BOWLING

BOWLING	A.A. Donald	G.C. Small	T.A. Munton	D.A. Reeve	N.M.K. Smith	R.G. Twose	A.F. Giles	J.D. Ratcliffe	A.J. Moles	D.P. Osler	T.L. Penney	M.A.V. Bell	P.A. Booth	P.A. Smith	Asif Din	M. Burns	Byes	Leg-byes	Wides	No-balls	Total	Wkts
v. Northamptonshire (Birmingham) 29 April–2 May	21–5–65–2	14–4–38–1	30–13–50–3	11.3–4–10–2	32–12–54–2												6	17	1	8	240	10
v. Derbyshire (Birmingham) 6–10 May	14–4–38–1 / 14–3–35–3	12–3–33–1 / 16–2–60–2	7–5–12–1 / 34–12–72–2	20–8–33–1	20.2–4–81–5 / 35–4–90–3	5–2–10–0											3 / 11	7 / 10	7	2 / 6	171 / 379	10 / 10
v. Kent (Canterbury) 13–17 May	20.2–1–93–2 / 16–2–60–2	12–5–12–1 / 11–4–24–1	22–5–41–7 / 19–8–28–1	15–9–23–1 / 13–5–16–1	13–3–61–0 / 46.1–11–122–6	1–0–1–0	12.3–3–33–1 / 14–2–31–1										4	6 / 6		2 / 2	177 / 231	10 / 10
v. Lancashire (Liverpool) 27–31 May	6–3–11–0	8–3–24–2	11–4–24–0	7–6–2–0	2–0–10–0	3–0–9–1		10–0–82–1	9–1–87–3	3–0–13–0	2.1–0–13–0							4			279 / 0	7 / 0
v. Sussex (Birmingham) 3–7 June	23–3–100–1 / 7–1–18–0	24–10–56–2 / 4–1–10–0	38–10–93–2 / 15–5–32–0	20.4–4–47–3 / 12–4–32–0	26–7–68–1 / 22–5–83–1	14–2–38–1 / 5–0–20–1											1 / 3	11 / 9	2	16 / 2	414 / 207	10 / 3
v. Australians (Birmingham) 9–11 June	10–4–67–0	13–3–40–1	20–4–57–1	23–5–55–2	15.5–4–55–3	8–3–27–0											1	15	1	10	317	7
v. Oxford University (Oxford) 12–15 June			5–3–6–1		10–4–16–1	6–0–34–3						5–0–22–0	11–5–16–1	6–0–21–0			2	1	1		118	6
v. Surrey (Birmingham) 17–21 June	20.3–6–56–1 / 6–1–11–2	15–5–39–4 / 6–3–7–0	21.3–7–54–1 / 5–2–14–0	4–4–0–2	4–1–12–2 / 5.2–1–30–0	1–1–0–0											10 / 9	4		14 / 3	175 / 71	10 / 2
v. Essex (Ilford) 24–8 June	17–4–57–0 / 21–2–56–0	17–4–34–0 / 7.4–2–16–1	26–14–54–1 / 25–3–80–2	13–1–47–1 / 9–2–33–0	28–2–126–1 / 12.2–3–42–2							10–3–53–1 / 10–3–27–2					5 / 5	13 / 14	1	16 / 16	384 / 273	4 / 7
v. Yorkshire (Birmingham) 1–5 July	17–6–31–3		20.9–36–3	17.8–38–3	4–1–12–1 / 31–16–47–1	3–1–3–0								8–0–47–0 / 13–0–52–0			5 / 10	6 / 3		20	178 / 282	10 / 10
v. Middlesex (Birmingham) 15–19 July	29–7–98–7		25–9–55–2 / 7–0–15–0	9–2–17–0 / 17–5–35–1	43.4–6–133–4 / 7–1–18–0			2–1–6–0				37–8–95–2 / 8.5–1–33–1		6–2–29–0			17	7	6	3	387 / 60	10 / 10
v. Leicestershire (Leicester) 22–6 July	25.2–9–57–6			20–12–20–2	27–6–54–1							8–3–13–0 / 15–3–28–1					3	13	4	6	188	10
v. Hampshire (Southampton) 29 July–2 August		11–2–32–1 / 4–0–15–0		21–5–43–2	40–7–85–2 / 33–9–93–4							16–5–47–3 / 17.3–6–43–5	23–4–81–2 / 15–4–52–1				6 / 1	6 / 7	1	4	294 / 208	10 / 10
v. Glamorgan (Cardiff) 5–9 August		14–0–53–1 / 21–4–43–2		16–8–22–0 / 1–1–0–0								23–2–86–5 / 8.5–2–34–0	14–5–16–2 / 10–1–22–0	12.5–4–59–3 / 10–2–35–4			9 / 7	9 / 13	1	36 / 14	236 / 138	9 A / 8
v. Gloucestershire (Birmingham) 12–16 August				17–4–28–1	21–6–42–3 / 21–8–45–0			3–1–6–1	5–1–10–1			20.1–5–48–7 / 27.4–6–95–2	12–6–17–0	1–1–0–0 / 17–0–56–1	3–1–10–0	7–4–8–0	5 / 3	5 / 8	3 / 2	6 / 16	145 / 263	10 / 5
v. Durham (Darlington) 19–23 August	31–8–56–3			18–9–27–0	25–10–51–0 / 11.3–1–48–0	34–4–85–4 / 10–2–46–0	11–1–37–0 / 4–0–27–1					31–9–96–2 / 11–3–48–0	26–6–69–3				6 / 6	18 / 11	2	32 / 10	369 / 243	1 / 0
v. Worcestershire (Birmingham) 26–30 August		37–15–73–1	4–0–17–0		48–18–103–5	12.2–1–29–1		1.3–0–2–0 / 2–0–10–0		3–1–3–0		42–11–111–1 / 2–0–6–0	29–12–36–2	11–1–57–0	1–0–2–0		6	12			397	0
v. Somerset (Birmingham) 9–13 September		5–1–20–0			4–1–12–0																11	0
v. Nottinghamshire (Nottingham) 16–20 September																					61	Ab.
Bowler's average	268.1–59–811–30 / 27.03	251.4–71–629–21 / 29.95	334.3–113–740–27 / 27.40	248.1–108–528–22 / 24.00	588.1–151–1593–48 / 33.18	102.2–16–302–11 / 27.45	41.3–6–128–3 / 42.66	18.3–2–106–2 / 53.00	14–2–97–4 / 24.25	6–1–16–0 / –	2.1–0–13–0 / –	212.1–52–649–25 / 25.96	174.5–49–396–12 / 33.00	130.5–16–505–14 / 36.07	4–1–12–0 / –	7–4–8–0 / –						

A D.L. Hemp retired ill

FIELDING FIGURES

47 – S.J. Rhodes (ct 40/st 7)
24 – G.A. Hick
21 – S.R. Lampitt
18 – D.A. Leatherdale
14 – T.S. Curtis
12 – D.B. D'Oliveira
8 – C.M. Tolley and P.J. Newport
7 – R.K. Illingworth
6 – W.P.C. Weston
4 – subs
3 – G.R. Haynes, N.V. Radford and M.J. Weston
1 – K.C.G. Benjamin and T. Edwards

WORCESTERSHIRE

Worcestershire won their last five matches of the season to claim second place in the Britannic Assurance County Championship.

A. Wylie made his first-class debut in the opening game of the season, but injury prevented him from playing again.

Wicket-keeper T. Edwards, formerly on the Somerset staff, made his first-class debut against Oxford University.

W.P.C. Weston and G.R. Haynes made their maiden centuries in first-class cricket.

K.C.G. Benjamin made his first appearances in county cricket, but the West Indian pace bowler will not be with Worcestershire in 1994.

WORCESTERSHIRE CCC — BATTING (Season Averages)

Player	M	Inns	NO	Runs	HS	Av
T.S. Curtis	19	32	3	1553	127	53.55
W.P.C. Weston	13	21	2	610	113	32.10
G.A. Hick	15	24	2	1266	187	57.54
D.B. D'Oliveira	15	24	1	513	94	21.37
A.C.H. Seymour	7	11	1	237	54*	23.70
S.R. Lampitt	16	25	2	438	68*	19.04
S.J. Rhodes	18	27	8	848	101	35.33
R.K. Illingworth	18	26	10	401	58	25.06
P.J. Newport	17	26	6	630	79*	31.50
N.V. Radford	13	14	5	106	29	11.77
A. Wylie	1	1	–	0	0	0.00
C.M. Tolley	18	24	7	381	78	22.41
K.C.G. Benjamin	11	13	3	85	26	10.62
G.R. Haynes	9	11	2	383	158	29.46
D.A. Leatherdale	11	16	2	354	119*	25.28
T. Edwards	1	1	1	–	–	–
M.J. Weston	7	13	1	277	59	23.08

BOWLING

Match	A. Wylie	P.J. Newport	S.R. Lampitt	R.K. Illingworth	G.A. Hick	N.V. Radford	D.B. D'Oliveira	C.M. Tolley	W.P.C. Weston	K.C.G. Benjamin	G.R. Haynes	D.A. Leatherdale	T.S. Curtis	M.J. Weston	Byes	Leg-byes	Wides	No-balls	Total	Wks
v. Nottinghamshire (Nottingham) 29 April–2 May	17-3-50-1	24-7-50-3	17-5-33-3	26-13-39-2	9-3-25-0	4.3-1-8-1	1-0-8-0								5	15	16	2	233	10
	5-0-23-0	22-3-63-6	22-3-85-2	27-5-67-0		11-2-56-1										1	1	2	295	10
v. Australians (Worcester) 5–7 May		22.5-6-59-3	16-3-47-2	15-2-52-2	6-0-33-0	7-1-56-1		16-5-36-2	2-0-10-0							5	1	2	262	10
		15-1-58-1	6-3-18-0	14.4-5-33-0	4-0-17-0			9-2-40-0								4	8	2	287	5
v. Yorkshire (Bradford) 13–17 May		10-1-31-0					1-1-0-0	18-4-39-2		16-3-54-2						4	1	4	196	4
v. Somerset (Worcester) 20–4 May		13-3-26-0	12-4-24-1	18.4-6-28-6	6-3-15-2	11-2-42-2		13-2-37-1		26.5-5-70-6	6-1-25-0				1	11	2	6	236	10
		22-7-31-4	6-1-22-0	13.2-2-34-3		6-0-24-1	2-1-2-0	25-6-55-3		5-0-9-0						8	1	4	151	10
v. Gloucestershire (Gloucester) 27–31 May		9-3-11-0						3-0-8-0		16-7-32-2					2	5	1	6	101	10
		11-5-20-2						13-6-14-1		18-5-35-4					3	10	1	16	116	10
v. Northamptonshire (Northampton) 3–7 June		30-7-91-0	31-5-110-0	31-6-63-3				18-4-60-0		30-4-103-1	18-3-51-2				3	13	6	2	494	4
				10.3-0-43-0				1-0-5-0		12-0-54-2					5	3	2		110	Ab.
v. Leicestershire (Worcester) 10–14 June			18-5-44-3	19-7-32-1		17-3-64-2	8-4-11-0	18-4-46-2		25-4-65-5	6-0-23-0	1-1-0-0			5	4		8	229	8
			12-2-35-3	24-9-58-2		8-1-42-0	9-1-37-0	4-2-12-0	3-0-13-1		5-1-27-0				4	6		4	249	6
v. Oxford University (Worcester) 18–20 June		12-8-10-1	10-2-26-1	9-3-19-2				14-2-44-1		24-1-80-3	3-1-7-0		6-2-15-0		2	14		10	187	10
v. Durham (Stockton) 24–8 June		24.2-5-75-3	22-4-102-0	22-8-44-2	8-2-26-1	9-0-33-1		5-1-28-0	2-0-2-0	20-1-84-3	3-1-7-0				12	9		8	355	10
v. Derbyshire (Kidderminster) 1–5 July		12-2-47-3	11.3-0-48-3	42-24-53-2	8-4-13-0	19-2-85-3		11-4-35-1		18-0-81-4					6	5	1	6	251	10
		14-2-60-0	4-0-24-0	12-3-27-0		12-2-34-1		25-6-80-3		32-5-99-4						5	4	8	358	9
v. Hampshire (Portsmouth) 15–19 July		29-6-80-1	6-1-23-0												4			6	355	10
v. Glamorgan (Worcester) 22–6 July		19-5-55-3	5-0-15-0	6.4-4-2-3	3-1-9-0	7-0-35-0		21-3-67-4		21-3-67-4				5-0-14-0		1	2	2	184	10
		21-4-60-2	26-5-84-3	26.3-3-81-1	6-1-19-0	8-0-26-1		10-3-42-1								8		12	334	9
v. Essex (Chelmsford) 29 July–2 August		4-1-14-0	19-3-43-3	35-16-54-2	18.1-5-58-2	5-0-25-0	4-2-6-0	22-7-86-2					1-0-7-0		7	7	1		305	6
		8-0-32-0	5-3-48-1	32.5-4-85-2	27-3-97-0		12-0-36-3	7-1-12-1							4	18	1	4	286	1
v. Sussex (Hove) 5–9 August		31-7-83-3	17-3-48-1	17-5-49-0	12-4-39-1		2-0-13-0	36.5-9-90-4		18-3-65-0				8-4-15-1	2	7			424	10
		7-0-31-0	10-3-28-0		4.3-0-29-0			12-6-19-0						6-1-36-1	18	7	2	6	167	10
v. Surrey (Worcester) 12–16 August		33-11-86-4	21-4-71-3	25-4-77-0	10-2-41-0	31-8-85-2		19-8-42-0		8-4-12-0	16-5-29-2				3	7	2		427	10
		12.1-1-48-2				14-0-64-2		6-0-18-2			3-1-8-0			1-0-4-0		3	1		227	9 A
v. Kent (Worcester) 19–23 August		15-4-33-1	10-1-53-1	18-7-34-3		19.1-8-53-2	9-3-24-2	21-5-55-5			16-5-29-2			3-2-9-0	1	2	2		189	10
v. Warwickshire (Birmingham) 26–30 August		18.4-3-49-3		34-16-68-4	10-3-19-1	16-2-67-2	6-1-13-0	14-4-32-1							8	8	1	2	249	10
		16.1-7-38-4		20-8-29-1	29-17-41-1	20-3-62-2	1-0-5-0	16-4-29-3								6	3		206	10
v. Lancashire (Worcester) 31 August–3 September		25.4-9-55-3		35-19-55-4	10-0-54-1	7-0-28-0		11-5-18-1		15-0-68-1	11-3-37-0			6-2-18-0		12	1	6	320	10
		31-7-73-3		38-14-91-4				14-6-21-1			16-2-36-1				2	9	3		201	8
v. Middlesex (Worcester) 16–20 September		7-0-20-4		47-20-84-3		7-1-21-2		16-1-72-0								1	1	5	330	10
		12-7-17-1	14-4-27-2	6-2-18-1		16.1-3-49-6		12-2-35-0							2	2		6	148	10
Bowler's average	22-3-73-1 / 73.00	546.5-135-1454-60 / 24.23	332-62-1062-34 / 31.23	645-219-1404-55 / 25.52	178.4-51-551-10 / 55.10	269.5-44-1012-33 / 30.66	55-13-155-5 / 31.00	437.5-115-1194-37 / 28.42	7-0-25-1 / 25.00	283.5-42-911-37 / 24.62	87-18-250-5 / 50.00	1-1-0-0 / –	7-2-22-0 / –	29-9-96-2 / 48.00						

A M.R. Benson absent hurt

FIELDING FIGURES

46 – R.J. Blakey (ct 41/st 5)
21 – D. Byas
14 – C. White
11 – R.D. Stemp
9 – M.D. Moxon and R.B. Richardson
7 – J.D. Batty
6 – A.P. Grayson
4 – S.A. Kellett
3 – D. Gough and P.J. Hartley
2 – A.A. Metcalfe
1 – P.W. Jarvis, M.J. Foster, C.E.W. Silverwood and sub

YORKSHIRE

R.B. Richardson, the West Indies Test captain, and R.D. Stemp, formerly of Worcestershire, played for Yorkshire for the first time.

M.J. Foster, M.P. Vaughan and C.E.W. Silverwood made their first-class debuts.

C. White hit a maiden first-class century and returned his best bowling figures, 3 for 9.

D. Gough had an outstanding season, was chosen for the England 'A' tour of South Africa and returned career-best bowling figures of 7 for 42 against Somerset.

P.W. Jarvis left the county and will play for Sussex in 1994.

YORKSHIRE CCC — BATTING (season averages)

	M	Inns	NO	Runs	HS	Av
M.D. Moxon	18	31	2	1251	171*	43.13
A.A. Metcalfe	10	16	1	467	133*	31.13
S.A. Kellett	5	9	0	301	85	33.44
C. White	19	32	6	896	146	34.46
R.J. Blakey	19	33	3	859	95	28.63
D. Byas	19	33	3	1073	156	35.76
D. Gough	16	24	3	248	39	11.80
P. Carrick	15	19	2	221	50	13.00
J.D. Batty	9			45	16*	22.50
S.M. Milburn	1				—	—
P.W. Jarvis	16			207	76	15.92
R.D. Stemp	17			265	37	15.58
M.A. Robinson	10			53	16*	4.41
A.P. Grayson	14			386	64	22.70
R.B. Richardson	13			759	112	34.50
M.J. Foster	1			6	6	6.00
C.E.W. Silverwood	1			0	0	0.00
P.J. Hartley	13	21	6	400	102	26.66
M.P. Vaughan	2	4		118	64	29.50

Match results

#	Opponent	Venue	Date	Result	Points
1	Cambridge University	Cambridge	17-19 April	D	—
2	Lancashire	Leeds	29 April-3 May	W	—
3	Essex	Chelmsford	6-10 May	W	24
4	Worcestershire	Bradford	13-17 May	D	4
5	Hampshire	Southampton	20-4 May	W	20
6	Glamorgan	Middlesbrough	3-7 June	L	5
7	Derbyshire	Chesterfield	10-14 June	D	0
8	Gloucestershire	Sheffield	17-21 June	D	6
9	Kent	Leeds	24-8 June	D	5
10	Warwickshire	Birmingham	1-5 July	L	3
11	Northamptonshire	Harrogate	15-19 July	W	20
12	Somerset	Taunton	29 July-2 August	W	21
13	Nottinghamshire	Nottingham	5-9 August	L	5
14	Middlesex	Scarborough	12-16 August	D	4
15	Lancashire	Manchester	19-23 August	W	21
16	Durham	Leeds	26-30 August	D	7
17	Leicestershire	Leicester	31 August-3 September	L	5
18	Sussex	Scarborough	9-13 September	D	6
19	Surrey	The Oval	16-20 September	D	8

BOWLING

The bowlers' header runs (left→right): D. Gough, M. Broadhurst, S.M. Milburn, J.D. Batty, C. White, P. Carrick, M.D. Moxon, P.W. Jarvis, M.A. Robinson, R.D. Stemp, C.E.W. Silverwood, M.J. Foster, P.J. Hartley, R.B. Richardson, M.P. Vaughan, A.P. Grayson; then Byes, Leg-byes, Wides, No-balls, Total, Wks.

Bowling analyses (by match; two-innings figures joined by "&")

Match	Gough	Broadhurst	Milburn	Batty	White	Carrick	Moxon	Jarvis	Robinson	Stemp	Silverwood	Foster	Hartley	Richardson	Vaughan	Grayson
v. Cambridge University (Cambridge) 17–19 April	18.4-7-37-2 & 6-3-9-0	1.1-0-7-0	11.5-7-18-0 & 6-1-17-0	25.7-7-36-5 & 6-1-10-0	8-0-13-2	12-6-14-1 & 5-5-0-0	4-2-7-0	13.3-4-20-3 & 16-2-41-0		25-10-55-3 & 42.3-13-92-6						
v. Lancashire (Leeds) 29 April–3 May	12-3-24-0			18.3-3-75-3	2-1-5-1					1-0-2-0						
v. Essex (Chelmsford) 6–10 May	12-6-31-0			32-8-83-3				19-3-64-2	8-1-14-0 & 6-3-8-1	6-3-12-1						
v. Worcestershire (Bradford) 13–17 May	14.2-1-53-3			14-3-43-3 & 5-0-21-0	5-1-15-1 & 7-3-9-3 & 10-3-13-0			20.4-2-76-4 & 21.2-3-56-2	17-5-34-1 & 19-5-45-3							
v. Hampshire (Southampton) 20–4 May	11-1-52-0			5-2-13-0					26-7-47-7	25.2-10-52-3 & 22-9-47-2						
v. Glamorgan (Middlesbrough) 3–7 June	21-5-45-0			25-4-76-0 & 22-5-72-2	4-2-6-0			25-4-61-3 & 14-3-52-1	26-8-49-0 & 17-6-30-1	30-10-51-3 & 28-4-84-0						
v. Derbyshire (Chesterfield) 10–14 June	23-4-90-1								22-5-52-3 & 23-4-68-0							
v. Gloucestershire (Sheffield) 17–21 June	17.3-3-50-5			31-15-27-4 & 18-3-51-0	16-6-32-2 & 6-0-15-0			34-12-78-3 & 17-3-33-0	32-14-48-0 & 12-4-52-1	13-4-13-0 & 21-7-47-1			19.1-1-39-1 & 7-1-22-0	2-0-5-1		
v. Kent (Leeds) 24–8 June	20-3-65-1				11-4-26-2 & 5-2-9-0			22-7-51-4 & 18-7-33-1	16-3-36-1 & 12-3-24-2	36-8-97-2 & 12-8-27-0			14-2-41-0 & 9-1-21-0			
v. Warwickshire (Birmingham) 1–5 July	8-3-19-0			17-5-32-0 & 7.2-1-25-0	8-2-23-0 & 3-1-6-1			30.1-7-95-3 & 7-3-8-0		38-19-43-3 & 6-2-18-0		15-3-39-3 & 2-0-11-0	19-5-63-2 & 10-3-21-3			
v. Northamptonshire (Harrogate) 15–19 July	16.5-3-40-1 & 18.3-5-47-3			27-8-89-2	6-2-21-0			3-0-16-0 & 7-2-21-0	14.2-3-37-9 & 28.5-6-87-3	9-2-29-0	14-2-56-0 & 6-1-19-1		17-6-37-1 & 23-6-51-5			
v. Somerset (Taunton)	26-5-75-2 & 9-1-32-0			26-7-80-4					12-3-36-0 & 3-1-4-0	17-7-33-1			10-2-29-1 & 11.2-4-19-1			
v. Nottinghamshire 29 July–2 August	17.4-4-54-3			28-10-72-2 & 10-1-41-1					18-6-51-1 & 11-2-44-0	19-10-24-0 & 25-4-68-3			15-1-89-1			
v. Middlesex (Scarborough) 5–9 August	21-7-42-7 & 20.2-4-52-3			18-4-44-2 & 9-1-47-0					26-9-95-1	39.5-14-89-5 & 30-10-107-0			14-6-36-2 & 23-4-85-1			
v. Lancashire (Manchester) 12–16 August	19-7-44-0 & 22-4-78-3				6-1-16-0 & 10-1-27-1	13-7-16-1 & 30-11-54-1			11-1-27-1 & 33-14-62-6	15-3-48-1 & 12-3-46-0			16-5-62-4 & 10-1-50-2		4-0-19-0	
v. Durham (Leeds) 19–23 August	12.1-3-46-4 & 25.5-4-101-1			9-3-15-0 & 2-0-8-0	6-2-17-1 & 5-2-20-1				24.5-1-89-2 & 15-1-36-2	1-1-0-1			32-15-50-1 & 19-7-35-3			
v. Leicestershire (Leicester) 26–30 August	28-6-79-5								17-6-31-2 & 23-4-71-1				17-4-53-3			
v. Sussex (Scarborough) 31 August–3 September	22.4-4-68-1 & 15.4-2-44-3			9-2-35-0	1-0-8-0				20-5-78-0	31-19-33-3			19.1-1-49-2	5-0-18-0	9-4-23-1	4-3-4-0 & 1-0-3-0
v. Surrey (The Oval) 9–13 September	22-3-88-3 & 28-10-82-3			25-6-83-1		17-6-38-0			21-3-81-1	26.2-6-63-2			29-5-97-2			
16–20 September	19.2-4-70-3												18-2-78-2			
Bowler's average	507.3-115-1517-57 — 26.61	1.1-0-7-0 —	17.5-8-35-0 —	383.2-97-1065-51 — 34.35	132-36-328-15 — 21.86	77-35-122-3 — 40.66	4-2-7-0 —	267.4-62-705-26 — 27.11	514-134-1346-49 — 27.46	540-188-1207-40 — 30.17	20-3-75-1 — 75.00	17-3-50-3 — 16.66	351.4-91-1027-37 — 27.75	7-0-23-1 — 23.00	13-4-42-1 — 42.00	5-3-7-0 —

Byes / Leg-byes / Wides / No-balls / Total / Wks (as read, innings order)

Byes	Leg-byes	Wides	No-balls	Total	Wks
4	8	1	4	137	10
	1		3	62	0
2	7	1	2	200	10
4			14	261	10
	10	2	10	250	10
3	4		8	215	10
4	16		18	192	10
4	8	4	12	307	8
1	8	3	22	162	9
	8	2	8	323	10
3	4		16	304	3
4	10	1	10	241	Ab.
4	4	3	14	235	10
4	6		14	298	3
6	11	1	10	167	10
2	3		2	346	6
2	3		16	115	10
2	6	2	6	97	4
7	1		2	305	10
4	7		2	235	10
9	15		21	170	10
9	4		2	316	10
4	6		26	259	9 A
7	8	2	8	439	5
	10	1	16	167	10
6	6		4	314	10
8	3		10	332	10
9	6	1	4	229	7
9	9		18	158	10
4		2	22	271	10
3	6		18	397	8
7	9	1	18	359	9
					7

A M.G. Field-Buss absent hurt